Formative Britain

Formative Britain presents an account of the peoples occupying the island of Britain between 400 and 1100 AD, whose ideas continue to set the political agenda today. Forty years of new archaeological research has laid bare a hive of diverse and disputatious communities of Picts, Scots, Welsh, Cumbrian and Cornish Britons, Northumbrians, Angles and Saxons, who expressed their views of this world and the next in a thousand sites and monuments.

This highly illustrated volume is the first book that attempts to describe the experience of all levels of society over the whole island using archaeology alone. The story is drawn from the clothes, faces and biology of men and women, the images that survive in their poetry, the places they lived, the work they did, the ingenious celebrations of their graves and burial grounds, their decorated stone monuments and their diverse messages.

This ground-breaking account is aimed at students and archaeological researchers at all levels in the academic and commercial sectors. It will also inform relevant stakeholders and general readers alike of how the islands of Britain developed in the early medieval period. Many of the ideas forged in Britain's formative years underpin those of today as the UK seeks to find a consensus programme for its future.

Martin Carver was an army officer for 15 years, a freelance commercial archaeologist for 13 years and Professor of Archaeology at the University of York for 22 years, retiring in 2008. From 2002 until 2012 he was editor of the global archaeology journal *Antiquity*. He has researched post-Roman towns in Britain, France, Italy and Algeria and excavated large sites of the first millennium AD at Sutton Hoo (Suffolk) and Portmahomack (north-east Scotland). He has produced numerous articles, lectures and broadcasts on the peoples of early Britain, and his latest books are *Sutton Hoo: Encounters with Early England*, *Portmahomack: Monastery of the Picts* and *Archaeological Investigation* (for Routledge).

Routledge Archaeology of Northern Europe

The British Palaeolithic
Human Societies at the Edge of the Pleistocene World
Paul Pettitt, Mark White

The Neolithic of Britain and Ireland
Vicki Cummings

Iron Age Lives
The Archaeology of Britain and Ireland 800 BC–AD 400
Ian Armit

The Mesolithic in Britain
Landscape and Society in Times of Change
Chantal Conneller

Formative Britain
An Archaeology of Britain, Fifth to Eleventh Century AD
Martin Carver

For more information about this series, please visit: www.routledge.com/Routledge-Archaeology-of-Northern-Europe/book-series/ARCHNEUR

Formative Britain

An Archaeology of Britain,
Fifth to Eleventh Century AD

Martin Carver

LONDON AND NEW YORK

First published 2019
by Routledge
2 Park Square, Milton Park, Abingdon, Oxon OX14 4RN

and by Routledge
52 Vanderbilt Avenue, New York, NY 10017

Routledge is an imprint of the Taylor & Francis Group, an informa business

British Library Cataloguing-in-Publication Data
A catalogue record for this book is available from the British Library

Library of Congress Cataloging-in-Publication Data
A catalog record for this book has been requested

ISBN: 978-0-415-52474-2 (hbk)
ISBN: 978-0-415-52475-9 (pbk)
ISBN: 978-0-429-44913-0 (ebk)

Typeset in Times New Roman
by Apex CoVantage, LLC

Contents

List of figures

Abbreviations

ADS:	*Archaeology Data Service* (York) http://archaeologydataservice.ac.uk/
AC:	*Aelfric's Colloquy* ed G N Garmonsway 1947 (London: Methuen).
ASC:	*The Anglo-Saxon Chronicle* trans and ed D Whitelock 1961 (London: Eyre & Spottiswood).
AY:	Addyman, P V (ed) *The Archaeology of York* fascicule series (York: Council for British Archaeology for The York Archaeological Trust.
Bede:	*Opera* trans B Colgrave. ed J McClure and R Collins 2008 (Oxford: Oxford University Press).
Beowulf:	trans and introduction by S Heaney 1999 (London: Faber).
Bible:	*The Bible designed to be read as literature* ed Ernest Sutherland Bates with an introduction by L Binyon 1944 (London: Heinemann).
BL:	British Library.
CCCC:	Corpus Christi College Cambridge.
CAR:	Complex Atlantic Roundhouse.
Corpus:	Corpus of Anglo-Saxon Stone Sculpture I (Cramp 1984), II (Bailey and Cramp 1988), III (Lang 1991), IV (Tweddle 1995), V (Everson and Stocker 1999), VI (Lang 2001), VII (Cramp 2006), VIII (Coatsworth 2008), (IX Bailey 2010), X (Bryant 2012), XI (Preston and Okasha 2013), XII (Everson and Stocker 2015).
Fm:	Formative period, 1, 2, 3.
The Gododdin:	trans and ed K H Jackson 1969 (Edinburgh: Edinburgh University Press).
HE:	*Historia Ecclesiastica* in Venerabilis Baedae *Opera Historica*; ed C Plummer 1969 [1896] (Oxford: Clarendon Press).
LC:	Life of St Columba.
Lives of the Saints:	(Brendan, Cuthbert, Wilfrid) trans J F Webb 1965 (London: Penguin).
The Mabinogion:	trans and ed G Jones and T Jones 1949 (London: Dent).
Sagas:	*The Sagas of Icelanders*, preface by J Smiley, introduction by R Kellog, various translators 2001 (London: Penguin).
SFB:	Sunken Featured Building.
Trioedd Ynys Prydein:	trans and ed R Bromwich 1961 (Cardiff: University of Wales Press).

Picture credits

The author and publisher are grateful to the following colleagues for courteously providing permission to reproduce the following images:

David Adams 2.40
Derek Alexander 4.37, 4.38
Anthony Barton, artist 2.4, 2.15, 2.16
Bill Britnell 4.45
Ewan Campbell 3.42, 3.43, 3.44
Tim Champion 3.81
Linda Clarke 4.99
Rosemary Cramp 3.74, 3.75, 3.76, 4.79, 4.80, 4.81
Tania Dickinson 2.10
Steve Dockrill 3.40
Steve Driscoll 3.41, 3.50
George Eogan 4.97
James Eogan 4.98
Chris Evans 3.64, 3.65, 4.64, 4.71
Chris Fern 4.23
Andrew Fitzpatrick 4.2
Katherine Forsyth 5.26A
David Freke 4.86, 4.87
Michael Fulford 5.34
Joyce Greenham 5.23A
Dawn Hadley and Julian Richards 3.98
Mark Hall 5.37, 5.60A
Denis Harding 3.3, 3.5, 3.39
Heinrich Härke 2.2
Stephen Harrison 4.82
Candy Hatherley 4.43
Jane Hawkes 5.54
Gillian Hey 3.29, 3.30, 3.31, 3.32, 3.33
Catherine Hills 2.14, 4.15, 4.16
John Hines 4.62, 4.63
James Holloway 4.93
Cliff Hoppitt 4.24
Jane Kenney 4.45

Andrew Langdon 5.23A, 5.23D
Chris Lowe 3.67, 3.68, 3.70
Adrián Maldonado 4.36, 4.39
Finbar McCormick 3.66
Jacqueline McDowell 3.115, 3.116
Tom McErlean 3.77, 3.79
Bob Meeson 3.91
Martin Millett 3.84, 3.85
Richard K. Morris 6.3
Kenneth Murphy 4.46, 4.47
Gordon Noble 3.53, 5.27B
Tomás Ó Carragáin 5.76, 5.79
Tim Pestell 2.14, 3.95, 4.69, 4.70
Dominic Powlesland 3.62, 4.56
Ann Preston-Jones 5.23B, 5.23C, 5.23D
Edwina Proudfoot 4.40, 4.41, 4.42
Michael Quinn 5.51
Mark Redknap 2.13
Andrew Reynolds 4.95
Warwick Rodwell 4.94
Chris Scull 3.93
Mick Sharp 5.56
Neil Sharples 3.97
Roger Stalley 5.75
Graham Sumner, artist 2.18, 2.22
Gabor Thomas 2.40, 3.94
Mark Thomas 2.2
Nicola Toop 3.71
Sam Turner 3.57
Bjorn Varenius 4.101
John Waddell 6.1
Penelope Walton Rogers 2.3, 2.4, 2.15, 2.16, 2.17, 2.18, 2.19
Lorna Watts 3.92, 3.100, 3.101, 3.102, 3.103
Howard Williams 4.72
David Wilson 3.96, 5.3B, 5.3C

Thanks also to the following institutions who have permitted reproduction of their copyright images under licence, with fee waived:

Aberdeenshire County Council 5.28
Anglesey Antiquarian Society 4.5, 4.6
Boydell and Brewer 2.14, 3.108–113, 4.17–21
British Museum Press 2.24B
Cambrian Archaeological Association 4.45
Cambridge Committee for Aerial Photography 3.20
Cambridge University Press 5.81
Canterbury Archaeological Trust 4.65, 4.66
Cornwall Archaeological Unit 4.35

Corpus of Anglo-Saxon Stone Sculpture 2.37, 2.38B, 4.92, 5.3A, 5.34, 5.44, 5.46, 5.48, 5.49, 5.50, 5.52, 5.54, 5.55, 5.56, 5.57, 5.58, 5.62, 5.63, 5.65, 5.66, 5.69, 5.71, 5.72, 5.73
Cotswold Archaeology 4.49, 4.50, 4.51
Durham University 3.58
Dyfed Archaeology 4.46, 4.47
East Anglian Archaeology 4.16, 4.23
Environment Agency 3.98
Gwynedd Archaeological Trust 4.45
Historic Environment Scotland 2.34, 2.35, 2.36, 3.49, 3.51, 4.10, 4.83, 5.27, 5.29, 5.36, 5.38, 5.41, 5.42, 5.61, 5.80
Leicester University Press 3.107, 5.53B
Manx National Heritage 3.96, 4.84, 4.85
Museum of Cultural History, Oslo 4.103, 4.104
Museum of London Archaeology 4.68
National Museum of Wales 2.13, 5.19, 5.21
Norfolk Historic Environment Service 2.14
Norwich Castle Museum and Art Gallery 2.24A
NPS Archaeology 2.40
Ordnance Survey/Crown Copyright 3.11, 3.12, 3.13, 3.17, 3.94, 3.98, 5.27B
Oxbow Books 3.54, 3.55, 4.44
Oxbow Books (on behalf of Windgather Press) 3.119
Oxford Archaeological Journal 1.11
Perth and Kinross Countryside Trust 3.46
Royal Archaeological Institute 3.84, 3.85, 4.48
Society of Antiquaries of London 3.105B–D, 5.53A
Society of Antiquaries of Scotland 3.69, 4.40, 4.41, 4.42, 5.2
Society for Medieval Archaeology 2.40, 3.105A
Society for Roman Studies 4.3, 4.4
Suffolk Archaeological Service 3.87, 3.88, 3.89, 3.90
Suffolk County Council 3.7, 3.59, 3.60, 3.87, 3.88, 3.89, 3.90, 3.93
Tees Archaeology 3.72, 3.73, 4.57, 4.58, 4.59, 4.60, 4.61, 4.77, 4.78
Trent Peak Archaeology 3.86
University of York 4.22, 4.25, 4.26, 4.27, 4.28, 4.29, 4.30, 4.31, 4.32, 4.33
Uppsala Universitets Museum för Nordiska Fornsaker 4.100
Valerie J. Keeley Ltd 3.117
Vikingeskipmuseet, Roskilde 1.7
Wessex Archaeology 4.2
York Archaeological Trust 3.36
York Museums Trust 2.25B

Finally, thanks to the following institutions and contractors who have permitted reproduction of their copyright images under licence, with fees paid:

Flemming Bau, artist 3.120
British Library Board 1.8, 2.38A, 4.33, 5.91B, 5.91C, 5.92, 5.93, 6.2, 6.4
FAS Heritage, York 1.1, 1.12, 1.13, 1.14, 2.7B, 2.28, 3.1, 3.11, 3.12, 3.13, 3.14, 3.15, 3.16, 3.17, 3.18, 3.34, 3.47, 4.1, 4.67, 4.92, 5.1, 5.6, 5.7, 5.10, 5.11, 5.24, 5.35, 5.40, 5.59, 5.70, 7.1

Preface

The subject of this book is the island of Britain and what happened there between the 5th and the 11th century AD, from 1,600 to 900 years ago. This period has suffered unjustly from professionals and public alike, being accorded the ambiguous category of the 'early middle ages' and accorded a personality only by being 'Dark'. The 'Middle' Ages refers to the long period that separates the glory of Rome from the glory of the renaissance (400–1600), but of course it was no tedious interval to those alive then. To some extent its latter centuries (from the 12th to the 16th) have been largely liberated from romantic cliché and now almost appear as a civilisation of their own. The earlier part, our period (the 5th to the 11th century), still has little more status than a pause within an interval, in which men and women waited inscrutably for more famous times. However, as I hope to show, far from being inscrutable, it was ambitious, intellectual, experimental, mobile and creative – an arena hosting a collision of ideas between deep prehistory and the Christian Roman Empire, a bubbling cauldron that would result in something new, different, remarkable and enduring. Never before, and seldom again, were the people of Britain exposed to such a startling variety of ideological programmes and the political freedom to choose and exercise them. The resulting debate, conducted with words, clothes, spears and monuments, gave us both the countries we still have and the convictions and prejudices that are still embedded in them. In that sense, the period was formative.

The picture to be painted here has emerged largely through archaeology, and in particular through the archaeology of the last 30 years. It is not a book that could have been written before, and if archaeological investigation is allowed to flourish in the next 30 it will soon be replaced and regarded as much an agenda as a synthesis. Archaeology in Britain has benefitted enormously both from the courageous funding of field research and from the rich harvest of large-scale investigations made possible by preventative projects in advance of development. This has shown us life and death at the human scale, as opposed to the small trenches and big theories of earlier explorations. It has brought many surprises, and the new story presented here is more the result of new discoveries than new theory. At the same time that the vista has been broadened by large-scale investigation, it has been deepened by science, especially the biological sciences and refined radiocarbon dating. In some cases, we can give the people we dig up a persona: not the vivid fame of the written record but access to the intimate experience of an individual.

The objective of the book is to discover what drove this early society into changing, distinguished here not so much as wars and chance but as the competing strategies of lordship, spirituality and wealth creation. Aspects of these forces are present in every century, and some would say they are always with us and always operate in uneasy union. However, the investigation presented here reveals them as competitive ideologies in which the pull of the past, the pressure of the neighbours and the gravitational field of the *zeitgeist* combine to privilege one and then the other and then the third, at different places and times. This process produced the monuments that remain, archaeology's long-term literature.

Space

A framework of space and time has been devised to be as neutral as possible. The island has been divided into seven 'natural' areas, which can sometimes also claim individual and collective identities that are familiar: Anglo-Saxon, Welsh, Celtic British, Scottish, Christian, non-Christian. However, ethnic and national labels can be misleading, mainly because they are artefacts of today defined at a distance and not necessarily realities of the past. Moreover, even when these attributes are appropriate they may vary with the passage of time, as languages and cultures mingle or divide. On the other hand it is irritating to read (and to write) 'the inhabitants of the south-east part of the mainland', when everyone knows you mean 'the English'. Accordingly, the seven regions, like most of us, have alternative names to be used as and when greater or lesser precision is required. The western part of modern Scotland is for most of this period just *Scotland*, in contrast to the north-east part, which is *Pictland*. *North-west England* is the area of modern England that runs from the Solway Firth to the Mersey. *Wales* is Wales. *South-west England* is the peninsula from Wiltshire to the Scilly Isles. *Northumbria* in the north-east runs from the Forth to the Humber. The area to the south of it, stretching from the Humber to the Channel and from the North Sea to Wales, is not culturally equivalent to England for most of our period, so is termed here *Southumbria*. I will use these words in italics as shorthand for geographical terms but will often fall to using 'north and west' as opposed to 'south and east' to describe larger cultural contrasts. If readers want to adjust these mentally to mean the traditional zones assigned to Celtic Britain and Anglo-Saxon England, I can't stop them. But it should be clear from the outset that we are in pursuit of more exciting quarries. The variegated personalities illustrated by the monumental zones are not merely rooted in landscape and language but are held to express more elusive qualities of culture and belief.

The smaller islands round Britain's shores are included, with a little inconsistency: for the present purpose, the northern and western isles, Man, Anglesey and Wight, are taken as part of Britain; the Channel Islands are not. Ireland is not treated jointly with Britain, as it sometimes has been in the past, mainly because its early medieval archaeology is relatively advanced in comparison with that of Britain, and has been the subject of a recent and exemplary overview.[1] But the Irish experience will be needed and cited at every stage. Britain is surrounded by four seas, separating it from important neighbours at no great distance by boat. Of these, Scandinavia, Ireland and the Rhineland exercised a powerful and continual influence, like three suns shining on a single planet. The archaeological narrative makes frequent trips to these places to help explain what is happening at home.

Time

The descriptor 'formative' has been borrowed from Mesoamerican archaeology, where it has been in service for generations as a successor to the archaic and a prelude to the 'Classic' period of the great Mayan centres. The origins of Mayan civilisation has been chronicled with ever increasing precision by tracking the establishment of agricultural, religious and social systems and the emergence of states[2]. Britain's formative follows rather than precedes the 'Classical' in Europe, but the term is still apt: here too religious, social and economic

Table 0.1 Formative periods in relation to other British and Continental time divisions. The Formative period as a whole is known as the early medieval ages, *Das Fruhmittelalterzeit, La haute Moyen Age, Altomedioevo, la Alta Edad Media.*

BRITAIN *400–1100*	*Formative 1* *400–675*	*Formative 2* *675–825*	*Formative 3* *825–1100*
South and east Britain 400–1066	*Early Anglo-Saxon* *600–675 Conversion*	*Middle Saxon*	*Late Saxon/Anglo-* *Scandinavian*
North and west Britain 400–1050	*Late Iron Age/Early* *Historic*	*Early Historic*	800–1050 *Historic/* *Norse*
Ireland 400–1100	*Late Iron Age*	[400–800] *Early Christian*	800–980 *Viking*
France	481–687 *Merovingian*	687–751–840 *Carolingian*	840–1039 *Ottonian*
Scandinavia	*Migration*	*Merovingian*	*Viking*
Denmark	400–575	575–800	800–1050
Sweden	400–550	550–750 *Vendel*	750–1050
Norway	400–570	570–800	800–1000

forces formed new political structures, albeit on the ruins of empire. The time span of the British Formative is defined as the 5th to 11th century. The sequence of events is constructed from agreed dates, drawn from scientific measurement where possible and otherwise from the cultural framework worked out by generations of European scholars. For convenience, or as a shorthand to aid navigation, the Formative period as whole is divided into three: Period 1–5th to 7th century, Period 2–7th to 9th century and Period 3–9th to 11th century. As can be seen, they overlap, allowing a prudent cushion of vagueness between them. These period divisions emerge quite readily from the dated sequence, and by the end of the book it will be possible to propose more precise figures for the points of transition. One motive for devising this scheme is to resolve the confusion caused by having so many names for the segments of this part of European history, in many cases with names drawn from site types (e.g. Vendel), languages (e.g. p-Celtic) or principal events (migration) (see Table 0.1).

Scope

The material assembled here has been recovered by numerous researchers over several centuries. No one life is long enough to master the primary records of the archaeological sources, which are already vast and now multiplying faster than anyone can write. In this it is not (at all) like a history book in which sources held in common can be reduced to a manageable size by a magisterial synthesis. The output here consists of partial overviews, into which life is breathed by puffs of interpretation of greater or lesser plausibility. Many archaeologists, especially those in the early medieval period (and especially me), suffer from the unfortunate ailment known as *PGS* (premature generalisation syndrome). In some ways this is inevitable, since the period is markedly underdeveloped in comparison to most others, whether prehistoric, proto-historic or historic. The arbiters of academic excellence tend to make no distinction between one period and another, so we are driven to try and keep up by synthesising what we have so far. While the result is always premature, other disciplines like us to do this, since it treats their needs with courtesy and common sense. By contrast, those in the game sometimes regard attempts to reinterpret their findings and incorporate them in an overview as an intrusion into their personal fiefdom. I can't do much about this, having the broader audience in mind. Nevertheless, knowing that I should control PGS to a supportable itchy state, I have usually attempted to put data before overview, so that the reader is briefed before a new model is presented; which it is, to a greater or lesser degree of invention, in every chapter. To those whose work is omitted or its significance distorted I offer a blanket apology: selection was needed, the choice was mine, the loss is to the reader.

Structure

The narrative is delivered with the aid of a three-draw toolbox: each chapter is focused on a particular kind of evidence (artefacts, settlement, burial, sculpture, texts), inside each of which the reader follows a sequence of the three predefined periods (Fm 1, 2, 3); and within each of these, trends and responses are explored making use of the seven predefined regions. The Table included in this preface (Table 0.1) shows the framework.

The structure is designed to be as simple to navigate as possible, though it might not always seem like that. The first chapter, *Inheritance*, sets the scene by pointing out the varied character of the island's geography and the permanent affect that its soils and climate had on everyone living there. This has been highlighted expeditiously by a succession of geographers, and archaeologists, but ignored by most scholars since. It is worth restating, since the natural landscape is the silent force behind much of what happened. The other silent force is prehistory, which may act through actual memory, more than we may suppose, or from interaction with its monuments on the ground.

Four chapters follow, exploring four major aspects of existence coupled with four major ways of understanding them archaeologically: *Looking for personhood* is about the distinctions in human biology and appearance and how that appearance was embellished with clothing and ornament. This is the single most common and effective way in which people could express their times and be distinguished from each other. *Working from home* encompasses settlements of all sorts including villages, towns, ports and monasteries, their assets and idiosyncrasies. *Addressing eternity* investigates the contribution of cemeteries, their plans, their rites and rituals in the development of thinking about this world and the next. *Monumentality* is focused on standing stones and buildings, especially crosses and churches, which in many ways succeeded cemeteries as the principal form of abstract investment after Christianisation took hold. Illuminated manuscripts, argued to be monuments too, make a guest appearance here.

From these four sequences, a general narrative is composed, and explanations offered. There are plenty of gaps: many sites of the greatest importance are unpublished, some indeed still languishing in private cupboards. The invaluable *Corpus of Anglo-Saxon Sculpture* was not complete at the time of writing. However, it is never a good time to write a synthesis in which everything is included, and this book does not try. In general, a series of well-excavated, well-published multi-period examples opens each chapter and provides the framework for each study, while other more partial evidence feeds the developing case.

I am aware that arguments based on archaeology alone will be new to many and distasteful to some. Where are the verses and anecdotes and heroes of history? I am far from immune to the charms of the written record and celebrate them in Chapter 6 (*Materiality in words*), which is placed towards the end for several reasons. Firstly, the obvious one that I do not claim competence in the analysis of written texts and would rather not use them than abuse them. Secondly, I want to convince my readers that archaeology can tell its own story, supported by its own witnesses in periods that have no written words, or in periods that have plenty, or, as in this case, periods which have little, and obscure at that. Lastly, in the nature of things, early authors describe events that have already happened or they thought had happened or wished had happened, and their testimony is retrospective and ingenious. The use made of this material is, perhaps perversely, not as a source for history but as a source for archaeology: it is poetry's revelations of materiality that are sought and spotlit.

Overview

Robin Fleming was one of the first scholars to attempt an account of early medieval Britain as a whole, in an excellent book that makes vivid use of both archaeology and documents. But she delivers a rueful verdict on the period: 'so diverse were the experiences of people living through these years that no master narrative, no matter how compelling, does justice to the lives of those who experienced them'.[3] While I accept the wisdom of this judgement, the present book does attempt a master narrative summarised in its final chapter (Chapter 7) and drawn from the models devised in the others. The economic inequality between the Jurassic plain, broadly the area occupied in succession by the Romans and then the English, and the less fertile and less accessible broken land of the rest of the island pervades the whole of our period. If the 'English' area (the south and east) was naturally richer, it was also less in touch with its indigenous prehistory, primarily because it was dominated by immigrants who took several centuries to settle in. In *Formative 1*, the Southumbrians, who had all the best land, were arable farmers living in open villages served by communal cemeteries of cremations and inhumations furnished with grave goods of characteristic Germanic type. The rest of the island was populated by communities operating from small family forts and living off stock, especially cattle. Their burial places showed much continuity in form, location and practice with their prehistoric predecessors. They signposted their routes and holdings with erect stone pillars inscribed with personal names. None of the peoples, either in the north and west or the east and south, appear to have invested in monuments or performance that was overtly Christian, but their upper classes were in contact with each other and maintained their own, separated, overseas alliances.

Towards the end of Formative 1, in the early 7th century, a more socially stratified society advertises its arrival in the south and east in the form of monumental burial mounds dedicated to individual males and multi-purpose 'magnate farms'. By the mid-7th century, it is the turn of the women to be celebrated in richly furnished burials, suggesting a need to express their leadership in both proprietorial and religious affairs. By the beginning of Formative 2, and specifically about AD 675, England finally begins its archaeologically visible Christian conversion, a process intimately interwoven with British integration and the creation of rich estates and ever larger kingdoms.

By contrast, the inhabitants of the north and west, including Northumbria, were swept up in a revived Christianisation programme shared with Ireland, marked by multi-purpose monasteries, stone crosses and illuminated manuscripts. Well into Formative 2, in the mid-8th century, Northumbria leads the charge for the conversion of the rest of the island into a monastic nation, leaving a trail of markers, the Victory Crosses, strung out across the land. At the same time, the English in Southumbria enhance their opposing project of royal control with the creation of a set of dedicated international trading places, the *wics*. The difference in the political agendas of the south-east and the rest of the island during Formative 2 emerges ineluctably from the examination of clothes, settlement, burial and monumentality, and it highlights both the pivotal position of Northumbria and the anomalous character of the early English monastery.

These two parallel, and sometimes confronted, programmes, the one driven by religious fundamentalism and the other by centralised kingship, had little time to compromise or confront each other before both had to deal with the arrival of the Vikings: the Danish in the east and south and the Norse in the north and west. Archaeologically this initiates *Formative 3*. Alfred of Wessex in the south and Macbeth of Moray in the north confronted the Viking incursions separately in a hundred years of war. The Vikings did not unite them, however; rather, the English used the cessation of hostilities to invade and attempt to subdue the other occupants of the island, eventually defining the space of a kingdom equivalent to the England of the present day. Under the radar of this new regime, archaeology finds the surviving substrate of local cultures. The material traces left by the Vikings mark their trajectory from conquest to settlement and the adoption of a secularised version of Christianity, with local churches and hybrid sculptures. The older cultures represented by Scots and Picts, Northumbrians and Southumbrians, peoples of Cornwall and Britons in every part, persist alongside the ghosts of prehistoric beliefs, Roman regulation, micro-religions and early kingdoms. Force and ideology create new identities, but earlier identities never wholly go away, their cultural footprints never entirely erased.

Readers will see that the archaeological analysis undertaken here accepts the English as developing out of immigrant communities from areas of the Rhineland, north Germany, Denmark and Norway. They largely hold themselves apart until the later 6th century, when they blend increasingly, even in the east, with the indigenous Britons, leading to a second definition of the Anglo-Saxons as Anglo-British. A third definition comes from the assimilation of the Danish and Norse, resulting in a population that can be broadly described as Anglo- or Scotto-Scandinavian. As will be appreciated, the English are a heterogeneous people and by no means always the principal players in this island story, for a large part of which the peoples of the north, south, east and west were equally matched. Nevertheless, the English work at being culturally English and were still attempting to dominate the other inhabitants of the island when they were conquered by Continental Normans and our period ends. Maybe the essential foreignness of the English in Britain is an issue that has yet to be resolved today – but that is for others to say. What will be noticed here is that in economics, art, ideology, engineering, stockbreeding, food production and trade – in everything, in fact, apart from power politics, it is the integration of the English with the other inhabitants of the island that generated advances of great originality and permanent value.

The author

Seamus Heaney's introduction to his translation of *Beowulf* contains an encomium for the happy accident that brought together so many different kinds of language and of poetry to develop cheek by jowl in a pair of European offshore islands. He describes his excitement at discovering that the common Irish word *uisce* (water) appears in British river names (Usk) and of course in 'whisky':

> so in my mind the stream was suddenly turned into a kind of linguistic river of rivers issuing from a kind of Celto-British Land of Cockaigne, a riverrun of Finnegans Wake-speak pouring out of the cleft rock of some prepolitical, prelapsarian, urphilological Big Rock Candy Mountain – and all of this had a wonderfully sweetening effect on me. The Irish/English duality, the Celtic/Saxon antithesis were momentarily collapsed.

A similar moment accompanied his rediscovery of the old English word *thole* used by older Ulster people: 'they'll just have to learn to thole' remarked his aunt of some family that had suffered an unforeseen bereavement.[4] This is a moment I can share: as a 17-year-old I was enraptured to note that *thole* deployed by James Joyce in *Ulysses* ('thole and bring forth bairns') was also inscribed on the dinner plates at home '*Thole and Think on*' – the motto of my mother's Border family.

My early education was neither archaeological nor academic, but military. I was born into a principled but anachronistic family which expected me to know how to saddle a horse, shoot a duck, catch a trout and risk my life fighting people I did not know for reasons I was not told. At the time I was impressed (and later alarmed) to find that signing up for war on the vaguest of pretexts did nothing to diminish the adventure – rather the opposite. No one today should underestimate the incomprehensible, reprehensible, exhilaration of going into battle, or believe that it is confined to fundamentalists. It is this unspoken joy of trying one's hand against fate that makes young people so easy to manipulate for politically moronic ends.

At 18, I was also induced into the deep narcissism that dwells in regiments of the line: the dressing up and preening with blue serge, shiny metal badges with their symbolic animals, the skeuomorphic chain mail, the formal greetings, the long loud dinners, the drinking challenges aimed at the youngest subaltern least likely to achieve them, the pipes playing round and round the table, as the diners sank into an alcoholic stupor, sobbing silently at the pibroch; the burst of activity afterwards when the sofas were up-ended and all the officers fell upon each other in a wild game of rugby without a ball, heads were broken, blood flowed and hundreds of pounds worth of hand-stitched uniforms were torn into shreds and delivered in the morning to delighted tailors. It is likely that a resurrected Fergus, or Cú Chulainn, the companions of Maelgwyn or Raedwald or the young man buried in Sutton Hoo's Mound 17 would have found much that was familiar in a 20th-century British officers' Mess.

Genesis of the book

This book arose from a basic need to try and understand better a period that I have loved for 50 years – since I first read the *Problem of the Picts* in the military library at Celle in 1969 and bought Jackson's translation of the *Gododdin* at the Edinburgh festival in 1970. In effect my introduction to the early middle ages was via poetry. I took up archaeology after leaving the army in 1972 and soon realised not only that it had penetrative powers of its own but also that it happened out of doors; so, better than poetry in some ways. I was urged to write the book by colleagues in Scandinavia, frustrated at having no accessible overview of early medieval Britain and, in England, by fellow academics working in early medieval history and literature, looking for a description of how archaeology works. The consequence is that this is an archaeological book: I make no pretensions to write history. My hope is that real historians will write new history using such parts of it that they find convincing.

My dearest friends will know that I had set my heart on a vivid rollicking book in a bid to popularise the period, encourage more people to learn from it and see how it still steers events today. By using a rhetorical and reckless approach to the task I hoped to attract more readers other than those already embedded, readers who in real life are politicians, teachers, children and pensioners. But more than ever today there is a sceptical gap between the labour of reason and the primrose path of conjecture. If the gap is to be bridged, the foundations must be laid. So the hard work has to come first, and its outcome has to be a serious book full of verifiable detail.

Among those friends, Rosemary Cramp, Catherine Hills and Madeleine Hummler are those who have taught and guided me most. Drafts were read by Steve Driscoll, Nancy Edwards, Helen Geake, Catherine Hills and Madeleine Hummler, and I am most grateful to them. Nancy's astute assessment in particular resulted in a major reconstruction that has made the whole thesis easier to follow, if not necessarily easier to accept. As always, I owe a debt of gratitude to Cecily Spall for her astute critique and to our company, FAS Heritage, for the production of the illustrations. I offer special thanks to Matthew Gibbons, Molly Marler and other staff at Routledge for their guidance, patience and faith in the project; to Jo Tozer and Autumn Spalding for invaluable help in getting the book to press; and especially to Madeleine Hummler for more than 40 years of encyclopaedic insights and shared adventure.

Ellerton, York
1 August 2017

Notes

1 O'Sullivan et al. 2014a.
2 Willey and Phillips 1958, 144ff; Renfrew and Bahn 2008, 506–514.
3 Fleming 2010, 240.
4 Heaney 1999, xxiv, xxv.

1 Inheritance

Landscapes and predecessors

Introduction

Britain and Ireland, two lands equally blessed with natural assets, are the largest members of an archipelago off the north-west edge of continental Europe that also includes smaller offshore islands in the south, west and north. The whole has been referred to as the 'British Isles', inaccurately since Ireland was never British.[1] This book is focussed on the island of Britain, as opposed to Britain and Ireland, mainly because a magnificent compendium on early medieval Ireland has just appeared, following a period of intense archaeological investigation.[2] The present survey has required frequent glances across the Irish Sea, and the two studies together will hopefully reveal something of that special power of difference that can inspire mutual admiration in close neighbours.

Since Britons also lived in Brittany, the term 'Great Britain' referred to its larger land mass, rather than its magnificent achievements on the world stage, a tenderly nurtured delusion.[3] The Britons themselves were a heterogeneous people, composed of several groups, including the Picts, the Welsh and the Britons of the south-west, seasoned by four centuries of immigration from the parts of the Roman empire, soon to be joined by the English in the south-east and by the Irish in west Wales and Scotland. Britain was already a mixed race in the 5th century, this being probably the basis for its ingenuity and resilience.

This chapter sets the scene for an exploration of Formative Britain by reviewing the legacy that its peoples inherited: the natural assets of the land and the seas and the relict landscape of the earlier inhabitants. We will find that terrestrial regions define themselves quite easily and that they are still with us; that their character was determined by nature and prehistory, and their experience in the Formative period was modulated by neighbours across the nearest sea, neighbours who were often immigrants and sometimes invaders; and that Britain, far from being a self-contained entity, was a frontier zone where vigorous cultures met.

The natural inheritance: the seas

Britain is surrounded by three seas, the North Sea, the Channel and the Irish Sea, plus the Atlantic Ocean, and these are divided into 14 inner 'sea-areas' surrounding Britain, all bearing names familiar to late-night listeners to the BBC shipping forecast (Figure 1.1). To get a feel for the seas, we can take an imaginary trip on the 30 m-long ship found in Mound 1 at Sutton Hoo, which had up to 40 oars and probably a sail.[4] Although small by yachting standards it remains the largest vessel known to early medieval Europe before the 11th century; it was open to the sky, had a simple steering oar (a 'steerboard' on the starboard (right-hand) side) and a freeboard (distance from the gunnel to the waterline amidships) of half a metre.

Figure 1.1 Britain and its neighbours with the location of sea areas (in italics), showing main rivers and principal points of entry.

(FAS Heritage)

Proposing a departure from Portmahomack in Easter Ross, we pass down the east coast of Britain, from north to south, through Cromarty, Forth, Tyne, Humber, Thames – all these names reporting the main gateways into the island via firths in the north and estuaries in the south. We take a right turn down the Channel through Dover, Wight, Portland and Plymouth, although only Southampton water, protected by the Isle of Wight, provides a well-protected entry point. Around the perilous cape of Land's End we head up the Irish Sea through sea areas Lundy, Irish Sea, Malin and Hebrides, passing the major gateways of the Severn, the Mersey, the Solway Firth and the Clyde, through the dense patterns of the western isles to the northern isles (Fair Isle) and round John O'Groats back to Cromarty. The outer sea areas report districts known to more adventurous, far-ranging mariners: Viking, Utsire, Forties, Fisher, Dogger, German Bight in the eastern sea; Fastnet, Shannon, Rockall in the west; Bailey, Faeroes and south-east Iceland in the north.

Wind and water

The politics and prosperity of the archipelago were contingent on how easy it was to travel by sea; and this in turn was dependent on a mariners' package comprised of the natural environment, the technology of boats and navigational skills. We know a little bit about each of these. Situated between the continent and the ocean, the natural forces of swell, current, tide and wind tend to create thoroughfares that differ with the time of year. In the North Sea, winds in spring favour the traveller from Scandinavia, and in autumn they blow them home[5] (Figure 1.2). But in winter, while winds theoretically favour northward travellers, the seas are dangerous. The strongest storm force winds (7–10) are recorded for the months of October to December, and they blow from the west, south-west (in the Channel) and north-west (in the north).[6] An open boat would be threatened by winds of Force 5 or more, so North Sea travellers did not generally put to sea after October. The early English sailors put to sea again in March, traditionally prompted by the arrival of a perennial spring visitor: 'the cuckoo calls, urging the heart onto the whales' road '.[7] The physical effects of these winds,

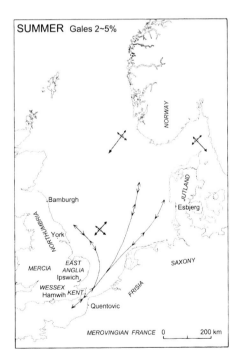
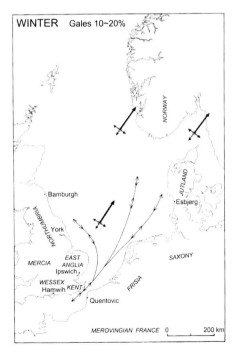

Figure 1.2 Tide and currents (narrow lines) and seasonal prevailing winds in the North Sea.
(Carver 1990, Fig 15.2 © author)

Table 1.1 Beaufort Scale of wind speed, with effect on a sailing smack

Name of wind	ON LAND	ON SEA	Speed of a FISHING SMACK
0 Calm	Smoke rises vertically	Like a mirror	Becalmed
1 Light air	Smoke shows wind direction	Ripples	Just has steerage way
2 Light breeze	Wind felt on face	Small wavelets. Crests look glassy	Sails filled speed 1–2 kn
3 Gentle breeze	Leaves in motion	Crests begin to break	Smacks tilt at 3–4 kn
4 Moderate breeze	Raises dust	White horses fairly frequent	Carry all canvas with good list
5 Fresh breeze	Small trees sway	Moderate waves, some spray	Smacks shorten sail
6 Strong breeze	Whistling heard in wires	Large waves. White foam crests everywhere	Double reef in mainsail
7 Near gale	Whole trees in motion	Sea heaps up and white streaks show direction of the wind	Smacks lie-to or stay in in harbour
8 Gale	Twigs broken off trees	Long waves, spindrift, well-marked streaks	All smacks make for harbour
9 Strong gale	Chimney pots blown off	High waves topple, tumble and turn over. Spray may affect visibility	–
10 Storm	Trees uprooted	Very high waves; whole sea looks white; poor visibility	–

so pertinent to travel and survival in the early middle ages, are today summarised by the Beaufort scale (Table 1.1). The North Sea is thus a thoroughfare rather than a barrier, but it is a thoroughfare that favours Scandinavian traffic. The tidal currents are at their fiercest where canalised in the Straits of Dover. The North Atlantic Drift, a spin off from the Gulf Stream, brings warm surface water past the Iberian peninsula through the Irish Sea to the Orkneys, marking out an ancient thoroughfare that has carried people and ideas from the south to the north of Europe since the Neolithic.[8]

Navigation

Wind, tide and current thus conspire to keep mariners off the deep water in the winter months, and then favour northward travel in the Irish Sea and westward travel in the North Sea (but not of course exclusively, or all the time). The 'haven-finding arts' have many natural signals in our region.[9] The whole of Britain stands on the continental shelf, with a depth of surrounding water of less than 100 metres, with characteristic estuarine outflows of broken shell and sand that can be picked up on a plumb-line. The sun is lower at midday the further north you go, so a mark on the mast gives a crude measure of latitude. As modern coastal dwellers know, the winds feel different depending on their direction: cold and dry (from the north, a 'northerly'), cold and wet (an easterly), warm and wet (a westerly), warm and dry (a southerly). The coastline, as viewed from the sea, has a profile that mariners learn to recognise, and early medieval people used burial mounds and standing stones as seamarks to indicate the entrance to estuaries and firths.[10] It is said that the sea breaking on certain rock formations makes a characteristic sound that can be heard in fog or by listening for it on the gunnel. The edge of the continental shelf is where fish congregate, marked by a feeding frenzy when the herrings or mackerel are in: the sea is flecked with a wavy line of fish fragments and seen from a distance as a ribbon of diving birds. In the western seaways, birds are especially useful: the nightly rush of fulmars indicates the direction of land. Geese go north in spring to feed and nest, and can be seen, skein after skein, through the day and sensed by night from their reassuring yelps. Since they must eventually land, the geese lead the way from the Irish Sea to the northern isles and beyond, to St Kilda, Faeroes and Iceland. These were the escorts of the firmament that led the early Christian wanderers in leather boats to remote islands in mid-ocean.[11]

Types of boats

The third component of the mariners' package was the type of boat available, owed to tradition and (some) invention. Tradition dies hard in boat building, where experience and superstition maintain a stubborn alliance.[12] In the western sea, boats had been constructed since the Bronze Age (or before) from stitched leather stretched over a wickerwork frame and made watertight with butter; these were observed by Julius Caesar and still formed the template in the early middle ages as the Irish *curragh* and the Welsh coracle.[13] They were light and so could be the more easily carried over short necks of land separating seaways, using wagons.[14] These 'portages' cut journey times or avoided turbulent water.[15] The shorter distances between landfalls and the numerous islands favoured a type of pottering itinerary from cove to cove in inshore waters.[16]

As seen in rock art, Bronze Age boat builders in the eastern seas also used a skin-over-frame build, possibly inspired by seeing seals and whales. Dugouts, made of a single tree trunk hollowed out, are the ancestral craft of lake and river. In the later Iron Age, small boats of about 3 m in length used for burial have been excavated on the island of Bornholm (Dk) and at Snape in Suffolk (p. 400). These appear to have been one-man log-boats carved out of tree trunks, with a thin-walled boat-shaped profile.[17] The larger sea-going boats were built hull-first, a shell being made by tying planks together edge to edge with sinews or roots tightened by wedges (a 'sewn boat'). A frame to support the benches was then placed in this timber shell and lashed into place. The Bronze Age Ferriby boat which took people and cattle across the Humber estuary would appear to have been one of these. The Hjortspring boat deposited in a bog with a cargo of weapons c. 350 BC has a hull of sewn planks. It was reconstructed as the sea-going craft *Tilia*, which could cruise at 4.7 knots and 'charge' (the beach or another boat) at 7.6 kn and could travel 74 km in a day paddled by the same crew.[18] In later shells, the planks (strakes) were laid overlapping and held together with iron clench nails, and the frame fastened to the shell with iron bolts, so that the construction resembled an upside-down timber-framed roof. In the northern seas, well–preserved excavated boats appear to have provided an evolutionary sequence from edge-built to clinker-built, from sewn planks edge-on to overlapping planks fastened with iron clench nails.[19] This mention of their development is intended to show that water transport and sea crossings were no novelty in the early middle ages.

The introduction of the sail is more controversial; the Romans had filled the seas with sailing ships, so neither the eastern nor the western seafarers would have found them strange. On the other hand, the boats we have found (and they are very few) seem to have been unstable and vulnerable to side winds. *Edda* was a replica of the ship found in the Oseberg mound on the Oslo fjord, a burial attributed to Queen Åse, who died about 825. Like all ships of the Viking era and before it had no keel, and the side rudder (the steerboard on the starboard side) was liable to come out of the water when the ship listed (Figure 1.3). *Edda* was designed to

Figure 1.3 Edda, a replica of the Oseberg ship under sail, shortly before it capsized.
(Carver 1995b © author; photograph by B. Marden-Jones)

reveal aspects of performance under oars and under sail and to test the notion that a Viking ship could tack.[20] This research question was significant: if the Vikings could tack they had a wide choice of journeys, less restricted by wind and tide; they would need to row less and carry less crew and, by corollary, could carry more cargo. At the end of this line of reasoning is the social and economic implication that slaves could be replaced by a voluntary crew united by their mission. The performance of the *Edda* answered some questions with certainty, others less so. Under the use of oars it was sluggish, perhaps feasible on a lake or in a river but laborious at sea. As soon as the sail was erected, the ship took off like a rocket, running before the wind. The hull jumped, even aquaplaned, like a wind surfer; it also writhed, giving a live body to the carved beast's head at the prow and the snake's tail at the stern. Excitement was at a maximum, control below the mean. The Oseberg ship had featured two pairs of sockets bolted on to the inner gunnel forward, and a long pole with a forked end had been found in the burial. By fitting the base of the pole into one of the sockets and the fork onto the bottom corner of the square sail, it could be held out against the wind, making a belly that acted, or might have acted, like a jib, to allow a side wind to push the ship forward rather than pushing it over. The experiment was not entirely successful; after dipping the gunnel into the waves a few times, the ship capsized, throwing the crew into the water. There was snow on the hills and the water was freezing. Many Viking crews will have been less lucky then we were.[21]

Our experiment did not demonstrate whether the Vikings could or could not tack, only that it was challenging to a modern crew. There was a debate about whether the ship had carried too much sail, since the height of the mast had been calculated not by the Viking rule of thumb (the girth amidships) but by the angle of the stem and stern stays, as indicated by the angle of the iron fitting on the gunnel. However, detailed survival of the vessel could not compensate for the lost skill. The early days of sailing must have been rather like the early days of hang gliding, often fatal, until the knowledge had been built up on how the 'play' the ship. An 8th-century Gotland picture stone shows a network of sheets handled by several members of the crew suggesting that together they could cradle or spill the wind, taking advantage of light airs and absorbing the shock of sudden squalls. Human beings are depicted here as part of the rigging (Chapter 5, p. 566). It can be deduced that Viking ships were very fast before the wind, required high levels of skill to handle them and that a wrong move could be fatal. This experiment opened a window onto a sailing tradition that relied on long-term survivors hoarding their experience and teaching the young.

Ease of passage has an effect on journey times, and these in turn on the exercise of policy, war and size of profit. As a rule of thumb, a ship can make up to 80 miles a day under sail and 40 miles a day under oars. This compares with land times of about 30 miles a day on a horse and about 15 miles a day on foot or pulling a cart, depending on the state of the road (Figure 1.4).[22] Water provides the quicker surface for diplomacy, soldiers and cargos. But the sea is also capricious; even in high summer, storms can bring a trip to an untimely end. For this reason, it seems to be common sense that coastal voyages, using seamarks, were preferred to 'blue water' crossings, out of sight of land. We can imagine that the seabed is littered with the buried wreckage of innumerable light vessels that put to sea, or could not escape it in time. On the other hand, sailors know to avoid a lee shore, and it is better to ride out a storm at sea than head for land and risk ending up on the rocks. Given the conjectured skills of navigators and skippers, it is likely that the range and frequency of blue water crossings has been underestimated.[23] To make a landfall, the preferred method is to beach the boat or make an entry into a firth or estuary. These are the front doors to the island of Britain, but they may not open easily. A wind blowing towards the shore can carry a boat onto the rocks; one blowing the other way prevents you getting in. Once on the river, you must row against the current and, if timed wrong, against the tide. These variables form a vital part of the manual mariners carried in their heads, making a ship's captain an indispensable player in society, then as now.

For the first 200 years of our period, the evidence (such as it is) points to an immense amount of ad hoc and adventitious voyaging, with planning heavily dependent on local knowledge and even omens. On the east coast, which would become the province of the Anglo-Saxons, havens are few and far between. But in low-lying regions, like East Anglia, the foreshore is laced with creeks where a ship can float in and ground itself, departing again with the tide. Fairweather landings are possible on shingle beaches. Once in a river a boat can make its way inland and beach on mudflats along the tidal reach. But mudflats are not convenient for unloading cargos. This is only to say that while water is the best carrier, it is not an ubiquitous connector, and settlements probably mark favoured river routes, implying that routes determine settlement, not the other way round. Bede's (rather limited) world was no doubt determined at least in part by the ease of travel afforded by the North Sea coast and the rivers that it gave access to.[24]

Overseas contact

In the 6th century, imported amphorae and red slip plates showed that sea contact was evident between the eastern Mediterranean and the Irish Sea area. In the 7th century, a slightly enlarged Irish Sea was receiving domestic crockery from south-west France.[25] There were no natural obstacles preventing the ships carrying these cargos from heading up the Channel and round Kent and into the Thames – but they did not (Figure 1.5). In some readings, this

TRAVEL TIMES FROM SUTTON HOO/IPSWICH

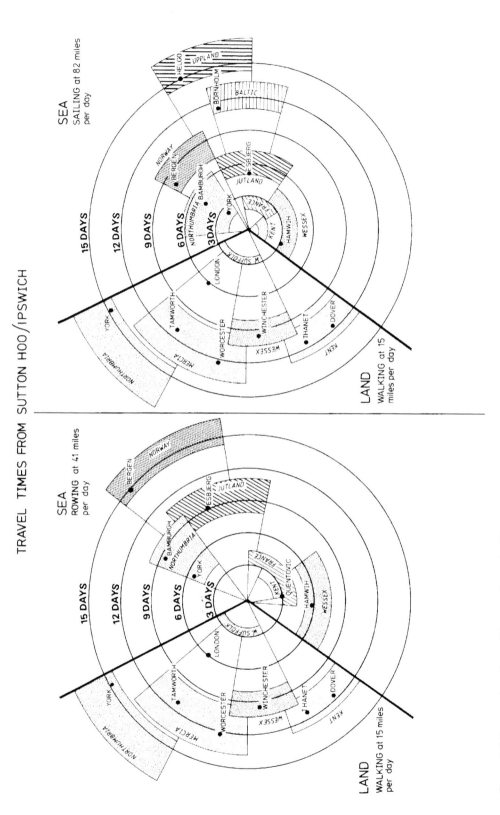

Figure 1.4 Journey times by walking, rowing and sailing.

(Carver 1990, Fig 15.3. © author)

is because the rewards for 7th century merchants were greater in the Irish Sea, and in western Scotland in particular.[26] Others feel that France sufficiently answered English demand for prestigious goods.[27] However, an alternative viewpoint is that international contact and long-distance exchange are encouraged or restricted as much by ideological as by economic drivers. In the southern North Sea, pottery and metalwork found in graves indicates contact in East Anglia and Kent with north-west Germany in the 6th century, and in East Anglia, Humberside and Kent with north-west Germany, Demark, Norway and Frisia in the 8th. Placenames and ogham stones show that the Irish were occupying parts of west Wales and of western Scotland (assuming they were not already there). These would seem to signal changes in international allegiance rather than changes in maritime opportunity.

In the 5th–6th century, it can be surmised that several 'offshore polities' populated the Irish Sea, the Channel and the North Sea. These have yet to be systematically mapped but can be lined up for investigation: the Cornish-Munster, the Leinster-S Wales, the Anglesey-Man-N Britain, the Ulster-Dal Riada, the South-west British-Atlantic/Acquitaine and the English- Danish, English-German and English-French maritime hybrid communities.[28]

In the late 7th and 8th century the surge in monasticism and its consequent literary output lit up new lines of communication with France and the Mediterranean. Many of the contacts were not so much initiated by Christian alliances as enhanced by them, as can be seen by comparing the sources of the objects buried in Mound 1 at Sutton Hoo with the sites of known scriptoria (Figure 1.6).[29] The journeys of enterprising British clerics increased in ambition during the 8th century. Willibald, a monk from Hampshire later to become bishop of Eichstätt, travelled across the Mediterranean to Syria in 720–3, stopping by the volcanic

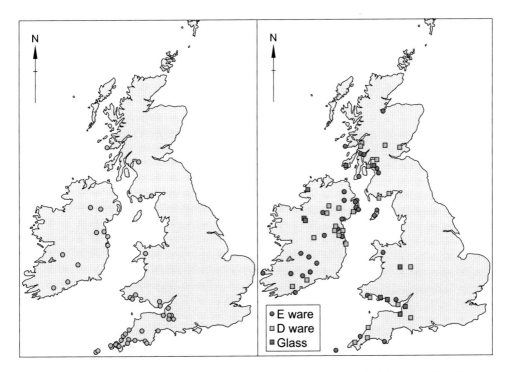

Figure 1.5 Destinations of pottery imported in the 6th century (left) and the 7th century (right).
(Carver and Loveluck 2013, Fig 6.7 after Campbell 2007; © authors)

Lipari Islands to collect pumice needed for smoothing parchment. While in Tyre he filled a calabash with balsam and succeeded in smuggling it through customs by disguising its scent with petroleum.[30] McCormick used this and other types of evidence to detect multiple lines of exchange and communication in a Mediterranean long thought to have been nearly deprived of traffic during the 7th–9th century.[31] Richard Morris' review of exotic objects found in Britain shows that, even if not economically engaged, the island was far from isolated. A pilgrim flask from Egypt was found on the seashore at Meols; Whithorn received glass and pottery from Tunisia, the Levant and Turkey. The monasteries themselves formed an internal network and were sited with a view to sea travel. By the 8th century, many points

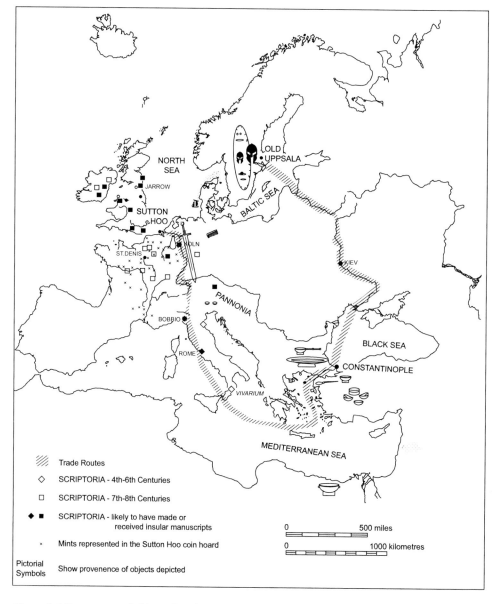

Figure 1.6 Provenance of objects found at Sutton Hoo.
(© Author)

of entry on the east coast were marked by a monastery. Once abroad the monasteries provided a staged itinerary with hostels, at least for those carrying references.[32] For non-urgent summer travel the approximate journey time from Canterbury to Rome was 7–8 weeks.[33]

The old Roman waterfronts did not suit the shallow draft vessels. Thus, Formative 2 mariners still used beaches and tides to land their cargoes: and a move towards the greater regulation of trade began to restrict the places where unloading was permitted, namely the *wics*. At *Lundenwic*, the 7th/8th century landing place was located on the Thames foreshore, remembered as The Strand. But by Formative 3, in the 9th and 10th century, the technology had adjusted to serve even tighter regulations and returned to the Roman prescription: heavy bottomed vessels were moored against robust timber waterfronts to discharge commodities on which tax was presumably payable. The beaches meanwhile became the preserve of fishermen and smugglers. Sea travel boldly expanded in this period. North Sea fishermen began risking their lives in deep sea fishing expeditions, the Vikings were discovering America and the travellers Ohthere and Wulfstan reported the reality of bringing furs from the Arctic Circle[34] (Figure 1.7). These reports were delivered to the court of Wessex, where in the 10th century the descendants of the seaborne Anglo-Saxon immigrants produced an idiosyncratic world map (Figure 1.8). But this was no navigational chart or commercial route-finder, such

Figure 1.7 Ohthere (Danish *Ottar*) was a 9th century merchant living near Lofoten, north of the Arctic Circle. The map shows his journey times east and south by ship, as reported to the court of King Alfred around AD 900.

(Drawing by Anton Englert. Bately and Englert 2007, Fig. 6. With permission from Vikingeskipmuseet, Roskilde)

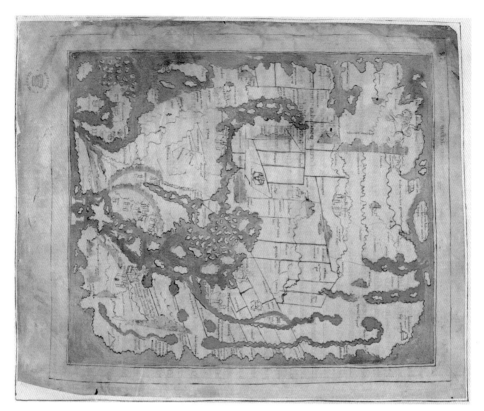

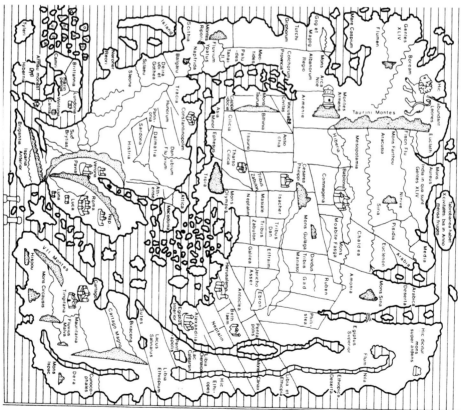

Figure 1.8 (Top): The Anglo-Saxon world map and (Bottom): a transcription by David Hill.

(BL Cotton Tiberius BV, Part 1. f56v, image licensed by the British Library Board; Hill 1981, 3)

as was to be made in Norman Sicily. The 'world' in question was the world according to the Bible, not the mariner.[35] Jerusalem lay at its centre, lands were allocated to the twelve tribes of Israel, Norway was called 'Scithia' and a note above the Taurus Mountains declared 'here lions abound'. This 'mental map' was no doubt important to a court for which Rome was now the principal destination and scholarly Christian discourse the principal passport. The implication is that real seafaring was a separate, perhaps hereditary business powered by practical knowledge, seasoned with ancestral salt.

The implication is that wherever and whenever the sea provided a higher conductivity than the land, then coastal peoples looked to each other for trade, ideas, marriage and inheritance. But while wind and current, technology and experiment show us what was possible and advantageous, the actual use of maritime space was restricted by enmities or promoted by political alliances. The weather might inhibit travel around certain capes at certain times of year, but politics and religion were also forces that wrecked ships or prevented goods from reaching harbour. Then, as now, maritime highways were thoroughfares, except when ideology or politics made them into barriers.[36]

The island of Britain

Britain has the charm of an island and the variety of a continent: an island unites the destinies of those living on it, but Britain is large enough and made up of regions sufficiently distinct 'to have cradled nations of their own'.[37] Scotland, England and Wales derive initially from areas proscribed by nature: England on the Jurassic deposits has all the most fertile land, Scotland and Wales have the ancient geology and most of the rain. Britain's invaders, the Romans and the Anglo-Saxons, knew this well enough and chose to occupy the productive lowlands of the south-east. While politicians might agonise today about the uneven distribution of wealth between the kingdoms, it is not something that has just happened. We may move our industries, but we cannot move the rocks. Within the kingdoms are older regions, uplands, valleys, coastlands and sea areas, equally drawn by nature's pencil, which new formations may overlay but never wholly erase. Until new kinds of provender are invented, the south and east will always be richer, and the north and west always need subsidies. The tensions are destined to endure.

The ancient rocks of Scotland and Wales are the highest surviving parts of a land mass otherwise largely submerged. To their south and east lie the Jurassic deposits laid out like an extensive beach curved in arcs bounded by escarpments[38] (Figure 1.9). The geology generated the soils, which, together with the climate, determined the arable yield, in terms of the length of the growing season. This in turn favoured different emphases on the type of farming that was most productive. Scholarly appreciation of the immutable aspects of this land prompted Mackinder in the early 20th century to propose a simple division between an upland and a lowland zone, which were credited with differences in agricultural strategy: cattle and sheep on the hills, cereals on the plain.[39] Common sense requires that these regions have different innate productivity, and the sources of inequality can be assigned to them.[40]

The lowland zone has since been further divided into a western, central and eastern belt, partly based on its escarpments and partly on the variations in vegetation and the types of settlement that it inspired.[41] Early medieval references to woodland and the measurement of tree pollen from samples indicate the tripartite division, with a central belt curving down from The Wash having the least trees and most arable cultivation.[42] The areas are endorsed by an assessment of the degree of settlement dispersal, the central belt being that most disposed to nucleated villages.[43] The use of open field systems also marks out the same central

Escarpments of the
'English plain'

Mountains and Platedux over 2000ft (ca. 600m)

High Platedux, 700-2000ft (ca. 210-600m)

High Hills. 700-2000ft (ca. 210-600m)

Low Platedux, 350-700ft (ca. 105-210m)

Low Hills. 350-700ft (ca. 105-210m)

Lowlands and valleys

Figure 1.9 The Jurassic plain (or 'English Plain') and its escarpments.

(Ferriday 1955, Fig 72, superimposed on Wreford Watson and Sissons 1964, Fig 12)

belt in the later middle ages.[44] The settlement provinces and subprovinces defined in the 19th century also remember the same divisions.[45] The question naturally arises, how far back can we reliably trace this template of natural productivity? The coincidence with the distribution of 5th century Anglo-Saxon burial indicates the incomers were already aware of it.[46] The distribution of Roman villas suggests that Roman incomers realised that the most profitable places for factory farms was towards the warmer end of the central belt, as well as around the northern edge of the Weald (Figure 1.10).[47] In this analysis, the eastern and western belts of the lowland zone emerge as woodland, farmed in small enclosures or strip fields from dispersed settlements. In contrast, the central belt was farmed in open fields from nucleated settlements, with greatly increased productivity. This too may have originated in a version of strip cultivation, but by the 5th century, or more likely by the 4th or possibly even by the Iron Age, it was the breadbasket of Britain.

The central belt as mapped from these parameters stretches from Gloucestershire into Norfolk (apart from the Fens) and up to the Yorkshire Wolds.[48] The two wooded belts either side had little in common except, apparently, trees, and by the 20th century the west was

Figure 1.10 The Jurassic plain, showing the distribution of Roman villas and the presence of woodland, c. 730–1086 (Roberts and Wrathmell 2002, Fig 3.11), overlaid with the zone of the
open two- and three-field system (between the lines; Simmons 2001, Fig 4.3).

largely devoted to dairy and the east to arable.[49] Thus in the Formative period, the area settled by the English was divided into two: the central belt, highly productive for cereals and grazing, stretched from Gloucestershire to the Wolds beyond the Humber and the eastern belt that stood between this and the North Sea. Between them these regions included all the most productive land in Britain and all the putative Anglo-Saxon kingdoms, except Bernicia and part of Mercia.

Productivity

Three basic earners can be proposed for the lowland zone: grain on open fields, cattle and sheep on pasture and woodland management.[50] Banham and Faith detect a 'cerealisation' process: spelt and bread wheat are grown in the Roman period; early Saxon settlers grow emmer and einkorn, but the emphasis is on barley, as in prehistoric times. In Middle Saxon England, bread wheat returns with rye and oats, perhaps indicating 'the spread of Mediterranean practices under the influence of the church'.[51] In emmer, einkorn and spelt, the edible protein is bound into glumes ('hulled') and must be pounded to realise the grain. Bread wheat is 'free-threshing': threshing releases the grain from the chaff. A basic mode of production applies: plant, harvest, dry out if need be, separate the grain from the straw by cutting and threshing, grind and mill the grain to make flour, mix the flour with water to make dough. At this point it can be baked on a flat grill to make flat pizza-like flans (bannocks). Or the dough can be encouraged to ferment with yeast and so expanded to produce an aerated loaf which is less dense, easier to digest and can go further.[52] To make beer, a grain, e.g. barley, can be spread out on a flat surface in the warm where it will begin to sprout (malt). The germination can be halted by toasting (toasted malt), then ground, pounded and boiled in water (making ale). Flavoured with some hedgerow plants, such as hops, to offset the sweetness, it became beer. It was left to ferment and after a few days contained enough alcohol to act as a preservative while being suitable for children (small beer; now 'mild'). Other batches were allowed to rest and ferment on their way to becoming stronger brews suitable to fuel midwinter and springtime celebrations. Wheat straw and hay was fed to the animals as fodder.[53]

In the uplands, cattle are run on different ground depending on whether they are being weaned (on the hills), fattened (foothills) or used for dairy (on the plain), each stage requiring the cows to graze at lower altitudes on richer grass.[54] Cattle were especially prized because they were an unmatched source of vital commodities in large quantities: milk, butter, cheese, beef, blood and leather. The leather hides made not only shoes and jackets but belts, straps, bridles for horses, bags, coverings for tables, beds and shields, tankards, water bottles, wineskins, thongs to lash buildings and cladding for boats.[55] The more delicate skins of calves and sheep were used to make the pages of illuminated manuscripts.[56] In the highland zone, the hide was the principal medium of currency until the 12th century (p. 652). While sea fish were a rare commodity until Formative 3, salmon and trout were available in the highland zones and eel, pike bream, perch, tench and carp (of which pike and perch are the most edible) in the lowland zone.[57] Sea fish only became a significant part of the diet from the 9th century, not only in Britain but in northern Europe more generally. Research by James Barrett and others showed that in Orkney marine diets were first seen among men buried with Viking grave goods but increased for both men and women in unaccompanied (probably Christian) burials of the 10th and 11th centuries. By the 11th century, there was a rising export market for dried fish.[58]

The woods supported a wide range of essential foods and materials. The distribution of native species was lime in the lowlands and oak and hazel on the uplands, with pine and birch on the highest or most northerly land.[59] By Formative times most of the wild wood had been cleared or managed, surviving only in patches. Managed woodland was farmed, offering wood pasture or parkland and a harvest of coppiced and pollarded trees producing rods of willow (osiers) for making baskets and hazel (wattle) for making animal-proof fences and infilling timber-frame buildings. Meanwhile, pigs ate the fungi and nuts on the forest floor. Charcoal-burners baked wood in slow-burning clamps to produce the fuel for the metalworkers. The timber itself was the basis of most manufacture. Katherine Woods, who recorded the rural crafts in England between the wars, noted how woodland was cared for and cultivated to produce a prodigious variety of objects from the appropriate wood[60] (Table 1.2). At that time, baskets, hurdles, handles, wheels, oars, chairs, pulleys, bowls, brooms, cabinets, tent pegs, buildings and boats were still being fashioned from willow, hazel, oak, ash, beech, chestnut and yew, by the hands of perhaps the last generation with a direct line of descent to first-millennium craftsmen. Every wood had its own character and competence, some to be split (oak planks), some to be chiselled (elm wheel hubs), some to be spun on a lathe (beech

Table 1.2 Character and use of British timbers (after Woods 1949)

Wood	Character	Use
Oak	Hard, strong, durable, resistant to water; can split longitudinally; gnarled grain	Frame buildings, joists, floors, ships (planking), carvings
Elm	Hard, heavy, tough, durable, does not split easily; twisted grain	Wheel hubs, ship's keels, pulley blocks, mallets, water-pipes; bowls and chair legs on lathe
Ash	Hard, tough, specially flexible; with straight grain	Handles, hafts, shafts, oars, barrel hoops; pegged tools; hay rakes, ladders; scythe sneads
Alder	Soft, weak, perishable when dry; durable under water	Revetments; platters
Birch	Tough, moderately hard, fine grained; specially good for turning	Lathe-turned vessels and legs, furniture; Besom, brooms [twigs]; bark for making boats, writing
Beech	Soft, brittle, prone to warp and woodworm	Lathe-turned vessels and chair legs; hay rakes, ladders, tent pegs
Chestnut	Soft and open, easy to cleave, withstands weather	Posts, fencing; substitute for walnut and fruit woods in cabinet making
Willow	Soft and straight grained; shaves into thin strips and cultivates into wands or osiers	Basket making
Hazel	Only the young growths are usable	Baskets, thatching spars
Yew	Technically a softwood, but heartwood is hard, close-grained and flexible	Bows

bowls), some to be steamed and bent into shape (ash scythe handles or sneads). Trees, like animals, were still part of the world's mysterious and inexhaustible beneficence, consoling the mind as well as arming the hand.

Surveys of wild plants were conducted during World War II in anticipation of starvation by siege. Members of my generation will recall nettle soup and be familiar with rosehip syrup, a sticky source of vitamin C, and chewy 'radio malt' eaten with a spoon. Marmite, from the dredging of brewers' barrels, is also a legacy from those days. Hedgerows offered numerous varieties of edible berry; the woods were full of fungus, a surprising number of species being safe to eat. Other surveys have broadened the range: 112 plant species have been recorded in Polish cooking since the 18th century, including two green vegetables and 15 species of fruit.[61]

Plants eaten or used in some way in the Formative period have been more directly recorded from archaeological excavations, most vividly from anaerobic sites where plant fibres were preserved as well as seeds. Species preserved in a 10th-century midden under Durham City included flax, blackberries, raspberries, sloes, plums, apple and fat hen (a precursor to the introduction of spinach from Asia). Plants thought to have been collected for their medical properties (being mentioned in herbals) included the opium poppy, yarrow, meadowsweet, self-heal, buttercup and wild radish.[62]

Agricultural strategies

The rural economy was adjusted to suit the natural properties of the land. Cattle herding and dairy products were the staple of the uplands, grain of the central lowlands and wood pasture of the east and west lowlands, but such simplification masks a number of significant and ingenious variants. Grain/sheep combinations suit acid sand, like Suffolk, where the crop is rotated between fields or strips and the sheep are folded on those that are lying fallow. In some areas, such as the Breckland, farming practice appears continuous with that of the Roman predecessors, perhaps because there was no other way of making the sandy soil work.

Farming in southern and eastern Britain experienced 'a general direction of travel': in Formative 1, farmsteads with small rectangular fields ploughed with an ard grew hulled cereals, emmer, einkorn and barley, but livestock was likely the principal resource. Animals, domestic or wild, were grazing in large numbers – sufficient to prevent Roman fields from re-afforesting. Formative 2 saw the reintroduction of free-threshing bread wheat and the expansion of arable land into heavier soils worked by ploughs with mould boards. The new fields were often strip cultivation, equitably allocated. Animals were now more closely associated with the settlements, so their dung could be collected to fertilise the fields. Oxen for drawing the plough were part of the livestock contingent. Cows and sheep were milked, and wool began its career as a cash commodity. Since this was a gradual process governed by opportunity, dispersed farmsteads and strip fields do not show a regional preference but survive where the evolutionary process stopped. In some places the process may have continued by the late formative into the highly organised, high-earning open-field farms served by nucleated settlements.[63]

The archaeological implication is that once we leave aside the inferences of later mapping, the forms of settlement and their agricultural landscapes are mostly still to be determined for the Formative period in every region of England, Scotland and Wales. While a confection of medieval evidence gives us a plan like Wheldrake, we are excavating in a period in which no settlement plan is complete, and the parts we have of one settlement rarely resemble any other[64] (Chapter 3). The benchmark for early medieval settlement in the western archipelago is now provided by Ireland, with 47,000 known sites, 900 of them excavated. In Britain, the number of comprehensible settlements is scarcely out of single figures.

Nevertheless, dated tree pollen does confirm the existence of a relatively treeless central belt by the 5th century, which persisted in a reduced area, including Norfolk and the Vale of York in the 6th to 9th centuries and expanded into the western belt in the 9th to 11th centuries.[65] In a sample area of southern England, some corroboration for these generalities of production has been recently obtained by analysing animal bone and charred grain recovered from excavations.[66] Cattle, sheep, pigs, wheat, oats, barley and rye occurred in most samples, but there were discernible trends: cattle did best on heavy soils in river valleys; sheep on chalk and limestone upland, pigs on Jurassic clay equated with woodland. Oats grew well in wet areas and dominated in the south-west: the one site examined had oats at 91%. Rye grew on heathland, barley on the chalk, while wheat dominated the boulder clay and Jurassic clay. Some chronological trends were observed: by Formative 3, cattle had declined as a proportion of livestock to 40% and wheat dominated the cereal output, leaving oats in the river valleys and barley on the chalk. The analysis went on to explore the later medieval assemblages in the same area, finding a good correlation with the regional and chronological patterns known from documents, so lending support to the interpretations of the early medieval period.[67] The sample area was confined to East Anglia, the Thames valley and the south-west of England, and variations were studied against surface geology: clays, chalk and limestone, river valleys, marsh.[68] Animal bone assemblages and charred grains provided the data, which was recovered from excavations (especially by commercial archaeology) up to 2013. The numbers of taxa from sites of each period were uneven: 67 livestock and 42 cereals in Formative 1; 15 livestock and 9 cereals in Formative 2 and 19 livestock and 17 cereals in Formative 3.[69]

Within these differing levels of confidence, it seems safe to suppose that a central belt of lowland England, including Norfolk and the Vale of York, offered the best arable in Britain, exploited by the Romans and then by the Angles who entered via The Wash; and it was in this zone that most progress had been made towards an open field system by the start of the middle ages. The implication is that during the Formative era there was a steady lifting from subsistence and mixed farming to the commodification of wheat as a taxable cash crop, something which perhaps had its impetus in the reforms of the 7th/8th century (pp. 16, 303n.). This general trend was favoured or restricted by the symbiotic relationships between livestock and crops and their underlying geology and topology. Farmers still exercised varied and appropriate strategies: wetlands were colonised with a range of open and enclosed fields and nucleated or dispersed settlements. This variety of initiatives on the same terrain 'can only be due to social agency'.[70]

The social forces created, or aligned with, different kinds of community, drawing another distinction between upland and lowland and also between the earlier and later part of the formative period. A herd of cows can be led to milking and back to pasture by a child with a stick; a flock of sheep can be managed by a child and a dog. Pigs look after themselves until they are slaughtered. Whatever the landscape and its resources, livestock husbandry is a much smarter choice for a small independent group than the cultivation of fields, making better use of a family and freeing up the adults to make artefacts or make trouble.[71] By contrast, arable enslaves. The sequence of settlement deduced at Witton (Norfolk) began as small-scale cultivation in Fm 1, which doubled in Fm 2 and again in Fm 3, presumably at the expense of pasture. One explanation might be that more grain was needed to meet obligations of tribute or tax. But the change in the livestock/arable balance might alternatively reflect an increase in the population, itself a result of farming success. At the least, the way the land was farmed implies a changing mood from Formative 1–3, in which a life of herding and hunting was gradually replaced with one of commodification of crops and land management, where production was maximised and profit monetarised. The distribution of soils and climate meant that this process was largely confined to England south of the Yorkshire Wolds, leaving the uplands of England, Scotland and Wales to maximise an animal-based economy and to hold on tight to the freedoms that went with it. The differences in the soils had a long legacy.[72]

Bread, meat, milk, butter, cheese, apples, hedgerow and woodland fruits, beer and cider were the staples on which early British communities were built, and were theoretically in reach of all. On these one could live well. If some fed on largely on dough and others on blood, neither party starved. Luxuries, principally wine and olive oil from the Mediterranean, were not needed and anyway available only to a few. Economists assume that people are eager for such things and led by demand. However, there is no necessary advantage of wine over beer and cider or oil over butter, and imports will have been driven, initially, by a strong political imperative associated first with Rome, then with Christianity (the rituals of which required them) and latterly (from the 8th century) with both. Thus, wine and oil are players in a different part of the story (Chapter 2–5).

Entry points

So Britain was, is, a heterogeneous space surrounded by three disconnected sets of neighbours – Scandinavian, Irish, French – across three seas – the North (or German) Sea, the Irish Sea and the Channel. One way of determining the way a map has come about over the *longue durée* is to start with the least moveable elements and build on them. In this case the least moveable are the mountains and the sea and, although these are not exactly static, the courses of the main rivers. This provides the stage setting, the template on which humans and animals can exercise their urge to move. The movement creates routes and the routes create settlements; the settlements develop regions.[73] This may be an odd principle to accept and will not be true always and everywhere, but it is implied at a primitive level: animals make routes to follow food, humans follow them; humans settle where animals gather or drink or routes cross; regions develop where settlements are strong. This groups the 'natural' explanations together without excluding the rogue effects of war, ethnicity and religion that can overpower them, at least momentarily. In this chapter we are exploring the chains of nature and so should be content to drift a little in the navigable streams and linger on the tracks, well aware that more furious chariots will bear down on us in later chapters.

In the early middle ages, all three seas could be easily crossed, as we have seen, with some natural advantage to the Scandinavians arriving at the east coast, and the shorter crossing points at the straits of Dover and the Irish North Channel marking thoroughfares where ferries still run. Winds and tides encouraged a clockwise periplus from Cornwall to east coast Ireland to the Hebrides and the Orkneys, and from Orkney down the east coast to Kent. This is not inescapable, but in an age of boats it would encourage interaction along each coast, in general pulling the Irish north and the Picts south. In an age of boats, travel along the east and west coasts and across to their nearest maritime neighbours is also more attractive and more practical than travel overland between the two coasts. This division of the island into two regions with their backs to each other facing different seas is accentuated by its topography, which essentially divides it into two, lengthways along a Pennine watershed that separates east-draining from west-draining rivers. Travellers coming to Britain by sea, even well-armed invaders, well-motivated monks or well-capitalised merchants, will have an incentive to develop their projects within the half they land in.

Rivers

The eastern half of this frontier zone is entered by a number of well-signed estuaries: Moray Firth, Tay, Forth, Tyne, Tees, Humber, Wash, Thames. In many cases the rivers will lead them far into the interior. On the western side the points of entry are fewer – Clyde, Solway, Lune, Ribble and Mersey – but include one of the most significant: the Avon-Severn. On the western seaboard the landing places are numerous: a sea of numerous opportunities, hard to control, regulate or restrict. For light boats, travel is eased by the large number of islands and the narrow isthmus where boats can be dragged across, providing a short cut (a portage) between laborious sea voyages. Some of those that saw most use have the place-name *Tarbat* (G. *tairbearht*; pull-across). With one exception all the *tarbats* are on the west side; the Great Glen provides a serious throughway from east to west, Inverness to Iona, saving weeks at sea.[74]

Travel by river must always have been the oldest and most reliable method of crossing land. Looking now at a weed-choked stream or muddy channel canalised by floodbanks and drained for irrigation, it is hard to imagine the extent of inland waterways that must have once covered Britain and their capacity for creating arterial highways and communities from those that shared them. In France, regions still proclaim shared valleys (*Seine et Oise*); in Britain this is masked by later attempts to unite territory around the towns that administered them. That does not prevent us from noticing the obvious importance of the Severn/Avon, the Thames valley, the Trent or the Tyne in the creation of communities in the Marches, the Midlands or Northumbria. In 'Why Wessex?' Andrew Sherratt showed how three rivers, each called Avon, provided a short cut between the Bristol Channel and the (French) Channel, with Stonehenge at its nodal point (Figure 1.11).[75] Similarly, Gordon Noble showed that the monumentally endowed Upper Clyde valley was a nodal high point connecting the Irish Sea via the Clyde, the Solway Firth via the Nith and the North Sea via the Tweed.[76] A river system irrigated early medieval society in more ways than one. If these 'natural' arteries that encourage trade and marriage are thwarted, then we have some specific impedance to search for and explain.

Trackways

Quiet incest flourished where roads were bad.

Laurie Lee[77]

Ancient natural tracks such as The Ridgeway have long been cited as part of a prehistoric infrastructure. They can certainly be brought into the service of the formative period where there is evidence for it, although mainly for foot and horse, and the river network, which required little organised upkeep for carriage, must surely take pride of place.[78] The

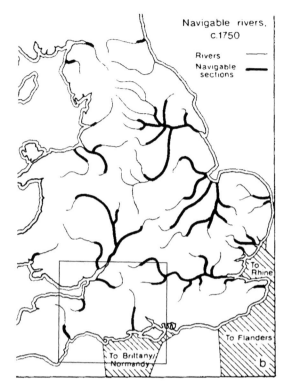

Figure 1.11 Navigable rivers and (Right) the Stonehenge shortcut.
(Sherratt 1996, Fig 2b, 3b; permission granted through RightsLink)

Romans used the rivers but also provided a road system, initially for the rapid movement of armies and scouts and latterly for the use of merchandise. In theory they could have neutralised the east/west divide but never quite managed it. The westward routes run out in Wales, the south-west and the north-west. Only in the east does the metalled road trickle on into Fife.

There were some level land routes connecting east and west, very few and so very important. One of these was bequeathed by the Romans themselves: Hadrian's Wall connecting Tynemouth to Solway. Others are prehistoric and well tried: the Loch Ness route runs along the Fault between the northern and eastern highlands, a sea passage from the Moray Firth to the River Ness, Loch Ness, Loch Lochy and sea-Loch Linnhe. In Columba's day, some portage would be needed between Loch Lochy at Invergarry and Fort Augustus on Loch Ness. When the Scots began to penetrate into eastern Scotland in the 6th/7th century, their principal routes appear to have been out of Argyll via Strathearn to Perth, via Loch Tay to Aberfeldy or from Mallaig via Lochaber, Loch Rannoch and Tummel into the Pictish heartland at Pitlochry (the 'road to the isles'). This pioneering route required a chain of fortified houses all the way. The Forth-Clyde route, now a twisted cable of railways, roads and motorways, was the main connection between the Britons of Strathclyde and those of *The Gododdin*; the rivers met at the Stirling gap.

South of the Peak district, the Trent runs round to join the Humber and Ouse north of Scunthorpe. The source of the Trent in Biddulph Moor, just north of Stoke on Trent, is only

5 miles south of the Dane/Weaver river that leads to the Mersey. This was the arterial route that connected Northumbria with Mercia and Mercia with the north-west British territories. This system was later all joined together as a navigable throughway for narrow boats linking the ports of Liverpool and Hull. The upper Trent, Warwickshire Avon and upper Thames lie relatively close together; if they do not facilitate travel, they do not inhibit it. In the south the barriers between east and west become the Severn and the foothills of Wales, the Mendips and Exmoor.

There have been a number of attempts to see ancient trackways in the maps of today, which may or may not be validated as relevant to the early middle ages by archaeology one day.[79] One of the more suggestive is the system of drove roads, whereby cattle were collected from the highlands to be sold off to the south. Using a combination of field survey, documentary references in the Edinburgh libraries and contact with some of the last drovers then living, A.R.B. Haldane compiled a map that showed drove roads from north and north-west (including the isles) converging on Inverness and Fort Augustus and thence threading through the Highlands east and west via strath and glen to converge on the Stirling Gap and unite at Falkirk ('The Falkirk Tryst'). This was the main exit from cattle country. The successive sites of the Falkirk Tryst were Polmont, Roughcastle and Stenhousemuir. From Falkirk a single delivery route ran over the Pentland Hills to Romannobridge, thence into England east to the Tyne or west via Carlisle.[80]

The drove roads as recorded belong to the 18th and 19th century and represent the apogee of a long history of cattle breeding, cattle trading and cattle raiding. Assuming that cattle, beef and hides represent the gilt-edged economy of the highland zone, the struggle was to gain control of the profit or at least not lose it all on the journey to the southern markets. An attempt at regulation in the 12th century under the Scottish king William the Lion included the branding of cattle, and the sale of beef was prohibited without the hide. When the trade enters the history books, we can see that the numbers are large: Exchequer Rolls for 1378 show the number of hides being exported as nearly 45,000. Henry VIII raided the Borders in 1544 and stole 10,386 cattle and over 12,000 sheep.[81] The cattle could be taxed where they had to pass over bridges at Linton in East Lothian or Auchendinny Bridge at Glencorse, the only direct passages between Edinburgh and the south.[82] It was also easy pickings for the border rievers over whose territory this mass of livestock had to pass.

These routes were mostly for professionals.[83] Droving provided highlanders with employment in the summer months, and the drovers, like their near contemporaries in the American west, had an interest in delivering the cattle to the buyer. They bought the cattle, 50 to a drover, at local *trysts* and needed to sell them at a profit to get their fee. Many an obstacle lay between, loss of condition en route, the relentless rustling and the vacillating price on arrival. Drovers, like cowboys, were licenced to carry arms to protect their herds, and like cowboys became the subjects of romance and admired for their legendary stoicism. A late 18th-century assessment by Sir John Sinclair, quoted by Haldane, illustrates the almost aboriginal impact that the cattle-herding highlander made on the gentrified intelligentsia of the day:

> he has felt from his early youth all the privations to which he can be exposed in almost any circumstance of war. He has been accustomed to scanty fare, to rude and often wet clothing, to cold and damp houses, to sleep often in the open air or in the most uncomfortable beds, to cross dangerous rivers, to march a number of miles without stopping and with but little nourishment and to be perpetually exposed to the attacks of a stormy

atmosphere. A warrior, thus trained, suffers no inconvenience from what others would consider the greatest possible hardships, and has an evident superiority over the native of a delicious climate, bred to every indulgence of food, dress and habitation, and who is unaccustomed to marching and fatigue.[84]

The drovers are described as dressed in shaggy homespun tweeds with kilts showing bare thighs and half the leg. Their provisions consisted of oatmeal, onions, sheep's cheese and whisky; the cattle could also be bled and the blood mixed with onions and oatmeal to make a black pudding.

We now operate under the inky blanket of that raconteur of historic Scotland, Walter Scott, so it does not follow that the past can be seamlessly extrapolated backwards, so assuming that 'highlanders were always like this'; we shall see that they were better off in many ways a thousand years earlier. Nevertheless, a close association with cattle, the appreciation of cattle as a major source of wealth, the bleeding of cattle to make blood pudding, the long Scots miles and the ability to get through the night in the open on oatmeal and wake up with a plaid covered in dew or frost, these paint a picture both of intimate association with their land and of the differences prevailing between their land and that of the southerners.

Horses

The droveways also teach us that a multiplicity of routes could be known and leave little permanent mark on the landscape, in this case not even a string of settlements, since the cattle live outdoors. A map of the hosting of the clans, converging on Stirling, might follow similar routes without needing a single signpost. The signposts were in the memory. The options widen still further when the traveller was mounted on horse back, as many of the highland people of the formative period certainly were. If the hide boat and plank boat were the queens of the seaways, the horse was king of hill, dale and plain, opening up numerous short cuts over ridge and across col. An understanding of the beauty and movement of horses is most evident in Pictish Art, where they walk, trot and gallop across the landscape. Their size relative to riders and their long legs and delicate fetlocks show that these are not ponies but horses of perhaps 13–15 hands in stature (p. 397). We encounter horses in Anglo-Saxon art too, but very stylised, in the form of fighting stallions; and buried in Anglo-Saxon graves, where they are sturdy and robust. The horse was dressed up by the equestrian class with as much care as one of their own (Chapter 2, p. 99).

Other animals

The Picts also celebrated bulls, deer and dogs and depicted hunts and fights in which these were players. Man is a herd animal and has deep empathy with other herd animals led by alpha males: cattle, deer, wolves; their companionship explains how the officious and superstitious ways of small human groups could be made bearable, especially among the young. The Picts at least had byre-houses in which humans lived at one end and cattle or sheep the other (p. 212). The moods and poise of animals, their mating, births, milking, health and deaths for the common good were intimately interwoven with those of their human companions, creating relationships between mammals of emotional richness somewhat distant from that of a shopper taking a plastic packet from a supermarket fridge. One can see that Christian priests would have their work cut out weaning the unconverted, especially children, away from the companionship of their beloved calves and piglets and lambs and superseding it with the cerebral metaphor of the crib in which animals are displaced in importance by humans, divine or not. It may not be until the later formative period that children were successfully trained to accept Jesus as a lamb rather than lambs as divinity. By the 11th century, the teacher in Aelfric's colloquy asks the class: – *Why do you want to study?* – and they dutifully reply: *We don't want to end up like the brute beasts that think of nothing but grass and water.*[85] The real blessing is that, long before it knows about a religion, every child up to the present day continues to rediscover, unbidden, deep fellow-feelings for their animal companions.

Natural territories

There are 5,000 islands in the British/Irish archipelago, disposed over three seas. The nature of land and sea has dictated that the experiences offered will be different, north and south, east and west, in climate, in productivity, in ease of communication. Is this unfair to the occupants? Does it skew history? The answer is yes, but only if the expectation is of a united land with a single history, a political artifice that actually lay several centuries in the future for the formative people. Archaeologists as well as historians have, one might argue, started their history at the wrong end, with Britain as part of a united kingdom, selling its story to an enormous English-speaking diaspora in the American, Australian and other continents. But what if the differences *were* the story? What if the extraordinarily wide range of terrain and maritime spaces offered us a laboratory to examine how people, language, wheat and cattle can produce quite different, if complementary, results in contiguous territory? In this case the 'formative process' will be different in each case and may have a different outcome. As we will see, the 'state' is not to be the destiny of all parts of this island. To force them, and north-west Europe in general, into that mould is to miss the interest and perhaps enlightenment that lies in political experiment.

That is for future chapters to convince. An important task in this one is to propose, define, group, justify and name the natural areas of the British island that seem to have shared a common experience. This will always be risky because it will appear to be defining these areas by their current cultural and even demographic identity, the very thing we are trying to escape. For the regions on land, the first defining attribute must be natural: topography, productivity, communication and, as this chapter has tried to demonstrate, natural differences matter. In this case, the principal dividers are the mountains and the river drainage, things that naturally reinforce each other. The result is to divide the island into seven parts (Figure 1.12). These could be given some neutral names of geography, reflecting these divisions: The north-west of the island shares a broken hilly terrain, inundated by ancient seas, leaving numerous inlets and islands. The sea regime suggests that as well as including the Hebrides (the future 'Lordship of the Isles') it embraces the north coast and the isles of Orkney. We could include the Faeroes and Shetland too, since these are in the Gulf Stream corridor. This region thus runs from the isles to the Clyde, and for most of our period it is associated with the Scots and then the Norse. To the east lies the most fertile part of the Scottish peninsula, running in a north-south ribbon along the east coast, indented by Firths (Dornoch, Cromarty, Moray, Tay, Forth) and broad rivers attractive to salmon and trout. Wheat was grown as far north as the Dornoch Forth in the 7th century. This is Pictland, which endured throughout Formative 1 and 2 with one of the most distinctive, if short lived, cultural signals anywhere in Europe.

From the Clyde to the Mersey is a coastal region of rolling hills and forests, with major inlets at the Clyde, the Solway and the Mersey. At its centre is the Lake District and Cumbria. We shall characterise this as mainly British territory, include the Isle of Man and name it north-west England, although it had a Norse personality in Fm 3. Two peninsulas define the southern part of Britain, Wales between the Mersey and the Severn, which has remained culturally British to this day, and the south-west peninsula comprising Cornwall, Devon and most of Somerset, which was also 'Welsh' (foreign) in the eyes of the incoming English until they conquered it in Formative 3. In the 5th to 8th century it would have been possible to ride from Lands End to John O'Groats without ever leaving Celtic-speaking areas, but the variants, especially Welsh, Pictish and Scottish, were not necessarily mutually comprehensible.

On the east coast, from the Forth to the Humber is another land of rolling hills, Lothian, Northumberland and County Durham, with entry points at the Forth, Tweed, Tyne, Tees and Humber. The northern part (Bernicia) is culturally British throughout most of our period, but the southern part (Yorkshire) experiences a strong English and then a Danish presence. English interest in the Vale of York and the slopes of the Wolds (i.e. Deira) appears early. So that although Northumbria as a whole shares more of its culture with the British regions to the north and west (pp. 369, 522), the English element, the 'tail in the Vale', is a long-lasting and determinant Germanic influence. Northumbria will be seen to vary in its cultural emphasis through time and from north to south as British, Anglo-British, English, Danish and Anglo-Danish gain the upper hand: a primary hybrid area, which fused, with brilliant results.

South of the Humber-Mersey, the east and south of Britain forms a single block of low-land, with the Jurassic soils divided into three sweeps by escarpments (p. 14). This is the English plain, with entry points at the Humber (Trent), Wash, Deben/Orwell, Thames and Hamble. As will be noted in the study that follows, the equation between language, culture and nature is by no means perfect, since people move, expand, conquer, impose control and adopt each other's expressions. For much of Formative 1, this zone, referred to as 'South-umbria', is composed of numerous communities derived from different places across the North Sea, with a British substrate that is occasionally evident. In Formative 2, it begins to coalesce as a cultural entity and adopt a version of Christianity, although one distinct from that of Northumbria.

These arbitrary regions are shown on the left of Figure 1.12, together with their order of citation in the chapters that follow; and on the right the likely focus of the kingdoms and communities, whose names we know better than their locations: (1) *Argyll and the Hebrides (Scotland)*, (2) *Firthlands and northern isles (Pictland)*, (3) *North-west England (Cumbria, Lancashire)*, (4) *Western peninsula (Wales)*, (5) *South-western peninsula (Devon and Cornwall)*, (6) *Tweed to Humber (Northumbria)*, (7) *Jurassic plain (Southumbria)*.

This brief tour through Britain's physical geography will seem like a statement of the obvious to many Britons, but even they may be unaware of the severe distinctions that nature has drawn in the wealth of the land and ease of communication, as between the territories of the east and south of the island on the one hand and the north and west on the other. It is clear that these differences cannot be laid at the door of ethnicity. If we knew nothing about Romans, Britons, Angles, Saxons or Scots, if there had been no change in demography or culture for the previous millennia, these distinctions of relative advantage would still obtain. Some of this is evident from the experience of prehistory, which will make frequent appearances in the next four chapters and in the second half of this one.

Figure 1.12 (Left) The seven regions used in this book, showing (numbered) their normal order of citation in Chapters 2–5. (Right) The focal areas of documented kingdoms.

(FAS Heritage)

The prehistoric inheritance

Just as the formative era was played out on the uneven platform provided by nature, so its players were guided and inhibited by the cultural geography left by the previous inhabitants. This inheritance, like any other, contained a variety of legacies, some expected, some baffling. The first millennium population of Britain was itself derived from diverse origins, some very ancient and static, others – like the Romans, Angles or Scots – rather more recent. These survived and were passed on in a number of properties that formative people could not see or touch or sometimes could not even sense: language, music, a sense of kin. Their traces are still more elusive for us but are thought to have left an imprint on the modern country – placenames, DNA, folk culture.[86] The archaeology of previous peoples is more tangible, and its rich material sequence shows where ideas, if not peoples, held sway at different times: Mesolithic shell mounds, Neolithic passage graves, Bronze Age standing stones, Iron Age forts, Roman roads. Although we do not know how much of this monumental furniture could still be seen by the inhabitants of the first millennium, we can be sure it was not less than we can see now. The relict pattern is a real pattern, reflecting earlier territories, earlier clusters of allegiance.

If prehistoric and Roman monuments are to play a role in the making of the formative period, we need to know how significant they were then felt to be. Understanding responses to prehistoric monumentality has made giant strides in recent years, showing that the different regions of Britain not only had different sets of surviving monuments but behaved differently towards them. A certain indifference is to be expected in the case of the recent arrivals; the English who buried their dead in barrows also buried them in natural mounds showing that they had no precise memory of the landscape. The Scots who held their medieval courts on top of burial mounds also sited their *comhdhail* on natural hills.[87]

These observations have tended, in our sceptical age, to replace the general concept of a continuous and sentient response to the landscape with a perception of the reuse of prehistoric monuments as simply a legitimation exercise, in which the users exploited ancient monuments for political purposes in their own day.[88] But these things are likely to have a graduated rather than a single meaning, as has the idea of continuity itself. While the use of megalithic sites may be little removed from the use of any other quirky natural feature, in other cases, even in England, we must suspect a basic ability to read its vocabulary, along the lines of 'these mounds are burials and those in them are ancestors of the land, even if not ancestors of ours'. These gradations can help explain why reactions to monuments vary from place to place and through time. In certain examples we are entitled to assume that major monuments such as Stonehenge or Knowth always had some meaning for those that came afterwards; indeed, it can hardly be otherwise, since people are not the mental equivalent of grazing cattle. Although 'the proponents of ritual continuity are forced to make imaginative leaps across impossibly long periods of prehistoric time', this is still mental continuity of a kind, and different from the exploitation of an alien heap of stones for political purposes.[89] A case can be made that stone circles retained a meaning that mattered to those that hosted them, even if the meaning is elusive and made no use of conventional archaeological knowledge. This will bear on the question of why early Christianities varied.

The case for responses that betray closer understanding becomes stronger when we consider the more recent monuments, not megalithic, but those belonging to the Iron Age. The numerous prehistoric forts distributed over British hills can be assumed to have formed part of the formative theatre, at some time and in some way. Some at least of these sites and the practices that went with them can be legitimately constituted as living memory. Living memory becomes still more widely acceptable in the case of the Roman inheritance, as huge as it was reusable. This inheritance was at its most dense in the area subsequently occupied by the English, so even if these Germanic speakers had not themselves migrated they would have been immersed in a landscape of towns, villas and roads they could hardly ignore. For immigrants, the first landscape they encountered was mainly one of Roman fossilised affluence. It would be a sharp English eye that privileged the traces of a prehistoric country over those of an abandoned Roman province. Added to this intimate daily association was the rising European clamour for the return of Christian imperial Rome. In England, Rome rather than prehistory provided the ancient wisdom to emulate or reject. Responding to the past was not a brief phenomenon of the first formative decades. People went on doing it. If the pagan English of Formative 1 buried their dead in Bronze Age barrows, by Formative 3 these barrows had been demonised as the entrance to hell, fit only for felons. While Christianity in Formative 2 naturally brought to England a new dose of Rome, it can be argued that Christianity in the western and northern regions still had their fingers entwined with their own prehistoric practice.

Ancient memory: the early prehistoric inheritance

By 'ancient memory' I do not mean to imply that early medieval people actually remembered the early prehistoric period, only that prehistory had already structured the territory of the islands in a way that the first millennium occupants could recognise. The Mesolithic period, 10,000 years previously, probably left nothing that could be seen above ground except shell mounds, but it is interesting that modern knowledge of the Mesolithic period marks out the area of Ulster as a significant zone.[90] This is a sign that post-Pleistocene communities were already etching their own use-patterns on the natural theatre and so feeding long-term demography. Cummings claims loyalties to successive landscapes of the Mesolithic and Neolithic that demonstrate continuity between them, with specific forms of monuments matched to particular landscapes.[91] These ideas encourage us to believe that monuments and territories build together in a non-random way that maps associations of people with similar world views.

As suggested by their survival, megaliths, that is, large stone monuments of the Neolithic, occupy a particular zone. They are confined to Ireland and the west and north of Britain, and their distribution should indicate more than the availability of rocks or the use of the Gulf Stream: common origins from migration via the Atlantic coast, a region of shared belief or some mixture of the two.[92] Within these generalities, tomb-territories have been mapped: Clyde and Court tombs mark an area spread between Argyll and Ulster, pre-echoing our Dal Riada.[93] The passage graves cluster in the southern Irish Sea, connecting eastern Ireland, west Wales and SW. Chambered tombs in east Wales and Cotswold-Severn area and Wedge tombs in SW Ireland create other territories recognisable in the first millennium, since they are today.[94] If the early churches of Ireland develop regional styles, and these regions echo those of the tomb-territories 4,000 years earlier, this need not be a coincidence to be shunned with an irritated *pshaw*, but neither must they become obsessions of deep time pseudo-links. A great deal has yet to be discovered from DNA about static and mobile patterns of descendance at the regional scale. The landscape can have a DNA of its own into which successive peoples are inserted.

The stone circles also have a limited distribution, being notably sparse in the 'English' area. These have their subdivisions too, such as the groups in north and south Ireland and the recumbent stone circles of Aberdeenshire. These do not have to pre-echo first millennium cultural zones, or indeed create them. However, to disregard prehistoric territories that could be still easily seen seems unnecessarily coy on our part and assigns an unjustified insensitivity to formative people. We are on more shifting ground when making use of artefacts. The distribution of carved stone balls, apparently Neolithic in date, pre-empts the later Pictland no less precisely than its symbol stones[95] (Figure 1.13). The mutually exclusive distributions of stone circles and grooved ware suggested an east-west divide to Barry Cunliffe.[96] A north-south cultural divide also appears in the 8th century BC, suggested by the distribution of Gundlingen swords (most in Ireland, Britain, France) versus continued deposition of votive bronzes (southerly part of Ireland, SW Wales, SW, Armorica).[97] The distribution in this latter region pre-empts the pillar habit of the 5th–7th-century Britons. Which causes what is matter for debate and for much more investigation. But the long reach of geography should not be too readily dismissed.

Taking a tour through the megalithic, Iron Age and Roman inherited landscapes, in that order, does not imply that formative people knew their relative antiquity, although it would be arrogant to assume that they knew nothing. At the least, we can allow that they theorised on the origin and meaning of prehistoric monuments much as we do. Their knowledge depended on their familiarity with the monuments in question, which in turn depended on how long they and their ancestors had lived alongside them. Some indication of first-millennium attitudes can be gained from evidence of subsequent frequentation, reoccupation and reuse. In Ireland, Neolithic tombs and Bronze Age standing stones were used to

Figure 1.13 Distribution map of prehistoric ornamented carved stone balls (grey) and Pictish symbol stones (black).

(Author/FAS Heritage, drawing on Carver 1999; Edmonds 1992; Marshall 1977, 1983; McNeill and MacQueen 1996)

host early medieval burials. A cross was carved on the Findermore standing stone, a prehistoric monument located next to three ring barrows. Crosses were carved in the kerb stones of Neolithic passage grave at Lough Crew.[98] Knowth, a passage grave 85 m in diameter, was converted into a double-ditched ringfort in the 7th/8th century and used as a cemetery (Chapter 4, p. 438). The ditches were backfilled, incorporating a rich assemblage of early medieval animal bone.[99] In the 10th century the site was re-exploited as a settlement with 15 lozenge-shaped houses, nine souterrains and five metalworking areas. These three kinds of acknowledgement can indicate that the status of prehistory varied with time and politics. John Carey has made a good case that the type of Christianity that developed in Ireland in the 4th to 8th centuries was in close sympathy with the natural world and the ghostly residents of ancient monuments.[100] This line of reasoning is related not only to the reading of myth (Chapter 6) but the much later treatment of witches (relatively benign in Ireland in comparison to England).[101] Thus while crosses and burials at megalithic sites may relate one way of thinking with another, by the 10th century the colonisation of the site is more suggestive of topographical convenience.

In Scotland, early medieval Pictish symbols were etched onto stones belonging to prehistoric stone circles (Creichie) or standing stones (Edderton). The form of the standing stone monument was extensively borrowed into the Christian era, evolving into sophisticated forms such as the Irish high crosses, the Anglian Victory crosses and the Pictish cross slabs (Chapter 5). In the northern Borders, the 6th-century inscribed stone at Whitfield, Yarrow, is pre-empted by a prehistoric stone of similar form, a few hundred metres down the same valley (p. 501). The largest and most elaborate of the Christian standing stones are situated in the less Romanised areas, which suggests that it is the Bronze Age monuments, not the later Roman examples, which provided their basic potency. Exploitation of barrow sites was prevalent in Wales,[102] implying a 'British tradition of reuse with its roots in prehistoric practice'.[103] Here, the early medieval monuments may occasionally involve the actual reuse of a prehistoric standing stone, but proven instances are rare.[104]

In England, the practice of burying early medieval people in prehistoric monuments became widespread, although in the majority of cases the monument used was the Bronze Age barrow.[105] By contrast, Semple finds that 'examples of 5–7th century burials associated with standing stones or stone circles are . . . virtually non-existent',[106] although extant stone circles are themselves rare in the eastern 'English area', where such monuments may have been fashioned out of timber and were no longer visible. They are however present in Wiltshire, where the 80% of early medieval burials associated with prehistoric monuments mostly targeted round barrows. None was associated with Roman remains, and few were associated with standing stones or henges. In East Yorkshire 70% of the early medieval burials were positioned in relation to prehistoric monuments, with a majority on the southern slopes of the Wolds. In Sussex, 60% of the secondary burials were in round and long barrows. A fondness for barrow burial was manifested in two phases, one in the 5th/6th century AD and one in the 7th, when the inhabitants themselves built barrows *de novo*. This leaves open the question of what was intended by the choice. Sarah Semple's study suggests that there was more to it than gravediggers attracted by easy digging; there were 'perceptions' of the past. Although modern authors hasten to assure us that ethnicity was not relevant, the interpretation depends on how the burial party is tacitly identified. If these were 'Anglo-Saxons', then the argument that a burial rite has been imported has some substance.[107] Mounds were prevalent in the landscape of Jutland and north Germany, just as they are in the pages of *Beowulf*. However the immigrant community is deemed to be composed, Britons are also present in the community, and perhaps especially in Wiltshire, where the first documented kings of Wessex have British names. In this case, rather than importing a ritual, burial parties recognised barrows as ancestral resting places and added to them. In either event, the reuse of prehistoric monuments is thought to signal advanced levels of cognition.

This thesis is strengthened by the changing patterns of use. In Fm 1, there is secondary burial, mainly in round barrows. In Fm 2 the secondary association (where there is one) is with the more monumental barrows, but from the late 6th century to the late 7th the English (i.e. the Anglo-Britons in the English region) are building high status barrows of their own. From the 8th century to the 10th, the secondary burials are of quite a different type, namely victims who fell foul of new laws and were executed by hanging or decapitation. These have been interpreted as judicial punishment but with a strong element of Christian damnation.[108] These new perceptions of the prehistoric burial mound belong to the late formative period, when Christianity is exercising its power as an exclusive ideology:

> it can be no coincidence that in the same era that such monuments were becoming synonymous with demons and monsters and hellish connotations, they were put to new purpose as *cwealmstow* or killing places for the execution of felons, the display of their remains and the interment of their bodies.[109]

Of 27 known execution sites, 13 are associated with mounds or barrows of various date, eight with linear earthworks and three with hillforts.[110] Good examples of the changing attitude of English communities to the prehistoric mounds and their reflection of the contemporary zeitgeist are provided by the sequences at Wasperton (3rd–7th century) and Sutton Hoo (6th to 11th century) (Chapter 4).

Living memory: the Iron Age inheritance in Ireland

In the less Romanised areas of the isles there is likely to have been a stronger link of understanding between the early middle ages and the preceding Iron Age past. The next group of monuments, dating from the Iron Age, can claim a closer kind of association with their early medieval successors in Ireland and in west and north Britain than in England. One reason could be that the English, being post-Roman immigrants, had no particular association with the British Iron Age and little need to acknowledge it, in comparison with the more evident Roman inheritance. But another might be the lack of prominent hillforts in an area poorly furnished with steep hills. It is possible that even in the Romanised area there are sites in which early medieval people made direct reference to Iron Age predecessors, and if England were to experience the kind of large-scale investigation that the National Roads Authority gave to Ireland, it would open the door to discoveries of this kind.

The study has received a continuing impetus from Ireland's rich inheritance of stories that seem to refer to its own heroic Iron Age; this equation has been called into question (p. 605), but in combination with a 20th-century political imperative to equip the independent country with a richer past, the exploration of named sites has been irresistible.[111] The early 9th century, *Félire* named four great pagan royal cult centres and explained that they had been superseded by four great Christian monasteries: Tara by Armagh, Rathcrogan by Clonmacnoise, Ailem (Dún Ailinne) by Kildare and Emain Macha (Navan Fort) by Glendalough (Chapter 6, p. 606). Although there could hardly be a more attractive blueprint for the investigation of ideological change, there are two persistent problems. Firstly, the assumption that these are the only four candidates. Brian Lacey also cites Rath Bécc (Rathvilly) and finds three more cult high places and their hinterlands in Donegal.[112] Secondly, there is the difficulty of recognising the Irish Iron Age on the ground and distinguishing it from the preceding Bronze Age and succeeding early medieval cultures.[113] There are some candidates: a cluster of monuments in the area of Uisneach in County Westmeath included a ceremonial enclosure 50 m across of 5th/6th century date, which was then incorporated (while still visible) into a ringfort 90 m across in the 7th/8th century.[114] Teltown, County Meath, was documented as an assembly place of the Uí Neíll kings during the festival of Lugnasad at least from the 6th century. Here there was an earthwork originally 100 m long, with radiocarbon dates in the 7th/5th century BC, the 7th/8th century AD and the 9th/10th century AD.[115] These examples constitute a manner of successive exploitations of a central place.

The late Iron Age central place would appear to have been a circular enclosure up to 50 m across with an adjacent mound: the Rath of Kings and Rath of the Synods at Tara were such enclosures;[116] more than 60 monuments are visible from the Rathcrogan mound (dated 4000 BC), which was succeeded by an early medieval ringfort with a souterrain inside;[117] at Navan a building of concentric wooden posts 40 m across was constructed in 95 BC;[118] at Dún Aillinne the excavators defined a timber circle 42 m in diameter;[119] and an isolated example was found on a road scheme at Lismullin, County Meath.[120] While none of these was directly succeeded by churches, their form was moderated into the 7th century. Their true successors, as Oengus states, will have been the monastic foundations coming into force in the later 7th or early 8th century, although at new sites. But the continuous potency of a ritual site can be acknowledged in subtle ways. The deposition of early medieval brooches in wetland contexts at Knowth, Newgrange and Tara has been seen as a continuation of Iron Age votive practice.[121] Women are recorded as offering their jewellery on Christian altars as a successor ritual.[122] Betty O'Brien has shown how in Irish burial, Iron Age to early medieval ancestral continuity took precedence over the effects of Christian conversion.[123] A recent example has been excavated at Ardsallagh I (County Meath), where 30 inhumations of 5th–7th century date were laid in a penannular ring ditch containing cremations of the Bronze and Iron Ages.[124]

The Iron Age inheritance in Ireland may be elusive, but it shows certain repeating signs in the immediate pre-Christian period: large circular palisaded or banked enclosures, massive figure-of-eight constructions, burial grounds, often with Bronze Age or Neolithic predecessors, and some use at least up into the Roman Iron Age. In addition to being celebrated in early medieval literature (see Chapter 6), these sites survived as clusters of monuments and spaces evoking assemblies, musters, hostings, sporting events and a feeling of ancient and inherited centrality. They have yet to be excavated at a large scale, in comparison with the early first-millennium central places and cult sites of Scandinavia (see p. 284), but a similar role in a socially flat society dominated by spirituality can probably be envisaged. The rise to prominence of the fighting kings would follow in the post-Roman Formative 1, with another strong wind of spirituality ready to blow in thereafter.

In Britain

Analogous Iron Age references can be seen among the Scots, Picts and Welsh, if less strongly signalled. Dunadd is an early medieval fort with a prominent symbolic role overlooking the long-used prehistoric monumental centre at Kilmartin Glen. The Picts also built strongholds in the lee of former Iron Age hillforts (Chapter 3, 186). A first cult site has been identified at Rhynie in Aberdeenshire, where a tall palisade surrounds a timber hall and pits containing incinerated ox bone. Nine Class I symbol stones are associated with the valley leading to the site.[125] For some, these stones with their distinct geometric and animal symbols are inspired by Roman art.[126] For others, the Pictish forms are revivals of Iron Age art and the symbols themselves, featuring caricatures of Iron Age objects and an iconography of mainly local animals, have roots in the pre- Roman, pre-Pictish Iron Age, where they replace grave goods with their images.[127] Pictish long cist graves, some under mounds that may be round or square, begin before the arrival of Christianity and may even refer back to the shorter slab-sided burials that are Bronze Age in date.[128] Similar early medieval burial rites in Wales are unproven regarding their religious affiliation but often focus on prehistoric monuments. The use of stone linings, often rather peremptory, is also found sparsely scattered in the English region, where it has seen as commemorating Britons or aligned to British practice (Chapter 4, p. 330).

Inherited language

Bede reports five separate languages being spoken in Britain (in the 8th century): Old English, Old Irish, Welsh, Pictish and Latin.[129] The Latin-speaking Augustine required an interpreter, obtained among the Franks, to communicate with the English.[130] The Irish cleric Aidan used King Oswald as his interpreter when he arrived in Northumbria.[131] Agilbert, an Irish-speaking Frank, asked Wilfred to present the case for the Roman party to the English at the Synod of Whitby rather than use an interpreter, something that members of the Irish party had also found necessary.[132] Columba needed an interpreter to preach to the Picts and to convert two young men on Skye, who were presumably Picts at that date.[133] Welsh and Pictish are listed as two separate languages by Bede but are currently thought to represent two branches of p-Celtic on the basis of placenames, kings' names and ogham inscriptions.[134] There is still a persistent but unconsummated desire to give the Picts a more exotic origin, preferably one that is not Indo-European.[135] Recent analysis of the river names cited by Ptolemy found 41 to be of Celtic extraction, with the remaining six not Indo-European, all of them in north-east Scotland, which is 'indeed what one might expect on the far edge of an island on the far edge of Europe'.[136] According to Sims-Williams,

> There is nothing un-Celtic about the ogam inscriptions in Ireland or Wales, but Scotland is different. Though it is fashionable for scholars to ignore it, a non-Indo-European language does seem to be visible in the inscriptions of Scotland, which have never convincingly been interpreted as Celtic.[137]

However, as we will see, the archaeology of Pictland favours an interpretation, presenting a people who are close to its preceding Iron Age and remain artistically affiliated to the other enduring British areas in Strathclyde, Wales and south-west Cornwall.[138]

Jackson's classic analysis of the British languages concluded that, in spite of the laboured discussion of religious matters between the peoples, there was very little permanent linguistic cross-fertilisation. His famous river map is held to show the relabeling of the landscape by the English immigrants in the 5th and 6th century. Going from east to west, in his Area I Brittonic names are confined to major rivers; in Area II, more small rivers retain their British names, especially between Tees and Tyne. In Area III, Brittonic names are common including those of mere streams; this area corresponds to the later expansion of the English in the 7th and 8th century, in which renaming was no longer an imperative. Area IV (Cornwall and Wales) has only British names, implying the use of Brittonic speech until the Norman conquest or later.[139]

The presence of Britons in the 'English' zones is not thereby linguistically excluded, since physical cross-fertilisation is likely. Placenames suggest surviving British enclaves in Bernicia, the Pennines, the North York Moors, the Chilterns, the heath and forests of West Sussex and Essex, and in the Fens.[140] Intermarriage, including at the highest level, as in Wessex and Lindsey, led to the naming of children in both languages.[141] This is likely to have increased as hostility eased and differences blurred in the third century of English occupation (see Chapter 4). But British seems to have had no effect on English, and vice versa.[142]

According to Jackson, Latin remained a formulaic language, kept at arms' length by all insular parties. He reports that there is no evidence for the survival of spoken Latin in the lowland regions once the [Roman] army had gone and the Saxons had come, but equally, 'no-one suggests that Latin was widely spoken in the Highland zone'.[143] The English borrowed many words from Latin but virtually none from British – a paradoxical situation explained as a lack of common interests,[144] although it also endorses the argument for an apartheid (Chapter 2). The verdict would seem to be that the languages of Britain remained distinct, but that did not inhibit intermarriage, trade, religious debate and the contest of arms. In each of these, the passions of shared experience could potentially generate creative new forms of expression: this is certainly what happened in the realm of material culture. Language, like landscape, does not by itself change quickly and may not change for long. In this sense, the peoples of Britain still spoke their Iron Age languages throughout the Formative period and still remember some of them today.

Religious practice (and other relics)

A number of early medieval practices traditionally thought to be Christian, or at least Roman imports, are betraying signs of origins within the Iron Age or some even older inheritance. Votive deposits are clearly part of the Irish, British and Scandinavian pre-Roman world. Wet places are preferred, but caves and mounds also provide portals to the underworld. Regarded as points of access were lakes, wells, groves, hills and tumuli and the royal stronghold; but not the sea, so far as we know.[145] Finds of weapons in rivers is seen as emulation of the practice in early medieval Britain, and particularly impressive is the long-term magnetism of the River Witham in Lincolnshire, where votive deposits seem to have moved from the river to the monastery as late as the 13th century.[146] The cult of relics has been long claimed as a Roman import but was already recognised as 'not specifically Christian' by Charles Doherty.[147] New work has found examples of the hoarding of body parts in the Neolithic and the Bronze Age, as at Cladh Hallan in South Uist, where skeletons, some composite, were kept in a bog and reburied in a house after an interval of 500 years.[148] The relationship to ancestor cults is self-evident, and a transfer of attention from the curation of revered ancestors to heroes and then saints is to be expected. The use of relics recorded in the early medieval period included the curing of ailments by touching, their perambulation to bring rain or ward off disaster, the winning of battles by ensuring the remains of a saint/hero was on hand to give advice and stiffen backbone.[149] It would be eccentric to regard this ethos as a Mediterranean import, and it sits uneasily within contemporary Christian doctrine as outlined by Bede.[150] A less tortuous argument would cite the role of Christian relics as evidence for the survival of a previous non-Christian anthropologically validated belief system.[151]

The visiting of relics or of holy places was also probably a legacy of prehistory. The routes traced in the Dingle peninsular are prehistoric in origin but emerge in the early middle ages as routes favoured by pilgrims.[152] Andrew Sherratt's 'Avon route', which provided a short cut from the Bristol Channel to the south coast, had Stonehenge as its pivotal point and stopping place, seen in its most recent interpretations as a centre for Neolithic and Bronze Age worship and healing.[153] Gordon Noble mapped henge-based itineraries for Dunragit and Kilmartin Glen and defined an Upper Clyde monumental cluster that provide a pivotal landmark for a route from Clydeside to the south coast and east coast via the Nith and Tweed respectively. He also noted that henge monuments cluster along the same routes as the modern main roads.[154] Here the henge monuments, the river routes and the sacred are packaged in a travellers' formula that combines a sense of geographical, cultural and spiritual direction that pilgrims of all faiths and none would recognise today. Whatever the specious explanations of early medieval and later commentators, neither preacher nor audience could escape the thud of the prehistoric heartbeat.

Other deep roots are suspected to lie behind early medieval religious schisms. The conflict of practice between the western and eastern churches that came to a head at the Synod of Whitby had a geographical distribution that echoed the east-west divides of prehistoric monuments. The Synod focussed on the form of the tonsure worn by monks and the date of the Spring Festival (Easter). The Roman tonsure (in the form of a dinner plate) was contrasted with the Celtic tonsure, where the hair was shaven forward of a line drawn from ear to ear, exposing the bare forehead of the thinker. This is claimed as the form of haircut worn by the druids and thus an inheritance from the Iron Age.[155] Differing opinions on the date of Easter are also distributed geographically as an echo of prehistoric monuments, in this case stone circles (see p. 28). The two modes of calculation are usually explained by different scholarly access to Mediterranean sources, each imported at different times into Ireland and Britain respectively. That may be so, but this would hardly explain the geographical division in an age of high clerical mobility. At the 664 Synod, Aidan, champion of the Celtic cause, remarked: 'The Easter customs which I observe were taught me by my superiors, who sent me here as a bishop; and *all our forefathers*, men beloved of God, are known to have observed these customs'.[156] Admittedly *omnes patres nostri* – could mean church fathers rather than forefathers, and Colman was unlikely to bring forward an argument based on prehistoric rituals at a church synod. More appropriately to the meeting, he claimed authority from St John the Apostle and Anatolius. His adversary Wilfrid retorted that the Columban church followed neither John nor Anatolius and that 'the only people who stupidly contend against the whole world are these Scots and their partners in obstinacy the Picts and the Britons, who inhabit only a portion of these, the two uttermost islands of the ocean'.[157]

A similarly intemperate attitude to the relevance of prehistory prevails among some Christians and early medieval scholars today. Our archaeological instruments of inference are weaker and less precise but entitled to be tabled. It is no longer controversial that stone circles had a calendrical function and were used to calculate pivotal moments of the year, of which the onset of spring is the most valuable.[158] There is a case for expecting similar structures to imply similar calculations, whatever they were. A current expert, Clive Ruggles rightly urges us to reason carefully and not give way to eager guessing and imaginative leaps. Nevertheless, he finds consistency of usage among the constructors of the recumbent stone circles of NE Scotland and the axial stone circles of SW Ireland, both of whom aligned their monuments with lunar events.[159] Many years separate the period of construction of stone circles and the Synod of Whitby. But these stones nevertheless stood then in the landscape, because they still do. If the arguments of archaeology are at all valid then there is a *prima facie* case that the areas with stone circles were accustomed in the first millennium AD, as in the fourth millennium BC, to calculate the date of their spring festival using a local method rather than one imported from the Mediterranean.[160]

British and Irish contact with Rome and the Mediterranean through the 5th/6th century is evident from imported pottery (above). The red plates, some with Christian symbols stamped upon them, and the amphorae, containing wine and olive oil, suggest a package designed to support the Christian project in opposition to the pagan English, in whose territory none have been found. This should imply a targeted intellectual contact, and the wine and olive oil were no doubt accompanied by sacred texts in Latin and Greek, together with early Christian art, advanced iconography and ideas. If so, the showing is weak; the imports are few, and in the

5th–6th centuries the few signs of Christianity are of the Old Testament, Davidian mentality, and the monumentality less devoted to saints than heroes or kings (Chapter 6, p. 602). However, this route from the Mediterranean via the Pillars of Hercules, Biscay, Brittany and Finisterre into the Irish Sea was already old by the Roman period.

Formative 2 sings a different song, led by Gospel books from Rome and pottery imported from neighbouring Aquitaine. While the message of the New Testament is now clear, its materiality expressed in vellum and stone is novel and home-grown. The Christian fundamentalist phase might frequently refer to Rome, but the British and Irish areas of the islands had their own driving force, couched in their own idiosyncratic style (see especially Chapters 4 and 5).

Living memory 2: the Roman inheritance

The Anglo-Saxons and their residual Britons claimed the lion's share of the territory colonised by Rome and took note of the extensive road network, the ordered fields, the villae, the temples and the forts that punctuated the land they were farming.[161] Nevertheless there are few signs of the exploitation by the 5th/6th-century English of Roman infrastructure either in town or country. In the aftermath of the campaign that made claims for continuity at Wroxeter (p. 263), the upper levels of villa sites have been examined minutely, and every urban excavation in former Roman towns, now numbering in the thousands, has been trowelled, brushed and sieved in the search for post-Roman continuity. But in spite of this diligent peering, the evidence remains as exiguous as it was 30 years ago: a water pipe in Colchester, sunken-featured huts in Canterbury, a burial by the gate at Winchester. Even in the imperial heartlands of Italy, continuity in the 5th/6th century has been hard to demonstrate, although easy to infer, for example in the survival of a street plan or a sewer. Large-scale studies such as Verona, Brescia and Crypta Balbi in Rome make it clear that major social changes are under way after the 6th century and that the new prescription had neither the resources nor the political will to continue with the old. The incidence of Christian burials within the former infrastructure is widespread, in the amphitheatres, in the rooms of houses and public buildings.[162] In Northumbria the excavations under York Minster were decisive: 250 interventions and thousands of tons of archaeological strata failed to deliver any convincing activity, even burial, between the 4th century and the 7th.[163] By contrast, in the west country and Wales the use of Roman temple sites continued into the 5th and even the 6th century. Striking evidence comes from Uley, where a temple complex serving the cult of Mercury in the Roman period was refurbished for devotees in the 5th century and superseded by a plausible if ephemeral Christian church, basilica and baptistery on the same site in the 6th/7th century.[164] Roman monuments, as well as prehistoric, provided foci for burials in Wales in the 5th–7th centuries, for example at Capel Eithin (Chapter 4, p. 312).

The 7th/8th century, our Formative 2, presents a very different picture. Roman establishments are the targets of the new Christian *Romanitas*. While Sarah Semple found no convincing deliberate association of a church or a Christian burial with a recognised *prehistoric* monument in the English region, Tyler Bell identified 250 medieval churches in association with *Roman* buildings.[165] Some of the earliest surviving ecclesiastical sites (Burgh castle, Bradwell on Sea, Escomb) are built at former Roman sites, and often out of recycled Roman materials. Seventh-century cemeteries took advantage of ex-Roman sites, either deliberately or by virtue of a favoured position, as Westhampnett (p. 305) and Lowbury Hill, where a male of over 45 years old was buried with sword, spear, knife, sugarloaf shield boss, shears, comb, bronze and iron buckles and a bronze hanging bowl. The burial stood next to a Roman temple and was covered by a mound, as if in deliberate reversion to earlier non-Roman ancestors. The burial was located near the junction of the Ridgeway, Icknield Way and the Roman road to Dorchester and had the best views in the area.[166] At the same time, although driven by a different ideological impetus, the towns reawoke, and their diocesan function was established or restored at York, Canterbury, Winchester and Gloucester, corroborated by dated archaeological features. In this later phase, female adornment also drank from the Mediterranean spring.[167]

In Formative 3, the 100-year-long Viking wars affected both islands and took their toll of both their wealth and their will to pursue the intellectual conquest of Europe. England and Scotland both won their battles, against Danes and Norse respectively, but still arguably succumbed to the Viking argument. When institutionalised uncompromising Christian orthodoxy revived in 10th-century England, it did so again under the Roman banner. In sum, the 5th-century end of empire seems to have been followed by a 200-year 'rest from Rome', followed by at least two moments of renaissance, in the 7th century and the 10th, both re-seeking the ethos of Rome in technology and politics. The latter episode also introduced something of Rome's ruthless military rule.[168]

Living memory 3: the German inheritance

The long discussion about how far the south-east side of Britain (aka England) was Germanised in the 5th/6th century has currently settled on the opinion of 'quite a lot'. Current researches have convinced all but the most obdurate that the massive language shift from British to English, the high-profile burial rites, the shunning of Roman towns, the new clothing, accoutrements, weapons, life style and gods, together with the lack of a detectable hierarchy, imply a large number of immigrants of both sexes into 5th- and 6th-century England from areas in modern Denmark, north Germany, Holland and Norway.[169] The degree to which Germanic practice came in with the migrants is a big topic to be explored in each of our reviews of material culture: in appearance (Chapter 2) it seems likely that a considerable amount of symbolism, belief and self-regard came in with the migrants and was expressed on the pots and brooches, swords and by the burial rites themselves (Chapter 4). The contribution of Germanic building techniques and styles to Anglo-Saxon settlement is debated (Chapter 3); there was certainly some. In stone monuments the Germanic signature is not marked, and it was some time before the idea of sculpture was adopted in the Anglo-Saxon region (in Formative 3: Chapter 5). To pre-empt the broader argument, it will be proposed here that differences in speech and culture were strong for the first two centuries of English and Irish occupation but began to blend in the 7th and 8th century. In the 9th–11th centuries, the triumph of the English language ensured that the Germanic inheritance remained powerful, not only in the areas where the Anglo-Saxons first settled but in the territories they conquered. While the archaeology is less vocal, there is enough in buildings and in art to recognise a 'Late Saxon' signature which is neither Roman, Viking nor British.

Attitudes to the past: FM 1, 2, 3

As we have seen, the 'royal cult centres' of Ireland had been retrospectively reduced to four in 9th-century literature, when their demise was recorded (p. 32). The archaeological evidence suggests that such central places were more numerous in the Iron Age and still active in the 7th/8th century, when they were redeveloped as ringworks (Uisneach, Teltown, Tara) or giant figure-of-eight structures (Dún Aillinne, Navan). These are not yet firmly labelled as princely centres, cult centres or Christian cult centres. The large crop of 'cemetery settle-ments' harvested by NRA archaeology showed the majority to have no churches and to be neither certainly pagan nor certainly Christian. This suggests that these were communities with family cemeteries that adapted to their own version of godliness.[170] At this time the con-tinuity between Iron Age and early medieval burial practice was marked, although in neither case indicating allegiance to a recognisable creed.[171] It is not impossible therefore that the figure-of-eight structures provided cult centres for those of a non-Christian persuasion. Early investment in Irish megalithic monuments in the 5th/6th century gave way to exploitation in the 7th/8th century, plausibly as feasting sites. During the 8th–10th centuries, burial began to migrate to communal cemeteries as 'a more extreme social hierarchy took hold'.[172] When in the 10th century the old centres, such as Knowth, were reused for settlement, it can be argued that their spiritual residue had worn thin.

The uses of prehistoric barrows in the English region changes gradually: secondary burial in the 5th/6th century, purpose-built mounds in the late 6th century, small at first and inte-grated with the communal cemeteries (Spong Hill, Wasperton) but gradually growing larger and proclaiming an independent and dominant identity (Sutton Hoo, Swallowcliffe Down, Taplow). The excision of the mound from its ancestral roots began in the 8th century. It remained a place of entry to the other world, but the other world was now hell. By the 10th century the mounds had become places of execution, where those guilty of anti-Christian behaviour were both hanged and damned.[173] That this was not simply a dismissive rejection of an unknown past is shown at Sutton Hoo, where the apparatus of execution was set up on or beside mounds that had been constructed for East Anglian kings only a generation before. The throttled dissidents were dumped in graves that ringed a mound, the occupant of which was probably well known to those condemned to the gallows.[174] Nevertheless, the occurrence of an execution burial at Stonehenge, as well as at barrows, hillforts and linear earthworks, shows a broader awareness of the vocabulary of landscape.[175]

Where ideas came from

It will already be apparent that in the story about to unfold, dominant families and politi-cal groups can take their cue from a wide range of sources, some nearby, some far away, some recent, some long ago, some only theorised fossils in the landscape. If we take the case of Western monasticism, there is a wide spectrum of sources from home and abroad from which this particular version of a new ideology was constructed (Chapter 3, p. 207). Certain beliefs and principles remain anchored to the soil; others are exotic and adopted; others are invented in the excitement of the new ideas. In the case of immigrants, some practices and images come in with them and are gradually relinquished unless ideologically revived. Others were acquired on marriage to locals, others proved politically prudent. In this kind of deconstruction, the contribution of prehistory is likely to be elusive but no less powerful for that.

It is a major premise of this book that the intellectual allegiance of the formative peoples vacillated and that it can be detected archaeologically. The basic theory is that high-profile sites, monuments and objects have received 'added investment' and so are more likely to carry political messages for public consumption. The messages themselves are deduced from the references made by the material culture. Plenty of examples will be encountered in the pages that follow, but here are four that can act as 'overture and beginners'.[176] At the site of Wasperton (Wa), burial began in the 3rd century AD. The women were buried with neck rings, the men with studded boots. An incoming late 5th-century group was buried in cremation urns. In the mid-6th century, a few inhumations were laid on adjacent prehistoric barrows; in the late 6th century, a few purpose-built barrows joined them. All these different burial rites were enacted within the same location, an abandoned Roman agricultural enclosure. One part of this enclosure was maintained a discrete area for W–E graves without grave goods, from the 4th to 7th century. This was a community that continued from the Roman period to the 7th century, respecting each other's graves but performing different rites. Apart from the apparently Christian enclave, the allegiance shown was to the Roman empire (3rd–5th century), to Germanic rites (5th/6th century), to British traditions (5th/6th century), to the prehistoric landscape (mid-6th century) and finally to the new leadership cult of late 6th- and early 7th-century Britain (Chapter 4, p. 324).

The new cult, or its heightened expression, was dramatically displayed at Sutton Hoo, where a 6th-century family cemetery was superseded in the early 7th century by a short-lived cluster of high-ranking mound burials that made references to Frankish horse burial, Scandinavian ship burial and (in its grave goods) to north Britain and Rome. This episode was followed in the 8th to 10th centuries by a reuse of the cemetery as a place of execution by hanging. Here the signals describe the progress of a local aristocracy from local lords to pagan kings to Christian kings with a penchant for punishing deviance (Chapter 4, p. 331).

At Portmahomack in the north-east of Scotland an equally sophisticated transition was recorded over the same period. In the 6th/7th century the place was a burial ground associated with a high-ranking equestrian family who left us a gilt bronze disc very similar to that worn by the horse at Sutton Hoo. In the late 7th century, the site was reorganised as a monastery, with workshops making vellum and church plate and erecting stone grave markers and cross slabs 3 m high. The cultural markers were Pictish in their symbols but insular in their art, with references primarily to Ireland and Northumbria but also to the British west. Between AD 780–810 (in radiocarbon years), the monastic workshops were burnt down and stone monuments were broken up and laid as hardcore and drain linings. Metalsmiths were soon in business, using the techniques previously applied to make chalices and patens to make belt buckles, pins and weights (to regulate trading). This phase lasted until the 10th century, by which time the Moray Firth had become a war zone between Norse and Scots (p. 148).

My fourth example, Stafford, was also created in a war zone, the wars of Aethelflaed of Mercia against the Vikings. As Alfred's daughter she was well aware of the ethos that drove the family not only to keep the Danes out of Wessex but, in a planned counter-attack, to clear them from Anglo-British regions in the north. This campaign was modelled on the Roman invasion of Britain. Aethelflaed and her husband, Ethelred, and brother Edward built rectangular forts. Aethelflaed initiated an industry at Stafford making Roman-style pots, and mistakes were punished by beheading (Chapter 3, p. 269).

This may seem a motley group to introduce the great variety of early medieval material we have, but these were all sites that carry the imprint of their ideology. Here the references are made to local prehistoric, Germanic, pagan, Roman and Christian inheritance. A reader might comment, 'That is not entirely unexpected.' This would be just, but archaeology is offering a little more than that: it is saying what allegiance, which intellectual current is being signalled where. Because the way people thought is a compendium of messages delivered by settlement, burial, objects and symbolic language, disentangling it is not straightforward, but disentangle it we must if the past is going to make sense. For the present, we have four examples where characterisation is reasonably clear; for the future we are about to plunge into the thickets of meaning left by every type of cultural material.

It is not accidental that the word ideological has popped up from time, since in my view it is the principal game-changer of the first millennium. That is, the influence of the environment, of resources, of disease, plague, even of violence is of minor consequence compared with the upheaval caused by the imposition of new ideas claiming a universal mandate. Individual visions, happily, are always with us, and we can hopefully encounter them in every site and work of art. Ideology by contrast is the blanket application of a single group of ideas and the closure of the mind against every alternative. This is Europe's curse, and it begins in the formative period. Archaeology often gives us a clue on where these ideas come from, or where they were last seen in action. From this we can enter the heads of our protagonists and learn something of what was driving their actions at that time and place and how they expressed it in material terms.

The seven regions as cultural areas

The seven 'natural' regions match reasonably well to the pattern of their diverse inheritance. The present Celtic areas – Scotland, Pictland, Cumbria, Wales and the SW – all retain prehistoric patterns that have some currency in the formative period, although not always manifested with equal strength. As in Ireland, there is continuity in the form of burial in Wales and Pictland and some attention given to henges. All areas embrace the standing stone as an emblem of shared values and recolonise prehistoric foci to a greater or lesser extent (Forteviot, Kilmartin, Cumbria, Wales, SW). Claims have been made here that early Christian fetishes – the cult of relics, the tonsure and the date of Easter – are derived from prehistoric practice and that the variation in the Christian mode seen in the different regions reflects variations in previous prehistoric worship. It is in Ireland that the shared prehistoric experience and the changing attitudes to its legacy are most evident.

The area of England that maps onto the Jurassic plain is distinct from the remaining regions in prehistoric times and distinct in its response to prehistoric monuments, the greater focus being on Bronze Age earth barrows. This region also harboured the majority of the Roman inheritance in its territory but took a few hundred years to acknowledge it in its own monumental agenda. It was after the English embraced a 7th-century Roman version of the Christian project and a special relationship was contrived with Rome that the inhabitants began to signal ownership of Roman remains, and prehistoric monuments were rebranded as gateways to doom.

Northumbria, which has a strong personality in formative and in modern territory, is a less perfect fit with its inheritance, because the characteristics of the English plain reach north of the Humber into the plain of York from the beginning of our period. One possibility would be to extend 'England' accordingly; another would be to accept the 'Anglo-British' tag.[177] From the 5th century until the arrival of the Vikings in the 9th, it is sensible to agree that northern England east of the Pennines and south of the Forth is a frontier zone populated by British, Anglian or Anglo-British kingdoms, and thereafter it becomes partly Anglo-Danish. A similar hybridisation sequence will be noted in north-east Scotland, where a Pictish region became Picto-Scottish and then Scotto-Norse as successive invaders altered the balance of power.

The premise offered is that each of the seven natural regions were also sufficiently distinct culturally, at least in regards to their inheritance, as to act as characters in our island story. They were reflected in the fuzzy borders of the known Iron Age territories and the Roman dioceses (Figure 1.14), and the same zones glimmer with faintly different colours in their language zones, religious affiliations and even in the games children played in the school playgrounds up to the 20th century (Chapter 7, p. 668). Other more subtle territories were signalled by pottery types, house types, styles of stone crosses and forms of churches, and we will see whether these can be justly cited as 'intellectual territories'[178] (Chapters 3, 4 and 5). It would be expected that association will be signalled in a wide spectrum of different colours and intensities, from a weak but persistent local glow from prehistory to the strong lights of newly imported peoples and arts. These latter need not map directly on to the territories of the *longue durée*, but our regions can serve as points of reference with which to compare them. In this respect the regions are arbitrary but firmly defined, lines on a map over which spill the trends of successive ages.

The structure of the book

As proposed in the preface, this book attempts to construct a narrative of the 5th to 11th century in Britain. It will be an archaeological narrative constructed from four general categories of archaeological evidence: objects (Chapter 2), settlements (Chapter 3), burials (Chapter 4) and stone monuments (Chapter 5), each enlivened with imaginative and probably injudicious interpretations. The task is to investigate the evidence in each category for the whole island over three periods (Table 0.1, p. xxiv).

The geographic structure is largely result of the considerations of the inherited natural and prehistoric character outlined in this chapter, which suggested the seven regions sketched in Figure 1.12. For each investigation, the evidence is reviewed by period; and within each

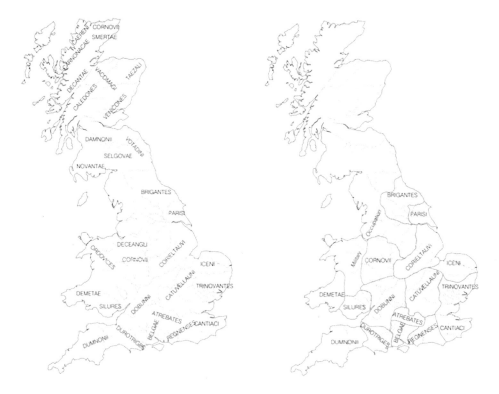

Figure 1.14 Iron Age (left) and Roman territories (right).

(FAS Heritage)

period the itinerary through the seven regions starts at the top left of the island, in 'Scotland', then goes east to 'Pictland' and then south to 'NW England' and thence to Wales and SW. Then it returns to the north to visit Northumbria and lastly returns south to the territories of south-east England, which are referred here as 'Southumbria'.

This system of citation has the advantage of a routine but has also to allow for the considerable variations and gaps in the evidence. So whereas Southumbria has no sculpture to speak off before Fm 3, its Fm 1 cemetery evidence is so rich that it has to be reported in four sub-periods. Similarly, settlement evidence is sparse in Fm 1 Pictland and in all three periods in Wales. These gaps and bulges will be addressed in their turn. Because Ireland and Scandinavia are so much part of our story, we will often visit them too, so as to have a haversack of comparative materials when the British material has been organised for comparison. In the case of the settlements and cemeteries, multi-period sites provide a particular asset, one that is responsible for most of the narrative framework of the book as a whole. So Chapters 3, 4 and 5 begin with a Field Trip taking a close look at a handful of these fieldwork projects that were ground-breaking in every sense.

One result of these discoveries is to reveal a set of drivers – leadership, spirituality and wealth creation, which operate in every period and region but at different levels of intensity. These differences of emphasis give each period its flavour. In Fm 1 leadership and land ownership in various forms generate signs of governance and control. In Fm 2 spirituality rises to the level of fundamentalist religion, embraced by the British and Anglo-British regions but less so in England. In Fm 3, wealth creation takes centre stage, initially under the Vikings, expressed as bullion, manufacture and trade and latterly as coinage syphoned into the treasure chests of the military and clerical overlords. A theme of the book is that these differences through time represent the outcome of conflicts between ideologies rather than good weather or good luck, even if these varied too. The thesis unrolled here suggests that it is these conflicts that characterised the Roman-Medieval transition and generated its material culture. Chapter 7 presents the narrative derived from archaeology in a form that is designed to aid its deployment by historians, at least of those parts they find acceptable or enlightening. A final coda invites the reader to appreciate, hopefully with curiosity mingled with affection, the legacy of the Formative period, its adventure, experiment, broad deep thinking, poetry, closeness to nature and the inspiration it can still give to individuals who feel themselves shackled by the universalisms of our own millennium.

Notes

1 It was declared an English possession by Henry VIII in 1542, subsequent colonisation being long resisted especially in Northern Ireland, a territory definitively settled by the English after the Battle of the Boyne in 1690. On the formation of the independent Irish state (now republic) in 1922, the six counties of Northern Ireland opted out, becoming part of the UK. Peace between north and south was eventually achieved in 1999 at a time when both Britain and Ireland were part of the EU. At the time of writing, archaeology operated in Ireland largely without borders.
2 O'Sullivan et al. 2014a. This survey covered the whole island of Ireland.
3 Coined by Geoffrey of Monmouth in his *History of the Kings of Britain* c. 1136. While the history itself is unreliable, there were Britons in Brittany at the time it was written.
4 Evans 1975.
5 Taylor 1956, 18; easterly and north-easterly winds driving across the Norway sea towards Iceland and Shetland 'could be counted on with the greatest certainty early in the sailing season in late April and May'; Taylor 1956, 75; McGrail 1998, 260; Carver 1990; Carver 2014b.

6 Based on modern data from Admiralty Pilots 1979/82, 1973, 1983, Admiralty Chart of the North Sea (HMSO, 1979); see Carver 1990, Fig 15.2; Lamb and Fryendahl 1991, 25–27.

7 Marcus 1980, 101; McGrail 1998, 259–260, citing the Old English poem *The Seafarer* line 62–63.

8 Cunliffe 2001, 558.

9 Eva Germaine Rimington Taylor's *Haven-Finding Art* (1956) remains the classic work for early navigation.

10 Taylor 1956, 31.

11 The Voyage of St Brendan in *Lives of the saints*, 55; Taylor 1956, 76–77; Carver 1990; Binns 1980; Tim Severin (1978) describes a successful experimental voyage in a leather boat from the Irish Sea to Iceland.

12 Westerdahl 2008: 'Maritime societies and individuals develop cosmologies and rituals, not only strategies for sustenance, which to them are supposed to be as necessary for survival.'

13 Miles 2005, 86 summarises recent evidence for Bronze Age sea travel around Britain.

14 Marcus 1980, 5–7; the sea-going curragh, the latest descendant of the hide craft, is deemed much more seaworthy than a logboat.

15 McCullough 2000; Phillips 2006; Westerdahl 2006.

16 Eileen Wilkes (2007) identifies 40 Iron Age landing places on the south coast indicated by favourable tides, shelter from winds, seamarks, beaching points and access to rivers. Ewan Campbell (1991, 2007) mapped the distribution of Fm 1 post-Roman imports and felt (1996, 79) that 5th–7th century exchange systems used a number of short journeys and successive cargos, as described in Neil Munro's *Tales of Para Handy*. See also Wooding (1996); Campbell and Bowles 2009 for Byzantine connections.

17 Crumlin-Pedersen 1991c; Filmer-Sankey and Pestell 2001.

18 Crumlin-Pedersen and Trakadas 2003, 239.

19 Crumlin-Pedersen 2010, 65–94.

20 Crumlin-Pedersen 1997.

21 Carver 1995b.

22 Carver 1990; Bill 2008; the 'Sea Stallion from Glendalough, a reconstructed Viking ship based on Skudelev 2 could make 11 knots (20km/h) under sail in a fresh wind and 5 knots (10km/h) under oars. It took three days to sail from Jutland to England' (Viking Ship Museum 2007, 63).

23 Taylor 1956, 4, comments that historians have invented 'coastwise creep' not believing in navigation, but that actually the last thing a mariner wants is a lee shore.

24 Morris 1989, 11.

25 Campbell 1991; Doyle 2009; Kelly 2010. With the pottery came glass, probably from south-west France (Campbell 2000, 42). Different types of glass reached the English areas from the Rhineland (Evison 2000, 90–91). The most easterly British find of pottery imported from the Mediterranean is probably Bantham in Devon, where imported amphorae of the 5th/6th century (LRA1) were found in association with a hearth and stake holes (Reed et al. 2011).

26 Ewan Campbell (1996, 87–88) argues that trade was attracted to western Scotland in the 6th to 7th century because it was further along the road to coordinated kingship than other parts of Britain or Ireland.

27 Wickham 2005, 809, 815.

28 Barry Cunliffe discerned several maritime communities indicated by the use of similar coarsewares opposite each other either side of The Channel during the Iron Age (5th to 1st century BC): the south-east with the Belgic area, the centre south with the Seine, the south-west with Brittany (Cunliffe 2013, 315, 331, 335).

29 Carver 1986a.

30 Levison 1946, 44; Jenkins 1949, 68.

31 McCormick 2001. Compare Bowden and Hodges 2012.

32 Levison 1946, 39.

33 Morris 2004, 2, 4, 5, 13.

34 Bately and Englert 2007; Englert and Trakadas 2009.

35 BL Cott. Tib. B.V f56v; Hill 1981, 3; Barber 2006, 4–8; Foys 2007, 120; Carver 2014b, 34. The map is thought to derive from a Roman original copied in the 9th century and modified in the 11th century – to reflect Archbishop Sigeric's journey to Rome in 990 via Pavia, Verona and Lucca.

36 Westerdahl 1992, 2005; Crumlin-Pedersen 1991a; for English waters see Carver and Loveluck 2013; Carver 2014b.

37 Wreford Watson 1964, 1.
38 Ferriday 1955, 173, Fig 72.
39 Mackinder 1915, 33; Fox 1952.
40 A similar division is apparent in the soils of Ireland, where poorly drained soils dominate the north and west, and the more fertile soils chiefly in the south-east. The latter maps the distribution of Anglo-Norman boroughs (Mitchell and Ryan 1998, 308–310, Figs 154, 155).
41 What follows makes use of studies by Ferriday 1955; Wreford Watson and Sissons 1964; Roberts and Wrathmell 2002; Rippon et al. 2014.
42 Roberts and Wrathmell 2002, Fig 3.11; Rippon et al. 2014, Figs 4.1, 4.2.
43 Roberts and Wrathmell 2002, Fig 1.2.
44 Simmons 2001, Fig 4.3.
45 Roberts and Wrathmell 2002, Fig 1.4.
46 Roberts and Wrathmell 2002, Fig 3.9. EngLaID is a project currently attempting to map early medieval settlement density using archaeological evidence (Green et al. 2017). It does not reflect these zones (which refer to agricultural strategies rather than population).
47 Allen et al. 2016.
48 Simmons 2001, 83; Rackham 2000, 174–176.
49 Ferriday 1955, Fig 116.
50 Rackham 2000.
51 Banham and Faith 2014, 33, 269.
52 Yeast is present in the air or in fermented wine or beer.
53 Hay loses one third of its protein due to fermentation in the rick, but drying in kilns gives a winter feed 50% richer in protein then cereal grains. Storage of freshly cut grass in shallow pits makes a silage (fermented feed) with a protein value twice that of hay (Ferriday 1955, 295–296).
54 Ferriday 1955, 291–292.
55 Kelly 2000, 54–55.
56 Parchment in the north was generally termed vellum from Latin *vitellus* calf. In the south, sheep-skin was more commonly used for mss.
57 Simmons 2001, 101.
58 Barrett and Richards 2004; Barrett 2008; Barrett et al. 1999, 2000, 2004.
59 Rackham 2000, 70.
60 Katherine Seymour Woods was born in Oxford in 1887 and published her invaluable book in 1949.
61 For example: *Rumex acetosa* leaves for soups and *Oxalis acetosella* as a children's snack; 15 folk species of fruits and seeds (*Crataegus* spp., *Corylus avellana, Fagus sylvatica, Fragaria vesca, Malus domestica, Prunus spinosa, Pyrus* spp., *Rosa canina, Rubus idaeus, Rubus* sect. *Rubus, Sambucus nigra, Vaccinium myrtillus, V. oxycoccos, V. uliginosum, V. vitis-idaea*) and four taxa used for seasoning or as preservatives (*Armoracia rusticana* root and leaves, *Carum carvi* seeds, *Juniperus communis* pseudo-fruits and *Quercus* spp. leaves) (Łuczaj and Szymański 2007).
62 Alison Donaldson in Carver 1979, 56–58.
63 Banham and Faith are less sanguine than Roberts and Wrathmell that it did so within the Formative period. Rather, the central belt defined earlier (p. 13) represents evidence of the middle ages: Banham and Faith p. 284: 'Evidence for early open field zone influenced by the evidence for open-field system at its fullest extent, often based on enclosure awards'; and p. 295: 'if open field farming as seen in English local records from the thirteenth century onwards was not yet in operation, the elements were available – the crops, the tools, the techniques – which allowed its development after the Conquest'.
64 Banham and Faith 2014, Fig 12.3 for Wheldrake village, strip fields and ings.
65 Rippon et al. 2014, Fig 4.
66 Rippon et al. 2014.
67 Rippon et al. 2014, 243.
68 Rippon et al. 2014, Fig 3.
69 Rippon et al. 2014, 218, 231–232. However, the Fm 1 sites included some Fm 2, since they were dated 5th–7th or 5th to 9th. Thus, only broad-brush conclusions have been cited here from a very detailed study.
70 Rippon et al. 2014, 242; also Banham and Faith 2014, 291.
71 Banham and Faith 2014, 294.

72 This is a distant echo of the zig-zag beginnings of agriculture, where hunted animals are herded, then impounded and fed wild cereals, then cereals are cultivated to keep the herds to hand; and as the population increases cereal production is required not only to make beer but to be fed to humans too in solid form. This powered the 12,000-year old congregational site of Göbeckli Tepe in Turkey (Dietrich et al. 2012). Another assembly place of similar date has been found at Wadi Faynan in Jordan (Mithen et al. 2011).

73 Sherratt 1996.

74 Westerdahl 2006. The east coast exception is Tarbat Ness in Easter Ross.

75 Sherratt 1996, 214.

76 Noble 2007.

77 *Guardian* 15 May 1997.

78 Pelteret 2009.

79 E.g. Taylor 1979.

80 Haldane 1997.

81 Haldane 1997, 7.

82 Haldane 1997, 14.

83 The 13th-century map of Scotland by Matthew Paris labels the regions of the north and west as 'marshy and impassable, fit for cattle and shepherds'.

84 Haldane 1997, 21.

85 *Aelfric's colloquy*, 226–251.

86 The basis for the arguments in this book is archaeological. Only some minor and general use is made of the specialist discipline of toponymy (placenames) for linguistic mapping. See Gelling 1978 for an introduction.

87 O'Grady 2014, 107.

88 Bradley 1987 was a seminal article.

89 Bradley 1987, 15, 1993, 117.

90 Cunliffe 2013, 119, Fig 4.13.

91 Cummings 2009, 187–196.

92 Henderson 2007, 299–302.

93 Mitchell and Ryan 1998, 166; Cummings 2009, 86.

94 Mitchell and Ryan 1998, 195; Cummings (2009, 193–194) links the passage graves under the generic title of dolmens and shows they are sited by a mobile maritime community that wishes to reproduce similar views for their dead.

95 Marshall 1977, 55, 1983; Edmonds 1992.

96 Cunliffe 2013, 195, Fig 6.12.

97 Cunliffe 2013, 298, Fig 9.5.

98 Swift 2000, 31; Herity 1995, 297.

99 McCormick and Murray 2007.

100 Carey 1999.

101 Hutton 2011a.

102 James 1992; Petts 2002a.

103 Petts 2009, 88–89.

104 Petts 2002b.

105 Semple 2013, 14.

106 Semple 2013, 110.

107 Thäte 2007.

108 Semple 2013; Reynolds 2009; Carver 2002a.

109 Semple 2013, 190.

110 Semple 2013, 197.

111 Waddell 1998, 2005, 2011.

112 Lacey 2011.

113 Mitchell and Ryan 1998, 237–245; Waddell 1998, 2011, 194.

114 Uisneach lies at the meeting point of the four ancient provinces of Ireland. Schot 2006, 2011, 87.

115 Waddell 2011, 195–198.

116 Newman 1997, 225–230; Newman 2011.

117 Waddell et al. 2009, 197. This was the legendary site of Queen Maeve and the rival bulls of the Cattle Raid of Cooley (Chapter 6, p. 603).

118 Lynn 2003; dated by dendrochronology.
119 Johnstone and Wailes 2007, 198.
120 O'Connell 2013.
121 Ó Floinn 2001, 7.
122 Swift 2000, 21.
123 O'Brien 2009; see Chapter 4.
124 Clarke and Carlin 2009, 16–19.
125 Gondek and Noble 2010; Noble et al. 2013. The excavations have still to be completed at the time of writing. See Chapter 3, p. 187; Ch 5, p. 494.
126 Hunter 2007a, 41.
127 Hunter's chronological scheme is given in his 2007a, 20, 36: ERIA 75–160; MRIA 160–250; LRIA 250–400; EH 400–1100. Harding 2016, 266.
128 See Chapter 4, p. 349.
129 Bede I.1; McClure and Collins 2008, note to p. 10 on p. 361.
130 Bede I.25.
131 Bede III.3.
132 Bede III.7and notes; III.25 and note, p. 357.
133 Adomnán II.32, I.33.
134 Forsyth 1995a, 1997a/b, 1998.
135 McClure and Collins 2008, 261.
136 Isaac 2005; Sims-Williams 2012, 431.
137 Sims-Williams 2012, 431.
138 See Chapter 5.
139 Jackson 1953, 220.
140 Jackson 1953, 197, 236.
141 Jackson 1953, 244.
142 Jackson 1953, 245: 'Britons learned the language of their conquerors, and they acquire its sound system and vocabulary very completely, their own phonetics having no discernable effect of the new language and their vocabulary very little.'
143 Jackson 1953, 248, 256: 'The possibility of contact between Latin speaking Britons and the English cannot be excluded, though it is not likely to have been more than trifling (p. 249). 'The heavy accumulation of negative evidence does seem to suggest strongly that the English met very few people who talked Latin of any sort at all during the course of the occupation of Britain' (p. 261).
144 Gelling 1993, 56.
145 Carey 1987, 5.
146 Bradley 2000; Stocker and Everson 2003.
147 Doherty 1984, 89; see Carver 2009a for prehistoric origins for the cult of relics, the tonsure and the date of Easter.
148 Woodward 1993; Parker Pearson 2005, 2007.
149 Doherty 1984, 96.
150 *contra* Thomas, e.g. 1971, Ch 5, p. 144.
151 Insoll tracks the curation of body parts back to the Mesolithic; 2011b, 1047.
152 Ó Carragáin 2003.
153 Sherratt 1996; Darvill and Wainwright 2009.
154 Noble 2007.
155 Venclova 2002.
156 *HA* III.25, Plummer 1969, 184.
157 Carver 2008b; Carver 2009a.
158 'Religious specialization is now hardly to be doubted at the stone circles of Stonehenge and Avebury . . . observation of the sun and moon at such sites was part of the calendrical interest seen . . . over much of Britain, especially in the highland Zone. Even if the megalithic unit of measurement was related to the pace or span rather than to a fixed universal standard there can be no doubting the precision and geometrical skill with which they were laid out. . . . Specialist observers or seers – in effect a priesthood – were a feature of this society' (Renfrew 1973, 555, cited by Ruggles 1999, 81).
159 Ruggles 1999, 100. These same well-separated regions have the later ogham in common.

160 In general, a new optimism that archaeologists can study ancient ways of thinking using material culture alone was initiated by Colin Renfrew's *Towards an Archaeology of Mind* (1985).

161 Millett estimates that 3.6 million people lived in Roman Britain, most of them in the countryside and 10% of them in villas (2016, 9).

162 Carver 1993, 46–50.

163 Phillips and Heywood 1995.

164 Woodward 1992, 74–76, 112, 118. Fully published in Woodward and Leach 1993. Other temple sites that saw use in the 5th century are Lydney and Bath.

165 Semple 2013, 112–117; Bell 1998.

166 Williams 1999.

167 Geake 1997, and see Chapter 4.

168 Chapter 3, p. 272.

169 Härke 2011; Hills and Lucy 2013; see Chapter 2, for comments on DNA.

170 Ó Carragáin 2009a.

171 O'Brien 2009.

172 Ó Carragáin 2009a, 357.

173 Semple 2013, 16, 50.

174 Mound 5; Carver 2005a.

175 Reynolds 2009; Semple 2013.

176 Summarised in Carver 2010a.

177 Lucy 2009, 141.

178 Carver 2011a, c. The zones are pre-echoed to some extent by Barry Cunliffe's Iron Age groupings (2005, 599): in the *west* petty chieftains with fortified enclosures, inhumation cemeteries and votive offerings in bogs; in the *east* large agglomerations in open settlements with votive deposits in rivers; and between them a *hillfort* culture with ritual fertility pits. He expects the hillfort culture to be more innovative, less conservative than the other two, perhaps because of its exposure to the continent.

2 Looking for personhood

Physique and adornment

Introduction

Personal identity is layered, deep and wide: language, looks, eyes, hair, stature, agility, clothing, equipment and the impression produced by modifying and decorating the body all play a part. Physique and its adornment, the body and the clothes, are two concentric shells of the person, two categories that leave archaeological lineaments of 'personhood'. *Physique* is increasingly in reach of archaeological science, which comes at it through anatomy – the bones that imply the flesh – and through isotopes and DNA, which characterise diet, origin and consanguinities and promise (in the future) to tell us details of colouring and inherited anomalies. By contrast, *appearance* may be captured from artefacts and from art, but by inference rather than measurement, and it is a slippery craft. Clothing and accoutrements may have been designed to prompt instant recognition ('he's a Pict'), but this is an assumption already filtered through three minds: that of the wearers, their contemporaries and of the bystanders of a later age (us). In all likelihood the messages of clothing were more varied, more subtle – and more ambiguous (Figure 2.1).

Accordingly, the first part of the chapter deals with the biology of formative people, known to us but mostly not to them, and then their own cultural self-presentation, clear to them but elusive to us. So, although the catch-all term 'identity' has been a useful way of defining social groups and their membership, there are really two identities, biological (given) and cultural (assumed), in every person. 'Ethnicity' is something attributed to a person by others on the basis of both physical and cultural markers. Up to now archaeologists have had mainly cultural markers to work with, and the advancement of science reveals that biological and cultural signals do not necessarily equate. Given the huge amount of mobility in the first millennium and the sexual energy of the players, the fail-safe position is to accept a signal of ethnicity but assume nothing about biological descent from what people wear.[1] Britain in the first millennium, containing a demographic mix created by four centuries of the Roman empire, was then invaded by groups of culturally and linguistically defined Scots, Anglo-Saxons, Danes and Norse. No one today can realistically claim a single biological ancestry, since we are all descended via a first-millennium melting pot. On the other hand, our *cultural* diversity is the first millennium's gift, the glory of the island and the celebration of this book.

Selected items of adornment have provided archaeology's staple diet since its inception, in the form of brooches and buttons and, in lucky cases, surviving cloth. Clothes provide the material language of the individual with which people express how they feel about themselves or how they want the world to see them. But some don extravagant amounts of clothing, some deliberately few, some adopt the uniform of a group, for some uniformity proclaims dominance, some aggression, some poverty, some humility; some

Figure 2.1 Heroic figure – 21st century image of the 7th century warrior from Mound 17 at Sutton Hoo.
(From an original painting by Kelvin Wilson 2017)

say they would welcome your attention, others that their emotional life is dead or given to God. It follows that clothes may report only a moment in a person's life or may disguise reality, as in a non-combatant warrior or a well-fed monk. The language of clothing, like other languages, has a local dialect, a broader usage, a tendency to deceive and a respected universality, between all of which we are obliged to navigate. And as if this were not enough difficulty to place between the wearer and the distant voyeur (namely ourselves), we are granted only a snapshot, at the moment of death in the case of grave goods, or some idealistic evocation in the case of drawn or sculpted images, or an abstract rhapsody on the written page. Furthermore, between the 5th century and the 11th, the character of the surviving evidence is exasperatingly uneven, making the matters we are most eager to compare – changes through time and contrast between places – the most elusive of all. Between the 5th and 7th century, we may find clothing and its ornaments in graves, sometimes of a wonderful quality, but they are located only in the south-east part of Britain where the grave-good habit was practised. Usable representations of clothing in images on sculpture and manuscript occur only in the Christian areas and only after the 8th century; even then they are hard to pick apart from their ritual exemplars until the 9th century, when ordinary men and women start to make their appearance on the page and on the stones – but only in the work of certain individual artists.

So is it worth it? Will every attempt to see how people used clothes in Britain's formative period end in 'occasionally', 'not necessarily' or 'perhaps'? This is an occupational hazard of archaeology of course, but not everything need remain ill defined and uncertain. Provided we do not assume that graves, images and words must represent a norm, there are ways and means of delving and testing in the attempt to make the acquaintance of a person. 'We are what we wear' should perhaps be modified to 'they were what they were wearing', so acknowledging the nature of the brief encounter. Nor can we assume that clothes are necessarily at the command (or to the taste) of the wearer. Whether they like it or not, a person laid out for burial is arrayed by the burial party in their traditional 'Sunday best' and festooned with antiques so that the ancestors will more easily identify the newcomer in their midst.

The types of evidence also vary in their authenticity: written descriptions are inflated, images on sculpture and manuscripts are often copied from elsewhere or make antique references. Burial is the richest source of real clothing but the hardest to interpret. The casual finds recovered by metal-detectorists are usually without context but in some ways are the best indication of what active people really wore: the buckles and strap-ends that fell off as they galloped across the turf or rolled in the long grass. After making our way through this gallimaufry of discarded costume jewellery and working out some ground rules of interpretation, the main investigation will begin: how appearance changed from the first post-Roman centuries, to the emergence of kingdoms and institutional religion, to the invention of greater England. It is a journey with many gaps and numerous blind spots but holds the promise of continuous and ever-increasing discovery.[2]

Evidence for the human – the bodies we inherit

Analysis of skeletons has shown that the stature of early medieval people is not greatly different to that of adult men and women in Britain today. But putting flesh on the bones requires a certain amount of conjecture – influenced, at least in part, by the distribution of personal attributes in the modern population but modified by archaeological reasoning and supported by a fast-developing range of sciences designed to characterise humans from their skeletal morphology, diet, ancestry and migrations: craniology, stable isotopes of bones and teeth, and the analysis of modern and ancient DNA (aDNA), the latter surviving best in the *petrus* bone of the skull.

The primary archaeological mode of defining human beings is the well-tested science of osteology, able today to evoke the live appearance of the person reconstructed from their skeleton, as well as writing a biography from their anatomy and trauma.[3] The analysis of skeletons reports age at death, sex, height (always a strong social attribute), childhood suffering, disfigurement through disease, rotting teeth, occupational hazards such as broken legs, and inherited or circumstantial injuries resulting in hunchbacks or arrested and lopsided growth. Other likely distinguishing characteristics remain elusive; for example, minor deformities like that suggested by the name Campbell (twisted mouth) or the claw-like hand traditionally attributed to Viking descent – and there must have been many more of these oddities and mannerisms – would have been influential in the building of identity.[4] Prejudice due to physical differences was likely in formative Britain and no doubt had numerous local opportunities to flourish, but the facial difference most readily noted at the time was probably that between the incoming Scots, English, Danish and Norse and the native Britons.

Signals of origin

Archaeology has a long tradition of associating the material remains of humans or the objects buried with them with peoples named in the historical record, and the reported presence and movement of such peoples has naturally enough been equated with invasions and nation building. Leaving aside the message of the objects for the time being, the scientific analyses of the bodies of those found in the cemeteries has added some substance to the debate. Three relatively new methods have been mobilised to address the matter or origins. Among some archaeological scientists there has been a return to **craniology** as a method of distinguishing people of different descent. 'Geometric morphometric analysis of cranial and dental morphology' relies on the shape of the teeth and the head, especially that of the neurocranium and in particular the temporal bone, which seem to be genetically controlled.[5] The method has perhaps remained in the shadow in Britain, where it nevertheless has potential, given the large number of excavated skulls surviving from the Formative period.

DNA, the current demographic power tool, comes in two models.[6] Until recently, genetic studies have relied largely on DNA samples taken from the *modern* population. This gives a distribution that reflects modern territories but is not wholly reliable as a proxy for the ancient population, for reasons put forward by Patrick Sims-Williams: the 'power law' means that if one man has more children than others, eventually that surname (and those Y-chromosomes) will predominate.[7] In other words prolific males can skew the descent – the 'Atilla effect'. In England it could be a 'Hengist and Horsa' effect, in Ireland a 'Niall of Nine Hostages effect', or in Scotland a 'Somerled effect'. So 'only a tiny and possibly unrepresentative proportion of people have bequeathed their patrilinear and matrilinear DNA to modern times', the remainder meeting dead ends before the present.[8]

In an attempt to anchor the results of modern DNA sampling in a more secure past, a recent Oxford University study used DNA taken from 2,039 middle-aged individuals, each with all four grandparents born within 80 km of each other, the idea being to reach back into the 19th century, when the British population was supposed to be more genetically local (even though then engaged in building an empire on four continents, with its inevitable, if surreptitious, liaisons). European DNA groupings were derived from 6,029 samples taken on a similar basis. All 17 of the British groups featured contributions from all the European (i.e. Continental) groups but were then clustered on the basis of a particular genetic emphasis.

Unfortunately, the report did not include the greater part of Ireland. The result showed a distribution of modern genetic groups much the same as the geography and landscape would predict, especially in the Celtic areas north and west; people bred locally by preference.[9] One of the participants in this project expressed surprise that there were a number of different genetic groups in the north and west of Britain; but it is clear enough from archaeology, and from Bede, that Irish, Scots, Pictish Britons, Cumbrian Britons, Welsh Britons and Cornish Britons, although all 'Celts', were culturally distinct from each other and did not even speak a mutually comprehensible language. The idea that to a large extent they also married within their local group does not appear unduly startling.[10]

A later critique has highlighted the limits of what is currently possible using modern DNA samples. The PoBI project had decided that an admixture event involving people from north-west Germany was due to Anglo-Saxon incomers and noted that there was no evidence for a genetic contribution from Danish Vikings. However, the critique noted in turn that the event was held to have taken place 38 generations ago, which (using a generation length of 28 years) put it in the 9th century, and since the Danish and Anglian homelands were pretty similar, the admixture was just as likely to be owed in whole or in part to the Viking episode. The authors of the critique offered the following salutary verdict:

> Distinguishing between a fifth-sixth century north and north-west German/southern Danish (Anglo-Saxon) genetic contribution to the modern English population and a ninth-century north German/pan-Danish (Viking) one will, however, probably remain exceedingly difficult, as it will involve populations that, based on their partial geographic overlap and temporal proximity, are unlikely to be genetically very distinct.[11]

At the present broad scale of inquiry, models show that while there is evidence for Norse settlers in Orkney and for Saxon or Danish settlers in East Anglia, these models do not easily distinguish closely dated population movements.[12] Current scientific opinion is that the principal episode of immigration into Britain so far detected occurred much earlier. Research published in *Nature* in 2018 determined that around 90% of the population of Britain was replaced by incomers from the Russian steppes in the third millennium BC.[13] This result was obtained from 400 dated aDNA samples, a method that also points the way forward for higher precision mapping of the movements of population. The new science made possible by the extraction of aDNA is moving at a relentless pace as related in David Reich's 2018 book and should also relieve anxieties about the misuse of ancestry by providing detailed stories of much human mobility. Evenso the most difficult populations to map with aDNA remain those of the last four thousand years.[14] Most narratives start with aDNA but still rely on the genome of modern people. Researchers used genetic markers on bones thought to belong to Richard III excavated under a car park in Leicester and found evidence for blonde hair – at least in childhood – and almost certainly blue eyes, resembling one of his earliest surviving portraits in the Society of Antiquaries, London.[15]

Stable isotopes also characterise the physical person and their travels, if less directly.[16] The carbon/nitrogen isotope signature is an indicator of diet, distinguishing access to different food sources within and between communities. Oxygen and strontium isotope signatures have the potential to show where people have moved since birth, since the variation found in layers of the teeth reflects the access to groundwater at different stages in their lives. Also in the teeth are traces of calculus and micro-debris, which contain identifiable plants that may not be native and so indicate mobility of the people or the plants.[17] In theory, the advent of stable isotope signatures of oxygen and strontium (O/Sr) as indicators of population movement should provide a sharpened focus to the pictures painted by exotic grave goods and documentary statements, for example, bearing on the question of Germanic immigration.

In a way it does, but recent results do not so much complement the existing models as refashion them. At Lankhills in Winchester the excavation and analysis of the late Roman cemetery initially offered a tidy account of 473 ordered burials in rows progressing from west to east from the 4th to the early 5th century; in its final stages two separate small populations were detected through their grave goods as belonging to Hungarian and Anglo-Saxon incomers (dated 350–410 and 390–410 respectively).[18] This cemetery was revisited during a development opportunity in 2000–2005, unearthing a further 307 inhumations and 25 cremations. O/Sr analysis was carried out on 40 skeletons, including several from the intrusive group, as defined by grave goods. This confirmed that 25% of the sample consisted of incomers, including at least one from the area of Pannonia, but by contrast virtually all the persons equipped with exotic grave goods were isotopically British.[19] At West Heslerton in North Yorkshire, four out of 24 skeletons sampled, all women buried without brooches, had origins in Scandinavia. A further 13 originated west of the Pennines, and the remainder were local. In northern Pictland we will encounter in the generation before the Vikings a case of two men of Scandinavian origin buried in a monastic cemetery in the manner of the monks (Chapter 4, p. 317). Some people at least dressed (or were dressed) to match the exigency of their survival or pursuit of profit.

The peopling of Britain

The make-up of the native population and the degree of migration into the island of Britain during the 4th–5th century (the 'migration period' on the continent) has been long in contention and is now a target in the sights of scientific analyses. The fact that the English speak a Germanic language and the description of the arrival of Anglo-Saxons written by the Venerable Bede some generations later led initially to expectations of a mass migration, something that has subsequently been much questioned, modified and deconstructed. The hope was that furnished Anglo-Saxon graves would confirm Bede's account of the arrival of Angles, Saxons and Jutes through classification and mapping of types of grave goods, especially weapons and brooches.[20] But subsequent studies showed that these 'nations' were not imported intact but rather were created and named in England out of disparate groups of immigrants. Catherine Hills showed that it is among second or third generation settlers that distinctions appear in women's brooches between areas in Britain ascribed to the Angles, Saxons and Jutes.[21] John Hines showed that the Anglian wrist-clasps distributed in Norfolk and Lincolnshire (around the Wash) emanated from 6th-century Norway.[22] Sam Lucy showed that in the later 6th century the Anglian areas in Northumbria were emulating British burial rites, while the Kings of Wessex sport British names.[23] These and other studies revealed something of the subtlety with which the actual movement of people and their proclaimed identities intertwine.

For the hot topic of the Englishing of England, the pendulum has swung from seeing the furnished Anglo-Saxon graves as evidence for large-scale immigration to interpreting them as expressions of political strategy among the indigenous Britons, and back again.[24] New research at Spong Hill, where the presence of a substantial immigrant population has been endorsed by the latest study, has given the pendulum another nudge.[25] Keynote research published in 2011 explored the demographic composition of the English area in terms of British and Germanic cultural and biological signals and offered a new vision.[26] The mapping of *modern* Y-chromosome DNA (the male line) showed a genetic origin for the English in Dutch Frisia, northern Germany and Denmark, the immigrants having a variable impact on the genetic map of Britain (Figure 2.2). On one reckoning, the regional difference in

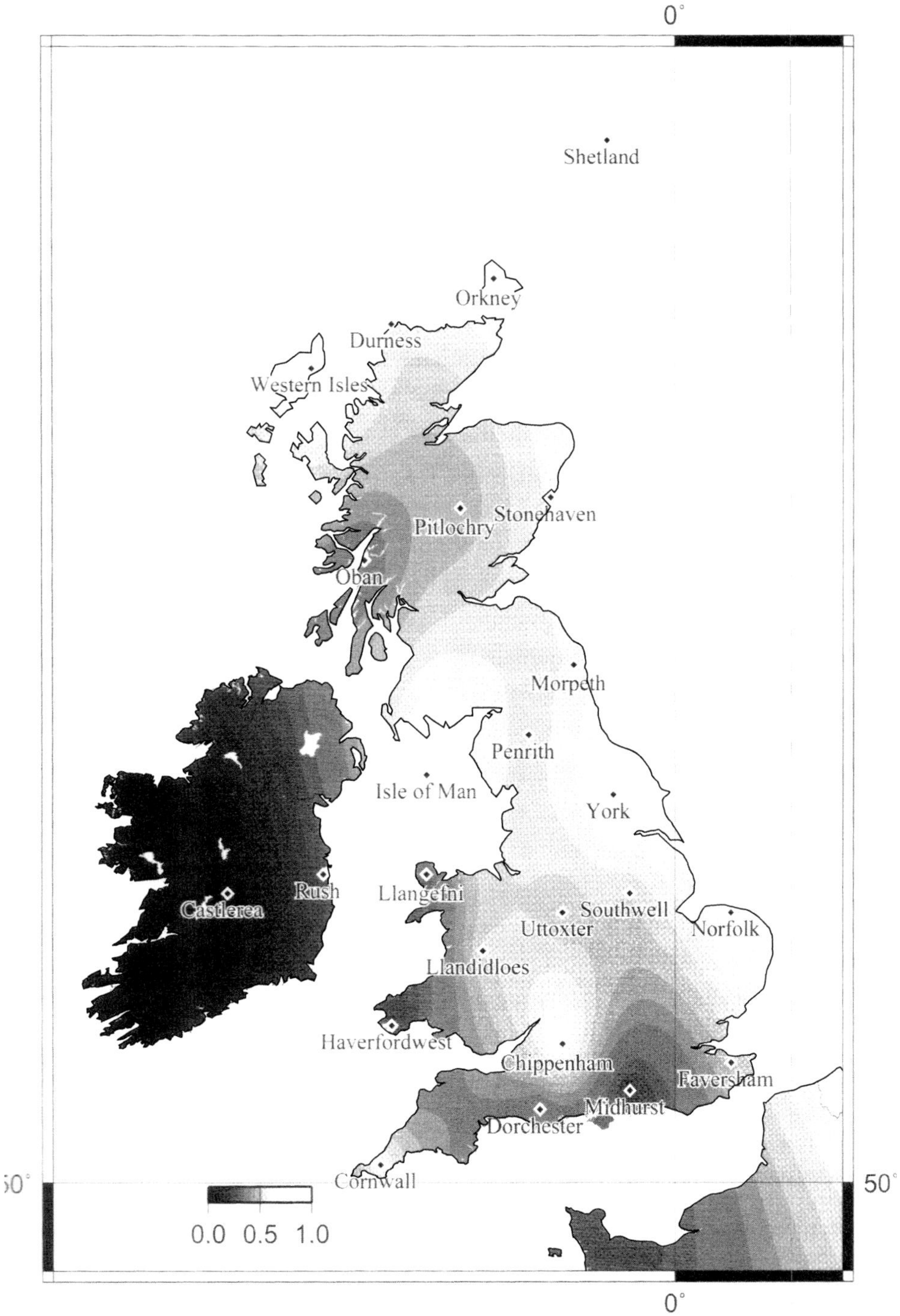

Figure 2.2 Trend map purporting to show the estimated Continental admixture proportions in Britain using Y chromosome data (1 = 100%). Admixture proportions were estimated using data from North Germany and Denmark as a Continental proxy and from Castlerea in Ireland as the indigenous British proxy.

(Härke 2011, Fig 3, after M. Thomas; with permission)

admixtures between Briton and German lay between 24.4 and 72.5% Anglo-Saxon, and the overall immigration was calculated as between 250,000 and 500,000 men and 100,000 women, in an estimated population of around 3.7 million. The *adventus saxonum* is here reprieved as a game-changing demographic event.

Aligning the genetic evidence with that of the physiognomy of skeletons and the nature of grave goods presents a moderately consistent picture. In the cemeteries, the cultural recognition of a German presence was accorded to taller-than-average weapon-bearing males, and of Britons by the distribution of penannular brooches which permeated virtually the whole English area.[27] The implication is that incomer and native were present in the eastern population at about 50/50% and had contrived various modes of coexistence. In one of these, Germanic immigrants and their descendants lived alongside Britons but kept in separate groups, an 'apartheid model' (example: Berinsfield). In the second, immigrant males arrived in a group and intermarried with British women, a 'war band model' (example: Stretton on the Fosse II). And in the third, a small group of Germanic immigrants took over a kingdom of Britons and ran it themselves, the 'elite transfer model' (example: Bernicia). For Heinrich Härke this acculturation was essentially a one-way process: English trumped British in culture as in language. An exception in Bernicia is seen as due to influence from western England and Ireland.[28]

Future research will undoubtedly make use of aDNA and ask more local and less overarching questions of a type that can be reliably answered. Such a micromapping of British demography should advance with the analysis of aDNA taken from skeletons in dated cemeteries in the seven different regions defined here – although at the time of writing systematic research in this field has scarcely begun. Ten individuals were analysed from a cemetery at Oakington, Cambridgeshire and found to have signatures related to *modern* Dutch and Danish populations. The authors calculated that the modern eastern English population owes 38% of its ancestry to the Anglo-Saxon migrations.[29] The analysis of nine genomes from cemeteries in north Britain showed continuity between Iron Age and Roman period populations, except for one exotic Roman from the Middle East and a different genome for the Anglo-Saxon population.[30] It would appear that aDNA requires a great deal of empirical data from many sources before a theory can be developed that relates its readings to the size and mobility of communities; the nature of power laws means that there will always be a few large families of connected kin.[31] It can be hypothesised that when immigrant Germanic groups met and (eventually) mated with a mixed British population, both parties being well supplied with genes from throughout the former empire, the chances of obtaining a representative sample of indigenous or immigrant groups would be fairly small.

However, what follows here in Chapters 3, 4 and 5 suggests not a single snapshot of the impact of the English but an unrolling demographic film. As the centuries went by, the composition and demeanour of the population changed overall, so that by the 7th century the men of either origin were of equal average height, and the erstwhile incomers adopted a 'nativist' attitude to kingship and to the past.[32] When the monastic movement arose in the late 7th and 8th century (our Formative 2), the archaeology indicates that it was led by Northumbria into the lands of the north and west, with a dominating culture that was hybrid in nature ('insular') and bypassed the English heartland (here 'Southumbria'). While the Northumbrian rhetoric may have promoted 'the English', the material culture manifests a spiritual movement rooted in the Celtic west and the prehistoric past.

An English immigration from the continent into Britain was thus achieved over 100 years or so, with various admixtures of native and immigrant and various types of encounter. The bigger kingdoms recognised in the 7th century by ancestral British or Anglo-Saxon names thus had different kinds of origin, created by those who had achieved power without any detailed knowledge of their genetic ancestry. In future studies, both cultural and biological, it is not excluded that the British contribution to the making of Britain will gain a more prominent reputation.[33] However, in the story that follows there is no doubting the privileged resources and unrelenting ambition of those that occupied the south-east part of the island, the part called England.

A précis of the present consensus might run as follows: peoples arrived from Frisia, Denmark and northern Germany in the 5th century in significant numbers, and immigration probably continued during part of the 6th century from other parts of the continent. By the third or fourth generation a German identity was being celebrated under the catch-all banners of 'Angle' and 'Saxon', terms used to label the nascent kingdoms, which were forming in emulation of Celtic practice. By the 7th and 8th centuries, shared identities were being constructed with the native Britons, using first burial rites, then insular art, as the primary binders. However, at the same time that Christianity endowed the peoples of the island with a common philosophy, its international nature encouraged the appointment of a wide variety of foreigners in prominent positions. Admittedly most of those we know about were clerics and so presumably had little effect on the gene pool.[34] But for each imported archbishop there will have been a number of sexually active secular companions and marriageable princesses of whom vigorous reproduction may be expected. In this aspect too, the demographic and social consequences of this second Romanisation will have been felt. Thus during the 7th and 8th centuries, the gene pool may be expected to have been enriched by French, Italian and possibly southern and eastern Mediterranean blood, just as it would be by Scandinavian blood in the Viking immigrations of the 9th and 10th century.

Prospects

The current debate on the composition of the population of Britain is bedevilled by wishful thinking on the question of ancestry, and there is a natural desire to suppose that being 'English' or 'British' or 'Scottish or 'Welsh' is a genetic fact and deserves to be ratified by DNA. The atmosphere is unlikely to be improved by the latest state-of-the-art DNA result mentioned above, which carries the inference that in the Bronze Age the population was almost entirely replaced by incomers from the eastern steppes. This has yet to have the impact it deserves in the popular press ('we are all Russians, say the scientists').

In this book my purpose is primarily to define the astonishing range of diverse cultural attributes associated with different parts of our island without laying two much emphasis on the traditional names inherited by the regions. That is not to say that the meaning of this diversity will prove to be any less stimulating.[35] On the other hand, whether using aDNA or any other method it may be that we are asking the wrong questions about demography for the present age. While it can be acknowledged that the English were immigrants into Britain, we still know rather little about where they came from, how their communities were composed, or how their identities were created. The English and the British represent a certain level of distinction, but not an explanation of the diversity of what happened. Common sense currently sees the immigrants as coming mainly from the north-western continent but in varying groups and as individuals. The Roman period with its high levels of mobility would have already introduced genes from all over Europe, parts of Asia and north Africa; to the innate differences that already prevailed between the different Celtic-speaking occupants of Britain due to geography was added a large and varied external range of descendants.[36] Neither should we forget that in some parts of Europe the most mobility in the first millennium, and the most genetic transfer, was probably due to the trade in slaves, especially trafficked women purchased from diverse sources and leaving children in new homelands.[37]

Studies of the Huns in central Europe reveal how mobility, especially of women, was a feature of the formative age, but cannot be neatly boxed in terms of exogamy, let alone of 'invasion' or 'migration'. The Huns arrived from central Asia in the 4th century, and it has been argued that the Hunnic intrusion penetrated far to the west and north of Europe under Atilla (d. 453), reaching as far as Sweden and provoking an ideological response in the 5th century with the building of monumental mounds and the adoption of monotheistic religion in the form of 'heroic Odinism'. It might also be supposed that the Huns made a significant genetic contribution to the European population.[38] A skeletal attribute of the Huns was an elongated skull deformed by binding and in central European cemeteries was a clear physical reminder that a person was foreign or had a history of migration.[39] Studied in association with grave goods, Susanne Hakenbeck's research has shown that their occurrence was the result of two different kinds of migration. In an eastern group, movement had taken place on a large scale over a long period of time, resulting in a new hybrid identity in members of both the receiving and the incoming population. In the western group, there was directed long-distance movement of a small number of individuals, mostly women, which may have been prompted by exogamous practices. In the first mode of migration, the encounter with different material culture practices and lifestyles is thought to have generated a transformation of identities, but in the second, the journey itself was transformative.[40] In other words, 'migration' is a confection of group movements and individual movements with different motors that quickly loses focus through contemporary or historical generalisation.

It may therefore be helpful if we could stop using the term 'migration' as a catchall for demic change in the debate over modern Europe no less than the debate about early Britain. A new approach might be to deconstruct 'migration' into its imperatives, using correlates and proxies. *Demic invasion* (mass movement of bodies) for both humans and animals can be assessed by aDNA and the isotope signatures of oxygen and strontium; *human trafficking* (including marriage) is a subset of these results, as is *ethnic* cleansing, but it will require much scientific ingenuity to distinguish between economic, sexual and predatory migrants. *Trade* may be tracked by the provenance of wooden objects (using dendro) and mineral objects (using thin sections); we have nothing for metal as yet (apart from their form and style). *Embassy* should be detectable from high-status gifts. *Ideological invasion* should offer a marked material signature, but the consequent movement of people can be at a trivial level. *Ethnic/political/ideological emulation* should be visible in settlement, structure and artefact styles. But here again there is no need to suppose that, in a period of high mobility and intellectual invention, every exotic idea implies a migrant.

The new bioarchaeological methods report on genetic admixture, degrees of kindred and demography, as well as the effects of diet and mobility and inherited pathogens – matters of which early medieval people themselves would often be blissfully unaware. Thus, while of great interest to the archaeologist, these things would not necessarily contribute to the agency of the social theatre, which relied on provocative observations such as 'he has his uncle's nose' that could only be resolved by bloodshed or complaisance. The skulls suggest a myriad diversity of faces, then as now, and a basic individual shape can be recovered using digital and plastic modelling techniques. But the unique and unmeasurable individuality that makes our hearts beat faster or our hackles rise, that mysterious weaver of affection or aggression, that causer of love, prejudice and war, will probably stay beyond the reach of science for the foreseeable future.

The body we prefer

Since early medieval people knew little of each other's DNA, expressions of identity relied heavily on speech and appearance to proclaim or accept the perceived ancestry of a stranger. We are not above such recourse today, so we are hardly entitled to remonstrate with our forebears for their prejudice or credulity. Speech, dialect or accent are likely to have provided the first divider, since such indications as we have suggest they were distinctive of origin and class. But appearance is the front-line weapon, not only because it dominates the first encounter but because it can be manipulated to display the intended identity, even to the degree that it will trump speech. Three components of appearance, in increasing ease of rediscovery, are the decoration of the body, clothing and accoutrements. Each of these invites or assumes recognition of class, of origin, of belief, of fertility, of ability, of attitude. In the age before the routine use of written records, the dressed-up human was its own walking CV.

People often sought to modify their appearance so that, even without any clothes on, they present a self-portrait; for this purpose, the principal palettes are skin and hair, especially tattoos and facial hair.[41] Few aspects of make-up have survived the long millennia, so we rely on indirect pointers: pictures, descriptions and objects used to manage a look, such as hair pins or tresses and (possibly) needles used to lay colour under the epidermis. Tattooing in the north is inferred from the Roman nickname 'Picti' (painted people) and constitutes a possible explanation for the fully formed emergence of standard Pictish symbols in 5th–7th-century stone carving.[42] It seems unlikely that tattooing, an adornment that was cheap, permanent and expressive and known globally from the Neolithic would have been confined to the Picts. At the time of Caesar's invasion: 'All the Britons dye themselves with woad (*vitreus*) giving them a blue colour, and they wear their hair long but shave all the rest of the body but the head and the upper lip.' This distinction was probably maintained longer in edge-of-empire north Britain.[43] The Celts of history manipulated their flowing locks. Strabo said their hair was naturally blond and made blonder by washing it with lime and drawing it back from the crown to the nape of the neck so that 'it differs in no way from a horse's mane'.[44] We will be on the lookout for beards and moustaches of various levels of pretension and for tresses, lock rings, hair pins and hair bands. There are likely to be some currently elusive links between the plaiting of the hair, the plaiting of wool in garments and the interlace seen in manuscripts and on sculpture, each of which would seem to celebrate the disciplining of nature.

Pictures, documents, burials and a mass of artefacts connected with spinning and weaving leave little doubt that all the peoples of Britain and Ireland invested enthusiastically in their appearance. We have Celtic men in fine cloaks and Saxon men in tunics and trousers. The Celtic women are more elusive, but Anglo-Saxon women were the subjects of adornment equal and often surpassing the men. The alpha female was dressed in flowing robes secured with necklaces, bangles and brooches that for the first two centuries of the formative period were the primary cultural markers, indicating rank, identity and date. The alpha male was a high-ranking warrior who rode a horse and carried a sword and shield. He wore a special 'warrior jacket' ultimately copied from Persian cavalrymen.[45] An iron helmet protected his head. His horse was also dressed and adorned, as were his servants. By the end of the 7th century, we also have sightings of the uniform adopted by those serving the church.

Evidence for dress

Verbal evocations

Written descriptions do not stint themselves in their use of rhetoric, but some contain credible details of textile colours and accessories. Here is an Irish princess, in whom beauty and wealth compete to engage the attention of an onlooker:

> He saw a woman at the edge of the spring, with a bright silver comb ornamented with gold, washing her hair in a silver bowl with four golden birds on it, and little flashing jewels of purple carbuncle on the rims of the bowl. She had a shaggy purple cloak made of fine fleece, and silver brooches of filigree work decorated with handsome gold in the cloak; a long hooded tunic on her, stiff and smooth, of green silk with embroidery of red gold. Wonderful ornaments of gold and silver with twining animal designs, in the tunic on her breast and her shoulders and shoulder blades on both sides.[46]

The voice of the poet resonates with *topos*, inviting us to take it all with a pinch of salt; but, given a suitably eclectic approach, virtually all the details in this eulogy could be paralleled to a credible degree somewhere in the corpus of metal objects and shreds of textile known from Britain and Ireland before the 9th century.[47] We will meet another striking woman, this time a spiritual authority, at the end of the chapter.

Images in art

This kind of status, the corpus of the not-impossible meta-evidence, is shared by that other seductive source, the images of people seen on sculpture, in manuscripts, on brooches and on coins. In practice, both texts and images can be used to dress real people, but only by applying a type of retrogressive analysis. The copying of earlier images was a positive virtue in the early middle ages, carrying none of the stigma of today's protection of intellectual property; nor is the 'original artist' necessarily viewed with admiration, as opposed to being seen as unlearned. The might of art history is engaged in deconstructing images in terms of their inspiration, aspiration and origins, the meaning often interpreted in terms of what they made of their 'exemplars'. The archaeological approach is appropriately more down to earth, its purpose being to isolate and define those fragments of authenticity that are embedded in the pictures and can be extracted, so to speak, stratigraphically.

The analytical technique is simple: the image is tested by searching for its occurrence as an image in an earlier medium or a dated object and eliminating as untrustworthy those images that could be copies. What is left may have represented a contemporary object. The method was originally evolved by comparing the Frankish Utrecht Psalter (9th century) with the Late Saxon psalter Harley 603, which was a copy of it made at Canterbury by various hands from AD 1000 onwards, and noting where the English scribes had amended the original. The retrogressive (or rather progressive) method found that the principal realists of Harley 603 were 'Hand 1A' and 'Hand 1F', both of whom drew from contemporary life and offer us a wealth of objects that they knew – some, like the weathercocks on church roofs, still unknown to archaeology. Although they had no surviving exemplars, the same methods were used to make a short list of those few manuscripts in which realists were active.[48] An outstanding example lies just outside the Late Saxon corpus – the Bayeux Tapestry, where the portrayal of real events helps us to distinguish between the abstract (blue and yellow horses) and the believable – tunics, swords and ships.[49] Using these as our escort we can the more easily accept King Edward's unkempt beard and his aristocracy sporting its 'English moustaches'; in contrast, the Normans have shaven lips. This gallery of contemporary life constitutes only a small part of all the thousands of images produced. It referred only to England and was very short-lived: 1000–1050 – perhaps into the 1060s. But it is rich and informative.

The same principles can be applied, although with less precision, to the northern artists of Northumbria and Pictland. The David in the Durham Cassiodorus wears his hair in tight curls, while the Vespasian psalter's David has ribbed hair bunched at the back.[50] One of the Pictish Davids on the St Andrew's sarcophagus carries a knife sheath ornamented in insular style; another on horseback wields sword with an ornate scabbard and carries a hawk; a spearman on foot caries a miniature shield of an Iron Age type dating to before 200 BC. The two major figures in the David sequence have flowing curly locks that would not disgrace a Jacobean monarch (see Figure 5.42). Isabel Henderson's verdict is that 'a review of the artefacts depicted on the surviving side panel of the sarcophagus suggests that the sculptor, faced with exotic models, did substitute contemporary or at least more familiar types'.[51] Giving David a hairstyle that reflected a Pictish royal fashion would be a credible indication of the deployment of the contemporary and familiar.

Evidence from artefacts – textiles

Textiles survive rarely on settlement sites and poorly in cemeteries, but the occasional find of fragments preserved by waterlogging or absence of air or by fossilised imprints on metal shows that the range of cloth was prodigious in weave and quality and included imports of fabrics (silk) and garments (cloaks). The value of these robes was on a par with swords and jewellery. Textiles were largely home-made from wool or flax spun into yarn using a spindle and weight ('whorl'); the terms 'Z' and 'S' represent the direction in which the yarn was twisted to give it strength. The yarn was woven on a loom that stood upright: the warp threads were kept taut by weights ('loom weights'), and the weft was threaded between them with a shuttle and made tight with a batten ('weaving sword'). There were numerous possibilities for interweaving the weft on the warp, giving rise to textiles of different patterns and strengths (Figure 2.3). The most commonly encountered were the tabby weave (straight criss-cross) and twills, where the weft is passed over stepped pairs of warp threads, resulting in a diagonal pattern. Flax was used to make fine linen and wool to make warm tunics and cloaks. Braids, cloth belts, tapes and edgings were made using sets of perforated tablets, which were moved to vary the weft and so produce long patterned strips – tablet weaving.

The Sutton Hoo burial ground has provided striking examples of the textile repertoire. The Mound 1 burial chamber, dated to about AD 625, contained evidence for 27 different kinds of textile recovered in 67 fragments, some preserved by replacement, where they had been in touch with metal, others conserved in a pad, like the pad of unburnt newspaper that survives in parts of a bonfire deprived of oxygen. From this remarkable collection it can be inferred that embroideries were hung on the walls and a carpet laid on the floor, linen was used to wrap weapons as a mark of protective respect, and a yellow tufted cloak imported from Syria was spread on top of the coffin.[52] Inside the coffin were three heaps of clothes. That furthest from the likely position of the dead man's feet ('Heap A') consisted of a leather garment, a horn cup and two little hanging bowls, a wooden bowl and, on top, a goose down pillow in its blue pillow case. On either side of the pillow were placed two pairs of indoor shoes, the length of one measurable at size 7 (or size 40 Continental): the Mound 1 hero

soumak

twills

Tabby weave

Spin direction

Z and S spun thread

Tabby weave with spaced pile

Tablet weaving

Warp-weighted loom

Figure 2.3 Types of textile weave.
(Courtesy of Penelope Walton Rogers)

was short and stocky. The heap nearest to the feet ('Heap B') began with a piece of folded twill on which a mail coat was placed, together with many coils of tape, perhaps for binding objects, cross-gartering or fastening garments. On top of these two heaps, another (Heap C) was loaded, beginning with a leather garment with a double buckle and then a toilet set in a fluted silver bowl, including burr-wood bottles, combs and four knives with horn handles, also something made of cowhair and an otter fur cap.[53] All this is personal paraphernalia, contrasted with the more ceremonial objects outside the coffin associated with parade dress and the business of government. The occupant of Mound 1, thought to be Raedwald, king of the East Angles, would have presented an impressive spectacle had he worn these garments: an international manifestation of power reinforced by Germanic and Roman symbolism.[54]

The woman buried about AD 650 under Mound 14 at the same site was laid in a chamber, possibly on a couch (indicated by a large number of small 'upholstery' nails). The chamber had been ransacked, but parts of a châtelaine and silver ornaments survived together with some precious fragments of textile, preserved through their contact with metal. The crumpled condition of the textile suggested that the clothes had been buried on a person rather than placed neatly in the grave. The most informative fragment, attached to the châtelaine, revealed a sequence of four layers, the primary one being actually a piece of human skin, followed by an inner gown of medium-weight linen, an outer gown of fine linen, and an outermost layer consisting of a fragment of a wool blanket or cloak. The textiles included embroidery and tablet-weave, each making ornamental bands worn probably around the sleeves (Figure 2.4). The embroidery was similar to that found on Bathild, the Anglo-Saxon wife of the Frankish king Clovis II, who died 680/1; and the tablet-woven bands recall the ornamental cuffs found on the forearms of Queen Arnegunde, who died c. AD 600 and was buried at St Denis, in France. Researcher Penelope Walton Rogers concluded that the woman had worn an inner chemise of medium-weight linen with long sleeves and embroidered cuffs and over it a gown of fine linen, also long-sleeved and also with patterned cuffs, this time tablet-woven. The Mound 14 textiles were made locally but using techniques known in Scandinavia. She also noted that the tablet-woven cuffs anticipated the gold-brocaded bands of later church vestments, for example those of St Cuthbert, who died in 687 and was later disinterred in the 10th century when his coffin lay in Durham Cathedral.[55] The main message of these examples (and of Walton Rogers' researches as a whole) is that the textiles and clothes of the early Anglo-Saxons aspired to sophisticated styles and achieved superlative quality. The careful preparation of smooth wool and flax thread, the minute detail and variety of the weave, the sense of colour, the geometric virtuosity of embroidery and brocade leave no doubt that, in spite of its meagre survival, the dressing of the upper classes was a major, perhaps the major, signal of wealth and excellence in the formative period.[56]

Metal accoutrements

Cloth was secured on the body with metal brooches, which offered an opportunity to declare rank, identity and the fashion of the day, decorated in a manner that incidentally allows us to date them. Both men and women wore brooches, but the trend was towards mainly men in the north and west and mainly women in the south and east.[57] In addition, men in burials were often armed with spear, shield and sword, which formed part of their identity, and women had a number of important accoutrements: the necklace of beads and especially the *châteleine* – a cluster of keys, rods and rings suspended from a belt. The buckle also sometimes offered an opportunity for expression in both sexes. These metal objects belonged to a repertoire that evolved over the formative period.

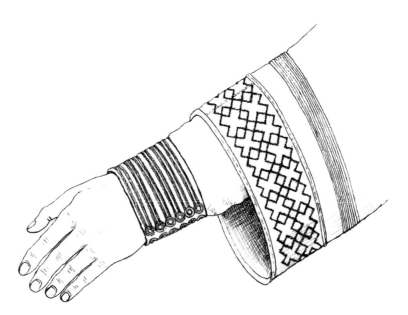

Figure 2.4 Part of a woman's garment of embroidered tabby weave found in Mound 14 at Sutton Hoo; with a reconstruction of the sleeve that it probably embellished, c. AD 650.

(Walton Rogers 2005, Plate 43, 2007, Fig 5.41; courtesy of Penelope Walton Rogers; drawing of the sleeve by Anthony Barton)

Most of the early brooches were made from copper alloy, using the lost-wax process: a detailed model was made in wax, clad in clay and baked until the melted wax ran out to leave a hollow to be filled by molten metal. In the Anglo-Saxon zone, a primary canvas was provided by the square-headed brooch of the 6th century, its bright gilded facade covered with broken limbs and isolated eyes, seeming to use the ambiguity of the fragments to celebrate human-animal alliances.[58] A woman who wears such a brooch commands the natural world (Figure 2.5). In the Celtic areas of the north and west, the complement to copper alloy was red enamel, seen on the terminals of 6th century brooches and on the escutcheons (decorated discs) of 7th century hanging bowls (Figure 2.6A). In the grandest of examples, bundles of

Figure 2.5 Square-headed brooch from Chessel Down, Isle of Wight in 'Style 1'.

(Reproduced under licence from the British Museum © The Trustees of the British Museum, and Style 1 images, Leigh 1984, Fig 1 and 2; Courtesy of Society of Antiquaries of London)

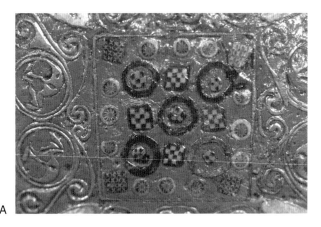

A

Figure 2.6 A: Ornament from a hanging bowl from Sutton Hoo. Top: Hanging Bowl no.1. Centre: Circular escutcheon from underside of the bowl. Bottom: Detail of the central part of one of the square escutcheons. The bowl is made of sheet bronze, and the escutcheons have reserved bronze scroll-work filled in with red enamel set with clusters of coloured glass (millefiori). The rim of the escutcheons is made of copper alloy enriched with tin (© The Trustees of the British Museum; licenced by British Museum).

B

Figure 2.6 B: Carpet page from the Book of Durrow. The interlace and the roundels with their ornamental spirals are rendered in orange and beige against a black background. Trinity College Dublin MS57, f3v; c. AD 680.

(Reproduced under licence from Trinity College Dublin)

minute coloured glass rods may be thin-sliced and floated on the hot enamel to provide a
dazzling collage.[59] The spiroform pattern is an ornamental theme that permeates the north
and west of Britain. Within the 7th century, the peltaic rhythms seen on the hanging bowls
transfer onto the earliest insular Gospel Books (Figure 2.6B). Here the knotted ornament

recalls the leatherwork seen on book covers (Chapter 5) or the embroidery seen on the garment worn by the woman buried in Mound 14 at Sutton Hoo (above).

High status 7th-century objects were fashioned of solid gold, in which red polished cut garnets were set into 'cages' (*cloisons*) soldered to the base. Throughout the 7th century, the animals of the insular (i.e. Anglo-British) repertoire evolve and are mobilised in new ways. Now whole bodied, they may take positions in tableaux, like the two wild boars crossed in a heraldic gesture on the gold and garnet shoulder clasp at Sutton Hoo (Figure 2.7A,B)

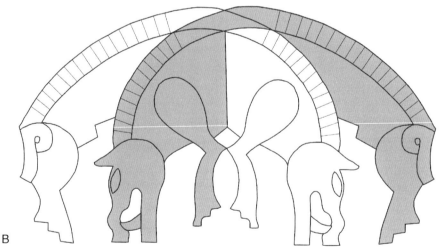

Figure 2.7 Animal ornament in the 7th century. A: Sutton Hoo shoulder clasp, c. AD 625 century. B: outline of the wild boar motif on A.

A: © The Trustees of the British Museum; licenced by British Museum; B: (FAS Heritage)

Figure 2.7 C: One end of the Sutton Hoo great gold buckle (c. AD 625). D: Ribbon animals from the Book of Durrow Trinity College Dublin Ms 57, f192v, c. AD 680 (detail). The central animal has a green body and is linked between two others with yellow bodies and green legs.

or cluster together in ribbons or chains ('Style 2'). Again the 7th century witnesses their changing roles. The animal (biting its own leg and bracketed by the jaws of death) on the foot of the great gold buckle of Mound 1 at Sutton Hoo joins a chain on a Book of Durrow carpet page (Figure 2.7C and D). Animals already stand alone in poll position on the Sutton Hoo shield (dragon and hawk) or helmet (see below), and the grandeur of such protective beasts is reprised in Christian contexts as the eagle, calf and lion of the evangelists' symbols of the first Gospel books. During the 8th century, animals (and birds) maintain a protective role in illuminated manuscripts (Figure 2.8A), but by the 9th century they have been assigned fun roles decorating the text (Figure 2.8B). The Vikings brought with them a new batch of beasts, both ribbon (Figure 2.8C) and stand alone, and bred them further in England during the 9th and 11th centuries (Figure 2.8D).

The chronology of this zoomorphic progression has been worked out using a chain of ornamental elements, where one is linked with the one before and anchored with independent chronological landmarks: association with dated coins, ascription to a named person (e.g. the Alfred Jewel or Aethelswith ring)[60] and, in rare cases, radiocarbon dating of the find-spot. In this way successive generations of scholars have built up a framework on

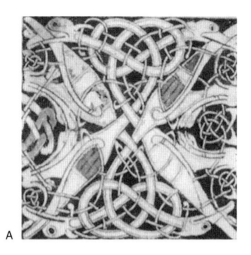

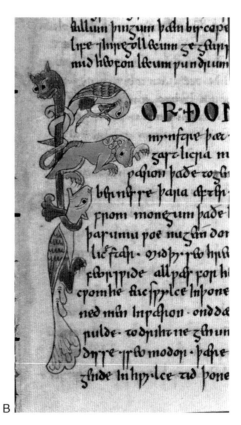

Figure 2.8 Animal ornament in the 8th to the 11th century. A: Birds in formation on a Carpet page in the Gospel Book of St Chad, mid-8th century. B: Initial (letter F) from a version of Bede's History in Old English. The animal has dark orange fur, and the two birds have beige bodies and brown feathers (first half of 10th century). C: Ribbon animals on the Jellinge cup (c. 900–975). D: The 'great beast' in Mammen style on the original Cammin Casket (960s–c. 1025). E: Figurehead on the Viking-style Noah's Ark (see also Figure 6.93).

(A: Lichfield Cathedral, p. 220; B: Oxford Bodleian Tanner 10, f79, licensed by and © The Bodleian Library Oxford; C: Permission National Museum of Denmark; D: courtesy of D M Wilson; E: BL Cott. Claudius BIV f14)

C

D

E

Figure 2.8 (Continued)

which early medieval Britain still largely relies for its chronology, especially that of artefacts (Table 2.2).[61]

Animal language

In this sequence there seems to be a gradual domestication, from mystical and fragmentary creatures, to symmetrical ribbon animals to individual beasts with proud heads. In the 7th century they begin to stand alone, on shields, on helmets, on parade gear, as a king stands alone in his task of acquiring territory and defending his people. The insular animals are pre-empted in 7th-century metalwork and are by no means inhibited by the arrival of imported Christian iconography: they are put to work even on the pages of Gospel books. By Fm 3, animals in English manuscript art are relegated to the margins and play at constructing initials; they have lost their magic and are here to serve man, as determined by the Christian God. The animals unleashed during the Viking interlude were no pets but servants of protection and power, from the gripping beasts of Borre, to the running ribbons of Jelling and the great beasts of Mammen, to the stressed and tangled creatures of the Ringerike and Urnes styles.[62]

Is there a meaning to these animal forms beyond social fashion? They may betray the influence of contemporary neighbours or the legacy of Rome (which comes and goes), but these 'references' to other cultures rarely dominate the idiosyncrasies of formative Britain. Fm 1 animals are broken up into kaleidoscopes of animal and human body parts: eyes that stare and limbs that cling and grip, forming a kind of tribal music, a mental map that is widely shared. Towards the end of Fm 1, as the animals are marshalled into chains of beasts hooked together like elephants, it is not too fanciful to see here the onset of a more managed human herd as folk gives way to kingdom. The stand-alone animals of Fm 2 soon acquire a new authority as spokesmen and ambassadors from the other world, notably in the form of the evangelist symbols. At a deeper level, animals appear to have a long-valued identity restated periodically as reified metaphors: the belligerence of the wild boar, the merciless pike, the nobility of the lion, the all-seeing eagle, the dominance of the serpent in the realm of death. In the north, the Pictish animals of Fm 1 are realistically drawn and have been seen as signifiers of names, families or peoples. This does not disqualify the animals from both serving as names and representing attributes: 'strong', 'fertile', 'proud'. Such ideas are suggested by anthropological studies, for example the iconic images deployed on the Gold Coast.[63] In contrast to the Vikings, the English artists of Fm 3 largely switched their attention to the human figure as the no.1 symbolic animal, acting under the tutelage of the Christian God, no longer as the colleague but as the master of all the animals, birds and plants (Figure 2.9). This short aside does not begin to deconstruct the complexity of animal language as used in the first millennium. But this is an archaeological book, and the intention is only to emphasise the changing roles of animals, especially as performers in human narratives. They express the moods of the age, they recall the deep certainties of the past – they have personhood themselves.

Masters of this vocabulary, top-rank metal-smiths, were in demand at the court of kings and later in the workshops of monasteries, changing their repertoire and techniques as demand reflected the intellectual preoccupations of the age. They were therefore the material equivalent of court poets: spokesmen and confidantes and masters of the oblique reference. The grave found at Tattershall Thorpe in Lincolnshire is a rare example of a smith buried with the tools of his trade: hammer, tongs, snips, drawbar, anvil, scrap metal box, a scale pan and weights. Among the grave goods were a blue glass jar, scabbard fittings, an openwork disc,

Figure 2.9 The Fuller Brooch is made of silver inlaid with black niello (silver sulphide), the two materials being polished together to give a deep sheen. The dished face (diameter 114 mm) portrays five vignettes representing the five senses surrounded with a border of 16 roundels in four groups of four with an animal, a bird, a human and a plant in each quadrant. The senses depicted are (clockwise from the top left) taste, smell, touch, hearing and, in the centre, sight. Of the nine human faces, two have curly hair and seven hair parted in the middle. The central figure (sight) wears a robe with a dangling textile marked with cross and resembling a stole and holds a V-shaped array of flowers which recalls the Alfred Jewell and perhaps the Pictish 'V-rod' symbol. The other figures are more down to earth and wear belted tunics with long sleeves and bare legs with leather shoes. Made in the 9th century, this celebration of the living world seems never to have been buried.

(Wilson 1964, 91–98, 211–214, Plate XLIV; Image © The Trustees of the British Museum; reproduced under licence)

a button with silk residues and an iron bell. He was a successful smith, it seems. Archaeologist David Hinton, who published the find, calls the Tattershall Thorpe smith 'a worker of great skill, perhaps one with a personal reputation'.[64] Whether working for lords in Scottish forts or abbots in Pictish monasteries, for farmers, kings, warlords, Vikings, commoners, or princesses in the English lowlands, the smith was a craftsman of considerable influence and outstanding knowledge not only of what pleases but of its significance for each member of the socially active community – a professor of appearance.[65] As shown in the examples above, descendants of those producing objects in precious metal must have found new roles with compass and quill in the scriptoria making illuminated manuscripts.

Interpretation of clothing

Evidence for dress found in graves is confined to the English region, which is therefore disproportionately representative of early Formative fashions as a whole. Moreover, it was confined to only a short part of the early middle ages, c. 400–670. Nevertheless, it offers us a glimpse of a comprehensive wardrobe and the industries that supported it and indicates something of the enormous labour, ingenuity and investment that went into dressing up.

The question to be considered is whether the clothing found in graves represents everyday life, a 'best dress' for special occasions only, or a uniform appropriate to particular occupations or people of a certain class or ethnic group. From the moment of their recognition in the 18th–19th century, the dressed-up dead of south and east Britain were put to work in defining the coming of the Anglo-Saxons in the middle of the 5th century, as described by Bede.[66] Attempts to unlock the furnished graves and their costumes from this historical context have punctuated the development of early Anglo-Saxon archaeology itself. While early commentators sought equations between the form of grave clothes and an ethnic group, later scholars have emphasised the agency of the burial parties, who may have used the funeral to express current aspirations and anxieties.

Some social drivers will also be active in determining the composition of the grave. Wealth at some level is necessary to manufacture the grave goods and to afford their loss. Governance, i.e. status and degree of power, will affect the degree of expression: a high investment grave is more likely to reflect the politics of the day. Spirituality provides a wild card: status can be overruled by a new dogma, such as Christianity, which causes a king to be buried naked in a winding sheet instead of in a chamber laden with treasure.[67] Graves speak from their local context: some have material signals that are low-powered through poverty, inferior status or religious inhibition. Others are blazing with rhetoric and have released a full voice of commentary on the past and the future – burial as eulogy, epic and elegy.[68] These differences are interesting but inhibit interpretation. Many of the Anglo-Saxon graves lie somewhere in between: there are precious objects, some of them probably or certainly heirlooms or antiques, some symbolic objects, some objects carrying symbols.

The special messages of these graves are probably best seen as individual expressions using a common language. Threads and themes can be picked up in the grave goods and burial rites – 'Romanness' 'Angles' 'Woden', 'Christ' – but there are few moments and few encounters when we are actually entitled to designate a grave as Anglian or Christian. Paradoxically, the messages are strong, but we cannot necessarily read them because they are local or even individual and may vary with the current ideological conversation. The position taken here needs to be distinguished from the two that have dominated the last few decades: on the one hand that the messages refer only to affiliations known to literature, such as Angles or Christianity; on the other, the nihilistic conclusion that graves have no useful relationship to expressions of belief.[69]

This still leaves us with the question: how far can we use the clothing found in graves as evidence for appearance? At one level there is no doubt that we can: the clothes were in use at the time of burial: they represent what that individual wore, at least once. A kind of traditional wear has survived in Germanic and Celtic countries, as *tracht* or folk costume, where it comes out at weddings and other public occasions at which the display of one's personal affiliation is socially welcome. As well as appearing aggressive when worn routinely, such costume might appear rather fancy or inconvenient for everyday use and ought to have scattered large quantities of fixings over settlements and the fields as they broke or dropped off. In fact, such finds *are* made from time to time (see below), but this need not imply that the whole burial outfit was everyday wear. Anglo-Saxon textile expert Penelope Walton Rogers concludes that the basic part of the dress encountered in Anglo-Saxon graves is that worn routinely by the people, but the full get-up was probably reserved for stepping out, getting married, parading or going to join the ancestors.

That being so, the dress tells us something about the tastes and inheritance of the dead person, something about their affiliations, to family, to kin, to local folk, to the broader Germanic *kulturkreis*, but not their biological relatives; something about their views of this world and the next, but little about allegiance to specific gods. The grave is rich with the ideas of a person, but equations with historically known groups – pagan, Christian, Angle, Briton – is more difficult and should not be allowed to drown out or dismiss the special character being celebrated, which, for those at the graveside and arguably for modern scientists too, is more individual and informative.

PAS

The Portable Antiquity Service (PAS) has provided a new source for the appearance of people of the early middle ages and indeed for earlier periods of the past. It records the objects found by metal-detectorists pursing their hobby of searching for treasure and now by voluntary agreement submitted to the PAS investigators. The result of relaxing the age-old prejudice against non-specialists looking for archaeological objects has been explosive: hundreds of thousands of objects have been submitted for recording in this voluntary scheme, the opening of a Pandora's box containing the products of centuries of hidden pillage and accidental loss. There are three limitations: first, the great majority finds are made of metal, since the instrument does not easily find glass or ceramics; second, the retrieval follows the instincts of the detectorists, who tend to follow each other's tipoffs like bird twitchers. Third, the new source of evidence is still unfortunately confined to the English administrative area, a small part of the British island. So the differences in historic prominence between the English region and the rest is destined to be artificially enhanced yet again. However, the advantage for researchers, and the one likely to persuade those countries opposed to the scheme on ethical grounds eventually to join it, is that it represents a whole new source of archaeological data, that of random loss. The scheme does occasionally allow sites to be inferred or hoards to be located, but its strength lies in the patterns of ordinary objects that have accidentally found their way onto the surface of land, the majority of which was then fields, woods or tracks. These casual losses will eventually provide a statistically valid account of what was in use among living people engaged in routine activities.

At the time of writing, the database contains 2,685 early medieval objects, of which 2,427 were brooches (or fragments of brooches), the great majority being copper alloy and found in the Anglo-Saxon heartland of Suffolk, Norfolk and Lincolnshire. Brooches, buttons, wrist-clasps, pendants and horse fittings predominate, so that while disturbance of a cemetery is always a possibility, the corpus as a whole reinforces the impression of casual loss. Whatever may have been eventually selected for burial, these objects were part of the apparel of the everyday Anglo-Saxon and their horse.[70]

Values

Much of the value that wearers put on their own clothes and accoutrements remains unknown, but we would love to hear something of their biography: 'It was my mother's'; 'Athelfrith gave it to me'; 'I won it on sports day'; 'My father won it on sports day'; 'My grandmother always kept it, as she said, for me'; 'It was my very first knife'. Others are identifiable, although not costly: a monk's hooded gown. But wealth spoke volumes, then as now. In both the Celtic and the Anglo-Saxon world value was related to a cattle standard. In Ireland the other currencies in use were female slaves and silver.[71] The Anglo-Saxon scale is specific: an ox is worth 1 *mancus* = 70 grains of gold = 30 silver pence. A sheep is worth 4 or 5 pence. The lesser denominations varied: 1 shilling = 20 pence in early Kent, 4 pence in Mercia and early Wessex and 5 pence in later Wessex. But 1 pound = 240 pence. In the Viking period, 1 mark [Danish] = 8 ores; 1 ore = 20 pence or 16 pence.[72] Compensations payable for the murder of a man varied with his perceived value (man-price), between 200 shillings (a churl), 600 shillings (a *gesith* or thane) and 1,500 shillings or 30,000 pence (a king's ransom). These 'wergilds' were payable at the open grave in Kent. A slave also had a price, usually around eight oxen (240 pence). Slaves were sold, like other goods, before witnesses, and tax was paid on the purchase.[73] The great gold buckle from Mound 1 at Sutton Hoo weighed in at 412.7 gm, equivalent to 90 mancus, 2,700 silver pence, 90 oxen or 11 slaves.

The arrival of institutionalised Christianity enlarged rather than developed the existing system, and with increased records, clothes emerged from the wardrobe, so to speak, to display their role in barter and legacy. Benedict Biscop gave two silken robes from Rome to buy three hides of land from King Aldfrith. Wilfred divided the treasury of Ripon and Hexham on his death bed into four piles of gold and jewels. A book from Rome acquired eight hides for Jarrow, and Richard Morris comments:

> The fact that a book could be worth eight family farms suggests that Roman souvenirs were also used to provide working capital for the new monastery. . . . Treasure . . . was part of the stock-in-trade of monasteries like Hexham, Ripon and Jarrow.[74]

Uneven evidence

The uneven survival of evidence and adornment is fundamental to the difficulty of representing the peoples of early medieval Britain fairly today, a problem with us throughout these pages. The archaeological record has conspired in favour of the English, who have the furnished graves in Fm 1, a rich gallery of manuscript images in Fm 3 and now an annual harvest of portable antiquities. The Celts of Ireland have a surviving literary inheritance, which we trust it is permissible to borrow in a spirit of analogy, however remote. The Pictish region has images on the Class II slabs (Fm 2) and a few examples of clothed persons can be found on stones in Fm 2 in Northumbria and in Fm 3 in the south-west.[75]

This uneven record must unbalance our story (Table 2.1); however, as a point of departure it can be surmised that such systems of investment can be extended across the seven regions, and we occasionally glimpse examples which confirm that the zeitgeist is shared, and with it a switch in the goals of personal appearance. After the Christianisation of the English, it can be surmised that many of the detailed fashions applied across the country.

Costume stories – Formative 1 (400–675)

We can now set out on a tour of Britain, and a tour through time. As explained at the end of the last chapter, the basic framework is provided by the three formative periods, and the

Table 2.1 Preferred symbolic vocabulary, 400–1000

Region	Fm 1	Fm 2	Fm 3
Scotland		Insular	Scotto-Norse
Pictland	Late Iron Age	Insular	Scotto-Norse
Cumbria			Isle of Man
Wales	Romano-British	Insular	
SW			Anglo-Celtic
Northumbria	Anglo-British	Insular	Anglo-Scandinavian Borre Mammen Jelling Ringerrike
England	Anglo-Saxon Style 1, Style 2 (from late 6th century)	Insular	Winchester school Anglo-Scandinavian Borre Mammen Jelling Ringerike Utrecht school

Table 2.2 The uneven representation of evidence for personal appearance from the seven regions

Region	Fm 1	Fm 2	Fm 3
Scotland			Brooches Viking
Pictland	Metalwork	Brooches Sculpture	Brooches Sculpture
Cumbria			
Northumbria		Sculpture	
Wales			
SW Britain			Sculpture
England (Southumbria)	Clothes in cemeteries brooches, fittings and textiles in cemeteries and PAS	Clothes in cemeteries brooches, fittings and textiles in cemeteries and PAS	Pictures Urban deposits (e.g. shoes). Metal accoutrements from PAS

tour happens within each of these following the same itinerary from north to south-west and from north-east to south. Where the information is thin or not accurately located, the text will treat larger regions, as 'north and west' and 'east and south'. Hopefully this will become a familiar and a pleasurable mode of travel through the island. The principal survival common to Britain as a whole is the brooch, from which cross-regional comparisons are possible. The common culture implied by the penannular brooch occupies Ireland and much of Britain and coincides with the distribution of Celtic-speaking people (see below). Some penannulars intrude into the south-east region, which is otherwise dominated by the wide range of brooches associated with incoming Germanic peoples. All these types are distinctive and show a difference in both the diversity and the rhythm of change between the two regions. As might be expected, the penannular (Celtic) region is more homogenous and conservative, while the Germanic region shows style zones around The Wash and to north and south of it. Change in appearance through time is also more noticeable in the east. Status appears in both areas from the 6th century in the form of larger, richer brooches.

Fm 1 in the north and west

Between the 5th and 7th century the material culture of the west and north of Britain is meagre in quantity and quality, an impression enhanced by comparison with the English area, with its richly furnished graves and its harvest from the Portable Antiquities Scheme. However, there are signs that the post-Roman poverty of the Celtic areas is a real one: metal-working at Dinas Powys employed recycled bronze from the English area, and even iron was in short supply.[76] A more pertinent indication is the NRA archaeology campaign in Ireland, in which a large amount of earth was moved in advance of road schemes, with a potential harvest of finds as significant in its scope as the Portable Antiquities Scheme in England. But here too the tally was not great.[77] The number of sites where copper was worked increased, but they are still fewer than iron. While small scale iron-working is present on many sites, copper alloy and glass working is still confined to high-status settlements.

We look to the Iron Age first, hoping for some pointers, but the gleanings are meagre.[78] Buffer torcs were worn by men and women around the neck, fibulae of bronze or iron were used to fasten a garment at the shoulder. Belts could have elaborate and ornate fittings, and armlets, wristlets and anklets, beads of glass, amber and other materials provided adornment. Men wore a shirt or tunic with trousers, the women long dresses. Both had heavy cloaks of sheep's wool of a type also exported to the Mediterranean.[79] These general and necessary provisions for a northern climate were no doubt continued in some measure into the early middle ages, but by then we gain assistance from new types of evidence. The brooch series from the 4th century to the 11th provides the key archaeological framework: a widely shared and datable cultural signal. Ring-headed pins were gradually replaced as the principal dress fastener in the Iron Age to Formative transition in the west, but dress pins continued in use into the 5th century.[80] There are some exceptional survivals, like the Orkney hood (below) and the embroidery from Llan-gors crannog in Wales (p. 124, note 212), but a review in 2007 showed that textile finds are sparse and uneven. Scotland (including Pictland and the Isles) had 34 find-spots, Ireland 17, the Isle of Man eight, Wales two. England, with the advantage of grave goods and anaerobic town sites, had more than 180 find-spots.[81]

The penannular brooch was a long-serving favourite way of securing clothes.[82] It had a pin on a hoop with a gap. The pin fastened two hems of cloth together and then locked them by rotating the hoop and tucking one of its terminals under the point of the pin. The early form had a small hoop (5 cm across) and a short pin (just a little longer), so these could secure thinnish cloth or linen. The brooches emerge from longer traditions of the pre-Roman to Late Roman periods, where they survive on both sides of the Irish Sea as small wire hoops with coiled terminals (Iron Age), then 'omega' shaped hoops with stylised bird's head terminals (Post-Roman Irish), a hoop with flattened terminals with stylised beast heads (4th century, west country) and brooches with flattened terminals inlaid with enamel (Dinas Powys, 6th century).[83] The 5th–7th-century Irish finds include numerous examples of penannular brooches with flange terminals, often with red enamel inlay. They are found suggestively distributed along the roads leading to the main Iron Age cult centres, which probably remained in use for ceremonial meeting and fairs. Finds on the ground and moulds show that metalworkers' output in Ireland was mainly dedicated to the production of stick pins, penannular brooches and ingots.[84] The western (British) parts of Britain also made extensive use of penannulars (Figure 2.10), and the occurrences in the more easterly parts of the island have been used to infer that Britons were interspersed with Anglo-Saxons in the English area.[85]

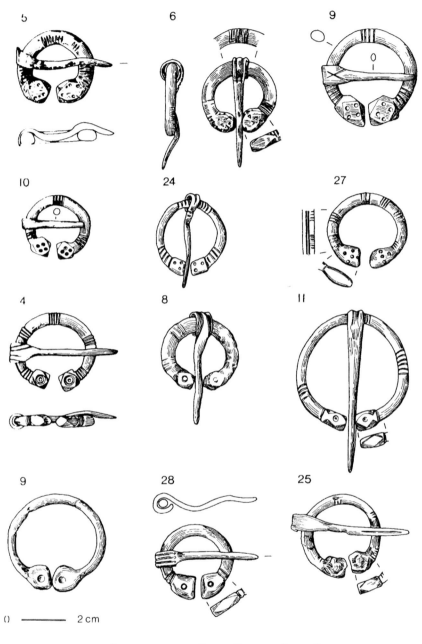

5, 6, 9, 10, 24, 27: type G1 1; 4, 8, 11 19, 28: type G1.2; 25. type G1.3. Scale 1 1 11 not to scale

Figure 2.10 British G-type penannular brooches of the 5th–7th centuries.

(Dickinson 1982, Fig 1, 3; with permission)

Both islands also made use of hand pins and stick pins, some of which could be truly grand. The Gaulcross hoard in Pictland had a silver hand pin with a 'finger-head' decorated with inlaid spirals, a length of silver chain and a silver bracelet. Similar pins occurred in the Norrie's Law hoard, along with a torc and silver leaf-shaped plaques that resemble pendants or earrings but had a boss at one end rather than a hole for suspension (Figure 2.11).[86] The Norrie's Law hoard included late Roman material, and late Roman material, probably belonging to the Gaulcross hoard, was excavated at the find-spot in 2013: Roman coins of the 4th century, spoon handles, a strap end or belt fitting, two small hollow hemispheres, the flattened terminal of a penannular brooch, a more complete penannular brooch with zoomorphic terminals, a lunate pendant and a silver ingot. The excavations at Gaulcross and at 5th/6th century Rhynie have served to pull the use of the Pictish symbols and the symbol stones back towards the end of Roman Britain.[87] Thus the silver pins, torc, bracelet and (sewn-on) plaques may be allowed to suggest what the upper class Pict was wearing in Fm 1.

Stick pins occur in many forms, and it is not excluded that some were used to secure the hair. They could be sturdy, plain and made of iron, like those found at Portmahomack (Easter Ross), or copper alloy, with cubic heads, round head or a ring; or silver fitted with lavish decorated heads.[88] Other examples, such as the Londesborough pin, have a solid disc at the head and a decorated shaft. Objects surviving from the Fm 1 period also included 'latchet' dress fasteners and bracelets.[89]

The clothes secured by these brooches and pins are drawn from a wide range of sources in use for centuries: pelts of foxes, martens (and maybe bears in Pictland), fleeces of sheep and hides of cattle, sheep, goats and red deer.[90] Most commonly, textiles were made from the wool of sheep, or linen from flax for undergarments. In Scotland, Ireland and Northumbria, the main fleece types are *hairy* and *hairy medium*. In Scotland the fleeces come in black, brown, grey and white. In Ireland, shades of brown are the norm.[91] The garments are made from spun wool thread, woven on a loom and cut to shape, the pieces sewn together and the hems sometimes finished with silk, linen or wool strips, woven with tablets and embroidered with coloured or gold or silver threads – to make a brocade.

Only a few textile fragments have been found that had been dyed, since burial in the ground leaches the pigment. Purple dye (Tyrian purple or imperial purple) is obtained from predatory sea snails of the Muricidae family (murex) in the Mediterranean. They could be extracted locally from the dog whelk *Nucilla lapillus*, found at a number of places along the west coast of Ireland. A workshop thought to be dedicated to dyeing cloth using dog whelks has been found on the island of Inishkea, County Mayo. It had a 'vat' and a pile of smashed dog whelk shells.[92] Traces of bromine, indicating whelk-dye, were found on the parchment of the Barberini Gospels (8th/9th century).[93] Cloth dyed with dog whelks was apparently known to the English, although no surviving example has been found.[94] Purple could also be extracted from lichen or by mixing blue indigo with red madder. Islamic dyers used indigo and lichen to obtain purple.[95] The survival is exiguous and late but enough to show that in the Celtic regions, as in England (below), the people were not dressed in rags but in tailored clothing of rich natural or artificial colours.

The one surviving garment from the British Celtic regions is the 'Orkney Hood', a fringed and hooded woollen cape using two shades of natural wool (brown and black), with a tablet-woven strip sewn along the hem (Figure 2.12). It had been recycled from other pieces to construct a weather-proof hoodie for a child. Found on Orkney, it has been radiocarbon dated to AD 250–640, so belongs to the earliest Pictish period.[96] This is a reminder that the hood itself was a practical garment and not necessarily a sign of office, as it has become for monks today. But we shall meet hooded clerics in Pictland in Fm 2.

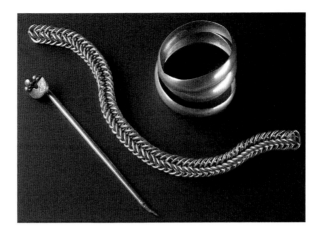

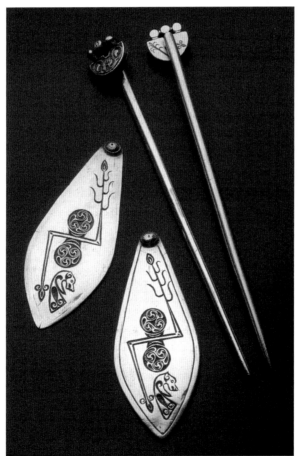

Figure 2.11 Items of Pictish apparel. (Top) Silver bracelet, chain and hand pin from the Gaulcross hoard. (Bottom) Silver hand pins and ornamental plaques (earrings?) bearing Pictish symbols from the Norrie's Law hoard. One of the plaques is a 19th century copy.

Figure 2.12 The Orkney Hood.

(X.NA3; Image © National Museums Scotland reproduced under licence)

There are some wonderful pen-pictures of dressed-up people, especially from Ireland, often difficult to place in the appropriate reality, but the brooches help to make the links. There are a few pictorial images that can be placed in Fm 1. The Rhynie man with belted tunic and pointed beard has been given a new context by the find of a cult centre at Rhynie, which includes a miniature version of the axe hammer carried over his right shoulder and should refer to the ritual sacrifice of cattle at the same site.[97] An animal-headed figure from Mail in Shetland, also carrying an axe hammer, wears a belted, pleated robe.[98] The figures etched on stone at Rhynie and Mail have a menacing air and may represent ritual specialists. They wear belted robes with ornamented hem or cuffs and carry axe-hammers. Finds of combs and the images of combs and mirrors that form such a prominent role in the Pictish symbolic language imply, if a little obliquely, that management of the hair was considered an important part of appearance. The double-sided comb resembles a modern nit comb and no doubt had a similar function. Most inhabitants of the north and west seem to have worn a plaid fastened at the shoulder with a penannular brooch or stick pin and presumably had a belted undergarment, probably with a hood. Without clothed burials, it is hard to tell if men and women had different styles of dress. Status is implied by the silver hand pins and by the enamelled terminals of penannulars, and these must express precedence over toggles and pins of bone, antler or wood.

Much of this personal materiality, in the form of combs, pins and brooches, was shared with Wales (Figure 2.13). The symbolic properties of the penannular is implied by its long

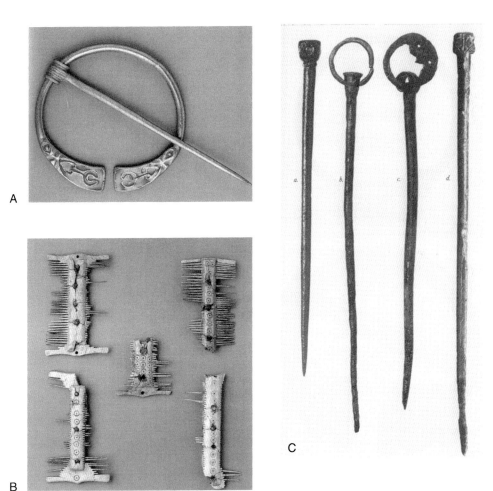

Figure 2.13 Welsh dressers. A: Enamel penannular brooch and B: combs from Dinas Powys; C: ringed pins from Wales; 5th/6th century.

(Redknap 1991, 18, 19, 33; By courtesy of Mark Redknap and the National Museum of Wales ©Amgueddfa Genedlaethol Cymru; © National Museum of Wales)

history of use, and not least by the attention that was to be lavished on the artefact in the 7th century and later.

Formative 1 in England

The period from the 5th–7th centuries in England is blessed with the richest evidence we have for male and female appearance thanks to the objects included in burials during this time, many of which related to personal clothing and equipment. The arrival of the Anglo-Saxons is currently accepted as having begun in the early 5th century, with The Wash then acting as the principal conduit. Its progress is illustrated by the incidence of cruciform brooches and the artefacts found at the 5th to mid-6th-century cemetery at Spong Hill, which originate in various lands across the North Sea.[99] A second wave, which came in via The Wash and the Humber, was indicated by wrist-clasps, metal links for wrist and ankle cuffs. These have been placed 'with considerable precision' as a female-only dress item originating in 4th-century southern Scandinavia and expanding northwards and southwards in the 4th and 5th centuries, and then 'the last major stage of expansion in Scandinavia is concurrent with a dramatic leap across the North Sea into Britain'.[100] In Britain, their eventual distribution is from the mouth of the Humber, from the Fens spreading inland via the Trent or along the Foss Way to Leicestershire and Rutland, Grave 155 at Sleaford (Lincolnshire) being one of the earliest. The type then morphed into two: Class A, only on female dress, and Class B, also worn by men. Their distribution represents a close relationship between the Humber and The Wash, both points of entry for Class B.[101] The wrist-clasps thus represent a secondary immigration and settlement pattern into the Anglian area, probably from Norway, in the later 5th century. Hines' thesis was published in 1984, but this distribution has not been much altered by PAS.

The repertoire of brooches subsequently expanded, and they were distributed over the English territories: cruciform, saucer, button, square-headed, small-long, composite. The overlap between different types in an eastern (Spong Hill) and a western cemetery (Wasperton) (Figure 2.14) gives a warning that many variables other than regionality or time or even the potential movement of people control the distribution of these brooches.[102] Annular and penannular brooches also came into use in the English areas, arguably under local British influence.[103] The brooches were cast in copper alloy from clay moulds, often intricately patterned and sometimes gilded. These are the star players of early Anglo-Saxon typology and chronology. The *Great square-headed brooch* is the primary emblem of the Anglo-Saxon alpha female. It provided a larger canvas for artists to exercise the enigmatic variations of 'Style 1' animal art in which heads, eyes, mouths, limbs and feet fragment and intertwine (see above). This type of brooch was brought into England from Denmark and continued to develop here. It was probably a badge of religious allegiance as well as rank.[104]

The textiles in graves report their own version of the Anglo-Saxon immigration in two waves.[105] The first, which appeared to originate in Denmark and appeared from c. 450 AD, used ZZ spun twills made on a warp-weighted loom with annular loom weights. The second, in c. 500 AD, originated in Frisia and north Germany and brought in ZS spun twills and the plano-convex mainly hemispherical spindle whorl. Women were well represented among the early settlers and introduced a distinctive pinafore dress fastened at each shoulder: the

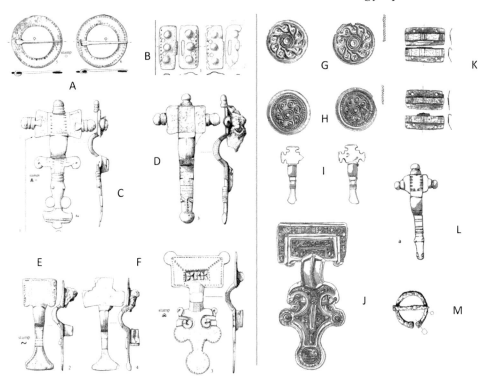

Figure 2.14 Fm 1: Types of Anglo-Saxon brooches, from Spong Hill (Norfolk) (A–F) and Wasperton (Warwickshire) (G–M). The brooches often occur in matching pairs. This example illustrates the overlap in types that occurs between eastern and western England. The types shown here are annular brooches (A, M), saucer brooches (G, H), small-long (E, I); cruciform (C,D,L), square-headed (F, J) and wrist-clasps (B, K).

(Spong Hill: Hills et al. 1984, Inh 55 (A), 37 (B), 45 (C) 46 (D) 2 (E), 18 (F); courtesy of Norfolk Archaeology Unit, © Norfolk Historic Environment Service; Wasperton: Carver et al. 2009, Inh 4 (G), 24 (H), 24 (J), 53 (K), 111 (L), 161 (M), 116 (I); reproduced under licence from Boydell & Brewer)

peplos[106] (Figure 2.15). The cloth, woven from wool, was of a natural light colour that might be dyed.[107] The evidence for *headscarves*, used by women to protect their hair and perhaps for modesty and fashion, is found as replaced textile, where it rested on metal brooches. During the 7th century these extended into long veils, perhaps under the influence of Christianity (Figure 2.16). Among the rich harvest of finds at Winchester, it was in Fm 2 that dress and hair pins were most numerous.[108]

By the 6th century, regional patterns of dress can be seen within the English area, indicating a gradual coalescence of allegiance within a growing population. In her classic survey, Penelope Walton Rogers defined four regions of early Anglo-Saxon costume (Figure 2.17): *Region 1* was the Anglian area and the earliest to be settled, comprising The Wash and Humber, East Riding, Lindsey and Norfolk. Here there was some Roman survival of textile technology in the form of spindle whorls, type of twill, tubular selvedge (the sealed edge that

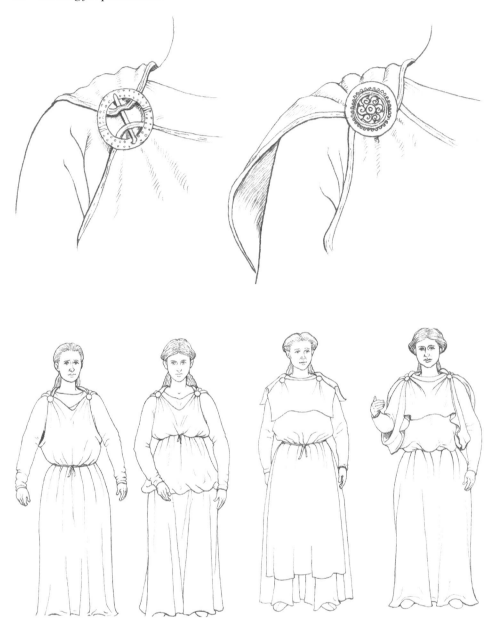

Figure 2.15 Four ways of wearing the *peplos* and methods of securing it at the shoulder.
(Walton Rogers 2007, Fig 5.5, 5.11; courtesy of Penelope Walton Rogers. Drawing by Anthony Barton)

keeps the cloth from unravelling) and soft-finishing with teasels. The *cruciform brooch* was an early marker, arriving from north Germany and Scandinavia in the 5th century (above). It was generally worn singly rather than in pairs, perhaps to fasten a cloak over the breast as in the north and west. *Annular brooches* were worn at the shoulder. Necklaces were sported by women from age 17 upwards.

Figure 2.16 Veils. A: Short veils of early Fm 1. B: Longer veils that came into use in Christian times.
(Walton Rogers 2007, Fig 5.29, 5.30; courtesy of Penelope Walton Rogers; Drawing by Anthony Barton)

The individual in Scorton (North Yorkshire) Grave 31 is a Region 1 representative (Figure 2.18A). She wore wrist-clasps and had matching annular brooches on the shoulders under the cloak, with a necklace of amber beads slung between them. A cruciform brooch lay crossways at the throat, and there was a large iron buckle near a knife at the midriff. The peplos was of a natural brown colour, and a cloak of coarse fabric was worn over it. Up near the head was

Figure 2.17 Textile zones.
(Walton Rogers 2007, Fig 3.37; courtesy of Penelope Walton Rogers)

Figure 2.18 Well-dressed women from Scorton (North Yorkshire) (left) and Snape (Suffolk).

(Reconstruction paintings by Graham Sumner; Walton Rogers 2007, Fig 5.38, 5.39; courtesy of Penelope Walton Rogers and Graham Sumner © Graham Sumner)

a fragment of the fine weave of a veil. She was buried prone (the brooches were found face down). Snape (Suffolk) G5 (also Figure 2.18B) wore an overdress and peplos made from medium-weight wool twill, one dyed dark blue with woad, the other dark brown (probably dyed with oak gall or bark). The peplos cuffs were Scandinavian style tablet-woven bands, with a soumak pattern worked in natural shades of horse hair, fastened with sleeve clasps. The sleeve slit was edged with a guilloche plait. She wore a single large amber bead at the neck and carried a knife in a calfskin sheath.

Region 2 is middle England, an intermediate area between Regions 1 and 3 and influenced by both, with an admixture of *penannular brooches* popular in the west and the Severn region. The River Severn also acted as an entry point to England, used to introduce Syrian summer-and-winter coverlets.[109] *Region 3* contains the Saxon areas and is very conservative. Amongst the Saxons the wearing of the peplos coincided with the child-bearing years, from late teens to maturity. The peplos is fastened at the shoulders by pairs of *saucer brooches*, a type originating in Lower Saxony in the 5th century and introduced into England from there. Necklaces with numerous beads are acquired after 30 years old. There is a maintenance of old traditions and age-related dress codes 'reminiscent of Victorian society'.[110]

Regions 4a (Kent) and *4b* (Isle of Wight, IoW) are the most affluent areas, featuring fine weaves, gold thread textiles and up to four brooches of silver, silver gilt and garnet. Frankish fashions are adopted in the early to mid-6th century, but Schleswig/South Jutland origins are remembered in gold-brocaded bands with patterns of squares and rectangles.[111] The figure shows two women dressed in the Kentish fashion: (a) wearing an inner dress with two brooches and (b) a shirt jacket with two crossways brooches (Figure 2.19).

Prima facie, the costumes would thus appear to endorse an ethnic model: Jutes in Kent and the Isle of Wight, Saxons in the south and Angles in the east, the Anglian area being periodically refreshed by more incomers from Scandinavia. To the north, centre and west edges are blurred where incomers and the British population merge. Naturally, like most ethnicity, these regions and social groups are self-defined or applied by neighbours; but it may be accepted that identity-seeking, even in death, was achieved, partly at least, by costume.

a   b

Figure 2.19 Ladies from Kent. (a) An inner dress with two brooches one above the other and (b) a shirt
jacket with two brooches worn sideways.

(Walton Rogers 2007, Fig 5.44; courtesy of Penelope Walton Rogers)

Dressing to signal their social standing, women carried a large number of accessories, especially bags and a range of objects denoting their rank and defining their role, such as mistress of the household, suggested by keys and girdle hangers. The overall set can indicate something beyond wealth and poverty. The **Bidford-on-Avon Cunning woman**, discovered in a 6th-century cemetery in Warwickshire, was one person whose apparel clearly suggested she was a specialist. She was a young adult aged 18–25, about 1 m 60 tall (5 feet 4 inches), who lay on her back with her head turned to her right. She was wearing a robe – her *peplos* – fastened by two brooches at the shoulder and, festooned between them, a necklace of 39 beads, of red, green and yellow glass, gold foil and amber. She had a linen belt decorated with beads of blue glass and amber, and there was a shawl thrown over the top of everything, fastened under the chin with an iron pin. The brooches were each of both British and Saxon type, perhaps reflecting the westward location of the site (Figure 2.20).

So far, this just displays a person who is well dressed and reasonably well to do. But there were some curious additions. A leather bag had hung down by her right hip with iron and copper rings – used to close and suspend the bag. Inside it – the tip of an antler and a stud. Beside the bag hung a knife with a short blade and a long, decorated bone handle, resembling a surgical instrument. Slung behind her shoulder – but originally dangling in front over her chest – was a kind of leather bib to which was sewn 12 tiny buckets with curved handles. This strange contraption had been suspended around her neck with leather thongs; their copper lace tags survived. Some of these objects seem to have a magical or amuletic purpose. A concentration of such objects in a female grave leads to the conjecture that here was a woman with special powers, variously known as a shamaness, a 'cunning woman' or a spiritual specialist.[112] The tiny containers at Bidford would scarcely admit the tip of the tongue, but there are suggestions of herbs and potions. If these and the scalpel were the symbols of an expertise, then we can guess that her role was curative of the body or the spirit. To suppose the Bidford-on-Avon lady to have been a mistress of the dark arts at 25 might seem a bit fanciful, but in the generation that followed men would be monks at 18 and priests in their twenties. Besides, the arts can be learnt, especially from a practitioner mother. Less directly, but more vividly, there is an echo of the Anglo-Saxon cunning woman among the better-documented *volva* of the later Viking age (see p. 401). The Bidford-on-Avon lady encourages us to believe in the Anglo-Saxon female shaman too, also expert in the healing business, perhaps escorting others out of the world as well as into it, with death as with birth. With the advent of Christianity, she was also to disappear – although it is perhaps reasonable to regard England's early abbesses, famous for their spirituality and wisdom, as her natural successors (see Chapter 4, p. 105).

Walton Rogers is sure that the clothing worn in the grave reflects the property and the biography of the individual, not grave gifts from mourners. Women adopted the veil, secured with a pin, at the age of 18 and bound up their hair on marriage.[113] Older women mix old fashions with new, reflecting how they dressed in their youth. Bequests written in wills in the later Formative show that women owned their clothes and linens and inherited them from their mothers, and so travelled with them when they moved. Thus, the time span of her belongings can be 30–40 years, or more if inherited objects are present. Walton Rogers also notes that while brooches were regionalised, textile technology spread from region to region, perhaps because women made the textiles and men made the brooches.[114]

Men in Anglo-Saxon graves were also buried in clothes, which ranged from tunics with hose (i.e. trousers with sewn-on socks), the laced sleeveless working tunic, and the tunic with

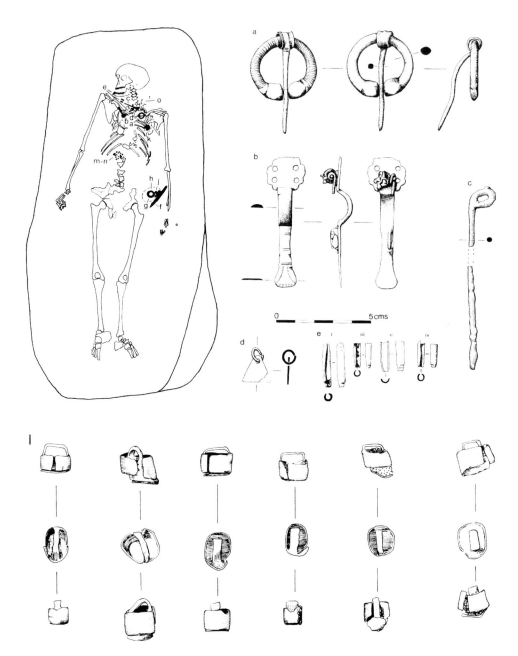

Figure 2.20 The 'cunning woman' from Bidford-on-Avon (Warwickshire); a bast-fibre dress was fastened by two brooches, a penannular brooch at the left shoulder and a small-long at the right (a, b). A shawl or cloak was fastened under the neck by an iron pin. A necklace of glass and amber beads (o) lay on the left shoulder, and another cluster just below the rib cage (m–n). A bag on the left hip had contained a knife with a decorated bone handle, an antler cone and two metal rings, probably to close the bag (f–j). At the back, but originally at the front, was a group of 12 miniature buckets, probably suspended on a leather 'bib' (i–k).

(Dickinson 1993b, Fig 6.1, 6.2, 6.4; courtesy of Tania Dickinson)

fascia ventralis under the belt and leg binding over trousers (Figure 2.21). The symbolic badge was not a brooch but the belt buckle, which varied from simple clasps to elaborate belt sets for those of higher rank, implying warrior fraternities.[115] A hierarchy of weapons – knife, spear, shield, sword – proclaimed warrior status. Older men, claiming higher status, were accompanied by more weapons, but this did not mean that they were actually battle worthy.[116] The 6th-century Anglian spearman from G157 at Morningthorpe in Norfolk wore a long-sleeved tunic and trousers, and a leather belt with five gilded plaques fastened with a bronze buckle and carrying a pouch (Figure 2.22A). The 7th-century man adopted the 'Persian' wrap-around 'warrior jacket'. The warrior figure from Taplow wore white linen trousers and a 'warrior jacket' of dark blue wool, with red wool tablet-woven bands brocaded in gold thread and yellow wool, the gold section running from the left shoulder to the right waist. The belt was fastened with a pair of clasps. He carried a drinking horn and his sword was slung over his shoulder, the belt fastened with a triangular buckle ornamented with garnet and beaded gold wire (Figure 2.22B).

Chronological framework

A ground-breaking study published in 2013 by John Hines and Alex Bayliss reviewed the occurrence of all the artefacts in the furnished inhumation graves of east Britain and put them into a dated sequence using radiocarbon dating and correspondence analysis.[117] The grave goods were organised into four phases of female and five phases of male burial in time-bands that vary from 40 to 60 years in length. The grave-good custom is held to have terminated abruptly for both men and women before 680, and this is attributed to reforms following the arrival of Theodore of Tarsus as Archbishop of Canterbury in 669. This included, one must assume, the imposition of a nation-wide

Figure 2.21 Men in Fm 1 England, dressed in tunics (a,b) and trousers (c,d).

(Walton Rogers 2007, Fig 5.56; courtesy of Penelope Walton Rogers)

Figure 2.22 Men from Morningthorpe (right) and Taplow: from reconstruction paintings by Graham Sumner.

(Walton Rogers 2007, Fig 5.63, 5.64; courtesy of Penelope Walton Rogers and Graham Sumner © Graham Sumner)

veto on furnished burial, effective before his death in 690. This is a result of the greatest importance, since it implies a close connection between burial practice and religion and the imposition of Christian behavioural rules that only came into effect in the late 7th century. It so happens that this same pivotal moment for the archaeological arrival of effective Christian authority is encountered elsewhere in this book, as we shall see, whether in the form of the northern monastery (Chapter 3), burial rites (Chapter 4) or monumental sculpture (Chapter 5), each of which take a new direction in material culture at the end of the 7th century.

The dates that have been used in the brief review of costume given above can be refined thanks to this study. Meanwhile, the periods of currency for the objects found in inhumations, many by implication worn by men and women in life, are shown in Table 2.3.

Iconic faces

There are few human images for English Fm 1, and most are cult figures and so are of questionable relevance to human appearance. But the act of displaying them signals identity.

Bracteates are gold discs modelled on late Roman solidi and depicting people and beasts, which mix Germanic and Roman themes in a way that shows that a common vocabulary

Table 2.3 Anglo-Saxon phase of grave-good usage in inhumations among females (F) and males (M), 6th to 7th century

Period	Dates (pde*, 95%)	Types of grave goods	Burial rite trends
WOMEN			
FA	400–550	*Brooches* Equal arm Saucer Button Cruciform	Cremations in pots
FB	510–585	Sq head brooch 1a,b,d,f Composite brooch 2a,b Annular brooch 3b,c Beads B	
FC	555–640	Brooch 2b Annular brooch 3b,c Beads B	Narrower range of grave goods
FD	580–650	Cowrie shell Cabochon pendant Key Brooch 2c,d Brooch 3d Penannular brooch 3f Beads C	Upsurge in numbers of burials Addition of new cemeteries Bed burials
FE	625–680	Garnets, cowrie shells, keys, workboxes, iron-bound boxes Cross pendant Brooch 3d,e Brooch 2c,d Wire-head pin Beads C	Mound burials Bed burials
MEN			
MA	400–550		
MB	525–565	Rectangular buckles Shield boss 1, 2, 3 Sword 1, 2b,3a,4	
MC	545–595	Triangular buckles Shield boss 3 Sword 3a,4	
MD	565–610	Triangular buckles Shield boss 4 Sword 3b,5b	
ME	580–610	Shield boss 4 Sword 3b,5b	Mound burials
MF	610–685	Shield boss 4 Shield boss 5 Sword 3b Scramaseax	

* pde = posterior density estimates.
For illustrations of the objects, see the second half of this chapter.
(Hines and Bayliss 2013, 460; Table 10.1, p. 561).

is being devised.[118] One series shows long-haired Germanic heroes or the triumph of Odin as the new Roman emperor, or more specifically (and controversially), Attila the Hun (C-bracteates).[119] Another series shows fragmented monsters, as on the Style 1 patterns on brooches (D-bracteates). More than 900 are known from Scandinavia, while in England they are concentrated in Kent and East Anglia (Figure 2.23). Initially probably gifted by leaders to supporters in the 6th century, they long retained their prestige as indicated by being fitted with loops for suspension on necklaces.[120] In Scandinavia, *guldgubbar*, small square gold plaques, are found on ritual sites from Borg on Lofoten to Uppåkra in Skåne (Chapter 3, p. 283). These also feature an Odin-like character licking his own thumb, but a large subset, in which a man and woman are seen kissing, seem much more quotidian, with a wide variation of representation. In this 'wedding scene' the men have short tunics that may be quilted and the women wear gowns that may be elaborately embroidered. The men have hair swept back from the forehead, and the women have their hair tied at the back in a knot, tress, tail or bun. Whether the figures are intended as gods or as ordinary persons plighting their troth, they are represented as clad in their best attire.[121] These have yet to be found in England.

Among the earliest human figures portrayed in England is the seated person realised in terracotta forming part of a pot lid found at Spong Hill and thought to be male (Figure 2.24A). The lid was not found on a pot, but Catherine Hills has confirmed its context in the earlier part of the cemetery, sees the narrow diameter of the lid as implying high status, noting that pot lids form part of the Germanic package and that this one dates before the end of the 5th century.[122] It has also been suggested that Spong man is holding a mask to his face and is wearing a Pannonian cap of a type seen on military figures in late Roman art.[123] With his

Figure 2.23 B-Bracteate from Binham (Norfolk).

(Behr and Pestell 2014, Fig 3d, 7; © Norfolk Museums Service; published under licence)

Figure 2.24 Pagan faces. A (left): Pot lid from Spong Hill (Ht. 145 mm). B (centre): Face on the sceptre from Sutton Hoo. C (right): Pendant from Carlton Colville, Suffolk.

(A: Hills 2014 © Norwich Castle Museum and Art Gallery; B: Bruce-Mitford 1978, Fig 238, A2; British Museum;
C: Reproduced under licence from the British Museum © The Trustees of the British Museum)

wide open eyes and hands holding his head, he has a shamanistic look. Faces which have the
stylised leonine look of a god or ancient ancestor are portrayed in relief on the Sutton Hoo
whetstone-sceptre and feature both male (bearded) and female faces in equal prominence, so
acknowledging the importance of both sexes in the pantheon and in determining the ancestry
(Figure 2.24B). The figure on the Finglesham buckle is naked except for his belt, with its
own large buckle; his two spears suggest a warrior god, no doubt Odin.[124] The Bloodmoor
Hill pendant shows a man with a pointed beard and drooping moustache wearing stockings
and knee-length 'knickerbockers' that hide a substantial penis. He probably has a belt and
buckle, but the area is screened by his right hand. His left hand covers the top area of the
tunic, but there is a hint of a V-neck below the beard. On his head – a dome-shaped helmet.
The object is made of a nearly pure silver, and the trousers, hands and face are gilded. This
tiny figure with a suspension loop was no doubt an amulet with divine connotations serving
some aspect of a pre-Christian belief system (Figure 2.24C).[125]

In the seventh century, the coinage takes over the task of flying the banner of allegiance,
in a primary phase (c. 675–710) imitating the icons of Rome and Francia in the form of
imperial heads, hair and drapery and the cross, and those of Frisia's 'porcupine heads'. In
a secondary phase (c. 710–750), a greatly enlarged range of designs include crosses, vine
scroll and posed animals such as lions.[126] For Anna Gannon, these have a common message, namely the promise of salvation, and she proposes that they were minted by clerical
authorities at minster sites. However, it is doubtful that many ecclesiastical sites south of the
Humber were monastic, or even religious in a way that would be understood to the north of
it. The example of the group of coins depicting the five senses, to be seen also on the Fuller
Brooch, seems to match 'the worldly sophistication of these establishments' and leave the

Figure 2.25 Helmets from Sutton Hoo, Suffolk (7th century) (left) (© The Trustees of the British Museum; licenced by the British Museum) and Coppergate, York (8th century).

(Image courtesy of York Museums Trust)

royal power in control of the coin supply – as was to be more clearly declared from 757 on the coins of Offa.[127]

The end of Formative 1

The first half of the 7th century sees an upsurge of exceptionally wealthy burials and a decrease in the furnished graves of more ordinary rank (Chapter 4). The clothing represented is at a higher level of extravagance initially for men and, later in the 7th century, for women. Both were influenced by the fashions of Rome and Byzantium, as they were perceived.[128] This is by no means the last time that the ghosts of Rome will be on hand to tend a major social change in Britain.[129]

Male assertion in the early 7th century

In the late 6th century, a warrior culture flourished among the men, leadership and individual prowess being celebrated by the display of weapons, the use of barrows and the concentration of wealth into fewer graves. The grave goods also increased in variety. The new high-ranking warrior rode a horse and carried a sword and shield, and an iron helmet protected his head. The occupant of Mound 1 at Sutton Hoo was provided with a helmet, a baldrick (sword harness) with gold and garnet shoulder clasps, a sword, shield, numerous spears and a large heap of clothing. Fierce creatures stood guard on the shield and protected the wearer of the Sutton Hoo helmet, essentially a Roman parade helmet recast for a Germanic leader: a dragon covers the crest and a bird of prey the face; warrior figures brandishing weapons are active on plaques[130] (Figure 2.25A). He wears Roman-style shoulder clasps, presenting the viewer with Style 2 ribbon animals chasing each other's tails and pairs of heraldic wild boars with blue tusks, perched on the warrior's shoulder and threatening enemies with their native belligerence (Figure 2.7, and see Chapter 4, p. 339 for other items in the coffin). In Christian times the message of the helmet remains similar, but the wearer has a new protector: the Coppergate helmet found at York carried a Latin inscription (bracketed with crosses) along the crest that called on all the saints to lend their aid (Figure 2.25B).[131]

The early royal burials did not include silk, which seems to have first appeared in England with Christianity.[132] Red dye was obtained from the roots of madder (*Rubia tinctorum* L.) which was used in Roman Britain, disappeared in the 5th century and reappeared at Sutton Hoo, Taplow and Siberswold in the 7th century. It was almost certainly imported: sherds of E ware stained with madder have been found at sites in northern Ireland and western Scotland.[133] The members of the rising belligerent upper class were buried with the emblems of their principal pride, horses and weapons, and the toys of their leisure hours, drinking horns, playing pieces and musical instruments.

Dressing one's horse

The young horseman under Mound 17 at Sutton Hoo was laid in a tree-trunk coffin with a sword, two spears and a shield. He also had a camping kit: a bucket, a small cauldron and a bag containing food. At his head was laid his horse's bridle and saddle, while the horse itself was buried in a parallel grave beside his.[134] The horses were dressed up too: the Mound 17 horse lay in a separate grave, its saddle and tack stacked at the head of the coffin of its master. The bridle had a head piece, brow band and snaffle bit with decorated bit rings with integral terminals (Figure 2.26). The roundels were of gilded bronze and carried ribbon animals; and the strap-ends carried images of stylised men in a nice sign of synergy: just as men carry animals, animals carry men, on their strap-ends as well as on their backs (Figure 2.27). The horse also had a body harness, with little silver-axe shaped pendants. This horse will have glinted in the sun as it trotted by, gold around the head and silver around the body. Other horses are coming to light as the fragments of bridles are recognised. A roundel very similar to Sutton Hoo was found at Portmahomack in north-east Scotland, Dunadd in the north-west and (as a mould) at the Mote of Mark, implying the development of an equestrian class with shared values crossing demographic zones over the length of the island (Figure 2.28).[135]

Staffordshire hoard

The wealth that was in circulation among the emerging upper classes of the early 7th century was stupendous, as illustrated especially by Sutton Hoo and endorsed by a find in south Staffordshire far to the west of the Anglo-Saxon heartland. This was an apparently random collection of metalwork buried as a hoard around the mid-7th century in a small wood overlooking the Roman Road to Wales (now the A5). The loot was probably carried in a sack and thrown into a shallow pit, later scattered by ploughing and eventually rediscovered by a metal-detectorist in 2009. It consisted of more than 3,000 gold and silver pieces weighing 5 kilos in all and including fragments of a shield, a helmet and – at last count – parts of 97 sword handles. The hoard also included Christian crosses and parts of a shrine or reliquary. The objects had been ornamented with ribbon animals of Style 2 showing close affiliations to Sutton Hoo and East Anglia and to early Christian Northumbria, and datable to the mid-7th century (Figure 2.29). The links with the east and north are strong, so the hoard is not necessarily native to Mercia. Every one of the sword pommels differed from the others, showing that the sword was a personalised weapon with a personality of its own. Tiny scraps survive from scenes showing warriors fighting and fallen that had probably decorated helmets like

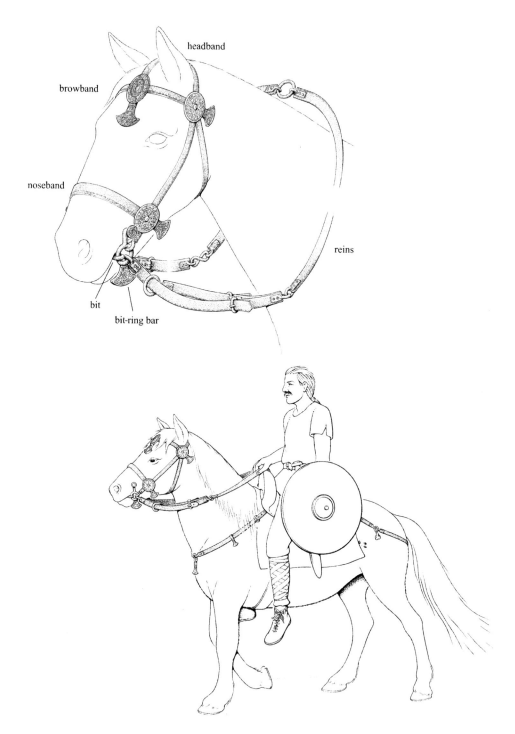

Figure 2.26 Sutton Hoo: Mound 17 Bridle as assembled by Angela Evans.
(Carver 2005a, Fig 115; British Museum)

Figure 2.27 Sutton Hoo: Bridle fittings, Mound 17.

(Carver 2005, colour plate 12; British Museum)

that at Sutton Hoo. The hoard as a whole is notable for containing predominately gold and silver: the iron blades of swords (for example) had been removed. It was thus intended to be a consignment of bullion.[136]

The motive and circumstances of the deposition of the hoard are unknown, and the mode of recovery did little to illuminate them.[137] A smith's hoard intended for recycling is one possibility, material collected from a battlefield is another, but both cases are inconsistent with the degree of fragmentation and absence of iron. The weight of gold and silver (5 kg, equivalent to 30,000 silver pence (see p. 76), suggests that the hoard represents a *wergild* – a compensation payment for the killing of a warlord or to buy peace – in this case collected from the secular and ecclesiastical aristocracy. There is a possible historical context for this. The mid-7th century was a time of much Mercian aggression against East Anglia and

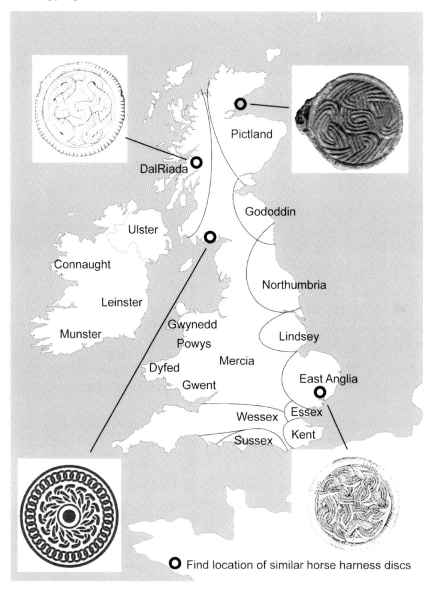

Figure 2.28 Finds of harness fittings in 7th-century Britain – signs of an island-wide equestrian class? (FAS Heritage)

Northumbria, led by Mercia's king, Penda, and in 655, Oswiu king of Northumbria tried to buy him off with 'an incalculable and incredible treasure'.[138] Penda refused and was subsequently killed by Oswiu at the Battle of the *Winwaed* (near Doncaster). So Oswiu decided the treasure would be 'given to God'. If the Staffordshire hoard was the consignment in question, it was never delivered to the monastery it was promised to. In England, as in Pictland, we are not visiting a country of ignorant chieftains from the sticks but proud aristocrats wearing high impact costumes, glittering jewellery, great manes of flowing hair and access to luxuries from all over Europe.

Figure 2.29 Items from the Staffordshire Hoard: sword pommel and fittings and a crumpled ceremonial cross, gold inlaid with garnets and white glass.

(© Birmingham City Museum, reproduced under licence)

Female assertion in the mid-7th century

As the celebration of individual men in rich graves under barrows began to come to an end in the first half of the 7th century, a celebration of individual women began. For the next 50 years, coincident with the conversion process in England, women were remembered in a series of elaborate tombs under mounds up and down the country, from Uncleby in the north to Swallowcliffe Down in the west. Its sartorial theme, as demonstrated by Helen Geake, was the adoption of types of high-ranking accessories and attire popular in the Mediterranean (see p. 98). According to Walton Rogers, they are 'almost certainly wearing fashions that represent the development of the Roman full-length tunic, fastened with a woven girdle or sash and combined with a long veil and *pallium* or mantle'. Like the longer veil, the adoption of a woven sash-like girdle with its symbolic connection to chastity was probably inspired by eastern exemplars, if not the precepts of Christianity.[139] The women now sported a distinctive new range of jewellery – composite brooches inset with coloured precious stones, necklaces with amethysts, metal beads and polished garnet pendants, twin pins linked by a chain, and finger rings – and, in the grave, canisters, caskets and workboxes. These evoke the dress of the upper classes in contemporary Byzantium.

   The group of rich mid-7th-century female graves are high investment, with evidence for costly possessions, interment on a bed or couch, wooden chambers and memorial mounds.

The young woman found at **Swallowcliffe Down** had been buried in the later seventh century in a pre-existing Bronze Age barrow that has come down to history as *Posses Hlwaewe* (Possa's mound). She was laid in a box-bed with maplewood casket containing silver brooches, knives and a comb and a bronze sprinkler. She had a leather satchel ornamented with a highly decorated gilt roundel (Figure 2.30, and see Chapter 4, p. 405). At Street House, Loftus, the young woman had two cabochon garnet pendants and a scutiform pendant, and her grave was surrounded by a large number of others in a regimented square. At Coddenham Grave 30, the woman was buried with a coin pendant, bag and latch-lifter in a chamber, also surrounded by other graves. At Trumpington, a young woman of around 16 years had a gold pectoral cross, originally sewn onto the robe she was wearing. The lady at Ixworth also wore a gold and garnet pectoral cross. The 'dowager' at Sutton Hoo 14 was buried on a couch and wore silver, but here the burial was much disturbed.[140]

Figure 2.30 Badge on the purse of the Swallowcliffe Down woman.

(Speake 1989, cover; image licensed by Historic England)

Some commentators feel that these graves belonging to the mid-7th century ought to be those of Christians, even though the rituals of burial give out a traditional, non-Christian signal. The analysis of Hines and Bayliss (Table 2.3) shows that Christianity need not be much manifested in material culture or spiritual practice before about AD 675. From that point of departure, Helena Hamerow has described how this group of privileged women redesigned their appearance and their attitude to personal possessions. The emphasis was now less on brooches and long strings of beads and more on shorter, lighter necklaces and objects that were concealed in bags and caskets. As advanced by Geake, dress accessories also lost the regional diversity characteristic of the 6th century and became comparatively uniform. Hamerow goes on to show that the known bed burials precede the establishment of nunneries and concludes that the clear Frankish and eastern Mediterranean influences signal elite status and 'an allegiance to new systems of power, rather than the adoption of Christianity per se'.[141] These women were documenting their status as the custodians of family property in uncertain times in the time-honoured manner and may have been expressing deeper intellectual allegiances. We will return to this important monumental episode in Chapter 4.

The **Franks Casket** with its five picture sequences reporting stories from the Germanic and the Roman worlds seems also to capture this period of open expression, intellectual curiosity and ideological transition. It dates art-historically from the 7th or early 8th century and (being a casket) is implied by the evidence of the graves to be the property of a woman; we can imagine that (like the Swallowcliffe casket) it contained accessories, amulets, ornaments and mementos.[142] The captions that label the actors and run round the edges of each picture frame are in Anglo-Saxon (runes) or Latin (letters). On the lid, the early 6th-century hero Egil defends the Swedish queen against the Geats. The front panel is shared, on one side, by Wayland the Smith, protagonist of a tale of rape, murder and revenge, and on the other by the birth of Jesus Christ, with three magi following the star to the stable. The other long panel shows the Romans storming Jerusalem in 70 AD as reported by Josephus; the ark of the covenant lies inside the temple, guarded by seraphim (*'Here Titus and a Jew fight: here its inhabitants flee from Jerusalem'*) (Figure 2.31). One short panel shows a horse named *Bita*, a burial mound and three cloaked figures, reminiscent of the weird sisters (*'Here Hos sits on the sorrow-mound'*). The other shows Romulus and Remus suckled by a wolf and discovered in the woods (*'Romulus and Remus, two brothers, a she-wolf nourished them in Rome, far from their native land'*). The front panel records the death of a giant fish on the shingle, presumably the whale that provided his bone for the box.[143]

Naturally the iconography has inspired a number of interpretations, most in favour of an essentially Christian object that makes pre-Christian references. Richard Fletcher was in no doubt that it signified the benefits of conversion: 'The front panel contrasts a non-Christian order with a Christian one: there can be no disputing that. . . . The narrative moves from left to right, so a Christian order has superseded a pre-Christian one.'[144] Leslie Webster sees the casket as delivering moral strictures on good and bad kingship and thought it might have contained a copy of (a small) Psalter – 'a very suitable gift for an Anglo-Saxon prince, especially one who was learning to read the sacred texts'.[145] Thus in seeing it as the constructed compendium of an intelligent upper class woman, I am going somewhat against the grain. The context for such audacity is the greatly increased evidence for female agency in the mid- to later 7th century, which can be seen as a prelude to its transformation, to my mind in a demoted form, in the nunneries of the next period.

Figure 2.31 Franks casket, front panel.

Costume stories – Formative 2 (675–850)

The rise of territorial leadership and the arrival of institutional Christianity converge in the late 7th century. Although this applies to the island as a whole, there is a difference of emphasis between the regions. The north and west sees the birth and expansion of the monastic movement, and the production of illuminated manuscripts and pictorial sculpture provides evidence of clothing on clerics as well as the privileged secular classes. Southumbria has not only lost its grave goods but has very little sculpture or imagery, which might offer a substitute. In Formative 3, some of these benefits will be reversed.

A glance at Irish texts

In Ireland at least, documents show that garments were not only dyed but colour-coded by rank, only a king's son being permitted to wear purple and blue. In the *Cattle raid of Cooley*, Cu Chulainn is described as 'a great dark man. His hair is dark and full. A purple cloak is wrapped about him, held by a gold brooch. He wears a red-embroidered hooded tunic'.[146] Niamh Whitfield's analysis of the story of Becfhola and Flann allows her to dress them both.[147] After Becfhola makes a mysterious appearance at a ford, she sets her cap at Diarmaid, his foster son Crimthann and finally Flann, who agrees to be seduced after he has organised his claim on a distant island. This he duly does, returning a year later to claim the lady too. The lovers are described by their clothes, rather than their natural features – like the actors they are. Becfhola wears a tunic of linen, with embroidery of red gold. On her feet are sandals made of 'white bronze with two natural stones'. Whitfield reads this as a pair of leather shoes with bronze buckles, probably set with pieces of amber. A cloak is thrown over the tunic, dyed purple, the mark of royalty, and secured by a brooch of precious metal, studded with 'variegated' gems – the term being suggestive of the inlaid cloisonée studs seen on the Tara brooch. She wears neck rings, perhaps of gold, and on her head a *mind*, a coronet, or a headband brocaded with gold foil. This could have secured a long veil, as became the fashion in Christianised England, as well as on the Continent (see p. 103). Flann had long flowing curly hair with gold hair ornaments, with a headband ornamented with gold silver and crystal and ribbons wound with gold foil to control the locks at the back. At his parting he carried two large (symbolic?) gold balls. He wears a tunic decorated with rows of circles reminiscent of Carolingian ornamentation. He had a cloak of many colours, interpreted here as a plaid, which also wrapped him up at night when on exercise: attempting to seduce him, Becfhola 'slipped beneath his cloak, between him and the wall'.[148] His two arms were laden with gold and silver bracelets, and his fingers possibly with rings. But here we have Viking paraphernalia.

This story occurs in the 14th-century *Yellow Book of Leinster*, but its references purport to describe an earlier time. Diarmaid, the instigator of the action, was king of Tara from 642 to 664. As described, Becfhola and Flann appear to belong to different centuries; she to the 7th/8th and he to the 9th/10th. Becfhola is a bit of a fantasy character, and her description (as well as her actual appearance) was no doubt richly embroidered. Practical embroidery was a high-status craft: 'the woman who embroiders earns more than a queen'. The verbal embroidery is equally prized, and it seems likely that the references to the 7th century – the brooch, the gold – would be accepted as being that early by a reader. Flann's apparel has more of the Viking in it, and maybe the contrast is intentional – the woman is a visitor from wilder times, if not a golden age, even a deep-rooted acculturating force. Such feelings are not inappropriate to a time of social, economic and ideological upheaval.

While Ireland is the richest source of textual evocations of well-dressed persons, investing in their appearance and using it to articulate society, it is not alone. In the *Gododdin* clothing is striped, spotted and chequered (possibly tartan). Men and women both wear purple. Amber beads and gold ornaments are worn, gold torques and possibly brooches. Ywain wore crimson, Gwaednerth wore silk and men (e.g. Blaen 'from the city') and women (the daughter of Eudaf the Tall) both wore purple.[149] Silk is found in Viking towns but may have arrived in Ireland in the 7th century, as it did in Britain, from sources already exploited by the Franks: 'Arnegunda's tomb' at Saint Denis contained a knee-length silk tunic. The Virgin portrayed in the Book of Kells is probably intended as wearing a silk gown, since its transparency reveals her breasts and legs.[150]

West and north Britain in Formative 2

From the late 7th century in this area, the series of formal brooches appears to split into two separate streams, Pictish and Irish. The Pictish brooches became large and ornate but remained true penannulars with a sliding pin which could be locked against one of the broad terminals, which may be floriate or beast heads, as those from Rogart and St Ninian's Isle Shetland (Figure 2.32). Those of the Irish series become *pseudo-penannular* or *annular*, the expanded terminals being joined by a bar or panel, so that the object functioned as a sturdy dress pin with a giant head. Designs became more elaborate and referential, as with the Tara brooch with its miniaturised decoration comparable with the finest contemporary manuscripts, or the Hunterston brooch, designed using mathematical ratios and implying the widespread insular theme of 'Christ between two animals' with a subtle (or secretive) equivocation[151] (Figure 2.33). The rise of these sumptuous brooches from the later 7th century coincides in Ireland with the rise of the monastic centres, where a new range of high-quality reliquaries, crosses and illuminated manuscripts joined the repertoire. The monastic phase at Portmahomack of the late 7th/8th century suggests that this was also true of Pictland. For a

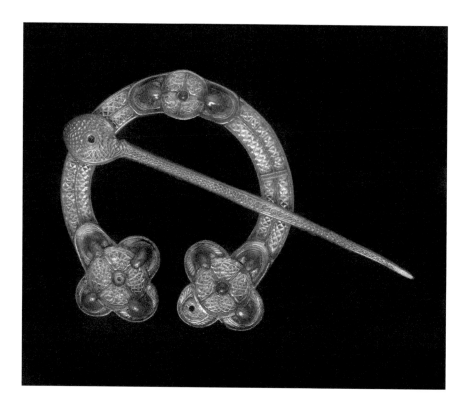

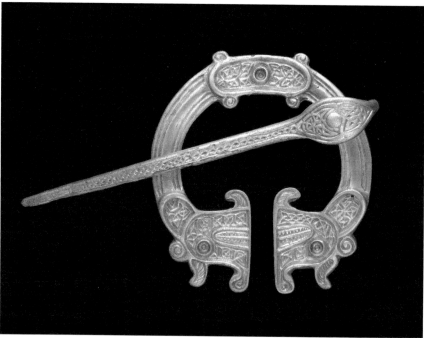

Figure 2.32 Pictish penannular brooches from Rogart (top) and St Ninian's Isle Shetland (bottom). (X.FC.2; X.FC.295; images © National Museums Scotland reproduced under licence)

Figure 2.33 Hunterston brooch, with (opposite) a view of the metrics by Niamh Whitfield, and (below)
an interpretation of the iconography by Alice Blackwell.

(X.FC.8 Image © National Museums Scotland; Blackwell 2011; Whitfield 1999; with permission)

century or so, it seems, the sacred and the secular each benefitted from this flourishing of
the arts. It is not excluded that the grander clerics wore lavish brooches, expressing their
right to the new authority or their own royal descent. Christ as depicted on the Muiredach
Cross at Monasterboice and the Virgin as rendered on the High Cross at Durrow sport large
brooches.[152] Since the high-flown descriptions recorded in stories were also products of
monasteries or known to them, the literary nostalgia for a lost corpus of aristocratic finery in
a previous generation is the more credible (Chapter 6, p. 606).

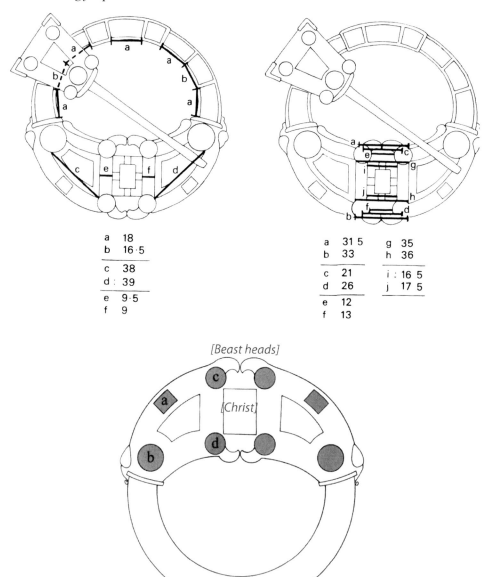

Figure 2.33 (Continued)

Pictures of Picts

Images show that the larger penannulars fastened a cloak: on the left shoulder for men and in the centre over the chest for women. This position is recorded in the Irish Laws (on the safe way to wear a brooch) and is seen on the male warrior on a stone pillar on White Island Co Fermanagh.[153] There appears to be no tradition of impressive belt buckles. In Irish manuscripts of the 8th–9th century the portraits of the evangelists introduce credible details of ceremonial robes pre-echoing the official dress of a priest: a long undergarment (the alb), an overgarment (the chasuble), a scarf around the neck (stole) and a hand cloth (maniple). Pictures also feature slipper-like shoes and well-managed hair. The principles of determining authenticity in these images are the same as with the stories and the later manuscripts (see p. 60); that is, examples are accepted as representative of their time where known contemporary objects (e.g. penannular brooches) are shown. An alternative, if weaker, test is to search for objects previously known or illustrated in earlier media.

The rich Pictish corpus of images has yet to be systematically tested, but scholars have long been aware of its archaeological potential.[154] The hunt, a favoured Pictish theme, features horsemen (and women), hunting dogs and trumpeters, all in pursuit of a deer that sometimes has a spear lodged in its flank. The female huntress on the Hilton of Cadboll slab on the Tarbat peninsula, Easter Ross, is preceded by a mirror and comb and wears a large penannular brooch over a pleated robe. The huntsmen on Kirriemuir 2 wear coats with raised ribs that may be intended as quilted (Figure 2.34).[155] While the mirror and comb are widely used symbols of Iron Age origin, the brooch could bring the trumpets, bridles, spears and shields with it into the realms of reality. This does not preclude the scene from being symbolic or allegorical, or even making reference to Classical or Biblical themes.[156] Here we are more concerned with

Figure 2.34 Pictish hunting scenes: Hilton of Cadboll (left) and Kirriemuir 2.

(Henderson and Henderson 2004, Ill 50, 263. Tom and Sybil Grey Collection. © Historic Environment Scotland, reproduced under licence)

the degree to which the scene, however formalised, reflected the cultural material of the land in which they were created. The answer must be cautiously affirmative, and it is noticeable that, as with the Anglo-Saxon manuscripts, there is a tendency of realist artists to bunch together: the same ateliers keep coming up (St Vigeans, Meigle, the Tarbat peninsula). An attempt has been made to reconcile the Hilton hunt with its strongly ecclesiastical, actually monastic, context by proposing it as a scene drawn from the life of a saint rather than an aristocratic patron, although the Hilton lady could have been both. This means that while the image can remain, in a sense, allegorical, the archaeological detail is relevant and contemporary with the artist.[157] Pictish archaeology is notoriously meagre in its current provision of sites and objects, so that ratification of reality and the identification of objects not yet found remains elusive; but in many of the images rendered in stone we have a gallery of daily life that is, *prima facie*, authentic.

A summary of the repertoire might be allowed as follows: the contemporary actors on the slabs are predominately warriors, fighting or hunting, or clerics holding books or sitting in chairs. *Warriors* may be spear-carrying foot soldiers or riders. The slab from Birsay (Orkney) shows two spearmen with square shields dressed in long robes led by a person of senior rank with a more decorated shield and a brocaded hem to his robe. He has a pointed beard and curly hair gathered behind a headband.[158] The two horsemen on Meigle 4 also have pointed beards and wear short cloaks with the sword showing.[159] The three riders on St Madoes (Perthshire) wear short cloaks with hoods[160]; on Kirriemuir 2 they wear pleated or quilted short tunics, one in britches with the cloak folded. The St Madoes and Kirrimuir 2 horses have bridles with a brow piece and bit rings.[161] In Meigle 3, 4 and 5 and Kirrimuir 2 (back), the horses have saddle cloths.[162] The Aberlemno churchyard warriors (assumed to be Picts) carry circular shields,[163] but then so do the attendants on Hilton of Cadboll who are taking part in a hunt.[164] On the Dupplin Cross the facial hair appears to be ranked: the spearmen are clean shaven, led by two officers with moustaches, while the cavalryman, probably Constantin, king of Picts, has the full facial drooper of beard and moustache (see Chapter 5, p. 542). Long gowns, short tunics, brocade, cloak, long hair, a pointy beard and a horse are distinguishing if not universal attributes of the Pictish warring and hunting, that is equestrian, classes, attributes too often repeated and too local in occurrence to require us to cite Mediterranean sources.

Thanks to the survival of Hilton of Cadboll, it can be accepted that *high-status women* would be active in the upper echelons of society, as also indicated by the stories (below). The lady is preceded by the mirror and comb symbol, generally interpreted as signifying the female gender.[165] She rides side-saddle, wears a pleated cloak secured by penannular brooch, and has a great head of hair that might be intended as a coife but more likely represents hair that fans out in braids or locks behind a headband. A man riding next to her, signalled by his horse's legs and his large protruding nose, is clearly intended as her companion, and the officers of the hunt sound the trumpet for 'gone away' and control the hounds that pursue a red deer (Figure 2.34). There is little to cavil about the *prima facie* reality of such a scene, which could have been enacted on the estate of any castle or country house in Scotland up to the early 20th century, an intrinsic, even ritual, passion of aristocratic life. All that is missing is the child who will be 'blooded' by wiping the freshly dead meat over his cheek to mark his first attendance at a kill.[166]

Priests in their robes

The curious figures with axes may represent pre-Christian spiritual figures, and probably refer to Fm 1 (see above, p. 82; and Figure 5.28). Scenes intended to evoke contemporary Christian activity in Fm 2 offer a clear enough contrast both with the hunting and fighting scenes and also with the iconographic extracts from the Old Testament featuring David and Daniel. At Dunfallandy, Perthshire, seated clerics in long robes face each other with symbols above them and a cross between them, while a third rides a horse.[167] At Fowlis Wester two sitting clerics and two standing clerics wear robes of decorated textile with braided hems and high collars at the back. Those facing each other sit in decorated high-backed chairs, wear round caps and one (the more senior?) is accompanied by floriated staffs[168] (Figure 2.35). The clerics often hold a square object in the folds of their tunics, usually identified as a book (Kirriemuir 1, Aldbar, Invergowrie, St Vigeans 11, Tarbat 20).[169] In the modern Catholic service, the priest at the altar carries the chalice in his left hand with the paten covered with a cloth and a burse on top, all held in place with the right hand. From a distance it is the square burse that catches the eye. This apparatus marking priesthood might have been intended for some

Figure 2.35 Pictish clerics; Dunfallandy (left) and Fowlis Wester.

of the figures, such as St Vigeans 11 (front). At Lethendy (Perth) two clerics are dressed in pleated tunics with braided hems. One carries a book. Below them are musicians with a harp and pipes.[170] At Papil, four clerics with long robes with peaked hoods and carrying croziers walk towards a cross while another in a short cloak rides on horseback.[171] If these are correct readings, then it is monks (rather than bishops) that carry the shepherd's crozier. One might look for a representation of the Celtic tonsure, where the head is shaved forward of a line connecting ear to ear, but these remain elusive. At St Vigeans 7, seated clerics face each other, wearing boots and high collars, probably meant as cowls.[172] They are sharing a loaf – so either represent or make references to Saints Paul and Anthony, as seen on the Nigg stone.[173] These founders of the monastic movement have superseded the earlier sacrificial procedures, seen immediately below them on St Vigeans 7, where a man stabs a bull and licks the blood.[174] This is a juxtaposition of images marking the passing from one ideology to another as powerful as the Félire's remembrance of the conversion of Ireland: 'heathendom has been destroyed, though fair it was and widespread' (Chapter 6, p. 606).

The sacrifice of the Mass, in which the re-creation of the flesh and blood is held to be real rather than symbolic, is thus depicted as a successor to the sacrifice of cattle. It is likely that this replacement of an ox by a human saviour would have been understood more easily than the imposed morality, especially in sexual matters, and the demotion of women from their roles in healing and leadership. By contrast, the stage props for the new arena of performance that form attributes of the new priestly personhood link with Roman ceremony: the chasuble, alb, maniple and stole reflect late Roman dress. The holy water sprinkled from its bucket at the start of Mass to the singing of *asperges me* remembers the laying of dust in Mediterranean *villae* and other grand places. The *thurible* (censer) with its smouldering charcoal and incense grains is a device used to fumigate the rooms before the entry of important guests. The round host remembers the round pieces of unleavened bread (like a pizza) eaten in the empire. The host used at the elevation of the host is stored in a *pyx*, a small circular box, not unlike the 'workboxes' found in female graves; the small versions used for communion are kept in a *ciborium*, a circular cup on a pedestal.[175] Pyx and ciborium are stored in a (locked) tabernacle and taken out for the Mass. The host is laid on a plate (the *paten*). During the transubstantiation, when the host is elevated, all other hosts in range are also transformed. Since every crumb of the wafers is potentially an element of Christ's body, great care is taken to sweep up all the fragments and ingest them. The wine is mixed with water, both poured from glass cruets into a goblet (*chalice*) and strained to remove insects and other impurities. Once consecrated, every drop must be consumed, and receptacles and the priest's mouth wiped clean with a white cloth (*purificatorium*) folded and placed when not in use in a stiffened cloth envelope (the *pall*) which lies on the chalice.[176] Deacons, subdeacons, acolytes and torchbearers complete the cast that performs in the chancel at the east end of the church, an area separated from the public by a stone fence, the *cancellum*. The church militant equipped its leaders with the crozier, the shepherd's crook, and their spiritual capital is stored in *reliquaries*, which contain the bones of the holy or artefacts that have touched them (Figure 2.36). Last, and certainly not least, is the codex, containing the four *Gospels*, the epistles – the letters of St Paul – specific extracts of which are dedicated to each Mass in the canonical year and detailed in the *missal* containing the script of the Mass in Latin.

The priest's robes were themselves adapted from late Roman aristocratic costume and appear in similar guise in Carolingian manuscripts, so it seems logical that those who took Christian orders in 7th century Pictland would be required to dress in the same way.[177] However, the Pictish clerics depicted on stones exhibit a variation of the layered dress of alb and chasuble seen in Irish manuscripts. Rather they are clad in a one-piece ankle-length robe

Figure 2.36 Monymusk reliquary, exterior and interior.
(H.KE 14, Images © National Museums Scotland, reproduced under licence)

with a hood or cowl visible at the back of the neck. The garment may be embroidered along the hem at the bottom or over the whole, as at Fowlis Wester. In other words, they are dressed as monks rather than priests, albeit with a level of embellishment to the monkish garb that would have startled members of medieval and later communities. These observations hint at differences between western churches as well as with those in the east.[178]

Northumbria and Mercia in Formative 2

Northumbria and Mercia, outside the English heartland, are arguably still part of an Anglo-British *kulturkreis* and deeply involved in the monastic movement. In Northumbrian sculpture, Rothbury 1 and Jarrow show individuals in pleated or quilted tunics. On Rothbury 1A a young Christ with swept-back hair parted in the middle and no facial hair is seen under a niche, holding a book. He wears a cloak of heavy tubular folds over a smooth undergarment.[179] On face 1C Christ heals the blind man and the woman with an issue of blood, as described in the Gospels. The blind man has a heavy moustache (paralleled on other non-divine figures on this cross) with empty slits for eyes. The woman in the same vignette has her head covered with a veil, with curls of hair showing.[180] On Jarrow 20, an athletic bare-foot young person heads through branches or undergrowth pursued by a beast. The figure is executed with a human rather than a symbolic model in view:

> His hair falls in a lock behind his ear. His features are conveyed lightly, his eye by a single punch mark. He is dressed in a short kirtle with what seems to be a fold around the waist, which passes over his shoulder and flies out behind him (Figure 2.37A).[181]

The secular figures conversing in St Mary Bishophill junior 1 (York, mid-9th century) wear plain tunics with a hood and belt, one with a horn and one with a sword[182] (Figure 2.37B).

Further south in Mercia we have a mounted warrior from Repton, carved probably on a cross shaft. The horseman is shown mounted on a stallion, sitting on a saddlecloth, with his right hand brandishing a two-edged sword and his left a small shield. The reins are looped over his right arm, and a seax, perhaps in a sheath, is at his waist. He wears an 'imperial' fillet on his head and a coat of ringmail over a knee-length pleated kilt, from under which a leg with criss-cross bindings emerges. He sports a drooping moustache. In the Biddles' analysis, the image is derived from a Classical exemplar (the stance, headband and the kilt), mutated by the choice of weapons and the ringmail so as to 'mirror contemporary Germanic practice'. The moustache and the corpulent rendering of the body suggest that, for all its references to antique and eclectic sources, this is portrait of an 8th-century figure. Not least through its likely date and location at Repton, it is claimed as a portrait of Aethelbald, Offa's predecessor, who was murdered by his own bodyguard in 757 (Figure 2.37C).[183] Also in Mercia is the

Figure 2.37 Fm 2 clothing: (top left): Jarrow; (right): St Mary Bishophill Junior York (*Corpus* III, 83–84, ill.216); (bottom left): Repton.

(Courtesy and © Corpus of Anglo-Saxon Stone Sculpture, photographer T. Middlemass (top left, right), photographer J. Hawkes (bottom left))

Breedon angel standing under a niche holding a trilobed rod and with right hand raised in blessing. He is clad in a ribbed garment with an extensive train looped over the left shoulder and forearm, resembling the Classic toga. As with its contemporaries in France, it is not clear whether this is a borrowed image or an actual item of dress that is being represented; but in either case the message should be one of learning and authority.[184]

England in Formative 2 (the long eighth century, 675–825)

In terms of archaeological visibility, the Christianising of the east of Britain would appear to have remained in abeyance for some 75 years after Augustine's mission. It then took place rapidly, signalled by the end of furnished burial in the south and east and the first recognisable monasteries in the north and west. The process of transition was roughly bracketed between the arrival of Archbishop Theodore in 669 and the publication of Bede's history in 731.[185] Even so the positive signs of this ideological change and the introduction of informative new media (sculpture and manuscript illustration) occur most clearly outside the English heartlands, that is, north of the Humber and west of the Pennines. This leaves us short on evidence for people's appearance in Fm 2, compared, for example, to Pictland.

Nevertheless, there are some indications. A glimpse of fashionable England of the late 7th and early 8th century embraced both by the laity and the new clergy is found in a disapproving text written by Aldhelm of Malmesbury:

> This sort of glamorization for either sex consists of linen shirts, in scarlet or blue tunics, in necklines and sleeves embroidered with silk; their shoes are trimmed with red-dyed leather; the hair of their forelocks and the curls at their temples are crimped with a curling iron; dark-grey veils for the head give way to bright and coloured head-dresses which are sewn with interlaces of ribbons and hang down as far as the ankles.[186]

Finds from excavations and from the PAS show that elaborate stick pins, sometimes linked, are features of English dress: a set of three linked pins were found in the River Witham at Fiskerton in a dry summer, decorated with the elegant, lively, bounding, sprawling animals that characterise 8th-century Mercia.[187] The three Witham pins could presumably have been employed to secure either hair or clothing. The site of Brandon in Suffolk produced 328 artefacts relating to dress, mostly stick pins of various types and sizes, suggesting the operations of a considerable industry. Most were cast copper alloy, but some were silver and others antler or bone. Pin heads were globular, biconical, polyhedral and disc and range in affluence from the utilitarian to rare examples gilded and decorated in relief. The ornament belongs in the late 8th century with Witham. Glass beads were also found, and the assemblage as a whole has something of a female signature, reinforcing the interpretation of the site as a magnate farm.[188]

Further south still, from the Christian enclave in Canterbury, comes the Vespasian psalter, whose frontispiece shows King David with six musicians and two dancers.[189] All have neat ribbed hair parted in the middle, which recalls the Celtic use of butter, and loose tunics brightly coloured. David's lyre recalls the one found in the Sutton Hoo Mound 1 burial ship, and the scene has some claim to be a quotation of 8th-century English court life (Figure 2.38A). Carved on a cross shaft at Codford St Peter in Wiltshire is another lively figure that Professor Cramp describes in these terms:

> His curly hair is bound with a filet and he is dressed in a short long-sleeved tunic with a cloak over, which is belted at the waist and clipped together at the top by a T-shaped

pin. . . . His shoes are cut away to leave a short tongue and a high back. . . . His left hand holds a globular object with a long tube or handle. . . . [His right hand] holds a plant with small triangular and long curling leaves, and is topped with globular berry bunches.[190]

In form and motion he resembles a dancer, perhaps keeping time by shaking a variety of rattles of the type of maracas or castanets in the manner of Morris dancers, and plausibly including the shaken branch (Figure 2.38B).

This small number of examples opens a window on a world of highly varied attire, from the sternly ceremonial to people having fun, from warm outdoor costumes that are padded or quilted to kilted warriors with weapons. Together with the mischievous animals that are released into the margins of illuminated manuscripts during the 9th century, these pave the way to the carnival of invention that is England in Fm 3.

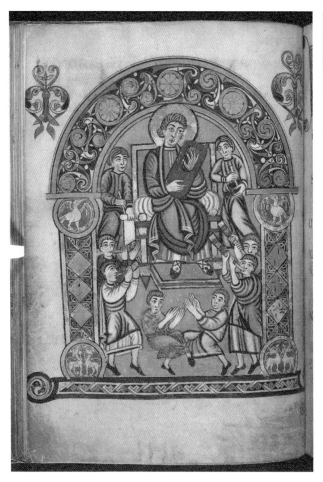

Figure 2.38 David with musicians and dancers in the Vespasian psalter (left) and a dancer on a cross shaft at Codford St Peter (right). The Vespasian scene employs a wide range of colours – gold, blue and white for the roundels in the arch, a light blue background for the birds and animals on the pillars either side, while the musicians and dancers sport tunics of vermillion, green, and light blue.

(*Corpus* VII, Ill. 425; courtesy and © Corpus of Anglo-Saxon Stone Sculpture, photographer K. Jukes)

Costume in Formative 3 (850–1075)

Vikings (9th/10th century)

The Viking intrusions from the 9th century affected the north and west (destinations of the Norse) and the east and south (the Danes) and revitalised the appearance of secular dress just as they re-energised trade and extolled the virtues of self-determination over those of prayer. The sources for costume are finds in settlements, especially those with organic preservation, from graves (not numerous in Britain), the PAS, some images carved on stone and a vivid set of sagas, which, while not preserved in contemporary documents (they are 12th century and later), offer details appropriate to the 9th to 11th centuries.

Viking textiles included a rich variety of twills, initially brought with them and soon made locally in north and west Scotland and Ireland. *Nålebinding* was a form of knotless netting producing an elastic fabric, found in York and Dublin and used in York to make a sock. Silk headdresses have been found in York, Lincoln and Dublin. The Vikings developed *wadmal*, a tightly spun, matted, water repellent fabric found in Orkney, Shetland, Iceland and Greenland.[191] A rich harvest of cloth and leather has come from the anaerobic deposits of Viking towns: York and Lincoln in England, Dublin and Waterford in Ireland; there are 2,340 leather objects from the Coppergate site in York alone. Sheaths include types that enclose the whole knife and its handle, types that are suspended from a belt, and types that are decorated on the flat side, the decoration marking the outline of the blade that lies hidden inside. Shoes made in the English tradition, where the sole and upper were made separately and stitched together, and in the Scandinavian tradition, where the sole is dovetailed into the upper, were on sale together in Anglo-Scandinavian York.[192] By Fm 3, if not before, leather was used to make a wide variety of essential items and helps to explain what happened to the thousands of cattle hides produced annually (Chapter 3, p. 288). Here is the leatherworker making his pitch in Aelfric's Colloquy:

> I buy hides and skins and use my crafts to make them into footwear of various kinds: slippers, shoes, chaps and ankleboots as well as bags, bridles, harness, bottles or wine-skins, satchels, stirrups, halters, purses and wallets; nobody could get through the winter without my skills.[193]

The Viking man is eulogised by the description of Skarp-Hedin at the Althing: 'his hair combed well back and held in place by a silken headband, looking every inch a warrior'.[194] Viking warriors carried spear, sword, shield and at least some of their wealth as ready cash in the form of armbands.[195] In the Norse area, the Irish/Scottish series of brooches continues, with giant silver penannulars using pins with thistle heads. The prevalence of Thor's Hammer pendants, e.g. in Grave 511 at the Repton winter camp or three examples from the Torksey winter camp, suggest a shifting of allegiance from Odin to Thor by the 10th century.[196] Rather than being imported, these pendants seem to have been made in Britain for a Scandinavian clientele, who maintained a strong Scandinavian cultural or political presence in Norfolk and Lincolnshire with their own dress and religious amulets and bullion exchange system, even while Christian Wessex was trying to roll them up.[197]

On the evidence of graves, the women wore a peplos-like garment secured with 'tortoise-shell' brooches and accompanied by a necklace, earrings and a variety of pendants, including the cross. Others appear in copper-alloy models wearing a long trailing gown that probably signified a higher rank.[198] On the picture stones we see images of dead Vikings arriving at

Valhalla greeted by women with flowing gowns and their hair in a bun, carrying drinking horns. This presumably evoked the real life of the hall.

As illuminated by Neil Price, the Viking way of dressing revealed the Viking way of thinking, most vividly perhaps the power of Viking women in their shamanistic role. Here one of them makes a spectacular entrance in Erik's saga:

> When she arrived in the evening, together with the man who had been sent to escort her, she was wearing a blue or black cloak fitted with straps, decorated with stones right down to the hem. She wore a string of glass beads around her neck. On her head she wore a black lambskin hood lined with white catskin. She had hairy calfskin shoes, with long sturdy laces, and they had great knobs of tin on the end. On her hands she wore catskin gloves which were white and furry inside.

And then we are introduced to some of the tools of her trade:

> Around her waist she had a belt of tinder wood, on which was a large leather pouch. In this she kept the charms that she used for her sorcery. And she carried a staff with a knob at the top.[199]

This is a medieval description written in Iceland – but archaeology has some contemporary Viking examples to offer too: the lady buried in a wagon-body at Fyrkat had silver toe-rings, a knife and whetstone, numerous silver pendants, a bronze bowl and miniature chair. By her side was a meat spit, a wooden staff and an oak box containing a pig's jaw-bone, seeds of henbane and owl pellets.[200] This seems a potent image of the female shaman, successor to the 'cunning woman' of Bidford-on-Avon (p. 401).

The sartorial expression of Viking men and women was a throwback to Saxon times: the men armed and dressed as warriors, the women in a peplos-like garment secured with extravagant 'tortoiseshell' brooches and wearing a variety of symbolic pendants purloined from warring religions. This cavalier appropriation of what others regard as sacred recalls the 7th-century young aristocrats at Sutton Hoo. The dressed-up Vikings must have provoked an atavistic response in the Germanic areas, including England, that had not seen the like for two centuries. The British were again the victims of the renewed hostilities from across the North Sea, and the Picts were all but eliminated from history.

English idyll, 10th/11th century

For much of the 10th and 11th century, and indeed after the conquest, the English aristocracy and clergy shared their adopted island with Britons, Scots, Norse and Danes, and for most of it they were at war, and not always on the winning side. And yet their cultural vitality during this period has seldom been exceeded. English painting entered its first triumphant international phase, producing work of such breath-taking quality that it continues to excite admiration today. As we will see, the imagery of a number of late Saxon manuscripts can also be relied on for archaeological purposes.

Material culture also offers an account of how people dressed and appeared. Although we have no grave goods, excavations in towns have provided a dazzling repertoire of objects for personal use, especially where anaerobic deposits have allowed organic materials – wood textiles and leather – to survive. It was at Coppergate in York that the 8th century helmet was deposited in a timber-lined pit. The subsequent occupation of the site in the Anglo-Scandinavian period (9th–11th century) produced a mass of material, including jet and amber jewellery, silver, copper and lead alloy disc brooches, a tin-coated spoon, wooden bowls spun on a lathe, boots and shoes, leather sheaths, a silk hood, a silk purse, a wool sock, combs of bone and antler, bone skates, dice, a bone whistle, wooden pipes and a gaming board.[201] Further north in Durham, the 10th–11th century Saddler Street site featured a cobblers' workshop making and mending a variety of shoes and boots, including a sandal. Shoe sizes in Saxo-Norman Durham varied from child size 7 to adult 11 (Figure 2.39). The Durham assemblage was also notable for a textile with a combination of a fine warp with a lumpy weft, giving

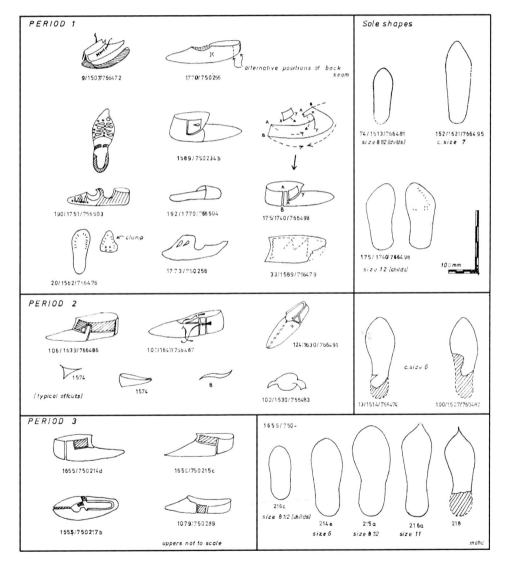

Figure 2.39 Shoes from the cobbler's workshop at Saddler Street, Durham.
(Carver 1979; © author)

a 'close warm surface'.[202] Further south at Winchester, a grander range of personal effects was retrieved. Material assigned to Formative 3 included linen, gold braid and red and gold silk imported from Byzantium, Syria or Persia, probably worn by high-ranking churchmen or members of the nobility, found in 9th–10th century burials in the Old Minster cemetery. Domestic refuse from Lower Brook Street offered a cornucopia of objects lost or jettisoned by the inhabitants of the town: textiles, buckles, toggles and clothes fasteners, shoes and boots, bone skates, jewellery, combs, tweezers, toilet equipment, games and toys, musical instruments, writing equipment, fragments of books and a small spherical cover apparently belonging to a 10th-century cricket ball.[203] York, Durham and Winchester all produced keys for barrel padlocks and mounted locks: locked chests and cupboards were the order of the day. In these communities, men women and children were well fed and well dressed, with recreational playthings and personal possessions kept in secure places.

Chance survivals of artefacts in the countryside, listings in wills and illustrations in art also reveal something of the current investment in personhood. The Portable Antiquities Scheme has provided a rich harvest of strap-ends: decorated metal sleeves made in bronze or silver that were designed to slip easily into a buckle and prevent the end of leather straps from fraying. Some look flashy and expensive, but what with strenuous galloping and the spring-time passions of the hay field, the strap-ends were prone to drop off and get lost (Figure 2.40). But the dates of those retrieved by the PAS are predominantly 9th century and later, and they are found in areas associated with the English and the Danish Vikings, suggesting that war too produced its detritus.[204] The PAS holds a thousand records for bronze or silvered strap-ends – undoubtedly a small fraction of the total. Stirrups, and presumably their suspending straps, were introduced into England by the Vikings (along with spurs), but not until the mid- to late 10th century.[205]

It is possible that some of the most treasured possessions, amongst the laity as amongst the monks, were never lost or buried but passed from person to person until finding their way into a 19th- or 20th-century museum. The Fuller Brooch is an outstanding article of adornment with a secular theme, so large and beautiful it is almost more worthy of the mantelpiece (Figure 2.9). It is 'scutiform', gently domed like a shield, and made of polished silver inlaid with niello. Within a circle of busts with hair parted in the middle, it shows portraits of four agitated individuals around a central figure holding a V-shaped pair of flowering rods. Look closer, and you can see that each figure represents one of the five senses, taste, smell, hearing and touch, and the central figure with big round eyes, sight.[206]

The records of precious items left in wills show not only the range of aristocratic possessions but the fact that many of them had extensive 'biographies' already well conserved by their owners. Here is an extract from the will of Prince Aethelstan, written in AD 1014:

> First . . . to Christ and St Peter . . . the sword with the silver hilt, which Wulfric made; and the gold baldric (*fetels*) and the armlet (*beh*), which Wilfric made and the drinking-horn, which I bought from the community at the Old Minster. . . . And to my father, King Æthelred, . . . the silver-hilted sword which belonged to [Earl] Ulfketel. And to my brother Edmund I grant the sword which belonged to King Offa and the sword with the pitted (*pyttedan*) hilt. . . . And I grant to my brother Eadwig a silver-hilted sword. . . . And I grant to Ælfmar, my dish-thegn, . . . the sheared sword (*sceardan swurdes*). . . . And to Siferth I grant . . . a sword. . . . And I grant to Eadric, the son of Wynflæd, the sword on which a hand is marked (*þe seo hand is gemearcod*). And I grant to Æthelwine,

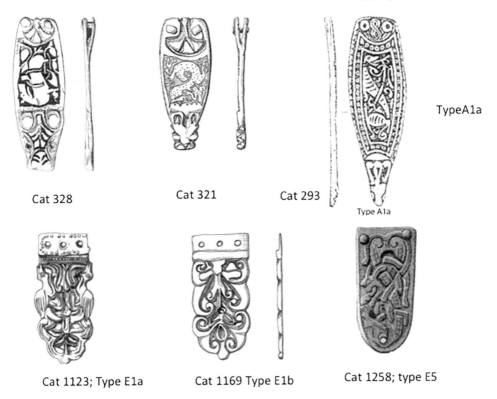

TypeA1a

Cat 328   Cat 321   Cat 293   Type A1a

Cat 1123; Type E1a   Cat 1169 Type E1b   Cat 1258; type E5

Figure 2.40 Examples of strap-ends classified by Gabor Thomas 9–10th century (left to right and top to bottom): Cat 328, 9th c, Norfolk; Cat 321, 9th century unprovenanced; Cat 293, late 9th century, N Yorks; Cat 1123, 10th century, Hertfordshire; Cat 1169, 10th century, Suffolk; Cat 1258, 10th century, Winchester.

(Thomas 2000; with permission of G Thomas (321,1123,1169,1258), *The Society for Medieval Archaeology* (293) and David Adams and NPS Archaeology (328))

my cniht, the sword which he previously gave to me. And I grant to Ælfnoth my sword polisher (*swurdhwita*), the sheared pattern-sword (*malswurd*).

Aetheling Aethelstan, this sword enthusiast, was the son of Ethelred the Unready. Apart from land, he also left a silver cross, a silver trumpet, a silver cauldron and numerous horses. The sword he left to his brother Edmund was more than 200 years old.[207] It can also be seen from this text that by Formative 3, the English regarded their monasteries as less of an institution for ritual intercession and more of a bank for the investment and redistribution of treasure.

Material rewards were sought and given in every working relationship, as indicated by two of the interviews in Aelfric's Colloquy:

– What about you, merchant?
– I am useful to king, leaders, tycoons and everybody else.

– In what way?

– I board a ship with my cargo, and navigate to places over the seas. There I sell my wares and buy things we don't have here and bring them to you – at the risk of getting shipwrecked, losing everything overboard including almost my own life.

– What do you bring?

– Purple cloaks and silks, precious gems and gold, dyed cloth, wine and oil, ivory and copper, bronze and tin, sulphur, glass and the like.

– Why do you want to buy them over there and sell them over here?

– I don't want to! . . . but how else can I make a profit?[208]

The hunter is asked: What do you make from hunting?

– Everything I kill I give to the king, because I am the king's huntsman.

– And what does he give you?

– He gives me food and smart clothes, as well as a horse or arm rings and so I can follow my craft freely.[209]

In a characteristically pithy passage, Dorothy Whitelock takes a snapshot of the fashions of the late Saxon upper echelon:

> That the upper classes cared for fine apparel we know mainly from the homilists' diatribes against it, especially against the priests, monks and nuns who emulated the laity in this respect. Men wore a mantle over a knee-length tunic and trousers and sometimes bequeath silken robes and fur cloaks (in their wills). The mantle was fastened by a brooch, often of beautiful workmanship and great size, the tunic held by a belt that might have richly ornamented clasps and mounts. Gold and silver finger-rings, armlets, and collars might be worn and much interest was taken in the elaborate ornamentation of weapons and of horse trappings. The verse literature, which never describes clothes, can spare several lines to depict a helmet, a sword hilt or a coat of mail.[210]

The manuscript ateliers suffered during the long Viking wars, but in the early 10th century, human figures begin to creep into the vegetation curling around the initials of ecclesiastical service books. Soon human actors appear as portraits in full colour. In the frontispiece to the *Life of Cuthbert*, dating before 937, Cuthbert wears a square-neck russet brown chasuble over an alb of a form that a modern-day Catholic priest would recognise. King Athelstan (presenting him with a copy of Bede's book) wears bright red leggings under a short grey belted tunic with brocaded cuffs and neckline, under a cloak pinned on the right shoulder by a small circular brooch, its modesty perhaps a mark of the authentic[211] (Figure 2.41). This picture offers a classic contrast between the different kinds of authority professed by bishop and king, both clad in rich garments. The colours should be significant, in that the colours that the church required at different seasons of the liturgical year for altar cloths, frontals and the vestments of the celebrant at Mass were aligned: white and gold for the feasts of Christ, purple for Lent, red for Palm Sunday, Good Friday, the martyrdom of the apostles and Pentecost, green for ordinary days. In Gospel books, insular-period evangelists appear in white, green, violet, blue and rose robes.

More standard liturgical costumes of the reformed priesthood can be seen on the gold-embroidered silk maniple and stole that were placed in Cuthbert's coffin on the same occasion.[212] The *Aethelstan Psalter* refers to the hosts of martyrs, confessors and virgins, depicting the first two categories as men, some, but not all, monks with the Roman tonsure

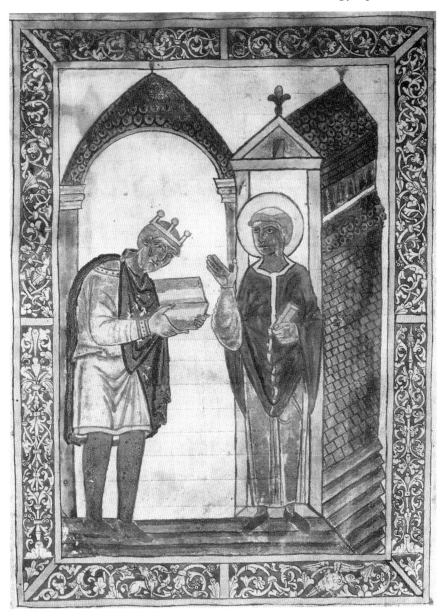

Figure 2.41 King and bishop in the early 10th century. King Aethelstan presents St Cuthbert with a copy of his life, written by Bede.

(Corpus Christi College Cambridge, ms183, 1v; Temple 1976, 29; © The Master and Fellows of Corpus Christi College, Cambridge, reproduced under licence)

and stoles. The virgins are well buttoned up, with close-fitting veil; the garments of the whole assembly are coloured red, green, blue and buff.[213] Formal figures with sacred roles are represented in sympathetic detail: less awe, more affection. Beards, hair, gowns and colours carry that 'whisper of authenticity' that allows several figures to be accounted as well-executed portraits.[214]

The principles developed on Harley 603 have allowed us to fill a wardrobe from the Late Saxon corpus. Harley 603's Hand IA (1000–1025) shows us swords with trilobed pommels, riveted shields, twin winged spears and floriated staffs as contemporary artefacts, while Hand 1F (1025–1050) offers a king and queen wearing crowns and a large Goliath in knee-length chain mail and conical helmet.[215] Harley 603's Hand 1A also allows a glimpse of the Late Saxon countryside: churches with pilaster walls, a shingle roof, gable finial and a weathercock.[216] Other realist pictures show us long-and-short work,[217] baluster shafts[218] and a range of musical instruments: triangular harp, viol, lute, rebec and xylophone.[219] Elsewhere, foresters load a cart with tree trunks[220] and harvesters cut grass with scythes, sharpened with whetstones.[221] These workers wear short kirtles, probably with a belt; their hair is blonde, black or balding, and one has a forked beard.

The picture gallery of late Saxon manuscripts is stunning, but the principle of pictorial deconstruction means that not all the images can be used to inform the archaeology. A natural delight in colour gives some wayward results. In the Anglo-Saxon Hexateuch, exotic figures assume exotic looks: the Pharaoh (with a 9th/10th century sword) and his courtiers (clutching drinking horns) wear cloaks and undertunics of green, blue, red and pink.[222] In the Tiberius Calendar, where one of our realists has depicted ploughmen in grey and blue tunics with red leggings, it will be objected that the plough has blue wheels and the unploughed grass is also blue.[223] Noah's family in the Hexateuch also sport blue hair, allowed to 'fashion' by the 19th-century commentator Thomas Wright.[224] But the colours on the ark, with its Ringerike style figurehead, are judged by a modern expert to be 'beautifully painted in blues, reds, yellows and greens, much as actual carved wood prows would have looked'.[225] The principles of analysing pictures is based on the artist making repeated references to objects known to be contemporary; but it does allow for some caprice.

The illustrators of some copies of Prudentius' *Psychomachia* qualify with honours for the company of artistic 'realists'.[226] The lively pen sketches in Cambridge ms CCC23 include a woman in a long dress and wimple (f17v), a man in a short kirtle and cloak with a disc brooch (f37v) and horses with body harness (f2). But it is the group scenes that provide masterly vignettes of young people socialising: there is a stand-off between the boys and the girls, and at a table, two young men and two young women share a drink and explore interests (Figure 2.42). The women, as always, wear headscarves, and one states her views to the others, earning a reception all attentive, all different. They could be university students in the pub today. Elsewhere *Luxuria*, an important allegorical character in the *Psychomachia*, dances barefoot to a powerful beat, while appreciative men look on. Her story does not end well, but the underlying message of the late Saxon idyll is unmistakable: young people had fun, and in ways as old as the earth (Chapter 5, p. 587).

For all the perils of the political situation, the artistic climate became sunnier in the 10th century, and it is as though the greater part of the English population, not just princes and prelates, had suddenly been let out to play. With their mixture of mischief and marvel, these Late Saxon artists are the unsung heroes of early English art. We can see their last flourish in the Bayeux Tapestry, full of colourful clothes in a figurative embroidery. In telling the story of the Norman invasion and the arrival of a more oppressive institutionalised religion, it also spells the end of one of Europe's greatest art movements, as surely as the Great War did, 900 years later.

A brief reflection on gender

In comparison with the Celtic zones, women's experience in Britain is more evident in the English region in all three periods, in both documents and archaeology, and may not

Figure 2.42 Young people socialising in the late 10th century.

(Corpus Christi College Cambridge 23, f37v, 17v; Temple 1976, 156, 158; © The Master and Fellows of Corpus Christi College, Cambridge; reproduced under licence)

be typical of the island as a whole. Christine Fell's keynote study turned mainly on documentary evidence, especially laws, but provides a solid thesis, a wide range of evidence and an important point of departure for archaeologists. She shows that a liberated role for Anglo-Saxon women had been appreciated by scholars since the early 19th century, based on their independent holding of land, property and wealth.[227] In 1956 Doris Stenton concluded that 'The evidence which has survived from Anglo-Saxon England indicates that women were then more nearly the equal companions of their husbands and brothers than at any other period before the modern age'.[228] Stenton defined two major setbacks for the rights of women, the first through Christianisation and the second through the coming of the Normans. Fell's own researches endorsed these views but felt that the Christian conversion did not disempower women, at least at first, as indicated by their frequent appointment to lead and administer religious houses. In the climate of the later 20th century, she also advises her readers 'to remember that scholarship does not require us to read only, always and inevitably a history of oppression and exploitation of the female sex. The real evidence from Anglo-Saxon England presents a more attractive and indeed assertive picture'.[229] She was indeed convinced 'that the average Anglo-Saxon wife was both valued and respected, enjoying economic and marital rights, her independence safe-guarded and her interests protected'.[230]

However, it is clear that the trafficking of women formed part of the slave trade, although she found no strong evidence for prostitution.[231] Sexual misdemeanours seem to have been addressed through the compensation system. The tariff for fornication and adultery was dependent on the class of the offended patron (seduction: 20 shillings for the maidservant of an earl, 6 for the maidservant of a ceorl). Seduction was distinguished from assault, and the compensation graded: touching a breast 5 shillings, throwing her down 10 shillings; throwing down and going the whole way 60 shillings. In the case of the rape of a ceorl's slave, 5 shillings is paid to the ceorl plus a 60 shilling fine. The fines are doubled for interfering with a nun.[232] Notably, in the case of a free woman, compensation was paid directly to her.

Judith Jesch demonstrated that Scandinavian women were similarly equal players in the Viking project, accompanying the men on raids, often admired as warriors, and being closely involved in manufacture and production.[233] There is a puzzling gender balance in the Swedish cemeteries: at Valsgärde in the Vendel period (7th–9th century) there were 18 cremations (50% female) and five boat burials (all men), and in the Viking period (9th–11th century) there were 11 cremations (70% female) and 10 boat burials (all men).[234] However, one female cremation buried c. 700 stood at a primary vantage point (no. 57), and Viking-period cremations included two of richly furnished women. At Tuna in Badelunda, by contrast, the 70 graves identified in the Vendel period were poorly furnished cremated men, but the eight richly furnished boat burials were all dedicated to women.[235] The Oseberg ship grave, one of the richest (and best preserved) of all Viking burials, was composed using the feminine vocabulary of bed, textiles, silks, embroidery, together with a four-wheeled wooden cart and four sledges contained within the power mode of a buried ship under an earth mound. Even if the inmate had not been identified as the Norwegian Queen Åse, there was no doubt about her status, indicated both by the grave goods and by the subsequent desecration of the grave (Chapter 4, p. 446). Evidence from runestones in Eastern Sweden shows women as landowners and road and bridge builders, with responsibilities passing from mother to daughter. The Dynna stone in southern Norway was raised by Gunnvor, an 11th-century mother who built a bridge in memory of her daughter, Astridr, 'the handiest girl in Hadelund'.[236] Scandinavian women are also credited with leading the assessment of Christianity as a socially useful ideology, and the same can be inferred for Anglo-Saxon women.[237] It would seem that men and women had equal access to power, or at least that Scandinavian women were not prevented from exercising power when the occasion and their character and incentive demanded they did so. This was not to be the norm in the subsequent European centuries.

Genetic histories would surely be influenced by the asymmetry of Anglo-British society, as well as the existence of trafficking. Under Viking influence, Northumbrian priests also took wives, although they were discouraged from having more than one. Although families may sometimes have remained ignorant of their own genetic descent, they clearly proclaimed it proudly in some cases. The immediate descendants of Ealdhun Bishop of Durham 995–1018 sported four Celtic, nine English and nine Old Norse names.[238]

Archaeology offers a specific material gloss derived from burials, both the sex of the skeleton and the gender signalled by grave goods (see Chapter 4). In a sample of over 3,000 Anglo-Saxon inhumations, Nick Stoodley found a strong equivalence between biological sex as determined from the skeleton and gender as implied by the grave goods: broadly, weapons for men, brooches and beads for women. However the gender statement was limited to a proportion of those buried: 60% of sexed females and 45% of sexed males.[239] Weapon injuries and cut-marks were overwhelmingly associated with males; but for women childbirth provided a risk of equal danger.[240] Since women equipped with brooches had been subject to less physical labour, perhaps Christine Fell's cheerful verdict should be qualified as not so much applying to the 'average Anglo-Saxon wife' as to women in the privileged 60% class.

While men and women had different roles, reflected (apparently with pride) in their appearance, the cemetery evidence suggests that the gender-emphasis changed through life and through the times. At a personal level, female grave goods broadly accompanied those of sexually active age (late teens to middle age), while men continued to carry arms symbolically probably long after they were able to wield them.[241] The emphasis on gender distinction also varied through the centuries. Catherine Hills identified gender-specific packages among the cremations at Spong Hill, implying that this form of expression was already important in the 5th century.[242] Within the standard repertoire, it is suggested that the expression of personhood became more subtle and varied through the 6th century, women using combinations of brooches to assert individuality and self-identifying groups within the same cemetery.[243] Gender is emphasised on the *guldgubber*, which represent couples, whether human or divine. Sixth-century women in both England and Scandinavia wore bracteates that proclaim their high social standing and religious authority. During the 6th century, there are indications that women performed influential roles as shamans and the supervision of burial, an inference endorsed by later and clearer evidence from Viking period Scandinavia.[244] In the early 7th century, male gender expression became more strongly stated through wealthy graves under barrows, while the female repertoire was diminished and included accoutrements of more Byzantine type.[245] In the later 7th century, male signalling was reduced, but the female expression of gender became more emphatic.[246] In this later phase, some children were also awarded adult feminine grave goods,[247] something that perhaps finds an explanation in the emulation of British practice, for example at Hallow Hill and Cannington, where selected young persons, probably female, were accorded special reverence (Chapter 4, pp. 308, 354). On Christianisation, there appears to have been a readjustment in the role of males, who were accustomed to serve as leaders in both war and cult. Märit Gaimster suggests that the emergence of abbesses supplied by aristocratic families indicates a key role for women in the transition: following a brief experimental phase in which kings performed as monks and saints, 'the double task of cult specialist and guardian of sacral kingship appears to have been taken over by royal women . . . successful because it followed a tradition of powerful women in this sphere'.[248]

From the 7th century, veils also got longer and covered more, a modesty that might be associated with a censorious new religion. Nevertheless, by the 10th/11th century, manuscript images show young people, men and women, at ease in each other's company. These variations must have had some social meaning, and perhaps reflected the way that men and women were valued by the opposite sex or by themselves at different periods. It seems likely that men and women would have applied different, if complementary, kinds of intuition to the events of the day and come up with different responses. The altercation between Raedwald king of East of Anglia with his unnamed queen in the matters of Christian conversion and loyal alliance provides a useful instance. Their marital affray was reported by Bede, who reviled the queen's opposition to instant acceptance of Christianity but admired her morality and her political wisdom on the handling of allies, of whatever persuasion.[249]

The impression that this brief review is intended to convey is that it is unwise to generalise on the subject of the relative freedom of women and of men. Both men and women have obligations that they may share or appropriate. We can see no gender distinctions in daily life except that men were better with heavy implements and women were better at embroidery and other kinds of intricate manufacture. However, when it comes to the exercise and signalling of power, both sexes were capable and acknowledged as such. The chief criterion was to be wealthy, and wealthy in one's own right, and this English and Scandinavian women plainly were. Who actually got to rule depended on wealth, character and circumstance, then as now. It is possible that in Tuna i Badelunda and in eastern Swedish runestones we see some formation of female groups; but this would be just an adoption of the kind of loyal bonding long practised by men. And both sexes were probably equally adept at betraying members of their own, as well as of the opposite sex.

Conclusions

Gathered together, these 'artefacts of personal agenda' present us with a diverse panorama of folk from across the island and through 700 years. It has to be admitted, of course, that our fashion parade offers only a sample of a sample, an archaeological sample of a social sample. Whether reflected in shiny brooches, sexy stories, on the painted page, carved in stone or even lying in a grave, these people are all dressed up, selected for display. We can be sure that clothing and accoutrements formed some of the most important investments and social and political instruments in early Britain, and even in its rough, discordant and provisional form there are intimations of value for the wider purpose of this book. Graves, documents, images and artefacts have to be woven together and harmonised, like instruments in the orchestra, so that they may sound singly but create a vibrant picture.

In Fm 1 there are marked differences in dress, insisting on separate regional or group identities. So far as we have seen, the northern and western areas appear at that time closely linked, and the evidence is not well mapped (as we might have expected) onto a diversity of Celtic peoples: the stories stay in Ireland, the brooches move. But the English identity is strongly asserted as equal and opposite. All regions experience the assertion of the male aristocracy from the mid-6th to early 7th centuries, whether in brooches, burial mounds, or personal pillars in the landscape. In the English areas in the later 7th century there is a flowering of female independence and intellectual originality, with strong references to upper-class Byzantium.

From the late 7th century, our Fm 2, the monastic movement takes off in Northumbria and Pictland, rich, proud and with a wide following. The Pictish monks, warriors of Christ, rode horses and wore padded or embroidered gowns with hoods. They were different but equal to the warriors and hunters of their laity. After the 670s, as grave furnishing ceased, the upper echelons in the regions lose their cultural differences and gain cohesion in fervent Christianity expressed in the insular style.

In the 9th century, insular goes Frankish, whether in England or in the Celtic west (Book of Kells), but an equal and opposite ethos is offered by the Vikings. The Celtic areas and Anglo-British Northumbria are Scandinavianised, while the English reinvent themselves as pre-eminent Roman Christians and commence the English idyll, where kings, priests and workers are all members of the cast. Women also reappear on stage, in principal or ancillary roles, dressed now in the headscarves that have become an obligatory sign of the new orthodoxy.[250]

The selective moments prompted by the dressing-up box will be important for our arguments as to when, or whether, governance, spirituality or personal wealth is driving the drama in each act. But a lot more context is required before the argument can stand on its feet unaided. As if we have dressed the actors, but have yet to find the script, the further significance of all these costumes will have to be left until they reappear on stage in Chapter 7.

Notes

1 'Ethnicity is a loyalty exercised in the heart not in the blood' (Härke 2011, 4). Distinctive burial does not prove immigration or descent but may imply intended ethnicity: the people who buried their dead in a culturally Anglian manner 'probably thought of themselves as Angles' (Woolf 2000, 100). 'Medieval people were capable of retaining a whole series of separate identities on a variety of scales, each valid within its own context' (Woolf 2007, 108). See Frazer and Tyrrell 2000; Gillett 2002 for overviews. For a succinct discussion of the relationship between ethnicity, identity and material culture, see Hakenbeck 2011, 25–6, 143–6.

2 Although it concerns the more richly documented later medieval period (c. 1050–1540 AD), Roberta Gilchrist's *Medieval Life* (2012) offers a model of what may one day be possible for the early middle ages.

3 See Roberts 2009; Roberts and Cox 2003; Gilchrist 2012, 43–67. For facial reconstruction see Wilkinson 2008.

4 G. *Cam Bèal*; Dupuytren's disease, which produces a flexion deformity of the finger, has its highest incidence in Iceland and Norway (Flatt 2001).

5 Sherwood et al. 2008; Johnson and Paul 2016.

6 See Brown and Brown 2011, Ch. 2 for an overview.

7 Y-chromosomes track descendance from father to son and mitochrondrial DNA (MtDNA) from mother to daughter.

8 Sims-Williams 2012, 429–430; cf Thomas et al. 2006.

9 The PoBI project (People of Britain and Ireland). Leslie et al. 2015. See *Nature* 18 Mar 2015, Fig 1.

10 Cf. a comment from a member of the research team: 'I had assumed that there was a uniform Celtic fringe from Cornwall through to Wales into Scotland – and this has very definitely not been the case': Prof Mark Robinson, University of Oxford, in a 'puff' for the *Nature* article (at www.bbc.co.uk/news/science-environment-31905764).

11 Kershaw and Royrvik 2016, 1674. See also Nash 2015, Ch 3.

12 Hills 2009.

13 'In Britain . . . the spread of the Beaker complex introduced high levels of steppe-related ancestry and was associated with the replacement of approximately 90% of Britain's gene pool within a few hundred years' (Olalde et al. 2018, 190).

14 David Reich (2018, 277) describes this gap 'like a highway overpass still under construction and ending in mid-air'. For the justifiable anxieties that using modern DNA is misleading see Nash 2015

15 For Richard III see (www.cam.ac.uk/research/news/richard-iii-case-closed-after-529-years). See Chapter 4, p. 392 for a pair of sword-bearing brothers at Dover identified by aDNA.

16 See Brown and Brown 2011, Ch 6 for an overview.

17 Examples: Mays 2000; Budd et al. 2004; Bentley 2006; Richards et al. 2006; Radini et al. 2017 for calculus.

18 Clarke 1979, 433; Kjølbye-Biddle 1992, 216–217.

19 Booth et al. 2010, 308–309. Ten out of 40 skeletons were identified as having non-British origins. Of these, one adult male, without Hungarian grave goods, was identified as possibly Pannonian (Ay21–1119). Of five children with 'Pannonian' grave goods, four were raised in the Winchester area. One woman with Pannonian grave goods was from the southern Mediterranean, as were two others without Pannonian grave goods, one perhaps originating from Egypt (Chenery et al. in Booth et al., 427–428).

20 Leeds 1945.
21 Hills 2003, 104–106. Angles and Saxons are distinguishable from brooches in England but do not map onto their supposed Continental homelands. 'The simplest explanation remains the arrival of successful invaders whose descendants celebrated their genuine Germanic ancestors, together with those of any surviving Britons who would have found it expedient to take on an Anglo-Saxon cultural identity' (Hills 2003, 111); cf Myres 1936, 363: 'the Jutish nation . . . was made in Kent'.
22 Hines 1984; Hines 1994.
23 Lucy 2000, 172.
24 For summaries see Hills 2003; Woolf 2007, 99; Lucy 2000, 2002, 147–150; Härke 2004, 456: 'There is some evidence that the pendulum of academic debate is swinging back. . . . The most modern technique returns us to the oldest model.'
25 Spong Hill is the only large Anglo-Saxon cemetery to have been completely excavated. Hills and Lucy 2013; see Chapter 4, pp. 321–4.
26 For what follows, Härke 2011, trailed in Härke 2002, 147–150, 2004 and Thomas et al. 2006.
27 For the British associations of penannular brooches: Dickinson 1982 and Campbell 2001. Another possible cultural marker not used by Härke is the burial rite without grave goods but with stone inclusions; see Chapter 4, Wasperton.
28 Härke 2011, 17: 'As far as the archaeological evidence can tell us, acculturation in the settlement areas of continental immigrants was a one-way process: the common culture being created was essentially Anglo-Saxon, not mixed or hybrid Anglo-British.'
29 Schiffels et al. 2016.
30 Martiniano et al. 2016.
31 Sims-Williams 2012.
32 The family kingdom model that prevailed among the British as a mode of governance from the 5th century was adopted by the English in the 7th century. See Chapters, 3, 4, 5, 6.
33 In this book the force of change will be seen as springing from the choices and traditions of the native population in aspects of settlement (Chapter 3), burial (Chapter 4), sculpture and art (Chapter 5) and legends (Chapter 6).
34 The first five archbishops of Canterbury were Italians (Augustine, Lawrence, Mellitus, Justus, Honorius), the eighth (Theodore) from Tarsus (modern Turkey).
35 The eventual effect of aDNA analysis on the modern population is likely to be the widening of origins to the point where it loses any meaning for us today. A yearning for ancestry is still understandable but will perhaps remain out of reach, a matter discussed at length by Catherine Nash in her book *Genetic Geographies* (2015).
36 Cunliffe 2002, 133 'the mobility of the population was very much greater in the Roman period than at any time in Britain's prehistory'.
37 Pelteret 2001; McCormick 2001, 738–777; Abulafia 2011, 248–249.
38 Hedeager 2011. However, see Näsman 2008. DNA specialists have observed no major genetic input from outside Europe after the early Bronze Age (see above).
39 Hakenbeck 2009, 64.
40 Hakenbeck 2009, 79–80. She remarks that 'The movement of women was a widespread phenomenon across all social strata and was not primarily linked to known historical migrations.'.
41 Ashby 2013, 2014 for social signals generated from hair 'technologies', especially as indicated by combs.
42 Fraser 2011, 36.
43 J Caesar *De Bello Gallico* Bk V, Ch 14. 'Omnes vero se Britanni vitro inficiunt, quod caeruleum efficit colorem, atque hoc horridiores sunt in pugna aspectu; capilloque sunt promisso atque omni parte corporis rasa praeter caput et labrum superius.'
44 Raftery 2000, 127.
45 Walton Rogers 2007, 244.
46 Jackson 1971, 181–182; Irish; anon; 9th century original.
47 For the realities of early gold and silver accoutrements, their production and context of discovery, see Graham-Campbell 1995, 2002, Hinton 2005, 2011; Spall 2006.
48 Carver 1986b, 141. The short list of English 'realist' output was Harley 603, Hands 1A-F, Ox Bod Jun 11, Cott. Claudius BIV and Cott. Tib BV. To these can be added the Bayeux Tapestry. See Wormald 1952 for the derivation of the individual hands in Harley 603 and Noel 1995 for a more recent description and analysis of this ms.

49 Stenton et al. 1957, especially Nevinson, 'The Costumes'.

50 Both dated to the second quarter of the 8th century: Alexander 1978, nos, 17, 29.

51 Henderson 1998, 164, in a fine review of the artefacts depicted, pp. 156–165. The notched shield was suggested as a distinctive Pictish type by Ritchie 1969, but the discovery of a number of miniaturised examples in the 1988 Salisbury hoard, where the objects were dated no later than 200 BC (Stead 2000), suggests that David or a member of his troupe was assigned a shield of the 'old style' in recognition of his ancestral persona (Carver 1999). A similar cross-cultural reference is seen in the Goliath dressed as a Norman with chain mail and conical helmet by Harley 603's Hand 1 F (Carver 1986b, 129, Fig 12).

52 Fine cloth, especially imported silk, was used in the west to wrap relics (Brubaker 2004).

53 Crowfoot 1983, Fig 325, pp. 457–462; Evans 1983; East 1983; Carver 2005a, 187; and see Chapter 4, p. 331ff for a description of the burial.

54 Bruce-Mitford 1978, 532–535; Filmer-Sankey 1996; Geake 1999, 212.

55 Walton Rogers 2005, 262–268.

56 Making a set of hand-made replica clothing for the incumbent of Mound 1 at Sutton Hoo was one of the most costly items of the complete burial chamber that was displayed to the public in the early years of the 21st century.

57 The men of the Gododdin wear brooches, and possibly torcs (Chapter 6, p. 610). But rank was perhaps a more decisive factor in the north: the Hilton of Cadboll woman wears an ostentatious penannular brooch.

58 Leigh 1984.

59 Carroll 1995.

60 Wilson 1964, 117, 1984, 110.

61 From a huge literature I would select, for precision and pleasure, Kendrick 1949; Wilson 1964, 1984; Wilson and Klindt-Jensen 1966; Alexander 1978; Speake 1980; Henderson 1987; Redknap et al. 2001; Henderson and Henderson 2004; Hinton 2005; Webster 2012; Graham-Campbell 2013.

62 See Graham-Campbell 2013 for an expert and entertaining road-map of Viking art.

63 See the *linguist* staffs carried by the Ebrie people, which take the form of animals with known meaning (e.g. tortoise = foresight) or groups representing a proverb (Garrard 1989, passim).

64 Hinton and White 1993; Hinton 2000. For a detailed survey see Hinton 2005.

65 Or even magical powers; see, for example, Heald 2003, 160–163.

66 Bede I.15. Following an initial invitation from the British leader Vortigern, the Saxons from North Germany (Saxony) settled in Essex, Sussex and Wessex, the Angles from south Jutland settled in East and Middle Anglia and Northumbria and the Jutes from north Jutland settled in Kent and the Isle of Wight. Following the first arrivals in 449, 'hordes of these peoples eagerly crowded into the island, . . . and became a source of terror to the natives who had called them in' (McClure and Collins 2008, 27). See above p. 56 for current views of the *Adventus Saxonum*.

67 Carver 2009b.

68 Carver 2000 on the subject of Sutton Hoo.

69 For helpful overviews see Lucy 2000 and Williams 2006. Burial rites here are the subject of Chapter 4.

70 https://finds.org.uk/database, accessed 22 Mar 2015.

71 McCormick and Murray 2007, 111; Kelly 1988, 122–126. See Scull 2011 for a discussion of social value in Anglo-Saxon grave goods.

72 Whitelock 1968, 9.

73 Whitelock 1968, 40, 84.

74 Morris 2004, 13.

75 In 2007, there were 166 find-spots of preserved textiles (all early medieval periods) in England, including 13 in Fm 3 York alone; this compares with 34 in Ireland, 32 in Scotland, two in Wales and four in the Isle of Man. Coatsworth and Owen-Crocker 2007, 149–151.

76 'Whereas a single lump of iron cinder from a Roman site might weigh 80 lb, the sum total of ore, slag, cinders and blooms collected in five seasons of excavation at Dinas Powys amounted only to 50 lb. Here is a measure of the degree to which material culture and technology had declined since 400' (Alcock 1973, 232).

77 And in English Britain too: in 2015 the PAS recorded only 84 early medieval penannular brooches as opposed to 249 of Roman date. See Hunter 2007a and b for artefact regions of the later Iron Age.

78 Raftery 2000.
79 Raftery 2000, 127–128.
80 Newman 1995, 23; ornament of the pins can be tracked from Iron Age La Tène and the penannulars from Roman-British types.
81 Coatsworth and Owen-Crocker 2007, 143–148.
82 Kilbride-Jones 1980; see Laing 2006, 153–162 for a guide.
83 Fowler 1960; Alcock 1973, 236–237; Kilbride-Jones 1980; Redknap 1991, 30, 19.
84 O'Sullivan et al. 2014b, 86, 111; O'Sullivan et al. 2014a, 227, app. Tables 6.2, 6.3.
85 Tania Dickinson (1982) showed that the Type G brooches probably had an origin-centre in the Severn Valley (G1) and were current from the 4th century into the 6th century. Later types (G2, G3) are found in north-west Britain, and a workshop for Type G3 was found in Dunadd (Campbell 2001, 287; Lane and Campbell 2000, 106–118).
86 Henderson and Henderson 2004, 87–90. They argue that the plaques may have served as tokens (p. 222).
87 Noble et al. 2016. These authors also note that one of the pins and one of the plaques from the Norrie's Law hoard are 19th-century copies.
88 Redknap 1991, 33.
89 Youngs 1989, 20; Laing 2006, 162–168.
90 Ritchie 2005, 28–29.
91 Henry 2004, 445.
92 Henry 1952.
93 Porter et al. 2002.
94 Biggam 2006a, b.
95 Whitfield 2006, 12.
96 Wood 2003.
97 Henderson and Henderson 2004, Fig 180.
98 Henderson and Henderson 2004, Fig 181.
99 Hills and Lucy 2013, 301–320, Fig 5.1, 5.8. The argument is subtle (pp. 305–306), reporting 'a consistent picture from all sources, which shows that cruciform brooches are rare south of the Thames, apart from Kent, and where they do occur they are of simpler varieties, not the elaborate "florid" types. They are absent southwest of Hampshire and very thinly spread in the western and northern counties of England, but concentrated in large numbers in east of England from Kent to the Humber, except for Essex, where very few have been found.' 'The regional concentration of this type, which coincides with the distribution of other artefact types within late fifth- to early 6th century inhumations, supports their interpretation as defining identity.' But 'the antecedents of this brooch type in southern Scandinavia and Schleswig-Holstein have distributions which overlap with some, but not all, of the sixth century "Anglian" artefact types: wrist-clasps also originate in south Scandinavia but annular brooches and girdle hangers do not.' This argues for more than one region of origin for the East Angles. See also Martin 2012.
100 Hines 1984, 2013, 23.
101 Hines 1984, 2013, 23–24.
102 These brooches have generally been the subjects of individual study by type: Suzuki 2000 (quoit); Mortimer1990 (cruciform); Martin 2012 (cruciform); Evison 1977 (equal arm and supporting arm); Bruns 2003 (equal arm); Evison 1978a, b (applied disc); Dickinson 1991, 1993a (saucer); Dickinson 1979 (disc); Avent 1975 (composite); Avent and Evison 1982 (button); Hines 1997 (square headed); Hines 1993 (clasps).
103 Fowler 1960; Dickinson 1982.
104 Hines 1997; Leigh1984 for an interpretation of the Style 1.
105 Walton Rogers 2007. The information and deductions paraphrased in the following section are principally owed to this accomplished and comprehensive work.
106 Walton Rogers 2007, 229.
107 Henry 2004, 445.
108 Biddle 1990, 552.
109 Harris 2003.
110 Walton Rogers 2007, 232–233.
111 Walton Rogers 2007, 323–323.
112 Meaney 1981; Dickinson 1993b.

113 Walton Rogers 2007, 241–243, who suggests that 'German women had learned the practice of covering the head on marriage from the Romans'.
114 Walton Rogers 2007, 234, 244. Hinton 2000, 111–112 for metalworkers as men.
115 Marzinzik 2003 C. Fern personal communication.
116 Härke 1990.
117 The methods used were to show the likely order of use of artefact types by correspondence analysis of grave assemblages and compare these with radiocarbon dates on the skeletons they accompany. Hines and Bayliss 2013. The results of this study are summarised and discussed in Chapter 4, pp. 383–7.
118 'Roman imagery was adapted to express Germanic mythological ideas' Gaimster 2011, 867; Hedeager 1999.
119 Gaimster 2011; Hedeager 2011.
120 Gaimster 2011, 874.
121 Watt 2004.
122 Hills 2014. The lid was found in a rabbit hole amongst cremation burials (Find 3324). At the time it was unassigned to a particular cremation but confirmed as dating from the time of the cemetery by thermoluminescence. Hills 1980.
123 Walton Rogers 2007, 209.
124 Webster 2012, 38–41.
125 Webster L in Lucy et al. 2009, 178. The object is 43 mm long and weighs 12.2 gm.
126 Gannon 2003, 184–185.
127 Gannon 2003, 187–192. See Chapter 3, p. 248 for a discussion based on the archaeological nature of minsters.
128 Crowfoot 1967; Campbell 1986, 67; Geake 1997.
129 As Jim Lang put it: the habit of resurrecting the Classical past returns like Halley's comet throughout Christian art (2000, 113).
130 Dickinson 2005 for shields; the role of animal guardians, terrestrial, aerial and aquatic, well equipped with claws, beaks and teeth was carried on to Christian crosses and illuminated manuscripts.
131 Hall 1984, 35; Tweddle 1992; Webster 2012, 32–33. The translation of the Latin inscription is disputed but appears to invoke the protection of the Father, Son, Holy Spirit and all the saints for one Oshere, presumably the owner of the helmet (Binns et al. 1990).
132 Walton Rogers 2007, 240.
133 Walton Rogers 2005, 238.
134 Evans 2005; Carver 2005a, 115–137.
135 Carver et al. 2016, 95. See Chapter 4, p. 396 for horses in Anglo-Saxon cult.
136 Leahy and Bland 2009.
137 Webster et al 2011; Carver 2011c.
138 Bede III.24.
139 Walton Rogers 2007, 245.
140 These burials are discussed in Chapter 4, p. 408.
141 Hamerow 2016, 427.
142 The casket is in the British Museum and is named after Augustus Franks, who donated it. It measures 22.9 × 19 × 10.9 cm (height).
143 Webster 2012, 91–97, 235–236; The British Museum Collection online www.britishmuseum.org/research/collection_online (26 April 2016).
144 Fletcher 1997, 270.
145 Webster 2012, 97.
146 Caerwyn Williams and Ford 1992, 100; see Ch 6, p. 603.
147 Whitfield 2006; all the following section is based on Whitfield's tour de force.
148 Whitfield 2006, 27.
149 Jackson 1969, 33; Ritchie 2005, 30; Chapter 6, p. 608.
150 Whitfield 2006, 25; Dublin Trinity Coll. Lib A.1.6, f7v.
151 Whitfield 1999; Blackwell 2011; Whitfield 2014/5. See also Leigh 1984 for ambiguity among the pre-Christian English, also perhaps a form of ritual concealment.
152 Ó Floinn in Youngs 1989, 89; Whitfield 2006, 12–14.
153 Ó Floinn in Youngs 1989, 89.

154 Alcock 1993; Ritchie 2005; Fraser 2011, 36: 'possibly a careful study of the representations of Picts on monumental sculpture would reveal aspects of Pictish ethnicity, since perceptions of ethnic difference in the early middle ages could relate to arms . . . dress . . . and hairstyle'. For the examples of Pictish carving see Allen and Anderson 1903 and Henderson and Henderson 2004, where they are indexed by location, described and placed in context.

155 Reid 2014 for some recent thoughts on the depiction of horses and the hunt in Pictish Art.

156 Alcock 1993, 235 argues that the absence of hunting scenes from western art makes the derivation of the Pictish hunts from Continental sources unlikely. For Henderson and Henderson 2004, 179, the image was derived, perhaps, from Rome ('it is hard to overestimate the importance of the hunt as an image in Late Antiquity'), and the Hilton woman is a queenly figure taking part in a literary hunt. In Henderson 2008, 189, she is held to represent the Virgin Mary in allegorical mode, with the animals providing metaphors for the virtuous life.

157 Carver 2008a, b.

158 For convenience the figure references are to Henderson and Henderson 2004, where authoritative descriptions and interpretations will be found. This is Fig 78.

159 (Fig 35).

160 (Fig 79).

161 (Figs 79, 183).

162 (Figs 35, 89, 91, 183).

163 (Fig 82).

164 (Fig 50).

165 Henderson and Henderson 2004, 128.

166 This is not as disagreeable as it sounds and certainly experienced routinely by my generation (including me), if with lesser quarries.

167 (Fig 77).

168 (Fig 222).

169 As depicted in insular manuscripts, Alexander 1978, Figs 204–213.

170 (Fig 210).

171 (Fig 301).

172 (Fig 48).

173 (Fig 203).

174 (Fig 204–205).

175 The workboxes may themselves have been intended as portable reliquaries; see Hills 2015.

176 The essential equipment for the Mass is therefore a chalice and paten, to which may be added a bowl to wash the priest's fingers and a strainer to remove intrusive material from the wine. These were components of the Derrynaflan hoard found in 1980 at the monastery of Derrynaflan, Ireland. Other items of the priestly kit are a thurible for burning incense, a reliquary and perhaps a hanging bowl, a bowl with drop handles which may have been set up on a tripod as a mobile holy water stoup (Youngs 1989, 130–140; Ryan 2005; Ryan and Ó Floinn 1983; Redknap 2009, 364–365 for a reliquary from Llan-gors, Wales).

177 For a later image, see the First Bible of Charles the Bald, Paris BN Lat.1 f423r, where tonsured prelates gather round the king.

178 Sharpe 1995, 37. And see Chapters 3–6.

179 Cramp 1984b, 219, where the cloak is referred to as a pallium. Strictly speaking a pallium is a narrow symbolic vestment worn round the neck, leaving open the interpretation of the ribbed garment so popular in Britain.

180 Cramp 1984b, 220; Owen-Crocker 2004, 159.

181 Cramp 1984, 115.

182 Lang 1991, 83.

183 Biddle and Kjølbye-Biddle 1985, 262, 264–265, 271–272, 290. Andrew Thompson http://thethegns.blogspot.co.uk/2011/10/repton-warrior-saxon-scale-armour.html; accessed May 2016.

184 Cramp 1977, 218: 'it seems a strange mixture of the antique and the late 9th century'. See Chapter 5, p. 534 for more about Mercian carving.

185 See note 117 above for dating by Hines and Bayliss. Chapter 4 for burial. Chapter 5 for the earliest Christian monumentality.

186 Fell 1984, 125.

187 Wilson 1964, 12.

188 Tester et al. 2014, 371; and see Chapter 3, p. 239 for discussion of the nature of the site.
189 BL Cot Vespasian A1, f.30v.
190 Cramp 2006, 210.
191 Henry 2004, 453.
192 Cameron and Mould 2004, 457–461.
193 AC, 170–174.
194 Whitfield 2006, 29, quoting Njal's saga.
195 Redknap 1991, 35.
196 Pestell 2013, 237–420.
197 Blackburn 2011, 242, 254.
198 Owen-Crocker 2004, 164.
199 Price 2002, 168; Eirik the Red's saga. trans. Keneva Kuntz. *Sagas*, p. 658.
200 Fyrkat 4. Price 2002.
201 Hall 1984, Ch 7. The publication of the York finds is ongoing, for example: MacGregor 1985; MacGregor et al. 1999; Mainman and Rogers 2000; Morris 2000.
202 Carver 1979.
203 Biddle 1990, 707 for the cricket ball.
204 Always remembering the limited geographical extent of the PAS. Thomas 2001; Thomas 2000, 28: they may extend back into the 8th century.
205 Seaby and Woodfield 1980; Biddle 1990, 1037–1038, 1042.
206 Wilson 1964, 211–214. Backhouse et al. 1984, 30–31. The diameter is 11.4 cm and the date is 9th century.
207 PASE *Athelstan 62*.
208 AC, 153–163.
209 AC 80–86.
210 Whitelock 1968, 95.
211 CCCC 183, f1v.
212 Wilson 1984, 154–156. These embroideries are seen as made between 909 and 916 and among the earliest examples of the Winchester School of art. Among the other rare embroideries of the age is the fragmentary linen and silk garment from Llan-gors crannog in Wales, which carried eastern designs but was made in Britain, perhaps in Wessex, in the late 9th or early 10th century (Granger-Taylor and Pritchard 2001).
213 BL Cott. Galba A xviii, f21r.
214 See Carver 1986b, 120.
215 f73v.
216 f2v, 3v.
217 Bod. Jun 11, p. 17.
218 Cot. Claud BIV f30v.
219 Cam Univ Lib Ff I.23, f4v.
220 BL Jul A VI f5. See Chapter 5.
221 BL Cott Tib BV f6v.
222 BL Cott. Claudius BIV, f 63r. Webster 2012, 191.
223 BL Cott. Tib BV f.3r.
224 BL Cott, Claudius BIV, f 14v. Carver 1986b, 118.
225 Webster 2012, 223.
226 Carver 1986b.
227 She cites Sharon Turner's *History of the Anglo-Saxons* (1799–1805).
228 Stenton 1957, cited by Fell 1984, 13.
229 Fell 1984, 21.
230 Fell 1984, 72.
231 'many a frightened white-cheeked woman had to go trembling into a stranger's embrace'. From the *Old English Genesis*, cited by Fell 1984, 67.
232 Fell 1984, 63, 124 (Laws of Alfred).
233 Jesch 1991, 204–207.
234 Ljungkvist 2010, 30 Table 6.
235 Schönback 1983, 128.
236 Gräslund 2003, 491; Page 1987, 52.

237 Carver 2003b, 9; Bierbrauer 2003; Staecker 2003, 478–480; Gräslund 2003, 489–492.
238 Fell 1984, 139.
239 Stoodley 1999, 136.
240 Roberts and Cox 2003, 168–169.
241 Härke 1990.
242 Hills and Lucy 2013, 234.
243 Fisher 2004 – a statistical study based on 106 female burials, discerning 'individual autonomy within community conformity'; Lucy 2011, 693.
244 Dickinson 1993b; Geake 2003; Price 2002.
245 Geake 1997.
246 Geake 1997, 128; Hamerow 2016 and see Chapter 4, p. 405.
247 Lucy 2011, 688–689.
248 Gaimster 2011, 880–881.
249 Bede II.12, 15; Carver 2017.
250 See Anne-Sofie Gräslund 2003 on the loss of female visibility on the political stage after conversion.

3 Working from home

Settlement and economies

Introduction

Formative people have left us a prodigious variety of settlements, which nevertheless still reflect the generality of the two main zones proposed from the natural and prehistoric inheritance sketched in Chapter 1. In Fm 1, those in the west and north were fortified and family-sized, while those in the east and south were open and extended in the landscape. In Fm 2, the west and north devised a new kind of settlement to meet the demands of the monastic movement; but in the south and east, the dispersed villages were largely superseded by magnate farms and trading places (wics).[1] During the Viking wars of Fm 3, the repertoire was revised again, introducing a series of forts (burhs) and ultimately the town. This outline story, with its twists and turns, is greatly illuminated by the contemporary sequences in Ireland and Scandinavia.

The inhabitants applied their expressive energies to the buildings, their materials and shapes, with results that also differed markedly through Britain. This 'kaleidoscopic' character, a strong sensation of this chapter and the next, presents a formidable task to the archaeologist anxious to get everything classified and marshalled, whether houses or graves. But this is the challenge we face in understanding a period in which so many people were empowered, on which a normative behaviour for the age was so slowly imposed. Local solutions were contrived to different degrees by the social structure, the circumstances of peace or struggle, the natural resources and materials to hand. The results were individual, in settlement, housing and the use of space. Every village had its voice. Trends and patterns will be proposed, but individuality is not lost, and as with much else in formative Britain, the variety turns out to be its own reward.

We have a further challenge in engaging with this period. The remains of settlements are notoriously elusive: there is often little more than a plan to work with, formed by ribbons of stones or sockets for wooden posts. The imposing elevation of Beowulf's *Heorot* (Chapter 6) is mostly missing. Nevertheless it is important to persevere, since it was inside these buildings that most livings were made, most feelings were felt, most relationships negotiated. Similarly, to know something of the economy and the driving ideas behind a settlement and its development over time, it is important to see the extent of the whole settlement and the material remains left by the occupants. Unlike a Roman villa or a medieval village, its component parts are difficult to predict from a small test trench. This requires the exposure and mapping of complete settlement plans and the recovery of all the surviving assemblage, something that rarely happens. This failing is to some extent the fault of archaeologists themselves, a matter that will be raised again (see Critique, p. 289).

Aspects of the natural resources and the inherited landscape were touched on in Chapter 1. The monuments generated in the formative age, especially cemeteries, standing stones and churches, are the subjects of Chapters 4 and 5. In Chapter 6 we will glance at what early

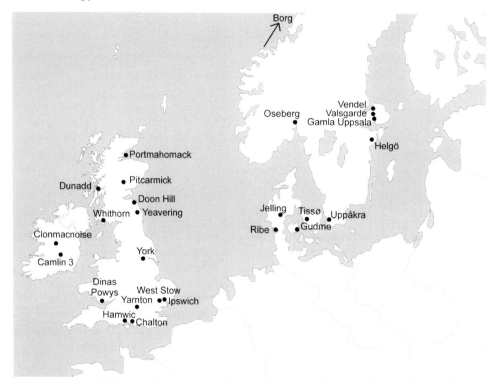

Figure 3.1 Places featured in this chapter.
(FAS Heritage)

authors expected of life in the hall. Here the focus is on the settlements and the stories they can spin from what survives. With this in mind, the examples will be highly selective (Figure 3.1).

Materials: stone, turf and timber

The materials available for house-building were limited to stone, turf and timber, with a division from the Tees to the Severn. In the highlands and islands, stone from naturally fissured outcrops can be levered free in slabs or blocks to make a dry stone wall or raised in overlapping stacks to make a corbelled roof. These methods of construction had been known since the Neolithic. 'Freestone', that is, mostly sandstones and limestones, was cut into squared blocks (ashlar) for churches in England: but more often builders recycled building stone from Roman ruins. Lime mortar reappears in Britain in the 8th century at Northampton and Jarrow, probably destined for churches. By Formative 3 English churches are using copious quantities of mortar to bond rubble walls. There was suitable stone available in Roman ruins or quarries throughout the English area, so the lack of stone buildings and the predominance of timber should represent a cultural preference.[2]

Many buildings traced on the ground seem to be lacking wall fabric altogether, and for these, cobbles, timber and turf are supposed. Ancient turf walls are more often inferred than observed, but later survivals of the 19th century and experimental reconstructions show what robust buildings are possible; they usually have an internal timber frame or a set of crucks with their feet set into the walls (Figure 3.2).[3] Turf construction on a large scale would have

Figure 3.2 Reconstruction of a turf building at the Highland Folk Museum.
(Author)

been familiar to the north Britons, since the Romans had built the ramparts of their marching camps and the Antonine Wall out of turf blocks.[4] Turf cut into slabs and laid grass to grass makes a substantial wall; an internal revettement of timber staves or dry stone keeps the water and bugs out. Turf was also used in partnership dry stone walling, in which rubble and turf were used in alternative layers.[5] Earth was used with cobbles for the same purpose (clay and bool). Vanished turf walls may be detected from patterns of finds[6] or timber or stone uprights (Bornais).[7] It is likely that the uplands were populated with buildings made of turf or peat, although few have been defined. Those at Pitcarmick in Perthshire were sufficiently robust for the surviving turf hulk to have been reoccupied in the middle ages (p. 212). Walls were also raised in cob – mud mixed with straw and bonded with puddled (squeezed) clay – and these may endure if well founded and roofed.[8]

Timber buildings were ubiquitous but rarely survive above ground and have to be inferred from post-holes, stake holes or stone patterns that indicate where a timber frame or floor had been. The majority of timber uprights used to make houses were natural round poles set in a pit, resting on a stone pad and supported by 'packing stones'. Wattles – that is, straight branches of willow or hazel – were split and woven into panels plastered with mud to make the walls (wattle and daub). Squared timbers of oak appear in the west in Fm 1 and in the east by Fm 2; these were first set individually in pits and later side by side in a trench. Later infilling used plank walls rather than wattle panels. The timbers have generally vanished, but the pits and trenches show as dark patches, especially against sand and chalk subsoils, with the rotted timber sometimes as a still darker mark (a 'ghost' or 'pipe') within the pit or trench fill. Earth-fast timber structures were roofed with slighter rafters lashed at head and foot with roots or withies. More sophisticated structures used squared timbers that are joined to each other by mortice and tenon to make a rigid box (the timber frame) which can rest on a sill beam, a dwarf stone wall or on just a piece of levelled ground. Frame buildings have usually disappeared and have to be inferred from surface patterns: although more sophisticated (than earth-fast buildings), they are harder to see. Timbers are occasionally preserved – as in the lake dwellings (*crannogs*) found in Ireland, Scotland and Wales – but in a collapsed state the buildings are not necessarily comprehensible.[9] The preservation encountered in such sites does sometimes offer hard evidence of materials used to make roofs: reeds, heather, turf.[10]

Whatever buildings were originally made of, they are clearly vulnerable to decay and dispersal, and we mostly retrieve little more than a plan. Even these may be equivocal: stone and turf walls notoriously leave anomalous patterns in the ground from which archaeologists attempt to contrive buildings. The objects and food waste that betray the use of a building are often piled in middens and subsequently scattered in the neighbouring topsoil. It is this material that is lost when sites are stripped by machine – a common modern practice designed to save time and money. Microscopic decay products are harder to lose and may be detected and mapped, and this 'chemical mapping' provides a signpost for the future. The method plots the acidity, geophysical responses and the pattern of elements, such as phosphorus, calcium and potassium, residual in the floor, together with small fragments of artefacts and bone. The resulting map shows something of what had happened in the building and the way men and women used their space.[11]

Iron Age prelude

A tradition of building roundhouses is widespread in Britain from the Bronze Age into the Roman period and endures into the 7th/8th century in the north and west, as also in Ireland. A round building requires vertical posts, a wattle, mud or stone infilling wall and a radial set of rafters to form bays and support the roof. The rafters were timbers with their feet on the wall top (wall-plate) and their heads collared or bound at the apex like a tent. These basket structures can bear a considerable weight of roofing in the form of wet heather or thatch.[12] The ground plan of such a building is easily laid out on the ground in a circle with a cord of appropriate length. The bays can be placed at regular intervals by laying out two lines at right angles by eye and then dividing the right angles in equal slices. Round buildings encountered in the ground may take the form of one or more circles of stakes, a groove, a drip trench or an internal ring ditch. These imply walls of wattle and daub, mud or turf. Inside there may be a circle of upright posts, a single post or none (Figure 3.3). A pair of posts may stand in front of the doorway, usually interpreted as implying a porch – although these could equally indicate that the entrance ran through a thick turf jacket (see p. 152).[13] Entrances traditionally face south-east or east.[14] This design offers the maximum protection from wind coming from any direction and provides for piecemeal repair and replacement in advance of collapse. Inside there are bed spaces against the perimeter wall and a central hearth, the smoke escaping from the apex, the highest point. These circular buildings offer a special form of social space: there is equal access to the fire and to the sleeping places (Figure 3.4). This does not necessarily imply an egalitarian community: the inference from both archaeology and written sources is that roundhouse people were dominated by powerful men and women (Chapter 6). The roundhouse may stand alone or be found in clusters, with or without enclosures, accompanied by four-post structures interpreted as granaries. Some of the grander circular buildings are ascribed to leaders, other to cult ('gods and heroes').[15]

Two roundhouse cultures with separate antecedents endured in formative Britain: the 'Atlantic' tradition, shared between northern Ireland, western Scotland and the western and

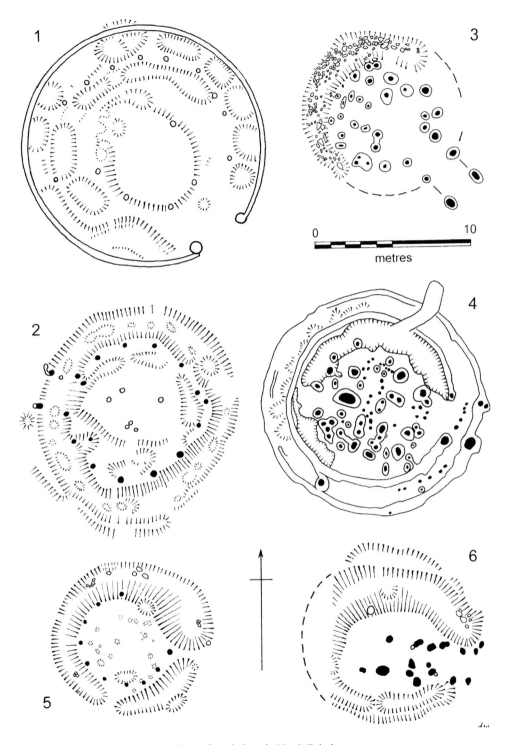

Figure 3.3 Iron Age timber roundhouse foundations in North Britain.
(Harding 2009a, Fig 15; courtesy of Denis Harding)

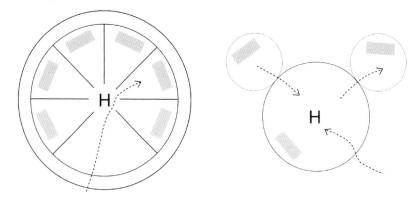

Figure 3.4 Diagram showing use of space in a roundhouse.
(Author)

northern isles, comprised stone buildings that drew on the prehistoric traditions of brochs and wheelhouses. These latter were built in the last centuries BC and first centuries AD but could still be used and modified in the formative period (some still stand today). By contrast, the rest of mainland Britain built its roundhouses in timber and turf, as it had from at least the Bronze Age. On Scottish late Iron Age sites the roundhouses were accompanied by underground storage galleries ('souterrains'), but these seem to have been abandoned in the early first millennium, perhaps following the invasion of Septimus Severus in the 3rd century.[16] The inheritance from the Iron Age takes two forms: the reuse of upstanding ruins and continuity of social and economic practice, which is suspected but requires more detailed study than is given here.

Roman prelude

Our two distinct settlement zones (north/west and south/east) have long been recognised by Romanists in Britannia, where they were roughly separated by a line from the Tees to the Bristol Channel and from there to the River Exe at Exeter. Traditionally, the upland area to the north and west of this frontier is termed 'military', and the settlements are often 'vici' associated with forts, while the lowland region to the south and east is 'civilian' and includes the majority of villas and open villages, laid out with multiple farmsteads, field boundaries and trackways.[17] In practice, this division is owed mainly to the natural distribution of soils suitable for arable production, which coincide broadly with the zones occupied by villas[18] (Chapter 1, p. 15).

The inhabitants were put to work by the new regime by means of coercion or economic inducement, which also seems to have generated a marked social division. Villa life saw the expansion of the aristocracy and the degradation of the extended family, a division into owners and workers, and the separate billeting of women and men. This degradation of kin members to estate workers was most advanced in the wealthy home counties, and by the late 3rd and 4th century the estate workers 'had become little more than slaves'.[19] This may well have affected the attitude of those that remained after the army had departed. Nor should we underestimate the ideological alignment of the immigrants, who were to build settlements out of simple houses and sheds rather than occupy the country seats of their departed landlords.

Thus the differences between the NW and SE regions were already well established before the Anglo-Saxons came and are likely to have reflected a different way of doing things, sharpened by the Roman experience. Hingley paints a picture in which the Iron Age peoples of the north and west were organised into local families in compounds using a cattle-based economy; they could generate enough surplus to pay tribute and invest any remaining wealth in retaining followers. The result looked different depending on perspective: in the Roman mind, the Britons of the military zone chose to remain poor; in the British mind they chose to remain independent. By the time we reach the 6th century, the most recognisable settlement in the north and west at present is the 'family fort' perched on a rocky knoll.

Round and rectangular

One notable characteristic of first-millennium housing is the change from round to rectangular plans. Such a transition already took place during the Roman occupation, for example at Whitton (south Glamorgan), where roundhouses were superseded (or perhaps joined) by rectangular buildings after the mid-2nd century (Figure 3.5).[20] In the formative *north and*

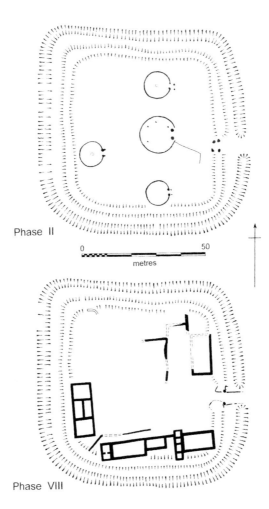

Phase II

Phase VIII

Figure 3.5 Round to rectangular at the Iron Age-Roman site of Whitton (Glamorgan).
(Harding 2009a, Fig 33; courtesy of Denis Harding)

west (including Ireland), the rectangular tendency arrives in the 7th and 8th century. It is noticed in the isles and Caithness in the form of rectangular modifications to stone round-houses, in the Pictish areas as rectilinear buildings of stone slabs (Wag of Forse) and rectilinear turf buildings with round ends (Pitcarmick), and in the Borders as buildings with straight sides and an apsidal end. Although none of these is yet claimed as a church, Christianity is likely to have been an important driver. In the *south and east*, by contrast, a repertoire of rectangular buildings was developed by the Anglo-Saxons from the 5th century in the form of small 'halls' surviving as sets of post-holes (Figure 3.6) and smaller sheds also built with vertical timbers but sited over a rectangular pit, the 'sunken-featured building (SFB)' (Figure 3.7). The rectangular form carries an implication of a social framework different to that of the roundhouse dweller: an internal organisation that defines activities with partitions and has a focus towards one of the short ends (Figure 3.8). However, like the roundhouses, the rectangular buildings generally seem to represent family units, and the degree of hierarchy was implied by the relative size of buildings that are grouped together. The Anglo-Saxons encountered in the Roman landscape the remains of four centuries of construction predominately in rectangular form; but whether they imported a pre-existing type of house from the continent, emulated the Roman exemplars they found in Britannia, or invented something new is still open to debate.

By the 9th century, virtually all dwellings in Britain and Ireland were rectangular, and this reports not only a change in construction and the impact of ideologies but the stresses on communities and their ingenuity in reconciling loyalty to the old with the aspirations of the new. In this sense, the settlement process in Britain is 'formative'.

Figure 3.6 Post-hole rectangular building at Chalton, Hants (Rescue 1974).

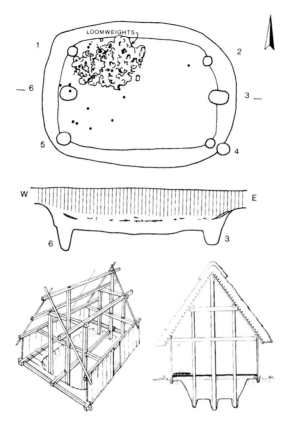

Figure 3.7 A six-post sunken-featured building (SFB) excavated at West Stow, Suffolk: plan and reconstructed frame based on SFB 21, a probable weaving shed. The internal area measures 4.9 × 6.4 m.

(West 1985, Fig 90; West 2001, 52–53; © Suffolk County Council)

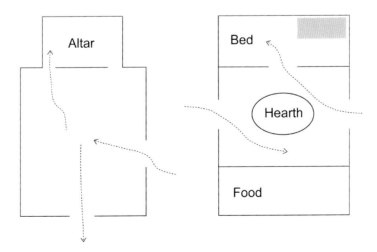

Figure 3.8 Diagrams showing use of space in rectangular buildings.

(Author)

A field trip

This book is intended for everyone who would like to know a little bit more about Britain in the first millennium. As will be appreciated from the introduction, prior knowledge is not assumed, and even those who are well informed may experience the occasional surprise that comes from looking out of a different window. The viewpoint being presented here tries to embrace not only the whole people of Britain but also some parts of the neighbouring lands across the seas that meant so much to them. Since these lands are explored to a greater or a lesser degree, we are some way from an overall archaeological context to work from. The results of this chapter will therefore generate more of an agenda than a synthesis.

One way of breaking the ice, always popular with students and leisured persons, is to go on a field trip, a tour with commentary that shows something of the range of material that we are to study and the questions that spring from it. Our trip will be virtual (avoiding long journeys in a coach) and will target specific places that introduce the repertoire. We will cherry-pick sites in Scotland, Northumbria and England, and their criteria for inclusion is that more than one period was represented. In this way we offer not a series of 'type sites' but examples of trajectory or transition.

Portmahomack (6th–10th century): elite centre-monastery-trading place

The site at **Portmahomack** on Tarbat Ness consisted of four successive settlements in the same place, offering a narrative stretching from the 6th to the 16th century. The object of attraction was the redundant church of St Colman standing on a ridge above a beach overlooking the Dornoch Firth in north-east Scotland (Figure 3.9). There was no surviving

Figure 3.9 Portmahomack (Easter Ross) with the church of St Colman (the white building), looking west across the Dornoch Firth and the coast of Sutherland.

(Author)

documentation for the origins of the church, but indications of early occupation came from antiquarian discoveries of pieces of 8th-century sculpture, one of them inscribed in Latin. In 1984 aerial reconnaissance by Ian Keiller and Barri Jones spotted a curved ditch surrounding the church, which added another hint that here was an early monastery. The purpose of the project was to encounter and explore a Pictish settlement – at that time a rarity – with the aim of throwing light on state formation in north-east Britain. Excavation was restricted by the land available, which did not include the churchyard. The resulting design was a T-shaped sample of the enclosure, together with the excavation of the church itself that was to be converted into a museum and visitor centre (Figure 3.10). The project was financed mainly by the Heritage Lottery fund; it began in 1994; excavation was concluded in 2007 and published in 2016.[21] The four settlements defined were an elite estate centre (5th/7th century), a monastery (8th century), a trading place (9th century) and a medieval township (12th–16th century) (Figure 3.11). On this occasion we will stay in the first millennium.

In *Period 1*, 5th–7th century (in radiocarbon years), an estate centre was established on the ridge above the beach facing the Dornoch Firth. It comprised a cemetery of men, women and children in long cist graves, a workshop making objects of iron and copper alloy (four iron dress pins and a harness mount were among the finds) and evidence for the cultivation of wheat, rye and barley (Figure 3.12). Around 680 the land occupied by this estate centre was appropriated, or more probably gifted, for the construction of a monastery (Figure 3.13). It resulted in a major landscaping operation. A ditch 5 m wide defined an area D-shaped in plan and 8 ha in extent against the edge of the Dornoch firth. The inland stream behind the ridge was dammed and a large pool created. A Roman-style paved road led from the hilltop

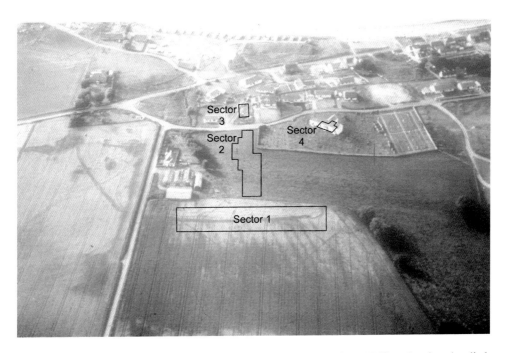

Figure 3.10 Portmahomack. Aerial photograph by Barri Jones and Ian Keillar showing the ditch around the monastic, with (superimposed) the 1996 excavation design.

(Carver et al. 2016, Ill 1.9; © authors)

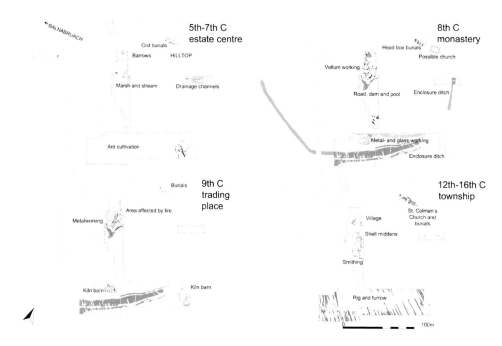

Figure 3.11 Portmahomack: the four settlements.

(Map extract Crown Copyright, all rights reserved; FAS Heritage)

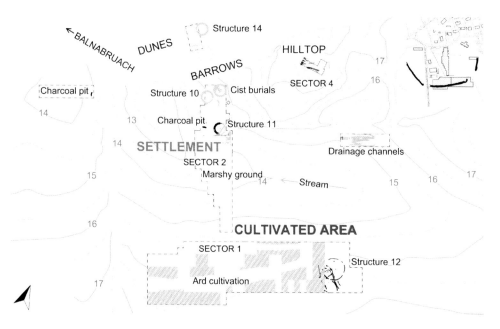

Figure 3.12 Portmahomack: Period 1: the elite estate.

(Map extract Crown Copyright, all rights reserved; FAS Heritage)

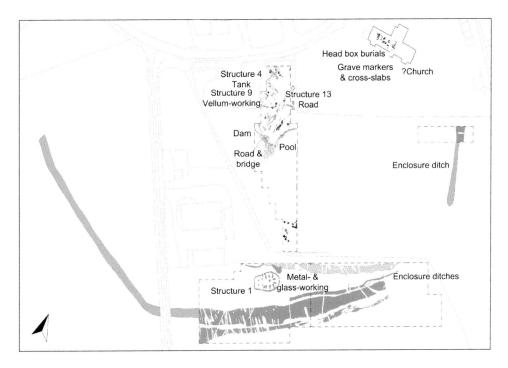

Figure 3.13 Portmahomack: Period 2: the monastery.

(Map extract Crown Copyright, all rights reserved; FAS Heritage)

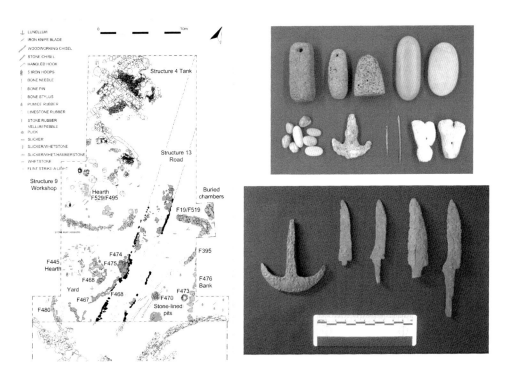

Figure 3.14 Portmahomack: the vellum workshop. (Left) plan of the features and the distribution of diagnostic finds. (Right) Pumice and stone smoothers, pebbles and bone pegs for fastening hides on a frame, needles for stitching; (below) knives and crescent shaped trimmer.

(FAS Heritage)

across the valley via a bridge towards the edge of the enclosure. Beside the road, craftsmen prepared leather and parchment for books from slaughtered cattle and calves, and beside the enclosure ditch other craftsmen made church vessels out of precious metals and glass (Figure 3.14).

The metalsmiths here worked in a remarkable building (S1) laid out with precise symmetry in the form of a semicircle joined to a trapezium and constructed with timber posts and a turf wall. The building was exceptionally well preserved; it had a ground plan formed of a semicircle sharing its diameter (10 m) with the long wall of the trapezium. It contained an array of post-sockets supporting a roof and was originally clad by a turf or stone and turf wall about 1.5 m thick (Figure 3.15). The timber posts were supported on pads

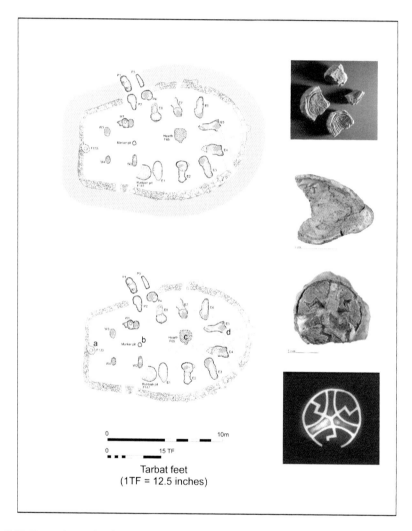

Figure 3.15 Portmahomack: the metalsmith's workshop, showing the turf-clad building (top), the mathematical layout of the building (bottom) and metalworking debris: three moulds for glass escutcheons, a heating tray for working opaque yellow glass and two glass studs (the lower one is an X-ray).

(FAS Heritage)

in pits packed with blocks cut from the same stratum of sandstone and were laid out with geometrical precision, making use of the ratio of the 'golden number'. This was the work of an architect who was spiritually inspired.[22] The cemetery, with many stone grave markers, continued on the hill, the likely site of the 8th-century church, and standing cross-slabs or crosses stood at the edge of the surrounding enclave (Figure 3.16). By the later 8th century, monumental cross-slabs also stood at key landing paces around the peninsula, providing seamarks and boundary marks and indicating that the monastic estate has expanded to the edge of the sea on every side (Figure 3.17).

Between 780 and 810 (in radiocarbon years) the monastery was raided, the vellum workshops were burnt down and the monumental sculpture was broken up and used as hardcore to level up the surface beside the road, which was soon to be redeveloped as a new workshop for metalsmiths (Figure 3.18). Although these used the same techniques as the monks, they were now engaged in serving a secular constituency, making copper-alloy buckles, brooches and weights, presumably for trade. This workshop continued to thrive until the end of the 9th century, at which point the site remained inert during an extended period of conflict between the Scots and the Norse Vikings. The Pictish hierarchy disappeared at this time, probably because of the irreparable damage suffered by their aristocracy in the wars. Portmahomack was revived in the later 12th century as a village and parish church, which remains to the present day.

The Portmahomack story provides something of a parable for the north, in that it revealed the importance of the monastery as a major episode of investment and influence but at the same time showed it to be just one political prescription, and a short-lived one, in a succession of others. The first period, equivalent to Fm 1, shows the far north in contact with the rest of Britain: the harness disc was paralleled at Dunadd, Mote of Mark and Sutton Hoo; the dress pins paralleled at Chalton in Hampshire. The monastic phase, belonging in Fm 2, makes references to both Irish and Northumbrian practice, but its use of Pictish symbols shows there was a strong local involvement. After the monastic workshops were burnt down, the revival

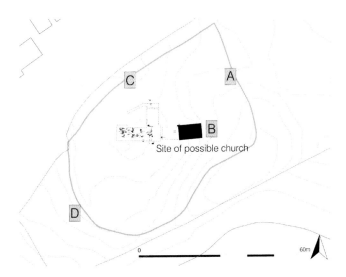

Figure 3.16 Portmahomack: St Colman's Church, showing hypothetical locations of four monumental crosses (A–D).

(FAS Heritage)

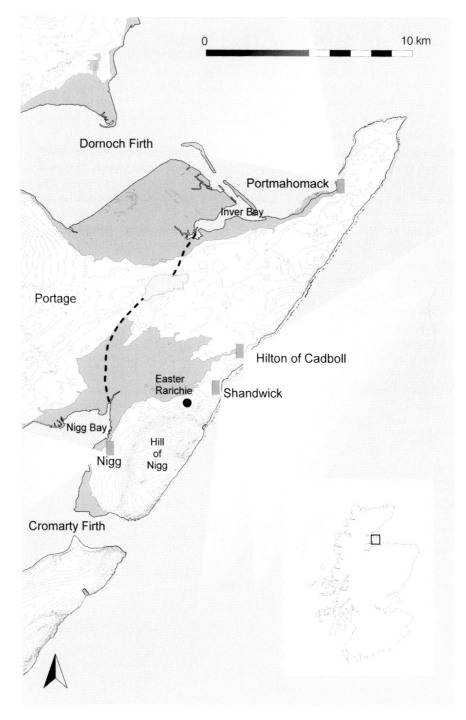

Figure 3.17 Portmahomack: a contour map of the Tarbat peninsula, showing low-lying land, the probably course of the portage ('tairbeart') and location of the principal Pictish stone monuments with their viewsheds.

(Map extract Crown Copyright, all rights reserved; FAS Heritage)

Figure 3.18 Portmahomack: Period 3: Metalworking after the Viking raid, early 9th century. Metalworkers' tools, moulds for acorn-shaped weights and (lower) a small hearth being lifted.

(FAS Heritage)

seemed to have remain in the hands of the monks or their compatriots: the same techniques
would be employed in the successor workshops of Fm 3, but to serve a non-monastic clientele. This theme, of local people adapting to changing ideologies, is echoed in other sites of
the north and west. Study of the human remains in the cemeteries also revealed the changing
beliefs and circumstances of the people and the presence of incomers from both the west and
the east across the sea (see Chapter 4, p. 315). The settlement is thereby portrayed as a complex living organism, adapting to the moods, pressures and intrusions of the day.

Yeavering (6th–8th century): centre of ritual and governance

Yeavering is situated deep in the Scottish borders on a whaleback ridge beside the River
Glen (a tributary of the Tweed) beneath the Iron Age hill fort of Yeavering Bell (Figure 3.19). The site was discovered from the air by J. K. St Joseph in 1949 (Figure 3.20)

Figure 3.19 Yeavering Bell Iron Age hillfort (Northumberland), seen from the site of the early medieval palace.

(Author)

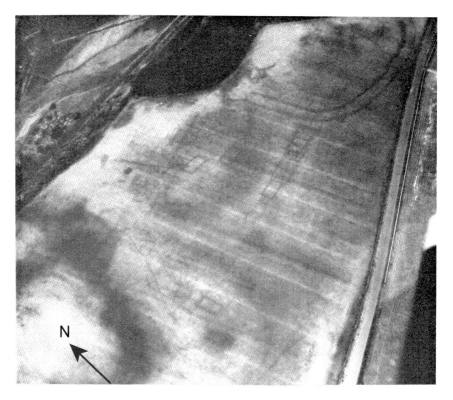

Figure 3.20 Yeavering. Aerial photograph taken by J.K. St Joseph in 1949.

(Hope-Taylor 1977, Plate 3; © Cambridge Committee for Aerial Photography)

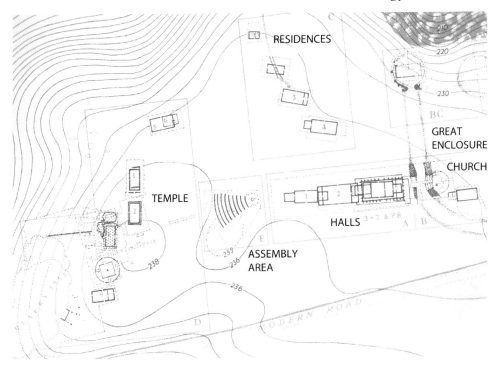

Figure 3.21 Yeavering: plan of excavations 1953–1962.
(Hope-Taylor 1977, Fig 12; image licensed by Historic England)

and excavated between 1952 and 1962 by Brian Hope-Taylor for the Ministry of Public Buildings and Works in advance of an encroaching sand quarry.[23] The whole of the summit of the whaleback ridge was explored in four open areas (Figure 3.21, A–D), this still being one of the largest-scale archaeological investigations to be undertaken in Northumbria. The technique of excavation was also exemplary, generating a sequence of activity in exquisite detail. The approach, innovative in its day, was, even more unusually, expounded in detail in the final report.[24] The surface of the natural subsoil was cleared with shovels, and the negative fills, scarcely perceptible at first, were revealed by a gradual process of definition: at ground level by brushing and sensing the diverse feeling and sounds of the trowel as it passed over them and from above by differential drying after rain viewed from a tower (Figure 3.22). It proved possible to make a sophisticated reading of the structural sequence based on myriad shades of grey and to tell the story of individual posts and slots that had been set in trenches, burnt in situ or pulled out of the ground. The build-ings revealed were far more varied, precocious and ambitious than anything seen in early medieval Britain up to that time.

Bede had mentioned *Ad Gefrin* (At the Goats) beside the river Glen as the *villa regalis* (royal centre) of King Edwin and his queen Aethelburh, where they welcomed Paulinus and were baptised by him along with many others in the early 7th century.[25] Without radiocarbon dating (then only recently invented) or datable finds (apart from a single 7th-century gold coin) Hope-Taylor understandably used Bede to provide his site with a historical framework, and this will be used here in a modified form.[26]

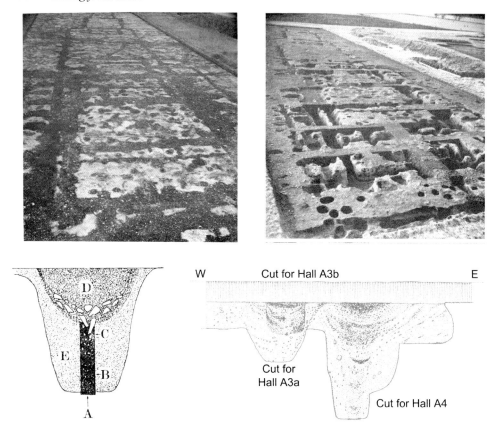

Figure 3.22 Yeavering: primary horizontal section of hall foundations in Area A. (Top left) cleaned horizon as photographed; (top right) as excavated; (lower left) diagram of section through a post-pit showing timber slot (A–B), packing (E) and demolition trough (D); (lower right) sequence of Halls 4, 3a and 3b as seen in section across the wall trenches.

(Hope-Taylor 1977, Plates 17, 18; Fig 8; Fig 18; images licensed by Historic England; Plates 17, 18 © Cambridge Committee for Aerial Photography)

The *prehistoric site* had a trackway along the centre of the whaleback, with a cluster of burial mounds to the south on the summit of the local high point. There were two prominent ring ditches harbouring cremations, one to the west (Western Ring Ditch, WRD) and one to the east (Eastern Ring Ditch, ERD), which were to prove influential in the layout of the later settlement (Phase 1). This prehistoric burial ground was developed in the 6th century as a post-Roman British central place focused on these ring ditches (Phase II, 'WRD', 'ERD'; Figure 3.23). The western ring ditch was transformed into a square-ditched shrine, acting as the initial focus for the post-Roman inhumation cemetery. Two large and sophisticated plank-in-trench buildings sited end to end (D1 and D2) were erected immediately north of the burials. A deposit of animal bone, dominated by ox heads, had been buried immediately north of the east door of D2, which was interpreted as a temple.[27] A third building, D3, sited to the west of D2 was seen as its kitchen, serving feasts as part of the pre-Christian ceremonies. In the centre of the whaleback was a remarkable wedge-shaped array of rising posts, deduced by the excavator to have been a type of grandstand (Figure 3.24). Still unique in the archaeological record, it wins credence by its derivation from the roman *cuneus*, segment of

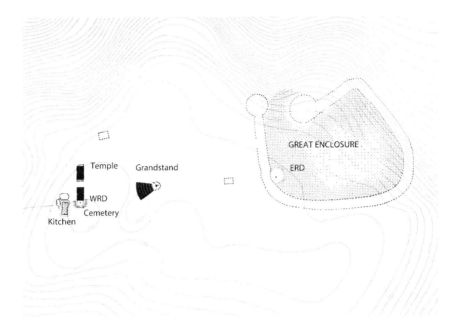

Figure 3.23 Yeavering: Phase II: late 6th–early 7th century.

(Hope-Taylor 1977, Fig 75; image licensed by Historic England)

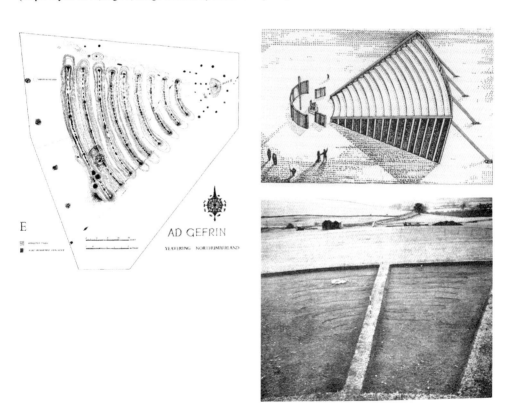

Figure 3.24 Yeavering: Building E, the 'Grandstand'.

(Hope-Taylor 1977, Fig 55, 57; images licensed by Historic England)

an amphitheatre, rendered in timber. No halls are assigned to this phase, which seems to have arisen in prominence as a largely ritual centre.[28] This phase was assigned by Hope-Taylor to the later 6th century and associated with Aethelfrith, the infamous anti-British and anti-Christian king of the Bernicians between 592 and 616. However, new studies of the burials now see Phase II at Yeavering as essentially a British site, albeit of the same period (late 6th to 7th century), its affiliations lying with the monumental burial grounds of south Pictland (Hallow Hill), Wales (Capel Eithin) and the south-west (Cannington).[29]

In Phase IIIa-b, the 7th century, the settlement begins its history as a *villa regalis* (Figure 3.25). Temple, kitchen and inhumation cemetery continue as the western focus, and in the east the first hall appears (A2) attached to a palisaded enclosure. The halls develop and supersede each other on the same footprint in Phase IIIc (Halls 1a and 4, either side of a rectangular palisaded enclosure) (Figure 3.26). Next to this was built the massive penannular 'Great Enclosure', formed of parallel ditches with circular terminals. This phase is assigned to the rule of the Anglian king Edwin (616–633), and includes the moment in 627 when Edwin and his court, no doubt seated on the grandstand, heard Paulinus' case for joining the Christian alliance and the response of his followers. This *villa regalis* had been largely destroyed by fire, perhaps in 633, marking the year that Edwin's reign ended, when he was killed by Penda of Mercia.

The settlement was shortly resurrected in a new guise under his successor Oswald (Phase IV; Figure 3.27). This is the first serious Christian phase. The pagan temple and its cemetery on the summit in the west have gone, as has the Great Enclosure in the east. The

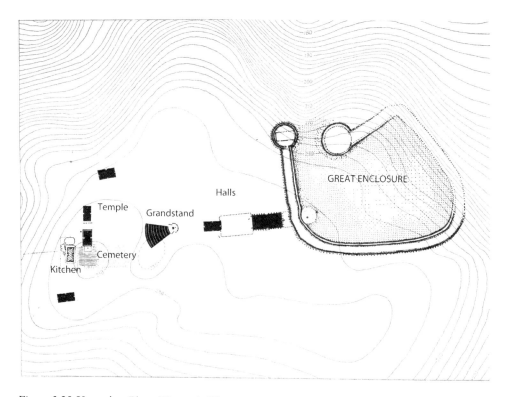

Figure 3.25 Yeavering: Phase IIIc: early 7th century.

(Hope-Taylor 1977, Fig 77; image licensed by Historic England)

Figure 3.26 Yeavering, the extent of Hall A4, Phase IIIc, marked out by visitors, at c. 120 × 60 feet (c. 36 × 18 m).

(Author)

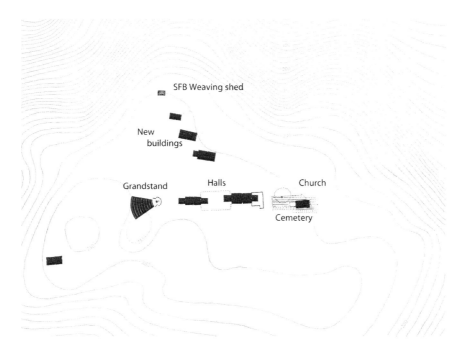

Figure 3.27 Yeavering: Phase IV: mid-7th century.

(Hope-Taylor 1977, Fig 78; image licensed by Historic England)

focus now is on the enlarged grandstand and the suite of halls (A1b, A3, both with double annexes) that stand beside it. Four additional halls were arranged in echelon on the northern part of the whaleback, probably the sign of an enlarged high-status community. A new cemetery appears to the east of the halls over the filled-in ditches of the Great Enclosure, and within this cemetery was a rectangular building on a W-E orientation with a western annex (Ba). Among the innovations of the Anglian phase is an SFB of a rather grand kind that had been burnt down, so revealing details of its construction and subsequent collapse (Figure 3.28). The bottom edges of the pit were lined (on at least three sides) with a double skin of planks on edge, and a floor of prepared clay was laid in the space between them. The fire had filled the pit with the remains of a wattle-and-daub screen, carbonised timber planks and ash. This building of the mid-7th-century preserves details that suggest the intricate carpentry probably employed in the 5th–6th century examples further south.[30]

These features are seen as markers of the resurgence of the site following its conversion to Christianity under Edwin's successors Oswald and Oswiu, and it is deemed to have lasted

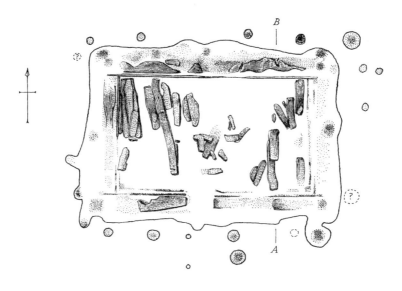

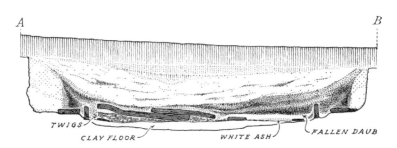

Figure 3.28 Yeavering: Sunken Featured Building (SFB) C1, plan and section.
(Hope-Taylor 1977, Fig 37; image licensed by Historic England)

Table 3.1 Yeavering redated

Phase	Structures	Burials	Associated ruler	Events	Likely date range
I	Assembly place Great enclosure	Western cemetery	British		5th/6th century
II	Assembly place Grandstand	Western cemetery Shrine, temple	British	Ida at Bamburgh 547	5th/6th century
IIIA, B	Villa regalis Great Halls	Western cemetery Temple	Aethelfrith c. 592–616	Catraeth c. 600 Degsastan 603	Early 7th century
IIIC	Villa regalis Great Halls	Western cemetery Temple	Edwin 616–33	Fire due to attack by Penda and Cadwallon 633	Mid-7th century
IV	Villa regalis Great Halls Subsidiary halls	Cross at AX, BX Eastern cemetery String graves Chapel?	Oswald 634–42	Foundation of Lindisfarne 634 Fire due to Penda 651–5	Mid-7th century
V	Monastery? Halls	Eastern cemetery Chapel	Oswiu 642–670	Bede mentions Ad Gefrin c. 735	Late 7th–8th century

until 651, the year of another of Penda's raids, coincident with another destruction of the site by fire. It revived in diminished form for a short period after the death of Penda in 655 and was probably abandoned finally by 685, the year that King Ecgfrith perished with his army at the hands of the Picts (Phase V).

Modern archaeological readers will baulk at the alignment of these historical dates and their spurious precision with the structural phases, and it is probable that they will be further modified in years to come. The account of the excavation argues for the long life of Yeavering as a congregational site and identifies Iron Age, Roman, British and Anglian influence in the evidence retrieved (mainly architecture). Assigning religious affiliation is more controversial, but it is clearly more subtle than a transition from British to English Christianity. The site is distinguished by its ritual variety, its possible temple, the attraction of prehistoric burial mounds, its 'Roman surveyors' layout, its grandstand and great enclosure. The review of burial rites in Chapter 4 (p. 370) places the first phases of the Yeavering settlement (Phase I–II) firmly in a British funerary and ceremonial context, and it could be that the Anglian domination is not expressed materially until Phase IIIc or even IV. Given the burden of the arguments in this book, there would be some logic in moving the Phase IV development, with its clear Christian affiliations, later in the 7th century, and it might even be seen to have taken on some monastic airs.[31] This would bring it into line with the advent of the monastic movement, which was about to begin (Table 3.1).

Yarnton (6th to 9th century) village to magnate farm

In the English area, until the foundation of the *wics* and *burhs* in Fm 3, settlements are predominantly rural and can be spread over large tracts of land. The high speed and low impact demanded by rescue archaeology means that areas affected by development are examined only where they need to be rather than the whole settlement. But there are exceptions. **Yarnton** was a settlement area examined with determination and skill at a landscape scale, not only providing an exemplary sequence of structures but a history of the environment they occupied.

The site lay on a gravel terrace beside Cassington near Oxford about half a mile from the confluence of the River Evenlode with the River Thames. Patches of gravel and alluvium were interlaced with former channels (Figure 3.29). Emergency salvage excavations in advance of gravel extraction began in 1989, followed by an evaluation using 393 trenches, each measuring 2 × 30 m (Figure 3.30). Although 'many of the diagnostic finds were recovered from the ploughsoil and presumably once came from ground or floor surfaces',[32] the ploughsoil still had to be stripped off by machine. Structured investigations continued until 1998, examining an area of 4.5 ha, revealing settlement evidence spanning the 5th to 9th centuries. Only 117 sherds of early and middle Saxon pottery were found in situ. The sequence was largely determined through a study of spatial patterning, anchored by 28 radiocarbon dates.

The early Saxon period (Phase 1, later 5th to 7th century) was represented by a scatter of SFBs, recovered during the salvage operation (Figure 3.31). The halls and the focus of the early village probably lay elsewhere, but there was good-quality environmental evidence for the period. The Middle Saxon Period (7th to 9th century) dominated the centre of the area opened and was divided into two phases. In Phase 2 (8th century), two post-built houses (B3619, 3959) and a 'grand hall' (B3620) were flanked by an animal enclosure and a paddock connected by a droveway, while a group of sheds was situated to the west, where they may have run on from the activities of Phase 1. In Phase 3 (9th century), the Grand Hall was embellished, and the business end of the farm moved east and reappeared as a pair of post-hole buildings (B3348, 5067) within a deep-ditched enclosure attached to a new paddock. The eventual tally rose to four or five carpentered halls, nine post-built structures, 10 SFBs and pits and wells lying in fenced and ditched enclosures. Hall B3620, the most imposing building encountered, began as a rectangular post-hole structure, which was then twice enlarged and subdivided, implying a growing hierarchy of space (Figure 3.32).[33] The feeling is that the family had gone up in the world.

The source of the wealth, then as now, was presumably successful farming, and indeed the environmental sequence showed a minor revolution in agriculture between the early and middle Saxon periods (i.e. Fm 1 and 2; Figure 3.33). The data from the earlier period implies much land under pasture in the river basin, providing grazing for cattle and sheep, with patches of arable above the edge of the river terrace, the most abundant crop being hulled barley. In the middle Saxon landscape, the area under the plough was greatly enlarged, and the lower-lying pasture had been converted to hay meadow.[34] Cereals included barley and emmer wheat, possibly superseding bread wheat; flax fibres to make linen were extracted by retting (soaking in water). The harvesting of hay suggests stalled animals, perhaps to facilitate the collection of manure. The expansion of cereal production implies a surplus.

The sequence reports a rise in productivity and increase in affluence over the 7th/8th century that is reflected in a concentration of settlement into a smaller, more ordered space with larger halls. At the same time, more land is given over to cash crops that presumably generate a surplus or a profit. The Yarnton sequence is echoed at many sites, although none have been excavated with such precision, on such a large scale or published with such clarity.

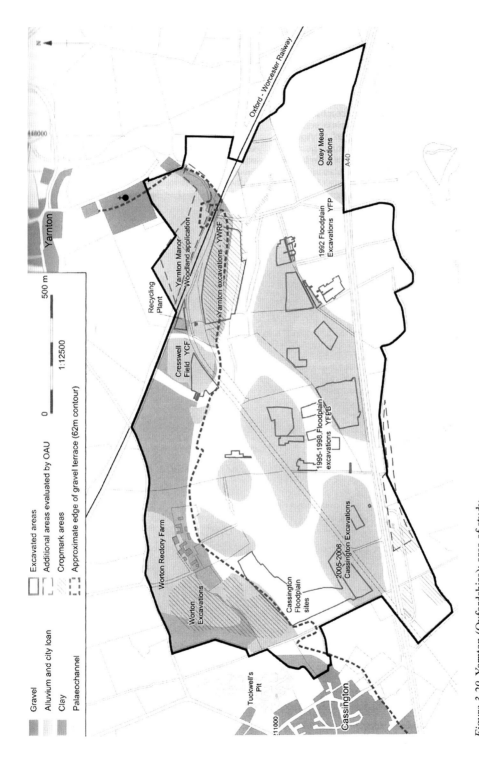

Figure 3.29 Yarnton (Oxfordshire): area of study.

(Hey 2004, Fig 1.4 with author's permission)

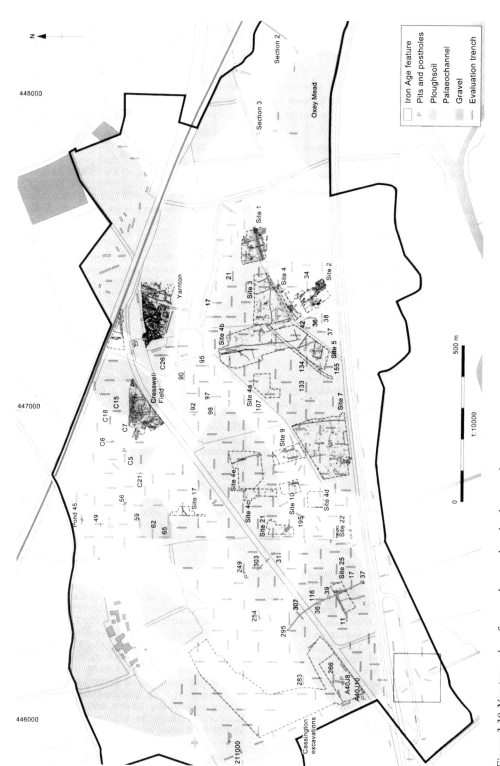

Figure 3.30 Yarnton: subsurface geology and evaluation trenches.
(Hey 2004, Fig 11.10, with author's permission)

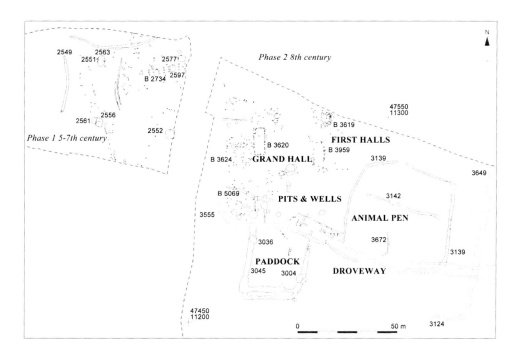

Figure 3.31 Yarnton: Phase 2 site plan.

(Hey 2004, Fig 6.2, with author's permission)

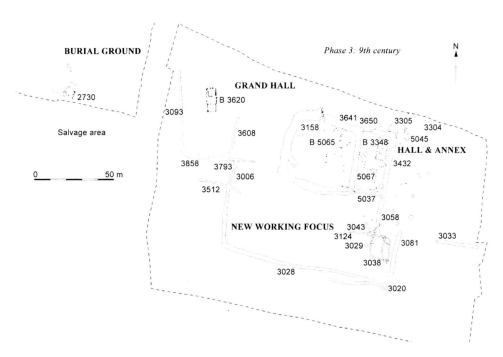

Figure 3.32 Yarnton: Phase 3 site plan.

(Hey 2004, Fig 7.2, with author's permission)

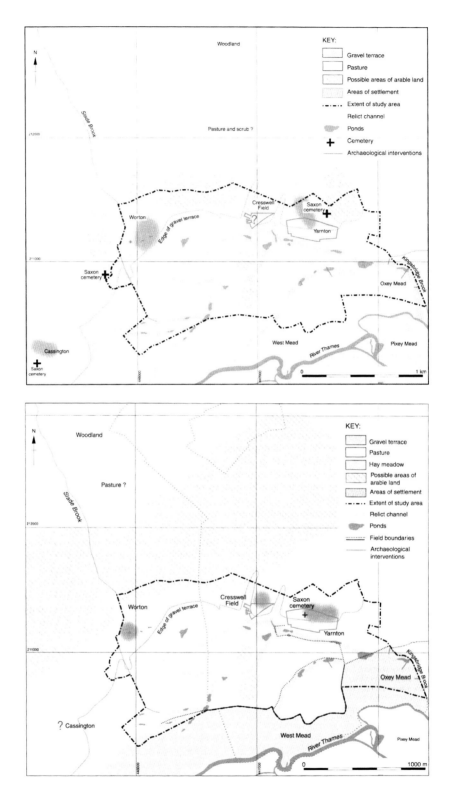

Figure 3.33 Yarnton land use: (top) Phase 1, 5th–7th century; (bottom) Phases 2 and 3, 8th–9th century.
(Hey 2004, Fig 2.5, 2.7, with author's permission)

York (1st to 11th centuries) Roman fort to Roman town to Viking trading place to English town

York was a Roman town, founded in 71 AD, that has endured to the present day, although not continually active to the same degree. The 'six Yorks' consist of the Roman legionary fortress and the 'colonia' settled by ex-soldiers (*Eboracum*, c. 80–c. 400); the Anglian settlement outside the walls at Heslington (mid-6th to 7th century), an Anglian port on the left bank of the Ouse (*Eoforwic*, 8th/9th century), a Viking port at the confluence of the Ouse and the Fosse (*Jorvik*, 9th–10th century) and the late Saxon burh constructed within the former legionary fortress (10th–11th century) (Figure 3.34). The exploration of the town has owed a lot to casual observations made over 150 years, accelerating in 1965 with the threatened collapse of York Minster through subsidence and in 1971 with the creation of York Archaeological Trust. The York Minster excavations offered an important challenge to British urban continuity, demonstrating that there was no structural occupation on that site between the collapse of the Principia building in the early 5th century and the arrival of an Anglo-Scandinavian burial ground in the 9th century[35] (Figure 3.35). During this interlude,

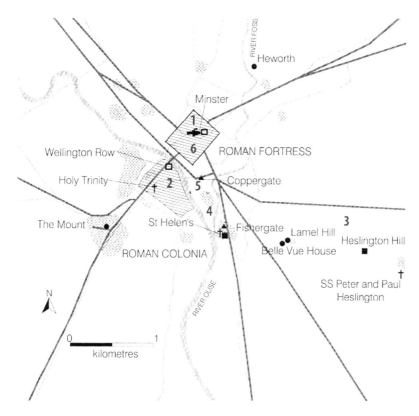

Figure 3.34 York city. The six Yorks: (1) *Eboracum*, Roman fortress. (2) *Eboracum*, Roman Colonia. (3) Anglian villages, 6th–7th century. (4) *Eoforwic*, Anglian trading place, 8th century. (5) *Jorvik*, Anglo-Scandinavian trading place, 9th–10th century. (6) Late Saxon burh, 10th/11th century.

(FAS Heritage/author)

Figure 3.35 Underneath York Minster: collapsed column of the Roman Legionary basilica, with the Anglo-Scandinavian burial ground above it.

(Phot. John Bassham: Phillips and Heywood 1995, Plate 5; image licensed by Historic England)

Figure 3.36 Viking York: excavations at Coppergate.

(With permission ©York Archaeological Trust)

Anglian activity was distributed at a number of sites around the old walled town, including a 6th/7th-century settlement on Heslington Hill and an 8th/9th-century trading place on the left bank of the Ouse at Fishergate, *Eoforwic*.[36] In the 9th century, Vikings created a new nucleus of residence and settlement at Coppergate (*Jorvik*), where notable excavations by York Archaeological Trust brought to light a suite of wattle or plank-lined houses (Figure 3.36) with a wealth of well-preserved artefacts including wooden bowls, leather shoes and clothing.[37] An Anglian (8th century) helmet was found in a pit in the lower strata at the same site.[38] The now derelict buildings in the Legionary fortress were reoccupied in the 10th century by a series of poorly defined structures with finds of pottery, glass, coins and bone objects (Figure 3.37).[39] The Norman minster was constructed over the Principal building in 1070 on an E-W alignment, and the operation appears to have begun with the extraction of Roman stone down to the pillar bases (Figure 3.38). Thick layers of 'ashy silts' were thought to derive from scraping the Roman mortar off the ashlar.

As with many long-lived European towns, the reading of this sequence has proved a major challenge to generations of archaeologists who have studied York's deposits. A wealth of detail has already been published, in particular by York Archaeological Trust, and there is more to come. Nevertheless certain conclusions can be drawn. It is clear that towns, no less than rural settlements, require to be investigated on a wide scale, since the remains of any one period can lurk in an area that has yet to be explored. Taking the larger site as a whole, the town has acted as a theatre for a series of social, economic and political strategies that reflect different approaches to governance, spirituality and trade. In this sense, it is not just the story of a community but a barometer of much broader agencies of change. It is a military

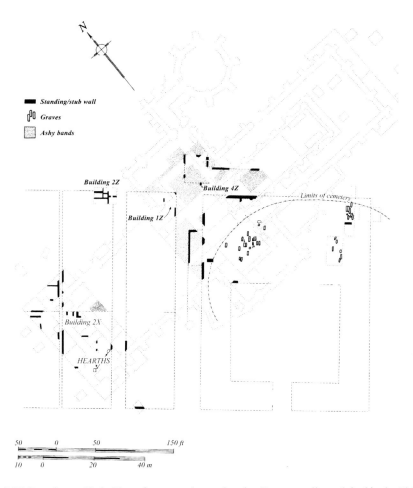

Figure 3.37 Late Saxon York: Plan of excavated area showing Roman walls exploited in the 10th/11th century and probable limit of the Anglo-Scandinavian cemetery. The 'ashy bands' originate from the cleaning of extracted Roman ashlar prior to reuse.

(Phillips and Heywood 1995, Fig 83; Courtesy of the Department of Archaeology, University of York; image licensed by Historic England)

Figure 3.38 York Minster. Section from Roman floor level up to the construction level of the Norman
Minster. A robber pit for the extraction of Roman building stone has been cut down to the
column base, disturbing the Anglo-Scandinavian cemetery.

(Derek Phillips: Phillips and Heywood 1995, Plate11; image licensed by Historic England)

fortress, to which is added a high status suburb (the *colonia*), and expands into a major town
known all over Europe as one of the most northerly outposts of Rome. When the Roman
empire ceases to operate in Britannia, *Eboracum* also ceases. The incoming 5th/6th century
English settle in the neighbourhood and farm. A measure of interest in the old Roman towns
returns in the 7th century when Christianity awards them a historical value, but there is
apparently no immediate reurbanisation. However, in the 8th century a parcel of land on the
left bank of the Ouse is given over to merchant activity (*Eoforwic*). This function is enhanced

by the 9th-century Vikings, who establish their trading station and commercial motor in the Ouse/Fosse confluence. It flourishes until the conquest of York in 918 by an English army under Aethelflaed, lady of the Mercians (p. 269). Then something resembling a *burh* is installed in the old Legionary fortress. Each of these changes in regime is labelled with a different emphasis, indicating whether it is governance and social control, spirituality or wealth creation that is driving the agenda, a theme to which we shall often return.

Return from a field trip: a debrief

Variations in visibility, archaeological opportunity, time, funds and specialist availability mean that the acquisition of settlement data can be an uneven if not a random affair. Some sites in open country, like Yarnton, reveal a plan quickly, but the assemblage is often diminished by ploughing, stripping topsoil and lack of time. Understanding urban sites requires access to the deposit, which is often opportunist and spread over decades, as at York. The generation of archaeological information is continuous, so it is never a good time to attempt a synthesis. But without a synthesis it is difficult to appreciate the meaning of what has been found or to construct a pathway for future research. So one must try.

The field trip offered several pointers. Portmahomack in the far north revealed a change of settlement form, from an estate centre with island-wide contacts in Fm 1 to a purpose-built monastery in Fm 2, which was superseded by a trading place at the start of Fm 3. Yarnton in the English Midlands showed that the Fm 1 dispersed village was superseded by a magnate farm of increasing grandeur in Fm 2 and 3. In the hybrid 'Anglo-British' area of Northumbria, the settlement at Yeavering straddled Fm 1 and Fm 2, at first dedicated to ritual and burial and then morphing into a 'villa regalis' associated with the Northumbrian kings and, at the end of its life, possibly, a monastery. York was a central place in which no urban life survived the Roman period, but nevertheless it continued to exercise a gravitational pull on 6th/7th-century Anglian occupation gathered outside its walls. Interest in the Roman fabric revived with Christianity in the 7th century. In the 8th century, a *wic* was found on the bank of the Ouse at Fishergate, in the 9th a Viking trading place at Coppergate and a further centre in the ruins of the Principia in the 10th.

There are some trends here that will require endorsement from other examples, and we shall proceed to do this by exploring the settlements of the island by period, in each case visiting the north and west first and then the east and south. We shall be looking for signs of prosperity and surplus, regional preferences and leadership agendas, whether driven by political ambition, spiritual conviction or the creation of wealth.

Formative 1 (5th–7th century)

Family forts in the north

In **north and west Britain** the number and size of settlement excavations remains very small, and so trends are still hard to determine. In this area, British settlement forms stem from roots in their local Iron Age, where individual family farms constituted the primary economic unit. These households could generate a surplus (for example in cattle and cheese), and their leaders could increase their influence and outreach through feasting and sexual relations. The society as a whole has been defined as *segmentary*, where the independent units could gather or 'host' from independent homes for purposes of ritual, joint defence or aggression.[40]

The present area of Scotland is divided by nature into a western and eastern part, which geographically can be termed the Atlantic zone and the Firthland or North Sea zone

(Chapter 1). For purposes of cultural mapping, they correspond more or less to the Scottish area and the Pictish area, at least up to the 9th century. Houses and settlements do differ as between east and west, but the evidence is exiguous, and more precise and more subtle zonation is expected from future research.[41]

Atlantic zone

The cultural marker of this zone is the *complex Atlantic roundhouse* (CAR), of which the most obtrusive examples are stone-built and circular, with internal radial divisions (wheelhouses) or alcoves (intramural cells).[42] The CAR is mainly Atlantic in distribution, that is, in the northern and western isles, Argyll, Sutherland and Caithness.[43] Prehistoric stone wheelhouses and brochs are modified in the 6th/7th century, producing roundhouses inside brochs (e.g. Clickhimin), cellular divisions inside roundhouses[44] or new free-standing cellular buildings which are variations on curvilinear themes as at Buckquoy, Orkney (Ritchie) or Bostaidh, Lewis[45] (Figure 3.39). The site of Old Scatness on Shetland exhibits a variety of

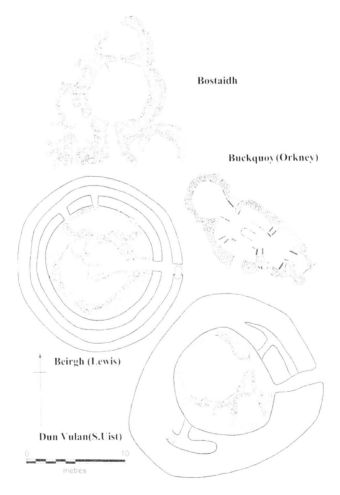

Bostaidh

Buckquoy (Orkney)

Beirgh (Lewis)

Dun Vulan (S.Uist)

0   10
metres

Figure 3.39 Examples of Atlantic houses.
(After Harding 2009b, Fig 40, with permission)

Figure 3.40 Old Scatness (Shetland): multi-lobed building of 6th–9th century (S7) constructed inside
  pre-existing broch.

(Dockrill et al. 2010, 33; courtesy of Steve Dockrill © S. Dockrill)

these themes in its Phase 7 (5th–9th century): an oval walled space (S25), a cellular building
within the broch tower (S7), a figure-of-eight building (S5) and a roundhouse with added
piers (S11)[46] (Figure 3.40). In this stone-using zone, secondary occupation and recycling of
the existing Iron Age stone settlements may be regarded as a norm.[47] Some rectangularity
begins to creep in at the edges, finding expression as 'wags', long buildings with round ends
divided into stalls, like a wheelhouse stretched out, as at The Howe, Orkney, and the Wag
of Forse, Sutherland.[48] Buckquoy can be seen as a roundhouse elongated by a cellular hall[49]
and the 'sporran-shaped' S1 at Portmahomack as half a roundhouse attached to a giant porch
also see below. Echoes of these spatial patterns can also be observed in timber roundhouses,
but these are less easily detected.

Irish Sea zone

One feature shared between Scotland and northern Ireland is the *small fort* – 'fortified
outcrop' in County Antrim, 'dun' in Argyll.[50] Like other artefacts, they have been used to
argue an intrusion from Argyll into Antrim – or Antrim into Argyll – and to constitute a
shared transmarine kingdom called Dal Riada.[51] It seems likely that human and material
traffic would be intense and continuous between these coastal lands, unless prevented by

political or ideological action. The form of the dun is that of a walled area at a summit, sometimes small enough to cover with a roof, with other enclosure walls defining defended spaces on the terraces below. Actual houses are hard to define on these rocky outcrops. At **Dunadd**, a capital place of Dal Riada situated in a prehistoric landscape, the primary dun was oval in plan, measuring c. 25 × 15 m (Figure 3.41). Difficulties of dating thin strata on rocky terrain leaves open the question of whether these 'nuclear forts' are creations of primary design or organic growth (Figure 3.42).[52] On the one hand they might be seen as a large sprawling Atlantic roundhouse laid over an uneven surface; on the other, as an Irish-type ringfort laid over a prominent knoll obliged to extend its defensible areas as political pressure increased.[53] Dunadd was more than a fort, since incised animal images and a carved out footprint on the summit suggested some kind of ritual role, and the site looked over the long-lived prehistoric monumental centre in Kilmartin Glen (Figure 3.43). There was evidence for metal- and glass working on the site, and in the 5th–7th century it was receiving pottery and other commodities from the continent and the Mediterranean region (Figure 3.44). These also suggest lines of alliance, in this case with the Christian imperial centres of the Mediterranean and south-west France. Dunadd blows away some of the mists of apparent isolation in Formative 1: its pottery shows it was in touch with post-Roman south Europe, the metalwork that Celtic and Germanic styles met in its workshop.[54]

Figure 3.41 Dunadd fort (foreground) in Kilmartin Glen (Argyll and Bute). Aerial photograph.
(Driscoll 1998, Fig 1; courtesy of Steve Driscoll)

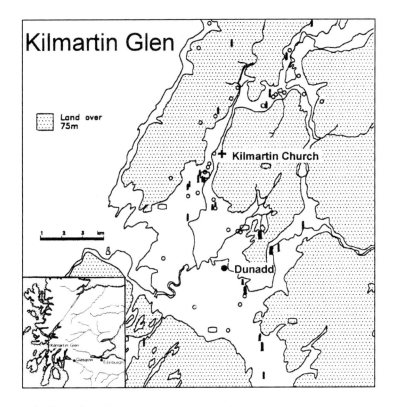

Kilmartin Glen

Land over 75m

✝ Kilmartin Church

● Dunadd

| Standing Stones, Henges and Stone Circles

○ Cairns

▢ Neolithic Chambered Cairns

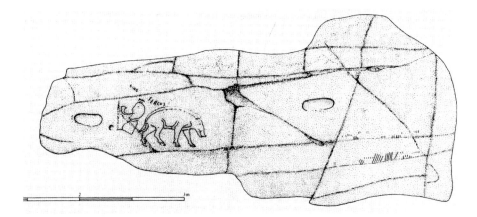

Figure 3.42 (Top): Location of Dunadd in relation to the prehistoric corridor of Kilmartin Glen. (Bottom): The incised carvings on the summit.

(A: Driscoll 1998, Fig 2; B: Lane and Campbell 2000, Ill 1.29; courtesy of Ewan Campbell)

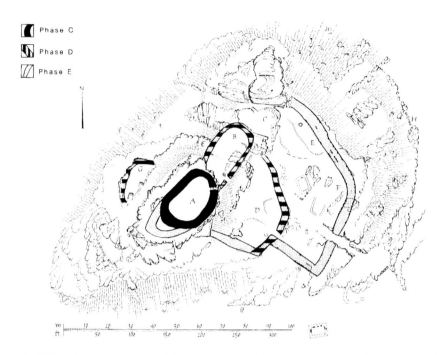

Figure 3.43 Dunadd composite plan of the sequence: with Early Medieval occupation (Phases C, D, E). The carvings are located at the south end of enclosure B.

(Lane and Campbell 2000, Ill 7.14; based on an original RCAHMS drawing with amendments; courtesy of Ewan Campbell)

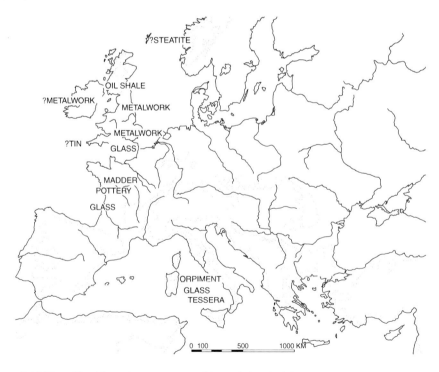

Figure 3.44 Dunadd catchment area: sources of imported material.

(Lane and Campbell 2000, Ill 7.5; courtesy of Ewan Campbell)

Up the glens

The large circular *fortified farmsteads* also relate to the concept of a family-sized strong-hold. When found, they consist of a ring of large blocks on flat ground, which are the remains of roundhouses encased by a very thick perimeter wall with a tunnel entrance (Figures 3.45–3.46). The example excavated at Queen's View above Loch Tummel was 16.5 m in diameter with walls 4 m thick and an entrance through the wall 1.5 m wide. There were post-holes inside, and most commentators believe that the whole structure was roofed. Finds included a yellow bead, assigned to AD 700–900 by Peggy Guido, and a stone lamp paralleled at Crossnacreevy, County Down, where it was dated to the 7th/8th century AD.[55] At a fortified roundhouse investigated nearby at Litigan, a radiocarbon date from clearance above the subsoil gave a *terminus ante quem* of 840–1020.[56]

The distribution spreads from the west up the glens until it meets the River Tay at Atholl on the threshold of the Pictish heartland (Figure 3.47).[57] This distribution is trustworthy, D.B. Taylor argues, since such massive structures 'are not easily overlooked or readily destroyed'.[58] He notes that an early name for them was *Caisteilean nam Fiann*, 'castles of the Feinn', and deduces that they originated in the west.[59] Atholl, the region where they congregate by the Tay, derives from Old Irish *Ath-fhotla*, or New Ireland. A number of *kil-* placenames, denoting Irish church sites, clusters on the west side of the River Tay. The architecture of the 'fortified farmsteads' certainly refers to an Atlantic or Irish Sea tradition, and we can agree *pro tem* with Ralston that 'Taylor constructs a reasonable case for seeing them as a later first millennium AD phenomenon in Atholl, with a background in the west, and thus as perhaps indicative of Scottic penetration eastward'.[60]

Figure 3.45 Fortified homestead at Queen's View, Allean at Loch Tummel (Perth and Kinross). (Author)

Figure 3.46 Reconstruction of the Queen's View fortified homestead.
(Strachan 2013, Ill 89; © Perth and Kinross Countryside Trust, with permission)

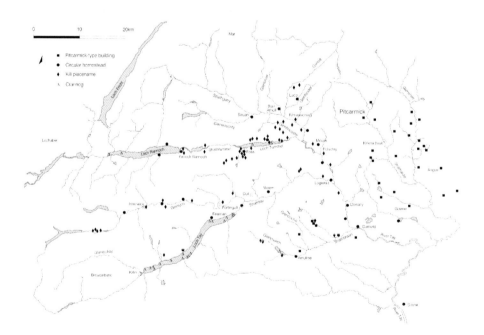

Figure 3.47 Distribution of fortified circular homesteads, crannogs, *kil-* placenames and Pitcarmick type buildings, the River Tay marked as a frontier.
(FAS Heritage, after Hooper 2002, appendix 9, plan 5)

However, the evidence is much in need of further precision and better dating. Dave Strachan's excavations at Black Spout, near Pitlochry, defined a fortified farmstead constructed in the last centuries BC, a dating he also applies to the extended family of thick-walled roundhouses in north-west Perthshire as a whole, including Queen's View, Litigan and the Argyll duns.[61] This would effectively remove the fortified farmsteads from any early medieval dynamic. However, half of the excavated Perthshire sites, including those mentioned, show evidence of a second life in the later first millennium AD.[62] The exploitation and enhancement of the Iron Age duns from the 7th century is not in doubt (cf Dunadd). Moreover, Strachan is well aware of the significance of the western link: Argyll has 'close geographical links to Highland Perthshire

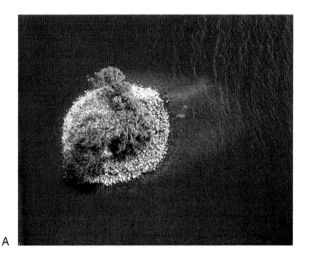

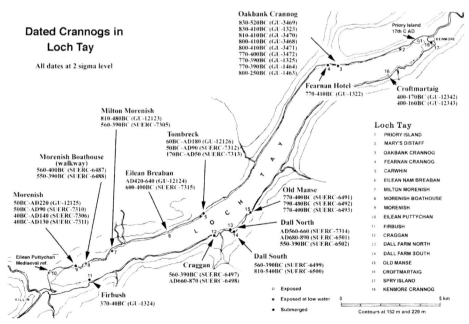

Figure 3.48 Crannogs (A. Top): Eilean Breaban, Loch Tay; (B. Bottom): dated crannogs in Loch Tay; (C. Next page): plan of the excavated crannog in Loch Glashan (Argyll and Bute).

(A: M. Brooks; Dixon 2004, Plate 9; B: Dixon 2007; C: Crone 2007, Fig 1; with permission of the authors)

Figure 3.48 (Continued)

through terrestrial routes such as Glen Orchy and Glen Dorchart to Glen Lyon and Loch Tay'.[63] The glens of the upper Tay constitute an area of Gaelic (i.e. Irish) placenames (and legends).[64] A precursor to an Irish penetration in the 6th/7th century might have been an Irish penetration at the dawn of the millennium. This receives some corroboration from the distribution of the principal Pictish identifier, the primary symbol stones, which appear to confine 'Pictland' to an area north of the Forth and east of the Tay in Fm 1 (see Chapter 5, p. 491). This implies that, by the time of the Roman conquest, the south-west quadrant of modern Scotland was already Irish (Gaelic-speaking Scots), the remainder being British (Brittonic-speaking Picts).

The Scottish *crannogs* provide a water-borne analogue to the duns and fortified farmsteads; they have a similar distribution, and the majority date to the early Iron Age (c. 800–400 BC) but come back into use in Fm 1 (Figure 3.48A).[65] The two types of settlement are related – the fortified farmsteads along the sides of the glen and the crannogs in the loch – and are a similar shape and 'family-sized'.[66] At **Loch Glashan**, Argyll, the successive occupying episodes were in the 6th/7th centuries, the 9th century and the medieval period, with (less certainly) an initial phase in the 2nd–4th centuries[67] (Figure 3.48B). Although the site had few comprehensible structures, there was an assemblage of E-ware imports, a copper-alloy penannular brooch and iron axe head, debris from working copper and silver, wooden artefacts and leather (including shoes and a book-satchel) that suggested access to an upper-tier society, either as consumer, client, manufacturer or cobbler.[68]

Once established in the landscape, crannogs also offer opportunities for short-term repossession and reinvestment responding to political and family dramas that we know nothing of. Anne Crone has proposed three periods of use for the 44 Scottish crannogs so far examined (more than 80% of them excavated before 1920): a prolonged phase in the first millennium BC, a resurgence in the early medieval period and, after an interval of nearly six centuries, a period of renewed energy from the 13th to the 16th century.[69] Ian Morrison paints a vivid picture of the intermittent post-medieval use of crannogs as garrisons and prisons up to the 17th century and thereafter up to our own day for fishing, illicit distilling and secret assignations, being in plain view but inaccessible and obscured from prying eyes.[70]

The early medieval usage is less intensive than that of the Iron Age but still most revealing. Out of 12 crannogs dated by radiocarbon in Loch Tay, 11 have earliest dates between 880 and 400 BC, and three of these were reoccupied in the early middle ages: Eilean Breaban (AD 420–640), Dall North (AD 560–890) and Craggan (AD 660–870). At **Buiston**, a seasonally submerged crannog in Ayrshire, two main building phases were determined by dendrochronology: initial construction in the 1st/2nd century AD and a main occupation within a defensive perimeter between the late 6th and mid-7th century AD.[71] (Figure 3.49) Within this overall framework, expert deconstruction of the sequence and dendro dating of timbers has provided Buiston crannog with a historical precision that can scarcely be claimed of any other excavated settlement in Britain.[72] The island originally created in the 1st/2nd century AD was revived with branches and trunks laid to consolidate the surface and protected with various timbers cut between AD 520–565. After these collapsed, the site was levelled and a new circular stockade built with timbers cut in AD 584 and 585. Erected within was a roundhouse made from concentric circles of wickerwork which stood for five years (589–594), during which it was flooded and its hearth replaced three times. In AD 594 the crannog was enlarged and a new palisade built containing House B, the hearth and floor of which was replaced four times before the final floor was laid, in alder, cut in AD 609. In AD 608 the palisade was equipped with a walkway. The days of House B were ended in AD 613. In 614, builders started to fell timbers to be used in new palisade keyed into the island by radial beams, the construction of which was completed by AD 620. From then on the crannog was in active use: the defences were maintained until the mid-7th century and occupied until the late 7th century – but no later.

The assemblages did not suggest that any part of this eventful history was purely military. The artefacts certainly indicated a high status and a wide cultural range: an early 7th-century Anglo-Saxon coin, an annular brooch of Anglian type, cup bindings, a hanging bowl, imports of E ware (from south-west France), glass vessels, decorated beads, combs, iron tools and a fragmentary shoe cut from a single piece of leather to fit a small foot (size 3½). Anne Crone points out that relative status in this period is hard to measure, since high-status objects constitute the principal means by which early historic sites can be identified. Nevertheless, it can be safely argued that these are members of a social upper tier in a stronghold demanding considerable investment. She paints a convincing portrait of the social standing of the occupants:

> the snapshot of early seventh century life presented [here] portrays a wealthy farming community which is relatively self-sufficient in foodstuffs and crafts, making and repairing most of the equipment and clothes required by the community, but which

produces enough of a surplus to acquire additional services, goods and manpower when needed. This, alone, may have guaranteed the community access to the socio-political hierarchy of Strathclyde.[73]

The Pictish house

The Firthland region between the firth of Forth and the Moray Firth is the Pictish heartland. As so far known, its settlements and housing culture are certainly different to those of the neighbours, which are cellular in the north, round, complex and fortified in the west, and

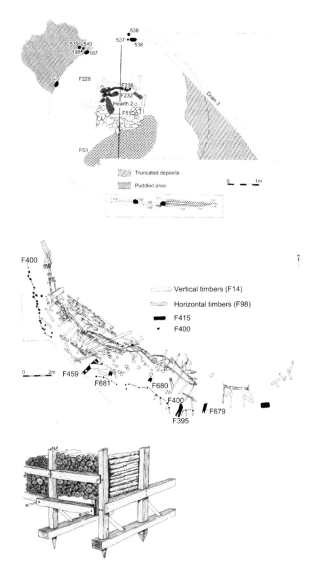

Figure 3.49 Buiston Crannog (Ayrshire). (Top): General plan and section of House A in Phase III. (Centre): Plan of palisades in the south-west corner. (Bottom): Reconstruction of the palisaded walkway.

(Crone 2000, Fig 7; Fig 22; Fig 81; Fig 113; licensed by and © Historic Environment Scotland)

rectilinear in the south. But we will struggle to define a Pictish brand. In the Bronze Age and Iron Age, the Firthlands have a roundhouse culture, but it remains unclear how long this continued into the early historic period. Cellular forms also occur,[74] and the continuation of some round and oval forms is in evidence for example at Easter Kinnear.[75] Rectilinear forms appear in stone in Caithness (Wag of Forse), curvilinear forms at Portmahomack and byre-houses have been claimed at Pitcarmick.[76] In brief, the examples are very few and all different from each other, offering us at least five different points of departure: the roundhouse, the dun-house, the hall-house, the byre-house and a monastic workshop.

In southern Pictland, people in the first centuries of the first millennium AD are living in roundhouses with a variety of souterrains (underground stores). At Dalladies 2, the settlement took the form of numerous meandering ditches associated with curvilinear post-hole buildings, with occasional stone paving.[77] These rather ad hoc constructions are not like their namesakes across the Irish Sea. While in Ireland souterrains occurred in Formative 3 and in association with rectangular buildings, their use in Scotland died out half a millennium earlier (in the 3rd century AD), and none has been linked to a rectilinear structure.[78] On Tayside, the Iron Age ring-ditched roundhouse is thought to have survived 'well into the first millennium'.[79] At Aldclune, the latest roundhouse was oval and ringed by a stone wall. It was built in the 2nd/3rd century but thought to have been used or reused for longer.[80] In what might be its final manifestation, the roundhouse transmogrifies into a sunken-floored flat-bottomed oval pit 1 m deep, revetted with a stone wall, as at Easter Kinnear and Hawkhill R, dated mid-6th to mid-7th century.[81] (Figure 3.50)

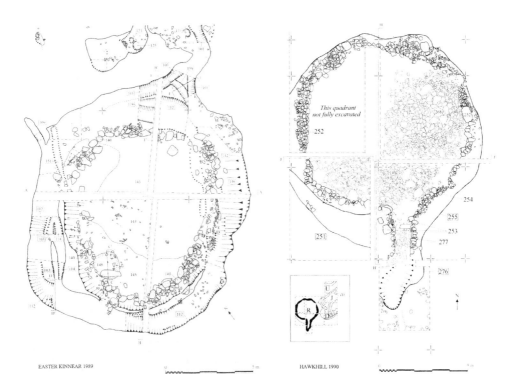

Figure 3.50 Sunken-featured buildings from southern Pictland. (Left): Easter Kinnear (Fife). (Right): Hawkhill R. (Angus).

(Driscoll 1997, Ill 11, 17; courtesy of Steve Driscoll)

Pictish hilltop and promontory forts known in documents, for example at Dunollie, Dundurn and Dunottar, were the subject of reconnaissance operations by Leslie Alcock in the 1970s, which confirmed their early medieval date and suggested their potential.[82] In Aberdeenshire, small fortified enclosures have been defined and radiocarbon-dated at Mither Tap Bennachie (340–540, 640–780); Maiden castle (430–570, 535–620, 540–600); Hill of Barra (480–540); and Cairnmore (480–540, 535–600) (Figure 3.51).[83] This move into fortifiable locations is thus dated between the 4th to 7th century AD, a period which Murray Cook noted was characterised by desertion in his extensive settlement excavations on lower-lying ground at nearby Kintore.[84] No structures have been defined in the small forts, unless they are themselves roofed like the fortified homesteads of Atholl.[85] Larger versions of the 'dun' were built in Pictland by the coast (e.g. Dunottar) or at the head of glens (e.g. Dundurn[86]; Figure 3.52). The promontory fort offers an early formative alternative to the small hill fort: at **Burghead** on the Moray Firth, the triple-banked enclosure featured '*murus gallicus*' type timber-laced ramparts, but the site was in active use in the 5th–7th centuries, as shown by

Figure 3.51 Mither Tap o' Bennachie; occupied 340–540 and 540–780 (radiocarbon dates).

Figure 3.52 Dundurn (Perthshire), a possible Pictish inauguration site at the head of Strathearn, occupied 6th–9th centuries.

(Author)

its famous symbol slabs, each showing a single bull[87] (Chapter 5, p. 492). Internal plans and structures are elusive and hard to date. Investigating the promontory forts of this coast, Ian Ralston excavated one internal structure at **Portknockie,** describing it as 'a single course of water-rolled stones defining the inner and outer margins of what may have been a turf-cored wall defining a building some 4 m wide with rounded corners'. This building also appears to have had a post-pad.[88]

The nature and form of even the larger examples of Pictish stronghold currently remain enigmatic, largely owing to the atavistic professional practice of attempting to understand them with small trenches. Research at a more informative scale has been carried out at **Rhynie** in central Aberdeenshire. Here a multivallate circular ditched and palisaded enclosure has been defined in association with the Craw Stane, a Pictish symbol stone standing in a field beneath the shadow of Bennachie (Chapter 5, p. 495). The enclosure contains a number of features (unexcavated at the time of writing), including a rectilinear building measuring at least 9 × 5 m, while a line of timber slots implies the additional presence of a hall 20 m long (Figure 3.53). Finds at this remarkable centre included imported Late Roman amphorae (LR1 & 2 *aka* 'B ware'), imported glass drinking vessels, burnt animal bone and a miniature bronze 'souvenir' of a sacrificial axe hammer. The construction and use of the site have been radiocarbon-dated to the 5th/6th century.[89]

Reoccupation and rectangularity

In the search for connections between the different forms of the Firthland repertoire and between the round and rectangular tendency, a key element of transition in the north and west is that of the reoccupation and adaptation of existing abandoned buildings. Examples

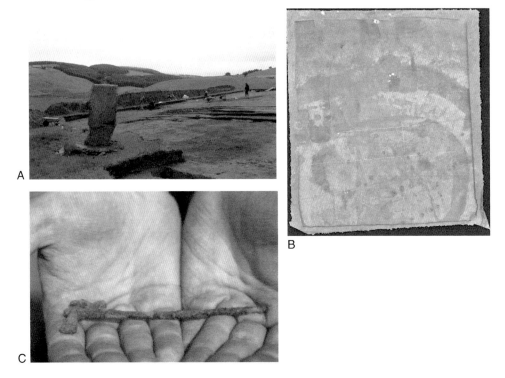

Figure 3.53 Rhynie (Aberdeenshire). A: Excavations in progress in 2012, with the Craw Stane in the foreground (author). B: Surface map of hall, pits, palisade and ditch. C: Miniature axe-hammer.

(Noble et al. 2013, Fig 5, 8; courtesy of Gordon Noble)

of the transmogrification of single buildings through time, or leaping over time, have been cited earlier, at Old Scatness. Periodic reoccupation of large stone buildings should come as no surprise; indeed, we know now that in this part of Britain 'secondary occupation is the norm'.[90] However, it was not confined to large stone structures. The intermittent use of crannogs has been securely demonstrated (p. 642).[91] But secondary occupation of turf houses (as at Pitcarmick) and the reoccupation of settlements themselves present a greater challenge and demand greater credibility.

A model for the prehistoric north is provided by the **Lairg** project, which examined 60 hectares of Achany Glen, recording its environmental sequence and defining 55 hut-circles, of which six Bronze Age and two Iron Age houses (1–8) were excavated.[92] Thirty-two rectangular buildings were also defined, of which two were excavated (Houses 9 and 10). Within the excavated sample of 10 (out of 87) buildings, the change to rectangular plans took place, but at a considerable interval. House 9 was built of stacked and stone turf laid directly on the ground; it was interpreted as a byre-house typifying 'the main form of the vernacular architectural tradition of the Highlands', albeit it in more recent times. Radiocarbon dates from charcoal from the turf wall suggested a 15th-century date. House 10 was a small rectangular building that stood nearby. The finds were mainly 19th century.[93] In the absence of strong material signals the earlier use of the buildings remains equivocal. House 9 resembles the Pitcarmick byre-house E1, which was assigned to the 7th–9th century but was nevertheless reoccupied in the 13th century.

The sensitive excavation applied in conjunction with copious radiocarbon dating at Lairg exposed a major factor in the understanding of settlement over the entire upland zone. The realisation that buildings of turf and stone could be revived after an interval of 300 years as at Pitcarmick seems to beggar belief and yet is likely to be true, given that these same buildings were still visible from the air and on the ground in 1993. In the judgement of experienced Scottish archaeologists, settlements are less likely to have been continuously occupied than periodically revisited and their dwellings refashioned, drawing on never-forgotten common-sense techniques of the local *longue durée*.[94] This has important implications for the things that field archaeologists must not do: no more trenches or partial excavations – these can only provide the answer you first thought of: the real history lies within and between the buildings. The concept of 'settlement shift' requires a more careful definition in this terrain: a settlement zone may be added to (Lairg), revisited (Pitcarmick), redeveloped (Portmahomack), revived (Carn Dubh) or, exceptionally, removed (the Highland Clearances). Above all it can be seen that only the liberal application of radiocarbon dating or dendrochronology (where wood survives) can hope to construct a useful historical narrative.[95]

In the west

In this section, Cumbria, Wales and the south-west are lumped together as the best candidates for British versions of settlement and economy, at least in Formative 1, 5th–7th century. Northumbria, being the most precociously Anglicised, is visited after this, so it can lead without too much stress on to Southumbria, the English region. Cumbria, Wales and the south-west have not yet been favoured with an indicative settlement sequence, which is unfortunate since, as with burial and sculpture, the principal signals of the repertoire of diagnostic British practice in settlement building are suspected to lie in these regions.[96] In Fm 1 the expectation is that hilltop sites act as central places for British kingdoms, an expectation endorsed by the structure and finds of those that have been excavated, but like the crannogs they are characterised by intermittent occupation.

The exiguous group of west British settlement spreads from Cornwall to Strathclyde and includes Trethurgy, Tintagel, Cadbury Castle, Dinas Powys, Mote of Mark, Dumbarton, Doon Hill, Trusty's Hill and Tynron Doon.[97] They have in common a need for protection, some metalworking and access to imported pottery from the Mediterranean, as well as glass, during the early 6th–7th century.[98] At the **Mote of Mark** in Dumfries and Galloway a mould found in pieces in the Mote of Mark 'central hollow' had been used to make a copper-alloy bridle strap distributor with axe-shaped pendant, matching examples from Portmahomack, Dunadd and Sutton Hoo, implying the existence of a common Fm 1 equestrian class (Figure 3.54). As Anne Crone argued for Buiston, the majority of diagnostic objects are high status, giving the impression that all the sites belong only to the upper tier of the settlement hierarchy. Following documentary expectations, farmers are likely to occupy *trefs* (Old Welsh; farmsteads), and it is possible that a species of unenclosed site of modest means awaits definition. However, it is equally possible that the economy was managed in its entirety from a network of forts, as implied from the density of their distribution around Mote of Mark (Figure 3.55). A generality of settlement for the age can encompass the fort on Dunadd, the reuse of Atlantic stone roundhouses, the ringforts of west Perthshire, and the hillforts of Aberdeenshire. The trend is perhaps especially to be associated with the deep traditions and landscape memories of the Britons.

Dinas Powys (Welsh, *fort of Powys*) in the Vale of Glamorgan was among the first sites to reveal the type and remains a valuable example. A knoll occupied in the Late Roman and

Figure 3.54 Mote of Mark (Dumfries and Galloway). (Left): View of the fortified hill from the estuary (Solway Firth). (Top right): Plan of the fortifications with the central hollow. (Bottom right): Metalworking moulds from the central hollow. Items of harness with reconstruction.

(Laing and Longley 2006, Fig 2, 1, 21 (2273), 30 (1104), 56 (2273/1104); with permission of Oxbow Books)

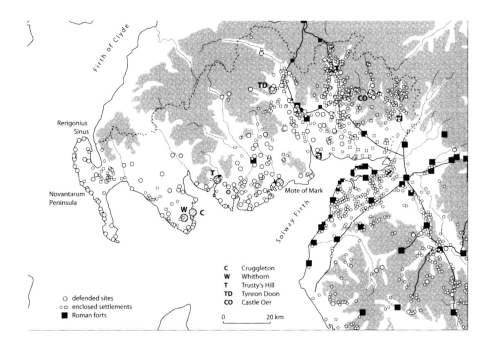

Figure 3.55 The Solway Firth area showing the plethora of defended sites.

(Laing and Longley 2006, Fig 58; with permission)

Iron Age periods was possibly occupied from the 5th century, fortified in the late 6th century to create a small stronghold (0.1 ha) and abandoned by c. 700. The site was later adapted as a Norman-period ringwork (Figure 3.56). In the 5th–7th century (Phase 4), the living space contained a rectilinear building with earth-fast timbers replaced in stone (possibly stone and turf) to give a lozenge-shaped plan. It was accompanied by a small building of square plan. Both buildings were largely implied from the shape of curvilinear drainage channels and were proposed as a 'hall' and a 'barn'. The space was protected on its shallow side by a single bank and ditch (Bank II on the plan).[99] The assemblage included imported fine ware and amphorae from the Mediterranean and fragments of insular metalwork, painting a picture of a minor chieftain attempting to maintain a little of the dignity of Rome in straightened circumstances. Cattle, sheep and pig contributed to the food supply in almost equal proportions. Animals were brought into the settlement on the hoof and butchered there. The irregular dairy pattern of the cattle and the absence of a peak for the slaughter of young male animals suggest that they were unlikely to have belonged to a dedicated local herd and had been supplied from elsewhere. This supply may have been tribute or indicate an exchange of animals within the region.[100] Alcock defined a second tier of 'native site' at Pant-y-Saer, an enclosure with roundhouses that was occupied in the Roman period and probably into the 5th century, and another five sites with pottery (including Dinas Emrys) that suggested occupation into the 6th.[101] This is also the period in which the landscape was marked with stone pillars inscribed with the name of a person and his ancestors, with a primary function in the claiming of land (Chapter 5, p. 462).

The site at **Trethurgy** in Cornwall might offer an analogous model for south-west Britain. Here a circular stone enclosure (a 'round') was occupied between the 2nd and 6th

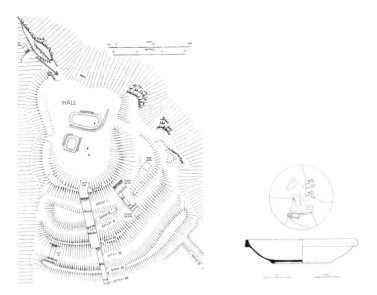

Figure 3.56 Dinas Powys (Glamorgan). (Left): Plan of the fortified site with the putative buildings superimposed (after Alcock 1963, Fig 10, 13). (Right): Imported Mediterranean pottery ('A' Ware).

(Alcock 1963, Fig 25; licensed by University of Wales Press)

centuries, peaking in the 6th when there was major redevelopment, with a new building X4 with an oval plan. The settlement received a wide range of imported pottery: 40–50 sherds of LR1 (Bii) imported from the Mediterranean in the late 5th to early 6th century, 15 sherds of LR 2 (Bi) 4th to early 7th, and two sherds of LR3 (Biv) from south-west Turkey (5th/6th century) and one sherd of E ware from south-west France, (dated 6th to early 8th).[102] Elsewhere in Cornwall, the site of **Tintagel** offers a naturally protected offshore knoll; it was thought by its excavator in the 1930s to be a primitive monastery but has now joined the set of 5th/6th century strongholds.[103] Similar promontory forts are found along the coast of Cornwall and Brittany and in general assigned to the pre-Roman and Roman Iron Age. At **Cadbury Castle** (south Cadbury) was a multivallate hillfort built about 400 BC. It was the site of a Roman temple and was still occupied or reoccupied in the 5th/6th century when imported pottery arrived from the Mediterranean. A large timber hall is assigned to this period.[104] **Cadbury Hill** (Cadbury Congresbury) is another Somerset hillfort reoccupied c. 300–600. Excavation there has produced 173 A-ware and 547 B-ware sherds and around 48 glass vessels.[105]

Sam Turner's analysis of settlement in the south-west demonstrated that the 5th–6th century defended enclosures ('rounds') and the reoccupied Iron Age hillforts at the edge of rough ground on the uplands were superseded in the 7th/8th/9th century by a number of lowland settlements indicated by *tre-* placenames, among them monasteries which created new settlement foci that endured into the medieval period (Figure 3.57). The monasteries later spawned daughter settlements that left their footprints in the form of oval churchyards.[106] In a broad sense the south-west therefore reflects the Formative 1 – Formative 2 transition (see also Chapter 5, p. 487).

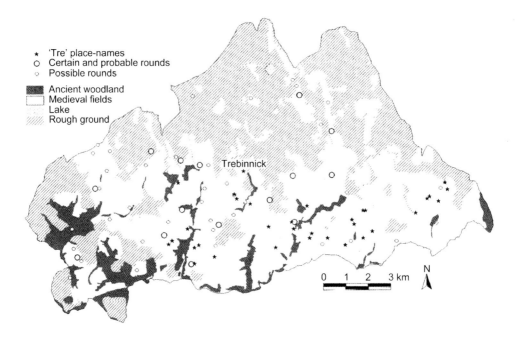

Figure 3.57 The movement from the Fm 1 'rounds' to the adjacent lowlands to make a new Christian landscape in Fm 2. Study by Sam Turner of the St Neot area in Cornwall using a backdrop supplied by Historic Landscape Characterisation.

(Turner 2006, Fig 29, with permission)

Northumbria

Being built up on an Iron Age British territory, Northumbria was familiar with the round-house and its small-scale settlements. The Anglian intrusions began in the 6th century as a logical extension of their campaign to possess all the best arable land, and thereupon they introduced a new pattern book for settlements and housing. By the later 6th century, the structures at **Yeavering**, although not yet necessarily culturally 'Anglian', exemplify and celebrate the rectilinear possibilities, including long halls, short halls, square shrines and a wedge-shaped theatre (p. 158).[107] At **Doon Hill**, Lothian, Brian Hope-Taylor excavated a timber hall within an enclosure that conformed in many particulars to the Yeavering blue-print. Similar halls have been defined at Dunbar and are expected to creep further north, led by aerial reconnaissance.[108] Gordon Maxwell reported a number of timber halls located from the air in the south-east; up to 30 m long and 9 m wide, comparable with the largest halls at Yeavering (e.g. A3), if of less robust appearance.[109] For Hope-Taylor there was a Roman inspiration in these buildings, and he called their design 'Anglo-British'. In many ways, it was the excavation of the Yeavering settlement that revealed the transition between the British and English aristocracy in Northumbria.

Ian Smith found examples of British architecture of a more equivocal kind in his investigations of the Tweed Valley kingdoms: Traprain Law, The Dod, Cow Green and Huckhoe all produced ephemeral stone rubble ground plans that were rectangular but apsidal at one end, recalling the form assigned to the early church at Icklingham in East Anglia[110] (Figure 3.58). The story in the north will be frozen at this point, to be linked up again in Fm 2, when the cultural exchange is enriched from both sides: Anglian halls meet British spiritual enclosures to create the miraculous innovative force of Northumbrian monasticism.

East and south

Anglo-Saxon immigrants took over the most fertile part of Britain, which had previously been farmed as a Roman province (Chapter 1, p. 37). Such takeovers of Roman imperial infrastructure were happening all over Europe in the 5th century, but judging by the lack of interest shown by the Anglo-Saxons in the Latin language or Roman towns, forts and villas, one can place the degree of intended integration with imperial ways well below that of the Vandals in Africa, the Goths in Italy or the Franks in Gaul. Although the ratio of immigrant to native is reckoned to average at 50% or so, the agenda of the English was domination (see Chapter 2, p. 56). Even if the supply of agricultural produce to the imperial granaries were disrupted, we would expect some continuities, in animal husbandry, crops, fields, orchards, irrigation, reclaimed fen, river embankment, roads, bridges and landing places – much of which could be exploited or restarted by immigrants drawing on experience fighting for or against the Roman army, with or without the cooperation of the sitting tenants. There is some evidence for this continuation, for example in the livestock, but it is not strong.[111] The Anglo-Saxons effectively recolonised the province and gave it their own branding, a process of 'Anglification'. In a few centuries this force would diminish, on the back of institutional Christianisation and the conquest of the rest of Britain, but in Fm 1, Roman villas, forts and towns did not provide a built environment that the Anglo-Saxons chose to imitate.

Settlements in the south and east consist mainly of buildings constructed from upright timbers that leave rows of holes where the timbers were seated (Figure 3.6). Other examples,

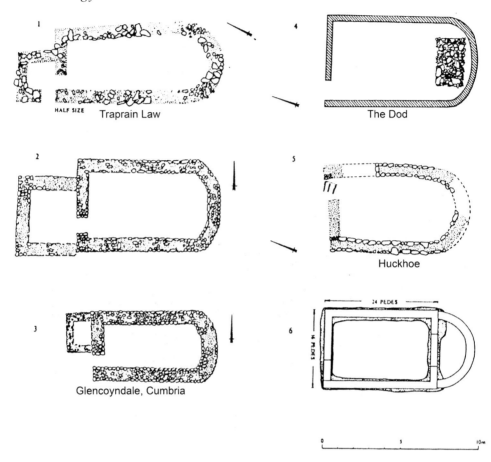

Figure 3.58 British round-ended buildings from the northern borders: 1. Traprain Law. 2. Cow Green, Cumbria. 3. Glencoyndale, Cumbria. 4. The Dod. 5. Huckhoe. 6. (for comparison) is the reconstruction of the church building at Icklingham (Suffolk).

(Smith 1990, Fig 4.19; with permission of Durham University)

mostly later in date, use posts or planks set side by side in trenches ('post-in-trench') as at Chalton. These 'halls' are often accompanied by smaller structures consisting of two, four or six posts at the edges of a rectangular pit. Such buildings are known on the continent as *Grubenhäuser* (dug houses). In England we use the more general term 'sunken-featured buildings', or SFBs, coined by Philip Rahtz, which reflects the fact that they too are post-hole buildings, but with a sunken area.[112] Reconstructing SFBs is contentious because the evidence is slim and tends to rely on analogy and experiment. Analogies range from nomadic pit-houses in the American north-west where pits were covered by simple tent-like structures[113] to sophisticated plank buildings over a cellar. Experiments to date have preferred the latter: tall plank buildings making use of timber sills, floors and carpentry of the type expected from Anglo-Saxons who built timber boats (see the later example with preserved timbers from Yeavering, p. 162).

Early English settlements also have ditches, usually seen as boundaries marking out property or fields. There may also be pits, although the villagers, especially in the early years of their occupation, stacked their rubbish in midden heaps and so made it available to spread on the fields as fertiliser. These settlements have been most easily rediscovered on the sands and gravels and chalk downs of southern and eastern England, land of high attraction to later arable farmers, who have largely erased them. However, on the credit side, the negative features cut into the natural geology can be spotted under the thin topsoil as cropmarks. Under the topsoil, the post-holes, SFBs and ditches show up well as dark patches or strips of fill against a background of yellow sand or gravel or bright white chalk. Definition on clay soils is more challenging.

Nevertheless, settlement and housing form is not imported wholesale with the Anglo-Saxon package. Some aspects are shared between the timber-building cultures either side of the Channel: a rectangular form, posts set in holes or trenches, sunken-featured buildings (the *grubenhaus* and the SFB), and (probably) a range of skilled carpentry that is largely now lost. More characteristic Continental living units have been elusive in England. The longhouse – a multi-functional buildings up to 25 m long in which space was divided between people and animals – had been a strong cultural marker of Denmark since the Iron Age and endured into the 7th century. Grand halls 30 m long or more succeeded them in Scandinavia, containing people only but still divided into spaces.[114] With the solitary exception of Pitcarmick (not in an Anglo-Saxon area), longhouses and byre-houses are conspicuously absent from early medieval England as well as from Britain and Ireland as a whole.[115] It may be that the Anglo-Saxon peoples did not have the means to erect these large buildings,[116] or that the communal life style implied by the partitioned longhouse and hall was more readily expressed as a gathering of small halls and huts. This is the likely inheritance in British and Irish communities at least, where the hierarchy of roundhouses was transferred to a hierarchy of rectangular buildings of similar capacity. Insofar as the smaller halls and SFBs are paralleled on the continent, they may indicate some transfer of a tradition from north-east Continental Europe.[117]

Once in England, this tradition was even so confronted by that of Roman construction, which survived in full view as courtyard villas and rows of barrack blocks. The Anglo-Saxon hall often takes the form of a rectangular building composed of two contiguous squares with an overall plan in the ratio of 2:1, originally thought to derive from Roman or early post-Roman forms.[118] But perhaps for technical reasons, or perhaps for ideological, the Roman building style did not enter the architectural repertoire until Formative 2, which saw its expression in churches and the first large secular halls at Yeavering in Northumbria.[119] To some extent, this is paralleled on the continent, where by the 7th century the longhouse was superseded as a living unit by settlements focused on halls, a change described as being one of the 'most significant of the early middle ages'.[120]

The Scandinavian settlement sequence might also lead us to expect a series of central places: from early cult sites where votive deposits are made, to more ordered spiritual destinations equipped with temples and shrines, to secular trading places and eventually to towns. The Anglo-Saxon settlement repertoire does not appear to include formalised cult sites in the pre-Christian period, although it is not excluded that their cemeteries could act in this capacity.[121] However, the arrival of magnate farms with a hall as focus, of trading places (wics) and prototype towns (burhs) is a leitmotiv of English Fm 2 and 3, as we will see. It is not improbable that some of these developments were prompted or inspired by Scandinavian example, especially as the Vikings became active in the North Sea (see 'Continental analogies' later in this chapter).

The English repertoire in Formative 1

The small group of four early Anglo-Saxon settlements so far completely excavated (West Stow, West Heslerton, Mucking, Bloodmoor Hill) consisted of varying numbers of houses and SFBs and one or more cemeteries. They are each different from the other in plan (and interpretation), something that probably reflects both their location in different parts of the island and the approach to their excavation. All were 'rescue' sites that are now being bent to the service of research.

West Stow was found in 1940 by Basil Brown, the year after he excavated Mound 1 at Sutton Hoo, and was fully excavated by Stanley West between 1965 and 1972 (Figure 3.59). A neighbouring cemetery had been encountered in the mid-19th century during the extraction of ballast, and local collections of finds were made between 1849 and 1852, from which around 340 items have survived.[122] While not sufficient to reconstruct the spear and brooch sets of c. 100 graves that were then brought to light, the material provides a parallel to that found in the settlement – which was itself unusually rich in objects. The village occupied a slight rise; it had been ploughed in the middle ages, sealing it beneath a thick black layer ('Layer 2'), and then buried in sand blow in the 14th century

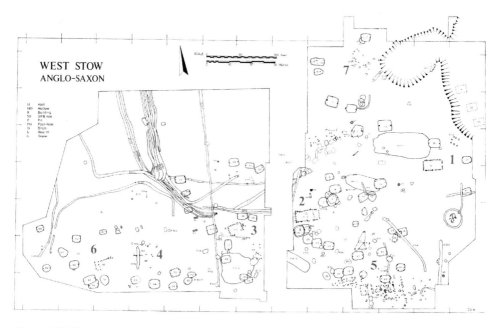

Figure 3.59 West Stow (Suffolk). Plan of excavated buildings with numbered groups, dated as follows: 1. (destroyed in sandpit); 2. c. 440–480; 3. c. 440–500; 4: c. 500–550; 5. c. 480–600; 6. c. 550–600; 7. c. 550–650.

(West 2001, Fig 2; dates from West 2001, 28 (Table 17), 43–47; with permission © Suffolk County Council)

('Layer 1'). In this way the Anglo-Saxon structures and artefacts were preserved to some degree, extending over an area of 1.8 ha. Layer 2 was extremely rich and up to 14 inches (36 cm) deep. It contained the churned up remains of the Anglo-Saxon village, but the Anglo-Saxon ditches were not truncated. For this reason, the association between finds and buildings in the abandonment phase was unusually good, good enough, it seems, to associate assemblages with each of the seven houses (halls) and 67 sheds (SFBs). However, there are understandable disclaimers since, in spite of the rich survival encountered, Layer 2 was still largely removed by machine.[123]

There was no continuity from a Roman predecessor – Roman pottery bases and coins had presumably been acquired by 'gleaning', and some sherds had been reworked as spindle whorls. The Anglo-Saxon occupants cultivated spelt, as had the Romans before them, together with barley, rye and wheat. There had been large flocks of sheep, but cattle were also numerous and red deer accessible. All the pottery, textiles and bone artefacts were made locally, but imports of brooches and glass beads began to arrive in the 6th century.[124]

The hall-houses were built of posts set in pits supporting a building rectangular in plan with a hearth in the centre and an annex at one end (Figure 3.60A). In the neighbouring ploughsoil were finds such as pins, toggles, combs and the occasional knife and axe head. The sheds (SFBs) were rectangular pits with curved corners and two, four or six posts set symmetrically at the short ends. As found, the backfill of an SFB was generally defined in two layers: a lower fill containing objects and traces of planking deriving from the structure and an upper fill that was essentially the dished-in medieval ploughsoil (Figure 3.60B). Studies of these profiles led to the proposal that these buildings included suspended wooden floors over the pit. The excavator supported this idea with two vivid examples: the find of a dog skeleton under planking on the base of SFB 16, articulated but with the head detached as though rotted in an open space under flooring ('dog 2'), and hearths laid at the interface between the lower and upper fills (e.g. SFB 16, 44). Experimental work conducted over several decades has supported the idea that the SFBs not only had floors but plank walls founded on sill beams and thatched roofs supported by rafters.[125]

In addition to the captured 'Layer 2', the SFBs contained a wealth of finds in their lower fills: a total of 199 Roman coins, 48 beads, 67 combs, 40 spindle whorls and Anglo-Saxon pottery assemblages ranging from 25 to 900 sherds. The nature of these assemblages encouraged the deduction that the sunken-featured buildings were not simply working sheds but were lived in. By contrast it was noticeable that the pattern of artefacts associated with the locations of the halls was meagre. The disposition of the buildings and the finds associated with them led to the deduction that the site was organised in seven groups of buildings, which superseded each other between the 5th and 7th centuries. Each building group consisted of one hall and 8–10 SFBs, representing a community of about 30 people.[126]

A later study by Jess Tipper has questioned the relationship between the SFBs and the finds they contained: 'Most of the material in *Grubenhäuser* fills has no direct association with the use of the original buildings and was the result of tertiary deposition from temporary surface dumps.'[127] The stratified section across the fill of an SFB, even when it shows traces of timber, can suggest different interpretations. In SFB 16, 'dog 1' is plainly deposited after the pit is refilled, and this can be true of the hearths laid elsewhere on top of the lower fill. The sections do show that the lower fill of the SFB was not the result of ploughing, unlike the upper fill, and if not *in situ* must have been transported from somewhere. A scenario in which the SFB was backfilled after it was disused and its planking collapsed would better match several cases.

However, the effects of such disassociation should not be exaggerated. In theory, several types of discard could have been practised: objects placed beneath a floor and remaining in situ, objects remaining on the floor, objects thrown onto middens in the adjacent area, objects transported to middens remote from the buildings, objects returned to the SFB pit after it was abandoned and the floor removed, objects lying about in the vicinity incorporated in later ploughsoils and pressed into the cavities left by former sunken areas. Common sense suggests that the backfilling of a disused SFB is likely to have been an insouciant rather than a rigorous activity. Carting away rubbish and putting it on the fields is documented behaviour, but bringing it back from the fields or from remote dumps to tip into an abandoned SFB at a later date is more implausible. The average SFB at West Stow most likely contained in its lower fills material that was in use in the buildings with or without a floor or pushed in from local dumps or discards, while its upper fill contained discards from scrambled middens dished-in by later ploughing, but still local to the buildings. In this, the assemblage is no worse and generally much better than the contents of pits used to date occupation and determine activity in any other prehistoric period. At West Stow, objects were also deposited as primary contexts in graves but distant at several removes from their users in the settlement, and made distant again by the trashing of the cemetery in the 19th century. Thus the status of finds may vary by one, two, three or six removes from their 'systemic' context, but that is no reason to disqualify them as irrelevant to the people who made and used the buildings.

The question that remains is how SFB assemblages and their distribution support the phasing of the site and the social implications that result. At West Stow the composition of the assemblages varies between SFBs, so they were less probably extracted from a common dump (cf Bloodmoor Hill). They may have derived from local middens or been pushed in by clearance before the later ploughsoil that sealed them. Alternatively, they may represent use contemporary with the building, especially where there was no evidence for a floor or where fragile objects remained whole. Leaving aside the stratified dogs and hearths, we can note the complete combs at the base of SFB 21 and 22 and the discrete bone masses in nine SFBs.[128] Thirty-one SFBs had remains of loom weights, which were primary in seven cases and explicit where the building had burnt down, as in the case of SFB 15 (Figure 3.60C). Loom weights, pin beaters and spindle whorls were distributed in the SFB clusters attached to Halls 2–7.[129] These were added arguments for a model of a 'shifting hamlet' in which one building group supersedes another. In his later publication, Stanley West refined his house-groups into six overlapping periods (Table 3.2). The overall period of occupation was also lengthened. Judging by the distribution of Ipswich Ware on the east part of the site, either the settlement (House 7) continued in use into the 8th century, or an 8th-century settlement elsewhere disposed of midden in the abandoned early Saxon village.[130]

The use of timber floors in the English version of the *grubenhaus* has since commanded general support.[131] But that does not mean all SFBs had them: the example excavated at Yeavering shows that the base of the pit could be used as a floor, and this is likely to have been the case where loom weights were found in an ordered pattern on the pit base, as at Upton.[132] Whether it originates in the roof, walls or floor, the timber planking rarely survives and most sites have even less hard evidence than West Stow.

Stanley West not only conducted meticulous research at West Stow but pioneered the public understanding and visualisation of early Anglo-Saxon buildings. The reconstructed village has inspired many to continue research, while others perhaps now retain an image of the period that is hard to shake off (Figure 3.61). As will shortly emerge, discussion continues on whether SFBs were houses to live in or sheds for weaving and whether Anglo-Saxon

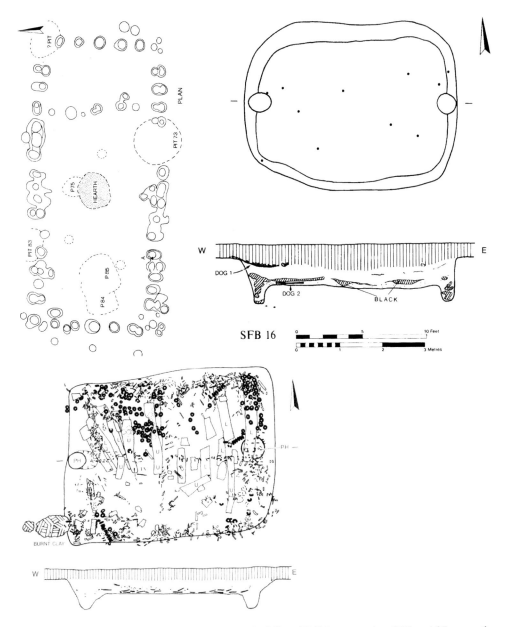

Figure 3.60 West Stow. (Top left): A post-hole building (Hall 2; measuring 9.75 × 4.27 m on the ground). (Top right): A Shed (SFB 16) plan and section showing the position of the two dogs in the stratigraphy. (Bottom): A weaving shed, SFB 15, its internal details preserved by burning. The planks are interpreted as belonging to a suspended floor.

(West 1985, Fig 75, 2001, Fig 4, 6; with permission © Suffolk County Council)

Table 3.2 Model of West Stow sequence

	440	450	480	500	520	550	600	650
2	-------	-------	-------					
3	-------	-------	-------	-------				
4				-------	------	-------		
5			-------	-------	------	-------	-------	
6						-------	-------	
7						-------	-------	-------

(derived from West 2001, Table 17).

Figure 3.61 West Stow: part of the reconstructed village seen in 2014.
(Author)

villages were composed of contemporary zones or successive hamlets. These are important matters, although still hampered by an unjustifiable expectation that all Anglo-Saxon villagers will have behaved in the same way. Obviously, it is better to discover what happened at each site rather than assume a common method of construction and use, or even less justifiably a standard site formation process and degree of survival.

West Heslerton is the largest excavation of a piece of English landscape to date (20 ha) and is provided with context by an intensive aerial and surface survey of the Vale of Pickering in north Yorkshire, in which it lies. Excavated between 1978 and 1995, the Anglian settlement and its cemetery occupied a strip of the gravel terrace running south-north for a thousand metres, with a maximum width east-west of about 400 m (Figure 3.62). Settlement began around a spring at the southern end in the Late Roman period, expanded either side of the stream in the early Anglian period (i.e. Fm 1) into a settlement measuring 400 × 300 m arranged in three large zones. Another 300 m north is the contemporary 5th–7th century cemetery of 200 burials, focussed on a small group of prehistoric monuments.[133] In Fm 2 (7th to 9th century), the settlement contracted and returned to the south end, where it overlay the

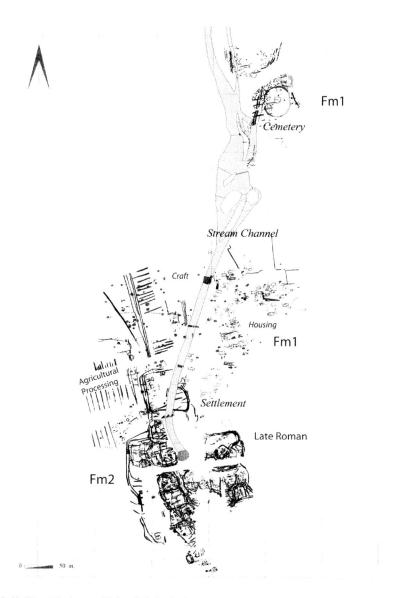

Figure 3.62 West Heslerton (Vale of Pickering). General plan.

(After Powlesland 2000, Fig 3.1, 3.2; courtesy of Dominic Powlesland, annotated by author)

Late Roman centre.[134] The post-excavation study of this settlement is still ongoing at the time of writing, but the special interest of the interim conclusions lies in the idea that the Fm 1 settlement zones indicate not a 'shifting hamlet' as at West Stow but contemporary areas distinguished by different kinds of activity.

The *Late Roman settlement* had its initial focus at a spring at the south end from which flowed a stream. A large structure built on rammed stone rafts lay adjacent. Bread ovens and large amounts of food waste were found here, including spreads of oyster and mussel shells. Crude Roman-style hand-made pottery found in pits was dated to the late 4th and 5th century. The preliminary interpretation is that this was a ritual destination of some kind, visited by pilgrims.[135] The site developed with a series of sub-rectangular stock enclosures, one with a roundhouse, laid out either side of the stream, to east and west.

The *Anglian village* may have been attracted to the late Roman centre or its spring as the initial rationale for settlement and subsequently spread northwards to encompass several hectares. To the east of the stream was a group of 35 houses and 20 sheds (SFBs) situated on a chalk knoll. This is interpreted as a *housing zone*. On the west side of the stream were two other areas of SFBs: an *agricultural processing zone*, with evidence for butchery and malting, and further north a *craft zone* with evidence for metalworking. The total tally is given as 90 post-hole buildings and 135 SFBs, clearly not all in use at once, since post buildings were seen to replace one another on the same footprint. There has been much discussion on the use of the material deposited in the SFBs for phasing the site, with the assertion, which began at West Heslerton, that the backfills are all tertiary and do not relate to the use of the building; this is based to some degree on conjoining sherds found some distance part.[136] However the verdict of the interim publications is that all the SFBs had wooden floors, and that their contents, tertiary or not, have been used as the basis for the stability of the zones and the activities practised within them.[137] Thus grain found under the floor horizon of an SFB is certainly assigned to its contemporary use.[138]

Given the numbers of burials in the cemetery, this is a small (12 ha), stable, well-ordered village, relatively short-lived at 250 years. It comes to an end sometime in the 7th century, when it is succeeded by a group of three post-in-trench buildings within enclosures, placed on the enclosures of the former Late Roman ritual centre but overlooking the early village. A well ('constructed in or soon after 724') and a series of *stycas* suggests that this focus remained active, perhaps reviving its former spiritual role until the middle of the 9th century.[139]

The site at **Mucking** (Essex) was excavated from 1965 to 1978 by Margaret and Tom Jones, who recorded 203 SFBs and 53 post-hole buildings spread over an area of 18 ha of the Thames gravels, mainly within the 100-foot contour (Figure 3.63). The site was one of the first in which Anglo-Saxon settlement and burial were excavated in the same place: there were two cemeteries, one containing c. 480 cremations and c. 274 inhumations (Cemetery II) and the other 62 inhumations, but incompletely excavated (Cemetery I).[140] The Jones's were led to the site by a cropmark on an area scheduled for quarrying; they fought for and applied a now commonplace excavation strategy whereby the topsoil (and often the subsoil) was removed in controlled conditions by a mechanical excavator and the exposed surface shovelled clean by labourers and students until the features showed against the surface of the natural geology.[141] Mucking was also one of the first projects to reveal the density of occupation that could occur on the gravels. Here was a Late Bronze Age enclosure (the 'South Rings') that provided the initial target of the excavations and proved to have been accompanied by post-hole buildings and pit clusters.[142] *South Rings* was superseded by a multivallate

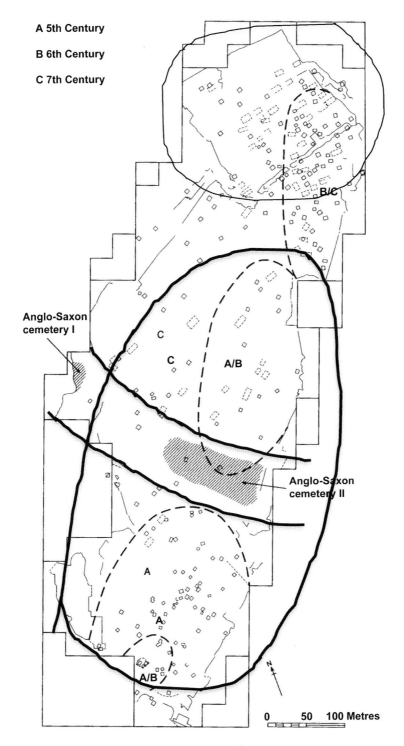

A 5th Century

B 6th Century

C 7th Century

Anglo-Saxon
cemetery I

Anglo-Saxon
cemetery II

B/C

C

C

A/B

A

A

A/B

N

0   50   100 Metres

Figure 3.63 Mucking (Essex). Phased Anglo-Saxon settlement.
(Hamerow 1993, Fig 50, p. 87; image licensed by Historic England)

earthwork in the Iron Age, while in the same period appeared a rectilinear enclosure 1 ha in extent, an open settlement of about 110 roundhouses and cemeteries including two small groups of square-ditched barrows. After the Roman conquest the settlement area was parcelled up into a series of ditched enclosures serving farmsteads. But later Roman evidence was 'surprisingly slight'. Thus, although the terrace had already seen several thousand years of settlement evolution, the 'incoming Saxons would have found themselves on a landscape that had been allowed to return to scrub for a substantial period, perhaps as little as 50 but probably more like 75 years'.[143]

The settlement of the Anglo-Saxon period was analysed by Helena Hamerow, who recognised an uninterrupted occupation from the first half of the 5th century to the beginning of the eighth century. The settlement was broadly zoned in three consecutive phases, each of a different size and focussed in a different place. This was deduced from the location of 42 diagnostic metal and pottery finds, two radiocarbon dates, seven instances of stratification, the distribution of dateable finds, pottery fabrics and the relative alignment of the larger buildings.[144] The net result was explained as a movement from south to north of a 5th-century group consisting mainly of sheds, a 5th–6th century group mainly of houses and a 6th–7th century group of houses and sheds mixed together. Mucking therefore appeared to follow the West Stow model in seeing a settlement formed by groups of buildings superseding each other: 'Mucking is thus best described as a shifting hamlet, at times perhaps more than one.'[145] However this is seen as a 'gradual process', perhaps representing the coexistence of only 'one or two farmsteads at a time'.[146]

Assuming the phasing is representative, the virtual absence of houses from the south part of the site raises the image of a 5th-century population that lived in SFBs. This would square with the arrival of a relatively large number of people using a type of building that is easy to erect: earth walls and head space are provided by excavating the pit, and the only timbers required are a ridge pole supported by a post at each end and rafters that leaning against the earth walls and the ridge. This type of building is, moreover, well-known on the continent in the area of the Anglo-Saxon homelands.[147] However, other interpretations are possible, as Hamerow would acknowledge.[148] On the grounds that 5th-century material occurred south of the cemetery zone and 6th/7th material both north and south, Tipper proposed two contemporary long-lived settlements based north and south of the cemeteries.[149] It is noticeable, however, that the central zone (north of the sheds) has few chronologically diagnostic finds and a preponderance of aligned houses; it is therefore possible that this distinction is one of function as opposed to one of time. They lived in the houses but worked in the sheds, where the finds of lead and slag are common. This would imply that Mucking, like West Heslerton, was essentially a zoned 5th/7th century settlement at the southern end. The two cemeteries, which both begin in the 5th century and contain nothing later than the early 7th, would seem to relate to this first settlement that lies astride them. Also, like West Heslerton, this extensive occupation was succeeded by a 7th/8th century settlement with boundary ditches that lay elsewhere, in this case further north. The cemetery for the 7th/8th settlement has not yet been found.[150] There are therefore two phases of settlement, defined by period. The early arrival and military references implied by finds in the cemeteries has encouraged a history-friendly vision of immigrant pioneers or mercenary soldiers making a landfall.[151] If this is the case, it must be judged successful: the community was here to stay and might have been planned from the outset.

Bloodmoor Hill was an almost complete settlement dating from the 6th to the early 8th century and represents a notable advance in the way these sites should be studied. The site

was initially evaluated by Suffolk Archaeological Unit using the standard commercial pro-
tocol of trenching, so missing some matters of consequence.[152] Subsequent area excavation
by CAU took place from 1998 to 2001, extended over 3 ha and recovered 38 SFBs, eight
post-hole buildings, a post-in-trench building, 270 pits and several large areas of spread
middens that had been captured by the previous Roman trackways and other hollows. The
site was stripped, as is customary, by a tracked excavator using a toothless ditching bucket,
but the spread middens (termed 'surface deposits') survived in situ and were examined by
a chequerboard of alternating metre-square pits.[153] This meant that the material discarded in
middens could be compared with that deposited in SFBs, with revealing results.

The phasing was achieved by stratification (where one feature cut another), 59 radiocarbon dates of carbonised residues on pottery sherds, and artefact typology. This allowed
features and structures to be gathered into three 'initial phases'. There followed a detailed
analysis of the content and formation of the surface deposits (i.e. spread middens), showing that they were dumps that had been added to over time and that successive dumpings
(recovered in spits) bore an artefact signature ('assemblage profile') that could in turn be
related to time periods. Assemblages with similar signatures found in pits and SFBs could
thus be added to the phases by proxy. These same signatures also indicated areas of dumps
that had been used to backfill features. Thus, for example, SFB 16, 17 and 5 had fills that
closely resembled the surface deposits under which they were located; S31 and Pit M were
backfilled with deposits that lay adjacent; and S14 was backfilled with adjacent deposits that
lay to the north or east. Its large group of tools, including chisels and punches, a spearhead,
a knife blade, shears and sickle fragments imply that this coincided with the end of metalworking in that area.[154] These ingenious analyses led to three revised 'Final site phases' from
which the story of the site could then be told.

In Phase 1 (500–580) a group of seven post-hole houses, aligned or orthogonal, occupied
a central area (40, 44, 46) (Figure 3.64). To the north was a strip of SFBs (4, 16, 17, 36, 37)
associated with a bank of midden already containing Roman debris to which more rubbish
was added, notably pottery, animal bone and oven debris. An SFB to the west (5) was concerned with metalworking, while others to the south-east (33, 34) were working with textile.
In Phase 2a (600–650), the new dwellings kept to their zone (41, 43, 45, 47) but drew the
attendant SFBs more tightly around them; some of these to the east (27, 29, 30) were involved
in crop processing. The 'village midden' to the north now acquired dumps of waste from
metalworking, butchery, spinning and weaving. In Phase 2b (660–700) (Figure 3.65) a high-
status post-in-trench house appears (42) with its own satellite SFBs (12, 13, 14, 15). A second
cluster of SFBs to the east (25, 26, 28, 20, 21) provided services that include the working of
metal, antler and textile. Between the two groups, an inhumation cemetery developed, with
dates consistently in the 7th century.[155]

This excavation and especially its inspired stratigraphic analysis have raised the understanding of a settlement and the activities within it to an entirely new level – but without any
insistence that the result has provided a normative template for early Anglo-Saxon behaviour.

The early English sequence

The message from the small group of early Anglo-Saxon villages so far examined at a useable scale is that they not only survived in different ways but were different to begin with:
well-designed and purpose-built analytical procedures are needed, as at Bloodmoor Hill,

Figure 3.64 Bloodmoor Hill, Carlton Colville (Suffolk). The excavated village in Phase 1.
(Lucy et al. 2009, Fig 6.35, with permission)

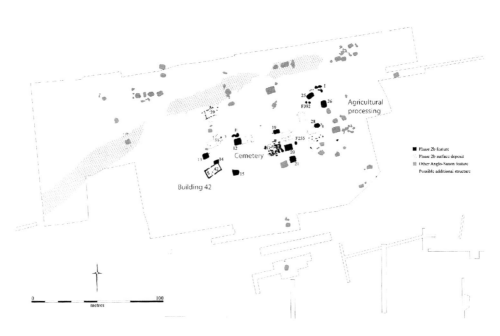

Figure 3.65 Bloodmoor Hill. The excavated settlement and cemetery in Phase 2b.
(Lucy et al. 2009, Fig 6.37. With permission. See Chapter 4, p. 402 for the cemetery)

in order to determine their most elementary properties. The story from Bloodmoor Hill is quite different to that at West Stow, although both are contemporary and in the same county. Mucking and West Heslerton are at opposite ends of England but may have had a similar layout. Given the state of survival of the Anglo-Saxon village, its vulnerability to later ploughing and the peremptory approach to excavation that is apparently forced upon us, the most important attribute for observing social and economic change is the evolution of the settlement plan. The question of the relation of post-hole buildings and SFBs to the finds recovered in their vicinities bears on the structure of an Anglo-Saxon settlement and whether it consisted of house clusters that replaced each other along a ridge (as first proposed for Mucking), or a small settlement in which houses shifted in a restricted area (like West Stow on its knoll), or a stable settlement within which houses are periodically replaced (suggested for West Heslerton). It goes without saying that the new research era needs to start with a radical improvement in the time and care invested in investigating these settlements (see *Critique* at the end of this chapter). Some progress has also been made in appreciating the larger landscape that the settlements belong to.[156]

In each case the Fm 1 settlement had a development of the 7th century that was different in character: a smaller offshoot at the edge of the village (Mucking north end, Hall 6 and Hall 7 at West Stow), or back at its late Roman origin (West Heslerton), or a larger building in the centre, accompanied by a cemetery (S42 at Bloodmoor Hill). These shapes of things to come are clearly portrayed at Yarnton (p. 167), where the 'grand hall' and its adjacent enclosure succeed the Fm 1 village in the 8th and 9th centuries. We will resume this itinerary later in the story of the English area in Fm 2.

Formative 2 (7th–9th century)

The monastic movement, magnate farms and the wics

A radical change occurs in settlement archaeology in Britain between the 7th and 8th centuries. However, the destination of the change is different in the upland and lowland zones. In the north and west, a new kind of settlement appears which can be ascribed to the monastic movement. In Scotland and Pictland, as in Ireland, these take the form of curvilinear enclosures usually divided into concentric zones, in which cattle pens and monastic crafts (the making of sculpture, vellum and metal vessels) surround a sacred precinct containing a church and cemetery (e.g. Portmahomack). The Northumbrian prescription takes the form of a large courtyard establishment resembling a Roman villa on the one hand and the later medieval type of monastery on the other (e.g. Jarrow). These settlements borrow elements of the dominant places of Fm 1, such as Dunadd and Yeavering, to serve a new type of community that is unusually well documented, that of the early medieval monastery of the British north and west.

This early monastic movement is less evident archaeologically in the east and south. Here, on the other hand, settlements continue the process of reducing their extent and increasing their wealth to create smaller, richer concentrations, called, for want of a better term, 'magnate farms' (as Yarnton, p. 173). Other new centres of concentrated economic energy are also created in Fm 2: the informal markets inferred from artefact scatters hitherto known (to metal-detectorists) as 'productive sites' and the emporia or gateway trading places or *wics*. Looking back at Fm 2 over Britain as a whole, it will appear that the wic and the monastery have analogous but contrasting roles, the one driven by the enlargement of royal power, the other by dedication to a theocratic alternative.

North and west – the monastic movement

The increased harvest of evidence over the past 20 years is conspiring to show that the advent and spread of monastic establishments in the north and west of Britain between the late 7th and early 9th centuries can claim to be one of the most significant trends, economic, political and ideological, of the whole formative period. In contrast to what came before and what was to follow after, it represents an unusual attempt to brigade all kinds and conditions of people not under a king but under a single spiritual authority. The people of the north and west are supposed to have already been Christian in the 5th/6th century, and the expectation has long been that these areas will be studded at that time with Christian monasteries dedicated to local saints, some associated with fortified sites (e.g. Saint Congar at Congresbury). Clerics writing in the 8th century also recorded memories of this distant missionary age (Chapter 6). However, although there are indications that the people were probably Christian, hard evidence for a monastic movement before the later 7th century has proved elusive. The standing stone monuments with inscriptions in Cornwall, Wales, Strathclyde and the Borders provide evidence of Roman thinking in their dedications and are now seen primarily as markers of inherited land (Chapter 5). No churches built before the 12th century have been recognised in Scotland, Wales or Cornwall (with the possible exception of Presteigne).[157] Adomnán's *Life of Columba* purports to describe the daily life of a community of the mid-6th century when Columba was alive, but its details have proved hard to substantiate for the earlier period and are not easily distinguished from those of the late 7th when the *Life* was actually written.[158] In Cornwall, the landscape is now seen as Christianised in the 8th century with the replacement of *rounds* by *trefs* and the implantation of monasteries, followed by the later budding off of villages manifested by standing stone crosses and oval churchyards.[159] The evidence of archaeology, acting beneath the documentary radar, reports monasticism not as an evolutionary process initiated by missionaries but as a revolutionary episode provoked by a new ideology initiated in the late 7th century, one that spread like wildfire over the next 100 years.

Its point of origin may have been in Ireland or Scotland or Wales, or all three, and an equally potent and influential partner was Northumbria, a hybrid Anglo-British territory with its own take on what monasticism meant. In practice, the each of the main players had a slightly different way of expressing their allegiance to the cause, but what unites them, as is clear from Chapter 5, is their monumentality, especially the standing stone monuments and churches that were erected. Also seen as a common strategy (where enough ground has been opened) are large formal cemeteries (Chapter 4) and a similar approach to the locations chosen, the layout of the settlement and the extensive evidence for the working of vellum and precious metal, collectively known as the monastic arts. It is striking that Southumbria can claim virtually none of these attributes. Even where named monasteries have been investigated in the south, monumental stone carving, the monastic arts and the ritual layout are barely detectable – at least so far. The English monastery, insofar as it can be defined, was a horse of a different colour to those of the principal monastic zones in the greater part of Britain. An explanation for this difference will be offered (later) when we visit the south-east. Here we focus on the monastic sites of Scotland, Pictland and Northumbria, their design, structures, economies and chronicles of investment.[160] In this area we are especially fortunate that a series of coherent large-scale investigations of monastic sites have been completed and, more importantly, published over the last decade. Notable are Inchmarnock in the Sound of Bute, Hoddom in Dumfries, Whithorn in Galloway, the Isle of May in the Firth of Forth, Portmahomack in northern Pictland and, in Northumbria, Hartlepool, Wearmouth and Jarrow.[161] We shall visit a selected number of these, guided by what they have to offer thus far.

In Scotland

A D-shaped boundary bank survives at **Iona,** still home to a Christian community and a site so famous from its associations with St Columba that it has attracted an uncountable number of excavations, many of them inexpert or unpublished or both.[162] For this reason Iona remains the poor relation of early monastic archaeology rather than its flagship. The line of the boundary bank tends to the rectangular in plan but is in fact a complex of earthworks, as shown by topographical survey and geophysics (Figure 3.66). Samples from different

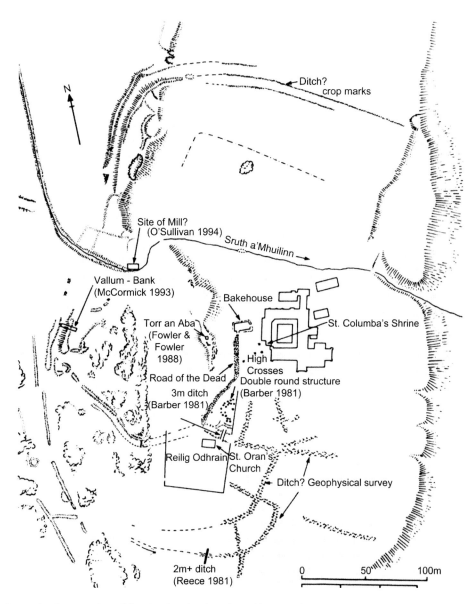

Figure 3.66 Iona. Plan of the site showing location of interventions.
(McCormick 1997, Fig 1, with permission)

parts of the ditch system have given dates in the pre-Roman and early Roman period and the mid-7th century.[163] Barber's excavations on the south side of the present monastery defined a ditch 5–6 m wide and 2.9 m deep, with a waterlogged lower fill containing turned wooden objects and leather from the hides of cattle, horse, red deer, seal and hairy sheep/goat. Finds from an adjacent pit (156) included metal and glass-working datable in a range from the 6th to the 9th century. The main feature was a large building c. 20 m in diameter formed from two concentric circles of timber posts.[164] Beyond the ditch segment lies the burial ground of Reilig Odhráin, which is still in use. Further south still, a working area adjacent to a ditch 3 m wide and 2 m deep produced 6th- and 7th-century imported pottery and radiocarbon dates between the 4th and 10th centuries.[165] Still further south lies St Ronan's medieval church, beneath which was a tiny predecessor in the form of a rectangle of clay-bonded stone walls, rendered inside and out with lime mortar and enclosing a space 4.5 × 3.3 m.[166] Women's burials were associated with the church in the post-medieval period, which may be a memory of an earlier tradition.[167] A shrine chapel, perhaps to house the remains of St Columba, has been defined beneath St Columba's House. It had evidence for *antae*, and historical documents suggest it was in existence before 849; like other shrine chapels in Ireland, it should date to the 8th/9th century.[168] A mill was located on the Sruth a' Mhuillinn which crosses half-way along the western boundary.[169] Apart from these sightings, archaeology has produced little evidence of how the site was used between the 7th to 9th century, when it is thought to have flourished. This is a site which probably produced the *Book of Durrow* in c. 680 and the *Book of Kells* in c. 800, and where the remains of more than a hundred grave markers and other crosses have been found, dated to the late 7th century and later.[170] In spite of its unusually harsh archaeological treatment, Iona retains a high potential for the understanding of Christian monumentality in the 5th–7th century (Formative 1), so conspicuously lacking elsewhere.

At **Inchmarnock,** the inner enclosure dates from c. 600 in radiocarbon years; a church survives at its centre, the earliest identified structure on the site (Church 1) being dated 800–900.[171] To the north of the church there was evidence for flimsy structures associated with metalworking dated mostly 650–780.[172] There were stone grave markers that imply an unlocated early cemetery; a burial ground, said to have been for women, was noted in the 19th century in a northern annex, 7th–11th.[173] The most exciting objects were recovered from the south-west corner of the church: a scatter of inscribed slates for practising writing, dated from their orthography to before 800 and perhaps even to the earlier 7th century.[174] This suggested a school-house located west of the church within an outer enclosure between the metal workshops and the residential cells (Figure 3.67). One of the slates, seemingly inscribed by a child, depicts an oared galley, mailcoated persons and an object that resembles a house-shaped reliquary suspended from an arm: the components of a raid, perhaps, recollected in trauma (Figure 3.68).

In Pictland

Now that we have had sight of a multi-functioning monastic settlement at **Portmahomack,** it seems probable that many others will be found, perhaps where today only a few broken pieces of monumental sculpture lie in a churchyard or on a window sill in a church. On this premise, the monastic network in Pictland, as in Scotland and Ireland, would have been extensive. Presumably not every settlement was a monastery, but other types of residence are currently even more elusive. The duns and crannogs of Fm 1 continued into the late 7th century (radiocarbon years) but apparently not much longer. One suggestive candidate

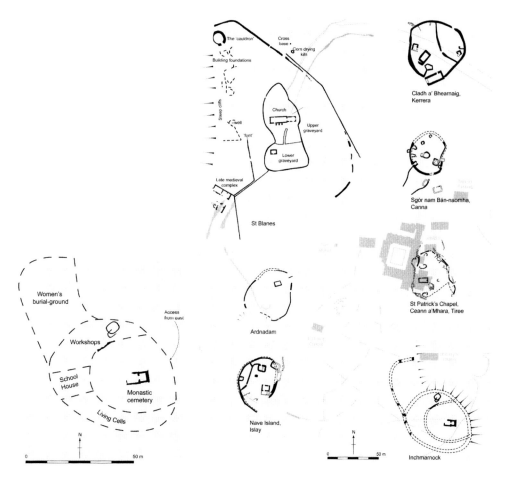

Figure 3.67 Inchmarnock, Clyde estuary. A: Model of the monastic settlement. B: Monastic settlements of the west of Scotland, with the site of Iona at the same scale as background.

(Lowe 2008, Fig 9.6, 9.3, with permission)

Figure 3.68 Inchmarnock: slate with armed figures and ship.

(Lowe 2008, Plate 6.6, with permission)

for upland settlement is vested in the houses of **Pitcarmick** type, named after Pitcarmick in Strathardle in NW Perthshire, where anomalies first noted from the air were identified as deriving from rectangular buildings with characteristic rounded ends. Their occurrence on the ground, between stone roundhouses, usually Bronze or Iron Age, and rectangular buildings, usually medieval or post-medieval, suggested that an early medieval date would not be improbable.[175] Excavation by John Barrett and Jane Downes of two examples revealed the lines of the buildings, and subsequent research showed them to be byre-houses measuring 18 × 4 m (C1) and 22.5 × 4.5 m (E1) internally, built of turf and stone, with the residence at the western end and the animals at the east served by a paved walkway[176] (Figure 3.69). Radiocarbon dates placed their construction between the 7th and 9th century. Both Pitcarmick byre-houses were reoccupied in the later middle ages (11th–13th centuries), implying a 200- to 300-year survival of a turf and stone building.[177]

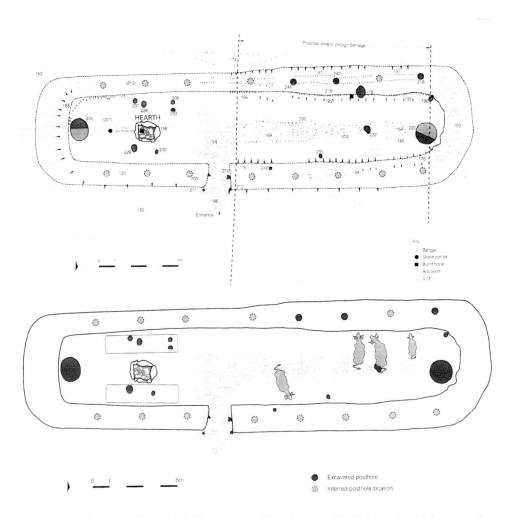

Figure 3.69 Pitcarmick (Perthshire). The excavated byre-house at Site E (above), with interpretation (below). The hearth gave radiocarbon dates of 540–690, 640–890, 690–980, 670–870, 680–890.

(Carver et al. 2012, Ill 22, 27; with permission of the Society of Antiquaries of Scotland)

These examples of byre-houses are currently not paralleled in Britain or Ireland, and their nearest relatives are in Scandinavia, where the tradition of sharing one's accommodation with herd animals is a long one. How far this represents a locally generated prescription or an international connection is an open question. There is some expectation that the longhouse should turn up more widely in early Scotland, as has been surmised at The Howe, and it would occasion no great surprise if it did.[178] Rectilinear turf houses also assigned to the 8th century have been found at the other end of Britain: at Hound Tor in Devon. The Hound Tor turf houses here were also imposed on a Bronze Age stone enclosure with roundhouses and superseded by stone longhouses in the mid-13th century. Each group of occupants farmed at over 1,000 feet above sea level. The turf houses were inferred from lines of stake holes and may themselves have been byre-houses, but this function was clearer in the 13th century, when there was a complement of four stone-built longhouses and three kiln barns. One Bronze Age roundhouse had been adapted as an animal pen and another as a barn. House 7, at least, was a stone byre-house with a central drain imposed on a sequence of earlier turf buildings. The excavator concluded that the use of the byre-house, here as elsewhere, indicated the altitude at which the climate permitted arable farming and successive periods.[179] The byre-house is associated with dairy animals (not excluding sheep), and its purpose is believed to involve keeping cows warm in winter, either to improve milk yield, to facilitate breeding or to foster family bonding.[180] It is not excluded that there were shielings on the summer uplands of the Highlands or that they were constructed in the service of the monastic movement.

Portmahomack's S1 and the Pitcarmick buildings are members of a still tiny corpus of buildings in a misty Firthland landscape. Is there a connection between them? Might they have a shared ancestry? Some particularly robust Iron Age roundhouses have been excavated at Birnie southwards from Tarbat Ness across the Moray Firth, so we need not doubt that there were northern exemplars to hand.[181] Even more evident to Pictish builders were Bronze Age stone roundhouses, such as those at Pitcarmick, which are still visible above the heather today. It was noted there that the Bronze Age and early medieval builders, although working to different ground plans in widely separated periods, used the same basic technique of construction: boulders and turf laid in a many-decker sandwich, with posts set either in the open space between the walls or within the walls. The Pitcarmick byre-houses also had a large post-hole central to each end thought to indicate a principal support for the hipped gable. This interpretation, requiring the liberal use of turf, is bolstered by many analogies from Iceland and Scotland in the form of photographs, site studies and reconstructions.[182] Given the ubiquity and endurance of such practice it is easy to imagine the Portmahomack building as contrived from ideas already to hand – essentially as a half a turf-built roundhouse with a giant trapezoidal extension, while the Pitcarmick building could be seen as a roundhouse cut in two halves and stretched to provide a linear corridor between them. At Carn Dubh, Moulin, Perthshire, the previous Bronze Age roundhouses were joined in the mid-first millennium AD by a rectilinear building (House 8) contrived from the remains of Bronze Age Houses 2 and 3, providing echoes in its plan of both Pitcarmick E1 and Portmahomack S1. It was radiocarbon dated to the bracket AD 655–960.[183]

Nevertheless, the impetus for such original building plans, however technically feasible, demands a better explanation than this. At Portmahomack, the design is argued to stem from early Christian ideology, enhanced by long-established theories of natural symmetry.[184] It may thus be seen as Insular art in the same way as a chalice or reliquary – indigenous in execution but provoked by incoming Christian ideology. The Pitcarmick buildings on the other hand are startling because they do have close parallels, but not in Scotland or indeed in Britain or Ireland, but on the Continent (see 'Continental analogies' later in this chapter).

In the borders

At **Hoddom** a ditch enclosed 8 ha against the bank of the River Annan, where a historic church building still stood (Figure 3.70). The archaeological excavations were limited to the part of the enclosure farthest from the river, an area mainly concerned with grain drying. The first form of the enclosure was a palisade and ditch, radiocarbon dated between 600 and 680 AD.[185] A series of kiln barns (S8–11) dated by carbonised grain developed over three

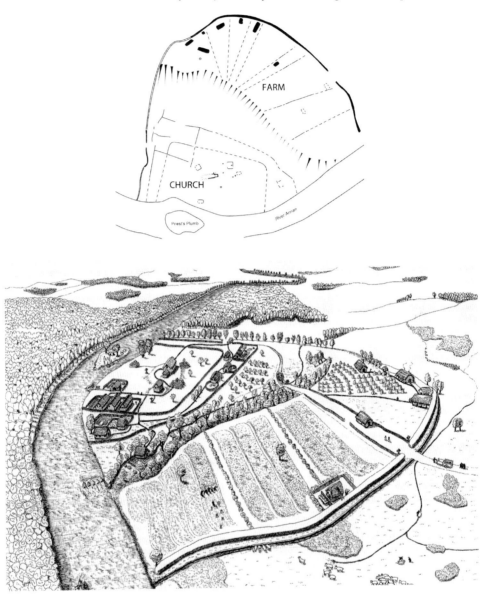

Figure 3.70 Hoddom (Dumfries and Galloway). (Top): General model of the monastic site. (Bottom): Artist's impression.

(Lowe 2006, Ill 4.31, 4.42, 8.11, 9.1, with permission)

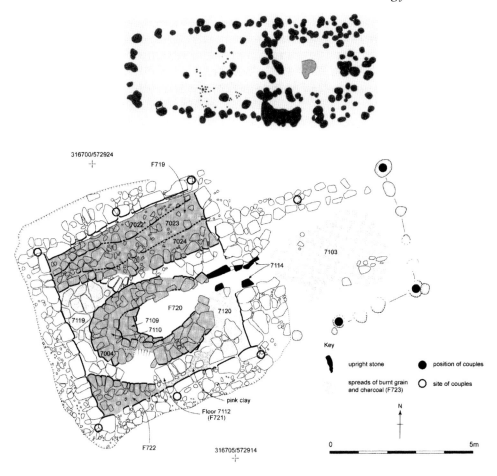

Figure 3.70 (Continued) (Top): Grain drying kiln within a timber building (S6.1, 7th century). (Bottom): Stone-built multi-phase grain drying kiln (S11.2–3, 9th–10th century).

phases (1–3) between 650 and 750. These were built with stone floors and mud walls, the roof supported by pairs of crucks.[186] More sophisticated structures followed in Phase 4 built in stone; one of them, probably dedicated to tanning (S1), incorporated two pieces of 2nd-century-inscribed Roman stone, probably originating from the fort at Birrens.[187] Grain dryers also continued to be built in this phase and through the 9th–11th century (Phases 5–6). Chris Lowe (the excavator) saw the first three phases (7th/8th century) as culturally British and monastic, Phase 4 (later 8th century) as Northumbrian and monastic, and Phase 5–6 (9th–11th century) as belonging to an estate centre. In practice, the monastic attribution in the first three phases is owed to the installation of the enclosure (as a *vallum*) and in Phase 4 to the sculpture found in association with Hoddom, which has Northumbrian links and is mainly 8th/9th century in date.[188]

   Whithorn on the south coast of Galloway offers a transition of roles before and after the installation of a monastery of a type better defined in Northumbria (Figure 3.71). The archaeological investigation and its publication was dominated by the documented figure of St Ninian, a holy man of the 5th century who had his headquarters at *Candida Casa*, a place identified as Whithorn.[189] The narrative developed by the late Peter Hill, its excavator,

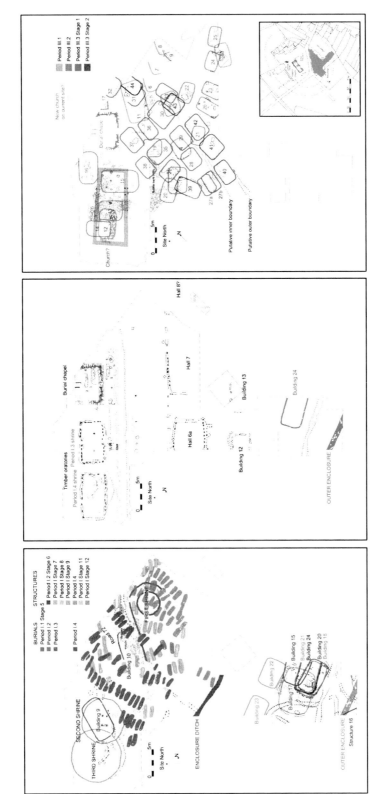

Figure 3.71 Whithorn (Dumfries and Galloway). The settlement sequence by Peter Hill 1997, modified by Nicola Toop 2005. (Left): Period 1; (Fm 1, 5th to 7th century): (Centre): Period II (Fm2, 7th to 9th century); (Right): Period III (Fm 3, 9th to 11th century). Inset: excavation area.

(Toop 2005, Fig 8.5, 8.6, 8.8, 8.11, with author's permission)

was framed by the expectation of a developing cult centre, beginning with a 'monasterium' in the 5th–7th century, adopting the form of a Northumbrian monastery in the 8th/9th and becoming a 'monastic town' in the 9th/10th. Subsequent students of the site have argued for a more secular role for the 5th/7th phase.[190] However, the settlement plan in each phase was not easy to determine. The main excavation took place some way from the site of the present ritual centre and the likely location of the early church. Enclosure ditches were proposed but not substantiated and the thin stratification that developed on broken stone in clay made the definition of buildings very challenging.[191] Nevertheless, thanks to some skilled and determined excavation, structures were defined and a sequence deduced. It is presented here with modifications owed to Nicola Toop (Table 3.3).

The 5th/6th century phase (Hill I.1, I.2; Toop Phase 1) consisted of a number of huts with evidence for cultivation and craftsmen, working glass and metal, with imported Mediterranean pottery. The early site is not overtly monastic or Christian in material terms. The *Latinus* stone, an inscription reworked in this period on a prehistoric standing stone, has been interpreted as commemorating a local leader with Roman aspirations (Chapter 5, p. 501). In the 7th century (Hill I.3; Toop Phase 1) there is some evidence that the site is being ritualised, with the arrival of a cemetery and three circular shrines.[192] Some Christian ideas are also being aired: to this century belong the later inscribed stones with ecclesiastical connotations

Table 3.3 The Whithorn phasing

Period	Buildings	Assemblage	Interpretation (Hill)	Interpretation (Toop)
6th century I/1 Before 550 I/2 550–600	Oval enclosure Small rectilinear stake-walled buildings Latinus stone	Plough pebbles, millstones Amphorae, Roman glass, claw beakers, smelting and smithying	'Monasterium'	1. Estate Centre or cemetery – settlement
7th century I/3 600–700	Oval enclosure, three successive shrines; stone-lined (Phase 2) and log coffin burials (Phase 3–4; Irish?) workshops	Glass working, metalworking	'Monasterium'	
8th century I/4, II 700–845	Guest quarters; oratories (before 800); 'unique' church (after 800); chapel with burials	8th/9th century coins, window glass, chest coffins; little evidence for manufacture or trade	Northumbrian monastery; burnt down	2. Northumbrian monastery; burnt down
10th century III 845–1000	Restored church and chapel; huts	Whithorn school of late sculpture; Comb making, spindle whorls	Monastic town	3. Secular town

(Toop 2005).

(the *Petrus* stone at Whithorn and the neighbouring Kirkmadrine stones) (Chapter 5, p. 501). This phase was published as an early monastery ('monasterium'), but taken together these findings approach more nearly to the model of the cemetery-settlement, as seen across the Irish Sea. It is not excluded that such settlements provided the residential template for an early monastic community, but without evidence for community life, or at least for Christianity, there is risk of retro-reasoning from what came later.

The second phase, beginning in the late 7th or early 8th century, sees the elements of a Northumbrian monastery transported several hundred miles to the west (Hill II; Toop Phase 2). The excavation area lay outside the precinct of the present (and perhaps the earlier) church, but the excavated rectilinear structures echo those at Jarrow and suggested an interpretation of end-to-end chapels or oratories and halls. This site was burnt down at a moment dated by coins to c. 845 AD. It quickly recovered: in a third phase (Hill III; Toop 3), the site was redeveloped with a new church and a plethora of huts. A minster church is supposed, and a continuation of ecclesiastical influence and authority is implied by the stone monuments of the Whithorn School found in the vicinity.[193] The assemblage suggests continued contact with Anglian (stycas), Anglo-Scandinavian (combs), Irish (souterrain ware) and, from the 10th century, Norse Viking culture (steatite bowl, ring money).[194] The revived site was commercially active, and its mixed urban and monastic signals align with those of the trading monasteries then active across the Irish Sea (p. 282). In sum, the evidence from Whithorn, a site with very difficult stratigraphy, can be read as showing an emphasis on lordship in the 5th/7th century, monasticism in the 7th/9th century and a more mercantile profile in the 9th/10th.

Northumbria

Thanks in part to the Venerable Bede and in part to the researches of Rosemary Cramp, the monastic identity is more sharply defined in Northumbria than anywhere else. Bede explains what a monastery in the 8th century was expected to be and lists a large number of foundations, singling out certain abbots for special praise (Table 3.4). According to this list, the movement arose in the 640s in the reign of Oswiu and accelerated in influence in the 680s in the reign of Ecgfrith. Archaeologically, the development of the Northumbrian monastic movement can be divided into two: a foundation phase from the late 7th century and an expansion phase from c. 750, the latter most evident from the advance of the 'Victory Crosses' (Chapter 5, p. 472).

At **Hartlepool** an establishment founded c. 646 was taken over and reorganised by the Abbess Hild in 649. The site is a natural harbour, with a promontory on its northern side (Figure 3.72). Marshy plants and signs of inundation show it to have been almost an island in the 7th century. Traces of a prehistoric predecessor were elusive, but there may have been a Roman signal station at the high point.[195] Three main sites have been examined on the promontory, within what continues as a living town: *Cross Close* on the seafront, encountered during building operations in the 19th century, was the primary focus, where 10 name slabs were recovered in unscientific conditions, loosely associated with skeletons resting on pillow stones and aligned north-south. Men and women are named in Latin and runic letters, confirming that this was an Anglian initiative of the 7th century (Chapter 5, p. 528). A second cemetery lay further inland at *Church Walk*, south of the present church of St Hilda. Here were buried men, women and children; a cist grave indicated some presence of a British tradition.[196] North of the church, at *Church Close* and *Lumley Street*, a group of excavations contacted a residential area (Figure 3.73). Some 28 small rectangular buildings were defined,

Table 3.4 List of monastic foundations recorded in Northumbria[197]

Oswiu 642–70
Hartlepool c. 646 (HE iv, 23)
Old Melrose c. 650 (VCB 6, HE iii, 26 & iv 27)
Tynemouth pre-651 (VCB 3)
Wall pre-653 (HE iii 21)
Gateshead pre-654 (HE iii 21)
Whitby 657 (HE iii, 24)
Lastingham 659 (HE iii 23)
Gilling late 650s (HE iii, 24)
Ripon c. 660 (VW 8, HE v, 19)
Coldingham pre-664 (VCB 10, HE iv 19)
12 unnamed 10-hide royal foundations created by Oswiu after his victory over Penda at the Winwaed in 655
Ecgfrith 670–685
Hexham 672–8 (VW 22, HE iv, 12)
Wearmouth 674 (HA4)
Jarrow 681 [685?] (HA 4)
Hackness c. 680 (HE IV.23)
Abercorn 682 (HE IV.26)

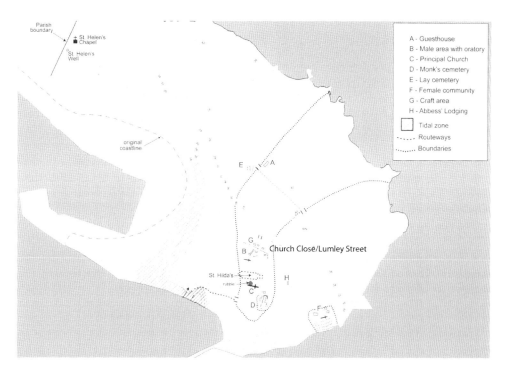

Figure 3.72 Hartlepool (Co Durham). Plan of the monastic settlement with interpretation.

(Daniels 2007, Fig 8.12; image courtesy of Tees Archaeology)

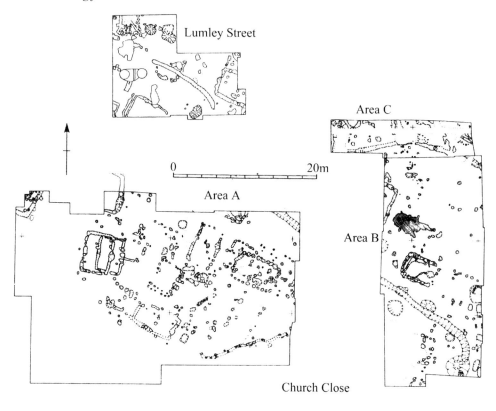

Lumley Street

Area C

0   20m

Area A

Area B

Church Close

Figure 3.73 Hartlepool. Buildings excavated at Church Close and Lumley Street.
(Daniels 1999, Fig 9.2; image courtesy of Tees Archaeology)

with an average of 4.4 × 2.7 m in plan and interpreted as cells serving the monastery. They were not directly dated but appear to follow an architectural sequence of earth-fast post, post-in-trench and timber frame on stone footings consistent with 7th/8th century English practice.[198] Evidence for metalworking included a mould of the symbol of St Luke the Evangelist.[199] A zonation can be proposed in which the ritual area in south was enlarged to enclose a residential and workshop area in the north.

The north-south burials, the cist grave and the family composition of the main cemetery lend Hartlepool a multicultural air, as befits the earliest documented monastery in Northumbria. British collaboration and un-ascetic regulation seem likely in this pioneering phase. But there is no doubt about its Anglian branding, the first of many signs that in Northumbria it is the English who take the lead in promoting its monastic movement.[200]

Wearmouth and Jarrow

The monasteries at **Wearmouth** (on the Wear) and **Jarrow** (on the Tyne) were founded 10 years apart, Wearmouth by the widely travelled nobleman Biscop Baducing in 673 and Jarrow by the equally enterprising Benedict Biscop in 682. Both were granted 40 and 70 hides respectively by the Northumbrian king (Ecgfrith) of land lying at the mouth of estuaries. There was no good evidence for prehistoric or Roman predecessors at either site, and both the new developments were planned *de novo* with a rectilinear layout, reflecting the form of a Roman villa.[201] To build Wearmouth, masons and glaziers were brought in from Gaul, while the later Jarrow was built by 22 Northumbrian monks with no hint of foreign craftsmen.[202]

Jarrow comprised two stone churches built end to end, with two large stone halls (A and B) also end to end and parallel to the south. Further south were Building D and a contiguous building, their joint plan reflecting the curve of the River Don leading to the Tyne (Figure 3.74). Building A was expertly constructed with walls of mortared ashlar on foundations of cobbles in clay, a floor of *opus signinum*, glazed windows and a roof of stone slabs with lead flashing.[203] An annexe was later added to the south. A polygonal column set into the floor was probably intended to support a lectern where readings were made (p. 525). Building B was also stone-built and glazed; it had a main hall space with a clay floor and an eastern annex, including a lobby with an *opus signinum* floor (Figure 3.75). These high-status buildings, resembling the halls of Yeavering reworked in stone, were interpreted as a refectory with an added kitchen and a dormitory above (Building A) and a multi-purpose hall, also with a dormitory above and a private cell at the east end (Building B). The Building

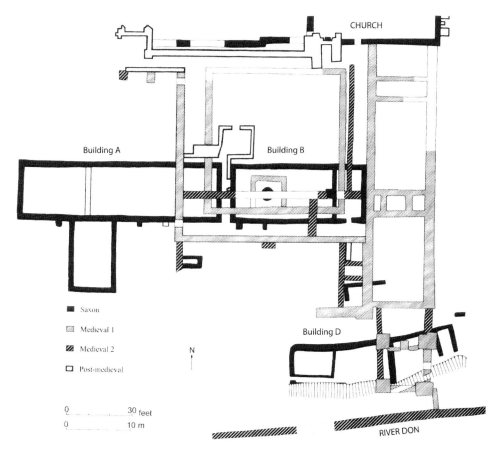

Figure 3.74 Jarrow (Tyne and Wear), monastic site. The main features of the Formative period monastery (in black) overlaid (in grey) by the walls of its medieval successor.

(Cramp 2005, Fig 22.5; © R. Cramp, drawing by L. Bosveld)

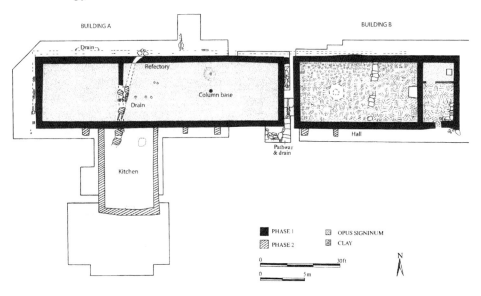

Figure 3.75 Jarrow: Building A (left) and Building B (right), plan and interpretation.
(Cramp 2005, Fig 16.37; © R. Cramp, drawing by N. Emery)

D suite was constructed on a platform cut into the slope overlooking the river Don. The face of the cut through the slope was revetted with large square blocks, perhaps obtained from a Roman site, and the building, which was found in a fragmentary state, was defined by dry stone slabs and a beaten clay floor, with some stone flagging. It may have been timber-framed. Finds suggested a domestic function, and the building was interpreted as a guest house. The excavation was not central to middens or refuse deposits, but the monks exploited cattle, sheep and pigs, of which sheep were the most important, together with horse, dog and cat (seen as 'working animals'), and they had access to roe deer, salmonidae (salmon and trout) and shellfish.[204]

Wearmouth and Jarrow had a strong Roman air and initiated a villa-like layout which pre-echoed the plan adopted by the Carolingian re-Romanisation two centuries later, as exemplified in the St Gall plan[205] (Figure 3.76). The monastic phase was ended by Viking raids, active from 794.[206] In the later 9th century, Building D and its adjacent riverside building and an area south of Building A showed evidence for a new phase of use, where items of dress were dropped or made and crucibles were used to melt glass and lead.[207] While the detailed post-use of the Anglian site was obscured by the construction of the medieval monastery, it is not excluded that Jarrow's window glass and lead flashing were being recycled for the benefit of more secular clients of the 9th century and later.

Materiality of monasticism in north Britain

It is clear from these archaeological examples that there were slightly different approaches to monastic planning in the north and west, as opposed to Northumbria. The curvilinear forms of the western enclosures refer to prehistoric roots, and there is a case for seeing monasteries as a special development of the cemetery-settlement, as seen in Ireland (p. 280) and as

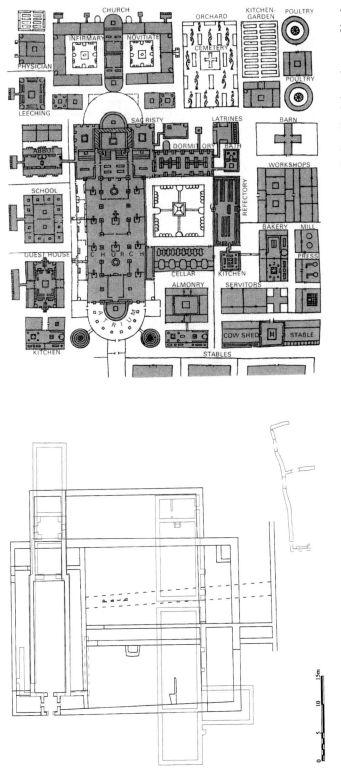

Figure 3.76 The quadrilateral plans of Monkwearmouth and Jarrow overlaid, with (right) an image of the 9th-century St Gall plan. North is at the top of both images.

(Cramp 2005, Fig 24.3; © R. Cramp, drawing by A. MacMahon; St Gall plan: Porcher 1970, 342)

proposed at Inchmarnock and Portmahomack (Figure 3.77). By contrast, those of Northumbria adopted a Roman template, perhaps derived from survivals in the Midlands of Britannia or imported with jobbing masons or in the form of travellers' notes from visits to Rome, or from learned engagement with the former empire. Both territories held in common a monastic package that combined a church, monumental sculpture, a cemetery, a range of crafts (of which metalworking is the most easily detected), a residential area and a farm. Of the attributes of the package, some are obvious imports, like the Christian story itself and its Mediterranean iconography, some are home-grown, like burial, and some are mixtures of the two, like church buildings, stone carving, metalworking and the making of manuscripts. Stone carving and burial belong to changing cultural theatres of such importance that they will be visited separately (in Chapters 4 and 5).

Apart from the surviving fabric at Jarrow, Wearmouth and Escomb, churches constructed before 1100 remain to be discovered. O'Carragáin's study of contemporary Ireland offers exemplars, but at the same time suggests that any imported template will be modified by regional preferences.[208] Monasteries did not introduce bronze casting into Britain, nor did they have exclusive use of metalworking, but they did host a particularly sophisticated version of the craft. What survives are crucibles, moulds, cuppelation dishes for separating silver from lead, tongs and a variety of whetstones for finishing copper alloy objects, and occasionally a touchstone for assaying gold. At Portmahomack, studs also survived, which together with the moulds gave a strong indication of what was being made: objects to serve the church, such as chalices, patens and reliquaries (Chapter 2, 113).[209] The

Figure 3.77 The monastery at Nendrum on Strangford lough, Northern Ireland: in the centre of the picture is the settlement on its promontory with its two concentric enclosures. At the left of the picture is an inlet, with the dam of the pond of the tide mill.

(McErlean and Crothers 2007, Fig 12.9E; with author's permission)

metalworkers there were housed in their own symmetrical bag-shaped building, and the quantities of metalwork, vellum and sculpture being produced suggest that this was a centre of production, perhaps to equip later foundations in the area with the essential tool kit of a codex, carved stone and sacred vessels.[210] Glass for windows was also in circulation in the 8th/9th century, but its use was probably not exclusive to monasteries or churches.[211]

Writing, especially the writing of Latin, is an undoubted import, although stones inscribed in both Latin and ogham were erected in the British areas of Wales, the Scottish borders and the south-west between the 5th and 7th centuries (see Chapter 5). At Hartlepool, on the threshold of Anglicised monasticism, slabs inscribed in both Latin and runes marked the early graves. Direct evidence for literacy is charmingly offered at Inchmarnock before 800, where children were taught to write on slates and encouraged to draw, famously recording a Viking raid and the possible theft of a reliquary.

The survival of codices dating (stylistically) to the 7th and 8th century, such as the Gospels at Durham (of c. 650) and the Cassiodorus, also at Durham (725–750), is proof that illuminated Gospel books of unparalleled beauty were produced in monastic settlements from their earliest days.[212] Better-appointed scriptoria were probably available at Lindisfarne, where the famous Gospels were produced in c. 698.[213] At Jarrow, three giant pandects containing the Old Testament and the New were prepared around 700, perhaps in Building A or B (see Chapter 5, p. 580).[214]

Horizontal mills also form part of the monastic package in the north, but the best example to date is in Ireland, the tide mill at Nendrum[215] (Figure 3.77). The water was trapped in a pool from a rising tide and released through a drilled oak penstock which played a jet of water onto the paddles of a horizontal wheel (Figure 3.78). The wheel turned the upper of two millstones against a static lower stone to grind the grain into flour. Such an investment implies a wide catchment, and no doubt it was seen as a way in which the monastery served a wider community. In the English regions, by contrast, the mills that have been found operated within royal estate centres, at Offa's Tamworth or Old Windsor.[216]

The use of standard measures and ratios has been detected at Portmahomack, where the plan of S1 was proposed as using a standard length of 12.5 modern inches and the bays set out in ratios of the Golden number (1.613). Although apparently anachronistic, since the Fibonacci series that tends to this number was not discovered until the 13th century, the ratio does exist in nature, for example in the increasing radii of a spiral shell.[217] The dimensions employed in monastic buildings and in carpet pages of manuscripts and on brooches are also candidates for the use of standard measures and ratios with esoteric meanings.[218] This kind of metrology might have had either a local or an overseas origin.

Monastic sites of the northern kind are expected to be enclosed with a bank and ditch, as seen at Iona, Hoddom and Portmahomack. In addition, a hinterland or *termon* may be marked out by monuments to provide bounds to their estates. In Ireland both shrine and standing cross or ogham stones were used. On Innismurray, altars (*leachta*) were used to provide the stages of perambulation (p. 565). Prayers for protection and good fortune would be said at each one as an act of both piety and insurance. On Tarbat Ness, the monastery at Portmahomack was one of four sites marked by giant cross slabs looking out to sea, which marked the edge of the monastic estate, the landing places and probably sites for periodic procession in the Irish manner. Together, the material attributes amount to a distinctive package, with the mix of the local and the exotic creating a strongly bonded structure (Figure 3.79).

However, the monumental signals, though necessary to the monastic movement, were not sufficient. Like other settlements, monastic sites needed an economic strategy, and the

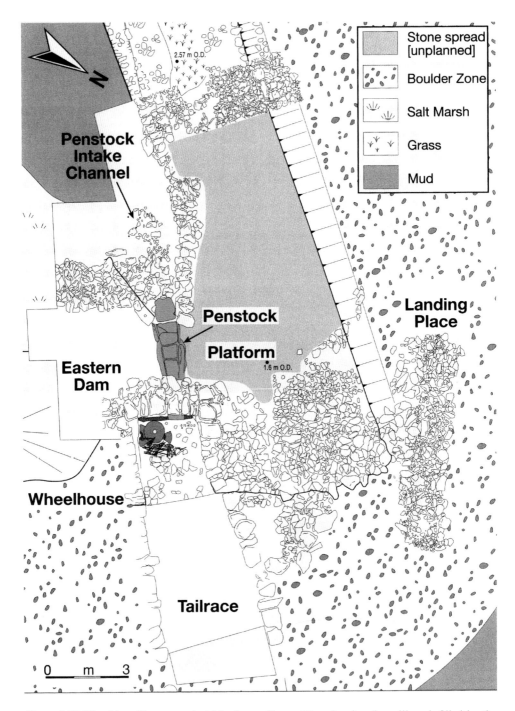

Figure 3.78 The tide mill excavated at Nendrum. Above: Plan showing the millpond, filled by the
tide (top left), the penstock that focuses the water into a jet that plays on the horizontal
paddlewheel, and the tailrace that evacuates the water.

(McErlean and Crothers 2007, Fig 1.6, 3.1b, 7.1; with author's permission)

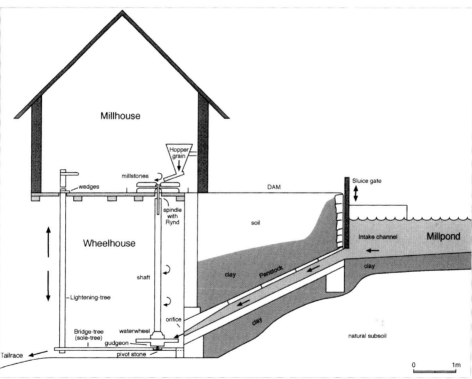

Figure 3.78 B: The wheel-pit with a millstone in situ (top) and cutaway side view of a model showing how the wheel-stones are driven (bottom).

(McErlean and Crothers 2007, Fig 1.6, 7.1; with author's permission)

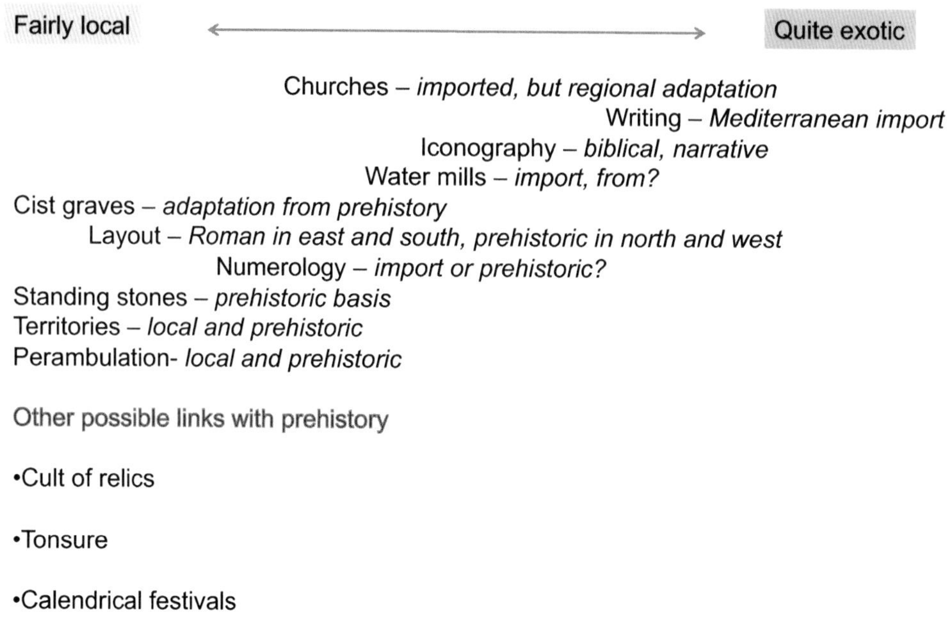

Fairly local ⟵————————————————————⟶ Quite exotic

Churches – *imported, but regional adaptation*
Writing – *Mediterranean import*
Iconography – *biblical, narrative*
Water mills – *import, from?*
Cist graves – *adaptation from prehistory*
Layout – *Roman in east and south, prehistoric in north and west*
Numerology – *import or prehistoric?*
Standing stones – *prehistoric basis*
Territories – *local and prehistoric*
Perambulation- *local and prehistoric*

Other possible links with prehistory

•Cult of relics

•Tonsure

•Calendrical festivals

Figure 3.79 Monastic materiality.
(Author)

evidence so far, from faunal remains and stable isotopes, is that theirs was an economy based on cattle (pp. 19, 282). The monastic settlement was initiated with a gift of land (as Jarrow and Wearmouth), and it is a justifiable leap in the imagination to suppose that the gift included a herd of cows. This is a self-enlarging resource, particularly if the primary consumption was of dairy products rather than beef. However, as the herd increased in size, so did the need for grazing, so that the monastic estate, if successful, would expand. It might do this by increasing its holding, as at Portmahomack, or by founding daughter-houses and so enlarging the territory over which the monastic movement held sway. A case can be made that the capital assets represented by cattle were stored in the form of hides, which could serve as a unit of currency as well as a commodity with numerous practical applications (e.g. clothing, shields, chariots and boats). The *hide* was a unit of wealth and a measurement of productive land from the 7th century and provided liquidity for the early Scottish burghs in the 12th century. Within the ethos of their regime, monasteries had other ways of attracting wealth: endowment ensured the eventual survival of the donor's soul, and paying for a blessing on marriage, burial, a long journey or success in war was advisable. It is less likely that manufacturing output created wealth, since it appears to have been dedicated to stone buildings and sculpture, church plate, glass windows and holy books – an output better fitted to founding new monasteries than the marketplace. Nevertheless, these crafts did require the import of other resources: dyes for manuscripts, glass cullet, copper, silver and gold, for example. If not gifted for the good of the soul of the donor, these would be acquired by purchase with food or hides from the monastic farm. The monastery therefore operated a 'salvation industry' in which divine protection and favourable futures were purchased with gifts ranging from a cheese to an estate. In this it could be accounted a sophisticated adaptation of prehistoric and Roman votive systems.[219]

A contrast between the monastic initiatives in Northumbria and the rest of northern Britain is evident. In the British regions, the movement grew in the deep soil of prehistoric practice to which Christianity had been added without making a revolutionary impact on the monumental landscape or relying on imports from Rome. But the changes of the late 7th century at least demanded an awareness that the new ideological allegiance was no longer to be ancestral and local but intellectual and universal. For its part, Northumbria was by this time heavily Anglicised, at least at aristocratic levels, and the English began their new deal with a characteristic refusal to learn anything from the natives and marched forward with a Romanising agenda to the fore. This was expressed in material culture as well as polemic. It is perhaps surprising that the differences, surfacing as a dogmatic dispute at the Synod of Whitby in 664, were quickly resolved and that the two sides combined to generate the first triumph of insular synergy. Much of the credit should perhaps go to Oswiu, the long-reigning Northumbrian leader, who could understand the merits of cooperation in what had become a European issue. But some role had also been played, so to speak, under the counterpane: the exiling of unwanted heirs to foreign parts meant that English princes in waiting learned to understand the language, traditions and attitudes of their neighbours at first hand, in the only effective way there is to reduce ethnic tension and weave peace.[220]

East and south – magnate farms, markets and wics

The 200 years from the later 7th century to the later 9th are the most fundamental for the development of settlement, as for much else in the English region of Britain. The village becomes a gathering of bounded farmsteads with trackways, as it had some years earlier on the continent and indeed in later Roman Britain. There are occasional signs of a larger building set apart, assumed on the continent to be a sign of hierarchy, a 'leader farm' or magnate farm, but here we shall have to argue the case that they are not communal.[221] In addition to the magnate farm, a series of specialist settlements emerge during the period, somewhat distracted by the roles of kingship, Christian congregation and commerce that are now documented. Thus, there is an expectation of rural 'palaces', the *villa regalis*, of monasteries and of trading places (*wics*), some of which are mentioned by the contemporary commentator, Bede, even if his first-hand knowledge was largely confined to Northumbria. There is also an expectation of monasteries or ecclesiastical settlements of some kind called in this region by the Anglo-Saxon abbreviation of *minster*. We shall need to address the question of how comparable such places were to the northern monasteries just reviewed. Archaeologists and historians have naturally striven to bend the sites we have into the service of these categories, but except in the few places that are as having a suggestive placename (Ipswich, Hamwih) England (i.e. Southumbria) has very little to offer that is certain: no central place that resembles Tissø, no monastic settlement that can hold a candle to Nendrum or Portmahomack.

We rejoin the road towards increasingly wealthy lordship where we left it after Bloodmoor Hill (p. 204). The process was well illustrated at Yarnton, where a 'grand hall' appeared in the 8th century and a more ordered and enclosed estate centre in the 9th (p. 167). Here we rewind back into the 7th century to observe the nucleation of a settlement in Hampshire (Chalton) and the development of the form into that of a magnate farm at nearby Cowdery's Down.

The value of the site at **Chalton** is that it represents a new village of the 7th century. Standing on the top of Church Down, a whaleback ridge on the Sussex/Hampshire border, the village was discovered in 1966 by Barry Cunliffe and the local landowner, John Budden. It was manifested on the surface of the ploughed field in the form of grass-tempered pottery of a type previously seen in the Porchester excavations and there dated 5th–8th century. The sherds, together with loom weights, iron slag and two glass beads, were scattered over some 6 ha.[222]

Excavations by Peter Addyman for the University of Southampton took place in 1971–72. A survey was carried out with a proton gradiometer, but most anomalies proved to be natural. An area of about 0.5 ha was stripped and the surface of the chalk brushed with churn brushes and watered to bring out the dark patches of the features (Figure 3.80). Over 50 rectangular

Figure 3.80 Chalton (Hampshire). Aerial photograph of excavations in progress in 1972, looking south. Building AZ1 in the foreground.

(Photograph by Rescue 1974)

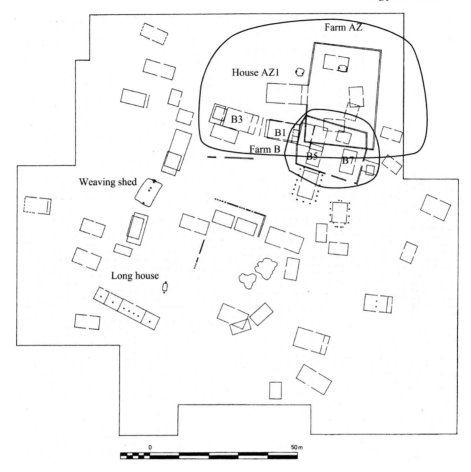

Figure 3.81 Chalton: rise of the magnate farm: *Farmstead B* (smaller circle) superseded by *Farmstead A* (larger circle).

(Champion 1977; with permission)

buildings arranged in a quadrilateral formation were excavated (Figure 3.81). The houses were mostly of post-hole construction (e.g. A20, Figure 3.6), two with buttresses on all sides (A10, A12). The point of departure appears to be a group of three buildings (B1, 2 and 3), the largest of them (B1) attached to an enclosure containing three other buildings set orthogonally to each other (B5, 6 and 7). B1 and B3 were replaced on the same footprints by A1 and A2/3, and the settlement thence expanded west and south with buildings on a similar alignment (WNW-ESE) set around a square (A4–20). In a third phase, building AZ1 was erected on a W-E alignment attached to its own enclosure, containing buildings AZ2 and AZ3. A single two-post SFB accompanied AZ1 on its northern side (Figure 3.82). AZ1 had a ground plan formed of continuous trenches that were demonstrated to have contained posts set side by side (Figure 3.83). The building had a central hearth area with stake holes suggesting a cowl, two opposed doorways with posts to the side on which to hang a door, an annex at the east end little more than 1.5 m wide, and a pair of slots at the west end perhaps intended to support stairs to the roof space. The enclosure was defined by a fence of vertical posts set alternately so as to anchor a barrier of horizontal planks (see Figure 3.83).[223]

Figure 3.82 Chalton: Building AZ1 under excavation.

(Author; photograph by Peter Addyman/T.J. Hurst)

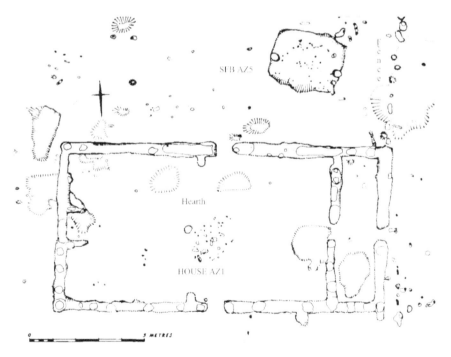

Figure 3.83 Chalton: Field drawing of AZ1 with its adjacent SFB (AZ5) and fence.

(Field record)

On the departure of Peter Addyman to York in 1973 the investigation remained in the care of the Department of Archaeology at the University of Southampton, which carried out further seasons of excavations in 1973–6 under the supervision of Tim Champion, extending the area to 2 ha and revealing an estimated additional 30 buildings. These continued the theme of houses aligned around a square or 'village green'. The new buildings included a longhouse (measuring 24.4 m × 5.1 m) subdivided into four rooms and a giant SFB, with no suspended floor but with annular loom weights stacked on the base; these together with timbers, wattle and daub had been preserved in a fire. The new excavator, an Iron Age specialist, was not impressed by the Chalton assemblage: 'With the exception of the sunken floored buildings and two small pits, the total volume of [finds from] all excavated features is less than that of two average Iron Age pits'.[224]

Nevertheless, the assemblage, when it is eventually published, promises to be of considerable value. It includes the grass-tempered pottery that led to the site's discovery, sandy hand-made pottery, wheel-turned pottery imported from France, animal bone, charred grain, metalworking debris, hammerscale, whetstones, fragments of lava querns, loom weights, spindle whorls, glass fragments, worked bone, combs, thread pickers, iron knives, an arrowhead and a variety of bronzes including pins, needles and small ornaments. Datable finds include flat-headed pins with parallels in the 7th century, a length of chain that had probably connected linked pins and a 7th-century hanging bowl escutcheon. There is a notable absence of material from the earlier (6th) or later (8th) centuries.[225] The impression is that the village had expanded in sight of two successive farmsteads (B and A) into a major complex probably dedicated to agricultural production, all this development taking place within the 7th century.

Also situated on the chalk of Wessex is the settlement at **Cowdery's Down**, a multi-period cropmark excavated in advance of housing development between 1978 and 1981. The pride of the findings was a series of rectangular timber buildings of the 6th–8th century (Period 4; Figure 3.84). Two enclosed planned farmsteads (Farmsteads 1 and 2) of post-hole buildings (Period 4A and 4B) were succeeded in Period 4C by nine buildings of Farmsteads 3 and 4, mainly post-in-trench, strung out along the ridge (C7–C15), one of them (C12) of notable size and advanced carpentry (Figure 3.85). The development of the site was chronicled by stratigraphy and spatial order, with valuable sequences seen at A1-B4-B5-C8 and A2-B6-C7.[226] Dating was hindered by an almost total lack of cultural material: half a kilo of coarse ware, most of it referring to phase 4C, and 'all that can be said for the date range of this pottery, based on form and fabric types, is that it is likely to lie between the early 6th and mid-8th century'.[227] Three samples for radiocarbon dating were taken from each of Buildings A2, C9 and C12. Calibrated dates for A2 centre in the early 6th century and for C12 in the late 7th/early 8th century. The samples were of oak, and the three dates from C9 ranging over 150 years suggests that old wood was involved.[228] The sophistication of the buildings tends to push the dates later, say late 6th for A, early 7th for B and late 7th/early 8th for C. There is no suggestion of a hiatus between these phases, although each constituted a planned and incremental rebuild: A1–3, B4–6, C7, 8,16 and C9, 10,11 formed successive courtyard farms. Fences in all three periods took the form of staggered posts supporting horizontal planks or wattle, as at Chalton.[229]

Understanding of the settlement was greatly enhanced by the well-preserved and expertly excavated details of the buildings themselves. The buildings of Farmstead 1 are post-in-hole with central doorways; A1 had doorposts, a narrow end room and two 'stair lobes', as Chalton AZ1. The Farmstead 2 buildings begin to use planks or pairs of planks rather than posts (B4).[230] In Farmstead 4, external posts (as C9, 12, 13) may imply the use

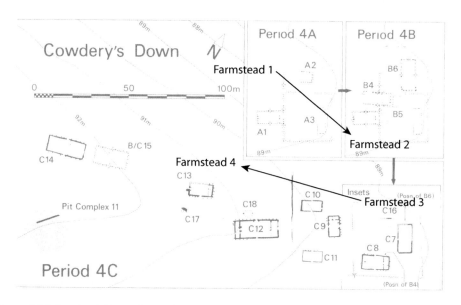

Figure 3.84 Cowdery's Down (Hampshire): development of the settlement towards the magnate farm (7th–8th century): Farmsteads 1–4.

(Millett and James 1983, Fig 27, with additions; courtesy of the author and Royal Archaeological Institute)

Figure 3.85 Cowdery's Down: the imposing timber frame building C12 of farmstead 4 with its raised floor.

(Millett and James 1983, Fig 70; courtesy of the author and Royal Archaeological Institute)

of crucks. In some of the other C group buildings (C9, 10, 14), the planks are set side by side in a trench. In Farmstead 3 and 4 (buildings C7, 8 and 12), the planks are staggered like a fence, and it was demonstrated that wattle panels ran between them.[231] This device means that a daub wall was clutched by offset vertical planks on either side. The appearance created inside and out would have been 'mock Tudor': rows of vertical oak studs separated by daub panels that were probably whitewashed. C12, the largest building at 22.1 × 8.8 m, had rooms at each end with arrangements of posts around their doorways that suggest 'stair lobes' leading to upper floors or galleries at either end.[232] At the northeast corner of C12, the foundation trench was found to have been incompletely backfilled at the time of construction and to have remained open until the building was destroyed by fire. This implied the existence of a suspended floor, as shown in the artist's drawing. The sophisticated carpentry of this reconstruction seems well justified by the evidence and could be extended to include the upper floor galleries and studding proposed earlier. In this sense, we are already in a medieval hall.[233]

In keeping with the epoch in which these buildings were brought vividly to light, special explanations were sought. Spiritual roles were proposed for some features: Building A1 had an annexe with a central pit, which has been suggested as having ritual airs.[234] Pit 6 outside one end of C13 contained a partly butchered and almost complete skeleton of an adult cow, thought unlikely to be coincidental and assigned 'some ritual function'.[235] More soberly, the settlement has some claim to be a 'magnate farm' in the Continental sense (p. 283) but (being in royalist England) has attracted the 'palace' epithet.[236] At the least, the excavator declares it 'not a normal village like Chalton' and holds C12 to be of sufficient grandeur to be used by a peripatetic aristocracy.[237] These are matters hard to judge without a more comprehensive assemblage.

The material culture might have been exiguous, but the story is consistent and signals the rewards and pretensions of increasing affluence. The settlement found at Cowdery's Down began as a farmstead, probably in the 6th century, that was enlarged in the 7th. In the later 7th century it began to adopt a more imposing presence, stringing out larger buildings along the skyline, C12 in particular having the trappings of high status; however, with its attendant shed (C18), it need be no more than what a wealthy landowner-farmer aspires to in the fertile home counties of the 7th century. These events, indicating the rising profile of lordship, took place while neighbouring farms, as at Chalton, emerged and declined.

The enclosure trend has been noted at other southern sites: West Fen Road, Ely (early 8th to mid-9th, eight enclosures along a trackway); Pennyland in Buckinghamshire (four enclosures and three droveways); Higham Ferrers, Northamptonshire (an idiosyncratic horseshoe-shaped enclosure, twice modified).[238] The current champion of enclosure is probably **Catholme** in the Trent Valley, where 10 contiguous 'farmstead zones' were defined surrounded by enclosure ditches and connected by trackways (Figure 3.86). The cropmarks were located by aerial photography on the gravels of the River Trent where it joins the Thame. Attempts to define the site by resistivity did not succeed, so the site was stripped, and an area of 3.4 ha was examined in a pioneering and revealing excavation between 1973 and 1980.[239] The formation of the deposit was studied in a series of sections at right angles along an 85 m stretch of the slope to the river, which showed the successive ploughing regimes.[240] There were 47 post-hole buildings and 18 SFBs (all two-post) defined by negative features; it was estimated that the top 30 cm of all features had been turned into ploughsoil. The sequence could be deduced from the spatial pattern, some stratigraphy and 19 calibrated radiocarbon dates, five before 680 and 14 between 680 and 900. The principal ditches that created the overall framework (D39, 40 and 47) were cut into a layer of alluvium

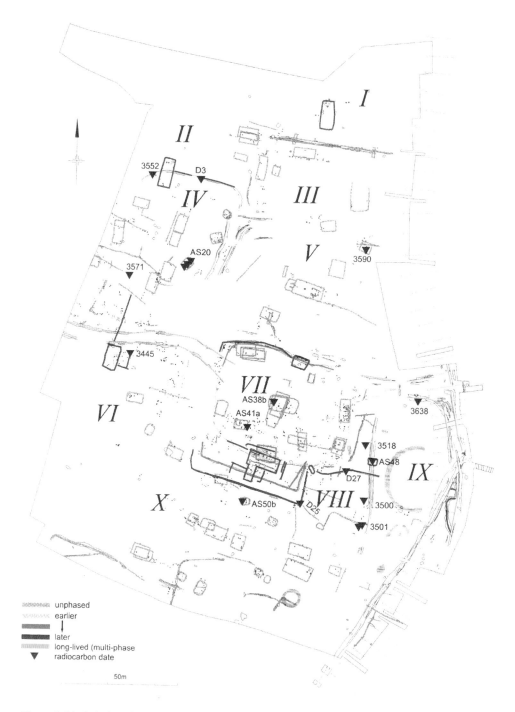

Figure 3.86 Catholme (Staffordshire) where the Rivers Trent, Mease and Thame meet: the village extends to 3.7 ha and takes the form of a cluster of enclosed farmsteads contained within a framework of tracks. It has been dated from the 7th to the 9th century (Fm 2).

(Losco-Bradley and Kingsley 2002, Fig 3.97; courtesy of Trent Peak Archaeology)

that buried the early features. For this reason the authors of the final report place Catholme in the 7th to 9th century (our Fm 2).

Catholme has the repertoire of post-hole and post-in-trench houses and SFBs seen further south at Bloodmoor Hill and further north at West Heslerton, and its combination of enclosures and trackways continue the themes seen at Chalton, Cowdery's Down and Yarnton.[241] The excavated size, at 150 × 250 m, is comparable with the central enclosures at Yarnton, and although settlement at Catholme no doubt continued along the terrace, it seems to provide a representative excerpt of the landscape. The farmstead at zone IV was bounded by ditches D3, D7 and D10 and served by trackways or droveways T2 and T3. At its centre was the long building AS15, constructed of posts or staves in holes at its south end and in trenches at is north end. Adjacent were two SFBs containing evidence for weaving with the loom standing on the base of the pit: in AS16 there were loom weights and patches of unburnt clay along the north side and stake holes along the south; the same pattern was seen in the neighbouring AS20. This would appear to be a large farmstead. A neighbouring long-lived enclosure is evident in zone VII, bounded by ditches D20 and D21 and served by trackways T4 from inland and T5 to the river. Within this enclosure there are many examples of buildings replacing each other on the same footprint (AS35, AS47 and the central AS38). There is a ribbon of sheds to the south that may be connected. In its latest phase, this farmstead sees a development of a new centre on its south side bounded by ditches D24 and 25. It contained the unusual building AS43, which resembles a large barn with an orthogonal annex and probably represents a new focus of the working area.[242] Other farmsteads are centred at zones III, IV and X, with appropriate banks and droveways, but the survival of cultural or datable material was insufficient to place them in a sequence, and they may have all been contemporary for a time. We do not have the strong environmental sequence or bold structural phasing of Yarnton, but similar developments may have been afoot. Catholme demonstrates that by the 7th–9th century the English style of high productive agriculture had reached the Midlands, and it is legitimate to claim comparable indications of rising status for the Trent valley, as for the Thames.[243]

The level of affluence that had been attained by English farming estates in the 8th century is also revealed by settlements at Flixborough and Brandon. Both have been claimed as monastic but whoever was the local driving force, the distinction of these sites lies in their high degree of preservation. In the case of Flixborough, rescue excavation chanced upon a major 7th–9th century dump; Brandon, of similar date, was more fortunate in revealing the buildings of a probable estate centre.

Flixborough is situated on the south side of the Humber and the east side of the River Trent on a belt of wind-blown sand, which had also buried and preserved the archaeological strata to a depth of up to 2 m. After the site had been exposed in a sand quarry and trial trenched, the sand overburden was removed by machine and excavation was conducted by hand between 1989 and 1991; additional surveys continued until 1995.[244] Parts of 40 buildings were defined in seven periods, of which the most significant were Periods 3–6 (8th to 10th century; summarised in Table 3.5). In Periods 3 and 4 two rows of modest buildings end to end stood either side of a shallow depression in which there had accumulated an enormous amount of refuse. Building 1A was built on a gravel platform and associated with six graves, but in general the buildings are not grand in any period, and the sequence of dumps surely refer to estate centres that lay elsewhere. A major change of land use in the late 9th/early 10th century (Period 5) saw the site cleared and levelled and the previous dump in the hollow built over with peremptory structures, including possible granaries and ovens. Between the early and mid-10th century (Period 6) these were demolished and superseded by two larger

Table 3.5 Flixborough summary

Period	Date	Interpretation	Artefacts	Fauna
1 & 2	7th century	Unidentified		
3	8th century	High status consumption at magnate centre International supply	Imported glass vessels	Cattle (imported?) Game birds and mammals, dolphins
4	early – mid-9th century	Production – for monastery [or elite centre] Regional supply	Iron, wood, leather, textiles, decorated dress accessories, styli, inscription, Ipswich ware Stycas, coins	Sheep, calves
5	mid- to late 9th century	Site clearance followed by low level of production No trade		
6	10th century	Production for elite centre Regional trade	Iron smelting and smithing Woodworking tools (boat building?) Transactions in weights; lead weights	Cattle, game, dolphins

buildings (B7, 12) which produced a set of woodworking tools, evidence for iron smelting and smithing and weights for trading.[245] The quantity and variety of the stratified material culture recovered at Flixborough provided evidence for a vivid sequence of use by communities of high-status settlement in the vicinity, broadly attributed to lordly estates (Period 3), a monastery (Period 4) or commercial activity (Period 6).

In Period 3, the verdict is that the site expressed 'feasting, hunting and conspicuous consumption'. Hunted animals included roe deer and hare, and cranes, wild geese, duck, black grouse; dolphin was thought to be valued as a contribution to elite feasting (rather than for its oil). In this period 'there is nothing to suggest the necessity for a monastic element on the site'.[246] The monastic attributes are assigned to Period 4, where there were 27 styli made of iron, copper alloy and silver, a silver gilt ring with the letters A to L around its band and a lead plaque inscribed with a cross followed by seven names in Old English, males Ealdwine, Ealdhere, Eadwine, Eanbeorht and Eadhaeth, with female names Aethlegyth and Aethelwine.[247] However, while the middens of Period 4 produced styli, they also contained the largest quantities of highly decorated 8th/9th-century dress accessories and fine quality textiles. There was a lunular knife, but here interpreted as for leather working.[248] There was no carved stone, no argument for vellum manufacture and no production of metal objects relating to Christian ceremony. The monastic interpretation appears to rest mainly on the styli and inscriptions, with some inferential associations.[249]

It may be that the main function of the excavated settlement zone was to provide agricultural and industrial services to a neighbouring estate centre through the 8th–10th centuries and that its activities reflected its fluctuating fortunes at one remove. Whether that estate was in the hands of the clerics or the laity depends on our current sensitivity to the spiritual significance of certain artefacts. It is not excluded that a monastic community was active in the neighbourhood, although a *floruit* in the mid-9th century would be unusual, and without the site itself it is hard to judge. Flixborough's reputation as a measure of especially high status may depend on the prodigal discards encountered in what was essentially an early English landfill site. This fortunate discovery may one day to be seen as an exceptional survival of an unexceptional estate, comparable to the less well-endowed Catholme, Bloodmoor Hill and Yarnton. Following the excavations at Jarrow, Portmahomack, Inchmarnock and Nendrum, it is clear that none of these southern sites conform to what is meant by a monastery in the regions of Britain north of the Humber and west of the Pennines. Indeed, the principal author of the report finds his most convincing parallels with secular aristocratic centres in western and central Europe.[250]

The site at **Brandon** ('Staunch Meadow') lies on the edge of the Fenland in Suffolk on a raised island of wind-blown sand (Figure 3.87). Middle Saxon pottery from molehills indicated the promise of the site, and the find by a metal-detectorist of a gold plaque with an image of St John the Evangelist raised expectations of a monastery. The area of 1.2 ha that was excavated in 1979–1988 (to make way for a sports field) coincided with the greater part of a 7th–9th century settlement; its medieval successor lay further east. The summary of the report tells us that the excavations revealed 35 post-hole buildings, some with timber still present, two cemeteries, two churches, a wooden bridge, evidence for textile dyeing and bleaching, a smithy and a bakery, with 20 Anglo-Saxon coins, numerous bronze and gilt bronze pins, window and vessel glass and 100 bone objects (Figure 3.88).[251] Evidence for literacy comprised runic inscriptions on a knife handle, silver tweezers and the back of an oval headed gilded silver pin, together with the Latin inscription of St John, three copper-alloy styli and fragments of eight glass inkwells and an antler inkhorn.

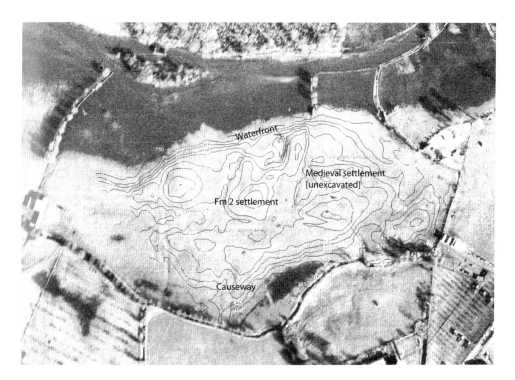

Figure 3.87 Brandon, Staunch Meadow (Suffolk), looking north during winter flooding, showing the areas of occupation.

(Tester et al. 2014, Plate 1.3; courtesy of Suffolk Archaeological Service © Suffolk County Council)

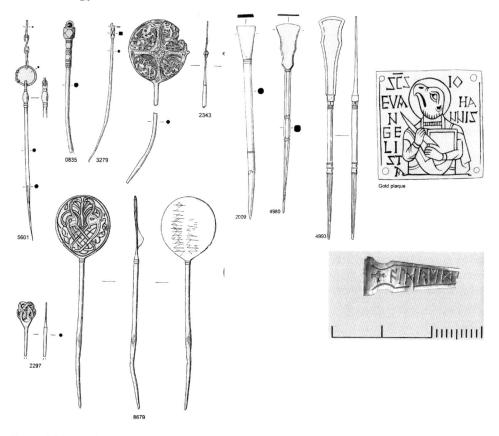

Figure 3.88 Brandon: styli, dress pins, gold book plaque with symbol of St John (stray find) and silver tweezers with runic inscription.

(Tester et al. 2014, Fig 8.16, 8.7, Plate 8.10; courtesy of Suffolk Archaeological Service © Suffolk County Council)

Although earthworks were visible, in the first year of the investigation, the site was stripped by machine 'to the natural subsoil' on the assumption that only negative features would survive. The number of finds that ended up on the spoil heaps led in subsequent years to a more appropriate strategy in which the turf, topsoil and subsoil were removed by hand down to the surface of the natural sand.[252] The finds distribution maps that were then possible produced a convincing picture of midden heaps that had contained the bulk of the rubbish, especially of the later periods, within the north-east part of the excavated area. The distribution maps also offered some trends of association: Ipswich ware in the area next to the waterfront, horse bone in the area of the halls, glass, slag, lead and tiles on the waterfront. The iron slag and tools were concentrated at the north (waterfront) end and the cattle bone at the area of the supposed churches.[253] Twenty-seven radiocarbon dates were refined by Bayesian analysis, the *a priori* knowledge in this case being supplied by the date of coins and other objects, stratigraphy and dendrochronology of timbers. The resulting posterior density estimates propose the settlement beginning after 680 and ending before 890.[254]

The published synthesis strives to show that Brandon was a monastery or minster. This is by no means self-evident, whichever definitions are applied. The earliest development probably comprised two or three 7th-century farmsteads within ditched enclosures, approached from the south via a trackway (Phase 1). A major reorganisation followed in the early to mid-8th century (Phase 2.1, Figure 3.89A). A ditched area to the south-west contained four post-hole buildings, aligned or orthogonal (2926, 2925, 1096, 1094), delineated by ditches 0681 and 8143. Unfortunately, this lay outside the zone served by the finds distribution map, but a sample area over buildings 1094 and 1096 showed a concentration of animal bone, Ipswich ware, slag and fired clay, with evidence for cattle urinating. Finds recovered from features in the area included burnt malt grist, a horseshoe and a fragment of vitrified hearth lining. These might be considered diagnostic of a farm. To the north of this enclosure was a building (8139) containing an oven at its north end and designated as a bakery. To the east of the enclosure was a group of two post-hole houses and a hall (7098) running east-west with an annex at each end (designated as a 'church'). To its south was a cemetery, completely excavated, with graves running W-E and SW-NE. On the south side, a causeway gave access to the 'island' represented by the raised hump of the site, surrounded by land prone to flooding.[255]

Phase 2.2 is dated from the middle of the 8th century into the 9th and represents an enlargement of activity, particularly in the form of an industrial or workshop zone next to the waterfront on the north side (Figure 3.89B). Here were numerous small post-hole buildings, including the continuation of the bakery and a smithy (4491). Their alignment suggests a planned facility, and the area (well served by the distribution mapping) was noted for an abundance of Ipswich Ware, glass, copper objects, pins, window glass, slag and iron tools.[256] There was also a partially excavated cemetery (Cemetery 2). To the south of this workshop area was a row of three parallel houses (0734, 7500, 8892) built wholly or partly post-in-trench, all with hearths and on a north-south alignment. They are separated by a ditch (8135) from the W-E building (7098), the 'church' of the previous phase, itself now replaced by a rectangular W-E building with no annexes (8851). This successor building was also designated as a 'church' by the authors of the report.[257] A row of other buildings stands further east, including one (1391) designated as a stable. This is the area richest in horse bones.[258] The south-west area was also reordered. The previous boundary ditch has gone, and a post-hole building, 11.5 × 5.75 (2923), is surrounded by its own enclosure, while a long building (1095; 18 × 4.4 m), perhaps a barn, has superseded 1094 and 1096.

During its long gestation after the investigations had ended, Brandon had been fancied as a monastic site, but now that the report has appeared it begins to conform more closely to the model of the farmstead clusters of increasing affluence seen at Cowdery's Down, Bloodmoor, Yarnton and Catholme, its additional assets being the industrial area and the large number of finds. The identification of the site as monastic depends on certain associations and analogies. The Phase 2.1 building (7098) is argued to be a church on the grounds that it looks high status and is adjacent to a cemetery (Figure 3.90). The case for this identification was thought to be strengthened by the burial of a horse within, or in a pit beneath, the post-pit for the door of the eastern annex.[259] The building is high status in that it resembles hall A1b at Yeavering, but the graves are not consistently aligned with it, and cemeteries can be present in these estate centres (as at Bloodmoor Hill) without presuming that an adjacent building is a church. Its successor is even less convincing as anything other than a hall, in this case with adjacent stables. The concentration of discarded cattle bones that is focused on this area would also suit a feasting hall rather better than a church. Ritual activity was also supposed further north, in the form of two buildings within a fenced enclosure 'incorporated into cemetery 2', interpreted as 'monastic buildings'. One was small, so a 'cell' (4531), with a burial (4584) found within it; the other (4669) was a rectangle of clay, declared a shrine. But burials oversailed the walls of both buildings.[260]

Apart from the three styli and the St John plaque, there are few potential monastic correlates as we know them to be from Jarrow or excavations in Scotland and Ireland. Styli alone are not now thought to be diagnostic of a monastery.[261] There was no sculpture and no

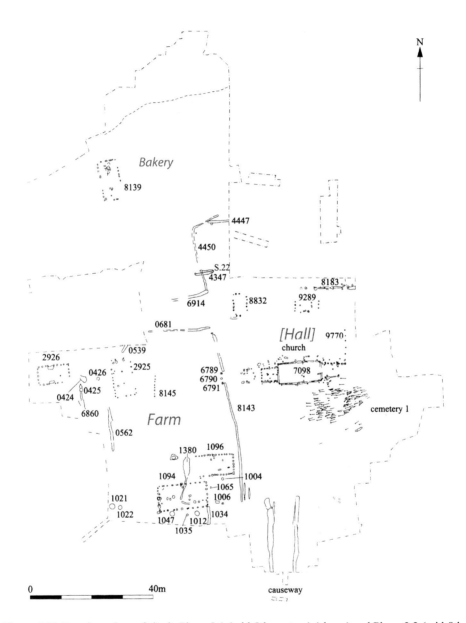

Figure 3.89 Brandon: plans of site in Phase 2.1 (mid-8th century) (above) and Phase 2.2 (mid-8th to 9th century) (below).

(Tester et al.2014, Fig 4.13, 4.23, courtesy of Suffolk Archaeological Service © Suffolk County Council; with author's additions in italics)

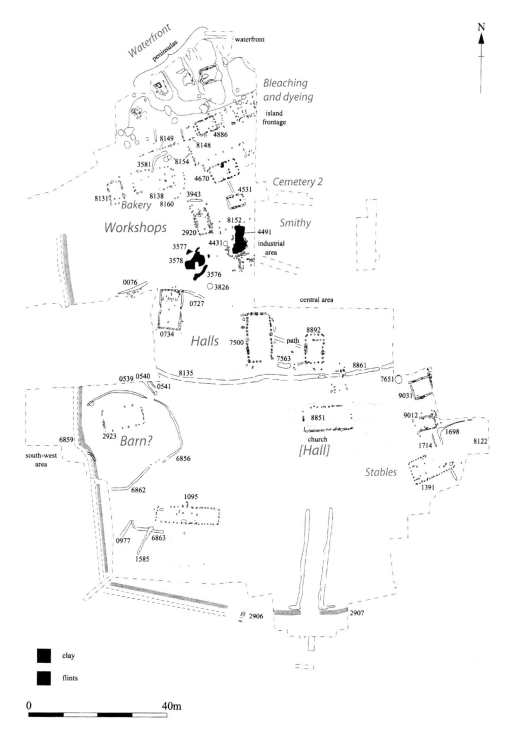

N

Waterfront

waterfront

peninsulas

Bleaching
and dyeing

island
frontage

8149

8148

4886

8154

3581

4670

Cemetery 2

4531

8131

8138

8160

3943

Bakery

Workshops

2920

8152

Smithy

4491

industrial
area

3577

4431

3578

3576

3826

0076

central area

0727

0734

Halls

8892

7500

path

7563

8861

8135

7651

0539 0540

0541

9031

9012

1698

8851

1714

8122

2923

Barn?

church

[Hall]

Stables

6859

south-west
area

6856

1391

6862

1095

0977

6863

1585

2906

2907

clay

flints

0   40m

Figure 3.89 (Continued)

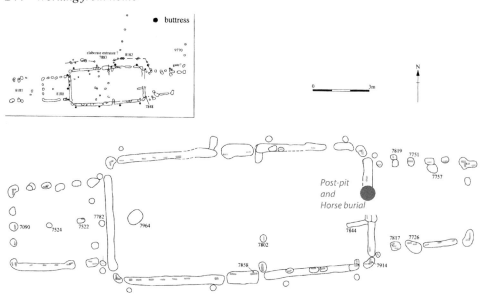

Figure 3.90 Brandon: the church in Phase 2.1, showing position of post-hole and horse burial.

(Tester et al. 2014, Fig 4.14, courtesy of Suffolk Archaeological Service © Suffolk County Council; with author's additions)

evidence for the manufacture of Christian church plate.[262] The three inscriptions are runic. The disc head of a pin (sf8679) carries the *furthorc* plus other letters; the silver tweezers (sf0836) are inscribed +*Aldred* and the deer antler inkhorn (sf9879) reads *wohswildumdeo . . .* perhaps *wohs wfldurn deor* 'I grew on a wild beast'.[263] The animal bone assemblage shows that sheep were prominent, and the cattle included fewer calves than West Stow.[264] There was none of the material associated with vellum making.[265] The population was hardly typical of a monastery: Cemetery 1 had a ratio of 60:40 males to females, and in the incomplete Cemetery 2, 20 out of 31 burials were those of children.

The case that Brandon was a monastery, a minster or even ecclesiastical in emphasis is unconvincing, and it is certainly not a monastic site in any sense that might be understood in Northumbria or the rest of Britain.[266] On the other hand, the evidence for an affluent estate centre in which a large family or a group of families enjoy increasing wealth generated by agriculture is consistent. As we have seen already, the 8th century in Southumbria seems to be characterised by rural properties of upwardly mobile Christian aristocrats, referred to earlier as 'magnate farms', of which Brandon would seem to offer a particularly well-preserved example.

The site of Offa's palace documented at **Tamworth**, Staffordshire, is mostly inaccessible beneath the modern town, which is unfortunate, as it must represent the 8th-century magnate centre *par excellence*. A raised area around St Editha's church detected from the air has been proposed as indicating the palace enclosure, but no artefacts or structures of the period have been located within it[267] (Figure 3.91). The clearest sign of Fm 2 occupation (although late in the period) is the horizontal timber mill excavated by Philip Rahtz that stood 150 m to the south-east on a presumed earlier course of the river Anker (Figure 3.92). A fire had affected some timbers and waterlogging had preserved others, giving a rare sighting of English carpentry and allowing the form of the mill to be reconstructed: it consisted of a timber-lined millpond feeding a timber platform on which the horizontal

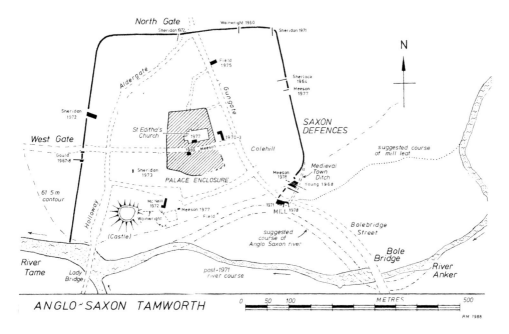

Figure 3.91 Tamworth (Staffordshire), showing St Editha's church on a raised part of the town, the site of Offa's Palace; the horizontal mill excavated in 1978 and the 9th–10th century defences of the burh.

(Rahtz and Meeson 1992, Fig 2; with permission, Bob Meeson)

Figure 3.92 Tamworth: timber platform for a watermill driven by a horizontal wheel in use in the 9th century.

(Rahtz and Meeson 1992, Plate 3; permission courtesy of Lorna Watts)

wheel set on a fine steel bearing was spun by a jet of water. Dendrochronology showed that timbers used to make the mill were felled between 855 and 859; it was still being refurbished before the end of the 9th century. Environmental evidence suggest that oats and barley were the cereals being milled.[268] It has been suggested that the space outside the 'royal' enclosure and the river would have been infilled by other buildings of the time, an idea that would be in line with the farmsteads at Chalton and Cowdery's Down. A parallel suggestion is that there was an outer enclosure coincidental with the line of the later burh. However, little evidence has emerged to support this to date. Thirteen sections have been cut across the putative line of the defences, and the findings, such as they were, are compatible with the expected date of the founding of the later *burh* in 913.[269]

Informal markets

The rise of the magnate residences in Fm 2 is no doubt due to more ambitious and successful farming, as indicated at Yarnton, but wealth is also being generated through an increased capacity and control of trade. Two forms of trading site have been defined: one consists of scatters of coins and fragments of metal, owed largely to discovery by metal-detectorists, and the other is large, planned and often best appreciated at a place termed a *wic*. Suitable nomenclature for the first of these is challenging. The metal-detectorists themselves called them 'productive sites' in that they have produced lots of treasure. 'Scatter sites' describes the normal form of discovery, as an amorphous area where coins and metal fragments survive in the ploughsoil. Those tested by archaeologists seemed to lack traces of structures, so they have been seen as resulting from informal open-air markets or fairs. The distribution of the sites so far is almost entirely confined to the east of England and to East Anglia in particular.[270] The PAS operates over the whole of modern England, so this is likely to be a real pattern and may indicate a precocious trade network in that part of England. The exceptional numbers of sceattas recovered point to a monetarised economy.[271]

However, more recent investigations have located some of these scatters at sites with settlement evidence, suggesting that they are not so much special in their function but rather in their poor survival and rediscovery.[272] As exploration broadens, the scatters are beginning to focus as major estate centres with rich burials. Coddenham in Suffolk has yielded not only five early sceattas but three tremisses and 12 English thrysmas, suggesting a start in the early 7th century or before. Excavations at Coddenham have found settlement evidence including a hall-type building and metalworking accompanied by a 7th-century inhumation cemetery with a number of high-status graves, including a bed burial. This implies that the centres of wealth were being created in a pre-Christian context.[273] Similarly, Bawsey in Norfolk was an economic focus from the 7th to 12th century. Tim Pestell paints a picture of a Fm 2 England connected by trading centres, engaged with the continent and using a coinage which at the height of its volume of circulation in the early 8th century was to be unsurpassed for another 500 years.[274]

An exciting new investigation with results that could fit this mould has taken place at **Rendlesham** in Suffolk near Sutton Hoo. Here a combined team of archaeologists and detectorists has recovered numerous finds that range by date from the later Roman period through to the 8th century – without a break – spread over an area of 50 ha. An aerial photograph has located a possible hall, and surface collection has defined zones dedicated to agricultural processing and manufacture (Figure 3.93). The deposit was exceptionally rich: the team has found 25 gold coins of c. AD 580–675 and 168 *sceattas* dating from AD 675, the number falling away after c. AD 720. These exclude those gold coins that were fashioned into jewellery. Rendlesham has thus been revealed as a central place growing in stature over a

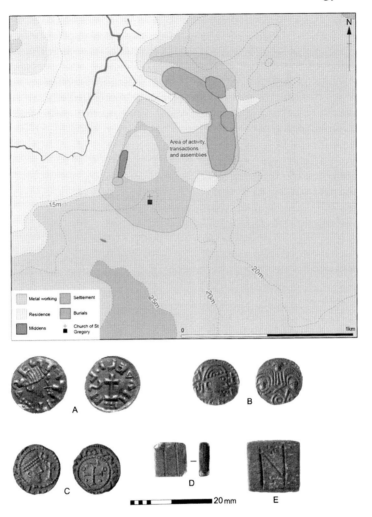

Figure 3.93 Rendlesham (Suffolk). Preliminary findings from surface survey showing (above): likely areas of high-status residence (including the site of a hall), metalworking, assembly, settlement, burials and the church of St Gregory and (below): examples of coins and weights from the assemblage: A: Merovingian tremissis; B: Anglo-Saxon gold shilling; C: Silver sceat; D: Copper-alloy coin weight inscribed with letter H (= 1 tremissis); E: Copper-alloy coin weight inscribed with letter N (= 1 solidus).

(Scull et al.2016, Fig 11, 8; courtesy of Prof. C. Scull and Suffolk County Council)

lengthy period between the late fourth century and the early eighth. Sutton Hoo would have counted as one event in its long history. Chris Scull and his colleagues conclude:

> Our preliminary interpretation of the sixth- to eighth-century complex is that it was a farm, a residence and a tribute centre where the land's wealth was collected and redirected, major administrative payments made, and important social and political events transacted.[275]

This place therefore fits with a model in which landed proprietors start accruing capital. They may do this by trade or through gift, marriage, rent, tax or toll[276]; in any case there is little doubt about the high level of disposable wealth. The idea of wealthy estates trading on their own behalf has been mooted elsewhere. A case has been made that the lords of Wessex were trading directly with the near continent from their estates (such as Dorchester), with a peak between 650 and 750, after which trade with Frisia seems to have declined sharply.[277] A growth of similar places has been proposed for the northern European coastlines and in Frisia, where the well-furnished cemetery is also an indicator of the activities of a rich estate.[278]

A general definition for the scatter sites to date is that these were places that attracted and discarded coins and other tokens of wealth, began in or before the mid-7th century and featured wealthy furnished burials. In this regard, the metal detectors' assessment is accurate. We could perhaps call them 'wealth traps', which leaves open the question of whether the affluence is owed to the promotion of merchants, clerics or landlords. The idea of an economy in which coin and bullion ran alongside each other was recently suggested for the Vikings for their first two generations in England; bullion was valid for overseas trade and did not attract tax.[279] This would have equally served the economic stage of the lords of Rendlesham, two centuries earlier. At first sight a more general interpretation for the 'productive sites' would be trading places or informal or private markets, but it is not certain that they were all necessarily involved in trade. A simpler deduction is that they represent enterprising aspects of the aristocratic estate or magnate farm – since such places must have been implicated in any wealth creation system. There is no good archaeological case that the church is yet involved – this, like the lack of sculpture, being another part of the contrast between the English regions south of the Tees and those of the British north and west where the monastic movement was in full swing.

Did the English have monasteries?

The previous discussion has led to the conclusion that although monasteries of Fm 2 are documented south of the Humber, for example by Bede, they have proved difficult to locate and characterise archaeologically on the ground. In particular, the candidates have so far failed to reveal the full monastic livery of the north and west: enclosure, watermill, manufacture of vellum, sacred vessels of precious metal and above all standing stone sculpture of diverse kinds. Gabor Thomas suggested that the problem was one of archaeological strategy, since the cherishing of heritage has discouraged the investigation of sites documented as monasteries at an appropriate scale. Accordingly, he launched a project at **Lyminge** in Kent, a village about 8 km from the Channel coast, to try and define the nature of the ecclesiastical settlement that was implied in surviving charters.[280] Eight seasons of excavation (2008–2015) defined a sequence in two main periods (Figure 3.94). A settlement of the late 5th to late 7th century was contacted in two areas 200 m apart, either side of the present church of Saints Mary and Ethelburga. The southern area contained SFBs and rectangular post-hole buildings (**1**), while that to the north featured a set of grand halls (**2**). The first of the halls to be defined was aligned approximately W-E, measured 21×8.2 m and had double-planked walls and opposed doorways (Hall A). It was associated with vessel glass and a gilt bronze bridle fitting as well as a large assemblage of animal bone, leading to its being dubbed a 'feasting hall'. Adjacent to the north, two more areas 30×30 m were opened, revealing another hall sequence at right angles using a single plank wall with raking posts and ultimately measuring 13.6×7.4 m (Hall B).[281] In a third sequence to the east (Hall C), two halls succeeded, each on the same footprint, using construction techniques of Hall A and Hall B respectively.[282] Two cemeteries of the period mark valley routes of approach to the settlement. One of them (Lyminge II; **3**) included a horse burial and a female accompanied by bracteates. Although the evidence was partial, the excavator makes a good case that

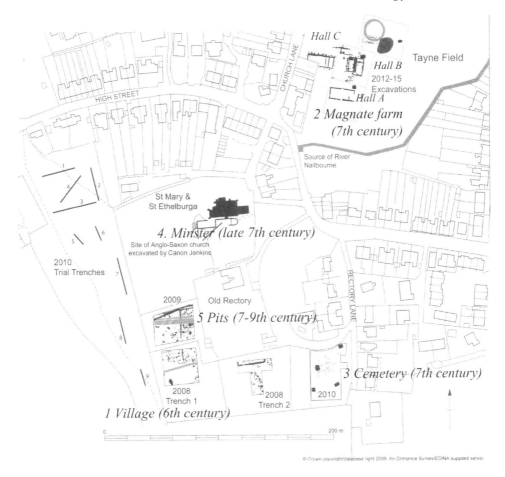

Figure 3.94 Lyminge (Kent). Plan and results of the investigations.

(Thomas, G. 2017, Fig 2, with additions by current author; with permission; base map © Crown copyright/database right 2009. An Ordnance Survey/EDINA supplied service)

this settlement had evolved from a sprawling layout in the 6th century to a more ordered 'magnate' establishment with grand halls and burials in the 7th century. In this it follows the trajectory seen at Chalton and Cowdery's Down and outlined earlier.

A 'major spatial rupture' was reported to have occurred in the second half of the 7th century. Archaeologically this comprised an occupation of the 7th–9th century situated adjacent to, but apart from, the magnate farm on slightly higher ground around the present church. It consists so far of foundations immediately south of the present church (that may belong to a Middle Saxon predecessor) defined by the Canon Jenkins in 1853 (**4**), and, further south, a cluster of pits, post-holes and ditches suggesting a granary, small buildings and rectangular enclosures, together with a rich assemblage of animal bone, especially sea fish (**5**). These collected attributes were somewhat optimistically claimed as 'the first detailed view of spatial organization of the outer precinct of an Anglo-Saxon Kentish double monastery', an interpretation largely prompted by documentary expectation.[283] However it has yet to produce any of the diagnostic correlates of the monastic movement itemised earlier; as it stands a northerner would be hard put to recognise it as a monastery of the kind with which he was familiar. Suggestive, however, is the transition from a high-status settlement site in the later 7th century, as previously demonstrated at Whithorn and Portmahomack.

John Blair encapsulated the documentary evidence as: 'The Kentish royal nunnery at Lyminge may also have replaced or coexisted with a royal estate centre.'[284] This describes what the excavations have found without, however, revealing the form or attributes of a nunnery (or a double monastery).[285] The options would appear to be either that the attributes that have been seen so graphically in the north have yet to be seen at Lyminge (for example they all lie nearer the church) or that the present result is what a 7th–9th century Southumbrian religious establishment actually looks like. The former is of course possible even though the excavations have been on a generous scale. The latter is perhaps a more prudent conclusion, its corollary being that 'monastery' means something rather different north and south of the Humber: in the English area it may refer to an estate in clerical hands rather than a citadel of the church militant. Meanwhile, attempts to shoehorn the documented English ecclesiastical settlements into the mould of the monastic movement will be fruitless if it was a movement in which (as the archaeological contrast suggests) the English did not take part. This should in no way slacken the mission for larger-scale examination of potential sites in England, for which Gabor Thomas rightly calls. It may be that the minster-monastery standoff can be resolved by continuing to use 'monastery' for settlements shown archaeologically to have been equipped with the monastic signature (lying mainly north of the Humber) and confining Blair's term of 'minster' to those, mainly south of the Humber, that lack it.

Wics

An economic foil for the minster is perhaps provided by a type of strategically placed centre of production, exchange and wealth creation that so far occurs only in the English regions, namely the *wic*. The term (borrowed into Old English from Latin *vicus*) provides us with a short list of placenames, indicating the most fully investigated targets so far: Lundenwic (London), Eoforwic (York), Ipswic (Ipswich) and Hamwic (by Southampton) (Figure 3.95). Much of the crucial material lies beneath modern towns, so that encounters with them have been necessarily piecemeal, and the picture must be assembled from fragments.[286] At Hamwic, a rich 7th-century burial ground was excavated at St Mary's Stadium, and the planned town began c. 700 and eventually spread over 47 ha, with a grid of metalled roads providing the framework.[287] The cemetery is seen as the point of departure for the *wic* and having no rationale unless 'those buried there were involved in Hamwic's emergence as a commercial centre'.[288] Lundenwic, which also had rich cemeteries, was a planned site on the banks of the Thames (at The Strand) extending over 55–60 ha.[289] At Ipswich the wealthy Buttermarket cemetery was established around 600 and abandoned a century later in the face of the expanding *wic* that would eventually cover 50 ha. The graves had included Continental material, implying a role for foreigners in the early development of the trading place. Pottery is imported during the 7th century, while locally made Ipswich ware appears in about 725.[290] Chris Scull has determined the way that these sites develop, from a local higher-status settlement 'with economic central place functions some of which involved monetary exchange' to a target of foreign investment, and then to an ordered and planned facility created by a regional authority with long-distance exchange, as controlled by elite groups.[291]

All these sites made use of a river within navigational reach of the sea. In the 8th century, laden ships floated up on the tide and discharged their cargos on a foreshore of sand or mud before being taken off by the tide for a new journey. It is likely that such a system was

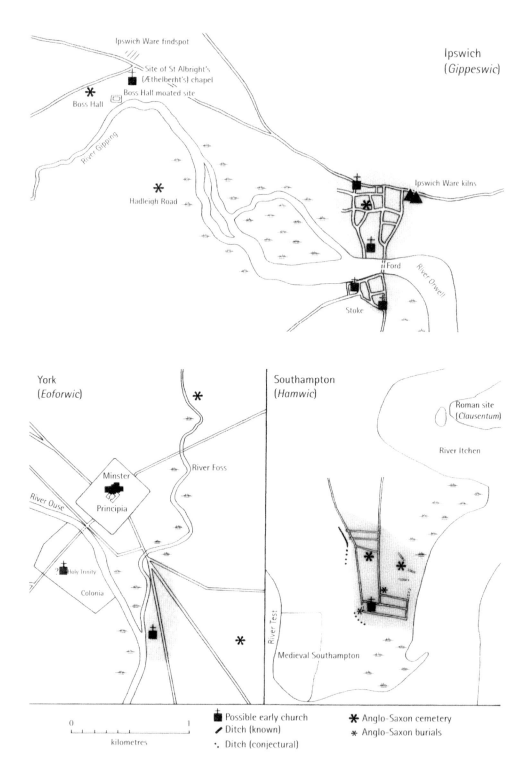

Figure 3.95 Wics in context: plans by Tim Pestell.
(Pestell 2011, Fig 29.3, 29.4; with author's permission)

already in use on the Thames in the early 7th century at London, which Bede refers to as a 'mart of many nations'.[292] Behind their waterfronts, *wics* were equipped with residential areas, light industry and probably warehousing. Pottery, lava querns and coins are among the identifiable imports. What was going out is less clear, but traditional exports such as wool and cloth probably figured highly. The character of the food waste raises the possibility that occupants of the *wics* might be beholden to sponsors or dependant on food renders from outside. Eighty percent of the faunal remains at Hamwic, Ipswich and Eoforwic were beef from older animals, and Ipswich was receiving cleaned grain from outside the settlement.[293] But low-value bulk commodities like lava querns show that there was a supply and demand relationship within the agricultural motor. That *wics* served, or were served by, some kind of hinterland is suggested by the distribution pattern of pottery made there.[294]

If imports, exports, sea traffic, planning and subsidies represent the *wic* signature, then few of these places have been defined so far. This increases the possibility that development and control after 700 had moved, by force or by agreement, away from the magnate entrepreneurs into the hands of a higher authority. This implies in turn that a lively period of free trade had been superseded by one restricted to authorised landing places. Here trade could be controlled and taxed, for the benefit of either the king, a ruling elite or, more altruistically, to benefit the kingdom as a whole.[295] Frisians were present in London (Bede IV.22) and Frisians or Franks at Ipswich.[296] This supports the idea that the ruling elite recruited long-distance traders to prime the English venture.

It can be seen that the scatter-site and the *wic* are beginning to converge: both emanating from high-status sites with rich burials and spreading over 50 ha or so, together constituting a formidable network for creating wealth. As the archaeology stands, the Southumbrian minster is a minor economic player, and as a corollary the *wic* initiative has yet to appear widely in the rest of Britain, where it is the monastery that turns to wealth creation. The case can be made that the *wics* and the monasteries represent two equivalent 8th/9th century developments from different parts of the island, which had a similar function but were ideologically opposed.[297] Both were affected by the activities of Danish and Norse invaders: where they survived, notably in Ireland, the monasteries turned their attention to pragmatic coexistence with the secular power, as monastic towns. The *wics* were also the targets of Viking attack and seemed rarely to have outlived the 9th century.[298]

Formative 3 (9th to 11th century)

The Viking impact

The Danish Vikings began to intrude into southern England and Yorkshire in the early 9th century, culminating in the arrival of the Great Army in 865. In the north the pressure came from the Norse, who targeted the monasteries. Pressure from Scandinavia continued for more than a century and had a major impact on the settlement repertoire in Britain. Settlements influenced by Norse approaches and material culture have been explored in Orkney (Birsay), in the Western Isles (Bornais),[299] in the Isle of Man (Braaid),[300] in Wales (Llanbedrgoch)[301] and in Ireland (Figure 3.96). The investigations at Bornais assembled good evidence for a construction in turf walls revetted internally with stone and planking (Figure 3.97). The longhouses with rounded corners formed the focus of farmsteads with byres and huts and middens, as in the Norwegian uplands. The buildings were predominately of turf, as survive in Iceland, revetted with stakes or dry stone walls. The interior of the houses had benches along the walls and a central hearth. Chemical mapping has indicated something of the distribution of activities that took place inside, here as in Iceland, where the techniques are

Figure 3.96 The Braaid, Marown, Isle of Man. Viking house with benches in the foreground, with a byre building behind, right. Behind, left is a pre-Norman roundhouse.

(Wilson 2008, Fig 46; courtesy of David Wilson and Manx National Heritage; © Manx National Heritage)

being refined on Viking sites that are seemingly susceptible to the method.[302] In Ireland, raiding was initially based on military ports (*longphorts*) such as Dublin, Limerick, Waterford, Cork and Wexford which morphed into trading towns, with their own Hiberno-Norse assemblages and architecture.[303]

In Northumbria the chief Viking foundation was by the Danes at York and further south in the 'Danelaw', the five boroughs: Lincoln, Derby, Nottingham, Leicester, Stanford. All these employed slimmed-down versions of the Viking house, employing wattlework and mud or planks, long and adding cellars as in York or smaller and more square as in Dublin. The economy based initially on the acquisition of bullion and the manufacture of ornaments soon expanded into the profitable exercise of long-distance trade, involving the transportation of commodities in exchange for coinage, ingots, pins, rings and hacksilver.[304] The actual commodities are elusive. Hiberno-Norse farms produced grain and cattle products, but these were widely available elsewhere. Timber for building would be needed in the north. Amber and steatite for carved receptacles would be in demand in the south. A dried fish industry was initiated in the northern isles in Viking times.[305] Not to mention the least visible and most valuable commodity of them all – slaves (Chapter 2, p. 58).

That this was more than a land-grab or a trade mission can be seen from the experience of the monasteries; the Vikings did not (only) burn them down: they would seem to have encouraged some establishments to align with their way of thinking. Something of the process can be glimpsed in some of the responses of the major monastic houses (Table 3.6). The

Figure 3.97 Bornais (South Uist, Outer Hebrides) House in Trench D. (Top left): Excavation in progress (1999). (Top right): Hearth. (Bottom): Conjectural reconstruction of the turf building.
(Sharples 2005, Fig 106, 38, 107; with author's permission)

Portmahomack experience is the clearest, where metalsmiths, using techniques identical to
those of the monks, set up shop on the ruins of the vellum workshop to manufacture objects
useful to a new secular clientele. Whithorn also recovered swiftly and became a player in
manufacturing and the coin economy. Even at Jarrow, 9th-century craftsmen in Building D
were making strap and dress hooks and apparently selling them for coin.

Wilfred's monastery at Ripon has only been examined on a small scale but provides an
indication of the ephemeral nature of the monastic project. The 7th/8th century monastery
was thought to be located in a precinct formed by a curved *vallum* cutting off the confluence of the rivers Skell and Ure. This contained the main church with its crypt, a subsidiary
chapel at Ladykirk and, 200 m east of the minster, the natural mound of Ailcy Hill. This
mound was used as a cemetery in three main phases: up to the late 7th century (i.e. during
Fm 1) there were graves of men and women, including some aligned N-S and one grave with
a late 7th-century iron buckle. In the 7th/9th century (Fm 2), the graves were aligned W-E,
and 9 out of 10 identified were adult males, some buried in chests; in the 9th/10th century
(Fm 3) the burials adopted slight changes in alignment and included men, women and children. This burial ground began before the documented date of the monastery on a feature no
doubt thought to be a prehistoric burial mound, and it was adapted to the appropriate ritual
over the monastic and subsequent period. Statistical tests were run to investigate changes in

Table 3.6 Monastic trajectories: before, during and after

Site	6th century	7th century	8th century	9th century
Inchmarnock	Burial?	Metalworking	Slates and schooling	Stone church [after Viking raid]
Portmahomack	Elite burials	Elite estate centre/ cemetery-settlement	Pictish monastery Vellum, glass, metal, sculpture	Trading and secular manufacture
Iona	Ditch	Metalworking Sculpture	Metalworking, sculpture	?
Hoddom		?British monastery	Northumbrian monastery	Estate centre
Whithorn	Cemetery-settlement	Irish cemetery-settlement	Northumbrian monastery	Restored monastery Whithorn school of sculpture
Hartlepool	British princely burials	Anglian monastery	Anglian monastery; grave markers	?
Ripon (Ailcy Hill)	[early burials?]	Community burials on a mound	Monastic burials	Community burials
Wearmouth		Built 674. Like Roman villa	Northumbrian monastery	Abandoned
Jarrow		Built 685. Like Roman villa	Northumbrian monastery Glass, metal, sculpture	Secular manufacture

demography, but none of significance was found.[306] This sequence shows something of the strength of tradition that operates while ideologies come and go, even in the headquarters of one of monasticism's most vigorous proponents.[307]

The narrative of the Danes in England is provided by the *Anglo-Saxon Chronicle*, which mentions many places, locatable today, that were involved. King Alfred and his children played starring roles and have earned a place in the national story. The Norse confrontation in Scotland is less well documented, but the written and the material evidence suggest that the struggle was harsh. The local hero Macbeth was just as hard pressed and, in some estimations, just as valiant.[308]

The Viking wars lasted for more than 100 years and profoundly affected the material culture of both north and south. Their target was not apparently Christianity *per se* or even the peoples of Britain but monasticism as a restrictive political regime. The objective was to replace an ideology seen as oligarchic and stifling with a more basic one in which enterprise was rewarded with wealth, land and progeny. The burden of the change was therefore political, rather than religious or ethnic: a swing from left to right. Viking Norse forces were defeated and converted. But there was no survival of fundamentalist Christianity as a mode of governance. If the Vikings became Christian, the Christians became entrepreneurs. In Britain the Vikings lost the war but won the argument.

The most convincing direct evidence of how a Viking army campaigned in England (and in Europe) has been brought to light through intensive archaeological investigations at the site of **Torksey** in Lincolnshire, where the Viking Great Army was reported to have overwintered in 872–3. Here a rich assemblage of early medieval artefacts has been found scattered over the surface of a prominent bluff, that, especially in the winter months, would have formed a virtual island in the River Trent.[309] The site was defined by test trenching and topographic and geophysical survey, combined with a map of 1,572 early medieval objects located by metal-detection, allowing an area of occupation to be proposed over some 55 ha (Figure 3.98A). The dates of the coins showed a strong peak between 825 and 875, consistent with the documented

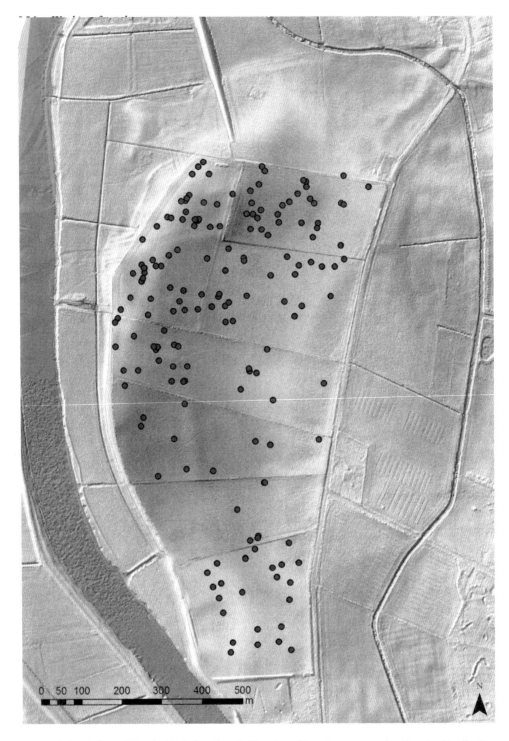

Figure 3.98 Torksey (Lincolnshire). (A, above): The site of the winter camp, showing the distribution of the early medieval finds and low-lying ground.

(Hadley and Richards 2016, Fig 11, 14 and 20; with authors' permission; Fig 11 is derived from 2m LiDAR data, Environment Agency © 2014, all rights reserved; field boundaries from Ordnance Survey Master map © Crown Copyright/database right 2014, an Ordnance Survey/EDINA supplied service; general map of GB derived from Ordnance Survey Miniscale map)

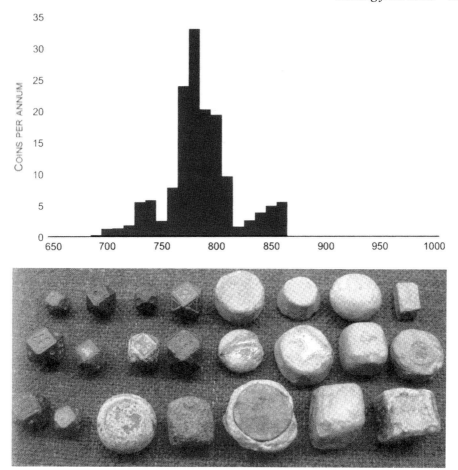

Figure 3.98 (B, top): Dating pattern of the Anglo-Saxon coins. (C, bottom): Copper-alloy weights from the Torksey site, possibly reflecting the design and standards of Arab types.

presence of the Great Army (Figure 3.98B). The extensive area and the short time span point to occupation by a large and homogenous community. The occupants appeared to have relied on the natural defences provided by the steep slope of the island perimeter, accentuated by the marshy conditions and natural inhibitions of winter warfare. As well as coins, the metal finds included silver ingots, hack-gold and more than 350 weights, of which nearly 100 were copper alloy, implying the circulation of bullion and exchange of commodities (Figure 3.98C). Tools suitable for the manufacture of metal ornaments, playing pieces and the repair of clothes or sails were found on site, together with numerous dress accessories, including 133 copper-alloy strap-ends that were Anglo-Saxon in style and late 9th century in date. These findings from the early stages of a promising research project paint a new picture of the Viking army as a lively community engaged in fending for itself, in contact with the wider British Isles and perhaps hosting contingents of English slaves.[310]

Discoveries at **Repton** in Derbyshire at one time provided a model for the footprint of the Great Army, excavations there leading to the suggestion that the site of St Wystan's church had been adapted in the 9th century as a Viking fort in which the church acted as the gatehouse to a D-shaped enclosure.[311] However, the area enclosed only 0.4 ha, sufficient to serve a war band of modest size.[312] The Torksey model not only shows that the Great Army was, in fact, large but that it provided encamped residence for men, women and children, was self-servicing and engaged in trade. It is not excluded that the Viking site, on a dry ridge with access to a river but protected by marshy ground, influenced strategists such as Alfred of Wessex and Athelflaed, Lady of the Mercians, in the location of defensible areas at Athelney and Stafford. However, the English response to the Viking war machine was to follow a different path, guided by different principles. The successor to the Viking camp at Torksey was an Anglo-Saxon defended enclosure constructed immediately to the south and on the same side of the river. This was a new kind of site and a member of an extensive network of English forts by means of which the south of Britain was defended and the Midlands eventually conquered: the *burhs*.

Country estates

Some indication of where the aristocracy holed up during the Viking campaign in the west is provided by the excavation of a crannog in Llan-gors lake in south Wales overlooked by the Brecon Beacons (Figure 3.99). The artificial platform was 40 m across and dated by dendrochronology to the late 9th or early 10th century. Finds included a fragment of embroidered cloth, and the site may have been the *Brecenanmere* raided and destroyed by Aethelflaed Lady of the Mercians, who captured the wife of king Tewdwr and 33 retainers.[313] In England, the magnate farm continued its development towards the medieval manor, as at Bishopstone (Sussex), where a courtyard range of three halls and a tower dating to the 8th–11th century was excavated on the north side of the church of St Andrew.[314]

Excavated by Philip Rahtz between 1960 and 1962, the **Cheddar** 'palace site' remains one of the best expressions of Fm 3 rural investment so far seen. It is situated on a promontory above the River Yeo in Somerset near the entrance to Cheddar Gorge (Figure 3.100).[315]

Figure 3.99 Crannog at Llan-Gors, Brecon, South Wales.
(Author)

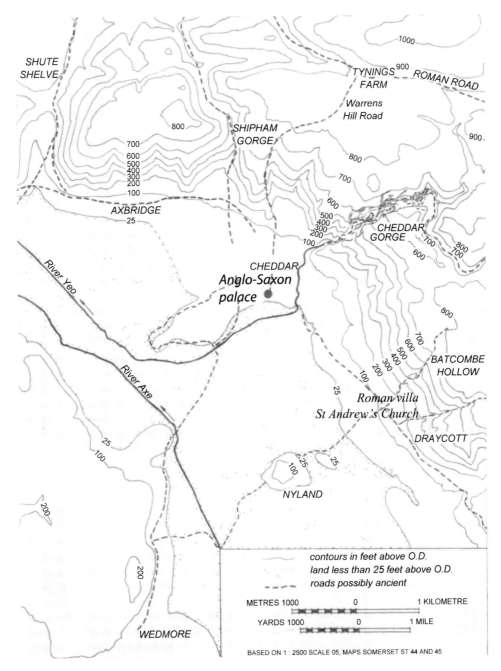

Figure 3.100 Cheddar (Somerset): Location of Fm 3 site ('palace site') and the location of a nearby Roman villa and medieval church of St Andrew.

(Rahtz 1979, Fig 3; permission courtesy of Lorna Watts)

Opportunity for the investigation was owed to the construction of a new school, and the excavation extended to 0.8 ha around the extant remains of a medieval chapel. In a characteristically expert and meticulous operation, Rahtz wrote the story of the site in seven periods from the 9th to the 17th century, using stratigraphy and assemblages. Cheddar was documented as the site of royal activity, and in the spirit of the age, the building phases were attributed to kings. In Period 1 (c. 850–c. 930) the promontory was selected for development, its neck (uphill) protected by a wide storm drain (Figure 3.101A). Adjacent was a bow-sided hall 24 m long and 5.5–6 m wide, with central opposed doorways and a hearth on one side. The walls were constructed from 91 posts of squared timber set in trenches, and an upper floor is implied (Figure 3.102A). Three smaller ancillary buildings stood to the west of the long hall and a fenced enclosure to its south. This phase is attributed to the time of Alfred and Edward the Elder.

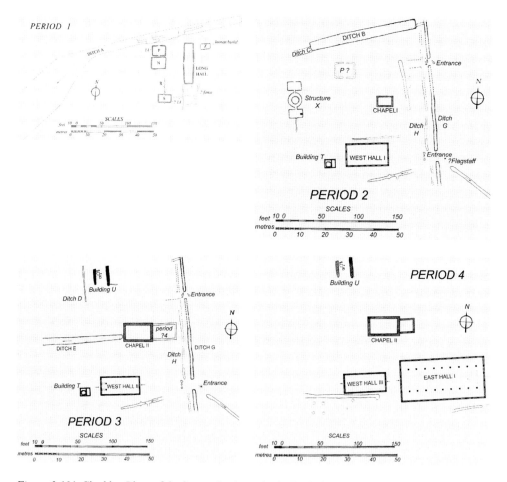

Figure 3.101 Cheddar: Plans of the four main phases in the Fm 3. (From top left): Period 1 c. 850–950. Bow-side long hall and possible bower. There is no chapel in this phase. Period 2. c. 930–to 1000. A chapel is constructed with new West Hall. This phase has an enclosure, a flagstaff and the poultry house. Period 3. Late 10th to 11th century. West Hall II continues on same footprint. Chapel II replaces Chapel I. Period 4. Late 11th to early 12th century. West Hall III is joined by the grand East Hall.

(Rahtz 1979, Fig 6, 12, 13, 15; permission courtesy of Lorna Watts)

In Period 2 (c. 930 to c. 1000) a chapel was founded with narrow stone footings, giving a plan (3.2 × 4.1 m) inside the extant ruin (Figure 3.101 B). It had stone ashlar walls and a monolithic window head, with holes for rods to key into the stone walls. This first version of the chapel was built across the foundation trench of the demolished long hall, and a new sequence of halls was constructed to the south. The first of these, West Hall I, measured 17 × 9.1 m externally and was built of square timbers set in post-pits (Figure 3.102 B). The settlement was now bordered by a linear double ditch with two points of entry. One of these was marked by a giant post-pit 1.25 m in diameter, originally holding a circular post measuring 90 cm in diameter and interpreted as a 'flagstaff' (Figure 3.103 A).[316] Building T was a small rectangular building containing a large straight-sided pit and may have been the (royal) latrine. Building X was constructed by two concentrated circles of stakes (surrounding a

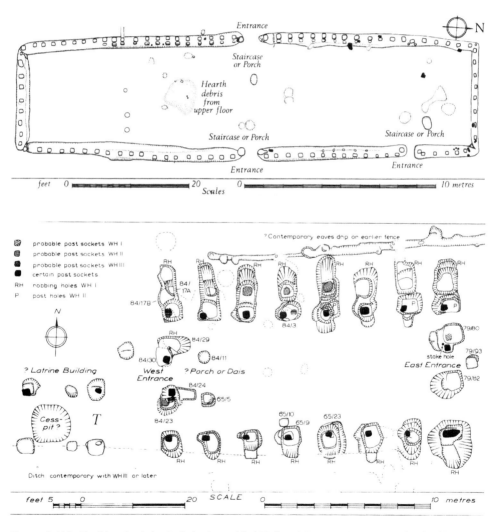

Figure 3.102 Cheddar: (top) the Period 1 bow-sided Hall and (bottom) the West Halls (detail).

(Permission courtesy of Lorna Watts)

blank area 2.5 m across) with rectangular annexes either side and was interpreted as a fowl-house on the basis of comparison with that illustrated (and labelled) on the St Gall Plan (Figure 3.103 B).[317] The Period 2 settlement was attributed to the time of Athelstan and his successors, with meetings of the court recorded in 941, 956, 968.

Period 3, also probably pre-conquest (late 10th to 11th century) in date, saw the construction of West Hall II (on the same footings) and Chapel II (on the enlarged (present) footings) (Figure 3.103 C). This is credited to the last of the Anglo-Saxon kings, Ethelred and Edward the Confessor. There is little sign of a change of form or function in the Norman period (Period 4 late 11th to early 12th) (Figure 3.103 D). The West Hall (III) was reconstructed

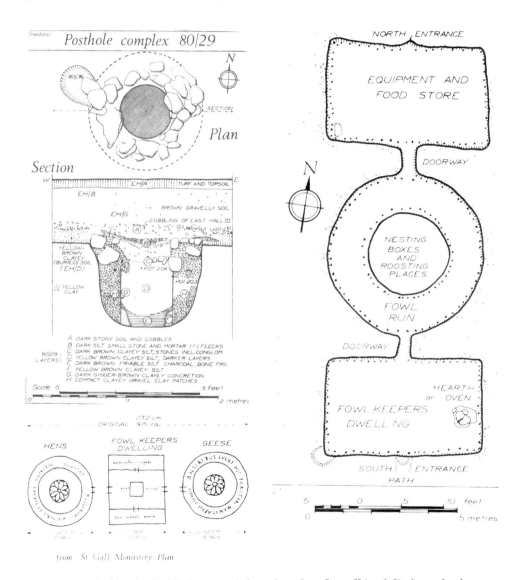

Figure 3.103 Cheddar: detail of the large post-hole, perhaps for a flagstaff (top left); the poultry house or dovecote (right) and a poultry house redrawn from the 9th century St. Gall plan (bottom left).

(Rahtz 1979, Fig 41; permission courtesy of Lorna Watts)

on the same footprint, using timbers, and a new grander aisled East Hall I built to the east in 10 bays, with an external ground plan measuring 33.5 × 18 m. This is assigned to the time of the Norman kings. Henry I visited in 1121; Henry II in 1158. The 'hunting lodge' arrives with the first stone hall in Period 5 (early 13th century) and an enlarged chapel in the 14th century, when the estate became the property of the Bishops of Wells.

In presenting the site as a sequence of palaces, Rahtz was probably influenced by the size of the buildings, the survival of the church as a 'Royal Free Chapel', the recent discovery of Yeavering (in 1953–1962), the meetings of the king's *witenagemot* documented at Cheddar, and the apocryphal story of King Edmund's repentance on a hunting expedition, written down in the 15th century (by which time the early palaces found at Cheddar had probably been long forgotten). He also cites the description of a Carolingian court at Annapes as providing useful analogies for the buildings, fixtures and economy.[318]

Leaving the ascription of 'palace' to one side and with the archaeological perspective of another 40 years, Cheddar fits well into the evolving courtyard magnate farms of England that have been sketched for Fm 2. Whoever owned it, Cheddar is a grand version of Cowdery's Down and Bishopstone, taking the story through the 9th century to its apogee as a 13th-century stone-built manor. It may be anticipated that in future years we will build up an extensive web of these proto-manorial centres, each with courtyard, church and burial ground, with roots in the 8th or 9th century. If this web remains elusive at present, it may be because its nodal points have often continued to be living villages with restricted access to archaeology.[319]

The gestation of towns

The gestation of the English town and its possible continuation from the models implanted by imperial Rome has been a strong theme of English archaeology for many decades.[320] Paradoxically, while the case for administrative continuity has diminished, the case for a Roman revival has improved.[321] The search for continuity is heroically exemplified by Phil Barker's campaign at Wroxeter (Shropshire), where the surface of the abandoned Roman town was dissected and its anomalies hypothetically resurrected in the form of a giant timber-framed successor.[322] While not credible as the footprint of a vanished 5th-century town, these patterns have not been systematically explained. However, the sequence at York Minster, with its deep robber trenches and scraping of mortar off ashlar, suggests an alternative interpretation for the anomalies discovered by Barker, rooted in the systematic extraction and cleaning of building stone.

Even in London, the evidence for the actual occupation of Roman towns is still mostly absent until the later 7th century, as the coins indicate (Figure 3.104). At this point, Christian interest provokes a revisitation of the old Roman towns, as at Canterbury and Winchester. At York a series of revivals then follows, resulting in manifestations of the *wic*, the Viking trading place and the *burh* (p. 169). Of these the *burh* is the newcomer, first appearing in the late 9th and early 10th century.

Development of the burh

Burh (plural *byrig*) is an Old English term for a fortified site, cognate with burg and borg in other Germanic languages, where it also carries the meaning of a defence.[323] The names of the earliest English *burhs* are known, since they were listed in the *Burghal Hideage*, a census of early towns that survives as a document of the early 11th century, and most of the sites have been

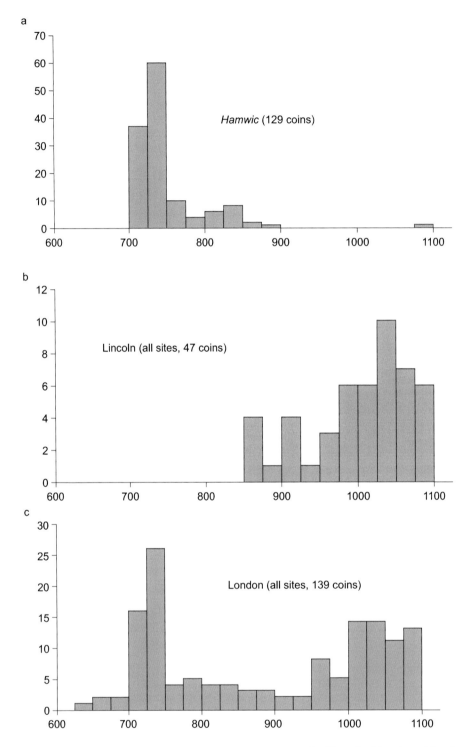

Figure 3.104 Coin loss (by numbers of coins) by quarter-century for Hamwic, Lincoln and London. (Blackburn 2011, Fig 30.2; licensed by Oxford University Press)

identified from their placenames, shared with those of modern towns.[324] The locations of those listed suggest a strategic system of early warning and defence, such that nobody was more than 20 miles from the nearest burh (Figure 3.105A).[325] Initially the system served Wessex, the part of England south of the Thames-Avon line. The burhs are assigned a 'hideage', which would normally imply an amount of land, for example the amount of land required to provision the garrison. In this case, there is a codicil to the document that explains that the hideage equates to the number of defenders required to man the walls, at one man for a length of 4 feet.[326]

David Hill used the formula to work out the length of the defences for a number of burh sites, and so to locate them on the ground.[327] However, there are problems. Where the defences of a burh can be seen, their extent does not always match the hideage. Winchester at 58.2 ha and Wallingford at 41 ha are both assessed at 2,400 hides. The burghal hideage at Exeter proposes a wall c. 912 m long (724 hides), but the Roman and medieval wall was some 2,316 m; this suggests that only part of the Roman defence (or none of it) was used.[328] At some promontory sites, the predicted length of the wall does not equal either the neck or the perimeter of the promontory, for example Christchurch, 591 m for a 400 m neck, or Lyng, 126 m for a 219 m neck. This shows that the hideation, while it may assess the manpower needed to defend a place, repair a place, garrison a place or operate from a place, does not need to reflect the length of the extant outer perimeter wall, although it may. The short lengths can refer, for example, to square forts that are sited on the promontory rather than the promontory itself; these would range from c. 30 × 30 m (Lyng) to c. 150 × 150 m

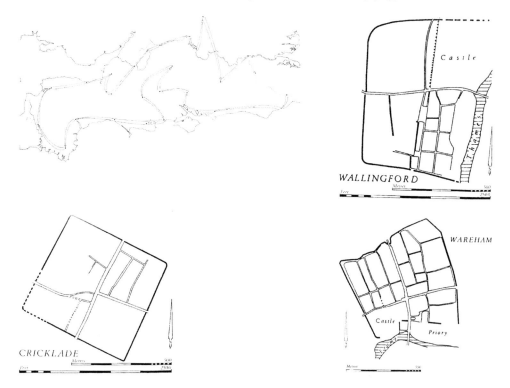

Figure 3.105 The Wessex burhs. (Top left) The order of citation of burhs in the Burghal Hideage. (Right and below). Outline forms of burhs at Wallingford, Cricklade and Wareham.

(A: Hill 1969, Fig 37; © Society of Medieval Archaeology; B–D: Biddle and Hill 1971, Fig 4; © Society of Antiquaries of London)

(Christchurch). There is some rationale in this, since all the burhs where the line of the defences is reasonably certain have a characteristic quadrilateral shape (Figure 3.105B-D).[329]

Winchester was the capital of Wessex and the target of major urban investment. Between the 7th and 9th centuries, the site of the former Roman town housed a royal centre with an episcopal church, an elite enclave that its excavator Martin Biddle memorably contrasted with the neighbouring *wic* at Hamwic.[330] At this point it was not a town but a large open space occupied from the mid-7th century and providing for adjacent royal and episcopal estates and their servants. The *burh* was created in the late 9th century (880–86), its defensive circuit based on the refurbished walls of the Roman town. The disused Roman south gate was blocked and a new gate inserted west of it. The palace and episcopal centre (now the 'Old Minster') retained their estate in the south-east corner. Elsewhere, a new grid was laid out, using 8,000 tons of cobbles to form 8.63 km of streets.[331] The streets formed small parcels against the main east-west concourse, with an extensive backland in each case. These 'quarters' pre-echo the medieval tenement system, but they may have served as refuges for groups of people at first, when the impulse was seen as defence and the protection of the hinterland a primary duty. By the 10th century, street names suggest that these spaces were being used by craftsmen to make and sell goods.[332]

Beyond the pioneering works at Winchester, the new burhs were protected initially by a purpose-built ditch with a rampart of turf, in some cases fronted by a palisade but later by a stone revetment wall. At Cricklade, there was a dump rampart of clay and turf fronted by a turf wall, later (in the 11th century) revetted with stone, with a double ditch dug before it. At Wareham the bank faced with a stone wall survives, measuring 16.8 m wide and 5 m high, fronted by a ditch.[333] These sites appear to have had little residential occupation within their defences, raising the likelihood that they were, in origin, camps.[334]

London, another old Roman town on an estuary and tidal point of entry for North Sea traffic, had a different kind of formative experience and became the jumping-off point for the second phase of burh building. Between the 5th century and the 7th (Fm 1) it was documented as a place of refuge or ritual, while the accumulation and probably the importation of humic soil (dark earth) suggests there were urban farms within the walls in this period. In the later 7th century (as the coin count rose again), clearer signs of life (and death) have been detected. Excavations on the site of the Royal Opera House turned up burials, huts, wells and fences.[335] In a period dated by the excavator to 675–730, there was evidence for a smithy, tanning, weaving, making bone objects and much imported pottery: this was the London described by Bede, writing before 731, as a 'metropolis' featuring an *emporium* frequented by people coming from land and sea.[336] The emporium was situated north of The Strand, this being the foreshore of the Thames where boats could come in, beach and unload on the tide. After 725, the date that Ipswich wares arrive, there was a rapid growth in this London-on-the-Strand, otherwise *Lundenwic*, with property divisions and service industries such as butchers and bakers. It declined in the later 9th century, and by 900 this particular landing place was redundant.

In 898, at a pivotal moment in the Viking Wars, Alfred held a planning meeting in London to decide what to do about its defences, the waterfront and the bridge to the south bank. Present were Plegmund, archbishop of Canterbury, Waerfrith, bishop of Worcester, Edward, heir in waiting, Ethelred, earl of Mercia, then governor of London, and his new wife, Aethelflaed, Alfred's daughter. They met in the old Roman town, and the clerics were given property for development in *Ethelred's Dock* (now Queenhithe), where the Millennium Bridge today makes its landfall in the city. So the business end of London returned to the Roman dockland, and with it the art of mooring against a jetty, thus loading and unloading at all hours, irrespective of the tide. Early in the 10th century the Roman bridge was rebuilt and fortified with *burhs* at both ends.

However, it was not until the late 10th or early 11th century that deep-water unloading was fully viable, Billingsgate was first documented as a port, and the assemblage of artefacts declares that international trade had returned to London.[337] As at Winchester, the royal palace and the principal abbey were established side by side, but on a new site, west of the Strand on Thorney island, where the Tyburn met the Thames. This West Minster became a new centre of power. The abbey was built between 959 and 971, and the royal Great Hall was built on reclaimed land from c. 1090–1099. It measured 72.8 × 20.7 m and was then probably the largest in Europe. This is now the site of the British parliament. There were therefore five Londons before the middle ages: a Roman fortified town (Londinium), a wic on the Strand (Lundenwic), a Late Saxon town in the old Roman city (Lundenburgh), another at Southwark and a royal place and abbey at Westminster.

Going north

Alfred's grown-up children, Edward and Aethelflaed, and his son-in-law, Ethelred of Mercia, all present at the London meeting in 898, took responsibility for the war after Alfred's death in the following year. The plan was to roll up the Viking and native opposition on two flanks (east and west), using the burh as the instrument of advance. This set of events provided a framework for the genesis of the burh (Figure 3.106). The army of the right

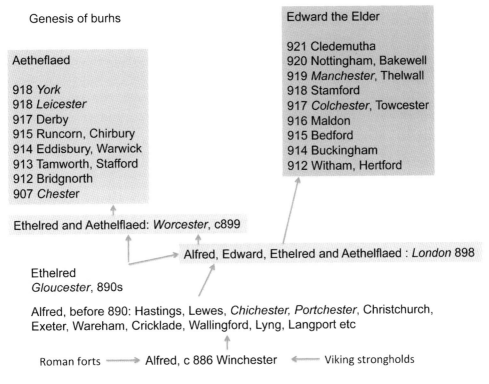

Figure 3.106 Genesis of the burh. The Wessex burhs from 886 and the second phase following the London meeting in 898, with the pincer movement led by Ethelred and Aethelflaed (west flank) and Edward the Elder (east flank).

(Author)

flank, commanded by Edward the Elder, took on the East Midlands, building burhs from Hertford to Nottingham. The left flank, addressing the West Midlands, had to cope with the Welsh and the Irish as well as the Danes and recalcitrant Mercians. Here the campaign was commanded by Ethelred and Aethelflaed, who built their first burhs in the Roman towns at Gloucester, Worcester and Chester (Figure 3.107).[338] Ethelred was Mercian himself, popular and brave, but was fatally wounded at the battle of Tettenhall (910). His wife,

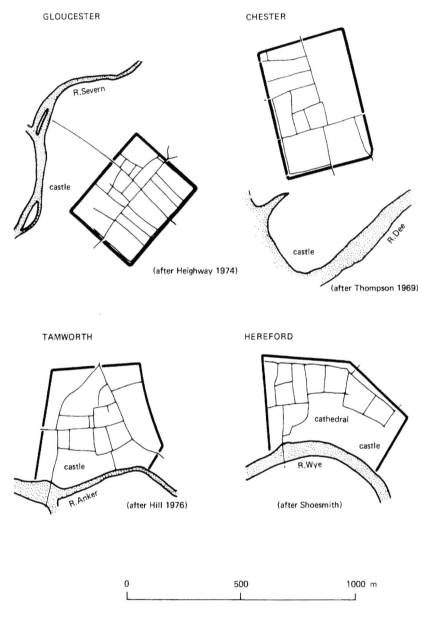

Figure 3.107 Examples of West Mercian burhs.

(Rahtz 1977, Fig 22; Leicester University Press)

Aethelflaed, then took over and proved herself an able and successful commander; more-over hers was an offensive not a defensive operation.[339] Now taken to the heart of the locals as 'The Lady of the Mercians', she built five more burhs and reinforced Leicester and then York, where she took the surrender of the Scandinavian town in 918 and shortly afterwards died exhausted.[340] This remarkable woman has yet to get the novels and films she deserves. Here I can offer her a modest tribute: the large-scale investigation of one of her minor burhs, Stafford on the River Sow.

Stafford was one of the later county towns to be redeveloped in the late 20th-century boom, so it was possible to plan and execute an archaeological campaign of three major area excavations (1975–81) plus an eventual tally of 52 sample excavations in areas that were accessible up to 1988.[341] (Figure 3.108). The Late Saxon burh proved to lie on a pen-insula formed by a marshy loop in the river, crossed by a Roman road. The river was not a formidable barrier and by Aethelflaed's day could be presumably crossed by a ford (Staf-ford). River and marsh combined, however, to present a defensible promontory, especially against those arriving by boat or on a horse. Activity before the 10th century took the form of granaries of late Iron Age type at a site north of the church, the same area that was to be used for grain processing by the burh. In spite of diligent searching and well-argued infer-ence, there has been no convincing evidence for a Middle Saxon (Fm 2) church or strong-hold, although neither is unlikely. The first development in historic times with any material impact was that of the Late Saxon army.[342] At that time the Roman road was probably viable, since the burh was divided by it: to the west (the highest point) lay the Late Saxon church of St Bertelin, with its charcoal burial and the grain processing area to the north. To the east was an industrial area with pottery kilns and, at the edge of the marsh, a town tip, with large consignments of animal bone and pottery wasters (Figure 3.109). The kilns were making a type of pottery ('Stafford Ware') which bears a strong resemblance to Roman pottery used in the same area (Severn Valley Ware). A pottery workshop was excavated in the vicinity, having two kilns, numerous pits and a well and gulley. In one of the pits with wasters from unsuccessful firings was the skull of a severed head, and this was not the only example (Figure 3.110).

Aethelflaed's burh at Stafford was a relatively simple affair, if hinting at a severe regime. Its main products were pottery – mostly orange jars of a regular capacity, but with a range of bowls and cups (Figure 3.111). It was also concerned with the processing of meat, pre-dominately of adult cattle, and grain, mainly wheat, oats and barley, which was ground and baked into loaves and bannocks in low temperate ovens at a specific location north of the church[343] (Figure 3.112). Sightings of Stafford Ware show that the whole peninsula was in use in the 10th century, but the spatial organisation hints at an industrial area to the east and a more privileged enclave to the west. The latter was the site of the Late Saxon church and the bread supply, and the surviving street plan would accommodate a square defensive enclosure measuring about 150 × 150 m in this area.[344] Such an arrangement appears to imitate that of the Roman fort and its vicus. Stafford Ware is found over the area of the West Midlands, but predominately in the form of jars and in the sites of other burhs. This endorses its ini-tial connections with the military campaign. Some of the Late Saxon wheel-thrown pottery industries – Thetford Ware, St Neots ware in the east, shelly ware and Cheddar E ware in the south – and arguably the glazed wares of Stamford and Winchester – also imitate Roman pottery and serve specific regions of England (Figure 3.113). The regions, which appear to be supplied with their pottery via rivers, equate broadly to Mercia, East Anglia, Wessex and the Thames Valley.[345]

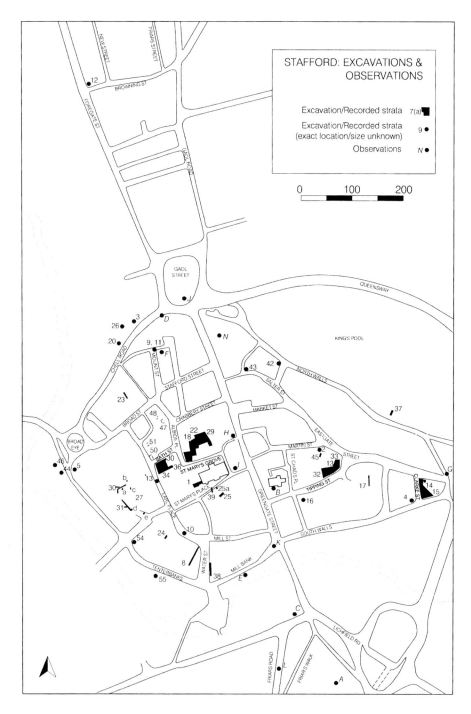

Figure 3.108 Stafford Town showing interventions 1975–1985. Major excavations in black (left to right): Bath Street (edge of burh), St Mary's Grove (bakery), St Bertelin's Church, Tipping Street (potters' workshop) and Clarke Street (town tip). The King's Pool (centre right) was marshy ground in 1975 providing a pollen sequence.

(Carver 2010b, Fig 1.2; courtesy of Boydell and Brewer)

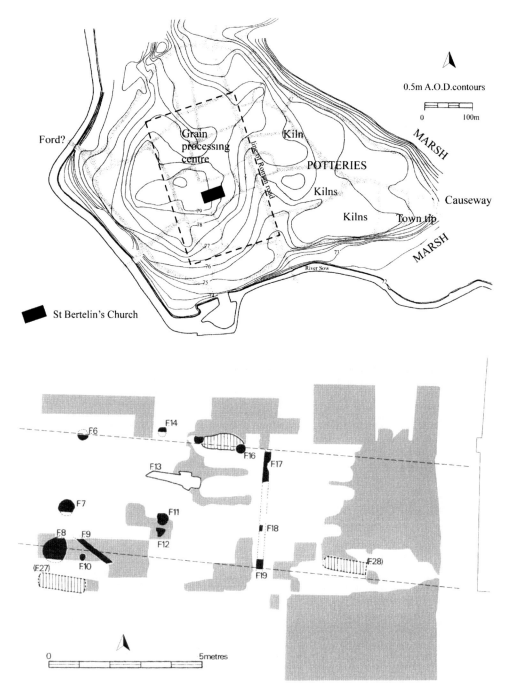

Figure 3.109 (Top): Plan of Stafford, showing the possible form of a rectangular Late Saxon fort. The peninsula site is divided into two by the line of a Roman road: to the west is the fort with a grain processing area and the church of St Bertelin, and to the east is the 'vicus', with extensive potteries and the town tip containing animal bones and pottery wasters. (Bottom): Plan of Late Saxon features from the excavation of the ruin of St Bertelin's church in 1954.

(Carver 2010b, Fig 1.3; courtesy of Boydell and Brewer)

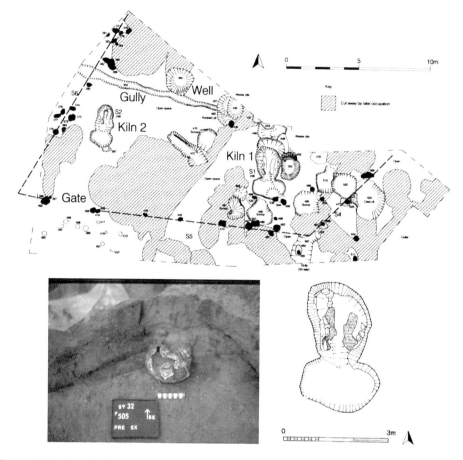

Figure 3.110 (Top) Stafford: Potters' workshop at Tipping Street, showing location of the fenced area, the well, two pottery-firing kilns and waster pits around Kiln 1. (Bottom left): A human skull in a waster pit. (Bottom right): Plan of Kiln 1.

(Carver 2010b, Fig 4.18; courtesy of Boydell and Brewer)

Figure 3.111 Examples of Stafford Ware, including jars, bowls, cups and lamps.

(Carver 2010b, Plate III, 4.20, 4.21; courtesy of Boydell and Brewer)

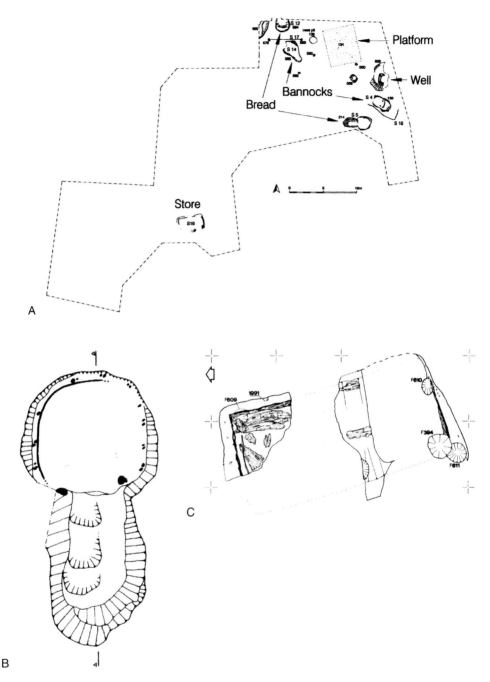

Figure 3.112 A: The industrial bakery north of St Mary's Church. The platform was formed of rammed pebbles and might have been a place for unloading carts. B: The bread was baked in ovens on a circular shelf under a clay and wattle dome. A distinction was observed between the baking of loaves (wheat) and bannocks (oats). Chaff was used as fuel. C: The grain store was a sunken-floored shed lined with timbers, and had been destroyed by fire and cut by later pits.

(Carver 2010b, Fig 4.18, 4.10, 4.11; courtesy of Boydell and Brewer)

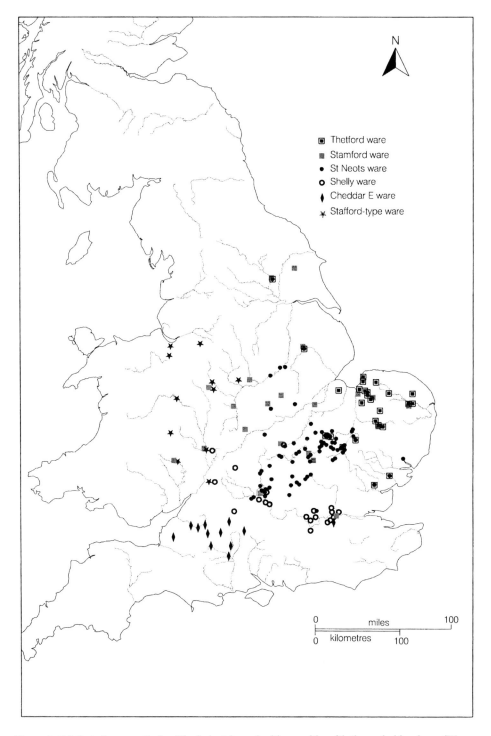

Figure 3.113 Late Saxon potteries. The industries coincide roughly with the early kingdoms (Wessex, Mercia, East Anglia) but perhaps relate more to the river system, reflecting the modes of delivery.

(Carver 2011b, Fig 47.10; courtesy of Boydell and Brewer)

Origins of the burh

Most theories on the origins of the burh focus on the types of settlement that were known to have preceded them. H. M. Chadwick saw the choice of site as guided by the presence of royal estate centres.[346] For Brooks, their roots lay in Mercian forts of the 8th century. Hill proposed that burhs were either intended as forts (if small) or towns (if large). For Blair, they were formed around previous minster sites.[347] The discussion about how the burh was created and used has been broadened in the last decade. Alan Vince's study of late Saxon pottery and Continental imports showed that while silver pennies were in circulation in the 10th century, there was no movement of international traffic until the 11th. In his view, burhs underwent a three-stage development: forts in the 9th century, centres for local government (and putative tax collection) in the 10th and trading towns in the 11th.[348] Even in Mercia, no convincing fortified centres have been encountered in the pre-burh period. The two hopefuls, Hereford and Tamworth, have not produced any well-dated defences before the mid-9th century.[349] That is not to say they were not occupied. Hereford had a corn dryer, and Tamworth is documented as the site of Offa's palace. Most if not all of the burhs had a minster church. But few of these appear to have been certainly earlier than the 9th century, and none to date was preceded by a monastery in the northern sense.[350] Chadwick also felt that the design of the eastern burhs may have reflected the Danish presence.[351] But although the Scandinavians had military forts in their homelands, the pre-9th-century examples are circular or curvilinear, and even so are not thought to have influenced later Viking design.[352]

In the reading advanced here, the English town is the result of an experimental sequence, in which the English aristocracy combined the 8th-century experience of increasing settlement hierarchy, lucrative trading ports, and a system of tribute or taxation with a new model for the defence of the island derived from a learned study of Roman Britain, perhaps seasoned with knowledge of an archaeological kind observed in old Roman forts and towns (Figure 3.114). As the term implies, a *burh* was primarily a fort, and in this case was adopted and developed by the royal family of Wessex as an instrument to defend the Wessex homeland and used to conquer much of Britain thereafter. If we are looking for a source of inspiration, the imitation of Rome is a strong theme to emerge from the Stafford excavations, and one that can be readily attributed to Alfred and his family.[353] The Wessex initiative adopted the rectangular or subsquare enclosure of the Roman marching camp, provided with two orthogonal streets and internal divisions. The lack of buildings in some examples indicates that the most likely occupation of the enclosure in the early days was that of a militia under canvas. In a raising of the game, the advance into the Midlands was achieved using a series of rectilinear forts to house shock troops along protected supply lines. Some burhs were based in former Roman forts; others were built anew using ditches, palisades and dump ramparts. Even on promontory sites, it is not impossible that a rectangular fort was the basic unit of defence. Each fort was manned by a garrison supplied with bread and meat. The pottery, itself of Roman type (orange in the west and black in the east) presumably contained other, vanished, rations – butter, cheese, honey. Here is a professionalised army on the move, executing a rerun of the Roman conquest.

Only after the political situation became more stable in the 10th century were some of the burhs adapted as regional centres and charged with the administration of shires. The third stage in which some of these, mostly those with access to the sea, became nodes of international trade did not generally arrive until the 11th century. At this point, on the eve of the Norman Conquest, it could be said that England had its first towns.[354]

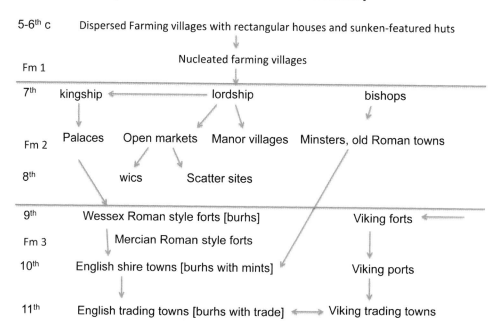

Figure 3.114 The urban trajectory in England. The verdict here is that there was no continuity from Roman towns but some reinvestment prompted by Christianisation in the 7th century and a revived interest in Roman fort building and military strategy in the 9th century. Selected forts became regional administrative centres in the 10th century and trading centres in the 11th century.

(Author)

Comparanda

Contemporary sequences in Ireland and Scandinavia

As a coda to this sequence of settlement designs in Britain, I propose very brief visits to similar trajectories in Ireland and Scandinavia. The primary purpose of these is to stress the influence, or potential influence, of neighbours to west and east. If we had begun the chapter with such a trip, or interwoven its examples with the main text, that might have brought confusion; and siting them here should make it possible to point out periods and places where that influence has been exercised, or seemingly ignored, in Britain.

The settlement experience in **Ireland** is an especially useful source of analogy in the north and west, much of which, like Ireland, did not pass through the Roman mill. The Iron Age in Ireland is famously elusive, and remains so up to the 7th century.[355] This root feeling has received endorsement from the recent period of intense research promoted by the Irish government. This was executed first by a national research initiative – the 'Discovery Programme' – intended specifically to illuminate the formative years of their island, and second by effective legislation designed to reap the dividends of rescue digging, culminating in the archaeological research programme managed by the National Roads Authority.[356] This fruitful period of research has confirmed that the majority of more than 50,000 ringforts (raths) located by survey are early medieval in date. At last count more than 900 of the early medieval settlements located by research survey or encountered during landscape rescue had been excavated.[357] There is a boom of settlement building from the 7th century, accompanied by an increase in cereal production (mainly oats and barley) and, presumably, an increase in population.[358]

In general those buildings where the plans have been securely documented are at first round and then rectangular.[359] Documentary descriptions of the 7th/8th century refer exclusively to roundhouses, and this is the story so far on the ground.[360] Roundhouses in Ireland are generally between 5 and 7 m in diameter and are most commonly recognised as a single perimeter of stake holes, or two concentric rings indicating a turf wall. Turf walls are also implied by arcs of upright stone slabs.[361] At Illaunloughan, huts A and B were circular buildings joined together, their turf walls implied by a circle of tall flat stones thought to have acted as revetments. The roofs were conjectured after Irish custom as made of turf strips pegged to wattle and straw panels.[362] There are no known examples of longhouses, byre-houses or halls, and the roundhouses are single ring or figure of eight; none are cellular.[363] The majority of settlements were concerned with farming, an activity producing a wide range of other structures besides dwellings: pens, barns, industrial areas, middens, grain dryers, horizontal mills, curvilinear fields (for crops) and rectilinear fields (for livestock).

From the later 7th century (our Fm 2), the country also abounds with new types of settlement: ringforts (raths), crannogs, monasteries and 'cemetery settlements', villages in which residence, light industry and burial are combined. The *raths* or *ringforts* present a type of circular banked and ditched enclosure up to 50 m in diameter, containing roundhouses. The grandeur and wealthy of assemblage of large-scale sites such as Garranes prompts the interpretation that they are royal in status.[364] Stout sees the ringfort as a form of dispersed settlement, although connected by intervisibility into associated clusters: they are found only in areas that support farming, especially of cattle.[365] For Chris Lynn, the ringfort is the base of 'middle-class homesteaders who saw themselves as small chiefs, drawing attention to their status and keeping out unwanted visitors (including sometimes their own animals) rather than having serious regard to military defence'.[366] The raised rath at **Deer Park Farms** was a flat-topped mound heightened by gravel layers built between about 660 and 760 and abandoned before the 9th century (Figure 3.115).[367] The wattle walls of the houses were fashioned from hazel, and heather, bracken and moss were found within the cavity walls, but there was also some evidence for turf walls. The beetles suggested that the interiors of these buildings were warm and dry. At this site, the largest roundhouse was located at the entrance and smaller roundhouses clustered behind it (Figure 3.116).[368] This site also had evidence for the burning of seaweed, water-rolled pebbles, an iron hook, a trough and possible parts of a stretcher frame, all components that were interpreted at Portmahomack in Pictland as indications of parchment-making (p. 151).[369] Curvilinear 'plectrum-shaped' enclosures may be a variation on the ringfort.[370] At Twomileborris, County Tipperary, a late Bronze Age enclosure with a circular house preceded a plectrum-shaped enclosure 42 m across containing a circular structure and 27 pits. The settlement was reorganised in the 7th/8th century, when it took the form of a circular enclosure containing three roundhouses, and the plectrum-shaped enclosure became the cemetery.[371] At Newtown, County Limerick, Bronze Age houses and a cemetery preceded an early medieval enclosure 50 m across containing a figure-of-eight building.[372] By the 10th century (Fm 3), the assertive individuality of the ringfort had faded.[373]

Figure 3.115 The raised rath at Deer Park Farms, occupied from 660 to 760.

(Lynn and McDowell 2011, frontispiece; courtesy of Jacqueline McDowell)

Crannógs (lake dwellings) are the wetland equivalent of the rath, famous examples being Ballinderry 2 and Lagore. Like Garranes, these rich sites, excavated in the early 20th century and encountering exceptional preservation and retrieving rich assemblages, were influential in creating a Gaelic or Celtic narrative for the formation of an Irish state.[374] More recent investigations at Moynagh Lough revealed a dominant 8th-century roundhouse 10 m across internally as well a rich assemblage that led its excavator to call it an aristocratic residence.[375] The start dates of Irish crannogs have been disputed or revised under the lash of scientific dating, but the 7th/8th century would seem to be the important moment of lift off.[376] The crannog excavated at Drumclay, County Fermanagh, has produced rectilinear buildings and homely objects up to the 17th century and is currently thought to have been founded as early as the 7th century.[377] Ballinderry 1 was occupied mainly in the 10th and 11th century and, by contrast with those mentioned, had no evidence at all for craft activity apart from waste products of iron-working, and an assemblage resembling that of Viking Dublin.[378] The crannog was to prove a useful type of settlement in certain places until the 19th century.[379]

Fm 2 also saw the appearance of the Irish *monastery*, ostensibly a species of rath concentric in form but dedicated to spiritual authority (see for example Nendrum). The current appreciation of the dates suggest that the numerous raths (ringforts) and monastic enclosures coexisted between the 6th and 9th century, although monasteries built before the 7th century remain elusive.[380] Those settlements identified as monasteries or 'ecclesiastical settlements' can generally claim several attributes of a defining package: circular or concentric enclosures (the *termon*), a church in the central enclave, a cemetery with incised grave markers and boundaries marked by high crosses, outdoor shrines and altars (*leachta*); and in the outer areas monastic crafts, of which working in precious metals is often the best survivor.[381] Clonmacnoise, Nendrum and Reask have been extensively excavated, while Illanloughan,

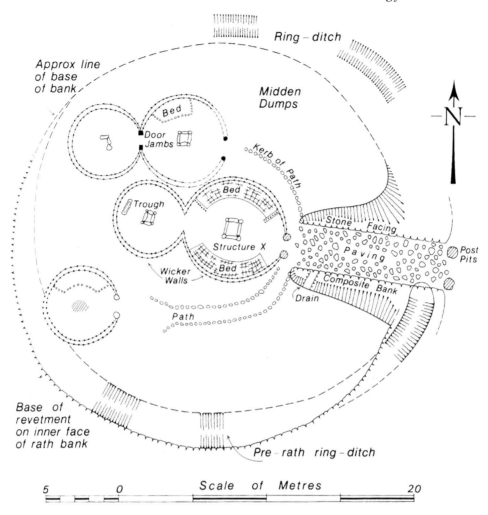

Figure 3.116 Plan of the Deer Park Farms rath.

(O'Sullivan et al. 2014a, Fig 3.11 after Lynn and McDowell 2011, Fig 7.11 courtesy of Jacqueline McDowell)

High Island and Innismurray have been subjected to illuminating surveys.[382] The economies generally exploit cattle, but grain was also a staple: **Nendrum** has produced the best defined example of a horizontal mill, in this case driven by the tide.[383] The ongoing investigations at **Clonmacnoise**, County Offaly, have contacted a 7th-century settlement of post and wattle buildings concerned with bone- and iron-working which were reorganised in the later 7th century. By this time it was importing gold, silver, copper, amber, lignite and E-ware pottery along with wine from south-west France, showing the place to be 'part of both an inter-regional and international trading network'.[384] Another major expansion occurred in the 8th/9th century when the enclosure covered 13 ha and was approached by a timber bridge across the River Shannon. By Formative 3 it was functioning at a level described as urban.

Thomás Ó Carragáin sees the original design of these monastic cult sites as inspired by eastern sacred places of refuge, notably Jerusalem.[385] Assuming a monastic site is dated by its church, the clearest evidence comes from the 7th century and later. Early timber churches are inferred but have not yet been clearly encountered on the ground; but three turf buildings are known, that on Church Island, County Kerry, probably maintained from the 7th to the 10th century.[386] Dry stone churches appear from the 8th century, and church buildings in mortared stone are known from the 8th and 9th. The *shrine chapel*, dedicated to the veneration of the relics of Irish saints, seems to be a development of the late 7th century and refer to the idea of the Holy Sepulchre.[387] Examples include that at St Columba's House at Iona (p. 210). The larger type of monastic site is thought to have emerged from local roots and to have dominated its own territory, and was perhaps affiliated with secular power. Dating remains challenging, but the possibility is that the larger centres were primary and arrived only in the 7th century, their independence boosted in the 8th century through the competitive status of relics.[388] The monastic movement, in which all the British and Irish regions took part, later spawned daughter-houses on peripheral islands and headlands, some with gardens and mills in enclosures linked by dry stone walling.[389]

The type of multi-purpose village provisionally entitled *cemetery-settlement* (or settlement-cemetery) was among the prime fruits of the NRA harvest.[390] They are distinguished by having burials and settlement in the same place but no church.[391] The cemeteries are enclosed and central to the settlement (Carrigatogher), integrated within the settlement (Johnstown) or contiguous with them (Camlin 3, Figure 3.117). Camlin also shows in stratified form a transition from round to rectangular housing thought to have taken place in the 9th century.[392] Many have evidence for iron-working as well as farming and one or more horizontal mills.[393] Tomás Ó Carragáin has interpreted these villages as potentially long-lived family farms at a time (or in a district) where worship was focussed on monastic sites and there was no overall provision of pastoral care in Ireland.[394]

Rectangular buildings appear in Ireland around the 9th century in raths, monasteries and villages.[395] They may be fashioned in timber and turf or of dry stone construction with the interiors frequently paved. The impetus for the change from round to rectangular is unclear. It is possible that the practice was led by the need to construct rectangular church buildings required by the Roman rite. The appearance of the technique is a little late to be credited to the arrival of Christianity, although it might be thought to coincide with the more rigorous version of Christianity that was imposed from the 8th century. The form is not obviously owed to Viking influence: in Dublin they are home-grown – there is nothing like them elsewhere in the Viking world.[396] It is with the advent of rectangular houses in Ireland (by contrast to Scotland), that souterrains first appear.[397] An excavated example at Tateetra Dundalk had two corridors 30 m long and 1.5 m wide, equipped with air vents and sumps, braces and bolt-holes.[398] The poky space suggests a hideaway, and 'souterrain ware' – a home-made tub-shaped coarse ware – suggests storage, although some are sooted, so used for heating the contents.[399] This suggests storage of grain, milk, cheese, honey and meat products.[400] For Chris Lynn the appearance of the rectangular house and the souterrain after c. 800 marks the watershed between the late Iron Age and the early Christian period in Ireland:

> by about AD 1000, we find most people living in rectangular houses pre-occupied in some areas with the need for personal defence, including being captured and taken into slavery. . . . It is possible that social patterns, the rules of land ownership and warfare had so changed partly as a result of the Scandinavian raids and settlements, as to render the bravado of ring-fort occupation inappropriate for all but the most powerful.[401]

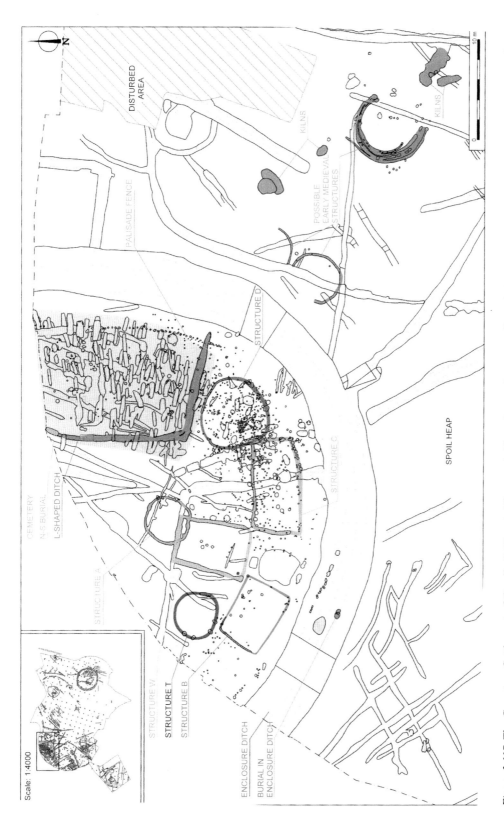

Figure 3.117 The Cemetery-Settlement of Camlin 3 (County Tipperary). The orientated cemetery lies within a rectilinear enclosure. The form of houses changes from round to rectangular around 800. The full circle of the enclosure was confirmed by geophysical survey.

(Flynn 2009, Ill 3; courtesy of Colm Flynn; with permission © Valerie J. Keeley Ltd)

It was probably the need for personal protection from the slave trade that led to the adoption of the stone-lined souterrain.[402]

The flight from ringfort culture is also reflected in livestock. At Knowth the ditches of the enclosure built around the passage-grave mound in the 7th/8th century contained an animal bone assemblage whose study has been determinant.[403] At 60% cattle, 20% pig and 20% sheep, it had (with Clogher) the highest cattle count in early medieval Ireland, accounting for 80% of the meat consumed. These figures are held to reflect a value system in which 'cattle, particularly dairy cows are the basis of wealth' and implied that the ringwork enclosures were primarily designed for the protection of herds. By contrast the following period (the 10th century) sees a marked decline in the proportion of cattle, as it does in the occupation of ringworks.[404] At the same time drying kilns and extensive iron-working appear in settlements. Ireland is affected by the Viking realpolitik: even monasteries begin to assume commercial roles and have been termed 'monastic towns'.

Ireland offers a model in which some kind of ideological change occurs roughly every two centuries. The three material periods correspond well to our Formative 1 (5th/7th century), Formative 2 (7th/9th century) and Formative 3 (9th/11th century); the second of these involved a religious initiative and the third an invasion. If Fm 1 is not strongly manifested, Fm 2 is a period of rapid growth, as seen in the number of ringforts, crannogs, monasteries, and villages. It is primarily a cattle economy. Fm 3 sees a switch from the ring-fort–roundhouse–cattle culture to one of settlements with underground storage or protection (souterrains) and less dependence on cattle and more on sheep, pig and cereals. In this period the larger monasteries also start functioning as centres of manufacture and trade. Here we have parallel to the transition from warrior-led, to spiritually led to commercially led initiatives noted in north and west Britain.

If Britain emulates Ireland, then the Irish equivalents should have primacy. As will be seen, this is only partly the case. Fm 1 connections are poorly represented. The souterrain, the crannog and rectangular buildings all flourish later than they do in Scotland.[405] On the other hand, Ireland provides templates for the ringfort, the monastery and the multi-functional village that are of the greatest value for understanding those in British territory, where the evidence is generally more exiguous.

Continental analogies for settlement in Britain (mainly south and east)

As the north and west of Britain look to Ireland for parallels and explanations, so we might expect eastern Britain to catch some its preferences and changing moods in the experience of the north-west continent and Scandinavia. The sequence is longer, stronger and more widely explored than that of its British cousins. In north-west Continental Europe, farms in the Rhine delta during the 3rd to 1st century BC consisted of pits, silos and rectangular buildings enclosed by an irregular ditch. Status was indicated by the number of houses enclosed and by the number of trees growing on the bank of the enclosure (which provided an indication of how long it had been there).[406] From a distance these were said to resemble a small wood.[407] In the Low Countries, the prevalent prehistoric living unit is the longhouse, many of which were byre-houses where an extended family shared the space with its animals, particularly cows. The late Iron Age examples were shorter (at 10–15 m) than their Bronze Age predecessors, implying the residence of a nuclear (as opposed to an extended) family. These served unenclosed farms mainly dedicated to cattle breeding which also featured four- and six-post granaries, wells and silos. New sites were frequently initiated, and central cemeteries served the corpus of wandering farms.[408] The longhouse was a complex unit that combined family life, animal husbandry and spirituality.[409] That at Grøntoft had stalls for

12 cows. The cow was the chief symbiotic companion, but there were others: at Ginnerup, where the house had burnt down, the stalls had contained four sheep, one pig and one cow; at Nørre Tranders there were seven cattle, five sheep, two lambs, two horses and one pig. The longhouse also stored cereals: a burned cellar at Overbygård contained c. 60 vessels and over 100 litres of grain. Also found were 10 balls of clay, five burnishing stones, two swords, two iron axes and some wooden objects, including the remains of a stool. Objects are also found under the floors and hearth, in the foundations and in post-holes – for example pots with food and animal bones – while an axe, a dog and a sea urchin fossil seem to converge on entrances. Leo Webley sees these as having a spiritual purpose – offerings to *vaetter* and *nisser* (spirits of hearth and home). Such votive deposition appears to increase in the Roman Iron Age. By the late Roman Iron Age, longhouses have partitions in the dwelling areas that seem to pre-echo the social divisions to come.[410]

In the 5th/6th century, the length of buildings decreased further and there was a change of living strategy in which man and cow parted company and the human living space was redesigned to create the open span 'hall'.[411] The change from the self-sufficient family unit to the central hall and attendant outbuildings implied a loss of independence or changes in individual and social structures that must have been deeply felt.[412] It is possible that climatic variation was the prompt, since the longhouse had already disappeared and reappeared in the course of prehistory.[413] Another possibility is migration, for example to England, which broke up families and mutual obligations. Another is a huge increase in the demand for cattle as tribute – for example by the Franks.[414]

The absence of the longhouse from early England might appear puzzling and has been explained by a lack of corporate energy (or 'social capital') to build them and the precocious adoption of the hall.[415] The widespread presence of the byre-house in the Britain of a much later period tends to presuppose that they were there in the early middle ages too. But up to now it has been conspicuous by its absence from Southumbria,[416] the only examples in the Formative period so far being those at Pitcarmick in southern Pictland and Hound Tor in Devon.[417] We can conclude that the incomers had a broad legacy on which to draw all variations on suitable domiciles.

In Fm 2, previously dispersed settlements began to 'nucleate', clustering around a hall of increasing size, denoting more ambitious social controls and termed 'magnate farms' (see p. 229). In Sweden, the farms were supplemented by *shielings*, residences serving summer grazing, and the making of dairy products. The system there appears to have been operated exclusively by women, implying the absence of the men on other business (such as fishing). The shieling zone ran from Uppland to Bohusland, separating areas of cattle herding to the north and arable farming to the south.[418]

In Norway and Sweden, important aspects of community cohesion have been revealed by the excavation of some outstanding sites, grouped under the general term 'Central Places', in which all centuries between the 2nd and 10th are represented: examples are Gudme on Fyn, Tissø on Sjaelland, Uppåkra in Skåne, Helgö on Lake Malar, Borg on Lofoten and Kaupang in Oslo fjord. In spite of their air of permanence, these settlements do appear to evolve through time.

Wealth is accrued initially through votive deposits in lakes and bogs, to the benefit only of the deity, but develop into donations retained on dry land: small gold foils, *guldgubber*, which are found scattered at the site and often lead to its discovery (Figure 3.118). This suggests that many of these places first gained prestige as cult sites.[419] In a second development, wealthy imports arrive (such as an Irish crozier and a Buddhist statue at Helgö). Votive deposits dry up, but the sites are apparently enriched with other offerings found in hoards that can be seen as contributions from pilgrims, supporting spiritual specialists, or as tribute to secular lords. In a third phase, wealth creation through the exchange of goods is more evident.

Figure 3.118 Uppåkra (in southern Sweden) a prominent long-lived cult site (3rd to 11th centuries). (Top left): The temple building showing the distribution of gold foil figures (guldgubbar) marked as spots. The area of the floor deposit is light grey (1) with the white space in between marking the extent of the clay floor of House 14. The four great post holes were surrounded by bow-shaped stave-built walls (2). In the centre was a hearth (3) (Top right): Shamanistic figure with staff, crew cut, torque or necklace and thumb in the mouth. (Centre left): Male figures cut out of gold. (Bottom left) Three of 11 die-identical female figures. (Centre) Male-female couple. (Bottom centre) Male-female couple from Toftegården, Sjaelland. (Bottom right) Male-female couple on modern replica die from National Museum Copenhagen.

(All images except G (author) from Watt 2004, with figure numbers indicated; courtesy of Margrethe Watt)

Dagfinn Skre proposed an evolutionary commercial model whereby markets were served by networks of increasing size from local to nodal to urban. The apparent multi-purpose nature of these sites led to the use of the neutral terminology 'central place', although perhaps 'congregational sites' is a better description, since their common denominator is the power to attract people, whether due to cult, governance or a market, for spiritual, social or financial benefits. It is possible that what is being manifested on the ground is a change of emphasis: Gudme and Uppåkra are primarily cult sites; Borg is the headquarters of a regional leader; Tissø changes from votive deposits in the lake to contributions associated with shrines and ultimately with hall sites[420] (Figure 3.119). As the communities dedicated themselves more to wealth creation through exchange, new sites are established with access to the sea and the greater networks of the 9th century, Skre's nodal markets and eventually towns: Ribe, Dorestad, Hedeby and Kaupang (Figure 3.120).[421]

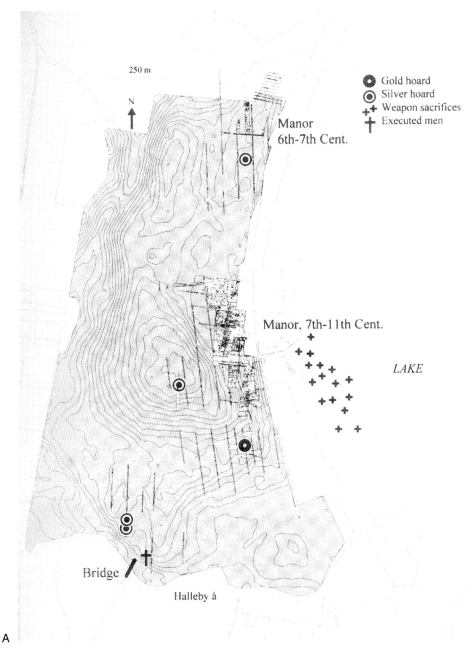

250 m

N

Gold hoard
Silver hoard
Weapon sacrifices
Executed men

Manor
6th-7th Cent.

Manor, 7th-11th Cent.

LAKE

Bridge

Halleby å

A

Figure 3.119 The site at Lake Tissø (Denmark). A (above): The location of the settlements, hoards and votive deposits. At least 10,000 metal finds have been recovered, including 50 swords from the lake. B (opposite top): The Phase 3 settlement (9th/10th century).

(Jørgensen 2003, 183, 191; licenced by Oxbow press on behalf of Windgather)

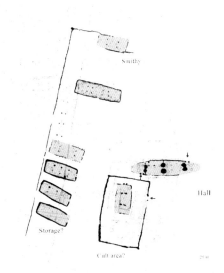

Smithy

Hall

Storage?

Cult area?

B

Figure 3.119 (Continued)

Figure 3.120 Ribe (Denmark): reconstruction drawing of the early town, organised into merchant tenements.

(Feveile 2010, Fig 117; image licensed by and © Flemming Bau)

Frands Herschend has painted a vivid picture of the first of these transitions from spiritual to secular governance in which the authority of the bog is supplanted by the authority of the hall, a reformation that was reflected in allegorical form in the poem *Beowulf*.[422] On a more mundane note it can be suggested that the priestly authorities running cult centres soon recognised the advantages of selling spiritual benefits to pilgrims rather than supervising the disposal of votive objects that would otherwise end up in the lake.[423] As the wealth of these cult sites increased, they would naturally attract the attention of the warrior class for reasons that went beyond theology. Thereafter Skre's model shows how sites are added to the repertoire as dependence on commerce grows.

Reflections

There are intermittent echoes and some unexpected silences in the conversation between England and the continent (Table 3.7). Sunken-featured buildings are common in England, longhouses currently absent. The hall is present from the outset, in a modest form. Larger halls are built from the 7th century, and the layout resembles that of the 'magnate farm', with enclosures and connecting tracks. Even though there are finds of bracteates, with their pagan iconography, no *guldgubber* have been found, and there are no convincing signs of the cult centres or ritualised central places like Gudme or Tissø, with the possible exception of Rendlesham (p. 246). On the other hand, in the northernmost part of the English region, in Northumbria, we see the rise of a type of site that in many ways is an analogue to the Scandinavian central cult site, namely the monastery. The scatter sites ('productive sites') find a parallel in Stavnsager and the 'creek sites' noted by Loveluck and Tys.[424] With the arrival of the wics we are on a convergent course with 8th–9th century Scandinavia but part company again after the Viking raids, when the English invest in forts and centres of local government in the context of the conquest of a greater England. Vikings employed mobile 'thing sites' as places of assembly, government and judgement and imported them into Britain – the Tynwald in the Isle of Man being an example.[425] In the hunt for home-grown assembly places, attention has been drawn to hundred meeting places and other documented spots, some of which have a prehistoric ancestry.[426] But many other settlements, cemeteries and monuments may have acted as congregational sites, central places and assembly points for a variety of reasons, as noted in this chapter and the next.

Table 3.7 Four sequences in parallel

Timespan	Ireland	N&W Britain	S&E Britain	NW Europe
Formative 1 5th–7th century	Enclosed circular villages (raths) with roundhouses Central places (ex-Iron Age)	Family forts on hilltops and crannogs using roundhouses	Extended all-purpose settlements using halls and SFBs	Extended villages using longhouses
Formative 2 7th–9th century	Monasteries Cemetery-settlements	Monasteries Upland villages with byre-houses	Magnate farms and trading places (wics)	Magnate farms Great halls Temples, cult sites, trading places, central places
Formative 3 9th–11th century	Monastic towns Viking forts, trading places and towns	Trading places	Viking forts and towns English forts and towns (burhs)	Viking forts and towns Overseas trading ports

Conclusions

This chapter has been concerned mainly with settlements powered by farming, and our tour round the island has shown up the farmer as a principal architect of settlement form. The differences of agricultural practice are those predicted in Chapter 1: in the north and west (the British zones) staple income is invested in cattle, managed in herds and stored as hides. The domestic food store is augmented by hunting, especially deer (the 'wild cattle'), and the people rely on dried meat, blood pudding and dairy products for their rations in hard times or on the move. Like the cattle, people also live in family groups led by an 'alpha male' willing to confront others and steal their cows. The settlements (so far) comprise curvilinear strongholds, roundhouses, former prehistoric stone dwellings and crannogs, sites where smiths can be put to work providing men with weapons, women with jewellery. By Fm 2, the monastery is a key settlement type in which herds grow, and a surplus is created to provide clerics with books and ritual vessels of precious metals with which to serve the new universal lord.

In the English plain, by contrast, the immigrants inherited a vast tract of fertile farmland where cereals (wheat and barley) and wool provided the main staples and working capital. In the early Saxon period, mixed farming, with equal reliance on cattle, sheep and pigs, appears to have been the order of the day. The story (so far) is of family groups in living in rectangular houses in individual farmsteads, each with its own weaving shed (West Stow), or gathered into larger kampongs (West Heslerton, probably Mucking) where the houses cluster in a residential area and the cellared sheds, used for storing grain, weaving or forging iron, are gathered in an adjacent industrial estate. These early Anglo-Saxons are organised for agriculture, and by Fm 2 they appear to have restarted the Roman grain machine and are generating large surpluses.[427] The Witton Survey showed that land under arable doubled every 150 years in this part of early, middle and late Saxon Norfolk.[428] The wealth commanded and handled by the rising Fm 2 aristocracy was considerable. The English had the luck to discover that the richest part of Britannia was also the least well defended, and within two centuries or so they were as favoured as Romans and living in magnate farms akin to villas.

Few parcels of land were all cereals or all cattle, so the discussion is about emphases. If the west of Scotland and the east of England show the differences in high profile, the extensive buffer zone between the two would naturally have reflected the local terrain as well as the cultural frontier: this is the Anglo-British belt. Northumbria, Cumbria, Mercia, even Wessex have something of a British legacy and mixed animal and cereal strategies. In 8th-century Pictland, byre-house confronts roundhouse either side of the River Tay. Farming cannot survive if it is wholly cultural, but it is unlikely to have been wholly pragmatic and environmentally determined, especially in a land of mobile peoples.

It is a fairly safe generalisation that there was no overarching authority in Formative 1 in any part of Britain, and so any governance happened at family or kin level, always allowing for the process of hosting where ethnic or religious difference drove crowds into confrontation and bloodshed. As the end of the 7th century (and the beginning of Fm 2) approached, the peoples of the north and west abandoned their family forts in favour of the divine protection of the Christian deity under the leadership of specialists in ritual philosophy. Nobody today should doubt the power of this leadership, which delivered a bloodless coup over a country of warriors, technical progress in farming and milling and a shared affluence in the name of the greater glory of God. All that was necessary was to share power, or give it, to the spiritual specialists.

However, the English in Fm 2 were engaged in the creation of their own version of an affluent country, mainly on the back of agricultural success. The wealth was attracted into the hands of a new aristocracy who concentrated their assets by rent, tolls or trade into magnate farms. In the early 7th century, some of the wealth was invested in the hereafter by being buried in a barrow.

At the end of the 7th century, as the English areas were Christianised, this practice should have been superseded by a new method of supernatural investment. However, it is not archaeologically evident at present that this included investing in monasteries of the type seen in the north and west. Enrichment was focussed on the magnate farm. However, from the early 8th century there was investment of another kind, consisting of ordered settlements in designated places dedicated to the creating of wealth through trade, national and international – the *wics*.

When the Vikings came in Fm 3, they burnt the monasteries, and the wics soon ceased to trade. The ensuing wars prompted the English to create forts that would, by the 10th century, become seats of regional government, tribute and monetised exchange after the manner of Rome, 1,000 years earlier. By the 11th century, that trade would be said to have again been international.

The wars for the control of the island persuaded most that religion should take second place to governance and the creation of usable wealth. In the north, monasticism in its inspirational 8th-century form was dissolved, its sites morphing into trading places under worldly abbots and bishops. The forms of Christianity preferred in the English areas were probably similar to that adopted by the Vikings, with the priest and chapel integrated into the local lordship (Chapter 5). Christian revival when it came in the later 9th century was mediated through secular power, with palace and minster working in tandem as in Byzantium or Aachen. It became an instrument of statehood and a node of guidance for this world as well as the next. The politics of tribal governance, spiritual propitiation and wealth creation alternate, and as they do, settlement forms hitherto thought long term light up and mutate. Admittedly, this is a cloth woven from shreds and patches; holes and rotten threads are everywhere. It will be interesting to see if similar trends are to be observed in burial and in monuments (Chapters 4 and 5). If so, we are some way along the track to a broader narrative and its explanation.

Tailpiece: the archaeology of settlement in early medieval Britain: critique

Because stone buildings and earthworks survive much better than timber, and shiny metal objects better than woodwork, they can give an impression from the settlements we know that everyone either lived in grand places or were invisibly poor. Archaeology is repairing this inequality of representation and also showing (through exceptional excavations such as Yeavering) the grandeur that could be realised in timber. However, this is happening slowly. A survey of Anglo-Saxon settlements in 1976 celebrated the progress that had been made since the Yeavering excavations of 1953–62 and the wider recognition that post-holes indicated timber structures.[429] But in Britain since then, with certain exceptions such as West Heslerton and Chalton, the parts of settlements that have been excavated have remained small. In Ireland, by contrast, the tally of excavated early medieval settlements has reached levels that equate or exceed those of any other period. Many of these sites have been wholly excavated, or their plans mapped by using geophysical survey, as part of the heritage response.[430]

However, even when opportunities are presented to investigate settlements in Britain, the response has been startlingly weak. During their life, settlement features often become redundant and acquire rubbish that may have originated nearby or further afield; in other cases houses are demolished or burnt down and are replaced with holes for new posts that can include objects then lying about in close vicinity. These are important moments for the story of a village, since they represent rare opportunities to capture material that had been in contemporary use. The legacy of the past in this case is not at all complete: the timbers have usually decayed. Ploughing has usually shaved the occupation surfaces down to the 'natural geology', converting the floors, hearths and all the material that lay on them into topsoil. Medieval and later ploughing also continues the business of spreading the midden that contained the bulk of the assemblage. Hardly any artefacts are in primary contexts, although the vast majority now in the topsoil do of course refer to the life style and economy of the village as a whole.

In spite of the fact that archaeologists have long known this to be the case, it has not prevented them machining off the topsoil after only a superficial examination, purely for reasons of cost. Only archaeologists who have not rejected the services of volunteers can afford to examine the topsoil by hand. But the commercial profession is not in favour of volunteers and cannot afford the cost of large-scale digging by hand. The current economic norm is to locate an area of settlement from the air, attempt to define it by geophysical survey or by collecting pottery on the surface of the fields, lace it with evaluation trenches, and then strip off the topsoil with a mechanical excavator, thereby removing and discarding most of the finds. However, it is fair to remark that in the rare cases where the topsoil and subsoil have been examined, the assemblage is often markedly sparse, increasing the risk of a poor return for money.

The upshot is that the characterisation of Anglo-Saxon buildings and their interpretation as social and economic theatres is dependent to a large degree on their ground plans. An interpretation of the settlement as a whole is fraught, since the 'settlement as a whole' is rarely obtained, the extent of excavation being controlled by the area threatened with damage, the funds available or, more reprehensibly, by heritage-induced timidity. We are obliged to add to this catalogue of deprivation the non-publication of many important excavations. Altogether this frustration has driven the scholarly community into many an irresolvable impasse.[431] Considering the wealth of the English part of Britain and its vast university and government resources, it is not to the credit of Anglo-Saxon archaeologists that the settlement record compares so poorly to that of the rest of Europe.

In Scotland and Wales, where soils are often less revealing and large scale development and the resulting excavation opportunities are less frequent, the tally of large scale settlement is also depressingly meagre. This is what an official review of early medieval Scotland concluded in 2011:

> Beyond the Atlantic zone, the evidence of buildings in the first millennium AD is minimal after c. AD 200, and has even been suggested to represent 'tableaux of desertion'. . . . This reduction in evidence may also reflect a change to non-earthfast building techniques. Whatever the cause of this apparently sharp diminution of structural settlement evidence, it means that obtaining a coherent idea of the range of settlement forms and the social structure that lay behind them, is going to be profoundly challenging.[432]

The reduction in evidence may reflect a change in building techniques to turf, timber and boulders. It does not mean there were no people there.

Thus, a combination of uneven resources, evanescent materials, undeveloped excavation techniques, piecemeal investigation and non-publication has delivered unflattering verdicts on the islanders' achievements as house builders. Unfamiliar design, inaccessible places, the recycling of abandoned sites, the use of ephemeral materials, and depleted assemblages – especially the loss, in nearly every case, of the organic objects that powered the settlement – these have also contributed to their poor showing. The result has been a coverage of early British society at home that is so uneven as to require a great deal of imagination to fill the gaps. We are not yet therefore in a good position to determine the distribution of status within settlements or between them.[433]

This question of the degree of representation of the settlement corpus as we know it is crucial for the more ambitious interpretations. In the early formative we appear to be missing the 'peasant' component in the major British regions that is widely assumed to be there, while in the early English region we have peasants and nobody else. We have seen that the identification of the settlements in west Britain, whether fortified farmsteads, crannogs or forts, is based not only on prominent and/or documented sites but the discovery of high-status objects. This gives the impression that all the known settlements belong only to the upper echelon of society (p. 189). One answer to the question 'Why are the peasant settlements missing?' might be that they are not: it is not impossible that the unequal members of a community lived together rather than in separate settlements. A similar imbalance is noted in south-east Britain in its mid- and late formative periods, when most excavated settlements display at least some of the trappings of high status in terms of their layout and buildings and finds, a proportion of the whole that has been thought 'unfeasibly high'. The discovery of discard at a profligate level (as at Flixborough) may be more a sign of good preservation than of high status.[434]

It might be thought that one of the results of this brief review would be to propose that we should abandon the concept of the 'type site' because there are too many variables to define them. The lesson is rather that types of settlement certainly exist, but the emphases of their components may differ: this puts a premium on places where a number of 'types', with different forms and functions, succeeded each other. Not only are forms of settlements related to the landscape, agriculture, social organisation, culture, and ideology, but these forms change as the ideology changes. We have seen this chameleon-like adaptation to the times at Yeavering, Whithorn, York, Portmahomack, Winchester and Bloodmoor Hill – anywhere in fact where the investigation has been at a sufficient scale. And this perhaps is the principal message for the future. Settlement studies require a new seriousness, as in the breaking of the stranglehold of commercial trenching, the professional excavators' default response, and the substitution of designed fieldwork projects appropriate to the opportunity, aimed especially at multi-period sites. This would approach more nearly the goals of archaeology, which are not to rescue scraps of culture but to enlarge history.

Notes

1 This term for a high-status rural farmstead with a hall building is borrowed from Danish archaeology, where it is applied, for example, to the 3rd–6th century settlement at Gudme (Jørgensen 2010, 275), or more commonly in the 10th century, where it is used to label a 'completely new type of agricultural unit' (Randsborg 1980, 5, 60, 66).
2 Jope 1964; see also Chapter 5 for a similar observation on the lack of stone sculpture in this area.
3 Fenton and Walker 1981, 45.
4 Walker 2006.
5 Fenton 1968; Fenton and Walker 1981, 73–77; Brunskill 1982, 134.
6 Crone 1993a, 379 argued that pottery and flint concentrations around three hearths were originally contained in houses built of turf.
7 Sharples 2005.
8 For earth buildings see Walker 1977; Walker and McGregor 1996; Noble 2003.
9 Anne Crone (2007) emphasises the amount of post-depositional disturbance experienced by crannogs underwater, scrambling the structural sequence, stratification and thus the history of occupation, even if organic materials are simultaneously preserved in lacustrine mud. See also Crone 1993a and b; Barber and Crone 2001; Barber et al. 2007.
10 Brunskill 1982, 137; Fenton and Walker 1981, 59.
11 Milek 2012.
12 Noble 1984, 2003; Walker et al. 1996. See Harding 2009a, especially Ch 3, for a comprehensive review of roundhouse forms in Britain.
13 Harding 2009a, 50–51. See Illaunloughan for a reconstruction of a turf roundhouse.
14 Harding 2009a, 139, 157.
15 Harding 2009a, Ch 9–11.
16 Armit 1999.
17 Hingley 1989, 133. See also Taylor 2007 for the 'two Roman Britains'. There is not a hard frontier between them: Hingley proposes a buffer zone between the two (including the future Mercia and Northumbria) in which there are some villas; and a similar grading is expressed by Taylor's (2007) division between enclosed and open settlements. Taylor 2007, Fig 4.6, 7.2.

18 See Chapter 1, p. 15; Allen et al. 2016 for the online resource of rural settlement in Roman Britain with interactive maps.
19 Hingley 1989, 153–156. This thesis is largely argued from the forms of houses and settlements.
20 Hingley 1989, 33; Harding 2009a, 155–158.
21 Carver et al. 2016; see Carver 2016a for a summary account.
22 Carver et al. 2016, Ch 5.9.
23 Hope-Taylor 1977, xvii, 5.
24 Hope-Taylor 1977, Ch 2.
25 HE II.14.
26 Hope-Taylor 1977, 276–277. The coin is a gold-washed copper imitation *triens* of Bertoldus of Huy dating between 630 and 660; Lafaurie and Kent in Hope-Taylor 1977, 182–183.
27 Hope-Taylor 1977, 98.
28 Fragments of crucibles and a loom weight said to be 'Anglian' were found during the excavation of a henge ditch 100 m to the south-east of the great enclosure in 1976 (Tinniswood and Harding 1991).
29 See Chapter 4, pp. 348, 312, 308.
30 Hope-Taylor 1977, 88–91.
31 A suggestion owed to Rosemary Cramp, personal communication.
32 Hey 2004, 41–43.
33 Hey 2004, 139–149. The first version measured 13 × 4 m; the second 13.2 × 5.8 and the third was 14 m long in two contiguous segments measuring 9.5 × 6.5 and 4.5 × 5 m.
34 The principal indicator of the switch from pasture to hay was the type of beetle encountered in the samples. Hey 2004, 42, 47–49, Figs 2.5, 2.7.
35 Phillips and Heywood 1995; Carver 1995c. The archaeology of the city of York has been explored by York Archaeological Trust, initiated by P. V. Addyman and published in a fascicule series (eg Kemp 1996; Hall 2014).
36 Kemp 1996; Tweddle et al. 1999; Spall and Toop 2005, 2008.
37 Hall 1984, 2014; Ottaway 1992. See Chapter 2, p. 119.
38 Tweddle 1992; see Chapter 2, p. 98.
39 Phillips and Heywood 1995, 177–195.
40 Hill 2011, 245, 253, 256, 259.
41 The work of Alexander Fenton on pre-industrial Scotland offers vivid analogics for living and farming in the Highland Zone; see Fenton 1999 for an overview.
42 As defined and mapped by Tanja Romankiewicz (2011).
43 Romankiewicz also maps examples in the lowlands, including Angus and Fife (2011, Illus. A10).
44 Beirgh, Isle of Lewis, 3th–6th century, Harding and Gilmour 2000; Dun Vulan on South Uist 500–750, Harding 2009a, 188).
45 Harding 2009a, 172–192.
46 Dockrill et al. 2010, 28–46.
47 Harding 2009b, 472–473.
48 Harding 2009a, 192–194.
49 Brundle et al. 2003, 95.
50 McSparron and Williams 2011.
51 Campbell 2001; McSparron and Williams 2011.
52 Lane and Campbell 2000, 252.
53 For Irish ringforts and raths see p. 276.
54 Campbell and Lane 1993.
55 Taylor 1990, 21, 27; Taylor 1990, 29; Harding 2009a, 186; Ralston 2004, 9.
56 Taylor 1990.
57 Also 'circular homesteads' (Taylor 1990); 'monumental roundhouses' (Strachan 2013) or more simply 'ringforts' (Morrison 1985, 79), adopted here.
58 Taylor 1990, 41.
59 Taylor 1990, 62–63.
60 Ralston 1997, 25.
61 Strachan 2013, 77–85.
62 Strachan 2013, 36.
63 Strachan 2013, 78.
64 Taylor 1996; McNiven in Strachan 2013, 69–75.
65 Dixon 1982, 2004; dates of crannogs in Loch Tay, Dixon 2007.

66 Circular or oval at about 20 m across. Morrison 1985, 76.
67 Crone and Campbell 2005, 117. Jack Scot's excavations took place in 1960 and were brought to press by Anne Crone and Ewan Campbell in 2005. Crone 2007, 224.
68 Crone and Campbell 2005, 120–125.
69 Crone 2000, 1.
70 Morrison 1985, 22–25.
71 Crone 2000, 160. In its final form it was oval and measured 19 × 15.5 m.
72 Crone 2000, 51, 64–66.
73 Crone 2000, 165–166.
74 E.g. Ardestie; Harding 2004, 240–242.
75 Driscoll 1997.
76 Carver et al. 2012.
77 Watkins 1980.
78 Fraser and Halliday 2011, 309; Cook and Dunbar 2008, 19; 'However it is clear that underground storage continued to be used into the early Historic period' Ralston 1997, 26.
79 Harding 2009a, 186; see Dunwell and Ralston 2008 for the sequence.
80 Hingley et al. 1997.
81 Driscoll 1997, 115 'the artefacts suggest dwellings of people of modest and servile status'; Rees 2009; Harding 2009a, 185–186.
82 Alcock and Alcock 1987; Alcock et al. 1989; Alcock and Alcock 1992.
83 Cook 2011, 209, 217.
84 RCAHMS 2007, 217; Cook 2011, 211.
85 Type 6, out of six types of hillfort; RCAHMS 2007, 215.
86 Alcock et al. 1989; Alcock 2003, 211.
87 Summary in Alcock 2003, 192–197.
88 Ralston 1997, 27; Ralston 1987, Fig 3. The nature and form of even the larger examples of Pictish stronghold currently remain enigmatic, largely owing to the ancestral practice of attempting to understand them with trenches.
89 Gondek and Noble 2010; Noble and Gondek 2011; Noble et al. 2013. The excavations have still to be completed at the time of writing. See also Chapter 5, pp. 494–8.
90 Harding 2009b.
91 Barber and Crone 2001.
92 McCullagh and Tipping 1998.
93 McCullagh and Tipping 1998, 61–66.
94 Halliday 2007.
95 Historic Scotland has led the way in the routine collection of numerous high-precision radiocarbon dates as government policy; see Ashmore 1999, 2000.
96 Newman and Brennand 2007, 81: [In Cumbria] 'Many of the problems regarding settlement studies of the period stem from the perceived lack of chronologically diagnostic artefacts, coupled with a timber building tradition, at least in the southern part of the region. This has rendered much of the evidence for human occupation difficult to detect, particularly in these lowland parts of the region, or to be seemingly invisible.' Mytum 1996, 127: 'In south-west England and Wales, elite sites of the period up to the 7th century have been identified, with some burial sites and ecclesiastical centres, but the mass of settlement remains unknown. From perhaps the late 7th century onwards, however the amount of archaeological information dramatically decreases, and few settlements are known.' Edwards et al. 2005, 33: 'It is difficult to talk in terms of strengths regarding the settlement archaeology of early medieval Wales. The number of dated sites remains tiny.' And in Edwards et al. 2011: 'There has been little change.'
97 Quinnell 2004; Morris 1996; Morris and Harry 1997; Alcock et al. 1995; Alcock 1963; Laing and Longley 2006; Alcock 1976; Hope-Taylor 1980; Toolis and Bowles 2013; https://canmore.org.uk/site/65300/tynron-doon.
98 Batches of imported Mediterranean pottery (A ware plates and B ware amphorae LR1) arrive in the Irish Sea zone in the early 6th century, and glass of Campbell's C and D type from the mid-6th into the 7th century. Glass correlates well with E ware and probably comes from the same area (south-west France). Glass has been found at 44 sites, 58% of all vessels at forts. Of the remainder, 80 sherds were found at Whithorn Phase 1: if this is also a lordship site then 81% of all imported 7th-century glass is high status secular (as opposed to religious) destinations (Campbell 2000, 35–36, 42, 44). Compare window glass which is mainly destined for monasteries.

99 Alcock 1963, 26–73. The phase is referred to as 'Dark Age' and 'Early Christian' and the one that followed as Early Medieval or Norman. The dating has been revised forward by radiocarbon (Seaman 2013, 6–7).
100 Respectively Alcock 1987, 82; Gilchrist 1988, 60.
101 Alcock 1963, 51 Fig 9, 66. Longley (1997) suggests that there were citadel-like sites in North Wales that fall into 'Alcock's class of hierarchically organized fortifications with high status associations'.
102 Quinnel 2004.
103 Burrow 1973, 1981; Rahtz 1982, 190.
104 Alcock interpreted his excavations as an 'Arthurian' stronghold with a central hall and a later Saxon church (Alcock 1972; Alcock et al. 1995). Barrett et al. 2000 rephased the prehistoric occupation, noted the coincidence of the hall (L1) with a late prehistoric iron-working area and identified the late Saxon church as a likely Roman temple. However, the close association of the footprint of the hall (L1) with the concentration of imported 5th/6th century pottery remains a good argument for a high-status centre at that date.
105 Rahtz et al. 1992.
106 Turner 2006, 35–46, Fig 29, 143 Fig 48. A similar conclusion was reached for Wales (Petts 2002a, 30). Charles Thomas asserted that 'full monasticism was introduced first to south-west Britain, apparently directly from the Mediterranean, in the later part of the 5th century'. This suggestion was aligned with the arrival of imported pottery from the Mediterranean, 5th–7th century (1971, 22). Oval/circular churchyards were identified as the likely sites of the consequent primary Christian establishments (Thomas 1971, 53). These associations are thought less probable now. See also pp. 192, 508.
107 Hope-Taylor 1977.
108 Hope-Taylor 1980. Undated examples of rectangular hall-like buildings in enclosures have been located from the air, for example at Monboddo (Ralston 1997, 29).
109 Maxwell 1987.
110 Smith 1990, Fig 4.19; Smith 1991; Smith 1996; Thomas 1981, 192.
111 Crabtree 1994, 50: 'While there may be some continuity in animal husbandry practices from the Iron Age and Romano-British sites . . . the patterns of trade and exchange in animal products seen at Late Roman sites . . . do not continue into the early Anglo-Saxon period.'
112 Rahtz 1976a, 70–81. See Tipper 2004 for a monograph on the SFB.
113 Snow 2010, 261.
114 For example Feddersen Vierde (Haarnagel 1979), Borg (Munch et al. 2003).
115 O'Sullivan 2014a, 47; Harding 2009a, 245; Hamerow 2012, 17.
116 Hamerow 2012, 21, 2002, 50–51.
117 Hamerow 2002, 48, Fig 2.22.
118 Marshall and Marshall 1993.
119 Millett originally ascribed the form of the Anglo-Saxon hall to Romano-British models (James et al. 1985) but has subsequently noted that the diversity of the 3,200 Roman sites explored to date makes this derivation unlikely; he now prefers the adoption of an idealised form in the spirit of 7th-century Romanisation (Millett 2016, 9, 14).
120 Hamerow 2002, 15.
121 Williams 2002; and see Chapter 4.
122 West 1985, 65.
123 West 1985, 10; 'This general cultural layer covered the entire area of occupation and considerable quantities of pottery, food bones and artefacts were recovered from it, in spite of the practical necessity to remove most of it by machine. . . . The small finds listed for each building cannot be positively associated with the structure in the way that objects from sealed deposits can from pits or SFBs.'
124 West 1985, 167–170.
125 West 2001, 68.
126 West 2001, 73: 'with so many personal items in the SFBs how can we define use for "domestic" or "workshop" purposes?'
127 Tipper 2004, 184.
128 West 2001, 23.
129 Walton Rogers 2007, Fig 2.33, pp. 42–43.

130 West 2001, 17, 22–23, 41, 43–47; House 6 thus follows House 4, not the other way round, as in West 1985, Fig 301. For the Ipswich Ware see West 1985, 28, Fig 15; it is currently dated early 8th to early 9th century (Blinkhorn 2012).

131 West 1985, 23, 12. In his review, Tipper concludes (2004, x, 185): 'most of the archaeological evidence [from England] points towards grubenhäuser as ground level buildings that possessed a suspended floor supported above a pit.'

132 Tipper 2004, 68: 'It seems reasonable to assume that large groups of intact loom weights were deposited close to where they had been used.' The sunken-featured building at Upton (measuring 9.1 × 5.5 m) was destroyed by fire, contained more than 60 loom weights, some in ordered rows, and was described as a weaving shed (Rahtz 1976a, 76; Jackson et al. 1969).

133 See Chapter 4, p. 376.

134 Unfortunately the Anglian settlement at West Heslerton was still unpublished at the time of writing (2017), so this summary account is drawn from interim statements (Powlesland 1999, 2000, 2003). The cemetery is published as Haughton and Powlesland 1999a, b.

135 Powlesland 2003, 30 shows a reconstruction of this 'shrine' complex as a barrack-like building with a central grand entrance leading via open spaces with food stalls to a temple at the top.

136 Tipper 2004, xi. The idea of backfill from remote places is suggested by vessel links more than 100 m apart. At West Stow, vessel links and stamp links are shorter range (less than 100 m) operating within house groups (Tipper 2004, 142–145, Figs C25, 26, 29).

137 Whether this will be maintained in the final publication remains to be seen. The excavator prefers a static rather than a mobile development of the 5th/6th century village 'If this is supported by the finds analysis currently in progress' (Powlesland 2000, 22).

138 Tipper 2004, 164.

139 Powlesland 1999, 63–64. Powlesland 2003 elaborates: 'In one location (12AE) a large Early Anglo-Saxon building had been replaced by a Middle Saxon building located on a raised platform that overlooked the whole village and was surrounded by a timber fence on three sides.'

140 Published by Hirst and Clark 2009. Their tally was 'more than 800 individuals over a period of 200 years' (p. 760).

141 Margaret Jones in Clark 1993–2009, 6–7; see also Hirst and Clark 2009, 9–12, where the precision of the Jones' machining is endorsed.

142 Etté in Clark 1993–2009, 19.

143 Going in Clark 1993–2009, 19–21.

144 Hamerow 1993, 5–6, Table 1, Fig 3, 7, Table 3, 7, Table 2.

145 Hamerow in Clark 1993–2009, 21.

146 Hamerow 1993, 86–87, Fig 50.

147 Hamerow 2002, 29; Tipper 2004.

148 Hamerow 2002, 91: 'The situation at Mucking . . . remains enigmatic and a matter for speculation'.

149 Tipper 2004, 52.

150 Hirst and Clark 2009, xxiii, 762.

151 The first cultural affinities of the cemeteries are with the Elbe-Weser area. During the 5th/6th century, others are noted: Saxon, Anglian, Kentish, Alamannic and Frankish, 'but whether this represents immigration, intermarriage or trade is not always clear'. Mucking is reckoned to have stood on an ancient route leading to a Thames crossing and so accessible to river traffic and prompting the appearance of a 7th-century trading place on its banks at East Tilbury (Hirst and Clark 2009, xxiii, 771, 774–776). See Chapter 4, p. 388 for the parallel history drawn from the Mucking cemeteries.

152 Trenches understandably passed over SFBs and through the cemetery without recognising them: Lucy et al. 2009, 12.

153 Lucy et al. 2009, 17–19.

154 Lucy et al. 2009, 340–357.

155 See Chapter 4, p. 402.

156 Dominic Powlesland (2003) has mapped a large part of the Vale of Pickering using aerial photography, surface collection and geophysics. Mary Chester-Kaldwell (2009) has constructed a geography for early Anglo-Saxon communities in Norfolk by combining the evidence from known settlements and cemeteries with the surface scatters recorded by the Portable Antiquities Scheme.

157 Davies 2009, 44; Pritchard 2009, 249.

158 The *Life of St Columba* makes useful references to the cultivation of barley (LC II, 3), barns for storage (LC III, 23), enclosures for flocks and herds (LC III, 23), the milking of dairy cows (LC II, 16), the slaughter of beef cattle (LC II, 29) and the hunting of seals (LC I, 41).

159 Turner 2006; Banham and Faith 2014, 274; Petts 2003, 2009.
160 See p. 278 for a brief note on monasticism in Ireland. There are few excavated monasteries in Wales, but Welsh monumentality (the cross-marked stones) suggests that a conservative version of monasticism, perhaps on a British foundation, was adopted (Edwards 2015, and see Chapter 5, p. 502).
161 O'Sullivan 1999; Lowe 2008; Lowe 2006; Hill 1997; James and Yeoman 2008; Carver et al. 2016; Daniels 2007; Cramp 2005, 2006.
162 John Barber found 15 trenches cut by academics before 1964; there may have been more than 40 (O'Sullivan 1999, 227). Professional accounts and assessments of useable archaeology will be found in Barber 1981; McCormick 1997; O'Sullivan 1994, 1999.
163 McCormick 1997a, 49–50.
164 Barber 1981, 328–346; McCormick 1997, 62.
165 Reece 1981.
166 O'Sullivan 1994, 332, 354–355.
167 O'Sullivan 1999, 236.
168 Ó Carragáin 2010a, 66–70.
169 O'Sullivan 1994.
170 Alexander 1978, no6, no52; Fisher 2001, Argyll 4, and see Chapter 5.
171 Lowe 2008, 82, 255.
172 Lowe 2008, 78.
173 Lowe 2008, 98–104, 157.
174 Lowe 2008, 254–255.
175 RCAHMS 1990; Stevenson 1991.
176 Carver et al. 2012.
177 Carver et al. 2012, 188–195.
178 Harding 2009a, 245.
179 Beresford 1979, 102–104, 125–127, 144–146; see also discussion under 'Continental analogies' later in this chapter.
180 Zimmerman 1999, 326. And see p. 282, for the byre-house and use of shielings in Scandinavia.
181 Hunter 2007a and 2007b; Romankiewicz 2011, A56, 57.
182 Fenton and Walker 1981; Brunskill 1982, 134; Walker 2006; Sigurthardottir 2008; reconstructions in Highland Folk Museum (see Figure 3.2).
183 Rideout 1995, 159.
184 Carver 2008a, 126–133.
185 Lowe 2006, 171–172.
186 Lowe 2008, 242.
187 Lowe 2006, 115–123.
188 Craig in Lowe 2006, 124–133.
189 Hill 1997.
190 Campbell in Hill 1997, 299, 2007; Toop 2005, 2011, 91; McComish and Petts 2008; reviewed by Maldonado Ramírez 2011, 183, who endorses this conclusion.
191 Hill 1997, 69, 130 names only two datable horizons: that containing imported Mediterranean pottery of the mid-6th century and that associated with Building I/24, dated by dendrochronology to c. 700 AD or later.
192 The shrines relate to examples seen in the British and Irish late Iron Age in association with cemeteries (see Chapter 4).
193 Hill 1997, 183. Chapter 5, p. 469.
194 Hill 1997, 50–51.
195 Daniels 2007, 190, 82.
196 Daniels 2007, 74–93; Loveluck in Daniels 2007, 187.
197 Cramp 1995. Large-scale archaeological investigations have taken place at Hartlepool (Daniels 2007), Whitby (Peers and Radford 1943; Rahtz 1976b), Wearmouth and Jarrow (Cramp 2005).
198 Daniels 2007, 69.
199 Daniels 2007, 127.
200 The burials are discussed in Chapter 4, including their relationship to the nearly contemporary cemetery at Street House across the Tees (p. 382).
201 Cramp 2005, I, 111.
202 Cramp 2005, I, 34.
203 Cramp 2005, I, 189–191.

204 Cramp 2005 II, 560–561. Cod bones were also found but may have derived from Late Saxon deposits.
205 Horn and Born 1979.
206 Cramp 2005, 34.
207 Cramp 2005, I, 229 and 344: 'the evidence for a different kind of occupancy during the 9th c is reinforced by the dress fastenings from that area, which included silver dress hooks and strap-ends as well as 9th century coinage'; see also, I, 360; II, 230. The assemblage included a coin of Eanred (810–41) and Athelred II (841–850). For the riverside workshop see pp. 234–241 (Phase 4). For the workshop south of Building A see p. 214. The assemblage here included a coin of Eadred (790–30).
208 Ó Carragáin 2002; see also Chapter 5, p. 569.
209 Carver et al. 2016, Chapter 5.7.
210 Spall 2009.
211 Window glass is known from at least 18 sites, all Fm 2 and later: in the north it comes from late 7th to 8th century monasteries (Monkwearmouth, Jarrow, Whithorn Phase 2 and Whitby). In the west, from Uley and Glastonbury in the same period; in Southumbria from Flixborough and Brandon and could be later, 8th/9th century. Examples from Barking and Winchester are 10th century and later (Cramp 2000).
212 Durham Cath. Lib. A.II.10; Durham Cath. Lib. B.II.30 Cassiodorus Commentary on the Psalms.
213 The Lindisfarne Gospels are in the British Library in London, BL Cotton Nero DIV.
214 Bede *The Greater Chronicle* 4671 (McLure and Collins 2008, 339); The surviving volume is the *Codex Amiatinus*, now in Florence. Bruce-Mitford 1969.
215 Mills, especially the vertical ones. 'are clearly implants of a late Roman building tradition'. Rynne 2000, 1; McErlean and Crothers 2007, 10.
216 Rahtz and Meeson 1992; Hope-Taylor unpublished.
217 Carver 2016a, 139–140.
218 The Hartlepool 'cells' also tend to the Golden Number: see scattergram in Daniels 2007, 70; Whitfield 1999 for the metrology of the Hunterston Brooch.
219 See Carver et al. 2016, 221–228 and references. Campbell 2009, 52–56 for the history of the hide in Britain (including England); Ekelund et al. 1996, 86 for the 'salvation industry'. Spearman 1988b, 105–107 for food renders to later monasteries and early towns in Scotland. Spearman 1988a for the larger thesis: 'It was in fact the processing of hides and skins for regional use and export that provided the major economic and industrial stimulus to Scottish urban development' (1988a, iv). '. . . one of the main sources of estate revenues were renders of hides and skins . . . these revenues had long been raised in an organised manner from the ancient regional divisions of the country both north and south of the Spearman' (ibid., 76).
220 E.g. Both Oswald and Oswiu were fostered in Scotland by the Pictish and Irish kin of Domnall Brecc. There was at least one marriage between Oswald and an Irish/Pictish lady, that produced Oswald's son Oethelwald (d.655). The Anglo-Saxons used the term *freothuwebbe* 'peace-weaver' to describe the skill of loving women in suppressing violence and improving judgement.
221 Wickham 2005, 371, 495–497.
222 Cunliffe 1972, 1–4.
223 Addyman et al. 1972; Addyman and Leigh 1973; Selkirk in *Current Archaeology* 37, 1973; plus personal observations and notes of the present author (who excavated building AZ1).
224 Champion in *Current Archaeology* 59, 1977. It will be obvious that a book on Early Medieval Britain is unthinkable without Chalton, but unfortunately a report on the site has yet to appear. Details culled or recalled here will probably require future moderation.
225 Addyman et al. 1972; Addyman and Leigh 1973, 19; Champion 1977, 367. See p. 153 for comparable dress pins made of iron from Portmahomack.
226 Millett and James 1983, 195, Fig 28, and 203, Fig 33.
227 Millett and James 1983, 195; Brisbane in Millett and James 1983, 255.
228 Millett and James 1983, 199, Table 6; AML Report 3434.
229 Millett and James 1983, 202, Fig 32.
230 Millett and James 1983, 208, Fig 37. B4 measures 13.8 × 6.2 m with staves of 400 × 100 mm scantling.
231 Millett and James 1983, 238, 230–231, Fig 60–61.

232 Millett and James 1983, 217–218, Fig 46; the excavator raises the possibility that these posts signify a hipped gable.
233 Millett 2016 allays criticisms of the Cowdery's Down architecture (Alcock and Walsh 1993).
234 Hamerow 2011, 137.
235 An association inspired by Yeavering; Millett and James 1983, 221.
236 Marshall and Marshall 1993, 400.
237 Millett and James 1983, 248, 249.
238 Mortimer et al. 2005; Williams 1993; Hardy et al. 2007, 205, Plate 5.4 by Rosalyn and Peter Lorimer.
239 Losco-Bradley and Kingsley 2002, with a comment by Helena Hamerow, pp. 123–129.
240 Losco-Bradley and Kingsley 2002, 13, Fig 1.7.
241 *pace* Hamerow pp. 123–126 who appears to be comparing Catholme with villages of (earlier) FM1, especially Mucking.
242 Dixon, in Losco-Bradley and Kingsley 2002, 96 defines this as a two-phase post-in-trench building with main hall and south wing, forming an L-shaped building with a cross passage at the junction of the arms. The spaces measure 8 × 5.5 m and 4 × 5.5 m with 4 × 3.5 m at the junction.
243 Hamerow, in Losco-Bradley and Kingsley 2002, 128 successfully argues that Catholme, with its culturally Anglo-Saxon cemetery at Wychnor belongs to the English cultural zone.
244 Loveluck 2001 for a summary. The report was published in four volumes by different authors: Loveluck and Atkinson 2007 (Flixborough 1); Loveluck and Evans 2009 (Flixborough 2); Dobney et al. 2007 (Flixborough 3) and Loveluck 2007 (Flixborough 4).
245 These periods are divided into a large number of sub-phases (Loveluck and Atkinson 2007) but it is noticeable that the buildings of Periods 3–6 inclusive maintain the same alignment, suggesting a change in fortunes rather than a change in function or ownership.
246 Loveluck 2007, 148–150.
247 Evans and Loveluck 2009, 140. In *The Making of England*, (Webster and Backhouse 1991, Fig 7) the caption adds: 'two of the names are feminine and three may be of people referred to by Bede as Lindsey clerics'. However Brown and Okasha in Evans and Loveluck, 138 write: 'All the personal names are recorded Old English names: many indeed are common names. None of the persons named can therefore be identified securely'.
248 Evans and Loveluck 2009, 278.
249 Loveluck 2007, 152–153: 'the life style witnessed in 9th century Flixborough is certainly far more similar to that seen amongst the documented monasteries in England and on the continent, rather than secular aristocratic or royal residences'. Specific sites are not mentioned. But see Evans and Loveluck 2009, 130 where Pestell makes the case that styli were actively used in secular contexts; and ibid., 140, where the inscriptions are not held to imply a local monastic context.
250 Loveluck 2007, 159.
251 Tester et al. 2014, xii
252 Tester et al. 2014, 6–8. In archaeological terms the 'topsoil' is the most recently developed humus (A to B horizon) and the 'subsoil' the previously developed usually much paler soil (B to C horizon). The 'natural' is the geological deposit which the human activity has marked. The natural sand or chalk with its bright and consistent colour provides a clear backdrop against which to define the dark patches of features, which is why it is the horizon by archaeologists in a hurry. Features, especially post-holes, are hard to see in the subsoil or topsoil; but these layers of course contain the vast majority of the cultural material.
253 Tester et al. 2014, 106–125. This analysis is owed to William Filmer-Sankey (Tester et al. 2014, xi).
254 Marshall and Bayliss in Tester et al. 2014, 16–19.
255 Tester et al. 2014, 55–61.
256 Tester et al. 2014, Fig 44.61, 4.63, 4.69, 4.71, 4.72.
257 Tester et al. 2014, 49–52, 63–66.
258 Tester et al. 2014, Fig 4.59.
259 Tester et al. 2014, 361–363. The horse pit is not marked in the plan of the church (Fig 4.14). It was on the north side of the door to the east annexe, subsequently disturbed by the ditch 8919 (Plate 4.2, p. 51). The deductive connection between a horse and a church is not explained.
260 Tester et al. 2014, 364, 370, Fig 7.12.
261 Pestell 2004, 41–48 makes a good case for a literate laity in England. 97 styli are known from 31 sites in England of which only 11 are documented *monasteria*.
262 Tester et al. 2014, 277.
263 R I Page in Tester et al. 2014, 260.

264 Tester et al. 2014, 304.

265 Tester et al. 2014, 283–284; see Carver and Spall 2004 for diagnostic objects.

266 The report relies on some curious logic: citing San Vincenzo as a parallel (a little like comparing High Wycombe with Rome), the author argues that the lack of ecclesiastical material 'does not necessarily mean that a site is secular at that point, particularly when we so rarely find the decoration and adornment of structures that so readily defines their character.' (p. 383). By p. 393 'the evidence would seem to support the suggestion that a minster church was imposed in Phase 2.1 with an associated burial ground possibly connected with a parent monastery at Ely [35km away as the crow flies]. The expansion from Phase 2.2 bears the hallmarks of a proprietary monastery with high status residents and complex zoning including rich material culture alongside a significant monastic presence'. By contrast, Tim Pestell's search for monasticism in East Anglia suggested that the role of the church has been exaggerated, and 'we face the dangerous possibility of seeing an emerging Anglo-Saxon landscape governed at all its key, nodal, points by the Church, rather than the aristocracy and secular rulers who lived and died in the pursuit of power, and who were the church's sponsors.' (2004, 59).

267 Meeson 1979, Fig 12; SCC 2011, 25.

268 Rahtz and Meeson 1992; SCC 2011, 27; Leahy 2011, 441–442.

269 Biddle 1976, 121; SCC 2011, 29. The verdict of Hall (2011, 605) was: 'Bassett (2007, 2008) reviewing the archaeological evidence from Tamworth, Hereford, Winchcombe and Worcester suggested their earliest medieval defences can be assigned to the period of Mercian overlordship in the eighth and early ninth centuries. Evidence for the nature of contemporary activity or occupation within the substantial areas enclosed by these defences. . . . is virtually absent.'

270 Newman 1999; Pestell 2011, 563, Fig 29.1.

271 Pestell 2011, 562.

272 E.g. Cottam in East Riding: Richards 1999, 2003.

273 Found by John Newman (2003). Pestell 2011, 569; 'The fact that Coddenham had subsequent minster church should not blind us to its origins as a secular centre that maintained itself within the landscape.' See also Hamerow 2016 and Chapter 4, p. 405 where the role of the bed burial as a proprietorial marker is discussed.

274 Pestell 2011, 573.

275 Scull et al. 2016, 1605.

276 Pestell 2011, 563; Richards 2003, 166; Loveluck and Tys 2006, 146.

277 Costen and Costen 2016, 20.

278 Jørgensen 2003, 175; Ulriksen 2004, 11; Loveluck and Tys 2006; Loveluck 2012, 152; Theuws 2004, 2012; Fiedel et al. 2011; cf Callmer 2002, 153: 'Around 700 large sites with ample evidence for large numbers of craftsmen, artisans and traders living together, perhaps not all of them throughout the year, but certainly for long spells of time, are known from North-western and Northern Europe'.

279 Kershaw 2017.

280 Thomas 2013, 2017 and www.lymingearchaeology.org/the-project/the-excavations/ for what follows.

281 See Chalton Building AZ1 which measured c14 × 7 m, was aligned E-W, was post-in-trench built, had opposed doorways, an annex at the east end and an SFB at its north-east corner.

282 Thomas 2017, 106–108. There was also fragmentary evidence for a third phase for Hall C.

283 Thomas 2013, 132.

284 'though the evidence is ambiguous.' Blair 2005, 186.

285 In his interim report at the end of the investigation Thomas laments 'it is true to say that the most recent campaign of excavation has added barely a scrap of new evidence relating to Lyminge's 'monastic phase" (Thomas 2017, 110).

286 That at Ipswich, one of the largest-scale excavations at a *wic*, was still largely unpublished at the time of writing (2017). Much data will be found at archaeologydataservice.ac.uk/archives/view/ Ipswich_parent_2015/overview.cfm. And see Wade 1988, and Scull 2001, 2002, 2009, 2013.

287 Birbeck 2005, 86–89, 196–197.

288 Pestell 2011, 570.

289 Leary and Brown 2004, 8, 142–143.

290 Scull 2002, 304. This is a new model; the previous model had Ipswich ware begin a century earlier and the settlement expansion a century later. See also Scull 2009, 2013; Ipswich Ware is now dated c720–850 (Blinkhorn 2012, 8).

291 Scull 2001, 2002, 312, 314; Scull 2013, 219, 228. cf Hodges 2012.
292 Bede II.3.
293 The faunal assemblages suggest royal control (Saunders 2001, 12–13), or at least 'some sort of command economy' (O'Connor 2001, 60) and a subject population with no rich merchant class (Bourdillon 1988, 189, 1994).
294 Ipswich is the most convincing to date (Newman 1999; Blinkhorn 2012, 70). Although logic suggests that each Anglo-Saxon kingdom should have a *wic* (Hodges 1982, 55), the picture has become richer with the recognition of scatter sites on coasts and inland and the wider involvement in trade (Newman 1999; Hodges 2012).
295 Carver 1993; Hodges 1982, 2012b.
296 Scull 2013, 223–224.
297 Doherty 1985; Soderberg 2004b.
298 ASC records attacks on Southampton in 840, York in 867, London in 842 and 851. An attack on Quentovic in 842 suggests that *wics* were targets. Ipswich (and probably Sandwich) appear to have been still worth attacking in 991.
299 Graham-Campbell and Batey 1998; Sharples 2005.
300 Wilson 2008, 96.
301 Unpublished. See Redknap 2004.
302 Sharples 2005, 149–152, Fig 51. Milek 2012, and references to her geochemical work cited there.
303 Wallace 1992.
304 Graham-Campbell and Batey 1998, 226–247; Kershaw 2017.
305 Barrett et al. 1999, 2000, 2004.
306 Hall and Whyman 1996, 117, 121.
307 ie St Wilfred; see Bede Bks III and IV passim.
308 Cowan 1993; Aitchison 1999; Carver 2008c.
309 Hadley and Richards 2016, Figs 2, 3, pp. 31–33.
310 Hadley and Richards, p. 57. The Torksey project was continuing at the time of writing.
311 Biddle and Kjølbye-Biddle 1992; see also here Chapter 4.
312 Hadley and Richards 2016, 26.
313 The excavations by Mark Redknap in 1989/90 are unpublished, but see Redknap 1991, 16–25 for a note and Granger-Taylor and Pritchard 2001 for the embroidery.
314 Thomas 2010.
315 Rahtz 1979.
316 Rahtz 1979, post-hole 80/29; pp. 166–167.
317 Horn and Born 1979; the image takes the form of a rectangular fowlkeeper's dwelling with two circular pens on either side. A better analogy might be provided by a dovecote which comes in both round and rectangular forms.
318 Rahtz 1979, 11, 8.
319 A Roman villa was located on lower ground nearer the river near the site of St Andrew's church 200 m to the south-east of the promontory (Rahtz 1979, 48, 371–372; endorsed by Evans and Hancocks 2005, 120 in the light of further excavations in 2001). John Blair (1996, 2005) has proposed a 9th century monastic site on the basis of the mention of a 'community at Cheddar' in King Alfred's will, conjectured to have been on the site of St Andrew's church. Blair relates his vision as 'a monastic site built on a Roman villa and later transformed into a secular site . . . The hunting lodge was the cuckoo in the nest, founded on the edge of the Cheddar community's precinct in about Alfred's reign and effectively absorbing it over the next two centuries' (2005, 326–327). However, as can be seen, this cuckoo was an independent bird, and the neighbouring nest has yet to materialise.
320 Brühl 1977; Biddle 1976, 110–112.
321 Carver 2010b, 127–145.
322 Barker et al. 1997.
323 Oxford English Dictionary 1887 cited in wikipedia under 'burh'.
324 Hill 1969. The earliest surviving text is The *Nowell Codex* of c1025, the remainder being 13th century.
325 Biddle 1976, 124.
326 'If every hide is represented by one man, then every pole of wall can be manned by 4 men' (Hill 1969, 90). A 'rod, pole or perch' is reckoned at 6 ½ yards or 16.5ft, making each man responsible for 4.125ft or 1.26 m.

327 Hill 1969.

328 Hill and Rumble 1996, 204.

329 Brooks comments that many of the hideage assessments require 'much interpretation and many favourable assumptions' to achieve even a 5% margin of accuracy (Brooks 1996, 130–131). See also Haslam 2009, 111–114 for an argument against the validity of the burghal hideage equation using a study on Christchurch.

330 He saw them as 'two complementary settlements, the one royal, ecclesiastical, ceremonial, heir of an ancient and still lively dignity; the other bustling, crowded, commercial out-ward-looking, from which the shire was named' (Biddle 1976, 114).

331 Barlow et al. 1976, 450.

332 Stenton 1971, 264; Barlow et al. 1976, 454.

333 RCHME 1959.

334 Haslam 2003.

335 Middle Saxon London was located on the Strand by Alan Vince (1984, 1990) and Martin Biddle (1984). The Opera House excavations revealed a sizable chunk of the settlement Malcolm et al. 2003. See also Blackmore 2001; Cowie 2004; Cowie and Blackmore 2012.

336 Bede HE II.3: *multorum emporium populorum terra marique venientium.*

337 Watson et al. 2001, 52–55; Vince 1985, 1994.

338 Rahtz 1977.

339 Griffiths 1995, 84.

340 Wainwright 1959; Walker 2000.

341 The campaign and its results are described and interpreted in Carver 2010b.

342 Carver 2010b, 61.

343 Moffett 1994.

344 This correlates with the size of the rating of the burh in the County Hidage (500 hides equivalent to a perimeter of 630 m). The edge of a linear enclosure was contacted at the Bath Street excavation; Carver 2010b, 100, 73.

345 Hurst 1976; Kilmurry 1980; Carver 2011b, 938. The inspiration for the glazed pottery could be lead glazed Forum Ware first identified in the Roman forum (Whitehouse 1965) and associated by Christie with the 8th/9th century re-establishment of Papal control (Christie 1987).

346 Chadwick 1905, 255: 'In earlier times most of the places mentioned in the burghal hideage must have been merely royal estates or villages.'

347 Chadwick 1905; Brooks 1971; Biddle and Hill 1971; Blair 1996, 2005.

348 Vince 1994, 114 [Based on pottery] 'I would suggest as a hypothesis that the inland towns of southern England mainly came into existence as forts in the 9th century, developed local marketing roles in the 10th and early 11th century and only later became part of the network for distributing goods to the coast in one direction and circulating imports inland in the other'. See also Astill 2000, 2006.

349 Thomas and Boucher 2002; Hall 2011, 605.

350 To date. See Carver 2010b, Ch 6 for the documented argument.

351 Chadwick 1905, 225: 'it seems clear that most of the boroughs of the East Midlands – Lincoln, Stamford, Nottingham, Derby, Leicester, Northampton, Huntingdon, Bedford, Cambridge and Colchester, perhaps also Norwich, Thetford and Ipswich – acquired their burghal character during the period they were under Danish government.'

352 Eketorp was built in the 4th century AD, one of a number of stone ringforts on Öland (Borg et al. 1976, 9, 34). For Randsborg 1980, 96: 'Earlier ring-forts in Denmark are but poor 'proto-types' for the Trelleborg type [of the 10th century].'

353 The inspiration for the Romanisation project and the building of burhs may have had an origin or spur in Alfred's visit to Rome in 853 (Howe 2004, 158, 168; Hill 2003).

354 In this three-stage sequence of fort- regional centre – international centre I follow Alan Vince's model derived from pottery (Vince 1994). Vince died in 2009.

355 Raftery 2000; Waddell 2011, 194 ('the problem remains the near complete absence of Iron Age settlement in Ireland'); Becker 2011, 449; O'Sullivan et al. 2014a reviews the discovery of early medieval Ireland to 2014.

356 Discovery Programme// NRA).

357 Expertly and expeditiously presented up to 2014 in O'Sullivan et al. 2014a, b.

358 O'Sullivan et al. 2014b, 110–111.

359 Lynn 1978; O'Sullivan et al. 2014a, 92–93.

360 Lynn 1994, 82.
361 Lynn 1994, 87, 90; examples at Deer Park Farms are buildings 40/122, 31/122 and 13/122.
362 White Marshall and Walsh 2005, 15, 23, 25.
363 For a comprehensive review, of which what follows is the briefest summary, see O'Sullivan et al. 2014a, 2014b.
364 O'Sullivan et al. 2014a, 325–326; O'Riordan 1942.
365 Stout 1997, 21, 106–107; Comber 2008.
366 Lynn 1994, 93.
367 Lynn and McDowell 2011, 233–234.
368 Lynn and McDowell 2011, 417, 434, 508, 511, 513; Lynn 1994, 92.
369 Lynn and McDowell 2011, 116, 424–425, 618; Carver et al. 2016, Ch 5.6.
370 O'Sullivan et al. 2014a, 95, Fig 3.14.
371 O'Droma 2008.
372 Coyne 2006.
373 Lynn 1994, 93.
374 O'Sullivan et al. 2014a, 16. The excavations at Ballinderry 1 and 2 and Lagore were undertaken by Harvard University on a large scale with expeditious publication (Hencken 1936, 1942, 1950).
375 Bradley 1993, 2011, 32.
376 Ballinderry 2 was dated by its excavator to the 7th c (Hencken 1942) but redated to the 6th by Conor Newman 2002. The 7th century foundation date accorded to Lagore (Hencken 1950, 115–117) was questioned by Lynn's (1986) detection of an earlier crannog. But Comey (2003/4, 35) suggests a start date of cAD700. Moynagh Lough was a prehistoric fishing platform adopted as a crannog in the 7th/8th century, (Bradley 1991). O'Sullivan et al. 2014a, 68 summarise: 'Dendrochronology suggests an intensification of crannog construction in the seventh century . . . making the typical early medieval crannog synchronous with the primary occupation of the univallate and multivallate raths.'
377 Work is in progress at Drumclay (Bermingham and Moore 2015). It is unusual in seeming to have been continuously occupied, see the discussion on Scottish crannogs in this chapter.
378 Hencken 1936; O'Sullivan et al. 2014a, 245, 332.
379 For overview see O'Sullivan 1998.
380 Ó Carragáin 2010a, 58–59.
381 See the processional circuit defined at Inishmurray: Jerry O'Sullivan and Tomás Carragáin 2008
382 Reask: Fanning 1981; High Island: White Marshall and Rourke 2000; Illaunlougham White Marshall and Walsh 2005.
383 McErlean and Crothers 2007; Soderberg (2004a) makes a case for a monastic fondness for red deer ('wild cattle').
384 King 1998, 2003, 2009, 344–345; O'Sullivan and Boland 2000; Murphy 2003. Some 700 carved stone grave markers are known from this site – see Chapter 5. See Doherty 1985 for the concept of the monastic town, Wheatley 1971 for its inspiration and Valante 1998 for reservations.
385 Ó Carragáin 2010a, 85.
386 By C14 dating; Ó Carragáin 2010a, 17. Excavation by M J O'Kelly (1958).
387 Ó Carragáin 2010a, 50, 57, 78–79.
388 Ó Carragáin 2003, 130, 143.
389 Rules governing the behaviour and diet of the 7th/8th century Irish monks are known in some detail (O'Maidin 1996) as well as the desired reforms of 750–900 (O'Dwyer 1981).
390 Kinsella 2010.
391 O'Sullivan 2014a, 303, 306.
392 Carrigatogher: O'Sullivan et al. 2014a, 309; Johnstown: Clarke and Carlin 2008; Camlin 3 Flynn 2009.
393 See Jackman et al. 2013 for a fine example of a mill at Kilbegly.
394 Ó Carragáin 2009a, 349.
395 Nendrum (Lawlor 1925), Rathmullan (Lynn 1981–2), Camlin 3 (Flynn 2009); Roundhouses are associated with imported E Ware pottery, but not rectangular, implying a post-7th century date for the latter (Lynn 1994, 85).
396 Lynn 1994, 85.
397 Hayes 2006, Seaver 2006.
398 Hayes 2006.
399 Edwards 1996, 72–73.

400 McCormick and Murray state that there are no souterrains in 7th/8th century Ireland (2007, 112).
401 Lynn 1994, 93.
402 After 800 slaves were sold in the Dublin market and silver began to appear in quantity (McCormick and Murray 2007, 112).
403 For Knowth and other revived prehistoric cemetery sites, see Chapter 4, p. 438.
404 McCormick and Murray 2007, 105–110.
405 O'Sullivan et al. 2014a, 34, 107; Clinton 2001; Crone 1993b, 250.
406 Mathiot 2011, 364.
407 Caesar *De Bello Gallico* VI, 30, 3.
408 Mathiot 2011, 368.
409 Rasmussen 1999.
410 Webley 2008, 39, 48, 50–54, 62, 115, 137.
411 Hamerow 2002, 15, 19, 2012, 26.
412 Olaussen 1999, 321; Hamerow 2002, 15 calls the transition from longhouse to hall one of the 'most significant of the early middle ages'.
413 Arnoldussen and Fokkens 2008, 13.
414 By the mid- 6th century the Saxons were paying an annual tribute of 500 cows to the Frankish king (Royman 1999, 295).
415 Hamerow 2012, 21, 2002, 51.
416 Hamerow 2002, 26, 2012, 21–22; cf Beresford 1979, 125–127; the Anglo-Saxon 'long-house' reported recently from Eye is a long house but not a longhouse nor a byre-house: Caruth 2013.
417 See p. 213 and Carver et al. 2012.
418 Nyman 1993, 108–109. For Scottish shielings see Fenton 1999, 130–142.
419 E.g. Hedeager 2002.
420 Arrhenius and O'Meadhra 2011 (Helgö), Munch et al. 2003 (Borg), Larsson 2004, 2007 (Uppåkra); Nielsen et al. 1994 (Gudme); Jørgensen 2003, 2010 (Tissø); Słupecki's study of Slavonic sanctuaries (1994) shows the range of monuments that can cluster at important pre-Christian cult sites. See Fabech 1994, 1999 and Fabech and Näsman 2013 for the genesis of the Scandinavian late Iron Age central place.
421 Skre 2010, 2012; Feveile 2012 (Ribe); Willemsen and Kik 2010 (Dorestad); Skre 2008 (Kaupang). See Müller-Wille 2010 and Fabech and Näsman 2013 for valuable overviews. Carver 2015 for analogies with Britain.
422 Herschend 1992; Herschend 1993, 193; Fabech and Näsman 2013, 82, 94. These ideas were revisited and extended by Battaglia 2009.
423 Carver 2015.
424 2006; and see p. 207.
425 Darvill 2004.
426 Meaney 1995; Semple 2004; Pantos 2004; Sarah Semple has pointed to the Bronze Age site at Scutchmer's Knob (Berkshire) as an example of a possible Anglo-Saxon assembly site, although not a Central Place in the Scandinavian sense: Sandmark and Semple 2008; Semple 2013, 1.
427 Banham and Faith 2014, 293–295 describe the equivalent of Formative 1 farming in England as back to the Iron Age, with hulled cereals and large herds, while Formative 2 saw the return of bread wheat and the expansion of arable, with a simultaneous increase in wool and dairy products.
428 Wade 1983.
429 Rahtz 1976a, 51. The tally was 187, the majority from small samples of whole settlements.
430 As practised in Ireland by the National Roads Authority (NRA). O'Sullivan et al. 2014a and 2014b, introduction. 241 of these sites have been described in print. For examples see p. 280.
431 Hamerow 2012; Carver 2013; Katerina Ulmschneider (2011, 167) makes these points still more forcefully: 'The pitiful evidence provided by this key-hole archaeology lies at the bottom of many of the present disputes, be it the nature of the Flixborough settlement, the lack of royal sites or the current debates about "productive sites". . . . In addition, many key sites and surveys, such as . . . West Heslerton, and Wicken Bonhunt (Essex) still await publication.' Another pivotal example is Chalton, Hampshire, publication of which has apparently defeated the University of Southampton since 1976.
432 SCARF 2012, 5.10, accessed 21 Mar 17.
433 Hamerow 2011, 121.
434 Hamerow 2011, 125–126.

4   Addressing eternity

Cemeteries as ritual places

Introduction

Of all the forms of expression in our period, burial offers the most inventive and most emotional repertoire. As with the settlements, its manifestations have largely disappeared under the ground; but once upon a time the landscape was furnished and ornamented with the remains of countless obsequies fresh in the mind or still in plain view, epitaphs of deaths and celebrations of lives. Naturally one important motive for these monuments was memory of the dead, and yet more than memory and more than that of the dead, since the audience of the grave was in the future as well as the present, communal as well as personal, seen as active both in the next world and in this one. The breadth and depth of the repertoire required to express these layers of aspiration is potentially enormous, drawing on deep prehistoric roots, current politics, local tradition and incoming ideas. Burial rite varied not only from period to period and region to region but from person to person, and there are long-distance links that seem presently to defy any logic of allegiance.

Investment in Formative burial varied in intensity from the richly caparisoned and highly individual to anonymous and faceless. We need to move on from making assumptions that burial will report the same kinds of things, always and everywhere, and listen instead to what the graves have to say, speaking from their own platform. Graves do not contain supportive material for our preferred version of history; they are material for their own version of history, not linear but layered; not disciplined accounts like annals or a diary but emotional and multi-textual like the internet. A cemetery is not a phalanx of the dead marching under a single banner but a chorus of voices talking at the same time, some calm and factual, some histrionic and fantastical. However, the one thing we can be sure of is that graves never mean nothing. Our task is not to tell the dead that they were Christian or pagan but to ask them what they believed, and not to assume we will understand the answer.

The factual messages now available from the dead resemble those that are obtained from the living by doctors: the scientific tests may not give the right answer, but they are in a different order of wrongness to the condition of the patient as explained by the bizarre (but essential) anecdotes of their relatives. So mourners design a burial that may or not reflect the assumed allegiances of the dead in this world and beyond; that is one story. The more factual story is provided by the scientific analysis of the human remains, which show, through osteology, stable isotope analysis and aDNA, their biological characteristics, what they had suffered from, what they mainly ate, where they resided and their place in genetic history. These substrates in the human identity build a picture of a person and their origins and the health and movement of communities. Both these kinds of evidence, the physical biography of the dead and what was intended by their burial, are essential parts of the interpretation, with neither right on its own. These matters were touched on in Chapter 2. In this chapter the theme concerns the grave and the cemetery as monuments, and the emphasis is on what was done, where and when, in order to celebrate lives and reassure successors. The individual and their ornamentation form part of this, but only a part. We are equally concerned with the actions and thoughts of the grave makers. For this purpose, all the burials of formative Britain are eligible, whether or not they had grave goods.

The expedition before us is daunting. We stand like Pier's Ploughman surveying a 'a fair field full of folk', wondering on what basis and following which system we can conduct socially scientific inquiries about what they thought of the world and each other, knowing in advance that while some will relate their views honestly, some will always lie, and others will be unsure which they do. Our sample of the folk is somewhat random, since only a few hundred cemeteries have been found in Britain belonging to these 700 years, and of these only a dozen have been fully investigated (Figure 4.1). These latter are the most valuable, since every social question about the relative treatment of men, women and children, or the display of wealth, or the variations in health or the presence of locals and incomers, and any question about change depends on having a large sample of the whole community. However, even partially excavated cemeteries make an increasing contribution to patterns of understanding, as knowledge builds.

I propose the following approach. First, to take another 'Field Trip', focussing this time on seven of the best-explored cemeteries in longest use in different parts of the island. What these offer is an overview of changes through time at a particular place, showing that the interest lies less in their role as 'type sites' and more in their role as barometers of the ideological winds that blew. We will start in the south, head for the west country, loop north through Wales to Pictland and come back south to the Anglo-Saxons. This preliminary exploration should allow us to line up a collection of attributes that will describe the funerary monument: location and plan of cemeteries, structures of graves, references to other cultures and so on. Armed with this 'vocabulary', we will then tour Britain and chronicle the preferred rituals of burial in each region through time, beginning in the Iron Age. Following this empirical reconnaissance, we will see how far how these varying attributes compose a narrative of practice and can be bent to serve the more general themes of this book: governance, spirituality and wealth creation. And, finally, I will attempt to compose a narrative of what happened where and what it might be contrived to mean.

A field trip

Westhampnett is a long-used cemetery discovered in a commercially funded investigation on the route of the Westhampnett bypass 3 km east of Chichester during improvements to the A27 trunk road. The burials were located on a low hill, which was to be removed to install a roundabout and slip road. The Wessex archaeologists carried out a desk-based assessment, followed by a field evaluation consisting of surface collection, test pits and machine-cut trenches. The gravely subsoil was covered by a brown loam that disguised the burials, and 45 of the graves were recognised only by their emerging contents (e.g. rims of pots). Formal excavation was extended to the whole area thought to include the cemetery, and 200 burials were excavated that proved to be of Iron Age, Roman and Anglo-Saxon date. A large ring ditch of a BA barrow (20882) was located and rapidly defined on the penultimate day of the field contract, so extending the life of the cemetery – but not the excavation (Figure 4.2).[1]

Figure 4.1 Map of places mentioned in this chapter, with those visited on the field trip in italics.
(FAS Heritage)

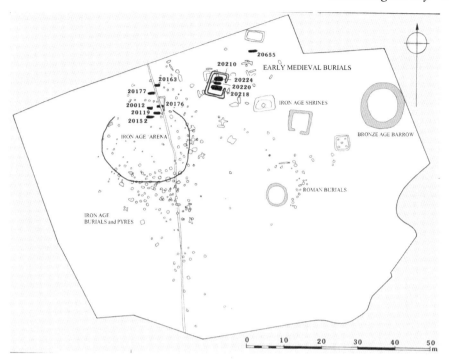

Figure 4.2 Westhampnett (West Sussex). Iron Age cremations, pyres and shrines, Roman cremations and early medieval (Fm 1) inhumations (black lozenges, numbered).

(Graphical compilation from Fitzpatrick 1997; courtesy of author and Wessex Archaeology)

The Iron Age phase consisted of 140 cremations, mainly in urns, clustered around a circular or oval area measuring 17 × 12 m. The rim of this 'arena' was well defined by an initial ring of older persons (45 years +, dubbed the 'elders'). The burials around the arena were cut into or covered by a layer of loam interpreted as generated by 'repeated turning of the soil during grave digging'; but it may have been the result of dispersing a mound that had stood on the arena and provided a focus for the first cremations.[2] Surrounding the cremations to east, south and west were 20 small shallow-ditched structures with one, two, three or four arms containing charcoal and interpreted as funeral pyres. The numerous directions of these trenches implied that they were sited to take advantage of the different directions of the wind – those with three or four arms implying pyres that were used more than once. To the northeast of the cremations was a row of four quadrilateral structures interpreted as shrines on the basis of their small size, rectilinear shape, east/south-east orientation and entrances.[3] They were thought to have been constructed of planks, close-set in the wall trenches and daubed with clay. They would have provided access (and shelter) to a group of mourners wishing to compose the urn, enact rituals or wait for the weather to clear. The end enclosure (706) was 4.4 m square and, unlike the others, had an internal post at each corner and a central cremation of an adult in a red-slipped pot, dating just before the Roman conquest.[4] This structure, marking a special burial, recalled Continental practice, especially in France, where 'small four post structures with a cremation centrally placed are well known'.[5] Roman cremations followed those of the Iron Age and were focussed on a small ring ditch to the east that may also have been the remains of a Bronze Age barrow. There were 36 in number, interred over a period of 80 years (70–150 AD), and were thought to represent the burials of one family.

The Anglo-Saxon burials consisted of 10 inhumations, six clustered on the north side of the Iron Age 'arena' and possible barrow and three set in a quadrilateral enclosure, imitating but overlying and cutting the most north-westerly Iron Age shrine. Only five graves were excavated as the contract ran out of time, and, in those, little bone survived in the acidic soil.[6] The grave goods, a spearhead and some knives, and the enclosed inhumations suggested a 7th-century date.

The gravitational force exercised by earlier burials on later is a theme of this cemetery and of many others we will visit; and the attraction exercised by Bronze Age barrows (among the most widespread and prominent monuments in the early medieval landscape) for Roman shrines and Anglo-Saxon cemeteries has been noted over many years of study.[7] Here the view from the low rise with one or more Bronze barrows attracted an Iron Age community which began by celebrating their senior figures around a circular arena – perhaps itself once the site of a barrow. Since the pyres respected the edge of the eventual cemetery, it seems likely that its extent was largely pre-planned. The positioning of the shrines, in a row to the north-east, show that this was also pre-planned. They were connected with the cremation ceremony, since pyres migrated into their vicinity, but whether one succeeded the other or all four functioned together (for example in the service of different deities) are matters for conjecture. The 'special burial' in structure 706 should have celebrated some prominent person intimate with the ceremonial place, perhaps a spiritual specialist.

The Iron Age community was no doubt all attracted to the spot by the vista (the land visible from the place) and by the ubiquitous icon of the Bronze Age barrow. The Roman family may have responded to the same attraction or have had some memory of the Iron Age community that was superannuated one or two generations earlier. The 7th-century family arrived 500 years after the last previous burial and used a different burial rite (inhumation) from their predecessors. Nevertheless, it seems likely that they could see at least two, possibly three barrows and possibly the earthworks of the Iron Age shrines. These were 'read' and reproduced in their burial rites. Although termed 'Anglo-Saxon', these need not be the graves of immigrants, especially by the 7th century in the south of England.

The reuse and imitation of prehistoric practice is an important and indicative aspect of early Formative burial. It clearly involves a response to the visible landscape, but not always, or not only. Ideas applied to graves can also have been obtained from knowledge of the past, but not necessarily ideas handed down directly from person to person. Rather they can be drawn from some common mental inheritance and reified to produce something remarkably similar to those of predecessors, but predecessors too remote in space and time to have been live contacts. Ship burial, horse burial, chamber graves, mounds, slab-linings and quadrilateral shrines are all examples we shall encounter. Their use is spasmodic and discontinuous, neither contiguous nor even cognate. They show that the human mind is at work, drawing on its knowledge or mis-knowledge to create each grave.

Cannington

Cannington cemetery is in Somerset and stands on high ground overlooking the Parrett estuary, with the Bristol Channel beyond. It shared its hill of carboniferous limestone with a hillfort occupied in the Iron Age and refortified in the Roman period. Being made of limestone, the hill has been intensively quarried for building stone and mortar; and it was the northern rim of Cannington Park quarry that retained the last part of the post-Roman cemetery. In 1962–3, 542 burials were excavated there by Philip Rahtz, perhaps twice as many having already been lost to the quarry without record. The cemetery was in use from the late Roman period until the late 7th century AD, thus embracing the whole of Formative 1. In addition to

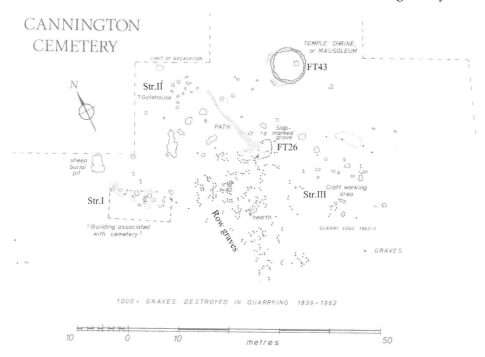

Figure 4.3 Cannington (Somerset) Roman and Fm 1 inhumation burials, with location of temple (FT43), shrine (FT26) and other structures (Str. I-III).

(Rahtz et al. 2000, Fig 251; with permission, Society for Roman Studies)

the graves, the excavators defined a number of significant ritual features and incorporated them in a detailed sequence of use through three centuries (Figure 4.3). The results were published following some 30 years of analysis in a comprehensive monograph that redefined – and greatly illuminated – the post-Roman period in the west of Britain.[8]

The surface of the limestone was broken and blocky; shallow graves, ditches and pits had to be distinguished from natural fissures, and man-made surface features (a path, slabs covering a grave) needed to be distinguished within the random scatter of rubble. This was achieved with considerable skill, given that much of the ritual repertoire was unfamiliar. Dating was by Roman and post-Roman artefacts found mainly in the thin topsoil, together with radiocarbon measurement on the bones in 31 graves, both agreeing on a period of use from the late 3rd to the late 7th centuries AD.[9] A ring ditch (FT43) with a central grave (424) stood at the northernmost and highest point, both closely associated with late Roman finds (Figure 4.4A). The central grave was that of an adult male, and the tumble of stones that lay over and beside it suggested that the ring ditch had circumscribed a small mound.[10] A grave (409) perhaps also originally under a mound (FT26) offered a later focus, an interpretation reinforced in this case by the definition of a pebble path that approached it from the north and the marking of the grave on the surface by a row of four lias slabs and a kerb (Figure 4.4B).[11] A post and a triangular marker of red sandstone had also stood on the mound. The path appears to have begun 20 m or so to the north at a point marked by a set of rock-cut post-holes which were interpreted as supporting a gatehouse or reception area (Structure II). The destination in this case was a young person of about 13 years old, and the location had

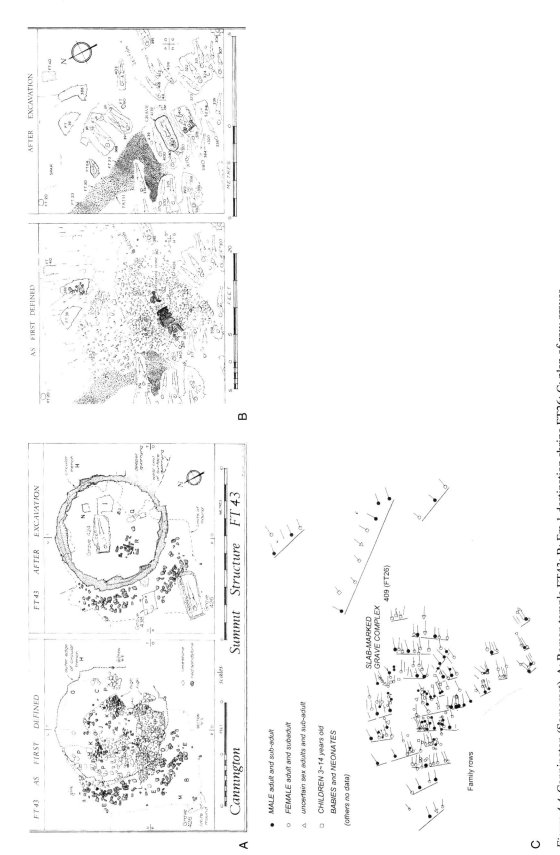

A Cannington

Summit Structure FT 43

FT 43 AS FIRST DEFINED

FT 43 AFTER EXCAVATION

- ● MALE adult and sub-adult
- ○ FEMALE adult and subadult
- ◔ uncertain sex adults and sub-adult
- △ CHILDREN 3–14 years old
- ▢ BABIES and NEONATES
- (others no data)

B AS FIRST DEFINED

AFTER EXCAVATION

C

SLAB-MARKED GRAVE COMPLEX

409 (FT26)

Family rows

Figure 4.4 Cannington (Somerset). A: Roman temple FT43; B: Fm 1 destination shrine FT26; C: plan of row graves. (Rahtz et al. 2000, Fig 25, 28, 252; with permission, Society for Roman Studies)

proved attractive not only to visitors on foot but to later burials. Situated immediately to the east and south-east of Grave 409 were three long rows that included graves with 7th-century objects within them. Stones had been deliberately placed in 30 burials (5.5%), in one case around the perimeter of the body (Grave 123); in five cases a stone was place beside the head, and in two cases beneath it.[12] These were symbolic measures and did not employ slabs as in the more protective cists at used in the northern cemeteries of Fm 1. The main cemetery stretched on the south side of FT26. Here the inhumations were laid out feet to east, and many appeared to have been organised in short rows (Figure 4.4C). Given that each row tended to include men, women, children and neonates, they were interpreted as representing family plots.

Two structures were defined either side of the main cemetery: Structure I was a group of closely associated blocks of limestone or spar; it had been partly cut away by the quarry but appeared to have had a rectilinear footprint that ran east-west and was duly interpreted as a church or guest house. Structure III to the east was defined by a set of post-holes implying some kind of linear building; it was associated with a high-temperature hearth and a scattering of craft debris: smithing slag, goat horn cores and pieces of antler including pins, combs and handles, perhaps for knives.[13] Other metal finds included a child's copper alloy tubular bracelet from Grave 407 and a trilobed penannular brooch from Grave 405. These date to the 7th or the latter even into the 8th century,[14] and their location in a row adjacent to Grave 409 shows that the reputation of the young person commemorated remained potent up to the point the cemetery was discontinued.

The overall sequence was determined thus:

1   During the 4th century AD, a shrine, temple or mausoleum was established on the summit of the hill (FT 43), with a central grave 424 containing an adult male but with only three others in the vicinity.

2   4th–6th century AD. The focus was on Grave 409 and slab-marked Mound FT 26. A path was created by visitors to this grave. Structure II provided a gatehouse or collecting point for the visitors.

3   4th–6th century AD. Development of a multi-focal cemetery with elements of row planning, indicating family plots. Structure I serves the cemetery, perhaps as a cult centre (church) or guest house.

4   7th–8th century AD. Graves were added in the main area and on the eastern periphery, which featured a strong row of furnished graves (for example 405, 407). Structure III was a possible building associated with the manufacture of objects in metal and horn.

5   Late 7th or 8th century. Cemetery abandoned.[15]

The authors make a clear case that the site began as a late Roman ritual destination (FT43) and developed in the post-Roman period with a new cult focus (FT26). This latter consisted of Grave 409 marked by a mound, with a row of slabs on top of it, a post and triangular marker beside it and a path leading to it, the whole interpreted as the resting place of a holy child that attracted pilgrims over a lengthy period. There is some uncertainty about whether the cemetery was joined by the focal grave or largely initiated by it. On the one hand, the spread of radiocarbon dates and finds suggested a span of late 3rd to late 7th century, and the date for Grave 409 was assessed as 620 at the earliest.[16] On the other, the cemetery plan strongly suggests that the grave 409/ST26 monument was the starting point for laying out a majority of the excavated graves, most being to the south and very few to the north of it.

The refreshed radiocarbon dates from the Harwell laboratory show that the cemetery should have been in continuous use from the 3rd–4th century, but those dated 5th–7th century correlate with the grander rows on the north-east side.[17] There is therefore a case for placing the establishment of the child's Grave 409 earlier in the post-Roman period and associating it with the adoption of family rows, which continue to be valid until the end of the 7th century.

Although the authors designate Structure I as a possible church by virtue of its alignment, they appreciate that this is a time when pagan and Christian signals can be interwoven. The absence of any Christian symbolism on metal or stone even as late as the 7th century would seem to suggest that deeper roots prevailed.[18] The authors also note that the reception of visitors implied by the focal grave and the path leading to it and the metalworking and antler-working 'may be associated with the making or selling of objects to visitors': this aligns Cannington with the 'congregational sites' that attracted visitors in pagan Scandinavia and in pagan and monastic Scotland and Ireland.[19] We shall meet others as the concept of a cemetery is enlarged from a burial place to a cult centre in other places we visit.

Capel Eithin, Anglesey

Let's now move north through Wales into Anglesey to visit a cemetery discovered in a field on a low promontory with views to the south-east over the Menai Strait (Figure 4.5). The outline of a stone-lined grave was discovered here by a farmer in the course of ploughing,

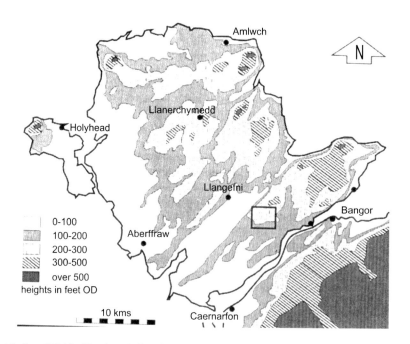

Figure 4.5 Capel Eithin (Anglesey): location (box).

(White and Smith 1999, Fig 1A; reproduced from *Trans. Anglesey Antiq. Soc*, 1999; with permission, Anglesey Antiquarian Society)

Figure 4.6 Capel Eithin (Anglesey): plan.
(White and Smith 1999, Fig 40, with additions of groups and phases (by author); reproduced with permission from
Trans Anglesey Antiq Soc, 1999, with additions; with permission, Anglesey Antiquarian Society)

and excavations by Gwyneth Archaeological Trust followed in 1980/81. An area of 55 ×
55 m exposed a group of Bronze Age cremations, a Roman period quadrilateral structure
in a circular banked enclosure that acted as a focus for graves of the 5th/6th century and
a quadrilateral foundation, perhaps for a shrine, that had acted as a focus for graves of
the 7th/8th century (Figure 4.6).[20] After this time the cemetery was abandoned. A 6th-
century stone inscribed *Devorigi* (of Devorix) was recorded at Capel Eithin in c. 1699 but
is now lost.[21]

The Bronze Age group of cremations consisted of 15 urned burials, 16 charcoal-filled
pits and 26 groups of cremated bone. A mound in this position is implied by the alignment
of later (post-medieval) field boundaries.[22] The Roman period enclosure was composed
of a bank of stony soil enclosing an area c. 32 m in diameter. On the top of the bank at its
eastern side was a linear stone setting resembling a cairn.[23] In the centre of the enclosure
was a large pit (134) cut into bedrock, which, given its position, may have supported a
wooden post or a monolith. It was superseded by Building 194, which had a foundation
trench up to 1.6 m wide containing footings of rounded boulders. The building was dated
to the 2nd century from the inclusion in its backfilled trench of fragments from three clay
moulds implying 'the small scale production of small trinkets', including a penannular

brooch. This date and the square form of the building led to its identification as a signal station.[24]

Building 617 at the north end of the excavated site measured 4.9 × 3.4 internally. Its square foundation trench had a dark organic sludge at the bottom, which indicated a rotted horizontal sleeper beam, to which vertical plank walls, now vanished, had presumably been mortised. It had been provided with a clay floor, which lifted off cleanly to reveal the central grave (66) that had been lined with planks and a child's grave (67) beside it. An entrance had been included in the east wall, subsequently the site of a third grave (74) placed exactly over the ingress passage.

The graves had been refilled with the excavated claysoil of their upcast, making them very difficult to see other than when drying after rain. Ninety-eight graves were defined, in none of which were any traces of finds or human remains. Seven types of grave structure were defined, varying from those with stone lintels (A), stone floors (B), stone walls (C), some stone inclusions (D and E), with a headstone and footstone (F), a headstone only (G) and a simple dug grave with no stones (J). In total, 40 had some stones and 58 had none. The graves were assessed in six groups; Groups 1 and 2 focussed on building 617 and Groups 3–6 on the Bronze Age and Roman features to the south.

The cemetery was sequenced on the basis of its plan, the grave types and their parallels (radiocarbon dating of samples of the planks in Grave 66 gave contradictory and unusably wide dates, from 5 to 1035 AD). This gave three main groups of burials.[25]

The earliest are likely to have been those on the south side (Group 3–6). Ten of these on the east side could be determined as aligned on the Bronze Age barrow, three along the outside of the bank and two within it, and the remainder (c. 17) were focused on the stone cairn on the north-east part of the Roman bank. These graves were mostly of the plain dug kind. Three (28, 30 and 32) featured wisps of wood implying timber placed in the grave; five had some stone inclusions; only one had a complete cist.[26] In Group 1, the 18 E-W graves associated with Structure 617 were dominated by full or partial cist graves. In Group 2, by contrast, the majority were plain dug, and their orientation was varied but mostly north of east. Their southern edge is curved as though the area commanded by the building 617 was originally fenced.

Without direct dating, this sequence remains somewhat floating. The authors use the former presence of an inscribed stone of 6th-century date that may have stood in the pit 134 or to mark Grave 66 as a key point in the use of the cemetery, and the 9th–11th century crosses at nearby Llanfihangel Ysceifiog, seen as Capel Eithin's successor, as suggesting its end date.[27] Parallels with the radiocarbon-dated cemeteries at Llandough and Tandderwen and elsewhere would place the use of stone-lined graves in the period 5th–7th century (p. 367). Therefore, it seems plausible that the cult centre at Capel Eithin began to develop during the Roman period, although not necessarily as a Roman site. It has little of the Roman cult apparatus, and the first burials are probably those aligned on the Bronze Age barrow. The Roman ringwork, with its central pit, square building and cairn, can belong with its attendant simple burials to the 4th/6th century (Phase 1). The construction of Building 617 with its special grave is a major new expression of intention and belief belonging, most probably, to the 7th century. The attendant graves are now full cists, aligned east to west and privileged by proximity to the holy man or woman commemorated at its centre (Phase 2). The graves that follow, of simple type and disorganised in their orientation, mark the last days in which, as at Cannington, allegiance to the revered subject takes precedence over Christian orthodoxy (Phase 3).[28] If the successor phase of a local parish church is accepted as valid, this stage will be over in or before the 9th century.[29]

Portmahomack, Easter Ross

Continuing the journey north brings as to the Moray Firth and the site of Portma-homack. Here we are in Pictland but still in the cultural region of stone-protected burial, and there was a rare opportunity to observe the transition between the burial rites of Formative 1 and those of Formative 2 on the same site. The Portmahomack site, on the Tarbat peninsula and overlooking the Dornoch Firth, hosted four consecutive settlements of different kinds (Chapter 3, p. 148). The first was an estate centre of the 5th–7th century, the second a monastery (late 7th to early 9th), the third a farm that also trades (9th century) and the fourth a medieval village with parish church (12th–16th century).[30] In each of these phases there was a group of excavated burials that referred directly to the excavated settlement. Cemetery and settlement provided each other with context, and it could be seen that although there were times when the primary function of the settlement was ritual (Periods 2 and 4), at other times it was more down to earth (Periods 1 and 3). Apart from a small gap between the 10th and 12th century, the cem-etery continued alongside the settlement and provided a vital commentary on the health and beliefs of its community. The burials were examined in two contiguous areas – along the ridge that separated the site from the sea and within the church of St Colman, the monastic centre that was readopted as the parish church (Figure 4.7). Since many of the burials succeeded each other in the same place, it was possible to put them into a

Figure 4.7 Portmahomack (Easter Ross). St Colman's Church (centre, right) and the monastic enclo-sure ditch as cropmark (foreground). The Fm 1 cemetery is spread over the ridge between the road and the firth and was contacted at the north end of the excavation and at the west end of the church. The Fm 2 cemetery was contacted within the nave of the church.

(Carver et al. 2016, Illus. 1.9, with additions; copyright authors)

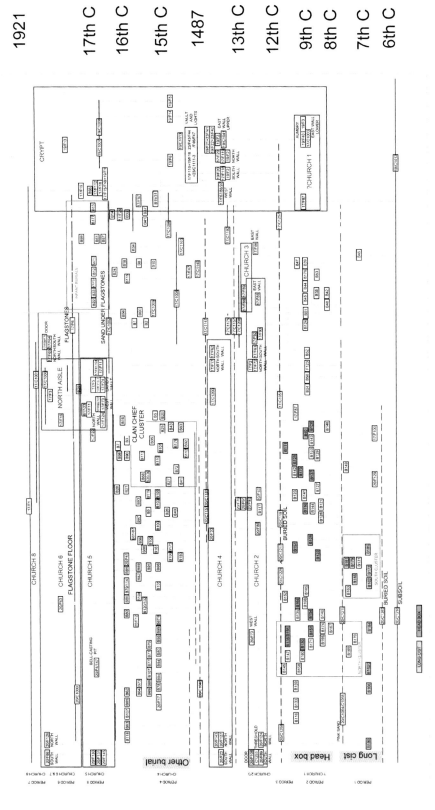

Figure 4.8 Portmahomack cemetery, excavations in St Colman's Church. Stratigraphic sequence of 6th- to 16th-century burials and churches. (Carver et al. 2016, Ill. 3.21; copyright authors)

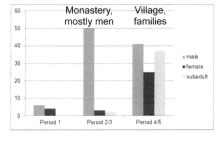

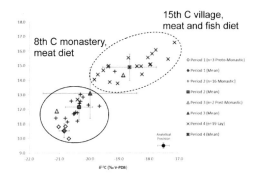

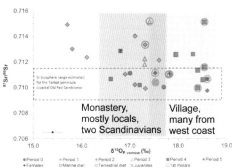

Figure 4.9 Portmahomack people: sex, diet, mobility in the 8th and 15th century compared.
(Carver et al. 2016, Ill. 3.24, 3.25, 3.26; copyright authors)

stratigraphic sequence (Figure 4.8), and the good preservation of bone allowed them to be assigned to decades by radiocarbon dating refined by Bayesian analysis. The human remains were also examined for their diet and their mobility since childhood, assessed from stable isotope ratios in bones and teeth (Figure 4.9). This was a research project, although there was an element of rescue in the excavation of the church in advance of its being made into a museum.[31]

The Period 1 burials were contacted inside the west end of the church and outside on the dunes of the shore. Originally they had formed part of an extensive cemetery in which many of the graves appear to have been marked by mounds (Figure 4.10). The principal form was the cist grave, built from large slabs that surrounded the body with the occasional survival of a floor or lintel piece. Partial cists and plain dug graves were also present in the Period 1 group, which was dated to the 5th to late 7th century. These were burials of men, women and children, local to Scotland and fed on meat, wheat and barley. Iron flat-headed dress pins and a gilt bronze harness disc found in the settlement could place them in the ranks of the affluent (p. 150). The Portmahomack burials were one of several groups of cist graves on the coast of the peninsula at this time (Figure 4.11). Beaker period and Bronze Age burials have also been contacted. The Portmahomack cemetery was thus added to a long pre-existing burial tradition on the Tarbat peninsula.

In Period 2 the site was redesigned as a monastery. New burials budded off from those of the previous period, but they were now laid in rows (Figure 4.12) and took a different form: small stones were included in the grave, often either side of the head (head-support burials)

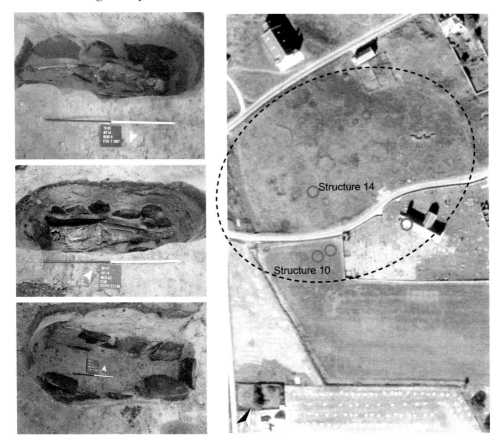

Figure 4.10 Portmahomack. (Left) Excavated Fm 1 cist burials and (right) putative barrows seen in
an aerial photograph of 1945. Cist burials of Fm 1 (circles) were encountered at the north
end of the excavation area ('Structure 10') and at the west end of the church of St Colman
(the building on the right).

(Carver et al. 2016, Ill. 4.8, 4.11; copyright authors; aerial photograph by RCAHMS 106G/UK751 flown 31 Aug
1945; licensed by and © Historic Environment Scotland)

or either side and over the top (head box burials) (Figure 4.13). There was also a comparable
number of burials in plain earth. Those interred were predominately middle-aged and elderly
men, representing a population of monks (Figure 4.9). Their diet was mainly meat and their
origins local, apart from two of Scandinavian extraction indicated by their oxygen/strontium
signature. Several of the graves had been marked on the surface by small slabs bearing a
cross, which had subsequently been disturbed and reused as building stone. At least four
large stone monuments had also been erected on the margins of the burial area. Only one of
these carried an inscription, in Latin, commemorating an unidentified person. The names of
other persons of high rank were commemorated in the form of Pictish symbols (see Chapter 5, p. 493).

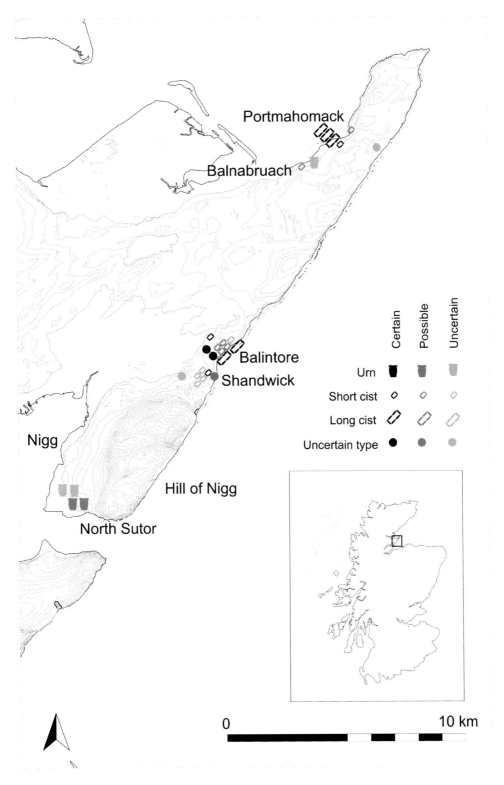

Figure 4.11 Portmahomack. Prehistoric and Fm 1 burials on the Tarbat peninsula.
(Carver et al. 2016, Ill. 4.28; copyright authors)

Figure 4.12 Portmahomack, St Colman's Church: Fm 2 row graves with head-support burials.
(Carver et al. 2016, Ill. 5.2.2 copyright authors)

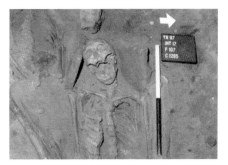

Figure 4.13 Portmahomack, head-support burials excavated in the church.
(Carver et al. 2016, Ill. 5.2.3 copyright authors)

The three large stone cross-slabs and one cross shaft were broken up at the turn of the 9th century in a raid attributed to the Vikings which also burnt down the vellum workshops. The community recovered quickly, and in the early part of Period 3 (the 9th century) was dedicated to making and probably trading personal accoutrements of copper alloy and silver. Burial continued in the church using the same rites as before, but in lower numbers, eventually blurring the rows. Very few burials could be assigned to the 10th–13th century, after which burial began again in the nave of what was now the parish church. It was not continuous even then. There was a low period in the cemetery (and the settlement) between 1350 and 1450, and a resurgence in the mid-15th century, when burial recommenced with a focus on a large man buried in front of the crypt steps accompanied by four heads – a medieval head cult. It was in this period that the Tarbat peninsula experienced its main influx of west coast people.

A sequence stretching beyond the formative has been presented in this case, firstly because it was possible to do so and secondly because it provides more support for the idea that a community can make a sensitive response to current events. While a close association between early medieval cemeteries and prehistoric predecessors (especially in the west and north) was fundamental to them, they nevertheless adapted their ideological allegiance to the times and expressed it in burial rites. An extended period of affiliation to a single conviction would appear to be unusual.

Spong Hill

It is now time to turn our tour southwards, into the territory that was settled in the 5th century by people from Frisia, Denmark and north Germany, the 'Anglo-Saxon immigrants' whose descendants became the English. Their funerary world in Formative 1 could hardly be more different from that of the north and west. Here many of the graves are furnished with objects signalling gender, rank and identity, and both cremation and inhumation are practised. Spong Hill is one of only two Anglo-Saxon cemeteries that has been completely excavated (the other being Wasperton, coming next).[32] It lies in open country on a low hill near North Elmham at a convergence of Roman roads by the upper reaches of the River Wensum. The excavation took place in a quick-draining sandy gravel under topsoil and extended over a hectare, in which 2,323 cremations and 57 inhumations were recorded, together with seven sunken-featured buildings and at least four rectilinear post-hole structures ('PG' on Figure 4.14). The bone was poorly preserved in the inhumations. Cremated bone was not attacked by the acid soil, but there had been disturbance, truncation and dispersal of many cremation urns and their contents (Figure 4.15). Nevertheless, a well-dated demographic and cultural picture could be drawn in detail from this, the largest sample of an early English community so far examined.

The cemetery was in use during the period 400–550, and for the first 75 years it was used for cremation only. The urns were decorated with stamps, cordons and bosses in relief and some were provided with lids – in one case taking the form of a thoughtful person in an ornamental chair (Chapter 2, 97). Potentially, there were many more totemic clay models of this kind, but their frail materials and height rising on top an urn rendered them especially vulnerable to plough damage. Inside the pots were cremated bones of men, women or children, together with animals including sheep, goat, dog and horse. Grave goods (not always burnt) took the form of combs, gaming pieces, spindle whorls, brooches, tweezers, glass beads, needle cases, needles, sword fittings, spears, tools and hones. Some of the objects had been produced in miniature versions, perhaps to fit into the pots.

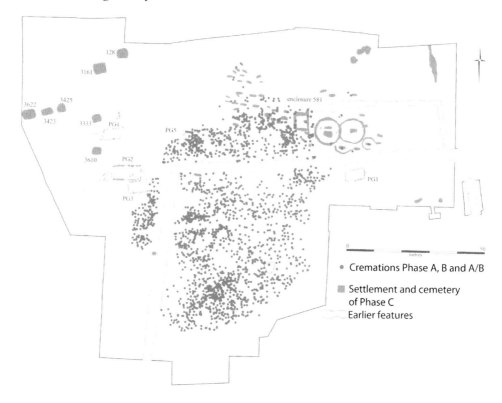

Figure 4.14 Spong Hill Cemetery (Norfolk) The rectilinear ditches marked in outline belong to the preceding Roman settlement; the locations of the cremations suggest that this boundary remained visible to those creating the cemetery. The Group A and B cremations south of the main ditch belong to the period c. 400–475. To the north are Group C cremations and the inhumations (in light grey) dating c. 475–550. Within the small northern enclosure are four ring-ditches indicating burial mounds that had covered high-status graves. In light grey to west and east are SFBs and post-hole buildings that are also assigned to Group C.

(Hills and Lucy 2013, Fig 1.15; Figs 3.20–3.27; image courtesy of authors)

The cremations were organised into three groups determined from pot stamps and artefact styles where these were clear. Groups A and B represent the first phases of the cremation cemetery, 1,686 cremations serving a community of an estimated 826 persons over a period of 70 years (400/420–470/490 AD). Group C comprised 180 cremations and 57 inhumations, serving a population of 140 persons over 60 years (470/490–530/550 AD).[33] Arriving in the later stages of the cemetery's development, the inhumations took up their station on the north-east flank: a ribbon of graves of both sexes with a general west-east alignment trailing from a mostly male enclave of two large and two small burial mounds at the east end (31 and 40; 41 and 46; Figure 4.16). Burial 40 contained a sword, shield, spearhead and bucket; Burial 31 a spearhead, buckle and shield, with a pair of fishes, each resembling a pike, as fixtures on the shield board. Rich female graves included no. 24, with amber beads, a square-headed brooch, bronze keys, a bronze bowl and an iron weaving batten, and no. 2, with a pair of

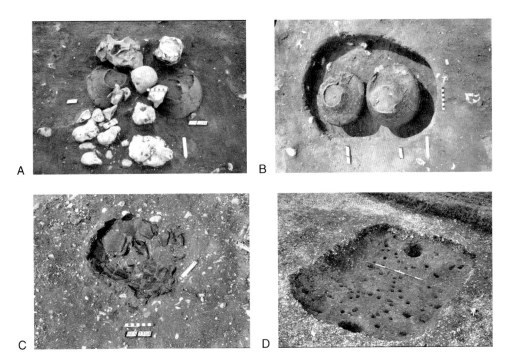

Figure 4.15 Spong Hill characteristics. A: Cremations 2696 and 2697 as found under a heap of flints. B: Cremations 2696 and 2697 excavated in their shared pit. Their stamps belong to Stamp Group 2 and include swastikas. C: Cremation urn 3304 crushed by later agricultural traffic. The grave goods included the remains of cruciform brooches, 20 or more glass beads and fragment of ivory. D: A sunken-featured building from the settlement.

(Photos courtesy of Dr Catherine Hills)

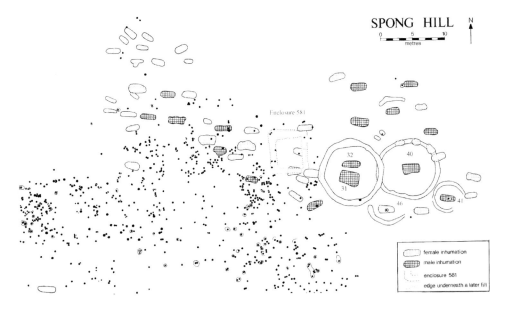

Figure 4.16 Spong Hill: plan of the Group C inhumation burials.

(Hills et al. 1984; image courtesy of Dr C Hills and *East Anglian Archaeology*)

florid cruciform brooches. These icons proclaiming gender and rank are maintained in the funerary record in Southumbria throughout the period of Formative 1 (5th to 7th century).

Did Spong Hill have any other function, religious or social, other than disposal of the dead? On analogy with Scandinavia, it has been proposed that larger Anglo-Saxon cemeteries could have functioned as 'Central Places', that is, cult centres, assembly places or congregational sites.[34] In this case, the expectation would be a wet or dry area of votive deposits and hoards resulting in a surface scatter of precious metal as at Gudme or Tissø and/or a hierarchy of buildings with a monumental centre as at Uppåkra (see Chapter 3, p. 284). This type of site is so far elusive in England. At Spong Hill, the site chosen was apparently a former Romano-British farmstead. Although the assemblage was not rich (by Roman standards), it included brooches, bracelets, glass and more than 10,000 sherds of Roman pottery, retrieved after stripping.[35] Judging from the plan, the Roman field boundaries had survived, in least in part, in the north to contain the barrows and in the west perhaps to inhibit the spread of cremations. Roman buildings should still have been standing in the early 5th century, and the scatter of Roman objects might have proved attractive to northerners seeking the familiar face of a cult site. However, the match is hardly convincing.

The SFBs and post-hole buildings form a cluster on the north-west side of the cemetery, all aligned approximately east-west. A further post-hole building lay on the east side (PG1). There was a deposit of loom weights inside the south door of PG2 but few other indications of activity, function or date; ploughing had removed all but the lowest parts of the post-holes.[36] The authors of the synthesis volume see these buildings as the survivors of a settlement relating to the later burials (Group C), although is not excluded that the settlement continued with a longer date span to the west of the excavated area.[37] The small group of buildings excavated seem to have respected the limits of the cemetery (which may have been fenced), and some of them (e.g. PG1–3) perhaps provided some service to burial parties and visitors, as suggested for Cannington and Westhampnett.[38]

The analysis applied by Hills and Lucy to the Spong Hill material offers a persuasive model, drawn from parallels in pottery styles and early brooches, of a cemetery of immigrants from north-western Europe who arrived via The Wash in the early decades of the 5th century and rapidly colonised the area of Norfolk and south Lincolnshire. Here they expelled or absorbed the inhabitants and took over working Romano-British farmland with a network of smallholdings managed from small villages. Their cemeteries were arenas in which allegiance to ancestors was restated, without any noticeable sign at first of acculturation or appreciation of the newly possessed landscape or its occupants. However, events associated with Group C show a dramatic increase in exhibited rank and a corresponding decrease in the size of population served. While Groups A and B are seen as providing burial facilities for 25 or so neighbouring villages of 35 persons, Group C might be seen as referring to something more local or, possibly, the patronising of the cemetery by far-flung descendants who have come up in the world.[39] The new generation of later 6th- and early 7th-century cemeteries will continue this process: an increased empathy on the part of the Anglo-Saxons with the British population and its kin, customs, ideas and perceived prehistoric ancestry, together with more demonstrative statements of wealth and class on the eve of Christian conversion.

Wasperton

Wasperton lies on the western border of the Anglo-Saxon cultural zone beside the Warwickshire Avon. By taking a trip there as our penultimate port of call in this introductory section, we have made a loop round the island and returned to the south-west, where we began. The

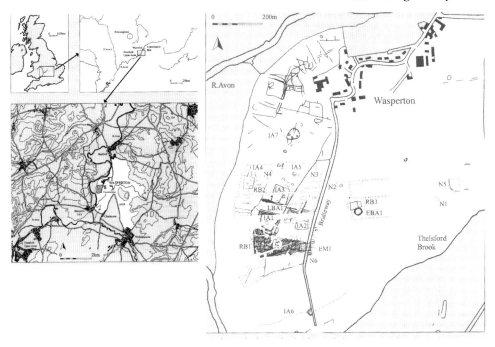

Figure 4.17 Wasperton (Warwickshire) location and extent of the excavations. The Formative 1 cemetery is marked 'EM1' at the east end of the Romano-British settlement (RB1).

(Carver et al. 2009, Fig 2.1, 2.3; reproduced under licence from Boydell & Brewer)

cemeteries visited on the west and east sides of Britain are so different that we seem to have visited two separate countries with little in common, a division that will be repeated in the chapter about sculpture (Chapter 5). Wasperton has the merit of reflecting a meeting of cultures, preserved as a fossilised encounter in a shared space.

The cemetery lay within a prehistoric and Roman landscape, of which 10 hectares were stripped and excavated in advance of gravel extraction between 1981 and 1985 (Figure 4.17).[40] From this we can be fairly sure that no contemporary settlement lay nearby. The burials were focussed on a pair of ditched and banked enclosures belonging to a late Roman agricultural complex, with the remains of a Neolithic long barrow on the south side and two barrows on the north side, which are argued as being still visible in Anglo-Saxon and Roman times. Two hundred and fifteen inhumation graves and 26 cremations were excavated, and (given that the area around was also fully explored) it is thought that these comprise the total of all interments relating to this place in the late Roman and early medieval periods (Figure 4.18). Although the campaign was under constant pressure from the gravel extraction, the edge of which hurried ever nearer, the definition of features, including graves, was made possible by horizon cleaning by large volunteer teams of students (Figure 4.19A). The subsoil was an acidic sand and gravel, so bone was poorly preserved, but it was often sufficient for anatomical and biochemical analysis. The cemetery was sequenced using a combination of the stylistic dating of grave goods, radiocarbon dating of the surviving bone, stratigraphic ordering where graves cut each other and spatial ordering that deemed neighbouring graves

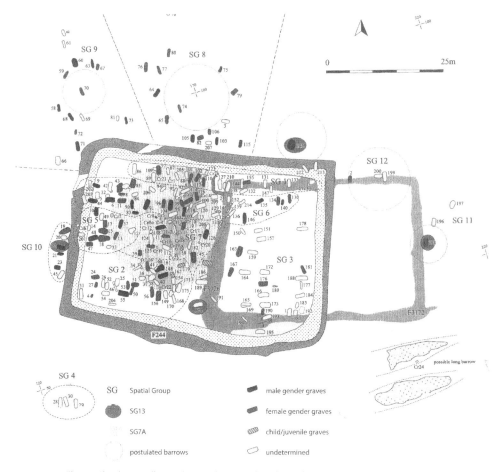

Fig. 5.1 Plan showing all graves by spatial group and gender, marking male, female and child

Table 5.3 Ordering of culturally Anglo-Saxon assemblages (from Tables 4.24, 4.25)

Period	Date (century)	Male	Female
2	5th		Cr 26
3	late 5th / early 6th	Inh. 9, 21, 33, 44, 48, 64, 73, 90, 115, 148, 161, 83, 107, 108	Inh. 13, 17, 39, 47, 59, 72, 111, 116, 145, 163
4	6th	Inh. 6, 10, 91, 103, 104, 146	Inh. 2, 11, 15, 18, 43, 50, 65, 70, 82, 85, 96, 97, 99, 114, 155, 167
5	later 6th	Inh. 60, 63	Inh. 24
6	late 6th / early 7th	Inh. 22, 55, 135, 142	Inh. 4, 58, 77, 198

Figure 4.18 Wasperton: Plan of the Fm 1 cemetery, 4th–7th century.

(Carver et al. 2009, Fig 5.1; reproduced under licence from Boydell & Brewer)

Figure 4.19 Wasperton characteristics. A: Excavations in advance of the dragline and conveyor belt used to extract gravel. B: Roman bracelets in situ in Inh.190 (4th century). C: Saucer brooches from Inh 11 and small-long brooch from Inh 39 (early to mid-6th century). D: Square-headed brooches from Inh 24 (left) and Inh 65 (late 6th century).

(Carver et al. 2009, Plate 1b, Plate II, Fig 4.2; reproduced under licence from Boydell & Brewer)

that shared an alignment to be contemporary. These latter measures allowed graves that had no grave goods to be included in the sequence.

Six periods were distinguished (Figure 4.20). In Period 1 (4th century), 22 inhumations and one cremation (Cr 23) were distributed over the inside of the main enclosure in a manner that suggested the pre-allocation of family areas or plots.[41] In these earliest graves the culturally diagnostic objects were hobnails, bracelets (Figure 4.19B) and neck rings, and the

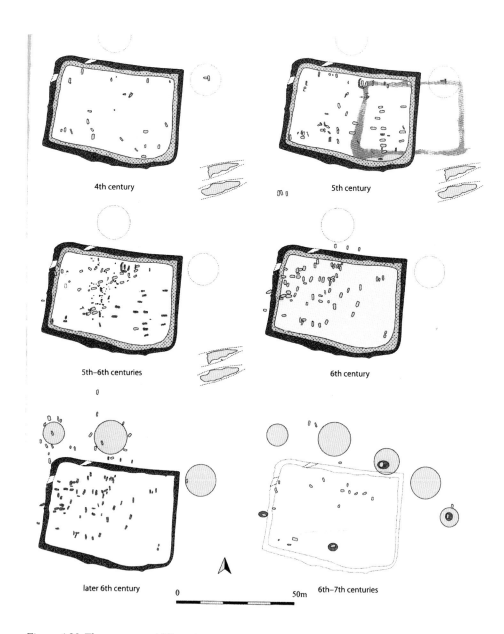

Figure 4.20 The sequence at Wasperton.

(Carver et al. 2009, Fig 1.2; reproduced under licence from Boydell & Brewer)

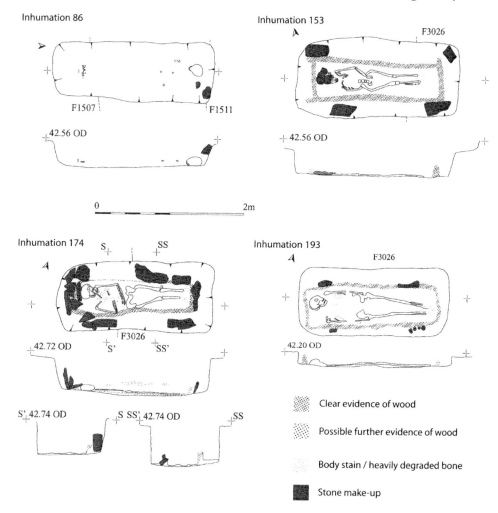

Inhumation 86

F1507   F1511

42.56 OD

Inhumation 153

F3026

42.56 OD

0   2m

Inhumation 174   S   SS

F3026

42.72 OD   S'   SS'

S' 42.74 OD   S SS' 42.74 OD   SS

Inhumation 193

F3026

42.20 OD

Clear evidence of wood

Possible further evidence of wood

Body stain / heavily degraded bone

Stone make-up

Figure 4.21 Stone and timber-lined graves at Wasperton proposed as culturally British.
(Carver et al. 2009, Fig 3.10; reproduced under licence from Boydell & Brewer)

burial rites included decapitation with the head placed between the legs. Burials assigned to Period 2, the 5th century, consisted of 40 inhumations and two cremations. All the inhumations here were without grave goods, the most distinctive being the 14 burials of SG3, which were orientated W-E and 12 of which had stone or timber linings and occasionally both (Figure 4.21). Period 3 saw the arrival of 24 cremations in urns, inserted in a circular area in the western half of the enclosure, possibly defined by a stake fence (SG13) and mutually exclusive to the burials of SG3. One cremation (Cr 24) was inserted in the remains of the long barrow. The dates suggested by radiocarbon and grave goods for this small-scale intrusion were after 480. Period 4, dated to the 6th century, was the heyday of furnished inhumation, the 65 examples inheriting their space from the previous cremation zone and spreading over the western half of the enclosure. The burials included pairs of saucer brooches (Figure 4.19C), and the affiliations of the objects were determined as East Anglia and the upper Thames. At this stage the family plots can still be seen as operative.

It was the later 6th century, Period 5, that saw the internal discipline break down, the boundaries disappear and the first graves migrate outside the enclosure. These were aimed at two pre-existing prehistoric or Roman barrows (SG8, SG12), a new barrow (SG 9) was created to cover a culturally Anglo-Saxon burial (Inh. 70). Two of the new generation of rich females sported great square-headed brooches (Inh 24 and 65) (Figure 4.19D), and the artefact affiliations were now towards the Upper Thames and the Wessex area.[42] By the final period, Period 6 (the late 6th/early 7th century), the old enclosure ditch had disappeared beneath the surface and the focus was on the postulated mounds, which now number five and have acquired a sprinkling of satellite graves. One other high-status 7th-century grave appeared in the SE corner of the Roman enclosure: it was oriented W-E and lined with large stone blocks and planks. Its inmate was of Mediterranean extraction. All the burials in this area (SG3), with the single exception of a S-N woman with a bead necklace, lacked grave goods and were lined with wood or stones and generally aligned W-E.

There has been a long tradition of making assumptions of direct connections between burial rites, ethnicity and religion, modified in our day by a contrarian trend to deny or diminish them. Both these positions are inhibiting in using cemeteries to make history. However, the evidence from Wasperton is strong and convergent because it offers good data for cultural change, in the form of burial rites, artefacts and childhood origins (as indicated by oxygen and strontium isotopes) in a cemetery that was completely excavated. The burials with neck rings and hobnail shoes are culturally Roman and dated to the 4th–5th century. The 5th-century burial rites with planks or rough stone linings relate to those in the (British) west and north.[43] Of those dated to the 4th and 5th century, three had a childhood home in the Mediterranean, four were from West Britain, and eight were local. The late 5th cremations and early 6th-century furnished inhumations are culturally Anglo-Saxon, relating to similar burials in East Anglia and Wessex; the four measured for isotope signatures were of local origin. After the mid-6th century, a few culturally similar people exhibit higher status in their grave goods and an engagement with the local prehistoric landscape in their mode of burial in mounds. The artefact affiliations are now to Wessex. All through the life of the cemetery, the south-east corner of the enclosure was populated by W-E unfurnished graves, some using 'British' signatures of stones and planks. The latest member of the group (174, Figure 4.21) was especially well constructed, and its 7th-century occupant had an origin in the Mediterranean.

These results are consistent with locals and incomers sharing a cemetery and allowing for differences in custom and belief. In the later years, cultural differences were to some extent maintained in death, even if they all experienced a trend to display rank. The impression is that of competitive coexistence in which differences in origins and morals are eased by prosperity and achievement; much like the home counties today, one might say. Allocating labels to individuals remains risky, but cultural distinctions between Roman, British and Anglo-Saxon affiliations seem clear enough. Some religious affiliation is evidently signalled by burials, composed as they are on the threshold of eternity. But it is probably a mistake to assume we know what that religion was. Material signals may equate with belief but not necessarily with any of the religions we know how to recognise today, including Christianity. According to the material culture, especially as manifested in cemeteries, Christianity in the first millennium varies in both time and place, as of course does 'paganism', a similarly coarse and pre-emptive label for a highly creative, inquisitive and free-ranging intellectual repertoire.

Sutton Hoo

Our last port of call takes us to Sutton Hoo (Suffolk), which offers not just incomparable treasures and a dazzling array of burial rites but an overview of how the English funerary experience developed after the 6th century. The site lies on the 30 m contour above the River Deben, overlooking the town of Woodbridge (Figure 4.22). The subsoil is an acid sand that leaves wood in graves as dark smears and the body as a dark brown deposit with traces of bone. Three consecutive cemeteries are known: (1) a 6th/7th-century family cemetery with cremations and inhumations; (2) a 7th-century royal cemetery consisting of 18 burial mounds and a handful of lesser graves; and (3) an 8th–10th-century execution cemetery with 39 victims of hanging, organised in two groups, one around Mound 5 and the other around the footprint of a gallows. The period covered includes Formative 1, 2 and 3 and shows that significant changes of thinking occurred between them.[44]

Graves belonging to the *first cemetery* (Tranmer House Cemetery) were excavated near Tranmer House before the Visitor Centre was constructed, and the area opened contained 13 cremations and 19 inhumations (Figure 4.23). The burials were laid within enclosures that had formed part of an extensive Iron Age field system which should still have been visible. They included a high-status cremation in a hanging bowl with an amethyst bead (Cr. 8) and

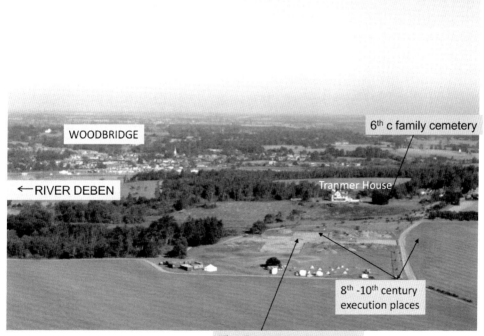

Figure 4.22 Sutton Hoo (Suffolk). An aerial photograph looking north, showing the relative locations of its three cemeteries, with the River Deben and Woodbridge in the background.

(Photo: University of York)

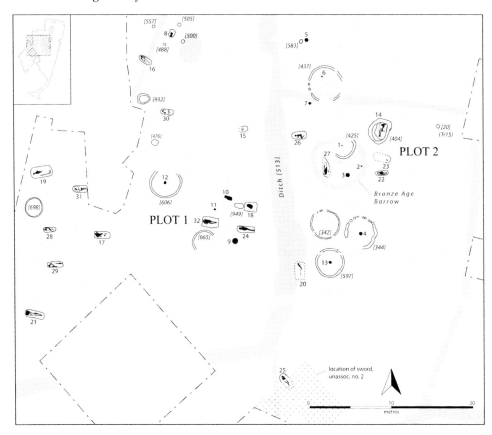

Figure 4.23 Plan of the Tranmer House cemetery.
(Fern 2015, Fig 3.1; courtesy of Chris Fern and *East Anglian Archaeology*)

two groups of high-status inhumations interpreted as family groups, Plot 1 and Plot 2. The burials of Plot 2 were focussed on a Bronze Age barrow in which secondary burials were made. All the graves that could be dated by grave goods or radiocarbon were generally of the 6th century, with cremation and inhumation being practised side by side. Prominent artefact types of the early migration period were missing, as were objects typical of the 7th century. Using correspondence analysis for the artefacts and Bayesian for the radiocarbon dates, it was possible to propose two main stages of use. Phase A between 510/20 and 550 featured the cremations in urns without ring ditches (2, 3, 9, 10, 11) and five inhumations, including one in a plain log coffin (19).[45] Phase B from 550 to 580/600 contained cremations with animal offerings within ring ditches (1, 4, 6, 7, 8, 12, 13). The Bayesian date for the end of cremation at Tranmer House and its start at Sutton Hoo (Mound 5, 6, 7, 3 and 4) was c. 580 AD.[46] Fern therefore identified two cardinal moments at Tranmer House: c. 550, when a family began to bury around a Bronze Age barrow (in Plot 2), and c. 580, when cremation ceased and the first barrows were constructed at Sutton Hoo 300 m to the south.[47]

There were several connecting traits between the Tranmer House cemetery and its successor to the south: in Phase A, a coffin fashioned from a tree trunk contained an inhumation.

Figure 4.24 The Sutton Hoo cemetery looking west in 1983.

(Courtesy of Cliff Hoppitt)

In Phase B, the idea of the Bronze Age barrow was imitated by the ring ditches containing cremations in urns; the grandest of these used a bronze bowl wrapped in cloth to contain the cremation. Fern also argues for a third phase at Tranmer House after 580, Phase C, in which there were just two inhumations: Inhumation 26, a woman, was placed in this date range by her amber and glass beads, and Inhumation 27, a man, by his sword, spear and shield.[48] On this reasoning, these individuals were laid to rest in the old family plot while the large mounds were being constructed in full view on the ridge to the south.

This *second cemetery* (the Sutton Hoo cemetery) consisted of an elite group of 18 burial mounds (Figure 4.24). Once these barrows are reconstructed (virtually) to their original height, it can be appreciated that they formed a considerable landmark visible from the far side of the River Deben and to traffic coming upstream from the sea. Excavations in 1938, 1939 and 1965–71 contacted a Neolithic and Bronze Age landscape, the Mound 1 ship burial, robbed cremations in Mounds 3 and 4, and the first Anglo-Saxon sand bodies. Basil Brown, the first excavator of modern times, contacted traces of a ship in Mound 2 and defined a full-length ocean-going vessel 27 m long in Mound 1. The latter had a robust timber chamber amidships in which the celebrated 'million pound treasure' had survived, now in the British Museum. The latest campaign at this cemetery (1983–1991) began with a design phase two years in duration in which the nature of the site was explored and assessed and a proposed programme of investigation was drawn up and published in advance (Figure 4.25). This was a research project that had the independent backing of national bodies and could go at its own pace, aiming for maximum information with minimum damage. Such opportunities remain very rare.[49]

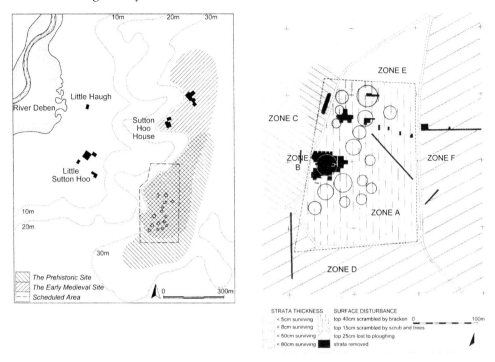

Figure 4.25 Sutton Hoo evaluation: predicted extent of prehistoric and formative sites (left) and predicted survival of archaeological strata (right).

(Author; published in Carver 2005a, Fig 10 11; University of York)

The excavation design applied a cruciform transect of just under a hectare to the centre of the site, focussing on areas already trenched by the British Museum. The mounds, quarry ditches and chambers of seven mounds were excavated together with the spaces in between them (Figure 4.26).[50] With the exception of Mound 17, all had been visited and plundered by excavators before – in the case of Mound 2, on three occasions between the 16th and 20th centuries. The previous content of plundered mounds was inferred from scraps of artefacts surviving in the backfills, enhanced in the Mound 2 chamber by chemical mapping. Although timbers had largely disappeared, enough remained to map chambers and coffins from dark lines in the sand (Mound 14 and 17), and in the case of ships (Mounds 1 and 2) from rows of corroded iron rivets. The excavated mounds were put in order using the stylistic date of the remaining finds, the stratification implied by the quarry pits and ditches, spatial logic and, to some extent, the burial rite.

The first burials at the Sutton Hoo site were determined as cremations in bronze bowls wrapped in cloth and originally placed in pits beneath Mounds 5, 6, 7 and 18, around 580–590 AD. Of these, Mound 5 was the only one built out of soil taken from quarried pits (as opposed to ditches) and was stratigraphically earlier than Mound 6, its neighbour to the south, and stylistically earlier than Mound 2, its neighbour to the north. Mound 5 was thus designated as the 'founder mound', and the cremation group as a whole developed themes that emerged at the Tranmer House cemetery. These cremations contained the remains of men and selected animals and playing pieces. In the case of Mound 5, the occupant had died of blade wounds to the head, and the funeral rites had included feasting on oxen.

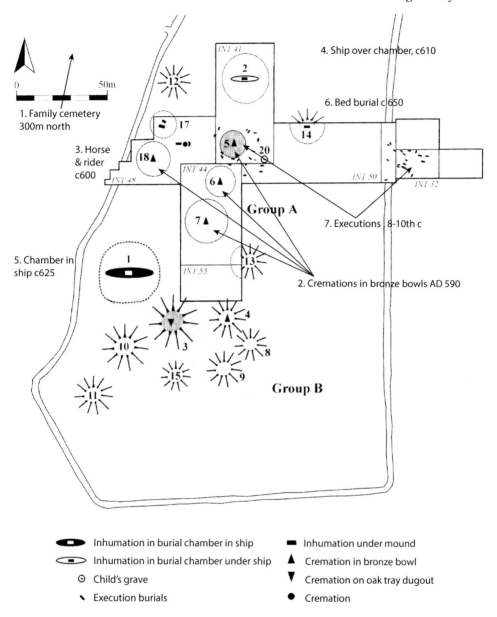

Figure 4.26 Sutton Hoo: map of princely burial ground.
(Carver 2005a, Fig 219; University of York)

Next came the inhumation of a horse and rider in separate pits under Mound 17, dated to c. 600 AD (Figure 4.27). The rider was a young man placed in a tree-trunk coffin, its lid secured with curved iron clamps. With him in the coffin were a sword and a purse containing trinkets. Alongside the coffin to the north were two spear heads, a shield, a bucket, a small cauldron and pottery vessel and what had originally been a bag contained ribs of lamb and possibly some bread, topped by a bronze drinking bowl. In a pile outside the head end of the

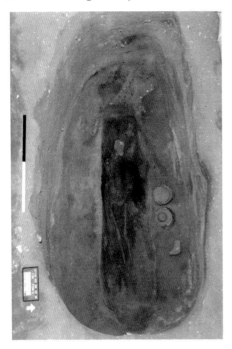

Figure 4.27 Sutton Hoo Mound 17: Young man in tree-trunk coffin accompanied by bucket and cauldron and harness (at top end of grave), with the horse buried in an adjacent pit.

(Photograph: author)

coffin were the remains of a saddle and a bridle with gilded and silver ornaments (Chapter 2,
p. 99). The horse had been in laid in the adjacent pit.

The next stages saw another new rite and escalating investment between 600 and 625: a
ship placed over a chamber in Mound 2 and a chamber placed in a ship in Mound 1. The
centre of the much-pillaged Mound 2 left a series of cavities relating to successive visitations
and an extensive scatter of nautical clench nails that had been dispersed. Some were gathered
up and sold off to a blacksmith during the 1860 excavation (Figure 4.28).[51] The chemical
mapping of the chamber floor allowed a recomposition of the burial tableau to include the
minimum complement of the body of a person, a sword, shield, drinking horn, blue glass
jar, cauldron and bucket (Figure 4.29).[52] The form of burial was that a body was placed in a
well-furnished underground plank-lined chamber, and a ship 20 m long was then drawn over
it at ground level, the chamber covered by the hull amidships.

The ship and burial under Mound 1 had been spared the depredations of earlier looters and
the wilder excavations. The 27 m long ship had in this case been laid in a west-east trench, with
the stern nearest the river. It had been a working vessel with at least one repair: there was no
trace of a mast, but along the gunnel there were indications in the sand of tholes for the pulling
of oars. The chamber was designed in four zones, each apparently displaying a different area
of public or private life (Figure 4.30). At the west end, items of rank and regalia were stacked
against the chamber wall: a shield with ornamental plaques, spears, a lyre, an iron 'standard',
a stone sceptre. At the east end was a row of three cauldrons, one with an ornamental chain for
its suspension from a roof beam. The central area was a rectangular zone of metal objects sand-
wiched in layers of collapsed wood, all much compressed by the weight of the mound. A row

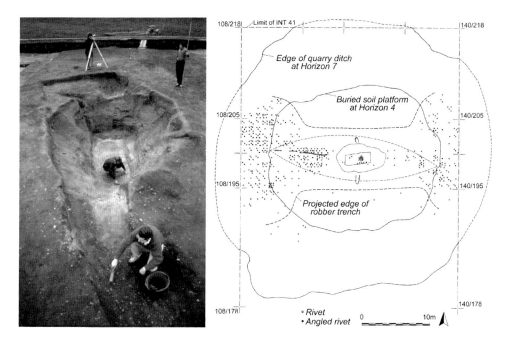

Figure 4.28 Sutton Hoo Mound 2: (left) the primary cut for the Mound 2 chamber and the three known interventions of c 1600, 1860 and 1938; (right) the excavated mound, showing the distribution of ship rivets, the likely position of the ship with the chamber beneath and the cut for the 1860 excavations.

(University of York; photographer Nigel MacBeth)

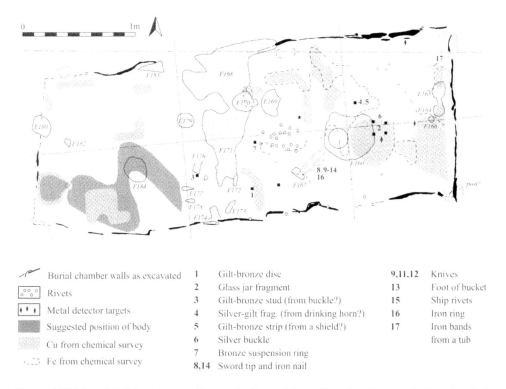

		1	Gilt-bronze disc	9,11,12	Knives
	Burial chamber walls as excavated	2	Glass jar fragment	13	Foot of bucket
	Rivets	3	Gilt-bronze stud (from buckle?)	15	Ship rivets
	Metal detector targets	4	Silver-gilt frag. (from drinking horn?)	16	Iron ring
	Suggested position of body	5	Gilt-bronze strip (from a shield?)	17	Iron bands
	Cu from chemical survey	6	Silver buckle		from a tub
	Fe from chemical survey	7	Bronze suspension ring		
		8,14	Sword tip and iron nail		

Figure 4.29 Mound 2: Map of anomalies on the floor of the robbed chamber revealed by chemical mapping, with an interpretation.

(Carver 2005a, Fig 77; University of York)

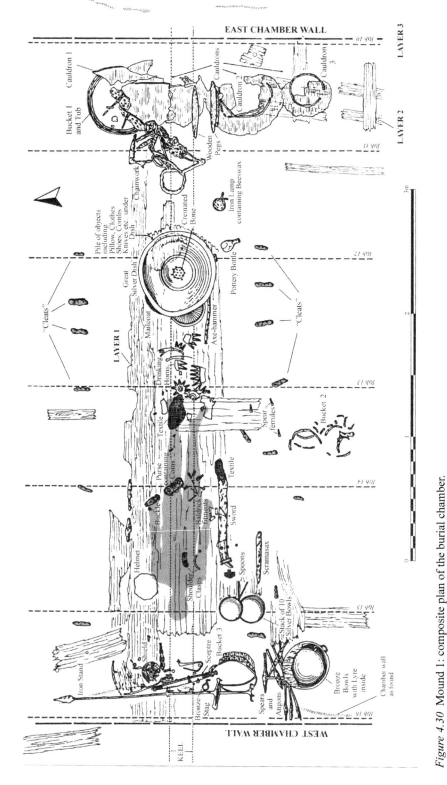

Figure 4.30 Mound 1: composite plan of the burial chamber.

(Author: assembled from Bruce-Mitford 1975, Fig 111, 112 redrawn by Elizabeth Hooper and published in Carver 2005a, Fig 88. © University of York)

of up to 12 curved clamps on either side showed that this zone had been dominated by a large tree-trunk coffin. On its flattened lid were spread one or more tufted yellow cloaks, and on these were placed, at the regalia end, a helmet, sword and baldrick (suspension harness) with a nest of 10 silver bowls, and at the feasting end a group of aurochs drinking horns and maple-wood drinking bottles and a great silver dish of Byzantine origin stamped with the monogram of the Emperor Anastasius (491 × 518). Outside the coffin, on its south side, was a scramasax (oversized knife), an iron lamp containing beeswax and an iron axe-hammer of a kind used to kill and butcher cattle – and so probably a ritual weapon marking out the leader of spiritual ceremonies. The fourth zone was within the coffin: at its east end was a stack of personal effects including a mail coat, two pairs of shoes, a pillow, a leather garment, a cap lined with otter fur and a toilet set in a coptic bowl. The remains of a body were not recorded and had probably been rendered invisible through the workings of a hostile subsoil. But phosphate tests showed that it was located in the central area, and the locus of the wood and objects suggests its likely position to be at the west end of the coffin, extended with the feet to the east, as customary in East Anglian burial of the 7th century. The chamber was erected amidships, and the ship itself placed in a deep trench. It is likely that the chamber roof was left off for a short period so that respects could be paid and ceremonies performed (Figure 4.31). Thereafter a large mound was piled up over the ship and burial; the nature of the subsequent fragmentation suggests that the roof of the chamber held up to form a hollow space for a few years underground.

The date of this burial has been reckoned as c. 625 AD, and its occupant identified as Raedwald, a king of East Anglia mentioned by Bede. Although not based on scientific measurement, this date and identification have not been seriously challenged.[53] This assemblage, of a

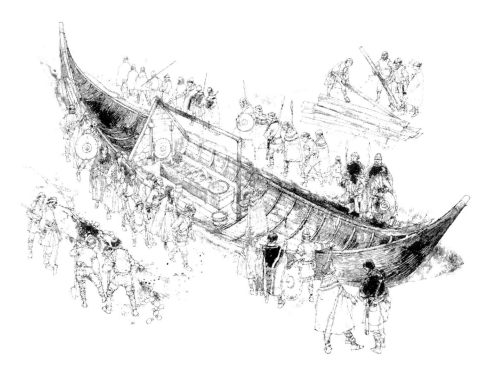

Figure 4.31 Mound 1: artist's impression of the day of burial by Victor Ambrus.
(© University of York)

richness and variety so far unsurpassed in Britain or Ireland, belongs to a monumental grave at the top of the range of investment and should therefore represent a high level of ideological expression at a pivotal political moment. This has been deconstructed, on analogy with epic poetry, as recording an aspiration to a kingdom of Britain united under English kings retaining strong links with the ancestral homelands in Scandinavia while exploiting new relationships with the continent of Europe and remaining plural in its religious alignment.[54] Of burials later than Mound 1, three were children or teenagers with minimal grave goods, and one, dated to c. 650, was a woman bedecked with silver and laid on an upholstered couch within a chamber under Mound 14.[55] This, the mound furthest from the river, should signal the last use of Sutton Hoo as a royal burial ground.

However, this was not the last use of the site for disposing of the dead; the *third cemetery* developed over and beside the royal burial ground. It was manifested in two groups of burials, one around Mound 5 and one on the eastern periphery of the mound cemetery. They were detected as three-dimensional 'sand bodies' placed in graves in a variety of postures. Some had their wrists or ankles laid together as if tied, others had detached heads or broken necks, in one case stained with a collar of rope. The inference is that these unfortunates were killed by hanging and deposited unceremoniously in grave pits, perhaps after *rigor mortis* and exposure on a gibbet (Figure 4.32). They were mainly young men buried singly, but there were cases of a man and a woman (and one case of a middle-aged man and two

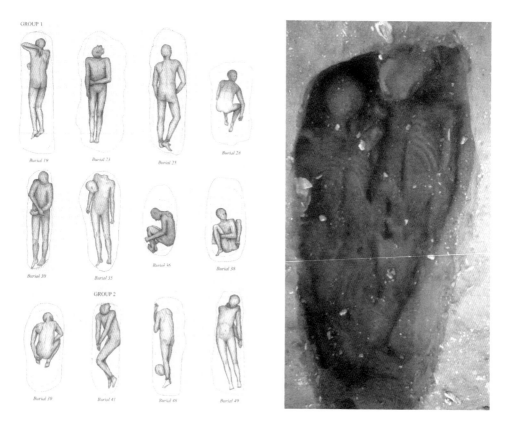

Figure 4.32 Execution cemeteries: body positions of victims recreated; (right) Double burial 32/33.
(Author; © University of York)

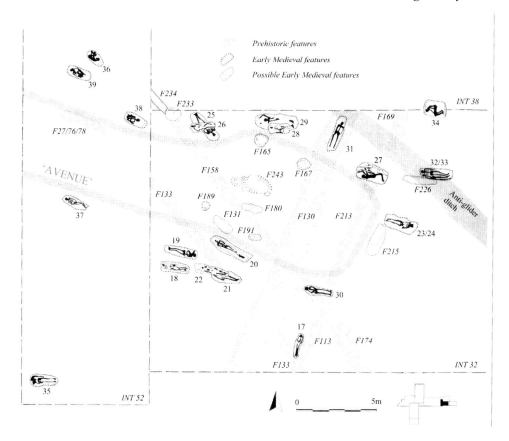

Figure 4.33 Plan of execution cemetery 1, showing the 'avenue' leading to the gallows indicated by post-holes.

(Carver 2005a, Fig 141; ©University of York)

women) buried together (Figure 4.33). The radiocarbon dates of traces of bone in the sand bodies placed both groups in the range 8th–10th century, a time when the kings of East Anglia are recorded as Christians. The crimes for which they were punished are unknown, but the Laws of Ine and the writings of Bede mention practices, particularly those of sexual nature, that had been criminalised as result of Christian conversion. It seems possible that in a time when Christianity was in its fundamentalist phase (i.e. the 8th century), victims guilty of dissent or offences against the new morality would merit death by hanging, and the former high-ranking pagan burial ground might be an appropriate place to do it.[56] The implication that the Mound 5 founder-mound was the site of a gallows chimes with the conversion of the burial ground of the former pagan regime to a place of Christian execution. The site on the eastern periphery, where the graves surrounded a tree pit and the post-holes of a timber structure, suggest that a gallows had been erected here, on the site of a routeway in use along the ridge since prehistoric times. The 11th-century image of the gallows depicted here is taken from a scene that also shows a reigning monarch and his advisers, placing execution in its context[57] (Figure 4.33).

These three cemeteries in the same place, each one reasonably well-defined and dated, are very different from each other. The Tranmer House burials suggest relatively well-off families operating at a local level, and those that were cremated and celebrated with a bronze bowl in a mini-barrow offer a suitable pre-echo for what came next. On the other hand, it is almost certainly part of a much large cemetery, so earlier burials and the large barrow graves supposed in the adjacent fields, if duly found and excavated, would present a picture of greater complexity. The use of the elite barrow cemetery at Sutton Hoo was a very brief (70 years) if glorious episode coincident historically with the arrival of Augustine in Kent and the reign of Raedwald in East Anglia. But the historical equations are neither certain nor determinant. The archaeology is sufficiently vocal on its own to express a period of confronted ideologies, celebrated in successive obsequies that are almost dramatic in their intensity (Figure 4.34).

Given the disposition of the mounds and the public nature of mound burial, the barrow cemetery should have had some function as an assembly place. But there is no direct evidence that it was one. The adoption of cremation, followed in rapid succession by horse burial, ship burial and bed burial, suggests continual twists and turns in the ideological screw. Christianity is acknowledged by these burial parties, but only as one intellectual position among several, and there is no justification in labelling any of the burials as Christian. The contrast is sharpened by the third cemetery, a series of execution burials interred intermittently in small numbers over the 8th to 10th centuries, a time that East Anglia, nominally at least, had been converted to Christianity, with the building of churches and burial in a churchyard. In common with the other multi-period sites we have visited, Sutton Hoo offers

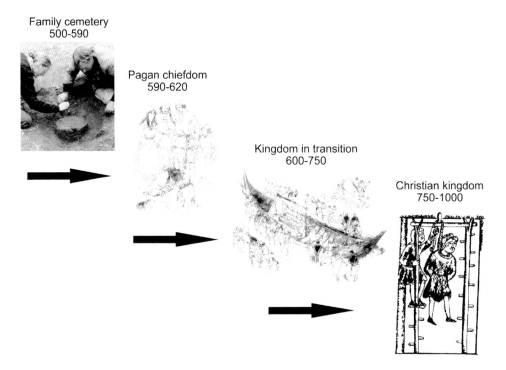

Family cemetery
500-590

Pagan chiefdom
590-620

Kingdom in transition
600-750

Christian kingdom
750-1000

Figure 4.34 Model of social transitions between the three Sutton Hoo cemeteries.

(Author; the image of the gallows is from BL Ms Cott. Claud BIV, f59v; licenced by British Library)

a political weathervane indicating the direction taken by aspiration and allegiance at traumatic moments in the destiny of its community.

Debrief and agenda

This trip round Britain stopping at selected points throws up several trails and cautions. The Iron Age cremation cemetery at Westhampnett (West Sussex) showed us how to recognise pyres, what a shrine might look like and a close association with previous monuments, especially barrows, that acted as a magnet to later episodes of burial. Cannington (Somerset) gave us a cemetery where people were buried in family rows that continued into the 7th century or later and focused on a holy child, although with no direct signs of conventional Christianity. Further north in Anglesey, Capel Eithin had foci for graves that shifted from a Bronze Age barrow to a Roman tower to an early medieval shrine. At Portmahomack in Easter Ross a long tradition of burial on the shores of a peninsula formalised above the best beach in the region as a high-status cluster of cist graves in Fm 1 that gave way in Fm 2 to a monastic community laid out in organised rows. In the south-east region, Spong Hill chronicled the arrival of the Anglo-Saxons, newcomers from across the North Sea. Within a century they had begun to express their social differences, culminating in the advent of furnished inhumation. At Wasperton we returned westward and found a small complete cemetery founded in late Roman times, in which culturally British and Saxon, pagan and Christian people coexisted and shared their memorial space. Sutton Hoo opened a window on the rise of socio-economic power from a local well-to-do family to a national leadership with international pretensions. In Fm 2, this 'burial ground of kings' became a place dedicated to the judicial killing of opponents to the new Christian regime.

With these first-hand encounters in mind, we could draw a few preliminary conclusions on what to look for and develop an agenda to guide us towards an overall appreciation of what burials were practised where and when on this island, and why they were. The western cemeteries have clear prehistoric roots and familiarity with the prehistoric landscape. There were some indications that burial was combined with cult centres rather than tied to settlements. In the absence of grave goods, the main diagnostic attribute of the grave seems to be a fondness for stones arranged in various ways, formal and informal. This is also the region where the celebration of the dead and their property is signalled by an alternative means: the inscribed pillar. The east by contrast has grave goods, providing an exhilarating potential to deduce date, wealth, gender, rank and signals of belief. This has provoked the development of important skills, in which the knowledge of the rich, varied and enormous corpus of Anglo-Saxon burial artefacts has almost generated a profession of its own. Can eastern and western cemeteries ever be usefully compared?

Seen from an appropriate distance, the island presents examples of individual brilliance, but the monument makers also share themes and changes through time. Grave goods are present in the south-east part of Britain, but not always: they illuminate the 5th–7th century but little more. The end of grave goods has actually been determined by radiocarbon as being around the year 675, coincident with a new Christian purism.[58] This is also the start date of the fundamental monastic movement in the north. We will see that Fm 1 displays very different strategies of mortuary celebration and belief between east and west, and a distinction is maintained within Christian burial in Fm 2; Fm 3 will report the brief flowering of the Viking memorials. Now the Christian zone exhibits more of a shared destiny, but there are outbreaks of special mortuary groups that remain unexplained: for example, late cist graves, charcoal burials and hogbacks (Chapter 5).

The observation of trends in all regions is best illuminated by cemeteries that are excavated on a large scale and were used over a long period. And yet not many of these were strictly continuous, even at a church site like Portmahomack. The moment is all – moments of fear, moments of triumph, moments when a community is confronted by the champions of yet another unforgiving god. At no time should we regard the disposal of the dead and their commemoration as a pragmatic routine. There is also a strong case building that the majority of people never reached a cemetery, not only in the Iron Age but long into the first millennium. Even in the later middle ages at Portmahomack there were long gaps in mortuary investment, when memorial at one place was only for the few. This makes a burial ground richer symbolically if less representative biologically.

We also notice that the records of cemeteries, like settlements, are extremely uneven, and thus pretty challenging when it comes to making generalisations. Some of this has natural causes – acid sand eats away at organic matter and metal, sometimes wiping the slate almost clean. Some of it is of our own making: a very limited ability to map cemeteries while they are still under the ground, whether through aerial photography or geophysics. This means that we cannot plan a sensible response to the threat of destruction (other than dig the ground that will be disturbed) or plan a sample of a conserved and protected site that is both sparing and meaningful. From excavation itself, we suffer incomplete records made in the rush of rescue, and from an obsession with the grave rather than the site of which it forms part. Ancient cemeteries are sites from which the living have largely been excluded by archaeologists, and yet it is their actions that have created this most informative arena.

So much for the caveats; none of this should deter us from attempting a synthesis, or we would never make one. Our reconnaissance trip has introduced us to things to watch out for and a basic vocabulary by which to describe them: the parameters of a grave: cremation, inhumation, skeleton, posture, grave goods; parameters of structure: plain earth, coffins, wood-lined, stone-lined; parameters of above-ground monuments: mounds, markers of stone or timber. There will be points of contact with other chapters: the source for the biology and the biography of the person and the appearance that they gave themselves is the subject of Chapter 2. The incidence of cemeteries in central places of various kinds means a link with Chapter 3. The standing stone monument that became such a feature of Formative Britain and was often (but not always) connected to burial is reviewed in Chapter 5. The major tasks that fall to this chapter are to review burial practice over the regions of Britain and then compose a narrative that describes their use, from 400 to 1100. This will arm us for the disputatious viewpoints and new theses of Chapter 7. The sequence of burial practised in Ireland and Scandinavia will again be useful foils for the interpretation of the British experience. In this case we will leave them to a 'field trip' of their own at the end of the chapter.

Formative 1 (5th–7th century)

Iron Age Britain

A starting point in the British Iron Age is necessary and useful; necessary because a practice that has already occurred on the island is a potential inheritance and useful because there are many practices in clearer contexts that provide analogies for the Formative. The burial of the dead does not always have deep roots, but it is a reasonable starting point that in confronting eternity, people will most likely do what they think has been and still is the right thing to do. Iron Age burial practice included cremation, inhumation, weapon burial, horse burial, head cults, feasting, drinking and artefacts ornamented with La Tène art – all things that will turn up in some form in early medieval Britain. However, it remains a question whether they are inherited within a direct genetic 'Iron Age transmission' or from a broader repertoire of European ancestral practice.

In a thesis of 1979, Rowan Whimster defined five kinds of Iron Age cemetery in Britain: four groups mark practice particular to separate regions, and one a particular but thinly spread burial rite. Group 1 practitioners, on the chalk downs of southern England, bury within settlements, the body placed on its left side, crouched, facing north and laid in former storage pits or ditches. Group 2 is confined to South Dorset in the territory of the Durotriges. Here the body is laid in a plain dug grave, on its right side, crouched and accompanied by pottery and joints of meat in organised cemeteries. These began in the later 1st-century BC. Group 3 is confined to the south-west, especially the coasts of Cornwall and Isles of Scilly, and flourished from the 2nd century BC to the 1st AD. These were cist graves using rough granite boulders or flat slabs of slate. The skeleton is crouched within the cists, on its left side, with the head to NNE. Grave goods include metalwork from south-west Europe and southern England. Famous examples include the cemetery of cist graves on the beach at Harlyn Bay and the sword burial at **Bryher** in the Scilly Isles, its mirrors reprised in Pictish carving (Figure 4.35a).[59]

At **Harlyn Bay,** the cemetery lies on a gentle slope 200 m from the present seashore and was discovered in the early summer of 1900 when well-diggers revealed a stone cist buried under more than 4 m of sand.[60] Extensive excavation was carried out during the remainder of that year and in 1901–05, noting a total of more than 130 individual inhumations. However, no formal report on the excavations was ever published, and modern understanding relies on Rowan Whimster's study of notes made by the Rev. Ashington Bullen up to 1912, valuable work, since this was a key site, and not only for the Iron Age (Figure 4.35b).[61]

The bodies were almost invariably placed in a crouched position within cist graves lined and covered with flat slabs of slate and measuring about 1 × 0.5 m in plan. The skeletons of men and women were buried side by side or one on top of the other, and there were at least seven juvenile burials. Almost all the cists are aligned on a common NNE–SSW axis and were apparently laid in rows, with bodies added to pre-existing cists or cists being superimposed. Whimster quotes the Rev. Bullen:

> The graves are placed methodically in regular lines and in some cases four cists have been put one above the other. Probably through the centuries during which the place was used for interments, the sand encroached and covered up the lower levels.

This implies that the geography of the rows was maintained as far as possible through time, even when they had been buried by sand blow. The loss of any plan made at the time is frustrating, as is the absence of detail in some intriguing observations; for example, in one grave (no. 10) four skulls had been arranged in a square formation, with a fifth placed over them. Surviving finds certainly associated with the cemetery include two disk-footed brooches that together with three other Cornish brooches were identified as Iberian imports brought in about the 3rd–2nd century BC. Other finds of a ring-headed pin, bronze wire bracelets and bow brooches take the use of the cemetery up to the 1st century AD.

Other cemeteries in the south-west of England share a similar material culture and the rite of crouched burial in cist graves with the head to the north.[62] Unfortunately, most of the discoveries were made in the 19th century and the records piecemeal, so the

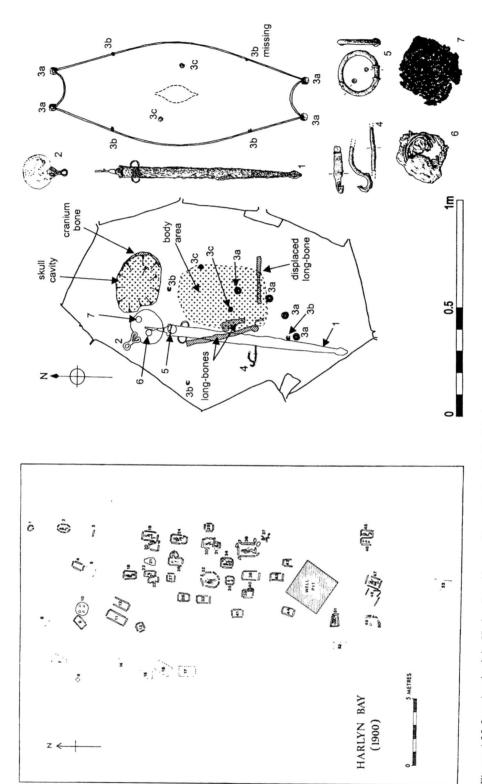

Figure 4.35 Iron Age burials: Harlyn Bay (Cornwall) and Bryher (Scilly Isles).
(Whimster 1979, Fig 25; Johns 2006, Fig 13; with permission © Cornwall Archaeological Unit)

degree to which these were laid out in rows is hard to assess. However, observations at Trevone and Stamford Hill (Devon) reported that cist graves here overlay each other, even though at a given moment they altered their axis from N-S to E-W. If this could be confirmed at a larger scale in persistent examples, it would be a neat demonstration of how families might handle an incoming ideology while maintaining their mortuary allegiance.

Group 4 is confined to the chalk wolds of east Yorkshire, where the skeletons were laid on their sides, crouched and head to north in square pits under barrows marked by square ditches. They date to the 1st–2nd century BC, and some included carts, resembling the cart burials of the Marne, but the skeletons are extended with the head to the east or west. Whimster's Group 5 consists of 23 sword burials not confined to a particular region but spread widely and occur as solitary examples that adapt to local customs. This supports their interpretation as members of a warrior or leader class.[63]

Clearly the Iron Age burial corpus cannot represent the totality of the Iron Age population, since the cemeteries all have a short lifespan, and other parts of Britain yet to produce Iron Age burials were certainly settled. In a recent review, Dennis Harding has produced an updated and refined account of Whimster's model.[64] While Whimster proposed that the missing population was buried in topsoil and has been ploughed away, Harding suggests that they were excarnated and exposed, then fragmented or cremated and afterwards dispersed in natural places or husbanded in small packets and added to particular deposits in settlements. Naturally these deposits of the 'dead among the living' are not easy to find, but large-scale excavation and high intensity plotting can pick them out. At Phantassie in Lothian, while attempting to define traces of structural remains, Lelong and MacGregor recorded an abundant scatter of burnt human remains dating to the 4th–1st century BC – comprising at least 62 individuals scattered in buildings, around hearths, in trackways and in middens.[65] Harding makes a convincing case that this kind of dispersal (which we might term 'Group 6') was actually the norm and accounts for the absence of a representative sample of the population in the Iron Age of Britain and Ireland. He calls this 'dividuality', whereby 'cremated remains could be distributed in and around the settlement to the continuing benefit of kin and the community'.[66] The same reasoning can be extended to early medieval Britain, bolstering the case for ancestor participation in the fortunes of settlements and for the special status of those for whom burial in a dedicated cemetery was thought appropriate; the use of stone monuments is also thought have been selective, based on land ownership or spiritual privilege (see Chapter 5). Location in the landscape was an important aspect of Iron Age monumentality, as it was in the early medieval period, and both used the enduring beacons of Bronze Age mounds. The coincidence of burials from both periods in the case of Westhampnett some 500 years apart is a reminder that landscape continuity can operate independently of human ancestry.[67]

In the ultimate years of the Iron Age, the area of Suffolk, Essex and Kent became a 'favoured region', building *oppida*, importing wine in amphorae and using stamped coins of precious metal. They also cremated their selected dead and buried them in chamber graves lined with timber and richly furnished.[68] This coincides with the arrival of immigrants from the area of France and Belgium via The Wash and the Thames, people who opened up new areas of agricultural opportunity, creating wealth and increasing social difference.[69] The development of the special Thames region (southern Anglian and Kent = Trinovantes, Cantiaci) also has analogies for the Anglo-Saxon development of Suffolk, Essex and Kent. Immigration via The Wash, the Thames estuary and Kent is also a feature of the Anglo-Saxon incursion, and its eventual socio-economic consequences were not dissimilar. This area also had richly furnished chamber graves (Sutton Hoo, Prittlewell) and a coinage (*sceats*) and possibly also ritual groupings (as bracteates) in the Anglian period.

Roman burial practice provides a more ready source of emulation for early medieval gravediggers, although the choice of site was focused on the town or outside it rather than the prehistoric landscape. For this reason, if no other, the transmission was most powerfully seen within and explained by the Christian religion. Special graves were destinations for visitors in rural cemeteries, as at Cannington and Hallow Hill, but it is in the extra-mural cemeteries of Roman towns that holy persons were buried in what became focal graves for a new generation of pilgrims. Evolved versions of Roman signature burials – the sarcophagus, the mausoleum and stone memorials – are found in early medieval Britain, especially in that favoured late Iron Age area, the main point of maritime entry, which was also the region most exploited by Rome and after them by the Anglo-Saxons. Transmission from Roman to British populations noted at Wasperton is paralleled in transition from Romano-British to Anglo-Saxon communities in more easterly parts of the Roman heartland of Britannia.[70]

In our travels through the regions, we will be on the alert for Iron Age roots; the emulation of Roman style (especially in a Christian context); the practice of incomers, especially of Angles and Saxons in the east and Irish in the west; new directions constructed locally; and grandiose experiments inspired by pivotal events, such the claiming of kingship and positive or negative responses to exotic ideologies.

Scotland and Pictland

The two great cultures of the north differ in their burial rites, as with much else, but both belong to a 'cist grave zone', as do Ireland and Wales. They have recently been the subject of a comprehensive study which has collected and assessed all the early medieval burials in modern Scotland that could be radiocarbon-dated.[71] The present section will follow this valuable model (the first for any part of the island), while pointing out the cultural differences that persisted in the north-east (i.e. Pictland), western (i.e. Scotland) and south-east (i.e. British) zones. In Formative 1 the main problem up to now is the relative lack of excavated burials in the west with which to make comparisons.

In the first characteristic burial rite, known throughout the first millennium AD, the body is crouched or flexed. This is virtually displaced between the 5th and 7th century (i.e. in Formative 1) by the extended body in a stone-lined cist ('long cist'), the barrow and the cairn (Figure 4.36). Cist graves occur from the 5th century, with a big spike in the 8th. Children are largely absent before the 7th century, endorsing the idea that the populations of Formative 1 cemeteries are selective.[72] 'Barrows' include the circular mound, the square mound, and the square-ditched enclosure, these two last not easy to distinguish without excavation. Barrows and cairns gather in cemeteries of small clusters or short alignments and are mainly found in the north and east (Pictland) and south-west (Galloway). Large cemeteries containing cist graves laid in rows, without mounds or cairns, are currently known mainly in the south-east. The distribution of the cairns and mounds on the one hand and the row cemeteries on the other is different, with a zone of separation somewhere on the boundary of Fife and Angus.[73] However, cist graves are also found under barrows, and the map looks less specific if it includes Roman mounds south of Hadrian's wall or the square mounds seen from the air in Dumfries and Galloway.[74]

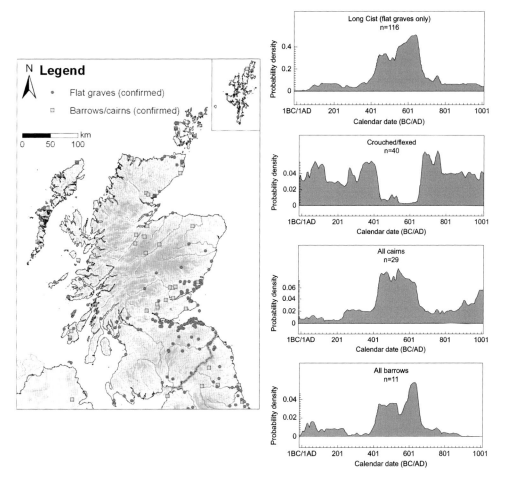

Figure 4.36 Pictland: Map of flat graves and barrow cemeteries (left) and averaged radiocarbon dates
for the occurrence of crouched, long cist, cairn and barrow burials.

(Maldonado Ramírez 2011, Fig 5, with author's permission)

Square-ditched features (mainly known from the air) are distributed in Pictland, Wales
and the south-west, suggesting that they constitute a British attribute. An example at Thornybank (Grave 62) had a timber slot in the fill suggesting a timber structure. At Plas Gogerddan in Wales the wood survived. Those excavated at Tandderwen and Stoneage Barton had
entrances, recalling Iron Age Westhampnett.[75] All so far date to the 7th century. Log coffins
made from hollowed-out tree trunks, known in the Bronze Age (especially in Denmark), also
re-emerge in the first millennium AD and are spread across Scotland and beyond.[76] Tree-trunk
coffins were also used in 7th-century East Anglia at Burrow Hill and notably at Sutton Hoo,
where they were employed for the well-furnished and well-preserved graves under Mound 17
and Mound 1.[77] Burial rites in Scotland thus feature long-term island-wide practices (crouched
burial), a Formative 1 preference for long-cist graves (clustered on the east coast), barrows
and cairns (mainly up the rivers in the east) and with square-ditched enclosures and tree-trunk
coffins making a spasmodic and currently dispersed appearance towards the end of the period.

Maldonado toils over demographic affiliations and the detection of Christianity in this material and ends up sitting on the fence: 'The distribution of new burial practices across such a wide area precludes any ethnic or religious affiliation.'[78] However, the geographical divisions do seem still to hold: 'the fact that barrow and cairn cemeteries are distinctly absent in the Lothians and Borders despite comprehensive aerial reconnaissance indicates a real absence there'.[79] The distribution of the barrow and cairn cemeteries, as we have it, also maps well onto the distribution of the Class I symbol stones (pp. 349, 491), which are the same date (5th–7th centuries), while the row cemeteries without mounds or symbol stones are currently more a feature of the south-east and south-west.[80] These are the zones of Scotland that coincide with regions known from Bede onwards to relate to those attributed, respectively, to Picts and Britons.

As for the vexed subject of Christianity, the premise adopted in this book is that while we cannot know the last thoughts of a person before they are laid in a grave, the form of burial and the layout of a cemetery do have some ideological and social significance and are worth studying. Scotland unquestionably became Christian, but it took time. The ideas being professed in the 5th–7th century (our Formative 1) are certain to include a system of belief of some kind, if not one we can as yet give a name to. Christianity may have been a factor in the intellectual mix, but, as will be repeatedly noted, specific archaeological evidence for Christianity in Scotland, Wales or England (or even Ireland) is vanishingly sparse before the later 7th century.[81] However, an archaeologist's job is to still explain differences, and there are plenty in early medieval Scotland that require explanation, in burial as in settlement and sculpture, even if our vocabulary is soft and arguments easy to overturn with singular exceptions.

Mounds have been mapped from the air and dissected in modern times at Inverkeilor in Angus, Garbeg above Loch Ness and Durness in Sutherland.[82] The **Garbeg** mounds include examples that are square and round, and they survive as (just about) visible mounds today. The larger round ones have a narrow gap in the quarry ditch, probably indicating a causeway for loading the mound, as at Sutton Hoo. The square barrows are composed of four short ditches with a gap at each corner. Part of a symbol stone was found in association with cairn no. 1. At **Dunrobin** there was a cist grave under the cairn of stones, in which was incorporated (in its northern edge) the symbol stone Dunrobin 2.[83] At Sangobegand, Loch Boraillie, the inhumations were laid on stone and covered with clean sand before being buried under the cairn. At **Redcastle** in the dunes overlooking Lunan Bay in Angus, Derek Alexander excavated 16 graves, five under square barrows, two under round barrows and nine others (Figure 4.37).[84] Four square barrows covered long cists; one (SB5) was a possible tree-trunk burial. At least six unenclosed graves had cists or stone settings. The ditch of SB1 measured 10 × 10 m and originally bordered a low earth mound topped with pebbles brought from the beach (Figure 4.38). It also had low external banks. Inside was a cist grave made of large slabs, forming sides, a roof and a floor. The body was dated to 400–560 AD. In the few examples excavated to date, the mound cemeteries are clustered with a tendency to align and apparently contain just mounds. In this they presumably refer to a privileged group and present a contrast with the row cemeteries.

The row cemetery at **Thornybank** in Midlothian contained over 100 burials and flourished in the 6th century. It featured numerous long cists, two graves within square-ditched enclosures (one possibly with a wooden structure over it), dug graves with log coffins, and pebbled lined or long cists with a infant burials.[85] It was established to the south of a Bronze Age pit alignment, probably using its surviving bank (Figure 4.39). A parallel palisade and a ringwork formed part of the prehistoric repertoire but were not necessarily still visible. The Fm 1 graves were oriented with their feet to the NE at right angles to the Bronze Age

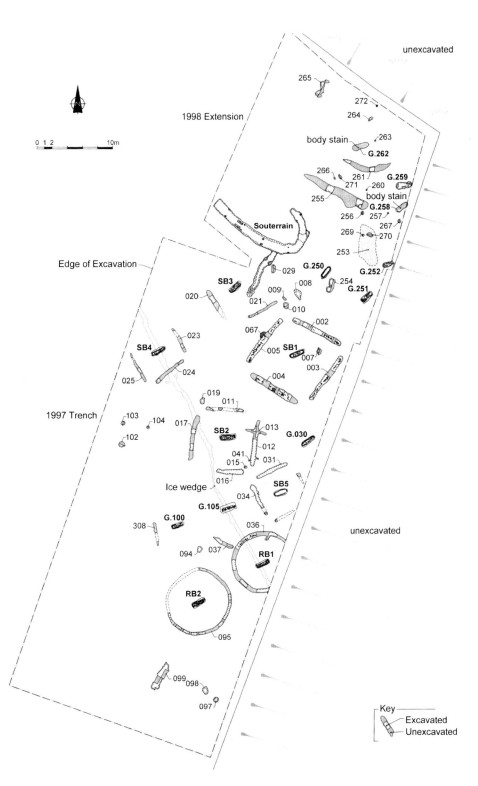

Figure 4.37 Redcastle, Lunan Bay (Angus). Plan of Pictish burials.

(Alexander 2005, Ill 3, with the author's permission)

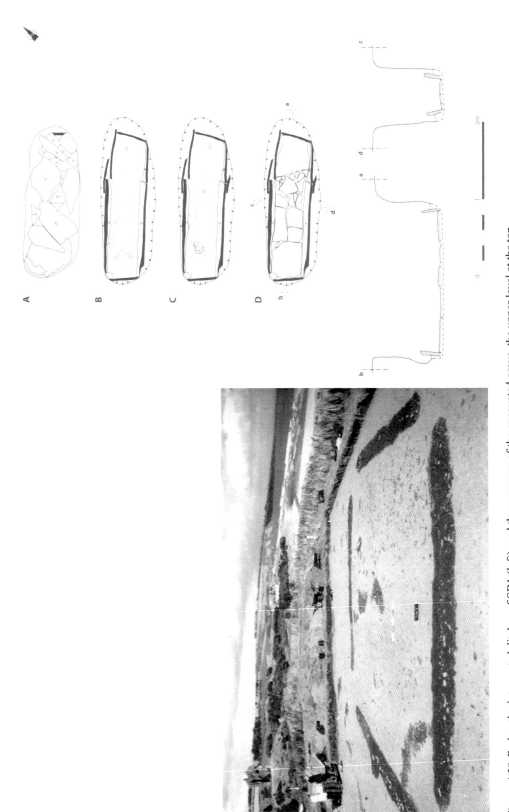

Figure 4.38 Redcastle: interrupted ditches of SB1 (left), and the sequence of the excavated grave, the upper level at the top.
(Alexander 2005, Ill. 26, 28, with the author's permission)

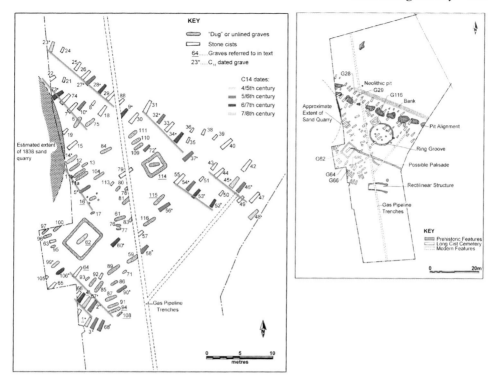

Figure 4.39 Thornybank (Midlothian); plan of cemetery.

(Rees 2002; Maldonado Ramírez 2011, Ill. 6.15; with permission; 'family rows' added by present author)

bank and mostly set in rows. The long cists were narrower at the feet than the head, and their construction was described thus:

> Initially a pit approximately 10% larger than the cist was excavated, into which upright side and end slabs were placed and chocked by numerous small pebbles between the cut of the grave and the slab. After the corpse had been interred, lintel slabs were laid across the tops of the upright slabs prior to the backfilling of the grave over the capstones. Judging by the position of many of the skulls relative to the body skeletons, it is likely that the burials were placed within shrouds, which covered the head before *rigor mortis* set in. This resulted in the chin lying tight against the chest.[86]

Grave 62 was surrounded by a square ditch measuring 5.6 × 4.4 m in plan, and its fill revealed the profile of a slot, suggesting a wooden superstructure; the grave contained a wooden coffin. Grave 16, also a grave with a coffin, had four posts, two at the head and two at the feet, perhaps to support a covered chamber. The human remains reported a healthy population with a normal sex and age distribution. The excavator felt that the long cists and lack of hierarchy indicated an egalitarian and Christian community.[87] Radiocarbon dates analysed by Adrian Maldonado showed that the rows contained individuals buried at different dates.[88] This implies that the rows were probably dedicated to family groups. They are perhaps the origin of the 'lairs' that remain effective in Scottish churchyards to this day.

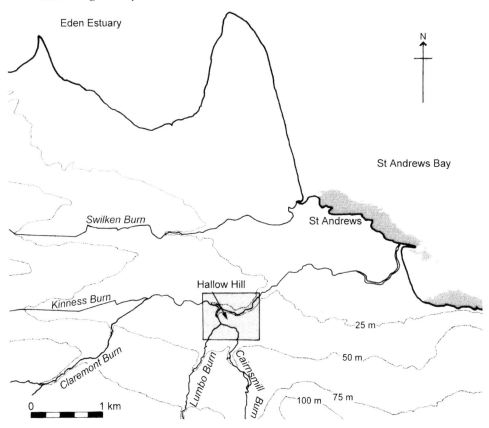

Figure 4.40 Hallow Hill, location with respect to St Andrews (Fife).
(Proudfoot 1996, Ill 1; courtesy of the Society of Antiquaries of Scotland)

Hallow Hill ('holy hill') stands on a spur between the Kinness and Cairnsmill Burns 4 km west of St Andrews, its location implying a strong Christian association (Figure 4.40). Here Edwina Proudfoot excavated 145 long cist burials (Figure 4.42) and other graves.[89] The excavated area was crossed by metalled trackway running SE-NW. To the north-east of the road was a set of row graves on a similar orientation (Group 1), with a tight cluster set among them (including Graves 119 and 51a-c) that may originally have been under a cairn. To the southwest of the road was another set of row graves similarly aligned and beyond that another set of graves not in rows and on a broadly E-W alignment (Group 2) set about a building (F92) composed of six posts (Figure 4.42). Within the Group 2 cemetery was a double-decker grave (Grave 54), the lower deck containing the cist of a child of about 5½ years old accompanied by grave goods, including pebbles, cattle teeth, a fragment of a silver bracelet, a Roman ring, a brooch, a bronze and millefiori seal box and a Samian sherd, all probably in a purse.[90] The space around this grave suggested that it too was originally covered by a cairn. The 19 radiocarbon dates recorded burials in the range 6th to 9th century, but the majority were encompassed by the 7th century. Grave 51 was dated from a composite bone assemblage to 600–730.[91] Building 92 provided an alternative focus for a small group of graves, and all were aligned E-W (3 on plan). One radiocarbon date was obtained of 600–730 (for Burial 56), but the situation of the building on a high point suggested an early Christian use.[92]

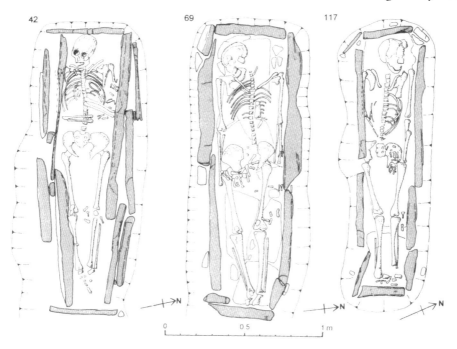

Figure 4.41 Hallow Hill, St Andrews: examples of long cists, Burials 42, 69 and 117.
(Proudfoot 1996, Ill 15; courtesy of the Society of Antiquaries of Scotland)

The cairn-covered graves 119/51 and 54 did not act as foci for the cist grave rows, which were following some other logic. As at Thornybank, Maldonado's radiocarbon analysis showed that the dates were spread over the excavated rows, offering no clear axis of growth over the cemetery as a whole.[93] Such a layout could only work if the rows were pre-allocated to a family, the most likely continuous social unit, and this would explain the diverse dates.[94] The same kind of association was noted at 5th–7th century Cannington where the rows were noted to contain persons of different ages and sexes, again suggesting a family group. Cannington might also provide an explanation for the special graves, since the tomb of the 13-year-old child accorded special treatment there was approached by a path in use until the 7th century and possibly later. At Hallow Hill the cairns 54 and 119/51 were in easy reach of the road. The excavator decided that the dates for long-cist cemeteries 'all indicated origins in pre-Christian or late prehistoric times . . . with changes in site use and burials developing in the 8th century'.[95] The latter trend might suit the installation of Building 92 and the new alignment. A provisional model of the mechanism for this kind of cemetery is therefore that of pre-planned family rows for cist and other graves, punctuated by clearly marked special graves, which arrived in the course of its life but were excluded from the rows. The properties of such people, set apart but clearly not military leaders, were most probably spiritual at Hallow Hill and Thornybank as at Cannington. Whether nominally Christian or not, the community is following a traditional and widespread indigenous practice to create a cemetery in which only the marginal Group 3 perhaps indicates some attraction to a new orthodoxy.

In this light, it is worth drawing attention to the cemetery at Monfode, **Ardrossan**, which echoes some of these characteristics, since it is one of the few to have been excavated in the Scottish south-west (Figure 4.43). It contained 60 graves within, or over-running, a

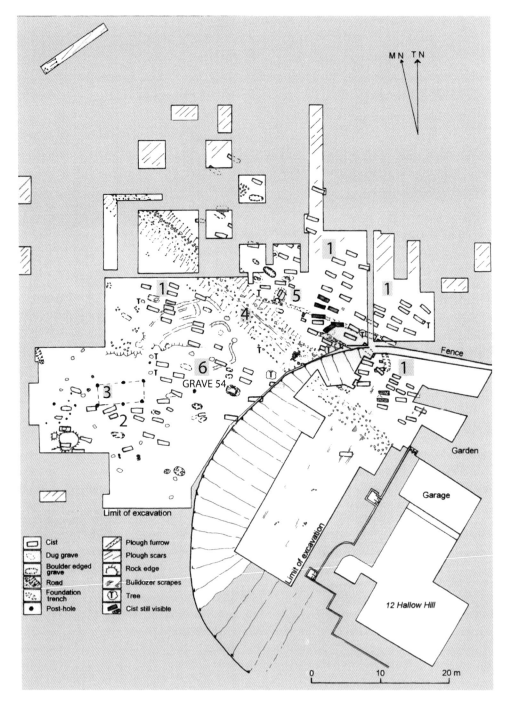

Figure 4.42 Hallow Hill, St Andrews: plan of cemetery. 1: Row graves. 2: E-W graves. 3: Building F92. 4: Road. 5: Focal group 51/119. 6: Grave 54.

(Proudfoot 1996, Ill 5; courtesy of Society of Antiquaries of Scotland; legend added by author)

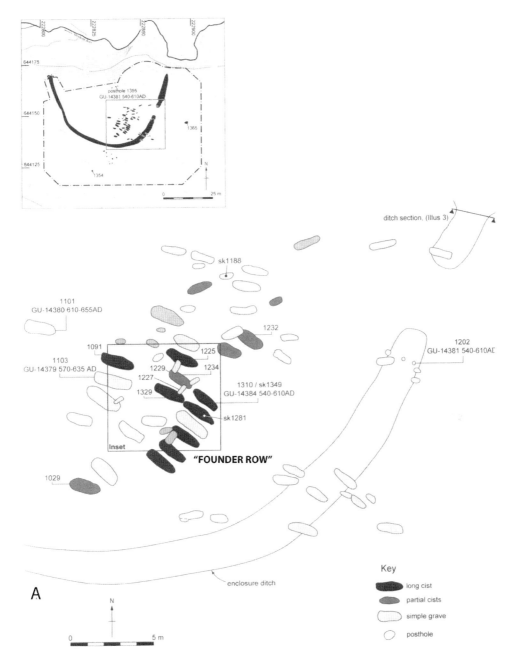

Figure 4.43 Montfode, Ardrossan (Ayrshire): A: plan; B: long-cist grave 1310; C: the 'founder row'; D: locations of early cemeteries in south-west Scotland.

(Hatherley 2009, Ill 4, 5, 6, 8; with author's permission)

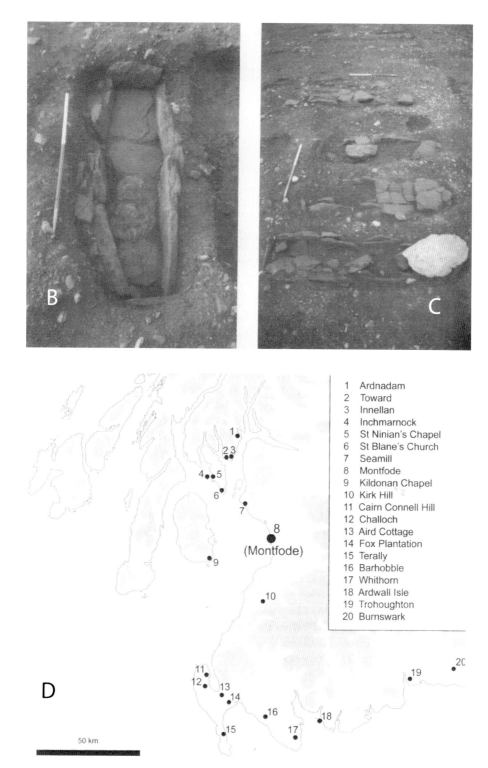

1 Ardnadam
2 Toward
3 Innellan
4 Inchmarnock
5 St Ninian's Chapel
6 St Blane's Church
7 Seamill
8 Montfode
9 Kildonan Chapel
10 Kirk Hill
11 Cairn Connell Hill
12 Challoch
13 Aird Cottage
14 Fox Plantation
15 Terally
16 Barhobble
17 Whithorn
18 Ardwall Isle
19 Trohoughton
20 Burnswark

50 km

Figure 4.43 (Continued)

previous semi-circular enclosure built against Montfode Burn. They included eight stone-lined long cists, six partial cists – with sides or lids only – and 49 plain dug graves. The latter type cut the other two types and the enclosure ditch and indicated those longest in use. The sequence began with a 'founder row' of five long cists and one plain grave datable to the mid-6th century. Two subsequent rows of cists, partial cists and plain graves were added, and then a number of scattered plain graves. The excavator decided that 'the short, well-defined rows may well be the primary burials and represent related individuals or family groups' and identified Monfode as one of at least 20 early medieval cemeteries along the south-west coast, none of which featured a chapel until the 8th or 9th century.[96] This verdict would appear to endorse the idea of local burial grounds with a prehistoric ethos that were 'converted' to more specified Christian ways, although not until the 8th century.

Wales and the west

To continue the burial story into the early medieval west, our best itinerary will take us to Wales and then back into south-west England, where we will meet many familiar and some inherited themes: prehistoric foci, cist graves, row cemeteries and rectilinear enclosures. Endemically with no bone and no artefacts we encounter chronic difficulties with the assignment of identity affiliation and dates, but these cemeteries still have plenty to offer. The site at **Tŷ Mawr** on Anglesey was investigated during the building of the A55 trunk road.[97] It occupies a prominent spot with views over the sea and to Caergybi (Holyhead), and the graves appeared to focus on and then overrun a double-ditched prehistoric barrow (or enclosure) with no central burial that occupied the highest point (Figure 4.44). There were four plain dug graves and 39 cist graves, of which 22 had floors, sides and lids, six were lidless, one lacked a floor and 10 had timber linings with some stones (a total of 43). There were no bones, other than fragments, and no artefacts, and thus no dates; but the cemetery would seem to belong in the early middle ages.[98] The graves were oriented to the east and set in interrupted rows running N-S. The stone linings are here varied by linings purely of timber or of timbers and stone together. This cemetery seems to have adopted the row grave framework, with graves of different levels of investment.[99]

Ysgol yr Hendre was a cemetery investigated by Gwynedd Archaeological Trust in 2010–11 in advance of the construction of a new school (Figure 4.45). Within the area assigned, a square-ditched enclosure had been spotted from the air that proved to belong to a cemetery spread over an area 200 × 100 m in extent, lying 500 m east of the Roman fort of Segontium in Caernarfon. In the main area, three rectangular ditched enclosures were excavated with east-facing entrances, one with three graves and the other two with a grave apiece. They stood amidst 40 graves oriented NE-SW, the more southerly being disposed in one or two segmented rows. Although these were not cist graves, many were lined with boulders that are thought to have been used to provide packing for a plank lining, as at Tŷ Mawr. There were no bones or artefacts, but hazel charcoal from one enclosure ditch returned a date of 6th–7th century.[100]

The cemetery at **Plas Gogerddan**, Dyfed, discovered and investigated during the installation of a gas pipeline, was focused on prehistoric standing stones, one of which is still standing (Figure 4.46). The area also hosted a sequence of Neolithic pits, a round barrow probably of the Bronze Age and three ring ditches of the first millennium BC with Iron Age crouched burials. The 22 early medieval burials were in plain dug graves without surviving

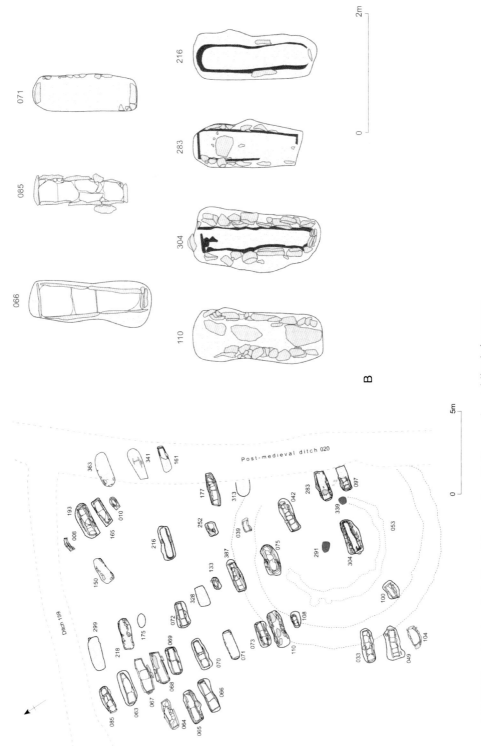

Figure 4.44 Tŷ Mawr (Anglesey). A: Plan of the cemetery. B: Stone and wood-lined cist graves. (Cuttler et al. 2012, Fig 6.9, 10.5; reproduced courtesy of Claire Litt and Oxbow books)

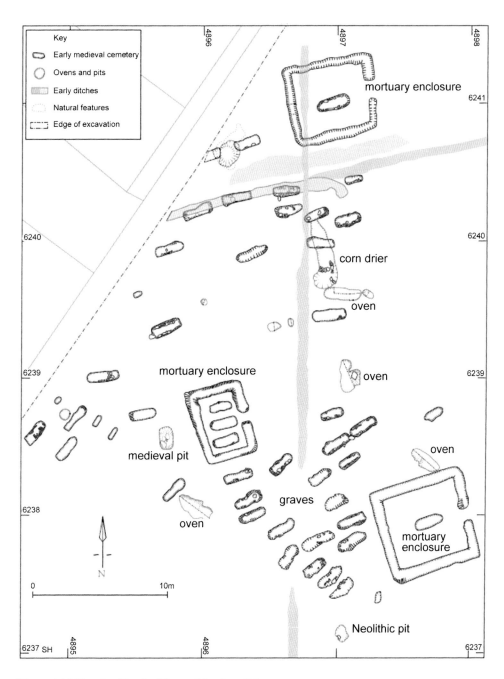

Figure 4.45 Ysgol yr Hendre (Gwynedd), plan of the cemetery.

(Courtesy of Jane Kenney, Gwynedd Archaeological Trust, Bill Britnell and Cambrian Archaeological Association)

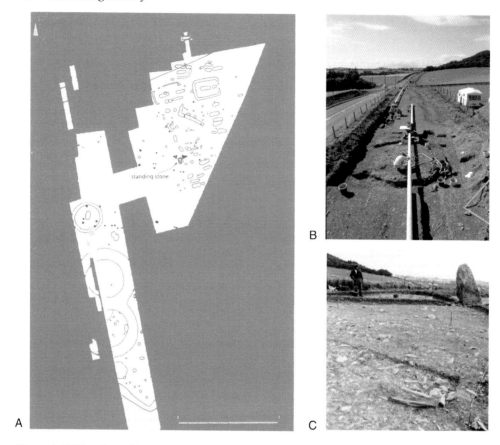

Figure 4.46 Plas Gogerddan (Ceredigion). A: Plan of excavated area. B: The pipe trench with the small ring ditch 237 under the pipe, looking north. C: The standing stone.

(Murphy 1992; Ill 3; courtesy of Kenneth Murphy and Dyfed Archaeology)

bone and occupied a roughly rectangular area which had adopted the standing stone on its western edge. All were aligned W-E and set in rows. Three of the burials were surrounded by rectilinear ditched enclosures with an east-facing entrance. In one of them, S373, 'a dark soil stain ran through the centre of the trench'; this almost certainly represented decayed timbers, apparently thick and thus hypothetically robust (Figure 4.47). Two post-holes stood either side of the entrance, and inside was a stone-lined pit and a grave with a coffin stain that was radiocarbon-dated to the 3rd–7th century AD. This would appear to be a secure plank-built shrine with a special grave and a pit, perhaps for libations. Similar structures have been found on other Welsh cemeteries such as Capel Eithin (p. 314), Tandderwen and Arfryn, with prehistoric ancestors perhaps represented at Westhampnett. At Landegai a rectangular trench 4.2 × 3.6 was considered to be the foundation for a small timber building on which 30-plus graves were aligned.[101]

At **Tandderwen**, Clwyd, the site of a Beaker inhumation cemetery and two Bronze Age barrows was colonised by an early medieval cemetery of 38 E-W inhumations in plain dug graves with no surviving bone, but a high proportion had contained coffins of oak planks

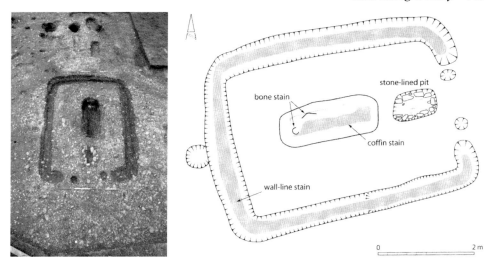

Figure 4.47 Plas Gogerddan. Burial enclosure 373: photograph and plan showing timber slot.
(Murphy 1992, Ill 11; courtesy of Kenneth Murphy and Dyfed Archaeology)

(Figure 4.48).[102] Eight single burials and one cluster of three were enclosed in rectilinear structures. Two had east-facing entrances, but there was no evidence that the ditches had supported planks or other timbers. The excavators considered the possibility of a central mound or an inner bank and concluded the most likely form of these monuments was an inner ditch and an outer bank, an interpretation encouraged by the spaces without graves outside the line of the ditches.[103] Decayed coffin wood from grave 29 was dated 560–655, and from grave 233, 886–1012 (at one sigma). The spatial patterning was obscure. The predominant orientation was ENE-WSW, and while long rows were not evident, there were three clusters of parallel contiguous graves on the east side. Six of the enclosures appeared to run in NE-SW rows, decreasing in size to the west. The site of the larger of the two Bronze Age barrows had been modified with the addition of a square causewayed ditched enclosure placed around it (feature 576). There was no direct dating evidence, but the enclosure had superseded 'a prolonged period of silting' in the Bronze Age quarry ditch, at a time when the barrow was still visible. The excavators' verdict was that this was an assembly place and can most plausibly be referred to as 'a date between the Iron Age and early medieval periods'.[104] In contrast to Capel Eithin, Tandderwen offered no buildings, cists, row graves or focal monuments. This would imply that an assembly place at a prehistoric burial mound gave the cemetery its rationale.

The cemetery at **Llandough** lies to the north of the church of St Dochdwy in Glamorgan and is the largest with the longest use so far encountered in Wales (Figure 4.49). To the south of the site are the remains of a Roman villa, and a near neighbour to the west is the early formative site at Dinas Powys (see Chapter 3, p. 189). The modern version of St Dochdwy's church is considered to overlie the site of a monastery recorded in the Llandaff Charters, and for this reason the findings were published as a 'monastic cemetery'.[105] Some 1,026 inhumations were recorded, of which 425 were well-preserved, with 30% male, 25% female and 26% children. The graves were unprotected, but 2% (about 16) had stone inserts. There were 122 'burial pebbles' deliberately deposited in 40 graves (Figure 4.50). Residual material

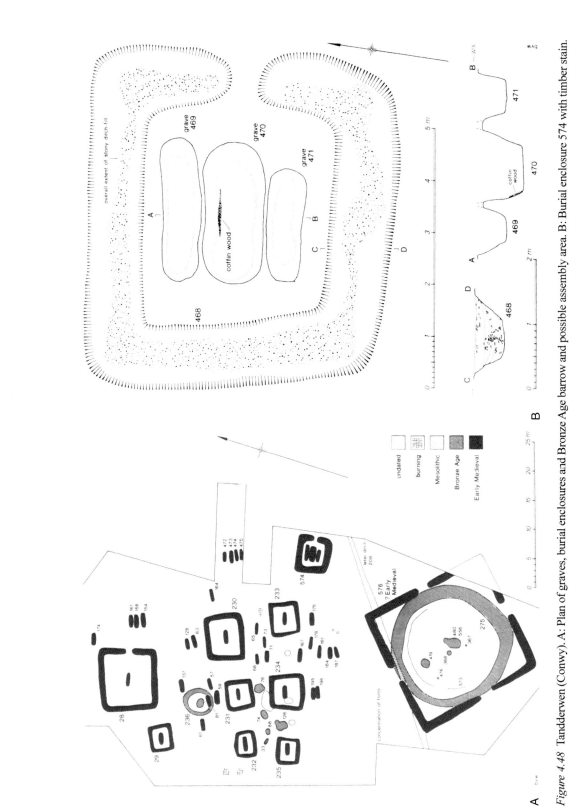

Figure 4.48 Tandderwen (Conwy). A: Plan of graves, burial enclosures and Bronze Age barrow and possible assembly area. B: Burial enclosure 574 with timber stain. (Brassil et al. 1991, Fig 2, 10; courtesy of the author and the Royal Archaeological Institute)

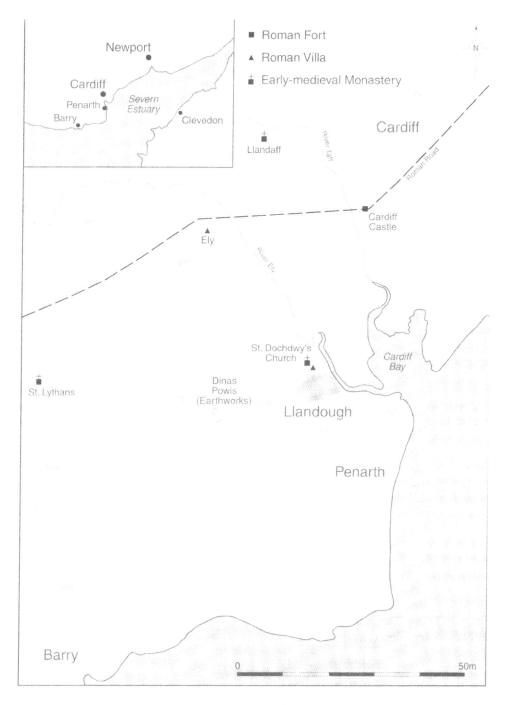

Figure 4.49 Llandough (Vale of Glamorgan): location of the site and (next page) of the 1963, 1979 and 1994 excavations.

(Holbrook and Thomas 2005, Fig 1, 2; courtesy of Cotswold Archaeology)

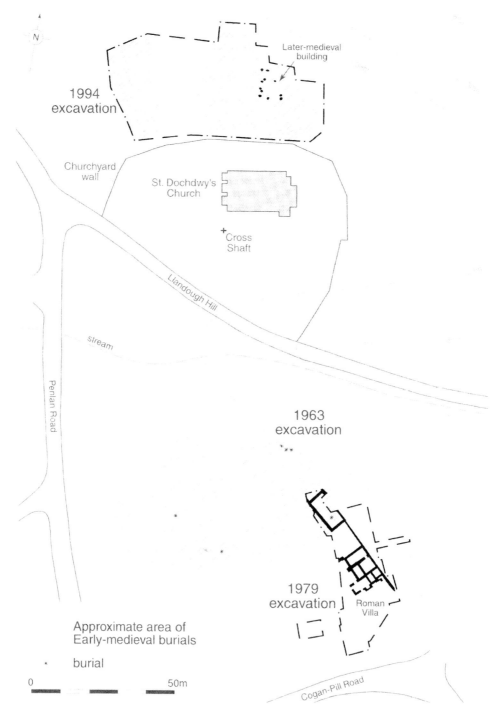

Figure 4.49 (Continued)

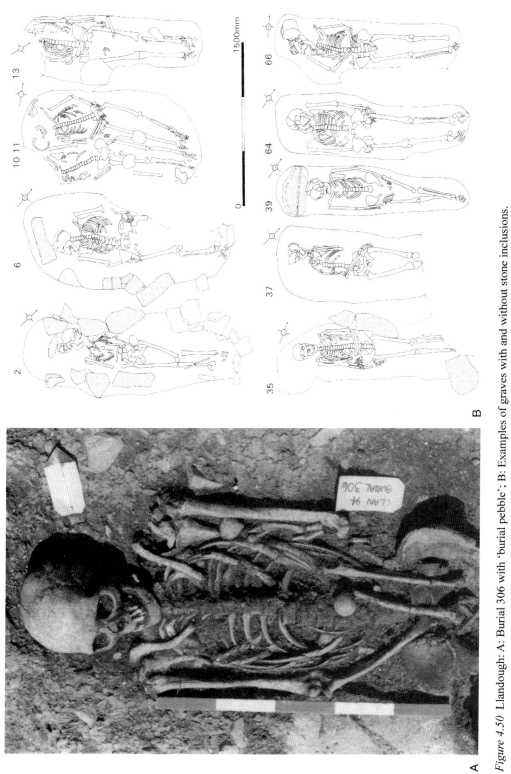

Figure 4.50 Llandough: A: Burial 306 with 'burial pebble'; B: Examples of graves with and without stone inclusions. (Holbrook and Thomas 2005, Fig 16,7; courtesy of Cotswold Archaeology)

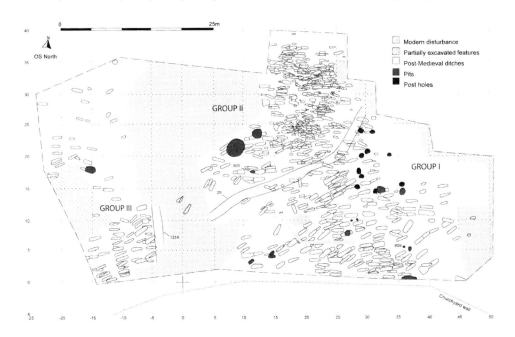

Figure 4.51 Llandough: plan showing locations of Groups I, II and III.

(Holbrook and Thomas 2005, Fig 5; courtesy of Cotswold Archaeology, with group numbers inserted)

included hobnails (Roman) and sherds of Bii amphorae of the 5th/6th century comparable to those found at Dinas Powys.

The graves were arranged in three groups, of which Group II showed the clearest indications of row allocation (Figure 4.51). Of the 12 radiocarbon dates, three were pre-650, one each in Group I, II and III. The remaining nine were 8th to 10th century, within the monastic period. However, the number of radiocarbon dates was insufficient to determine secure chronological or spatial trends. Burial B631 in Group II was a robust adult male who had apparently worn two narrow iron bands around his waist. The section of the (2–3 cm wide) band was curved with a concave outer surface retaining textile traces and a convex inner surface that was featureless. The skeleton was dated 340 × 660 AD. Since the bands were fastened at the back and worn under the clothes and next to the skin, they were proposed as a device for counteracting a hernia – or were perhaps a mode of penitential self-torture. On the whole, the evidence from this large sample converges on the existence of some kind of cemetery-settlement contemporary with Dinas Powys in the 5th–7th century, with graves already grouped by kin, which was adopted in the late 7th or 8th century as the cemetery for a monastery and kept in use until the 10th or 11th century.

An indication that the square-ditch and row grave trends reach into Somerset has been noted at Cannington, and another example was encountered in a small excavation at **Stoneage Barton**, in the same county. Here were three W-E graves in a row, one of which had posts at three corners and was placed within a rectangular enclosure with an eastern entrance. Sufficient bone survived in one of the graves to give a combined radiocarbon date of 600–690 AD.[106] The excavators understandably considered their discovery in the context of other rectilinear features in cemeteries from Poundbury to Redcastle. However, when flattened and truncated by ploughing, the square enclosures, the square structures and the square barrows are not easily distinguished on the ground, although they imply different structures and uses, and the study of their anatomy in the field must be placed on the archaeological to-do list.

For the present, it seems plausible to propose a cultural zone for burial (as for sculpture) in Formative 1 encompassing the south-west, Wales and southern Scotland that can be legitimately labelled as 'British' and a related zone in north Scotland that is allowed the shorthand term 'Pictish'. Both zones have cemeteries where the graves may be arranged in 'family rows' or focused on pre-existing monuments and may include rectilinear shrines or 'special graves' marked by cairns.[107] These practices probably signal different kinds of loyalty, to distant ancestors, to family and to individuals revered outside the family but within the community. The best two examples of the latter (at Cannington and Hallow Hill) were both children, so discounting the focal graves as necessarily those of warriors or Christian leaders, although the holy child is not excluded as an object of reverence.

Further east, the signature is detectable in the late Roman period, for example at Poundbury, where 69 out of 1,114 burials (7%) had stone inclusions arranged along the sides, the numbers increasing in the later stratigraphic sequence, while most others employed coffins or planks.[108] The graves were set in regular rows around 10 square-ditched or walled enclosures described as mausolea. However, only three graves were stratigraphically post-Roman, although the excavators felt that the stone linings and lack of grave goods were pointers towards a post-Roman contingent.[109] Even further east, in the late Roman cemetery at Lankhills at Winchester, there was a small number of graves (38) where flints or tiles had been deliberately placed in association with the body; this was 'an extremely late development', after c. 370.[110] At Wasperton (p. 324) the stone-lining/row-grave tendency superseded Roman practice in the 5th century AD and continued, especially in the south-east of the cemetery, a part that remained largely free of culturally Anglo-Saxon burials.[111] It seems reasonable to allow these diagnostic properties as signs of a continuing, submerged or resurgent indigenous British practice.

In Formative 2 there will be major changes, especially in the north, in burial as in sculpture. As noted at Llandough and Portmahomack, successor cemeteries of the late 7th to the 9th centuries are mainly monastic, although others may continue up to the point at which the parish church arrives, in the 11th or 12th century (see p. 411).

Northumbria

Our Formative 1 review now covers eastern Britain south of the Forth, beginning in Northumbria and arriving finally in the Anglo-Saxon heartland. Northumbria is a fairly uniform geographical area consisting of the parallel valleys of the Tweed, Tyne, Wear and Tees, which empty into the North sea, bordered by the large estuary of the Forth in the north and the Humber in the south (Chapter 1). From the viewpoint of burial archaeology, the region is exceptionally diverse. Attempts to identify the zones of preference have been somewhat obfuscated by the documented existence of the three kingdoms of the Gododdin (around the Forth), Bernicia (from the Tees to the Tweed), and Deira (from the Tweed to the Humber), to which Ian Smith's research added a fourth, the kingdom of the Tweed valley.[112] The burials have been successfully used to construct cultural zones of their own, if not to explain them. Sam Lucy showed that the zones were not only strongly marked, but neither were they static.[113] In her recent thesis Celia Orsini defined three areas of different burial activity between Forth and Tyne (namely the Tees, Derwent and Humber).[114]

The rivers do provide useful axes for areas of burial practice. In the 5th–6th century, the Forth lies in the region of row grave cist cemeteries that we met at Thornybank and

Hallow Hill, south of Smith's line through Fife, which makes a boundary with the Pictish barrow cemeteries that lie further north (p. 73). In the Tweed valley, burials furnished with knives and buckles were found in rows in association with a henge at Milfield and in plain earth graves in radial formation at Yeavering. A row grave cist cemetery is currently being explored adjacent to the Castle Rock at Bamburgh which has produced three radiocarbon dates that lie between 560 and 780.[115] Cist graves associated with barrows or cairns have been contacted at Blackhall, Castle Eden, Cornforth and Houghton-le-Spring, all in County Durham. None of these have specifically Anglo-Saxon grave goods. All may be expected to have had a start date in the 6th century and represent the indigenous fraction at that point. We lose sight of this fraction south of the Tees, which provides a convenient 6th-century frontier at present, with the Anglo-Saxon burials coming up the other way. This movement begins in the North Humberside region south of the Derwent with the cremation cemetery at Sancton and reaches as far north as Norton in the Tees valley before the century ends.[116]

Yeavering in the Tweed Valley is probably the most important early cemetery, as well as settlement, in Northumbria (Figure 4.52). At first sight, its burials appear to be individual, if not eccentric, but they can be placed without too much stress into a 6th/early 7th British phase superseded by a late 7th/8th-century phase that is led by a more Anglian agenda.[117] All the burials, excluding some prehistoric cremations, were inhumations in a very poor state of preservation. It was not the least of Hope-Taylor's many pioneering achievements as a field archaeologist to show how the form and orientation of bodies of which only the teeth had survived could be determined from the locus of powdery traces and sand colour. At

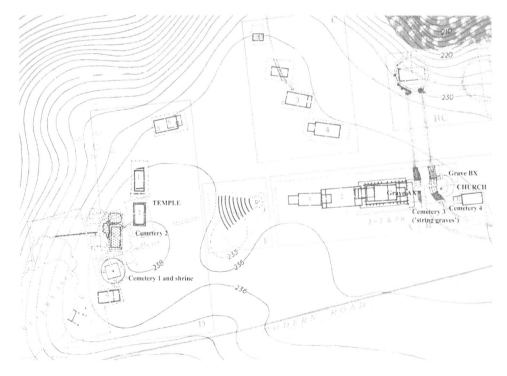

Figure 4.52 Yeavering (Northumberland), showing the four cemetery areas.

(Hope-Taylor 1977, Fig 12; with emendations by author; image licensed by Historic England)

the west end, standing on the spur, was the *western ring ditch (WRD)*, with graves arranged radially within it (Cemetery 1), and the *temple* (Building D2), and between them at the highest point was a group of unaccompanied burials (cemetery 2). At the east end was the *eastern ring ditch (ERD)*, containing *Grave BX* with to the west *Grave AX* and, between the two, a set of so-called *string graves* (Cemetery 3). To the south was a group of tightly clustered E-W graves in a fenced enclosure (Cemetery 4) associated with a *timber building B* proposed as church. Of these four cemeteries, the western pair belong to the earliest phases of the site (broadly the 6th/7th centuries) and the eastern group to the later phases (7th/8th centuries), when the Great Enclosure ditch has been backfilled and the graves overrun it.

The *western ring ditch complex* began life as a stone circle with a central monolith which, by the time it was used for burial, had morphed into a circular bank with a central wooden post (Figure 4.53). Twenty-eight graves were dug within the bank, all set radially

Figure 4.53 Yeavering Cemetery 1, western ring ditch, shrine and burials.

(Hope-Taylor 1977, Fig 50; image licensed by Historic England)

towards the centre (Cemetery 1). Four cases of graves cutting others showed that the lay-out kept its meaning over a period of time. At a given moment this arrangement was succeeded by a square structure with clay-daubed walls supported by timber posts, probably open to the sky, which has been interpreted as a shrine.[118] Three more graves were added that respected this structure, aligned W-E. The *western cemetery* (Cemetery 2) which lay to the north of this shrine and probably succeeded it was associated with Building D2, noted for its large deposit of ox skulls and interpreted as a temple (Chapter 3, p. 158). Near the south-west corner of this building was the crouched grave of a child accompanied by an ox tooth, probably originally an oxhead. Although only 35 graves were examined, Cemetery 2 is noted as having extended eastward from this point, covering an area of c. 40 × 20 m.[119] Hope-Taylor appreciated the original size of this burial ground, calling it a great aggregation of native graves and arguing that 'Yeavering's early unfurnished inhumation burials are both unchristian in their associations and at odds with pagan Anglo-Saxon custom and are far more economically accounted for in native-British than in intrusive Germanic terms'.[120]

The *eastern burial ground* (Cemetery 3) had two components. The *string graves*, so called, were seen in three adjacent areas and were characterised by their arrangement in lines of graves head to tail (Figure 4.54). They were phased with great ingenuity by examining the charcoal in their fill: those with no charcoal were the earliest; those with fresh charcoal pieces picked up from the topsoil after a major fire came next; and a third phase was evident in graves that contained charcoal in the form of weathered pellets, thus dug sometime after the fire. The earliest graves appeared to form, or aim for, certain landmarks, of which the most ancient was the burial mound originally covering a cremation (34) that had been partly overlaid by the inner ditch of the Great Enclosure.[121] Once these ditches had been filled in, the mound was still visible, since it became the setting for one or more timber posts known as BX, on which two graves butt-ended. A second focus or starter-grave may have been provided by the early burial AX that lay in an attendant position end-on to the doorway of the hall A4. It contained a flexed skeleton with a goat's skull and a decayed wood and bronze object identified as a form of *groma* or Roman-style surveying instrument (or possibly a standard). The later string graves that followed the fire appeared to use Grave AX as their point of departure, but two or three other wooden posts appeared to have generated new strings.[122] The final string graves joined the group but no longer conformed to its geometry. The *far eastern cemetery* (Cemetery 4) around Building B was of a very different character: 250 burials densely packed inside a rectangular timber building or outside it to the south, within a fenced enclosure (Figure 4.55).

While the stratigraphic ordering of the structures at Yeavering is argued in convincing detail by its gifted excavator, their dating necessarily relied on inferences drawn from archaeological and historical sources. This was hard enough given that very few artefacts were discarded and radiocarbon dating was only invented three years before Hope-Taylor started digging, and even so, here as elsewhere in the north, the surviving bone was minimal. His tools are still largely our tools, but we have the advantage of discoveries made since 1977, which, it so happens, tend to confirm his reading of the site: a native-British central place with a stone setting, shrine, temple and burial ground at the west end and a cemetery at the east end, perhaps also British, respecting a barrow and a special grave, developed as the string graves. The final cemetery in and around Building B, which oversails the string graves, was for him unambiguously Christian. These four cemeteries were located in history using Bede. The Western shrine is assigned to the later 6th century (Hope-Taylor's

Figure 4.54 Yeavering Cemetery 3. A: Grave AX (the surveyor). B: The phased 'string graves'. Post AX can be seen in both images. (Hope-Taylor 1977, Fig 25, 31; images licensed by Historic England)

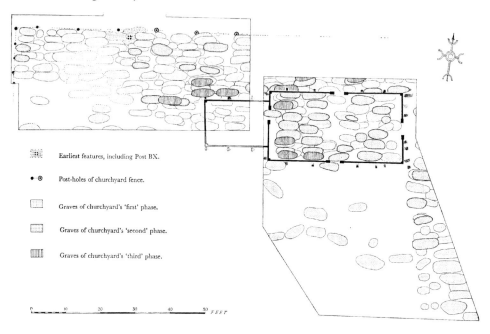

Earliest features, including Post BX.

Post-holes of churchyard fence.

Graves of churchyard's 'first' phase.

Graves of churchyard's 'second' phase.

Graves of churchyard's 'third' phase.

Figure 4.55 Yeavering Cemetery 4 with Building B, a putative church.
(Hope-Taylor 1977, Fig 33; image licensed by Historic England)

Phase 1). The temple and its cemetery belongs to the early 7th century, during the reign of Aethelfrith (605–616) (Phase II). The string graves are native Britons buried in the reign of Edwin (616–633) (Phase III); and the church to the reign of Oswald (633–651) (Phase IV). This sequence only sets up tensions by aligning each phase to a people or a king who has a biography provided by Bede. If Phase 1 relates to Britons, why are they not Christian already? If Aethelfrith is the ruler in Phase II, why is he providing the Britons with such a large cemetery? Who are the native Britons buried after the fire of Penda's raid in 632, when Edwin and then Oswald are supposedly in residence?

These contradictions can be eased if we park the kings for a moment and just consider the people. If early Yeavering were a 6th-century Anglian village, we should expect the graves to be English too, unless burial is reserved for some kind of native serf.[123] Sam Lucy and Helen Geake have made detailed surveys of Anglian artefacts in graves that show that they are found in the Tweed area by the late 6th century and that we would recognise them if there had been any at Yeavering.[124] Lucy concludes: 'The Yeavering burials fit more comfortably into a northern British context than they do in a more southerly Anglo-Saxon one, unless they do in fact date to the late seventh century and beyond'.[125]

The question of religion also initially favours Angles for the first cemeteries with their shrine and temple; after all, who could be more pagan than Aethelfrith? It has been claimed that square enclosures with central posts had their origins in pre-Roman prototypes, Romano-British shrines and large ditched enclosures imposed on prehistoric monuments. This is not in dispute; the less safe assertions are that the form was adopted by the English as shrines, and the corollary, that such shrines are therefore English. John Blair puts the Yeavering western ring ditch into a group with New Wintles Ox, Slonk Hill, Shoreham and the annex to Cowdery's Down A1, so claiming the Yeavering shrine as 'unambiguously pagan Anglo-Saxon'.[126] Sam Lucy, for one, is not convinced by Blair's attribution, pointing out that the New Wintles structure is not necessarily contemporary with the Anglo-Saxon settlement and concluding that 'there is little evidence that these square and rectangular structures at Yeavering belong to an Anglian pagan tradition, rather than a sub-Roman milieu'.[127]

That sub-Roman milieu is in fact distinctly non-English, as argued in the preceding part of this chapter, which has identified rectilinear shrines in Scotland, Wales and North Britain. These seem to stem from an indigenous Iron Age tradition and marked places that had a spiritual or congregational function and served the occupants of the 'family forts' of Chapter 3 by providing both assembly and burial.[128] The arrival of the Halls ushered in a new era.[129] As relentlessly stressed in this book, part of the problem has been the assumption that 8th-century authors were right in retrospectively assigning the Christian religion (as they understood it) to the generations that had flourished in the 5th to 7th century. The archaeology is quite consistent on this point: there is virtually no investment of a Christian character in the north and west of Britain, or in Ireland, in the 5th to 7th century, whether in sculpture or in burial; the monumentality is rooted in the prehistoric past and its function in the 'ancestral present'. We could also add, linking Rhynie and Sutton Hoo with Yeavering, that the sacrifice of oxen played an important part in the 5th–7th century ethos, island-wide, if not Europe-wide (p. 650). This would mean that when Briton met Saxon, their belief systems were not so far apart, and both would be targets for institutionalised Christianity. This was to come, but only in the later 7th century, when it took a more assertive form.

The densely packed eastern cemetery and its 'church' do seem to belong to a later period when the parish church arrived and circumscribed burial. In north Britain this was generally much later, the 11th or 12th century. There is, however, a northern context in which burial in rows was practised in connection with a church; we met it at Portmahomack (p. 320) and will meet it again at Wearmouth (p. 415). It is not impossible that towards the end of its life in the 7th/8th century, Yeavering adopted a monastic posture.[130] This would be in keeping with the trajectory that has been sketched out in Chapters 3 and 5 and here: elite leaders with ceremonial duties dominate the 5th–7th century but are overshadowed in the late 7th by the spiritual overlordship of the monastic movement. If we suppose that Yeavering was essentially a British central place that hosted regional leaders as they gained power, we have accounted for the British character of the burials and ritual structures, the sacrifice of cattle and the role of English kings in Phases I-III. Without archaeological dates to the contrary, it seems reasonable to allot a span to this cult centre of the 5th to the late 7th century. A local leader may have presided over the ritual routines here without attracting the attention of Bede. But kings such as Aethelfrith and even Edwin and Oswald will have been aware that to govern a people one must be seen to serve their gods and will have been familiar with the rite of sacrificing cattle and stacking their heads, whether they had learnt it in Pictland or in north Germany. By Oswald's time, the 'timber posts' that anchored the string graves may have been crosses. But it was probably not until the time of Oswy (642–670) or his successor Ecgfrith (670–685), at any rate after the synod of Whitby (664), that serious Christian investment began. Since Bede mentioned Yeavering, it would be reasonable to suppose that it had survived into the 8th century.[131] By that time it would be appropriate for it have a Christian church and burial ground, and since the prime ecclesiastical instrument was then the monastery, it is not impossible that the halls of Yeavering were adapted to serve this end. In the context of wider British practice, Yeavering's ritual apparatus thus suggests two phases: a Formative 1 role as a centre of pagan cult and governance and a Formative 2 role as a Christian monastery.

The most extensive and fully published Anglicised 6th-century cemetery in Northumbria is at **West Heslerton** by the River Derwent in the Vale of Pickering. This site contained 201 cremations and inhumations focussed on a Neolithic circle of massive posts, a henge and three Bronze Age round barrows, a small cemetery of Iron Age crouched burials and a late prehistoric pit alignment (Figure 4.56A). It was estimated that the more robust of these monuments would still have been visible when the Anglian cemetery was planned.[132] The cemetery was bisected by the A64 trunk road, but otherwise all graves were excavated. Poor bone survival inhibited radiocarbon dating, but the graves were reckoned to run from AD 475 to 650 based on their grave goods, and the development was seen as springing from five focal or family groups (A-E), each with men, women and children and covering the whole date span (Figure 4.56B). The graves had a wide variety of orientations, with an emphasis on west and south-west. Over half were flexed or crouched, and only 18% extended where the body position was observed. There were 12 prone burials, which, added to three at Sewerby and seven at Norton, gives the northern fringe of the Anglian cultural zone the preponderance of this rite.[133] The material culture from the grave assemblages is distinctively 'Anglian' in nature and includes links with Scandinavia in particular. Analysis of stable isotopes revealed incomers at West Heslerton – in this case incomers from the west of Britain.[134] The archaeological effort to prove or disprove the immigration of persons from the Germanic continent has perhaps obscured a more interesting story – the human mixing that results from targeted exogamous marriage and slavery in all its forms.

A natural assumption for explaining the Northumbrian cemeteries in the 5th–6th centuries is that incoming Angles are modifying their mortuary behaviour due to close contact,

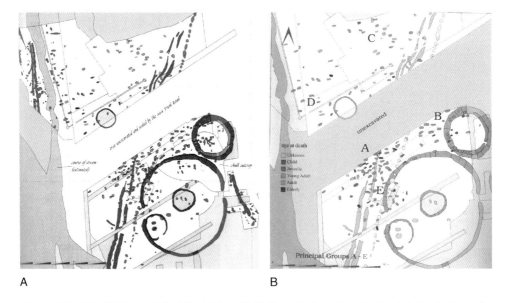

A   B

Figure 4.56 West Heslerton (North Yorkshire). (left) General plan of Anglian burials in relation to the stream channel and prehistoric features (right) The age-sex distribution of individuals buried in the cemetery, with probable foci of family groups (labelled A to E).

(Haughton and Powlesland 1999a, Fig 44, 49; with author's permission)

including intermarriage, with the native Britons.[135] Sam Lucy has argued against this assumption in that the supposedly ethnic markers, crouched burial and association with prehistoric monuments, come later in the Anglo-Saxon period and are unlikely to be a response to a contact period.[136] However, both these things can be true at the same time, if one navigates adroitly. At Spong Hill we can see what the earliest incoming Angles looked like in the ground – a field full of 5th-century cremations. Sancton shows that something of the kind was tried, not much later, north of the Humber. The example of Wasperton opened a window on another frontier, where burial rites that should equate with Anglo-Saxon and Briton continue side by side in the same cemetery from the 5th century to the 7th. In Northumbria the proximity of a major British area and the experience at Norton and West Heslerton makes an eventual acculturation more likely than not. Crouched burial is a known Iron Age form (see p. 345) which marks 50% of the graves at Norton and a higher proportion at Heslerton, further south. The engagement with prehistoric monuments is certainly an indigenous propensity, as we saw in Wales, Scotland and Tweedside. Both these attributes are absent at first (as at Sancton) and arrive later; but this does not imply that there were no Britons or no Saxons. It means rather that at Heslerton and Norton we have already arrived in the 6th century. Perceived ethnicity in some form was real, ever present and the curse of human existence in the first millennium, as it often is today. Ethnic assimilation in Northumbria is real enough and affects the Angles with increasing impact on burial practice as they move north, not necessarily, but most likely, due to intermarriage. The Anglian burial signature coincides with the best arable land, suggesting that the objective of the incomers was simple enough – to possess, farm and govern it. This signature weakened as they moved north, and the most likely reason is that they were marrying the best land rather than killing for it, at the same time that the best land was running out.

Acknowledgement of the spiritual power of local prehistoric monuments is a consequence of this acculturation, and from the mid-6th century this is also an aspect of Anglo-Saxon burial in southern England. The fact that it is nothing like as strong or as early in the century as it is in Northumbria can be due to the nature and timing of the contact between Angle and Briton. The cemeteries indicate how and when ethnicity was negotiated, not that it was insignificant; in this compromise we have hopefully squared modern anxiety about ethnicity as causation with a real-world clash in which people recognised their differences and eventually dealt with them – but only after several generations had come and gone.

South of the Tees and on a bluff of the North York Moors looking to the coast of the North Sea was the remarkable 7th-century cemetery of **Street House**, where a layout of unusual regularity was combined with a distinctly feminine emphasis. The site was found during the investigation of an Iron Age settlement seen from the air as the cropmark of a rectangular enclosure ditch (Figure 4.57).[137] The enclosure proved to contain a cluster of nine or 10 roundhouses, later cut by Anglian-period graves which would not have seen them. The cemetery took a rectangular form, measuring 36 m E-W by 34 m N-S, but it was set skew to the Iron Age enclosure, although the entrances of both enclosures were in line, implying the later was aware of the earlier. The site is at a high point (170 m) above the sea, marked by a Bronze Age cairn and other prehistoric monuments.[138] The location and setting thus belong with the set of ancestor sites that we have already discussed in this chapter as a feature of Formative 1.

The graves and the prehistoric features were defined on the surface of a boulder clay subsoil under 25–30 cm of ploughsoil – a difficult terrain to excavate, but the particularity of the plan (Figure 4.58) gives a high level of confidence that most aspects of the cemetery were skilfully retrieved. All the graves were oriented east-west and had been laid out in single

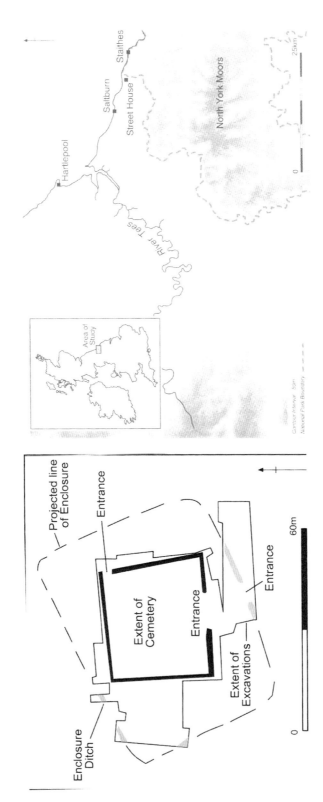

Figure 4.57 Street House, Loftus (North Yorkshire). Location and map of principal enclosures.
(Sherlock 2012, Fig 1.1, 1.6; images courtesy of Tees Archaeology)

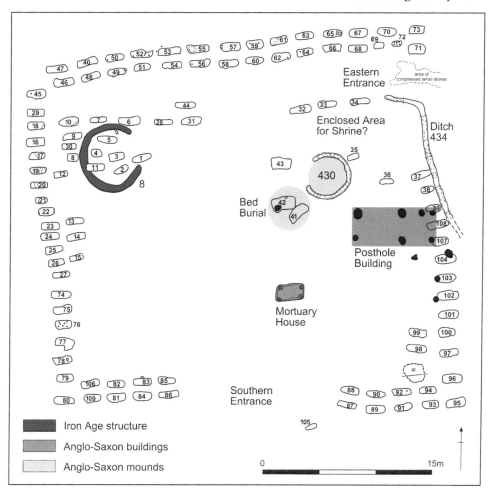

Figure 4.58 Street House; plan of graves and other early medieval features. Bed Burial 42 is in the centre of the site.

(Sherlock 2012, Fig 42; image courtesy of Tees Archaeology)

or double rows, like an army around a parade-ground. On the south side were 16 graves in two groups of four pairs, either side of an entrance-way 14 m wide. Thirteen pairs of graves formed the north side, except that the penultimate grave at the east end had two small partners rather than one, making 29 in all. The east and west sides were mostly in single file. The 21 graves on the west side had been joined at random points by four partner graves, and there was a cluster of 15 in the NW corner around a circular structure (F8). On the east side were 13 graves joined by two partner graves. A narrow ditch (F434) continued the rank northwards and then turned west, where its line was continued by the three graves 34, 33 and 32. This left a gap 6 m wide between the east and north ranks that had been used as a thoroughfare, as indicated by a patch of compressed small stones.

The north-eastern corner of the interior defined by the ditch formed a rectilinear zone containing, in its northern part, a penannular ring ditch with a west facing entrance, enclosing an

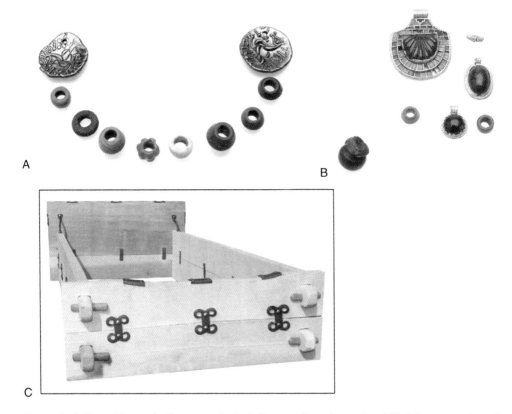

Figure 4.59 Street House. A: Grave goods, including two Iron Age coins drilled for suspension of a necklace of beads (from Burial 21). B: Grave goods from Bed burial (Burial 42). C: Reconstruction of the bed from Burial 42.

(Sherlock 2012, Plate 2.3, 2.4, Plate 4.5; images courtesy of Tees Archaeology)

orange clay floor (F430, said to have been a mound) and a group of special graves outside the ranks, amongst which was Grave 42, a bed burial. In its southern part were a set of post-holes and a sunken-featured building. The cut for the bed burial was abnormally shallow, implying that a mound had covered it. There is a good case that the north-east zone was central in importance to the cemetery as a whole.[139]

No human bone survived, but there were artefacts contemporary with the burial in 41 graves (out of 108). The bed burial (42) contained nails, cleats and rails of twisted iron sufficient to infer the headboard, footboard and canopy of a bed. The grave goods included two blue glass beads, a gold wire bead, a small circular gold cabochon pendant, an oval gold cabochon pendant, and a shield-shaped gold and cloisonée pendant worn together in the chest area (Figure 4.59). The neighbouring grave 43 was also that of a wealthy female: it had a silver circular brooch, an annular blue glass bead, two beads of silver wire, three beads of gold wire and four silver *bullae*. Eight other assemblages marked the graves of affluent women (10, 12, 21, 52, 55, 66, 67, 70), and nine other graves had beads or pendants. Burial 21 had two Iron Age coins drilled to make pendants. Five of the graves contained objects interpreted as amulets (55, 62, 67, 70 and 73). The datable objects were the *bullae* and a

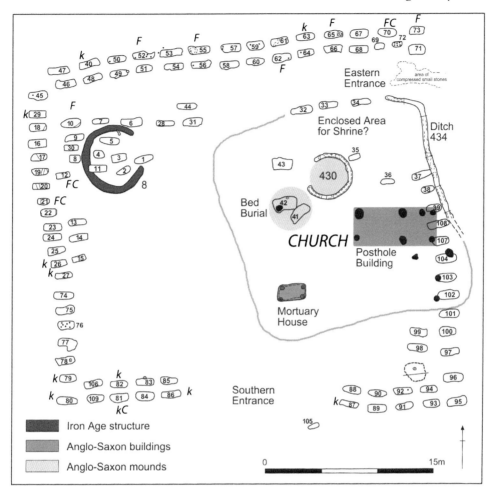

Figure 4.60 Street House. Model following the excavator's interpretation of the cemetery as a largely Christian site (after Sherlock 2012, 121–131; Fig 42. Plan courtesy of Tees Archaeology). Annotated by present author as follows: F – wealthy female grave; k – grave with a knife only; C – grave with a suggested Christian symbol.

cabochon of the later 7th century and a circular gold pendant dated to 650–670. The beads were all dated typologically to the 7th century.[140] Twelve graves had only a knife; two only a buckle; one with a knife and buckle. There were no specifically male-related objects.

In his interpretation, the excavator strove to normalise Street House and decided it should be Christian, royal and dedicated to both men and women (Figure 4.60). He allowed bed burial as a Christian rite, interpreted the post-holes as belonging to a church and detected Christian messages in the amethyst bead 12.1, the Iron Age coins 21.1, the scallop shell (a precocious symbol of St James, 42.6), a cross pattern on the gold pendant 70.6 and the knives and whetstones placed to make a 'cross' in grave 81.[141] Although the grave goods were overwhelmingly female and the graves themselves generally short, he suggested that certain objects were male in this site and that the short graves could be explained if the men

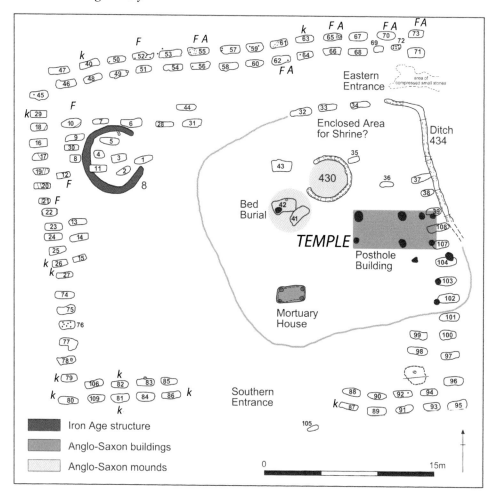

Figure 4.61 Street House. Model following a largely pre-Christian or non-Christian interpretation. (plan courtesy of Tees Archaeology after Fig 42). Annotated by present author as Fig 4.60; A – grave with suggested amulet.

had been crouched.[142] Sherlock also notes that the burial site is contemporary with Hild's monastery at Hartlepool, on the coast on the other side of the Tees, and urges (in spite of their numerous dissimilarities) that both should be Christian.[143]

In the light of the lack of positive evidence for the presence of men or of Christianity, and following corroboration from other sites reviewed in this chapter, Sherlock's conclusion might seem unnecessarily contrived. There are no direct signs of Christian belief at Street House. On the other hand, it can be aligned without too much strain with the non-specific 7th century cult centres with burials we have already visited in Pictland, Wales, the West Country and Northumbria (Figure 4.61). The central feature 430 was unlikely to have marked a mound since it had an entrance and a clay floor, but if contemporary can have served as a shrine. Similarly, the scatter of post-holes is no less realistically a temple than a church, albeit more unusual. The domination by artefacts of the female gender may be a matter of date, since the male equivalents disappear from the Anglo-Saxon record before 650 (see p. 641). But the domination can still be real, and the presence of the amulets is suggestive. The basis of the attribution of some graves to men is not at all convincing, but the graves with only knives do have an interesting distribution nevertheless. The cemetery may easily be believed to celebrate a company of women (why not?) or, if we must revert to cliché, a company of leading women attended by male guards.

Street House lies in an Anglo-British region, and its strongest signal to date is of a British non-orthodox alignment, combined with an Anglian non-Christian alignment. The proximity with Hartlepool, a documented female-led Christian establishment from the mid-7th century, is of undoubted significance, chiefly by virtue of the strong contrast offered by two establishments following closely on one another (see Chapter 3, p. 218; here Figure 4.77). The fact that both sites seem to have been led by women is another sign of female spiritual prominence in the later 7th century. Such an intriguing confrontation, typical of people who are alive, competitive and politically aware, deserves a high profile in the national story.[144]

Southumbria

The English zone of burial is mainly concentrated in the lowlands of Britain, stretching from the Humber to the Channel and in southern England from the land comprising the Thames valley and the upper Avon to the south coast. This is also broadly the same area that was fully exploited by the Romans, with the best arable land (Chapter 1). Early Anglo-Saxon burial was a strong and obtrusive brand; the cemeteries are large and contain decorated pots and ornamental metalwork that are easy to recognise and attractive to acquire. It also has a strong time-signature: the earliest manifestations, as we saw at Spong Hill are cremation urns with direct parallels across the sea which arrive via The Wash through the 5th century and suggest well-bonded closed communities. This colonising phase signalled by its segregated urns continues throughout the century, arriving at Wasperton in the west and Sancton, East Yorkshire, in the north by c. 480. Within the generalities of international parallels and regional groups, cremating people appeared to have designed the urn and its contents in symbolic memory of each individual.[145]

Chronological framework

The period of Formative 1 in Southumbria is punctuated by some remarkable social changes, as indicated by the cemeteries, the graves and the objects found within them. The appreciation of these changes has been inhibited by the lack of a chronological framework, whereby the dates of the manufacture of objects, of the use of burial rites and of the dead themselves can be independently known and compared. This was not an easy task, since the only absolute dating method, radiocarbon dating, has until recently not been widely applied and had had success only with inhumed and not cremated bone. The dates of grave goods have been largely dependent on typological studies and the occurrence of different types together in a grave as an assemblage. This has resulted in chains of association, anchored only by the occasional independently dated coin. The itinerary that leads objects to be associated with a person in a grave is uncertain but is unlikely to have been always the same. Objects can be treasured over several generations as heirlooms, like Aetheling Aethelstan's collection of swords (Chapter 2, p. 122), or take time to reach these offshore islands, as is suspected in the case of several retro treasures found at Sutton Hoo. The date of a grave and the use of a burial rite is therefore not an exact equivalent to the date of manufacture of the most recent artefact, even if we knew it. And without more precision, changes can remain blurred and their significance escape us.

Happily, the present decade has been blessed by some outstanding new scientific work that offers a more secure chronology to Anglo-Saxon modes of burial and their meaning. The new study of Spong Hill has provided a sturdy chronological framework for cremation, combining a correspondence analysis that produced a sequence of favoured attributes for the grave goods and the pots with the spatial grouping of burials, pot stamps and styles. The resulting model indicates that culturally Anglo-Saxon cremation begins in England at the end of the Roman occupation in the early 5th century and endures as a generally active rite until the mid-6th century in three phases:[146]

    Phase A: 400/425–430/460, say 400–460
    Phase B: 430/460–470/490, say 430–490
    Phase C: 470/490–510/530, say 470–530

Inhumations with Anglo-Saxon grave goods appear towards the end of this sequence. The uncertainties inherent in stylistic dating and correspondence analysis mean that the periods (which are 60 years long) overlap and that the start and end dates for each phase have a span of 20–30 years. Now that cremated bone can be radiocarbon-dated, more precision could be achieved by reconciling the probable spans of the correspondence analysis of artefacts with those of the radiocarbon dates of human remains using Bayesian analysis.[147]

This was the procedure that has been undertaken for the furnished inhumations countrywide, resulting in a ground-breaking work of chronological analysis and historical interpretation by John Hines, Alex Bayliss and others.[148] The whole corpus of furnished Anglo-Saxon inhumations was addressed, but the chronological framework was based on assemblages selected for their range of artefacts together with the presence of bone from the skeletons. The skeletons (and by implication the graves) were dated by radiocarbon to a certainty of 95% and given greater precision through Bayesian analysis. This method refines the radiocarbon dating by applying 'prior knowledge' such as stratification, which shows that the graves were dug in a particular order.[149] However, Anglo-Saxon graves of Formative 1 are rarely stratified, so in this case the prior knowledge had to be provided by the relative age of the objects as determined by stylistic study and refined by correspondence analysis of the assemblages. Bayesian analysis was thus used to reconcile two model sequences: the probable date ranges of death provided by the radiocarbon dates of skeletons, and the probable date ranges for the deposition of the grave goods offered by the seriation of objects. The Bayesian statistical method provides the best fit for these two estimated time spans.[150] The combined model suggests that female inhumation graves could be defined as belonging to four phases and the male graves into five (Figure 4.62; Table 4.1).[151] In sum, furnished inhumation burial begins after 510 for women and 525 for men and ceases for both by the last quarter of the 7th century.

The resulting chronological framework was refined by removing outlying objects that did not fit into it as being older than they should be.[152] These 'anomalies', indicative of heirlooms, are integral parts of burial practice and not its least interesting aspect, but their removal can be justified, since without a master framework based on objects supposed contemporary, the heirlooms could not be identified. Although not strictly independent, because it assumed that all graves in Europe interred contemporary objects at the same time (objects ultimately dated by coins), the correspondence analysis produced a plausible sequence that

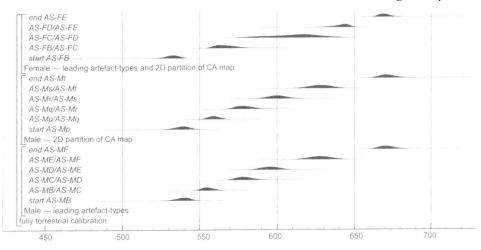

Figure 4.62 A new chronological framework for Anglo-Saxon furnished inhumation graves. Phases of graves associated by radiocarbon dates and grave goods are lettered AS-FB to AS-FE for women and AS-MB to AS-MF for men. The diagram shows the probable date range for the boundaries of each phase (e.g. the boundary between AS-FB and AS-FC lies in the range of *cal* AD *555/585* with a *probability of 95%*). Alternative phase boundaries were proposed for the male graves using leading types of artefacts (AS-MB to AS-MF) and by correspondence analysis (AS-Mp to AS-Mt).

(Hines and Bayliss 2013, 460–461, Table 8.2; Fig 8.1; reproduced by permission of the authors)

Table 4.1 Phases of Anglo-Saxon inhumation burial

FEMALE

FA [cremations] before 510/545
FB 510/545–555/585; [early to mid-6th]
FC 555/585–580/640; [mid- to late 6th]
FD 580/640–625/650; [late 6th to early 7th]
FE 625/650–660/680; [early to late 7th]

MALE

MA [cremations] before 525/550
MB 525/550–545/565 [early to mid-6th]
MC 545/565–565/595 [mid- to late 6th]
MD 565/595–580/610 [late 6th]
ME 580/610–610/645 [early 7th]
MF 610/645–660/685 [mid- to late 7th]

(after Hines and Bayliss 2013, 460, Table 8.2).

enabled the Bayesian analysis to give every grave a date. There remained a mismatch in some cases between the dates of graves computed by the Bayesian package and the dates given to coins in the same graves by numismatists. So, while seven of the 15 coin dates could be reconciled with the Bayesian dates (including Sutton Hoo and Prittlewell), seven other graves (including examples at Finglesham, Buttermarket, Ipswich, Lechlade, and South-ampton) contained *tremisses* or *sceats* that occurred with radiocarbon-dated skeletons that appeared to have died 10–30 years earlier than the earliest date of the coin contained in the grave.[153] These differences are all located in the second half of the 7th century where, it must be deduced, that the coins are being dated too late or the bodies too early.[154] This contradic-tion between the Bayesian dates of the later graves (latest 670–680) and some of the coin dates (latest 700–720) was left unresolved.[155]

There are therefore some anxieties with the model and its aspiring precision. But the researchers argued convincingly that the correspondence analysis was not depressing the deposition date by failing to take account of heirlooms and that the order obtained uses independent variables, and thus the model stands. The disagreement over the significance of the coins could inflict damage in one area only: that is the date at which furnished burial ceased. This late 7th-century date is perhaps the most significant result of the project and is understandably the subject of careful reasoning.[156] However, in the last resort the most persuasive indication that the model is correct on this point can actually be drawn from the radiocarbon dates themselves, without any need for correspondence or Bayesian analysis or indeed input from types of grave goods. With one exception there is a 95% certainty that all those persons buried in culturally Anglo-Saxon furnished graves died before 675 AD.[157] This provides support for a major conclusion of the research: that the deposition of grave goods in England ended between 670 and 680, half a century earlier than previously supposed.[158]

The phases revealed by the model show peaks of investment in furnished burial that are different for men and women (Figure 4.63).[159] The use of grave goods for both sexes rises rapidly from 530, peaks at 550 and plummets in the later 6th century. It remains low until 650, when there is a new peak (for women only) at about 660, and has diminished to noth-ing for all by 680. At the first peak for men (MB) there is a good correlation between the weapons being buried in England and those being brandished on the continent; for example, men have a succession of changes in the shape of shield bosses (which become taller) and the seax, which increases in size and importance, both keeping in step with those on the Con-tinent and in Scandinavia.[160] This boom in investment and strength of contact might almost be interpreted as another influx in the mid-6th century, although 'there is no consistently dominant centre of innovation and subsequent patterns of diffusion'.[161] Period MC features the first long-socketed spears, but the contact with the Continent diminishes in the later 6th century, and there are no artefact types in MD and ME with close parallel overseas. A revival of Continental contacts among the men is noted in the mid- to late 7th century, partly due to overseas communities in Ipswich, London and Southampton.[162]

The women experience a lower, flatter mid-6th century peak and a lower plateau until their rapid and dominant ascendency in and after the mid-7th century. In FB and FC, the range and position of women's accessories imply that they were buried fully dressed; but from FD and especially FE (the late 7th century) there is a marked shift to items in pre-cious metal, and more objects take the role of real grave goods, laid beside the body or treasured in caskets (p. 407). The artefacts buried on women exhibit a strong regionality and weak Continental contact, apart from a few types (e.g. amethyst beads) which are shared Europe-wide. But (in contrast to the men) even in the unparalleled richness of their later 7th century surge, evidence for Continental contacts does not appear markedly in the female graves.[163]

The trajectory seen in the combined levels of investment in male and females, as revealed by this study, is pronounced enough to suggest a four-fold division of Formative 1 in the Southumbrian region: Formative 1A, early settlement by cremators (400–530; FA, MA);

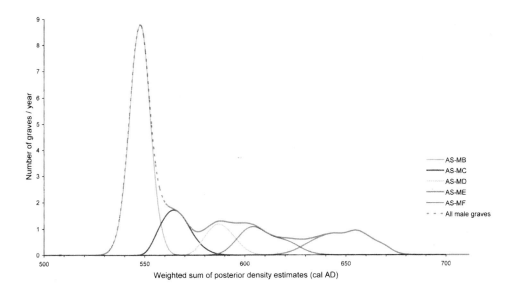

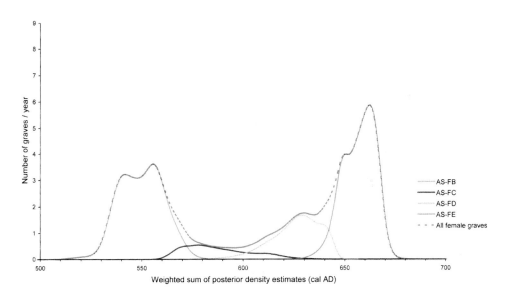

Figure 4.63 The contrasting histories of male and female burial rites. The illustration shows the
number of graves identifiable per year (determined by radiocarbon dating and Bayesian
modelling) partitioned into groups of affiliated grave goods defined by specific leading
types (by correspondence analysis). After c. AD 550 there was a precipitous fall in the
numbers of male graves of at least 80% (top). Furnished burial then continued as a succession of low peaks (Sutton Hoo mounds 17 and 1 belong in phase AS-ME) until 'the
practice came to an end during the 660s or 670s'. The female rate of furnished burial
(bottom) also drops by at least 80% after the middle of the 6th century and reaches its
lowest rate in the 580s and 590s. Investment then 'accelerates markedly from the late
630s and continues to rise sharply through the 640s and 650s'. Female furnished burial,
as male, ceases in the 670s.

(Hines and Bayliss 2013, Fig 8.14, pp. 476–479 reproduced by permission of the authors)

1B, adaption or settlement by inhumers (530–570; FB, MB); 1C, a phase of male assertive ranking (570–630; FC/D, MC/D); 1D, a phase of female assertive authority (630–675; FE). Each of these Anglo-Saxon burial phases should represent the trending of a new idea and a creative response to it. They are all positive steps into the future, and the scheme issues a final redundancy notice to the negative term 'the final phase' (p. 449).

These intriguing patterns are currently unexplained, and there are few historical analogies to help us. The patterns apply only to the area where the Anglo-Saxon grave-good ritual was practised, so the results are focussed on Southumbria.[164] Here, however, they endorse many of the basic models without strain, such as the rise of monumental mound burial for men in the later 6th century, its cessation in the early 7th, the 'dramatic upsurge' in the number of wealthy female burials in the second quarter of the 7th century, with a new range of objects strikingly different to those of Continental contemporaries but reflecting current Byzantine taste, and new cemeteries opened for the purpose.[165] The grave-good custom is held to have terminated abruptly for both men and women before 680, and this is attributed to the arrival of Theodore of Tarsus as Archbishop of Canterbury in 669.[166] This was followed, one must assume, with the imposition of a nation-wide veto on furnished burial, effective before his death in 690.

This is a result of the greatest importance, since it implies a close connection between burial practice and religion and the imposition of Christian behavioural rules that only came into effect in the late 7th century. Connecting burial rites with religion in Anglo-Saxon England has become unfashionable, but it so happens that this same pivotal moment for the archaeological arrival of effective Christian authority is noted consistently elsewhere in this book, whether in the form of the northern monastery (Chapter 3), burial rites (Chapter 4) or monumental sculpture (Chapter 5), each of which take a new direction in material culture in the last quarter of the 7th century. It is true that the factors at work here may be prompted by great men and events, such as the imposition of a more rigorous regime with the arrival of Archbishop Theodore, but it is noticeable that in matters involving ideological conversion, people need time. Richard Bulliet's study of the conversion of Christians to Islam in the eastern Mediterranean suggests that the take-up is logarithmic (or exponential), that is, very slow to start with and rapidly rising after an interval until, at 80% conversion, the curve flattens out and the process is deemed complete.[167] The interval in that case was computed at 75 years, which is a similar length of time between the arrival of Augustine in 597 and the formal beginning of the Christian era in c. 675, as argued here. We may thus be talking of a generational lag: it is the grandchildren of the 20-somethings that built Sutton Hoo who embrace the fundamentalist Christian wave of the late 7th century.

Exploring themes

It remains to explore some of these themes using examples drawn from the large corpus of Anglo-Saxon cemeteries. The focus will stay on *Formative 1*, the 5th–7th century, since that is the period when 'culturally Anglo-Saxon' graves flourished. We have already visited Spong Hill, which described the arrival of the immigrants (p. 321), Wasperton, which described interaction between Roman, Briton and Saxon on the western border (p. 324), and Sutton Hoo, which described the rise of kingship (p. 331). The following section visits a few of the more expressive cemeteries in the English region, addressing selected themes: *how cemeteries start*, (using Mucking as an example), *social change* (Mucking, Dover, Bloodmoor Hill), *heroic men*, considering barrow burial, horse burial and boat burial, and *heroic women*, using Bidford-on-Avon, Harford Farm and Swallowcliffe Down. There are more examples and better ones, but these are vivid and well-published sites of the kind that lodge in the memory and provoke ideas.

Where did Anglo-Saxon cemeteries take root?

Given that the Anglo-Saxons took possession of lowland Britain, that is, the same territory developed by the Romans as the heartland of their province, it might be expected that a Roman-Saxon transition would be visible in burials, as it is in settlement and agriculture. However, the actual continuation of a burial ground is only demonstrable so far at Wasperton, and even there, it was the Britons rather than the Saxons who succeeded the Romans. The Saxon arrival was relatively late (c. 480) and was hospitably allocated its own zone within the old Roman enclosure. Takeovers from Roman to Saxon might be expected further east, but there are few signs of any that could be called direct. At the late Roman cemetery of Lankhills, 16 graves (eight men, four women and four girls) were recognised as belonging to an intrusive group arriving after 350, although not convincingly claimed as Anglo-Saxon (Chapter 2, p. 54). More pertinently, stones and tiles were inserted in 38 graves in what was seen as 'an extremely late development', allied with sub-Roman practice.[168] Stone linings also arrived in the late Roman cemetery at Poundbury, although in small numbers. Here too they are among the latest graves and were compared to those in post-Roman cemeteries, like Cannington (p. 308). These observations suggest that Britons rather than Saxons were inheriting the late Roman burial places.

Thames valley cemeteries at Berinsfield and Queenford farm near Dorchester have been cited as candidates for Roman-Saxon continuity. Queenford was an enclosed late Roman cemetery laid out with an entrance onto a trackway. There were no grave goods or grave structures, but five radiocarbon dates seemed to allow the cemetery to span the 5th century and continue into the 6th.[169] At Berinsfield, four cremations and 114 inhumations shared relict Romano-British enclosures between the 5th and early 7th century. At least one grave with a N-S orientation cut one with an E-W orientation, and six graves had stone linings, suggesting that a Saxon succeeded a British contingent, as at Wasperton.[170] These two cemeteries were set to provide a scenario for a smooth Roman-Saxon transition. Complications followed. The excavators of Berinsfield decided that there was no conclusive evidence that burial continued at the late Roman cemetery at Queenford substantially later than the 5th century.[171] Using dental features, Lloyd-Jones found that the teeth from Berinsfield and Queenford had a very high statistical probability of being derived from the same population, while samples from the Anglo-Saxon cemetery at Lechlade showed a high divergence. He concluded that the Roman populations at Queenford and Berinsfield underwent a cultural change without pressure from an invasion.[172] Recalibrating the radiocarbon dates, Hills and O'Connell deduced that Berinsfield succeeded Queenford Farm in the early 5th century, although there could have been a short period of transition when both were in use. However, the change in burial rite and the Continental influence apparent at Berinsfield did suggest that there were significant differences between the two populations, teeth notwithstanding.[173] The story so far would appear to be that Britons went on using a Roman cemetery at Wasperton until they were joined by Saxons in the late 5th century. Elsewhere, Britons abandoned their cemeteries (Queenford) or joined cemeteries established by incoming Saxons (Berinsfield and Lechlade). This picture is consistent with Anglo-Saxons displacing Britons, although perhaps less thoroughly as they moved west. The modern sciences, although persuasive, have yet to answer historians' questions with the precision they would like.

A second question is whether the choice of site for an Anglo-Saxon cemetery was influenced by the presence of Roman or prehistoric features in the landscape. Here it is important to distinguish between cemeteries that target, respect and reutilise a prehistoric landscape and those that write over it without necessarily knowing it was there. The first case is clear when the graves lie inside an earthwork, encircle it, focus on it or dig into it: we have seen plenty of examples of this in the north and west during Formative 1 in the British regions: Yeavering, Capel Eithin or

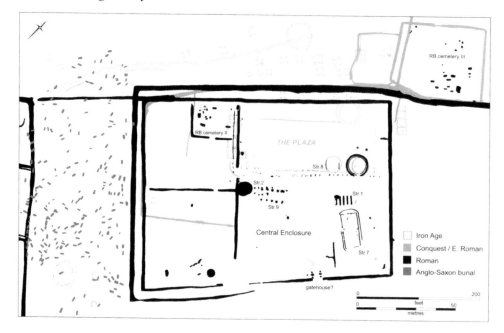

Figure 4.64 Mucking (Essex): prehistoric and Roman features that comprise the 'long-term hub', with the burials of the Anglo-Saxon cemetery.

(Evans et al. 2016, Fig 6.27; with permission)

Cannington. It would appear that the Anglo-Saxons, by contrast, did not begin to do this until some time after their arrival. We can discount Wasperton because the cremations were hosted within a going concern. At Spong Hill, founded at the end of Roman rule, the siting on an abandoned Roman farm was probably inevitable in an intensively farmed Roman landscape.[174]

At Mucking, the prehistoric landscape was dense and layered, as would be expected of a Thames-side site, but little of this earlier occupation had apparently shown itself above ground for at least 75 years before the arrival of Anglo-Saxons.[175] An exception is suggested by the line of the south-western edge of the Roman double-ditched enclosure, which had clearly acted as a boundary for Anglo-Saxon cemetery II (Figure 4.64).[176] Hirst and Clark suppose that the banks showed above the surface, but it is not impossible that the line of the ditch had survived as cropmark, visible at ground level in the 5th century as in the 20th.[177] Inhumation grave 765 was placed inside the locus of a roundhouse ditch (bottom left on Figure 4.64). But this is likely to have been fortuitous.[178]

In brief, it is hard to find an example of very early Anglo-Saxon acknowledgement of the ancestral potency of either the Roman or the prehistoric landscape. From the mid-6th century, however, attitudes to prehistory change. Anglo-Saxon burial parties begin to focus on prehistoric earthworks, especially Bronze Age barrows. In the 7th century, it is the turn of Roman places to re-exert their gravitational attractions.

Social change

Changing attitudes and their social consequences are most readily revealed by large excavations at long-lived cemeteries, and **Dover Buckland** provides an exemplary sequence. Bisected by a railway-cutting, it has been investigated in two halves (Figure 4.65). The

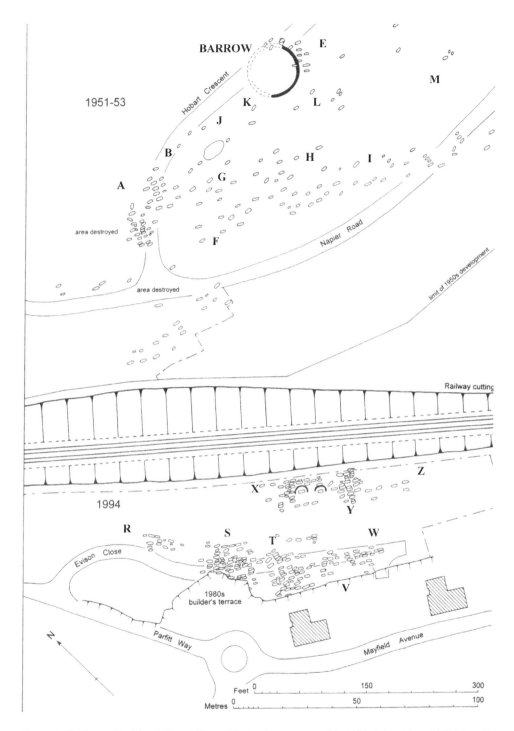

Figure 4.65 Dover, Buckland (Kent). Plan of the burials excavated in 1951–3 (north) and 1994 (south) either side of the railway.

(Parfitt and Anderson 2012, Fig 1.3, with additions by present author; with permission © Canterbury Archaeological Trust)

north-east half, excavated 1951–3, contained at least 171 inhumations dating between 475 and 750, with three notable foci (marked on the figure): **A** where burial began c. 450, **B** from c. 500, and **E** where burial began in the late 6th century, arranged with respect to a Bronze Age barrow.[179] The south-west half contained 244 burials, also from the mid-5th to mid-7th century and later.[180]

Household groups or family plots were proposed by both excavators on the grounds of the clustering of the graves, the empty spaces around the clusters and the presence of men and women and juveniles within each cluster (Figure 4.66).[181] This is a similar logic which led to the definition of family lines, for example at Cannington and Hallow Hill (pp. 308, 354), but

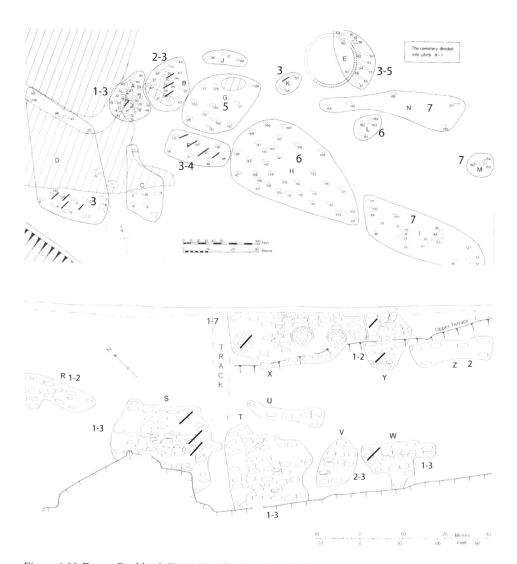

Figure 4.66 Dover, Buckland (Kent). Family plots (A–Z), showing occurrences of swords ('/') and phase of occupation (1–7).

(Evison 1987, Fig 98 image licensed by Historic England; Parfitt and Anderson 2012, Fig 2.4, with additions; with permission, © Canterbury Archaeological Trust (with author's additions))

in Southumbria we have the additional advantage of the grave goods, to endorse gender and indicate rank. Fourteen plots were defined in the north sector (A-N) and nine in the south sector (R-Z). The time frame adopted for the cemetery derived from artefacts included in the graves was:

Phase 1: 450–510/530
Phase 2: 510/530–550/560
Phase 3: 550/560–c. 650
Phase 4–7: after 650–750[182]

While the earlier date ranges align with the latest research by Hines and Bayliss (see above), we should be less confident now that furnished burial continues at Buckland after 675. The graves at Buckland showed good agreement with the remodelling for the men: for example, grave 323, assigned to Phase 3, radiocarbon-dated to 545–630 (89%), or grave 375 (Phase 3b) 545–630 (87%); but poor agreement for the women: Grave 222 (Phase 3a) 420–495 (64%) (i.e. Phase 1); grave 250 (Phase 3a) 415–555 (95%) (i.e. Phase 1); grave 391A (Phase 5–7) 585–660 (95%) (i.e. Phase 4).[183] Objects with Continental affiliations, mainly Frankish, are mostly featured in the earliest graves (Phases 1–2).[184] Buckland graves produced four coins: those in Graves 29 and 232 were counterfeit tremisses of Justinian 1 dated AD 518–527; both skeletons had dates modelled by radiocarbon 560–625 (95%), which showed the coins to be residual. Grave 110 contained two gold tremisses of Pada with numismatic dates of c. 680, placing the grave in Evison's Phase 6 (675–700). This grave lies in Plot H, and so Plots I and L, which succeeded it and had few or no grave goods, were allocated to Phase 7 (700–750).[185] The new study has pulled the date of grave 110 back to 640–675.[186] This exercise is not definitive: it is intended to demonstrate the potential precision of the new model, which can be used to revisit published sequences. The revision is most likely to be felt in the last stages of furnished burial.

On this basis, one plot in the north (plot A) and five plots in the south (S, T, W, X, Y) contained the earliest graves, suggesting that at least six family groups founded the cemetery sometime in the later 5th/early 6th century. Sword graves are thought to indicate both leading men and founder graves. Six early swords were found in northern groups and two in southern, but swords of the later 6th/early 7th century also seeded burial clusters. Groups B, D, F, S had three or more swords, implying peer groups. The sword graves in Plot S were close together, and aDNA showed that the two skeletons in graves 264 and 265B shared maternal ancestry and could have been brothers or cousins. Similarly, the men in graves 375 (Plot X) and 437 (Plot Y) were related through the female line. The woman in Grave 360 had a sword pommel, probably in a pouch laid on the left side of her pelvis.[187]

The graves 375, 393, 427, 413 in Plot X appear to have been covered by barrows, implied either by a ring ditch or an empty space around the grave. Grave 375 contained a sword, spear and shield boss and was dated 540–615 by radiocarbon. Grave 393 contained a spearhead and knife with two poorly preserved skeletons. Grave 427 contained two skeletons in a coffin indicated by flint packing. Fragments of copper-alloy wire and a pin with six segmented beads implies a female. Grave 413 contained a woman assigned to Phase 5–7, accompanied by a girdle hanger, knives, pins, three amethyst beads and glass beads, silver wire and silver gilt pendant with turquoise inlay.[188] These data suggest the rise of the barrow habit in Plot X in the late 6th/early 7th century. At a similar date, a group of graves are mustering in the east side of the Bronze Age barrow in the north (Plot E).

The story at Buckland is that half a dozen families arrive in the 5th century and found plots in open country north of the Roman lighthouse at Dover, near a Bronze Age barrow, but without making any reference to it. Each plot is initiated or anchored by the burial of a sword-carrying leader, and other members of the household – men, women and children and in two cases sword-bearing siblings (or close relatives) – are laid to rest in the same zone. There are examples of aligned graves, but the lines did not obviously endure. The cohesion seems to be due to the proximity of kin. In the early phases, graves rarely intercut, so were probably marked. In the later there were examples of graves dug coincident or close to one of the phase before, also suggesting ordered allocation of burial space.[189] In the later 6th century new centres of attraction were created by two or more burials under mounds in Plot X and by the appropriation of the prehistoric burial mound at the top of the hill (Plot E), where nine of those buried were female and five male (based on grave goods).[190] This implies a shift of allegiance from known and recent to unknown and more remote ancestors. Adoption of the new dating suggests that investment in furnished graves had ceased by around 675 and that later burials were plain and peremptory.

Mound, chamber, horse, boat and bed: 7th-century celebration of heroic men, 600–625

The 7th century is distinguished by a high level of investment in a stunning variety of burial rites, including mound burial, horse burial, boat burial and bed burial (Figure 4.67). In line with current thinking, this variety reflects an experimental phase in the expression of spirituality, variations both in ideas about eternity and the need to express them, probably connected closely to the arrival of St Augustine and ideological pressure from a Christian Continent.[191]

Burial under round mounds was practised from the Bronze Age, and there are examples from the Iron Age and Roman period in Britain. These littered the Anglo-Saxon landscape, and many were used for secondary burial by the immigrants in their fourth or fifth generation (e.g. Buckland, e.g. at Dover Buckland). The post-Roman surge of barrow building in northern Europe has been claimed as triggered by the arrival of the Huns and in particular the death and burial of Atilla in 453. This event has been connected to the rise of a 'cult of Odin' among the warrior and equestrian classes, superseding a more polytheistic cosmology. The earliest grand mounds appeared at Gamla Uppsala in Sweden in the 5th century and are thought to represent the furthest outreach of Atilla's influence.[192] In Chadwick's view, the ideology of the warrior underpinned by a single god provoked a new loyalty to a war band and led to the celebration of successful leaders by burial under a mound.[193] This supplanted long-term allegiance to the folk (tribe) and created a system of overarching single male control (monarchy) at national level that would survive conversion to Christianity.[194] Michael Müller-Wille also saw mound burial as receiving a boost from the funeral of the Frankish king Childeric at Tournai in 482, an occasion notable for the sacrifice of 21 horses in addition to the mount of the king.[195] Another hypothesis proposed that mounds in northwest Europe were erected in opposition to the rising pressure of Christianity.[196] This idea was originally suggested to explain the Sutton Hoo mounds and has been applied to the Krakow mounds where the context was appropriate, but it can have no general application.[197] V. Gordon Childe, like Chadwick before him, saw monumental burial as distinctive of a community at an early stage of social development 'suddenly irradiated from a much higher civilisation'. He found examples widely spread in world prehistory, including the European 'royal graves' of Sutton Hoo and Oseberg.[198]

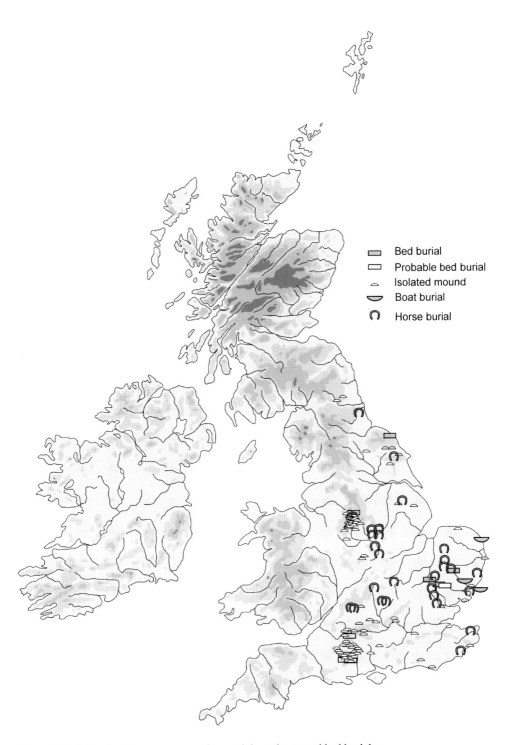

Bed burial

Probable bed burial

Isolated mound

Boat burial

Horse burial

Figure 4.67 Map showing occurrence of mound, boat, horse and bed burials.
(FAS Heritage after Shephard 1979, Fern 2007, Carver 1995a, Speake 1989, Fig 90, with additions)

In Britain, mound burial is a relatively late arrival. Many graves in 6th-century Kentish cemeteries (e.g. Finglesham) were covered by small mounds, and Apple Down in Sussex was noted for the large number of small quadrilateral ditched and posted structures around graves. On both these sites the superstructures become larger and fewer into the 7th century.[199] As already noted at Spong Hill, Wasperton and Dover Buckland, small mounds are incorporated into cemeteries in the 6th century. At Mill Hill, row graves were succeeded by barrows.[200] But only in the 7th do they raise their vistas above the local plot and address the wider landscape. At this point they become truly monumental. Some years ago, Jonathan Shepherd plotted this simple distinction on a map, showing that while the cemeteries with many small mounds were confined to the areas of Kent and Sussex, the use of larger more singular mounds spread west into Wessex and north up the coast via East Anglia to East Yorkshire. There is a group in the Peak district which may have more indigenous roots.[201]

The construction of these monumental mounds requires many more hands than a household can command: Mound 2 at Sutton Hoo involved the excavation and piling up of 543.17 cubic metres of earth, sand and turf, requiring the estimated labour of 80 people for 10 days.[202] They were erected in praise of male warriors and their contents are rich, varied and highly symbolic, suggesting less a biography or eulogy than a heroic poem setting out the credentials of the dead warrior for the instruction of a celestial audience.[203] Swedish monumental mounds are found in the 5th century at Högom and Gamla Uppsala, in the 7th and 8th century at Vendel and Valsgärde. There are plenty of examples in the Anglo-Saxon milieu, but like the other attributes we are about to review, they do not constitute any kind of diffusionary system. They pop up where and when they will. For this reason they are more realistically seen as taken from a 'sleeping repertoire' and prompted by a local impetus at a historical moment.

The purpose of such investments clearly extends beyond the disposal of the dead. Prehistory leads us to expect a pre-mound ritual involving a structure of some kind and a long afterlife in which the mounds were used as assembly places, where decisions were taken in the presence of the ancestors. Vivid examples are provided by the Mississippi mounds of the central United States and the Kofun of Japan.[204] Mounds were 'broken' – that is, dug into and the principal body removed in the 10th century from the 9th-century mound at Oseberg in Norway – a sign that it was still potent in the landscape (p. 446). But in Britain, apart from their landscape vistas, the evidence for these other properties remains elusive. Even at Sutton Hoo, where large-scale excavations scrutinised the surface of the mounds and the spaces in between, the suspected public functions of the mounds failed to materialise in support of the suspected link between mound building and state building.

Diverse arrangements are provided for the dead warrior. Some hold court in an underground *chamber*, as at Sutton Hoo Mound 1, 2 and 14. A 7th-century example found at **Prittlewell** in Essex revealed the dead man in a coffin, with feasting equipment hanging on the walls and a sword, shield and lyre lying on the edge of the rug beside him[205] (Figure 4.68). *Horses* have long provided the heroic companion for the warrior and were specially favoured by the line that led from Atilla to Childeric to the Rhineland, as well as from the British and Pictish Iron Age.[206] It was one of the most frequent offerings among the communities east of the Rhine, and recent research by Christopher Fern has given us a good pedigree for the distribution and varieties of horse burial in Britain.[207] Cremated horses occur in burials from the mid-5th century around The Wash and along the westward rivers from the early 6th.[208] Sometimes a rider is buried in a decorated urn, with the horse in a plain pot adjacent. Men and women and juveniles all had horses, and the horse motif was signalled on pots with miniature hoofprints.[209] Horses are constant players in Germanic cosmology, featuring in art, ritual and taboo, and so formed a 'crucial component of Anglo-Saxon pre-Christian

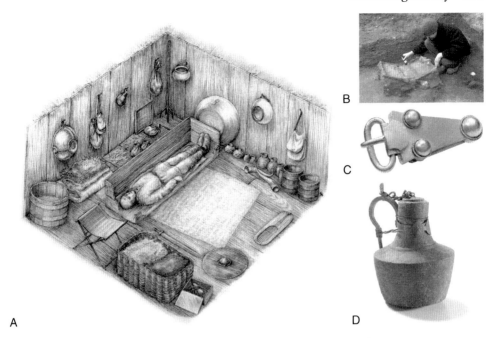

Figure 4.68 Prittlewell (Essex). Chamber grave of the 7th century. A: Reconstruction of the chamber and the burial tableau. B: Excavation of the chair. C: Gold buckle. D: Byzantine copper alloy flagon with medallions of figures on horses.

(Images from interim publication MoLAS 2004, with permission)

religion'. Moreover, 'Anglo-Saxon kings claimed equine blood in their veins'.[210] The horses found in graves were in general between 13.2 and 14 hands, the normal height for mature horses found on settlement sites, and were strong animals in their prime.

These ideas no doubt fuelled the second wave of horse burial in England, in the later 6th century, when the horse reappears as a companion in inhumation graves and is found in the expanding periphery of English settlement north and west. The sacrifice is now rare and special: 31 horse-and-rider graves and 38 bridle sets in England compared with 700 horse burials and 600 harnesses on the Continent.[211] In its new context it takes up its role as a war-horse in alignment with the ideology of the heroic male. Chris Fern sums up the distinction like this: horse burials in cremations refer to 'a funerary expression of communal animal-human shamanism' and look to Scandinavia; while horse burial in inhumations 'align with equestrianism, masculinity, leadership and military prowess and look to the Rhine'.[212] A change in the horse-burial scenario has been remarked to occur around 600, when the horse is buried in a separate pit to its rider. This may signify a change in their relationship: has the horse graduated from a possession, a grave good, to a companion? Or is the horse, still a disposable asset, too tainted with the old religion to share the grave of a reconstructed 7th-century pagan?[213]

At Sutton Hoo Mound 17, created about 590–600 AD, it is the rider who has the tack – saddle, bridle and bran tub – in a heap at his head, and the horse lies in a pit adjacent (Figure 4.27). Both were covered by a single mound. The young man's grave is furnished with considerable affection, with weapons, a little purse with trinkets, a comb, a bucket, a cooking cauldron and a haversack with traces of ribs of lamb. The horse too is decked in its best, with gilded strap-distributors and silver pendants. This seems like the ministrations of a family giving their young hero a sympathetic send off in the way they wanted him to be remembered and recommended to the future.

The horse burials at **Sedgeford** (Norfolk) offer an interesting late instance of buried horses, at least one of which is dated to the period 670–820 at 95%. The horses occurred in three contexts, the first a composite burial of a horse, a woman and a child in close association. The woman of about 40 years was laid with her head on the hip of a male horse with the child over the horse's head. Parts of other animals, cow, sheep, pig and chicken, were included in the grave pit. This was the horse radiocarbon-dated. A second burial was of a horse about 8 years old, on its own. And the third context was a quantity of horse parts that had been spread about in the area. This would appear to combine many of the aspects of divinity, ritual and taboo collected by Fern, but in a later and feminine context.[214]

Boats and ships also provide a particular vehicle for the heroic dead, and like other special rituals they appear, disappear and reappear at intervals. Bronze Age Scandinavia is notable for its ship settings which also act as cemeteries (for example at Anundshög, Sweden). In the Iron Age, Tacitus reports that the Suebi sacrifice to Isis (by burying ships), and in the subsequent early middle ages there are outbreaks of ship burial in the 1st to 3rd centuries at Slusegård on Bornholm, where the shell boat coffins are interpreted as the prerogative of priests; in the 7th/8th century Vendel culture, where the ship graves are found in male and female cemeteries; and in the Viking period (9th–10th century), where the ship graves of men and women are found on the coasts of their northern European maritime area of influence. Like the horse, the ship forms part of the persistent cosmology of northern Europe, appearing in rock art, stone settings and the burial of actual boats either in bogs or lakes (as Nydam) or in trenches on dry land, with a cargo of weapons, horses and dogs to accompany the dead (as at Vendel, Valsgärde; see p. 443).[215]

In Britain, the early medieval adoption of the practice is splendid but rare: five examples from the late 6th or 7th century and seven from the Viking period. So far, all the Formative 1 boats are from East Anglia: three at Snape and two at Sutton Hoo. An uncertain number of boats or boat parts were used as biers at Caistor-on-Sea in the 8th/9th century. They were deduced from the surviving clench nails used to hold the planks of the boat together, and since clench nails have been found in several graves along the coast, the practice may have been more widely spread.[216] There are several other sites where 'boat-shaped coffins' without nails have been supposed as dug-out boats; but it is fair to point out that it is not always easy to distinguish a decayed dug-out boat from a tree-trunk coffin. At Sutton Hoo Mound 1 and Mound 17, the tree-trunk coffins were identified from the curved iron clamps that secured the lid.

If we confine ourselves to the five examples where the boat formed an integral part of the burial rite, the most vivid and varied use is provided at **Snape** (Figure 4.69).[217] Here there were two types of vessel – the boat at 3 m long and the ship at 14 m long – in use at the same time (late 6th to early 7th century) and presumably signalling differences in rank. The smaller boats (in Graves 4 and 47) contained boat-shaped traces that appeared as thin black lines of decayed wood. There were no clench nails and no evidence for planks in the hulls (although planks were seen elsewhere as a bench in Grave 4). The deduction was therefore that these were 'expanded dugouts' similar to those found at Slusegård, where the tree-trunk is cut out in a boat-shape profile with thin upper walls. This gives extended height to the freeboard and makes a craft that is lighter and easier to handle than the prehistoric logboat.

The boat in Grave 47 was the best preserved (Figure 4.70). It was originally made of oak, was 3.09 m long, 0.62 m in the beam and could draw up to 0.35 m of water. Calculations suggested it had a weight of 58 kg and performed like a canoe, with the stability largely in the hands of

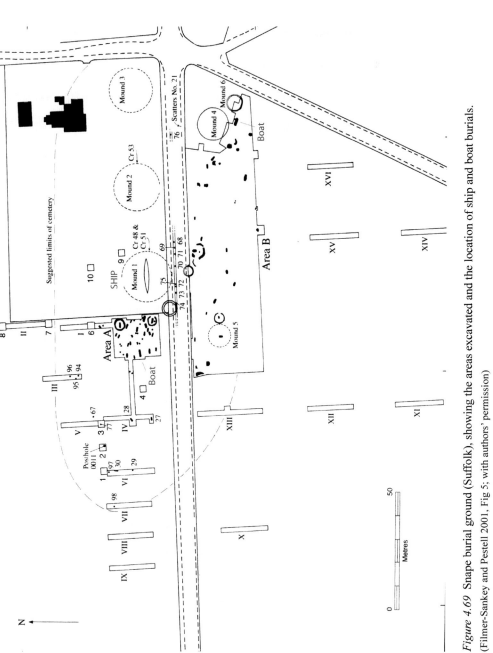

Figure 4.69 Snape burial ground (Suffolk), showing the areas excavated and the location of ship and boat burials. (Filmer-Sankey and Pestell 2001, Fig 5; with authors' permission)

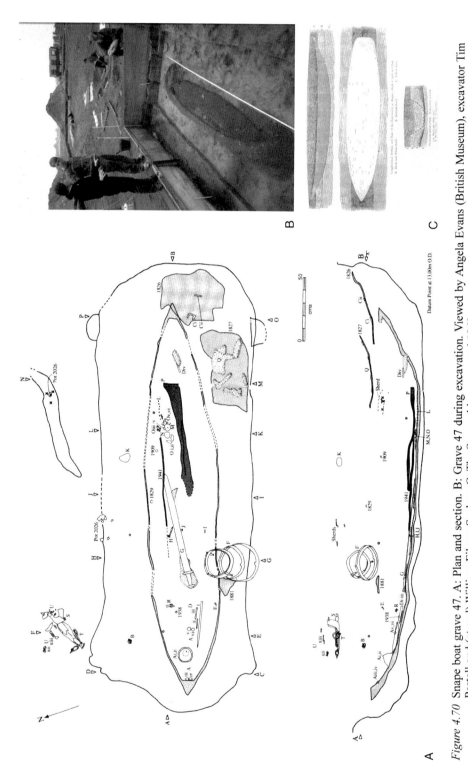

Figure 4.70 Snape boat grave 47. A: Plan and section. B: Grave 47 during excavation. Viewed by Angela Evans (British Museum), excavator Tim Pestell and (at end) William Filmer-Sankey. C: The Snape ship, excavated 1862.

(A: Filmer-Sankey and Pestell 2001, Fig 75; B: photo by present author; C: Filmer-Sankey and Pestell 2001, Fig 4; with authors' permission)

the paddler.[218] The boat had been laid in an E-W grave, covered with a textile, and a pillow was provided at the west end before receiving the body, of which no tangible traces remained. Grave goods were laid in the body of the boat: a shield covered the west end, a sword and two spears lay beside the presumed site of the body. There were unidentified personal effects, possibly in a box at the feet-end. There was a wooden stave bucket outside the boat but within the grave on its south side. The shadow burial of an animal (suggestive of a dog) was found adjacent. A horse's head had been added to the tableau but at a higher level: its jaw was horizontal and faced west, with the harness 'perhaps draped down into the main burial deposit'.[219] This suggests (though it was not claimed) that the horse's head had been placed above the grave at ground level or on a stake, to 'ward off malefactors'.[220] The ship at Snape was excavated in the 19th century, and little survived from the expedition apart from a sketch and a gold ring. It is likely to have been richly furnished, like Sutton Hoo Mound 1. The Sutton Hoo ships in Mound 1 and Mound 2 were 30 m and 20 m long, large enough to have conveyed a crew of 20–40 warriors. This is what sets them apart from the one-man scud-abouts. Grave 47 at Snape probably represented a social relation to Grave 1 (the ship), as the Mound 17 horseman at Sutton Hoo to the occupant of the Mound 1 ship; that is of a son to a father, a prince to a king.

There was certainly an ideological significance in boat burial, as in the other expensive obsequies in which 7th-century England specialised. It was previously spasmodic and widely spread in northern Germany and Scandinavia, but there is no satisfactory diffusionary trail either for the practice or for specific people to go with it. The theory has been advanced that the boat, as the most important machine in the maritime countries of 5th–8th century Europe, had an enduring role in its various cosmologies. While this is probable, the real question is why it was adopted when it was in Britain. Here the best bet is to discover a political context to go with the need for this ideological expression; in East Anglia, we can probably find it in the rise of kingship, loyalty to an overseas origin and the threat of the incipient Christian empire.[221]

Heroic women

The heroic phase in female burial began around 630, but like the men there was a long pre-lude that showed that their late dominant role did not spring from nowhere. Women were represented equally in cremation and inhumation through the 5th and 6th century. Their graves were notably well furnished, and even if the early phases were most informative about what they were wearing, there was no shortage of informative insignia in the formal dress adopted. The girdle hangers and châteleine (p. 63) were indicators of title, and the brooches were subjects of high investment in materials, artistry and symbolism. The great square-headed brooch could be regarded as the badge of the alpha female par excellence, with its central position on the body and mass of 'quoted' imagery (Chapter 2, p. 65). This implies that such women were held in esteem for their knowledge, perhaps arcane knowl-edge, as well as their more familiar social assets.

Certain women could be classed as not merely knowledgeable but as specialists in matters spiritual. Audrey Meaney saw this in a range of natural objects such as sea urchins or amethyst beads and manufactured items such as miniature buckets and pixiform workboxes containing traces of thread. All these objects, and many more, have been seen as amuletic.[222] The later version of the workboxes were reliquaries used to transport bone and other items valued by Christians, so it is likely that the earlier version had a curative or protective function too; the indications are that the cult of relics was a variant on the indigenous ancestor cults and not an idea introduced with Christianity.[223] The **Bidford-on-Avon** cunning woman is a pre-echo of the even more graphic examples known from the Scandinavian 9th century, such us that found at the fort at Fyrkat in Denmark (Chapter 2, p. 120). She wore brooches of British and Saxon affiliation, a necklace of beads, a shawl pinned with an iron pin and a linen belt. She wore a 'bib' festooned with 12 miniature buckets and had a bag at her hip containing a knife with a decorated handle, a stud, and an antler tip. These objects, which served to identify the metier of the Bidford cunning women, led to her being seen as having practised 'beneficent magic, healing, protecting and divining the future'.[224] The discoveries collected by Neil Price in his study of Viking religion makes it probable that the role of women as healers and shamans was prominent through the Anglo-Saxon period, peaked in the late 7th century and may have gone underground for a few decades after the 675, the date to be regarded as the threshold of serious Christian control.[225] Understandably, they were involved in both original religion and new ideas.[226]

The cemetery at **Bloodmoor Hill** (at Carlton Colville) provides an attractive entrée into this world. Here a tight group of 28 graves dating to the mid- to late 7th century were placed in the centre of a 6th- to 8th-century settlement.[227] Five rectangular buildings were aligned with the graves, and a large pit stood adjacent to the east (Figure 4.71). Of those human remains that could be identified, five were biologically male and four were female, but six other graves could be identified as women from their grave goods. The five

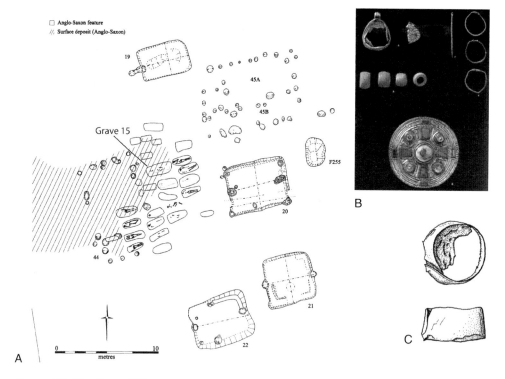

Figure 4.71 Bloodmoor Hill, Carlton Colville (Suffolk). A: The cemetery area, with the plan of the graves (grave is 15 marked), structures 20, 21 and 22 and pit F255. The hatched area marks the extent of metal-working waste in the surface deposits. B: Grave goods from Graves 22 and 23 and C: bucket pendant from the area of Building 20.

(Lucy et al. 2009 Fig 6.26; Colour Plate X; Fig 4.4; with authors' permission)

richest graves – 11, 12, 15, 22, 23 – were all of women. Reviewing them in order of symbolic complexity, Grave 12 contained iron shears, a key and a chatelaine complex, Grave 22 had a necklace of glass beads, silver rings and a gold pendant, and Grave 23 was probably also rich but had been robbed in antiquity (via a secondary pit cut down through the grave). Grave 11 had a necklace of silver pendants with a silver sheet cross at its centre and an iron girdle hanger, shears and a chatelaine complex of rings, links and rods. Grave 15 had a wooden casket placed at the feet inside the coffin. It contained a shell, a comb, a padlock key and iron ring with beads and pendant suspended from or mounted on it. There was a second iron ring and textiles originally folded within it.[228] There were no corresponding rich male assemblages: those identified biologically as men had a knife or tool, but women also had knives. The graves were set in five N-S rows. Graves 11,12 and 15 were in the central row that featured only women and children. Graves 22, 23 were in a row of four, one of which might have been a male. The feminine emphasis of this short-lived place was clear. Ten radiocarbon dates placed the cemetery as a whole in the mid- to late 7th century.[229]

Chris Scull, who reported on the cemetery for the published volume, emphasised the special character of Grave 15, judging from the layout of the burial and the lack of a chatelaine and dress accessories. He concludes that while graves 11, 12, 22 and 23 express 'authority in the nuclear family', Grave 15 with her casket expresses a different feminine identity with ' a status transcending, or outside of, the gradations inside . . . the household'.[230] He identified the burial ground as that of a small wealthy female community, linking it with the 7th-century aristocratic barrow (or barrow cemetery) some 250 m away to the south-west (demolished in 1758). He makes the plausible suggestion that this community was one of religious women, although less plausibly that they were Christian. The single Christian emblem is outranked by the other grave goods and the burial rites, and its inclusion is by no means more determinant than they are; the silver cross on a necklace in Grave 11 can equally be seen as a sign of the expected spiritual inclusivity of this period.

The immediate context of the cemetery seems rather to support an interpretation linked with the world of female spiritual specialists we have seen in action from at least the 6th century. Leaving aside the rectangular structure 44 (which was earlier), Buildings 19, 20, 21, 22 (and perhaps Building 45A and fence 45B) surround the cemetery to the east, were aligned with the graves and are seen as contemporary with them. The metalworking spread and pit F255 were also part of this contemporary complex. The 7th/8th century pit F255 was very large, at 2.6 × 1.85 m in plan, and contained one of the richest assemblages from the site: a massive amount of animal bone, with duck, chicken, goat, roe deer, eel and carp alongside more familiar species, and a big assemblage of pottery, loom weights, lava quern fragments and slag. There were two 7th-century knives and a major group of worked bone, including a 7th to mid-8th-century pin and a mid-7th to early 8th-century double-sided composite comb. There was a (probably curated) prehistoric flint awl.[231] Carlton Colville was also the find-spot for one of the most striking amuletic objects from Anglo-Saxon England, a silver gilt bearded male figure modelled in the round and featuring a prominent penis (Chapter 2, Figure 2.25). This pendant was found by a metal-detectorist, and its exact location was not reported.[232] Of the three pendants from the site, only one is located: a miniature bucket that was found in Building 20, the building closest to the cemetery (Figure 4.71).[233] This is the type of pendant interpreted as diagnostic of the Anglo-Saxon shaman or 'cunning woman'.[234]

Thus, the operating authorities of this cemetery seem to have had the use of neighbouring buildings and a metalworking facility to celebrate their obsequies and support their ceremonies, which probably included animal sacrifice. As well as Pit 255, all the graves but two contained animal parts (although it proved impossible to be sure that these were deliberate placements rather than incorporated in the backfill). These rites involved a wide-ranging repertoire of processed cultural material, both natural and man-made, and provide us with another small window onto the intellectual movement apparently being powered by women in the late 7th century.

In making these higher-level interpretations, we can see that there are clear advantages in large-scale excavations, as opposed to the broken windows with which we so often have to make do. At **Harford Farm** two groups of 7th-century burials were widely separated in a prehistoric landscape comprising Bronze Age barrows and rectangular enclosures, probably of Iron Age date.[235] Thirty-one east-west graves were arranged in tight rows at the north end next to a prehistoric barrow (North Group; Graves 1–31), and 15 others were found 160 m to the south, cut through ditches and ring ditches (South Group; Graves 32–46) (Figure 4.72). Human remains were too badly preserved to determine sex. Graves 11, 18, 22, 28 (in the northern group) and Grave 33 (in the southern group) were distinguished by their grave goods, all of gendered female type: Grave 11 had silver rings, a silver toilet set and a composite disc brooch inscribed on the back with entwined serpents and a runic inscription saying 'Luda repaired this brooch'. Grave 8 had a gold and garnet pendant, iron shears and pursemount, a cylindrical threadbox or relic box, as well as two

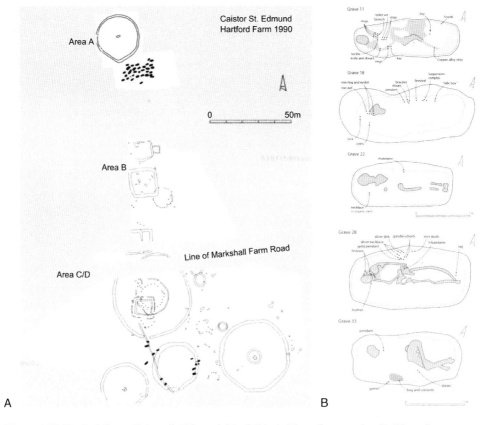

A   B

Figure 4.72 Harford Farm, Caistor St Edmund (Norfolk). A: Plan of cemeteries. B: Plan of graves.

(Williams 2010, Fig 2.1, Fig 2.2, 2.3; drawn by Sean Goddard; courtesy of Howard Williams)

sceats dated c. 690.[236] Grave 22 had the remains of a necklace and chatelaine. Grave 28 had the remains of a necklace of two dozen silver bullae and discs, an openwork gold pendant, a chatelaine and associated iron pieces and a festoon of 15 silver wire rings and a silver miniature bucket on a leather backing (recalling the Bidford-on-Avon bib). The woman in Grave 33 in the southern group wore a gold and carnelian pendant on her chest. Beside the body was a leather or textile bag containing the remains of a necklace of silver rings and amethyst beads, a toilet set and a possible chatelaine. The remaining 41 graves were unfurnished, or equipped with a chatelaine, a knife and buckle, or a knife. Graves 34–45 in the southern group were furnished with a knife alone, although an unstratified iron spearhead may have originated in Grave 43 or 44. Otherwise, no specifically male object was found.[237]

Howard Williams' verdict on this cemetery is that 'in the later seventh and eighth centuries, certain female-gendered artefacts used in regimes of body management and adornment accrued a mnemonic significance through their mortuary display and consignment through staged and sequential association with the cadaver'.[238] A simpler interpretation might be that here, as at Carlton Colville or Street House, women are running their own political and religious prescription in the face of a new authority that had placed spiritual welfare in the hands of a male god served by an attendant hierarchy – apostles, bishops and priests – that was also exclusively male. The loss of a previous female prerogative for the cure of bodies and souls may also have generated an important reaction amongst those who practised it. That is not to say that all late 7th-century burials need be those of female shamans, and in this briefest of reviews we have seen many that do not qualify. But once there is an ideological movement, however short-lived, one might expect it to be manifest in different ways. We should also bear in mind that, so far, we have only a few burials with tell-tale diagnostic features from large-scale excavations and revealing contexts comparable with Harford Farm, Carlton Colville or Street House.

One notable feature of the late female assertive phase is the use of *bed burial*, and one of the most graphic examples was found in excavations in 1966 at **Swallowcliffe Down** in Wiltshire (Figure 4.73).[239] The lady had been buried in the later 7th century in a pre-existing

Figure 4.73 Swallowcliffe Down (Wiltshire). Excavations by Faith Vatcher in progress in 1966.
(Speake 1989, Fig 6; licensed by Historic England)

Bronze Age barrow beside an ancient ridgeway – now the A30 trunk road. The Anglo-Saxon name of the reused barrow has survived as *Posses Hlwaewe* (Possa's mound), per-haps a reference to its incumbent (Figure 4.74). If so, 'Possa' was 1.6 m in height, with excellent teeth, and aged between 18 and 25 years when she died. She was laid on a bed, surrounded by a mass of costly things (Figure 4.75). The bed was a box-bed made of ash wood, deduced from 50 small iron fittings, which was all that was left of it. It measured 6 feet long and 2 feet, 9 inches across – a single bed, therefore. The sides were of two planks joined edge-on by metal cleats; there was a sloping headboard at one end and an iron rail on each side. The mattress was missing, but its support was made of ash strips, probably woven criss-cross to make a lattice with a little nail securing each crossover point. It appears to have been suspended inside the box frame using eyelets and cord. There is no doubt that this was a real bed with a real person laid upon it – maybe even her own bed. Tiny fragments of wool and flax and braid preserved on the nails give a hint of the bedclothes.

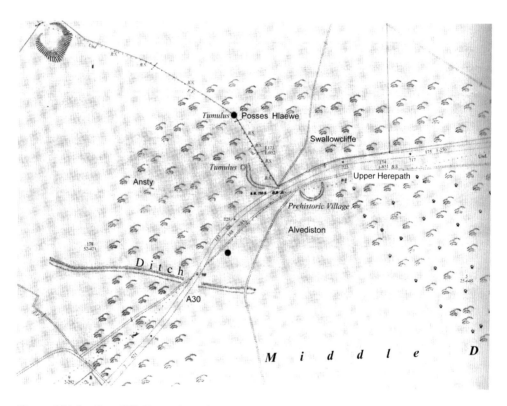

Figure 4.74 Swallowcliffe Down. Location of the tumulus termed *Posses Hlaewe* on an Ordnance Survey map of 1925.

(Speake 1989, Fig 3; licensed by Historic England)

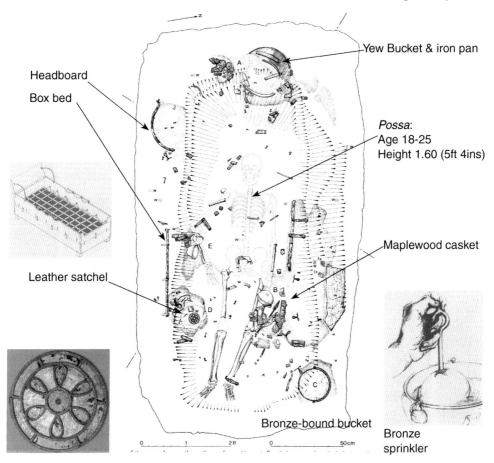

Headboard

Box bed

Yew Bucket & iron pan

Possa:
Age 18-25
Height 1.60 (5ft 4ins)

Maplewood casket

Leather satchel

Bronze-bound bucket

Bronze
sprinkler

Figure 4.75 Swallowcliffe Down. The excavated grave.

(Speake 1989, Fig 19, Fig 37, Fig 64, Fig 81 with additions; images licensed by Historic England)

On the bed beside her left thigh was a maplewood casket shaped like a miniature trunk with a curved lid and bronze hinges and a lockplate (Figure 4.76). Inside was a silver gilt spoon, four silver brooches like safety pins, two beads, two knives and a comb. And there was a bronze sprinkler that took the form of a hollow sphere perforated with little holes joined to a long hollow tube.[240] On her other side lay a leather satchel, stiff-sided and shaped like a sporran, made to contain something precious and flat – we do not know what. It was ornamented with a gilded disc combining Anglo-Saxon and British (i.e. early Insular) motifs (Chapter 2, Figure 2.32). Then there were the supplies: at the head-end of the bed, an iron-bound yew wood bucket and an iron pan. At its foot, a bronze-mounted bucket; these would contain wine or beer or milk or butter or apples. And on the bed, close to the right forearm, two little shallow glass cups of a bluey-green colour, a sign perhaps of desperate remedies administered during a last illness.

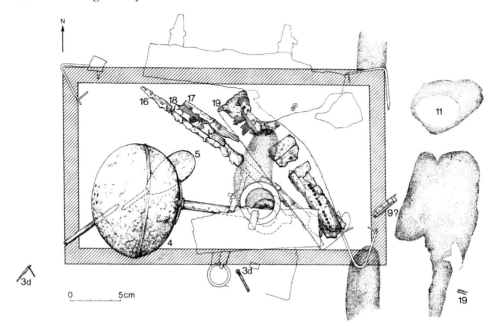

Figure 4.76 Swallowcliffe Down. The casket.

(Speake 1989, Fig 28; image licensed by Historic England)

The period of the dominance of Anglo-Saxon women in the funerary world in the mid-7th to late 7th century was signalled by furnished graves that provide the evidence of high investment and the rich spiritual influence. These have now been confined by radiocarbon dating in combination with correspondence analysis to peak in the period 650–675.[241] The influence of this single generation was felt all over the Anglo-Saxon zone, perhaps most readily appreciated by the talismanic practice of bed burial, which so far reveals intellectual territories in Wessex, East Anglia, with two in the Peak district, and a single but exceptionally vocal example at Street House in Cleveland (see p. 377).[242] There is a slight correlation with the use of amulets and animal food offerings, but at present the bed burials seem to present hot-spots within a broader geography of female-focussed mid-late 7th-century burials.

Various commentators have attempted to associate bed burial with Christianity, mostly on the grounds that they occasionally contain objects featuring Christian symbols, and sometimes on the intuitive grounds that the rich ought to have been Christian by this time.[243] Others suggest that the bed burials form part of a reactionary response of female spiritual specialists in the face of Christian pressure.[244] At best the evidence is equivocal. At Coddenham 30, the woman was buried with a coin pendant, bag and latch-lifter in a chamber, also surrounded by other graves.[245] At Trumpington, a young woman of 16 had a gold pectoral cross, originally sewn onto the robe she was wearing. The lady at Ixworth also wore a gold and garnet pectoral cross. The 'dowager' at Sutton Hoo 14 was buried on a couch and wore silver, but the burial was much disturbed. We are not able to know whether these late 7th-century women had signed up to the Christian doctrine in life and are presently restricted to

more general view, applying the balance of probabilities, being careful not to replace one kind of wishful thinking with another. The task is to reconcile the undoubted high investment with a mid-late 7th-century context, a date that now appears to precede the adoption of the formal Christian apparatus, at least in a material sense.

Helena Hamerow has produced a fine study of bed burial showing that a Christian affiliation was unlikely since most antedated the foundation of female Christian houses, and conversely there are good grounds for thinking that Anglo-Saxon women played a special role in pre-Christian cults, as well as representing family continuity in the ownership of land. She argues that that

> these well-furnished graves reflect a new ideology of investment in the commemoration of aristocratic females who came to represent their family's interests in newly acquired estates and whose importance was enhanced by their ability to confer supernatural legitimacy to dynastic claims,

concluding that:

> the archaeological evidence, when considered together with written sources, points to an undocumented tradition of females 'embodying the spiritual power' of landowning families, a tradition upon which the royal abbesses of the later seventh and eighth centuries were able to build.[246]

The fact that, at much the same time, some daughters of the rich were packed off to France for induction into the monastic life, while others were buried in their beds in prominent places, did not mean that they had signed up to a common ideology. On the contrary, the Anglo-Saxon aristocracy were well known for hedging their bets in the event of an ideological confrontation. The important thing was to adopt the appropriate convictions to ensure that wealth stayed in the family.[247] Thus, these aristocratic women were well qualified to provide pre-Christian leadership and continuity of inheritance during one regime and become abbesses and govern monastic establishments in the next. The archaeological evidence from the last phase of Formative 1 should give the lie to assumptions that women had no power in England a thousand years ago.

Future directions for Formative 1

The Formative 1 burials offer a kaleidoscope of monumental expressions and references to past and present that offer unparalleled access to communal belief and, especially in the late 7th century, to the thoughts of an inspired cadre of creative and assertive individuals. However, it is clear that in the future we will need better ways of exploring cemeteries than stumbling across them. The necessary improvements to remote mapping are nearly in reach, so that cemeteries can be sampled to address research questions and then conserved, rather than dug up at random in advance of quarries or road building. The radiocarbon dating of cremations is now possible, so the achievements of Hines and Bayliss for the 6th and 7th century could soon be extrapolated back to the 5th. The peaks of investment expressed through monumentality and their implications for the adoption of new ideology will be clarified by the new dating. A better definition of indigenous British signatures in burial rites and aDNA will help to join up the experiences of the different parts of the island and chronicle the local effects, or non-effects, of ethnic mixing. The exploration of the intellectual allegiances and their territories is perhaps the most exciting part of the future agenda. The years of negativity of the burial-means-nothing school are now behind us, but we still have to cope with the latter day saints who see Christians under every bed (burial). The discipline needs an acceptance that first-millennium belief is not divided into Christianity/not Christianity but presents a wide spectrum of ideas that has yet to break free of this binary framework. The formative is not a period of religious confusion resolved by Christian belief. It is a period of multiple intellectuality, which Christianity eventually reduced to a single world-view.

Formative 2 from ancestry to salvation

In 675–700 AD, things change in the world of British funerals. If burial is still a varied practice, there is a change in the way it varies. In Northumbria and the north and west of Britain, the monastic cemeteries reign until the Viking wars of the 9th century, when their populations and burial grounds dwindle. The subsequent homes of the local 10th–11th century dead are less well explored. The Norse Vikings brought a portfolio of their own, including weapon burial, mound burial (Heath Wood) and boat burial (Balladoole, Scar). These forms of investment merge with local practice through the 10th century, producing Anglo-Danish sequences (York Minster) and Hiberno-Norse sequences on the Isle of Man (Peel).

In Southumbria, from the 8th century, burial is thought to migrate to churchyards and minsters, although there are field cemeteries and burial within settlements too. Within these sites there is apparent uniformity of the grave, unfurnished and aligned west-east, but new research has shown that there was more individual expression than previously assumed.[248] The new type of punitive cemetery, with executions by hanging seen at Sutton Hoo, is found widely over the south-east, situated at assembly places or prehistoric landmarks.[249] England was wrested from Danish Viking control in the 10th century, when Alfred and his successors in the house of Wessex proceeded to push north and create a new English kingdom embracing East Anglia, Mercia, Northumbria and eventually the west country. But Norse control remained effective in the Irish Sea and the Western and Northern Isles. At the Norman conquest, the west and north of Britain on the one hand and the south and east on the other remained very different countries under the ground. If the burials have less to say than they did in Formative 1, their messages are nevertheless increasingly useful and often unexpected.

Formative 2 in Pictland and Scotland

By the late 7th century, barrow cemeteries and row cemeteries have had their day, and the new era in the north is dominated by the monasteries. Burial in Period 1 at in bold in Galloway, confined to the later 6th and early 7th century, was essentially a row-grave cemetery using cists and tree-trunk burials. In the early 8th century, the site took on the robes of a Northumbrian monastery. A small group of burials accompanied a possible chapel in the Glebe Field, and further north in Fey Field, head-support burials were found south of a boundary; but in its heyday of the 8th-century to the early 9th-century burial, the focus of burial had moved to the unexcavated area around the present church (Chapter 3, p. 216).[250] At Portmahomack, the privileged burial of the Fm 1 equestrian classes, in full cists under barrows on a seaside ridge within a 'cemetery-settlement', gave way to an equally privileged treatment of the new spiritual aristocracy of a monastery in Fm 2, in this case men buried using head-support and/or plain graves laid in rows. The new cemetery moved steadily east, since the first rows were laid next to the previous barrows and new rows are added inland, at a certain moment (the later 8th century) changing their orientation to reflect the arrival of a stone church. It might be argued that the rows employed by the monastic community apply an old formula to a new type of family.

In Scotland, the head-support rite, with two vertical stones either side of the head, has been so far a feature of ecclesiastical sites, beginning in the 7th century and enduring to at least the 12th.[251] As such it should be an indicator of Christian affiliation, at first restricted to professionals and latterly a sign of more widely shared devotion. The assumption is that those accorded the rights of formal burial but not buried in monastic cemeteries will be found in what are now parish churches. There is an example at Balblair to the south of Portmahomack on the Black Isle where 21 head-support burials were found along 58 excavated graves of the 11th–12th century.[252] Such contacts as have been made with 9th–12th century burial in Scotland has been on such a small scale that it would be hard to say whether they are successors to the monasteries or part of a cemetery-settlement that had endured alongside the monastic movement since the 8th century, or before and was maintained until the arrival of parish churches in the 11th century.[253] At present, the burials of the 7th–11th century, other than in monasteries, are mostly missing, presumed to be under parish churchyards.[254] A clue to the future tracking of burial through the late formative period can perhaps be found in the work of Hadley and Buckberry in England (see note 248).

Formative 2 in Northumbria

The Northumbrian sequence in the 8th century may be sampled from a number of important monastic cemeteries.[255] The proper place to start is probably **Hartlepool**, documented as founded in 640 and situated across the Tees estuary from the Street House cemetery described earlier. Hartlepool is a site of the greatest importance for early Britain, although one with a lamentable experience of archaeological investigation, especially in the matter of cemeteries.[256] Two main burial areas are known, neither published by their excavators. The one known as *Cross Close* lies adjacent to the southern seafront and was contacted during building operations in 1833, 1838, 1843, 1921 and finally by TV's *Time Team* in 1999 (Figure 4.77; and see Chapter 3, Figure 3.78). These diggings threw up 10 name slabs with crosses, incised or in low relief, and inscribed with the names of Anglo-Saxon men and women in Latin letters or runes. They are dated to the 7th or 8th century (Chapter 5, p. 528). The name slabs were given a robust reception by the townsfolk, being sold, given to museums in Durham, London and Ipswich, lost altogether or broken up and mixed with the builders' concrete.[257] One enterprising builder, noting the price the name slabs were fetching, made one himself, announced its 'discovery' in a railway-cutting at Sandy, Bedfordshire, and sold it to a lady who donated it to Bedford Museum.[258]

Okasha's penetrating analysis of the records that survive concluded that the graves were orientated N-S and arranged in rows. Skulls were reported as lying on *top* of name slabs, while other skulls lay on plain unmarked stones ('pillow stones'). This has remained a puzzle: modern authors have preferred to see the name-stones as upright grave markers or recumbent slabs so the inscriptions could be read, although it is (just) possible that the name of the buried person was intended for God alone and therefore buried intimately within the

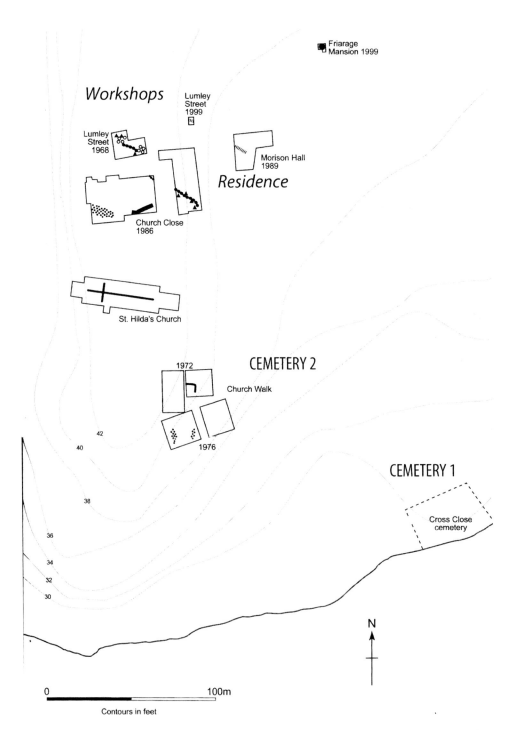

Figure 4.77 Hartlepool (Co Durham). General plan showing the locations of cemeteries at Cross Close and Church Walk.

(Daniels 2007, Fig 9.1; image courtesy of Tees Archaeology)

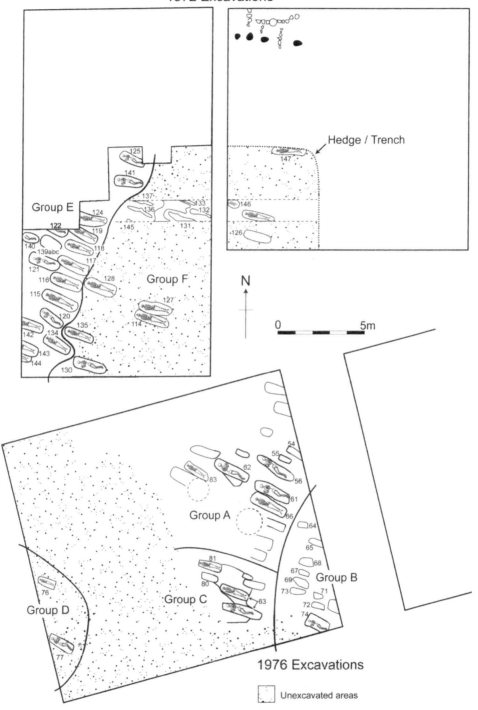

Figure 4.78 Hartlepool. Plan of the Church Walk cemetery.

(Daniels 2007, Fig 4.5; image courtesy of Tees Archaeology)

grave, like grave goods.[259] Given the nature of the investigations, the slabs may have been laid over a body, been used or reused as pillow stones or been covered by a later body. A monograph published in 2007 combined the antiquarian records with observations made in more modern times. This allowed a mapping of the locus of the cemetery, endorsed the N-S orientation, the 7th/8th-century date (from radiocarbon) and the likely presence of men, women and children.[260] None of these interventions has turned up artefacts that might imply the former presence of a furnished Anglo-Saxon cemetery of 5th–7th century date.[261] Daniels speculated that a 'long brass pin with an oblong head' found in 1833 was a square-headed brooch, but it sounds a lot more like a dress pin. Even in its garbled account, the Cross Close cemetery gives a good impression of a new cemetery founded in the later 7th century which employed traditional N-S row graves for men, women and children, as seen at Norton, but added some inventive rites inspired by the new ideology – pillow stones and recumbent slabs with crosses and Anglo-Saxon names.

The other cemetery lay inland to the north at a site known as *Church Walk*, the church in question being the present church of St Hilda. This was investigated in two areas in 1972 and 1976 (Figure 4.78).[262] Thirty-four individuals from the 1972 area and 54 from the 1976 area were analysed. Men, women and children were all present, in normal proportions: of those identified 27 were men, 12 women and 34 children; death was most frequent for women of child-bearing age (the 18–35 bracket) and for middle-aged men.[263] The distribution as encountered was uneven and divided into six somewhat arbitrary groups. It was noted that there was a majority of men in Groups E and F and of children in Group B in the south-east, while the enigmatic Group D in the west produced two graves edged with cobbles, probably at ground level (as Viking graves; see p. 419). Attempts have been made by various authors to confine the burials to male, female and juvenile sectors in homage to the documented presence of an early nunnery, but given the limited character of the excavation, its non-publication and the absence of a located church, the figures are hardly numerically or spatially significant.[264] There were no name-stones or pillow stones at Church Walk. However, here, as at Cross Close, the cemetery was the first activity on the site. The form of the settlement and its activities, including burial, was proposed in the 2007 overview (see also Chapter 3, p. 218).[265]

The identity of Hartlepool as a monastery founded in 646, reported by Bede (*HE* IV, 23), is supported by the 10 name slabs and endorsed by the workshops, where moulds were found for making an image of a ribbon animal and a trumpeting St Luke.[266] The burials as so far known represent a community of men, women and children with no convincing separation of the sexes, using some local practice (N-S orientation) but no Anglo-Saxon grave goods. The mixture is striking, but the 7th was an eventful and inventive century. One suggested explanation has been the presence of a British contingent implied by the N-S orientation and some flexed burials.[267] However, the British signature is not strong at Hartlepool, compared with the Anglo-Saxon branding of the name-stones. Both cemeteries actually present a credible picture of the first century of the monastic era, when the use of grave goods disappears suddenly and successors adopting a new ideology have a free hand to devise suitable successor rites, in this case perhaps opposed by equally inventive reactionaries on the hill at Street House. Both communities were apparently led by women, roles in keeping with their Scandinavian and especially their Swedish colleagues during a period of ideological challenge.[268]

The response of the lower Tees valley to the white heat of the conversion period was certainly precocious and individual, and we shall surely be digging up other inventive confrontations elsewhere. By contrast, **Wearmouth and Jarrow** belong to the fully fledged monastic movement and have some qualifications for being seen as its point of origin. The two sites, described as a paired monastery by Bede, were investigated by Rosemary Cramp in a targeted research programme on site between 1959 and 1988 and fully published in 2005.[269] Both sites were constructed on estuaries on new ground that had no prehistoric or Roman predecessor, apart from some cultivation.[270] At both sites there were indications that some burials may have preceded some parts of the original church, but the spatial patterns generally suggest that church and burial ground were used together.[271]

At **Wearmouth** the remains of 417 individuals of the 7th century and later were recovered, of which 168 were undisturbed, although preservation was poor (Figure 4.79). They were buried in plain earth graves with their feet to the east, some in segmented rows with the heads aligned along a northing. Out of 117 bodies whose position could be determined, 30 (25.6%) were supine, 79 (76.5%) were on their right side, six were prone and three

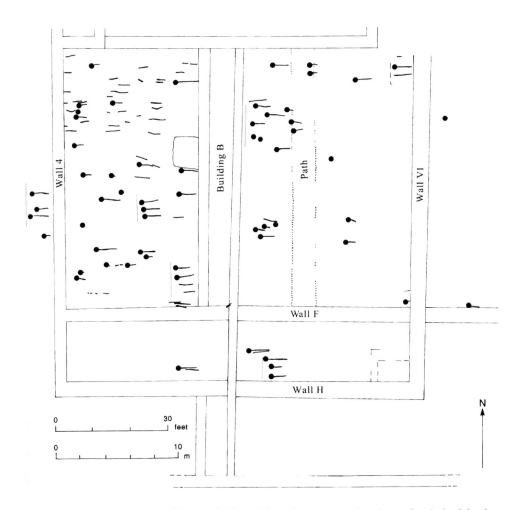

Figure 4.79 Monkwearmouth (Tyne and Wear). Monastic cemetery: locations of early burials, dug before the collapse of the Fm 2 buildings with lines indicating possible family groups.

(Extract of Cramp 2005, Fig 8.3; original image courtesy of Rosemary Cramp)

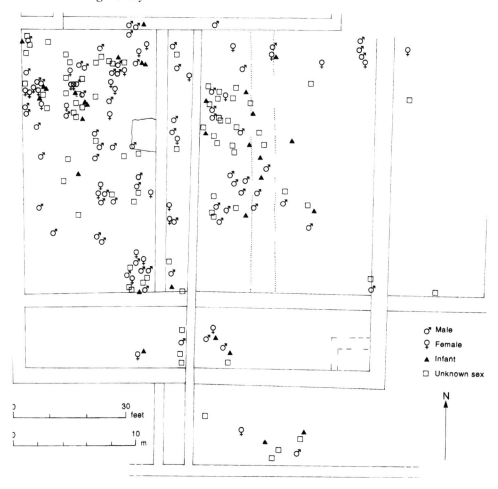

Figure 4.80 Monkwearmouth monastic cemetery showing distribution of men, women and children. (Cramp 2005, Fig 8.18; courtesy of Rosemary Cramp)

were crouched. The sex ratio was 63.6% male to 36.4% female, and there was some spatial emphasis, with the women mainly to the west and the men to the east, separated by a covered walkway ('Building B') (Figure 4.80). Many of the children were also buried on the east side; they may represent boys recruited to the monastery. Datable objects associated with burial were rare: three coins, one Roman and two Saxon; parts of a horse and boars' tusk may have come from disturbed burials. A piece of gold thread near a skull should have come from a veil, and the pins were most likely to have fastened shrouds. There were many coffins implied by fittings and wood stains. None of the name-stones at Wearmouth was found with a skeleton, but one plain headstone accompanied a grave cut through a mortar mixer assigned to the building of the first church of St Peter (Structure A). There were no cist burials, but 21 graves had deliberately placed stones outlining parts of the body, and four skulls rested on stone pillows. A group of flat stones laid in a square marked the position of five burials, two males and three juveniles.[272]

At **Jarrow**, 132 articulated burials in plain earth graves with the feet to the east were identified as Anglo-Saxon by their stratification, although here too the bones were poorly preserved. Most lay in the spaces between the church of St Paul and the monastic buildings aligned with it (Buildings A and B), although cut away by the foundations of the later medieval monastery; Figure 4.81). Of the 55 sexed adults, 64% were male and 36% female. Men, women and juveniles were intermingled in the cemetery. All the body positions were extended, either supine or on the right side, half in half; three were identified as prone. There were some indications of coffins and eight examples of deliberately placed stones, including one pillow stone and one head box which could be pre-Norman.[273] The graves were essentially unfurnished. A single polychrome bead was found in two graves, and other residual beads may have originally been worn on a body; these are likely to refer to items of dress. Other material in backfill was probably secondary: shells, pottery, window glass, plaster. There were hints of N-S segmented rows, but the excavation areas were interrupted by the walls of the later medieval monastery. However, nine examples of superpositioning and the occurrence of men and women and sometimes children together reinforce the idea of the use of family lines, as already observed from Cannington to Hallow Hill and at Hartlepool. Some additional formal zoning was inferred from the stratification. Burials south of St Paul's chancel (east) experienced less intercutting as compared with areas to the west, where burial sequences were longer. This might imply a zone of privilege opposite the midpoint of St Paul's church, with family plots outside it.[274]

Neither at Monkwearmouth nor Jarrow does the burial record show marked signs of sexual segregation nor of discrimination by rank, although the name slabs imply that some of the deceased had earned special celebration. The main signs of a persistent social practice are the segmentary rows, which seem to indicate family areas and the presence of men, women and children at both sites. Traces of indigenous practice can be seen at Wearmouth, with some use of stone inserts and possible objects placed in graves. The small numbers become smaller still at Jarrow. In general the strict orientation, the replacement of any prehistoric focus by a church, the plain unprotected graves and the near total absence of grave goods illustrate a

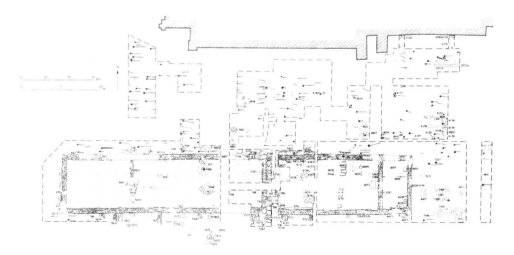

Figure 4.81 Jarrow (Tyne and Wear). Monastic cemetery and other Anglo-Saxon features.
(Cramp 2005, Fig 16.4; courtesy of Rosemary Cramp)

new departure in which people abandon allegiance to their land, ancestry and advertised self-worth in order to embrace sanctity and salvation. But they may still do this in families.

Formative 3

Estate cemeteries

In *Formative 2*, the late 7th to 9th century, we encountered the new world of 'thinking burial' most vividly in the monasteries of the north: Hartlepool, Wearmouth, Jarrow and Portmahomack. There should be a cognate series in English monasteries, but so far these sites seem to exist largely on paper in the pre-Viking period, and there are no large systematically excavated monastic cemeteries in Southumbria that have also been published.[275] At the time of writing the contrast between the excavated monasteries of Northumbria, Scotland and Ireland and the putative monastic movement in England, assuming there was one, is sharp. We do however have a number of field cemeteries and churchyard cemeteries (Raunds) which may originate as early as the 8th century.

In the 9th and 10th century the Vikings occupied parts of Britain that served their missions of colonisation and wealth creation, specifically in the northern isles and the Irish Sea for the Norse and in eastern Britain for the Danes. Another factor is that, as so far observed, there is a smoothing of differences between the regions, even if a new generation is showing us that the Late Formative burial rite contains much variety.

North and west

In Formative 2, the best-known burial sites in the north and west of Britain are currently those identified as monastic, for example, Portmahomack in Pictland or Llandough in Wales. The degree to which burial continued in these places after the 9th century is uncertain, although additional radiocarbon dates may lengthen their period of use, or identify reuse (see Period 3 at Portmahomack). At some stage the rite of burial may have been transferred to parish churches operating in the 10th and 11th centuries. But this is unlikely to be the whole story, since the degree of episcopal control will surely vary from place to place for the rest of the millennium. David Wilson summarised the situation as it applies to Britain before the 10th century like this:

> It must be stressed that at the beginning of the Viking Age, there was no such thing as consecrated Christian burial grounds in the rural areas of north-west Europe. The dead in all rural areas were buried either in a family cemetery (or a cemetery reserved for the community) by the family itself, probably without the assistance from the clergy and in almost every case without the benefit of an ecclesiastical building. Gradually this changed, and by the tenth century in much of Anglo-Saxon England, for instance, the presence of the clergy at burials became increasingly obligatory and cemeteries began to be consecrated.[276]

Such churchless and unfurnished rural burial grounds are hard to find, but the chance finds of rescue archaeology, driven by a new sensitivity to the interest of cemeteries without grave goods, means that the corpus is increasing in size. Rescue work at the Althea Library in **Padstow** in Cornwall exposed 17 graves in two rows. All were lined and capped with slate. There was no church, but the burials seem to focus radially on something still hidden to the south.[277] Three radiocarbon dates lay in the 8th–9th century. It is possible that what was contacted here is a monastic cemetery, typical of the north and west of Britain in the 7th–9th century, as at Jarrow or Llandough (p. 363). But equally it may be a chance encounter with a traditional burial ground using cists not associated specifically with Christianity or any religion and not now very noticeable in the ground. The large number of cemetery-settlements now revealed by the Irish road schemes encourages the view that these ritually neutral resting places were the norm, while deposition in monastic establishments was reserved for the privileged (Chapter 6, p. 515). The cist grave is no longer reliable as a signal of Christian belief. At Padstow, the lining of burials with slate goes back to the Iron Age, 1,000 years earlier, as seen in the neighbouring site at Harlyn Bay (p. 345).

Vikings

In burial, as in sculpture, the more visible aspects of Formative 3 monumentality were provided by the Vikings, who reintroduced the colonising of prehistoric burial, monumental mound burial, boat burial, a new type of stone-edged grave and gendered grave goods. A tally of culturally Viking graves published in 2007 showed a distribution focused on the northern and western archipelago, from Shetland to the Isle of Man, presumably with Norse affiliation, and on the rivers of the Humber, The Wash and the Thames, presumably Danish in affiliation (Figure 4.82).[278] Its author, Stephen Harrison, tries to wean us from seeing these

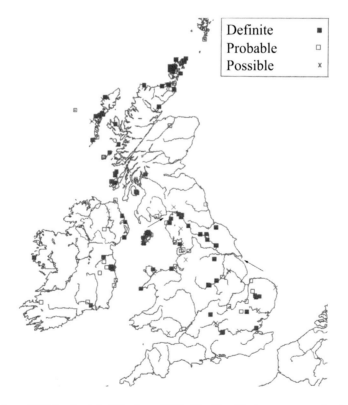

Figure 4.82 Map of Viking burials (Harrison 2007, Fig 1) with the current author's hypothetical 'Humber-Solway' linkway indicated by arrows.

(Map courtesy of Stephen Harrison)

monuments as marking sea routes as opposed to central places commanding territory. However, 113 of the 176 sites collected are on the coast, and, of these, 73% are situated close to the ends of beaches or on flanking promontories. While only three of the 35 sites in the eastern English area are on the coast, most of the others are on lowland sites and in reach of rivers. Of particular interest is the cross-country trail of burials that seems to connect east with west: it runs from the Humber to the Ouse, thence to the Ure to the Eden and to the Solway. The watershed between the sources of the Ure and the Eden at Great Shunner Fell is less than 1 km long (see also Figure 5.59, where the same route is marked by sculpture). There are some grounds for thinking that whatever the local control exercised (surely variable), the more visible burial monuments served as route finders and trail-claimers, as the Anglian grand crosses had before them (p. 529). In the interests of visibility, if not as acts of homage, legitimation, ancestral association or spiritual alignment, the Vikings commandeered prehistoric tombs, barrows, standing stones, burnt mounds and brochs (18%), especially in the north, or continued previous early medieval cemeteries, especially in the east (36%).[279]

Following the sea road from Orkney to the Isle of Man will give us a feel for the way the Vikings marked their maritime route, laying down a trail of monumental burials celebrating key figures, who though dead helped their descendants keep faith with each other and with their mission. Unfortunately, these monuments, mainly mounds, have been gnawed by the sea and attracted the attention of much serendipitous fossicking. Let's begin at the **Westness** cemetery on a promontory on the coast of Rousay, Orkney, discovered in 1963 when a farmer was burying a cow. Thirty-two graves were subsequently excavated by the Norwegian archaeologist Sigrid Kaland between 1968 and 1984. Of these, 16 were unfurnished, occasionally slab-lined and marked by headstones, and eight contained grave goods of the Viking period. Radiocarbon dating implied that the cemetery was in use from the 7th century to the 9th and was therefore a Pictish burial ground, probably Christian given the headstones, superseded in the 9th century by Vikings. At the time of writing (2016, 32 years later) the excavation remains unpublished, but it is known that the site included two burials in wooden boats, one a warrior with sword and shield, while others were in small boat-shaped stone settings. The grave of an important woman, the one that had led to the discovery of the cemetery in 1963, had contained a tortoise brooch, a bead necklace, two 9th-century Anglo-Saxon silver strap-ends and an 8th-century Irish silver brooch pin with gold filigree decoration.[280]

The boat burial at **Scar** on Sanday was rescued by modern archaeologists from the sea edge after half of it had been swept away; the remaining half was excavated and studied in 1991 (Figure 4.83).[281] The 7.15 m long clinker-built boat, originally of oak, contained a woman aged about 70, a man of about 30 and a child of about 10. The man lay at the prow with a sword, shield, a quiver with eight arrows and a battle axe either side of him, and a gaming board and a bag of playing pieces at his feet. The elderly woman and the child lay side by side towards the stern. The woman wore a rare and magnificent gilded equal-arm brooch and had a casket by her side containing a weaving and sewing kit and a small sickle. At her feet was a whalebone plaque with a smooth surface, possibly intended to press linen like an ironing board. The east end at her feet was filled with stone ballast.

The western isles continue the theme of mounds and boats. At **Cnip** headland on the Isle of Lewis, Viking Age graves joined earlier Bronze Age cairns and cist burials.[282] Edges of stone blocks were placed around three grave pits at ground level, marking the graves after backfilling. **Carn a'Bharraich**, 'Cairn of the men of Barra', lies in the dunes on the east coast of Oronsay. Explored intermittently with varied precision in the 19th and early 20th century, it appeared to consist of a man and women laid to rest in a mound on the remains of a burnt clinker-built boat. The woman wore oval 'tortoise' brooches of early type, and

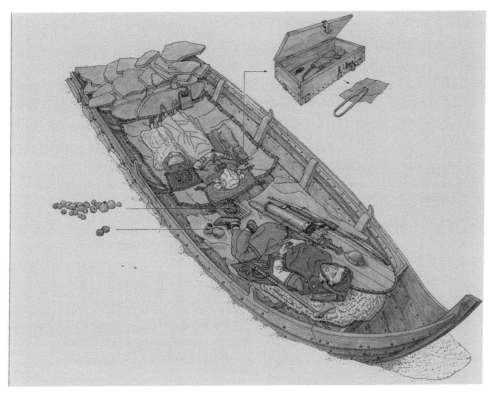

Figure 4.83 The Viking boat grave at Scar (Sanday, Orkney).

(Owen 1999, 30 reconstruction by Christina Unwin; reproduced with permission of the author and Historic Environment Scotland)

her cloak was fastened with a native-type Irish pin. The secondary burial of another woman seems to have been made at the edge of the mound, perhaps a generation later, but still within the 'raiding period': her dress was fastened with two brooches contrived from decorated pieces stripped off a house-shaped reliquary.[283] The grave opened at **Kiloran Bay** on Colonsay was lined with stones, apparently set upright, as in a cist grave. The burial was of a man accompanied by a sword with a silver-inlaid pommel, an axe, spear, shield, arrows and pair of scales with pans and lead weights. His horse was buried in an adjacent pit. A large number of ship rivets (i.e. clench nails) was recovered from the immediate area of the man and the horse, suggesting that both had been inside, or covered by, a boat.[284]

So we arrive at the Isle of Man, pivot point of the northern Irish Sea, around or through which all traffic will pass. The Vikings arrived there about 900 AD and have left at least four monumental mounds, at Ballateare, Cronk Moar, Ballachrink and Knock y Doon.[285] The boat burial at **Balladoole** at the south end of Man excavated by Gerhard Bersu (in 1944–46) may also have been covered with a mound (Figure 4.84). It contained the skeleton of a man laid in a clinker-built boat c. 11 m long set within a kerb of large stones capped with smaller stones. His costume and effects consisted of a shield represented by its grip and a conical boss, 2–3 knives, a hone, a flint strike, a light, a belt and a ring-headed pin of Irish type to fasten his cloak. With him in the grave were a horse's bridle and saddle with gilt bronze mounts and some of the earliest stirrups to reach Britain, closely paralleled by examples from France and

Figure 4.84 The early medieval cemetery at Balladoole, Isle of Man.

(Wilson 2008, Fig 14; courtesy of David Wilson and Manx National Heritage; © Manx National Heritage)

Moravia. The horse and boat conferred status in life and in death provided a metaphor for travel to the next world.[286] The construction of the boat grave had disturbed 17 or more cist graves oriented east-west and set in two rows (Figure 4.85). These were probably part of a larger 6th–9th-century cist grave cemetery that was established on the hill. It is possible that the Vikings had attempted some kind of legitimation or spiritual conquest but more likely that they wished to occupy the same vantage point.[287]

The sequence on St Patrick's Isle, **Peel**, offers a similar vignette of the passage of power (Figure 4.86). On this landmark site there was a cemetery of cist graves dated to c. 500–900 by radiocarbon. It was succeeded by Viking graves dated to 900–950 by coins and other artefacts. This was followed in turn by a 'conversion period' cemetery, dated to the late 10th century by radiocarbon. The cemetery continued in use through the 11th to the 13th century. The Viking presence was represented by seven graves accompanied by 10th-century objects: there was one adult male and one adult female in lintel graves, one adult and one child in nailed coffins, and two adults and one child, uncoffined. The female adult in a full lintel grave was one of the richest 10th-century woman's graves known from in the Norse world outside Scandinavia (the so-called 'Pagan Lady' (Figure 4.87).[288] She was middle-aged, bow legged and 1.65 m tall. Her accoutrements consisted of a work bag or pouch containing two needles (OV on plan], a necklace of 71 beads with pendant (chin), a pendant of two amber

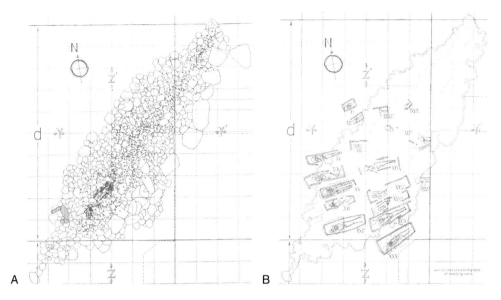

A   B

Figure 4.85 A: Viking cairn with ship rivets. B: Cist graves in the phase previous to the Viking ship grave.

(Bersu and Wilson 1966, Fig 4, 5; courtesy of David Wilson and Manx National Heritage)

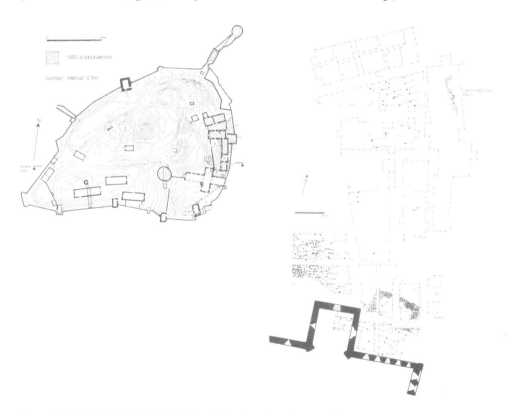

Figure 4.86 Peel, St Patrick's Isle, Isle of Man: location of excavations.

(Freke 2002, Fig 15; with permission)

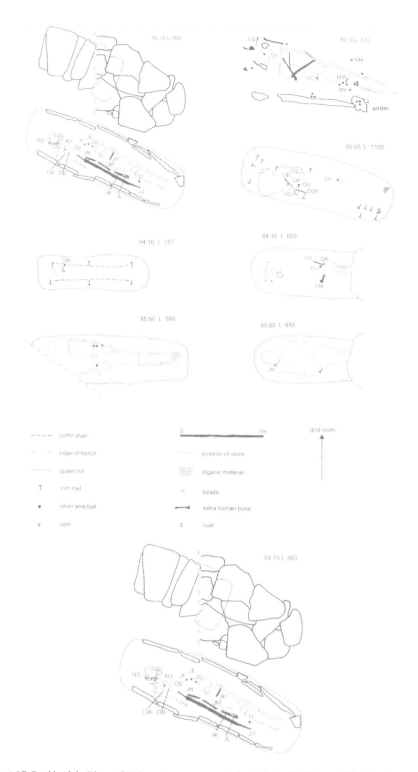

Figure 4.87 Peel burials. Plans of 10th century graves and (below) detail of Grave 483, 'The Pagan Lady'.
(Freke 2002, Fig 19, 20; with permission)

beads and a pierced ammonite (JE, JF, JG), an iron knife with a silver wire-inlaid handle and scabbard ([JM, JP]), an iron knife with wooden handle (JN), bone comb (JL), iron shears (JK), iron cooking spit (JJ) and a pillow with feathers (NS).

The man (in lintel grave 420) had a ring-headed pin and a buckle decorated with interlace, and he was wrapped in a cloak with at least 18 decorated silver wire balls (tassels) fastened with a ring-headed pin and a buckle. There was coin of Eadmund, 939–46. Disarticulated bones had been arranged over the corpse: two femurs and a tibia lay across the chest, and fragmentary arm bones framed the head. Although the burial rites changed, the cemetery was managed as a continuing concern. This was the excavator's verdict:

> the community on St Patrick's Isle seems to have lasted without a break throughout the Iron Age into the first millennium AD. . . . There were at least six episodes of construction . . . with no layers . . . which could be interpreted as turf lines which had developed over an abandoned settlement.[289]

The Danish impact on burial has been studied at few sites in the Danelaw. The barrow cemetery at **Heath Wood, Ingleby**, represents (so far) the only known Viking cremation cemetery in Britain.[290] The barrows stand on a promontory at the 100 m contour overlooking the River Trent (Figure 4.88). North-east is the village of Ingleby by the river, and a few miles to the west is Repton, where the Viking army wintered in 873–4.[291] In the late 9th century there should have been intervisibility between the Heath Wood barrows and the church of St Wystan at Repton on the flood plain.

There was some prehistoric agricultural activity on the promontory, but no prehistoric monument has been defined that might have served as an attraction. The site has up to 60 barrows, many of which had been trenched in antiquarian times. The recent professional area excavations (1998–2000) showed that some mounds had covered the remains of a pyre, spread across the base, while others covered a small sample of cremated material retrieved from a pyre elsewhere. Based on 16 controlled excavations, the ratio of pyre to 'token' barrows is about 1:2. Mounds were built by digging out a circular quarry ditch and piling the spoil within, leaving two or more causeways to assist in loading. The original grave goods were mainly destroyed on the pyre, but from some mounds there were diagnostic fragments of swords, shields, knives, personal ornaments and dress fittings. There were traces of fittings that could be attributed to chests or biers but not of boats. Mound 50 had covered a pyre in which were identified the remains of a possible female and juvenile, numerous nails and iron fittings and a fragment from a sword-hilt, together with a mass of animal bone including a horse and a dog and parts of pig, sheep and possibly ox. The cemetery as a whole dates to the late 9th and early 10th century. Julian Richards finds the burial rites of the Heath Wood Barrow cemetery appropriate for burial of members of the Viking Great Army.[292]

But the Vikings may also have invested ritual activity of some kind at the Mercian church of St Wystan at Repton, down by the river. Here was excavated a mass grave of at least 264 individuals, mostly male, stacked within a pre-existing building, perhaps in origin a Mercian mausoleum. The bone deposit had apparently been closed with the sacrifice of four young men and covered by a barrow.[293] Recent recalibration of the radiocarbon dating has indicated that the charnel was deposited in the late 9th century, so could be a spectacular Viking grave and a memorial of the campaign of the Great Army that overwintered there in 873.[294]

A sequence of 242 burials excavated around a medieval chapel at **Auldhame** in East Lothian provides a useful case study of a rural estate cemetery in the Fm 3 north. Divided into four phases by radiocarbon dating, the 18 burials assigned to Phase 1 (bracketed between

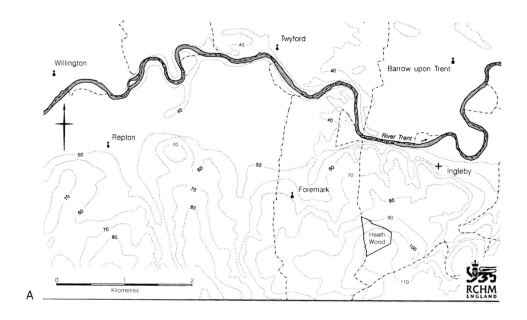

A

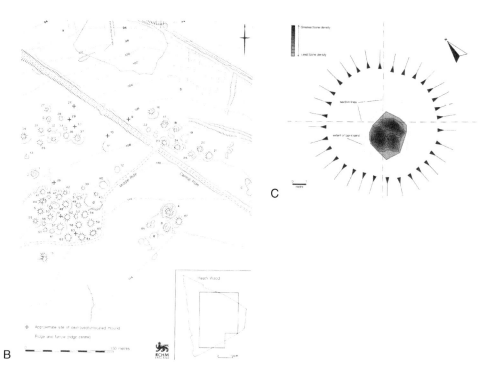

B

C

Figure 4.88 Ingleby (Derbyshire), the Viking cemetery. A: Promontories south of the Trent, showing the relative position of Ingleby, Heath Wood and Repton. B: Plan of the cemetery. C: Mound 50 showing the density of cremated bone.

(Drawing by Marcus Jecock; Richards 2004, Figs 1, 15, 21; images licensed by Historic England)

650 and 1000 AD) belonged to a community of men, women and children of local origin, all buried simply without coffins or stone linings. The one furnished grave was that of a Viking, with spear, belt-set and spurs. A large assemblage of animal bones, mainly cattle and sheep, was also radiocarbon-dated to Phase 1 and showed that the cemetery had served a settlement. A curving ditch provided its possible boundary, and the Phase 1 assemblage included a gilt bronze stud, fragments of a glass inkwell, a possible stylus (SF 356, described as a pin) and two socketed stones. A slot belonging to an earlier timber building, and stone foundations were discerned beneath the medieval chapel (but could not be confirmed by excavation due to constraints of conservation). The settlement and cemetery belonged to a mainly local community farming cattle, visited by Vikings and in touch with Northumbria. Its interpretation as an 'Anglian monastery' was fairly inferential but recalls the ambiguous versions of monasticism south of the Humber.[295] A nearer parallel is probably offered by the cemetery-settlements of Ireland or the estate churches of the south, as at Raunds (see below).

In the south

Open cemeteries that lacked grave goods and diagnostic buildings are archaeologically elusive, but it seems likely that they were very numerous between the 8th and 10th centuries, serving communities who were at least Christian in name. In this they resemble the cemetery-settlements of Ireland, which include dedicated graveyards in the settlements but no churches (p. 436). The Southumbrian examples are not inside contemporary settlements (as far we know): they have been discovered within prehistoric or Roman enclosures or early medieval bounded fields. These are likely to have been dedicated by a nearby settlement for the purpose and at times in the 8th/9th century, determined by radiocarbon dating.[296] The change came in the 10th century, when communities acquired stone parish churches (that have survived). The burial of the conformists was pulled into a 'churchyard', and soul-scot (a death tax) became payable at the graveside. Grenville Astill has explained how this development accompanied the emergence of a minor aristocracy (of thegns) and their creation of numerous manorial estates with proprietary churches, at a time when the gravitational pull of the regional minsters or mother churches was weakening.[297]

Raunds Furnells provides one of the few large-scale windows on a late first-millennium rural cemetery in the English area. The sequence begins with a small single-cell church 5.5 m long placed just outside the enclosure of an eventual manor house, some miles from the village of Raunds, no doubt intended to serve the occupants of a magnate farm (Figure 4.89). It shortly acquires a stubby chancel and begins to exercise the right of burial, probably initiated by a high-investment grave with a decorated grave cover and standing cross in its own plot at the east end, the so-called founder grave ('F' on Figure 4.90). Burials then accumulate in a progression that was well-documented by an ingenious excavator.[298] The first graves, laid out in short straight rows, occupy a band around the four sides of the church, extending 9 m north and south and 5–6.5 m east and west (Zone 1). Men and women have equal presence here. Subsequently, the exclusion area is filled in, especially with infants and children, who are preferentially sited under the eaves and west gable of the church (Zone 1B). Expansion then takes place to the east (Zone 2) and the west (Zone 3), with the groupings defined by more sinuous rows. Zone 4 represents an overspill to the east and Zone 5 an overspill to the south-east.[299] The rows, probably family groups here as elsewhere, are filled in piecemeal as the generations of a family succeed each other. Altogether 361 burials were excavated, nine samples taken from Zone 1 suggesting an overall time span of c. 978–1040. The ceramic assemblage gave

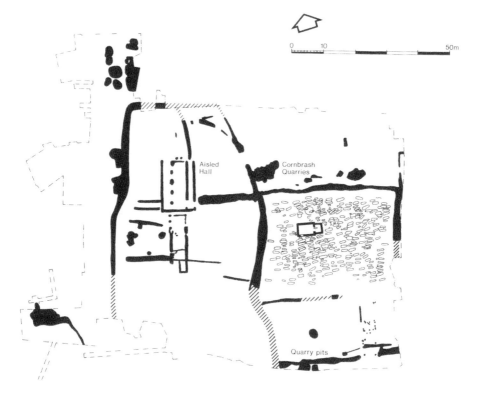

Figure 4.89 Raunds Furnells (Northamptonshire). The Fm 3 manor, church and cemetery.

(Boddington 1996, Fig 3; image licensed by Historic England)

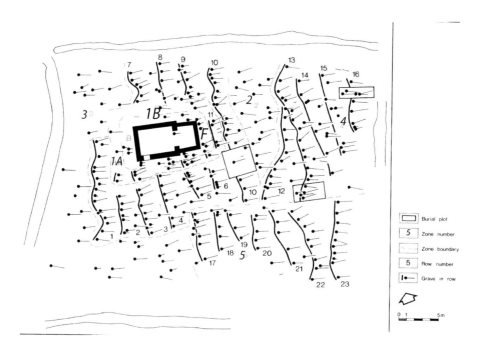

Figure 4.90 Raunds Furnells: development of the cemetery, showing the chapel, location of the founder grave (F), the early burials (ZONE 1, around the church) the children's area (1B) and subsequent zones with family rows marked.

(Boddington 1996, Fig 66; Historic England; image licensed by Historic England)

a likely date of the late 9th/early 10th century for the construction of the church, a mid-10th-century date for the addition of the chancel and the beginning of burial, and a late 11th to mid-12th-century date for the demolition of the first church and the construction of a second, four times the size. The change of regime after the Conquest was accentuated by the reuse of the shaft of the late Anglo-Saxon founder grave as a door jamb in the Norman church. At this point, burial ceases in the manor churchyard.[300]

During its life the cemetery served a population of around 40 persons, half of them children, implying that this was a private church particular to a leading family, their relatives and servants. The villagers were buried elsewhere. Standing upright and shoulder to shoulder, 20 adults could just about fit into the nave. The levels of investment in burial indicate that a class system was in operation. Those with highest status had a stone marker, stone or wooden coffins or a stone grave-slab and congregate nearest the church. The next tier down have uncut stone pieces lining the grave, graduated from all-over coverage to the insertion of a small stone about the head that is barely more than a token. Others have sewn shrouds, implied by the tight straight-sided posture of the body.

Revisiting the Raunds population, Elizabeth Craig and Jo Buckberry obtained a good correlation between reduced stress indicators (cribra orbitalia/tibial periostitis) and high-status indicators (graves with stone covers or coffins). Graves employing coffins or stone covers clustered near the church or south of it, showed fewer signs of stress in life. These also occupy the earliest part of the cemetery, implying that the founder's family and descendants were those initially favoured. Graves with no status indicators or with token stone inserts had high levels of stress and trended to the south-east corner of the churchyard, furthest from the church (Zone 5).[301]

These and other current studies triggered by Raunds have put paid to the idea that Christian burial was the great leveller, presenting everyone in death as equal before God. In a way, this row cemetery is focused more nearly on the ancestors in the manner of British Formative 1 than on the salvation offered by the monasteries of Northumbria. Although the language has changed and was more muted than the heroic burial mound, the rare survivals of carved stone monuments, the investments in coffins of wood and stone and the relative health of a well-fed life crystalised in the bones show that social stratification was alive and kicking in the 9th–11th-century England.

The parish church graveyard has been the traditional resting place for the English from the 8th century until today; but as so often, the Formative period has several tricks up its sleeve. Dawn Hadley has led the charge for the rehabilitation of the 9th–11th century cemetery as a highly informative social entity, emphasising the variety of burial forms and the widening range of places in which they are found. In addition to parish graveyards, there are 'field cemeteries' without any churches, execution cemeteries and burials within settlements at sites that at first sight seem random.[302] In addition to the expected mode of burial in a shroud in plain earth, burial under a slab, in a sarcophagus, in a coffin, burial with stone inclusions, charcoal burial and execution burial provide a varied repertoire that implies a consequent variety of social meaning.

The 9th–11th-century cemetery under **York Minster** and over the Roman legionary fortress is one of the few where stone memorials survive in situ with those they commemorated (Figure 4.91, and see Chapter 5, p. 554 for sculpture). There was one stone coffin or sarcophagus (Burial 55), which contained the mixed remains of four individuals, and nine flat decorated slabs (recumbent grave covers) laid over graves in situ with small upright marker stones at either end (Figure 5.67). One grave cover carried the ghost of a Roman inscription, but all the slabs were probably conjured from Roman memorials or masonry. All

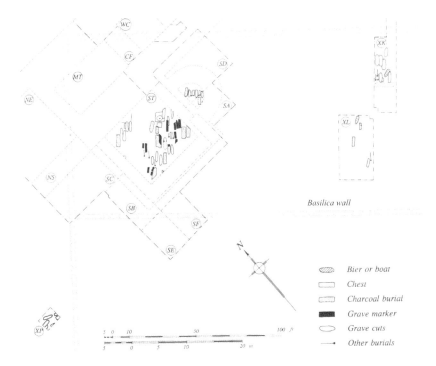

Figure 4.91 York Minster. Fm 3 graves in relation to the south transept of the Norman cathedral
church.

(Phillips and Heywood 1995, Fig 14; image licensed by Historic England)

the burials were aligned with the Roman principia (NE-SW), the stub walls of which were
presumably standing.[303] Jim Lang felt that earlier Anglo-Scandinavian memorials were here
being recycled, so that the ornamental grave covers (9th/10thc) are earlier than the burials
(10th/11th – i.e. the latest before the Norman minster was built).[304] Similar grave covers
have been recovered from elsewhere in the City of York (e.g. All Saints Pavement, St Mary
Bishophill Junior, St Denys, St Olave). Dawn Hadley cites three Late Saxon *sarcophagi*: at
Wirksworth, South Kyme and St Alkmund,[305] but of these, Wirksworth is a grave cover and
South Kyme consists of parts of an 8th-century slab-shrine. St Alkmund is a true sarcophagus – hollowed-out base and fragment of slab lid.[306] The recently discovered 11th-century
stone sarcophagus excavated at Lincoln Castle was intact with its lid and contained the skeleton of a man wearing leather shoes (Figure 4.92).[307]

  Winchester will eventually provide an outstanding case study of the sequence of burial in
a town, although it is currently only known in outline.[308] More than 1,000 graves are known
from the late Roman period outside the city gates. At Lankhills, the burials started in the
early 4th century and were marked and laid in rows, moving from west to east. Two sets
of intrusive graves were assigned to Hungarian and possibly Anglo-Saxon incomers (dated
350–410 and 390–410 respectively).[309] From the 7th century, well-furnished graves appeared
in positions that were probably significant: a richly dressed woman under an Anglo-Saxon
stone building at Lower Brook Street, two from the early 8th century outside the South
Gate. Burial at the Old Minster is thought to have begun in c. 673, when it was designated

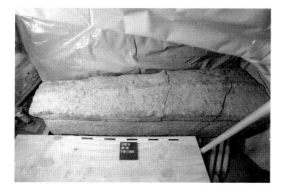

Figure 4.92 Lincoln Castle, 10th/11th century cemetery. Excavation of an intact sealed sarcophagus. For comparison (right), a coped grave cover of the 11th century encountered in the excavations under York Minster.

(*Corpus* III, no 44, Ill 184; FAS Heritage)

as the episcopal church, and soon exercised the sole right of burial. Preliminary analysis has divided this large cemetery into 22 phases or 'generations' reckoned as lasting 25 years each up to 800 AD (Generations 1–6) and 20 years thereafter. It initially served a community estimated at 650 persons. There were no coffins before the 9th century, but by Generation 7 (810–830) 40% had them, men dominating. In Generation 9 (c. 850–870) they began to be bound with iron strips. Charcoal burials appeared in the 9th century, and numbers increased during the 10th and 11th. These were all men until the mid-10th century, after which they were joined by some women. The Old Minster cemetery continued as the sole burial place until the 16th century, when once more burial migrated outside the city walls.[310]

As can be seen, high-status burial treatment in this period favours males. The most expensive looking wooden coffins are iron-bound or reused chests with keys and padlocks, as found at York Minster.[311] The 10th-century examples of such coffins at St Oswald's Gloucester were located very close to the church and were used by eight men but only one woman. The 16 burials clustered near the supposed grave of St Swithun at Winchester were mainly males.

Charcoal burials also declare status, and all those at Winchester for which sex could be determined were adult males.[312] Here the corpse or coffin is laid on or in a layer of charcoal, which needs to be distinguished in the ground from a carbonised coffin base or a tree-trunk burial, things that can leave a comparable deposit of rich dark matter. In burials so distinguished, the charcoal may be found under the coffin or packed around it as at Old Minster, Winchester, or on top of the coffin, as in some of the burials at York Minster and St Mary Major, Exeter.[313] In some cases the corpse is encased in charcoal, without a coffin, as St Helen's on the Walls York.[314] Charcoal layers have been found in thicknesses varying from 5 to 15 cm.[315] Some examples also had head-support stone inserts as at Hereford, and at Winchester there was a correlation between the use of charcoal and elaborate coffins with iron fittings at both the Old and New Minsters.[316] Over 300 hundred charcoal burials have been excavated, about 20 of which have been radiocarbon-dated, placing them in the 9th–11th century. They occur predominately in high-status urban minsters and are themselves generally high-status graves, using specially prepared charcoal.[317] The geographical distribution is very particular: they are almost absent from the English heartlands in East Anglia and Kent, but present in Northumbria, Mercia, Wessex and the south-west, in effect a 'Border region' distribution (Figure 4.93). This implies that their adoption in Late Formative Britain is not likely to be owed to an English initiative. The Viking link is more equivocal, since although absent from East Anglia, examples of charcoal burials have been found in Lund (Sweden) and the Viking town of Waterford.[318]

The most often repeated explanation for the rite is that the charcoal is an attempt, practical or metaphorical, to preserve the corpse in a pure form suitable for its resurrection at the last trumpet. Its preservative properties were observed by Sir Thomas Browne: 'Common tombs preserve not beyond powder: a firmer consistence and compaction of parts might be expected from arefaction, deep buriall or charcoal'.[319] Some archaeological support for this idea is given by the sequence of late Formative prelates excavated in the Chapter House at Durham in the 19th century, five of whom were charcoal burials.[320] Round-headed (Norman) skulls were there said to have succeeded long-headed (Anglian) skulls: the first of the latter being Ranulph Flambard (1099–1128), who was laid on a bed of charcoal. A successor (Geoffrey) was disembowelled and preserved in salt. These measures were probably deemed locally appropriate thanks to the influence of the cult of the incorruptible Saint Cuthbert, also buried in Durham Cathedral. The interesting distribution might prompt a search for a wider origin, less based on Christian theology, which after all was no less powerful in the Anglo-Saxon south-east, and more on the high-status burial rites of the Border zone, celebrating priesthood or knighthood. Unfortunately, these are little known as yet but are unlikely to include cremation.

These grand burials with their special containers and stone memorials may be found at private churches such as that at Raunds Furnells but more frequently near the major minster churches. They are usually taken to be high-ranking secular individuals, but it is likely that some commemorate (equally aristocratic) clerics, as at Durham. Sliding down the social scale a notch or two, to the minster church of St Peter's at **Barton-upon-Humber**, we have a well-preserved, well-excavated cemetery featuring wooden coffins with and without nails, planks supported by stone packing, stone slabs protecting the head and small stones added in the head area (Figure 4.94).[321] As demonstrated at Raunds, this latter rite was the bottom of the heap, always excepting the burial in plain earth containing nothing but body and soul. The inclusion of white quartz pebbles, wooden rods and animal bones, where not fortuitous, are attributed to superstitious or semi-magical beliefs that are accounted to lurk long in folk memory.[322]

Off the bottom of the social scale are the alienated and exiled, marked by their treatment and mode of deposition. The best studied so far are the *execution cemeteries* placed on boundaries or landmarks, some of which were originally monuments of the pre-Christian era.[323] The graves are often peremptory and the bodies dumped unceremoniously in them, but some were provided with coffins, as at Sutton Hoo. The method of execution appears to have been hanging from a gallows, with some evidence of exposure (and consequent

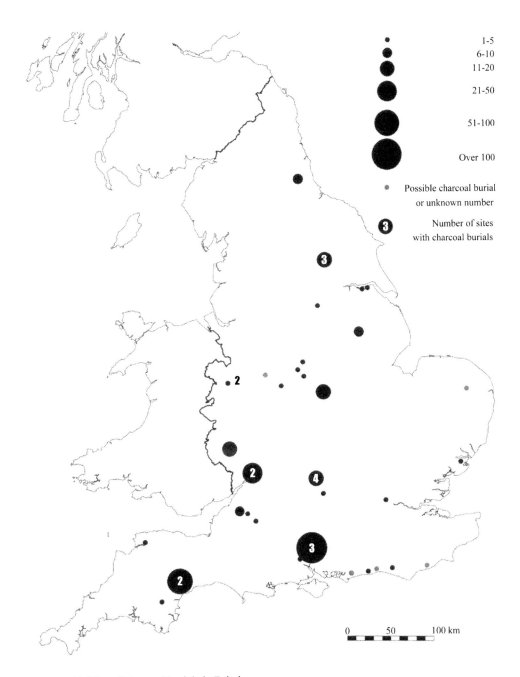

Figure 4.93 Map of charcoal burials in Britain.
(Holloway 2010, Fig 6.2; with permission of James Holloway)

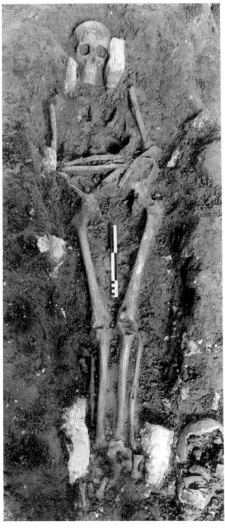

A   B

Figure 4.94 Barton-upon-Humber (Lincolnshire) burials. A: Burial F1464. The body was placed in the
           coffin with stones supporting the head and feet. B: Burial F3869, a well-preserved plank
           coffin in which was placed a long thin rod.

(Rodwell 2011, Fig 227, 230; with permission © W. Rodwell)

decomposition) on a gibbet (see Sutton Hoo, p. 340). These burials have been generally
dated 8th–10th century, with a surge in the 10th–11th century to match an extended reach
and increased rigour in the control of personal behaviour contemporary with the Christian
reforms. Victims may have transgressed against criminal laws, such as theft or murder, or
political laws such as betraying the king, or committed moral misdemeanours of a kind that
were not capital offences in the pre-Christian era but had lately become so, such as polyg-
amy or polyandry, or marriage of a son to his dead father's second wife.[324]

The distribution of execution cemeteries is focused on England, especially Wessex
(Figure 4.95). In his study, Andrew Reynolds proposed that a 'landscape of judgement'

Figure 4.95 Execution sites in England. The key to the numbered sites will be found in Reynolds 2009. (Reynolds 2009, Fig 39; licenced by Oxford University Press)

determined the itinerary of the condemned: first confinement at the magnate farm of a local lord, then to the court for the verdict and judgement, then to the church for the ordeal, testing veracity and guilt through hot iron or boiling water, then the last journey to the gallows and a grave located away from society's eternal protection in the churchyard.[325]

Burial outside the bounds of any formal cemetery is a phenomenon that may be wide-spread, but so far detected only on a small scale. C.M. Sofield found 30 examples of inhumations in Anglo-Saxon settlements between the 5th century and the 9th; half of these were laid out in 'deviant' postures and were located on or near boundary ditches; the other half were buried in a more normal manner alongside the walls of houses.[326] There were no substantial trends in the age or sex of those so interred. One hundred and twenty examples of animals or animal parts buried in settlements collected by the same researcher were interpreted as 'placed deposits' – that is, placed for the spiritual benefit of the occupants. The human burials could be seen as placed deposits too, and even the deviants buried on boundaries, although possibly suffering capital punishment, might be seen as helping 'to contain any danger thought to reside in liminal places' instead of, or as well as, being socially excluded.[327] It can be seen that the normative burials, at least, conform to a long practice that was especially prevalent in the British Iron Age, where bodies or body parts were buried in settlements as beneficial ancestors, in what was seen as the norm: those reaching the cemeteries were the privileged exceptions (see p. 344). It would not be surprising if the discovery of non-cemetery burial became increasingly common over the island as a whole. Meanwhile, the extent of execution burial has probably also been underestimated. The heads of potters tossed into mounds of wasters at Stafford shows summary execution in action; no doubt this was a feature of army life and the prerogative of the now full-time Christian aristocracy (p. 269).

Formative 2 and 3, the 8th to 11th centuries, in a nutshell

The overall sequence in FM 2–3 would tend to something of this kind: in the south and east, oriented burials without grave goods become the norm (even if it is not actually insisted on by the church) from the late 7th century. The English dead largely disappear at this point for 150 years, and it seems likely that they await discovery at the tail-end of the recognisable 7th century cemeteries (as at Sedgeford or Bloodmoor Hill), in other unfurnished and as yet undated field cemeteries without churches or in unfurnished and as yet unpublished phases of the minster churches, as at Winchester. By the late 10th century, churchyard burial has become the norm, and there are many churches to choose from.[328] In these cemeteries, whether rural or urban, the social hierarchy is vividly declared.

In the north and west the situation is very different. In the late 7th century, burial moves to the new monastic centres, such as Hartlepool, Wearmouth and Jarrow, with other candidates that have produced radiocarbon-dated 8th–9th-century burials, but are not certainly monastic establishments, such as Crayke and Addingham.[329] In the 9th century, the monasteries are 'dissolved', although their burial grounds may linger on. The Viking incomers – the Danes at Ingleby, the Norse at Westness and on the Isle of Man – introduce their retro brand of heroic burial along their routes but soon embrace a culture of the private church and the family-based cemetery at estate level. This solution to the problem of eternity, which harnesses ancestry, salvation and single male leadership in a single philosophy, is one that is found to suit most of the next millennium, bar the intermittent but regular outbursts of ecstatic spirituality led by fundamentalist soldiers of faith.

Comparanda – a visit to Ireland and Scandinavia

Before leaving Formative Britain with its many-sided funeral celebrations, it will be worth visiting Ireland and Scandinavia to glean a few examples and assess the connections. It will be little more than an overflying of the countries with view to picking up echoes – the international conversations of the dead deserve more research and more coverage than is possible here. The objective is to light a few beacons across the sea which show that the burials of Britain, varied as they are, reach out into still more varied and distant territory.

Ireland

The Irish selection is designed to provoke reflections on the gradual migration of the dead from ancestral cemeteries to the new community of Christians.[330] The dominant burial rite from the 4th century AD was an extended body in a grave lined with stone slabs, sometimes with a floor and sometimes with a surviving lid ('lintel grave').[331] Graves may also be lined with wood or contain a coffin, betrayed by a dark narrow line in the soil left by decayed wood. Human remains have also been encountered in house floors, caves, ditches and in drying kilns, implying that the elusive but probably widespread Iron Age practice of husbanding or dispersing fragments of ancestors for protective purposes was continued in the early middle ages. This same tendency accounts for the enthusiastic development of the cult of relics. A small number of cremations of 5th–8th-century date have also been found in a mound or with a standing stone. In the later formative centuries there is a trend to the use of a tightly bound shroud, holding the arms and legs together. Graves with stones either side of the head (ear muffs, head-support burials) are rare but found through the whole early medieval period. The less diagnostic simple dug graves with the body laid extended in the earth are widespread throughout the period in Ireland, as in Britain. Items of dress such as buckles and knives are occasionally found, which, while not strictly grave goods, indicate that a person was buried fully dressed.

In the 5th to 7th centuries (the first Formative period used in this book) people were buried in ancestral Iron Age burial grounds, near visible prehistoric monuments such as a mound or standing stone, actually within a burial mound or within the space defined by a ring ditch, where the ditch was still visible although the mound had gone. In some cases a natural mound had been chosen, perhaps in the belief that it was a burial place.[332] In the 7th century and earlier, purpose-built circular enclosures for use as burial grounds were constructed from scratch.[333] Some chronological sequences have been proposed: graves lined and floored and roofed with large slabs are found near prehistoric sites in the 5th/6th century; while graves lined with small slabs are found in cemeteries in the 7th/8th.[334] This has been seen as part of a social trend in which ancestral family burial grounds are superseded in the late 7th/early 8th century by communal cemeteries, as a more severe hierarchy takes hold.[335]

The continuous use or intermittent revisiting of monuments prominent in the landscape show that their broad meaning was never lost. The massive Neolithic chamber tomb at **Knowth**, County Meath, attracted Bronze Age tomb builders who placed mini-passage graves around its perimeter. At least 30 Iron Age cremations, dated 175 BC–250 AD, were inserted in these or next to them (Figure 4.96A; Tombs 2, 3, 8, 13, 14, 16, 17).[336] A scattering of finds indicated an interest in Knowth during the 4th–6th centuries AD, including two sherds of E ware (3962, 4030), an enamelled bronze mount (5257), a bronze decorated disc (4484), and a penannular brooch with zoomorphic terminals (4035). These were all secondary finds, without a structural context.[337] In the 7th/8th century the mound was enclosed, and 14 inhumations were added: in the main mound of the passage grave (Burial 33), in the Bronze Age mini-passage graves (Burials 27–29 added to Tomb 15) and in other sites around an outer perimeter in the form of cist graves and plain graves (Figure 4.96B, C). These were dated by radiocarbon from the 7th to the 9th century. The enclosure consisted of two concentric penannular ditches, one around the summit and one inside the kerb, with an entrance-way 6 m wide on the south-east side. The east and west passages were also brought into service: personal names were inscribed in well-formed letters on their structural stones. The ditches were backfilled with a massive consignment of animal bone, with a terminal radiocarbon date in the 8th century.[338] A century later, the mound was occupied again, this time as a settlement with 15 houses and 9 souterrains.[339]

The part of our period in which this famous and enduring monumental mound became attractive for burial and enclosure was the 7th/8th century. The top of the summit provides a splendid view with strategic benefits; the concentric ditches recall the form of the ringfort or the form of the monasteries that flourished in this period (p. 276). The excavator considered it a likely residence of the kings of North Brega, but there was no trace of a structure surviving within it. Given the presence of the tombs of ancestors, an interpretation as a cult centre or assembly place is perhaps more appealing, especially given the large quantity of cattle bones found in the upper ditch.[340]

Bettystown, also in County Meath, lies on the coast between the estuaries of the Boyne and the Nanny (Figure 4.97A). The famous Tara Brooch (p. 106) was discovered just to the south of it. The cemetery was revealed during archaeological investigations in advance of a new

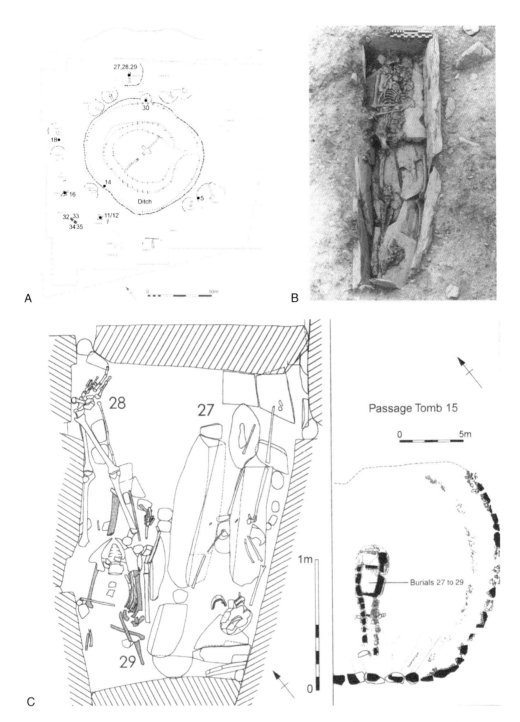

Figure 4.96 Knowth, Boyne Valley (Co Meath, Ireland). A: The Neolithic chambered tomb (centre) attracted Bronze Age mounds that in turn were exploited by Iron Age 'satellite' burials (2nd century BC to 4th century AD), which were in turn recolonised in Fm 2 (7th–9th century; numbered graves). In Fm 2 the Neolithic mound was separated from the later burials by a deep wide ditch. B: Burial 33. C: Burials 27–29 (detail) and position within former passage grave.

(Eogan, G. 2012, FIG 1.3, 1.4, 3.1, 3.4, 3.9, Plate 3.VIII)

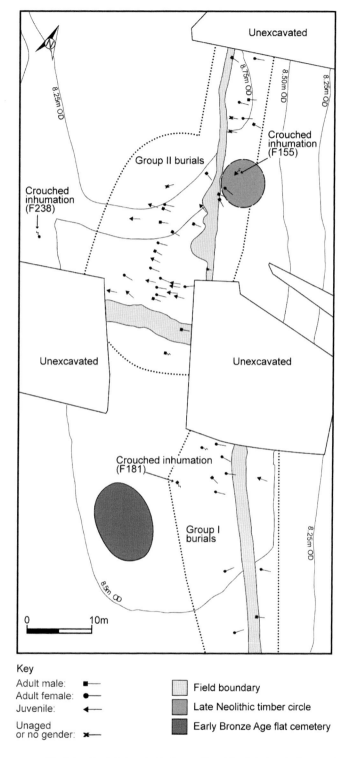

Figure 4.97 Bettystown (Co Meath). A (above): Early medieval burials in relation to a Late Neolithic timber circle and Early Bronze flat cemetery; B (opposite): examples of burial rites.

(Eogan 2010, Fig 9.2, 9.9, 9.10, 9.8; with author's permission)

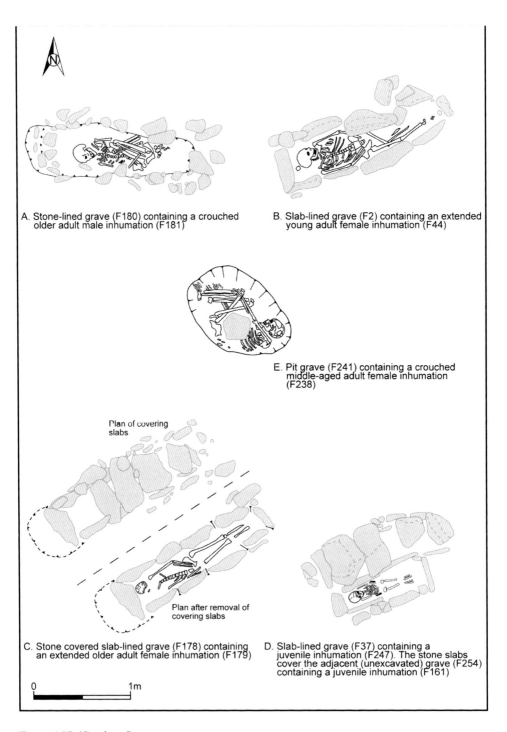

A. Stone-lined grave (F180) containing a crouched older adult male inhumation (F181)

B. Slab-lined grave (F2) containing an extended young adult female inhumation (F44)

E. Pit grave (F241) containing a crouched middle-aged adult female inhumation (F238)

Plan of covering slabs

Plan after removal of covering slabs

C. Stone covered slab-lined grave (F178) containing an extended older adult female inhumation (F179)

D. Slab-lined grave (F37) containing a juvenile inhumation (F247). The stone slabs cover the adjacent (unexcavated) grave (F254) containing a juvenile inhumation (F161)

0   1m

Figure 4.97 (Continued)

residential and retail development at 'The Anchorage', strung out along a ridge overlooking the sea. Less prominent in the landscape than Knowth, the place nevertheless attracted ritual celebration and burial over several millennia. In the excavated area was a Neolithic timber circle, a Bronze Age group of nine graves associated with a possible mound, two crouched burials of the later Iron Age (2nd to 1st century BC) and 61 inhumations mainly of the 5th and 6th centuries AD.[341] The graves came in at least five variants: in a pit (the crouched burials), slab lined, slab lined and lidded, partially stone lined, and stone lined with cobbles (Figure 4.97B). The 5th/6th century bodies were extended and laid feet to the east, and their distribution suggest three family groups taking post along the ridge. The excavator's verdict was 'The forms of the excavated burials reflect the influence of Christian practice, while the location of the cemetery in the landscape echoes long-established, non-Christian, indigenous practices'.[342] The Bettystown cemetery formed part of a continuing sequence, not just at that site but in the vicinity: a burial mound of the 5th–7th century at Ninch 1, enclosed secular settlements also used for burial at Ninch 2 and Colp 1 west in the 6th–8th century, and from the 8th century onwards, burial in churchyards.[343] Further inland, as we saw, the old monument at Knowth flares up as a starburst of spirituality and governance in the 7th/8th century.

In the multi-functional villages ('cemetery-settlements' or 'settlement-cemeteries', p. 280) the burials are usually sited within ditched enclosures. Some burials have been shown to begin in the 5th century, before the settlement; thereafter both expanded together (Raystown). Burial at Carrowkeel, County Galway, began in the 7th century, with the majority of graves dated between the 8th and 11th, and continued until the later medieval period, perhaps latterly as a *cillín*, a burial place for unbaptised children and persons alienated from the churchyard.[344] The cemetery at **Johnstown 1** endured from the 4th to the 17th century and was contained in three consecutive enclosure ditches constructed in the 5th to 10th centuries (Figure 4.98A). Burial began around the 4th century, when the disturbed remains of three adults were interred in a charnel pit under a low mound. Subsequent burial developed in at least seven curvilinear rows focussed on the mound or laid within its reduced platform. Sometime after AD 700 the burials began to cluster south of the mound, and after AD 1000 to the north (Figure 4.98B). Burial continued until the post-medieval period but remained related to the mound and the enclosure ditches, and there was no sign of a church in the large area opened (c. 0.7 ha). The settlement served by the cemetery was active between 500 and 1500 and was represented by linear features and cobbled areas with much domestic activity, arable production of wheat, oats and barley with grain dryers and a mill, and long-term ironworking. After 1700 a children's cemetery (*cillín*) was established over the backfilled mill race (Figure 4.98C, 'modern burial ground').[345]

These are the family cemeteries that ran in parallel with the great monastic burial grounds like Clonmacnoise, which, it can be surmised, were reserved for the great and good (Chapter 3, p. 279; Chapter 5, p. 563). Their ditched enclosures are probably the *fertae* (ancestral burial grounds) which clerics writing in the 8th century denounced in writing. The move to churchyard burial was a long-drawn-out affair, starting in the 8th century, whereby loyalty to the ancestors was slowly supplanted by a new allegiance to the eternal Christian community.[346] The majority of churches, initially associated with the cult of the saints and their relics, seem to have acquired dedicated burial grounds, often exploiting pre-existing *fertae*, from the 8th century onwards.[347] In practice, cemeteries present a range of variations on these themes through time, but perhaps a useful distinction may be made between cemeteries attracted to ancient monuments, cemeteries in prominent natural settings without settlements, cemeteries integrated with settlements and cemeteries integrated with churches.

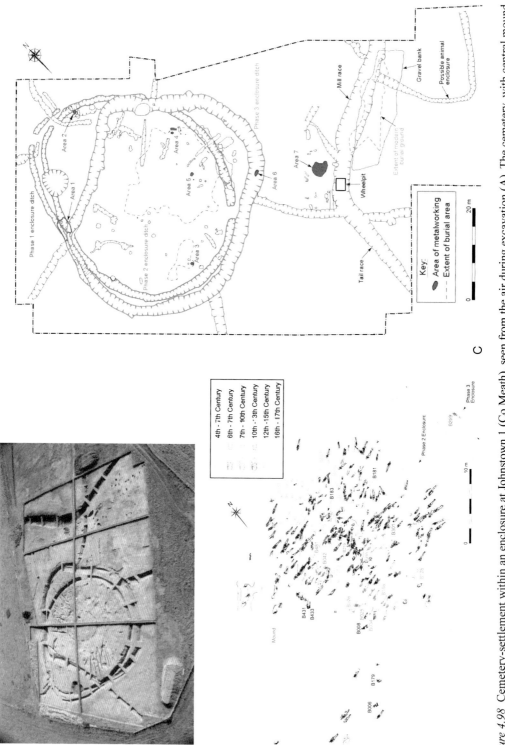

A

B

4th - 7th Century
6th - 7th Century
7th - 10th Century
10th - 13th Century
12th - 15th Century
16th - 17th Century

Phase 2 Enclosure

Phase 3 Enclosure

B269

B181

B183

B301

B431
B433

B008

B179

B006

Mound

0   10 m

C

Phase 1 enclosure ditch

Area 2

Area 1

Phase 2 enclosure ditch

Area 4

Area 5

Area 3

Area 6

Area 7

Phase 3 enclosure ditch

Mill race

Gravel bank

Possible animal enclosure

Extent of modern burial ground

Wheelpit

Tail race

Key:
Area of metalworking
Extent of burial area

0   20 m

Figure 4.98 Cemetery-settlement within an enclosure at Johnstown 1 (Co Meath), seen from the air during excavation (A). The cemetery, with central mound (B) is contained within the settlement area, which continued beyond the enclosure to the south-east, where there was a mill (C).

(Clarke 2010, Fig 6.2, 6.4, 6.9; with permission)

Scandinavia

The Scandinavian selection is intended to show how the massive levels of investment that we associate with a short, if brilliant period in 7th-century England continued into the later 7th, 8th, 9th and 10th century in Scandinavia. Moreover, this late flowering reveals something of the potency that these burials retained in the landscape. **Valsgärde** in Sweden is a monumental cemetery that has been almost completely excavated, in all revealing 62 cremations, 15 inhumations and 15 boat graves.[348] Its topography consists of ridges of high ground parallel to the River Fyris, which runs to the west of them (Figure 4.99). Burial began with four inhumations dating to the pre-Roman Iron Age (500–0 BC), placed at the highest point on the eastern side (57). In the 5th century AD, after a gap of almost 400 years, chamber burials appear on the next ridge to the west (27, 24, 20, 21). The main burial rite is now cremation, but elite burial adopts the form of inhumation in a ship, one on the foremost

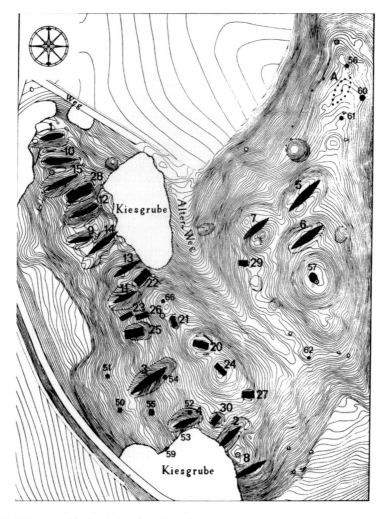

Figure 4.99 Valsgärde, Uppland, Sweden. Plan of cemetery.

(Arwidsson 1977, frontispiece; with permission © Uppsala Universitets Museum för Nordiska Fornsaker)

ridge (8) and three prominently sited on the east ridge (5, 6 and 7) dated between 620 and 700 (Figure 4.100). On the highest point of the east ridge, over the founder inhumations, an important cremation was placed (57). The burials of the 7th century are attributed to two leading families, but unlike Sutton Hoo (p. 333), it is not only a burial ground reserved for the elite. Apart from the ship graves, all ranks are present and are cremated, irrespective of

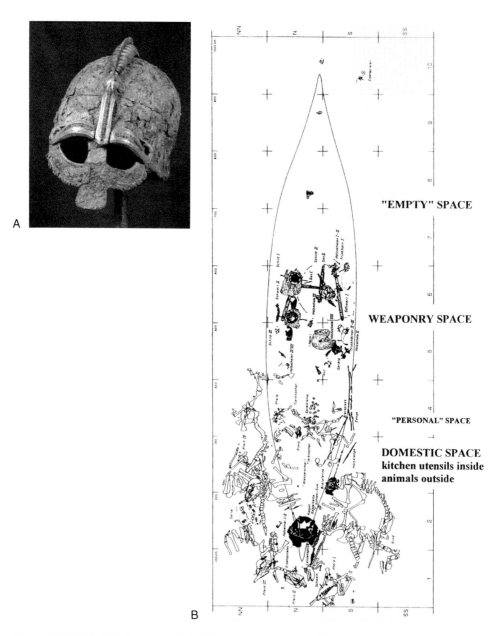

Figure 4.100 Valsgärde boat grave 7. A: Helmet from boat grave 7 in Uppsala Museum; B: plan with suggested apportionment of space.

(A: Author. B: Varenius 1995, Fig 4; with permission)

gender, age or status. In the Viking period a row of boat graves develops from south to north on the west ridge overlooking the river (e.g. 14–1).[349] The chronicle of the cemetery shows that burial is a dynamic business, the investment varying with the character and pressures of the age. The chamber graves and the ship graves only appear intermittently and appear to mark special moments in the four centuries that the cemetery is in use. These moments are likely to relate to specific historical events or ideological pressures.

Gamla Uppsala (Old Uppsala) in Sweden is known for its three giant burial mounds containing cremations of the 5th/early 6th century and measuring 50 m or more in diameter cut out of a ridge (the geological formation known as an esker), with a fourth 'the Thing mound' having no burials but a flat top level with the surface of the natural esker.[350] The cemetery also contained at least seven to eight hundred other mounds and was surrounded by an extensive settlement with specialised crafts. Hard up against the mounds was a sequence of monumental halls, the latest 50 m long and founded on a terrace made up of redeposited clay and midden. The finds included 550 garnets. The halls and all the excavated graves so far are dated to the 5th to 8th century.[351] As well as assemblies implied by the Thing, a general festival for all the provinces of Sweden was held every nine years that included animal and human sacrifices. These ceremonies were described by the 11th-century German historian Adam of Bremen, who also noted a temple. The temple has not been found, but it may lie adjacent to the mounds under the present church that inherited its ritual functions.

A famous cult centre for Denmark was at **Jelling** on Jutland, but its heyday was in the Viking period (Figure 4.101). Here a church stands between two very large mounds, and outside the church door is a massive boulder carved with an image of Christ as Woden entangled in branches and a dragon fighting a snake. A lengthy runic inscription explains that 'Harald Bluetooth ordered these monuments (i.e. the mounds) to be erected in memory of Gorm his father and Thyre his mother; He was that Harald "who conquered all Denmark and Norway and made the Danes Christians"'. The mounds were excavated in the 19th century, one containing a wooden chamber already ransacked in antiquity, leaving only a few bones and fragmentary finds, including the 'Jelling Cup' (Chapter 2). In the 20th century, parts of a male skeleton, apparently those missing from the mound chamber, were found during excavations in the

Figure 4.101 Jelling, Jutland, Denmark. The large runestone outside the door of the church. (Author)

Figure 4.102 Oseberg, Oslo fjord, Norway. Excavations of the ship burial in 1904.
(Brøgger et al. 1917; Museum of Cultural History, Oslo)

church, with grave goods recalling some in the chamber. It seems that the bones of Gorm had been removed from his mound and reburied in the church, so effecting his 'conversion'.[352] More recent investigations have shown that the whole ceremonial centre had an earlier origin as a massive ship-setting enclosed by a rhomboidal palisade.[353] The north mound stood in the centre of the ship-setting, while the south mound was laid over its south end.

The activities of Harald Bluetooth, as revealed also by archaeology at **Oseberg** in Norway, have proved highly instructive for the status of ancient mounds in the years following their construction. The body of a famous person, like holy relics, retained its power, and where that power was detrimental to a new regime the body needed to be dug up and neutralised. The Oseberg mound on Oslo fjord was the reputed burial place of Queen Åse, who had murdered her drunken husband and put their son on the throne, with herself acting as regent. Excavations in 1904 found a magnificently preserved and well-furnished ship, certainly the property of a woman, with a bed, sledges and tapestries and the ship itself, all preserved by the dense blue clay of the mound (Figure 4.102). The chamber had been broken into at some later date, and while the majority of the grave goods were left in place, the skeletons of two women had been removed and scattered just outside the mound. Jan Bill and Aoife Daly used dendrochronology to date the ship and chamber (AD 834), and also the wooden spades left behind by the desecrators of the tomb, which were over a century later, at AD 953–990 (Figure 4.103). A similar desecration happened to the ship burial at nearby Gokstad at much the same time – the time that Harald Bluetooth 'conquered all Denmark and Norway'.[354] This showed how long the power of a famous mound endured in the landscape, to the point where it became politically necessary to break it.

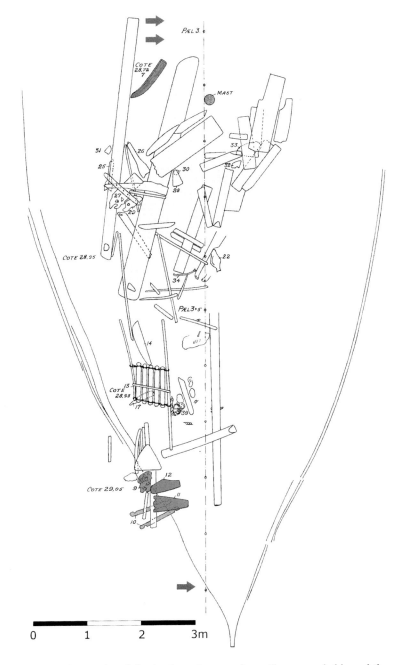

Figure 4.103 Oseberg: the results of dendrochronology on the well-preserved ship and the wooden spades left behind when the mound was 'broken'. (A): Plan of the layer formed at the bottom of the break-in trench. (B): Wooden spades. (C): The results of dendrochronology with lines marking the date of the Oseberg burial (summer 834) and the date of the break-in, calculated to AD 953–990.

(Bill and Daly 2012, Figs 2, 4, 6; permission from authors and Museum of Cultural History, Oslo)

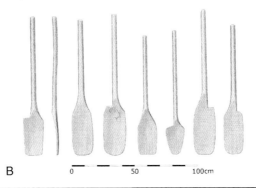

B

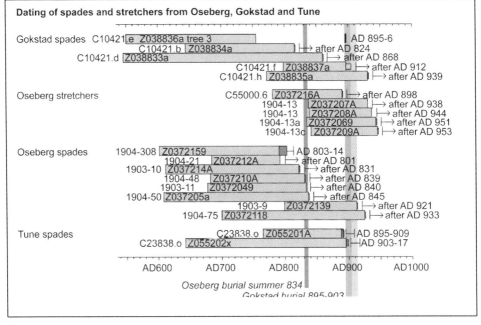

C

Figure 4.103 (Continued)

Conclusion

These patterns at home and abroad are sensed from a distance and high up. They are patchy patterns seen through clouds which screen parts of the country and sometimes shift and cover what we thought we knew. With more research, first impressions alter, trends are refined or modified or become no longer credible, but the past as a whole becomes more useful, part of us. The clouds are thickest over Scotland and the west, where the touch of modern development (and thus archaeology) has been a little lighter, metal-detection has been less active or less tolerated and there are fewer shiny finds to show where sites may lie hidden. There has also been a tendency countrywide to treat cemeteries as quarries to be sampled for burial rite, human statistics and artefacts, as opposed to sites with a geography and a history. Half a dozen fully excavated early medieval cemeteries in Britain is hardly a tally to be proud of. Naturally there are inhibitions owed to cost and conservation for the future, so a clear priority is to develop methods of locating and mapping cemeteries without damaging them, so that questions can be addressed to greatest effect and minimum loss.

Nevertheless, this imperfect and brief review has offered some themes worth sharing. In Formative Period 1 (5th to 7th century) there are separate shows running, as it were, in different parts of the island. In the north and west a leitmotiv is supplied by the unfurnished stone-lined grave, examples of which have been contacted from Cornwall to Caithness. Current observations show their numbers rising between the 5th and 7th century, but the practice has at least one foot in the Iron Age, as seen at Harlyn Bay, and may continue much later, as at Padstow. A second trend is a fondness for pre-existing monuments, especially those marked by the robust and enduring mounds of the Bronze Age. But there are intriguing if ill-defined variants in the way this basic vocabulary is applied. In Pictland they bury their cists under mounds that are round or square, as at Redcastle. In the British borders, including Lothian and the Forth, they arrange their cists in ordered rows, as Hallow Hill, but there are also examples of this pattern, seemingly family plots or lairs, further south at Llandough and Cannington. In north Wales they like to line their graves towards a prehistoric or a Roman focus, a barrow or a shrine. All these areas also have 'special graves', such as the child's grave with Roman objects at Hallow Hill (54) or the grave of a teenager, approached by a well-worn path at Cannington. Structures also punctuate the cemeteries, often small and rectangular. Some resemble the ditches around the Pictish square barrows, but others were structural, with vertical plank walls and an entrance, as at Tandderwen, echoing the Iron Age shrines of Westhampnett. The overall post-Roman expression would seem to relate to family cemeteries established in the monumental homes of ancestors, to which are added the bodies or relics of new persons who deserve to be revered. It is not excluded that these tiny rectangular 'houses', of which we have only the footprint, are what are represented by the portable reliquaries (as at Monymusk) and on the summit of the Irish high crosses. Nothing in the materiality of western and northern Fm 1 burial grounds offers us a specific Christian signal, but they are clearly central places concerned with cult at which congregation and assembly may be expected.

There is a faint murmur of some of these trends further east, as in the use of occasional inserted stones and planks at Wasperton or the use of prehistoric sites, little more than coincident at first but becoming more deliberate as the Anglo-Saxons integrate with British ways. At first sight the contrast between east and west could hardly be more stark. The eastern cemeteries are due to people coming from overseas in the early 5th century via The Wash and laying out large fields of furnished cremations in urns, as demonstrated at Spong Hill. In the 6th century they are joined by well-furnished inhumations, and by the mid-6th century selected persons are being placed under small mounds. Gender difference and relative affluence are strongly signalled in these graves and constitute an important aspect of Anglo-Saxon thinking; but in general terms, gender difference is matched by gender equality – women are no less respected than men, at least in the grave. Wealth difference on the other hand is terminal: poorer people are nearly invisible, at least to us.

In the later 6th century selectivity increases still further, with fewer but richer graves culminating in the highly demonstrative monuments at Sutton Hoo. Far from being a 'final phase' (called this by Leeds on account of it being the last period having grave goods), the first 75 years of the 7th century were a period of extravagant experiment, when the burial parties of Anglo-Saxon England were at their most declamatory. All bases were covered: there were bed burials, horse burials, boat burials, chamber graves, cremations in bronze containers; burials were laid out in rows, in linear alignments, in groups. It is as though for 50 years or so burial parties had access to a lexicon of burial practices from the Bronze Age and a range of examples from Hungary to Norway and were determined to use them to create a new spiritual orthodoxy, seasoned with a good deal of local invention. The men were on the stage first with their weapons, and the women followed closely with graves furnished with symbols of feminine power. At least some of these were spiritual leaders, as suspected of the earlier 'special graves' in the north and west; others were persons of influence in other ways sufficient to merit high investment memorials. The variety, quality and raw expression of these tombs should be acknowledged; they are the equivalent to books of sermons, hagiographies, eulogies and epic poems all rolled into one. It would appear that the incoming Anglo-Saxons gave emphasis at first to families led by a sword-bearing male, and/or women of equal status who gradually widened their influence and acquaintance to operate over larger communities. The burial grounds report the eminence of the alpha male war leader in the first quarter of the 7th century and the alpha female spiritual leader in its third quarter. Both were probably concerned to maintain the control of inherited land at a time of uncertain ideological principles.

The episode came to an end somewhat abruptly in the east in about 675 AD, with the cessation of the grave-good practice. However, a similar point in time marked the end of an era in the north and west too, in burial as it had in stone monuments, which changed their medium of monumental investment from inscribed pillars to crosses (Chapter 5). These are seen (and not only by this author) as responses to the late 7th-century rise of institutional Christianity and especially the militant form it took in Northumbria, Scotland, Wales and Ireland as the monastic movement. Before leaving Fm 1 we should call attention to the strong indication that, in burial as in sculpture and indeed in settlements and artefacts, there is still no clear expression of Christian allegiance or authority – no churches, no stone crosses, no church plate, no indigenous Gospel books surviving from this time. As it stands, we have to conclude that between the early 5th and the late 7th century, Britain was not a Christian country in the modern sense. As can be seen, it is much more interesting than that.

After the late 7th century, there is no doubt that material culture was Christianised, but even in Formative 2 it is only clearly visible in the regions of monastic fundamentalism, especially Ireland, Scotland, Wales and Northumbria. In other areas, including what is now southern England, there is currently little Christian materiality outside one or two partially resuscitated Roman towns, notably Canterbury and Winchester. The explosion for Southumbria comes in Formative 3, the 9th–11th century, when what is to become England rises to embrace Christianity and covers the countryside with churches and crosses. At this time the more overtly Christianised north and west are defending their monasteries and losing many of them in wars against the Norse and the Danes.

The southern English experience offers another varied and intriguing repertoire in the burial record. Rural cemeteries attached to estates recall the settlement-cemeteries defined in Ireland, raising the suspicion that this might be a hitherto undetected norm. Visibility increases in churchyards (like Raunds and Barton-upon-Humber), where careful analysis has detected changes of attitude through the 8th–11th century. Some new kinds of class-marks are visible underground: grave markers, special locations, coffins of wood and stone, charcoal layers apparently dedicated to the preservation of privileged bodies and very occasionally, grave goods. Outside, often on boundaries or former pagan cemeteries, victims who have fallen foul of the regime are executed by hanging and exiled not only from the extended family but from society itself. The prescription of Christian civilisation brings prosperity harnessed to intolerance. The puzzle of eternity is now to be addressed in a more orthodox, more regulated, more universal manner.

The message of the cemeteries would seem to be that they are places of cult and assembly for most of the Formative period. In the north and west, the example of Ireland shows that former prehistoric sites attracted special burial, while villagers tended their own dead. However early the impact of Christianity claimed to be, the migration from ancestral to communal Christian cemeteries took time and only began in the 8th century, and the monasteries were part of it. This would seem to be also the trend in north and west Britain. In the east the level of their investment, design and size implies that here too the cemeteries may have performed as the central places of their locality, although the evidence is still vague. The example of Scandinavia suggests that extravagant monumentality, using mounds, chambers and ships, was not a norm but expressed important political aspirations and crises at particular times and places. Moreover, the monuments continued to radiate policy long after the burial, until neutralised by 'mound-breaking' or superseded by still more extravagant monuments of the Christian kind. The presence of such a spiritually persuasive and closely connected neighbour across the North Sea may have encouraged the English to drag their feet in the long march towards Christian orthodoxy, only adopting churchyard burial in the 10th century.

If the treatment of the dead reflects the way the living were thinking, formative Britain was a forum of lively debate about past and future, this world and the next, current events and local loyalties. Christianity was slow to enter the cemetery and probably slow to persuade the bulk of the population of its merits. At the political level, there were more effective and obtrusive ways of indicating the dominance of the Church Triumphant – the stone crosses of the next chapter.

Notes

1   The work was undertaken by Wessex Archaeology and reported in Fitzpatrick 1997.
2   Fitzpatrick 1997, 14.
3   Fitzpatrick 1997, 231.
4   Fitzpatrick 1997, 236.
5   Fitzpatrick 1997, 236 with references.
6   Fitzpatrick 1997, 287.
7   Woodward 1992, 26–28; Evison 1987, 154; Williams 1997; Semple 2013.
8   Rahtz et al. 2000.
9   Rahtz et al. 2000, 391.
10 Rahtz et al. 2000, 46–47; it may alternatively have been an open structure, interpreted as a late Roman shrine or temple, pp. 50–51.
11 Thus, 'slab-marked grave' rather than lintel grave or cist grave, p. 54; the conclusion is that the path led to the slabs, which were on top of a low mound covering the grave, p. 57.
12 Rahtz et al. 2000, 105; the one dated grave with stone inclusions (259) was 3rd to 7th century (255–640).
13 Rahtz et al. 2000, 367–372.
14 Graham-Campbell in Rahtz et al. 2000, 354.
15 Rahtz et al. 2000, 129, with additions.
16 Rahtz et al. 2000, 54; however, the radiocarbon dates of 620–1020 were from an early uncalibrated measurement that proved impossible to rerun, p. 390.
17 Rahtz et al. 2000, Fig 93, 252; 'almost every row includes a grave that is likely to be later than the 4th century'; p. 111.
18 Rahtz et al. 2000, 413; 'we should . . . not regard the pagan/Christian alternatives as mutually exclusive'. The suggested indicative signals are reviewed on pp. 418–420. However, in his O'Donnell Lecture, Rahtz found that the evidence for Christianity in Somerset before 700 was tenuous (1982, 188).
19 Carver 2015; here pp. 284, 665.
20 White and Smith 1999. There were 102 early medieval graves in all.
21 Edwards 2013, 173.
22 White and Smith 1999, 49, 65.
23 Of the Bronze Age as proposed by the excavators; but a post-Roman feature is more likely, as suggested by David Longley (2009, 120).
24 White and Smith 1999, 123.
25 The excavators proposed six groups, their groups 3–6 being assessed together here (White and Smith 1999, 140).
26 White and Smith 1999, 132, 140.

27 White and Smith 1999, 157.
28 The authors propose that 'continuing kin beliefs' and 'some kind of social differentiation', are exhibited by this group, p. 156.
29 Recent discoveries on the Llangefni link road included 48 cist graves www.bbc.co.uk/news/uk-wales-north-west-wales-36322953.
30 Carver 2016a; Carver et al. 2016.
31 The project was carried out by the University of York in collaboration with FAS Heritage, Tarbat Historic Trust and Highland Council. It ran from 1994 to 2007 and was published in 2016.
32 Spong Hill was excavated between 1972 and 1981, from 1974 under the direction of Dr Catherine Hills, sponsored by English Heritage in advance of terminal plough damage. It was fully and promptly published in nine volumes of *East Anglian Archaeology*, concluding with the synthesis volume (Hills and Lucy 2013). The inhumations are described in Hills et al. 1984.
33 Hills and Lucy 2013, 294.
34 Härke 2001; Williams 2002, 2004; such a site has also been proposed at Binham on the basis of a distribution of bracteates: Behr and Pestell 2014.
35 Hills and Lucy 2013, 12–21.
36 C. Hills, personal communication.
37 Hills and Lucy 2013, 227–229, 267. The buildings and Group C also share a predilection for organic tempered pottery.
38 No in situ pyres have yet been found in Anglo-Saxon England (Fern 2015, 198).
39 Hills and Lucy 2013, 295.
40 This was before the advent of the planning procedure known as PPG16 (1990), which gave archaeologists the opportunity to excavate sites in advance of their destruction in the UK. In this case the excavation was carried out by the University of Birmingham's Field Unit and Warwickshire Museum and made extensive use of student labour and the Manpower Services Job creation scheme. The discoveries were finally brought to press in 2009 thanks to the studies of a German doctoral student from the University of Kiel (Jonathan Scheschkewitz) and the good offices of English Heritage, who procured a grant from the Aggregates Levy (Crowfoot 1988; Wise 1991; Scheschkewitz 2006; Carver et al. 2009; see Hughes and Crawford 1995 for the prehistoric site).
41 Called Spatial Groups (SG) by Scheschkewitz 2006. For family plots in Anglo-Saxon inhumation cemeteries, see examples at Dover (Evison 1987, 19–20) and in East Anglia (Penn and Brugmann 2007, 87).
42 Carver et al. 2009, 119, n23.
43 As for example at Llandough and Cannington; summarised in Carver et al. 2009, 131.
44 The royal burial ground was been explored on five separate occasions, the latest by the University of York in 1983–2005 (Carver 2005a). The Tranmer House cemetery was excavated in advance of the construction of the visitor centre in 2000 and published as Fern 2015. For recent overviews see Carver 2014a, 2017.
45 Fern 2015, 207.
46 Fern 2015, 189. This was one of the first Anglo-Saxon cemeteries to have its cremations radiocarbon-dated. The dating of cremated bone at other sites such as Spong Hill, Wasperton and Sutton Hoo could be revealing.
47 Fern 2015, 189, 217.
48 Brugmann type B2 (580–650), Fern 2015, 129, 187 for the weapons dated 580–610.
49 The campaign was funded by the Society of Antiquaries of London, the British Museum and the BBC. The work was carried out by the University of York for the Sutton Hoo Research Trust, a body representing the sponsors and academic advisors.
50 Carver 2005a. The excavation encompassed seven mounds (2, 5, 6, 7, 17, 18 and 14), touched 3, 4 and 13 and involved about a quarter of the known site. The designated Mound 16 remains uncertain, so the number of putative mounds is 17.
51 This was an excavation in 1860 reported in the *Ipswich Gazette*.
52 Carver 2005a, 153–177.
53 Bruce-Mitford 1975, 1978, 1983 for the detailed description of all the objects found in this grave, including the ship, and Carver 2005a, 177–199 for the revised burial rite summarised here. Dobat 2006 for the ritual axe-hammer.
54 Carver 2000. The author has also developed a model of the character and role of Raedwald's queen, who was credited with the political know-how that led to the composition of the burial (Carver 2017, 191–192).

55 Carver 2005a, 107–115.
56 See Formative 3, later in the chapter, and Reynolds 2009 for a study of the wider use of execution burials, especially in the Later Saxon period.
57 BL ms Cott. Claud. BIV f59, cited in Reynolds 2009, 29, Fig 6. In her survey, Temple comments of this manuscript, a late Anglo-Saxon Pentateuch, 'The scenes of Israelites' everyday life . . . depict usages and customs of 11th century England' (1976, 103). See also Carver 1986b, 141, where it is tested as a 'realist' manuscript.
58 Hines and Bayliss 2013; see p. 387.
59 Whimster 1979, 272; Johns 2006; Harding 2016, 79; See Chapter 5, p. 475 for the mirror depicted at Dunrobin.
60 Whimster 1979, 74–90; Harding 2016, 78–79.
61 Whimster 1979, 1981. Whimster's reconstituted plan locating 53 of the burials, his Fig 25, is reproduced here.
62 Whimster 1979, 272; His Group 3 (see FIG 75). Harding 2016, Fig 3.15.
63 Whimster 1979, 268–276; Mira 2011 for more conspicuous comparisons from Iberia.
64 Harding 2016; Harding was the supervisor of Whimster's thesis.
65 Harding 2016, 120, 267–270; Lelong and MacGregor 2007, 95, 195.
66 Harding 2016, 289.
67 Harding 2016, 291: 'it evidently did not require cultural continuity to preserve a sense of sanctity of place'.
68 Harding 2016, 152–154, for example Baldock, Aylesford, Gravesend, furnished with buckets and cauldrons.
69 Hill 2007, 37; Harding 2016, 87.
70 Philpott 1991 has reviewed burial practice in Roman Britain.
71 Maldonado Ramírez 2011; for overviews of Pictish burial see Ashmore 1980; Close-Brooks 1984; Foster 2014, Ch 5; Winlow 2011.
72 Maldonado Ramírez 2011, 174.
73 Smith 1996; Foster 2014, Fig 66.
74 Cowley 1996.
75 Webster and Brunning 2014; see above for Westhampnett and below for Tandderwen and Plas Gogerddan.
76 Maldonado Ramírez 2011, 103; a Welsh example is at Tandderwen in Wales (Brassil et al. 1991, 62).
77 Carver 2005a: 67–69. See also the discovery of 81 tree-trunk coffins of the 7th–9th century at Great Ryburgh, Norfolk (*Guardian*, 16 Nov 2016).
78 Maldonado Ramírez 2011, 46–48, 97.
79 Maldonado Ramírez 2011, 122.
80 As noted by Smith 1996, who suggested that a religious boundary was implied between Fife and Angus.
81 Having discovered that they were Early Medieval, previous generations hoped to link long cist graves with the Christianisation of Scotland (eg. Hutcheson 1903; Thomas 1971, 49–50). Maldonado's verdict (2011, 1) was that 'New radiocarbon dates show conclusively that these burial rites predate Christianity in Scotland'.
82 Brady et al. 2007; Murray and Ralston 1997; Wedderburn and Grime 1984.
83 Close-Brooks 1980, Fig 2, 1989, 1; Williams 2006, Fig 5.9.
84 Alexander 2005.
85 Rees 2002.
86 Rees 2002, 328.
87 Rees 2002, 335, 347.
88 Maldonado Ramírez 2011, Ill.6.15.
89 Proudfoot 1996.
90 Proudfoot 1996, 417–420.
91 Proudfoot 1996, 423.
92 Proudfoot 1996, 440–441.
93 Maldonado Ramírez 2011, 162, 163.
94 *contra*Maldonado Ramírez 2011, 260.
95 Proudfoot 1996, 447.
96 Hatherley 2009, 207.
97 Cuttler et al. 2012.

 98 Longley in Cuttler et al. 2012, 262, 265.
 99 Compare Capel Eithin. Also on Anglesey is one of the most important cemeteries of early medi-
     eval Wales at Arfryn, Bodedern, originally excavated by Richard White in 1971 but since lan-
     guishing in unpublished obscurity. Here 117 early medieval burials were reputed to have focused
     (improbably) on the ruins of a Middle Bronze Age house. There have been a few notices of the
     site, but its date and character remain elusive (White 1972; Longley 2002, 311; Longley 2009,
     118; Edwards 2013, 143–144).
100 www.heneb.co.uk/llanbeblig/earlymedcem.html accessed 7 March 2016.
101 Murphy 1992, 17 for the quote.
102 Brassil et al. 1991; Maldonado Ramírez 2011, 103.
103 Brassil et al. 1991, 64.
104 Brassil et al. 1991, 86–87).
105 Holbrook and Thomas 2005 is a comprehensive report.
106 Webster and Brunning 2014.
107 Petts (2009, 211) sees ogham and Latin inscribed stones as marking burials in the early 5th cen-
     tury and marking land thereafter and notes the two types of layout, row grave and focal graves.
108 Farwell and Molleson 1993, 61–63, 236.
109 Farwell and Molleson 1993, 83, 236.
110 Clarke 1979, 143, 428; see also Chapter 2, p. 54.
111 Carver et al. 2009, 116, and see p. 330.
112 Smith 1990.
113 Lucy 1999; for a map of cemeteries then known, see her Fig 2.1.
114 University of Durham PhD in progress 2016; my thanks to the author for letting me have sight of
     her work.
115 Groves 2010, 245.
116 At Norton some burials had a radial alignment to a vanished Bronze Age barrow, and a third were
     crouched (Sherlock and Welch 1992, 15–17). Lucy 1999, 16–18 for the group as a whole.
117 This section makes extensive use of Sam Lucy's analysis in her 1999 and 2009 articles (see also
     Lucy 1998, 2002). Her interpretation and support for Hope-Taylor's are richly endorsed by the
     examples cited in the previous parts of the present chapter. For the Yeavering settlement as a
     whole, see Chapter 3, p. 156.
118 Hope-Taylor 1977, 113; Blair 1995, 19; Lucy 2009, 140.
119 Lucy 2009, 130, Fig 42; the extent of the western cemetery (here Cemetery 2) 'is unclear from the
     publication'.
120 Hope-Taylor 1977, 250.
121 Hope-Taylor 1977, Fig 26.
122 Hope-Taylor 1977 Fig 31.
123 As Scull 1991; Scull and Harding 1990, 23.
124 Geake 1997; Lucy 1999, 2009; Howick and Galewood are 6th century Anglian. The two cemeteries
     excavated at Milfield lie north and south of the settlement known from APs, perhaps to be identi-
     fied as *Maelmin*, a villa regalis known to Bede. The northern one, in a henge, had five burials with
     annular brooches, buckles and knives, and dates to late 6th century; maybe all are 7th century. The
     southern one within and around another henge contained 45 burials, one with grave goods including
     knives, a buckle and a lace tag. This one is probably 7th/8th century (Scull and Harding 1990). The
     Bowl Cemetery at Bamburgh, with 100 inhumations of late 6th to 8th century, features both cists and
     plain earth graves, some furnished with knives and buckles, and a bone comb (Groves 2010).
125 Lucy 2009, 143.
126 Blair 1995, 19.
127 Lucy 2009, 141.
128 Driscoll 1998 argues that the idea of focussing a royal site on a prehistoric monument is typical of
     the north and west (Scotland and Ireland, but also Wales) but not of those areas further south that
     subsequently became Anglo-Saxon England.
129 Hope-Taylor (1977, 131) thought that wooden posts of pre-existing cemetery 3 (AX and BX)
     were used to lay out the halls.
130 A suggestion owed to Rosemary Cramp.
131 Hope-Taylor marks the end of Yeavering in 670, the end of Oswiu's reign. This would make a
     more appropriate beginning for its overtly Christian phase.

132 Haughton and Powlesland 1999a, 78.

133 I.e. 22 out of 33 cases from 24 cemeteries in the whole of Britain; Haughton and Powlesland 1999a, 91. Grave 49/41 at Sewerby was that of a young woman with an older woman buried in a sprawled prone position on top of her. The latter was interpreted as buried alive and punitive (Hirst 1985, 38–43).

134 Haughton and Powlesland 1999a, 93; Budd et al. 2004.

135 Eagles 1979; Faull 1979.

136 Lucy 1999, 2000, 2009.

137 Sherlock 2012.

138 Sherlock 2012, 10, 2011.

139 The published interpretation of this structure was a roundhouse converted into an Anglo-Saxon barrow; Sherlock 2012, 104).

140 Sherlock 2012, 44–48, 61.

141 Sherlock 2012, 131.

142 Sherlock 2012, 113: 'If there is more than one gender indicator, for example two knives or a knife and tool, this could suggest a likelihood of a male burial. . . . It is proposed that the males would include burials with tools or two knives'. On this basis, 15 burials were designated as male, randomly distributed, with one sharing the bed burial on the basis of its tool (sic). This was find 41.1, a small tanged gouge.

143 This is assumed rather than argued: p. 130: 'It is important that these events are not seen as conflicting ideologically or politically but instead viewed as part of the same movement for social, political and religious change at this time. Christianity was the accepted religion by AD650.' Why this generalisation is 'important', or for whom, remains unstated.

144 For bed burial and the assertion of female roles in the later 7th century, see later in this chapter; Chapter 2, p. 105; Hamerow 2016.

145 A statistical analysis of 2,440 cremation urns and their contents by Julian Richards (1987) found a general variation between those in the traditional Anglian and Saxon regions and correlations between the size of the pot and the age of the occupant and between the form and decoration of the urn and the grave goods they contained; for example, pots with bosses were linked with adults rather than children, males rather than females and cows rather than sheep (1987, 194–197, 1992, 143). He deduced that cremation was the subject of a commemorative 'language' applied, and that its specific references operated at a number of levels (1988, 147). Ravn 2003 also used multivariate analysis in an attempt to further enlarge the definitions of social identity.

146 Hills and Lucy 2013, 229, 232; the dates are taken from Figure 3.30; see p. 321 for Spong Hill cemetery.

147 See the Tranmer House cemetery, Fern 2015, for the method.

148 Hines and Bayliss 2013.

149 As used for example at Portmahomack Hamilton in Carver et al 2016, D7–19.

150 The *posterior density estimates*.

151 Hines and Bayliss 2013, 461, 491; FIG 8.1, Table 8.2; the 'A' phases refer to the period dominated by cremations, equivalent to the Spong phases A-C. The inhumations at Spong Hill are coeval with FB and MB.

152 'A series of steps was taken to try to refine the chronological trend in the initial data set by removing grave-assemblages that could be argued to be chronologically anomalous, for instance those where untypically late survival and burial of one or more artefact types could be suspected'. Hines and Bayliss 2013, 252.

153 Hines and Bayliss 2013, 500–506, nos 8, 9, 10, 12, 13, 14, 15.

154 Marion Archibald in Hines and Bayliss 2013, 512–515.

155 Hines and Bayliss 2013, 509.

156 Hines and Bayliss 2013, 510 (their italics):

> An alternative scenario . . . is that furnished burial in Anglo-Saxon England did not come to an abrupt end as assumed by the use of a uniform distribution to model the currency of this phenomenon, but that rather there was a measurable period of decline in its popularity. . . . However the closely comparable date-estimates for the end of furnished burial provided by *statistically independent* chronological models for the male and female series argue against this proposition (the medians of these distributions differ by only two years), as does the absence of late outliers with poor agreement in the preferred models.

157   Tables 6.1, 7.1; the one exception is St Peter's Tip, Grave 113 with dates of 670–730 (64%) or
      740–770 (31%), the single example of a 'late outlier'. Its date may be due to the isotope measure-
      ment: 'given the rapid change in the concentration of atmospheric radiocarbon . . . late outliers
      should be easy to identify' and 'only SPtip113 in the male series maybe such a case' p. 510. The
      modelled date is 655–680 Fig 6.53, p. 291.
158   E.g. Geake 1997.
159   Hines and Bayliss 2013, 478, Figs 8.14 a,c. I am very grateful to John Hines for checking and
      improving the captions to my Figs 4.62 and 4.63.
160   Hines and Bayliss 2013, 519.
161   Hines and Bayliss 2013, 489.
162   Hines and Bayliss 2013, 484–488.
163   Hines and Bayliss 2013, 490–491.
164   'What we are actually able to compare, distributionally, on the basis of our dataset and analysis is
      the south and east and thus we can barely consider the territory of the great emergent kingdoms
      of Mercia and Northumbria' (Hines and Bayliss 2013, 536).
165   Hines in Hines and Bayliss 2013, 520, 529, 530, 552; Geake 1997, 107–122.
166   Hines in Hines and Bayliss 2013, 464–465, 553. 'The end of furnished burial as we can detect it
      coincided closely with the key events of AD 664–9 that marked a threshold in the consolidation
      of the early English church.' Cf Bassett 2000, 110: 'Mortuary practices change for many reasons,
      most of which have nothing to do with religious beliefs.'
167   Bulleit 1979, 109.
168   Clarke 1979, 433, 143, 355–356; and see Gowland 2007.
169   Chambers 1987, 65, 58.
170   Boyle et al. 1995.
171   Boyle et al. 1995, 138.
172   Lloyd-Jones 1995, 72; at Lechlade, 219 inhumations and 29 cremations included six with stone
      inclusions; Boyle et al. 1998, 35, 38.
173   Hills and O'Connell 2009, 1105–1106.
174   Hills and Lucy 2013, 12–13, 21.
175   Hirst and Clarke 2009, 444 where it is described as *agri deserti*.
176   Evans et al. 2016, 524–525, Fig 6.27.
177   Hirst and Clark 2009, 759; Evans et al. 2016, Fig 4.44.
178   Hirst and Clark 2009, 124: the grave apparently cut a rectangular hollow associated with the Iron
      Age hut gully 9522.
179   Evison 1987.
180   Parfitt and Anderson 2012.
181   Evison 1987, 145; Parfitt and Anderson 2012, 372.
182   Parfitt and Anderson 2012, 344–351.
183   Parfitt and Anderson 2012, catalogue; Hines et al. 2013, 233, 341.
184   Parfitt and Anderson 2012, 378–381.
185   Evison 1987, 142.
186   Hines et al. 2013, 499–501, 504.
187   Parfitt and Anderson 2012, 48–49, 322.
188   Parfitt and Anderson 2012, catalogue.
189   Parfitt and Anderson 2012, 29, 325.
190   Evison 187, 147–148.
191   Even the choice between cremation and inhumation is now regarded as based in a system of belief
      (e.g. Hirst and Clark 2009, 759); see note 156 for Hines' endorsement of a positive view of burial
      as a reflection of religion and Carver 2001 for the relation between religious change and the need
      to express it through burial.
192   Hedeager 2011.
193   Chadwick 1912; Hedeager 2011.
194   Carver 2002b, 2016b.
195   Müller-Wille 1970–1, 16.
196   Van de Noort 1993.
197   Carver 1986a; Słupecki 1999; Lutovsky 1996. The 5th-century burial mounds at Högom in cen-
      tral Sweden, which included a bed burial in Mound 2, were unlikely to be reacting to a Christian
      mission (Ramqvist 1992).

198 Childe 1944, 96; Martin-Clark 1950, 111.
199 Hawkes and Grainger 2006; Down and Welch 1990, Fig 2.4.
200 Parfitt and Brugmann 1997, 120–121.
201 Shephard 1979.
202 Carver 2005a, 171.
203 Carver 2000.
204 Carver 1986a, 2002b, 2016b.
205 MoLAS 2004.
206 Harding 2016, 200, 264–265.
207 Fern 2007.
208 Müller-Wille 1970–71; Fern 2007, 92.
209 Fern 2007, 93–101.
210 Fern 2010, 154.
211 'It is highly probable that the origin of the horse inhumation rite in post-Roman England is, like that of weapon burial, to be sourced from the funerary symbolism of the Continental *Reihen-gräberzivilisation'* Fern 2007, 101.
212 Fern 2007, 102.
213 Oexle 1984.
214 Fern 2010; Cross 2011 for the Sedgeford burials with an overview of horse mythology.
215 For overviews, see Müller-Wille 1974, 1995; Carver 1995a. Crumlin-Pedersen 1991c for Slusegård.
216 Darling and Gurney 1993; Carver 1995a, Fig 1, and appendix.
217 Filmer-Sankey and Pestell 2001.
218 Pestell in Filmer-Sankey and Pestell 2001, 199; Marsden in Filmer-Sankey and Pestell 2001, 201.
219 Filmer-Sankey and Pestell 2001, 102.
220 cf Cross 2011, 197.
221 Carver 1995a, 119–121.
222 Meaney 1981; Hills 2015.
223 See Carver 2009a.
224 Dickinson 1993b, 53; Meaney 1981, 249–622.
225 Price 2001, 2002, Fig 3.27.
226 Carver et al. ed. 2010.
227 Lucy et al. 2009; see also Chapter 3, p. 204 for the settlement.
228 Lucy et al. 2009, 392–397.
229 Lucy et al. 2009, 386, 423, 415.
230 Lucy et al. 2009, 422–426.
231 Lucy et al. 2009, 364, 365.
232 Leslie Webster's Treasure Report dates it to the early 7th century; p. 178.
233 Lucy et al. 2009, no 43, pp. 176–177.
234 See p. 91; Dickinson 1993b; Meaney 1981.
235 Penn 2000, 4.
236 Penn 2000, 18; this date was modified to 640–675 by Hines et al. 2013, 513.
237 Penn 2000, 58. The excavator supposed that the presence of seax in Grave 25 and graves with a knife and buckle might indicate a male.
238 Williams 2010, 35.
239 Excavation by Faith Vatcher in 1966; published by Speake 1989.
240 Such sprinklers, used in Roman villas to lay dust and scent rooms, were later adopted by the church to initiate the Mass with the chant *asperges me*. Naturally, the presence of such an object in this grave does not make its occupant a Roman or a Christian.
241 Geake 1997. Her dates need drawing back from the 8th century, following Hines and Bayliss 2013; here see pp. 91, 105, 383.
242 Geake 1997, 262.
243 See Sherlock 2012, passim (above); Speake 1989, 126.
244 See e.g. Bierbrauer, Wicker, Geake, Yorke, Gräslund and Staeker in Carver 2003a.
245 Penn 2011.
246 Hamerow 2016, 425, 447.
247 Angenendt (1986, 749–754) argues that aristocratic families withheld selected heirs from baptism to ensure the succession if the conversion project failed politically; cf Hamerow 2015, 105–106.

248 Hadley 2002; Buckberry and Cherryson 2010.
249 Reynolds 2009.
250 This follows Toop's (2005) revision of the Whithorn sequence (see Chapter 5). Hill's (1997) Period I is c. 500–730, and Period II, 730–845).
251 Maldonado Ramírez 2011, 102–103. Maldonado uses the term 'head box' to describe these burials, since some have a stone over the face. The side stones are the more normal occurrence, called 'ear muffs' in Ireland. Here we stick to the more general term 'head-support' for the type.
252 Reed 1995.
253 Maldonado Ramírez 2011, 244 sees them as successors.
254 This piece of history is unlikely to be enhanced until the Scots overcome their inhibitions about excavating graveyards.
255 See Chapter 3, p. 219, for a list of dated monastic foundations.
256 See Chapter 3, p. 218 for an account of the plan of the monastery and its buildings.
257 Okasha 1999, 113–116.
258 Okasha 1999, 116; the experience of Whitby and the Hilton of Caboll stone reminds us of the down-to-earth attitude of many local inhabitants towards early medieval antiquities, the value of which was by no means self-evident. A Mr Smyth endeavouring to make records in 1921 was 'subject to the captious wit of a crowd imbued with prurient curiosity' (Okasha 1999, 121). See Sîan Jones in James et al. 2008 for a more sanguine view of local interest.
259 Okasha 1999, 125.
260 Daniels 2007, 79: C14 of 660–940 for the articulated skeleton, 640–780 for stratigraphically earlier disturbed bones, among which were those of a child.
261 Daniels 2007, 74–80.
262 Excavations by John Hinchliffe and Marilyn Brown, still unpublished at the time of writing (2016). Summarised in Daniels 2007, 82–93.
263 Daniels 2007, 97–107.
264 *Contra* Anderson in Daniels 2007, 99).
265 Daniels 2007, 174, Fig 8, 12; the plan is reproduced in Chapter 3 in a revised and amended version.
266 Daniels 2007, 134–136, 127.
267 Loveluck in Daniels 2007, 187; note that the stone-edged graves at Church Walk and Back Gladstone Street are not cist graves.
268 See note 244 above.
269 Cramp 2005 (site), 2006 (finds).
270 Cramp 2005, 23–26; there is no good evidence for a Roman signal station at these sites or at Hartlepool, cf Daniels 2007, 82.
271 Cramp 2005 75, 78.
272 Cramp 2005, 76–90 (with Pam Lowther).
273 Cramp 2005, 180; Graves 75/96, 70/161).
274 Pam Lowther in Cramp 2005, 173–186.
275 For example, the unpublished cemetery at the Old Minster Winchester; see p. 430 for a summary.
276 Wilson 2008, 46.
277 Manning and Stead 2006.
278 Harrison 2007.
279 Harrison 2007, 176–178.
280 Summarised in Graham-Campbell and Batey 1998, 135–138.
281 Owen and Dalland 1999.
282 Dunwell et al. 1995, 731–733; Close-Brooks et al. 1995.
283 Graham-Campbell and Batey 1998, 113–118.
284 Graham-Campbell and Batey 1998, 118–122.
285 Wilson 2008, 25, 27.
286 Bersu and Wilson 1966; Wilson 2008, 27–41.
287 cf Wilson 2008, 45–46.
288 Freke 2002, Grave 84.16/L 483.
289 Freke 2002, 57.
290 Richards 1995, 2004.
291 See Chapter 3.
292 Richards 2004, 107.

293 Biddle and Kjølbye-Biddle 1992, 2001; and see Chapter 3. This excavation had not been fully published at the time of writing (2016).
294 Jarman et al. 2018.
295 Crone and Hindmarch 2016, 18, 48; Viking grave: 60–68; and see Chapter 3, p. 248, *Did the English have monasteries?*
296 Astill 2009, 222, 225.
297 Astill 2009, 227; Blair 2005, 426.
298 Boddington 1996.
299 Boddington 1996, 54, Fig 66.
300 Boddington 1996, 70–86.
301 Craig and Buckberry 2010.
302 Hadley 2002, 2007, 2010; Buckberry 2007.
303 Phillips and Heywood 1995, 82–85; and Table 2, p. 88.
304 Lang in Phillips and Heywood 1995, Vol II, 440.
305 Hadley 2002, 211.
306 See also Wilmore 1939 for a series of Roman-Medieval stone coffins from Gloucestershire.
307 By FAS Heritage in 2016; personal communication Cecily Spall.
308 The following comes from a summary owed to Kjølbye-Biddle 1992.
309 Kjølbye-Biddle 1992, 217. Subsequent excavation and analysis of additional graves at the same site has shown that although there were skeletons suggested by stable isotopes to originate in Pannonia, there was little correspondence between these and the 'exotic' grave goods; see Chapter 2, 54).
310 Kjølbye-Biddle 1992, 224.
311 Kjølbye-Biddle in Phillips and Heywood 1995.
312 Hadley 2010, 104.
313 Holloway 2010, 84; Biddle 1969, 321; Phillips and Heywood 1995, 87; Henderson and Bidwell 1982.
314 Dawes and Magilton 1980, 16.
315 Holloway 2010, citing examples at Oxford and York.
316 Holloway 2010; Shoesmith 1980, 24; Kjølbye-Biddle 1992, 229–230.
317 Holloway 2010, 88.
318 Holloway 2010, 85.
319 Quoted by Holloway 2010, 87.
320 Carver 1980, 13.
321 Rodwell 2011. These burials belong to the later 10th and earlier 11th century, p. 234. 'The scientific dating programme carried out on a selection of the earliest identifiable burials suggest a date of cal AD 975–1010'. There may be some continuity with the neighbouring cemetery at Casteldyke, where the radiocarbon dates were 7th to 8th century. These dates are wisely qualified: 'it is highly improbable that the latest burial graves at Castledyke and the earliest graves at St Peter's have been found and scientifically dated'.
322 Hadley 2010, 104.
323 Reynolds 2009.
324 For examples of double and triple burials implying punishment for sexual deviance, see Reynolds 2009, 170–177; Hayman and Reynolds 2005, 238; for marriage to one's stepmother Reynolds 2009, 24–25; Whitelock 1968, 150.
325 Reynolds 2009, 232 (Fig 69), 240.
326 Sofield 2015.
327 Sofield 2015, 381.
328 Hadley 2007, 199.
329 Hadley 2002, 216–219.
330 For overviews of Irish burial see O'Brien 1992, 2003, 2009.
331 O'Sullivan et al. 2014a, 285–290.
332 E.g. Madden's Hill, Kiltale (Eogan J. 2010, 110).
333 O'Sullivan et al. 2014a, 285–300.
334 O'Brien 2003.
335 Ó Carragáin 2009a, 357.
336 Eogan 2012, Stage 6; Raftery 2000, 195.
337 Eogan 2012, Stage 7, p. 751.
338 McCormick and Murray 2007. This assemblage is definitive for early medieval Ireland.
339 Eogan 2012, 76; Stage 9.

340 Eogan 2012, 751–753; McCormick and Murray 2007, Ch 3.
341 Eogan 2010.
342 Eogan 2010, 114.
343 Eogan 2010, 112.
344 O'Sullivan et al. 2014a, 311; Raystown, Seaver 2010; Carrowkeel, Lehane et al. 2010.
345 Johnstown, Clarke and Carlin 2008; Clarke 2010.
346 O' Brien 1992, 136, 2009, 150; Ó Carragáin 2009a, 357, 2010b, 224.
347 O'Sullivan et al. 2014a, 304.
348 Ljungkvist 2008.
349 Ljungkvist 2008, 18.
350 Persson and Olofsson 2004.
351 Ljungkvist et al. 2011.
352 Krogh 1982.
353 Hvass 2011.
354 Brøgger et al. 1917; Bill and Daly 2012.

5 Monumentality

Sculpture, churches and illuminated books

Introduction

The word 'monument' has been used in this book to set apart cultural material of high investment designed to express the ideology, deliberate or unwitting, of its age and people. In the eyes of archaeologists, monuments are manifestos, branding allegiance and advertising agendas. Some monumentality has already been noted, in metal brooches (Chapter 2), in settlements in the form of the hall and planned layout (Chapter 3), and met again in burial with its earth mounds and cairns and references to the past (Chapter 4).

The monuments considered in this chapter are primarily stone sculpture, churches and illuminated parchment codices. Their archaeological interest may be defined as what their builders intended by their form, configuration and provenance, which taken together may be seen as their 'message'. Many of the later carved stones overtly proclaim their Christianity, deploying ingenious ornament and iconography laden with metaphor, allusion and allegory; but it is not their art or theology that is at issue here but their economics, social context and political purpose – archaeology's staple diet: not so much the deciphering of what is figured on the stones, its sources and references, but their role as signals of changing times and changing world views in different regions; in this they will prove to be very potent. The differences between the stone monuments erected in the different regions of Britain provide a starting point for the inquiry.[1]

All the same I have tried to learn how to behave correctly in the provinces of art history and epigraphy, because it is primarily their scholars who have gathered up the fragments, described and deciphered them with meticulous care and made them available in a series of publications of enduring value which are themselves monumental in every positive sense.[2] In these will be found detailed descriptions, images, interpretations and deconstructions of every piece and pattern, however little or large. Since the archaeological investigation of the sites of any monumental production has been minimal, this chapter relies greatly on these studies for date and context. Even so, in recent years the agenda has expanded to include the broader archaeological agenda, just as it has in burials, leading a new generation to include the landscape automatically in its studies.[3] Here attention is drawn to the property of the monument as an investment, its role in the geography of its contemporaries, its political and ideological signals (signals of power and statements of principle), the way those who erected them construed the pre-existing landscape and the experience of the monument in its long and chancy journey to the present day, ideas now characterised as 'materiality, biography and landscape'.[4]

While the matters to be treated are linked by their high investment, sacral quality and individuality, the carved stones are by far the most numerous of the three types of monument to be considered in this chapter. Archaeological examples of early churches are rare and cluster in Formative 3. The illuminated books, while just as striking as signals of the times, are no longer generally in their place of manufacture and had limited exposure to the community. Being portable and made of organic materials they were especially vulnerable to flood, fire and theft, and out of the many thousands of codices that must have once graced religious houses, their corpus represents only a few libraries, unevenly dispersed. Accordingly, the chapter is dominated by carved stone monuments, and the churches and picture books, so central to Formative thinking but so partial in their survival, are paraded briefly in a coda at the end.

The impetus for analysing carved stones as players in the landscape has come partly from studies of monuments within prehistory, partly from a feeling that they were often concerned with memory and so analogous to burial, and partly from a desire to highlight their social and political roles. They may express allegiance to a demographic group, an intellectual territory or a perceived ethnicity.[5] Monastic themes may relate to monastic precincts, secular themes to secular patronage, although these are not always easy to tell apart.[6] A stone monument has a social context, expressed by its cost of production, its relation to contemporary settlements and its location in the landscape, and an intellectual context expressed in its references to ideas, literature, other art forms and monuments near and far and in the past. In addition it has a legacy, since it will interact with those that see it so long as it remains standing.[7] The cognitive link of sculpture with the celebration of burial is clear enough and might lead to the conclusion that stone monuments take over where furnished burial leaves off. However, standing stone monuments are not only concerned with remembrance, or even memory, but also exercise functions of intellectual manifesto, land claiming and even conquest. Furthermore, the distribution of these monuments and their functions changed radically over the three formative periods and from region to region (Figure 5.1).

Definitions

In early Medieval Britain as it has come down to us, the overwhelming strength of the carved stone monuments lies in its pillars, slabs and crosses. In the 5th–7th century the incised pillars cluster in the British north and west, and their primary purpose is to structure the landscape for secular power. From the 8th century this same area is marked by standing crosses and cross-slabs, now carrying powerfully executed Christian messages, the sentinels of the monastic movement. From the 9th century these were superseded in the regions of north-east and north-west England by the hybrid creations of Anglo-Scandinavian carvers. From the 10th century it is the turn of the English regions of the south and south-east to demonstrate their own version of sacred art.

The monuments take many forms. An inscription may be made on an outcrop, flat rock or boulder, as with the Pictish symbols at Trusty's Hill and Dunadd. An 'inscribed pillar' means a roughly shaped stone intended to stand upright carrying an inscription in Roman or Ogham letters. A 'cross-marked pillar' is a stone of similar shape marked with a cross, with or without an inscription. A 'grave marker' means a small, usually square or rectangular stone, recognised because it carries a cross or inscription that was intended to lie on or stand at one end of the grave of a Christian. A 'grave-slab' is a larger version of a grave marker, lying on the surface ('recumbent'). A 'sarcophagus' is technically a solid hollowed stone coffin with a lid of a kind well known from Roman and Medieval Britain but rare in the early middle ages. The most famous example, 'The St Andrew's Sarcophagus', is really a slab shrine or even an elaborate cist grave constructed to stand above ground so that its carving

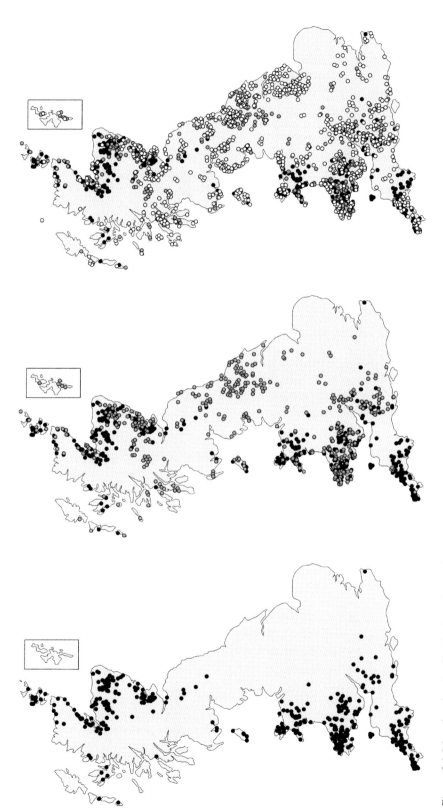

Figure 5.1 Map showing the distribution of carved stone monuments in the three Formative periods. From left, Fm 1 (5–7th century); Fm 2 (7–9th century); Fm 3 (9–11th century).

(FAS Heritage)

can be seen and the presence of its inmate felt. The 'cross-slab', mainly confined to Pictland, is a large rectangular slab with the proportions of a playing card or the folio of a Gospel Book. A 'cross' means a monument with a shaft, square or round in section, on a base and carrying a cross head with free arms, which may be supported by a ring. This form becomes tall and imposing in the 8th to 9th century in north and west Britain and in Ireland, where it is known as a High Cross, a variant of a more widespread 'Grand Cross'.[8] They are richly ornamented with motifs of Mediterranean and insular derivation carved expertly in relief and feature vignettes, many recognisably from the Old Testament (for example those concerned with David and Daniel), others apparently portraying people in action everyday life (see also Chapter 2). Where particular characters are displayed, they may stand in niches and are often (but not always) players in the Christian project (evangelists, apostles, desert fathers or other saints). Those celebrated on the Grand Crosses celebrate the holy rather than heroes, but none is known to mark a burial. Instead they use locations of high visibility to proclaim the arrival or progress of the Christian idea or mark the confines of a centre of the new omnipotence: the precinct of a monastery or the boundaries of its estates.

Dating

For the sake of simplicity, Fm 1, 2 and 3 are used to provide a chronological framework of real time to which the various monuments may be assigned with greater or lesser confidence. Archaeology has contributed very little to the dating of sculpture, with the exception of some stratified fragments in Pictland dated by radiocarbon (Old Scatness, Pool, Portmahomack). The dates rely mainly on art history – and the survey undertaken here would be impossible without its verdicts – and on three kinds of epigraphy: ogham, runes and Latin letters.

Epigraphy

Ogham, formed of combinations of lines, would appear to be the earliest non-Roman insular script, originating in Ireland in the 4th century or earlier and spreading widely into south Wales, western Scotland and Pictland.[9] It offers us a record of the names of post-Roman people and what they sounded like. The majority of the more than 360 examples are dated to the 5th, 6th and into the 7th century (our *Fm 1*). The ogham letters consist of groups of lines cut against or across an axial line or the edges of quadrilateral pillar stones (Figure 5.2). Later equivalences with Latin show us that this was an alphabet of 16 consonants and five vowels. Five 'letters' (*flesc*, the *forfeda*) were later added representing diphthongs. Because it is an alphabet, not a pictographic system (like the Pictish symbols, p. 473), the most likely origin of ogham is thought to be Latin, the nearest method of spelling out words with letters used in the island across the water during the time it was occupied by the Romans. Names with more or less the same spelling in Latin and ogham script on the same stone in Wales and south-west Britain reinforce the notion that this was a script that was on conversational terms with Latin. It is only a short stride to assume that the one was owed to the other.[10]

This explanation does not entirely satisfy: if Latin was the teacher, why not use the teacher's own tongue? The ogham letters do not progress in the order of the Latin alphabet, and they have quite different names (*beth, luis* . . .). It also seems counter-intuitive that a script could simply be invented rather than emerge from deeper usage. As we have often seen, the pre-literate past of Ireland and Britain is a deep dark thicket, and even small excursions bring anxiety. To derive ogham from Greek seems far-fetched to some, but in practice it is little

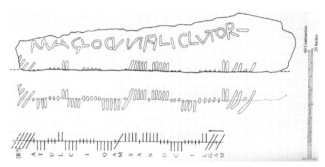

Figure 5.2 Ogham inscriptions. (Left): Brandsbutt Stone, Inverurie with Pictish symbols (crescent and V-rod and serpent and Z-rod) and with an ogham inscription reading IRATAD-DOARENS. (Top right): Slab from Nevern, Pembrokeshire (cat. P70) reading *Maglicunas maqi Clutar . . .* in ogham and Latin letters. (Bottom): Detail of inscription with the ogham alphabet.

(A: Wainwright 1955, Plate 12; © Society of Antiquaries of Scotland, with permission 8 Nov; B: MOHC; C: (diagram) Edwards 2007, 391; under licence from Royal Commission on the Ancient and Historical Monuments of Wales)

better than deriving it from Latin; it does not leave the confines of the Classical heritage. To refer to the signs of the pre-Latin Iberian *stelae* is at least to follow the trail likely to have introduced Celtic languages into the northerly isles; but these letters of the Phoenicians and Tartessians are already more sophisticated than ogham. Ogham's simple strokes, numbering one to five, suggest a sign language using the hands, where the fingers or the whole palm of one hand are placed against the palm edge of the other. We know Late Saxon monks also made use of sign language.[11] For obvious reasons, the currency of any sign language is hard to track, but it would make sense if such a one already existed in pre-literate Ireland. Inspired as it may be by neighbouring Romans, it could then be phonetically transliterated using the names of the letters, reified in the form of lines for the fingers and so displayed on stones to bring comfort that the new ideology had not erased the old.

The ogham message on the stones is a name and a patrynomic (X son of Y) in the genitive, where a possession is understood: 'The stone of', 'the land of', 'the grave of'. But no ogham stone has yet been found in association with a grave or a church that is contemporary. Only 14% also have crosses, and in some cases these can be shown to have been added at a later date. They mainly date from the 5th to the 7th century, with some inscriptions making a later appearance. The impression is that they are primarily concerned to name a man and his father, probably to signal the ownership of land during a period in which land was being claimed, or in danger of being claimed, by incomers, in this case the Irish.[12] They are neither overtly Christian nor necessarily non-Christian. This is a period in which the nature of the religion plays second fiddle to the ownership of territory, and we will be arguing this for western Britain and the Borders, where the names are generally Irish, and for Pictland, where the names are less easy to identify. Ownership has primacy not least because this is as much a migration period for the Irish as it is for the Saxons on the other side of the island. The occurrence of Irish names and the location of ogham stones is held to indicate the presence of Irish incomers, even as far afield as the Tweed valley and Aberdeenshire.[13]

Runes, a Germanic script, was in use on wood at least from the 2nd century AD; the 24 letters of the alphabet (the *futhork*) were formed by lines cut along or at an angle to the grain. They appear on metal as the name of the owner or nickname of the object (for example, 'stabber' on a spearhead). On coins they may spell the name of a king. Runic memorial stones occur fleetingly in Fm 1 (Sandwich), runes of Anglian type appear in Fm 2 (Hartlepool) and of Norse form in Fm 3, especially in the Isle of Man, where they long endured along with ogham[14] (Figure 5.3).

In *Latin epigraphy*, the task has been to marry the dates suggested by the comparative forms of the Latin letters (palaeography) with the comparative forms of the Celtic names (British, Irish or Pictish) that they spell (phonology). In general this has resulted in a consensus, allowing the assignation of Latin inscriptions and Celtic names to periods between the 5th and 7th century, with four or more subdivisions.[15] Enhancing Jackson's pioneering work of the 1950s, Sims-Williams found 28 sub-periods in which certain names or parts of names were prominent.[16] There are a few examples from the island in which a person named on a stone can be identified with one known from a text, although the parallels are perilous. In Fm 1, *Catamanus Rex Sapientissimus Opinatissimus Omnium Regum* on Anglesey (AN26) is identified with Cadfan ap Iago (wisest and most esteemed of all kings), active between 616 and 625 (see p. 502). In Fm 2 and 3 Latin inscriptions occur less frequently, but more persons and purposes can be identified; for example Constantine King of Picts on the Dupplin cross,[17] Hywel ap Rhys on a cross at Llantwit Major (G63), or the Eliseg pillar (see pp. 502, 550).[18]

In recent decades, early medieval art historians have achieved a broad consensus in devising a chronological framework for the 5th to 11th century in Britain, using comparative data drawn from the contemporary scene in Scandinavia, north Germany, Ireland, the Continent, and the Mediterranean as well as the legacy of the Roman empire and the British Iron Age. There naturally remain some grey areas, and every new find presents a challenge. While the motifs used in carvings have a long life, their manner of execution allows the most popular (interlace, spiroform, key patterns and vine scroll) to be placed in Fm 2 and 3 with some precision, in general changing in sculpture from geometric exactitude achieved with ruler and compass to more relaxed chunky examples. The animal forms provide a still more diagnostic evolutionary sequence. The Anglo-Saxon imported species ('Style 1' and 'Style 2') do not survive in sculpture, but their descendants interbreed with native species (bull, deer, dog, goose) and selected Mediterranean mythical beasts (centaur) to dominate the cultural landscape of the north and west, as the 'Insular Style' in Fm 2. Fm 3 sees the intrusion of a rich new menagerie from Scandinavia and new plants, notably the acanthus from Carolingian France.[19]

f u þ a/o r k h n i a s t b m l R e æ

Figure 5.3 Runic inscriptions. A. (Top left): Hartlepool no.1 Name-slab with alpha and omega and the name in Anglian runes: *Hildithryth* (a female name) *Corpus* I, Illus. 433. B. (Top right): Stone from Maughold in the Isle of Man (Maughold 145) showing inscription in Manx runes and in ogham saying 'John the Priest cut these runes' (12th/13th century). C. (Bottom): The Manx *futhork* (runic alphabet).

(A: courtesy and © Corpus of Anglo-Saxon Stone Sculpture, photographer T. Middlemass; B: courtesy D.M Wilson; Wilson 2008, Fig 38; C: courtesy D.M Wilson. Wilson 2008 Fig 36)

Sequences in outline

Pioneer scholars organised the monuments into groups, classes or categories, largely based on their form. Even as they were being advised against it, archaeologists have found it difficult to resist pasting these groups into a chronology. In practice the groups (which usually come in threes) are moderately consonant with the three formative periods, although there is a fuzzy boundary in each region over which individual sets may be held to spill. When more precise dates become available, for example by excavation combined with radiocarbon dating, it is likely that many more subgroups will begin to appear: but the overall sequence is assumed here to be reasonably valid. At least, using the general forms and the three periods, we will hopefully provide a *vade mecum* by which the reader can navigate.

The Pictish sequence (Figure 5.4) can serve as an example. The earliest type consist of unshaped slabs that carry Pictish symbols and no other ornament (Allen and Anderson's Class I). These belong to the 5th to 7th century (Fm 1) and are sited with a view to overseeing land. From the 7th century (Fm 2), simple cross-marked stones appear without Pictish symbols, some

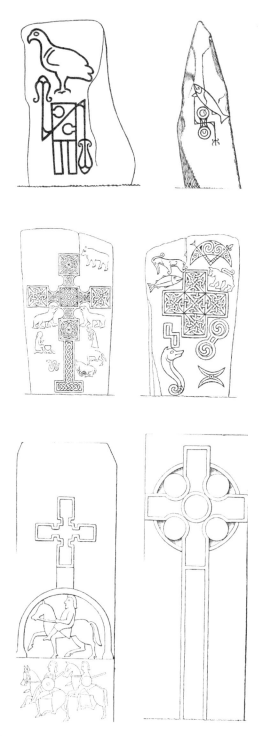

Figure 5.4 The Pictish sequence. (Top): Birnie 1, Edderton 1 (Class I). (Centre): Ulbster front and back faces (Class II). (Bottom): Edderton 2 front and back faces (Class III).

(Allen and Anderson 1903)

of these unshaped (Henderson's Class IV). From the later 7th or 8th century (also Fm 2), masoned upright stones come into use, showing the cross on one side and Pictish symbols accompanied by secular or Biblical scenes on the other (Allen and Anderson's Class II). Some of these at least are grouped at sites that have proved to be monasteries (Portmahomack). The fourth type (Allen and Anderson's Class III) and the fifth belong to the 9th–11th century (Fm 3), when the power of the Picts was broken and Pictland merged into Scotland. They have no Pictish symbols and may take the familiar local form of the cross slab, or the free-standing cross preferred in the west.

This sequence reports a change in the purpose and meaning of the stones as indicated by their location, size and iconography.[20] Meggan Gondek has measured the relative efforts required to extract the stone and carve it in south Pictland, Argyll and Galloway and showed that the corpus passed through three phases of investment: in her Phase I (6th/7th, i.e. Fm 1) the pieces are modest and dispersed, in Phase II (8th/9th century, Fm 2) investment is massive and concentrated at nodal points (Iona, Whithorn, St Andrews, Meigle, St Vigeans). Phase III (9th/11th century, Fm 3) shows a drop in the display of symbolic wealth in Dal Riada and Pictland. In Galloway it continues with the Whithorn school.[21] The building of sequences is assisted where large numbers of stones congregate in the same place (for example at Iona, Portmahomack, Margam and Wearmouth/Jarrow), and there are some cases of 'stratification', where a later ornamental or iconographical scheme overlays an earlier, as at Clydai in Pembrokeshire (Figure 5.5).

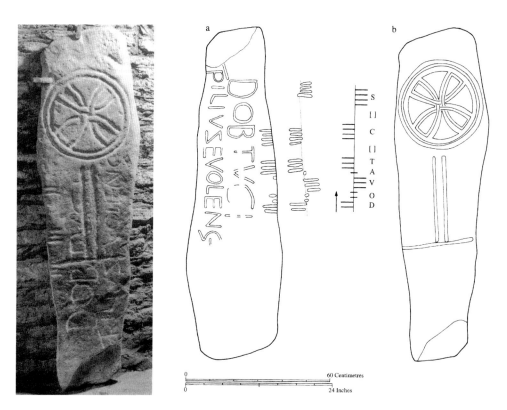

Figure 5.5 'Converted' stone from Clydai (Pembrokeshire); PHASE 1 (a): 5th/6th century inscription in Latin and ogham letters; PHASE 2 (b): 7th/8th century floriate cross.

(Edwards 2007, P15; under licence from the Royal Commission on the Ancient and Historical Monuments of Wales)

The survival of the monuments can be accounted relatively good: they are robust and heavy, and although recycled in medieval church foundations and as gateposts, we can guess that they seldom travelled far from their place of origin. Nevertheless, the corpus is unevenly distributed in time and space, and this needs explaining: whereas all regions and periods required apparel, settlement and burial, not all had the incentive or the wherewithal to carve stone. Its occurrence should have a strong symbolic significance. The corpus of Fm 1 consists mainly of inscribed stones distributed in the 'British' areas of Pictland, the Scottish Borders, Wales and the south-west. The crosses of Fm 2 are widely spread and of outstanding quality in Pictland and Northumbria, with a plethora of simpler crosses spreading from western Scotland to Wales. Grand Fm 3 monuments occur occasionally in the north and west, but the 9th–11th century is the time in which the Anglo-Saxon (and former Roman) heartland of Southumbria, which largely ignored sculpture for four centuries, leads the field in its range and quality of Christian carved stone monuments. It also has the largest set of identifiable stone church buildings, which, with rare exceptions, appear in the rest of the island only after the Norman conquest.

The corpus and other sources

The coverage of the island is complete and comprehensive in different ways and to different degrees (Figure 5.6; and see Table 5.1). An inventory of the stone monuments in Scotland and Pictland (Regions 1 and 2) was compiled by Allen and Anderson, who recorded and classified 508 stones in 249 locations.[22] This inventory was published with a comprehensive commentary in 1903 and reissued but not updated in 1993. For Western Scotland (Region 1), the Royal Commission published a new inventory with a detailed commentary by Ian Fisher in 2001, while the understanding of the references and meaning of the Pictish monuments (mainly in Region 2) has been developed and enlarged over 50 years by G and I Henderson, culminating in her 2004 work (with George Henderson) which reviewed the whole range of Pictish Art. Inscribed monuments in the Scottish Borders are mapped and discussed in Forsyth 2005 and the Isle of Man by Kermode (1907) in an edition updated by David Wilson in 1994. Wales has about 150 inscribed stones in Fm 1 and more than 400 other monuments. The corpus was reviewed by Nash-Williams in 1950 and has since been updated, revised and comprehensively published in three volumes.[23] The counties of modern England are being surveyed in Rosemary Cramp's monumental *Corpus of Anglo-Saxon Sculpture* and is complete apart from East Anglia and the East Midlands.

It will be seen in Table 5.1 that many regions already surveyed are blank in Fm 1 and that the English heartland south of the Humber is largely blank in Fm 1 and 2. In this chapter as in others the term 'Southumbria' refers to Lincolnshire, East Anglia and the home counties, Mercia and Northumbria being treated separately. The question of why Southumbria is poorly represented in Fm 1 and 2 will be confronted later (p. 508).[24] Meanwhile it can be noted that material gathered in the 'Corpus of Anglo-Saxon Sculpture' is in practice richest in the Anglo-British areas such as Northumbria, Cumbria, Mercia and the south-west, and the sculptural trends ride with some insouciance over the modern county boundaries.

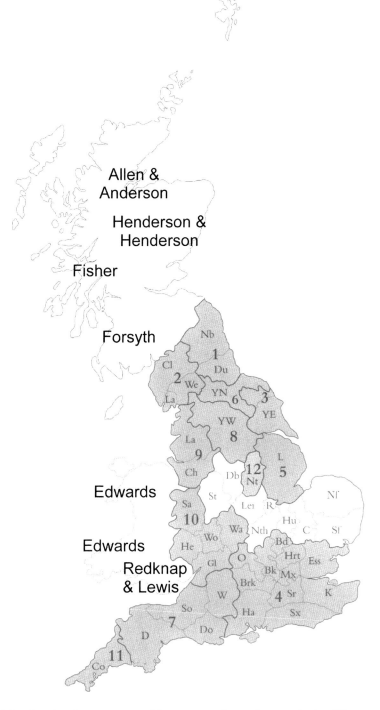

Figure 5.6 Map showing the areas covered by surveys of carved stones in the different regions of Britain to 2017. The counties of England have been covered by the *Corpus of Anglo-Saxon Stone Sculpture* 1984– (grey stipple) or will be (unstippled). Allen and Anderson covered the whole of modern Scotland; Henderson and Henderson's (2004) study focussed on Pictland, Fisher's on Argyll and the western Isles and Forsyth's on the Borders. Edwards 2013, Edwards 2007 and Redknap and Lewis 2007 have covered north, south-west and south-east Wales respectively.

(FAS Heritage)

Table 5.1 Sculpture in Britain

REGION	Period 1 (5th–7th century)	Period 2 (7th–9th century)	Period 3 (9th–11th century)
1. NW Britain[25]	[one ogham on Gigha]	Ogham and Pictish symbol outliers Grave slabs with crosses High Crosses with religious themes	Grand crosses and other Viking monuments; Hogbacks on Clyde
2. NE Britain[26]	Symbols prehistoric monuments	Cross-slabs with religious and secular themes	Scottish Victory slabs Viking hogbacks on Tay and Forth
3. Wales N[27]	Inscribed stones in Latin or ogham marking land	Plain Latin crosses on monastic and church sites	Grand crosses at sites of mother churches Eliseg's pillar
3. Wales SW[28]	Inscribed pillars in Latin and ogham with Irish names marking land	Cross-marked stones at large central and small local monasteries	Grand crosses at Bishops' seats and other churches
3. Wales SE[29]	Inscribed stones with British names marking land	Crosses at monasteries: Margam, Llantwit	Grand Crosses with elite donors at monasteries or other churches
4. SW Britain[30]	Pillar stones with Latin or ogham inscriptions marking land	Victory crosses at Anglian monasteries at Glastonbury, Bradford-on-Avon	Grand crosses at Penwith and Cardinham
5. Northumberland and Durham[31]	BLANK	1–Architectural sculpture, inscribed grave slabs (English names in Latin and runes) 2–Expansion using Victory crosses (Auckland, Rothbury)	1–Viking memorials (e.g. Sockburn) 2–Grand crosses (e.g. Durham)
5. N Yorks[32]	BLANK	Whitby crosses Anglian grave markers, crosses and Victory crosses	Anglo-Scand. crosses
5. E Yorks[33]	BLANK	Incised grave slabs and cross shafts	Anglo-Scand. crosses
5. W Yorks[34]	BLANK	Architectural sculpture at Ripon and Ledsham. Victory crosses at Otley, Ilkley, Dewsbury	Anglo-Scand. crosses and hogbacks
6. Scottish Borders[35]	Incised proprietorial stones	Anglian monasticism heralded by Victory Crosses at Bewcastle, Ruthwell Monastery at Whithorn	Grand crosses Viking hogbacks on Tweed
6. IoM[36]	Inscribed Latin and ogham proprietorial stones	Incised cross-marked small and large slabs Monastery at Maughold	Viking crosses with ogham and runes
6. Cumbria and N Lancs[37]	Addingham 4? Otherwise BLANK	Victory crosses at Anglian monasteries at Addingham, Bewcastle, Dacre, Irton	Viking crosses and hogbacks Gosforth

REGION	Period 1 (5th–7th century)	Period 2 (7th–9th century)	Period 3 (9th–11th century)
6. S Lancs and Cheshire[38]	BLANK	Victory Crosses in Lune Valley and Sandbach	Viking crosses
6. Mercia[39]	BLANK	Architectural sculpture, Grave slabs and grand crosses (Deerhurst)	Carolingian formal monuments in minsters (Gloucester)
7. Lincolnshire[40]	BLANK	Some grave markers and a Victory Cross at Edenham	Anglo-Scand. grave covers and crosses
7. SE Britain (Southumbrian England)[41]	Two pillar stones inscribed with German names in runes 6th/7th century Early 7th-century Imitation Roman architectural sculpture at Canterbury and Reculver	9th-century figurative sculpture at Reculver	Winchester School architectural and formal Less than 10% grand crosses

The numbers in the first column refer to the seven regions defined in *Chapter 1*.

A field trip

The carved stone monuments of Britain offer a diversity that is initially bewildering, but like a foreign language, slowly reveals something of its structure. Archaeologists like to start by meeting the material itself face to face, so rather than serving up too many initial abstractions, the procedure here, as in other chapters, will be to set out on a 'Field Trip' in which we will visit a number of destinations, selected for the number of the monuments and their relatively strong context. Our trip will start in the north in the Moray Firth and head south via the Isle of Man and Margam in south Wales, ending in Cornwall. This will hopefully present us with a wide range of monuments from the three periods placed in their landscape and their region. These four examples also have the asset of relative date, allowing them to be compared in chronological sequence.

In the Moray Firth

The 'Firthlands' in north-east Scotland have some claim to be the origin point of the Pictish symbols, and thus the early type of stone monument that carries symbols only.[42] A large group of these stones is to be found around the Moray Firth, positioned in general on the edge of good agricultural land in the straths or at the edge of the upland in the case of the narrow fertile Golspie strip that runs beside the seashore (Figure 5.7). The agricultural location of the simple symbol stones (Class I) suggests that they are intended to mark territory.[43] They may also mark burials in combination with round or square barrows, which have been used through prehistory for the same purpose. Following this analogy, the symbols themselves ought to indicate the person or the people to whom ownership or use of the land refers, through inheritance, and indeed there is some consensus today that the symbols represent names. The purpose of the Fm 1 stones can thus be seen as ancestral or 'proprietorial', following Forsyth.[44] The date of these monuments is between the 5th to 7th centuries, our Formative 1, a period in which such labelling of land apparently became important, perhaps goaded by pressure from outside, such as the Irish/Scots, who would soon introduce ogham into the same territory. The symbol slab from Dunrobin (**Dunrobin 1**) provides an example (Figure 5.8). It was found in 1854 half a mile east of

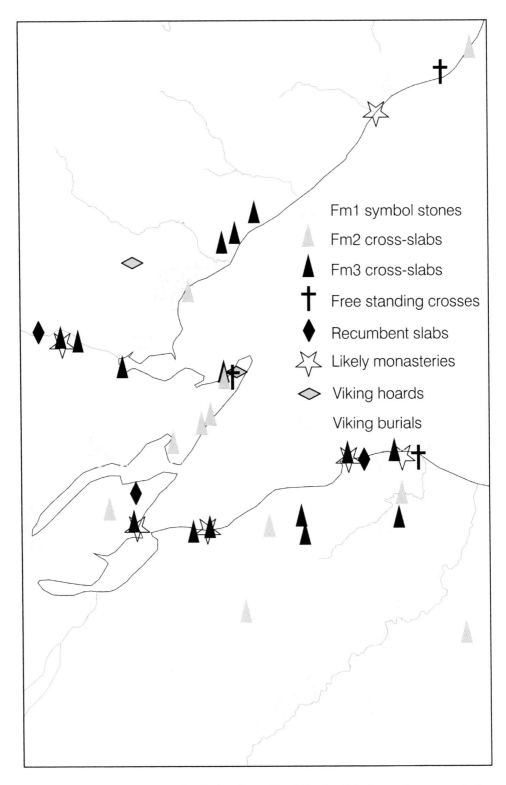

Figure 5.7 The Moray Firth, showing the locations of Fm 1, Fm 2 and Fm 3 carved stones, equivalent to Pictish Class I (symbols only), Class II (symbols plus crosses) and Class III (crosses without symbols).

(Carver 2008b; FAS Heritage)

Figure 5.8 Pictish symbols on Dunrobin 1 (Sutherland).
(Author)

Dunrobin Castle, one of three slabs used as the lid for a long cist grave containing two adult men.[45] On the flat face of the slab are carved symbols, easily recognisable as that of a salmon, a sword handle, a mirror and a comb. These symbols in combination are thought to represent names and the mirror and comb together to indicate the feminine: thus the symbols would read something like [the marker of] 'Mrs Swordfish' (the interpretation of the symbols is discussed on p. 473).

The successor stones of Fm 2 (7th/8th century) were larger, symmetrically shaped flat-faced rectangular slabs bearing on one side a cross and on the other Pictish symbols and a variety of animals, people and activities of a secular or sacred character – sometimes both combined, for example in the person of David.[46] A Moray Firth example is the slab from **Golspie** now curated in the summerhouse at Dunrobin Castle, which has a front face showing a (damaged) cross with a shaft and side panels bearing interlace and fretwork worked in low relief. The reverse face is incised and busy with symbols: from top to bottom, the rectangle, the Pictish beast, the salmon, the flower, a crescent and a double disc (Figure 5.9). In the centre, left, is a man with a beaked nose and pointed beard carrying an axe in his right hand and a knife in the other, reminiscent of the Rhynie man (p. 498). Facing him is a dog-like

Figure 5.9 Cross-slab from Golspie (Sutherland). (Left): Cross side. (Right): Symbol side.
(Source © Historic Environment Scotland, reproduced under licence)

creature with a curled tail. At the base are two aquatic serpents intertwined. Although it is not excluded that some of the lower symbols have been added, the whole resembles a composition placed within a frame. The edges of the monument are ornamented with continuous runs of double spirals, and incised on the roll moulding of the frame on the symbol side is a lengthy ogham inscription of at least 30 legible letters, including eight pairs; little is recognisable apart from the group spelling MAQQ ('son of' in Irish).[47] The edge of the cross side has been reworked in recent centuries to carry a more modern inscription 'Here is the burial place to Robert Gordon eldest son to Alex Gordon of Sutherland'. This is a monument with a complex history of use and reuse to which the term 'biography' may be justly applied.

The Fm 2 stones are clearly of Christian association and occupy a different location in their landscape to those of Fm 1, being gathered together at sites that were or subsequently became the sites of churches and/or monasteries (see Figure 5.7). These were sited less to command fertile land and more with a view to marking nodal points of communication by sea or land. The idea that they also mark the sites of monasteries has been greatly strengthened by research at **Portmahomack** on the Tarbat peninsula, where 263 fragments of carved stones were recovered in stratified sequences in a large-scale excavation. These sequences anchored by 71 radiocarbon dates showed that the monastery to which all the

Figure 5.10 Pictish carving at Portmahomack (Easter Ross). From top, left to right: Grave marker carved in relief (TR33), grave marker with simple scratched cross (TR25), corbel with human head (TR223/263); side view of sarcophagus lid (TR22), sculptor's chisel.

(Carver et al. 2016, Chapter 5.3; FAS Heritage)

stone monuments belonged was constructed on an elite secular site towards the end of the 7th century and attacked between 780 and 810, probably in a Viking raid, at which point the greater part of the monuments were dispersed or broken up. The collection as a whole is therefore independently dated to a short period equivalent to little more than a century (the 8th). The range of stone monuments in use includes grave markers carrying crosses of greater or lesser simplicity, which originally stood at the head or foot of rows of graves of a predominately male community (Figure 5.10). There was also the lid of a sarcophagus decorated with panels featuring a wild boar and a lion. Other fragments could be shown to have derived from shrines and a corbel and four large monuments that stood at the edges of the graveyard enclosure. All of these were incomplete, but three were cross-slabs and the fourth probably a shaft cross. Only the base survived of Cross A, which bore ornament of good quality vine scroll framing a scene possibly representing Daniel. Fragments of interlace panels were all that remained of Cross B. A large piece of carved stone belonging to Cross C was retrieved from the wall of the crypt under the present church (Figure 5.11). It showed a complex cross-form 'guarded' by a dragon-like creature, and on the other side a row of apostles holding books. This same cross originally incorporated a stone recovered from the garden

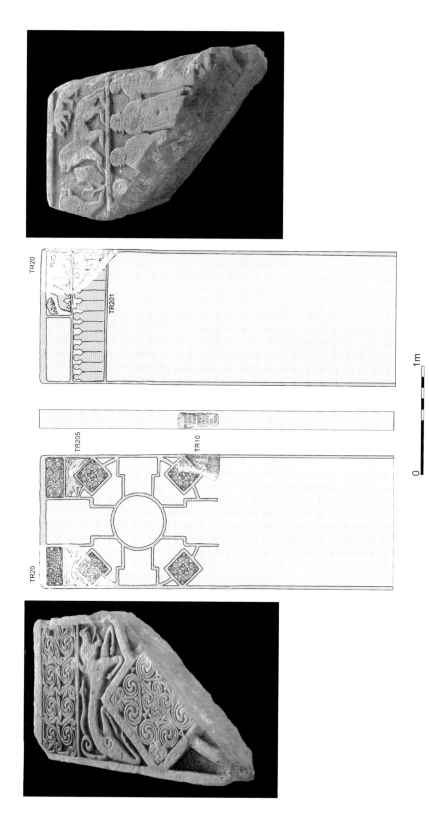

Figure 5.11 Pictish carving at Portmahomack: cross side (left) and reverse of TR20 with reconstruction including inscribed stone TR10. (FAS Heritage)

wall of the manse which, unusually for Pictland, carried an inscription in insular majuscules worked in relief long the edge of the stone, announcing that this was the Cross of Christ was erected in memory of . . (but the clear name of a dedicatee were missing). Cross D was too broken up for its form to be understood, but surviving sections suggested that this was a shaft cross, so probably of the later 8th or early 9th century rather than a cross slab. Judging from their find-spots, these four large monuments originally stood at or around the highest part of the churchyard, where the monastic cemetery and possible church were located (Chapter 3, p. 153).

The grandest of the Portmahomack cross-slabs were part of a set that stood at the edge of the Tarbat peninsula, looking out over different parts of the sea and marking landing places (Chapter 3, p. 154). Those surviving at Nigg, Shandwick and Hilton of Cadboll are richly decorated and are among the finest stone carved monuments not only in Britain but in early medieval Europe as a whole. Each shows, or originally featured, an elaborate cross on one side (originally facing the sea), and on the reverse sides a series of highly active scenes of inspirational composition and executed with virtuoso skill. The Nigg cross slab shows the Biblical king David as harpist and shepherd; Shandwick depicts a wild safari in which warriors duel and animals are hunted; and below this possible vision of a Pictish paradise is a symmetric explosion of spirals in rings of 4, 8, 16 and 16, a numerically magical big bang signalling the explosive start of the new life (Figure 5.12). One cannot deny the

Figure 5.12 Tarbat peninsula: spiroform 'explosion' on the Shandwick stone.
(Author)

exhilarated optimism of these works that celebrate the triumph of the church and its embrace of nature and science. At Hilton the scene shows a female rider wearing a prestigious brooch accompanied by a man with a big nose and huntsmen and hounds, together with the deer that is their quarry (Figure 5.13).

Figure 5.13 Tarbat peninsula: the Hilton of Cadboll stone in the National Museum of Scotland.

(X.IB 189; image licenced by and © National Museums Scotland)

Figure 5.14 Making the Hilton replica. (Left): Carving of the reverse face of the marked-out stone at
      Balintore. (Right): The replica erected at the site of St Mary's Chapel, Hilton with sculptor
      Barry Grove.

(Author)

The context of these grand and broadly contemporary monuments is the monastery of
Portmahomack and its associated estate. St Paul and St Anthony depicted on the cross face
at Nigg are desert fathers closely associated with the origins of the monastic idea.[48] Each
carries a set of symbols, held to represent names. These may be names of sponsors, but
given their role in the monastic landscape a more suitable subject might be a holy person,
celebrated by an incident in their biography. This is of course a conjecture, designed here
principally to illustrate the sophistication and intellectual depth of the Picts as highly original and accomplished pioneers of the new Christian monastic movement at the edge of the
known world. The challenges of making these great monuments were formidable. On the
Tarbat peninsula, good-quality freestone suitable for carving was available from the coastal
outcrop of Old Red Sandstone. Experimental work undertaken in connection with the stone
mason and sculptor Barry Grove extracted stone from the cliff, marked it out, carved it with
a hammer and chisel and erected at St Mary's Chapel at Hilton near the point at which it
once stood (Figure 5.14). The operation took seven years, including the time spent in raising
the money, deciding how to carve the missing parts of the replica and where to erect it, and
allowing time for visitors to see the carving take shape.[49]

A sequence on the Isle of Man

Fm 1 on the Isle of Man features stones inscribed with names in Latin and Ogham. An
example at Port St Mary marked in ogham on a boulder in the 6th century declares that
this is 'The stone of Dovaidu, son of the Druid' (*Dovaidona maqi droata*).[50] (Figure 5.15).

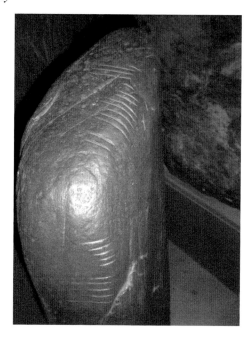

Figure 5.15 Isle of Man, Ballaqueeney, Rushen. Fm 1 stone inscribed in ogham.

(In Manx Museum, Douglas, RUSHN/1. In public domain at https://commons.wikimedia.org/wiki/File:Clagh_ Ogham_ec_Thie_Tashtee_Vannin.jpg Photographer Shimmen Beg)

Monasticism on the Isle of Man is signalled between the late 7th and 10th centuries and is notably focused at **Maughold**.[51] Modest cross-marked grave markers form one part of the repertoire and standing, incised, cross-marked slabs another (Figure 5.16). Maughold has two 8th-century inscriptions in Anglian runes.[52] The Latin inscription on Maughold 27 refers to a cross of Christ made in Christ's name. Another Maughold stone records an aspect of monastery foundation in an inscription in a Latin book hand of the 8th or 9th century: '[In the name of] Jesus Christ, Branhui brought water to this place'. Traditions lived on: Maughold (145) has a 12th-century inscription giving the Norse runic and half of the ogham alphabet and runic aside, saying 'John the Priest cut these runes'. This monasticism drew on many sources, but the geographical location, the use of ogham and carvings like the Calf of Man crucifix might encourage the view that its principal progenitors here were Irish.[53]

The Isle of Man has the richest vein of Norse culture, with probably the most precocious examples of Hiberno-Norse carving in the early 10th century. Gautr's Cross at Kirk Michael (74) announces the beginning of the monumental initiative: 'Mael Bridge son of Athankan the smith erected this cross for his own soul (and that of) his brother's wife. Gautr made this and all in Man' (Figure 5.17). Kirk Ballaugh (106), which shows the touch of Gautr, records that the cross was erected by Eric Liotulfson in memory of his son Ulf. The cross at Kirk Braddan (138) recalls that 'Hross-Ketill betrayed in a truce his own oath-fellow'.

The Sigurd cycle is also displayed in a number of the Viking monuments alongside the Christian cross, suggesting a complementary, rather than a confrontational attitude towards Christ (see Chapter 6, p. 625). At Kirk Andreas (121/95), Sigurd slays the dragon Fafnir with his sword and roasts its heart over a fire; licking the blood from his fingers enables him to

Figure 5.16 Isle of Man: Fm 2 carved stones from Maughold: Nos 15–19 (left) and no. 27 (right). The inscription on no 27 may read 'bishop of the island'.

(Kermode 1907, Plate VIII, X)

Figure 5.17 Fm 3 in the Isle of Man: Michael no.74, two faces and the inscribed edge. The runic inscription reads 'Gautr carved this and all in Man'.

(Kermode 1907, Plate XXX)

understand the language of the birds. His horse Grani (the grey one), who has carried the gold hoard, stands apart, while on the other side Gunnar, who purloined the treasure is being savaged in the snake pit. Sigurd makes guest appearances on the mainland too (see p. 544).

A sequence in South Wales

Another illustration of the way that stone monuments evolved for use over the centuries is provided by the site of **Margam** in Glamorgan, south-east Wales. This is an area on and below the foothills overlooking the Roman road from Caerwent to Neath (Figure 5.18). The central focus is the Iron Age hill fort of Mynydd y Castell (Castle Hill) with the site of Hen Eglwys ('Old Church') on a spur to the west. Below on the plain is the site of St Mary's Abbey. The earliest stones, dated in Fm 1 to the first half of the 6th century, were located on the Roman road (Figure 5.19). G92, found on the line of the road in 1839, was originally a Roman milestone, later inscribed on the back: *Hic iacit Cantusus pater Paulinus* (in this case, 'father of') (Figure 5.20A). G86, with a Latin inscription set vertically to match the ogham, commemorates a Briton named Pumpeius Carantorius[54] (Figure 5.20B). In the late 6th century, a stone (G77) was erected on Margam mountain on a Bronze Age cairn, one of four on the summit near a track. It is inscribed *Bodvici Hic iacit filius Catotigirni pronepus Eternali Vedomavi*: [The stone of] Bodovicus. Here he lies, the son of Catotigirnus and great grandson of Eternalis Vedomavus (Figure 5.20C).[55]

In Fm 2, the signature symbol is the plain Christian cross rendered in outline. At Margam, the example is the thick pillar incised with outline crosses found at Lower Court Farm (G89).

Figure 5.18 Margam (West Glamorgan): the Margam plain from the Old Chapel.
(Author)

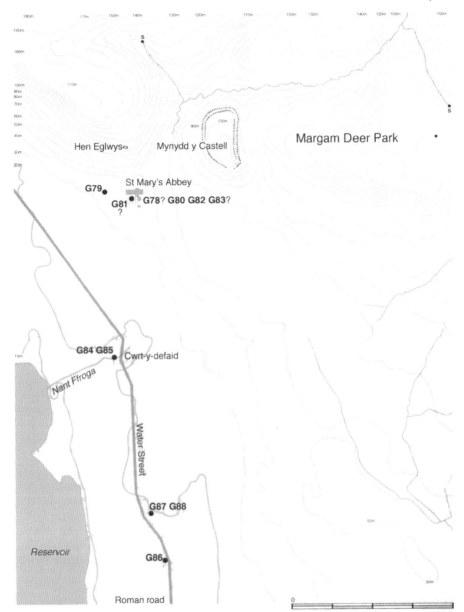

Figure 5.19 Margam: plan of the environment, showing Roman road and locations of monuments.
(Redknap and Lewis 2007, Fig 98; licensed by the National Museum of Wales)

There is an inscription, 'of Thomas' (thus the epithet 'Pillar of Thomas') (Figure 5.21). The pillar is dated from the double-outline cross (side B) and the inscribed letter-forms to the 8th/9th century, while the linear cross (side A) 'might be earlier'.[56]

In Fm 3 the stones have large cross heads and floriate ornament, and the majority were found near the later abbey (G78–85). G78, dated to the late 9th century, is a ring-headed cross in low relief, with a shaft and head decorated with plaitwork. The inscription proclaims

Figure 5.20 Margam (Museum). Inscribed pillars (Fm 1): (Left to right) G92, G86, G77.
(Author)

Figure 5.21 Margam (Museum). (Fm 2) Two of three crosses carved on 'Thomas's Pillar', G89 showing outline and incised forms.

(Redknap and Lewis 2007, p. 447; licensed by the National Museum of Wales)

that this is a cross of Christ erected by Enniaun for the soul of Guorgoret (Figure 5.22). G79, dated late 9th/early 10th century, is a disc-headed slab cross set in a rectangular base; it shows two figures, the Evangelist and the Virgin Mary, and two galloping horsemen pursuing a stag. It is inscribed 'Conbelin set up this cross for the soul of Ric'.[57] The 'cart-wheel cross' G84 (10th/11th century) had been reused as a footbridge; now somewhat worn, it was marked *Petrus Ilquic* (the stone of Ilquic).[58]

Figure 5.22 Margam (Museum). (Fm 3) Stones carved in low relief. (Left to right) G78, G79 and G84. (Author)

This site provides a neat illustration of some of the themes associated with each period: in Fm 1 (5th–7th century), the Latin- and ogham-inscribed pillars (situated on prehistoric landmarks or by Roman roads) exercised a primary function, with or without the added power of a buried ancestor, of marking land owned or controlled by individuals with Roman, Brittonic or Irish names, who if they were Christians did not feel the need to announce the fact. In Fm 2 (7th–9th century), a rising Christian movement used its monuments to redraw the landscape focussed on monastic centres. In Wales, the monasteries often continued into Fm 3 and the stone markers of monastic boundaries and focal points retained their potency. However, in Fm 3 lay patronage is on the increase: some of the monuments are highly decorated and carry inscriptions that emphasise their role in aiding salvation of the patrons through prayer. Some of the patrons are of Hiberno-Scandinavian extraction (e.g. Penmon 1 &2).

A sequence in Cornwall

Cornwall is an attractive region for finding and studying early sculpture, but by no means straightforward to resolve into an orderly sequence: its granite was difficult to carve and its products difficult to date.[59] Fifty-eight inscribed stones assigned to Fm 1 have been identified, the majority bearing names in Roman letters written downwards on the face of the roughly cut 'pillars'. Others bear ogham inscriptions as well as or instead of the Roman lettering and imply Irish intrusion. Several have the *maqq* conjunction, indicating an Irish person. The **Fardel** stone spells out FANONI MAQI RINI in Roman letters and MAQIQICI; SAFAQQUCI in Ogham. It refers to '[The stone of] Fanonus son of Rini'. **Lewannick II** is also inscribed in both ogham and Roman letters: 'Here lies Ulcagnus', an Irish name (Figure 5.23A). There are three ogham stones distributed on the east boundary of the county (St Kew, Lewannick, Worthyvale), joining others just the other side of the Tamar (Tavistock, Fardel).[60] Beyond this ogham cordon there are a few inscribed stones to the east, an empty zone east of that and then still further east we meet a concentration of sub-Roman sites in east Devon[61].

Stones carrying linear or outline incised crosses that might herald the arrival of Fm 2 are rare. There are nine examples in all, of which seven, including slates with incised crosses and a possible cross-of-arcs, have been found in excavations at Tintagel churchyard.[62] Crosses have been added to prehistoric monuments (for example a Neolithic chambered tomb at Mulfra Quoit). Monuments at St Just, St Endelion and Southill carry the chi-rho symbol.[63] But there is no strong body of material to imply a particular change of direction in the late 7th or 8th century, unlike Wales (p. 520).

However, there is a corpus of more than 40 sculptured free-standing crosses, all assigned to the 9th–11th century (Fm 3). This has been divided into three groups (Figure 5.23B–D). Group 1, the *Panelled interlace group*, has four stones: St Cleer 2 (The 'Doniert Stone') (Figure 5.23B), St Cleer 3 (the 'Other Half Stone'), St Neot 1 in East Cornwall (Wivelshire) and St Just in Penwith (extreme west). These are crosses with a nearly square cross-section, not located near each other but connected through their use of similar panelled interlace. This alone would make them likely candidates for linked monastic sites. One of the few to correlate with documentary records is St Cleer 2, which has an inscription to Doniert, equated with Dungart, a Cornish king who died in 875.[64]

Group 2, the *Penwith Group*, consists of nine crosses at the western limit of the peninsula. These are all ring-headed and have a crucifixion one side and five bosses on the other: Sancreed 1, Gwinear 1, St Buryan 1, Paul 1 and 2, St Erth 1 and 2, Ludgvan 1 and Phillack 1(Figure 5.23D). The crosses draw on multiple inspirations. The Penwith area has some of the tallest prehistoric standing stones in Britain, which must have had an influence. Ireland is the most likely origin of the five bosses motif. The ribbon animals on Gwinear and Sancreed are late 9th-century Danish Jellinge style. The use of double strand (median

Figure 5.23 The monumental sequence in Cornwall: (Left to right) A. Stone inscribed in Latin and ogham at Lewannick II (5th to 8th century). B. Cross base inscribed *Doniert* in St Cleer parish; C. Cross carved in low relief at Cardinham (Group 3; 10th century); D. Cross with crucifix carved in low relief at Phillack (Group 2; late 11th century).

(A: With permission © Joyce Greenham, courtesy of Andrew Langdon (with charcoal emphasis); B: with permission © Ann Preston-Jones; C: with permission © Ann Preston-Jones; D: with permission © Ann Preston-Jones and Andrew Langdon; Okasha 1993, no.24; Preston-Jones and Okasha 2013, Ill.51, 45, 197)

groove) interlace, found throughout Britain, is most common in Wales. St Buryan, Paul and St Phillack are potential early monasteries. The group dates to the 10th/11th century and probably springs from the foundation of an English monastic house at St Buryan.

Group 3, the *Mid- and East Cornwall group*, consists of 15 monuments headed by Padstow, Cardinham 1 (Figure 5.23C), and St Neot 3 and identified by their plant scrolls, trails and trefoil heads. St Petroc's at Padstow (i.e. Petroc's place) was the most powerful monastery in Cornwall from the 10th century. This group makes no reference to Wales or Ireland, but the sculptured foliage is paralleled in England, consistent with a period in which Cornwall, or at least St Petroc's, was coming under increasing English influence.[65]

The overall chronology is currently loose. Authorities agree on a date bracket of 5th–7th century for the majority of the inscribed pillars, but some must have been made later: that at Lanteglos-by-Camelford bears a vertical inscription in Old English.[66] Insofar as they occur, incised linear crosses (which can be 7th–9th century in Wales) are seen as part of a later continuing tradition in Cornwall, with none earlier than the 9th century. The more numerous sculptured free-standing crosses all date to the 9th century and later.[67] Thus the inscribed pillar stones flourish in Fm 1 but can still be made up to the 9th century, while incised crosses and crosses carved in relief share the landscape from the 9th–11th century (Fm 3).

The Cornish trajectory (so far) offers a differing slant on the use of sculpture from the sequences observed in Pictland, Scotland or Wales. In the 3rd to 6th century, imported Mediterranean pottery is reaching sites such as Tintagel, Chûn Castle and St Michael's Mount, sites that suggest a role as elite centres.[68] The inscribed stones would seem to be associated with this phase of small lordships with Iron Age roots. One of the sample areas used for detailed analysis by Sam Turner (centred on St Neot's) shows that the Iron Age settlement type known as a 'round' was associated with inscribed stones, for example, the cluster around Cardinham. By contrast, the *tre-* placenames had a mutually exclusive distribution and were associated with medieval sites. As a first step in mapping the monastic network, Turner used a list compiled by Lynette Olsen from 10th-century charters and the Domesday Book. While an origin for a few in the 7th century is implied, there is little historical or archaeological evidence for any of these sites before the 9th century.[69] The correlation between this list and sculpture is also somewhat weak: 2 out of 21 inscribed stones and 6 out of 21 sculptured crosses coincide with supposed monastic sites.[70] After the 9th century, sculpture returns to the front line: the Christian landscape is marked by standing stone monuments, with indications of English influence. Of these, the collections at Lanivet, St Neot, Padstow and Phillack must be strong candidates for players in a monastic movement. The monasteries listed cluster in valley bottoms at the focus of what became medieval farmlands.[71]

This distribution and the character and content of the inscriptions supports a model for 5th–9th century Cornwall as dominated by the agenda of an elite who are using stones to mark ancestral holdings or claim new land. As in Wales and the northern borderland, there is reason to believe that these were Christians, but equally that professing Christianity is not a principal or necessary purpose of their monumentality. Imported pottery shows that commodities from the Mediterranean and France are reaching these allied communities, who presumably have relationships of politics and kinship with Brittany, south Wales and southern Ireland, of which the story of Tristan and Iseult may be a distant relic (see Chapter 6, p. 607). Unusually this elite geography appears to continue through Fm 2. The monastic phase, so evident elsewhere in the 7th–9th century, seems to be established here only in the 9th–11th insofar as the finds of sculpture reflect it.

Thus the precocious monasticism of Cornwall, implied by dedications to uniquely local saints and sought by generations of antiquaries, remains elusive. A Christian community led by an elite, the norm in the 5th–7th century elsewhere, seems here to have prevailed until the 9th century, when a high investment institutional Christianity superseded it, preceded, accompanied or speedily followed by an English invasion. This later date should make continuity from this point into the middle ages easier to accept. It would not be the first time that a monastic network was used as an instrument in the administration of newly colonised land.

The sequences noted on our field trip show that in the north and west of Britain, which has the lion's share of the carved stones monuments, there is a general trend from simple to complex, from the agenda of lordship to that of the church, addressed first to local then to national and ultimately to international audiences. Within this overall narrative occurred episodes of unusual brilliance, marked by variations in intensity from high investment to nothing at all. Following the course of monumental development in different regions in each major period, as we now will, has the potential to throw open a window on a new piece of history.

Formative 1 (5th–7th century)

In Fm 1, as defined in this book (5th–7th century), the south-west, Wales and the Borders between the Roman walls invest in pillars inscribed with names and kin written in Latin, p-Celtic or q-Celtic ogham. In Pictland the analogous monuments use symbols which probably also represent named individuals, as well as the occasional inscription in ogham. All these stones are seen here as primarily proprietorial, marking territory and commemorating leaders, many of whom may have been of a Christian persuasion, but rarely making this affiliation explicit.[72] Lancashire and the eastern part of the country, from Northumbria to Kent to Somerset, have little or no monumental sculpture at this time (Figure 5.24). Accordingly, our itinerary will go from north-east to south-west.

Pictland

Pictland has the largest, richest, most original and most diverse sculptural repertoire on the island, and its achievements in carving are some of the greatest in the European post-Roman world. Moreover, it is a part of Britain where we are unusually dependent on sculpture to know what is going on. Many of the Pictish monuments still stand in the landscape, although in very few cases have their localities been investigated. Many others have been moved (without archaeological investigation) into museums. Although the excavations on Tarbat Ness in the Moray Firth have provided a dated sequence of unusual precision, they relate only to products of Fm 2. So while carved stones still form the spearhead of Pictish archaeology, knowledge of their context and of the relevant settlements and cemeteries lag behind.[73]

The Picts were Britons, and in their sculpture, along with that of Wales, can be heard the distinctive British voice sounding clear above those of Ireland, England or Rome, although in harmony with all. In any comparable history of a European territory, the equivalent of Pictland would be the place that the study begins, the part that was not conquered by the Romans, the English or the Vikings. Nevertheless, its role in Britain has remained strangely marginal, perhaps firstly because in the 9th century (before the end of the formative period) it was culturally and linguistically overwhelmed by Scots from the west, and secondly because it generated no surviving usable history in its own language. Bede counts Pictish as a language separate from Irish, English and indeed British, although it is currently recognised as a dialect of Brittonic.[74] The question of the date and period of use of the majority of the symbol stones found in the Pictish heartlands will be addressed shortly. First let's consider what these stones might have been for.

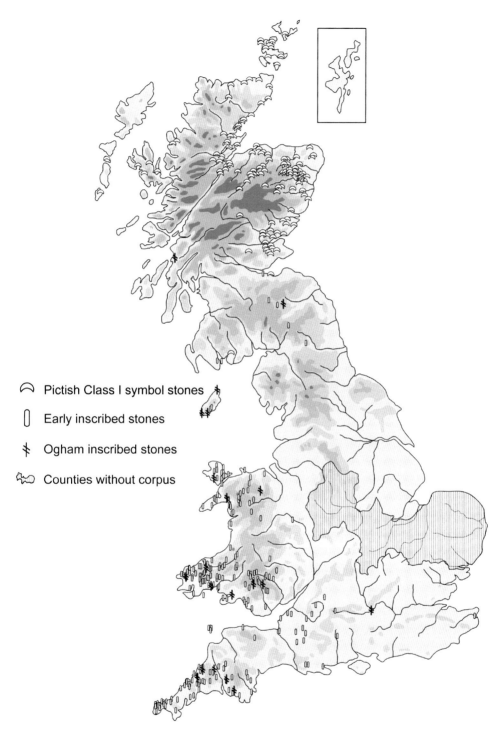

Pictish Class I symbol stones

Early inscribed stones

Ogham inscribed stones

Counties without corpus

Figure 5.24 Map showing the distribution of carved stone monuments in Fm 1.
(FAS Heritage)

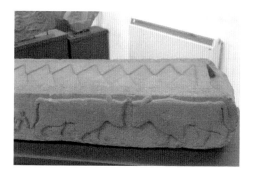

Figure 5.25 Pictish animals. (Top left) Ardross wolf; (Centre left) Portmahomack wild boar; (Bottom left) Burghead bull; (Top right) Portmahomack family of cattle; (Bottom right) Meigle bulls.

(Author)

Pictish art offers a frisson of authentic depiction in its treatment of animals, which are observed with a realist's eye that is unusual anywhere between the Roman and late Medieval periods. Animals on the earlier symbol stones – the stag, salmon, hound, cow and bull –are all executed with a single sure line with the eye of someone for whom these local creatures are intimate and familiar and who knew how to draw (Figure 5.25). In particular, their rendering of the movement of horses is extraordinarily lifelike, distinguishing the walk from the trot, and hard to parallel in Roman monumental art of the kind that survived in Scotland, where horses rear above fallen enemies, or even in such early manuscripts as are known to have been imported with Christianity. By contrast, animals that are not native to Scotland, like the lion, or belong to mythologies, the griffin, the dragon, the kelpie, are varied, ornamented with artistic flourishes and clearly not modelled from life. Other clues are given by the iconography of stories, such as Daniel in the Lions' Den, which carry the caveat of containing material that is inherited from the original source.

Several of the animals depicted singly on stone form part of the repertoire of *Pictish symbols*, which include a range of geometric compositions that are repeated over the whole Pictish corpus and indeed define it (Figure 5.26 [top]). In a series of studies, Katherine Forsyth has elucidated the structure, chronology and affiliations of the Pictish mode of visual communication insofar as it has survived and is currently knowable.[75] The symbols occur in sets on 160 unworked stones, and on 57 Christian cross-slabs, their currency stretching from the 6th century or before to the later 9th century, when the Pictish voice fell silent. Ogham occurs on 29 monuments in Pictland, the majority dated from the 7th to the 9th century; Roman-letter inscriptions survive in six legible examples, all on crosses of the 8th/9th century, apart from that on the silver sword chape of similar date from St Ninian's Isle. All these represent, or most probably represent, names. As noted in our visit to the Moray Firth, in Fm 1 they are distributed in the landscape in a manner that suggests landowners, and in Fm 2 clustered in places of a Christian and ecclesiastical persuasion and so likely to be names of clerics, artists or their sponsors. The trajectory of use in Pictland can be thus aligned with or deduced from that assigned to the sculpture in the other areas of Celtic Britain and Ireland.[76]

The earliest symbols occur on live rock, cave walls and on unworked boulders or slabs of stone (i.e. those termed Class I by Allen and Anderson). They are distributed in the east part of Scotland and along the valleys (straths and glens) in general in contact with productive agricultural land; and the territory marked by the stones includes not only Skye but the western and northern isles more generally.[77] Most modern analysts agree that the symbols ought to represent names, even if they can rarely be vocalised.[78] In putting them to work as a language system, Forsyth rejects those that occur rarely and/or singly, and organises the remainder in five groups on the grounds of their visual form, as with the five groups of ogham *fesc*.[79] Most of the Fm 1 symbols occur in pairs, typically one

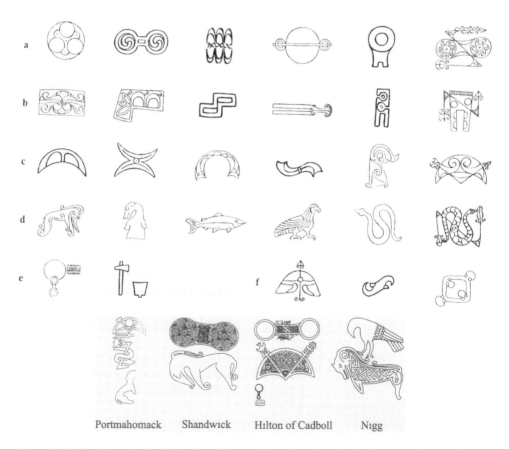

Portmahomack   Shandwick   Hilton of Cadboll   Nigg

Figure 5.26 Pictish symbols. (Top): Symbol sets from Forsyth 1997b, Figs1–3, with permission. (Bottom): Symbolic representation of 'names' on the Tarbat peninsula.

(Author)

above the other. If each symbol represents a syllable, then each pair is a name of two sylla-
bles; if each symbol is a name, then two names are displayed, recalling the formula used in the
south and west: X son of Y, or X member of kin-group Y; in Latin *filius* and from ogham using
Irish *MAQQ*. Those that occur singly may have another explanation (Figure 5.26 [bottom]).

However, none of these monuments also bears a date or a recognised name that could be
identified in the written record. We are left with the deductions that can be made from their
form and artistry. Charles Thomas deconstructed the form of a number of the symbols in
terms of Iron Age exemplars (sword, spear, shield, chariot) and deduced that the combinations
depicted on stones served to evoke furnished burials of the elites.[80] Henderson and Henderson
also noted that their designers 'thought within the conventions of Iron Age metalwork'.[81]
While some scholars note their Iron Age affiliations and push them back to the 5th century or
earlier, others note their ornament and exceptionally competent purity of line and tend to pull
them forward into the Christian period. Linguists see the proximity of literate Roman Britain
as being determinant, as with ogham, and so prefer a derivation somewhere between the two.
Historians and antiquaries look for a context in the (very meagre) written records.[82]

Forsyth sees the execution of the majority of the symbol-only stones as fitting into the
5th–7th century, the period also consonant with land-marking in the rest of Britain and Ireland (pp. 472, 503). While those that remained in the landscape are likely to have had a continuing relevance, 'many or most' of the 160 symbol-only stones had an origin earlier than
the cross-slabs.[83] Like ogham there must be a suspicion that any system that emerges fully
formed must have had a gestation in another medium, in this case perhaps carried by tattoos,
as implied by the Roman nickname *Picti*, the painted ones. The symbol-writing system also
resembles ogham in that, if derived from Rome, it appears to start a long way away from its
model.

Direct archaeological investigations have helped to secure the symbol-only group as the
primary sculptured monuments of Pictland and their date range as 5th to 7th century.[84] The
sites at Dunadd, and Trusty's Hill, occupied in the 6th/7th century, have symbols incised
on rocky outcrops so are not subject to the distortions of displacement.[85] An ox bone from
the broch at Burrian inscribed with two symbols was radiocarbon-dated to 570–655.[86] Most
significantly, the site of Rhynie, dated to the 5th/6th century by imported pottery and radiocarbon dating, is associated with a set of eight stones with a range of symbols. The location
and distribution of these 'symbol-only' stones set them apart from those that follow that are
marked also with a cross (Allen and Anderson's Class II); none of Allen and Anderson's
Class I is firmly associated with a cross-marked sculpture or with sites of later churches.

If the landmark/land-controlling function provided the impetus for a great many of these
symbol stones, other locations less clearly dedicated to this purpose are worthy of exploration. Symbols are found in caves at Wemyss in Fife and Covesea in Moray, accompanied by
other graffiti. These may represent 'early forms of the basic shapes', but whether they imply
a special use of the cave has yet to be determined. Meggen Gondek has identified 17 settlement sites with symbol stones, 10 of which are associated with enclosed or defensible places.
They are well spread from Shetland to Galloway: Old Scatness (Shetland), Broch of Gurness
and Knowe of Burrian on Orkney, Birkle Hill, Keiss (Caithness), Burghead (Moray), Rhynie
and Dunnicaer in Aberdeeenshire, East Lomond Hill (Fife), Dunadd (Argyll) and Trusty's
Hill (Galloway).[87] Four others from the group are notable as having more than one stone: Six
have survived from Burghead, but there were thought to have once been as many as 30; Old
Scatness has four; Dunnicaer six, of which four are certain; and Rhynie as many as eight.[88]
The sites in the north predominantly display animals: boar, bear and salmon at Old Scatness
and multiple bulls at Burghead.

At **Rhynie**, archaeological investigations have brought to light an enclosure with special features that have opened a new chapter on the purpose, status and meaning of the Period 1 symbol stones.[89] The enclosure is defined by a palisade with two concentric ditches, its interior taken up by large rectilinear post-hole buildings, and pits containing burnt cattle bone. The entrance is marked by a rough pillar with a salmon and a Pictish beast (the Craw Stane) and seven other symbol stones survive from Rhynie village, now displaced but once probably ranged along the valley of the River Bogie that gives the site its location (Figure 5.27). These appear to constitute an avenue of approach to a special place in a manner familiar from prehistory. Counted among these stones is the kite-shaped slab bearing an incised image of the human figure known as Rhynie Man (Figure 5.28). He has a pointed beard, ferocious pointed teeth and purposeful look, accentuated by the large axe hammer he carries over one shoulder.[90] An axe hammer of this type was found in the royal burial ship in Mound 1 at Sutton Hoo. Long thought to have been a weapon or a ship builders' tool, it has been shown to belong to a set of northern European ritual implements for poleaxing and butchering cattle.[91] In the present context, the incinerated cattle bone is relevant, and more so the find from the site of a miniature axe-hammer cast in bronze.

These findings converge on the deduction that Rhynie was a site with a ritual purpose in which a spiritual specialist (or a leader in a spiritual role) despatched cattle for the propitiation of a deity and the benefit of the people. Imported Mediterranean pottery (LR1 and 2) and vessel glass of the 6th to 7th century reached this site, hundreds of miles east of its supply route in the Irish Sea (see Chapter 1, p. 9). This anchors the activities observed, and by implication the symbol stones, within the 5th to 7th century AD.[92] Radiocarbon dates obtained from the site in 2016 place the life of the Rhynie site in a narrower bracket in the mid-5th/6th century.[93]

The discoveries at Rhynie invite us to credit an active pagan Pictish religion, although this possibility still generates anxiety today: to suppose that Christianity arrived in Pictland only in the 7th century has been dubbed a 'sinisterly late conversion'.[94] Clearly it was not 'late', since the stones are mainly pre-Christian; but why should a late conversion be 'sinister' rather than, say, 'prudent'? In fact, the date proposed here for the start of Pictish public expression of Christianity (the late 7th century) aligns with most other territories in Britain, who kept any Christian leanings before the 7th century under wraps and away from their carved stones and their burials until around the same date. It would be truly surprising if the Picts were the only people in Europe who had no developed pre-Christian religion or failed to invest in it symbolically.

However, even if certain symbols were put to work in the service of a public ritual, this does not preclude them from being used as names. It has long been recognised that within the corpus of symbols, certain animals form an interesting subgroup. Drawn with especial realism and easily recognised today, the bull, horse, bear and wolf occur alone on their slabs. All, like Rhynie man, face right, they do not feature on the later stones with crosses, and they seem to be preferred in the Firthlands and further north. They appear to concentrate in Ross, Inverness and Moray or along the Great Glen, although the finds at Old Scatness suggest a wider northerly usage.[95] On these grounds, Forsyth omits them from her list of ideograms that make up the symbol 'script' system, while certain other 'real' animals – fish (a salmon), stag, boar, eagle, serpent – that occur in combination with other symbols, and also on the later Christian stones, are eligible for inclusion. But all the animals are special in the reverential way they are drawn and the iconic demeanour they present.

Figure 5.27 Rhynie (Aberdeenshire). A. (Above): The Craw Stane. B. (Opposite): Map of Rhynie marking the locations of the excavated site and the location of six of the symbol stones.

(A: Henderson and Henderson 2004, Ill 76; Tom and Sybil Grey Collection; licensed by and © Historic Environment Scotland. B: Crown copyright. Ordnance Survey. See also Chapter 3, Fig 3.53, adapted from Gondek and Noble 2011, Fig 8.1; with permission)

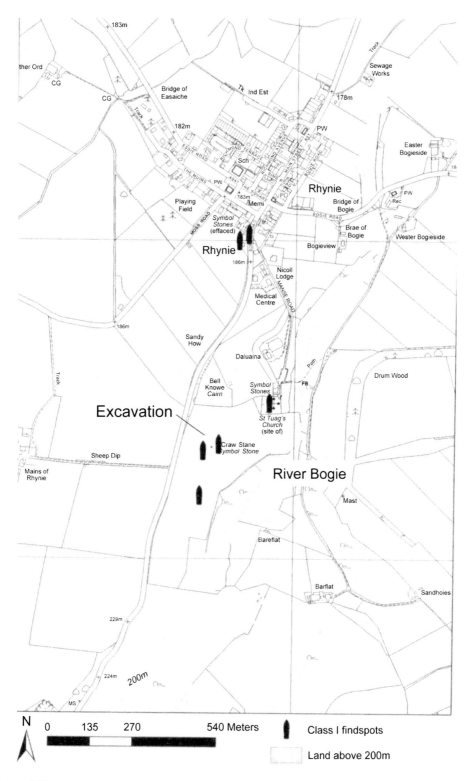

Figure 5.27 (Continued)

Figure 5.28 Rhynie; male figure carrying axe-hammer.
(© Aberdeenshire County Council; with permission)

Matters may be simplified by assuming that each symbol, even the animals, is a name rather than a syllable (see p. 492). In his seminal paper Ross Samson argued that the corpus of Pictish names could be constructed from a relatively small number of phonemes on analogy with those of documented Anglo-Saxons.[96] However, the small number of symbols would not be sufficient to account for the more numerous and more complex names recorded in the Welsh inscriptions – which are arguably close linguistically to their fellow Britons in Pictland.

The passage of time, or a localised usage, would be sufficient to account for the non-appearance of some symbols on the cross-marked stones. Thus it is not excluded that these animals too originally had a religious meaning, deprived of reverence once they had been incorporated into a common name. There are many Christian examples of this 'familiarisa-tion' process – names such as Gilchrist, Josemaria and so on, not to mention the countless men and women who are named after saints while not feeling themselves obliged to emulate saintly behaviour. Similarly, superannuated gods may linger on in the names of the con-verted, as the Vikings show. If animals may prove to be one indication of a spiritual focus, another is suggested by the sites in which stones are so far known to cluster. Whether there is a variety of images as at Rhynie and Old Scatness, or the same image repeated, like the bulls at Burghead, the superfluity suggests a purpose which is more votive than proprieto-rial. Thus we can propose a function of the Class I stones additional to their role in the labelling of land, one which is perhaps particularly apposite to cult centres. In some manner these 'central places' provide a pre-echo to the signature sites of Fm 2, where the stones are revered in a monastic setting.

Western Scotland

Eight examples of Pictish symbols have been found outside the Pictish heartland in western Scotland: one incised on an outcrop at Dunadd fort, three on upright stone slabs on Skye, at Gairloch, Poolewe and Pabbay on Barra, and on displaced stones on Benbecula and Fiscav-aig on Skye.[97] According to Adomnan in 700 AD, Argyll was thought to have been still Pictish territory in 563; Columba needed an interpreter when he preached to the Picts, and also when he visited Skye, then apparently occupied by Picts.[98] That ordinary people on Skye were Pic-tish in Columba's lifetime suggests that this was the date that could be given to these symbol stones. Skye was apparently part of a 'Gaelic milieu' by the later 7th century, with a mon-astery established on the mainland at Applecross by 672, and perhaps one on Skye itself.[99] Gairloch, with a salmon and possibly a goose, would fit in with a 5th–7th century date, but is the only one with animals (Figure 5.29A). However, there are perhaps too few to insist that they represent original Pictish territory. Like the oghams the remainder are dated 7th–9th century by Fisher, which would make them late arrivals in the Pictish corpus as well as distant from the heartland otherwise well-defined by the symbols.[100] On the stone at Pabbay the symbols share the space with an incised equal-armed cross, and on Raasay with a cross of arcs (Figure 5.29B). This is compatible with the idea that symbols represent the names of Picts, some of them Christian, buried or celebrated in this western territory.

The Scottish part of Scotland shared much of its early development with north-east Ire-land, the two making an area defined in the 6th/7th century as Dal Riata, a sea kingdom comprising Argyll (land of the Gaels) and Ulster with the islands in between. The Scots were people whose homeland was Ireland, but how many arrived in west-coast Scotland, and when, is as much of an issue in the north as the *adventus Saxonum* is in the south.[101] It seems likely that the archaeology of the formative period will eventually decide that the Scots are the significant immigrants into Scotland, just as they have decided that the English are the dominant immigrants into England (p. 56). There was a cultural shift in settlement form that appears to move down the glens and via the lochs in central Scotland from the west towards the east and into Pictland (Chapter 3, p. 179). The well-documented Irish intrusions into south-west Wales are corroborated by the arrival there of ogham inscriptions with Irish names from the 5th century (p. 225). It might be expected that a similar trail would light up demographic movement into western Scotland, but the material appears to be sparse. The Royal Commission's survey cites scarcely half a dozen sites with ogham inscriptions: on the walls of the King's Cave, Bute, on a pillar on Gigha, on a rocky outcrop at Dunadd and on a movable piece of stone at Potalloch. The examples at King's Cave and Gigha include

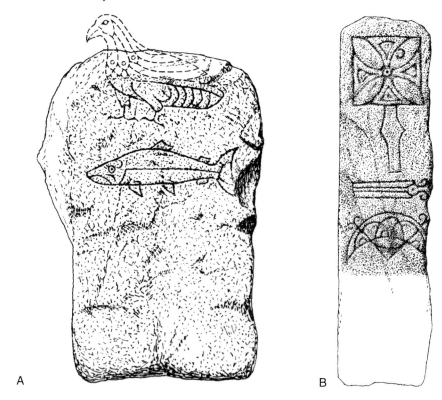

Figure 5.29 Pictish symbol stones in the west. A: Gairloch (Wester Ross). B: Raasay, Skye.
(Fisher 2001, 26 nos. W20, W34; licensed by and © Historic Environment Scotland)

the term *maq*; Dunadd seems to mention a 'Finn' and Potallach a 'Crónán', so that all these would seem to indicate an Irish presence.[102] A recent review of Scottish oghams counted 35 inscriptions in Greater Scotland, of which 29 are in Pictland, but only 20 are long enough to have any linguistic clarity. Those situated in Pictland remain impenetrable beyond the intimation that they could derive from one or more Brittonic dialects. However, the Irish patronymic term *maqq* can be recognised in seven of them.[103] The Irish penetration of Cumbria and the Border areas also seems surprisingly slight. One reason for this might be a difference in time. Ogham is in active use elsewhere in Britain from the 5th century, but in the north most examples occur after the 7th century, that is in Fm 2 contexts.[104] The use of the *forfeda* (the diphthongs) in some inscriptions also implies a later date. Ogham inscriptions that are legible appear to represent personal names: Dunodnat, Conmor, Edarnon, Talorg, Nectan.[105] This implies that they are the poor relations to the enormous and well-defined sculptural repertoire of Fm 2 with its Christian grave markers and, later, its Grand Crosses.

   Early sculptural action in this north-western part of Britain is therefore minimal or intrusive, and this will not be the last region presenting us with a near blank in Fm 1. In Fm 2 the numbers of monuments increase greatly, as does the range of expression. Grave markers carry hexafoils and crosses-of-arcs, linear-incised crosses, outline crosses and some relief carvings. These are joined by historiated grand crosses beginning in the 8th century at Iona, notable for their iconographic repertoire which, (apart from the Virgin Mary) is 'entirely of Biblical (OT) origin', featuring Cain and Abel, Abraham and Isaac and David and the

Lion.[106] Their arrival is seen as a response to innovations in Northumbria, especially no doubt the march of the Victory Crosses in the later 8th century (see below).[107]

Northern borders

To the east of these and connected with them in form and purpose are the inscribed 'proprietorial' stones found in Fm 1 (5th–7th century) in Galloway and the Tweed valley. There is a single late Roman example from Brougham (Brocavum), and these stones, like those of North Wales, are signals of direct transition from Roman to Formative Britain. The 5th-century stone at Whithorn celebrating Latinus, descendant of Barrovadus, aged 35, and his daughter, aged 4, has connections with stones remembering Celtic persons in 'extended Latinate' inscriptions at Maryport (Rianorix), Vindolanda (Brigomaglus) and Old Carlisle (Tancorix). Forsyth sees these, including Latinus, as local leaders with Roman roots, and argues against a Gaulish origin for the centre at Whithorn.[108] Other examples are sited further east in the Gododdin region, dated to the 6th century: the Catstane (now joined by Edinburgh airport) remembers Vetta and his/her father Victricius buried 'in this mound'. This was probably a Bronze Age standing stone recommissioned in the early middle ages and it is surrounded by long-cist graves.[109] The Brox stone in Liddesdale commemorates Carantius son of Cupitianus, and the Yarrow stone the 'most famous princes' Nudus and Dumnogenus. These three carry no Christian symbols and no direct associations with a church, their task being apparently to dominate landscape in the name of the family (Figure 5.30). Other stone monuments in the zone, Kirkmadrine 1 and 2 and the *Petrus* stone at Whithorn, are more specifically ecclesiastical and later in date – late 6th to 7th century.[110] Whithorn,

Figure 5.30 Scottish Borders: The Yarrow stone by Yarrow Water, a tributary of the Tweed.
(Author)

Kirkmadrine, with Aberdaron on the Hŷn peninsula in N Wales seem to represent some of the very few candidates for residential ecclesiastical communities in the west before the great age of the monasteries.

Welsh overview

Analytical research on the carved stones of Wales has been of exceptional breadth and quality, with an emphasis on the archaeological context argued from location and change in function, progress largely owed to the leadership and publications of Nancy Edwards at Bangor.[111] Three kinds of monument are defined, assigned broadly to three periods: *early inscribed stones*, which are stone pillars carrying inscriptions in Latin or ogham, characterise Fm 1 (5th–7th century). *Cross carved stones* appear in Fm 2 (7th–9th century) and remain current in Fm 3 (9th–11th century), when they are joined by *Sculptured Crosses and cross-slabs*, grander crosses carved in relief.[112] The first of these groups functioned as grave markers and/ or as signals of landowning (a 'proprietorial' function as in Pictland). Within Fm 2 (from the late 8th century), Wales experienced a version of the monastic movement, with crosses and cross-slabs clustered around monastic sites. However, specific Biblical or monastic images are largely confined to angels and references to the Crucifixion, and the nature of the corpus may imply that the Welsh Church adhered to British practice at least into the 8th century.[113] In Fm 3 monasteries continued to thrive, but with greater secular involvement, as in Ireland. Some monuments record the donation of land to the church, while others, famously the Pillar of Eliseg, reprise the role of documenting land.[114] While Margam (p. 484) provides a *sond-age* of the sequence as a whole, there are some interesting generalities and variations over the three periods (Table 5.2) and between the three regions of Wales (Table 5.3), where the uneven coverage indicates different levels of engagement in monumentality.

Table 5.2 Broad characteristics of the three periods in Wales

	[Formative 1] 400–700	[Formative 2] 700–800	[Formative 3] 800–1100
Forms	Inscribed pillars	Incised crosses	Sculpted crosses
Nash-Williams	Group I	Group II	Group III
Sims-Williams	Periods 1–16	Periods 17–19	Periods 20–28
Inscriptions	Ogham/Irish/Latin	Latin	Latin/Welsh
Dated monuments	Cadfan c. 625		Cyngen 854 Hywel ap Rhys c. 886
Sponsors	Elite landowners	Monasteries	Elite and monasteries

Table 5.3 Numbers of carved stones by region and period in the three regions of Wales

	North	SW	SE	Total
Fm 1 (landmarking pillars)	50	64*	33	147
Fm 2 (monastic)	21	84*	34	139
Fm 3 (monastic and elite)	44	60	90	194
	115	208	157	480

*Including 11 examples of reused Fm 1 in Fm 2.

Formative 1 in Wales

Between the 5th and 7th century, inscribed stone pillars or slabs were erected, and the post-Roman landscape was under construction. The British population could potentially have been assembled from a number of demographic sources: long-settled native families led by regenerated tribal leaders, some of whom still aspired to belong to the Roman upper class, Irish incomers from the west into the south-west and, possibly, some refugees from the east displaced by the Anglo-Saxon invasions of the 5th century, north-east Britons from Manau Gododdin intent on expelling the Irish from Gwynedd and perhaps some incomers from Gaul as part of the traffic between south-west Britain and Brittany.[115] These were the likely players from whom the leadership classes were drawn, whether warriors or churchmen. Their relative balance varied over the regions of Wales, the south-west being strongly Irish and the north and the south-east having Roman roots.

Dating

The form and ornament of the corpus provide a relative chronology which is anchored by the palaeography, phonology and historical references in the inscriptions. Kenneth Jackson counted 54 inscriptions from the British region south of the Tweed, of which 35 have ogham and Latin on the same stone. These were ordered using the implied sounds (phonology) of the Brittonic words into seven stages from the mid- to later 5th century to early 7th. None of the ogham stones in Wales was dated earlier than the 5th century, and the bilingual examples were placed after the mid-5th. This chronology has been refined by Patrick Sims-Williams into 28 stages from c. 400 to the first half of the 9th century.[116] Another chronological scheme relied on the forms of the Latin lettering and placed them in four phases, all contained in our Fm 1. While the earliest have similar forms to those of late Romano-British epigraphy, new letters and letter-forms join the canon in the first half of the 6th century, with insular forms evident in the later 6th century.[117]

Several inscriptions construct links between the stone monuments and historical references. *Memoria Voteporigis protectoris* at Castell Dwyran (CM3) has been equated with the tyrant Voteporius mentioned by Gildas c. 550, (though this identity has been questioned on linguistic grounds).[118] Gwynedd emerges into history before c. 540, since Gildas castigated its king, Maelgwyn. Maelgwyn's descendant, Cadfan ap Iago (fl. 616–625), is equated with the person commemorated on AN26 as *Catamanus rex sapientissimus opinatisimus omnium regum*, which was erected probably shortly after his death at Llangadwaladr, implying that it was a burial place of the kings of Gwynedd. Cadfan's son was the 'godless' Cadwallon who was besieged by Edwin on Ynys Seriol off Anglesey in c. 629, but in 633 Cadwallon and Penda killed Edwin at Hatfield. As well as being evidence for the ambition of the Gwynedd kings, the superlatives suggest knowledge of an Old Testament *topos*, Cadfan emulating Solomon as better than all the kings of the world.[119]

The location of the monuments is related both to former prehistoric centres and the Roman infrastructure. In the *south-east*, as already noted, several inscribed stones stood beside prehistoric trackways or Roman roads. In the same area, the *Macaritinus Stone* G7 stood on a Bronze Age cairn beside a Roman road. Vaynor 1 and 2 (B46, 47) were found built into farm buildings adjacent to a large cairn which later produced a Bronze Age burial and pottery. Aileen Fox showed that many pillars stood on false crests, visible within a farm territory rather than from the outside: the *Dervacus Stone*, Ystradfellte 1 (B50) 'was sited in relationship to the area around the farm of Coed y Garreg in a sheltered limestone valley beside the source of the River Nedd'. The *Bodvoc Stone* (Margam Mountain 1 G77) stood on one of a line of four prehistoric barrows in high moorland. The inscription was on the south face, 'visible from the uphill approach from the presumed settlement area'. The stone at Gelligaer (G27) still stands in its original site on the edge of a ruined Bronze Age cairn.[120]

In the *south-west*, prehistoric standing stones themselves carried post-Roman inscriptions, either in ogham as at Nevern (P70, 71) or in Latin letters, as on three stones at Brawdy (P1, 3, 4) which use *filius* as the patronymic linkword. It may be significant that some post-Roman monuments were made of Ordovician spotted dolerite from the Preselis, the quarry for the bluestones found at Stonehenge. The choice of prehistoric places was no doubt prompted by the need to emphasise quasi-ancestral land claims, something apparently reinforced by the incoming Irish users of the ogham script.[121] At Penbryn, Ceredigion, a stone inscribed '[The grave of] Corbalengus who lies here, an Ordovician' commemorates a person with an Irish name, belonging to an Iron Age tribe and having a Latin epitaph. The stone seems to have stood on a Bronze Age cairn that had been reused for a Roman cremation, overlooking the sea.[122]

In the *north* at least 12 stones were sited with respect to prehistoric monuments. On Anglesey AN12, AN1 and AN20 are sited in prehistoric cemeteries with wide views, with AN12 (Llanfaelog) reusing a Neolithic or Bronze standing stone still in situ. Llanor 2–4 (CN30–02) was associated with long cist graves and two prehistoric standing stones. Caerwys (F1) was sited close to a barrow. The one Period 1 stone in Denbighshire at Clocaenog 1 (D1), the only bilingual Roman letter and ogham stone in the north, is sited overlooking a valley adjacent to a barrow and a massive uncarved standing stone. This is a region in which a number of Iron Age hillforts were reoccupied in the post-Roman period.[123]

These investments use the vocabulary of landscape to stimulate social cohesion for incomer and native alike.[124] There is a clear difference between the north-west, especially in lowland Anglesey, where the Fm 1 stones are numerous, and the north-east, where the distribution is sparse and virtually absent altogether from the region that would become Powys. The land east of the River Conwy constitutes a different cultural zone that apparently did not require the landscape to be marked.[125] Whether this indicates stability or stress is a matter that also troubles those seeking to understand the use of burial mounds.

While most of those commemorated were probably (and some unequivocally) Christian, the purpose of the Welsh Fm 1 stones has been convincingly aligned with the secular control of land, as deduced by Nancy Edwards.[126] The main episode during this first period was the Irish intrusion implied by the ogham inscriptions, while the nature and impact of Christianity is a more open question. The Irish intrusion is focused on the south-west, where there are 65 examples of pillars, slabs and boulders with incised Roman letters (43) or oghams (eight) or both (17), distributed along the fertile valleys reflecting the presumed pattern of encroachment: the ogham distribution is held to be 'broadly indicative' of the areas settled by the Irish at the end of the Roman period. As a whole it is roughly equivalent to the early kingdom of Dyfed, with slight concentrations to the east of St Davids and between R. Nyfer and Teifi estuary. A significant proportion of the Latin inscriptions also bear Irish names.[127] In the south-east, by contrast, only three ogham and four bilingual inscriptions are known, and in the north, only three, all bilingual.[128]

The direct association of Fm 1 stones with contemporary churches remains elusive and inferential.[129] The association of later churches with inscribed stones may be indicative, but is variable. In the south-west, almost 70% of inscribed stones were linked with a church, compared to 40% in the north and 36% in the south-east.[130] In the south-east, many memorial stones stand in open country, and where there are churches, the church can be seen to have been added to the site of the stone (Gelligaer G28, Margam 1 G86).[131] C. A. Ralegh Radford proposed the (once-popular) theory that Christianity died out at the end of the Roman period and was reintroduced from Gaul, as indicated by the *Hic Iacit* formula.[132] A preferred model now is that it transitioned directly from Roman into post-Roman Britain.[133] Nevertheless, firm archaeological evidence has been hard to come by, largely due to few and earlier poor-quality excavations. Evidence for Roman Christianity has been mooted at Caerwent in the south-east region in the form of a cache of late 4th-century tablewares thought to imply a Christian ritual supper.[134] The existence of a Romano-British church might be implied by the placename *Bassaleg* (basilica). The conjunction of Roman villa estate centres with major early churches is thought significant at Llantwit Major and Llandough.[135] Another candidate is the parish church dedicated to St Peblig (Publicius) at *Segontium*, which is sited by the road just beyond the east gate near the Roman and post-Roman cemeteries.[136]

The Formative 1 dedicatees offer a panorama of early Welsh society in their landscape, among the most illuminating in early medieval Britain. Most are male leaders of some sort: 'Maglicu son of Clutorius' at Nevern (P70), 'Carausius lies in this heap of stones' buried by the side of a Roman road near Penmachno (CN38; Figure 5.31a). These were no doubt all powerful in their day – but it is possible to exaggerate: Cadfan was remembered at Llangad-waladr AN26 as 'King Catamanus, the wisest, most illustrious of all kings' (p. 466). Other actors suggest a diversity of status. *Cantiorix* at Ffestiniog (MR8) was 'a citizen of Gwyn-edd, cousin to Maglus the magistrate' (Figure 5.31b). The Roman infrastructure would have

Figure 5.31 North Wales in Fm 1: inscribed stones.

(Author)

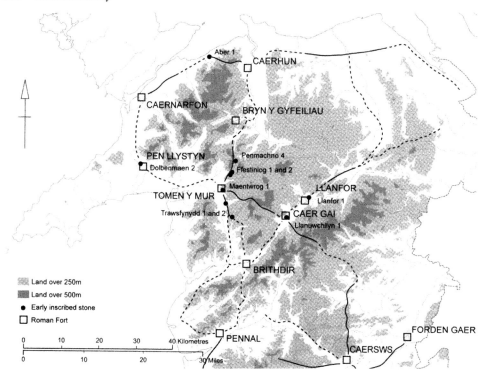

Figure 5.32 Map showing inscribed stones in relation to Roman roads.

(Edwards 2013, Fig 4.3, Royal Commission on Ancient and Historical Monuments of Wales)

provided a landscape template, recognised for what it had been, if not for what it still was. There is slight evidence for the continuing use of a Roman fort at Segontium.[137] Eight northern stones were sited with reference to Roman roads (Figure 5.32). The stone of *Voteporix the protector* (CM3) probably stood on the Roman road west of Carmarthen. The *Carausius stone* (**CN38**) was found while digging at Rhiw Bach quarry on site of the old Roman road at Cwm Penmachno and Cwm Tegl at 400 m above sea level. Ffestiniog (MR8), also now in Penmachno church, formerly stood beside a Roman road and mentions the Roman office of magistrate.[138] These monuments no doubt referred to the fertile valley of Penmachno (Figure 5.33).

On the Lyn peninsula, we meet two priests: 'Veracius the priest' was buried under Aberdaron 1 (CN2) near a chapel named after the man commemorated in the inscription, while Aberdaron 2 (CN3) announces that 'Senecus the priest lies here with a multitude of the brethren.' At the least, this implies the presence of a cemetery, if not a religious community. The area provided the traditional point of departure for pilgrims en route to Bardsey Island. A *sacerdos* in the 6th century can be a married ordained priest with sacramental functions, which perhaps typifies the clerical provision of the pre-monastic era. *Sacerdos* can also refer to a bishop.[139] More special still is the wife of a priest commemorated at Llantrisant AN46 on a 6th-century monolith (reused as a gatepost) found in the parish near chapel Bronwen and reused as a gatepost. She was 'a most holy woman, the most loving wife [coniux] of Bivatisus, servant of god,

Figure 5.33 Penmachno valley (Conwy).
(Author)

priest [sacerdos] and disciple of Paulinus, from Avdus by kindred, and [out] of all citizens and kinsfolk an example of character and wisdom better than gold and precious stones'. Some kind of congregational destination served by such spiritual specialists seems plausible. It is conceivable that these arrangements, and perhaps even the 'priests', formed part of the Roman Christian inheritance, tempered (as suggested in Chapter 4) by prehistoric traditions. So far, the sculpture offers little support for ecclesiastical centres in Fm 1, in contrast to those of Fm 2, which marked the sites of monasteries and were more overtly concerned with sanctity.

Formative 1 in south-west Britain

The Iron Age kingdom of Dumnonia, which included much of the present 'west country', the south-west peninsula of Britain, was not part of the regulated Roman province, so the old loyalties would have continued to exercise their pull after the demise of the empire and the coming of the Saxons in the east. In Cornwall, as noted on the **field trip**, the 'proprietorial phase' seems to have continued until Fm 3. The implication is that the early post-Roman population was composed of competing elites from ancestral local dynasties, incomers from Ireland and south Wales, and refugees from Roman Britain. This admixture, mitigated by demographic exchange with Brittany, would give the peninsula its dynamic until the 9th century, when the region was Anglicised. In Fm 1, the south-west belongs to the culture that erected inscribed pillars, their design looking both to Ireland (in their use of ogham) and aligning in date and content – and probably function – with those in Wales. Of the 79 inscribed stones examined by Elizabeth Okasha, 58 are from Cornwall, 21 from Devon, including one on the Somerset border, and one from Llanveynoe (Herefordshire). As suggested for the Borders and Wales, if these were Christians, their Christianity did not apparently require stating in stone, one reason perhaps why a 'British church' has so far escaped convincing archaeological detection.

The two earliest types of inscriptions use ogham, running vertically along the edge of an upright pillar, or Roman capitals, running vertically downwards on its face (Figure 5.2). Both of these scripts are used to state the name of a Celtic person and their father or a member of their extended family. Most names are identified as Celtic (53%), in general without distinction between Irish and British; 20% of the names are Latin.[140] Either side of the River Tamar is a band of six ogham stones, of which several have the *maqq* conjunction, indicating an Irish origin. The territory of the south-west peninsula appears to have been divided into three, with a 'late Iron Age' Cornwall separated from a sub-Roman area to the east by the band of ogham stones and a blank area. Mapping the inscribed stones thus paints a picture of a British monumental initiative confined to west Devon and Cornwall from the 5th century, eventually superseded by the first Anglo-Saxon inscriptions in the 9th century as the south-west peninsula came under English control.

Northumbria in Fm 1

There is no sculpture in Northumbria that can be assigned to Fm 1 (or we should have found it by now). There is an inscription from Chesterholm (Vindolanda) that reads *Brigomaglus hic iacit* (see p. 501), but otherwise there are no inscribed pillars from Period 1 (5th to 7th century) from this region recorded in the CISP (Celtic Inscribed Stone Project).[141] The square pillars at York Minster, along with other plain and smooth forms, would seem to belong to the Roman awakening of the later 7th century that begins Fm 2. Rosemary Cramp decided that there can be no debt to British or Romano-British craft in Northumbrian sculpture as it then emerges. Northumbrian grave markers are recumbent, as in Ireland, rather than upright pillars as in Wales and Pictland.[142] However, this is also a matter of chronology: Fm 1 in Ireland, as in Wales and Scotland, is characterised by upright pillars carrying inscriptions in Latin or ogham.

The Anglian intrusion is marked from the 6th century by settlements or cemeteries at Heslington, Heworth and The Mount in York, on the western edge of the Wolds (Sancton) and at West Heslerton in the Vale of Pickering, indicating that 'by the mid 6th century the Anglian presence was sufficiently dominant to establish this region as the nucleus of the kingdom of Deira'.[143] Although Angles are recorded as politically active at Bamburgh in the mid-6th century, there are few cemeteries known that can be classed as culturally Anglian north of the Tees, in other words in Bernicia (see Yeavering, Chapter 4, p. 370). The numbers of migrants remain to be determined by aDNA, but insofar as it can be read from the material culture, they varied from a high proportion of English south of the Wolds to a proportion north of Hadrian's Wall that was vanishingly small. By the 7th century, the Wolds may have provided a species of monumental frontier in that while Anglian barrow burial dominated its southern slopes, the Vale of Pickering which bounds it to the north was the location for the earliest monasteries and home to virtually all the early stone sculpture.[144]

Fm 1 in Southumbria

The presence of carved stone in Fm 1 in south-east Britain, south of the Humber and east of Dorset, is also sparse and dispersed, implying that the examples constitute strays and rarities not amounting to a cultural zone (Figure 5.34). These few examples offer meagre signs of British survival on the one hand and of intrusive people on the other. There are five plain pillars from Wareham (Dorset) inscribed with names of British origin. They are of uncertain

Figure 5.34 Fm 1 in Southumbria. (Top row from left): Wareham, nos 3B, 2C, 8A. (Bottom row): Sandwich 1A; Wroxeter 1; Silchester.

(B: © Corpus of Anglo-Saxon Stone Sculpture, photographer K. Jukes and D. Craig; C: Fulford et al. 2000, Fig 7, with permission; D: Courtesy and © Corpus of Anglo-Saxon Stone Sculpture, photographer D. Tweddle)

date but thought likely to have originated in a pre-9th century British burial ground.[145] Citing the later Wareham stones, Rosemary Cramp suggested that a British Christian community had here 'retained its identity and a certain status for a considerable time after the establishment of Anglo-Saxon rule in this region'. The British church in the south-west region may have survived into the later 7th century and the English 'swiftly followed up their victories with foundation of monasteries and churches, sometimes apparently in centres which had belonged to the British Church'.[146] This plausible suggestion of a precocious British church has so far had little support from archaeology. As elsewhere, the inscribed stones do not feature crosses and are not specifically marked as Christian, and in Cornwall and Devon, no monasteries, churches or church sites have been found that need be earlier than the 9th century (see p. 488). The argument from the Somerset cemeteries further east (for example, Cannington) is not indicative of an institutional Christianity but rather of a static sub-Roman, sub-Christian population that had its own form of unspecifically Christian worship. But this may be what the 'British Church' was like.

There are two inscribed stones from Roman towns, both probably representing Irish incomers. The *Cunorix* stone from **Wroxeter** is a piece of reused Roman stone inscribed with an Irish patronym, *Cunorix, son of [Macus] Maqqas-Coline* and dated to 5th/6th.[147] The ogham stone at

Silchester is the earliest memorial in stone in the region. Carved on a Roman dwarf baluster shaft and found in a well adjacent to a late Roman town house, it conforms to the expected 4th–5th-century date range for the type and probably represents an Irish traveller or resident in the city. The inscription reads 'Of Tebicatus son of the [. . .] tribe' using the Irish linkword *maqi* and conforming to the norm of the first name in the genitive, where 'the stone of' or the grave of' or the 'land of' or, in this case perhaps, 'the house of' is implied.[148] Two plain pillar stones were found in the 19th century on open ground near **Sandwich** in Kent. One was inscribed in runes representing a probable Anglo-Saxon personal name and dated to the 6th/7th century.[149]

Some other material within English Fm 1 can be attributed to the arrival of St Augustine's mission in 597 AD and dated to the early years of the 7th century. The key sites of activity were the former Roman towns of Canterbury, Rochester and Reculver, and the carving was focussed on architecture: two columns from Reculver, a column base from St Pancras Canterbury, a baluster shaft from St Augustine's and an inscription from St Martin's Canterbury. These architectural pieces are seen as original, if imitative, products of early 7th century-Kent.[150] This is the enclave where the church early acquired wealth and power and one that was little affected by the pagan revival of the 7th century, when power passed from Ethelbert of Kent to Raedwald of East Anglia.[151]

Why are some areas blank?

The gaps that have opened up in this brief review imply that all Britain south of Hadrian's wall and east of Avon-Severn had no memorial pillars or other carved stone in the 5th–7th century. This cannot be caused by a precocious Anglo-Saxon invasion in the 5th/6th century, since it is also true of regions thought to have had little or no Anglo-Saxon penetration before the 7th century, areas moreover that are thought to be as Christian as Wales or Galloway at that time, areas like Cumbria and Lancashire (see Table 5.1, p. 472). This will require further elucidation. It is worth noting that the common denominator for the regions with a blank Fm 1 (Northumbria, Southumbria, Cheshire, Lancashire, Mercia, Lincolnshire) is not so much that they came under early Anglo-Saxon influence but that they had been part of the Roman province. There was plenty of stone in these regions, if only the ubiquitous freestone in ruinous Roman buildings. This reinforces the idea that in Fm 1, the British appetite for erecting marker stones was most pronounced where Roman and Saxon reordering of the landscape was least effective, namely in the north and west. This suggests in turn that the urge to erect these stones was not an attempt to emulate Roman practice but more probably emerged from an older, prehistoric stratum, in regions where that stratum had remained fertile.

Formative 2 (7th–9th century)

In Fm 2, carved stone crosses more elaborate in size and execution appear in Pictland and Scotland and all over the north and west of Britain (Figure 5.35). Pre-eminent among the forms are the tall (3 m or more) free-standing crosses with elaborate iconography termed 'Victory Crosses' that spread from early examples in Northumbria into an Anglo-British border zone from Galloway to Gloucestershire. These are interpreted as the signals of a monastic movement that dominated the west and north of Britain, as it did Ireland, for nearly 150 years.[152] In Wales the introduction of cross-marked stones also indicates monastic centres, and the same may turn out to be generally true of Pictland. The occupants of south-east Britain (i.e. the English) had very few carved stone monuments until Fm 3, and, by that token at least, would appear to be less eager participants in the monastic project.

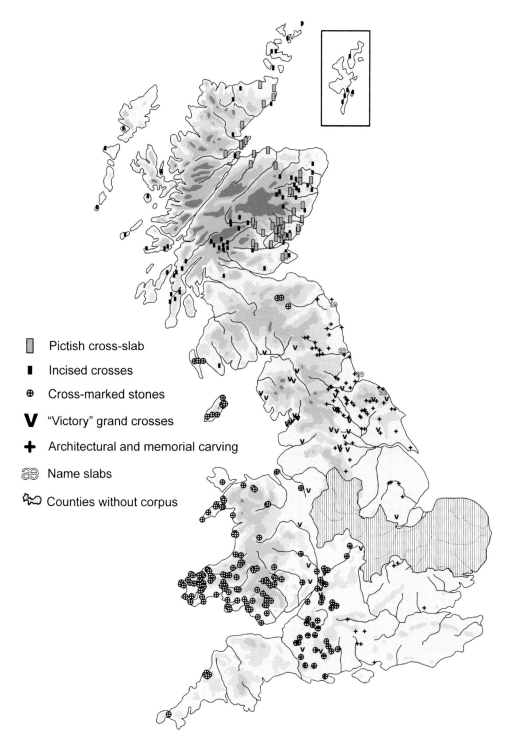

Legend:

- Pictish cross-slab
- Incised crosses
- ⊕ Cross-marked stones
- **V** "Victory" grand crosses
- ✚ Architectural and memorial carving
- æ Name slabs
- Counties without corpus

Figure 5.35 Map showing the distribution of carved stone monuments in Fm 2.
(FAS Heritage)

Western Scotland

Iona has the pre-eminent assemblage of sculpture in the north, with 108 monuments. The site was known to have been an ecclesiastical centre following the arrival of Columba in AD 563, but comparison with other material suggests that the carved stone corpus only begins to impact in the 7th century, after Columba's death.[153] Iona has suffered from numerous small excavations which have done little to elucidate the plan and development of the monastery or the date and roles of its sculpture (Chapter 3, p. 209). Adomnán's *Life of Columba* paints a picture of a busy and regulated establishment, but it may be that he is describing the settlement of his own day. In this case, it could be seen as serving a monastic institutional initiative that begins, as in all the other regions of Britain and Ireland, in the 7th century, with a major investment in the 8th.

The majority of the monuments recorded at Iona and in its region are incised linear and outlined crosses on stones of different shapes and sizes, some bearing names (Figure 5.36).

Figure 5.36 Examples of grave markers from Iona (Mull). (Top row from left) No. 10, waterworn boulder carrying a Latin cross; ht 0.39 m. No. 34, slab bearing an incised, ringed Latin cross; ht 0.39 m. No. 14, slab bearing a Latin cross and an inscription in Old Irish: 'A prayer for Mail-Phatraic' l. 0.84 m; 9th century. (Bottom left) No. 22, grave marker with compass-drawn cross and hooked terminal recalling the chi-rho; the inscription along the top edge marks it 'The stone of Echoid', an Old Irish name; ht 0.36 m; 7th century.

(Fisher 2001, pp. 127–128, nos. 10, 14, 22, 34; licensed by and © Historic Environment Scotland)

Dating is notoriously difficult, but those executed with incised lines probably represent an earlier stage than those that employ relief. Fisher's comprehensive study offers a sequence for Iona and its region that begins in the 7th century with *hexafoils and crosses-of-arcs*, (for example, on the Isle of Great Cambrae 3) and *incised linear crosses* (Iona 10; Eileach an Naoimh 1); this type remains current into the 9th century, an example being Iona 14, a Latin cross with forked terminals and an inscription in half uncial Old Irish, '+ A prayer for Mail-Phatraic'. *Outline unringed crosses* are also placed initially in the 7th century (Iona 22, Rona 2).[154] *Outlined ringed crosses* begin in the second half of the 8th century, together with *relief carvings*.[155]

Free-standing crosses (High Crosses) arrive at Iona in the 8th century and probably served as models for the region (Figure 5.37). They are elaborately ornamented with carving

Figure 5.37 Iona. St Martin's Cross.
(Courtesy of Mark Hall)

in high relief. St John's Cross has numerous bosses of domed or 'bird's nest' form, around which snakes coil. St Martin's Cross also has snake and boss ornament and features David harping, Abraham sacrificing Isaac, and Daniel between two rearing lions, while the roundel in the centre of the cross head features the Virgin Mary and her child. A high cross of this type stands at Kildalton on Islay, with snake and boss ornament and similar iconographical programme to St Martin's.[156] The high cross at Keills features Daniel holding a book and raising his hand in blessing his head set between two pairs of lions, one of which appears to lick it. A'Chill on Canna 13 features a snake biting a penis. This mixture of the sacred, the severe and the mocking, recalls the illustrative programmes of the Book of Kells, which may also have been an Iona product (p. 210).

In terms of concentrated monumentality, the current runner up to Iona is **Cladh a' Bhile** with 29 pieces, including a hexafoil and cross of arcs and a distinctive type of outline cross with four pellets under the arms, a pattern confined to the vicinity[157] (Figure 5.38, no 1). The proposed dating is 7th century, with none thought to be later than the 8th. Preliminary surveys of the immediate environment have conjectured a role for the site as a monastery or a centre for inauguration. The quantity of sculpture situated within a graveyard would suggest

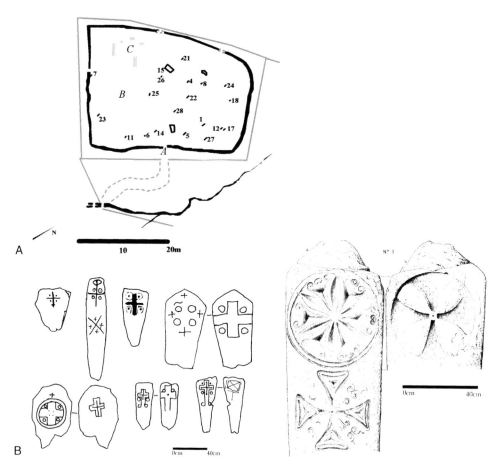

Figure 5.38 Cladh a'Bhile (Argyll and Bute). A: Plan of the cemetery. B: Outline drawings of grave markers.

(Gondek 2006b, Illus. 2, 3, 4, after Galloway 1878; by permission of the author and Historic Environment Scotland)

a privileged burial ground (like Iniscealtra, p. 564). Cladh a' Bhile would appear to be a good candidate for an early stage monastery that did not move to the higher institutional level. Eileach an Naoimh and North Rona are two more burial sites of unknown status, although the grave mound at the first and the curious anthropomorphic 'cross' at the second invite the possibility that these too began as sites of privileged burial, perhaps also serving a secular elite that never made the transition to full monasticism that beckoned in the late 7th and early 8th century.[158]

Sculpture in Period 2 is thus focussed on the monasteries, where the monks and their associates are buried under recumbent slabs of stone and the High Crosses stand around the monastic precinct, probably painted in bright colours, their panels like a permanent slide show to inspire, instruct and protect the faithful and proclaim the presence of an ideological power centre. Artistically connected with Northumbria, Scotland and Pictland, the Irish monasteries belong to the same overarching project that dominated the insular north and west through the 8th century (see *Ireland*, later in this chapter).[159]

Fm 2 in Pictland

The first group of carvings eligible for a place in Pictland's Fm 2 are those carrying ogham inscriptions, or where ogham inscriptions have been added to symbol stones, as at Brandsbutt (Figure 5.2). Unlike in Wales, the majority of the Pictish and Scottish ogham inscriptions are dated to Fm 2 and later, although it is not excluded that some, for example those on pillars, could have belonged to the earlier period and performed a proprietorial role. Of the 29 examples in Pictland, there are ogham inscriptions on two pillars and one slab with text only; four on Class I, 5 on Class II; four cross-slabs, five stone fragments, four building slabs, one free-standing cross, two knife handles and one on a spindle whorl.[160] Their secondary appearance could imply a Christian impetus even if it is placed somewhat later than Columba's 565 AD mission up the Great Glen.

Another group more clearly signals the Christian message: the roughly hewn stones carrying only a cross, initially termed Class IV by Henderson.[161] These seem to cluster in churchyards, such as Tullich in Aberdeenshire (Figure 5.39), but they also occur in sites otherwise known to have been monastic and dated to after the later 7th century (e.g. Iona, Portmahomack, Figure 5.40). At Tullich, the outline ring crosses etched on stones lying on the surface near the ruined chapel equate with those of Ireland and Argyll dated to the 7–9th century.

The principal Pictish monument of the new era is however the **cross slab**, an indigenous product stamped with the Picts' own identity-marking symbols but rising to international primacy in composition and execution. It takes the form of a large slab worked into a rectangular shape (for example Golspie, Figure 5.9). The front, back and edges are shaped and carved, either with incised lines, low relief or a combination of both; others are in high relief. The increasing impact of the carving may be a function of affluence, sponsorship and intended grandeur or driven by a new spiritual agenda. The normal composition features the display of a decorated cross on one face and on the reverse side a historiated medley in which Pictish symbols are prominent. A direct reference to the transition between the old world and the new can be seen in the right hand lower corner of St Vigeans 7 (Figure 5.41) where two clerical figures in chairs share a circular object that may be intended for the loaf shared by St Paul and St Anthony, pioneering desert fathers. Immediately below them is an image of a spearman killing a bull, perhaps in reference to the now superannuated sacrificial rite.[162]

Figure 5.39 Cross-incised grave markers at Tullich (Aberdeenshire).
(Author)

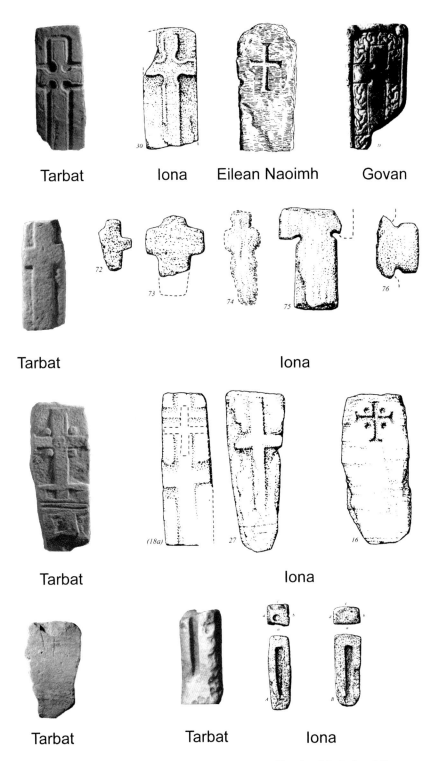

Tarbat   Iona   Eilean Naoimh   Govan

Tarbat   Iona

Tarbat   Iona

Tarbat   Tarbat   Iona

Figure 5.40 Grave markers and shrine posts from Tarbat, Iona, Eileach an Naoimh and Govan compared. (FAS Heritage; commissioned from FAS Heritage)

Pictish sculptors achieved astonishing levels of excellence in artistic composition and carving in less than a century, achievements exemplified by the monumental Tarbat cross-slabs and the St Andrew's Sarcophagus. The latter monument was found in fragments in 1833 and first reassembled in 1922, when it began to be termed a sarcophagus.[163] It takes the form of a composite stone shrine made of stone posts and slabs held together with a mortice and tenon construction. Such shrines were probably located inside a church at ground level and perhaps functioned as tombs or repositories of relics that could be accessed by the faithful. Fragments belonging to such structures have been found at St Ninians Isle, Shetland, Iona, Burghead and Ardwall in West Scotland and are suspected in England.[164] The pieces surviving at St Andrews' sarcophagus are three slotted posts, one side panel and one end panel, their surfaces all expertly carved in high relief (Figure 5.42). The end panels and posts carry mainly decorative motifs, but the surviving side panel is a continuous frieze crammed with symbolic citations: a standing figure rending the lion's jaws, a mounted lion-hunter, the first certainly and the second probably intended as David, and an attendant hunter on foot with a spear and notched shield and hounds. At the bottom of the picture a griffin attacks a mule. and in the top left-hand corner is a tree (or a thicket) inhabited by ambiguous animal and human forms.[165]

In her study of this magnificent shrine Isabel Henderson stressed the multiple sources accessible to the Pictish carvers: the 'classically draped' figure of the standing David seems

Figure 5.41 St Vigeans 7, showing (right) the 'conversion' scene (enlarged).

(Henderson and Henderson 2004, Ill.204, 205; Tom and Sybil Grey Collection; reproduced courtesy of Historic Environment Scotland)

Figure 5.42 The St Andrew's sarcophagus. (Top): Front panel. (Bottom): Three-quarter view showing form of construction.

(Courtesy and © Historic Environment Scotland)

to be extracted from 'some orientalizing Late Antique imported treasure'; the horseman lifts his sword against the lion 'like a Sassanian king'; two monkeys depicted on one of the end panels were 'originally waiting for a purchaser in a Roman shop window'.[166] Besides these Mediterranean references, commentators have found echoes of the work and thinking of peers in Northumbria, Mercia, Ireland and on the Continent.[167] There is little doubt of the international stature of this piece of monumental sculpture or the depth of current learning that its carvers have reified in an extensive stone metaphor on Christian kingship. Steve Driscoll pronounced it 'an important step on the road to statehood'.[168] Notwithstanding their high-flown agenda, the series of images also provides opportunities for the extraction of real Pictish artefacts that became embedded in the exotic iconography (see Chapter 2, p. 111).

The discoveries at Portmahomack open the possibility that the many sites known to have high-quality carving are likely to have been monasteries too, even if we have no specific documentary evidence. Among the most suggestive collections are those at Meigle and St Vigeans, but many others can be proposed on these grounds, especially round the Moray Firth. Some of these may have been Irish foundations, others may have had a Northumbrian input. Ireland, Scotland, Pictland and Northumbria were autonomous and equivalent players in the 8th-century monastic movement. Their sculpture displays 'unity in diversity', in which each region interweaves the message of salvation with the deep intellectual roots of its local prehistory. Although the contexts for the surviving cross-slabs have so far been only tentatively investigated, these observations suggest that in looking at their distribution in the landscape, we are also looking at the distribution of Pictish monasteries (Figure 5.7). They are located on the coasts, in the firths and on major rivers – so the theme is no longer the control of productive land but the heralding of a sanctified area, the reception of devotional traffic, the waystaging of a maritime network. Over Pictland as a whole, the sites cluster in two main areas, the Moray Firth and Tayside, coincident with the expected heartlands of operation of the emerging polities of the northern and southern Picts. Many of these establishments will have encountered hostility and damage during the 9th century, as at Portmahomack, when the incoming Norse rewrote the rules for the prevailing ideology of the elite.

Fm 2 in Wales

The decisive transition from Fm 1 to Fm 2 in Wales can be tracked in the form of the monuments and their locations: there is a major change in the landscape, with the development of new communities using cross-marked stones that can be defined as monasteries or 'mother churches'. While some Fm 2 stones may retain the simple pillar form of Fm 1, the difference is that they are now marked with an incised cross, which may be linear or outline, and most are anonymous. They may have functioned principally as grave markers, but some at least were employed to mark the boundaries or focal points of monastic estates or sacred precincts.[169] Some Fm 1 stones were recommissioned to serve the new prescription, for example Llandeilo Fawr 4 (CM21) and Llangyndeyrn 1 (CM29), which were 'Christianised' by the addition of crosses.[170] At Clydai (P15), a Fm 1 stone commemorating *Dob-tucus son of Evolengus* in Latin complemented by an ogham inscription (*Dovat..c-s*), was reworked in the late 7th/early 8th century with a cross formed of deeply incised intersecting arcs supported by two vertical lines for the shaft and standing on a horizontal line as the base (Figure 5.5).[171] On Caldey Island, an ogham stone (P6) was reworked to carry a Latin inscription of the 8th/9th century.[172] These 'conversions' may be serendipitous or serve to indicate that land has been gifted by a secular landowner to the church.

While there is some inevitable coincidence of locations and some continuity of form, the more specific indications of the inscriptions show how the agenda has changed: the new themes are the saving of the soul of the deceased and the protection of the land of the religious community. The inscription on P6 reads 'With the sign of the cross I fashioned on that (?) . . . I ask all walking there that they pray for the soul of Catuoconus'. The late 8th-century Latin inscription on a cross shaft G65 at St Illtud's Church, Llantwit Major, reads: 'In the name of God the Most High begins the Cross of the Saviour that Abbot Samson prepared for his soul, and the soul of King Iuthahel, and of Artma(i)l and Tecan+' . In the south-west at Llanllŷr in Ceredigion (CD20), a pillar incised with Latin crosses has an inscription dated by its lettering to before 800, recording the donation of land: 'The small waste plot of Ditoc (which) Aon, son of Asa Itgen, gave to Madomnauc' – the latter being an Irish saint.[173] Handley shows that this represents a gift of land to found a monastery and dates it to the 8th century from the use of the esoteric word 'tesquitus' (desert) which he attributes to Isidore of Seville.[174] The 9th-century inscription at Llanddewibrefi (CD9) – 'Here lies Idnert son of Jacob who was slain on account of the plundering of (the church of) St David' – implies a close connection between a landed family and a monastery with growing assets.[175]

In the northern region of Wales, all the Fm 2 stones occur on sites different to those of Fm 1 except for Penmachno (CN36) and Llandanwg (MR13). Nancy Edwards comments, 'this suggests that the ecclesiastical sites with the cross-marked stones were generally established after early inscribed stones went out of fashion'. The new sites are numerous, especially on Anglesey, where 'there is a dense pattern of small parishes with *llan* names and Celtic dedications whether to a saint or to a secular founder who was later regarded as one'.[176] Situated on Bardsey Island (Ynys Enlli), CN11, dated 7th–9th century, is a rough pillar, smooth on one face, which carries a Latin cross (Figure 5.43A). This was the site of a hermitage that became (or remained) an important pilgrimage destination. According to later sources, St Cadfan is supposed to have built a monastery dedicated to St Mary there on his arrival from Brittany in 516. There is some correlation between the location of Fm 2 stones and sites documented as 'mother churches', but it is not strong: of 26 named sites, five have Fm 2 and eight have Fm 3 sculpture.[177]

At the church at Tywyn (Towyn) (dedicated to St Cadfan), the Fm 1 mode of monumentality seems to have been adapted to serve Fm 2. There was an early stone here (now lost) inscribed with the Latin name *Pascent* (MR24, dated 5th/6th century).[178] The first of two surviving later stones took the form of a thin square pillar 2.44 m high incised with a simple linear Latin cross, (MR26, dated to the 7th–9th century). The second is a square pillar, once at least 1.72 m high, also inscribed with a simple cross but carrying Roman-letter inscriptions on all four faces (MR25, dated to the 9th century). These commemorate two women, Tengrumi wife of Adgan and Cun wife of Celyn, and constitute the earliest surviving examples of written Welsh.[179] At the same place is a sundial with two shallow incised circles (MR27). This stone had also performed as an 18th-century milestone and a gatepost, but 'sundials have been identified as important symbols of the liturgical life of early medieval monasteries'.[180]

In the south-west, only five well-documented monastic sites also have early inscribed stones, (Llanddewibrefi, Nevern, St Dogmaels, Caldey Island, and Llandeilo Fawr.).[181] This again implies that as the new ecclesiastical sites were established, inscribed stones were no

Figure 5.43 Wales: incised crosses of Fm 2: (Left): Bardsey, North Wales CN11; (Centre): St David's P93; (Right): St Dogmael's P112.

(Edwards 2013, 258; 2007, 434, 465; reproduced under licence from Royal Commission on Ancient and Historical Monuments of Wales)

longer carved, although those that remained in place did not necessarily lose their potency or relevance in the marking of land. The stones carrying crosses are widespread and cluster at some sites, though not yet in the large numbers seen at the monastic sites in Ireland, western Scotland and Isle of Man. There are very few on high ground, the preferred locations being on the more fertile soils and river valleys. A considerable number have *llan* names with a suffix naming a (probably) local saint. The form of the crosses suggests the involvement of a monastic initiative from Ireland, and the sites themselves are numerous in north Pembrokeshire on the 'Irish' coast. Assemblages of four or more stones suggest important centres at St Davids (Figure 5.43B), St Dogmaels and the five sites in between (Llanwnda, Llanllawer, Llanychaer, Llanychlwydog, St Edrins).[182] St Dogmaels 3 (P112) is a tapering pillar of the 8th to early 9th century, its small outline circular cross with slender stem recalling a *flabellum* or liturgical fan for dusting the altar, known in early medieval Ireland (Figure 5.43C).[183]

Fm 2 in Northumbria

Northumbria's 'Golden Age', as reflected by sculpture, is one of sophisticated artistry and ideological assertion.[184] It is of course possible that this was driven by the ambition of Northumbrian kings and thus just an inflated example of acquisitive lordship. But the material evidence at least suggests that the kings were subservient to a more fundamentalist Christian initiative. At the Synod of Whitby Oswiu, king of Northumbria, had accepted that spiritual dominance of the political agenda was essential. The question now was which agenda? After 664, the die was cast, and the Northumbrian monastic machine swung into action, soon bumping up against similar, contemporary and, inevitably, rival surges to north and west. Poised between prehistory and history, this is a precocious and naked example of the power of the irrationally-driven political convictions that have periodically redirected the world's thinking.

Within Fm 2 Northumbria, Rosemary Cramp has discerned two phases of production: in the late 7th to mid-8th century (her 'Phase 1'), the carving of monuments begins alongside the construction of stone churches and made use of imported masons.[185] In the mid-8th to 9th century ('Phase 2'), the carved stone industry expanded, diversified and moved beyond the Northumbrian heartland, principally in the form of grand free-standing crosses. Jim Lang detected a difference in the emphasis of endowment from the treasuries of secular sponsors in Phase 1 to the exploitation of the monastery's own wealth and the expression of its agenda in Phase 2.[186] The grand crosses have been termed 'Victory Crosses'[187] and may be associated specifically with a monastic initiative in the mid-8th century and held to signal its advance. Here what has been inferred in Pictland and Wales is made explicit.

Phase 1: the warm-up: late 7th to mid-8th century

The revolutionary movement that united Angle, Briton and eventually Scot and Pict under the banner of Rome was due partly to the skilled advocacy of exceptional politicians, such as Wilfred and Oswiu, and partly to the logic of strength through orthodoxy, something that required a single authority, in this case the Pope. Wilfred and Oswiu, the Trotsky and Lenin of their day, prevailed at the Synod of Whitby in 664, where the direction of travel was determined by force of argument, underpinned by the force of politics in the person of King Oswiu, the greatest power in the region.[188] There followed a period of ideological ambition and territorial control for which the sculpture offers strong corroborative evidence.

The material investment in the new project took the form of making not only carved stone monuments but illuminated manuscripts and richly ornamented church plate, their ateliers being based in a new kind of collegiate community called a monastery (monasterium) by Bede.[189] Archaeologically, these have proved to be identifiable on the ground by specific correlates, namely the presence of a church and cemetery contained by a *vallum* and the remains of three foundation industries: the making of vellum, the casting of precious metals and glass and the carving of stone monuments.[190] This kind of settlement is currently known only from Ireland (as at Clonmacnoise, p. 279), Scotland (Iona), Pictland (as at Portmahomack) and Northumbria (as at Wearmouth and Jarrow). It is strongly inferred in Wales, mainly on the basis of sculpture only. But whatever anticipations the documents may raise, such institutions have yet to make an archaeological appearance in English Southumbria. The distinction made here is between a place named as a monastery in a document (for example Bede's *History*) and the existence of a monastic settlement identifiable by its correlates on the ground. English candidates such as Flixborough and Brandon have so far failed these tests (Chapter 3, pp. 237–9).

Stone carving in Northumbria begins with the making of grave markers and the building of stone churches and their architectural embellishment in the late 7th century.[191] The region is distinguished by a group of surviving stone churches of which the foundation date is known: Hexham 673–4, Monkwearmouth 674 and Jarrow 682–5 (and see Chapter 3, p. 218 for other foundation dates derived from Bede).

Architectural fittings and embellishment

These churches were highly decorated with carved stone furnishings, some still surviving in the fabric, others recovered 'by controlled, and uncontrolled, excavation'.[192] About 50 fragments survive from the three last-mentioned sites alone. Examples include balusters, lintels, imposts and friezes. Some, like Wearmouth 14, carried red and black paint on gesso.[193] Roman inspiration is evident in animals fashioned in the round at Monkwearmouth (15) and Hexham (33, 34), a ceremonial stone chair (Hexham 41), a chair terminal (Monkwearmouth 16), a monolithic head window (Monkwearmouth 14), a corded pillar base (Hexham 40) and the Jarrow dedication stone (Jarrow 17) (Figure 5.44).[194] The dedication stone, now set in the west wall of the earliest upstanding church above an arch, is inscribed DEDICATIO BASILICAE S(AN)C(T)I PAVLI VIIII K(A)L(ENDAS) MAI(AS) ANNO XV ECFRIDI REG(IS); CEOLFRIDI ABB(ATIS), EIVSDEMQ(UE) ECCLES(IAE) D(E) O AUCTORE CONDITORIS, ANNO IIII ('The dedication of the basilica of St Paul on the 9th day before the Kalends of May in the 15th year of King Ecfrid; and in the 4th (*sc*. 'year') of Abbot Ceolfrid, founder, by the guidance of God, of the same church'). This records the dedication of the earliest church at Jarrow, which took place on Sunday, 23 April 685. Parts of this church remain (p. 576). Also at Jarrow are precise figurative carvings in high relief that belong to friezes originally set into the church wall. They show birds, beasts and a man inhabiting a plant scroll (Jarrow 19, 20) (Figure 5.45) (see Chapter 2, p. 116, Figure 2.37 for the dressed-up human figure in Jarrow 20).

The dramatic Roman take-off at Wearmouth, Jarrow and Hexham was compounded with some other elements both local to Northumbria and from across the Irish Sea and the Channel. The principal form shared between the three sites is the stone baluster, either the full-size grooved stone cylinders spun on a lathe or balustrade friezes composed of mini-balusters side by side. At Jarrow there are 25 lathe-turned full sized baluster shafts, all the same height (73 cm), implying they were used in a row, probably to enclose a space

Figure 5.44 Northumbria in Fm 2: Jarrow 17 dedication stone; Hexham 33, 34, 40, 41 (*Corpus* Vol 1, Illus. 524, 1007, 1012, 1022, 1040).

(Courtesy and © Corpus of Anglo-Saxon Stone Sculpture, photographer T. Middlemass)

Figure 5.45 Jarrow 19.

(Author)

Figure 5.46 Balustrade (Jarrow 25) and (right) baluster shafts from Monkwearmouth (14a,b).
(*Corpus* Vol 1, Illus. 540; © Corpus of Anglo-Saxon Stone Sculpture; photographer T. Middlemass)

like the Roman *scola cantorum* (choir) (Jarrow 30). Monkwearmouth has 35 balusters with a variety of diameters, two pairs flanking the opening of the porch (Figure 5.46). Jarrow, Monkwearmouth and Hexham all have friezes representing rows of mini-balusters. The use of a lathe to turn stone pillars recalls woodwork, as in the chest from the well-preserved 6th/7th-century cemetery at Oberflacht or the mini-balusters comprising the rails of beds at the same site and the Prince's cot at Cologne.[195] However, one suspects that much of northern Europe would be familiar with this kind of carpentry and joinery, and Cramp suggests that the immediate inspiration of balusters and balustrades in stone is seen in examples in situ at the 7th-century Hypogée des Dunes, Poitiers, or at 5th-century Nouaillé.[196] Architectural sculpture was not confined to the church building: Jarrow 22 is a pillar from Building A (a possible refectory), its base originally sealed by the floor, which was rendered in *opus signinum*. It is hexagonal in section, with vertical ribs separating ornament of interlacing plants, carpentered in appearance. Its location suggested a role as a column to support the roof, but it is now thought to have been part of a reading desk (Figure 5.47; see Chapter 3, Figure 3.75 for location). Input from the north and west includes stone 'butterfly' finials that grace the gable of a stone church. They have their origins in Ireland, and examples have been found at Whitby, Lastingham, Lythe and Heysham, as well as at Portmahomack.[197] Meanwhile, Buildings A and B at Jarrow resemble in plan, design and proportion the halls built in timber at Yeavering in the Borders (Chapter 3, 222).

Figure 5.47 Jarrow 22: column, octagonal in section, probably to support a lectern.
(Author)

Memorials

The grandest early Northumbrian name-slab would appear to be that dedicated to the
Anglo-Saxon priest Herebericht at Monkwearmouth (Figure 5.48). The inscription, in precise and formal Anglo-Saxon capitals, reads: HIC IN SEPULCRO REQUIESCIT COR-
PORE HEREBERICHT PR(ES)B(YTER), which can be paraphrased as *In this tomb lies the
body of Herebericht the priest*. Plainer smaller name slabs (marked only with a cross and a
name) are distributed over the Northumbrian heartland – at Lindisfarne, Wearmouth, Jarrow,
Hartlepool, Whitby, York (Figure 5.49). The cross-forms may also be seen in more elaborate
execution in the early Northumbrian Gospel books. The names are incised in Anglo-Saxon

Figure 5.48 Monkwearmouth 4: Grave marker (530 wide × 1040 mm high) inscribed 'Here in the tomb rests Herebericht the priest in the body'.

(*Corpus* Vol I, Illus 604; courtesy and © Corpus of Anglo-Saxon Stone Sculpture; photographer T. Middlemas; Cramp 2006 (vol II), 193)

capital letters or runes or both. Some, like Osgyth's stone at Lindisfarne, were designed to stand upright at the end of a grave; others were recumbent on top of it as at Hartlepool, the only slabs to have been found (loosely) associated with graves (p. 411). Those remembered at Hartlepool are Hildithryth (female, no.1), Hildigyth (female, no.2), Edilwine? (male, no.3), Vermund (*sc*. 'and') Torhtsuid' (male and female on same slab, no.4), Edilwine, Vermund and Torhtsuid on the same slab (no.5), Beorhtgyd (female. no 6), and ALEVB (not linked to any recorded form, no. 8).[198] Men (Aedberecht, Beanna) and a woman (Osgyth) are also present at Lindisfarne (Lindisfarne 23, 24, 25). An exhortation to pray for the soul is seen at York (21) and for the man and woman on Hartlepool (4).[199]

Thus, those first commemorated in Fm 2 have Anglo-Saxon names and include both men and women. While Hartlepool was a led by a woman and Oswiu's own daughter was an inmate, it does not appear to have been totally closed to men, and men and women lie together on name slabs elsewhere, as at Lindisfarne.[200] Of the 59 names recognised on

Figure 5.49 Name slabs: (Top left) Lindisfarne 25A (Beanna), (top right) Hartlepool 2A (Hildigyth), (bottom left) Hartlepool 6A (Beorhtgyd) and (bottom right) York Minster 22A (Wulfhere).

(*Corpus* Vol I, Ill.1122, 430, 444; III, Ill.91; courtesy and © Corpus of Anglo-Saxon Stone Sculpture; photographer T. Middlemass)

Northumbrian grave slabs, 25% were women.[201] While men no doubt controlled the lion's share of the resources, there is some indication here that the monastic movement was one in which men and women shared the adventure, at least initially. In the 9th century at Thornhill there is an example, so far unique, of a woman erecting a memorial stone to another woman: 'Gilswith raised up in memory of Berhtswith a beacon on a hill. Pray for her soul'. There is no surviving mound under the church, although there is one on the hill, as the placename implies.[202] Nevertheless, it would be intriguing to know the status of these two Anglian women and the context for their ritual, given that it melds ancient procedures for land-marking with the up-to-date liturgical exhortation to pray for the soul of the departed, and it took place on the eve of the Viking arrival.

The name-slab culture has roots in Rome and in Gaul and was taken up at much the same time in Ireland (see Clonmacnoise, p. 563). This was part of the large net of learning that was thrown outwards from Jarrow encouraging the rapid assimilation of Roman, Gaulish and Irish Christian experiments in one assertive hybrid. Jarrow (16) carries an inscription read as IN HOC SINGULARI SIGNO VITA REDDITUR MUNDO *In this unique sign life is returned to the world.* The 'unique sign' is the cross of Christ, recalling the dream of the emperor Constantine before the battle of Milvian Bridge (312), and the inscription offers a pre-echo of the role that the cross would play in the Northumbrian monastic movement.[203]

Phase 2: the break out: mid-8th into 9th century

Wilfred built the church at Ripon between 669 and 678, inspired by ideas from Gaul. Like the Hypogeum of Mellabaude at Poitiers, it was equipped with a crypt designed for the worship of relics by the faithful: its stepped ingress and egress survive. Wilfred spearheaded a militant form of monasticism involving the acquisition of land and the allegiance of territories newly won for the cause. He was given 309 hides when he became abbot of Ripon, some of it apparently land recently vacated by British clergy. After he became Bishop of York, he acquired estates into Elmet along the Roman routes along the river valleys leading up into the Pennines. Maintaining a strong association with the Deiran heartland, Ripon was a bridgehead to the west.[204] If Wilfred hoped to initiate a Northumbrian expansion with a fundamentalist programme, the sculpture suggests that in practice the breakout only took off 50 years later, in the mid-8th century, and continued only until the mid-9th. The expansion most likely involved the acquisition of monastic estates marked by the 'Victory Crosses'. It would arrive in the far west at Whithorn and in the south at Glastonbury.[205]

Prototypes for these evangelising monuments may have been provided by the stone cross at Hexham, dated 740 by the death of Bede's confidant Bishop Acca, and the free-standing cross erected at Lindisfarne for Bishop Aethelwold before his death, also in 740.[206] The map (Figure 5.35) shows an approximation of the progress of the subsequent campaign. Estates were founded from Ripon and in Ryedale in the late 7th century (Lastingham, Whitby), up Wharfedale in the 8th century (Ilkley and Otley Figure 5.50), up Uredale in the late 8th (Masham and Easby), across the Pennines to Galloway (Ruthwell and Bewcastle Figure 5.51), down into west Yorkshire in the 8th/9th century, culminating in the Dewsbury group in the 9th century. The crosses combine a refreshed classicism with a focus on Jesus Christ and his apostles, with some references to Old Testament themes. Coatsworth describes them as major monuments designed to 'proclaim and enhance the theological and liturgical programme of a literate monastic community'.[207] For Jim Lang, the Grand Crosses do not offer redemption, monasticism or 'even simple piety'. They are 'statements of ecclesiastical authority . . . of orthodoxy, perhaps ownership'.[208] The programme of the monuments thus combines a crusade with a return to the Roman empire, the Classical style pre-echoing Charlemagne's ideological project.

But neither the techniques nor the ideology had to wait for Charlemagne: Masham 1 and Otley 1 have recessed panels for captions in the mode of the pillars at St Mark's Venice (pre-8th century). At Otley 1, the sculptor adopted the Roman technique of modelling gesso over the roughed out stone, then applying paint. Sculptors working in Northumbria must

Figure 5.50 'Apostle pillars': (Left) Masham 1v, with apostles in the top register; (Right) Otley 1aA, with learned figures holding books.

(*Corpus* Vol VIII, Ill. 564; courtesy and © Corpus of Anglo-Saxon Stone Sculpture, photographer K. Jukes and D. Craig; *Corpus* Vol VI, 171, 218, Ill.601; courtesy and © Corpus of Anglo-Saxon Stone Sculpture, photographer R. Trench-Jellicoe)

Figure 5.51 The Bewcastle Cross (8th century), looking east towards the Northumbrian heartland. Detail of west face showing Christ as master of animals. Within the runic inscription have been read the female name Cyneburh and the words 'This token of victory . . . set up in memory of . . .'

(Page in Bailey and Cramp 1988, 63, 65; courtesy and © Corpus of Anglo-Saxon Stone Sculpture, photographer Rosemary Cramp) have seen this in Italy. At Bewcastle the claim of the Victory Cross is explicit, an inscription reading 'This victory cross Hwaetred set up in memory of . . . [missing]'. The cross features a male figure with beard and lamb, Jesus Christ holding a scroll and standing on the heads of two beasts; a figure with rod and bird on a perch and ornamental panes of vine scroll; and interlace. Each of the figures is thought to represent the adoption of the animal world by the new authority from their previous masters.[209] Writing of its cousin, the mid-8th century Ruthwell cross, Rosemary Cramp evokes the driving forces expressed by a new iconography, in which

> the explanatory Latin inscriptions with the figural panels combine in a great theological meditation on the recognition of the divinity and power of Christ, and the runic poem framing the animated scrolls emphasises with birds and beasts in the vine, the relation of creation to God, and man's position in the hierarchy of creation. No other cross illustrates so perfectly the intellectual background of Northumbrian Christianity.[210]

Lang conjured up an even more specific meaning in the group formed by Easby, Masham, Otley and Dewsbury, linked by their prominent display of apostles.[211] Otley 1 is a very distinctive monument in Classical style and had an enduring influence. The dress of the figures is Classical, with V-necked garments that became the alb.[212] Masham 1 has a columnar shaft with four horizontal registers and seven arcaded bays in each, with Old Testament scenes: David slaying the lion, David the psalmist and Samson at Gaza. Lang sees Masham as not especially related to Otley but an original creation of 'the Uredale master', a carver identified by a common style and some common themes, e.g. Samson carrying off the gates of Gaza, at Masham, Cundall/Aldborough and West Tanfield.[213] At Easby, a panel shows the risen Christ flanked by Peter and Paul celebrating the moment that Christ gives Peter the keys of the kingdom of heaven and the instruction to apply the new law worldwide. Dewsbury 5 shows the Baptism of Christ, the wedding at Cana and feeding of the five thousand with an inscription mentioning wine (Cana) and two fishes. The sources are late Classical/early Christian, but this time filtered through Carolingian France. 'The whole area south of Leeds and west of Wakefield has yielded no work earlier than the late 8th/early 9th century', suggesting this was a venture into new territory.[214]

James Lang also maintained that the 'pillar' represented by the shafts of these crosses also made reference to a triumphant conversion process: the apostles James, Cephas and John are cited by St Paul as 'pillars' in the confrontation with the heathen (*Epistle to the Galatians* 2.9). The *Book of Revelations*, which deals with a campaign to reform the seven churches (and cure them of fornication), promises 'He that shall overcome, I will make him a pillar in the temple of my God' (Rev 3.12). Lang also supposes that the erection of a cross near water implies the rite of baptism necessary to provide the gateway for the converted to join the new estate.[215] These specific messages apart, Lang's ingenious advocacy of the 8th/9th-century Grand Crosses adds to the case that they represent the imposition of a new, stricter Christian code, in which Christ's call to the apostles, 'Go ye and teach all nations', has become one of ideological conquest.

The 'Victory Crosses' mark the boundaries of the territory in which Northumbrian fundamentalism had been applied by the time the Vikings came. This stretched from Irton in the Lake District, to Halton, Heysham and Lancaster in the Lune Valley, to Sandbach and Overchurch in Cheshire (Figure 5.52).[216] Halton has a last judgement scene, and Heysham a bird head, probably from a chair. Lancaster has an Anglian runic inscription asking for prayers for Cynebald. These are seen as a 'ninth century group reflecting the artistic

Figure 5.52 Victory crosses reach the west. (Left): Halton 3A (Lune Valley, Lancashire). (Right): Sandbach 1C (Cheshire).

(Corpus Vol IX, Illus 481; courtesy and © Corpus of Anglo-Saxon Stone Sculpture, photographer R. Trench-Jellicoe; ibid. Illus. 248 © Corpus of Anglo-Saxon Stone Sculpture, photographer K. Jukes)

dynamism of many of the west Yorkshire monastic sites'.[217] The Grand Cross in the Market Place at Sandbach, dated c. 800, has an elaborate iconographical programme including evangelists and scenes from the life of Christ, influenced by intellectual advances in Carolingian France; it is seen as a totemic declaration of the salvation being offered.[218] At neighbouring Overchurch there is a runic inscription on a grave cover, asking for prayers for Aethelmund.[219]

However, in spite of the vigour of the stone markers in parts of the region, most of the large territory of Lancashire continued to be deprived of sculpture in Fm 2. This cannot be explained by a lack of stone, so an explanation has been sought in the notion that only certain types of monastic centre produced sculpture.[220] An alternative interpretation might be that the equation of carved stone with the monastic movement remains valid, but this area took no part in it. This would align it with other areas similarly sparsely furnished with 7th–9th century sculpture, such as west Mercia, Lincolnshire and indeed much of the English heartland.

Even in the more Anglicised southern part of Northumbria, the take-off of the monastic movement was more modest. In the East Riding of Yorkshire, 7th-century monumental barrows can be found occupying primary vistas on the south side of the Wolds, while the new monasteries cluster on its north side along the Vale of Pickering, also connected by lines of sight.[221] The implication is that the loyalties of the English settlers in East Riding remained linked to those of their kinsfolk south of the Humber, while those that had acculturated with the Britons in the north and west of Yorkshire became the standard-bearers for a well-founded Northumbrian Christianity.

Fm 2 in Mercia

Expert survey of the English Midlands was incomplete at the time of writing (see Table 5.1, p. 472), so that it is likely that the strength of Mercia as a game-changing agent is underplayed here.[222] The ateliers of the *East Midlands* appear to have been both advanced in their agenda and sophisticated in execution.[223] The church at **Breedon-on-the-Hill** in Leicestershire is ornamented inside with a magnificent if battered range of carvings, including intricately carved string-courses, friezes with insular ornament, now much weathered, a portrait of the Virgin and one of an angel in high relief (Figure 5.53).[224] **Hedda's tomb, Peterborough**, is the prototype for the Anglian shrine: solid, shaped like a building. Twelve figures are depicted on it: Christ (with cross-bearing halo), Mary with the palm given to her by Gabriel, St Peter with his keys, Andrew with his crazy hair, John looking youthful. The other seven are probably apostles. Further sophistication is expected from those admiring the **Wirksworth slab** (Figure 5.54). The crowded scene features Christ as the Lamb of God, ascending to heaven and harrowing hell, and the funeral of the Virgin Mary, with a Jewish high priest. Richard Bailey weaves this disparate drama into a single homily concerning the 'the glory to be achieved though humility'.[225] Nevertheless, it is hard to avoid the conclusion that the 'humility' is a little feigned: these were scholarly compositions aimed at fellow clerics and celebrated their mutual access to esoteric knowledge. As with the druids, the magic lay in the deep learning.

In the *West Midlands*, only two sites have produced sculpture in any quantity: Deerhurst (9th century) and Gloucester, St Oswald's (c. 890 to c. 940). There is a startling absence from Hereford and Worcester and from other monastic candidates, such as Leominster, Much Wenlock, Cirencester, Fladbury and Winchcombe.[226] Where carved stones occur, the quantities are still small: 271 recorded pieces, of which 164 are from Gloucestershire, 43

Figure 5.53 Carving at Breedon-on-the-Hill (Leicestershire). A. (Top): Ornamental frieze in the south face of the south porch. B. (Bottom): Angelic figure in a wall panel. Late 8th century.

(A: © Society of Antiquaries of London); B: Cramp 1977, Fig 58c; Jewell 1986, Plate LIa; photograph courtesy of Emily Howe)

Figure 5.54 The Wirksworth slab (Derbyshire). *Upper centre* is the cross with the lamb of God ('that takest away the sins of the world'), flanked by the four evangelists. *Left* shows Christ washing the feet of his disciples. *Right*: The funeral of the Virgin Mary preceded by her palm, confronted by the Jewish high priest whose hands stuck to the bier and was later converted by St Peter. *Lower centre*: Christ ascending in the mandorla flanked by angels. *Left*: The Harrowing of Hell, with Christ raising a diminutive Adam. *Right*: The annunciation and presentation of Christ in the temple.

(© Corpus of Anglo-Saxon Stone Sculpture; photograph courtesy of Jane Hawkes)

from Worcestershire, 28 from Shropshire, 24 from Herefordshire and 12 from Warwickshire. There is no shortage of suitable stone, either as freestone or Roman stones.[227] Of the various explanations put forward, the one proffered here is lack of enthusiasm for the monastic movement, which arrived too late for the Northumbrian mission to be still appropriate.

Bryant dates the appearance of carved stone monuments at the two principal centres of St Oswald's Gloucester and the Church of St Mary at Deerhurst in the late 8th and early 9th century and aligns it with the era of Mercian supremacy from AD 750.[228] Four crosses at **St Oswald's** show the development through late 8th to mid-9th century. All four were standing near each other at St Oswald's by the 9th century. Here, evidence for stone churches in the form of imposts, hood mouldings, string-courses, jambs, window heads and door heads began to appear, in this case shortly after the first of the stone crosses.[229]

At **Deerhurst**, the earliest carving was probably St Mary 2 of the late 8th century, reused as part of a triangular doorhead in late 9th or early 10th.[230] The church began to acquire the first phase of its rich assemblage of architectural adornment in the first half of the 9th century: beast-head label stops on doors and *prokrossoi*, protective beast heads projecting from the wall.[231] The large animal heads that terminate the chancel arch still carry traces of their 9th-century red, yellow, white and black paint.[232] At the same time, the figure of an angel was incorporated in the wall fabric, high on the exterior of the polygonal east apse, and a carving of the Virgin and Child on the west face of the central wall in the west tower above the door.[233] In a second phase of the late 9th/10th century, the church was fitted with triangular openings, originally painted red (Figure 5.55).

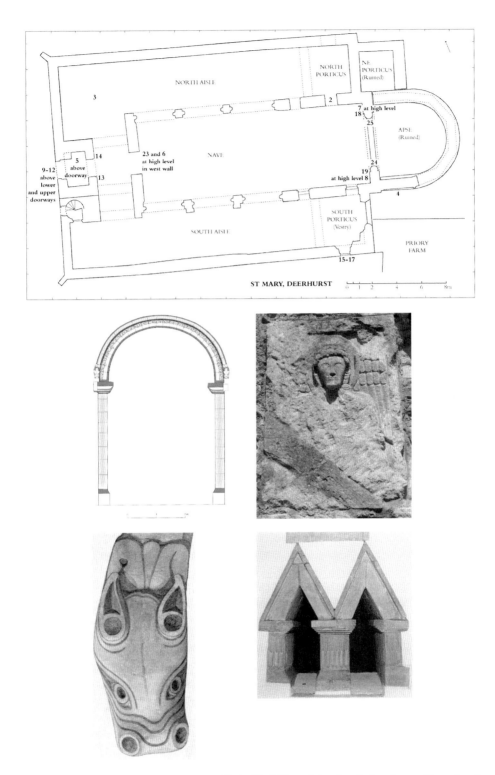

Figure 5.55 Deerhurst St Mary (Gloucestershire). (Top) Plan of the church showing position of sculpture; (Centre left) Chancel arch, showing location of beast head label stops; (Bottom left) Detail of beast-head label stop; (Centre right) Figure of an angel on the exterior wall of the apse; (Bottom right) Triangular-headed openings.

(Courtesy and © Corpus of Anglo-Saxon Stone Sculpture: A: Vol X, Fig 19; B: Vol X, Fig 36; C: Vol X, Ill. 145; E: Vol X, Plate 1, photographer R.M. Bryant; D: Vol X, Ill. 215, photographer Steve Bagshaw)

Figure 5.56 Cropthorne (Worcestershire) cross head (no 1A).

(Courtesy and © Corpus of Anglo-Saxon Stone Sculpture, photographer Mick Sharp)

Away from these this pivotal places, ambitious ornamental sculpture was achieved by sculptors creating the 'Cropthorne group', with examples at Acton Beauchamp, Wroxeter church and Gloucester St Oswald's as well as **Cropthorne** itself (Figure 5.56).[234] Further south, the monumental upsurge also dates generally to the mid-8th/9th century, although the geometric patterns derived from metalwork (like the Sutton Hoo shoulder clasps) of the altar frontal at Bradford on Avon might suggest an earlier date (8th century).[235] The dancing figure at Codford St Peter (Chapter 2, 118) is probably meant to be King David 'dancing before the Lord with all his might' and is dated late 8th/early 9th century, as are the lacertine animals at Colerne.[236] At Britford 1, a pair of corbels either side of the chancel arch could have supported a cross beam on which a cross stood.[237]

Such investments in high-quality pieces and richly appointed churches might suggest that these are the sites of monasteries, as elsewhere in Northumbria and the Anglo-British borders, but with so few excavated sites it is hard to be sure if the same kind of institution is intended. Some of the clusters occur at documented ecclesiastical centres. Bath, Glastonbury, Keysham and Ramsbury have collections of different forms and styles of monuments, and working from documents, Michael Hare assumes that sculpture marks the sites of 'minsters', although he offers no archaeological definition of what form these might take.[238] The negative evidence (lack of industries and infrastructure) seems to set the minsters apart from their monastic cousins in the north. It may be that a minster is not a dedicated central place like a monastery, only a church with the rite of burial, thus prone to produce memorials where they can be paid for, its ritual function subservient to that of a pre-existing central place. According to Teresa Hall, the majority of minsters in Dorset were founded at the centre of the large royal estates.[239] This of course does not make them monasteries in the sense used in this book. It seems that in the south-west, as on the Humber, we have found the interface where the furthest reach of the Northumbrian monastic movement meets the Southumbrian English prescription, in so far as it can be detected.

Fm 2 in Southumbria

The sculpture of the Southumbrian region, comprising Lincolnshire, East Anglia and the home counties, offers at present a meagre and disparate showing in Fm 2. Nine fragments of a mini-baluster frieze from Old Minster Winchester and one from Barking are dated to Fm 2, making comparison to those at Jarrow.[240] Winchester may have been an exceptional early Christian centre in the 7th century, like Canterbury (see Fm 1), or have revealed traces of a more generally hidden history, thanks to the intensity of its investigation. But there is very little sculpture in the English region assigned to the 8th century, although **Elstow** may be an exception (Figure 5.57A). The other candidates are Bedford St Peter, Steventon, Little Somborne, South Hayling – all cross shafts assigned to the late 8th/early 9th.[241] The *figurative* carving at Reculver, once thought to have been Roman or 7th-century work, is now seen as constituting five pieces from a cross shaft of the 9th century (Figure 5.57B).[242]

Figure 5.57 A. (Left) Carvings at Elstow (Bedfordshire) no. 1; and B. (Right) Reculver (Kent) no. 1e (Corpus IV, Ill.269, 120).

(Courtesy and © Corpus of Anglo-Saxon Stone Sculpture, photographer S.I. Hill. Photograph A is reproduced courtesy of Moot Hall, Elstow, Bedford)

Figure 5.58 Fm 2 stone carving in Lincolnshire: (Left) Edenham 1, the 'one fragment which is part of a pre-Viking cross-shaft'; (Right) South Kyme, fragments perhaps from a shrine.

(Everson and Stocker 1999, 27, 248; Lincolnshire; *Corpus* V, Illus 165, 339; courtesy and © Corpus of Anglo-Saxon Stone Sculpture, photographers P. Everson and D. Stocker)

In Lincolnshire too the candidates for late 7th to early 9th-century carving can be counted in single figures: there are grave markers from Lincoln St Paul in the Bail and St Marks (21 and 22), a possible 7th-century cross base from Bardney, fragments of 8th/9th century insular panels from **South Kyme**, and a monumental cross at **Edenham** (mid-9th c)[243] (Figure 5.58). Of these, the Edenham 1 cross shaft, now very weathered, seems to have depicted an evangelist and must originally have been a monument of great quality standing several metres high, in the style of the Northumbrian Victory Crosses.[244] This exiguous material implies some penetration by the monastic movement into Lincolnshire, albeit one that is half-hearted and late. The map suggests that the first penetration came from York rather than Mercia, following the Roman road south and founding documented monasteries to the east of it at Barton, Caistor, Bardney, Louth, Partney, South Kyme, Threekingham. Edenham, however, was an even later outlier, probably from Mercia.

Formative 3 (9th–11th century)

In Fm 3 (9th–11th century), the overall trend in the production of stone monuments was from monastic to secular patronage. Secular leaders sponsored carving, sometimes for their own aggrandisement in connection with their estates and kingdoms or to raise the status of their church. Anglo-Scandinavian sculptors took over the production of stone monuments in the regions that had previously had them (Northumbria, Scotland, parts of north Wales) and installed them liberally in regions where they had been previously sparse or absent (Lincolnshire, Lancashire) (Figure 5.59). In the north, the landscape borrowed the *tropheum* of the grand cross and the grave slabs of the sanctified from the monastic church and redeployed them in the service of a new Hiberno-Britto-Anglo-Scandinavian aristocracy. Even where

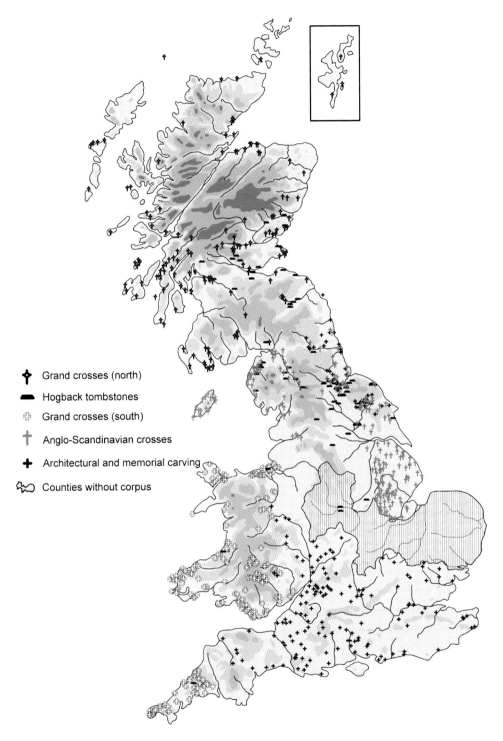

Legend:

- **Grand crosses (north)**
- **Hogback tombstones**
- Grand crosses (south)
- Anglo-Scandinavian crosses
- Architectural and memorial carving
- Counties without corpus

Figure 5.59 Map of places with sculpture in Fm 3.

(FAS Heritage)

monasteries continued, they are likely to have been secularised with a 'trading arm', as suggested for those in Ireland (Chapter 3, 278). In the south, the English carvers entered their own golden age, with a wealth of carving embellishing cathedrals and a plethora of parish churches.

Fm 3 in Scotland

From the 9th century, the expectation of history is that Picts and Scots will have got together under a single governance and that the north British peninsula will begin to function as one country. The sculpture does not insist that this has happened. The west coast monasteries continue to produce memorials, but a third player, the Norseman, is actively creating monuments with Viking themes: a sarcophagus and hogbacks at Govan on the Clyde and inscriptions on cross-slabs at Iona and Inchmarnock (remembering *Guthleifr*). These belong to the 10th to 11th century.

The 'eclipse' of the Pictish elite took place in the 9th century while they were being pressed by the Scots from the west and the Norse from the north. In practice these pressures were of different character, and the north and south of Pictland experienced them in different ways: more violent in the north, more insidious in the south. The Irish pressure had been active since the implantation of ogham and through the foundation of monasteries, so that it is reasonable to visualise much intellectual and biological mixing between Scot and Pict for several centuries before the north British peninsula was re-established as the kingdom of Scotland (Alba). The Pictish leaders suffered a number of defeats at the hands of the Norse, and by the later 9th century they constituted a much-diminished faction.[245] Gaelicisation followed, with no new erection of monuments with symbols and by implication the marginalising of the Pictish language. Deprived of their symbols, cross-slabs were still made, and the images of cowled monks (at Bressay and Papil in Shetland, Aldbar, St Vigeans 10, 11) or of armed warriors (Edderton, Kinnedar, Aldbar, Benvie) imply a collaborative secularised monasticism similar to that developing in Ireland. Although not always on exactly the same sites, the distribution of these slabs without symbols (Allen and Anderson's Class III) maps onto that of those of the Class II stones likely to signal the monasteries.

Some other monuments were particularly large and worldly and seem to have stood alone. In the south, the **Dupplin Cross**, once on the valleyside in Strathearn, Perthshire, also proclaims military might – a cavalry officer supported by a phalanx of spearmen led by two officers with moustaches (depicted on the side) (Figure 5.60). It is dated to the early 9th century and has been discovered to be inscribed with the name of Constantin, son of Fergus, king of Picts from 789 to 820.[246] Henderson and Henderson detect Northumbrian references in the cross head and suggest that its original siting enabled the cross to be seen against the sky in reference to the visions of Oswald and perhaps of Constantine the Great. However, apart from the cross head, the religious references are limited to David, the pre-Christian hero of early insular kings.[247] There seems no strong reason for doubting that this monument was driven by military rather than ecclesiastical triumphalism – a contrast to what had gone before and a sign of the 9th-century imperatives visited on the land. At Meigle to the east, where there was probably a monastic centre in the 8th century (p. 519), the making of stone monuments continued under lay patronage in the 9th and 10th centuries.[248]

In the north, at Forres on the Moray Firth, **Sueno's Stone** kept the design of the cross slab, if somewhat exaggerated in its height (6 m) to width ratio. In spite of this and the name it

Figure 5.60 The Dupplin (Constantine) Cross, Forteviot (Perthshire).
(A: Courtesy of Mark Hall; B: Allen and Anderson 1903, Fig. 334C, D)

subsequently acquired (that of the Norse king Sven), the teeming activity on the reverse face recalls an Irish rather than a Pictish (or Norse) format.[249] Henderson and Henderson stress the likely inspiration of Classical triumphal carving, although this should not disqualify the stone from celebrating a comparable local event, or indeed a comparable indigenous ambition.[250] It is certainly a Victory Cross, but not in the way used at Tarbat (or extensively in the Anglian sectors): its burden is not religious but political conquest, a battle followed by the systematic beheading of the prisoners. It might be a scene in the spirit of the Bible, but David is absent and we are spared the crude measures by which he liked to signal his triumphs (see Chapter 6, p. 616). The identity of the victims of this sad event has been buried with them, but there is little doubt about the identity of the victors. By the time this 9th- or 10th-century *tropheum* was erected, the Pictish kingdom of Fortriu had departed from history and the area had become Moray, a sea kingdom of the Scots.[251]

Many of the Irish monasteries survived the Viking onslaught and continued to develop during the 9th to 11th centuries. Iona and its hinterland also continued to produce monumental sculpture after the Norse raids in the form of *cross-slabs*, dated to the 10th/11th century.[252] **Iona 69** has a cross formed by a double ribbon with a Norse runic inscription along one edge 'Kali son of Ölvir laid this stone over Fugl his brother' (Figure 5.61A). The example at **Ardchattan 1** has a winged figure holding a book, three seated hooded figures playing instruments: harp, triple pipe and ?trumpet and a figure with a spear and notched shield who may be David (Figure 5.61B).

Vikings in the north-west

The strongest sculptural signature of the Norse Vikings is in the Isle of Man, but Viking period sculpture appears in other schools that are artistically related grouped on the mainland in Cumbria and Lancashire. The Beckermet group, with nine carvings from Beckermet (St Brigit and St John), Haile, Workington and Brigham, is situated just north of Gosforth, and the spiral-scroll school has 27 carvings spread along the west coast further north. Other groups further south lie in the Lune Valley, the Ribble Valley and the Wirral.

Although the Viking grip is firm and articulate, the sculpture shows that the Fm 3 territory is a genuine hybrid community: Christian/pagan, British, Anglian, Irish, Danish, Norse. Only Gosforth 4 and Lowther 4 and 5 carry no Christian symbolism (they have themes paralleled in Gotland).[253] Sigurd and Ragnarök feature on Christian crosses, in the case of Gosforth alongside a crucifixion tableau with Longinus and Mary Magdalene. British traits are visible in the nine circular cross heads, part of a signature distributed between Cumbria, Cheshire, North Wales and Cornwall.[254] Other cross heads are free-armed, in the Anglian tradition. Halton St Wilfred's 10th-century cross has a Sigurd on it but is 'strongly Anglian at heart'. The spiral scroll and Beckermet styles are 'essentially native art'.[255] No Irish influence has been detected in Cumbria, but Fm 3 contact is more evident in Cheshire and the Wirral.[256]

The high point of Viking monumentality is at **Gosforth**, Cumbria, with six products so similar that they have been attributed to a 'Gosforth master' (Figure 5.62 A-B). The Gosforth cross, tall, elegant and svelte, carries a crucifixion scene, together with three scenes from Ragnarök, the twilight of the (old) gods: the figure with arm and foot in a beast's mouth is Vithar, Odin's son, avenging his father's death. The figure with the horn is Heimdall, the watchman god. Loki, leader of the forces of evil at Ragnarök, is depicted bound. The Gosforth master who was active in the first half of the 10th century was also responsible for two

Figure 5.61 A; (Left) Iona 69, with runic inscription 'Kali son of Ölvir laid this stone over Fugl his
brother'; length 1.11 m. 10th/11th century; B: (Right) Ardchattan (Argyll 217), cross-slab
topped with a winged figure holding a book; height c. 2.0 m.

(Fisher 2001, p. 130; Fisher 2001, p. 120; licensed by and © Historic Environment Scotland)

hogbacks and a slab that shows Thor and Hyrmir fishing for the world serpent with a bull's
head for bait and a serpent wrestling with a deer as the surrogate of Christ.[257]

Hilda Ellis-Davidson has reminded us that hunting pagan mythology is a perilous business,
inhibited by two equally extreme attitudes: one claiming ubiquitous sightings of Odin, the
other assuming that every representation on a Christian monument must have a connection
with the church.[258] Nevertheless, certain stand-alone scenes from Scandinavian mythology and

cosmology can be recognised in stone carvings made in Britain, especially the tales of Sigurd and the events of Ragnarök. These provide strong parables with deep roots to which the messages of the New Testament could be grafted. For Ellis-Davidson it is 'beyond dispute' that the carvers of the Viking period were aware of the alignment between heathen and Christian parables: Christ saves the world from the serpent and the devil is bound for all time.[259]

As with Christian mythologies, the sculptor makes references in a series of 'clips' and assumes that the stories are well known to those looking up at a cross or down at a tomb. Sigurd's hunting and despatch of the dragon Fafnir is divided into a number of stages: he stands in a pit and thrusts a spear into the dragon's underbelly; he roasts its heart (cut into slices) on a stick over a fire; he puts his thumb in his mouth, tasting the dragon's blood, and now understands what the birds are saying. The sequence is displayed on stones on the Isle of Man, for example Andreas 121 (Figure 5.62C). At Ragnarök, Othin, Thor, Freyr and Tyr

Figure 5.62 Gosforth (Cumbria) A. (left): The Gosforth cross (Gosforth 1) ht 1.74 m. (B. Centre) Gosforth 6, part of a slab that depicts Thor's fishing expedition with the giant Hymir in which they caught the World Serpent using a bull's head for bait. C. (Right): Cross slab Andreas 121 from the Isle of Man celebrates Sigurd's valour: (left hand side, from bottom to top) Sigurd plunges his sword into the body of the dragon Fafnir; Sigurd roasts the diced heart of Fafnir and licks the blood off his fingers, enabling him to understand from the gossip of the birds that he is danger.

(B: Courtesy and © Corpus of Anglo-Saxon Stone Sculpture; C: Kermode 1907, Plate XLV, 95A)

perish at the hands of the wolf Fenrir, Jormungand the world serpent, Sutr the Fire-giant and the Hellhound Garmr. Loki, a shamanistic figure who fathered the wolf Fenrir and the hellhound as well as Sleipnir, the eight-legged horse, was bound with the entrails of his son and placed in a snake pit. His wife, Sigyn, tried to help him by catching the venom in a bowl; but the drips got him.

In south Lancashire there is a local group in the node where Mercia and Northumbria meet that includes Adlington 1, Cheadle and Macclesfield St Michael, and the extraordinary and particular cluster in the Peak District. One notable characteristic of these monuments is their form: a square-sectioned shaft on top of a round pillar, with hanging 'swags' at the join. The Gosforth cross is a particularly delicate example, but the type appears to have its pedigree in Yorkshire, in Anglian round shafts as at Masham, and the use of swags as at Dewsbury.[260] There are examples in Lancashire and Cumbria, but this has not provided the main impetus for the Peak group, none of which show an impact from Scandinavian art. Out of 24 examples, only four are associated with churches. The remainder offer a characteristic somewhat retrospective for their period of construction (the 10th/11th century): a location on hills, an association with prehistoric tumuli, tracks and parish boundaries.[261] In this they recall the kind of landscape dominance noted in the Fm 1 'proprietary stones' in Pictland, the Borders and Wales.

A prominent example at **Wincle Cleulow** stands on top of a large natural mound of glacial drift, dominating its local topography (Figure 5.63). There are two prehistoric standing stones within 2 km and a Bronze Age barrow within 1 km, a Bronze Age stone circle within 0.5 km. The mound lay close to several routeways. It is thought to have been an assembly place, although such a mound in such a location is liable to have had a long and varied 'biography' of which the erection of the pillar must mark a return to important priorities.[262] These have been seen as 'Victory Pillars', making reference to those of Rome.[263] But by the 10th/11th century in Mercia, an alternative and more potent model lay nearer at hand: the Victory Crosses that heralded the Anglian monastic intrusion of the previous two centuries. After its collapse in the post-Viking period, it would be understandable if certain areas were to make use of this symbolism in a reversion to a previous ideology in which the secular power offered the most immediate chance of salvation. A famous and more explicit example is offered by **Eliseg's pillar** in Powys, which overlooks the valley of Nant Eglwyseg.

Bailey makes the point that, like facial traits, the particular mix seen in each monumental grouping results from human encounters, which in turn depends on which people, where, are thrown together by history. But it will also depend on which viewpoints are suppressed by politics and which ancient substrates are extracted from the past in the name of change. Learning why these things happened and were pursued with such passion, and when, is a key source of history which perhaps has yet to be adequately quarried.

Fm 3 in Wales

Many of the Welsh sites with Fm 2 monuments continued without a break into Fm 3, so qualify as continuing ecclesiastical centres, and in this they resemble the trajectory in Ireland.

Groups of decorative motifs have been seen as indications of indigenous networks, with centres of gravity (for example) at St Davids, St Dogmaels, Llandeilo Fawr, Penally and Carew/Nevern.[264] Only at Penally (P82, 83) do vine scroll, acanthus-like plants and beasts indicate contact with Mercia or Wessex or perhaps directly with Carolingian France in the later 9th or 10th century.

Even so, from the 9th century there is a marked change of gear: investment increases, and the sculptural products are more lavish, even brash, and their messages become more

Figure 5.63 Wincle Cleulow (Cheshire). A 'Victory pillar' standing on a natural mound.

(*Corpus* IX, Illus 362; courtesy and © Corpus of Anglo-Saxon Stone Sculpture, photographer K. Jukes)

worldly. The monuments are crosses, some with massive heads richly ornamented with plaitwork in relief (see Margam G79, p. 487). They may also have been brightly coloured, using combinations of red, yellow, green, blue, black and white.[265] These Grand Crosses sometimes carry general exhortations to pray for the soul of the person celebrated, even if they were located at a distance from the grave. In this sense, the monastery is rewarding the family of a donor with spiritual benefits, in the manner of a reward for tribute.[266]

In the south-east, an 11th-century inscription (G99) at Merthyr Mawr records the donation of land using phrasing found in land charters.[267] The *Cross of Irbic* G42 at Llandough and the *Cross of Conbelin* at Margam G79 both bear the names of donors, implying secular involvement and a broadening access to spiritual benefits.[268] The early 10th-century *Illtud Cross* at St Illtud's Church, Llantwit Major (G66), records that King Samson set up a cross here for the sake of his soul. Some inscriptions anchor their monuments in history: Llantwit Major G63 carries the name of Hywel ap Rhys, someone mentioned by Asser as the ruler of Glywysiog who accepted the overlordship of Alfred, so should date before 886. In the south-west, the Fm 3 monuments are concentrated at documented ecclesiastical sites, including seats of Bishops.[269] At Nevern, a grand cross decorated with panels of median-incised interlace and chunky key patterns stands in the churchyard, probably in its original position dated late 10th or early 11th century (P73). An inscription on Side A reads 'Lord', and on the other side, at kneeling height, 'Hauen', a personal name.[270] This forms an artistic set with grand crosses at Carew 1 P9, Llanfynnyd 1 CM24, Llantwit Major G66, well separated from each other in space and so perhaps served by a peripatetic craftsman.

In the north, 60% of the new 'ambitious' sculptured monuments are associated with known church sites, although they have been found at only eight out of 35 documented 'mother-churches'. There is now an important presence in the north-east, in Flintshire on the coast between Clwyd and Dee.[271] The rectangular slab at St Dogfan's Church at Llanrhaeadr-ym-Mochnant (D7) carried a Latin cross in relief with interlace and key pattern decoration (of the 9th or early 10th century). An inscription added in the late 10th or 11th century labels this '(The cross of) Cocom son of Edestan', the latter bearing an English name.[272]

The evidence from inscriptions raises the expectation that Anglesey and to some extent Gwynedd were part of the Hiberno-Scandinavian political zone in the late 9th and 10th century. Some indications are seen at Penmon (AN51–2) with the appearance of Borre-style ring-chain ornament. Further along the coast in Flintshire, crosses at Meliden (F8) and Whitford (F12) not only sport ring knots but warrior images that refer to Scandinavian themes.[273] A Viking phase has been announced in the unpublished excavations at Llanbedrgoch.[274] At Llanddewi Aber-arth (CD6–7), the cross and hogback suggest Viking influence, and the coastal site itself resembles Lythe in Yorkshire (p. 555), with a landing place below the site, and so may imply mercantile activity.[275] However, the Viking impact on Wales is not as game-changing in terms of investment and iconography as that of the Danes in Yorkshire or the Norse in Lancashire.

In Powys, the to and fro of Welsh and English land hunger left one monument which is exceptionally well documented by its own inscription and most suggestively positioned in the landscape (Figure 5.64). The **Pillar of Eliseg** (D3) stands on a cairn, plausibly an early Bronze Age barrow, looking down the valley of the Nant Eglwyseg 1 km north of its confluence with the Dee, and just north of Valle Crucis Abbey (named after the pillar, which has now lost its cross head).[276] Its round shaft links it with those of an earlier generation in Yorkshire and a later generation in the Peak district, all noted for their land-dominating properties. Here we are left in no doubt of the role of the pillar in celebrating ancestry and the claim of territory in the immediate viewshed and to a wider allegiance beyond it. The

Figure 5.64 The Pillar of Eliseg (Powys), overlooking the valley of Nant Eglwyseg and the abbey of
Valle Crucis.

(Edwards 2013, D3 at Llandysilio yn Iâl; author)

inscription explains that Cyngen set up the pillar in honour of his great-grandfather Eliseg,
who had 'united the inheritance of Powys' and regained land from the English. That kingdom which emerged in the later 8th to 9th century was to disappear with the death of Cyngen
(= Concenn) himself in Rome in 854/5.

The full text, with its frustrating omissions, reads:

> +Concenn son of Cattell, Cattell son of Brohcmail, Brohcmal son of Eliseg, Eliseg son
> of Guoillauc. +Concenn therefore, great-grandson of Eliseg, erected this stone for his
> great-grandfather Eliseg +It was Eliseg who united the inheritance of Powys . . . how-
> ever through force. from the power of the English . . . land with his sword by fire (?)
> (+) Whosever shall read out loud this hand-inscribed . . . let him give a blessing (on the
> soul of) Eliseg + It is Concenn . . . with his hand . . . his own kingdom of Powys . . .
> and which . . . the mountain . . . monarchy . . . Maximus of Britain. Pascent . . . Maun
> Annan . . . Britu moreover [was] the son of Guarthigirn whom Germanus blessed (and
> whom) Sevira bore to him, the daughter of Maximus the king, who killed the king of
> the Romans. +Conmarch represented pictorially [*pinxit*] this writing at the demand of
> his king, Concenn +The blessing of the Lord upon Concenn and likewise(?) on all of his
> household and upon the province of Powys until . . .

Concenn is using the name of the supposed last emperor of Britain, Maximus, to state
his agenda for removing the English not only from Powys but from the island of Britain.

Concenn died in Rome in 854/5, and the mission (largely) died with him. The place, however, is likely to have continued to function as a focus of assembly and anti-English resolve.[277]

Eliseg's pillar provides an overt demonstration of how the form of sculpture, the vocabulary of inscription and the theatre of the landscape could be harnessed together in the service of politics. A recent GIS-based study showed that the Pillar of Eliseg not only overlooked the Valle Crucis but the corridor of the River Dee that led eastwards through Offa's Dyke and Wat's dyke into England. It therefore was a sentinel controlling a network of lookout points at the front door of mid-Wales, its viewsheds implying that it could be used to monitor movement between the two countries, whether of armies, traders, shepherds, animals or goods.[278] It must be assumed that many monumental sculptures were investments that potentially represented similar interests of land dominance, wayfinding and traffic control, and in this they were well suited for furnishing hilly country. While the details remain elusive, we can permit ourselves to believe that the changing character and location of the monuments may offer a deep narrative of the way those also politics changed, from century to century and region to region.

Anglo-Scandinavian Northumbria

Danish Vikings arrived in Lindisfarne in 793 and over the following century settled much of Yorkshire, leaving a highly individual legacy of carved stone monuments (Figure 5.65A).[279]

The clientele switched from the monastic network, soon effectively dissolved, to that of private sponsors on their estates (Figure 5.65B).[280] The impetus for change is naturally laid at the door of the Vikings, but as with other political trends then and now there was a 'bow wave effect'. Before the Viking wars took off in earnest, the church was already retreating from a dependency on the monopolistic monastic centres and allowing more spiritual authority to be abrogated by the episcopal administration.

Reading from the sculpture, Elizabeth Coatsworth puts it like this:

> the wide ranging connections of Ilkley 2, like those of Collingham 1, . . . show the growth in the number of centres with churches as the eighth century progresses: while many of these are on known ecclesiastical estates, or on sites known to be monastic; and while all work of the period shows strong ecclesiastical input in iconography, the picture is already moving away from the very narrowly focussed monastic network revealed by the earliest work. The strengthened role of the archbishopric with its regional and continental contacts probably played a part in this.[281]

The softening up of the monastic system was probably driven partly by the consequences of increased wealth from endowment, the delivery of spiritual benefits and land holding and thus a drift from social charity to benevolent aristocracy. The faith of the clientele may also have been weakened on the one hand by a diminishing confidence in the corporate power of intercession to deliver security and on the other by the authoritarian stance detected by Jim Lang (p. 529). The same trajectory had been followed in pagan Scandinavia some 200 years earlier, so that the Viking assumption of secular leadership roles in the church was already a familiar option (p. 282). The main losers were women, since local power rather than sanctity was now the qualification for high office in the church, not an advantage when much land was being acquired by force of arms rather than force of argument.

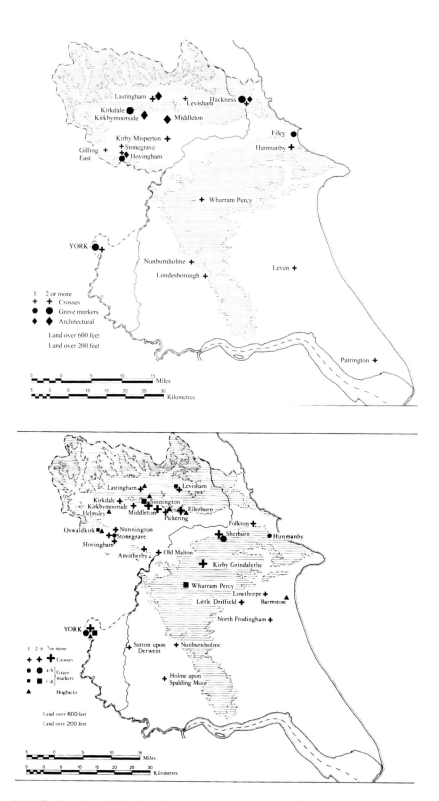

Figure 5.65 The changing distribution of carved stone monuments in Yorkshire's East Riding. A (Top): Pre-9th century. B (Bottom): Post-9th century.

(*Corpus* III, Fig 3, 4; © Corpus of Anglo-Saxon Stone Sculpture, photographer Y. Beadnell)

In Ryedale, numerous sites now boasted one or more monuments, but only at Hovingham and Stonegrave were previous monastic sites reused.[282] The creations of the new lords can be noted at **Middleton** and **Sockburn**, where the images of warriors are carried proudly and sometimes full face on the shafts of crosses, and at **Nunburnholme**, where the landlord is seen side view, clutching his sword[283] (Figure 5.66). In an era where patronage was dependent on the enthusiasm of one family rather than the fame of a saint, the number and quality of sculptural investments would be hard to predict. A rich collection of Scandinavian pieces is at assembled at **Sockburn**, an estate situated in a loop of the Tees. Sockburn 3 features a horseman with a bird and two other figures, depicted in interesting everyday detail; the horseman 'is either bare-headed or wears a tight-fitting cap, his eyes are punched with a lightly modelled surround and he appears to have a drooping moustache. He wears voluminous short breeches. In the lower scene showing the remains of two figures, the one on the left is a woman, facing right, but with head turned towards the front.

She holds a horn to the lips of the person opposite. She has smooth wig-like hair. Her eyes are punched and modelled. She wears a pleated over-garment cut away to a point. The rest of her dress is lost.[284]

Figure 5.66 Christianised Viking martial landowners (left to right) at Sockburn, Middleton St Andrew and Nunburnholme.

(*Corpus* I, Illus 726, *Corpus* III, Illus. 676); courtesy and © Corpus of Anglo-Saxon Stone Sculpture, photographer T. Middlemass; Nunburnholme: author)

Figure 5.67 Sculpture in action under York Minster.

(*Corpus* III, Illus. 417; © Corpus of Anglo-Saxon Stone Sculpture photographer D Phillips; Image licensed by Historic England)

Under **York Minster**, graves of the 9th–11th century were aligned with the Roman Basilica, perhaps reflecting the orientation of the lost Anglian episcopal church of St Peter.[285] Some of the decorated recumbent stone slabs had been placed over the grave with head and foot stones (Figure 5.67). These slabs were reworked from Roman building debris and sarcophagi, recarved in combinations of Anglian crosses and Viking zoomorphic interlace.[286] A less expected but highly significant cluster of nearly 40 Anglo-Scandinavian monuments has been noted at **Lythe** on the coast at the north end of the Whitby strand. It had both recumbent and upright slabs, as under York Minster, together with stumpy plain crosses that may have stood at the end of hogbacks. It is possible that this was a cemetery that served a wide hinterland.[287] Alternatively, given its position on a cliff above the beach and inlet, it served a landfall that had expanded into a coastal command or trading place (Figure 5.68).

The Viking stone-carving signature in Northumbria uses outsize twists, step patterns and meanders, loose rings, increased stylisation. Although it was first exposed to the Danes, the repertoire expanded with the arrival of the Norse-Irish and their takeover of York in the 10th century. With them come distinctive cross heads, circle heads and hammerheads otherwise found only in Cumbria, and a bold interweaving with traditional Scandinavian pagan themes. **Leeds 1** is an 'Odinisation' of Otley 1, featuring Weland escaping in his flying machine and Sigurd with a sword in separate niches. South of Leeds, Scandinavian influence is minimal.[288]

Figure 5.68 Lythe (North Yorkshire) The view from the present church towards the beach.
(Author)

Hogbacks

In addition to these, a monument of a wholly new kind was invented in Period 3 Northumbria, the hogback. It is not found in Scandinavia nor the Isle of Man, nor the Danish areas of Lincolnshire and East Anglia. It appears to have originated in Brompton, North Yorkshire, and spread north as far as the Firth of Forth and west as far as the coast (Figure 5.69). The basic form would seem to derive from the house-shaped shrine, already known in Ireland (on top of High Crosses) (p. 564) and in Anglian Northumbria (e.g. Hedda's shrine, p. 534). These house forms, whether local or not, also carried the meaning of a reliquary; so that the solid hogback on top of or beside a grave communicated the double metaphor of last home and ancestor relic. The arched niche seen in the side of some examples suggest an origin in the idea of accessible bones.[289] The bears that clutch the gables have no earlier exemplars, but may perform protective roles, as other beasts do, for example on jewellery. The bears are also the main providers of a typological sequence to archaeologists: their reality declines as time goes by. Some of the schemes celebrated also profess warrior status: on Sockburn 14,

> The riders hold what seem to be a snaffle and bit with short reins in their left hands and a spear in their right. The horsemen are without helmets but may wear close-fitting caps; they sit on high-backed saddles, and the one on the left is braced back against it.[290]

From Brompton, the monuments spread to Sockburn and down the Tees eastwards onto the North York moors and westward over Stainmoor into the Eden Valley, and down the

Figure 5.69 Brompton (North Yorkshire): hogback monuments.
(*Corpus* VI, Illus. 91; © Corpus of Anglo-Saxon Stone Sculpture, photographer T. Middlemass)

Lancashire coast to the Wirral (Figure 5.70). A secondary distribution spreads in southern Scotland, all close to maritime routes. It appears to bud off from a first arrival on Inchcolm and proceed to the banks of the Clyde, Forth, Tweed and Tay, with 'a string of sites from Berwickshire to the Firth of Forth culminating in a cluster of sites in the Alloa district'. There is one outlier in Orkney.[291] There are none in the Danish areas of Lincolnshire and East Anglia, one in Ireland, one in Wales, one in Orkney and none in the Isle of Man. So the derivation of their form, their origin, ethnic affiliation and meaning are not immediately obvious. The form was prominent, widespread and short lived in the early 10th century, perhaps between the Hiberno-Norse incursion of c. 920 and the English takeover in 954. It seems to have been popular for little more than 50 years, coincident with the supremacy of the Kingdom of York.[292]

For Jim Lang the adoption of hogbacks signalled a 'colonial' monument representing a network of wealthy communities.[293] Based on the way that other brands of stone carving seem to mark the lands, an alternative interpretation can be offered. A new ideology arises in the affluent inner Kingdom of York and expands east and west, and then by sea to the north-east (Forth and Tay) and north-west (Clyde). However, the enthusiasm for this innovative hybrid is limited to perhaps two generations. The ideology is not clearly defined but may have been one of a number that attempted to embrace the warrior as a religious role model after a period of intense clerical domination.

Lincolnshire in Fm 3

Out of an indifferent past, Lincolnshire in the Viking period experiences a great upsurge in the production of memorial sculpture in the form of grave covers, grave markers, recumbent grave slabs and cross shafts, widely distributed over the county. The Viking incursion began

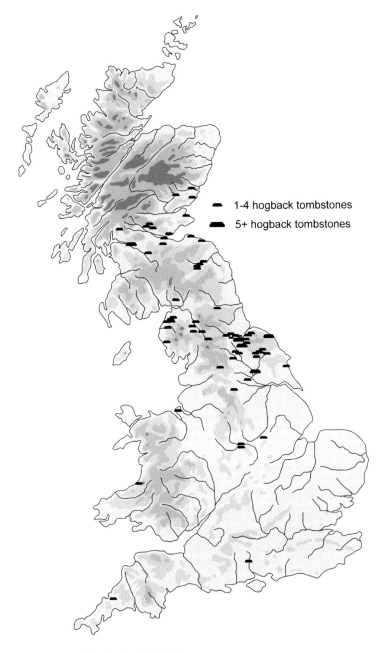

1-4 hogback tombstones

5+ hogback tombstones

Figure 5.70 Distribution of hogbacks in Britain.
(FAS Heritage, after Lang 1972 and 1984, Fig 1)

with penetration from York (Crowle 1, Thornton Curtis, Holton le Clay) and then flowered in the Hackthorne group (Hackthorne 2 and Lincoln St Marks 16A; Lincoln Cathedral 2A) that shows some influence of Borre style. These were 'evidently memorials of individual burials at parochial level'.[294] The authors of the *Corpus* survey note that the distribution of stone sculpture does not map onto that of documented minster sites. Although several designated senior 'minster' sites have produced sculpture, the 10th and 11th century produce of the county is certainly not confined to them: of a total of 96 sites with pre-Conquest sculpture, only 21 are sites that are potentially of minster status (c. 20%). Most examples are found at sites that became parish churches.[295]

The English region in Fm 3

In Fm 3, the south-eastern Anglo-Saxon lands finally embrace a prominent carved stone industry in their turn, and they do it in two phases. Between 800 and 950 there is a modest increase in production of idiosyncratic types: round shafts from Winchester, a memorial with a nimbed figure from Whitchurch, a crucifixion from Romsey and the figurative sculpture from Reculver, now claimed for the 9th century (p. 539). The second phase between 950 and 1050 features a massive increase of production associated with the 'Winchester School'. The Winchester School developed its admired style in manuscript art, both in magisterial, even monumental portraiture and in lively narrative sketches as seen in calendars, psalters and in homiletic tales like the *Psychomachia*. In addition to those in Winchester itself, 200 sculptures survive, of which 50% were architectural, 25% monumental and less than 10% free-standing crosses. Monumental work has survived at many parish churches, often built into walls. Crucifixions (six survive), figural panels, grave markers and grave covers are found at Breamore, Headbourne Worthy, Romsey, Oxford St Michael 2, Jevington 1, Sompting 13, Oxted, Bexhill Headbourne Worthy no. 2, Stratfield Mortimer and Dover St Peter, which has a runic inscription commemorating *Gilsheard* .[296]

With the development of the Winchester school, the dark forces tamed by Christ are reborn as fluttering angels and royal acanthus wreaths. The south-western region was a major beneficiary. Angels fly at Bradford on Avon, Winterbourne Steepleton and St Oswald's (Figure 5.71A-B).[297] At St Oswald's, a 'royal tomb', perhaps for Aethelflaed, Lady of the Mercians, or her husband, Eorlderman Ethelred, is capped by a tomb cover luxurious with 10th-century foliage.[298] As in the manuscripts, even formal figurative sculpture is now animated by personality. The images of St Peter seen at Daglingworth and Dowlish Wake are marvels of economic portraiture, people of character and probably of the locality drawn with affection (Figure 5.72).[299] The manuscripts also feed the architecture, as in the 24 capitals and bases reused in the slype at Worcester cathedral, all lathe turned and of a type depicted in the Benedictional of St Aethelwold.[300] A sense of victory returns to the Christian mission with iconic scenes such as the Harrowing of Hell at Bristol, Christ triumphant at Congresbury and the Virgin and Child at Inglesham and Langridge. When painted, as traces of red paint betrays that they were, the carvings presented the churchgoer with daunting reminders of being in the hands of God, and perhaps also the state.[301]

These are the signs and trophies of a southern England that sees itself as a European Christian country, a leader in art and in morals. But given the story of the house of Wessex from the time of Alfred to that of Cnut, it is not surprising that Scandinavian themes make an occasional appearance and do so in high-status contexts. The slab at London St Pauls carries a dragon vs. serpent combat reminiscent of the Jelling stone that commemorates Harald Bluetooth's conquest of Norway in the mid-10th century (p. 445); here the Ringerike style

Figure 5.71 Angels on the walls. (Top): Bradford-on-Avon (Wiltshire) over the chancel arch of St Lawrence. (Bottom): Angel fresco from St Oswald's Priory, Gloucester (*Corpus* X, Illus 791;

(A: *Corpus* VII, Illus. 405; © Corpus of Anglo-Saxon Stone Sculpture, photographer K. Jukes; B: Courtesy and © Corpus of Anglo-Saxon Stone Sculpture and Richard Bryant; drawn by Richard Bryant and supplied by the originator in October 2017 in a revised version to reflect a slightly earlier date)

Figure 5.72 A. (Left): Face of St Peter on a panel built into the north wall of the north aisle at Daglingworth (Gloucestershire). B. (Right): Dowlish Wake (Somerset), portrait in low relief with
inscription probably identifying the figure as St Peter. Found as a reused stone subsequently erected at a garden in Dowlish Wake. Seen by Rosemary Cramp in 2004 and later
sold at auction at Sotheby's.

(A: *Corpus* X, Ill.106, no. 4; © Corpus of Anglo-Saxon Stone Sculpture, photographer R.Bryant); B: *Corpus* VII,
p. 189, Illus. 380; courtesy and © Corpus of Anglo-Saxon Stone Sculpture, photographer K. Jukes and D. Craig)

offers a date in the early 11th century. A runic inscription reads 'Ginna and Toki had this
stone laid' (Figure 5.73).[302] The Sigmund stone at Winchester, installed between 1017 and
1035, depicts a scene from the Volsunga saga (Figure 5.73). Sigmund and his nine brothers
were captured and clamped in the stocks in the forest: every night an evil-looking old she-
wolf arrives and kills and eats one of the brothers, until only Sigmund is left. Sigmund's twin
sister smears honey on his face and tongue. The wolf licks the honey and puts his tongue
into Sigmund's throat: Sigmund bites it, and the wolf tears out his own tongue and breaks
open the stocks. It has been suggested that this gruesome anecdote formed part of a frieze
celebrating the shared origins of the two royal houses of England and Denmark, whose
ancestors probably lay in the Old Minster cemetery at Winchester.[303]

A discussion about sculpture

This trip around the monumental landscape of Britain has shown a variety of investment
over space and through time. The uneven distribution is evident, but as argued throughout
the chapter, this unevenness of distribution cannot be blamed on the ignorance of some

Figure 5.73 A. (Left): London St Pauls Churchyard. B. (Right): Winchester; the Sigmund stone.

(A: *Corpus* IV, p. 026–227, Illus. 351; © Corpus of Anglo-Saxon Stone Sculpture, photographer D. Tweddle; B: *Corpus* IV, Illus. 646; courtesy and © Corpus of Anglo-Saxon Stone Sculpture, photographer P.M.J.Crook)

demographic groups or their lack of resources and must imply the initiatives and reactions consequent on the appearance of new political ideas – the new ideologies and positive or negative responses to them expressed by different regions in different periods.[304] These are the signals we hope for from monuments, and if the stone carvings are to be believed, they are powerful and opinionated advocates.

The work of reviewing the sculptural corpus that remains to be done is liable to occasion further surprises and emphases. It is clear that the Midlands, for example, will have a lot more to say. But the story so far is reasonably consistent. The observations made on our tour suggest the following narrative of 10 episodes over the three periods:

Formative 1 (5th–7th century)

1 In the 5th century, the British, stemming from their prehistoric and Roman experience, erect stone markers. The context is Christian in the West (Wales) and non-Christian in the north (Picts). The emphasis is on land and ancestry. The need for land claiming in western Wales may have been prompted or accentuated by encroachment from Ireland. Pressure from Irish/Scots incomers may also explain the *floreat* of Pictish Class I.

2 5th/6th century: The Irish use ogham to express their own ancestry and land claims, including in newly occupied lands in Wales and (later) in Pictland. Some have roles as grave markers, though few are overtly Christian.

3 6th/7th century: Inscribed stone markers of different kinds multiply in Pictland, Skye, Galloway, Tweeddale, Wales, Isle of Man, Cornwall and Brittany.

4 None of these need be ritual. But their use in a pre-Christian cult site at Rhynie and at meta-Christian sites in Anglesey and Galloway suggests a role in also proclaiming sacred land.

5 On the arrival of Christian missionaries from Rome, 7th-century communities in Kent experiment briefly with Roman-style stone architecture.

Formative 2 (7th–9th century)

6 Spiritual leaders in late 7th century Pictland, western Scotland, the northern Borders and the late 8th-century in Wales promote the monastic movement in harness with Ireland, creating highly ritualised settlements richly endowed with carved stone monuments.

7 In mid-late 7th-century Northumbria, spiritual leaders in association with their kings promote monastic establishments in alignment with papal Christianity, creating villa-type settlements with stone churches, architectural sculpture and grave markers.

8 In the mid-8th to early 9th century, the monastic movement in Northumbria erupts north to the Forth, west to the Irish Sea coast and south to the Humber and the Severn, its reach indicated by tall Victory Crosses. These carry the fundamentalist message of total commitment to prayer, intercession and universality, with Christ as the single authority. A knock-on effect is seen in Ireland, west Scotland and Wales in the form of the High Crosses or Grand Crosses.

Formative 3: 9th/11th century

9 In the 9th century, Scandinavian incomers complete the supersession of the monastic movement in Northumbria and the west coast. They use the cross and the grave cover and distribute them in secular estates, on sites to be later associated with medieval parish churches. A short-lived home-grown heroic warrior movement marked by hog-backs beginning in north Yorkshire spreads west to Lancashire and north to the Tweed-Forth- Clyde-Tay region.

10 10th/11th century: England embraces carved stone culture with a high quality and inventive range of 'Anglo-Saxon' architectural embellishments and set-piece monuments, some using the Carolingian-inspired *Winchester School* of imagery. Some show Viking influence, as St Pauls, London and Winchester.

In summary, what the sculpture says about early medieval Britain is to report three very different intellectual worlds that succeed each other with rather little overlap.

Excursus: sequences from Ireland and Scandinavia

Ireland

This trajectory in Ireland complements that in Britain, especially western Britain. In Ireland, Fm 1 carving is mostly expressed in ogham, and the ogham distribution shows that Irish interest in Wales and Scotland increases, with the upright stones with their Irish names recording the acquisition of land. Although the Christianisation of Ireland is often held to begin with the arrival of St Patrick in the 5th century, the serious archaeological signalling of Christian affiliation in Ireland begins in the equivalent of Fm 2 (7–9th century).[305] Stones

Figure 5.74 Glimpse of the sequence in Ireland: grave cover from Clonmacnoise inscribed *'Pray for the soul of Thuathal the craftsman'*.

(Author)

marked with a cross and the occasional inscription (sometimes added later) then appear, distributed along the western seaboard from Kerry to Donegal (one of them, at Kilnasaggart c. 700 (County Armagh), refers to Ternoc, a priest, who died in 714 or 716).[306] Some stand upright and mark the edges of monastic territory; others are rectangular slabs intended to lie flat on a grave (Figure 5.74). Within the 8th century the High Cross arrives, probably inspired by the grand crosses in Northumbria, but with strong references to exemplars in metal – the stone bosses recalling rivets and panels in low relief.[307] They are typically constructed from three components: a square-section shaft stands on a chamfered base and carries a ringed cross topped with a little model house (Figure 5.75). The base refers to the hill of Calvary and the little house to a wooden or metal reliquary. The shaft and face of the cross are lavishly decorated with scenes carved in relief and presented in panels.

The first high crosses at Clonmacnoise and Ahenny were clad mainly in insular ornament.[308] By the 9th century, figurative scenes appear in the panels on high crosses in the Midlands and Boyne Valley. Castledermot, County Kildare, features David, hero of the Old Testament, playing his harp, Abraham about to sacrifice Isaac and St Paul and St Anthony, pioneers of devotional monasticism, meeting in the desert.[309] Others have clips from the New Testament: Christ baptised at Kells, mocked and crucified at Monasterboice, betrayed and buried at Clonmacnoise and the miracle of the loaves and fishes at Moone, County Kildare.[310]

Two sites offer Irish examples of sculpture in action. At Clonmacnoise, County Offaly, nearly 700 recumbent grave markers were laid down between the 8th century and the 12th, many bearing inscriptions in the Irish language, some mentioning names identifiable with abbots.[311] The lack of patronymics suggests that the majority buried in this way were clergy.[312] High Crosses appear towards 800, as the Viking raids begin in Northumbria and Scotland. Clonmacnoise was itself plundered and burnt three times in the 8th century and on at least nine occasions between 815 and 846; however, only two of these are attributed to the Vikings.[313] In Fm 2, the secular authority at Clonmacnoise is provided by the kings of Connacht, but from the mid-9th to the early 11th century (Fm 3), these are replaced by the Clann

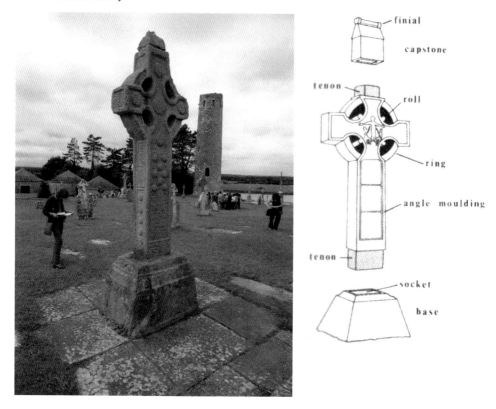

Figure 5.75 High Cross at Clonmacnoise (Co Offaly, Ireland); (right): the structure of a high cross.
(Author; Stalley 1996; with permission for carpentered construction see Maclean 1995)

Cholmain kings, whose sponsorship may account for a change in the recumbent slabs.[314] The Connacht kings returned in the 12th century when there were three monastic reforms, probably in response to previous secularisation.[315]

At Iniscealtra in County Clare, the remains of five churches, 70 cross-inscribed stones, 40 plain grave slabs, and several high crosses have been noted. Permanent habitation on the island began in the 7th century, and the first group of burial markers are dated 7th–9th century. These are small recumbent slabs with equal-armed crosses in a square surrounds, some with a name, a type seen at Clonmacnoise and Hartlepool in Northumbria. They are not numerous (less than 20, three with names), and all have been displaced.[316] In Fm 3 and later, there is an increase in the use of memorials, and over 100 survive, many still in situ side by side in rows.[317] Clíodna O'Leary deduces that Iniscealtra was a place of privileged burial for elite believers, in which few were granted a slab and fewer still a name. As at Clonmacnoise, this kind of privilege is the prerogative of the spiritual specialist and those closely associated with them. Even in the later period, where the grave covers were more numerous, this privilege prevails; the swelling company of monks naturally granted themselves increased chances of salvation, which in turn offered an incentive to join them. Recent advances in settlement archaeology have revealed where the unclerical majority were most probably buried: in the villages with cemeteries but without churches – the 'cemetery-settlements'.

Here people were buried with their kin without grave markers, their religious affiliations remaining unheralded and equivocal.[318]

Sculpture in Fm 2 is thus focussed on the monasteries, where the monks and their associates are buried under recumbent slabs of stone and the High Crosses stand around the monastic precinct, probably painted in bright colours; their panels like a permanent slide show inspire, instruct and protect the faithful and proclaim the presence of an ideological power centre. Artistically connected with Northumbria, Scotland and Pictland, the Irish monasteries belong to the same overarching project that dominated the insular north and west through the 8th century.[319]

Monumental 'added value' was given by church and stone monuments and landscape working in harmony. At the local level this was achieved by standing stones or *leachta* (altars) or slab-shrines marking out an enclave around the church (a *termon*). The community and its devotional visitors would perambulate around the territory so formed, offering prayers at each sacred staging point, as proposed at Inishmurray[320] (Figure 5.76). Such a

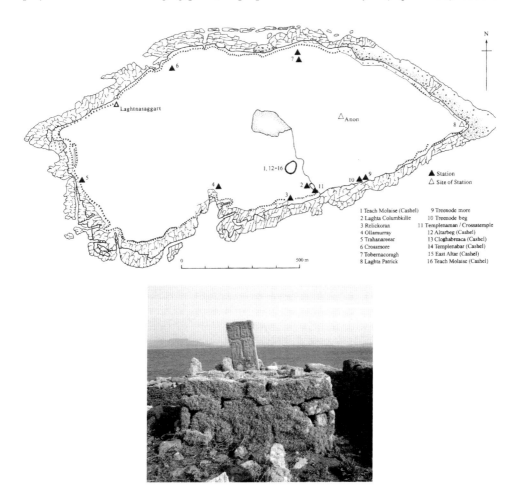

1 Teach Molaise (Cashel)   9 Treenode more
2 Laghta Columbkille   10 Treenode beg
3 Relickoran   11 Templenaman / Crossatemple
4 Ollamurray   12 Altarbeg (Cashel)
5 Trahanareear   13 Cloghabreaca (Cashel)
6 Crossmore   14 Templenabar (Cashel)
7 Tobernacoragh   15 East Altar (Cashel)
8 Laghta Patrick   16 Teach Molaise (Cashel)

▲ Station
△ Site of Station

Figure 5.76 Ritual perambulation at Inishmurray (Co Sligo, Ireland): the perimeter is marked at intervals by altar stations (leachta) of which Crossnatemple (inset) is an example (no.11 on plan).

(O'Sullivan and Carragáin 2008, Fig 4; Plate 44; with permission)

marking of territory could be performed on a wider scale, as Ó Carragáin showed on the Dingle and Iveragh peninsulas, within a still wider zone of attraction using a web of routes, which in some cases can be traced to prehistoric pilgrims.[321] Aspects of such nested catchments have also been detected in the British north and west.

There is a new mood in Fm 3 signified by closer collaboration between the spiritual specialist and the secular power.[322] The cross at Kinnity carries an inscription asking us to pray for King Maelsechnaill, who was king of the southern Ui Neill between 846 and 862. The inscription on the West cross at Clonmacnoise requests prayers for Flann (who was king of southern Ui Neill 879–916). Colman, who made the cross, may be identified with the Colman who was Abbot of Clonmacnoise, c. 904–21. To complete the statement of coalition, a panel on this cross shows two figures, probably king and abbot, planting a rod in the ground, 'thereby symbolising a pact between Church and state'.[323] Ireland therefore provides useful parallels and possible contexts for the monumental sequence in Scotland and in a more graphic form: the marking of family land, the labelling of the special families of the monasteries, the convergence of secular and clerical interests, still celebrated at the monastic central places that were perhaps now turning their attention to more worldly matters.

Scandinavia

The Scandinavians may have expressed their hostility to the monastic monuments in late 8th/early 9th-century Portmahomack, but in later years they were enthusiastic erectors of stone monuments, especially in Yorkshire and Cumbria. This can be seen as an indication that they were not against Christianity but preferred it in a more secular package. However, we can note that the Scandinavians had their own carved stone trajectory that expressed their responses to the times quite independently of Christianity, but in symbolic language that was not dissimilar. The sequence on Gotland begins in the 5th/6th century in the form of tall slabs with a curved top, featuring patterns and images that had been used in rock carvings since the Bronze Age (Figure 5.77A). Here the stone proclaims communal, probably ancestral, beliefs. In the 6th/7th century the stones acquire the well-known phallic profile and become more individual in the totems, such as lone animals, that they display. These could serve as markers of owned land (Figure 5.77B). In the 8th/9th century, Gotland creates its 'picture stones' – large slabs carrying elaborate stories. A ship sets forth with a crew who manage her, the dead hero rides home to be greeted by a divine lady with a drinking horn: he is in Valhalla. These images therefore appear to commemorate the great adventurers of the North Sea breakout (Figure 5.77C). By the 10th/11th century the picture stones are superseded by the runestones. While the death-defying phallic shape persists, the subject matter is now spelt out in runes written along the body of the serpent of death. The headline symbol is provided by the cross, depicted in forms derived from Northumbria[324] (Figure 5.77D). Those listed on the snake are men and women of status, commemorated by family members, and this form now extends over the whole of eastern Sweden. The adoption of these iconographies on home ground shows that the messages of the slabs are not so specific as pagan/Christian, Viking/English. In use is a general vocabulary of monumentality intended to correlate, comment on and steer the times.[325] It takes us from statements of prehistoric belief, to land markers, to celebrations of heroes served by women, into a hybrid world in which beliefs are adapted to family continuity and men and women have equal agency. This sequence provides a useful comparison and contrast to what was happening in Britain. Its 'heroic' third phase was pitched against the ideology of the monasteries, where the heroes were holy. Its civilising fourth phase with its hints of sexual equality and the primacy of the family also had

Figure 5.77 The sequence on Gotland using stones in Gotland's Museum. A: Väskinde 400–600 (Ht. 1.85 m). B: Smiss 500–700 (Ht. 73 cm). C: Broa IV 700–800 (Ht. c. 65 cm). D: Rune-stone G134: The inscription says that *Hróthvísl and Hróthelfr raised the stone in memory of their son Hróthfúss who was betrayed on a voyage by Blakuman. 'May God help Hróðfúss' soul. May God betray those who betrayed him'.* Two other sons are remembered on runestones G135 and G136.

(Gotland Museum; photos: author)

little impact in England of the 10th/11th century, in which the church promoting its family of Christ (under the king) had returned with renewed vigour.

The archaeology of sculpture

As will be clear from this review, up to now art historians have led the investigation of this material, and archaeologists and historians have relied on them for the date and meaning of the monuments. The labour has been intensive and subtle, and it was not part of my mission to supersede theirs. On the contrary, without the foundations laid by the analytical study of the last 50 years, the overview given here could not even have begun. Nevertheless, archaeologists do pursue a slightly different agenda, one intended to facilitate connections between this and other types of investigations, into settlement, economy and self-expression as well as attitudes to the divine.[326]

The making of a stone monument is a lot of work and so is closely dependant on the exigencies of the day.[327] Therefore, the size, date and distribution of stone monuments tell us most about the social and economic context of the builders. The stylistic links are more random, since a wide variety of ornamental vocabulary is available to satisfy a secular or clerical client; iconography might matter more, but precision sought by cross-referencing the messages will be hard to come by. For our archaeological purposes, the main measurables are the situation in the landscape, the degree of investment, and the associated settlement – something still difficult to locate in Britain (see Chapter 3).

The burial mound provides a useful analogy to the way that stone monuments could say more about the societies that made them and saw them, and the kind of evidence we need. Like the mounds, they were created in an intellectual context, erected in a geographical context, and used in a social context and retained their potency as long as they remained visible (Figure 5.78). In

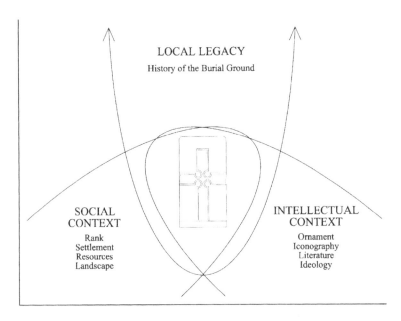

Figure 5.78 Sculpture in action – connections in space and through time.
(Author)

this they not only resemble burial mounds but echo the difficulties of discovering these things without fairly extensive investigations on the ground. The afterlife of the stones is perhaps one of the most interesting objectives to pursue. Many of these stones still stand: what did they continue to mean as they were superseded by other monuments? In the later formative periods, a landscape with many monuments of different dates presented a challenge to the inhabitants. Could they ignore the early stones, or did they still operate as landmarks? What factors or ownership allowed their survival? Were some moved to reflect a new landscape of ritual or of governance? Potentially, the assemblage maintained a grand complexity of records equivalent to a shared chronicle. Potentially it endured, at least until some became redundant and were made into bridges and gateposts.

The objective of the present study was to chronicle the ideologies of the different parts of Britain through time, with a view to telling the story of how people thought. The premise is that this can be reached through monuments, since monumentality is shorthand for an expressive medium. To know what kind of monument was erected, when and where, is in reach of archaeology for sure, but it does not tell the whole story or even the part of it of most interest to the hunter after ideologies. For this we do not merely need the assistance of art historians and epigraphers, we need to build teams with them. Guided by our experts, these have been used to reveal the essence of intellectual change. Not exactly what people believed, not their precise ideology, but the changes of emphasis indicated by words, images, size, status and numerous unexplained, repetitive, obsessive and intoxicating concatenations of figures, animals and symbols. As this chapter has sought to release these actors from their cages of stone, so the other chapters seek to give those actors a home and an agenda. And so begins a discourse too long delayed.

Coda: churches and manuscripts

In the matter of early church buildings, Ireland is (as so often) the pathfinder. Stone churches, there as elsewhere, were probably preceded (and succeeded) by buildings of timber and turf. Examples have been deduced at Iniscealtra, County Clare, where the walls were 2.5 m thick and enclosed an internal space of 5.5 × 4.4 m; at Illaunloughan, where upright stones remain that originally clad a turf wall; at Church island, where a turf church stood from the 7th/8th to the 10th/11th century (Chapter 3, 280); and at a number of sites where post-holes under later stone churches imply an earth-fast timber building.[328] Small and frail constructions implied by documents were made from woven branches or carpentered huts light enough to transport, or indeed to blow away.[329] It might be argued that such structures are hardly monumental, but monumental churches in timber are not excluded. The great church at Kildare described by Cogitosus in the 7th century was an 'oak house' with parallel aisles for men and women fronting onto male and female tomb-groups either side of the altar. Cogitosus refers to its many windows and awesome height.[330]

More tangible monumentality arrives with stone churches, which have been linked with the cult of relics, a development of the 8th century.[331] These were tall and narrow and employed 'megalithic' construction for the walls, enclosing a single room rarely larger than 6 × 4 m, with a single western door and an east window. The roof pitch could be as steep as 60 degrees and use stone slabs or oak shingles (Figure 5.79). Within the surviving corpus of stone churches collected, and subjected to a penetrating review, three early types were distinguished by Tomás Ó Carragáin as unevenly distributed across the island: *dry stone churches*, notably clustered on the Dingle and Iveragh peninsulae,[332] *mortared churches with antae* (extensions of the wall-plate that appear to remember timber techniques), plentiful

Figure 5.79 Early church buildings in Ireland. (A): Tighlagheany (Co Galway), Ó Carragáin Type 3. (B): Teach Molaise on Inishmurray, with radiocarbon dates in the 8/9th century. (C): St Columb's, Kells (Co Meath), Ó Carragáin Type 5 (with modern doorway).

(A: Ó Carragáin 2002, Fig 68a; B: O'Sullivan and Ó Carragáin 2008, 70–6, Plate 25, lower; C: Ó Carragáin 2002, Fig 75a; with permission)

in the Midlands and south, and *mortared churches without antae*, dominant along the west coast.[333] In that all these constructions implied elite investment, the distinct regional trends must have signalled a political allegiance or cultural preference of some kind.[334] The date range of both the dry stone and the mortared churches is 8th/9th for those associated with the cult of relics, especially the diminutive *shrine chapels*.[335] Such buildings could be as imposing and numinous in their landscape as a dolmen or stone circle. But the churches were also monumental in other ways. Firstly, there were often more than one of them erected on the same site, a puzzle that has been explained by the need to provide for both men and women or to segregate the celebrant clergy from the public, to celebrate more than one saint, or to add another devotional building to house a relic. The implication is that these Fm 2 church clusters, often marking a monastery, were geared to attracting investment and serving the interests of those with spiritual commitment – a class factor also noted in both Scotland and Wales (pp. 350, 410, 515).

After 900 until the 12th century (Fm 3) there was a widespread replacement of timber churches in stone, with larger buildings sponsored by kings.[336] The cost of building in stone was probably prohibitive until the 10th century, when powerful leaders fuelled by Viking bullion were active in church-building.[337] The churches of 10th/11th-century Ireland were sometimes accompanied by free-standing round towers many metres in height, reminiscent of north Italian *campaniles* and probably performing a similar function.[338] In the 12th century and after, grander stone buildings appear, having chancels or being double-vaulted, with a main focus on the east coast in County Dublin and County Wicklow.[339]

Churches in Scotland

Churches built in Scotland, Pictland or Wales, as in Ireland, probably represented responses to liturgical trends and local practice – or would do if we had them. In a recent review searching for physical traces of early churches in Scotland, Sally Foster concluded that there were no certain church buildings surviving from before the 10th century.[340] The earliest churches still standing (for example Abernethy, Restenneth, Edinburgh Castle) have been dated to the period 1090–1130 by Eric Fernie.[341] Many of the candidates for hermitages in remote places are now thought to have been later implantations symptomatic of medieval waves of sanctity. The corbelled buildings and a clay-bonded chapel at Eileach an Naoimh are likely to be 11th/12th century. The corbelled buildings on North Rona are 'unlikely to date before the 10th century'. The church buildings defined at St Ronan's on Iona, Isle of May (Fife), Inchmarnock (Bute) and Brough of Deerness (Orkney) – belong to the 9th or 10th century and later.[342] Nevertheless, the building of stone churches in 8th-century Scotland should have been achievable.

Excavations have located earlier walls beneath existing chapel sites, but these are difficult to substantiate as churches without removing the existing buildings (which are usually protected heritage). The wall stub at St Ninian's Isle (Shetland) may represent a stone church within which the hoard of 8th/9th century brooches was buried.[343] At the 7th–9th century cemetery and settlement of Auldhame (Lothian), a timber slot and stone foundations were glimpsed under the later medieval chapel, but could not be pursued owing to conservation restrictions (see Chapter 4, p. 425). Four phases of a church and its cemetery were excavated at The Hirsel, near Coldstream on the Scottish Borders, of which the earliest was placed in the 11th century by pottery and radiocarbon.[344] Irrefutable evidence has come so far only in the form of pieces of sculpture that were architectural in use and so must have originated in a stone church. The 8th/9th century Forteviot arch (Figure 5.80) certainly relates to a stone building, and the placing of a lamb at its central point indicates a pre-eminent role in a church (such as a chancel arch). Such a church must have stood somewhere in the vicinity of Forteviot in Strathearn, a known royal site overlooked by the Dupplin Cross.[345] The excavations at Portmahomack produced a large quantity of carved stone, among which were a flat-topped stone corbel with a supporter in the form of a human head and a butterfly finial of Irish type. The finial was a stray find, but the corbel was securely stratified, each of its three conjoining pieces being provenanced in layers deposited before the early 9th century. The siting of the church itself is most likely to be under the present medieval building, but there is no doubt about the wider context: a large number of other excavated finds and radiocarbon

Figure 5.80 Intimations of Pictish church architecture: the Forteviot solid arch.

(Henderson and Henderson 2004, Ill 211; Tom and Sybil Grey Collection; licensed by and © Historic Environment Scotland)

dates support the identification of the site as a monastery that flourished in the 8th century (see p. 148).[346] Other carved stone pieces found in association with the church site include grave markers, a sarcophagus or shrine lid, and a stone post and panel, perhaps from a shrine or *cancellum*.[347] Compared with the showing of 8th/9th century ecclesiastical architecture in Ireland, these are mere fragments, but taken in context suggest unexpected grandeur and leading artistry applied to the mainstream Christian project. This is all the more impressive for being encountered at an 8th-century monastic establishment at the extreme north-east of the island, 170 miles from Iona, 400 miles from York, 650 miles from Canterbury and 1,800 miles from Rome. It is sufficient to imply that the achievements of the short-lived Pictish church were outstanding and that much remains to be revealed.

Churches in Wales

As in Scotland, evidence for churches in contemporary association with the stone monuments is very thin. There are currently no upstanding church remains that can be attributed to the formative period. Stone churches might be expected from the 8th century as part of the monastic project, but there is currently little indication of tangible church fabric earlier than the 12th century. At Burryholms, there was a possible timber building measuring 3.35 × 3.05 m defined under the 12th century stone church. A pre-Romanesque church at Presteigne, although in Wales, is a culturally Anglo-Saxon construction.[348]

On its own, the sculpture has offered a sequence indicative of changing ideology but one that lacks a contemporary social context. Studies in other places with a strong sculptural repertoire show how a single site can dramatically change its allegiance according to the *zeitgeist*, and it is not easy to determine the rate of change using the surface finds of the assemblage alone. To read the signature of these partial collections demands the kind of chronological precision that can only come from comprehensive large-scale archaeological investigation – starting with sites that have churches today.

Churches in England

The last major survey of churches in the present territory of England was undertaken by Harold Taylor, a physics professor, and his wife, Joan, who collected their information by means of visits by train and on foot and bicycle over some 30 years. Their work was published in two volumes in 1965. A third volume appeared in 1978 summarising the characteristics of the buildings and the reasons why they may be seen as products of the pre-Conquest period.[349] Documentary references and visual analyses of building sequences were used to place the churches into three periods, each proving to have certain diagnostic architectural elements; Period A is 600–800, Period B 800–950 and Period C 950–1100. Each of these has also been subdivided into three (A1, A2 etc). In 372 churches, the Taylors found fabric that could be assigned to Period A in 43 (12%), to Period B in 7 (2%) and to Period C in 322 (87%), the majority of the latter assigned to Period C3, 1050–1100.[350]

Nine of the Period A churches are in Kent and 19 in Northumbria, with a further 17 spread over southern England and the Midlands from London to Glastonbury and Bishopstone to Repton.[351] Those claimed as retaining visible fabric earlier than 700 (i.e. Period A1, A2) are Jarrow, Monkwearmouth, St Peter and Paul, St Martin, St Mary and St Pancras at Canterbury and Bradford on Avon in Wiltshire. The list is underpinned by the arrival of Augustine at Canterbury in 597 and the foundation of the Monkwearmouth and Jarrow religious houses in 674 and 681, respectively.

Putting the documentary associations aside, the chief Period A characteristics are an apsidal chancel, small chambers used for burial ('porticus') flanking the nave, single-splay windows and side-alternate megalithic quoins (Figure 5.81).[352] The best preserved buildings are at Escomb and Jarrow in County Durham and Bradwell-on-Sea in Essex, contrived from the gatehouse of a Roman fort (Othona) (Figure 5.82). Many of these churches reuse Roman masonry or ashlar, but this is not diagnostic of itself: the tower of St Mary Bishophill Junior erected in the 10th/11th century is composed of building stone, drains and *pilae* of ruined adjacent Roman town houses. The form of the few early Northumbrian churches that survive is tall and narrow. Escomb, the most complete, is constructed from ashlar retrieved from the Roman fort at Binchester,[353] with monolithic head windows apparently made from recycled drains and a chancel arch formed from giant voussoirs similar to those used in Roman sewers (Figure 5.83A,B). Monkwearmouth had a west door, with imposts displaying interlaced bird-fish. At Jarrow, the walls are of recycled ashlar and the window embrasures have stone jambs and monolithic heads (Figure 5.84). In silhouette, the Northumbrian churches resemble the Irish, and like them may occur in small groups of two or three, as at Jarrow, where they were end to end. Rosemary Cramp's study of Monkwearmouth and Jarrow shows that each monastery had a rectilinear layout recalling that of a Roman villa with its courtyard and anticipates the Carolingian monastery with its cloister, epitomised in the St Gall plan.[354] Jarrow and Monkwearmouth, the style leaders of 8th-century northern monasticism, set their sights on a central European project. They drew material from Rome, Ireland and the Continent and encourage participants in the movement to do the same. The number of churches with fabric assigned to Period B is small, dispersed and not obviously diagnostic.[355] A Period B phase was identified at Deerhurst (St Mary) where the west porch was raised to three storeys, and animal-head terminals and triangular-headed openings are dated to the 8th/9th centuries (p. 573). It seems likely that churches built in this period were the most affected by the Viking raids.

The architectural features of the dominant group, of Period C, include pilasters, strip-work, hood moulds, slab-imposts and long-and-short-work quoins. Square towers and round

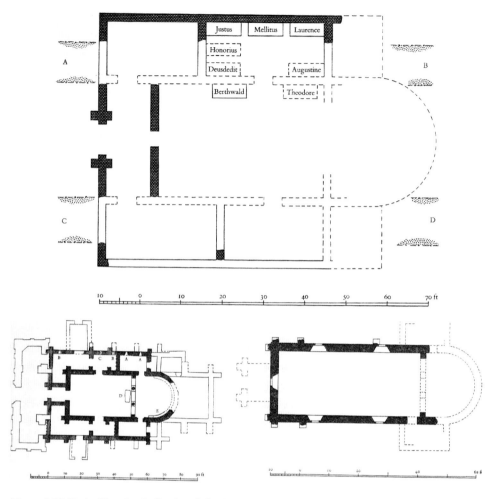

Justus | Mellitus | Laurence
Honorius
Deusdedit | Augustine
Berthwald | Theodore

A
B
C
D

10   0   10   20   30   40   50   60   70 ft

B   C B A A

D

E

0 10 20 30 40 50 60 70 80 90 ft

10 0 10 20 40 60 ft

Figure 5.81 Early Churches in Southumbria. (Top): Canterbury, St Augustine's. (Bottom left): Reculver. (Bottom right): Bradwell on Sea.

(After Taylor and Taylor 1965, Figs 62, 247, 40; Cambridge University Press, with permission)

Figure 5.82 Bradwell on Sea (Essex). Chapel contrived out of the gatehouse of a Roman fort in the late 7th, early 8th century.

(Author)

Figure 5.83 Escomb (Co Durham), 8th century church. (Top): South face. (Bottom): Interior.
(Author)

Figure 5.84 Jarrow (Tyne and Wear), south wall of chancel with monolithic head openings, Fm 2.
(Author)

towers spring up, and they have double belfry windows, both round-headed and gable-headed. These towers are likely to have performed both as bell-tower and treasury, as in Ireland.[356] Well-preserved examples stand at Earl's Barton and **Barton-on-Humber**, where the pilasters climb in a series of round-headed and triangular-headed arcades, later furnished with pillared double- openings (Figure 5.85). Internal plans pre-echo those of the medieval parish church. Inside the church at Breamore, Hants, the chancel arch is made of through-stone voussoirs, supported on slab-imposts and carries an inscription.[357] There are many variations and eclectic combinations: at North Leigh, Oxford (St Michael), the architectural work consists of balusters, side-alternate quoins and single-splay windows. At St Botolphs, Sompting, Hadstock and Langford there are long-and-short-work quoins and double-splayed windows (late 11th century). All these can be features, or are also features, of the later 11th century, when they are more properly called Anglo-Norman work.[358]

The drive to prove that the churches are Anglo-Saxon, that is, built before 1066, has perhaps obscured a more interesting aspect: like the early Irish churches, their chronological trends might have been trumped by regional ones. Double belfry windows with hood moulds are more popular in the north-east, round towers on the east coast, stone pilaster strips in the Midlands and south (Figure 5.86). This suggests that regional substrates still operate, or indeed resurface, even after the English state and church are institutionalised. Preliminary analysis suggests that regions display certain groupings, for example in types of openings preferred in Yorkshire and

Figure 5.85 Barton-upon-Humber, square tower with stripwork (11th century).
(Author)

Norfolk. These may imply a commissioning of parish churches that relates closely to a bishop
or diocese or to a fashioning of the new sense of the parish through a network of local lords.
Since the architectural properties of these churches apparently flow over the 'Norman barrier'
into the 12th century, there is perhaps some merit in alternatively supposing an expression at
the level of the mason, such that the regional variations represent artisanal 'co-operatives in
which ideologies and practices were shared'.[359] In any event there is no doubt that while the
church building had rather a specialist role in Fm 2, by the late 9th to 11th century the parish

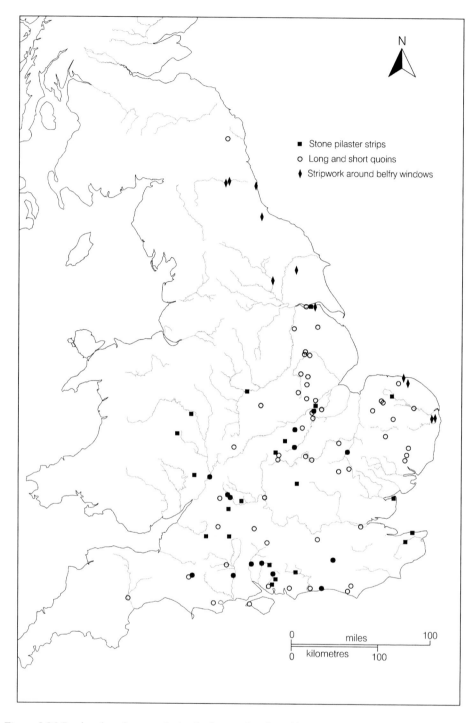

Figure 5.86 Regional preferences in Anglo-Saxon church architecture in Fm 3; distribution of strip-work on walls (pilasters), long-and-short quoins and stripwork around belfry windows. A black spot indicates pilaster strips and long and short work together.

(Map by FAS Heritage; Taylor 1978, 929 (Table 1), 944 (Table 1), 932 (Table 3))

system had released the expressive power of local monumentality, and at this point the Christian landscape was well and truly signed, and churches were ubiquitous.[360]

Illuminated books

The codex was a major instrument of Christian power in Fm 2, a necessity for any Christian foundation, more important than a church or stone monuments, as it contained the texts that governed a religion that essentially derived its authority from a book.[361] The texts were written on parchment, made from calfskin (vellum) in the north and mainly from sheepskin in the south.[362] A workshop for preparing vellum has been excavated at Portmahomack in Easter Ross, in which skins were cured using a seaweed ash, scraped with a curved knife, fastened to frames with bone pegs and white pebbles, rubbed with abrasive and smooth stones and (probably) 'pounced' with powdered lime to give a smooth surface for writing.[363] The treated parchments would be cut to size and sewn together in gatherings. The sheets would be pricked and ruled to guide the scribes, who wrote in oak gall ink with sharpened quills. Insular images were laid out with compass and ruler, and different dyes employed to colour them. Bibles and Gospel books were bound in leather over wooden boards.[364] (Figure 5.87)

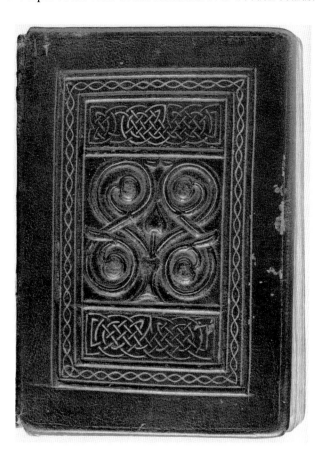

Figure 5.87 Sacred codices in Formative 2: The leather cover of the Cuthbert Gospels, late 7th century. Page size 138 × 92 mm. Compare the carpet page of the Book of Durrow (Figure 2.6B).

(BL Add Ms 89000; By Unspecified [CC0], via Wikimedia Commons)

The individual correlates of parchment-making are actually quite commonly encountered, and it is likely that other workshops and, by implication, makers of books will be swiftly found. Another correlate could be the stylus, a rod made of bronze or iron or bone, that was used to make notes on a wax tablet (with the pointed end) and erase them (with the chisel end). But these are now thought to be part of the standard equipment of any administrative centre (such as a magnate or manor farm) and not a sufficient or a necessary signal of book production.[365] The occurrence of items from the larger assemblage does also suggest that even in Fm 2 books may have been made at sites other than monasteries. The raised rath at Deer Park Farms (Ulster) produced evidence for the burning of seaweed, water-rolled pebbles, an iron hook, a trough and possible parts of a stretcher frame (Chapter 3, 277). At Dunadd, there were finds of seaweed, neonatal cattle bones, orpiment and madder dyes, leading Ewan Campbell to note the increasing importance of writing materials in lordship as well as monastic centres.[366] The leather book-satchel found in Loch Glashan is a reminder of how widely books travelled, whether to supply a new foundation or in an ambassadorial or devotional role. Study of the codices themselves shows that other materials, such as dyes, await detection in the ground (Table 5.4).

The 'monumentality' of the codex lies in the value of the materials used and the time taken to assemble them. Cattle and calves, which provided the parchment and the leather covers, were already a major asset and a measure of wealth in Fm 1, especially in the north and west. It has been suggested that the monastic endowments of Fm 2 would have included a herd of cows (p. 228). The average demand for making books was modest and could be met within a monastery's resources. The Salisbury library of 55 volumes of 100 folios apiece, would have required 28 calf- or sheepskins per year. A few major projects, judged by the size of the codex, would have required investment on an exceptional scale. Of the three complete Bibles made around 700 by Ceolfrid of Jarrow, one has survived, the *Codex Amiatinus*, which weighs 34kg and measures c. 490 × 340 × 180 thick mm closed. It opens to c. 490 × 680 mm, the size of a calf-hide. It required 515 calves to make, or 1,545 calves for the three pandects[367] (Figure 5.88). This represents a considerable outlay of a monastery's capital and a transfer of wealth to the new governance: *ad maiorem Dei gloriam*. The script was copied from an earlier Bible (the *Codex Grandior*) compiled by the 6th-century landowner Cassiodorus at the monastery he developed at his villa at *Vivarium* on the Gulf of Squillace in Calabria. The impeccable text of Amiatinus was copied from the original by seven scribes, each of whom was responsible for ruling, pricking and writing their own section, which was presumably pre-allocated so that all seven could work in parallel.[368] Fronting the Old

Table 5.4 Sources of colour used on the pages of the Lindisfarne Gospels[371]

carbon, from candles – BLACK
chalk, from the ground – WHITE
red lead = lead oxide; burn lead in air – RED
white lead = lead carbonate; burn lead and lime (shells?) – WHITE
orpiment = arsenic trisulphide – YELLOW
indigo – indigo or woad plants *indigofera* – VIOLET/BLUE
verdigris – copper acetate (put copper or bronze in vinegar, and scrape) – GREEN
folium – *crozaphora tinctoria* – PURPLE
binder – albumen (raw egg white)

Figure 5.88 The Jarrow Codex, a replica of the *Codex Amiatinus*. The original weighs 34kg and was made in Jarrow in the late 7th century but is now in Florence (Biblioteca Medicea-Laurenziana Amiatinus 1).

(Bib. Medicea-Laurenziana, Amiatinus 1; photo, author)

Testament is a double-page spread showing a plan of the Temple at Jerusalem, complete with a representation of the Ark of the Covenant. Introducing the New Testament is a celebration of Christ in Majesty. Placed originally as a frontispiece to the book was portrait of Ezra, the Old Testament scribe, precursor of those who had transmitted the Bible to that point: Jerome the 5th-century translator of the Bible into Latin, Cassidorus maker of the *Grandior* and perhaps Ceolfrid himself, who took the word to the northern kingdom. Ezra writes with a quill and has a footstool, a portable table with double inkwell, a pointer for pricking out, compasses and templates.[369] On f.1v and once opposite the portrait is the dedication of the work to Pope Gregory II by Ceolfrid of the Angles, 'abbot on the furthest frontiers'.[370] Ceolfrid left Northumbria in 678 with aim of delivering the book to Rome and presenting it the Pope, but he collapsed and died en route at Langres. The book subsequently went astray, turning up in Florence with its dedication altered to pretend it was a gift to the Saviour from Peter of the Lombards, abbot of Monte Amiato in the 9th/10th century. This vignette reveals a little of the time depth, international references, immense investment, dominant status and enduring kudos of the sacred books produced in Britain in Formative period 2. It is not excluded that similar tales and ambitions lay behind other great monumental achievements, of dress, burial and grand crosses.

Table 5.5 Stepping stones in Insular Mss production

Phase	MSS
FORMATIVE 1	
Phase 1 600–675	Dublin Codex Usserianus Primus (Gospels, early 7th century ?Ireland)
	Milan Orosius (Commentary on Isaiah, early 7th century Ireland)
	Dublin, Cathach of S. Columba (Psalter, early 7th century, Ireland)
	Durham AII10 c. 650 (Gospels, mid-7th century Northumbria)
	[Cambridge CCCC286 (Augustine Gospels, 6th century Italy)]
FORMATIVE 2	
Phase 2 650–720	Dublin Book of Durrow (Gospels, c. 680, ?Iona)
	BL Nero DIV (Lindisfarne Gospels, 696–698, Lindisfarne)
	Florence, Codex Amiatinus (Bible, c. 700, Wearmouth/Jarrow)
	Durham AII17 (St John's Gospels, 690–710, Northumbria)
Phase 3 720–800	Durham BII30 (Cassiodorus Commentary, c. 725, Northumbria)
	Leningrad Bede (Bede's History, c. 746, Wearmouth/Jarrow)
	Lichfield (Gospels, 725 × 750, acquired by Llandeilo-fawr in exchange for a horse)
	BL Vespasian A 1 (Psalter, 725 × 750, Canterbury)
	Stockholm Codex Aureus (Gospels, c. 750, Canterbury)
	BL Tiberius CII (Bede's History, 775 × 800, South England)
	BL Royal IEVI (Gospels, 775 × 800, Canterbury)
	Vatican, Barberini Lat.570 (Gospels, 750 × 775, York?)
	Leningrad Gospels (Gospels, 750 × 775, Northumbria)
	Cambridge University Library, Book of Cerne (Gospel texts, 800–850, Mercia?)
	Dublin Book of Kells (Gospels, c. 800, Iona?)
Phase 4 Frankish 800–900	Corbie psalter 770–820; *Rhine Group*; *Rheims Group*, *Tours Group*; Alcuin Bible; Vivian Bible c. 846 *Metz Group*: Drogo Sacramentary 850–5; *S. Denis Group*: Psalter of Charles the Bald 842–9 *Franco-Saxon Group*: Second Bible of Charles the Bald; *S Gall Group*
FORMATIVE 3	
Phase 5 850–1000	Bod Jun 27 (Junius Psalter, 925–950, Winchester)
	Bod Tanner 10 (Bede's History, 900–925, –)
	Cambridge CCCC 183, (Bede, Lives of Cuthbert, c. 937, Winchester)
	BL Galba A XVIII (Aethelstan Psalter 950–1000, Winchester)
	BL Vespasian A VIII (New Minster Charter, 966, Winchester)
	BL Add.ms 49598 (Benedictional of St Aethelwold, 971–84, Winchester)
	Rouen MsY6 (Benedictional of Archbishop Robert, c. 980, Winchester)
	Cambridge CCCC 23 (Prudentius, late 10th century, Canterbury)
	BL Cleopatra C VIII (Prudentius, late 10th century, Canterbury)
	BL Add. mss 24199 (Prudentius, late 10th century, –)
	BL Vitellius A XV (Marvels of the East, late 10th century, –)
Phase 6 1000–1025	BL Harley 603 (Psalter, 1000–1050, Canterbury)
	Bod Jun 11 (Genesis, c. 1000, Canterbury)
	York Minster (Gospels, late 10th/early 11th century, Canterbury)
	BL Jul AVI (Calendar, early 11th century, ?Canterbury)
	BL Add.ms. 34890 (Grimbald Gospels, c. 1020, –)
Phase 7 1025–1060	BL Stowe 944 (New Minster Register, ?1031, Winchester)
	Cambridge University Library, MS Ff. 1.23 (c. 1030–50, Winchcombe Abbey)
	Vatican Reg. lat 12 (Bury psalter, 1025–50, Canterbury)
	BL Claudius B IV (Aelfric's Pentateuch, 1025–1050, Canterbury)
	BL Tiberius B V (Calendar, 1025–1050, ?Winchester)
	BL Tiberius C VI (Psalter, c. 1050, Winchester)
	New York Pierpoint Morgan 709 (Gospels, 1025–1050, –)
	BL Caligula A XIV (Hereford Troper, c. 1050, –)
	Bayeux Tapestry

Note: Each entry gives the current place of curation, the common name, the type of book, and date and place of manufacture. (BL is the British Library; Bod is Bodleian Library Oxford; CCCC is Corpus Christi College Cambridge).

The trajectory of the codex

The types of book that were made and distributed in Britain varied markedly through time. Table 5.5 is an attempt to present an overview of this trajectory using famous books as stepping stones across the centuries, divided (in sympathy with the remainder of the book) into Formative 1, 2 and 3.[372] The earliest period, 'Before the Book of Durrow' (here *Phase 1*, 600–675, coincident with the conversion period in the last part of Fm 1) contains three books attributed to Ireland and one to Northumbria. The Milan *Orosius* was at Bobbio, the monastery founded in Italy by Columbanus, who died there in 615. This book contains the earliest known insular carpet page, a full page of colourful geometric decoration with the appearance of ornamental metalwork, leatherwork or indeed a carpet. Found at the front of a section of text, these decorative folios were likely intended as skeuomorphic book covers.[373] The decoration begins modestly: little red dots decorate the chi-rho symbol of Usserianus, and the opening initial of Mark's Gospel in Durham A II 10 is formed of colourful panels of blue, olive-green, yellow and orange. The *Augustine Gospels* were not made in Britain but arrived in Canterbury in 597 with Augustine's mission to convert the English. Made in Italy in the 6th century, it is a Mediterranean product, depicting scenes from the Bible in little square panels as though on marble columns or coffered ceilings, and has a portrait of Luke looking like a Greek philosopher. Although it was in the library at Canterbury all through the formative period, it seems to have had virtually no influence on insular codices.

In the late 7th and early 8th century, while the *Codex Amiatinus* made its own connection with the Mediterranean, the rest of the north produced outstanding works of insular art in the form of Gospel books illustrated with full-page carpet pages, evangelical portraits and decorated opening initials. The ornament mixed British and Germanic motifs to produce a vivid, almost psychedelic, vision of twisting ribbon animals within a precisely measured geometric template (Figure 5.89). The contrast between *Amiatinus*, which has almost no insular ornament, and the broadly contemporary and neighbouring Lindisfarne Gospels, with its bright colours and riot of animal life, is striking. In *Phase 3*, which overlapped with Northumbria's sculptural breakout, Gospels continued as the principal sacred book, with the magnificent *Codex Aureus* (Figure 5.90) of the mid-8th century to levels of wild fervour that were almost baroque with the Book of Kells of c. 800.[374] But other forms of literary output joined the repertoire. King David was a featured celebrity, as a warrior in Northumbria's BII30, as psalmist in Canterbury's Vesp. A1. Bede's *History of the English Church and People* had already achieved iconic status and has survived today in 8th-century editions from Jarrow and Canterbury. No books seem to have survived from Wales, although the 8th century St Chad Gospel book (now at Lichfield) was in Wales, probably at the monastery of Llandeilo fawr in the 9th century. An inscription comments that the manuscript was acquired by Gelhi son of Arihtiud in exchange for his best horse and offered to God on the altar of St Teilo.[375]

Phase 4 coincides with the Viking raids in Britain – one must suppose that it was the newer books that were on display and more vulnerable to damage or looting. Meanwhile, the flourishing of the codex may be seen in France, where it reached new levels of grandeur and of vivacy in a succession of brilliant ateliers.[376] Classical portraiture and realist animal styles were revived at Charlemagne's court,[377] and French artists at Hautvillers and Rheims developed an expressive style of line drawing, reaching its height in inventive panoramic illustrations of the Psalms.[378] These innovations would be studied and emulated in post-Viking England.

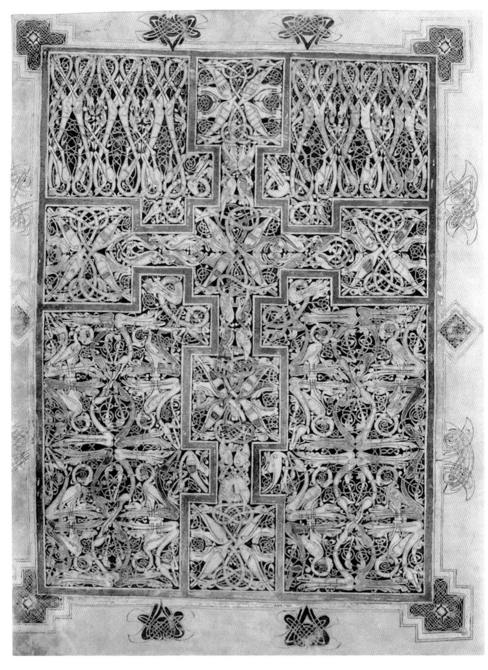

Figure 5.89 St Chad Gospels at Lichfield, c. 725–750, carpet page before St Luke's Gospel, p. 220. The birds are rendered in shades of pink and cream and the geometric cross is a rosy copper. This type of richly decorated page may stand for an ornamental leather book cover.

(Lichfield Cathedral, Gospel Book of St Chad. Image licensed by © Lichfield Cathedral).

Figure 5.90 Codex Aureus. The beginning of St Matthew's Gospel, the name of Christ initiated with the chi-rho: *Christi autem generatio sic erat* (So thus was the birth of Christ). The whole codex is lavishly ornamented with gold, thus its name. The spiroform ornament in red and blue recalls the escutcheons of earlier British hanging bowls, and letters are painted in orange and blue as well as gold. Made at Canterbury in the mid 8th century. The Anglo-Saxon inscription at the foot of the page records how the book was in the possession of the Vikings but bought back for gold by Aldorman Aelfred and his wife Werburg and given to Christchurch Canterbury, probably in the early 9th century (Alexander 1978, 57).

Now in Stockholm Royal Library Ms A.135, f11. (Reproduced by Wikimedia Commons https://commons.wikimedia.org/wiki/Commons:Licensing 21 July 2017)

When the production of books revived slowly in the later 9th century, it was almost entirely restricted to England, with Canterbury and Winchester as the best-represented scriptoria.[379] The first stirrings are the playful people and animals who form initials in Jun 27 and Tanner 10, a pre-echo of the realist exuberation to appear during the next century (Chapter 2, Figure 2.8B), and calendars which for all their Classical exemplars must offer us a frank report on late formative farmers at work (Figure 5.91A,B). A ceremonial tone and formal portraiture appears in the early 10th century, not in Gospel books but in psalters (for example Athelstan's), and Benedictionals (for example that of St Aethelwold). The psalms attributed to the biblical King David now serve as inspiration for the West Saxon aristocracy. Later in the century English artists try their hand at narrative line drawing, with breath-taking success, especially in illustrations of the popular *Psychomachia* by the 5th-century writer Prudentius. Here patience, chastity, and love do battle with anger, lust and greed in an allegory that was the *Pilgrims' Progress* of its day. The text is late Roman, but the figurative drawings

Figure 5.91 Illustrated life in Fm 3. A (Top): Cutting wood in June from an early 11th century calendar (pen and ink). B (Bottom): Mowing in August from a calendar dated 1025–1050. The mowers, dressed in brown, green and pink tunics are pictured against a field of golden corn.

(A: BL Cotton Julius A VI, f5v; image licensed by British library Board; B: BL Cotton Tib BV f.6v. (Temple 1976, 36, 199, 274; images provided and licensed by British library Board)

Figure 5.92 A scene from Prudentius' *Psychomachia*: Luxuria dancing, supported by her band and watched by admirers. Drawn in brown ink with touches of green, mauve and blue.

(BL Add Ms 24199, f. 18; image provided and licensed by British library Board)

disarmingly reveal aspects of the clothing, appearance and social attitudes that must have belonged to Late Saxon England (Figure 5.92; Chapter 2, 127). It is striking that the early English artists exercised their skills in representing emotion, beauty, charm, humour and even caricature throughout the long wars of the 10th and 11th century. Spread over *Phases 6 and 7*, **Harley 603** is a copy of the Utrecht psalter and was certainly inspired by it.[380] However, the special interests, attitudes, architecture and artefacts of the English can be extracted by comparing the two manuscripts, and isolating images that belong to contemporary life as opposed to being copies from previous exemplars, whether Classical or Carolingian. This 'regressive' method, reinforced by a comparison with images of artefacts that were known to have been in use, also spotlights particular scribes of a 'realist tendency' who may act as genuine witnesses of the world about them.[381] From the more realist of the several scribes of Harley 603 (Hand 1A and 1F), we learn that English churches had weathercocks, their monks had flails, their diners had a knife, fork and spoon, and their merchants had staved barrels and red-banded pots, as well as seeing images of items more familiar from archaeology: swords, helmets, a mail coat, an axe, a club hammer.[382] The storytelling skills of Late Saxon artists were displayed in other great works such as the Bodleian Junius 11, Aelfric's Pentateuch (BL Cot Claudius BIV). The latter had many quotations from the times, from the gruesome Anglo-Saxon gallows (Chapter 4) to the Viking ship full of animals piloted by Noah (Figure 5.93). One of the greatest achievements of English art in any century, it came to an end in a final flourish with the Bayeux Tapestry, which recounted the events that led to its own demise.

Figure 5.93 Noah's Ark, with Viking-style figurehead, loaded for its voyage. Noah and his sons have
          turquoise hair; the birds are pale blue and white and the animals pale blue and pale red.
          The Viking-type ship has scarfed planks and a figurehead and is equipped amidships with
          a gold church door fortified with iron tracery.

(BL Cott. Claud B IV, f.14; image provided and licensed by British library Board)

Reflections

The manufacture of illuminated manuscripts may appear to us a cerebral exercise, intended
to circulate the received doctrines of the new ideology. And so it was. But a glance at the processes of manufacture shows that the codex is in direct line of descent not only from Roman
but from prehistoric ritual practice. It begins with the sacrifice of a calf or sheep and continues with the deployment of themes of Iron Age, Roman and Germanic art that have already
featured in apotropaic roles on weapons and brooches of pre-Christian type. The artist-smiths
of Sutton Hoo bequeath their iconic language and their compositional skills to the scribes of
the Book of Durrow. The earliest books of Fm 1 and 2 are themselves amuletic, some, like the
Cathach of St Columba, clad in a shrine and taken to war to bend the outcome of battle using
its numinous powers. With its leather cover and plant dyes, the early book smells of deep
nature, of the bog; its layout uses the magical properties of lines and circles and a metrology
derived from nature that have been glimpsed in buildings, brooches and sculpture.[383]

In Fm 2, the talismanic Gospel books at first prevail, but as Northumbria's power rises and the
missionary project is launched in the mid-8th century, Bede's History joins the political forces.
The surviving corpus is dominated by Northumbria (in its 'Golden Age'), but Mercia may be
represented by the Book of Cerne and the Tiberius Bede, and south England by the Vespasian
psalter and the grand Gospel books, the sumptuous *Codex Aureus* and Royal I E VI from Canterbury.[384] In Fm 3, the baton is brandished by England, where artists find a new way of celebrating the human alongside the divine and a thousand flowers bloom. The illuminated manuscripts
thus provide a harmonious accompaniment to the sequence offered by sculpture and churches,
and some bright flashes of light to the stories told by clothing, settlement and burial.

Conclusion

The three types of monumentality reviewed here converge on a shared account of the intellectual history of Britain in the 5th to 11th century. In the first formative period (5th–7th century) we see an island in which there are territories of competing lordships in Scotland, Pictland, Galloway, Wales and Cornwall, which are strongly marked by proprietorial inscribed stone pillars. 'Greater Southumbria' has no sculpture from which to read the situation, although the Anglo-Saxon regions and landscapes are widely signed by burials and then by burial mounds (see Chapter 4). Some areas, such as Lancashire, that contain neither pillars nor furnished graves provoke considerable interest. What sort of societies are these?[385] The geographical gap (Cumbria, Lancashire, Cheshire) in 5th–7th century monumental activity in the lands that separate busy Pictland, the Borders and Wales is unexplained but seems likely to relate to post-Roman territorial claims being negligible or uncontested. By contrast Pictland, Manau Gododdin with Tweeddale and the kingdoms of Wales were, or had become by the sixth-century, proclaimed British heartlands.

In the early 7th century, at the end of Fm 1, church building begins at Canterbury in the context of the arrival of the mission of St Augustine. The same mission imported illuminated manuscripts, at least one of which has survived.[386] Archaeologically, these experimental initiatives appear to have remained isolated for the best part of 75 years. In the west of Britain, a flourishing of Christian sculpture, codices and churches is expected to accompany the 'Age of the Saints' in the 6th/7th century. Still taking an archaeological perspective, the evidence for this episode has yet to materialise with any conviction. Here too, as in the north, we have to wait until the late 7th century for a more public, widespread and emphatic Christian branding.

In Scotland, Wales and Northumbria, and in contemporary Ireland, this takes the form of three great expansionary monastic movements that span the period c. 675–825. The earliest overtly Christian sculpture, the earliest books produced in Britain and the earliest churches still standing would seem to survive from this region and this period. The interest of the rest of the island, including Lancashire and Cornwall as well as the Anglo-Saxon heartland, appears not have been engaged, or at least not at a sufficiently high material level to make the archaeological antennae tremble. There is little doubt about the devotional intensity of the investments made in Northumbria, Pictland, Scotland, Ireland and Wales in the period between 675 and 750, which run in tandem with the development of monastic sites of a particular kind: wealthy, productive, networked and proclaiming their mission in the landscape. These monasteries are of two kinds, the Northumbrian, Anglicised and aligning with Rome, and the others, different from each other but with shared deep roots in their indigenous past. Between them, the books and the sculpture share ornamental and iconographic vocabulary to such an extent they can be grouped together as 'Insular Art'. But variations show clearly in the sculpture produced, not only as between Northumbria and the north and west, but between Pictish, Scottish, Welsh and Irish practice. This cannot be dismissed as evidence that all their carvers are producing quirky or inexpert versions of the same belief system. The variants are more deliberate, more competent and more learned than that. Similarly, they do not carry signs of a conscious ethnicity. Judging by the indications of the cemeteries (Chapter 4), they are more likely to be a reflection of the inherited pre-existing regional systems of belief, whether Christian or pre-Christian. A distinction can be drawn between this first half of Fm 2 and what followed it: a monastic break-out led by Northumbria with its 'Victory Crosses' which affected the greater part of the north and west, if with increasing patchiness over the Severn Valley and little impact at all in south-east England. These potent landmarks are thought to indicate not only intellectual conquest but the acquisition of estates. Fewer books and even fewer church buildings survive from the late 8th and early 9th century, a deprivation we like to blame on the Vikings. But it may also be that, as with burial in the first half of 7th century, the trend was actually to produce fewer, although grander, examples, as the community of worshippers abandoned the ideology of equality and succumbed to the realities of class.

The new sculptural world created in Fm 3 Britain following the Viking impact is as busy as a waterhole where different herds meet in uneasy equilibrium. The monasteries of Northumbria have been largely wiped out and replaced by a secularised parish system with a strong Scandinavian flavour. Many ecclesiastical settlements survive in Wales and Scotland, but in a secularised form in which the aristocracy are major agents and the ethos is driven by trade and wealth creation. This can coexist, or at least align better, with the thinking of the Norse, which is heralded in numerous stone monuments in the Irish Sea region. The theatre is sufficiently fluid to allow smaller ideological movements to come and go. Some return to an older or refreshed ideological agenda on a larger scale, like the proprietorial landscape markers of Powys (Eilseg) or the Peak district, or the hogback tombs of north Yorkshire. Such a coexistence in general implies a cooling of the theistic temperature and the exercise of more worldly financial aspirations. The outstanding event of Fm 3 is probably the rise of the English south-east as a major monumental zone of artistic carving combined with a widespread campaign of church building. A tidal wave of artistic energy and invention is released into manuscript painting, in which all ranks and sectors of early English society take a bow. This is a phenomenon we will meet again in the next chapter, which is concerned with archaeology's kaleidoscopic relationships with the written word.

Notes

1 'In considering the national groups, Irish, English, Scottish, Welsh, Manx, what strikes one most is the independence of traditions' (Cramp 1965, 5). The question to be addressed can be summarised as 'why that, why there, why then?' (Carver 2001).

2 What remains in the modern English counties are collected in Rosemary Cramp's *Corpus of Anglo-Saxon Stone Sculpture* (12 volumes), complete at the time of writing apart from East Anglia and the Northern Midlands. The survey of the Welsh counties is comprehensively achieved in the three volumes of the *Corpus of Inscribed Stones and Stone Sculpture in Wales* (Redknap and Lewis 2007; Edwards 2007, 2013). Scotland's Early Medieval corpus was collected and assessed in unparalleled depth by Romilly Allen and Anderson in 1903, reprinted in 1993 and reassessed for more recent readers in Henderson and Henderson's *Art of the Picts* and Ian Fisher's *Early Medieval Sculpture in the West Highlands and Islands*.

3 Edwards 2001.

4 Williams et al. 2015. See Gondek 2006a for measures of investment, and for biography Hall et al. 2000; Hall 2012; for landscape Edwards 2001, 2007; Gondek and Noble 2010.

5 Driscoll 2000.

6 Driscoll 2000, 250; see Hilton of Cadboll on the Tarbat peninsular for secular vocabulary in use on a monastic monument (Henderson in James et al. 2008, 200–202; Carver 2016a, 199–200). Edwards 2015, 15 accepts that figures in hunting scenes may represent patrons or those commemorated.

7 Carver 2005b.

8 I use the term 'grand cross' here to encompass the western Scottish High Crosses, the Welsh free-standing crosses, the Northumbrian Victory Crosses and the major Pictish cross-slabs.

9 Harvey 2001, 49–50;.An ogham inscription naming Tebicatus son of (*maqi*) was carved on a dwarf baluster shaft from the 3rd–4th-century town of *Calleva Atrebatum* or a neighbouring geological zone and held to infer a contemporary late Roman Irish resident of the Roman town. Fulford et al. 2000, 17.

10 Edwards 1996, 103–104; Harvey 2001; Sims-Williams 2012.
11 Conde Silvestre 2001, see p. 630.
12 Edwards 1996, 103–104.
13 Okasha 1993, 37; Forsyth 1995a, 9; Fulford et al. 2000, 15.
14 Page 1987 for an introduction. Page 1998 for essays by the leading exponent of the day.
15 Sims-Williams 2003, 352; Tedeschi 2001 divided the palaeography into four phases: (1) 5th century has more or less the same letter-forms as British Late Antique epigraphy. Usually traditional layout in horizontal lines. Horizontal I still unusual. (2) First half of 6th century. New letters join the previous: ligatures F-I and L-I, uncial E.miniscule letters such as F, H, S and T. Horizontal Is increasingly common. (3) Second half of 6th century. Arrival of insular A, Insular D and G, trident shaped M, H-shaped N. Miniscules increasingly common. (4) First half of 7th century.
16 Jackson 1950, 199–205, 1953, 149–193; Sims-Williams 2003, 290–291.
17 Forsyth 1998, 47.
18 Higgitt (1986b, 142) discusses inscribed *crosses* (Fm 2 and later), counting 55 from England, 21 from Wales and 15 from Ireland. There is also a Latin inscription from Tarbat (Higgitt 1982).
19 For overviews see Allen and Anderson 1903, Henderson and Henderson 2004; Wilson 1984; Webster 2012; Wilson and Klindt-Jensen 1966; Graham-Campbell 2013. Detailed dates and diagnoses are drawn from the *Corpus of Anglo-Saxon Sculpture*, passim, and especially on the expertise of Richard Bailey and James Lang, and the volumes of the Welsh *Corpus*, Edwards 2007, 2013; Redknap and Lewis 2007.
20 See Henderson and Henderson 2004, 10–11 for an update on the utility of Allen and Anderson's 'classes'. A category of monument bearing crosses but no other ornament was proposed by Isabel Henderson in 1987.
21 Gondek 2006a.
22 Geddes 2011, 127. The number now known is about 1,800.
23 Edwards 2015; Redknap and Lewis 2007; Edwards 2007, 2013.
24 Some 72% of surviving 'Anglo-Saxon' sculpture comes from the north. So does 80% of the Roman-alphabet inscriptions. And 100% of all inscriptions from the 9th century or earlier come from the north. 'Yet no satisfactory explanation has been provided as to why Southumbria should be completely lacking in such monuments,' Forsyth 1998, 53. As Jope (1964) demonstrated for churches, the reason is not a lack of suitable stone.
25 West Highlands and Islands: Allen and Anderson 1903, 1993; Fisher 2001.
26 Pictland: Allen and Anderson 1903, 1993; Henderson and Henderson 2004.
27 Wales Corpus Vol III; Edwards 2013.
28 Wales Corpus Vol II; Edwards 2007.
29 Wales Corpus Vol I; Redknap and Lewis 2007.
30 AS Corpus VII: Wiltshire, Dorset, Somerset, Devon (Cramp 2006); AS Corpus XI: Cornwall (Okasha 1993; Preston-Jones and Okasha 2013).
31 AS Corpus I Northumberland and Durham Cramp 1984; Collingwood 1927.
32 AS Corpus VI; Northern Yorkshire Lang 2001.
33 AS Corpus III York and Eastern Yorkshire Lang 1991.
34 AS Corpus VIII West Yorkshire Coatsworth 2008.
35 Forsyth 2005.
36 Kermode (ed. Wilson) 1994.
37 AS Corpus II Westmoreland, Cumbria and North Lancashire Bailey and Cramp 1988.
38 AS Corpus IX Cheshire and Lancashire Bailey 2010.
39 AS Corpus X Shropshire, Herefordshire, Warwickshire, Worcestershire and Gloucestershire (The West Midlands) Bryant 2012; Staffordshire, Derbyshire, Nottinghamshire, Leicestershire, Rutland and Northamptonshire were incomplete at the time of writing. Cramp 1977 and Bailey 1988, 2005 provided interim overviews of Mercian sculpture.
40 AS Corpus V Lincolnshire Everson and Stocker 1999.
41 AS Corpus Vol IV (South-east England) Tweddle et al. 1995. The surveys of Norfolk, Suffolk, Cambridgeshire and Huntingdonshire were awaited at the time of writing.
42 Allen and Anderson's 'Class 1'. Henderson 1958 for the original hypothesis; the term 'Firthlands' is also owed to Isabel Henderson.
43 Alcock 1988.
44 Forsyth 2005, 119.

45 Allen and Anderson 1993, 42. This is Dunrobin 1. Dunrobin 2 was found at Dairy Park, also in association with a cist burial.
46 Allen and Anderson's 'Class II' stones, which appear in Pictland from the later 7th or early 8th century.
47 Allen and Anderson Vol 2, 48–50; Vol 1, pattern no.1045; Close-Brooks 1989 describes the stones from the Golspie area conserved at Dunrobin castle.
48 Ó Carragáin 1989. For Nigg and Shandwick, see Henderson and Henderson 2004, passim; for Hilton of Cadboll, Henderson in James et al. 2008.
49 See James et al. 2008, 251–257, 391–398. During this time, excavation at St Mary's located the missing bottom section of the Hilton stone.
50 Kermode 1994, no. 1. A recent example was found by Time Team in 2007; information by Andrew West.
51 The continuation of this monastery into the Viking period is argued by Trench-Jellicoe 2002, 28.
52 Kermode nos 25, 25A.
53 Wilson in Kermode 1994, 18 n5.
54 Redknap and Lewis 2007, 450–452, 438–441.
55 Redknap and Lewis 2007, 402–408.
56 Redknap and Lewis 2007, 448.
57 Redknap and Lewis 2007, 408–420.
58 Redknap and Lewis 2007, 427–433.
59 This section is based on Preston-Jones and Okasha 2013 and Turner 2006; the fact that these revise the pioneering research of Charles Thomas does not reduce the attraction of the latter's contributions, especially *The early Christian archaeology of Camborne* (Thomas 1967).
60 Okasha 1993, nos.13, 23, 24, 52, 61, 78; Higgitt in *Corpus* VII, 245–247.
61 Turner 2006, 142, Fig 48. See Chapter 6, p. 608 for the Tristan stone.
62 Preston-Jones and Okasha 2013, 257–258.
63 Preston-Jones and Okasha 2013, 53–55, 257–258.
64 Preston-Jones and Okasha 2013, 86.
65 Preston-Jones and Okasha 2013, 85–95.
66 Turner 2006, 140; Okasha 1993, 55–56, 141–145.
67 Preston-Jones and Okasha 2013, 50, 52, 56, 85.
68 Turner 2006, 54.
69 Turner 2006, 35.
70 Turner 2006, 35, 36, Fig 6.
71 Turner 2006, 46.
72 Forsyth 2005.
73 See essays in Pictish Progress (Driscoll et al. 2011); also Chapters 3 and 4.
74 Bede I.1; Forsyth 1997a; Rhys 2015, 346–347. These scholars allow the possibility that some pre-Celtic words may have been in use in the Roman period.
75 Forsyth 1995a, 1997a, 1997b, 1998.
76 Henderson 1971; Driscoll 1988, 1998; Thomas 1994, 20; Forsyth 1997b, 91; Forsyth 1998, 56–57 here, pp. 490, 513, 540).
77 Alcock 1988.
78 Samson 1992; Forsyth 1995a, 9, 1997b, 92, 1998, 56.
79 Forsyth 1997b, 91, Fig 3; she also proposes a derivative relationship between the two systems, something that is less easy to visualise.
80 Thomas 1961, 1963.
81 Henderson and Henderson 2004, 60.
82 Thomas 1961, 1963. Smyth 1984, 78–79 and Fraser 2009, 117 felt that the impetus was provided by the arrival of Columba in Inverness in the Pictish heartland in 565, the area that Isabel Henderson (1958) had designated on art historical grounds as the origin centre of the Pictish symbol stones; also Forsyth 1997b, 91.
83 Forsyth 1997a, 32, 1997b, 95, 1998, 57.
84 Gondek 2015.
85 Lane and Campbell 2000.
86 Clarke and Heald 2008, 293.
87 Gondek 2015, 92–93.
88 Gondek 2015, Table 4.2.

89 Noble and Gondek 2011; and see Chapter 3, p. 187.
90 Henderson and Henderson 2004, 123: 'his intimidating appearance will be his function, a ritual prophylactic one in which his tool or weapon plays some part'.
91 Dobat 2006.
92 Noble and Gondek 2011; Noble et al. 2013; Gondek 2015, 87; Maldonado considers that the relationship between burial and Class 1 stones remains ambiguous, but in most cases it is 5th/7th-century burials that incorporate them. Thus, as a group, the Class 1 stones are 5th/7th century or earlier in date and not in a context that could be called specifically Christian (2011, 257–258).
93 https://nosasblog.wordpress.com/2016/12/04/rhynie-season-4/ accessed July 2017.
94 Henderson and Henderson 2004, 168. But the same authors agree that the general forms of the symbols were established 'in the pagan period' (Henderson and Henderson 2004, 171) (for a reflection on Pictish Christianisation, see Carver 1998).
95 Forsyth 1997b, 88.
96 Samson 1992.
97 Fisher 2001, Gairloch (W20), Poolewe (W21), Raasay (W34), Fiscavaig on Skye (W36), Tobar na Maor on Skye (W37), Tote on Skye (W38), Pabbay Barra (W40), Benbecula (W44), Dunadd (281).
98 Adomnán, II, 32; I, 33. On a second visit Columba addressed an extremely large boar, presumably in his own language, inviting it to drop dead; II.26.
99 Fraser 2009, 204, 252, 208; Sharpe 1995, n.147, 148.
100 Fisher 2001, 11–12. This is the source for the numbered stones used here.
101 Campbell 2001.
102 Fisher 2001, 65, 117, 151–152.
103 Rhys 2015, 44–48, 347.
104 Rhys 2015, 44 follows Forsyth by giving them a date range of 7th–10th century.
105 Forsyth 1995a, 9.
106 Fisher 2001, 18, 22.
107 Edwards 1985, 1996; Dorothy Kelly (1993), however, argues that the West Scottish grand crosses all relate to Ireland and belong to a Dal Riada cultural zone that offers a separate tradition to that in the east.
108 Forsyth 2005, 116–117, 125; 'the chances are that Latinus was a local magnate, but with Irish ancestors'.
109 Cowie 1978 for the excavations.
110 Forsyth 2005, 124.
111 See Edwards 2015 for her most recent overview.
112 The periods are those used throughout this book, which generally fit the dates accorded to the individual Welsh pieces of each kind. There have been three major surveys of the material, each with its own numbering system, Macalister 1945; Nash-Williams 1950, and most recently the three regional volumes of the Corpus, Redknap and Lewis 2007; Edwards 2007 and Edwards 2013, which number by county: thus the Voteporius stone at Castell Dwryan in Carmarthenshire was numbered 358 by Macalister, 138 by Nash-Willams and CM3 in Edwards 2007.
113 The Roman Easter was adopted in Wales only in 768. Welsh carvers may have been inhibited by the Biblical injunction: 'thou shalt not make unto thee any graven image, or likeness of anything that is in heaven above', Edwards 2015, 4, 10, 18–10. The deep roots of the prehistoric past are likely to have also remained potent (Chapter 4, p. 462).
114 Edwards 2001, 15.
115 Edwards 2013, 6–7; these semi-legendary records may preserve some apposite memories. The influence or presence of Gauls from the south (Knight 2001, 12) is thought less probable.
116 Jackson 1950, 199, 205–206; Sims-Williams 2003, 290, 351–353.
117 Tedeschi 2001, 24–25; the four stages are c. 500–600, 500–550, 550–600 and 600–650.
118 Redknap and Lewis 2007, 140; Sims-Williams in Edwards 2007, 206, proposes that the Votepor in the inscription flourished in the 5th or early 6th century, rather earlier than Gildas's tyrant.
119 Bede III.1; I Kings 10.23; Edwards 2013, 8, 180–183.
120 Fox 1939; Knight in Redknap and Lewis 2007, 135.
121 St Dogmaels P110 Bridell 1 P5 and Llanboidy 1 CM13; Edwards 2007, 34.
122 Edwards 2001, 18, 21, 2013, 46.
123 Dinorben, Dinas Emrys, Degannwy; Edwards 2013, 10.
124 Edwards 2013, 48.

125 Edwards 2013, 41–42.
126 Edwards 2001, 27–28.
127 Edwards 2007, 30–31.
128 Redknap and Lewis 2007, 60; Edwards 2013, 56–57.
129 Edwards 2001, 28. Most Group 1 monuments are not associated with known churches.
130 Edwards 2013, 45.
131 Knight in Redknap and Lewis 2007, 134. 'Presumably' a cemetery lay near the stone.
132 Redknap and Lewis 2007, 132.
133 Petts 2003, 20–21; Edwards 2013, 15.
134 Knight in Redknap and Lewis 2007, 132–133.
135 Knight in Redknap and Lewis 2007, 133.
136 Edwards 2013, 15; ref. for post-Roman cemetery found in recent excavation.
137 Edwards 2013, 9.
138 Edwards 2001, 24, 27, 2013, 47, Fig 3.
139 Edwards 2013, 210–216.
140 Okasha 1993, 43.
141 www.ucl.ac.uk/archaeology/cisp/database/.
142 Cramp 1965, 2.
143 Lang 1991, 7.
144 Dobson 2008; Carver 2011b, 189.
145 Cramp 2006, 65 The Wareham stones are likely to have come from a Celtic burial ground which preceded the Saxon minster in existence by 802 when King Beorhtric was buried there. Yorke 1995, 69–72.
146 Cramp 2006, 65, 69, 31.
147 Bryant 2012, 318–319, ll571.
148 Fulford et al. 2000. Determined as Irish due to the use of ogham and the Irish linkword maqi for 'son of'. However, Sims-Williams points out that Tebicatos is a specifically p-Celtic (British) form (Edwards 2007, 205).
149 Tweddle et al. 1995, 17, 168.
150 Tweddle et al. 1995, 17. Meanwhile the figurative sculpture from Reculver has been redated to the 9th century (p. 539).
151 Brooks 1984, 64.
152 I.e. 675–825 – 'the long Eighth century'.
153 Fisher 2001.
154 Fisher 2001, 35.
155 Fisher 2001, 36, Fig 11, 13.
156 Fisher 2001, 133, 138.
157 Gondek 2006b.
158 Etchingham proposes an elite who enjoyed upgraded Christian privileges (and chances of salvation) and terms them 'paramonastics' (Etchingham 2006, 85–88).
159 Edwards 1996, 164.
160 Forsyth 1998, 48.
161 Henderson 1987.
162 Henderson and Henderson 2004, 140–142.
163 Foster 1998, 36.
164 Thomas 1971, 145–161; Thomas in Foster 1998; also now at Portmahomack.
165 Henderson 1998, 119–134, 152, 140, 160.
166 Henderson and Henderson 2004, 83.
167 Contributions in Foster 1998.
168 Driscoll in Foster 1998, 178.
169 Edwards 2007, 59.
170 Edwards 2007, 57 cf Fisher 2001, 8.
171 Edwards 2007, 318–321.
172 Edwards 2007, 294–299.
173 Edwards 2001, 32.
174 Handley 2001 has 'Occon son of Asaitgen gave this little piece of Ditoc's desert to Madomnuac'.
175 Edwards 2007, 152; Handley 2001.

176 Edwards 2013, 81.
177 Mapped in Edwards 2013, 16, Fig 1.3.
178 Edwards 2013, 421.
179 Edwards 2013, 425.
180 Edwards 2013, 432.
181 Edwards 2001, 30, 2007, 33, 56.
182 Edwards 2007, 56–57.
183 Edwards 2007, 465–466.
184 Hawkes and Mills 1999.
185 Cramp 1965, 4.
186 Lang 2000, 109: 'although kings undoubtedly endowed the Church during the eighth century, secular power only rarely served as patron for the monuments whose form and decoration speak of ecclesiastical aspirations – objectives with much wider European horizons.'
187 Cramp 1965, 4–7; Bailey and Cramp 1988, 63; Edwards 1996, 163; Everson and Stocker 1999, 157; Lang 2000; Hawkes 2009; Edwards 2013, 326; Kirton 2015, 52.
188 Bede III.25 describes the meeting and Oswiu's role in it.
189 Bede, passim. Plummer indexes the description of the monastery founded by Ethelthryth at Ely (HE IV.19) with the rubric: 'monastery . . . rigour of communistic rule in' (Plummer 1969, 244–245, 498; see Plummer 1969, xvii–xviii, xxx–xxxiii).
190 Carver et al. 2016, Ch 5.
191 Cramp 1965, 4: 'I would suggest that in the late 7th and early 8th century most of the efforts of English carving went into the enrichment of churches both internally and externally and the making of plain memorial crosses or recumbent slabs.'
192 Cramp 1984b, 23.
193 Cramp 1984b, 23.
194 The numbers used in this section refer to the catalogues of the *Corpus of Anglo-Saxon Stone Sculpture*, for Northumberland and Durham and Yorkshire Volumes 1, 3, 6 and 8).
195 Dopplefeld and Weyres 1980, and see http://www.koelner-dom.de/rundgang/domgrabung-rund/reconstruction-of-the-boys-and-the-womens-grave/info/; Paulsen 1992.
196 Cramp 1984b, 24, 2006, 164–166, 185–191.
197 Lang 1990; Ó Carragáin 2010a, 42.
198 Cramp 1984b, Hartlepool 1–7.
199 Lang 1991, 60–67.
200 Stenton assumes that monasteries led by a woman were double monasteries in which men and women were separated on the same site: 'it is doubtful whether any houses for women only were founded during this period' (8th century) (1971, 161). See Chapter 2, p. 405–9 for discussion on leading women.
201 Okasha 2001, 84.
202 Coatsworth 2008, 258–259.
203 Levison 1943, citing a translation of Eusebius by Rufinus. This text was known to Bede and so offers a live link between the scriptorium and the mason's yard; Cramp 1965, 4.
204 Coatsworth 2008, 14–15, 6–8.
205 See Toop 2011 for a proposed mechanism of the Northumbrian western takeover, read from monuments.
206 Cramp 1965, 6–7, 1984b, 27. The Lindisfarne cross influenced acolytes erected further north at Abercorn, Aberlady, Coldingham, Ruthwell, Bewcastle and Jedburgh. When they fled from the Vikings, the Lindisfarne community took it with them and re-erected it at Durham.
207 Coatsworth 2008, 72.
208 Lang 2000, 109.
209 Bailey and Cramp 1988, 63–71.
210 Cramp 1965, 8–9.
211 Lang 1999.
212 Coatsworth 2008, 69–70.
213 Lang 2001, 41–43, 168–171.
214 Coatsworth 2008, 72–73, 135–143.
215 Lang 2000, 114–118.
216 Bailey and Cramp 1988, 10–11; Bailey 2010.
217 Bailey 2010, 21.

218 Sandbach 1, Hawkes 2002; Bailey 2010, 99–113.
219 Bailey 2010, 93.
220 Bailey 2010, 19.
221 Lang 1991, 16; Dobson 2008; Carver 2011b, 189.
222 As a holding operation I have used reviews by Rosemary Cramp (1977) and Richard Bailey (1988, 2005).
223 Bailey 1988, 4.
224 Cramp 1977, 194–210; However, Jewell 1986 sees the friezes as essentially ornamental rather then religious.
225 Bailey 1988, 8–14.
226 Bryant 2012, 19, 20.
227 Bryant 2012, 23–24.
228 Bryant 2012, 46; cf Cramp 1977, 194 'we must agree with Kendrick, if we use comparative stylistic evidence, that the earliest Mercian sculpture does not appear until after the mid 8th century'.
229 Bryant 2012, 49, 52.
230 Bryant 2012, 46, 162, Ill 129–131.
231 Bryant 2012, 55, Fig 19.
232 Emily Howe in Bryant 2012, 112–115.
233 Bryant 2012 St Mary 4 Ill. 145, p. 99. The latter since defaced; St Mary 5, pp. 170–172 Fig 33E, Ill147–149.
234 Bryant 2012, 70, Fig 25, Ill 621.
235 Cramp 2006, 5a-c, Ill 409, p. 205.
236 Cramp 2006, Ill 425, pp. 209–211, 1aA ill 434, pp. 211–212.
237 Cramp 2006, Ill 411, pp. 206–208.
238 in Bryant 2012, 21; following Blair 2005, 215.
239 Hall 2000, 79.
240 Tweddle et al. 1995, 17, 32–33.
241 Tweddle et al. 1995, 35.
242 Reculver 1; Tweddle in Backhouse et al. 1984; Tweddle et al. 1995, 58–61, 161.
243 Everson and Stocker 1999, 69.
244 Everson and Stocker 1999, Ill 165, pp. 157–162.
245 Wormald 1996.
246 Forsyth 1995b.
247 Henderson and Henderson 2004, 135, 190–191.
248 Ritchie 1995.
249 Sellar 1993a;Jackson 1993, also argued for a monument celebrating a Scottish triumph over the Picts, in this case on the order of Kenneth MacAlpin himself. See also an online essay by Brigitte Geddes endorsing this idea in 2016 and urging 'that it be signposted to the viewing public'.
250 Henderson and Henderson 2004, 135–136.
251 Woolf 2006 for the relocation of Fortriu.
252 Fisher 2001.
253 Bailey and Cramp 1988, 29–30.
254 Bailey and Cramp 1988, 31–32.
255 Bailey 2010, 39–40.
256 Bailey 2010, 39.
257 Bailey and Cramp 1988, 33, 100–104.
258 Ellis-Davidson 1950, 123: 'To seek for illustrations of the legends and myths of the pagan past carved on the memorial stones and crosses of Anglo-Saxon England is to embark on a subject which has provoked wilder flights of interpretative fancy than perhaps any branch of Anglo-Saxon studies.' She quotes the influential negative view of J. Romilly Allen (1887, 7) that 'the representation of a purely secular or historical event having no connection with the church, is probably not to be found on any Christian monument'.
259 Ellis-Davidson 1950, 123–133, 138.
260 Bailey and Cramp 1988, 30.
261 Bailey 2010, 34–36.
262 Kirton 2015.
263 Hawkes 2009 proposes a Roman inspiration for Masham; Lang 2000, 114 sees it as metaphor of ideological conquest by the crusading apostles, as suggested by the Book of Revelations.

264 Edwards 2007, 84–89.

265 Redknap and Lewis 2007, 128. These show coloured casts in the National Museum. No evidence of surviving pigment has been found on monuments, although it is likely that they were coloured (Nancy Edwards, personal communication).

266 Petts 2003, 208.

267 Edwards 2001, 35; Redknap and Lewis 2007, 578–579.

268 Knight in Redknap and Lewis 2007, 137.

269 Edwards 2007, 60.

270 Edwards 2007, 396–401.

271 Edwards 2013, 83.

272 Edwards 2013, 340–344: 'An Old English patronym combined with an Old Welsh name would imply Anglo-Saxon penetration into this part of Powys or possibly intermarriage across the border.' This was a mother church (acc. to Fig 1.3).

273 Edwards 2013, 129.

274 Redknap 2004, 147–149.

275 Edwards 2007, 61.

276 Edwards 2009a, 149–151.

277 Edwards 2013, 326, 329–330, 333.

278 Murrieta-Flores and Williams 2017.

279 Cramp 1984b, Lindisfarne 37.

280 Cramp 1982.

281 Coatsworth 2008, 71.

282 Lang 1991, 26.

283 Lang 1991, 37.

284 Cramp 1984b.

285 This most likely stood within the courtyard of the principia, one of the few open spaces in the legionary fortress that was probably not encumbered by fallen stone work. Its position may be marked (intentionally or not) by the present Roman Catholic church, which is also aligned with the no longer visible basilica; Phillips and Heywood 1995.

286 Lang 1991, 26.

287 Lang 2001, 49.

288 Coatsworth 2008, 74–76, 202.

289 Lang 2001, 23.

290 Cramp 1984b, Sockburn 14.

291 Lang 1984, 87; Lang 1972, 209.

292 Lang 1984, 97.

293 Lang 1972, 1984, 2001, 20–23, 47–49; Coatsworth 2008, 28–30.

294 Everson and Stocker 1999, 70.

295 Everson and Stocker 1999, 72–77.

296 Tweddle et al. 1995, 73.

297 Cramp 2006, Ill 405, pp. 202–204, Ill 150, p. 125; Bryant 2012, Ill 791.

298 Bryant 2012, 83, Fig 30.

299 Bryant 2012, Ill 105, 106, p. 159; Cramp 2006, Ill 379, p. 189.

300 Bryant 2012, 26, 369, Ill 683, 686.

301 Cramp 2006, 73.

302 Tweddle et al. 1995, 1A p. 227, Ill 351.

303 Tweddle et al. 1995, Old Minster 88A Ill 646.

304 As Driscoll 1988, 54.

305 Patrick is said to have originated in Britain, perhaps from the north-west. However, the strongest links archaeologically were between Southern Ireland and south-west Britain (Ó Floinn 2001). The distribution of ogham inscriptions and penannular brooches may connect areas with similar forms of pre-Christian affiliation (Ó Floinn 2001, 7–8).

306 Stalley 1996, 9; Edwards 1996, 161.

307 Edwards 1996, 163.

308 Stalley 1996, 22.

309 Stalley 1996, 18.

310 Stalley 1996, 16, 8, 24, 20, 29.

311 Ó Floinn 1998, 90.

312 Swift 1999, 2003, 119.
313 Ó Floinn 1998, 91.
314 Ó Floinn 1998, 97–98. The first to be used are Type A in the 8th century, with Types B and C following but contemporary.
315 Ó Floinn 1998, 97; O'Leary 2015, 125.
316 O'Leary 2015, 116–175. These are her 'Group 1'.
317 O'Leary 2015, 125. These are her Group 2, dated to the 11th/12th century.
318 O'Leary 2015, 124; Ó Carragáin 2009b; Ó Carragáin 2010b.
319 Edwards 1996, 164.
320 O'Sullivan and Carragáin 2008.
321 For example Mount Brandon, Ó Carragáin 2003, 131.
322 Edwards 1996, 166–167.
323 Edwards 1996, 167.
324 Lager 2003; Karnell 2012.
325 Martin-Clark 1950, 112n; Nylén and Lamm 1988; Gräslund 2003; and see Chapter 2, p. 128 for the handy girl of Hadelund.
326 Carver 2005b; Gondek 2015.
327 Carver 2001.
328 Ó Carragáin 2010a, 17–19.
329 Ó Carragáin 2010a, 22–23.
330 Carol Neuman de Vegvar makes the case that this was a real church constructed with Irish technology but in a Roman image: 2003, 154, 156, 159, 165.
331 'The cult of relics goes hand in hand with architectural innovation' Ó Carragáin 2010a, 85.
332 Where there are 31 of the 36 examples (86%), Ó Carragáin 2010a, 52.
333 Summarised in Ó Carragáin 2010a, Fig 1, p. xi. There are also *indeterminate mortared churches* widely dispersed across the island.
334 Ó Carragáin 2010a, 55.
335 Ó Carragáin 2010a, 66. These measured less than 12 square metres and 'are always the smallest churches at a particular site'.
336 Ó Carragáin 2010a, 87.
337 Ryan 2005.
338 Ó Carragáin 2010a, 161–165.
339 Ó Carragáin 2010a, Fig 1, p. xi.
340 Cameron 1994, 1996 ; Yeoman 2009, 228 has mid-11th century as the earliest. Carver et al. 2016, 175–177; McGibbon and Ross 1896 for the first survey; Foster 2015 for the latest overview.
341 Fernie 1986.
342 Foster 2015, 72–74.
343 Barrowman 2003. But these excavations were on too small a scale to confirm or confront the conclusions of the 1973 publication by Small, Thomas and Wilson.
344 Cramp 2014, 72, 134.
345 Aitchison 2006.
346 Carver 2016a, 119; Carver et al. 2016, 149–154, 169. The excavators argue that the east wall of the present crypt represents the west wall of this 8th-century church.
347 As seen at St Ninians' Isle: Small et al. 1973.
348 Edwards 2013, 74; Taylor and Taylor 1965, 497–499; Davies 2009, 44; Pritchard 2009, 249, 258
349 Taylor and Taylor 1965; Taylor 1978. The work is entitled *Anglo-Saxon Architecture*, although it concerns only upstanding churches. Its motivation is revealed in its dedications 'to the Anglo-Saints' (Vols I, II) and to the

> one eternal and ever-loving [Christian] God . . . not only as a further contribution to the buildings themselves but also as confident expression of faith that these ancient churches will endure through the current years of unbelief and indifference until the dawn of those days when the Glory of the Lord will fill the whole land.

> (Vol. III, xii)

Volume III was produced with the collaboration of Taylor's second wife, Judith Samuel (Vol. III, xvi).
350 Taylor and Taylor 1965 (Vols 1 & II) and 1978 (Vol III).
351 Northumbria: Escomb, Hart, Jarrow, Monkwearmouth, Seaham, Sockburn, Staindrop; Bywell St Peter, Corbridge, Heddon on the Wall, Hexham; York Minster(?), St Mary Bishophill senior(?),

Skipwith, Masham, Whitby, Ledsham, Ripon, Kirk Hammerton; Kent: Canterbury St Martin, St Mary and St Pancras, Lyminge, Reculver, Rochester, Stone-by-Faversham, Whitfield; Elsewhere: Bradwell-on-Sea (Essex), Deerhurst (Glos), Somerford Keynes (Glos), Atcham, Much Wenlock, Wroxeter (Shrops), Glastonbury (Somerset), Bradford-on-Avon (Wilts) Repton, All Hallows by the Tower (London), North Elmham, South Elmham (Nor), Brigstock, Brixworth, Peterborough (Northants), Stoke-d'Abernon (Surrey); Bishopstone (Sx).

352 Clapham 1930; Taylor 1978, 767–772 lists the evidence upon which a church is claimed as Anglo-Saxon; not all those so dated in Volumes I and II are included. In practice his 'primary' group are mainly churches likely to be those documented by history. Those which are primary and assigned to Period A provide a platform on which the modifications of later Anglo-Saxon period can be identified. The *terminus post quem* is provided stratigraphically by stylistically Norman fabric. It should be noted that the archaeological analysis of buildings (as understood today) was in its infancy when the Taylors did their work.

353 Taylor and Taylor 1965, 236.

354 Cramp 2005, 351; Chapter 3, 223. The architecture of the visitor centre at Bede's World in Jarrow makes a deliberate visual reference to Roman inspiration.

355 E.g. some have megalithic side-alternate quoins, others have arches with through-stones; Repton, Titchfield Hants; Heysham Lancsx2; Edenham Lincs ?; South Elmham; Hackness, Kirby Hill (N Yorks).

356 Taylor 1978, 887–891 counted 62 square west towers and 21 round west towers, with 16 square towers placed otherwise than the west end.

357 Tweddle et al. 1995, 254, Ill 429.

358 Tweddle et al. 1995, 62–63.

359 Carver 2011a, 941.

360 Morris 1989; Jope's survey (1964) demonstrated that all parts of England were in reach of good quality building stone. In particular, south-east England had its own supply of exploited stone and 'should not really be seen as a non-stone-building area' (1964, 92). This is also relevant for the production of stone sculpture.

361 See Chapter 3 for the monastic production and Nieke 1988 for writing as a form of monumentality.

362 Gameson 2013b, for the manufacture of the codex.

363 Carver and Spall 2004; Spall 2011; Carver et al. 2016, 194–211.

364 Surviving examples include an Irish pocket Gospel book of the later 8th century now at Fulda in Germany (Alexander 1978, no.49) and the Cuthbert Gospels, dated to the end of the 7th century, when it was placed in St Cuthbert's coffin in Lindisfarne. It was retrieved in 1104 after the coffin had reached Durham. It was for many years in the possession of Stonyhurst College in Lancashire and is now Add. ms 89000 in the British Library, which bought it in 2012 for £9 million.

365 See Pestell in Evans and Loveluck 2009 2, 130, 140. Tester et al. 2014, 381 argue for an ecclesiastical association for Middle Saxon styli at Brandon.

366 Campbell 2010, 142.

367 Alexander 1978, 33.

368 Gameson, Jarrow lecture 2017, personal communication.

369 Bruce-Mitford 1969.

370 'extremis de finibus abbas' (Chazelle 2003).

371 Brown 2003, 281. The wish to reproduce the imperial purple dye of the murex shellfish probably led to attempts to extract a similar dye from the dog whelk *Nucella lapillis* (Biggam 2006a, b; Gameson 2013b, 89). In addition to getting more precise identification of pigments via chemical analysis (e.g. Brown and Clark 2004), aDNA analysis applied to fluff generated by cleaning has been used to determine the species of animal that provided the parchment. In one study, out of 1,000 English legal documents, all but one were made from sheepskin (Collins et al. 2015). See also Neate et al. 2011 for the study of books as artefacts.

372 The main sources are Alexander 1978 for the period to 800 and Temple 1976 thereafter. Chapter 1, 9 for European scriptoria. Chapter 2 made some use of the illustrations to argue for the way people looked. Chapter 3, 225, for monasteries.

373 Orosius was a 5th-century Spanish monk who wrote the influential *Seven books against the Pagans*.

374 Meehan 1994.

375 Alexander 1978, 49; Edwards 2015, 18.

376 Porcher 1970.

377 For example, the *Goldescalc Gospels* from Mainz and the *Gospel of Saint-Médard of Soissons*, which both also depict the classical 'Fountain of Life'.

378 For example, the *Utrecht psalter*.

379 Temple 1976, 241.

380 Noel 1995.

381 Carver 1986b.

382 Carver 1986b, 141.

383 See Alexander 1978, 11 (fig. 3). Building S1 at Portmahomack was thought to have been laid according the principle of the Golden Section (Carver 2016a, 140–141). See Whitfield 1999, 311; and Harding 2009a, 59 for use in the Iron Age.

384 Alexander 1978, 60.

385 Bailey and Cramp 1988; Bailey 2010.

386 The 'Augustine Gospels' was made in the late 6th century, probably in Rome, was once in Canterbury and is now in Cambridge (CCCC286) (Weitzmann 1977, 22).

6 Materiality in words
Myths and records

Introduction

The Formative Period has been defined here in terms of its material culture – material that is neither neutral in its original expression nor in our interpretation of it. That much is always conceded, notwithstanding our desire and our efforts to allow the matter of early Britain to speak for itself. I have tried to develop a principle of convergence in which observations accumulate and seem to point in similar directions, eventually raising confidence that they do or will support each other. This much can be contrived into an archaeological narrative. How then should we view the texts that survive from or purport to describe the same world we have encountered in solid form above and below ground?

A prudent archaeologist would leave them out altogether. The tradition of our study is that the lions of literature lead and the donkeys of archaeology follow, and there is no point in sending an ass to do a lion's work. I make no criticism of this, since it has in general been the legends of the period that first recruited archaeologists to the hunt, and I am certainly no exception: I approached the period not so much through poetry as because of it. But things have also changed over the last 50 years: the students of the texts have become more sceptical and the students of the soil more upbeat. We may not be entirely on message so far as the textual narrative goes, but inquisitive archaeologists have poked about in activities and attitudes, faces and faeces, quips and quiddities hitherto out of reach of everyone. This was the broad reason for letting the material culture speak first.

What follows is intended as a complement to the archaeology, in the same way as the archaeology was once regarded as a complement to the texts. I shall try to avoid both the pretension of any special expertise and the clumsy passion of a first love. I am hoping that by exposing some of archaeology's particular hopes we shall broaden the small-scale relationships that have flourished over the years in so many centres and conferences of medieval studies into something of a more general dialogue. The purpose of this book is to court the interest of historians of art and literature with what we have to offer and so earn the rights and pleasures of reciprocity.

At the same time, for the archaeological reader, the hope is not only to introduce the inspirational corpus that survives but a little bit of what it can do for us. The chapter addresses two questions that could be helpful in developing a valency of ideas. Does the text represent, with any degree of precision, the times it purports to describe? And if it does, in what way does it convey the activities and attitudes of the period? This is well-trodden ground, and by better boots than mine. The difference here is that we start with an archaeological framework (Chapters 1–5) and then see how the literature fits it, rather than the other way round. This was probably not possible up to now.

So the chapter divides, as ever, into sections on Formative 1, 2 and 3 and considers how the principal (or selected) texts relate to each. It will be seen that in Formative 1 we will have occasion to present examples of 'heroic' literatures of British, Anglo-Saxon and Irish origin and compare them with each other and with the Old Testament in which they often found inspiration. In Formative 2, it was the turn of the New Testament to provide the paragon and of a new generation of Scottish, Northumbrian and English chroniclers to provide the first exercises in biography and history. In Formative 3, Scandinavian incomers offer hybrid sagas, at once heroic and historical, while England expands its output beyond chronicles into histories, handbooks and sermons.

All of these have the power to enliven and enhance the archaeological picture and often match it in mood and substance. Heroic literature will be seen not only to speak of artefacts, halls and extravagant burials but to match their energy and expression. In some cases the synergy is close. As suggested at Sutton Hoo, the Mound 1 ship burial was not an emulation of Beowulf, nor was Beowulf a memory of Sutton Hoo. Both were poetic compositions drawing from the same world in different media. The historical and biographical texts of Fm 2 allow themselves more latitude in making eulogy and commentary specific, the more poetic role being carried on in the iconography and descriptive friezes of monumental stone sculpture. In Fm 3 literature has become a more normal artefact of life; it may have lost something of its hyperbolic glitter, but it has other rewards. The emergence of English writing as a descriptive, analytical, judgemental and almost journalistic companion of the times is matched by the vivacity of Late Saxon drawing and the proliferation of its products and contacts.

However, the texts are not just another kind of material culture but another kind of evidence altogether, and my purpose in reviewing a few aspects of them here is partly to show the older and more developed discipline of literary criticism that it has a new partner, and an informative or at least a chatty one. Some licence will be required. The first of the two questions that began this section requires us to connect artefacts and sites with citations in texts in a way that can be eye-opening; but the second, in which we attempt to use texts and materiality together to deduce the mood music and scenography of those times, may have to allow the deployment of some imagination and invention if we are to put the parallel expressions of both media in reach of us today.

The early medieval literatures relating to Britain are enigmatic, seductive and rarely refer directly to dated events. In this they resemble archaeology, but the surviving literary monuments are more isolated. They were made at different places and different times for different purposes and written down in four different languages: Irish, British, English and Latin. Bede (I.1) counts five languages, recognising Pictish as distinct from British. However, Pictish literature has not survived in any useable form, so we must be content with four. Knowing of five languages, Bede could make an equation with the Divine Law, namely the *Pentateuch*, the first five books of the Bible as found in the Latin version made by Jerome in the 4th century (Genesis, Exodus, Leviticus, Numbers, Deuteronomy). This probably provided the dominant canon for the generation of literature in the early medieval British Isles.

Relating to Formative 1

Heroic literature

Hector Munro Chadwick's definitions of 'heroic literature' were comparative in two ways: first, similarities in the content and style of the texts, and second, similarities in the belief and behaviour of those described. The earliest European examples that survive are the works of

Homer and certain books of the Old Testament, all originating in the Bronze Age. Chadwick and his wife, Nora, went on to explore the heroic literatures of Europe, Brittonic, Teutonic and Slavic, and showed something of the manner they connected with archaeology and with each other. The connections between the Greek and German canons were especially striking, and since there was no clear literary descent, the anthropological aspects were emphasised, proposing that 'similar poetry is the outcome, or rather the expression, of similar social conditions'.[1] The poetic voices in this case are those of vaunting males, which Chadwick characterised in a way that was not wholly sympathetic:

> That which they prized above all else is the ability to indulge their desires to the full – in feasting and every form of enjoyment for themselves, in unlimited generosity to their friends, in ferocious vindictiveness towards their foes. . . . The hero of the Odyssey, when his opportunity arrives, sets no limit to the vengeance which he exacts, from prince, goatherd or maidservant.[2]

The prevailing conditions are war and conquest, sometimes to be equated to a known invasion such as the Achaeans in Greece or the Huns in Europe. The protagonists who share this 'adolescent stage' (in both senses) engineer a social breakaway from the rigorous customs of the tribe to create the structured anarchy of the boy gang. Chadwick was among the first to discover that the peoples named in literature (Angles, Jutes, Picts, Vandals) were not tribes linked by kin but, on the contrary, bands of brothers in arms linked by excessive testosterone. In this sense, many of the peoples of 5th–7th century Britain and Ireland can be cast in the heroic mould, and its thinking may be detected within the tattered literature that has survived.

Three principal illustrative examples of the genre are the Irish *Táin Bó Cúailnge*, the British *Gododdin*, and the Anglo-Saxon *Beowulf*. All are thought to refer to historical events in the early first millennium but assumed their extant form well after the Bible had reached the islands. There are good reasons to think that a certain amount of mixing and accretion will have changed their character and thinking. In other words, like archaeological monuments, these texts have 'biography', and not only biography but consummated interaction with other texts. Of these the Old Testament was probably the most significant.

The Cattle Raid of Cooley

The *Táin Bó Cúailnge* – TBC (The Cattle Raid of Cooley) is a story found in Irish in the 12th-century *Book of Leinster* that appears to describe a saga of celebrated Iron Age heroes. In bed with her third husband (Ailill, prince of Leinster), at her hillfort of Rathcroghan in Connacht, Queen Medb (Maeve) plans to steal the stud bull Donn Cooley from the Ulstermen. Donn Cooley is the only rival to her husband's bull Finnbennach, and Maeve must have him since she insists on equality of wealth with her men. Aided by Fergus, former king of Ulster, Medb and Ailill set out to raid Donn Cooley's homeland and capture him. The men of Ulster had been rendered inactive by a spell when the raid took place, apart from their 17-year-old champion, Cú Chulainn, who proceeded to despatch the raiding warriors one after another in single combat at a ford, causing Maeve additional aggravation by also killing some of her handmaidens and pets. Donn Cooley is captured nonetheless, taken to Connacht and pitched into a lengthy battle with his rival in strength and fecundity at the ringfort of Rath na Darbh. After much roaring and bellowing, Donn Cooley drove Finnbennach into the lake at Crúachan and came out with his rival's loins, shoulder blade and liver on his horns. He then headed for Ulster and home, depositing parts of Finnbennach en route, but himself dropped dead on arrival. Meanwhile, Maeve's particular form of diplomacy continued unabated; she had found time to seduce Fergus, her collaborator in the raid, whom Ailill then murdered from jealousy before being murdered himself by Conall Cernach at Maeve's instigation, on the grounds that he was seeing other women (Figure 6.1).[3]

Figure 6.1 Queen Maeve by J.C. Leyendecker, 1907; published by Theodore Roosevelt in *The Century Magazine*.

(Courtesy of John Waddell)

This tale of sex, murder, power, deception and cattle breeding appears to have its roots in an ancient conflict between Ulster and the rest of Ireland. It is thought to have taken the form in which it survived in or after the 4th century AD and was probably composed in the mid-7th century by a professional poet *(fili)* 'who may have had some of the Latin learning of the monasteries and wished to record the native heroic tradition in a worthy form. He or a later redactor may have been familiar with the Aeneid'.[4] Like the Aeneid (and indeed the Odyssey), its stories create an intoxicating world of ambition and miracle that is better than life and consequently better than history. Gods and heroes plant an image in the mind that is hard to eradicate, at once gilding a nation's past and preventing access to it.

Nevertheless, a persistent historical question is how far the Cattle Raid evoked the world in which its characters lived. For Kenneth Jackson, TBC was 'a window on the Iron Age', showing us rival warrior-kings head-hunting, fighting from chariots, and being rewarded with the 'champion's portion' of meat.[5] Belief that the Irish Iron Age might have been like this has invited the enlargement of the repertoire of reality to include the ritual mating of a king with a horse, although mound-dwelling fairies have enjoyed a less enthusiastic following. However, it is now sad to relate that modern scholarship has 'stripped the *window on the Iron Age* of everything bar its memorable title'.[6] Some of the critique is down to earth: insofar as there is any match with materiality, the swords of the Tain are more Viking than Late Iron Age.[7] Others argue from analysis of the text, insisting that the 12th-century version that survives must have been transmitted and filtered by monastic scribes.[8] They must therefore represent what those authors thought then, motivated by whatever then drove them.

However, even if consumed in a predigested state, the striking revelations coming from the small group of Irish scholars who are editing, translating and deconstructing these texts have implications far beyond the boundaries of Irish linguistics, notably in archaeology. The monks who transcribed TBC were not repeating mindless garbage, reshaping ancient belief in the Christian image or even preserving the works of pagan poets in a spirit of liberal intellectualism.[9] Kim McCone observes the close parallels between TBC and the Old Testament[10] and concludes that the Ulster Cycle did probably represent the Formative period: 'the decapitation of enemies was more likely a contemporary early Christian practice, not a hangover from the Iron Age of which they "were quite unaware"'.[11] Not only do 'native mythological modes of thought and expression . . . resonate happily with those of the Bible',[12] but the early monks set out to give Ireland an Old Testament of its own.[13] McCone's suggestion is that the early days of the Christian conversion were dominated not by the teachings of Jesus but by the OT and the books of Samuel in particular. These provided a rational ease of passage between previous practice and the new thinking, particularly for kings. Pagan gods could be conveniently dressed up as heroes or saints. The OT could be reconciled with the church's mission through ingenious allegory; thus the overtly erotic *Song of Songs* could be recast as a hymn celebrating the church as the Bride of Christ.[14]

This critique does not remove the archaeological value of early Irish literature, which remains in a recent verdict 'an extraordinarily extensive corpus of myth, legend, law, genealogy and history – unique in its scope in medieval Europe'. It is described as 'robustly pagan in character', and even 90% of the hagiography is 'demonstrably or implicitly pagan in origin'. Thus, it 'cannot be disregarded and must have something to tell us about the prehistoric past'.[15] The professional mystic poet seems to have survived to some extent outside the monastic embrace. While it is not excluded that the *filid* (plural *filidh*) was the heir of the druid, only nine of the 50 or so *filidh* mentioned in early medieval annals are attached to monasteries.[16] *Filidh* hostile to the new faith constructed a religious hero (Mongán) and a pagan heaven of their own, the plain of pleasure. A quote from the preface to the Hymn of Fiacc shows that contemporaries were aware of what was at stake: 'What is attempted?' asked Fiacc. 'The tonsuring of Dubthach,' said they; the response was tinged with remorse for the replacement of an old mysticality with an new orthodoxy: 'That is foolish, for there is not in Ireland a poet of his equal.'[17]

Filidh convey some information that archaeologists feel confident to use: found in the *Book of Leinster* are histories of prominent places, the *dindsenchas*. These raise expectations of royal seats, ritual events, law giving and horse racing that it would be unwise to dismiss wholly as *topoi*. Locating any Iron Age correlates securely is befogged by the near complete absence of Iron Age settlement in Ireland,[18] but a fruitful archaeological inquiry has sprung from a later text, the *Félire Óengusso*.[19] This was written down before AD 824 (when the Oengus of the title died), and consists of a calendar of saints' days, with a prologue. It was not only composed in the bosom of the church but celebrates the demise of paganism and the triumph of Christianity: 'Heathendom has been destroyed, though fair it was, and wide-spread.'[20] The great hillforts were reported as succeeded in prominence by monastic sites: 'Tara's mighty burgh perished at the death of her princes: with a multitude of venerable champions, the great Height of Machae (Armagh) abides.'[21] 'Rathcroghan, it has vanished with Ailill, offspring of victory: fair the sovranty over princes that there is in the monastery of Clonmacnoise.'[22] 'Aillenn's proud burgh has perished with its warlike host: great is victorious Brigit: fair is her multitudinous cemetery.'[23] 'Emain's burgh it hath vanished, save that its stones remain: the cemetery of the west of the world is multitudinous Glendalough.'[24] The four principal pairs, Tara/Armagh, Rathcroghan/Clonmacnoise, Dún Aillinne/Kildare, Navan/Glendalough, have naturally been attractive targets for tracking the Iron Age through to the early Christian period, although not as yet revealing a monumental sequence at any site where Iron Age ritual enclosure morphs into Christian church on the same site (see Chapter 1). Other examples of royal cult high places are Uisneach, where 4th–5th-century and 7th–8th-century monuments lie adjacent,[25] and Teltown, County Meath,[26] with three more likely candidates in County Donegal.[27]

Tara gives a fine example of how archaeologists have fed on the lotus of legend and engaged in a classic confrontation of competing pasts.[28] 'British Israelites' investigated the Rath of the Synods between 1899 and 1902 looking for the ark of the covenant and the grave of Princess Tea Tephi, heir of the house of David. A massive and uncontrolled excavation began with the permission of Gustavus Villiers Briscoe, a freemason and enthusiast and the then-owner of the site. Naturally the Irish intelligentsia reacted, and among the many protesters was W. B. Yeats, who visited in 1902 and was threatened with a gun by one of Briscoe's employees. Yeats, Douglas Hyde and George Moore wrote to *The Times*, and the excavations were terminated before the site was destroyed. No records or finds survived, but the rath was later scientifically re-examined by Seán Ó Ríordáin. The sequence consisted of a large ditched enclosure (undated), then a series of Iron Age circular enclosures, flat graves and a barrow of 1st–2nd century AD, and a residential enclosure with associated domestic and industrial activity from the 3rd to 4th century AD. Roman pottery was present, probably supplied from the Severn Valley.[29] The site of Tara as a whole has been studied as part of the Irish Discovery Programme and resolved into a Middle Bronze Age phase with mounds and ring ditches (Phase 5), the Iron Age Rath of the Kings (Phase 6), the Roman Iron Age Rath of the Synods (Phase 7) and the early medieval 'Cormac's House' a ringwork built to incorporate the king's seat (Phase 8).[30] The present readings of this and other sites have shown how the monuments of Iron Age Ireland did indeed provide an inheritance for the Formative, if perhaps less colourful and less specific than was once expected.

This brief excursus into Irish territory instructs us that the heroic tales are lucky survivals of literary artefacts originating in the early first millennium AD. They have a biography that has marred them and marked them but probably retain some vivid memories of their early days. Those early days are Late Iron Age or *Formative 1* in the sense used in this book, that is, the 5th to 7th century. Although nominally preceding the 'Early Christian' period, the archaeology of the Late Iron Age takes place on the royal cult high places after Christianity has theoretically reached Ireland – in the 5th century.[31] Thus the cult of the king, assembly, cattle as wealth, the long struggle of the Ulster Cycle, head-hunting, fighting from chariots and the celebration of Old Testament values can all be equated with the known traditional monuments on the one hand and TBC on the other. All that is necessary is to acknowledge that, although both are termed 'Christian', Christ does not arrive as a political player until the 7th century: as noted in the previous chapters, the ideology of Formative 1 (400–675) is quite different to that of Formative 2 (675–850). The second conversion is to Christian values as expressed by metaphysical experts – no longer the poets, but the monks, their successors in title. Where details are given it is legitimate to use the 'retrogressive' method, as in art, to extract likely material aspects of the period, for example hairstyle, brooches and clothing.[32]

Heroic literature of Britain

Britain has preserved several collections of heroic literature, no less evocative (or less obscure) than that of Ireland. Surviving tales are to be found in the *White Book of Rhydderch* (AD 1330–1325) or the *Red Book of Hergest* (AD 1375–1425), the older ones being first written down in the 11th century but including material referring to personalities of the 6th century, famously Arthur and Maelgwn, king of Gwynedd.[33] Primary among the texts are the *Four Branches of the Mabinogi* which tell the story of Pwyll Prince of Dyfed, Branwen daughter of Llŷr, Manawydan son of Llŷr and Math son of Mathonwy.[34] These are much concerned with failed fertility (of all kinds), threatening downturn and the destruction of the kingdom. The players are kings, with gods (Maponus) and goddesses (Rhiannon) assuming disruptive and confusing interventions. Gods play havoc by substituting themselves in the action at awkward moments. Pwyll is to swap places with neighbouring lord Arawn, fight his enemy and lend him his wife. After a year they return to their own courts, where Pwyll's wife has apparently remained chaste. Sitting on a mound, Pwyll is attracted by a lady on a white horse and gives chase. He spends the rest of the story wooing her, a frustrating process since she is the goddess Rhiannon and something of a tease. The tales feature hunting, drinking and feasting and one-night liaisons, resulting in a trail of trouble. Ships arrive from Ireland and visits are made to Oxford, London and Kent in *Lloegr* (England). Branwen, the eponymous heroine, is successfully wooed (in one night) by the King of Ireland, Matholwch, who arrived with 13 ships. A family feud broke out, and Irish horses were attacked. Although new horses, a staff of silver as tall as the king, a gold plate as broad as his face and a magic cauldron that restored dead warriors were offered in compensation, the war eventually destroyed both islands. Other themes include the wronged wife, the seduced wife and the unfaithful wife.[35]

The story of Tristan and Iseult also appears to have been concerned with Irish-British relations in the post-Roman period, although the earliest version is preserved in a 12th-century manuscript.[36] In this account, Tristan is a Cornish knight sent to Ireland to fetch an Irish princess, Iseult, as a bride for his ruler King Mark, possibly with a view to moderating hostilities between the two countries. Tristan and Iseult fall in love on the voyage home after sharing a magic potion, so bringing strife into the Cornish court rather than peace with Ireland. Archaeologically, the Irish presence in both Wales and Cornwall is signalled by the distribution of monumental pillars with Irish names inscribed in ogham (Chapter 5, p. 466). The 'long stone' near Fowey was actually read as 'Drustan' by several scholars, thus strengthening the Cornish connection to a such a degree that it was renamed on maps.[37] However, a recent 3-D imaging of the inscription by 'ambient occlusion' read the name as *Cirisius*, as indeed had the earliest antiquaries, Camden and Borlase.[38] There is also a case that the Pictish warrior Drust son of Talorc was the original Tristan. None of this will inhibit the random seeker of romantic connections. But as this book attempts to demonstrate, the real formative Britain is both larger and much more interesting than a few names snatched from the thicket.

Five British poets are mentioned by the compilers of *Historia Brittonum* (para 63): Aneirin, Blwchbardd, Cian, Taliesen and Talhaearn. Of these, works purporting to have originated by two of the bards have survived: the Poems of Taliesen (*Canu Taliesin*, CT) and the Book of Aneirin (*Llyfr Aneirin*, LA). The 14th-century *Book of Taliesen* concerns Britons of the kingdom of Rheged, its king Urien, Maelgwn king of Gwynedd, who held court at Castell Deganwy, and Cynan Garwyn, king of Powys.[39] The *Book of Aneirin* contains the heroic poem *Y Gododdin*, in two versions (A and B) written on vellum in hands of c. 1250.[40] The older of the two (Text B) derives from a lost manuscript in Old Welsh, probably of the 9th or 10th century.[41] In the Brythonic literature, the big question is which texts (and how much of them) actually refer to the early first millennium.[42] J. T Koch's recent analysis resulted in a list of eight examples (Table 6.1) in which events of the 5th to 7th centuries seem to be reported.[43]

Besides being one of the sources richest in detail, the *Gododdin* is the primary candidate for a poetic product with roots in the 6th century.[44] The events that generated this outpouring of praise and grief have been attributed to an unsuccessful attempt by north Britons to stem the advance of Anglo-Saxon invaders.[45] English penetration north of the Humber had reached almost to the line of the River Tees when a band of Britons based at Dun Eidyn (Edinburgh) in Gododdin (i.e. Votadini) territory resolve to put a stop to the encroachment. They work each other up into a battle rage, and 300 warriors or possibly 363 (three hundred, three score and three) set off southwards and eventually encounter the army of the heathen Saxons at the old Roman camp at Catterick (Catraeth). Only one

Table 6.1 Texts containing material probably referring to events of the 5th to 7th centuries

1 *Marwnad Cunedda* National Library of Wales MS Peniarth 2 (Llyfr Taliesin) 69.9–70.15. Dealing with events of around 430 AD.

2 *Y Gododdin* Cardiff MS 2.81 (Llyfr Aneirin). Dealing with Battle of Catraeth mid- to late 6th century. Text B2, B1, A.

3 *Trawsganu Kynan Garwyn* Peniarth 2.45.9–46.5 (Ifor Williams *Canu Taliesin* I); referring to events of 570–610.

4 *Awdlau* (long poem) addressed to Urien of Rheged (Canu Taliesin II-IX); referring to events of 570–595.

5 *Eneit Oweinab Vryen* Penairth 2, 67.18–68.4 (Canu Taliesin X).

6 *Awdlau* addressed to Gwallawg fab Lleëmmawg (Canu Taliesin XI-XII); referring to events of 570–610.

7 *Moliant Cadwallon* NLW Add. Mss 14907; referring to events of 630–634.

8 *Marwnad Cynddylan* NLW Ms 4973b 108a–109a; referring to events from 5 August 642, when Oswald of Northumbria was killed, to 15 November 655, Battle of Winwaed.

(or three) survive the slaughter and return north, where Aneirin composed his elegy for the lost warriors.

These events were attributed by Jackson to c. 600 AD.[46] Recent analysis prefers a scenario in which the Gododdin's enemies at Catraeth were mainly fellow Britons under Urien of Rheged and Gwallawg of Elmet and the battle took place not around 600, but earlier, around 570.[47] Angles were also involved in the battle, fighting on the side of Urien. In the Northumbrian area, both Bernicia and Deira were seen as already Anglo-British.[48] The mixed character of the community at Catterick was sketched in a recent compilation of earlier observations and excavations. Cist burials were seen as British and Christian, small-long brooches, a great square-headed brooch and textiles as belonging to Anglian culture. The archaeological verdict was

> the fact that the early Anglian occupation evidence is dispersed suggests that by the late 5th and 6th centuries either the area was under Anglian dominance, or, more probably, that the Anglian settlement pattern was integrated with that of the indigenous population.[49]

Warlord animosity would explain why the men of Gododdin might trot down the line of the A1, apparently bypassing the Angles in Bernicia, not to fight their invading compatriots at Catterick Bridge in Yorkshire but to settle a score with other warlords. Ethnicity was not then determinant, since oppositions were built on temporary alliances and enacted in a 'highly volatile political scene in which warriors struggled for supremacy using hostages, treasure and cattle'.[50] Ethnic alignments only became important later: 'it is in the political and intellectual developments of the 7th century that we first see interests decisively polarise along English v non-English lines'.[51] This is one of the many changes that mark the 7th-century transition from a 'heroic' to a Christian Britain, in line with the attendant materiality (Chapters 2–5, passim).

The close conjunctures with archaeology are few, since metaphors rain thick and fast, and for some the poem is all the product of ideological hyperbole, full of sound and fury and signifying very little. But Jenny Rowland shows that a number of the elements of the story are historically acceptable, and without excessive elaboration: a band of hot-headed young warriors spend a year partying somewhere near Edinburgh, at the court of Mynyddog, a king of Gododdin at the height of his powers. Then they mount an expedition without him, but probably with his blessing, and go off to the south, looting and burning. They fight on horseback, charging with long lances, throwing-spears, stabbing-spears and slashing-swords from the back of horses, which were also intimately involved in the fighting. In this they resembled late Roman light cavalry – which might in the event have got its ideas from Celtic recruits. They are eventually cornered at Catraeth and massacred with only a handful of survivals. The style of the poem 'a consolation through panegyric' means that the objective of the expedition and the cause of its failure would not necessarily be mentioned. But Rowland thinks it is unlikely to have been a strategic move directed against English settlement or an expansionist expedition or a grudge encounter between British kingdoms; she sees it rather as 'a straightforward raid with no special mission', justified, as in the poem, by exuberance and adventure.[52]

The poem is also mediated in transmission, distinguished from the Irish by having a Roman tradition, but here too 'the waters of [the] native tradition have been muddied somewhat by the influx of classical and Judeo-Christian traditions', often self-evident: 'in the poem that Taliesen recites in response to the queries of Maelgwn Gwynedd . . . Old Testament,

Classical and Welsh traditions come together with a resounding thud'.[53] Although two of the warriors have Biblical names, the Christianity as far as it goes is Roman: after the battle there is to be a welcome in heaven 'in perfect union with the Trinity'.[54]

The Gododdin resembles heroic poetry in the way that a sleepover of teenage boys resembles parliament – rhythmic, repetitive, emotional, boasting and bonding. It is hard to grasp the kind of power that the recitation must have had without a modern rendering (and I hope I will be forgiven for trying). It is done by freely extracting and contracting the epithets applied to named but mainly unknown members of the war band and then imagining them shouted out by different voices to the beat of the drums:

> Neirthiad went to the front and fought
> Tudfwlch the Tall made a space in the spears
> Erthgi the lonely thinker
> Blaen the legendary drinker
> Rheithfyw solid as stone
> Cynon stung like a snake
> Cydywal splintered shields
> Breichior never runs backwards
> Llifau never gives up
> Buddfan the galloping colt
> Gwenaby preferred fighting to farming
> Isag the smoothest of killers
> Ceredig, well-mannered artist
> Caradog charged like a boar
> Eithinyn roared like a bull
> Crafty old Cadfannan strong as an ox
> Gwrfelling cut through the spears like a reaper
> Bradwen held on to the mane of the wolf – Died fighting like three
> Marchlew the fastest rider showered spears from the back of his chestnut horse
> routing the English rabble.[55]

References to the real

The warriors of the Gododdin ride horses with battle harness, accompanied by hounds, wear dark blue mail, carry spears and swords and lime-white shields; they dress in purple and sport brooches and gold torcs; they feast in a hall, drink the 'sweet yellow ensnaring' mead from silver goblets and wine from glass vessels. All of these are archaeologically possible. Four verses in a row start 'wearing a brooch'; 'Wearing a brooch, a warrior, the net of the enemy, with the swoop of the eagle'; 'wearing a brooch, in the front rank, like a wolf in fury'; 'wearing a brooch in the front rank armed in the battle shout'; 'wearing a brooch, in the front rank wherever he went, breathless in the presence of a girl'.[56] Jackson takes the breathless warrior (Madog) to be 'modest with women', but like the other epithets it seems more likely to be an aspirational norm rather than a quirk: Madog's response was that of a real man, highly susceptible to a woman's powers. The brooch was presumably of the penannular type, of which modest examples have been found in the British areas, and it was an elite badge of some significance. The expectation in the later 6th century would be a bronze penannular brooch with splayed terminals decorated with red enamel inlay (Chapter 2, p. 83). Jackson distinguishes between *kaeawc* in version A2–5 from the gold torques (*eurdochauc*) worn by the 300 in version B8.[57] The torque/torc is conventionally a neck ornament of the pre-Roman Iron Age, but a piece of twisted metal would be enough to give it the name. A silver hoop with flat terminals found in the Norrie's Law hoard (Fife) has been identified as a torc worn around the neck.[58] Alternatively, 'wearing gold torcs' might be a trope for a seasoned warrior, shorthand for any gold ornament, or, less usefully, 'an empty formula of archaic origin preserved in heroic poetry'.[59] What glitters in these fragments, more than gold in earth, is the love of comrades and defiance to the enemy. The rhythmic and repetitive strophes (W. *gorchanau*) have their analogy in the north British *pibroch*, variant ripples of dying cadence played on the bagpipes after a feast, in which the combination of grief, pride and alcohol still raises tears in the eyes of the diners of today.

A different kind of reality steals upon us from the recognition that these are people with families. The Gododdin text, as inherited, contains the famous lullaby to a child (called Dinogad) who is clearly enamoured of the family dogs, Giff and Gaff. It is of another time, being inserted by a later copyist, but it is perhaps semi-legitimate to share some of its family sentiment in the context of early Britain. Here is an attempt at an informal evocation in nursery rhyme mode:

Your father's gone hunting
Out on the sand
Spear on his shoulder
Club in his hand
Leathers and spur
Seek feathers and fur

You father's gone hunting
Up in the hills
Many eyes watching
For whatever he kills
Leathers and spur
Seek feathers and fur

Giff and Gaff, go, go!
Fetch, fetch, find, find
The springing hounds leap
On the staggering hind

What will he bring us
Your clever old man?
A wild boar, a roebuck
A hare if he can

Perhaps he will paddle
Where kingfishers drink
And spear us a salmon
All silver and pink

One thing is certain
And I don't tell a lie
It won't get away
Unless it can fly[60]

Of all the cultures in our island, those of the British (Cornish, Welsh, Cumbrian, north British) have fared worse from the scythe of time, and linguists are having to dig deep to rediscover them. It is certain that most of the island was once populated by p-Celtic speakers, who could probably understand the q-Celtic variants of vocabulary used in Ireland (e.g., map = mac, son of). The first five numbers *yan, tan, tethera, wethera, pimp* survive in Cumbrian sheep counts, and traces of the Welsh version: *ein, tein, tethera, wethera, pimp, sethera, leathera, overa, covera, dic* survived not only in Wales and Cumbria but also in the Lincolnshire Wolds and the Cambridgeshire Downs.[61] Some identifiable places earn a mention, such as those of the 'Three perpetual harmonies of the Island of Britain' listed in *The Welsh Triads* no. 90: one at the island of Afallach (Avallon, Glastonbury), the second at Caer Garadawg (perhaps Caer Caradoc in Shropshire, or Salisbury, but there are other candidates) and the third at Bangor (Bangor Is-coed, Flint). The harmonies in question refer to religious chanting: 'in each of these places there were 2400 religious men; and of these 100 in turn continued each hour of the twenty-four hours of the day and night in prayer and service to God, ceaselessly and without rest for ever'.[62] Later medieval literature captures certain administrative terms that may have some relevance for our period. The kingdoms of post-Roman Wales were divided into *cantrefs*, subdivided into *commotes*. Each kingdom had a central court with a timber hall for the royal family and 24 officers: judge (*ynad llys*), steward (*distain*), falconer (*hebogydd*), head huntsman (*Pencynydd*), head groom (*penwagstrawd*) and page (*gwas ystafell*) together with the bard, porter, butler, server, cook, priest and doctor. The people lived in *trefs*, farmsteads, obliged to provide food, horses, dogs and falcons to the court.[63] These open windows on vistas of uncertain date and limited focus but serve to emphasise that from Wales, as from Pictland and Cornwall, huge amounts await rediscovery. But archaeologists need to dig deeper still, and I hope we are.

Heroic Literature of the Anglo-Saxons: Beowulf

The contribution of the newcomers in the south-east of the island to the heroic canon was *Beowulf*, a poem of some 3,182 lines in Old English; however, it does not directly concern the English but the people of their homelands. The poem describes the adventures of the title character, a Geat hero (from east Sweden) who as a young man crosses the Baltic to visit the hall of the Danish king Hrothgar, which, at the time in question, was under repeated attack from a monster, Grendel, who dwelt in a nearby dark tarn. When Grendel attacks the hall (the building carried the name *Heorot*) Beowulf is ready for it and hacks off one of its arms, which he triumphantly nails to the gable. Grendel's mother then strikes back, inflicting more casualties. Beowulf pursues her down through the lake water into her lair and slays her in an underwater cave. He is rewarded for his daring and returns to his homeland among the Geats laden with gifts, which he gives to his own lord, the proud Hygelac. Beowulf is subsequently elected king of the Geats and rules peacefully for 50 years. However, in his declining years the old warrior is called out to defend his people against a rampaging dragon spreading contagion throughout the land. Ageing and deserted by all his lieutenants except Wiglaf, he succeeds in killing the dragon but dies of his wounds and is buried in a mound overlooking the sea.[64]

The poem survives in only one version written down in Wessex about AD 1000. Linguistic evidence suggests it probably assumed its present form in an Anglian territory at a date between 700 and 900 AD. Scholarly options include Northumbria before 735, Mercia at the time of Offa, 757–796, and East Anglia in the 8th century.[65] There are enough uncontroversial references in the poem to agree that the actual events it describes took place in the 5th/6th century in what are now south-east Sweden (Scania), land of the Geats, and Denmark. The temptation to bend Beowulf to the needs of history is therefore strong, but the metaphorical and mythical character of the language also invites interpretations focused on creative litera- ture and allegory. Its potential as an archaeological source is perhaps as strong as any in the genre. Many of the artefacts and cultural practices mentioned evoke the material culture of north-west Europe between 400 and 800.[66] However, as in previous examples, we shall note a confrontation, in text as in archaeology, between those who hail the surfacing of a cultural norm and those who view the poem, as they view burial, as an individual expression made at a particular conjuncture with a high level of rhetoric and drawing eclectically on a wide and deep cultural reservoir.[67]

The broader Germanic picture

Chadwick's survey of all the pre-Viking northern literature shows that it includes the doings of some characters otherwise known to history. There are remarkably few of them: Eor- menric (the Goth) who committed suicide at the imminent invasion of the Huns (c. 370); Attila (aka Aetla, Atli, Etzel), their leader, who died in 453; the Burgundian king Gunthere (Gundicarius) who was defeated by the Roman general Aetius in 435; Theodric the Ostro- goth (aka Dietrich von Bern) who ruled Italy 489–526; Hygelac, a Danish king who cam- paigned disastrously against Franks and Frisians in c. 520; and Theodberht the Frank who defeated Hygelac and ruled 534–548. The early literature reviewed by Chadwick makes no mention of anyone later than Alboin, king of the Langobardi, who died in 572.[68]

Chadwick concluded that the heroic literature of the Germanic north reflected a real historical process – the breaking of the Roman war machine, the rise of the reckless warlord and the achievements of the greatest of them, Attila the Hun.[69] This resulted in a radical change of ideological allegiance – from local deities to individual war leaders. About 70 passages in Beowulf refer to Christianity, but always to the Old Testament. The focus here is on Genesis, identifying Grendel and his mother with the clan of Cain who had been expelled from the Garden of Eden and the evil race of giants, most of whom God destroyed with the Great Flood. Even though Sutton Hoo was not to be discovered for another 27 years, Chadwick thought that the burial rites described in Beowulf (a ship burial and a mound burial) were determinant in placing the events in the 5th/6th cen- tury,[70] while the Christian allusions placed the composition of the poem after Caedmon's *Creation* of c. AD 660.[71] A hundred years after Chadwick, Lotte Hedeager developed the theme into a more specific thesis, claiming an intellectual and possibly a military take- over of the northern European political agenda by the Huns, reflected in art, burial rite and attitude.[72]

The magic and the monsters have inhibited many scholars from accepting the *Beowulf* poet as a descriptive witness to his/her times. J.R.R. Tolkien and many after him stressed that this was the work of a creative artist, able to call real things into service from wide sources to deliver moral verdicts and tragic cadences. The confrontation between Danish kingship and a relict race of giants suggests that an allegory was at work. For Tolkien, who was subsequently to try his own hand at heroic literature in *The Lord of the Rings*, the allegori- cal enemies were death and evil.[73] Michael Alexander stressed the epic (as opposed to the merely heroic) character of the poem and saw in Beowulf a defender of all mankind against its adversaries, with tragedy as the inevitable companion of triumph. While the model of good governance is the patriarchal ruler in the hall, lapses in loyalty to the warrior code mean that court and dynasty are subject to constant risk of destruction.[74]

A more specific allegory has been advanced by Frans Herschend, who sees the poem as a dramatisation of a religious war of the 6th century of which one outcome was that the rituals of votive deposits in a lake were superseded by a cult regulated by the leader in the hall.[75] Grendel and his female divine ancestor, resident in the marshes and lakes, represent the cult of votive deposits and accessible worship inferred at sites of bogs and lakes. Grendel's enemy is the new order of royal leadership, abrogating to itself the authorities of cult specialists. Spiritual benefits are now to be won by service under arms rather than votive deposits. In this way the arbiters of truth move from the marsh to the hall, but not without a struggle, since these matters are deeply felt. This narrative has also been revealed in some detail by the archaeological sequences at Tissø, Gudme and elsewhere (see Chapter 3).

References to the real

After the discovery of the Mound 1 ship burial at Sutton Hoo in 1939, its relationship with *Beowulf* became a hot topic, each using the other to redefine itself.[76] This relationship would have been warmed up by a mutually acceptable date, but while literary considerations put the composition of Beowulf into the 8th or 9th century, the Sutton Hoo burial tempted it back into the early 7th century.[77] However, as recent commentators continue to emphasise, *Beowulf* is not an annal but a work of the imagination using the conventional apparatus of heroic poetry, so 'no linguistic, historical, or archaeological fact compels us to anchor Beowulf within reach of Sutton Hoo'.[78] Potentially the poet can draw on anything that happened before its composition, so that any artefact identified in its corpus only offers a *terminus post quem*. A consideration of the latest researches at Sutton Hoo suggests that wealthy burials are subject to pressures of the same kind as poetry – they represent not a cultural norm but a selective and creative response to a historical event, drawing on a wide range of symbolic artefacts and actions from a common northern European stock; in other words, the rich and ritualised burials are poems themselves.[79]

The idea that the artefact repertoire of *Beowulf* was not confined to the England of the 7th century was understood by one of the first scholars who attempted to examine it archaeologically.[80] Rosemary Cramp used the known archaeology to assist the interpretation of the poem and the poem to enrich the meaning of the archaeology. Thus the Beowulf helmets conform to the type known from 7th/8th century Sweden and England (as opposed to the conical *spangenhelm* that remained in use from Roman times to the 11th century), so explaining its protective ridge and chain mail neck curtain.[81] Hrothgar's description of Grendel's sword as covered with gold plates engraved with runes and depicting the Flood overwhelming the Race of Giants is made credible by comparison with the Snartemo sword from Norway, dated c. 500 AD.[82] The real sword does not date the fictional sword or urge us to go looking for it; it only raises confidence that such a thing could have been made, whether in the time of Grendel's ancestors, the time of Hrothgar, or the time of the poet. At the time Rosemary Cramp was writing, Yeavering had yet to be published and the imposing hall at Borg had yet to be discovered (p. 96). But even with the materials then to hand, she could discern the nature of the hall and the *brydbur* set apart from it where Hrothgar and his queen retired for the night. The description of the hall *Heorot* aligns with buildings made from vertical planks clamped with iron and equipped with a porch to provide an entry without bringing in the weather. Some other features may have morphed into metaphor, but 'a gold-plated shingle roof is at least imaginable'.[83]

It may seem that the archaeology has become less specific as it has become more vocal. This is exactly so. The researches of archaeologists have illustrated a world that has become more complex as its repertoire has become richer and more varied. In no way does this inhibit its dialogue with literature; it has simply become a dialogue of equals by which both are enlarged. It should be emphasised that the dialogue on either side is very far from exhausted and can be enhanced, using Cramp's abstemious and disciplined approach, as archaeology adds year by year to its tally. Merely to flag up the possibilities suggested by equivalence, it can be noted that the Beowulf poet refers to buildings with beams, rafters, gables, a polished floor and doors with bars and hinges; outbuildings and sleeping arrangements; burial in a ship and in a mound; a ship with a snake-head prow, tarring, an anchor; spears, bows and arrows, patterned swords, chain mail, boar-crested helmets, shields with gold boss and wooden buckler; a gold standard with boar's head crest, a crown, gold banners, gold collars, horn, armlets, tapestry, saddle, a monstrous glove, lyres, necklets, heirlooms, ancient treasure, ale cup, wine flagons, goblets and dishes.[84] These are all accredited or plausible stage props for Britain in the 5th to 7th century.

Seamus Heaney's rendering of *Beowulf* is perfect for our times, as it has not only given us a great poem in modern English but reawakened the archaeological appetite by prompting the recognition, biography and significance of numerous objects. Serving for many other examples is the elegy uttered by 'the last survivor of a forgotten race' who had gathered up a treasure and buried it in a mound:

> Now earth hold what earls once held and heroes can no more . . . it was mined from you first by honourable men. My own people have been ruined by war; one by one they went down to death, looked their last on sweet life in the hall. I am left with nobody to bear a sword or burnish plated goblets, put a sheen on the cup. The companies have departed. The hard helmet, hasped with gold, will be stripped of its hoops; and the helmet-shiner, who should polish the metal of the war-mask, sleeps; the coat of mail that came through all fights, through shield-collapse and cut of sword, decays with the warrior. Nor may webbed mail range far and wide on the warlord's back beside his mustered troops. No trembling harp, no tuned timber, no tumbling hawk swerving through the hall, no swift horse pawing the courtyard. Pillage and slaughter have emptied the earth of entire peoples.[85]

The Old Testament

As many but by no means all readers will be aware, the Judeo-Christian canon is preserved in two collections, the Old Testament (OT) representing the history and opinions of the people of Israel and their stormy relationship with their single male divinity (Jehovah); and the New Testament (NT), which centres on the life and teachings of the prophet Jesus Christ, who lived and worked in Palestine between 4 BC–29 AD. The two collections are different in their burden: the New Testament is a moral programme which urges the acceptance of all humans as God's creatures, who should act with understanding towards each other under whatever government, motivated by a belief or hope of a better life to come after death. The Old Testament is a moral history of the Jewish people from the creation of the world (Genesis), to their development under various types of government (Numbers and Judges), their enslavement by the Egyptians and eventual escape (Exodus) and their arrival in Palestine, which they conquer from the occupants (the Philistines) under a number of successful male leaders claiming to enjoy a covenant with God (Samuel, Kings). The OT was not written down in the order it eventually took. Fragments of Exodus, Numbers and Judges originate before 1000 BC; the history of David (Samuel 2 and 1) in the 10th and 9th century BC, Kings in the 7th and 6th century, the Song of Songs in the 4th century, Jonah in the 3rd, the book of Daniel and the Psalms in the 2nd and the Wisdom of Solomon in the 1st century BC. The story line covers the arrival of Abraham from Mesopotamia in the Bronze Age, the enslavement of the Israelites in Egypt, their escape c. 1200 BC and the establishment of a kingdom in Judea in the 10th–9th century BC. It is the latter, the emergence of the kingdoms under Samuel, Saul, David and Solomon, that presents the clearest history and provided messages attractive for early medieval people. Often belligerent in tone, its ethos is essentially that of conquest and state building in the Late Bronze Age and early Iron Age, its events and thinking complemented, corroborated or adjusted in many cases by modern archaeology.[86]

It would seem that the Old Testament, and the figure of David in particular, provided matter most in tune with the 'heroic' ethos and dominated the Christian attributes of the British Isles until the later 7th century, when Christ and his teachings superseded them.[87] The islands therefore accepted two successive sets of ethics, the first emulating the conquering and state building of the Jewish peoples and the second equating more to the community-based teachings of Jesus. This appears to be reflected in the transition between Fm 1 and Fm 2 as seen in the archaeology of settlement, burial, sculpture and manuscripts outlined in earlier chapters.

For the post-Roman peoples of Britain and Ireland, it must have been a deep thrill to encounter an ancient text about the struggles of a people to survive, aided by a god, prophets, heroes and miraculous deeds. The texts also contain fundamental reflections on government which would have influenced the leaders of early Britain and Ireland. The moral theme of the 10th/9th century BC *Samuel* is an argument about whether a nation is best protected by fair judgement, the mollification of God or the election of a good war leader. This dilemma (still with us today) was particularly pertinent for communities newly bereft of the *pax romana*. In the Old Testament, lamentation follows the capture of the Ark of God by the Philistines ('*Ichabod* – the glory is departed from Israel'), and the people insist that Samuel find them a king. Samuel is hesitant about this strategy and warns them of the consequences: 'he will take your sons and make them instruments of war and your daughters to confectioners, cooks and bakers, he will take your fields and vineyards and olive groves and give them to his servants'.[88] This wise caution is ignored by the people, and Saul finds himself appointed as the first all-powerful king. Royal paranoia soon follows: the rise of David, son of Jesse, through success in battle and the smiting of Goliath presents a challenge. David increases his profile by making love to Saul's son Jonathan and marrying his daughter Michal, but the more potent edge of Saul's jealousy was directed at David's body count. He had to listen the jubilation of the women who danced as they sang: 'Saul hath slain his thousands, David his ten thousands.' David presented his prospective father in law with 200 Philistine foreskins as a bride price for Michal – double the number asked for.[89] David was a successful rather than a moral leader. He helps himself to more wives, including other people's, and occasionally runs amok. Returning from his successful recapture of the Ark of God, David 'danced before the lord with all his might' to the sound of numerous musical instruments. Reproved by his wife for leaping about naked in front of the handmaids, he countered that he did it before the lord, and as for the handmaids 'of them shall I be had in honour'. When he died in c. 837 BC, David had been a shepherd boy, head hunter (Goliath), war leader, poet, musician, promiscuous lover of both sexes and had established a dynasty. Most importantly, he was beloved of God, a lucky king. Given this key attribute, the others were no bar to his being adopted as a role model for early medieval kingship in the British Isles.[90]

That a move from warrior to spirit power was already on the agenda is probably indicated by the popularity of Daniel, another iconic figure. The Book of Daniel, probably written down in 165 BC,[91] describes someone who is more nearly priest than king and celebrates the obstinacy of the true believer and its rewards: the stories concern the effective power of a great invisible god over kings. Daniel is one of a number of captive Chaldeans taken to Babylon by the conquering Babylonian king Nebuchadnezzar along with their sacred vessels, in the early 6th century BC. Daniel out-performs other palace seers in the interpretation of the king's troubled dreams and is consequently made a great man and ruler of the Babylonian district, bringing his fellow believers Shadrach, Meschach and Abednego with him into the administration. From the first, Daniel maintains his own diet and his own form of worship to his own god, but survives through his talents in relieving royal anxiety. Nebuchadnezzar sets up a gold monument in the plain of Dura and demands that all worship it. When Shadrach, Meshach and Abednego refuse, they are cast into the burning fiery furnace but astonish the king by singing lustily in praise of their god. They emerge without a hair of their head being singed, and a decree ensures that any one speaking against them in future will be cut into pieces and their house made into a dunghill. Nevertheless, Nebuchadnezzar falls and is driven away to eat grass and grow nails like bird's claws. His son and successor Belshazzar subsequently held a great feast at which a hand appeared and wrote the words *Mene, mene, tekel, upharsin* on the wall. Daniel is brought in and interprets the words as referring to the kingdom itself: its days are about to be *numbered* and found to be *finished*, and the kingdom itself *weighed in a balance (and found wanting)* and thereafter *divided* (between the Medes and the Persians). Belshazzar is duly slain and succeeded by the Medean Darius. These monarchs never learn: Darius decrees that no-one shall make petition to anyone but himself on pain of being cast into the den of lions. But to the king's regret, it is Daniel who is denounced, and he is duly cast into the lions' den, since the Law of the Medes and Persians is irrevocable. However, the lions had their mouths shut by an angel, and Daniel comes out in the morning light untouched. In a vengeful twist, those who accused him, along with their women and children, are thrown to the lions, which 'break all their bones in pieces'.

Daniel was a shamanistic figure given to visions, sometimes brought on by fasting ('I ate no pleasant bread, neither came flesh or wine in my mouth, neither did I anoint myself at all until three whole weeks were fulfilled').[92] He saw strange beasts coming out of the sea: a lion with eagle's wings, a bear with three ribs in its mouth, a leopard with four heads and four wings on its back and a dreadful beast with iron teeth and horns, one emerging horn with eyes and a mouth 'speaking great things'. These powerful visions were construed as prophecies concerning the future political struggles of western Asia: during which only the people that 'do know their God shall be strong, and do exploits' can prevail. It is beyond my competence to assess the potency of this intoxicating text in later times. But it can be seen that for the historical people of first-millennium Britain the encounter with this allegory came at an excellent moment: as kingdoms formed, it showed how by invoking an absent but all-seeing power inspired clerics could tame local tyrannies. To mobilise the power of the divinity required a harsh asceticism that would be practised by the vanguard of the monastic movement in Syria, Egypt, Italy, southern France and eventually in Ireland, Scotland and the British west. The practices it promotes, especially the colleges of spiritual specialists, personal deprivation, the cult of relics, the programming of the ritual year, the magic of holy water – which powered the movement of insular monasticism – all seem closer to the prehistoric roots of the islands and more readily associated with the Old Testament than the new.

Relating to Formative 2

The New Testament

The results drawn from Chapters 2–5 suggested that Christianity in Britain was largely not signalled in material culture until the end of the 7th century, and it then leads the ideological field for 150 years. However, this was no Damascene revelation: Christianity was a belief system familiar to the British and indeed the English from Roman times. Knowing about it, accepting its precepts and institutionalising it within government are three separate stages of conversion, the first two barely detectable by archaeology. As seen in previous chapters, the materiality of Christianisation is not evident in artefacts, burial or sculpture until the third quarter of the 7th century, when it comes in a rush and drives the philosophy of politics in the form of northern monasticism until the 9th century.

Writing in Britain was largely (but not wholly) a gift of Christianity, a religion of the book, so it is understandable that the greater part of manuscript production and texts surviving from this period should be dedicated to Christian themes. Jesus Christ was a historical figure who lived in Palestine, then under Roman rule, and preached a doctrine of equality under a single omnipotent and all-seeing God. He made extensive analogy of God as a father and himself as His only son. This was probably the main reason that he fell foul of the Roman authorities and was executed by crucifixion between 26 and 37 AD, while Tiberius was emperor. His life and ideas were recorded in the nearly contemporary *Gospels* in four versions, written by the evangelists Matthew, Mark, Luke and John. These form the main components of the *New Testament* and are anthologised with the story of Christ's followers after his death (*Acts of the Apostles*), letters of the preacher Paul to various early communities (*Epistles*), and the *Book of Revelation* (the *Apocalypse*), a mystical tract predicting the downfall of Rome and written by John, a prophet of Ephesus at a time of Christian persecution under the emperor Domitian in the later 1st century. Since the four Gospels reported the events of the life of Christ through the eyes of different observers, the set of four was prefaced by a *concordance* which showed which stories were mentioned four, three, two times or only once. These 'Eusebian Canons' were presented in a series of illuminated arches that provided early medieval artists with an attractive display area.

Forty-three illuminated Gospel books and one Bible survive from Britain and Ireland, over half of all the 78 known illuminated insular manuscripts.[93] The Lindisfarne Gospels of c. 700 contains the four Gospels, and the Codex Amiatinus of c. 700 contains the Old Testament and New Testament in a single volume or *pandect*. The next most popular genre is the Psalter, containing an anthology of Jewish hymns (psalms), the earliest probably owed to King David himself. Nine psalters can be attributed to Fm 2 including the vivid picture of the Psalmist in action in BL Cotton Vespasian A1.[94] The early output is not all homily: there are two copies of Bede, a copy of Pliny's *Natural History* and even some extracts from Ovid's *Ars Amatoria* glossed in Old Welsh (Bod ms auct. F.4.32). Only 14 places of production of manuscripts in insular style have been identified, and of these only nine are in Britain and Ireland, emphasising the immense losses of all kinds of early manuscripts in the Viking wars.[95]

The Christian package rewrote the pagan rituals in words, music, symbol and iconography, absorbing some of the pre-existing religious attributes of the island and importing others that were embedded within the Christian canon. Examples of the former are the cult of relics, the tonsure and (more arguably) the date of Easter, the spring festival and the relationship of animal and man.[96] Examples of the latter are the evangelists' symbols: for

Figure 6.2 Evangelist portrait (St John), with his symbol of the eagle, clutching his book, from the Lindisfarne Gospels. St John wears a wine red cloak over a green shift and sits on a blue cushion.

(BL Cott. Nero DIV, f209v; Image provided and licensed by British library Board)

St Matthew the man, for Mark the lion, for St Luke the calf and for St John the Eagle (Figure 6.2). The behaviour patterns required by the Christian church were prescriptive and affected every part of life, every view of the landscape and every room in the house. These things may have been as much sought after as imposed, since people of a religious leaning would wish to adopt the whole package and even enlarge it. The documents make clear how the Ten Commandments and the fear of hell were used as an effective method of social control, exercised through laws about sex, property and personhood overseen by a hierarchy of priests and bishops. There were surely behavioural restrictions in pagan times, but the Christianisation of the insular communities must have required a fundamental revolution in living and attitudes to life.

The principal new ritual performance was the 'Sacrifice of the Mass' enacted by a priest every day of his life and attended by everyone once a week on Sunday, the designated holy day. This performance commemorated the life and death of Jesus Christ and reconciled the inherited need for sacrifice to propitiate the divinity and calm the worshippers, with the indoctrination of new social values. This was achieved by treating Christ's death as the last and greatest human sacrifice and prayer as the universal means of intercession. The congregation took part in the sacrifice (just as they would previously have done) by eating bread and wine that had been turned into the body and blood of Christ (through *consecration*), thus reinforcing the salvation metaphor.

The basic materiality that Christianity requires is therefore the four versions of the life and teachings of Christ (the *codex* containing the Gospels), a plate to hold the bread or host, the *paten*, and a goblet to the hold the wine, the *chalice*. Water, already vested with beneficial powers under paganism, is thrice blessed as 'holy water' and deployed by dabbing the hands and face on entry to the church via a *stoop*, sprinkling on the floor and people with a brush dipped in a bucket (the *asperges*) and washing the hands of the priest (*lavabo*). As well as having its dust laid by the asperges, the 'house of the lord' (the church building) was also perfumed by burning incense in a thurible, the job of the thurifer being to convey sweet odours to the building and its congregation. The laying of dust, the incense and the priest's vestments were all aspects of the inheritance of Rome.

The chapters before this one have cited the way that Mass was hosted in churches and the numerous ways that Christian images were selected, deployed and displayed on sculpture and other artefacts. The archaeology has also shown how the acceptance of institutionalised Christianity was slow, at 75 years, say three generations, from its introduction from abroad, and how the form in which it was embraced was clearest in the north and west and that this form was monastic, with pre-echoes in the form of collegiate spiritualisation which encouraged its adoption. In the south and east, meanwhile, Christianity appears as a more cerebral and politically expedient project of the upper classes, requiring war and capital punishment to impose and maintain it (Chapter 4, p. 340). Naturally, not all of this is reflected in the texts.

Monastic manuals

The time of the monasteries (centred on the 8th century) was one of commitment, orthodoxy and obedience, in which the logic of force was replaced as a political strategy, even among the aristocrats, by a commitment to the power of prayer and ritual. This is likely to have been a vacillation experienced through much of prehistory, as people put their faith alternately in pugnacious fighters, spirituality or wealth, investing in turn in weapons, monumentality and gold. In their transition from poet to priest, the Irish spiritual specialist still managed to discover a mystic compromise in which nature was not merely reconciled to God; it turns out that God lived in nature, much as he had before.[97] The body of devotional thought and celebration produced by the Céli Dé (servants of god) was not to reappear in Europe until Rousseau and Wordsworth, although it was always ready to break away from the central axiom the sturdier it became: Cistercians and Franciscans also sought God in nature, but with nothing like the sophistication of the Irish. The Irish nature poems are attributed to 'Mad Sweeney', king of Dal Riada, whose madness followed the battle of Mag Rath (AD 637), and he subsequently went and dwelt in the wilderness, mostly in treetops. His counterpart in Welsh literature is Myrddin Wyllt (Mad Merlin). The hermit Marbán explains to his brother Guaire, king of Connacht, why he lives in a wood, sleeping on the ground. He has a dwelling composed of two trees surrounded by fruit and animals. He can listen to 'the wind's voice against a branchy wood, on a day of grey cloud, cascades in a river; roar of rock. Beautiful are the pines which make music for me, unhired; through Christ I am no worse off at any time than you'.[98] The archaeology of these poems lies in their rejection of material culture. Thus, some of the deepest thinking in 8th-century insular life hardly leaves a footprint in the damp earth.

The Céli Dé brought in, or forcefully reapplied, new rules of comportment and deprivation that would help those to whom they might not have come naturally. The Rule of Ailbe (d. 534), which was imposed after 750, required monks not to wear red or blue or any kind of ornamentation, and, somewhat oddly, 'not to travel or leave your monastery . . . even though it be on business or to make request'. The rule of St Ciaran of Clonmacnoise (applied late 7th/early 8th century) expressed its disapproval of drawing persons into endless chatter and addiction to delicacies. The bread ration was a loaf 30 ounces in weight, but the Rule of the Céli Dé allowed for whole milk mixed with honey on the eve of festivals, although beer drinking and merry making were not allowed. Teachers fared better: a milk cow and a generous annual maintenance was the reward for teaching 150 psalms, the hymns, canticles, readings and the method of administering baptism and communion. When the students were examined, the panel before whom the psalms were recited were entitled to a supper of food and beer for five.[99]

Adomnán's Life of Columba

In the 7th century, the political focus of western Scotland was the northern territory of Dal Riada, centred on Kilmartin Glen. Being closely linked with Ulster, it was reflected in its annals, the *Annals of Ulster* and the *Annals of Tigernath* (AU, AT).[100] Perhaps the most interesting document from an archaeological viewpoint is the *Senchas Fir nAlban* (History of the Men of Alba), a short 10th-century document listing the genealogies of the Irish (Scots) settled in the British part of Dal Riada (Alba) in the 7th century. They are divided into the three clans (*cenel*) of Gabhrain, Loairn and Oengus. The document (of 70 lines) names a number of settlements and states how many houses they have (they vary from 150 to 20). Every village of 20 houses is expected to provide two seven-bench boats in the event of a call-up to battle.[101] Since the numbers are given, it is tempting to count them up and arrive at total muster for Dal Riada of 'a little over 2000 men' raised from a population of 10,000.[102]

There is some incidental detail in the *Life of Columba* (c. 521–597), written by his successor Adomnán (c. 628–704) (Life of Columba, LC). Columba (Columcille) founded the monastery on Iona in 563 and in 565 made a journey with companions up the Great Glen into the land of the Picts, presumably seeking permission to preach. On his journey they encountered the Loch Ness monster, which made its first appearance in history and tried to eat one of the holy company. Columba had a meeting with the king of the Picts, Bridei son of Mailchu, somewhere near Inverness. The text is much concerned with magic and miracles and is short on realist description or credible explanation. Columcille made white pebbles float on water and used them for healing, chanted the 44th Psalm in an unbearably loud voice, caused the gates of the royal fortress to spring open and took on Broichan, the king's wizard, in a competition to control the weather, and easily won.[103] His miraculous achievements are delivered with much gusto by his biographer, a fellow enthusiast for the new divinity. But this was after an interval of 100 years, in the course of which much had changed.

In his introduction to the edition of the *Life* published by Penguin, Richard Sharpe offers a master class in extracting historicity from saints' lives. The *Life* established the reputation of a charismatic figure of the 6th century at a moment useful to the major monastic expansion of the 8th. After his move to Iona, Columba had become a player in Irish politics.[104] He seems to have made little more than a dent in Pictish religion, although he was said to have established monasteries on that side of the Druim Alban that through his sanctity were unaffected by the plague of 664–8.[105] The references to the settlement on Iona must be those of the author, who lived and wrote there in the late 7th and early 8th century. Even so, they are thin and unspecific, noting a boundary bank, a garden, a hut, a chapel, a communal building with beams brought in from Loch Moidart.[106] There is much that is hard to grasp, but as in the case of overtly heroic literature, the reward is not so much to specify actions but to convey the 'mood and thought of the period'.[107] This is as much a benefit to archaeologists as their beloved 'incidental detail'. The lives of saints (hagiography) are full of great achievements and miracles and references to other great tales; in this they resemble a late flowering of heroic literature, the new heroes having no weapons but being immune to hardship and prone to visions.

Bede's History of the English Church and People

Bede's *History* is the acknowledged historical masterpiece of the age, being clearly written and assured in its faith. Although Bede, a monk of Jarrow, was writing a history of the English people, he was doing so in Northumbria, culturally, as we have seen, an Anglo-British territory. He travelled little (as far as we know) and the area he knew best was northern England, with authenticated documentation on church matters collected from Ireland, Pictland, Scotland, southern England, France and Italy from the late 7th century until his death in 735. He seems to have known little of Cornwall, Wales, Cumbria or Strathclyde, and he marginalised and diminished the achievements of the Britons, even though (or because) they were all around him.[108] But although championing the English takeover of Britain and its fledgling church, he seems to have been deliberately vague about contemporary Scandinavia or indeed the pagan English. His interests and records are partial: he can recount details of a dream experienced by Edwin when fugitive at the court of Raedwald of East Anglia but omits to mention the Sutton Hoo ship burial (c. AD 625), which must have constituted one of the most newsworthy and politically controversial events of the age. Nonetheless, all attempts at a historical account of the 5th to 8th century begin with Bede. The places he mentions have often triumphantly delivered their anticipated archaeological character, and the events he recorded continue to provide the historical framework for much of Formative 2[109] (Figure 6.3).

Annals and chronicles

The attraction of heroic literature for the archaeologist lies in its ability to evoke mood and purpose outside the Christian party line, and sometimes to see past the heavy censorship of the age in which it was filtered into the pre-Christian era. But annals and histories offer attractions of other kinds: they are more factual and have dates, so provide the basis of a chronological framework. Annals, as the name applies, are bare records of events noted year by year in the margin of Christian documents – such as Easter tables. The *Annals of Ulster* (vol 1 AD 431–1201) refer mainly to the area of the northern Irish Sea – Ulster and south-west Scotland, a combination known to the annalists as Dal Riada, but later entries include the Picts. The entries are often inscrutable: 626: 'A dark year'. 769: 'An earthquake and famine; and leprous disease attacked many. Abundance of oak mast.' Many concern battles, death and the burning of named but unspecific places: 672: 'The battle of Dúngal son of Mael Tuile; and the burning of Ard Macha and of the house of Taille son of Ségéne.'[110]

Figure 6.3 Places in Britain known to Bede.

(Morris 1989, Fig 3; courtesy of Richard Morris)

Easter tables were also annotated in Britain and were used to generate the two main British historical sources in Latin: *De Excidio et conquestu Britanniae*, written by a British monk, Gildas, between about 530 and 540 AD, and *Historia Brittonum*, assembled in north Wales by Nennius, a Welsh monk of the 9th century.[111] The first of these deals rather hysterically with the coming of the Saxons (*Adventus Saxonum*) and the threat to an obscure but passionate British Christianity, while the second declared itself 'a heap of all that I found, from the annals of the Romans, the writings of the holy fathers, the annals of the Irish and the Saxons and the traditions of our own old men'. So we know what to expect. In his ground-breaking research of 50 years ago, Leslie Alcock sifted through these documents in his search for King Arthur and a context for South Cadbury (Chapter 3, n.104), finding Gildas unhelpful but Nennius more revealing of 'British elements attached to Northumbrian history'. He concludes that there is a case for saying that a real, if elusive, Arthur fought battles in the south-west and perhaps in the Scottish borders.[112] However, more recent scholarship has cast doubts on the links he made.[113] The import is that the world of 6th-century Wales and Brittany was not dissimilar in its mood, ethos, customs and shifting alliances to the Irish west, the British north and English east, apart from an expected, but so far elusive, network of British monastic settlements.

Relating to Formative 3

The Anglo-Saxon Chronicle

The *Anglo-Saxon Chronicle* has a pedigree of several related versions, allowing its entries to be cross-checked and so assessed for their authority.[114] The *Chronicle* (ASC) describes the period from the establishment of the English in Britain to the time of Alfred and from there to the Viking wars and the Norman Conquest. It could be said that, together with Bede's *History of the English Church and People*, the *Anglo-Saxon Chronicle* itself contributed much to the conquest of Britain's history by the English. The text survives in six main versions (A-F), of which the oldest (A) is at Cambridge.[115] It begins in 494 and continues to the end of 891 in the hand of a single scribe – so it is a copy made around that time, probably in Winchester. For the early 10th century, it contains the only record of the later wars of Edward the Elder.[116] B and C are closely related and include *The Mercian Register*, which for the 10th century contains the record of the wars of Aethelflaed, Edward's sister.[117] D and E are also closely connected and include early northern events, so probably originate at York.[118] F is a bilingual Latin/English version made in Canterbury in the late 11th or early 12th century using A and E as its basis.[119]

The *Anglo-Saxon Chronicle* is a set of 'thick annals', in which the chronicler likes to put in the occasional aside:

> 604 Aethelfrith led his army to Chester and there killed a countless number of Britons. And thus was fulfilled Augustine's prophecy by which he said: If the Britons do not wish to have peace with us, they shall perish at the hands of the Saxons'. There were also killed 200 priests who had come there to pray for the army of the Britons. Their leader was called Brocmail, and he escaped with 50 men (E).

Examples can also be found where Northumbrians and Wessex and Mercians have different or less committed views of the same event:

> 641 – In this year Oswald, king of the Northumbrians, was slain. And Cenwealh succeeded to the kingdom of the West Saxons and held it for 31 years (C, A, B).

– In this year Oswald, king of the Northumbrians, was slain by Penda, the Southumbrian at Maserfeld on 5 August and his body was buried at Bardney. His holiness and miracles were afterwards made known in manifold ways throughout his island, and his hands are undecayed in Bamburgh. In this year Cenwealh succeeded to the kingdom of the West Saxons and held it for 21 years (E).

This priceless compendium, reviewing the experience of the English from their arrival to the Norman conquest (and beyond) and capturing the diverse viewpoints of the English kingdoms, provides a basis for a national history unmatched even by the Franks. Tensions are detectable between Northumbrian, Mercian and Wessex versions of the past, consecutively dominant kingdoms from the late 7th to the 10th century and anxious to subdue each other ('he who controls the past controls the future'). For a Germanic people, the English chroniclers knew very little about their ancestors. By the time the *Chronicle* was being compiled, the Scandinavians were the enemy.

The worlds of the *Anglo-Saxon Chronicle* and Bede are thus selective, one driven by battles and triumphant warriors, the other founded on the spiritual life and the triumph of the kingdom of God. One property of all the texts beloved by archaeologists is that they seem to provide a gazetteer of dated early medieval places, the great majority easy to identify, and this in turn presents an open invitation to go there and start digging. Even when excavations are well done, the disappointment of both parties, historical and archaeological, is due to the fact that documents, like sites, capture material of varied veracity, quality and relevance and survive variously from century to century. These sites have often inspired rough wooing, such that, thanks to their literary fame, Canterbury, Iona, Whitby were much mangled even before scientific archaeology got to them.

Sagas

The adventurers from Scandinavia who raided, settled and traded in Yorkshire and Atlantic Scotland and Ireland brought with them many aspects of their culture, religion, traditions and folk tales. These have survived in a retrospective written form largely from the 13th century or later and must be deconstructed like other anachronistic texts if they are to yield information of interest and relevance to the Formative Period. Neil Price has shown how the way that Vikings thought can be deduced from a convergence of the archaeological evidence (unspecific but contemporary), the sagas (deep and highly descriptive, but written down two–three centuries after the event), and anthropological observations of the 19th century (applied to much later people but using similar artefacts and likely to indicate similar behaviour).[120]

The Icelandic sagas describe the deeds of heroes and their manly virtues of ruthless slaughter, tricky trading, seduction of women and, more unexpectedly, sex with each other.[121] But the focus is less on kings than on farmers that make their way in the world by daring, courage, deception, prudent alliance and a sharp tongue. The actors settle Iceland (874–930) and expand into Shetland, Orkney, Caithness, the west coast and eventually Ireland. In addition to providing a basic chronology of numerous power struggles in these areas, the sagas offer an insight into Viking attitudes to the other world and to the business of this one. The quarrels are endless, mediated by combat, marriage, compensations paid in slaves and swords, and tireless voyaging. In this rich compendium of anecdote and intimate eavesdropping, one passage will have to serve for many. It is a description of how pre-Christian religion was invoked even as its experts diminished in number.

This was a very lean time in Greenland. Those who had gone hunting had had poor catches, and some of them had failed to return. In the district there lived a woman named Thorbjorg, a seeress . . . one of ten sisters, all of whom had the gift of prophecy, and was the only one of them still alive. It was Thorbjorg's custom to spend the winter visiting, one after another, farms to which she had been invited, mostly by people curious to learn of their own future or what was in store for the coming year. Since Thorkel was the leading farmer there, people felt it was up to him to try and find out when the hard times would let up. Thorkel invited the seeress to visit, and preparations were made to entertain her well, as was the custom of the time when a woman of this type was received. . . .

Late the following day she was provided with things she required to carry out her magic rites. She asked for women who knew the chants required . . . but such women were not to be found. The people of the household were asked if there was anyone with the knowledge. Gudrid answered 'I have neither magical powers nor the gift of prophecy but in Iceland my foster-mother, Halldis, taught me chants she called ward songs . . . but I intend to take no part because I am a Christian woman.' Thorbjorg answered: 'It could be that you could help the people here. and you would be no worse a woman for that.' The women formed a warding ring around the platform raised for sorcery, with Thorbjorg perched atop it. Gudrid spoke the chant so well and so beautifully that people there said they had never heard anyone recite in a fairer voice. The seeress thanked her for her chant and said that many spirits were attracted who earlier had turned their backs . . . and 'many things are now clear to me'.[122]

The Scandinavians left precocious interpretations of prehistoric burial: *Ynglinga saga* written by Snorri Sturluson in about 1225 records that Odin

ordained that all dead men should be burnt and brought on to the pyre with their property. In this fashion he spoke that every dead man should come to Valhalla with whatever property he had on the pyre; he should also enjoy what he had himself buried in the earth. But the ashes should be carried out to sea or buried down in the earth. A howe should be raised as a memorial to noblemen. And for all such persons as had achieved any distinction bauta-stones should be set up.[123]

Beliefs and images from the world of the Vikings have not been preserved in illuminated manuscripts, but a wealth of detail has been incorporated in the burials and the sculpture they left where they settled (Chapter 4, 5).

The most popular pagan hero depicted in Viking-period Britain is Sigurd the Volsung, slayer of the dragon Fafnir, both of whom later appear as players in Richard Wagner's music drama *Siegfried*. Among the scenes represented in Britto-Scandinavian art are: (1) Sigurd (Siegfried), wearing a helmet, stands in a pit and thrusts a spear into the dragon's underbelly; (2) Sigurd wearing a pointed cap roasts the dragon's heart on a stick over a fire, sometimes cut into slices; (3) Sigurd, with his thumb in his mouth, tastes the dragon's blood, so that (4) he now understands what the birds are saying; (5) Sigurd works in a smithy testing his sword and kills Reginn the smith (see Chapter 5, pp. 544–6). The choice of these episodes seems to imply that a popular poem on this theme was in circulation between about 1000 AD and the 12th century.[124] The Gosforth Cross also offers characters and episodes from Ragnarök, the downfall of gods and men. These themes of revenge and redemption are interwoven with the Christian messages carried by the crosses, notably the crucifixion scene on the Gosforth cross and the image of Woden as Christ carved on the Jelling stone. Anglo-Saxon and Viking craftsmen were aware of obvious parallels between heathen legends and Christian teaching and while the main inspiration of their art was Christian, the gods and heroes of a rich pagan past long had a voice.[125]

Pictures in books

One hundred and six manuscripts that were also illustrated survive from the England of the 10th and 11th century, and the range of topics is greatly increased beyond that of the 43 Gospel books of Fm 2. Gospels and Psalters are still the most numerous editions in circulation, but now we also have *Benedictionals* (for delivering blessings), *Calendars*, and works of Classical authors, including Boethius, Cicero and Virgil, the travelogue 'Marvels of the East', and commentaries of a phalanx of theologians. However, the number of identified scriptoria represented is still extremely small (15) and the output is overwhelmingly dominated by Canterbury and Winchester. Once again, the corpus of surviving illustrated books is unbalanced: the British and Irish regions and indeed much of the rest of England have apparently fallen silent.[126]

For archaeologists the illustrations in these manuscripts provide a rich and largely untapped source of images relating to daily life and work. The pictures still require careful deconstruction before assuming that the scenes, buildings and objects actually refer to contemporary life in Britain. In Formative 3, scribes and artists rise to the challenge of turning the Psalter's high-flown metaphors into pictures: 'Why do the heathen rage and the people imagine a vain thing?' 'Let them be as the grass upon the housetops that withereth afore it groweth up.' 'Except the Lord keepeth the city the watchman waketh but in vain.' In Harley 603, a Psalter copied at Canterbury in about AD 1000, characters rich and poor, holy and malign are depicted with equal flourish on a colourful stage[127] (Figure 6.4). Among more recent authors, another artists' favourite is Prudentius' *Psychomachia*, an allegory describing the battle for the soul with the aid of single combats between such role models as Lust and Chastity, attractive subjects for illustration.[128]

Handbooks

The English also produced two handbooks of great interest to archaeologists because they purport to describe how ordinary people went about their business. The first, *Gerefa* (i.e. reeve or overseer) is a guide to the duties of an estate supervisor, probably of Roman inspiration, parcelled with *Rectitudines Singularum Personarum* (RSP), which lists the obligations of farmworkers. These survive in CCCC 383, a 12th-century manuscript that refers to Anglo-Saxon practices. RSP adopts an officious tone:

> [24] One should in May and June and July during the summer [set land] to fallow, take out dung [from] the manure pile, build hurdles for the sheep folds, shear sheep, build, repair, set hedges, build, cut wood, weed, construct sheepfolds and make fish weirs and mills.

> [25] During autumn reap [fields] in August and September and October, mow [pasture], plant woad, gather cultivated products in to the home, thatch the thatch-roof, and to clean the fold and prepare the cattle-shed, and likewise the pigsty, before the harshness of winter comes to the estate, and also to go forth and to plough diligently.

Figure 6.4 Harley 603, f51v illustrates Psalm 103 (Vulgate), which equates to Psalm 104 (Hebrew). The text refers to *the Lord who stretches out the heavens as a curtain; sendeth the springs into the valleys, which run among the hills; gives drink to every beast of the field; and bread which strengtheneth man's heart, he planted the cedars of Lebanon, where the birds make their nests; as for the stork, the fir trees are her house; the young lions roar after their prey . . . There go the ships; there is that leviathan. These all wait upon thee, that thou may give them their meat in due season.* There are blue waves in the water and blue wisps in heaven. Green plants grow beside the lake and the landscape is marked with brown cliffs and clefts.

(BL ms Harley 603 f51v. Image provided and licensed by British library Board, fee paid)

The farmer's rental agreement makes the landlord of today's London student seem quite benign:

> tenants must pay ten pennies tax on Michaelmas day (29 September), and on the day of Martin's Mass (11 November) [he must give] twenty-three sesters of barley, and two hens; at Easter (a movable feast in March or April) [he must give] a young sheep or two pennies. And from Martin's Mass to Easter he must remain with the lord's fold as often as it comes around to him. And from the time when one first ploughs to Martin's Mass he must plough one acre each week, and collect the seed himself from the lord's barn. In addition to that, [he must plough] three acres as compulsory service on demand and two [acres] pasturage-ploughing. If he needs more grass then he may earn it in such way as one allows him to. . . . And [he] pays his hearth-penny. As one of a pair [he must] feed

a hunting dog. And each peasant pays six loaves to the lord's swineherd when he drives his drove [of pigs] to woodland-pasture.

The list of tools available would furnish a modern folk museum and leaves no doubt about the levels of competence that can be expected from an Anglo-Saxon builder, gardener or weaver:

[28] Axe, adze, billhook, chisel, plane, saw, joining iron, hook for earthenware vessels, auger, mattock, crowbar, ploughshare, coulter, and also a goad, scythe, sickle, weed-hook (hoe), spade, shovel, woad-dibble, barrow, broom, mallet, rake, fork, ladder, horse-comb, scissors, fire tongs, weighing scale and many spinning implements, a cord for hanging flax from, spindle, reel, yarn winder, weaver's slay, distaff, clothes' press, loom parts, wool comb, weaver's beam, shuttle, harness, shears, needle, mallet.

The 'Sagacious Reeve' is not a tyrant and the stipulations need not have the force of law; he is, however, running a tight outfit in a complex industry.[129]

Aelfric's Colloquy (AC) is an 11th century course-book to help Anglo-Saxon children learn Latin. The children practise their language skills by means of questions put to a wide variety of professions and trades. The Latin questions and answers are glossed in Anglo-Saxon. The text is wonderfully revealing of daily life, although this was not its purpose. Examples were given in Chapter 2, p. 123, and here is one more:

The carpenter says: 'Which of you does not need me? I make all your houses, tools and boats'

The blacksmith replies: Come off it carpenter, you couldn't bore a single hole without me. And the counsellor says: good workers, let's not argue, let peace break out and each share his skills with the others.

[AC 229–235][130]

Historical frameworks

Much of the information recorded in chronicles has been placed online (see e.g. Corpus of Electronic Texts, www.ucc.ie/celt) or gathered in landmark collections: *English Historical Documents* (EHD) or *Early Sources of Scottish History* (which includes Pictland).[131] Unlike the heroic literature, these are dominated for the most part by dated events that allow a chronological framework to be constructed. Anglo-British Northumbria and English Southumbria enjoy the lion's share of historical notice in Britain, largely focussed on themselves, from the 5th century to the 11th. Wales, Cumbria and Cornwall are scarcely noticed, and Pictland exists only as a king list and in comments by unsympathetic neighbours. The Scots do well, being closely aligned in language and politics to the Irish, who outscore all other early medieval people in north-west Europe in the intellectual range of their interests and the virtuosity of their exposition in literature. The early period is the most difficult, but commentators have made some attempt to cover Ireland and the six regions of Britain in the 5th and 6th century, even if mostly at second hand. In Britain from 600 there is a startling expansion of literary sources into Northumbria and south-east England. Thanks to Bede, this expands further in the early 8th century to Northumbria, but after his death in 735 we are feeding off scraps. The 9th century is all about the Vikings, the 10th about the triumph of Wessex over them and the 11th about the return of Viking/Norman control over much of

Britain, contended largely by the house of Wessex. This lopsided coverage obscures much of the key history of the first millennium. The old adage – absence of evidence is not evidence of absence – is always valid, but never more so than in Britain in the late first millennium. The wars with the Norse in the Moray Firth were no less catastrophic than those of Wessex against the Danes; and the leadership role of the much-maligned Macbeth in defending eastern Scotland was arguably no less admirable than that of Alfred, holding the line in southern England. But the caprice of history-writing has turned one into a national hero and the other into a theatrical villain, immortalised by Shakespeare. The dominant English story is a Churchillian saga in which threats are soberly assessed, defeats are not brushed over and the superiority of the English worn lightly. Luck is involved, but it is not necessarily dispensed by the Almighty. The Christian church is a permanent presence, sometimes well-run, sometimes degenerate, but not possessed of magical powers or even good advice. The church equates rather with 'cultural assets', and the struggle is a secular one. The English never give up; not because England's people are devoted to a dynasty but because, within the numerous little coteries each headed by a local lord, they refuse to be beaten. But in the form and quantity of their literary output, Irish, British and English writers grow ever further apart in the course of the first millennium.

Reflections

Between the 4th century and the 11th the land was full of language and languages, not all written down, not all even spoken. For example, the *Indicia monasteralia* was a sign language used to enable late Anglo-Saxon monks to communicate when silence was the rule.[132] For the refectory, 'place your three fingers as if you were putting food into your mouth'. For drinking, lay your index finger along your teeth. Hand flat over the belly means 'I need the loo'. 'The dean is coming': make as if ringing a small bell with one's hand hanging down. To ask for a book: use the right hand to turn over an imaginary page. For a martyrology, turn over the pages and make as if to cut your throat. And they could describe people. For a nun: draw a veil in the air; a layman has a beard; a laywoman has a headband or a fillet, drawn in the air by the fingers from ear to ear. A queen has an outsize veil with a crown shaped by the hands. These gestures are hard to guess, but they can be coaxed out with clues. Archaeology does this too.

Texts do not enjoy an innate primacy or set a direction for archaeologists to follow. On the contrary, the theme of this book is that literature has no prerogative to set an agenda for archaeology or vice versa; we are equal partners, equal in reward and potency. We report from parallel worlds and steal analogies at will. As Derrida used archaeology to define layers of meaning, so archaeology uses Derrida to deconstruct the messages of a monument.[133] This whistle-stop tour was intended to show how texts and illustrations reflect the preoccupations of the upper classes, the *zeitgeist*, the social drivers that leave a trail in the narratives that survive, as they do in the monuments. Perhaps as an accident of survival, they also show us a sequence of half a millennium in which the access and participation of those without history or political power emancipates and widens. The poets of *Beowulf* and the *Gododdin* and the artists of Harley 603 are not short of admirers who are confirmed in their opinion that the early tales and sketches of Britain and Ireland are among the greatest survivals from the islands. This book will succeed if it can add to this canon by drawing from archaeology a thousand more voices reporting, emoting and aspiring on every subject that was important to them.

Notes

1   Chadwick 1912, 76.
2   Chadwick 1912, 462.
3   Caerwyn Williams and Ford 1992, 12–14; Carson 2008.
4   Caerwyn Williams and Ford 1992, 97.
5   Jackson 1964.
6   Waddell 2011, 192.
7   Mallory 1992.
8   McCone 2000.
9   McCone 2000, 6–8.
10   McCone 2000, 29.
11   McCone 2000, 30.
12   McCone 2000, 83.
13   McCone 2000, 77.
14   McCone 2000, 158.
15   Waddell 2011, 201.
16   McCone 2000, 21–22.
17   Caerwyn Williams and Ford 1992, 29.
18   Waddell 2011, 194.
19   Martyrology of Oengus; Stokes 1905; Edel 1995.
20   Stokes 1905, l. 213.
21   Stokes 1905, l. 165.
22   Stokes 1905, l. 177.
23   I.e. of Kildare; Stokes 1905, l. 189.
24   Stokes 1905, l. 193.
25   Schot 2011.
26   Waddell 2011.
27   Lacey 2011.
28   Waddell 2005.
29   Grogan 2008; The 'British Israelites' formed a powerful lobby which attempted to prove that the heirs of ancient Israel resided in 19th-century Britain. Princess Tea Tephi was a daughter of King Zedekiah of Judah who had killed all his own sons, leaving her as the surviving heir of the House of David. In the 19th century she was hypothesised to have emigrated to Ireland and married a high king of the 6th century BC. The British Israelites extended this link to the British monarchy and constructed a chart connecting Queen Victoria to the House of David (so resurrecting the early medieval emulation of King David in a more fantastic form). The British Israel World Federation confirmed their belief in a link between the British monarchy and the House of David in 2001 (Wikipedia 2015–03–13).
30   Newman 1997, 225–230.
31   I.e. the later 5th century, when St Patrick, a Briton captured in an Irish raid, began preaching.
32   For example, the analysis of Irish Fm 1 appearance by Niamh Whitfield in Chapter 2, pp. 106–7. 'retrogressive' refers to the identification of contemporary objects in manuscript illustrations (Carver 1986b).
33   Ford 2008, 2.
34   Jones and Jones 1949.
35   See Hutton 2011b for pre-Christian Welsh gods.
36   Gregory 1991.
37   Radford 1951.
38   Spring and Peters 2014; Okasha 1993, 92, no.10.
39   Ford 2008, 164; Williams and Caerwyn Williams 1968.
40   *Cardiff 1*; The poem begins 'This is the Gododdin; Aneirin sang it' Jackson 1969, 22; Koch 1997.
41   Jackson 1969, 42–43.
42   Woolf 2013.
43   Koch 2013, 177–178.
44   Jackson 1969; Koch 2013.
45   Jackson 1969, Introduction.

46   Jackson 1969, 11–12. He argues for a date between 588 and 590 for the raid.
47   Koch 1997, xxii, xxiii; Clancy 2013, 163–164.
48   Hope-Taylor 1977, 282 et seq; Alcock 2003, 221, 255–266.
49   Wilson et al. 1996, 54.
50   Clancy 2013, 164.
51   Koch 1997, xliii.
52   Rowland 1995, and notes esp . 13–29, 32, 37, 39.
53   Ford 2008, 19.
54   Ford 2008, 37.
55   Author, freely abusing Jackson 1969, *passim*.
56   Jackson 1969, 116–117; Clancy 1998, 47–48 has 'betorqued' rather than 'wearing a brooch'.
57   Jackson 1969, 33–34, 101.
58   Alcock 2003, 314.
59   Jackson 1969, 34.
60   Freely fashioned by the present author after Clancy 1998, 94; Jackson 1969, 46–47, 151; Gwyn
     Williams 'Dinogad's petticoat' in Heaney and Hughes 1982, 128.
61   Rees 1963, 152.
62   Bromwich 1961, 217–218. The triads are evocative but formulaic and lacking in historical
     context.
63   Rees 1963, 153–154. The literature is 12th–13th century, and there is little evidence for the use of
     these terms before the 11th century (N. Edwards, personal communication).
64   Alexander 1973.
65   Alexander 1973, 11; Frank 1992; Newton 1993.
66   Cramp 1957.
67   Sam Newton (1993) argues for a specific link between the poem and Suffolk, the Wuffinga family
     and Sutton Hoo.
68   Chadwick 1912, 23–28.
69   Chadwick 1912, 31–40, 2010, Ch VI, VII.
70   Chadwick 1912, 52–55.
71   Chadwick 1912, 49.
72   Hedeager 2011.
73   Tolkien 1936.
74   Alexander 1973, 31–34.
75   Herschend 1992.
76   Frank 1992.
77   cf Whitelock 1951; Frank 1992; Newton 1993.
78   Frank 1992, 53–54.
79   Carver 2000.
80   Cramp 1957.
81   Cramp 1957, 61–62.
82   Cramp 1957, 65–66.
83   Cramp 1957, 71–73.
84   Wright 1957 is an accessible, down-to-earth prose translation for those tracking artefacts and
     activities.
85   Heaney 1999, 71–72.
86   The events in the story of Israel's early kings have been the subject of many excavations and
     radiocarbon dating programmes, published in *Antiquity*, e.g., Finkelstein and Piasetzky 2003; and
     reviews by Charlotte Whiting in *Antiquity* 81 (2007), 210–213.
87   The source used here is *The Bible designed to be read as Literature*, edited and arranged by Ernest
     Sutherland Bates (London: Heineman, c1944) Henceforward Bates.
88   Bates, 224.
89   First Book of Samuel; quoted by McCone 2000, 30. Presumably one ancient reason for circumci-
     sion is that an enemy cannot make away with your foreskin, assuming that is all they were after.
90   Eddius Stephanus compares Ecgfrith of Northumbria to David in the number of his victories, (*Life
     of Wilfred* Ch 20).
91   Bates, 799–824.
92   The use of fasting to bring on visions was also embraced by holy men of the formative era, but
     this may have been a prehistoric inheritance.

93 As catalogued by Jonathan Alexander (1978, 90, 216).
94 See Chapter 2, p. 118.
95 Jonathan Alexander 1978, 216.
96 Carver 2009a.
97 Carey 1999.
98 Caerwyn Williams and Ford 1992, 81–87.
99 O' Maidin 1996, 19, 31, 81, 94.
100 Anderson 1922; Bannerman 1974.
101 Bannerman 1974.
102 Alcock 2003, 50, 114.
103 LC I.1, I.37; II.33–35.
104 LC, 26.
105 LC II.46; n346.
106 LC, 66–68.
107 Tolkein 1936.
108 Alcock 2003, 9.
109 Notable examples of convergence between Bede and archaeology are the investigations by Rosemary Cramp at Monkwearmouth and Jarrow and by Brian Hope-Taylor at Yeavering.
110 Many of the sets of Annals, including *Tigernach*, the *Four Masters* and *Inisfallen* are now published on line (www.ucc.ie/celt).
111 BL Harley 3859; Alcock 1973, 22, 31.
112 Alcock 1973, 38, 81, 88, 1972, 18.
113 For a critical assessment of post-Roman sources and the significance of Arthur, see Dumville 1977, and now Halsall 2013, 85. For sources from Bede to Henry of Huntingdon (or their absence), see Woolf 2007, 1–3.
114 Whitelock 1961, foreward, xi–xviii.
115 CCCC 173.
116 Whitelock 1961, xi.
117 BL Cott. Tib Avi & Bi; Aethelflaed makes an appearance in Chapter 3.
118 BL Cott. Tib. Aiv and Ox. Bod Laud misc 636.
119 BL Cott. Domit. VIII.
120 Price 2002.
121 Halli agrees with the king that he has never seen a better axe. 'Will you allow yourself to be fucked for the axe?' said the king. 'I will not', said Halli, 'but it seems understandable to me that you would want to sell the axe for the same price that you paid for it.' *The Tale of Sarcastic Halli* in *Sagas* 2001, 711.
122 Eirik the Red's Saga trans. Keneva Kunzin in *Sagas*, 658–659.
123 Martin-Clark, 1950, 112 n1. 'bauta-stone (bautastein)' is a Scandinavian term for a standing stone or *menhir*.
124 Ellis-Davidson 1950, 124–125.
125 Ellis-Davidson 1950, 133, 138.
126 Temple 1976, 241.
127 Noel 1995; Wormald 1952.
128 Carver 1986b.
129 Addyman 1976; Harvey 1993; Wormald 1999, 387.
130 Garmonsway 1947 [Edited version of BL Cott MS Tib A iii; present author's trans.]
131 Anderson 1922 [1990].
132 Conde-Silvestre 2001.
133 Carver 2002b.

7   Narratives – reflections – legacies

Introduction

It can be seen that the labours of archaeologists, geographers, art historians and students of literature have produced new evidence in abundance, summarised in Chapters 1–6. At this stage most of this is undomesticated knowledge, offering us luxuriant growth rather than a rich harvest. It was originally collected with many different objectives and circumstances in mind – the resolution of texts, recollections or revisions of geography and environment, heritage surveys of sites, buildings and works of art, results from research excavations with local, national or theoretical agendas, results from rescue excavations that light on random parts of the island in advance of housing, car parks or road schemes, casual finds picked from the surface or detected by treasure hunters. It will be apparent that neither the yield, nor my coverage of it, is even-handed. I can only answer for the latter, an emphasis on the stories, natural assets and prehistoric legacies of Britain and Ireland (the *Inheritance* of Chapter 1) and on the high-status, high-investment creations of the people, captured in pictures, sites, monuments and, especially, in multi-period excavations. These constitute the results of Chapters 2–6. The aim has been to bring onto the stage the principal archaeological storylines of the 5th to 11th century in Britain in the hope that they will be of service to the historical sciences. Ours is a discipline that deploys many theories and theoretical approaches (see 'Reflections', later in this chapter), but the most potent agents of new narratives and new understanding are not based on new concepts but new discoveries: not so much 'thinking hard', more 'digging deep'. For this reason, archaeologists exercise a certain insouciance about the future; none of us will write the equivalent of the *Origin of Species*, since every generation will find fresh species of human behaviour and new ways of looking at it, a process that will never end so long as there are still humans on the planet.

Nevertheless, this book has an axial thesis, already referred to here and there, which will emerge from the process of assembling a narrative. For all its imperfections and random emphases, the material requires an attempt at concordance if it is to play a role in history making, even if its chief reward is mainly to show up areas of ignorance, mine or ours. The making of narrative comes first, then the thesis, then the critique. Accordingly a picture will be painted for each period, Formative 1, 2 and 3, and peering at them we will decide on a theme that suits all and deserves the epithet 'formative'. The thesis is that the events are not driven so much by the environment, the ecology or the economy as by the more elusive and insidious forces of ideology; these play on an island where the cultural geography lies deep and diverse. The result is to provoke a series of changes that from the vantage point of 1,500 years appears sudden and seismic, and their effects enduring. My coda concerns the place of formative Britain in the world today.

Narratives[1]

The principal message of Chapter 1 was that Britain and its islands are very diversely favoured by geology, geography and climate. In any agricultural economy, the south-east has a marked advantage over the rest; it has more fertile soil, a longer growing season and a greater repertoire of resources: woods, pasture, arable and well-watered meadows. If crops fail, there are cattle; if cattle fail, there are sheep and pigs. In the British upland regions there is mainly fish, cattle, fruit and kaleyards. The natural imbalance was greatly exacerbated by the Romans: their failure to invest in the prosperity of the upland areas and Ireland was matched by their pumping money into the British home counties and into raising its output to levels of mass profit. Nature, prehistory and Rome had bequeathed a communication system on land that also favoured the south-east: north of the Humber and west of the Pennines, the difficulties of bulk transport over land inhibited the development of markets and the amassing of wealth.

By sea, the advantages were not only with the English. The Channel had short crossing points encouraging interaction with the Rhine delta and the Low Countries. The southern North Sea connected East Anglia with Denmark and southern Sweden. The northern North Sea provided a passage between Norway, Shetland, Orkney and mainland Scotland. The Irish Sea exercised links between southern Ireland and Cornwall and south-west Wales, between central Ireland, Anglesey and the Isle of Man, between northern Ireland and the country that would become Scotland, and in the early period with the Mediterranean via the ancestral route to Iberia. Britain was never of no interest to its neighbours. Short cuts within the island also carved their own rat runs and frontiers: the Bristol Channel to Weymouth, the Thames to the Warwickshire Avon and the Severn, the Tay to Argyll via Loch Tummel; the Moray Forth to the Irish Sea via the Great Glen. All these were active long before the Formative period. The formative people inherited them and wore down the trails, reinforcing the regional advantages (and deepening their prejudices).

Refining the chronology

Three broad time spans were adopted here, called with traditional archaeological deadpan Formative 1 (5th to 7th century), Formative 2 (7th to 9th century) and Formative 3 (9th to 11th century). They have all the advantages of vagueness: they overlap and allow happenings in one part of the island to be out of sync with those elsewhere without elaborate use of numbers. However, the data-gathering exercise has shown that these periods are very different to each other, and there are definite *caesurae* between them. The proposed formative periods are aligned with traditional British and European time divisions in Table 0.1 (see *Preface*).

The pioneering work of Hines and Bayliss (p. 93) in finding a cut-off point for furnished burial in the English area can certainly embolden us to find others. Grave goods cease in the south and east in the same generation that the monastic movement takes off in the north and west, the one succeeding the other at a cusp around 675. In

Table 7.1 Refined chronology

Formative 1 5th to late 7th century

1A: 400–475 Migration period, into Southumbria (German) and into the west coast (Irish)

1B: 475–550 Land claiming period, all over Britain

1C: 550–625 Rise of male leaders in the east

1D: 625–675 Rise of female leaders in the east

Formative 2 Late 7th to early 9th century

2A: 675–750 Rise of the Monastic movement in Northumbria, Wales, Scotland (and Ireland)
Rise of the magnate farm in Southumbria

2B: 750–825 Expansion of the Northumbrian monastic movement in the west
Rise of the *wic* in the east

Formative 3 Early 9th to mid-11th century

3A: 825–900 The Viking Age in the south-east (Danish) and north-west (Norse)

3B: 900–975 The Wessex conquest of the Midlands, Cornwall and Northumbria; rise of the *burh* as a fort and administrative centre

3C: 975–1050 The late kingdoms; development of the *burh* as a trading centre

---

brief, the Hines and Bayliss trajectory proposes an early settlement phase by cremators (400–530); inhumation burial (530–570); increased ranking and integration with Britons (570–630); a final celebration of female authority and cessation of the grave-good rite (630–675) (p. 409). Although it applies to only a small part of Britain and only to the earliest part of the formative sequence, these periods of common practice separated by quantum leaps seem to present us with a framework more in keeping with human behaviour than a slow plod of imperceptible change. There is also some merit in the empirical observation that, in very general terms, human enthusiasm endures for only about 50–75 years before looking for change. It is coincidentally the average human lifespan or two to three active generations. The same period of three-quarters of a century was proposed by Richard Bulliet as the average time taken to convert a community to a new religion, in that case to Islam (p. 388). This tendency to periodic ideological renewal has been fought by conservative societies throughout history, but it seems too deeply embedded to respond to reason. Change comes as a *zeitgeist* regular as a puberty, as a communal heartbeat.

This suggests the adoption of the following periods, subdivisions and principal characteristics, as suggested by the cultural material (Table 7.1).

At first sight such precision seems reckless – and we surely do not know enough about the whole island to warrant it. So an 'early' and a 'later' have been held in readiness to counter any temptation to spurious exactitude. But absolute dates, where we have them, are given in what follows.

Interweaving the evidence

At the end of each of Chapters 2–6 there is a summary of the principal trends extracted from that particular kind of evidence, each reporting how it characterises the same three periods of time. It is probably premature to expect all five data sets to combine coherently, but the act of lining them up is suggestive. Table 7.2 offers a summary, not so much as a synthesis as an aid to navigation. There follows an attempt to paint a picture of Formative 1, 2 and 3, or at least assemble a set of sketches.

Table 7.2 Summary of trends

	Formative 1 *5th–7th century*	*Formative 2* *7th–9th century*	*Formative 3* *9th–11th century*
Personhood	1A All dress in accordance with regional, tribal or family allegiance 1C In S&E Male leaders adopt trappings of Roman warriors 1D In S&E Alpha females adopt Byzantine dress	New clerical dress for spiritual specialists Christian women don long veils	In N&W, return of the working warrior In S&E kings and bishops emerge, with clothing costly and symbolic In S&E the underclasses emerge into the light of day, elegant and playful
Settlement	N&W family forts, with wealth invested in cattle S&E open villages, with wealth in crops	N&W Monasteries S&E 2A Magnate farms 2B wics (trading places)	N&W War with the Norse S&E 3A War with the Danes 3B magnate farms The burh as a fort and administrative centre 3C The burh as a town
Burial	N&W: Ancestral row graves and shrines S&E: 1A Immigration 1B Land claiming 1C Male leaders 1D Female leaders	N&W Monastic S&E Village cemeteries	Church cemeteries Criminals (or dissidents) are executed and exiled from the community after death
Monumentality	N&W: Inscribed pillars Irish immigration signalled by ogham	N&W 2A 675–750 monumental Christian sculpture, codices, stone churches 2B 750–825 advance of Victory Crosses S&E Investment in timber halls	N&W Hybrid monumental sculpture (English/British/Irish/Norse/Danish/Christian/Odinic) S&E Monumental Christian stone sculpture, stone churches and codices Frankish influence Release of vernacular themes
Literature	Heroic poetry	Christian liturgy and hagiography	Christian and vernacular themes
Overall	Immigration of Scots (in the west) and Anglo-Saxons (in the east)	Rise of monasticism (in N&W) Rise of secular lordship (in S&E) Women disempowered	Marginalisation of the N&W; Anglo-Scandinavian conflict then dominance Continental alliance and emulation; signs that the role of women in governance, spirituality and wealth creation has diminished

Formative 1: early 5th to late 7th century

FM1A 400–475: migration period

Early Formative 1 is most easily seen as a migration period, comparable with the European migration period as a whole. But while Goths and Vandals could follow lengthy itineraries from northern to southern Europe, arrivals in the island of Britain had nowhere else to go.

An accommodation of the incomers with the British was necessary but took (or is taking) some time to achieve. The island attracted diverse peoples from the north-west continent ('Anglo-Saxons') to the east coast estuaries, and peoples from Ireland ('Scots') along a far more extensive landfall along the west coast. The populations that the Irish encountered in the west were sub-Roman, that is, Britons with a knowledge of Roman culture, and in the north 'Late Iron Age' Britons who had less first-hand experience of Rome. In the south-east, heartland of the Roman province, the Anglo-Saxon immigrants presumably found urbanised Romano-British subjects of the Empire; their subsequent traces in cemeteries, whether due to belief or to reduced social status, are modest: a few stones and planks set beside the body. But new scientific analysis of ancestry may change that.

Britain today still feels like a frontier zone between north and south and east and west, and this is likely to be an inheritance from the formative, but we are some way from writing a coherent genetic history. Modern DNA separates England and Northern Ireland from the Republic of Ireland and to a lesser extent from Scotland, suggesting that this demography is largely an artefact of recent centuries. We await a rather more definitive exercise using ancient DNA, but this is not the only factor inhibiting the discussion of the peopling of Formative Britain. 'Immigration' for that period (as for today) has become the plaything of prejudice, no less for those that deny it as for those that fear it. The movement of people is not the same as the reproduction of people, although one may lead to the other. The mixing of genes is an inevitable consequence of men and women who meet and mate, and this activity had already been in train for at least 3,000 years among the inhabitants of Britain and Ireland when the Anglo-Saxons, similarly of mixed origins, arrived. Language and taste in clothing are not transmitted via sperm (as far as we know), so there is little necessary equivalence between speech, appearance, belief and descent.

In Chapter 2 it was suggested that migration ought to be studied on the basis of what motivates the journey rather than assume an osmotic creep from one part of Europe to another promoted by pressure or vacuum. *Individual movement* of either humans and animals took place, then as now, to generate prosperity through political, social or economic advantage. It probably follows rules determined by the current climate, ecological or intellectual, so cannot easily be controlled by kings. Such varying mobility can theoretically be tracked by aDNA or O/Sr isotopes. *Human trafficking* (including marriage), a particular form of enforced mobility, might be inferred from the genetic history of an individual. *Ethnic cleansing* has been claimed for both early medieval Britain and Neolithic North Germany, but the scientific protocols for sampling aDNA are not yet routine. *Trade* may be tracked by the provenance of artefacts and materials – a well-developed procedure. *Embassy* may be implied by high-status gifts. The relationship between bulk trade and treasure in graves is not necessarily one of distance or value, so much as the political or spiritual benefits won by the journey. The demand for materials to serve major ideological change, such as the monastic movement, should have been immense and driven by the clerical branch of the elite. Such an *ideological invasion* could certainly have followed the rise of monasticism, resulting not only in a large number of invisible imports but a large number of invisible spiritual specialists. *Ethnic/political/ideological emulation* should be visible in settlement, structure, and artefact styles. But there is no need to suppose that every exotic idea implies a migrant. Unless prevented by moral or physical forces, mobility is a natural consequence of being alive and curious. A question for the times is which kind of mobility is prevalent.

The footprint of the migration period in the west is still elusive. The message of the cemeteries is mainly one of continuity from a real or perceived prehistoric past, as at Cannington or Capel Eithin. Evidence of Irish intrusion from portable artefacts and sites is slight, but it is fair to note that settlement evidence is also sparse in Ireland itself in this early phase. The detection of Irish presence on the east side of the Irish Sea still depends mainly on the dating assigned to the pillar stones, featuring Irish names inscribed in Irish ogham in south-west Wales and Cornwall. An ogham outlier in Silchester is thought to have been erected while the Roman town was still a going concern. Pillars inscribed in Latin in south-east and north Wales and the northern borders ought to have been in existence in the 5th century; Sims-Williams (phonology), Jackson (phonology) and Tedeschi (epigraphy) begin their series in 400, 450 and 500, respectively. Forsyth dates the Latinus stone in the 5th century and other more eastern stones to the 6th (Chapter 5). It seems that immigration in the west involved a number of q-Celtic-speaking peoples coming into p-Celtic lands, a process spread over the whole 5th and into the 6th century. We can legitimately equate this with Irish pressure on Britons at the same time as the latter were being squeezed by the English. The period is the one for which Gildas reported the groans of the Britons at Saxon intrusion, while the authors of the Mabinogion and Tristan evoked it as one of Irish pressure and danger to British potency. In the north, Irish pressure on the Picts is thought to be detectable in the arrival of ogham and in the occupation of robust stone roundhouses from the Atlantic region up the Glens that lead via Loch Tummel to the Tay (Chapter 3). It is not clear whether this was a trend of the earlier or later part of Fm 1.

The archaeological markers of the incomers in the east are predominately cremation cemeteries, and the pots and the brooches show unmistakable affiliations with the cult and cultures of the people of northern Germany. The English occupation strategy would seem to be to create dispersed settlements exploiting parcels of Roman farmland. The cemeteries would appear to have served more than one settlement, so providing a district with a common allegiance and, in some sense, a central place. The English occupation appears remarkably free of defended sites or monumentality.

FM1B 475–550: land-claiming period

The north and west and the south-east parts of the island then declared societies with rather different political agendas, although both are concerned with claiming and marking land. In northern and south-eastern Wales pillar stones are inscribed with Latinised or British names in Latin letters; in south-west Wales, Cornwall and the Isle of Man, they include Irish names and names in ogham. In Pictland they take the form of symbols incised on rocks, prehistoric stones or boulders. These symbols too also probably represent names and denote land ownership. There are no references to Christianity on these monuments, nor proven association with churches or with oriented burial. A few indicate a Christian alignment in the form of an inscription ('hic iacet'). However, direct references to the church of Christ come only in the 7th century. Whatever their religious affiliation, and it is likely to be that of inherited Roman Christianity, the 5th/6th century pillar stones are dedicated, it would seem, to the memory of a male ancestor and by implication their estate. Elsewhere, as in heroic poetry, we note a strong interest in the Old Testament, as opposed to the new.

The presumably Celtic-speaking areas of Cumbria, Lancashire, Cheshire and Mercia are enigmatically blank. Was there no land to be claimed there in the 5th/6th century? There was certainly freestone that could have been cut for monoliths, but the lands are unsigned until the later 7th century, and sometimes beyond. More puzzling is the case of Northumbria, where there were certainly intruders to challenge but no pre-existing stone pillar culture to confront the creep of Anglo-Saxon burial grounds. The paradox is that these incomers were later to pioneer and champion a range of stone monuments of unusual magnificence.

Settlements of this time are elusive in the north and west. Many of the fortified places about to come to notice after 550 may already have been occupied. Where there are burials of the 5th/6th century, as at Yeavering in Hope-Taylor's Phase I and II, the buildings are specialist rather than residential: the Great Enclosure, the Assembly structure, a shrine and a temple. This aligns more closely with the cemeteries in Wales and the west, which feature family rows punctuated by special graves or small square-ditched enclosures designated as shrines.[2] Dating is difficult in the absence of bone or artefacts but inclines to the 5–7th century. Cannington is one of the most graphic examples: graves in the 3rd–5th century focused on a Roman temple (FT43) superseded in the 6th and 7th centuries by family row graves focussed on the special grave of a child (FT26) approached by a well-worn path. Hallow Hill, at the other end of the British zone, also featured a 6th-century child in a furnished special grave amidst a cemetery of families buried in rows. Further north in Pictland, the preference is apparently for round or square-ditched burial mounds. Those at Redcastle in Angus are dated 400–560. Those at Portmahomack in Ross and Cromarty are dated 5th to late 7th century. Whether in rows, under mounds or within rectangular enclosures, the abiding grave structure is the long cist made of flat slabs placed vertically and horizontally. But the case is argued that, in all the British regions, only a selected few were buried in cists, and only a slightly larger cohort reached a cemetery at all (p. 314).

The identifying garment of the upper-class inhabitants of the Irish Sea area, including Wales and Pictland, was the cloak, secured at the shoulder by hand pins and small penannular brooches. Since the latter also occur in English Britain, we can probably assume a Celtic habit inherited from the Iron Age and once active over the whole archipelago. Some are rudimentary – the dress pins that Portmahomack shared with Chalton in the 6th/7th century resembled Roman nails with the head hammered flat. They would have secured clothing that was no less robust, made from fleeces that were brown in Ireland and black, brown, grey and white in Scotland. The one surviving garment from the British regions is not a cloak but a fringed and hooded woollen cape, using two shades of natural wool, brown and black, with a tablet-woven strip sewn along the hem. It had been recycled from other pieces to construct a weather-proof hoodie for a child. Found on Orkney, it has been radiocarbon-dated to AD 250–640, so belongs to the earliest Pictish period (p. 82).

Within the Anglo-Saxon burial zone, the cultural material is enriched by the presence of furnished inhumations, at Spong Hill from c. 475, culminating in 550 with two well-furnished inhumations under small mounds. The Sutton Hoo Tranmer House cemetery (phase A) had furnished inhumations and cremations and ran from 510 to 550. Reaching west, we have dates for cremations at Wasperton from 480 to 520 and Anglo-Saxon inhumations from c. 500 to 550. Reaching north we have family clusters at West Heslerton from 475 to 650. These show up a general trend to locate the dead in family groups, comparable to the rows of the British. All these are declared members of the Anglo-Saxon cultural zone, with some indigenous diagnostics showing in the more northerly latitudes and the later decades – crouched burial in 6th-century Norton, cist graves in 6th-century Bamburgh.

Settlement on the English plain is more visible than elsewhere: at West Stow dating c. 450–500 (Groups 2 and 5A) and c. 500–550 (Group 4). Mucking 1, a 5th/6th zoned settlement with cemetery I/II begins in 450 or more likely 475. West Heslerton village develops from a late Roman ritual destination into three zones, residential, agricultural and industrial, between 475 and 650. By the mid-6th century most of the territory of the former Roman province has been Anglo-Saxonised. There is no longer a vacuum but rather a pressure on *lebensraum.* Expanding German groups exert pressure on each other and on the larger area of western Britain. War is inevitable.

FM1C 550–630: rise of the warlords

By the late 6th century in the north and west, the Gaulcross and Norrie's Law hoard leave no doubt that there was a flourishing aristocracy, and the horse harness pieces from Dunadd, Mote of Mark, Portmahomack and Sutton Hoo show that there was, by the late 6th or early 7th century, an insular equestrian class, dressing itself and its horses (p. 102). These were also the wearers of quality penannular brooches – the Welsh with red-enamelled terminals, as at Dinas Powys, the Irish millefiori, as at Ballinderry Crannog 2. The upper class had now curdled into an aristocracy, equestrian and entitled, interacting with each other, fed by their homelands.

The settlement repertoire enlarges. It had probably been gradually enlarging over a longer period of time (namely through the previous 150 years), but *pro tem* the arrival the new settlement species are assembled in this date bracket, on the grounds that they reinforce each other and seem to compose a trend. It is moreover a trend that suits the mood of other parts of the island. One can assume that having erected the stone pillars in the previous sub-period, they remained effective in this one. In general, the role they were given as sentinels of landscape is not contradicted or questioned by the new surge in defended forts. There are fragments of inscribed stone in settlements here and there (e.g. Old Scatness in Shetland, Dunadd, Trusty's Hill), but there is no repeating coincidence between sentinel and citadel: so they probably did different things. The exception is Rhynie, where symbol stones were found in close association with a palisaded enclosure. But this is currently an unusual site, with strong element of cult in a poor defensive position.

Broadly speaking, the strategies in the north and west were to reoccupy Atlantic Iron Age circular stone houses, or crannogs, hill forts or promontory forts or build new forts on a smaller scale (as Dinas Powys). This was the period of Britain's *incastellamento*. Apart from rare radiocarbon dates, the diagnostic materials are imported pottery from the Mediterranean (red plates and amphorae, 5th/6th century) or from Aquitaine (cooking pots, 7th century), to which may be added the more elaborate enamelled brooches and items of harness. These objects are all sought after, if not high status, leaving the bulk of the population still living, as it were, in the shadows. Nevertheless, it is possible that these small centres, likely to prove numerous, are the habitats of family groups in which all ranks of society are represented. In that case, there will be no 'peasant villages' to find.

In Atlantic Scotland, the Formative 1 peoples moved into massive dry stone prehistoric wheelhouses and brochs in the 6th/7th century and modified them, like Grand Designers playing with a French farmhouse. They erected roundhouses inside brochs (e.g. Clickhimin), placed cellular divisions inside roundhouses or added lobes to create extra bedrooms. The site of Old Scatness on Shetland exhibits a variety of these themes in its Phase 7 (5th–9th century): an oval walled space (S25), a cellular building within the broch tower (S7), a figure-of-eight building (S5) and a roundhouse with added piers. The reuse of monumental houses extends to the 'fortified farmsteads' of Strath Tummel. There is a good argument that these thick-walled circular buildings are original structures of the Scottish advance into Pictland; however, if they were there already (and there are good arguments for this too), then they were reoccupied in the 7th/8th century. A large number of these early medieval buildings, even those of turf as at Pitcarmick, were refurbished and reoccupied again in the later middle ages.

Crannogs mostly built 800–400 BC in Scotland also attracted renewed attention in the formative period; three on Loch Tay were refurbished on occasions between the 5th and 9th century, and the detailed dendro dating of that at Buiston (Ayrshire) gave it a high precision biography. The 13 precisely dated episodes reveal the fluctuating pulse of local need and initiative, often unresolved on less favoured sites to a single occupation, dated '5th to 7th century'. It is nevertheless these modest family forts that are attracting the imported pottery and glass from the Mediterranean and then from south-west France. The targeting of the Irish Sea citadels might be attributed to the natural seaway of the Gulf Stream. However, it seems unlikely that merchants would fail to respond to a straightforward demand from England, if there was one. This would seem to be another case of a long-distance exchange being driven by ideology and politics rather than 'free trade'.

In Pictland, sunken-floored roundhouses of the 6th to mid-7th century at Hawkhill R were presumably those of free farmers. But at Rhynie in Aberdeenshire, the circular ditched and palisaded enclosure containing a rectangular hall has revealed new aspects of early Pictish life. This site also produced 5th/6th-century imported amphorae and glass drinking vessels and was associated with up to nine Class 1 symbol stones marking the site, the approaches to it and the territory around (Chapter 5). Pits containing calcined ox bone and a miniature axe-hammer of a type used to despatch oxen both emphasise the cult function of this place as well as its high status.

Also in the Pictish heartland we find early experiments with new forts, not so much the reuse of the grand prehistoric hill forts with their heads in the clouds but smaller protected areas on minor knolls, outcrops and promontories at lower altitudes. That on Mither Tap of Bennachie was active 480–600. The multivallate promontory fort at Burghead occupied in the 5th–7th century is also credited with ritual airs – Class 1 slabs originally more than 30 in number each depicting a single bull and a deep stone-lined well approached by stone steps reminiscent of the Iron Age site at Minehowe on Orkney. The majority of these sites, however, appear to be working forts providing a base for campaigns and herding.[3]

While not as imposing as the mighty Bronze Age hillforts or Iron Age *oppida*, these places were intended to be dominating and defensible in their day. The largest forts enclosed areas 200 m across (Burghead, Bamburgh, Dumbarton), and the next size down 100 m (Clatchard Craig, Crag Phadraig, Durdurn, Dunadd), while the smallest came in at 50 m (Mither Tap, Mote of Mark). But the status may relate to strategic location rather than capacity. Some were protected by dump ramparts and ditches,[4] others used timber-framing.[5] At Dundadd and Dundurn the fortifications grew through time, enclosing more people and animals, as their status, or their provocation, grew. Dumbarton, Dunadd and Dunollie hosted metalworkers and attracted imports. Dunadd and Dundurn had features supposed to indicate 'royal' inaugurations.[6] There is therefore *prima facie* evidence that these were the principal instruments of governance.

One can follow the trail of formative forts all the way down the western coastline from Dunadd in Argyll to Tintagel in Cornwall.[7] To the degree to which they have been examined, the occupation (or reoccupation) of all these places falls within the 5th–7th century and features elements of the lordship package: rampart, hall, metalwork and imports. Along the eastern seaboard, the hillfort habit gives way around Tweedale to more lowland solutions: Doon Hill – a hall within a palisaded enclosure – and Yeavering, initially a British cult site but changing in the early 7th century into an Anglo-British central place, apparently not fortified (unless the Great Enclosure acted as a refuge) and containing grand timber halls. The ranking declared by the Pictish symbol stones and forts is reinforced by burial mounds, some of which are thought to have been also marked with symbol stones. Although these tombs are not lavishly furnished, the slabs of the cist graves and the design of the cairns or barrows signal high investment.

In *Southumbria*, both settlements and cemeteries show a marked increase in the display of rank. At West Stow seven farmsteads, each with hall and sheds (including one weaving shed) succeed each other on adjacent sites c. 520–600 (Group 5B); c. 550–600 (Group 6) and c. 600–650: (Group 7). In the latter days of the settlement, fences begin to demarcate the extent of the properties. This process continues. Chalton is a large village of the 7th century in which a succession of two courtyard farms is surrounded by other buildings, many of them probably dedicated to agriculture. At Cowdery's Down, four well-fenced farmsteads succeed each other through the 7th century, each grander than the one before. The environmental research at Yarnton showed that the arrival of these 7th-century 'manors' was accompanied or made possible by something of an agricultural revolution. In the 5th/6th century, the natural properties of the land were exploited: much land in the river basin was devoted to pasture, grazing cattle and sheep, with patches of arable above the edge of the river terrace, the most abundant crop being hulled barley. By the 7th century, the lower-lying pasture had been converted to hay meadow, and the amount of land under the plough greatly increased, the harvests now including emmer and bread wheats. The productivity of the arable fields was most likely improved with manure, collected by feeding animals within fenced enclosures or stalls to facilitate its collection.

There is some comparison here to the Danish sequence of settlement nucleation that would culminate in 8th/9th-century 'magnate farms'. Up to the 7th century, the dispersed societies are to some extent united by a shared interest in cult sites: focused on lakes, as at Tissø or Gudme, where votive offerings of weapons are discarded. In the 7th century, control of these places is developed with suites of halls, shrines and a temple (at Uppåkra), and the emphasis shifts from personal devotion towards a more managed salvation industry. These cult sites will soon be overtaken by regional and then international trading places. We are led to expect that such 'central places' ought to be a concomitant of other pre-Christian Germanic societies. But in spite of two centuries of intensive archaeology and almost 50 years of metal-detection, no convincing case has been advanced for the existence of dedicated Anglo-Saxon cult sites in the 5th–7th centuries. The spiritual emphasis was apparently not on the supplication of gods but on the family and the ancestors, and the principal ritual investment was in the cemetery.

The spiritual accentuation of this tendency shifted in the late 6th and early 7th century so as to place more value on a militant aristocracy. English male villagers came from a tradition that liked to present themselves as warriors with sword, spear and shield, and the obsequies involved animal sacrifice and were no doubt of a ceremonial nature. Small mounds covering small chambers were seen at Spong Hill in the mid-6th century; at the Tranmer House cemetery there were cremations with animal offerings in and around previous and new-made barrows between 550 and 580. But the heroic burials after 580 were declarations of a different order: large mounds, chambers, coffins, boats and horses were recruited to these highly theatrical events. The upper class saw itself not so much as servants of the gods, more as their successors. Their deeds were proclaimed in verse by professionals in the hall, and in the grave by means of a magnificent set of stage props carefully selected to report the fame of the dead man to those who would receive him in the next world.

The Sutton Hoo burial ground offers a microcosm of the short-lived heroic ethos of early 7th-century England and the way it was reified. The cemetery begins in c. 580 with Mounds 5–7; these are the first 'monumental' mounds, but their use of cremations in bronze bowls refer back to the Tranmer House burial ground a few hundred metres to the north. In 590–600 (radiocarbon years) there is a pair of graves for a horse and a rider covered by a mound (Mound 17). The references here are to the Rhineland, where the presence of horses now signifies not religiosity but rank: 'masculinity, leadership and military prowess'.[8] Ship burial is a component of the next two burials; they represent the apogee of the Sutton Hoo rituals: a ship laid over a furnished chamber (Mound 2) and a ship laid in a trench with a chamber erected amidships (Mound 1). The creation of this latter tableau inspired the comparison of a rich burial to a celebratory poem and credited its composition to the unnamed widow of King Raedwald. These obsequies, public, lavish, large scale and long-lasting, belong to the period 600–630.

Insofar as we can place it in the itinerary of thought that we have tracked to this point, it converts ancestor appreciation to the celebration of current heroes. Chadwick, still the most reliable guide, describes the heroic character as 'adolescent': and he sums up the context of a heroic age as follows: 'the occupation of new lands; a cult of conquest; the weakening of tribal ties (and ties of kindred), emancipation from tribal law and a new reliance of bonds of allegiance between warriors'. This is achieved through

> the development of an irresponsible type of kingship resting on military prestige, the formation of kingdoms with no national basis and the growth of relations between one kingdom and another. In religion . . . the predominant characteristic is the subordination of previous chthonic [relating to the underworld] and tribal cults to the worship of a number of universally recognised and highly anthropomorphic deities, together with the belief in a common and distant land of souls.

The rewards of great deeds, even of unbridled savagery and revenge, are immortality in verse, on stone and under the ground.[9] In his study of the heroic poetry of early medieval Europe, Chadwick points out that it makes no mention of Christ or the New Testament; evil comes in the form of monsters whose fate is to be slain by heroes, a deed providing its own upbeat morality.

The urge to celebrate great deeds and illustrious ancestry in song is older than the formative period but must have become especially strengthening in the process of kingdom formation. At whatever date they were finally conserved on vellum, the stories plausibly relate to events that took place in the 5th to 6th century, and so were enacted or were recreated as fiction in the halls and houses of later Formative 1. Later renditions and the first written texts are naturally stained with the colours and cobwebs of their age, but the words of the *Gododdin* in the north, the *Mabinogi* in Wales and *Beowulf* in the south-east are alive with the shadows, smells and sounds of early Britain. The tellers of tales also cite the Old Testament to provide examples of heroic achievement drawn from the miraculous behaviour of its actors, David in particular. As war leader and psalmist, David exemplified a leader beloved of God, a king both skilled and lucky.

Following the events in Europe that rolled out after Chadwick's book was published (in 1912) we would not now assume that the peoples of the earth were on a journey from the primitive to the civilised or from childhood to maturity via adolescence. It seems that adolescent leadership can return at any time to wreck the laborious achievements of thinking generations and that its attractions are irresistible to those not so engaged (including other adolescents, of course). It is valid I think to use Chadwick's insights to connect the poetry, dress, settlements, monuments and burial rites of Britain in the 5th–7th century in order to reveal a shared culture with a particular ideology. The emancipation that Chadwick found in the Teutonic and Homeric societies released a mass of invention and experiment, in politics, religion and attitudes to treasure. This we see in the rich legacy of sites, monuments and artefacts from this period. It would certainly not be expected that its exponents would spring to embrace the trappings of a universalist religion. Although this is what was about to happen.

FM1D 625–675: women take the helm

Anglo-Saxon women, like their men, had celebrated their social roles through burial rites in cremation and thereafter in inhumation, where they are presented fully dressed, carrying certain symbolic artefacts, festooned with ornaments and in the later periods accompanied by caskets and food offerings. There is no case for saying that less care was invested in female as opposed to male burial; perhaps the contrary. There is also no case for saying that the smart appearance of the women is owed to a man, or at least the burials do not imply it. The idea that an Anglo-Saxon man has ownership of his wife appears to be claimed only in later writing, by which time Christian influence is *ipso facto* dominant.

The emergence of a specifically female role in burial iconology can be glimpsed in the sequence at Dover Buckland. The cemetery began in c. 450 and expanded in c. 500 in family clusters. The late 6th/early 7th century saw the arrival of sword-burials and mounds. As well as exhibiting their rank through grave goods, women connected two sword-bearing men through the female line. The woman in Grave 360 had a sword pommel, probably in a pouch, laid on the left side of her pelvis. The climax in Plot E was a group of 7th-century graves placed around a Bronze Age barrow. These included six rich female graves and three men with spears. Special status is implied for 6th-century women with great square-headed brooches; and special roles for them are inferred by the grave of the 6th-century 'cunning woman' at Bidford-on-Avon, with its amulets and miniature buckets. Parallels with pre-Christian Scandinavian women seem justifiable: these are shamans, they are landowners, they inherit land-rights and duties from their mothers.[10]

This background suggests that when the grand mound burials of women appear, which they do between 630 and 675, there was a long period of well-respected experience to drawn on. The upsurge seems particularly prominent because they are late – the last of the Anglo-Saxon furnished burials – and because in the immediately previous period 575–625 they had been eclipsed by the men. The female grand graves follow the male emphasis of display and the mound, but the importance of the leader is drawn in a different way: often on a bed in a chamber. At Sutton Hoo, the disturbed burial under Mound 14 originally contained a woman with silver pendants on an upholstered couch. The young woman at Swallowcliffe Down ('Possa') was laid clothed on a bed and accompanied by a casket containing a sprinkler and other luxuries. Others were more clearly aligned to ritual performance. At Bloodmoor Hill, a group of five women were buried in richly furnished graves, one with a casket, within a small cemetery in the mid- to late 7th century. There were men present, but no corresponding rich male assemblages. Biologically identified men had a knife or tool, but women also had knives. There were four buildings adjacent to the cemetery, with traces of metalworking and a large pit filled with a massive assemblage of animal bone, including duck, chicken, goat, roe deer, eel and carp alongside more familiar species. Other finds included a miniature bucket of the type carried by the Bidford-on-Avon cunning woman and a famous pendant figurine, a helmeted jacketed man with a prominent penis. The evidence here is of the 'convergent' kind – the women were the rich ones, the activities next to the cemetery imply animal sacrifice, and the dates fell in the later 7th century.

Even more graphically dominated by women was the cemetery at Street House, within a former prehistoric site, adjacent to prehistoric monuments, its idiosyncratic layout designed from the start. The principal target of devotion would appear to have comprised a cluster of assorted features: a woman in a bed burial (Grave 42) with a small group of other graves, a penannular ditched platform with an orange clay floor (F430) and a post-hole building. Around this focus marched 79 inhumation graves in pairs forming a parade-ground rectangle. Grave 42 contained a small circular gold cabochon pendant dated 650–670, an oval gold cabochon pendant and shield-shaped gold and cloisonée pendant worn together in the chest area. A neighbouring grave (43) contained a silver circular brooch, an annular blue glass bead, two beads of silver wire, three beads of gold wire and four silver *bullae*. Eight other assemblages marked the graves of affluent women (10, 12, 21, 52, 55, 66, 67, 70), and nine other graves had beads or pendants. Five of the graves contained objects interpreted as amulets (55, 62, 67, 70 and 73). Twelve graves had only a knife, two only a buckle, one a knife and buckle. Thus all of the diagnostic graves were female, and those with a knife may have been male or female. There was no certain sign of Christianity. Street House is a pivotal site marking the rise of feminine power at the end of the pre-Christian era. The feminine late burial programme, argued by Helena Hamerow to serve the interests of dynastic land-holding, was also one in which high-ranking women made an attempt to maintain the cosmological values that had defined the English settlers. While the maintenance of the family inheritance is certainly a credible driver, this is also the century of conversion, and it would be odd if there were no monumental or artistic signal intended to give warning that something was about to be lost.

Summary of Formative 1

The nine generations of formative 1 (400–675) naturally saw many changes, but there were some unifying trends over the island as whole. The east coast of the former Roman province was invaded by Anglo-Saxon immigrants in significant numbers; but so was the west coast, by immigrants from Ireland. Both established a foothold that was to lead to permanent occupation and demographic admixture. The Anglo-Saxons mainly occupied Southumbria, but with an increasing presence between the Humber and the Tees, the northern continuation of the fertile plain. The Irish had a much broader holding, from Cornwall, through west Wales to Argyll, the Northern and Western Isles. In due course their descendants, mixed to an unknown degree with the Picts, would occupy the whole of the north British peninsula and call it Scotland. Modern Britain began its formative process 1,600 years ago, at a time when the English newcomers were minor players and culturally backward compared with the Irish, the British and the legacy of Rome.

There followed a period of consolidating land claims, in the west using inscribed pillars, in the east using cemeteries, which kept the English and British apart, exercising their habitual social structures: the English as families living in dispersed villages and the Britons in dispersed family forts. Both used their cemeteries as central places in which family groups were signalled in rows or clusters. In the west and north, these cemeteries were bonded with the prehistoric landscape, and there were signs of more focussed supernatural devotion in the form of purpose-built shrines and 'special' graves among the family rows (Cannington in Somerset, Hallow Hill in Fife, both with children as the spiritual focus).

In the later 6th and early 7th century the rise of the upper-class warrior is a major feature of the Anglo-Saxon territories, where they are celebrated in death with weapons, horses, boats and mounds. From the mid-6th century, the westerners embellished their forts, and one or two emerged as leader sites (Dunadd in Argyll). The warriors of the Celtic lands, where the tradition had run for longer, carry richer, larger brooches on their cloaks, and the surviving concomitant literature suggests a level of luxurious clothing that would have had a stupendous impact. Even if little has survived, there is no good reason for seeing it as less lavish than the plethora of wealthy garments that graced the dead man in the Sutton Hoo Mound 1 ship burial. The theme is lordship, war and the acquisition of land, and its natural destination is kingship and the kingdom. In both the east and west of Britain this period is likely to have been concurrent with the formation of the two dozen kingdoms that were remembered (Figure 7.1A).

The last few decades of Formative 1 (c. 650–675) were especially noticeable for the rise of an expression of feminine thinking that took the form of richly furnished burials (including bed burial) and Byzantine accoutrements. There is some implication at Street House that this movement was driven by an ideological, perhaps religious, conviction. It ended suddenly, and with it the grave-good habit. If the leitmotiv of Formative 1 is enforced governance of increasing tracts of land, at its end is a sign of the rise of a spirituality that anticipates and leads to the dominance of institutional Christianity, although this would take different forms in the British and the English areas.

If belief reflects society and vice versa, there is clearly a marked contrast between the tribal communities supported by their pagan pantheon and the dominance of a single male leader favoured by the Christian God. In the English area, the celebration of male leaders under mounds presaged the passage of power from elders to warriors. By the last quarter of the century, the true point of conversion, the Christians had created a spiritual aristocracy run by a hierarchy of men in imitation of Christ and the saints. In the north and west the transition was still clearer, the new power (of the monks) resurrecting the old power (of the druids). Although abbesses are cited as examples of a (rare) continuation of female religious leadership, women were the overall losers here, as in Scandinavia. While the monastery was to become the new power-house of the pious north and west, in the south and east, the centre of right behaviour was the 'magnate' settlement abrogated by lordship that would eventually lead to the manor, the law of the land and social control in the hands of a male upper class. The 7th century not only saw a change in the balance of power between spirituality and violence but between men and women, two trends that reinforced each other to produce a revolutionary period in British history.

Formative 2: late 7th to early 9th century

In spite of a rich legacy of tales of early missionary triumphs, the real era of Christianisation in Britain, at least as reported by archaeology, began in Formative 2. The results of the Formative 2 studies led to the conclusion that the impact of the arrival of institutionalised Christianity was manifested in three different material forms: in Ireland, Scotland, Pictland and Wales as a monastic movement with prehistoric roots; in England south of the Humber (Southumbria) in a more Roman episcopal form; and in Northumbria as a hybrid of the two: a monastic movement but anchored in Rome. The driver of monasticism was the setting up of oligarchies of like-minded ideologues, tasked with a mission guided by the teaching of Jesus Christ to join all people in a single polity under God. The movement operated from specially designed enclosed settlements, where there was a church, a burial ground and a light industry dedicated to the production of equipment necessary for ritual performance: bronze and silver vessels for the essential unifying ceremony (the Mass), illuminated manuscripts, mainly Gospel books containing the underpinning texts, and sculpture. These are the archaeological diagnostics of the monastic package, and their manufacture was necessary for the founding of new monasteries and the expansion of the network. The monasteries were farms of a particularly intensive and progressive kind, likely to have been at least self-sufficient but arguably capable of generating a surplus of agricultural products, perhaps inspired by imported knowledge of Roman drainage and milling. There is some overlap with the princely sector (for example metalworking and writing), but archaeologically the package is distinct. The indication of documents is that the movement also affected Britain south of the Humber in some measure, although curiously, there is as yet no strong archaeological evidence that it did so, or at least took a similar form. The period dominated by the movement is the 'long 8th century' (i.e. century and a half) from about 675, when it achieved unity, until about 825, when it collapsed under the Viking onslaught.

The documentary model holds that Christian conversion began immediately after the end of Roman Britain and was promoted by a number of powerful advocates, Patrick in 5th-century Ireland, Ninian in 5th-century Galloway, Columba in 6th-century Argyll, Augustine in early 7th-century Kent, Cuthbert, Benedict Biscop, Wilfred and Ceolfrid in later 7th-century Northumbria, Curadan in 8th-century Pictland. This may be true, but we are concerned here with the rather different viewpoint permitted by archaeology, and particularly the archaeology of the last 20 years. This reports the development of a society that, while it may well have contained Christians, did not sound their material trumpet until nearly three centuries later, when Formative 1 was at an end.

In the north and west, monastic sites and stone crosses supersede the sentinel and citadel roles of the pillars and princely sites of the previous period and are the main story tellers of this one. Using the dates emanating from these studies we can distinguish two or perhaps three pivotal moments: a foundation period 675–750; a proselytising period, recruiting new territories to the cause in the north, west and south (750–800); and a coda (800–825) when the monastic establishments struggled to survive in the face of the Viking realpolitik.

FM2 A 675–750: rise of the monastic movement in Ireland, Wales, Scotland, Pictland and Northumbria

In *Ireland*, the monastic movement grew on the back of a 7th-century agricultural boom that accompanied the creation of more than 50,000 settlements, largely known from survey and excavation in advance of roadwork schemes. A large increase in population is implied. The new settlements took the form of small ringworks or *raths*, circular enclosures containing roundhouses (Deer Park Farms) and crannogs, founded in lakes. A variant of increasing importance is the 'cemetery-settlement', which might feature iron-working, intensive agriculture and mills, as well as a cemetery (Camlin 3). The settlement repertoire thus already contains many of the ingredients of the fully fledged monasteries, but apparently without their churches or grave markers. Both these monuments are enduring signals of monastic sites, especially when fashioned in stone. The construction of the churches appears to vary with the region in which they were built and to reflect the development of the liturgy. On grave markers, ogham inscriptions are superseded by a cross, but the investment subsequently moves to stone grave covers inscribed with a cross and the name of a person. At Clonmacnoise these memorials have been found in very large numbers but are still likely to commemorate only those eminent in the cause. In a second phase, in the late 8th century and into the 9th, the monasteries mark their territory with tall 'High Crosses' displaying homilies from the Old Testament or the Life of Christ and commemorating illustrious clerics or donors. The great monasteries of the 8th century, like Clonmacnoise and Nendrum, are multivallate enclosures, with the church and sacred precinct at the centre, residential cells in an inner ring and craft activities in an outer ring, perhaps also used to protect the monastery's cattle, its principal form of reproductive and moveable wealth. At Nendrum the mill lay beyond the enclosure, powered by the tide. Crosses or shrines marked the limits of the *termon*, the monastic territory, which might be signalled at the edge of the enclosure or. as at Inishmurray. at the edge of the island. These great cult centres were linked to each other by a common purpose exercised through the free movement of expertise; they provided the population with spiritual specialists dedicated to divine intercession for the good of all souls. In this, their role was probably not so different to that of the Iron Age druids, and Irish monasticism was noted for its particular empathy with nature and with the thinking of prehistoric ancestors.[11] There are also numerous examples of smaller ecclesiastical settlements with churches, mills and enclosures and a handful of cells, mostly on islands (High Island, Skellig Michel). These were once thought to be the simple prototypes where hermits began the ascetic life that would later lead to the more centralised communal foundations, following the itinerary set by the desert fathers. However, recent work, as in Wales and Cornwall, now prefers to see these as secondary developments budding off from the principal cult centres, in the manner of St Martin's retreat from Tours at Marmoutier.[12] Viewed from the 9th century *Félire Óengusso*, the triumph of the monastic movement was reported with a certain nostalgia: the destruction of paganism, 'though fair it was and widespread', and the passing of spiritual power to new central places, the monasteries: 'Emain's burgh it hath vanished, save that its stones remain: the cemetery of the west of the world is multitudinous Glendalough'.

In *Scotland*, documentary sources tell us that St Ninian founded a monastery at Whithorn in the 5th century. As argued here, this is not supported by archaeological investigation, which exposed a 6th-century 'cemetery-settlement' not specifically Christian, with a Northumbrian type monastery arriving in the 8th century. Documentary sources also report that Columba (Columcille), having been sent into exile by the authorities in the Boyne Valley in Ireland, travelled to Scotland in 563, where he founded a monastery on the island of Iona off Mull. Here the archaeological evidence suggests a precocious start for the settlement, unless the dates from the enclosure ditch indicate that it belonged to a previous (Iron Age) earthwork. As at Whithorn, there is imported pottery and glass of the 6th/7th century. There is also evidence for metal, wood and leather working and a large circular building. However, archaeology has produced little evidence as yet of how the site was used in the 5th–6th century, as opposed to the 8th century, when Columba's biographer, Adomnán, was writing. Objects that are specifically Christian are lacking until the later 7th century, when it is expressed in a profusion of grave slabs. And the scriptorium that produced the Book of Durrow in c. 680 was probably located at Iona.

The cutting of the enclosure at Inchmarnock has been dated to c. 600; there was metalworking on the site between 650 and 780. Sometime before 800 there was a school on the island where children were taught how to write and draw on slates. It lasted long enough for one of them to sketch a Viking raid. The enclosure at Hoddom in Dumfriesshire was also dated between 600 and 680, and excavation otherwise encountered a number of grain dryers, kiln barns and other agricultural structures. Between 650 and 750 it was thought to have served as a British monastery, transforming to a monastery of Northumbrian persuasion by the later 8th century, the date of the associated carved stones. In the 9th century it lost its monastic robes and became a large farm serving an estate. The large-scale excavations at Portmahomack in north-east Pictland produced a settlement sequence in which a regular change of role was seen as a determinant feature. Between 550 and 670 it was an estate centre or a cemetery-settlement with long cist burials, a metalwork shop and evidence for extensive arable farming. In c. 670 it was landscaped and redeveloped as a planned monastery with a paved axial road, roadside workshops engaged in making church vessels or preparing vellum and a cemetery of row graves with many 'head-support' and some head box burials. Carved stone crosses without names had been disturbed from the area of the cemetery. In the later 8th century, massive cross-slabs were erect around the precinct at Portmahomack and on the edge of the Tarbat peninsula at the neighbouring sites of Nigg, Shandwick and Hilton of Cadboll. The majority of these were marked with Pictish symbols, indicating both the cultural affiliation of this brand of monasticism and inferring that the monumental cross-slabs were intended to celebrate a prominent personage. The iconography, which includes an image of St Anthony and St Paul, the begetters of monasticism, emphasise the pure doctrinal sources and raise the possibility that these crosses, which form a devotional circuit as at Inishmurray, were designed to celebrate the lives of holy men or women. The Portmahomack monastery was raided between 780 and 810 in calibrated radiocarbon years, but the settlement there continued to function for another 70 years under new management as a manufacturing and trading centre using the previous monkish techniques. Thus the place is claimed as demonstration of the transition from lordship to monastery to trading place that provides the theme for the formative period as a whole.

Small slabs marked with crosses or small free-standing crosses cluster at some other sites (e.g. Tullich in Aberdeenshire). These may be satellites of major monasteries, secular equivalents, parish graveyards or long-lived family cemeteries: they are not easy to date and thus to put into context. The cross-slabs superseded the Class I stones of Period 1 that carry symbols alone and have a quite different distribution. While the Class I stones celebrate leaders and mark land, the cross-slabs (Class II) cluster on the coast and rivers, on major routes and landing places. The northern monasteries succeed a previous religious cult involving the sacrifice of cattle, now brought to light at Rhynie. There are images of this conversion on Pictish cross-slabs. St Vigeans 7 depicts figures in cowled clerical garb seated in chairs, while below them an official of an earlier cult cuts the throat of a bull and catches the blood. Early stone church buildings in Scotland remain elusive, but an anthropomorphic corbel at Portmahomack and a monolithic stone arch at Forteviot make it clear that such buildings existed. The cross-slabs in Pictland and the High Crosses in Argyll and the west mark the high point of monasticism in those regions, which arose in the later 8th century and endured until the repeated destructive attentions of the Vikings in the 9th.

In *Wales*, well-defined monastic settlements are elusive, but a monastic phase is claimed for the cemetery at Llandough in the 8th–10th century, and it is possible to track the advent of the monastic movement through sculpture. The inscribed pillars that celebrate land-owning families seem to remain current until the later 8th century, when they are succeeded by carved stones incised with a cross that cluster on lowland sites presumed or known to have been monastic (for example Margam, Llantwit or Llandough). The first series (Group II) carry a simple cross in single or double outline and the later series (Group III) a more elaborate curvilinear cruciform image in low relief carving. In Cornwall, this sequence is still more attenuated: the pillar stones inscribed with Latin or ogham inscriptions continue in active use until the 9th/10th century, when the cross finally arrives, probably heralding some kind of late monasticism, but now in the context of an English overlordship.

Northumbria

In its material culture, Northumbria emerges as a prime laboratory of insular monasticism and is precocious. According to Bede, 10 named monasteries were created in the reign of Oswiu (642–670), with a further 12 in gratitude for his victory over Penda at the Winwaed in 655. Under his successor, Ecgfrith (670–685), monasteries were founded at

Hexham in 672–8, Wearmouth in 674, Hackness in c. 680, Jarrow in 681 and Abercorn in 682. This has undoubtedly raised the Northumbrian profile mightily and may tempt us into spurious precision. Bede is a partisan, even passionate champion of the monastic cause and has prompted sceptical responses in modern critics. But it is fair to point out that the narrative is not of itself likely to be an attempt to deceive those reading his book in his lifetime; moreover, the independent chronology offered by radiocarbon dates from monastic sites and the semi-independent dating given by the stylistic studies of the sculpture provide a framework that is consistent with Bede's history. It can even be claimed, as I do later, that the archaeology has a rich tale to tell up to Bede's death in 735, and one that is more valuable still for the rest of the 8th and into the 9th century. The sculpture especially reveals Northumbria's political ambitions in the second half of the 8th century with unexpected clarity.

If Northumbria's prominence is not owed only to Bede, we are entitled to ask 'why there?' The territory in Formative 1 was heterogeneous, with an Anglian occupation between the Humber and the Tees and a stronger British materiality from the Tees to the Forth. The study of the burials has shown that people in the later pagan period turned towards a more indigenous mode, for example favouring prehistoric sites, rows and crouched burial. There is a case that English and British ways were converging in Northumbrian territory in the first half of the 7th century. The strongly stated female burials of the 650s–680s give this trend still greater momentum: the Anglian-leaning language of bed burial, amulets and Byzantine 'imperial' accessories combines with the indigenous-leaning language of body position and fealty to the prehistoric theatre.[13] There are enough points of synergy (as it seems to me) to suppose a female initiative in the debate that must have heated the anxious days of the later 7th century: what are we to do about the Christian pressure? Will we lose the coherence achieved over the previous century and replace it with antagonism? Or is there a way of going forward together? The situation recalls that sketched for the Alpine region and for Scandinavia, where readings of the cemetery archaeology and the standing stones have suggested a strong female agenda, and by no means a negative one, in the conversion process.[14] The juxtaposition of the mid-7th-century female-led cemetery at Street House with the mid-7th century female-led monastery at Hartlepool, either side of the Tees estuary, on the coast and 20 km apart as the crow flies, provides a frozen vignette of the debate between female intellectuals at a turning point in the politics of Britain.

Hartlepool was founded by Heiu, said to be the first woman in Northumbria to take the vows and vestments of a nun. The description of Heiu and of her successor Hilda implies that Hartlepool was a nunnery, although its excavated name slabs commemorated persons with both male and female names, and men, women and children were buried in its cemeteries. The 28 small rectilinear buildings defined there were consistent with English practice, and the mould for a trumpeting symbol of St Mark implied the production of illuminated manuscripts. Too little has been excavated to be sure of its plan or that of any others in the list of Oswiu's foundations.[15]

The later developments, Wearmouth and Jarrow, have a rectilinear layout markedly different to those of the north and west, one that must have been revolutionary in its day. It evokes the form of a Roman villa, makes references to the halls of Yeavering and pre-echoes, by several centuries, the more familiar medieval monastic plan focused on a cloister south of the church, previously thought to have been an invention of Carolingian France and captured in the St Gall Plan. As Bede describes, these late 7th-century monasteries of Northumbria could already profit from research undertaken by the early proponents of the movement who toured the continent looking for up-to-date models aligned to Rome, and no doubt found them in reused Roman villas, as that of Cassiodorus on the Bay of Squillace. They introduced technologies that included window glass, rectangular stone-founded halls sited end-to-end, one at Jarrow having a floor of *opus signinum* with a polygonal column planted, probably to support a reading desk, in what was then a refectory. Foreign craftsmen were employed at Wearmouth; but Jarrow, founded 10 years later, was built by Northumbrian monks, now proficient in the 'Roman manner'. Like Hartlepool, the cemeteries of Wearmouth and Jarrow contained men, women and children.

These communities practised the monastic arts, the production of illuminated manuscripts, and essential ritual items of church plate: the chalice, paten, ciborium, crozier and reliquary, and most importantly sculpture, of which more presently. Of the manuscripts that survive, probably a tithe of the whole, only a few are complete and can be assigned to their place of production. The scriptoria at Lindisfarne and Jarrow were neighbours and in contact with each other, and their manuscripts were products of the Northumbrian coast; but the contrast between the two codices is startling. *Lindisfarne* is lavishly illuminated with geometric and zoomorphic ornament parading the colourful joys of insular art. *Amiatinus* is more severe, its script perfect and its art so Mediterranean in aspiration that it is no wonder that crafty clerics were able to pass it off as an Italian manuscript, its Northumbrian attribution only rediscovered by analysing the counterfeit dedication under ultra violet light. This confrontation of two contemporary high status manuscripts remembers, without obvious antipathy, the deep roots of British religiosity (at Lindisfarne) and the Anglian striving for authenticity in accordance with adopted Roman grandeur.

The resources required to produce these books required the diversion of enormous wealth. The Codex Amiatinus alone has been claimed as requiring the hides of 515 calves, to which may be added another 1,030 for the other two pandects, not to mention numerous other Northumbrian manuscripts now lost or burnt in Viking raids.[16] Added to the costs of production are the dyes designed to emulate the colours of the late Roman and Byzantine purple and gold: purple possibly from the dog whelk or from the plant *crozaphora tinctoria*, blue from woad, green from verdigris, a copper-corrosion product, and yellow orpiment, a crystalline arsenic sulphide found in volcanos and traded in the Roman empire – it gave a deep yellow colour, imitating gold. The colours were mixed to give the astonishing range of pastel shades seen in the Lindisfarne Gospels.[17] The discoveries at Portmahomack, which included the use of incinerated shellfish to provide an astringent for preparing vellum, demonstrated the ingenuity with which insular communities adapted local resources to place their products on par with those of the Mediterranean world. Missing so far from the archaeological record but confidently inferred are the vestments, worn by priests and cloths hung on and behind the altar, richly embroidered, their colours changing like trees with the season of the church year.

The power declared by the monasteries and the exhortation to sign up to it was proclaimed in their layout, churches, fabulous portable art and wealth. At Portmahomack a case was made that the insular monastery received its initial investment not only in land but in the form of a herd of cattle; this provided the self-reproducing capital asset that could be exchanged and used to make cash purchases. It was conjectured that the currency employed was actually cattle hides, which could be stored, transported and adapted to a large number of practical uses, for example, to make tents, shields, boats and clothing. The principal income took the form of serial endowment – deposit of treasure and commodities in exchange for spiritual benefits, especially on the performance of rites of passage for birth (baptism), marriage and death. A rise in spiritual dependency therefore had the inevitable consequence of a demand for ritual comfort and of an increase in wealth for those that purveyed it. Capital assets could be employed to acquire more grazing but also to employ more monks to copy books, found new monasteries and acquire more followers for the greater glory of God. The effect of all this wealth was to show by how much the splendour of the aristocratic men and women buried in the early and middle 7th century could be exceeded by the new fundamentalist theocratic regime.

Perhaps the most powerful of all the instruments that were used to advance the monastic movement was sculpture, which unlike church vessels and manuscripts (and burial) was in the public eye and had the maximum artistic impact. The presence of vertical columns standing in the open air was not new: it was a prehistoric practice already ancient in Roman times and renewed in Formative 1, especially in the north and west. The Northumbrian version was new, not only in its outstanding quality but in the way it was used. In a first period (c. 675–750), carving focussed on the embellishment of the new stone churches: an inscribed dedication at Jarrow, lathe-turned balusters at Jarrow, Wearmouth and Hexham, a polygonal lectern pillar at Jarrow. Architectural sculpture was designed to replicate Classical interiors using entablatures of mini-balusters and friezes of animals and human figures running along the walls, many or all of them painted. Carved stone enters the cemetery as slabs that stood vertically or were laid horizontally on the grave and were incised with crosses and names (Hartlepool, Whitby, Wearmouth).

Break-out

In a second phase (c. 750–825), the carved stone takes to the landscape and marches north, west and south, superseding the princely pillars. These 'Victory' monuments seem consciously to have been used as instruments of conversion, signing monastic estates that supported the venture. The early stone Jarrow 16, which bears an inscription saying *In this unique sign life is returned to the world*, perhaps marks the origin point of the advance. The inscription on the cross at Bewcastle includes the incomplete phrase 'This Victory cross was set up by Hwaetred. . . .' The crosses are grand, expert and full of people and life. Some forms, e.g. Masham, recall the triumphal columns of Rome (Hadrian's); most are tall, rectangular in section and feature niches with busts of figures carved in relief bearing books, manifesting holiness and wisdom. They celebrate the apostles and their preaching to all nations. The monuments appear to start in west Yorkshire around Ripon, where Wilfred had his estates in the late 7th century, spread southwards, establishing new estates around Otley (8th century) and Dewsbury (9th century), and westwards up Uredale, via Bewcastle and Ruthwell to Whithorn and into the Lune valley. Signs of the march might also be seen in grand crosses at Glastonbury and Ramsbury and perhaps in the 9th/10th-century crosses of Cornwall.

Northumbria's participation and leading role in the monastic movement was culturally English and adopted a Roman rather than a prehistoric plan for its ritual centres. In this it draws a distinction both with English culture south of the Humber, where traces of a comparable monasticism are elusive, and British, Pictish and Scottish cultures to the north and west, where the form of ritual centres and some of their practices are more aligned with prehistoric tradition. Bede's attempts to write the Southumbrians into the monastic agenda are not corroborated, so far, by archaeological expression of an alignment with it on the ground. The Northumbrian initiative, driven by individual kings and prelates, is therefore an original and self-confident project of Northumbria, holding the balance of the political agenda during a long 8th century. Its priority in its expansion phase is towards the north and west, as opposed to towards its compatriots in the south and east. This could mean that that the

Northumbrian project is the child of an Anglo-British community or that, while committed to the primary governance of God, it is reluctant to abandon the English objective of secular dominion over the whole island. Embracing a new Roman Christian empire would appear to have been the logical compromise, acceptable to all but extremist factions in England and Scandinavia.

Dressing northerners in Formative 2

The rise of monastic wealth did not noticeably impoverish the aristocracy, whose families no doubt placed certain of their members strategically within the movement. The lords still dressed to kill and, if anything, increased their personal splendour, while clerics looked splendid too, each sporting the robes of their metier. At the end of the 7th century, the brooch culture splits into two: the Irish brooches are annular (Tara), the Pictish penannular (St Ninian's Isle). Both are equally lavish and include many masterpieces. The documentary and pictorial survivals suggest that the emergent leadership class on both sides of Britain are cranking up their aristocratic airs. We can now dress them more fully: tunics with brocaded hems, leather shoes with bronze fittings. The brooches, on the left shoulder for the men, over the breast for the women, fasten cloaks, coloured brown or black or dyed blue or purple. The leading men still have long flowing hair, kept out of the eyes with a headband. They carry spears and swords into battle and spears in the hunt.

They were shortly joined in the fashion parade by the new brand of high-status cleric, who were not above sporting badges of rank and wisdom. The Irish clerics wear circular brooches, perhaps indicating their superior calling, now at the service of the church. They proclaim their mission in long embroidered cowled robes, making references both to their aristocratic contemporaries and to the masters of pagan ceremonies who preceded them. Some aspects of the clerical dress no doubt came in with Christianity, whose desert fathers would have adopted a hood and overall coverage of the body against the sun. But the Orkney hood, certainly pre-Christian, shows that the adaptation to the northern climate had already resulted in a similar prescription against rain and wind. The Pictish monks, warriors of Christ, rode horses and wore ankle-length, richly embroidered surplices with hoods.

Southumbrian lords

It has been once or twice averred that the region south of the Humber, that is the area of primary English settlement, did not take an active part in the monastic movement. This needs to be carefully reconsidered when there is more and better archaeological evidence. At present we can address two main questions: are the religious characteristics of Southumbrian settlements in Fm 2 different to those of Northumbria, and if so can any of the former still be counted as monastic? However, I should emphasise that this has been addressed here using only archaeological evidence and does not employ arguments drawn from documents or from silence. Monastic status and saintly leaders are certainly claimed in documents for a number of settlements south of the Humber, some of which may have operated in 'federations'.[18] However, to date they have not produced more than a few elements of the northern package and are notably lacking in sculpture, stone churches, specialist crafts, and symbolic plans, whether of Jarrow or Nendrum type. To say that an English monastery looks the same as an English high-status settlement is to endorse the archaeological argument.

On the other hand, the English settlement sequence in Formative 2 is indicative in another way. It sees the introduction of self-contained farmsteads (Yarnton, Higham Ferrers, Pennyland, Catholme) of increasingly high-status villages (Cowdery's Down) that deserve a special title ('magnate farm' being the one chosen here). Some of these have already diversified into exchange centres (Rendlesham, Coddenham) when this role is superseded by a new kind of coastal international trading place or *wic* (Ipswich, Hamwic, Lundenwic, Eoforwic). None of these sites is enclosed, and there is so far very little sign of spiritual investment at any of them: no churches, no sculpture, no manufacturing of church plate, no vellum making, no oriented unfurnished graves.

Dedicated ecclesiastical sites remain elusive. There are churches or church fabric associated with Augustine's mission to Kent and a building that became a church at Bradwell-on-sea which was contrived from the gatehouse of the Roman fort there. Out of 51 surviving manuscripts illuminated in the British Isles before the 9th century, only nine are claimed to have had an origin in southern England; of these three are Gospels, two are Psalters and two prayer books. Very few pieces of sculpture from southern England are dated to Fm 2, although there are weak signs of penetration in Lincolnshire from Yorkshire (South Kyme) and from Mercia (Edenham). A case has been advanced for two settlement sites to have been monasteries or to have passed through a monastic phase, namely at Brandon in Suffolk and Flixborough in north Lincolnshire. On the face of it, Brandon has every appearance of a high-status farm that took to manufacture and trading in its Phase 2.2 (later 8th century). The presence of a cemetery does not imply a monastery, nor does it even demand a church, as we have noted from the Irish and Scottish cemetery-settlements. Flixborough had few buildings, and the mass of finds stratified in its landfill site certainly indicate a powerful establishment nearby, one that may have changed its allegiance through time. The evangelist symbol at Brandon and the seven names inscribed on a lead plaque do not need to indicate a monastic presence in the area – although it may. Finds of styli are not thought to be diagnostic of a clerical community on either site; these are standard tools for taking notes on wax tablets, not instruments for copying or illuminating manuscripts. Designed to address the question of the form of a Southumbrian monastery, the recently completed project at Lyminge, expertly planned and executed, revealed instead a very fine high-status farmstead, but 'added barely a scrap of new evidence relating to Lyminge's "monastic phase"'.[19] Thus a general response to the two questions posed earlier can be that although we have yet to see enough of them to be sure, sites claimed as monastic in Southumbria do not resemble the monasteries of the north, especially in respect of their lack of sculpture and monastic crafts. Insofar as there are indications, the communities are secular and family based; at least where there is a church the term 'minster' could be used to describe them, as it was of later convents serving a bishop.[20]

As well as the magnate farm, the 8th century in Southumbria was the century of the *wic*. with investigations in Hamwic, Ipswich, Lundenwic and Eoforwic allowing a broad characterisation: they are located on a river bank, they have a planned layout with houses and (probably) warehouses, and areas of manufacture. They receive goods from overseas and (probably) send others out. They rise probably under royal initiative and perhaps with the assistance of established Continental traders, Frisian or Frankish. They flourish during the 8th century and disappear in the 9th. They are supplied from a hinterland and possibly serve it, as indicated by the distribution of Ipswich ware. They align with the beachmarkets of Scandinavia but do not seem to belong to a similar trajectory, i.e. cult centre – local market – nodal market and town. Nevertheless the discovery by metal-detectorists of numerous surface scatter sites implies a network of inland markets, and it is not excluded that there will be additional coastal trade points, as is proposed for the Low Countries and Denmark. However, the present model is that *wics* were created or harnessed to generate wealth for the lords, and this required canalisation of trade through these designated places, maybe throttling the incipient trading activities of the magnate farms.[21] In this they emulated – and opposed – the control of incoming wealth achieved by the monasteries in the British zones of the north and west, to which they set up an English counterweight.

Summary of Formative 2

Given the domination of the landscape by the Victory crosses of the Northumbrian church militant, in combination with the High Crosses of Ireland and Scotland and the great cross-slabs of Pictland, an 8th-century traveller to the British Isles could be forgiven the conviction that monastic Christianity was there to stay. However, there were three unsettling signs on the horizon: the first was the lack of penetration of the new prescription into Southumbria, the second the beginning of the Viking raids in the late 8th century, and the third was the commercialisation of monasteries.

Although historians and art historians have delighted in bringing all the people of the British Isles together within one brilliant 'insular' programme, this can only been done by assuming that Northumbria can stand for the whole of England. Examined archaeologically, we come to a rather more subtle ideological topography. It is rather in the previous period, the late 6th to 7th century, in which the aristocracies of Ireland, Scotland, Pictland, Wales, Northumbria and Southumbria make common cause. They manifest a 'heroic' demeanour that is competitive, aggressive, egocentric and creates great art which extols the virtues of men and women achieving results in the real world. It is the new Christianity that splits them up, and it does this from the late 7th century to at least the mid-8th. Whether opinions about the date of Easter or the form of tonsure were really significant or merely masked opposing ideological convictions is not the central issue. The archaeology exposes real differences in monumentality on the one hand between the British regions and Northumbria and on the other between Northumbria and Southumbria. Neither does the British west and south manifest any great uniformity: Scotland, Pictland, Wales and Cornwall all react differently to the grand project of the age. The Border zones seem to opt out until the mid-8th century.

In the second half of the 8th century, Northumbria, already head and shoulders above its neighbours in wealth and the proclamation of the Christian project, bursts its boundaries to leave a trail of Victory Crosses west to Galloway and north to Abercorn, and possibly into the highlands in harness with the Pictish church. It is probably Northumbrian energy that galvanises the Borderlands from Cumbria to Devon and inspires an equivalent response in Mercia. The only territory that is barely affected is that of Southumbria, where penetration of the Victory Crosses is minimal and investment in monastic settlement is barely detectable, at least in any form that would be recognised north of the Humber.

There may be other explanations for this. In the light of the documentary evidence, and such materiality as we have, it would be folly to suppose that south-east England remained aloof from Christianity and from the new thrust that apparently brought furnished burial and its cognate ritual to a halt precisely in its territory in the late 7th century. On the other hand, it would not be unreasonable to look for Christian practice of a different kind, one that was focussed not on the communities of the blessed but in the rather more down-to-earth purview of the aristocratic landowners and within its control. This was the prescription that would follow the Danish takeover in Yorkshire in the 9th century. However, even the markers of that prescription, namely standing crosses and private churches, are still largely absent from Southumbria. One possible alternative, always conjectural, is that Christian practice was here in the direct control of the king. In this case we should find it in close association with the *villa regalis* or palace. If we have not dug up such combinations as yet, there is a hint of something of the kind at Foxley near Malmesbury, where an air photograph apparently shows church and hall adjacent, and in Martin Biddle's unpublished excavations at Winchester, where a putative palace, a 7th-century church and furnished 7th-century burials were succeeded by convents of male and female communities serving a cathedral.[22] If these communities show us what is intended by a 'minster', then the distinction is a helpful one: Southumbria has a Christian college that primarily serves the king. In Northumbria, Scotland and Pictland, it was the Christian college itself that provided the ultimate authority.

In this sense, it is legitimate to accord a different ideology to the English north and south of the Humber. If we go by the sculpture, we can accord further ideological variations within monasticism too, between the great midland bloc of Northumbria and Mercia, north and south Pictland, Scotland, Ireland and Wales, with Cornwall not taking part until the 9th century. The differences need not have been actively divisive but are politically significant, and they remain, so to speak, in the soil. Such diverse territories were encountered in the following century, by the Danes in the east and the Norse in the north and west, who will have provoked different responses to their invasions. The farms and *wics* in the south-east would have been much more familiar to them than the monasteries in the north-west. But even in Southumbria we need not assume a united response: in Wessex they were prepared to fight the Viking army. In East Anglia they provided it with horses.[23]

Formative 3: early 9th to mid-11th century

FM3A 825–900: the Viking Age in the south-east (Danish) and north-west (Norse)

The Vikings were at Lindisfarne in 793 and raided the coasts of Northumbria, Scotland and Wales intermittently for the next century, mainly targeting monasteries. In recent years, their impact has been sanitised by archaeologists, probably because the initial hostility suffered by monasteries has been harder to see than the civilised commerce of the later trading establishments. The excavation at Portmahomack has provided a clearer picture of such a raid, which involved the burning down of workshops and the felling and breaking up of the totemic grand cross-slabs, an event radiocarbon-dated around AD 800. Blade injuries were noted on skeletons in the monks' cemetery, resulting in immediate or later deaths. This conforms to what was reported at other places but attributed to clerical hysteria, and it was echoed at the Inchmarnock writing school, where a drawing seems to show a mailcoated Viking making off with a reliquary. While the attempts at white-washing may not have succeeded in persuading us that the violence was exaggerated, it has increased credibility in the political and targeted nature of the Viking campaigns. The violence was not mindless. It was aimed at monasteries, on the face of it the most innocuous part of British society, rather than the armies, halls and treasuries of the aristocracy. And it was aimed mainly at the north and west, where the monasteries were. This suggests that the real enemy was the monastic ethos and its methods of accruing wealth, no doubt perceived by non-believers as fraudulent.

Some corroboration that the Viking motives were primarily political is suggested by two other trends. In the first place, the invading Scandinavians readily accepted Christianity, but redesigned it to fit a more secular structure and embrace some of the morals of the familiar non-Christian tales. Thus the Christian landscape of East Yorkshire was soon repatterned in numerous lordships with standing crosses and a church, whether of Viking origin or not. The second trend concerns the fate of the monasteries themselves, which were not apparently left as smouldering ruins. Excavations have shown that in most cases recovery was immediate but resulted in a different kind of settlement. Hoddom reverted to being an estate centre, the guest house at Jarrow became a workshop making dress accessories and Whithorn turned to trade, as did Portmahomack, where secular masters were served by the manufacture of buckles, brooches and weights. Iona, which returned to the monastic life, was raided repeatedly between 790 and 880.

The Viking agenda was therefore to wean the people of Britain off their monastic dependence and get them trading. This is understandable, since it is more or less what they did in Scandinavia itself: that is, they placed the cult sites under secular control and superseded them with trading towns. The principle, that prosperity trumps prayer, was actually the unwitting message of the monasteries themselves as they accrued wealth. The commercialisation of the monasteries in Wales, as in Ireland, as in France was in one respect a way of maintaining their relevance in the new *zeitgeist*. In another, it was a sign that the Vikings had won the argument.

While they might have had sympathy with Viking policies, the English set out like any other Germanic competitor to make sure that it was their top families, rather than the incomers, that ended up in control of the island where they had settled. They were not about to be pushed aside as they had previously pushed aside the British. The British areas were more hesitant, and their self-determination less effective in consequence: what was the advantage in exchanging the promise of eternity and the peaceful coexistence of all peoples under Christ for a life of relentless commercial ambition? If this is a fair characterisation of their attitude, it was to lose them control, first to the Scandinavians and then to the English, over the next hundred years. In the 13th century, the Scandinavians were still governing the north and western isles and the English were pursuing their right, on family grounds, to dominate southern Scotland, Wales, Ireland and a large part of western France.

One example of the influence of 9th-century thinking on settlement was the change from round to rectangular house forms in Ireland. The adoption of the North Sea norm from c. 800 coincided with a flight from ringfort culture, the decline of cattle and an increase in drying kilns and souterrains, all probably indicating a rise in cereal production and the use of money.

While the monasteries turned to commerce and became quasi-urban, Viking beachmarkets and longphorts morphed into trading towns.[24] The Viking exchange system favoured the accumulation of moveable wealth, especially silver: out to the Continent and to the Mediterranean went cloth, amber, steatite, dried fish and slaves; in came coins, pins, rings and hacksilver, converted for portability into bracelets, arm rings and gross thistle brooches.

Settlements influenced by Norse approaches and material culture have been explored in the Orkneys (Birsay), in the Western Isles (Bornais), in the Isle of Man (Braaid) and in Wales (Llanbedrgoch). Llan-gors is a latter day Irish-type crannog, the headquarters of a lord who was active against Wessex in the early 10th-century war of conquest. These are dispersed strongholds in the local idiom, where settlements, cemeteries and stone monuments were all 'Vikingised' in the mildest of manners. Viking boat burials and richly furnished female graves were added to pre-existing cemeteries in Orkney, the Isle of Man and in York.[25] The burial of the heroes of the Great Army are probably to be seen at Ingleby, commemorated in mounds, while casualties of war were buried in a pit at nearby Repton.

The erection of stone monuments continued unabated but was now acting as a vehicle for the Formative 3 agenda. In Pictland, the giant cross slab at Forres (5.5 m high) is a Victory

Cross, but a victory of the Scots, probably over the Picts as well as the Norse. A latter day landowning monument is erected in Powys recording the family of Eliseg on a tall round pillar on a barrow overlooking a valley and stating its determination to reclaim Wales from the English. Other pillars, also seemingly serving land-claiming interests, pepper the Peak District. Elsewhere in Wales, in Cornwall and in Ireland, grand crosses are erected at the sites of mother churches, monasteries and bishop's seats sometimes remembering prominent prelates or elite donors. Anglo-Scandinavian, Hiberno-Norse, pagan-Christian hybrid monuments are erected in Northumberland and Durham, Yorkshire, Clydeside, Cumbria, Lancashire, Anglesey and notably on the Isle of Man. A particular sect appears to be mapped by the hogback stone grave covers, which combine the devotional character of an Anglian shrine and an Irish reliquary with the form and images of a warrior's hall – a cult of heroes adapted to its contemporary culture. It begins in Brompton in Yorkshire and spreads north to the Tweed and Perthshire, north-west to Clydeside and west to Cumbria, Lancashire and Cheshire.

There was no need to modernise the settlement pattern in England – it already consisted of magnate-type proto-manorial farms housing a social hierarchy of lords and labourers and was in tune with Scandinavian practice. From the 9th century, the English village took its characteristic form and modern location, each with a lord, manor, church and cemetery. Stone grave covers commemorate the earliest lords. The church at Raunds was built in the late 9th/early 10th century, and people were buried there in family rows between c. 978–1040. The variation in burial form and the health of those buried make it clear that a class system was operating. Remote from the family burial grounds and located in a 'pagan' ambience around a barrow or prehistoric standing stone are the burials of those who came into conflict with the regime or its ethos and were executed by hanging. This practice was noted in the 8th century at Sutton Hoo and reached a high intensity in the 10th. The victims were sometimes exposed on a gibbet, after which their remains were buried in an advanced state of decomposition. The majority of the victims were young men, but some young women and older men were executed and buried in combinations that suggested sexual 'crimes'. This is in keeping with the dates, which show that these executions were the work of Christian kings or prelates who are punishing those failing to conform to the new morality or to the absolute loyalty demanded by the crown.

Dressing up in Formative 3

Formative 3 keeps the dressy male leader on stage and provides us with some rare glimpses of smart women. On the picture stones, and in metal pendants, we see dead Vikings attended by women with flowing gowns and their hair in a bun. The men are exemplified by the description of Skarp-Hedin at the Althing: 'his hair combed well back and held in place by a silken head-band, looking every inch a warrior'. Viking warriors carried spear, sword, shield and at least some of their wealth as ready cash in the form of armbands. Their cloaks were fastened with an extravagant version of the penannular brooch, with a giant pin with the thistle-shaped head. Viking women wore a version of the peplos, secured on each shoulder with domed oval 'tortoise brooches'. Silk headdresses have been found in York, Lincoln and Dublin. The Vikings developed *wadmal*, a tightly spun, matted, water repellent fabric found in Orkney, Shetland, Iceland and Greenland.

The effete south had a more florid wardrobe. In the 8th-century Vespasian Psalter, King David wears a red striped undergarment with a sleeved mantle on top and is playing the lyre, while the boys in the band have tight cuffs to keep their hands free for the instruments and the two dancers wear green and rose belted tunics. David wears a pair of shoes with a tongue and cross straps, while the others wear cuffed slippers. The young musicians have their hair parted in the middle, the others have their hair in curls or contained in a cap, while David wears his slicked down, combed over the head and into a bunch at the back (p. 118). Military figures of the 10th century wear a cloak with a brooch on the right shoulder and carry a sword on a sword belt. The main garment is a kind of kilt, flat in the front and kicked up in folds at the back. The legs are clad in what look like 'compression leggings' with gaiters around the shins supported by suspenders. Women wear a long gown with a head scarf, lengthened from the days in which a *cuffie* set off the peplos, into a long veil (sometimes as long as a pashmina) so that the whole length of the body is covered. As can be seen in the 'realist' portraits of the *Psychomachia*, this was not confined to religious women but can be seen in pictures of young people socialising: the men show off their head, neck and legs, the women have their faces framed by the scarf, their sinuous forms hinted in folds of cloth with kicked up hems. The clergy too are nicely dressed, with no whiff of the hirsute hermit (p. 125). In the frontispiece to the *Life of Cuthbert*, a Winchester manuscript dating from before 937, Cuthbert wears a square-neck russet brown chasuble over an alb, – a form that a modern day Catholic priest would recognise. King Athelstan (presenting him with a copy of Bede's book) wears bright red leggings under a short grey belted tunic with brocaded cuffs and neckline, under a cloak pinned on the right shoulder by a small circular brooch, its modesty perhaps a mark of the authentic. Meanwhile workers in the woods and fields wear short kirtles, probably with a belt, tucked up to work with bare legs in mucky places; their hair is blonde, black, balding or with a forked beard. But few art forms offer us portraits of clerics as sympathetic and evocative as the St Peter relief busts from Daglingworth and Dowlish Wake. They might be every intelligent teenager's favourite Latin teacher (p. 534).

FM3B 900–975: the Wessex conquest of the Midlands, Cornwall and Northumbria

The third phase of Formative 3 is the war between the English, Danes, Norse, Scottish, Picts and Welsh and the concomitant conquest of the Midlands and the north by the kingdom of Wessex. This created a new version of England twice the size of that of Formative 2's 'Southumbria' and more or less coterminous with the one we have now. The war lasted just over 50 years, from about 866 when the Great Army landed in East Anglia to 918, when Aethelflaed took the surrender of York. The most useful archaeological contributions to the story, richly documented by the *Anglo-Saxon Chronicle*, have probably been the development of the *burh* and the emergence (or survival) of a number of regional industries, including wheel-thrown pottery and church architecture. Ironically, at the very moment of the (rather forceful) creation of a united England, the regional loyalties shine through. Other achievements were on the national scale: the introduction of coinage, the development of the Winchester School of carving and manuscript illumination, probably the most impish, appealing and humane art to ever to come out of England.

Few parts of Britain were untouched by the war. The Norse invaded the outer isles, Caithness and both sides of the Irish Sea. The Danes invaded East Anglia and Northumbria. The Scots invaded eastern Scotland and subsumed the remains of Pictish culture. The principal theatres of conflict were Wessex, where Alfred and the Saxons held off the Danes, and the Moray Firth, where Macbeth and the Scots held off the Norse. By the early 10th century, the invasions were in temporary remission, and the English reinvented themselves as the heirs of Rome, using Roman methodology to conquer the whole island up to the Forth-Clyde divide.

Their principal instrument was the *burh*, a rapidly erected rectangular fortress based broadly on the Roman marching camp.

In Chapter 3 I argued for the acceptance of Alan Vince's three-stage model of *burh* development, as a military fort (c. 886–918), as a regional administrative centre (918–1014) and as a place of national and international trade (1014–1066). The original inspiration of the burh continues to create discussion. My own feeling is that there was no influence as strong as that of Rome, gleaned by the family of Alfred the Great from serious study of the Roman military and from the ruins of Roman towns and forts spread liberally over the English plain. The Roman influence became evident in the character of Late Saxon coinage and the Roman style of Late Saxon pottery, the nature of which even varied in colour and style with their Roman predecessors, made half a millennium earlier. It had probably not escaped the attention of Alfred's studious entourage that the Roman army was successful and their subsequent administration had controlled an extensive territory for 400 years.

The driving principle of *burh* design consisted of patching the defences of former Roman towns where this was practical[26] and the building *de novo* of forts that were almost square.[27] These were protected by a ditch and a dump rampart that may have had a timber frame, where the soil demanded it (Hereford). Ramparts were later reinforced with a stone wall facing the enemy. There were hints of towers (e.g. Stafford). A third type seems at first sight to use the natural topography – a loop in the river (Durham) or a marsh (Athelney, Lyng). But a case can be made, as yet requiring proper demonstration, that all the forts had a rectilinear plan even when planted in a loop in the river, on a promontory or in a previous hill fort (Chirbury, Cadbury).

Burh development proceeded in four phases: the buildings of burhs for the defence of Wessex in the late 9th century; the building of burhs for the conquest of the East and West Midlands in the early 10th; the adaption of selected burhs to serve the shiring of the new English territories in the later 10th; and the development of some burhs as towns to promote the rise of national and international trade. The first phase, owed to Alfred, created the Wessex burhs, starting with Winchester in c. 886 and the principle of the system: each should be not more than 20 miles (a day's ride) away; each should have a dedicated garrison provided by the tenants of the hinterland. There was a way of working out the levy, depending on the size of contributing estates (number of hides), but attempts to correlate the number of men with the precise length of the defences have ultimately hit the buffers. However, the figures we have show credibly enough the sort of numbers involved. At Wallingford the line of the defences was approximately 2,500 m, enclosing 41 ha; it was rated at 2,400 hides, which may equate to the size of the garrison, 2,400 men (at 4 feet per man this would imply a defended length of 9,600 feet, 2,900 m). The sites of burhs were chosen on strategic grounds and used royal land (Wilton) or land requisitioned from church property (perhaps Cricklade). In general the *de novo* burhs have failed to produce much evidence for occupation until the later 10th century, suggesting that they functioned primarily as camps and were not developed further.

Stage 2 began with a meeting in the old City of London in 898 attended by Alfred, his son, Edward (the Elder), his daughter, Aethelflaed, her husband, Ethelred of Mercia, Waerferth Bishop of Worcester and Plegmund Archbishop of Canterbury.[28] London was redesigned between the Thames and Cheapside, the new work including a dock at Queenhithe and the rebuilding of London Bridge. Alfred died the next year, and the command passed to his son and his son-in-law. The agenda was now enlarged: not only to clear Scandinavian opposition but to absorb the previously occupied territories into an expanded kingdom of Wessex. As with the Roman conquest, the land would be secured by a trail of forts: Edward took the right flank, building burhs from Hertford to Manchester. Ethelred of Mercia took the left flank, starting with the burh he had already built at his home town at Gloucester and recommissioning other Roman towns at Worcester (899) and Chester (907). But in 910 he was fatally injured at the Battle of Tettenhall and died a year later. Aethelflaed, his wife (and Alfred's daughter), took control of the western army and built 11 burhs between 912 and 918 when she died, exhausted, at York. By this time her army had neutralised the Danes, the Norse and the Welsh, making her probably the most successful Anglo-Saxon battlefield commander.

The realities of this campaign were seen on the ground at Aethelflaed's burh at Stafford, where a peninsula surrounded by marshes, crossed by a Roman road and used since the Iron Age as a tribute delivery point was adapted as a military headquarters in which meat was supplied and grain was turned into bannocks in sufficient quantities to feed an army. At this time (the early 10th century), a pollen diagram from King's Pool showed a leap in cereal production. Stafford had its own potters making lamps, bowls, storage vessels and, in particular, the ubiquitous orange jars that travelled over a wide hinterland. The radiocarbon dates suggest that the camp got going in the early 10th century, consistent with the date (913) given by the *Anglo-Saxon Chronicle* for the foundation of the *burh*. The layout suggested a generous use of space: Stafford Ware was spread over the whole peninsula, being found in every site examined (32 trenches), but features were few and far between. Stafford was not the right place to fully test Vince's hypothesis, and yet it was consistent with it: the place was commissioned as fort; it served a military force; towards the end of its short life it was designated as the county town of Staffordshire and served as an administrative centre with a mint (Stage 3). It never arrived at Stage 4: there was no sign of trade of short or long distance before the town was crushed and abandoned in the scorched earth campaign of William I; then every part of the town died, to revive only in the late 12th century.

FM3C 975–1050: Irish, Welsh, Scottish, Norse kingdoms

Formative 3 saw the ultimate humiliation of the Britons, who were dispossessed by three powers: Scandinavians, Scots and English. The remaining British elements in the southwest, Mercia and Northumbria were eliminated or driven underground, and British self-determination survived only in Wales. This was the moment at which the island radically changed its character. Its new lords shared a competitive wealth-driven ethos in which money was theoretically more important than nationalism or religion; but the English had all the advantages, notably the most fertile land, proximity to the Continent and a successful new model army. The Irish and Scottish fleets were boxed in by the Scandinavians, making alliance with them the only strategy with a reasonable chance of success. In the 10th century, the English *burhs* were redesigned to act as nodes of regional government subsisting on tax; by the 11th century, the better placed *burhs* began to create wealth through manufacture and trade. All the *burhs* naturally contained one or more minsters, but these need not have provided their principal *raison d'etre*.

The paradox is that the conquest by Wessex of the rest of Britain, conducted in the Roman manner, succeeded not in liberating and uniting the island but in replacing one species of imperial tyranny with another. England stopped where Rome had stopped, at the limit of the good land. Beyond lay the troublesome Celts, worthy of correction and punitive raids but not for economic development. This view was to drive English political opinion for another millennium. Strategically, however, it made sense to attempt to control the whole island and to hold to account disaffected factions that might side with the Scandinavian-Norman-French aristocracy that represented the current threat. England had already been part of a Scandinavian overlordship when it shared King Cnut with Denmark; it would quite shortly be invaded by another Scandinavian kingdom-claimer from northern France, William I.

In spite of this, the century leading up to 1066 is noted archaeologically for its exuberant self-expression and for laying the foundations of English culture. In art one can argue about whether Carolingian emulation, as in the sprawling acanthus of the Winchester school, or Scandinavian superstitious vigour, as in the St Pauls' Churchyard slab, was determinant or even influential. The enduring legacy was neither the pomp of the court or the stiffness of the church but the vivacious humour of the ordinary citizen and the love of their landscape that pervade the corpus of drawings made in the years around 1000, a first informal sight of the untitled, unbuttoned English citizens at work and play. This is also the era of the first stone-built parish churches, with their regional variants; of the founding elements of the English village (Shapwick), of the streets in towns dedicated to markets (Cheapside) or particular trades (Bread Street), of Roman-style mass-produced pottery, of Roman-style coins with a lively symbolic language of their own, of the Law codes, the first attempts at official histories (the *Anglo-Saxon Chronicle*), of primacy in textiles and the miracle of narrative history that is the Bayeux Tapestry, – a 70 m-long linen strip where it is not the story that is embroidered but the embroidery that causes reality to leap to life presenting us with character actors, inventive vignettes, gossipy stories, threatening moods and tragic battles in a few deft stitches. This work of art was completed in c. 1100 after nearly 40 years of Norman rule. Just as the regionalism of late Saxon architecture and late Saxon pottery reflected the by now redundant kingdoms of Formative 2, so the English creative wit of Formative 3 continued to thrive beneath the cloak of Norman oppression.

Summary of Formative 3

The 9th–11th century in the north is a real dark age, archaeologically speaking, giving few material clues as to what drove it. The most revealing analogy is probably that provided by Ireland, where monasteries adapted to the new ethos by creating 'monastic towns'. Similar trends may be glimpsed not only in adjacent Whithorn but in an embryonic form in Northumbria. In the absence of adequate evidence for settlement, monuments or burial in the north, the Scottish intrusion comes across as a straight piece of aggression in pursuit of more fertile territory. Resistance was ultimately unsuccessful: the Norse were driven to the isles and the Picts were driven out of history. The new polity, Scotland, was here to stay, and the Scots have fought since for recognition as the 'original' inhabitants. This they were not, but their 9th-century conquest (and the disappearance of the Picts) gives them primacy in the north over that other acquisitive power, the English. It is certainly strange in our day to hear the English and Scottish nationalist causes claimed as owning the logic of history.

The period in the south is much better known, both because it was recorded in some detail at the time and because it has left the remains of settlements full of material character, especially *wics* and *burhs*. From the cultural material we draw a strong sense that the motivation of Wessex for defeating the Scandinavian and Hiberno-British armies was not simply the wish to control extensive territory. Here too there was an ideological driver, but a different one to the free-marketeers. Wessex wished to build a kingdom in the Roman image, a civilised kingdom which was well fed and a style leader in the civilised arts: architecture, sculpture, illuminated manuscripts, central places, trade and war. While coins, pots and burhs speak clearly of Rome, there are hints of a more profound allegiance to its methods of civic control: of a taxation, redistribution and welfare that was regionally based, not feudal. In this sense, Wessex was on its way to creating a state that was some way ahead of its time. The struggles of history make no sense if they appear generated by animal competition, a 'darkling plain in which ignorant armies clash by night'. The ideology is all: as the archaeology reveals, it can explain why alliances cross ethnic and regional boundaries, why the strongest can still lose, why some ideas keep coming back.

There is a possibility that we can assign a general ideological climate, if not a specific ideology, to the time divisions of the Formative period. The burden of the narrative is that in formative Britain changes of direction are prompted by a perceived need to embrace either belligerent leadership, the grace of God or wealth as the essential prerequisite for survival. Since all three promised success in different ways, the long trail from the 5th century into the middle ages and perhaps beyond is punctuated by attempts to combine them successfully. Without being overly prescriptive, it seems possible to associate Formative 1, 2 and 3 in most of Britain with a political agenda driven respectively by an emphasis on lordship, spirituality and wealth creation.

Reflections

Seven hundred years separate the beginning and end of the period defined in this book. A lot can happen – and plainly did – in seven centuries, 20–30 generations. With the assistance of scientific dating, the objective has been to chronicle changes in material culture and to attempt to read them as changes in the way people acted and thought. The changes appear to be quite sudden – quantum leaps – in which a people changed direction like fish in a stream.

Our narrative paints a picture of an island in which many peoples met at a time when a previous, almost omnipotent, regime had collapsed. In the first of our three periods, we see these peoples confronting ideas that they had inherited from their own prehistoric and Roman pasts pressed into conversation and comparison with each other. It is not so much the differences in speech or appearance or custom that would have made this such an interesting time to be alive as the differences in ideas about this world and the next. Since Rome had gone, there was no overarching intellectual authority to insist on a universal behaviour. Old ideas shared space with new. The vast range of early thinking is laid out for us brightly, if sometimes obscurely, in Formative 1's safari park of monuments, cemeteries, houses, settlements, clothes, faces and poetry.

These descriptions have been determined in the climate of the early 21st century, when Britain was questioning the large power blocks to which it then belonged, the EU and the UK, and redefining smaller polities, England, Scotland, Wales, Ulster, not only perceived as more manageable intellectually but as having an eternal and rightful identity. As we have seen, all these 'nations' have their roots in the Formative period and most are composed of a sizable proportion of immigrants. Indeed, in the case of the two largest, it was the immigrants that created the nation. This process was not confined to Britain: all over Europe in the later first millennium, peoples relieved of the universalist government of the Roman empire were building nations that are more or less the ones we still have and embedding variant sets of moral principles into their foundation. Most are less than a thousand years old in a human history that is five to 10 times as long. This was therefore not a biological process like the origin of a species but an artificial human construct, although no less interesting for all that.

Most if not or all of the countries established themselves as kingdoms, a community restricted to one territory governed by a single male leader, in contrast to a widely spread folk associated by a common world-view. The making of these kingdoms has been discussed in the better-developed prehistoric context of 'state formation', an itinerary whereby an amorphous community graduated from bands and tribes to a hierarchical and regulated group of people, perceived to act in history as a single entity. Such itineraries have been explored most successfully in prehistory, beginning with the vision of Gordon Childe, but we should be less sanguine now that it was a one-way journey.[29] The route from super-state *back* to tribe is a leitmotiv of Formative 1 in Europe as a whole. When the gravitational field of politics was again reversed, the immediate destination was the kingdom, but the establishment of a Christian super-state remained on the agenda.

The creation of kingdoms has been seen as having a number of drivers, internal or external, environmental, economic, social and ideological. The basic source of wealth is provided by agricultural produce, and the basic mechanism of change is the transition from subsistence to surplus and the consequent mobilising of privilege.[30] The north and west was already hierarchical on a local scale in the 'family forts' of Fm 1.[31] But the late 7th century saw the capitalisation of cattle and the concentration of assets into the central places provided by the monasteries with their extensive herds and stock-piled hides. In the east and south, the increasing productivity of the grain economy implies an increase in the taxable surplus, with the inference of a more effective ruling class.[32] These changes and the imposition of two alternative types of governance, devotional or proprietary, take place together at the start of Formative 2.

The rise of kingdoms did not take place in a vacuum, and since the environmental resources were reasonably static, the question arises: why then? External prompts that may kick-start social change will include a range of events in neighbouring lands – events promising new sources of wealth or new cosmological promises of life after death. Bjorn Myhre's 'chiefdoms' in south-west Norway seem to have been funded through the interception of increased traffic up the 'North Way' in pursuit of furs.[33] The Mediterranean fervour for a post-Roman Christian empire was obviously one of the most heady potions available in 7th-century Britain. The trajectory in the Scandinavian countries from cult site to regional markets to towns must have had a strong influence on eastern Britain, which shared much of its ethos. The Christian version of the congregational cult site, the monastery, was not only the flagship of change in Ireland and western and northern Britain: the monastery was a proto-town in the central and southern Continent too, accruing wealth, conducting restrictive practices and acting as the bank of royal hopes, so long as holiness could not be trumped by autocracy. Monasteries could grow directly from aristocratic domains, the pre-existing owners of surplus, or be founded by missionaries championing the theocratic state as an alternative to kingship.[34] The direction of travel of the kingdoms has been seen as governed by a perception that the Mediterranean was the core and the northern isles (the utmost limits) were the periphery of the 8th-century Christian project.[35] However, it is uncertain that such a panoramic superiority of mission was really accepted by all the small entities that were jostling for position. A better description is perhaps provided by 'peer polity interaction', where the competition between emerging neighbours results in change through contest and emulation in the manner of an academic seminar.[36]

Alternatively change emerges through conversation between equals, not impossibly an aspect of the Formative period. A contribution expected, whether to governance, spirituality or wealth creation, is the adoption of assembly places that offer relief from autocracy or orthodoxy with a forum for decisions made by popular acclaim. Archaeologically, this is a wished-for prescription, since it seems to liberate people to some degree from the shackles of hierarchy. We have met a great many potential Central Places or Assembly Places in the course of our journey, and their diverse interpretations exemplify the uncertainties. The ancient sites of Göbekli Tepe in Turkey and Wadi Faynan in Jordan, 10 millennia old, set the theme: these places acted as magnets that were initially spiritual, drawing crowds who expressed their need for catharsis through feasting in the shadow of giant carved stones (Chapter 1). These 'congregational' sites have their analogues in pre-Christian formats, as in Scandinavia (e.g. Tissø, Uppåkra, Helgö; Chapter 3), in Iron Age Ireland (e.g. Rathrogan; Chapter 1), in post-Roman Britain (at Uley transforming from temple to shrine and church (Chapter 1, p. 37), in Fm 1 at cemeteries on prehistoric monuments (Capel Eithin, Cannington; Chapter 4) or barrows (Sutton Hoo, Chapter 4) or at enclosures marked by cattle sacrifice and ritualised sculpture (Yeavering, Rhynie, Chapter 3). The Christian movement deployed the congregational package using monasteries and churches (Chapter 3), burial grounds (Chapter 4) or sculpture (Chapter 5). Regional powers used natural or man-made landmarks for collecting tribute (e.g. Stafford, Chapter 3), ritual violence and execution (Chapter 4) or (presumably) hosting for war.

Individual central places have some or all of these attributes, but the argument here is that they progress through use, from placing votive deposits in lakes and bogs to delivering them to formal reception areas with shrines and temples in which pilgrims seek spiritual benefits through endowment. No one is suggesting that these diverse cultures learnt directly from each other or that they operated in precisely the same way. But there is a driving force here requiring in people the expression of their altruistic beliefs, which can be served by aligning with doctrine, proclaiming allegiance, or submitting to shamans and priests – a psychological vulnerability commandeered in turn by the secular power or turned into markets. In reading these alternatives, we read a change in the political climate that explains the fate of a particular community at a deeper level than successes of production or the character of kings.

External forces stimulating change have been most diligently sought through the medium of long-distance trade, since goods ought to be a prime indicator of contact and thus influence. The goods that are most detectable, even the red plates and amphorae reaching western Britain and Ireland, tend to be high-class commodities rather than the bulk supplies that might indicate an economic dependence and a broader hegemony. For this reason (among others), Chris Wickham has pointed at the aristocratic deployment of agricultural surplus rather than trade as the primary motor of early medieval change, at any rate in the southern lands.[37] In the north, where imports glitter brightly in furnished graves or are found scattered on the fields, it is tempting to see them as providing a major signal of pressure from overseas, in a similar way that the late Iron Age polities of Britain responded to Roman feelers at the start of the millennium.

It is clear that not only political alignments change; change changes too. By Formative 3 (beyond the chronological range of Wickham's synthesis, which ends in 800), we are in a very different theatre of exchange, a world system even, where the seas and rivers are thoroughfares and the traffic in commodities is enormous, not excluding slaves.[38] The Vikings revitalised maritime traffic and reintroduced targeted trade between the new coastal towns.[39] New discoveries and new appreciation of the typology of 7th–12th century amphorae is extending the mercantile Mediterranean both backwards and forwards in time.[40] Formative Britain is a chapter in the story of Formative Europe.

Away from the fascination and tyranny of generalised process, the period discussed here can never escape the power that contemporaries attributed to events, or perhaps of fate. The invasions, battles, murders and marriages that obsessed early medieval leaders – and their many historians – can never be completely sidelined by archaeological argument: they are too potent to dismiss as agents of change, even if the changes are imperceptible and escape the neat classifications of archaeological method. I am conscious of trying to stay under the historical radar for two reasons, already rehearsed in the Preface. First, I do not feel competent to assess the historical models, and second, I want to offer archaeological models that in some measure will themselves serve 'big history' better.[41] However, it is still through archaeology's upbeat initiatives that we will eventually discern the social, political and economic character of early medieval communities more surely than contemporary commentators could know.[42]

Every time there is a new vision for the mechanism of change, we nevertheless fail to answer the 'why-then?' question; what caused the causes of change? It may be that the answer never arrives: one prime mover always conceals another. It may also be that whatever explanation one human dreams up, the next generation can easily demonstrate to be untenable, not through lack of logic applied to evidence of the past but by dint of new ways of seeing through fresh eyes. Ideology in the sense deployed here is also conviction politics and is not based on reason, even when it pretends to be, but by instinct and emotion. The formative period in Britain, and in Europe more generally, is spell-binding for the diverse and numerous ideas it held in play. Their properties can be tracked back to earlier belief systems and their variations deconstructed through the geography and history of the protagonists. This gallimaufry of ideas is our inheritance as Europeans.

Is it possible to see some emphases trending underneath or behind the political choices made at particular places and times? In arguing that first-millennium politics swung between the prioritisation of governance, spirituality and wealth creation, I am aware that the driver of change from the flying of one banner to another remains obscure. If there are changes in the *zeitgeist*, which seems to be the case, then everyone should change at the same time. If it sometimes seems that they nearly do this, as in 675 AD, this is not quite good enough. For the future, though, the archaeology undertaken by every generation does enlarge our perspective, so we should see further, and not only further back.

Legacies

How much does modern Britain owe to its Formative years? I would like to think the answer is 'a great deal'. But tracking the legacy of the 5th to 11th century through Shakespeare's kings and the early modern imperial politicians up to the year of the European referendum in 2016 requires a historian who is a lot more gifted than I am. It is easy to idealise or politicise later events as an echo of what had happened previously, and easier still to interpret the events of the first millennium as though they (as well as we) knew what was coming. But there are plenty of clues that the peoples of formative Britain and their ideas endured as a substrate into the present.

The Gaelic languages survive on signposts; and if the mother languages have died or been revived, they are reflected in the more subtle distribution of the regional accents in which English is spoken. Religion and politics play interesting variations on the 'conviction territories' of the first millennium. Catholicism survived in Ireland but in Britain was replaced by three non-papal Old Testament-based groups, Presbyterians in Scotland, Methodists, big in Wales and Cornwall, and the Church of England, the faith of Empire and the home counties – 'the conservative party at prayer' to quote an old adage. Together with the voting patterns in 1832, 1950 and 2010, all these evoke divisions that first arose through immigration and ideological difference in the 5th–10th centuries. The revival of Scotland as an independent-minded region reached its apogee in 2015, with the near total control of the northern peninsula of Britain by a nationalist party, claiming allegiance to a 9th-century kingdom, then new and largely built by immigrants.

The pluralism that has survived in Britain, in politics, in religion, in attitudes to wealth, is an inheritance from the Formative period. The people of this time, so often thought primitive by those now scarcely aware of their existence, were of diverse and penetrating intelligence.

They could see no problem in appreciating the merits of three conflicting viewpoints and supporting at least two of them. This does not make them easy to understand, but it should at least invite us to respect their intellectual powers. It was probably an accident of history that made such diversity of options and consequent resistance to dictators possible: there was, as yet, no overarching power by which a single leader could try to 'take control', although many tried and go on trying.

An appealing glimpse of the survival of the life force of Formative diversity is provided by Peter and Iona Opie's survey of children's games and songs, recorded all over the island after the Second World War but before television rubbed them out. When their book was published, it was hailed by Marghanita Laski in the *Sunday Times* as the record of 'a fantastic transmission' – and so it was. Games and language and songs were passed from child to child in the schoolyard up to the age of 12, thus from generation to generation under the adult radar. Among the Opies' collected data were *truce terms*, the words that children shout to win relief when set upon in the playground. The distribution of these terms bears an uncanny resemblance to the kingdoms of Formative Britain (Figure 7.1B).[43] How many more such regional variants survive? How many more will new communities of immigrants

Figure 7.1 (Left) Locations of early British kingdoms; (Right) Areas using specific truce terms recorded in British schools in the 1950s by Peter and Iona Opie.

(Left: FAS Heritage; Right: FAS Heritage, after Opie and Opie 1959, Fig 7)

add? When will we realise what a treasure house of variation and invention lies beneath the surface of the country we live in? Political decisions made today are too often short term and see history as irrelevant or only a few centuries old. But the original and inventive thinking of the 5th to 10th centuries is still with us and should still inform debate. The Formative period lives on, providing the basis for everything that happened since and is happening now.

Notes

1 All the statements made in the service of the narrative constructed in this chapter draw on material or argument presented in Chapters 1–6, and repeat some of it in detail to advance the argument. Rather than cross-reference every instance, I am hoping that readers will be able navigate to the source using the index, site name, period and subject of each chapter.
2 E.g. Capel Eithin, Tandderwen, Arfyn, Plas Gogerddan, Llandough 1.
3 Dunottar is on a rocky outcrop with adjacent beach, a situation resembling Tintagel. Dundurn is on a knoll blocking the head of Strathearn. Dunbarton sits high on the summit of volcanic plug on Clydeside. There were forts on the castle rock at Edinburgh and Bamburgh, on Traprain Law and on minor hills in the Borders such as The Dod.
4 Clatchard Craig, Craig Phadraig and Dunollie.
5 Burghead, Portknockie and Dumbarton.
6 Alcock 2003, 182–211; Driscoll 1998, 2011.
7 Mote of Mark, Trusty's Hill, Tynron Doon, Dinas Emrys, Dinas Powys, Cadbury Congresbury, Cadbury Camp.
8 Fern 2015, 154.
9 Chadwick 1912, 442–444.
10 Carver 2003b, 9–10; For a sample here, see Chapter 2, 128–9; Chapter 3, 258; Chapter 4, 434; Chapter 5, 482; Chapter 6, 607.
11 Burn 1969; Carey 1999; Carver 2009a.
12 'Many also of the brethren had, in the same manner, fashioned retreats for themselves, but most of them had formed these out of the rock of the overhanging mountain, hollowed into caves', Sulpicius Severus *Life of Martin* X.
13 Examples are Street House, Uncleby, Garton Station, Cheesecake Hill.
14 See the papers by Bierbrauer, Staecker, Gräslund and Lager in Carver 2003a.
15 Even the extensive excavations of 1925 at Whitby failed to produce a comprehensible plan. Reviewing the results in 1976, Philip Rahtz showed that a multi-period site had been encountered, which 'certainly does not consist of a group of individual buildings with empty spaces separating them' (i.e. as claimed for Hartlepool). He would suggest either large buildings with rooms, as at Jarrow, or elements of a medieval claustral range: Rahtz 1976b, 462; Cramp 1976, Fig 5.7.
16 Bruce-Mitford 1969.
17 Brown 2003, 281.
18 Stenton 1971, 160 mentions Peterborough, Breedon, Brixworth and Barking. These were hardly ardent pioneers of a new ideology, but they had tax advantages, and 'there was an obvious temptation for the head of a family to evade his duties to the state by converting his household into a pseudo monastery'.
19 Chapter 3, p. 250, 299n.
20 As advocated by Blair 2005 and passim. The term should not apply north of the Humber.
21 Cf Rendlesham, where the activities fell away around 720.
22 Hinchliffe 1986; Stenton 1971, 445: 'It is significant that the New Minster which Edward the Elder founded at Winchester was not a monastery but a house of clerks.'
23 ASC [C] s.a. 866.
24 E.g. Dublin, Limerick, Waterford, Cork, Wexford.
25 See Kjølbye-Biddle in Phillips and Heywood 1995, 500–505 for the Viking boat burial under York Minster.
26 E.g. Winchester, Gloucester, Chester, London, Colchester.
27 E.g. Wareham, Cricklade, Wallingford.
28 Brooks 1996, 143.

29 Childe 1942.
30 Wickham 1984, 2005.
31 Alcock 1988, 36–37.
32 As seen at Witton: Wade 1983; Carver 1989; Scull 1992, 1993, 2011.
33 Myhre 1987.
34 Brown 2013; Alciati 2011; Knight 2005; Angenendt 2008; Lebecq 2000; Henning 2007b.
35 Barrett et al. 2000.
36 Renfrew and Cherry 1986.
37 Wickham 2005, 818–819; 'it is the crucial importance of demand, above all for bulk products distributed internally to regions, which makes macroeconomic models of medieval historical change based on long distance exchange alone as not much wrong, as largely irrelevant.' Cf Hodges 1982, 2012.
38 Theuws 2012; McCormick 2001, 2007, 2012; Mango 2009; Henning 2007a, and2008.
39 Sindbæk 2007.
40 Especially the 7th–8th century site of Commacchio on the Po estuary Gelichi et al. 2012; Carver 2015 for summaries, *pace* Bowden and Hodges 2012.
41 For examples of stimulating guides, overviews and models of early Medieval British history: Yorke 1990; Wormald 1996; Wickham 2005; Smith 2005; Woolf 2007; Fraser 2009; Fleming 2010.
42 Urbańczyk 2010 ('what did early medieval authors know about structures of governance and religion in northern central Europe?').
43 Opie and Opie 1982, Fig 7. The term excluded is 'pax', used by the privately educated child.

References

Abulafia, D 2011 *The Great Sea. A Human history of the Mediterranean* (Oxford: Oxford University Press).

Addyman, P V 1976 Anglo-Saxon Archaeology and Society, in G de G Sieveking, I H Longworth and K E Wilson (eds), *Problems in Economic and Social Archaeology* (London: Duckworth), 309–322.

Addyman, P V and D Leigh 1973 The Anglo-Saxon Village at Chalton, Hampshire: Second Interim Report, *Medieval Archaeology* 17, 1–25.

Addyman, P V, D Leigh and M J Hughes 1972 Anglo-Saxon Houses at Chalton, Hampshire, *Medieval Archaeology* 16, 13–31.

Admiralty 1979 *Admiralty Chart of the North Sea* (London: HMSO).

Adomnán of Iona *Life of St Columba*, ed and trans and with an introduction by R Sharpe 1995 (Harmondsworth: Penguin).

Aitchison, N 1999 *Macbeth: Man and Myth* (Stroud: Sutton).

Aitchison, N 2006 *Forteviot: A Pictish and Scottish Royal Centre* (Stroud:Tempus).

Alciati, R 2011 And the Villa Became a Monastery: Sulpicius Severus' Community of Primulacrum, in H Dey and E Fentress (eds), *Western Monasticism 'Ante Litteram': The Spaces of Monastic Observance in Late Antiquity and the Early Middle Ages* (Turnhout: Brepols), 85–98.

Alcock, E 1988 Pictish Stones Class I: Where and How? *Glasgow Archaeological Journal* 15, 1–21.

Alcock, L 1963 *Dinas Powys: An Iron Age, Dark Age and Early Medieval Settlement in Glamorgan* (Cardiff: University of Wales Press).

Alcock, L 1972 *By South Cadbury Is That Camelot: Excavations at Cadbury Castle, 1966–1970* (London and New York: Thames & Hudson).

Alcock, L 1973 *Arthur's Britain* (London: Penguin).

Alcock, L 1976 A Multi-disciplinary Chronology for Alt Clut, Castle Rock, Dumbarton, *Proceedings of the Society of Antiquaries of Scotland* 107, 103–113.

Alcock, L 1987 *Economy, Society and Warfare Among the Britons and Saxons* (Cardiff: University of Wales Press).

Alcock L. 1988 The Activities of Potentates in Celtic Britain AD 500–800 a Positivist Approach, in S T Driscoll and M Nieke (eds), *Power and Politics in Early Medieval Britain and Ireland* (Edinburgh: Edinburgh University Press), 40–46.

Alcock, L 1993 Image and Icon in Pictish Sculpture, in R M Spearman and J Higgitt (eds), *The Age of Migrating Ideas: Early Medieval Art in Northern Britain and Ireland* (Edinburgh: National Museums of Scotland and Stroud: Sutton), 230–236.

Alcock, L 2003 *Kings and Warriors, Craftsmen and Priests in Northern Britain AD 550–850* (Edinburgh: Society of Antiquaries of Scotland).

Alcock, L and E A Alcock 1987 Reconnaissance Excavations on Early Historic Fortifications and Other Royal Sites in Scotland, 1974–84: 2, Excavations at Dunollie Castle, Oban, Argyll 1978, *Proceedings of the Society of Antiquaries of Scotland* 117, 119–147.

Alcock, L and E A Alcock 1992 Reconnaissance Excavations on Early Historic Fortifications and Other Royal Sites in Scotland, 1974–84; 5: A, Excavations and Other Fieldwork at Forteviot, Perthshire, 1981; B, Excavations at Urquhart Castle, Inverness-shire, 1983; C, Excavations at Dunnottar, Kincardineshire, 1984, *Proceedings of the Society of Antiquaries of Scotland*, 122(1992), 215–287.

Alcock, L, E A Alcock and S Driscoll 1989 Reconnaissance Excavations in Scotland, 1974–84, 3: Excavations at Dundurn, Strathearn, Perthshire 1976–77, *Proceedings of the Society of Antiquaries of Scotland* 119, 189–226.

Alcock, L, S J Stevenson and C Musson 1995 *Cadbury Castle, Somerset. The Early Medieval Archaeology* (Cardiff: University of Wales Press).

Alcock, N W and D Walsh 1993 Architecture at Cowdery's Down: A Re-consideration, *Archaeological Journal* 150, 403–409.

Alexander, D 2005 Redcastle, Lunan Bay, Angus: The Excavation of an Iron Age Timber-lined Souterrain and a Pictish Barrow Cemetery, *Proceedings of the Society of Antiquaries of Scotland* 135, 41–118.

Alexander, J J G 1978 *Insular Manuscripts 6th to the 9th Century* (London: Harvey Miller).

Alexander, M (ed) 1973 *Beowulf: A Verse Translation* (Harmondsworth: Penguin).

Allen, J R 1887 *Christian Symbolism in Great Britain and Ireland* (London: Whiting).

Allen, J R and J Anderson 1903 *The Early Christian Monuments of Scotland*, 3 volumes (Edinburgh: Society of Antiquaries of Scotland), reprinted 1993, 2 volumes (Balgavies: Pinkfoot Press).

Allen, M, N Blick, T Brindle, T Evans, M Fulford, N Holbrook and J D Richards 2016 *The Rural Settlement of Roman Britain: An Online Resource* (ADS: http://archaeologydataservice.ac.uk/archives/view/romangl/ accessed 12 March 17).

Anderson, A O 1922 [1990] *Early Sources of Scottish History, AD 500–1286* (Edinburgh: Oliver and Boyd).

Angenendt, A 1986 The Conversion of the Anglo-Saxons Considered against the Background of the Early Medieval Mission, *Angli e Sassoni al di qua e al di là del mare; Settimane di studio del Centro italiano di studi sull'alto Medioevo* 32, 747–781.

Angenendt, A 2008 *Donationes Pro Anima*: Gift and Countergift in the Early Medieval Liturgy, in J R Davis and M McCormick (eds), *The Long Morning of Medieval Europe, New Directions in Early Medieval Studies* (Farnham: Ashgate), 131–154.

Armit, I 1999 The Abandonment of Souterrains: Evolution, Catastrophe or Dislocation? *Proceedings of the Society of Antiquaries of Scotland* 110, 346–355.

Arnoldussen, S. and H Fokkens (eds) 2008 *Bronze Age Settlement Sites in the Low Countries* (Oxford: Oxbow).

Arrhenius, B and U O'Meadhra (eds) 2011 *Excavations at Helgö XVIII Conclusions and New Aspects* (Stockholm: Kungl. Vitterhets Historie och Antikvitets Akademien).

Arwidsson, G 1977 *Valsgärde 7* (Uppsala: Uppsala Universitets Museum för Nordiska Fornsaker).

Ashby, S P 2013 Making a Good Comb: Mercantile Identity in Ninth to Eleventh-century England, in L Ten-Harkel and D M Hadley (eds), *Everyday Life in Viking Towns: Social Approaches to Towns in England and Ireland c. 800–1100* (Oxford: Oxbow), 193–208.

Ashby, S P 2014 Technologies of Appearance: Hair Behaviour in Early Medieval Europe, *Archaeological Journal* 171, 151–184.

Ashmore, P 1980 Low Cairns, Long Cists and Symbol Stones, *Proceedings of the Society of Antiquaries of Scotland* 110, 346–355.

Ashmore, P 1999 Radiocarbon Dating: Avoiding Errors in Dating by Avoiding Mixed Samples, *Antiquity* 73, 124–130.

Ashmore, P 2000 A Radiocarbon Database for Scottish Archaeological Samples, *Radiocarbon* 42(1), 41–48.

Astill, G 2000 General Survey 600–1300, in D M Palliser (ed), *The Cambridge Urban History of Britain* (Cambridge: Cambridge University Press), 27–49.

Astill, G 2006 Community, Identity and the Later Anglo-Saxon Town, in W Davies, G Halsall and A Reynolds (eds), *People and Space in the Middle Ages, 300–1300* (Turnhout: Brepols), 233–254.

Astill, G 2009 Anglo-Saxon Attitudes: How Should Post-AD 700 Burials Be Interpreted? in D Sayer and H Williams (eds), *Mortuary Practices and Social Identities in the Middle Ages* (Exeter: University of Exeter Press), 222–235.

Avent, R 1975 *Anglo-Saxon Garnet Inlaid Disc and Composite Brooches* (BAR British Series11) (Oxford: British Archaeological Reports).

Avent, R and V I Evison 1982 Anglo-Saxon Button Brooches, *Archaeologia: Or Miscellaneous Tracts Relating to Antiquity* 107, 77.

Backhouse J, D H Turner and L Webster (eds) 1984 *The Golden Age of Anglo-Saxon Art 966–1066* (London: British Museum).

Bailey, R N 1988 *The Meaning of Mercian Sculpture* (6th Brixworth Lecture) (Leicester: University of Leicester).

Bailey, R N 2005 *Anglo-Saxon Sculptures at Deerhurst* (Deerhurst Lecture 2002) (Deerhurst: Friends of Deerhurst Church).

Bailey, R N 2010 *Cheshire and Lancashire* (Corpus of Anglo-Saxon Stone Sculpture Volume IX) (Oxford: Oxford University Press for The British Academy).

Bailey, R N and R Cramp 1988 *Corpus of Anglo-Saxon Stone Sculpture Volume II Cumberland, Westmoreland and Lancashire-north-of-the-sands* (Oxford: Oxford University Press for The British Academy).

Banham, D and R Faith 2014 *Anglo-Saxons Farms and Farming* (Oxford: Oxford University Press).

Bannerman, J 1974 *Studies in the History of Dalriada* (Edinburgh and London: Scottish Academic Press).

Barber, J W 1981 Excavations on Iona 1979, *Proceedings of the Society of Antiquaries of Scotland* 111, 282–380.

Barber, J W and A Crone 2001 The Duration of Structures, Settlements and Sites: Some Evidence from Scotland, in B Raftery and J Hickey (eds), *Recent Developments in Wetland Research* (Dublin: University College Dublin), 69–86.

Barber, J W, C Clark, M Cressey, A Crone, A Hale, J Henderson, R Housley, R Sands and A Sheridan (eds) 2007 *Archaeology from the Wetlands: Recent Perspectives* (Edinburgh: Society of Antiquaries of Scotland).

Barber, P 2006 Medieval Maps of the World, in P D A Harvey (ed), *The Hereford World Map: Medieval Maps of the World and their Context* (London: British Library), 1–44.

Barker, P, K Pretty and R White 1997 *The Baths Basilica, Wroxeter: Excavations 1966–1990* (London: English Heritage).

Barlow, F, M Biddle, O von Feilitzen and D J Keene 1976 *Winchester in the Early Middle Ages: An Edition and Discussion of the Winton Domesday* (Oxford: Clarendon Press).

Barrett, J C, P W M Freeman and A Woodward 2000 *Cadbury Castle, Somerset: The Later Prehistoric and Early Historic Archaeology* (London: English Heritage).

Barrett, J H 2008 Cod Bones and Commerce: The Medieval Fishing Revoloution Revolution, *Current Archaeology* 221, 20–25.

Barrett, J H and M P Richards 2004 Identity, Gender, Religion and Economy: New Isotope and Radiocarbon Evidence for Marine Resource Intensification in Early Historic Orkney, Scotland, UK, *European Journal of Archaeology* 7, 249–271.

Barrett, J H, R Nicholson and R Ceron-Carrasco 1999 Archaeo-icthyological Evidence for Longterm Socioeconomic Trends in Northern Scotland: 3500 BC to AD 1500, *Journal of Archaeological Science* 26, 353–388.

Barrett, J H, R Buekens, I Simpson, P Ashmore, S Poaps and J Huntley 2000 What Was the Viking Age and When Did It Happen? A View from Orkney, *Norwegian Archaeological Review* 33(1), 1–39.

Barrett, J H, A Locker and C Roberts 2004 Dark Age Economics Revisited: The English Fish Bone Evidence AD 600–1600, *Antiquity* 78, 618–636.

Barrowman, R 2003 A Decent Burial: Excavations at St Ninian's Isle in July 2000, in A Ritchie and J Downes (eds), *Sea Change: Orkney and Northern Europe in the Later Iron Age AD 300–800* (Balgavies: Pinkfoot Press), 51–61.

Bassett, S (ed) 1989a *The Origins of Anglo-Saxon Kingdoms* (London and New York: Leicester University Press).

Bassett, S 1989b In Search of the Origins of Anglo-Saxon Kingdoms, in S Bassett (ed), *The Origins of Anglo-Saxon Kingdoms* (London and New York: Leicester University Press), 3–27.

Bassett, S 2000 How the West Was Won: The Anglo-Saxon Takeover of the West Midlands, *Anglo-Saxon Studies in Archaeology and History* 11, 107–118.

Bassett, S 2007 Divide and Rule? The Military Infrastructure of Eighth- and Ninth-century Mercia, *Early Medieval Europe* 15(1), 53–85.

Bassett, S 2008 The Middle and Late Anglo-Saxon Defences of West Mercian Towns, *Anglo-Saxon Studies in Archaeology and History* 15, 180–239.

Bately, J and A Englert (eds) 2007 *Othere's Voyages: A Late 9th-Century Account of Voyages Along the Coasts of Norway and Denmark and its Cultural Context* (Maritime Cultures of the North 1) (Roskilde: Viking Ship Museum).

Bates, D and R Liddiard (eds) 2013 *East Anglia and its North Sea World in the Middle Ages* (Woodbridge: Boydell).

Bates, E S (ed)1944 *The Bible Designed to Be Read as Literature* (London: Heinemann).

Battaglia, F 2009 Not Christianity Versus Paganism but Hall Versus Bog: The Great Shift in Early Scandinavian Religion and its Implications for *Beowulf*, in M Kilpiö, L Kahlas-Tarkka, J Roberts and O Tomifeeva (eds), *Anglo-Saxons and the North: Essays Reflecting the Theme of the 10th Meeting of the International Society of Anglo-Saxonists in Helsinki, August 2001* (Tempe: Arizona Center for Medieval and Renaissance Studies), 47–68.

Becker, K 2011 Iron Age Ireland: Continuity, Change and Identity, in T Moore and X-L Armada (eds), *Atlantic Europe in the First Millennium BC* (Oxford: Oxford University Press), 449–467.

Behr, C and T Pestell 2014 The Bracteate Hoard from Binham – An Early Anglo-Saxon Central Place? *Medieval Archaeology* 58, 44–77.

Bell, T 1998 Churches on Roman Buildings: Christian Associations and Roman Masonry in Anglo-Saxon England, *Medieval Archaeology*. 42, 1–18.

Bentley, R A 2006 Strontium Isotopes from the Earth to the Archaeological Skeleton: A Review, *Journal of Archaeological Method and Theory* 13, 135–187.

Beresford, G 1979 Three Deserted Medieval Settlements on Dartmoor: A Report on E. Marie Minter's Excavations, *Medieval Archaeology* 23, 98–158.

Bermingham, N and C Moore 2015 The Drumclay Crannog-dwellers, *Current Archaeology* 299, 30–37.

Bersu, G and D M Wilson 1966 *Three Viking Graves in the Isle of Man* (Society for Medieval Archaeology Monograph 1) (London: Society for Medieval Archaeology).

Biddle, M 1969 Excavations at Winchester 1968: Seventh Interim Report, *The Antiquaries Journal* 49(2), 295–328.

Biddle, M 1976 Towns, in D M Wilson (ed), *The Archaeology of Anglo-Saxon England* (London: Methuen), 99–150.

Biddle, M 1984 London on the Strand, *Popular Archaeology* 6(1), 23–27.

Biddle, M (ed) 1990 *Object and Economy in Medieval Winchester* (Winchester Studies Volume 7.ii) (Oxford: Clarendon Press).

Biddle, M and D Hill 1971 Late Saxon Planned Towns, *Antiquaries Journal* 51, 70–85.

Biddle, M and B Kjølbye-Biddle 1985 The Repton Stone, *Anglo-Saxon England* 14, 233–292.

Biddle, M and B Kjølbye-Biddle 1992 Repton and the Vikings, *Antiquity* 66, 36–51.

Biddle, M and B Kjølbye-Biddle 2001 Repton and the 'Great Heathen Army', 873–4, in J Graham-Campbell et al. (eds), *Vikings and the Danelaw: Proceedings of the 13th Viking Congress* (Oxford: Oxbow), 45–96.

Bierbrauer, V 2003 The Cross Goes North: From Late Antiquity to Merovingian Times South and North of the Alps, in M O H Carver (ed), *The Cross Goes North: Processes of Conversion in Northern Europe, AD 300–1300* (Woodbridge and Rochester (NY): York Medieval Press), 429–442.

Biggam, C 2006a Whelks and Purple Dye in Anglo-Saxon England, *The Archaeomalacology Group Newsletter* 9, 1–2.

Biggam, C 2006b Knowledge of Whelk Dyes and Pigments in Anglo-Saxon England, *Anglo-Saxon England* 35, 23–55.

Bill, J 2008 Viking Ships and the Sea, in S Brink and N Price (eds), *The Viking World* (London and New York: Routledge), 170–180.

Bill, J and A Daly 2012 The Plundering of the Ship Graves from Oseberg and Gokstad: An Example of Power Politics, *Antiquity* 82, 808–824.

Binns, A 1980 *Viking Voyagers: Then and Now* (London: Heinemann).

Binns, J W, E C Norton and D M Palliser 1990 The Latin Inscription on the Coppergate Helmet, *Antiquity* 64, 134–139.

Birbeck, V 2005 *The Origins of Mid-Saxon Southampton: Excavations at the Friends Provident St Mary's Stadium, 1998–2000* (Salisbury: Wessex Archaeology).

Blackburn, M A 2011 The Viking Winter Camp at Torksey, 872–3, in M A Blackburn (ed), *Viking Coinage and Currency in the British Isles* (British Numismatic Society Special Publication 7) (London: Spink), 221–264.

Blackmore, L 2001 The Origins and Growth of Lundenwic, a Mart of Many Nations, in Hårdh and Larsson (eds), *Central Places in the Migration and Merovingian Periods* (Stockholm: Almqvist & Wiksell International), 273–301.

Blackwell, A 2011 The Iconography of the Hunterston Brooch and Related Early Medieval Material, *Proceedings of the Society of Antiquaries of Scotland* 141, 231–248.

Blair, J 1995 Anglo-Saxon Pagan Shrines and their Prototypes, *Anglo-Saxon Studies in Archaeology and History* 8, 1–28.

Blair, J 1996 Palaces or Minsters? Northampton and Cheddar Reconsidered, *Anglo-Saxon England* 25, 97–121.

Blair, J 2005 *The Church in Anglo-Saxon Society* (Oxford: Oxford University Press).

Blair, J and C Pyrah 1996 *Church Archaeology: Research Directions for the Future* (CBA Research Report 104) (York: Council for British Archaeology).

Blinkhorn, P 2012 *The Ipswich Ware Project: Ceramics, Trade and Society in Middle Saxon England* (Medieval Pottery Research Group Occasional Paper 7) (London: The Medieval Pottery Research Group).

Boddington, A and G Cadman 1996 *Raunds Furnells: The Anglo-Saxon Church and Churchyard* (English Heritage Report 7) (London: English Heritage).

Booth, P, A Simmonds, A Boyle, S Clough, H E M Cool and D Poore 2010 *The Late Roman Cemetery at Lankhills, Winchester: Excavations 2000–2005.* (Oxford Archaeology Monograph 10) (Oxford: Oxford Archaeology).

Borg, K, U Näsman and E Wegraeus (eds) 1976 *Eketorp: Fortification and Settlement on Öland, Sweden* (Stockholm: Royal Academy of Letters, History and Antiquities).

Bourdillon, J 1988 Countryside and Town: The Animal Resources of Saxon Southampton, in D Hooke (ed), *Anglo-Saxon Settlements* (Oxford: Blackwell), 177–195.

Bourdillon, J 1994 The Animal Provisioning of Saxon Southampton, in J Rackham (ed), *Environment and Economy in Anglo-Saxon England* (York: Council for British Archaeology), 120–125.

Bourke, C (ed) 1995 *From the Isles of the North: Early Medieval Art in Ireland and Britain* (Belfast: HMSO).

Bourke, C (ed) 1997 *Studies in the Cult of St Columba* (Dublin: Four Courts Press).

Bowden W and R Hodges 2012 An 'Ice Age Settling on the Roman Empire': Post-Roman Butrint Between Strategy and Serendipity, in N Christie and A Augenti (eds), *Urbs Extinctae: Archaeologies of Abandoned Classical Towns* (Farnham: Ashgate), 207–242.

Boyle, A, A Dodd, D Miles and A Mudd 1995 *Two Anglo-Saxon Cemeteries: Berinsfield and Didcot* (Thames Valley Landscapes Monograph 8) (Oxford: Oxford University Committee for Archaeology).

Boyle, A, D Jennings, D Miles and S Palmer 1998 *The Anglo-Saxon Cemetery at Butler's Field, Lechlade, Gloucestershire. 1. Prehistoric and Roman Activity and Grave Catalogue* (Thames Valley Landscapes Monograph 10) (Oxford: Oxford University Committee for Archaeology).

Bradley, J 1991 Excavations at Moynagh Lough, County Meath, *Journal of the Ryal Society of Antiquaries of Ireland* 121, 5–26.

Bradley, J 1993 Moynagh Lough: An Insular Workshop of the Second Quarter of the 8th Century, in R M Spearman and J Higgitt (eds), *The Age of Migrating Ideas: Early Medieval Art in Northern Britain and Ireland* (Edinburgh: National Museums of Scotland and Stroud: Sutton), 74–81.

Bradley, J 2011 An Early Medieval Crannog at Moynagh Lough, Co Meath, in C Corlett and M Potterton (eds), *Death and Burial in Early Medieval Ireland in the Light of Recent Archaeological Excavations* (Dublin: Wordwell), 11–33.

Bradley, R 1987 Time Regained: The Creation of Continuity, *Journal of the British Archaeological Association* 140, 1–17.

Bradley, R 1993 *Altering the Earth: The Origins of Monuments in Britain and Continental* Europe (The Rhind Lectures 1991–2) (Edinburgh: Society of Antiquaries of Scotland).

Bradley, R 2000 *An Archaeology of Natural Places* (London and New York: Routledge).

Brady, K, O Lelong and C E Batey 2007 A Pictish Burial and Late Norse/Medieval Settlement at Sangobeg, Durness, Sutherland, *Scottish Archaeological Journal* 29(1), 51–82.

Brassil, K S, W G Owen and W J Britnell 1991 Prehistoric and Early Medieval Cemeteries at Tanderwen, Near Denbigh, Clwyd, *Archaeological Journal* 148, 46–97.

Brøgger, A W, H J Falk and H Shetelig 1917 *Osebergfundet* (Kristiana: Universitetets Oldsaksamling).

Bromwich, R (ed and trans) 1961 *Trioedd Ynys Prydein: The Welsh Triads* (Cardiff: University of Wales Press).

Brookes, S, S Harrington and A Reynolds (eds) 2011 *Studies in Early Anglo-Saxon Art and Archaeology: Papers in Honour of Martin G. Welch* (BAR British Series 527) (Oxford: Archaeopress).

Brooks, N 1971 The Development of Military Obligations in Eighth- and Ninth-century England, in P Clemoes and K Hughes (eds), *England Before the Conquest: Studies in Primary Sources Presented to Dorothy Whitelock* (Cambridge: Cambridge University Press), 69–84.

Brooks, N 1984 *The Early History of the Church of Canterbury: Christ Church from 597 to 1066* (Leicester: Leicester University Press).

Brooks, N 1996 The Administrative Background to the Burghal Hidage, in D H Hill and A Rumble (eds), *The Defence of Wessex: The Burghal Hidage and Anglo-Saxon Fortifications* (Manchester: Manchester University Press), 128–150.

Brown, K L and R J H Clark 2004 The Lindisfarne Gospels and Two Other 8th Century Manuscripts: Pigment Identification by Raman Microscopy, *Journal of Raman Spectroscopy* 35(1), 4–12.

Brown, M P 2003 *The Lindisfarne Gospels: Society, Spirituality and the Scribe* (London: The British Library).

Brown, P 2013 *The Rise of Western Christendom: Triumph and Diversity AD 200–1000* (10th Anniversary revised edition) (Oxford: Blackwell).

Brown, T and B Keri 2011 *Biomolecular Archaeology: An Introduction* (Chichester and Malden (MA): Wiley-Blackwell).

Brubaker, L 2004 The Elephant and the Ark: Cultural and Material Interchange Across the Mediterranean in the Eighth and Ninth Centuries, *Dumbarton Oaks Papers* 58, 175–195.

Bruce-Mitford, R L S 1969 The Art of the Codex Amiatinus (Jarrow Lecture; reprint from the *Journal of the British Archaeological Association* 3S, 32, 1–25) (London: British Archaeological Association).

Bruce-Mitford, R L S 1975, 1978, 1983 *The Sutton Hoo Ship Burial Volumes 1–3* (London: British Museum).

Bruce-Mitford, R L S 2005 *A Corpus of Late Celtic Hanging Bowls* (Oxford: Oxford University Press).

Brühl, C 1977 The Town as a Political Centre: General Survey, in M W Barley (ed), *European Towns: Their Archaeology and Early History* (London: Academic Press), 419–430.

Brundle, A, D H Lorimer and A Ritchie 2003 Buckquoy Revisited, in J Downes and A Ritchie (eds), *Sea Change: Orkney and Northern Europe in the Later Iron Age AD 300–800* (Balgavies: Pinkfoot Press), 95–104.

Bruns, D 2003 *Germanic Equal Arm Brooches of the Migration Period: A Study of Style, Chronology and Distribution, Including a Full Catalogue of Finds and Contexts* (BAR International Series 1113) (Oxford: Archaeopress).

Brunskill, R W 1982 *Traditional Farm Buildings of Britain* (London: Gollancz).

Bryant, R 2012 *The Western Midlands* (British Academy: Corpus of Anglo-Saxon Stone Sculpture Volume X) (Oxford: Oxford University Press for The British Academy).

Buckberry, J 2007 On Sacred Ground: Social Identity and Churchyard Burial in Lincolnshire and Yorkshire c. 700–1100, *Anglo-Saxon Studies in Archaeology and History* 14, 117–129.

Buckberry, J and A Cherryson (eds) 2010 *Burial in Later Anglo-Saxon England c. 650–1100 AD* (Oxford: Oxbow).

Budd, P, A Millard, C Chenery, S Lucy and C Roberts 2004 Investigating Population Movement by Stable Isotope Analysis: A Report from Britain, *Antiquity* 78, 127–141.

Bulleit, R W 1979 *Conversion to Islam in the Medieval Period* (Cambridge (MA) and London: Harvard University Press).

Burn, A R 1969 Holy Men on Islands in pre-Christian Britain, *Glasgow Archaeological Journal* 1, 2–6.

Burrow, I 1973 Tintagel – Some Problems, *Scottish Archaeological Forum* 5, 99–103.

Burrow, I 1981 *Hill-fort and Hill-top Settlement in Somerset in the First to Eighth Centuries AD* (BAR British Series 91) (Oxford: British Archaeological Reports).

Caerwyn Williams, J E and P K Ford 1992 *The Irish Literary Tradition* (Cardiff: University of Wales Press).

Callmer, J 2002 North European Trading Centres and the Early Medieval Craftsmen. Craftsmen at Åhus, North-eastern Scania, Sweden c. AD 750–850+, in B Hårdh and L Larsson (eds), *Central Places in the Migration and Merovingian Periods* (Stockholm: Almqvist & Wiksell International), 125–157.

Cameron, E and Q Mould 2004 Saxon Shoes, Viking Sheaths? Cultural Identity in Anglo-Scandinavian York, in J Hines, A Lane and M Redknap (eds), *Land, Sea and Home: Settlement in the Viking Period* (Leeds: Maney), 457–466.

Cameron, N 1994 St Rule's Church, St Andrews, and Early Stone-built Churches in Scotland, *Proceedings of the Society of Antiquaries of Scotland* 124, 367–378.

Cameron, N 1996 The Church in Scotland in the Later 11th and 12th Centuries, in J Blair and C Pyrah (eds), *Church Archaeology: Research Directions for the Future* (York: Council for British Archaeology), 42–46.

Campbell, E 1991 *Imported Goods in the Early Medieval Celtic West, With Special Reference to Dinas Powys* (PhD dissertation, University of Wales, published online by EThOS, British Library https://ethos.bl.uk/OrderDetails.do?uin=uk.bl.ethos.281955) .

Campbell, E 1996 Trade in the Dark Age West: A Peripheral Activity? in B Crawford (ed), *Scotland in Dark Age Britain* (Aberdeen: Scottish Cultural Press), 79–91.

Campbell, E 2000 A Review of Glass Vessels in Western Britain and Ireland, in J Price (ed), *Glass in Britain and Ireland, AD 350–1100* (London: British Museum Press), 33–46.

Campbell, E 2001 Were the Scots Irish? *Antiquity* 75, 285–292.

Campbell, E 2007 *Continental and Mediterranean Imports to Atlantic Britain and Ireland, AD 400–800* (CBA Research Report 157) (York: Council for British Archaeology).

Campbell, E 2010 The Archaeology of Writing in the Time of Adomnán, in J M Wooding (ed), *Adomnán of Iona, Theologian, Lawmaker, Peacemaker* (Dublin: Four Courts Press), 139–144.

Campbell, E and C Bowles 2009 Byzantine Trade to the Edge of the World: Mediterranean Pottery Imports to Atlantic Britain in the 6th Century, in M M Mango (ed), *Byzantine Trade 4th–12th Centuries: The Archaeology of Local, Regional and International Exchange* (Farnham: Ashgate), 297–314.

Campbell, E and A Lane 1993 Celtic and Germanic Interaction in Dalriada: The 7th Century Metal-working Site at Dunadd, in R M Spearman and J Higgitt (eds), *The Age of Migrating Ideas: Early Medieval Art in Northern Britain and Ireland* (Edinburgh: National Museums of Scotland and Stroud: Sutton), 52–63.

Campbell, J 1986 *Essays in Anglo-Saxon History* (London: Hambledon Press).

Campbell, J 2009 Archipelagic Thoughts: Comparing Early Medieval Polities in Britain and Ireland, in S Baxter, C Karkov, J L Nelson and D Pelteret (eds), *Early Medieval Studies in Memory of Patrick Wormald* (Farnham: Ashgate), 47–61.

Carey, J 1987 Time, Space and the Otherworld *Proceedings of the Harvard Celtic Colloquium* 7, 1–27.

Carey, J 1999 *A Single Ray of the Sun: Religious Speculation in Early Ireland: Three Essays* (Aberystwyth: Celtic Studies Publications).

Carroll, J 1995 Millefiori in the Development of Early Irish Enamelling, in C Bourke (ed), *From the Isles of the North: Early Medieval Art in Ireland and Britain* (Belfast: HMSO), 49–57.

Carson, C 2008 *The Taín* (London: Penguin).

Caruth, J 2013 Is This the First Anglo-Saxon Long-house to be Discovered in England? *Saxon* (Woodbridge: Sutton Hoo Society), 56:1–3.

Carver, M O H 1979 Three Saxo-Norman tenements in Durham City *Medieval Archaeology* 23, 1–80.

Carver, M O H 1980 Early Medieval Durham: The Archaeological Evidence, in British Archaeological Association *Medieval Art and Architecture at Durham Cathedral* (Leeds: Maney), 11–19.

Carver, M O H 1986a Sutton Hoo in Context, *Settimane di studio del Centro italiano di studii sull'alto Medioevo* 32, 77–123.

Carver, M O H 1986b Contemporary Artefacts Illustrated in Late Saxon Manuscripts, *Archaeologia* 108, 117–146.

Carver, M O H 1989 Kingship and Material Culture in Early Anglo-Saxon East Anglia, in S Bassett (ed), *The Origins of Anglo-Saxon Kingdoms* (London and New York: Leicester University Press), 141–158.

Carver, M O H 1990 Pre-Viking Traffic in the North Sea, in S McGrail (ed), *Maritime Celts, Frisians and Saxons* (London: Council for British Archaeology), 117–125.

Carver, M O H (ed) 1992 *The Age of Sutton Hoo* (Woodbridge: Boydell).

Carver, M O H 1993 *Arguments in Stone, Archaeological Research and the European Town in the First Millennium* (Oxford: Oxbow).

Carver, M O H 1995a Ship Burial in Early Britain: Ancient Custom or Political Signal? in O Crumlin-Pedersen and B Munch Thye (eds), *The Ship as Symbol in Prehistoric and Medieval Scandinavia* (Copenhagen: National Museum of Denmark), 111–124.

Carver, M O H 1995b On – and Off – The *Edda*, in O Olsen, J S Madsen and F Riek (eds), *Ship-shape: Essays for Ole Crumlin-Pedersen* (Roskilde: Viking Ship Museum), 305–312.

Carver, M O H 1995c Roman to Norman at York Minster, in D Phillips and B Heywood, *Excavations at York Minster Volume I: From Roman Fortress to Norman Cathedral* (London: HMSO), 177–221.

Carver, M O H 1998 Conversion and Politics on the Eastern Seaboard of Britain: Some Archaeological Indicators, in B Crawford (ed), *Conversion and Christianity in the North Sea World* (St Andrews: Committee for Dark Age Studies, University of St Andrews), 11–40.

Carver, M O H 1999 Shielding Identity: Some Comments on Objects and Images in Pictish Carving, in S Bennett (ed), *Pictish Art* (Proceedings of a Conference held at Elgin) (Elgin: Elgin Museum), 7–9.

Carver, M O H 2000 Burial as Poetry: The Context of Treasure in Anglo-Saxon Graves, in E Tyler (ed), *Treasure in the Medieval West* (Woodbridge: Boydell), 25–48.

Carver, M O H 2001 Why That? Why There? Why Then? The Politics of Early Medieval Monumentality, in A MacGregor and H Hamerow (eds), *Image and Power in Early Medieval British Archaeology. Essays in Honour of Rosemary Cramp* (Oxford: Oxbow), 1–22.

Carver, M O H 2002a Reflections on the Meanings of Monumental Barrows in Anglo-Saxon England, in S Lucy and A Reynolds (eds), *Burial in Early Medieval England and Wales* (London: Society for Medieval Archaeology), 132–143.

Carver, M O H 2002b Marriages of True Minds: Archaeology with Texts, in B Cunliffe, W Davies and C Renfrew (eds), *Archaeology: The Widening Debate* (Oxford University Press for The British Academy), 465–496.

Carver, M O H (ed) 2003a *The Cross Goes North: Processes of Conversion in Northern Europe, AD 300–1300* (Woodbridge and Rochester (NY): York Medieval Press).

Carver, M O H 2003b Northern Europeans Negotiate their Future, in M O H Carver (ed), *The Cross Goes North: Processes of Conversion in Northern Europe, AD 300–1300* (Woodbridge and Rochester (NY): York Medieval Press), 3–14.

Carver, M O H 2005a *Sutton Hoo: A Seventh Century Princely Burial Ground and its Context* (Society of Antiquaries Research Report 69) (London: British Museum Press).

Carver, M O H 2005b Sculpture in Action: Contexts for Stone Carving on the Tarbat Peninsula, Easter Ross, in S M Foster and M Cross (eds), *Able Minds and Practised Hands: Scotland's Early Medieval Sculpture in the 21st Century* (Edinburgh: Historic Scotland), 13–36.

Carver, M O H 2008a *Portmahomack: Monastery of the Picts* (Edinburgh University Press).

Carver M O H 2008b The Pictish Monastery at Portmahomack (Jarrow Lecture for 2008; Jarrow, Parish of Jarrow).

Carver, M O H 2008c *Post-Pictish Problems: The Moray Firthlands in the 9th–11th Centuries* (Groam House Lecture) (Rosemarkie: Groam House Museum).

Carver, M O H 2009a Early Scottish Monasteries and Prehistory: A Preliminary Dialogue, *The Scottish Historical Review* 88, 332–351.

Carver, M O H 2009b On Reading Anglo-Saxon Graves, in A Jorgensen, H Conrad-O'Brien and J Scattergood (eds), *The Kemble Lectures on Anglo-Saxon Studies 2005–8* (Dublin: Trinity College), 81–103.

Carver, M O H 2010a Four Windows on Early Britain, in W North (ed), *The Haskins Society Journal* 22, 1–24.

Carver, M O H 2010b *The Birth of a Borough: An Archaeological Study of Anglo-Saxon Stafford* (Woodbridge: Boydell).

Carver, M O H 2011a What Were They Thinking? Intellectual Territories in Anglo-Saxon England, in H Hamerow, D A Hinton and S Crawford (eds), *The Oxford Handbook of Anglo-Saxon Archaeology* (Oxford: Oxford University Press), 914–952.

Carver, M O H 2011b Intellectual Communities in Early Northumbria, in D Petts and S Turner (eds), *Early Medieval Northumbria: Kingdoms and Communities, AD 450–1100* (Turnhout: Brepols), 185–206.

Carver, MO H 2011c The Best We Can Do? (The Staffordshire (Ogley Hay) Hoard), *Antiquity* 85, 230–234.

Carver, M O H 2013 Those Elusive Villagers, *Saxon* (Woodbridge: Sutton Hoo Society) 57, 9.

Carver, M O H 2014a [1998] *Sutton Hoo: Burial Ground of Kings?* (London: British Museum Press).

Carver, M O H 2014b Travels on the Sea and in the Mind, in S S Klein, W Schipper, and S Lewis-Simpson (eds), *The Maritime World of the Anglo-Saxons: Essays in Anglo-Saxon Studies* 5 (Medieval and Renaissance Texts and Studies 448) (Tempe: Arizona Center for Medieval and Renaissance Studies), 21–36.

Carver, M O H 2015 Commerce and Cult: Confronted Ideologies in 6th–9th Century Europe, *Medieval Archaeology* 59, 1–23.

Carver, M O H 2016a *Portmahomack: Monastery of the Picts* (Edinburgh: Edinburgh University Press).

Carver, M O H 2016b Mound-building and State-building: A Poetic Discourse, in T N Jackson (ed), *The Earliest States of Eastern Europe: Old Rus' and Medieval Europe. The Origin of States* (Moscow: Russian Academy of Science), 131–157.

Carver, M O H 2017 *The Sutton Hoo Story: Encounters with Early England* (Woodbridge: Boydell).

Carver, M O H and C Loveluck 2013 Early Medieval, AD 400–1000, in J Randlsey and F Sturt (eds), *People and the Sea: A Maritime Archaeological Research Agenda for England* (York: Council for British Archaeology), 113–137.

Carver, M O H and C A Spall 2004 Excavating a *Parchmenerie*: Archaeological Correlates of Making Parchment at the Pictish Monastery at Portmahomack, Easter Ross, *Proceedings of the Society of Antiquaries of Scotland* 134, 183–200.

Carver, M O H, C Hills and J Scheschkewitz 2009 *Wasperton: A Roman, British and Anglo-Saxon Community in Central England* (Woodbridge: Boydell).

Carver, M O H, A Sanmark and S Semple (eds) 2010 *Signals of Belief in Early England* (Oxford: Oxbow).

Carver, M O H, J Barrett, J Downes and J Hooper 2012 Pictish Byre Houses at Pitcarmick and their Landscape: Investigations 1993–5, *Proceedings of the Society of Antiquaries of Scotland* 142, 145–199.

Carver, M O H, J Garner-Lahire and C A Spall 2016 *Portmahomack on Tarbat Ness: Changing Ideologies in North-east Scotland Sixth to Sixteenth Centuries* (Edinburgh: Society of Antiquaries of Scotland).

Chadwick, H M 1905 *Studies on Anglo-Saxon Institutions* (Cambridge: Cambridge University Press).

Chadwick, H M 1912 *The Heroic Age* (Cambridge: Cambridge University Press).

Chadwick, H M 2010 [1924] *The Origin of the English Nation* (Cambridge: Cambridge University Press).

Chambers, R A 1987 The Late- and Sub-Roman Cemetery at Queenford Farm, Dorchester-on-Thames, *Oxoniensia* 52, 35–70.

Champion, T 1977 Chalton, *Current Archaeology* 59, 364–369.

Chazelle, C 2003 Ceofrid's Gift to St Peter: The First Quire of the Codex Amiatinus and the Evidence of its Roman Destination, *Early Medieval Europe* 12(2), 129–158.

Chester-Kaldwell, M 2009 *Early Anglo-Saxon Communities in the Landscape of Norfolk* (BAR British Series 481) (Oxford: Archaeopress).

Childe, V G 1942 [1971] *What Happened in History* (Harmondsworth: Penguin).

Childe, V G 1944 *Progress and Archaeology* (London: Watts & Co.).

Christie, N 1987 Forum Ware, the Duchy of Rome and Incastellamento: Problems in Interpretation, *Archeologia Medievale* 14, 451–463.

Clancy, T O (ed) 1998 *The Triumph Tree: Scotland's Earliest Poetry, 550–1350* (Edinburgh: Canongate).

Clancy, T O 2013 The Kingdoms of the North: Poetry, Places, Politics, in A Woolf (ed), *Beyond the Gododdin: Dark Age Scotland in Medieval Wales* (St Andrews: University of St Andrews), 153–175.

Clapham, A W 1930 *English Romanesque Architecture Before the Conquest* (Oxford: Clarendon Press).

Clark, A, H Hamerow, S M Hirst and D Clark 1993–2009 *Excavations at Mucking* (London: English Heritage).

Clarke, D and A Heald 2008 A New Date for Pictish Symbols, *Medieval Archaeology* 52, 291–296.

Clarke, G 1979 *Winchester Studies 3, Pre-Roman and Roman Winchester. Part 2: The Roman Cemetery at Lankhills* (Oxford: Clarendon Press).

Clarke, L 2010 Johnstown 1, Co. Meath: A Multi-period Burial, Settlement and Industrial Site, in C Corlett and M Potterton (eds), *Death and Burial in Early Medieval Ireland in the Light of Recent Archaeological Excavations* (Dublin: Wordwell), 61–76.

Clarke, L and N Carlin 2008 Living with the Dead at Johnstown 1: An Enclosed Burial, Settlement and Industrial Site, in N Carlin, L Clarke and F Walsh (eds), *The Archaeology of Life and Death in the Boyne Floodplain* (Dublin: National Roads Authority), 55–86.

Clarke, L and N Carlin 2009 From Locus to Focus: A Window on the Development of a Funerary Landscape, in M Deevy and D Murphy (eds.) *Places Along the Way: First findings on the M3* (Dublin: National Roads Authority) 1–20.

Clinton, M 2001 *The Souterrains of Ireland* (Bray: Wordwell).

Close-Brooks, J 1980 Excavations in the Dairy Park, Dunrobin, Sutherland 1977, *Proceedings of the Society of Antiquaries of Scotland* 110, 328–345.

Close-Brooks, J 1984 Pictish and Other Burials, in J G P Friell and W G Watson (eds), *Pictish Studies: Settlement, Burial and Art in Dark Age Northern Britain* (Oxford: British Archaeological Reports), 87–114.

Close-Brooks, J 1989 *Pictish Stones in Dunrobin Castle Museum* (Derby: Pilgrim Press).

Close-Brooks, J, M Harman, R Hetherington, B Denston and D Lunt 1995 Excavation of a Cairn at Cnip, Uig, Isle of Lewis, *Proceedings of the Society of Antiquaries of Scotland* 125, 253–277.

Coatsworth, E 2008 *Corpus of Anglo-Saxon Stone Sculpture Volume VIII Western Yorkshire* (Oxford: Oxford University Press for The British Academy).

Coatsworth, E and G R Owen-Crocker 2007 *Medieval Textiles of the British Isles AD 450–1100* (BAR British Series 445) (Oxford: Archaeopress).

Collins, M, S Fiddyment, C Webb, T P O'Connor, M D Teasdale, S Doherty, J Vnoucek, S Hall and J Finch 2015 Reading the Leaves: Sheep Parchment as a 1000 Year Genetic Resource, *Advances in Animal Biosciences* (Proceedings of the British Society of Animal Science 2015), 63.

Collingwood W G 1927 *Northumbrian Crosses of the pre-Norman Age* (London: Faber and Gwyer).

Comber, M 2008 *The Economy of the Ringfort and Contemporary Settlement in Early Medieval Ireland* (BAR International Series 1773) (Oxford: John & Erica Hedges).

Comey, M G 2003/4 Stave-built Wooden Vessels from Medieval Ireland, *Journal of Irish Archaeology* 12/13, 33–77.

Conde-Silvestre, J C 2001 The Code and Context of *Monasteriales Indicia.* A Semiotic Analysis of Late Anglo-Saxon Monastic Sign Language, *Studia Anglica Posnaniensia* 36, 145–169.

Cook, M 2011 New Evidence for the Activities of Pictish Potentates in Aberdeenshire: The Hillforts of Strathdon, *Proceedings of the Society of Antiquaries of Scotland* 141, 201–229.

Cook, M and L Dunbar 2008 *Rituals, Roundhouses and Romans: Excavations at Kintore, Aberdeenshire 2000–2006* Volume 1 (Edinburgh: Scottish Trust for Archaeological Research).

Corlett, C and M Potterton (eds) 2010 *Death and Burial in Early Medieval Ireland in the Light of Recent Archaeological Excavations* (Dublin: Wordwell).

Corlett, C and M Potterton (eds) 2011 *Settlement in Early Medieval Ireland in the Light of Recent Archaeological Excavations* (Dublin: Wordwell).

Costen, M D and N P Costen 2016 Trade and Exchange in Anglo-Saxon Wessex, c. AD 600–780, *Medieval Archaeology* 60, 1–26.

Cowan, E J 1993 The Historical Macbeth, in W D H Sellar (ed), *Moray: Province and People* (Edinburgh: School of Scottish Studies), 117–141.

Cowie, R 2004 The Evidence for Royal Sites in Middle Anglo-Saxon London, *Medieval Archaeology* 48, 201–208.

Cowie, R and L Blackmore 2012 *Lundenwic: Excavations in Middle Saxon London 1987–2000* (MoLAS Monograph 63) (London: Museum of London Archaeology.

Cowie, T G 1978 Excavations at the Catstane, Midlothian 1977, *Proceedings of the Society of Antiquaries of Scotland* 109, 166–203.

Cowley, D C 1996 Square Barrows in Dumfries and Galloway, *Transactions of the Dumfriesshire & Galloway Natural History & Antiquarian Society* 71, 107–113.

Coyne, F 2006 Excavation of an Early Medieval 'Plectrum-shaped' Enclosure at Newtown, Co Limerick, in J O'Sullivan and M Stanley (eds), *Settlement, Industry and Ritual: Proceedings of a Public Seminar on Archaeological Discoveries on National Road Schemes, September 2005* (Bray: Wordwell), 63–72.

Crabtree, P 1994 Animal Exploitation in East Anglian Villages, in J Rackham (ed), *Environment and Economy in Anglo-Saxon England* (York: Council for British Archaeology), 40–54.

Craig, E and J Buckberry 2010 Investigating Social Status Using Evidence of Biological Status: A Case Study from Raunds Furnells, in J Buckberry and A Cherryson (eds), *Burial in Later Anglo-Saxon England c. 650–1100 AD* (Oxford: Oxbow), 128–142.

Cramp, R J 1957 Beowulf and Archaeology, *Medieval Archaeology* 1, 57–77.

Cramp, R J 1965 *Early Northumbrian Sculpture* (Jarrow Lecture) (Jarrow: The Rector of St Paul's Church).

Cramp, R J 1976 Monastic Sites, in D M Wilson (ed), *The Archaeology of Anglo-Saxon England* (London: Methuen), 201–252.

Cramp, R J 1977 Schools of Mercian Sculpture, in A Dornier (ed), *Mercian Studies* (Leicester: Leicester University Press), 191–233.

Cramp, R J 1982 The Viking Image, in R T Farrell (ed), *The Vikings* (London: Phillimore), 8–19.

Cramp, R J 1984a *A Corpus of Anglo-Saxon Stone Sculpture: General Introduction* (Oxford: Oxford University Press for The British Academy).

Cramp, R J 1984b *A Corpus of Anglo-Saxon Stone Sculpture Volume I: County Durham and Northumberland* (Oxford: Oxford University Press for The British Academy).

Cramp, R J 1995 *Whithorn and the Northumbrian Expansion Westwards* (Whithorn Lecture) (Whithorn: Friends of the Whithorn Trust).

Cramp, R J 2000 Anglo-Saxon Window Glass, in J Price (ed), *Glass in Britain and Ireland, AD 350–1100* (London: British Museum Press), 105–114.

Cramp, R J 2005 *Wearmouth and Jarrow Monastic Sites Volume 1* (and Volume 2 [2006]) (Swindon: English Heritage).

Cramp, R J 2006 *South-west England* (Corpus of Anglo-Saxon Stone Sculpture Volume VII) (Oxford: Oxford University Press for The British Academy).

Cramp, R J 2014 *The Hirsel Excavations* (Leeds: Society for Medieval Archaeology Monograph 36).

Crawford, B (ed) 1996 *Scotland in Dark Age Britain* (Aberdeen: Scottish Cultural Press).

Crawford, B (ed) 1998 *Conversion and Christianity in the North Sea World* (St Andrews: Committee for Dark Age Studies, University of St Andrews).

Crone, B A 1993a Excavation and Survey of Sub-peat Features of Neolithic and Bronze Age Date at Bharpa Carinish, North Uist, Scotland, *Proceedings of the Prehistoric Society* 59, 361–382.

Crone, B A 1993b Crannogs and Chronologies, *Proceedings of the Society of Antiquaries of Scotland* 123, 245–254.

Crone, B A 2000 *The History of a Scottish Lowland Crannog: Excavations at Buiston, Ayrshire 1989–90* (Scottish Trust for Archaeological Research Monograph 4) (Edinburgh: Scottish Trust for Archaeological Research).

Crone, B A 2007 'From Indirections Find Directions Out'; Taphonomic Problems at Loch Glashan Crannog, Argyll, in J W Barber et al. (eds), *Archaeology from the Wetlands: Recent Perspective* (Edinburgh: Society of Antiquaries of Scotland), 223–230.

Crone, B A and E Campbell 2005 *A Crannog of the First Millennium, AD: Excavations by Jack Scott at Loch Glashan, Argyll, 1960* (Edinburgh: Society of Antiquaries of Scotland).

Crone, B A and E Hindmarch 2016 *Living and Dying at Auldhame, East Lothian: The Excavation of an Anglian Monastic Settlement and Medieval Parish Church* (Edinburg: Society of Antiquaries of Scotland).

Cross, P 2011 Horse Burial in First Millennium AD Britain: Issues of Interpretation, *European Journal of Archaeology* 14 (1–2), 190–209.

Crowfoot, E 1967 Appendix 1: The Textiles, in H R E Davidson and L Webster, The Anglo-Saxon Burial at Coombe (Woodnesborough), Kent, *Medieval Archaeology* 11, 37–39.

Crowfoot, E 1983 The Textiles, in A Evans (ed), *The Sutton Hoo Ship Burial, Volume* 3, Part I (London: British Museum), 409–479.

Crowfoot, E n.d. (1988?) Textiles: Wasperton, Warwickshire (Ancient Monuments Laboratory Report 6/88) (Unpublished Report, Historic Buildings and Commission for England, c. 1988).

Crumlin-Pedersen, O 1991a Ship Types and Sizes AD 800–1400, in O Crumlin-Pedersen (ed) *Aspects of Maritime Scandinavia* (Roskilde: Viking Ship Museum), 68–82.

Crumlin-Pedersen, O (ed) 1991b *Aspects of Maritime Scandinavia* (Roskilde: Viking Ship Museum).

Crumlin-Pedersen, O 1991c *Slusegårdgravpladsen III Gravformer og Gravskikke Bådgravene* (Jysk Arkaeologisk Slskabs Skrifter 14) (Aarhus: Jutland Archaeological Society).

Crumlin-Pedersen, O 1997 *Viking-age Ships and Ship-building in Hedeby/Haithabu and Schleswig* (Copenhagen: National Museum of Denmark).

Crumlin-Pedersen, O 2010 *Archaeology and the Sea in Scandinavia and Britain: A Personal Account* (Roskilde: Viking Ship Museum).

Crumlin-Pedersen, O and B Munch Thye (eds) 1995 *The Ship as Symbol in Prehistoric and Medieval Scandinavia* (Copenhagen: National Museum of Denmark).

Crumlin-Pedersen, O and A Trakadas (eds) 2003 *Hjortspring: A Pre-Roman Iron-Age Warship in Context* (Roskilde: Viking Ship Museum).

Cummings, V 2009 *A View from the West: The Neolithic of the Irish Sea Zone* (Oxford: Oxbow).

Cummings, V and R Johnstone (eds) 2007 *Prehistoric Journeys* (Oxford: Oxbow).

Cunliffe, B 1972 Saxon and Medieval Settlement-pattern in the Region of Chalton, Hampshire, *Medieval Archaeology* 16, 1–12.

Cunliffe, B 2001 *Facing the Ocean: The Atlantic and its Peoples* (Oxford: Oxford University Press).

Cunliffe, B 2002 Tribes and Empires c. 1500 BC–AD 500, in P Slack and R Ward (eds), *The Peopling of Britain: The Shaping of a Human Landscape* (Oxford: Oxford University Press), 115–138.

Cunliffe, B 2005 *Iron Age Communities in Britain* 4th edition (London: Routledge).

Cunliffe, B 2013 *Britain Begins* (Oxford: Oxford University Press).

Cuttler, R, A Davidson and G Hughes 2012 *A Corridor Through Time: The Archaeology of the A55 Anglesey Road Scheme* (Oxford: Oxbow).

Daniels, R. 1999 The Anglo-Saxon monastery at Hartlepool, England, in J. Hawkes and S. Mills (eds) *Northumbria's Golden Age* (Stroud: Sutton Publishing), 105–112

Daniels, R 2007 *Anglo-Saxon Hartlepool and the Foundations of English Christianity: An Archaeology of the Anglo-Saxon Monastery* (Tees Archaeology Monograph 3) (Hartlepool: Tees Archaeology).

Darling, M J and D Gurney 1993 *Caister-on-Sea: Excavations by Charles Green 1951–55* (East Anglian Archaeology 60) (Dereham: Norfolk Museums Service).

Darvill, T 2004 Tynwald Hill and the 'Things' of Power, in A Pantos and S Semple (eds), *Assembly Places and Practices in Medieval Europe* (Dublin: Four Courts Press), 217–232.

Darvill, T and G Wainwright 2009 Stonehenge Excavations 2008, *Antiquaries Journal* 89, 1–19.

Davies, A 2009 The Early Medieval Church in North-west Wales, in N Edwards (ed), *The Archaeology of the Early Medieval Celtic Churches* (Leeds: Maney), 41–60.

Davies, W, G Halsall and A Reynolds (eds) 2006 *People and Space in the Middle Ages, 300–1300* (Turnhout: Brepols).

Davis, J R and M McCormick (eds) 2008 *The Long Morning of Medieval Europe, New Directions in Early Medieval Studies* (Farnham: Ashgate).

Dawes, J D and J R Magilton 1980 *The Cemetery of St Helen-on-the-Walls, Aldwark* (The Archaeology of York 12/1 – The Medieval Cemeteries) (York: Council for British Archaeology).

Dey, H and E Fentress (eds) 2011 *Western Monasticism 'Ante Litteram': The Spaces of Monastic Observance in Late Antiquity and the Early Middle Ages* (Disciplina Monastica 7) (Turnhout: Brepols).

Dickinson, T M 1979 On the Origin and Chronology of the Early Anglo-Saxon Disc Brooch, *Anglo-Saxon Studies in Archaeology and History* 1, 39–80.

Dickinson, T M 1982 Fowler's Type G Penannular Brooches Reconsidered, *Medieval Archaeology* 26, 41–68.

Dickinson, T M 1991 Material Culture as Social Expression: The Case of Saxon Saucer Brooches with Running Spiral Decoration, *Studien zur Sachsenforschung* 7, 39–70.

Dickinson, T M 1993a Early Saxon Saucer Brooches: A Preliminary Overview, *Anglo-Saxon Studies in Archaeology and History* 6, 11–44.

Dickinson, T M 1993b An Anglo-Saxon Cunning Woman from Bidford-on-Avon, in M O H Carver (ed), *In Search of Cult: Archaeological Investigations in Honour of Philip Rahtz* (Woodbridge: Boydell), 45–54.

Dickinson, T M 2005 Symbols of Protection: The Significance of Animal-ornamented Shields in Early Anglo-Saxon England, *Medieval Archaeology* 49, 109–163.

Dickinson, T M and D Griffiths (eds) 1999 *The Making of Kingdoms* (*Anglo-Saxon Studies in Archaeology and History* 10) (Oxford: Oxford University Committee for Archaeology).

Dietrich, O, H Manfred, J Notroff, K Schmidt and M Zarnkow 2012 The Role of Cult and Feasting in the Emergence of Neolithic Communities. New Evidence from Göbekli Tepe, South-Eastern Turkey, *Antiquity* 86, 674–695.

Dixon, T N 1982 A Survey of Crannogs in Loch Tay, *Proceedings of the Society of Antiquaries of Scotland* 112, 17–38.

Dixon, T N 2004 *The Crannogs of Scotland* (Stroud: Tempus).

Dixon, T N 2007 Crannog Structure and Dating in Perthshire With Particular Reference to Loch Tay, in J W Barber et al. (eds), *Archaeology from the Wetlands: Recent Perspective* (Edinburgh: Society of Antiquaries of Scotland), 253–266.

Dobat, A 2006 The King and His Cult: The Axe-hammer at Sutton Hoo and its Implications for the Concept of Sacral Leadership in Early Medieval Europe, *Antiquity* 80, 880–893.

Dobney, K, D Jaques, J Barrett and C Johnstone 2007 *Farmers, Monks and Aristocrats, the Environmental Archaeology of Anglo-Saxon Flixborough* (Excavations at Flixborough Volume 3) (Oxford: Oxbow).

Dobson, L 2008 Landscape, Monuments and the Construction of Social Power in Early Medieval Deira (Unpublished PhD dissertation, University of York).

Dockrill, S J, J M Bond, V E Turner, L D Brown, D J Bashford, J E Cussans and R A Nicholson 2010 *Excavations at Old Scatness, Shetland, Volume 1: The Pictish Village and Viking Settlement* (Lerwick: Shetland Heritage Publications).

Doherty, C 1984 The Use of Relics in Ireland, in P Ní Chatháin and M Richter (eds), *Irland und Europa. Die Kirche im Frühmittelalter* (Stuttgart: Klett-Cotta), 89–101.

Doherty, C 1985 The Monastic Town in Early Medieval Ireland, in H B Clarke and A Simms (eds), *The Comparative History of Urban Origins in Non-Roman Europe* (BAR International Series 255) (Oxford: British Archaeological Reports), 45–75.

Dopplefeld, O and W Weyres 1980 *Die Ausgrabungen im Dom zu Köln* (Mainz am Rhein: Von Zabern).

Down, A and M Welch 1990 *Chichester Excavations VII: Apple Down and Marden* (Chichester: Chichester District Council).

Downes, J and A Ritchie (eds) 2003 *Sea Change: Orkney and Northern Europe in the Later Iron Age AD 300–800* (Balgavies: Pinkfoot Press).

Doyle, I W 2009 Mediterranean and Frankish Pottery Imports in Early Medieval Ireland, *Journal of Irish Archaeology* 18, 17–62.

Driscoll, S T 1988 Power and Authority in Early Historic Scotland: Pictish Symbol Stones and Other Documents, in J Gledhill, B Bender and M T Larsen (eds), *State and Society: The Emergence and Development of Social Hierarchy and Political Centralization* (London: Unwin Hyman), 215–236.

Driscoll, S T 1997 A Pictish Settlement in North-East Fife: The Scottish Field School of Archaeology Excavations at Easter Kinnear, *Tayside and Fife Archaeological Journal* 3, 74–118.

Driscoll, S T 1998 Picts and Prehistory: Cultural Resource Management in Early Medieval Scotland, *World Archaeology* 31(1) (*The Past in the Past: The Reuse of Ancient Monuments*), 142–158.

Driscoll, S T 2000 Christian Monumental Sculpture and Ethnic Expression in Early Scotland, in W Frazer and A Tyrell (eds), *Social Identity in Early Medieval Britain and Ireland* (London: Leicester University Press), 233–252.

Driscoll, S T 2011 Pictish Archaeology: Persistent Problems and Structural Solutions, in S T Driscoll, J Geddes and M A Hall (eds), *Pictish Progress: New Studies on Northern Britain in the Early Middle Ages* (Leiden: Brill), 245–279.

Driscoll, S T and M Nieke (eds) 1988 *Power and Politics in Early Medieval Britain and Ireland* (Edinburgh: Edinburgh University Press).

Driscoll, S T, J Geddes and M A Hall (eds) 2011 *Pictish Progress: New Studies on Northern Britain in the Early Middle Ages* (Leiden: Brill).

Dumville, D N 1977 Sub-Roman Britain – History and Legend, *History* 62, 173–192.

Dunwell, A J and I Ralston 2010 *Archaeology and Early History of Angus* (Stroud: The History Press).

Dunwell, A J, T G Cowie, M F Bruce, T Neighbour and A R Rees 1995 A Viking Age Cemetery at Cnip, Uig, Isle of Lewis, *Proceedings of the Society of Antiquaries of Scotland* 125, 719–752, fiche 4.

Eagles, B 1979 *The Anglo-Saxon Settlement of Humberside* (BAR British Series 68) (Oxford: British Archaeological Reports).

East, K 1983 The Shoes, in R L S Bruce-Mitford, *The Sutton Hoo Ship Burial Volume* 3, 788–812.

Edel, D (ed) 1995 *Félire Óengusso: Cultural Identity and Cultural Integration: Ireland and Europe in the Early Middle Ages* (Dublin: Four Courts Press).

Edmonds, M 1992 Their Use Is Wholly Unknown, in N Sharples and A Sheridan (eds), *Vessels for the Ancestors: Essays on the Neolithic of Britain and Ireland in Honour of Audrey Henshall* (Edinburgh: Edinburgh University Press), 179–193.

Edwards, N 1985 The Origin of the Free-standing Stone Cross in Ireland – Imitation or Innovation, *Bulletin of the Board of Celtic Studies* 32, 393–410.

Edwards, N 1996 *The Archaeology of Early Medieval Ireland* (London: Routledge).

Edwards, N 2001 Early Medieval Inscribed Stones and Stone Sculpture in Wales: Context and Function, *Medieval Archaeology* 45, 15–40.

Edwards, N 2007 *A Corpus of Early Medieval Inscribed Stones and Stone Sculpture in Wales, Volume II: South-West Wales* (Cardiff: University of Wales Press).

Edwards, N 2009a Rethinking the Pillar of Eliseg, *Antiquaries Journal* 89, 143–177.

Edwards, N (ed) 2009b *The Archaeology of the Early Medieval Celtic Churches* (Society for Medieval Archaeology Monograph 29, Society for Church Archaeology Monograph 1) (Leeds: Maney).

Edwards, N 2013 *A Corpus of Early Medieval Inscribed Stones and Stone Sculpture in Wales, Volume III, North Wales* (Cardiff: University of Wales Press).

Edwards, N 2015 *The Early Medieval Sculpture of Wales: Text, Pattern and Image* (Kathleen Hughes Memorial Lecture 13) (Cambridge: Hughes Hall & Department of Anglo-Saxon, Norse and Celtic).

Edwards, N and A Lane (eds) 1992 *The Early Church in Wales and the West* (Oxford: Oxbow).

Edwards, N, A Lane, I Bapty and M Redknap 2005 Early Medieval Wales: A Framework for Archaeological Research, *Archaeology in Wales* 45, 33–46.

Edwards, N, A Lane and M Redknap 2011 *Early Medieval Wales: An Updated Framework for Archaeological Research* (February 2011) https://archaeoleg.org.uk/pdf/reviewdocs/earlymedreview.pdf

Ekelund, R B, R F Hebert, R D Tollison, G M Anderson and A Braidson 1996 *Sacred Trust: The Medieval Church as an Economic Firm* (New York and Oxford: Oxford University Press).

Ellis-Davidson, H 1950 Gods and Heroes in Stone, in C Fox and B Dickins (eds), *The Early Cultures of North-West Europe* (Cambridge: Cambridge University Press), 123–139.

Englert, A and A Trakadas (eds) 2009 *Wulfstan's Voyage: The Baltic Sea Region in the Early Viking Age as Seen from Shipboard* (Roskilde: Viking Ship Museum).

Eogan, G 2012 *Excavations at Knowth 5: The Archaeology of Knowth in the First and Second Millennia* (Dublin: Royal Irish Academy).

Eogan, J 2010 Excavation of an Unenclosed Early Medieval Cemetery at Bettystown, Co. Meath, in C Corlett and M Potterton (eds), *Death and Burial in Early Medieval Ireland in the Light of Recent Archaeological Excavations* (Dublin: Wordwell), 103–116.

Etchingham, C 2006 Pastoral Provision in the First Millennium: A Two-tier Service? in E Fitzpatrick and R Gillespie (eds), *The Parish in Medieval and Early Modern Ireland: Community, Territory and Building* (Dublin: Four Courts), 79–90.

Evans, A 1975 The Ship, in R L S Bruce-Mitford, *The Sutton Hoo Ship Burial Volume 1* (London: British Museum), 345–435.

Evans, A (ed) 1983 *The Sutton Hoo Ship Burial Volume 3: Late Roman and Byzantine Silver, Hanging-bowls, Drinking Vessels, Cauldrons and Other Containers, Textiles, the Lyre, Pottery Bottle and Other Items* (London: British Museum).

Evans, A 2005 Seventh Century Assemblages, in M O H Carver, *Sutton Hoo: A Seventh Century Princely Burial Ground and its Context* (London: British Museum Press), 201–282.

Evans, C, G Appleby, J Appleby, S Lucy and M Brudenell 2016 *Lives in Land: Mucking Excavations by Margaret and Tom Jones 1965–1978: Prehistory, Context and Summary* (Oxford: Oxbow).

Evans D and A Hancocks 2005 Romano-British, Late Saxon and Medieval remains at the Old Show Ground Cheddar. Excavations in 2001 *Proceedings of the Somerset Archaeological and Natural History Society* 149, 107–122.

Evans, D H and C Loveluck, 2009 *Life and Economy at Early Medieval Flixborough, c. AD 600–1000: The Artefact Evidence* (Excavations at Flixborough Volume 2) (Oxford: Oxbow).

Everson, P and D Stocker 1999 *Corpus of Anglo-Saxon Stone Sculpture Volume V Lincolnshire* (Oxford: Oxford University Press for The British Academy).

Evison, V I 1977 Supporting-arm Brooches and Equal-arm Brooches in England, *Studien zur Sachsenforschung* 1 (Festschrift for A Genrich), 127–147.

Evison, V I 1978a Early Anglo-Saxon Applied Disc Brooches. Part I: On the Continent, *Antiquaries Journal* 58, 88–102.

Evison, V I 1978b Early Anglo-Saxon Applied Disc Brooches. Part II: In England, *Antiquaries Journal* 58, 260–278.

Evison, V I 1987 *Dover: The Buckland Anglo-Saxon Cemetery* (London: Historic Buildings and Monuments Commission for England Archaeological Report 3).

Evison, V I 2000 Glass Vessels in England AD 400–1100, in J Price (ed), *Glass in Britain and Ireland, AD 350–1100* (London: British Museum Press), 47–104.

Fabech, C 1994 Reading Society from the Cultural Landscape. South Scandinavia Between Sacral and Political Power, in P O Nielsen, K Randsborg and H Thrane (eds), *The Archaeology of Gudme and Lundeborg* (Copenhagen: Akademisk Forlag), 169–183.

Fabech, C 1999 Centrality in Sites and Landscapes, in C Fabech and J Ringtved (eds), *Settlement and Landscape: Proceedings of a Conference in Århus, Denmark, May 4–7 1998* (Moesgård: Jutland Archaeological Society), 455–473.

Fabech, C and U Näsman 2013 Ritual Landscapes and Sacral Places in the First Millennium AD in South Scandinavia, in S W Nordeide and S Brink (eds), *Sacred Sites and Holy Places* (Turnhout: Brepols), 53–109.

Fanning, T 1981 Excavation of an Early Christian Cemetery and Settlement at Reask, Co Kerry, *Proceedings of the Royal Irish Academy* 81C, 67–172.

Farwell, D E and T I Molleson 1993 *Excavations at Poundbury 1966–1980. Volume II: The Cemeteries* (Dorset Natural History and Archaeological Society Monograph 11) (Dorchester: Dorset Natural History and Archaeological Society).

Faull, M 1979 British Survival in Anglo-Saxon Yorkshire (Unpublished PhD dissertation, University of Leeds).

Fell, C 1984 *Women in Anglo-Saxon England* (Oxford: Blackwell).

Fenton, A 1968 Alternating Stone and Turf – An Obselete Building Practice, *Folk Life* 6(1), 94–103.

Fenton, A 1999 *Scottish Country Life* (East Linton: published 1976, reissued 1999 by Tuckwell Press, East Linton).

Fenton, A and B Walker 1981 *The Rural Architecture of Scotland* (Edinburgh: John Donald).

Fern, C 2007 Early Anglo-Saxon Horse Burial of the Fifth to Seventh Centuries AD, *Anglo-Saxon Studies in Archaeology and History* 14, 92–109.

Fern, C 2010 Horses in Mind, in M O H Carver, A Sanmark and S Semple (eds), *Signals of Belief in Early England* (Oxford: Oxbow), 128–157.

Fern, C (ed) 2015 *Before Sutton Hoo: The Prehistoric Remains and Early Anglo-Saxon Cemetery at Tranmer House, Bromeswell, Suffolk* (East Anglian Archaeology 155) (Bury St Edmunds: Suffolk County Council).

Fernie, E 1986 Early Church Architecture in Scotland, *Proceedings of the Society of Antiquaries of Scotland* 116, 393–411.

Ferriday, A 1955 *A Regional Geography of the British Isles* (London: Macmillan).

Feveile, C 2010 Ribe. Emporium and Town in the 8th–9th Century, in A Willemsen and H Kik (eds), *Dorestad in an International Framework: New Research on Centres of Trade and Coinage in Carolingian Times* (Turnhout: Brepols), 143–148.

Feveile, C 2012 Ribe: Emporia and Town in the 8th and 9th Century, in S Gelichi and R Hodges (eds), *From one Sea to Another: Trading Places in the European and Mediterranean Early Middle Ages* (Turnhout: Brepols), 111–122.

Fiedel, R, K Høilund Nielsen and C Loveluck 2011 From Hamlet, to Central Place, to Manor. Social Transformation of the Settlement at Stavnsager, Eastern Jutland, and its Networks, AD 400–1100, *Neue Studien zur Sachsenforschung* 3, 161–176.

Filmer-Sankey, W 1996 The Roman Emperor in the Sutton Hoo Ship Burial, *Journal of the British Archaeological Association* 149, 1–9.

Filmer-Sankey, W and T Pestell 2001 *Snape Anglo-Saxon Cemetery: Excavations and Surveys 1824–1992* (East Anglian Archaeology 95) (Ipswich: Archaeological Service, Suffolk County Council).

Finkelstein, I and E Piasetzky 2003 Recent Radiocarbon Results and King Solomon, *Antiquity* 77, 771–779.

Fisher, G 2004 Faces in a Crowd or a Crowd of Faces? Archaeological Evidence for Individual and Group Identity in Early Anglo-Saxon Eastern England, in J R Mathieu and R E Scott (eds), *Exploring the Role of Analytical Scale in Archaeological Interpretation* (BAR International Series 1261) (Oxford: Archaeopress), 49–58.

Fisher, I 2001 *Early Medieval Sculpture in the West Highlands and Islands* (RCAHMS and Society of Antiquaries of Scotland Monograph Series 1) (Edinburgh: The Royal Commission on the Ancient and Historical Monuments of Scotland and The Society of Antiquaries of Scotland).

Fitzpatrick, A 1997 *Archaeological Excavations on the Route of the A27 Westhampnett Bypass, West Sussex ii: The Late Iron Age, Roman and Anglo-Saxon Cemeteries* (Wessex Archaeology Report 12) (Salisbury: Trust for Wessex Archaeology).

Flatt, Λ E 2001 The Vikings and Baron Dupuytren's Disease, *Proceedings of the Baylor University Medical Center* 14(4), 378–384.

Fleming, R 2010 *Britain After Rome: The Fall and Rise 400–1070* (London: Allen Lane).

Fletcher, R 1997 *The Conversion of Europe: From Paganism to Christianity 371–1386 AD* (London: Harper Collins).

Flynn, C 2009 Camlin 3: A Cemetery-Settlement in North Tipperary, in M Stanley, E Danaher and J Eogan (eds), *Dining and Dwelling* (NRA Scheme Monograph 6) (Dublin: National Roads Authority), 133–141.

Ford, P K (ed) 2008 *The Mabinogi and Other Medieval Welsh Tales* (Berkeley (CA) and London: University of California Press).

Forsyth, K 1995a Language in Pictland, Spoken and Written, in E H Nicoll (ed), *A Pictish Panorama* (Balgavies: Pinkfoot Press), 7–10.

Forsyth, K 1995b The Inscriptions on the Dupplin Cross, in C Bourke (ed), *From the Isles of the North: Early Medieval Art in Ireland and Britain* (Belfast: HMSO), 237–244.

Forsyth, K 1997a *Language in Pictland: The Case Against 'Non-Indo-European Pictish'* (Utrecht: De Keltische Draak).

Forsyth, K 1997b Some Thoughts on Pictish Symbols as a Formal Writing System, in D Henry (ed), *The Worm, the Germ and the Thorn* (Balgavies: Pinkfoot Press), 85–98.

Forsyth, K 1998 Literacy in Pictland, in H Pryce (ed), *Literacy in Medieval Celtic Societies* (Cambridge: Cambridge University Press), 39–61.

Forsyth, K 2005 *Hic Memoria Perpetua*: The Early Inscribed Stones of Southern Scotland in Context, in S M Foster and M Cross (eds), *Able Minds and Practised Hands: Scotland's Early Medieval Sculpture in the 21st Century* (Leeds: Society for Medieval Archaeology), 113–134.

Foster, S M (ed) 1998 *The St Andrews Sarcophagus: A Pictish Masterpiece and its International Connections* (Dublin: Four Courts Press).

Foster, S M 2014 *Picts, Gaels and Scots: Early Historic Scotland* (Edinburgh: Birlinn).

Foster, S M 2015 Physical Evidence for the Early Church in Scotland, in P Barnwell (ed), *Buildings for Worship in Britain: Celtic and Anglo-Saxon* (Rewley House Studies in the Historic Environment 4) (Donington: Shaun Tyas).

Foster, S M and M Cross (eds) 2005 *Able Minds and Practised Hands: Scotland's Early Medieval Sculpture in the 21st Century* (Leeds: Society for Medieval Archaeology and Historic Scotland).

Fowler, E 1960 The Origins and Development of the Penannular Brooch in Europe, *Proceedings of the Prehistoric Society.* 26, 149–177.

Fox, A 1939 The Siting of Some Inscribed Stones of the Dark Ages in Glamorgan and Breconshire, *Archaeologia Cambrensis* 94, 30–41.

Fox, C 1952 *The Personality of Britain: Its Influence on Inhabitant and Invader in Prehistoric and Early Historic Times* (Cardiff: National Museum of Wales).

Fox, C and B Dickins (eds) 1950 *The Early Cultures of North-West Europe* (Cambridge: Cambridge University Press).

Foys, M K 2007 *Virtually Anglo-Saxon: Old Media, New Media and Early Medieval Studies in the Late Age of Print* (Gainesville: University Press of Florida).

Frank, R 1992 Beowulf and Sutton Hoo: The Odd Couple, in C B Kendall and P S Wells (eds), *Voyage to the Other World: The Legacy of Sutton Hoo* (Minneapolis: University of Minnesota Press), 47–64.

Fraser, I and S Halliday 2011 The Early Medieval Landscape of Donside, Aberdeenshire, in S T Driscoll, J Geddes and M A Hall (eds), *Pictish Progress: New Studies on Northern Britain in the Early Middle Ages* (Leiden: Brill), 307–333.

Fraser, J E 2009 *From Caledonia to Pictland. Scotland to 795* (Edinburgh University Press).

Fraser, J E 2011 From Ancient Scythia to the *The Problem of the Picts*: Thoughts on the Quest for Pictish Origins, in S T Driscoll, J Geddes and M A Hall (eds), *Pictish Progress: New Studies on Northern Britain in the Early Middle Ages* (Leiden: Brill), 15–44.

Frazer, W O and T Andrew (eds) 2000 *Social Identity in Early Medieval Britain* (London: Leicester University Press).

Freke, D 2002 *Excavations on St Patrick's Isle, Peel, Isle of Man 1982–88: Prehistoric, Viking, Medieval and Later* (Liverpool: Liverpool University Press).

Friell, J G P and W G Watson (eds) 1984 *Pictish Studies* (BAR British Series 125) (Oxford: British Archaeological Reports).

Frodsham, P and C O'Brien (eds) 2009 *Yeavering: People, Power & Place* (Stroud: The History Press).

Fulford, M, M Handley and A Clark 2000 An Early Date for Ogham: The Silchester Ogham Stone Rehabilitated, *Medieval Archaeology* 44, 1–23.

Gaimster, M 2011 Image and Power in the Early Saxon Period, in H Hamerow, D A Hinton and S Crawford (eds), *The Oxford Handbook of Anglo-Saxon Archaeology* (Oxford: Oxford University Press), 865–891.

Galloway, W 1878 Notice of the Ancient Kil or Burying Ground Termed 'Cladh Bhile', Near Ellary, Loch Caolisport, South Knapdale, *Proceedings of the Society of Antiquaries of Scotland* 12, 32–58.

Gameson, R (ed) 2013a *The Cambridge History of the Book in Britain Volume 1: c. 400–1100* (Cambridge: Cambridge University Press).

Gameson, R 2013b The Material Fabric of Early British Books, in R Gameson (ed), *The Cambridge History of the Book in Britain Volume 1: c. 400–1100* (Cambridge: Cambridge University Press), 11–93.

Gannon, A 2003 *The Iconography of Early Anglo-Saxon Coinage* (Oxford: Oxford University Press).

Garmonsway, G N (ed) 1947 *Aelfric's Colloquy* (London: Methuen).

Garrard, T F 1989 *Gold of Africa: Jewellery and Ornaments from Ghana, Côte d'Ivoire, Mail and Senegal in the Collection of the Barbier-Mueller Museum* (Munich: Prestel).

Geake, H 1997 *The Use of Grave-Goods in Conversion-Period England, c. 600–c. 850* (BAR British Series 261) (Oxford: British Archaeological Reports).

Geake, H 1999 Invisible Kingdoms: The Use of Grave-goods in Seventh Century England, in T M Dickinson and D Griffiths (eds), *The Making of Kingdoms* (Oxford: Oxford University Committee for Archaeology), 203–215.

Geake, H 2003 The Control of Burial Practice in Middle Anglo-Saxon England, in M O H Carver (ed), *The Cross Goes North: Processes of Conversion in Northern Europe, AD 300–1300* (Woodbridge and Rochester (NY): York Medieval Press), 259–270.

Geake, H and Kenny, J. (eds) 2000 *Early Deira: Archaeological Studies of the East Riding in the Fourth to Ninth Centuries AD* (Oxford: Oxbow).

Geddes, J 2011 The Problems of Pictish Art, 1955–2009, in S T Driscoll, J Geddes and M A Hall (eds), *Pictish Progress: New Studies on Northern Britain in the Early Middle Ages* (Leiden: Brill), 121–134.

Gelichi, S and R Hodges (eds) 2012 *From one Sea to Another: Trading Places in the European and Mediterranean Early Middle Ages* (Turnhout: Brepols).

Gelichi, S, D Calaon, E Grandi and C Negrelli 2012 The History of a Forgotten Town: Comacchio and its Archaeology, in S Gelichi and R Hodges (eds), *From one Sea to Another: Trading Places in the European and Mediterranean Early Middle Ages* (Turnhout: Brepols), 169–206.

Gelling, M 1978 *Signposts to the Past: Place-names and the History of England* (London: Dent).

Gelling, M 1993 Why Aren't We Speaking Welsh? *Anglo-Saxon Studies in Archaeology and History* 6, 51–56.

Gilchrist, R 1988 A Reappraisal of Dinas Powys: Local Exchange and Specialized Livestock in 5th to 7th-century Wales, *Medieval Archaeology* 32, 50–62.

Gilchrist, R 2012 *Medieval Life: Archaeology and Life Course* (Woodbridge: Boydell).

Gondek, M 2006a Investing in Sculpture: Power in Early Historic Scotland, *Medieval Archaeology* 50, 105–142.

Gondek, M 2006b Early Historic Sculpture at Cladh a'Bhile, *Proceedings of the Society of Antiquaries of Scotland* 136, 237–258.

Gondek, M 2015 Building Blocks: Structural Contexts and Carved Stones in Early Medieval Northern Britain, in H Williams, J Kirton and M Gondek (eds), *Early Medieval Stone Monuments. Materiality, biography, landscape* (Woodbridge: Boydell), 87–113.

Gondek, M and G Noble 2011 Together as One: The Landscape of the Symbol Stones at Rhynie, in S T Driscoll, J Geddes and M Hall (eds), *Pictish Progress: New Studies on North Britain in the Early Middle Ages* (Leiden: Brill), 281–306.

Gowland, R 2007 Beyond Ethnicity: Symbols of Identity in Fourth to Sixth Century AD England, *Anglo-Saxon Studies in Archaeology and History* 14, 56–65.

Graham-Campbell, J 1995 *The Viking-Age Gold and Silver of Scotland (AD 850–1100)* (Edinburgh: National Museums of Scotland).

Graham-Campbell, J 2002 *Pictish Silver: Status and Symbol* (H M Chadwick Memorial Lecture 13) (Cambridge: University of Cambridge, Department of Anglo-Saxon, Norse and Celtic).

Graham-Campbell, J 2013 *Viking Art* (London and New York: Thames & Hudson).

Graham-Campbell, J and C Batey 1998 *Vikings in Scotland: An Archaeological Survey* (Edinburgh: Edinburgh University Press).

Granger-Taylor, H and F Pritchard 2001 A Fine Quality Insular Embroidery from Llangors Crannóg, Near Brecon, in M Redknap, N Edwards, S Youngs, A Lane and J Knight (eds), *Pattern and Purpose in Insular Art* (Oxford: Oxbow), 91–99.

Gräslund, A-S 2003 The Role of Scandinavian Women in Christianisation: The Neglected Evidence, in M O H Carver (ed), *The Cross Goes North: Processes of Conversion in Northern Europe, AD 300–1300* (Woodbridge and Rochester (NY): York Medieval Press), 483–496.

Green, C, C Gosden, A Cooper, T Franconi, L ten Harkel, Z Kamash and A Lowerre 2017 Understanding the Spatial Modelling of English Archaeology: Modelling Mass Data, 1500 BC to AD 1086, *Archaeological Journal* 174, 244–280.

Gregory, S (ed. and trans.) 1991 Thomas of Britain, *Roman de Tristan* (New York: Garland Publishers).

Griffiths, D 1995 The North-west Mercian Burhs. A Reappraisal, *Anglo-Saxon Studies in Archaeology and History* 8, 75–86.

Grogan, E 2008 *The Rath of the Synods: Tara, Co Meath: Excavations by Seán P. Ó Ríordáin* (Dublin: Wordwell).

Groves, S 2010 The Bowl Hole Burial Ground: A Late Anglian Cemetery in Northumberland, in J Buckberry and A Cherryson (eds), *Burial in Later Anglo-Saxon England c. 650–1100 AD* (Oxford: Oxbow), 116–127.

Haarnagel, W 1979 *Die Grabung Feddersen Wierde: Methode, Hausbau, Siedlungs- und Wirtschasfts-formen sowie Sozialstruktur* (Wiesbaden: Steiner).

Hadley, D M 2002 Burial Practices in Northern England in the Later Anglo-Saxon Period, in S Lucy and A Reynolds (eds), *Burial in Early Medieval England and Wales* (London: Society for Medieval Archaeology), 209–228.

Hadley, D M 2007 The Garden Gives up its Secrets: The Developing Relationship Between Rural Settlements and Cemeteries, c. 750–1100, *Anglo-Saxon Studies in Archaeology and History* 14, 194–203.

Hadley, D M 2010 Burying the Socially and Physically Distinctive in Later Anglo-Saxon England, in J Buckberry and A Cherryson (eds), *Burial in Later Anglo-Saxon England c. 650–1100 AD* (Oxford: Oxbow), 103–115.

Hadley, D M and J D Richards 2016 The Winter Camp of the Viking Great Army AD 872–3. Torksey, Lincolnshire, *Antiquaries Journal* 96, 23–67.

Hakenbeck, S 2007 Situational Ethnicity and Nested Identities: New Approaches to an Old Problem, *Anglo-Saxon Studies in Archaeology and History* 14, 21–34.

Hakenbeck, S 2009 'Hunnic' Modified Skulls: Physical Appearance Identity and the Transformative Nature of Migrations, in D Sayer and H Williams (eds), *Mortuary Practices and Social Identities in the Middle Ages* (Exeter: University of Exeter Press), 64–80.

Hakenbeck, S 2011 *Local, regional and ethnic identities in early medieval cemeteries in Bavaria* (Contributi di Archeologia Medievale. Premio Ottone D'Assia e Riccardo Francovich, 5; Firenze: All'Insegna del Giglio).

Haldane, A R B 1997 *The Drove Roads of Scotland* (Edinburgh: Birlinn).

Hall, M A 2012 Three Stones, One Landscape and Many Stories: Cultural Biography of the Early Medieval Sculptures of Inchyra and St Madoes, Carse of Gowrie, Perthshire, Scotland, in S Dudley, A J Barnes, J Binnie, J Petrov and J Walklate (eds), *Narrating Objects, Collecting Stories* (London: Routledge), 85–102.

Hall, M A, K Forsyth, I Henderson, R Trench-Jellicoe and A Watson 2000 Of Makings and Meanings, Towards a Cultural Biography of the Crieff Burgh Cross, Strathearn, Perthshire, *Tayside and Fife Archaeological Journal*, 6, 154–188.

Hall, R 1984 *The Viking Dig* (London: Bodley Head).

Hall, R 2011 *Burhs* and Boroughs: Defended Places, Trade, and Towns, Plans, Defences, and Civic Features, in H Hamerow, D A Hinton and S Crawford (eds), *The Oxford Handbook of Anglo-Saxon Archaeology* (Oxford: Oxford University Press), 600–621.

Hall, R 2014 *Anglo-Scandinavian Occupation at 16–22 Coppergate: Defining a Townscape* (The Archaeology of York 8/5) (York: Council for British Archaeology).

Hall, R and M Whyman 1996 Settlement and Monasticism at Ripon, North Yorkshire from the 7th to 11th Centuries AD, *Medieval Archaeology* 40, 62–150.

Hall, T 2000 *Minster Churches in the Dorset Landscape* (BAR British Series 304) (Oxford: Archaeopress).

Halliday, S P 2007 Unenclosed Round-houses in Scotland: Occupation, Abandonment and the Character of Settlement, in C Burgess, P Topping and F Lynch (eds), *Beyond Stonehenge: Essays on the Bronze Age in Honour of Colin Burgess* (Oxford: Oxbow), 49–56.

Halsall, G 2013 *Worlds of Arthur* (Oxford: Oxford University Press).

Hamerow, H 1993 [2013] *Excavations at Mucking Volume 2: The Anglo-Saxon Settlement* (London: English Heritage).

Hamerow, H 2002 *Early Medieval Settlements: The Archaeology of Rural Communities in Northwest Europe 400–900* (Oxford: Oxford University Press).

Hamerow, H 2011 Overview: Rural Settlement, in H Hamerow, D A Hinton and S Crawford (eds), *The Oxford Handbook of Anglo-Saxon Archaeology* (Oxford: Oxford University Press), 119–127.

Hamerow, H 2012 *Rural Settlements and Society in Anglo-Saxon England* (Oxford: Oxford University Press).

Hamerow, H 2015 A High-status Seventh-century Female Burial from West Hamley, Oxfordshire, *Antiquaries Journal* 95, 91–118.

Hamerow, H 2016 Furnished Female Burial in Seventh-century England: Gender and Sacral Authority in the Conversion Period, *Early Medieval Europe* 24(4), 423–447.

Hamerow, H and A MacGregor (eds) 2001 *Image and Power in the Archaeology of Early Medieval Britain, Essays in Honour of Rosemary Cramp* (Oxford: Oxbow).

Hamerow, H, D A Hinton and S Crawford (eds) 2011 *The Oxford Handbook of Anglo-Saxon Archaeology* (Oxford: Oxford University Press).

Handley, M A 2001 Isidore of Seville and 'Hisperic Latin' in Early Medieval Wales: The Epigraphic Culture of Llanllyr and Llanddewi-Brefi, in J Higgitt, K Forsyth and D N Parsons (eds), *Roman, Runes and Ogham: Medieval Inscriptions in the Insular World and on the Continent* (Donington: Shaun Tyas), 26–36.

Hansen, I L and C Wickham (eds) 2000 *The Long Eighth Century* (Leiden and Boston: Brill).

Hårdh, B and L Larsson (eds) 2002 *Central Places in the Migration and Merovingian Periods: Papers from the 52nd Sachsensymposium Lund, August 2001,* (Stockholm: Almqvist & Wiksell International).

Harding, D W 2004 *The Iron Age in Northern Britain: Celts and Romans: Natives and Invaders* (London: Routledge).

Harding, D W 2009a *The Iron Age Round House: Later Prehistoric Building in Britain and Beyond* (Oxford: Oxford University Press).

Harding, D W 2009b Secondary Occupation of Atlantic Roundhouses: Problems of Identification and Interpretation, in G Cooney, K Becker, J Coles, M Ryan and S Sievers (eds), *Relics of Old Decency: Archaeological Studies in Later Prehistory. Festschrift for Barry Raftery* (Dublin: Wordwell), 471–484.

Harding, D W 2016 *Death and Burial in Iron Age Britain* (Oxford: Oxford University Press).

Harding, D W and S Gilmour 2000 *The Iron Age Settlement at Beirgh, Riof, Isle of Lewis: Excavations 1985–1995* (Volume 1, Calanais Research Series 1) (Edinburgh: University of Edinburgh, Department of Archaeology).

Hardy, A, B M Charles and R J Williams 2007 *Death and Taxes: The Archaeology of a Middle Saxon Estate Centre at Higham Ferrers, Northamptonshire* (Oxford: Oxbow).

Härke, H 1990 'Warrior Graves?' The Background of the Anglo-Saxon Weapon Burial Rite, *Past & Present* 126, 22–43.

Härke, H 2001 Cemeteries as Places of Power, in M de Jong and F Theuws with C van Rhijn (eds), *Topographies of Power in the Early Middle Ages* (Leiden: Brill), 9–30.

Härke, H 2002 Kings and Warriors. Population and Landscape from Post-Roman to Norman Britain, in P Slack and R Ward (eds), *The Peopling of Britain: The Shaping of a Human Landscape* (Oxford: Oxford University Press), 145–175.

Härke, H 2004 The Debate on Migration and Identity in Europe, *Antiquity* 78, 453–456.

Härke, H 2011 Anglo-Saxon Immigration and Ethnogenesis, *Medieval Archaeology* 55, 1–28.

Harris, A 2003 *Byzantium, Britain and the West: The Archaeology of Cultural Identity AD 400–650* (Stroud: Tempus).

Harrison, S H 2007 Separated from the Foaming Maelstrom: Landscapes of Insular 'Viking' Burial, *Anglo-Saxon Studies in Archaeology and History* 14, 173–182.

Harvey, A 2001 Problems in Dating the Origin of the Ogham Script, in J Higgitt, K Forsyth and D N Parsons (eds). *Roman, Runes and Ogham: Medieval Inscriptions in the Insular World and on the Continent* (Donington: Shaun Tyas), 37–50.

Harvey, P D A 1993 Rectitudines Singularum Personarum and Gerefa, *English Historical Review* 108, 1–22.

Haselgrove, C and T Moore (eds) 2007 *The Later Iron Age in Britain and Beyond* (Oxford: Oxbow).

Haslam, J 2003 Excavations at Cricklade 1975, *Internet Archaeology* 14.

Haslam, J 2009 The Development of Late Saxon Christchurch, Dorset and the Burghal Hideage, *Medieval Archaeology* 53, 95–118.

Hatherley, C 2009 Into the West: Excavation of an Early Christian Cemetery at Montfode, Ardrossan, North Ayrshire, *Proceedings of the Society of Antiquaries of Scotland* 139, 195–212.

Haughton, C and D Powlesland 1999a *West Heslerton: The Anglian Cemetery I. The Excavation and Discussion of the Evidence* (Landscape Research Centre Archaeological Monograph 1.1) (Yedingham: Landscape Research Centre).

Haughton, C and D Powlesland 1999b *West Heslerton: The Anglian Cemetery II. Catalogue of the Anglian Graves and Associated Assemblages* (Landscape Research Centre Archaeological Monograph 1.2) (Yedingham: Landscape Research Centre).

Hawkes, J 2002 *The Sandbach Crosses: Sign and Significance in Anglo-Saxon Sculpture* (Dublin: Four Courts Press).

Hawkes, J 2009 The Church Triumphant: The Figural Columns of Early Ninth-century Anglo-Saxon England, in H Hamerow and L Webster (eds), *Shaping Understanding: Form and Order in the Anglo-Saxon World, 400–1100, Anglo-Saxon Studies in Archaeology and History,* 16, 29–42.

Hawkes, J and S Mills (eds) 1999 *Northumbria's Golden Age* (Stroud: Sutton).

Hawkes, S C and G Grainger 2006 *The Anglo-Saxon Cemetery at Finglesham Kent* (Oxford University School of Archaeology Monograph 64) (Oxford: Oxford University School of Archaeology).

Hayes, A 2006 Archaeological Investigation of a Souterrain at Tateetra, Dundalk, County Louth, in J O'Sullivan and M Stanley (eds) *Roads, Rediscovery and Research* (Dublin: National Roads Authority), 53–61.

Hayman, G and A. Reynolds 2005 A Saxon and Saxo-Norman Execution Cemetery at 42–54 London Road Staines *Archaeological Journal* 162.1, 215–255.

Heald, A 2003 Non-ferrous Metal-working in Iron Age Scotland (c.700 BC to AD 800) (Unpublished PhD dissertation, University of Edinburgh).

Heaney, S 1999 *Beowulf a New Verse Translation* (London: Faber).

Heaney, S and T Hughes (eds) 1982 *The Rattle Bag* (London: Faber and Faber).

Hedeager, L 1999 Myth and Art: A Passport to Political Authority in Scandinavia During the Migration Period, in T M Dickinson and D Griffiths (eds), *The Making of Kingdoms* (Oxford: Oxford University Committee for Archaeology), 151–156.

Hedeager, L 2002 Scandinavian 'Central Places' in a Cosmological Setting, in B Hårdh and L Larsson (eds), *Central Places in the Migration and Merovingian Periods* (Stockholm: Almqvist & Wiksell International), 3–18.

Hedeager, L 2011 *Iron Age Myth and Materiality an Archaeology of Scandinavia AD400–1000* (London and New York: Routledge).

Hencken, H O'N 1936 Ballinderry Crannog No 1, *Proceedings of the Royal Irish Academy* 43C, 103–239.

Hencken, H O'N 1942 Ballinderry Crannog No 2, *Proceedings of the Royal Irish Academy* 47C, 1–76.

Hencken, H O'N 1950 Lagore Crannog: An Irish Royal Residence from the Seventh to Tenth Centuries, *Proceedings of the Royal Irish Academy* 53C, 1–247.

Henderson, C G 1987 *From Durrow to Kells: The Insular Gospel Books 650–800* (London and New York: Thames & Hudson).

Henderson, C G 2008 The Art-historical Context of the Hilton of Cadboll Cross-slab, in H F James, I Henderson, S M Foster and S Jones (eds), *A Fragmented Masterpiece: Recovering the Biography of the Hilton of Cadboll Pictish Cross-slab* (Edinburgh: Society of Antiquaries of Scotland), 127–204.

Henderson, C G and P T Bidwell 1982 The Saxon Minster at Exeter, in S Pearce (ed), *The Early Church in Western Britain and Ireland: Studies Presented to C A R Radford* (BAR British Series102) (Oxford: British Archaeological Reports), 145–175.

Henderson, C G and I H. Henderson 2004 *The Art of the Picts Sculpture and Metalwork in Early Medieval Scotland* (London: Thames & Hudson).

Henderson, I H 1958 The Origin Centre of the Pictish Symbol Stones, *Proceedings of the Society of Antiquaries of Scotland* 91, 44–60.

Henderson, I H 1971 The Meaning of the Pictish Symbol Stones, in E Meldrum (ed), *The Dark Ages in the Highlands* (Inverness: Inverness Field Club), 53–67.

Henderson, I H 1987 Early Christian Monuments of Scotland Displaying Crosses but No Other Ornament, in A Small (ed), *The Picts – A New Look at Old Problems* (Dundee: Graham Hunter Foundation), 45–58.

Henderson, I H 1998 Primus Inter Pares: The St Andrews Sarcophagus and Pictish Sculpture, in S M Foster (ed), *The St Andrews Sarcophagus, A Pictish Masterpiece and its International Connections* (Dublin: Four Courts Press), 97–167.

Henderson, J C 2007 *The Atlantic Iron Age: Settlement and Identity in the First Millennium BC* (London: Routledge).

Henning, J (ed) 2007a *Post-Roman Towns, Trade and Settlement in Europe and Byzantium: Volume 1 The Heirs of the Roman West* (Berlin and New York: De Gruyter), 233–270.

Henning, J 2007b Early European Towns: The Way of the Economy in the Frankish Area Between Dynamism and Deceleration 500–1000AD, in J Henning (ed), *Post-Roman Towns, Trade and Settlement in Europe and Byzantium: Volume 1 The Heirs of the Roman West* (Berlin and New York: De Gruyter), 3–40.

Henning, J 2008 Strong Rulers – Weak Economy? Rome, the Carolingians and the Archaeology of Slavery in the First Millennium AD, in J R Davis and M McCormick (eds), *The Long Morning of Medieval Europe, New Directions in Early Medieval Studies* (Farnham: Ashgate), 33–54.

Henry, F 1952. A Wooden Hut on Inishkea North, Co. Mayo (Site 3, House A), *Journal of the Royal Society of Antiquaries of Ireland* 82, 163–178.

Henry, P A 2004 Changing Weaving Styles and Fabric Types: The Scandinavian Influence, in J Hines, A Lane and M Redknap (eds), *Land, Sea and Home: Settlement in the Viking Period* (Leeds: Maney), 443–456.

Herity, M 1995 *Studies in the Layout, Buildings and Art in Stone of Early Irish Monasteries* (London: Pindar Press).

Herschend, F 1992 Beowulf and St Sabas: The Tension Between the Individual and the Collective in the Germanic Society Around 500 AD, *Tor* 24, 145–164.

Herschend, F 1993 The Origin of the Hall in Southern Scandinavia, *Tor* 25, 175–199.

Hey, G 2004 *Yarnton: Saxon and Medieval Settlement and Landscape Results of Excavations 1990–96* (Thames Valley Landscapes Monograph 20) (Oxford: Oxford University School of Archaeology).

Higgitt, J 1982 The Pictish Latin Inscription at Tarbat in Ross-shire, *Proceedings of the Society of Antiquaries of Scotland* 112, 300–321.

Higgitt, J (ed) 1986a *Early Medieval Sculpture in Britain and Ireland* (BAR British Series 152) (Oxford: British Archaeological Reports).

Higgitt, J 1986b Words and Crosses: The Inscribed Stone Cross in Early Medieval Britain, in J Higgitt (ed), *Early Medieval Sculpture in Britain and Ireland* (BAR British Series 152) (Oxford: British Archaeological Reports), 125–152.

Higgitt, J, K Forsyth and D N Parsons (eds) 2001 *Roman, Runes and Ogham: Medieval Inscriptions in the Insular World and on the Continent* (Donington: Shaun Tyas).

Hill, D H 1969 The Burghal Hidage: The Establishment of a Text, *Medieval Archaeology* 13, 84–92.

Hill, D H 1981 *An Atlas of Anglo-Saxon England* (Oxford: Blackwell).

Hill, D H 2003 The Origins of Alfred's Urban Policies, in T Reuter (ed), *Alfred the Great: Papers from the Eleventh-centenary Conferences* (Farnham: Ashgate), 219–233.

Hill, D H and R Cowie (eds) 2001 *Wics. The Early Medieval Trading Centres of Northern Europe* (Sheffield Archaeological Monograph 14) (Sheffield: Sheffield Academic Press).

Hill, D H and A Rumble (eds) 1996 *The Defence of Wessex: The Burghal Hideage and Anglo-Saxon Fortifications* (Manchester: Manchester University Press).

Hill, J D 2007 The Dynamics of Social Change in Later Iron Age Eastern and South-eastern England c. 300BC–AD 43, in C Haselgrove and T Moore (eds), *The Later Iron Age in Britain and Beyond* (Oxford: Oxbow), 16–40.

Hill, J D 2011 How Did British Middle and Late Pre-Roman Iron Age Societies Work (If They Did)? in T Moore and X-L Armada (eds), *Atlantic Europe in the First Millennium BC* (Oxford: Oxford University Press), 242–263.

Hill, P 1997 *Whithorn and St Ninian. Excavation of a Monastic Town 1984–1991* (Stroud: Sutton for the Whithorn Trust).

Hills, C M 1980 Anglo-Saxon Chairperson, *Antiquity* 44, 52–54.

Hills, C M 2003 *Origins of the English* (London: Duckworth).

Hills, C M 2009 Anglo-Saxon DNA? in D Sayer and H Williams (eds), *Mortuary Practices and Social Identities in the Middle Ages* (Exeter: University of Exeter Press), 123–140.

Hills, C M 2014 'Spong Man' in Context, in S Ashley and A Marsden (eds), *Landscapes and Artefacts: Studies in East Anglian Archaeology Presented to Andrew Rogerson* (Oxford: Archaeopress), 79–87.

Hills, C M 2015 Work Boxes or Reliquaries? Small Copper alloy Containers in Seventh-century Anglo-Saxon Graves, *Neue Studien zur Sachsenforschung* 5, 51–62.

Hills, C M and S Lucy 2013 *Spong Hill: Part IX Chronology and Synthesis* (Cambridge: MacDonald Institute).

Hills, C M and T O'Connell 2009 New Light on the Anglo-Saxon Succession: Two Cemeteries and their Dates, *Antiquity* 83, 1096–1108.

Hills, C M, K Penn and R Rickett 1984 *The Anglo-Saxon Cemetery at Spong Hill, North Elmham Part III: Catalogue of Inhumations* (East Anglian Archaeology 21) (Dereham: Norfolk Archaeological Unit).

Hinchliffe, J 1986 An Early Medieval Settlement at Cowage Farm, Foxley, Near Malmesbury, *Archaeological Journal* 143, 240–259.

Hines, J 1984 *The Scandinavian Character of Anglian England in the pre-Viking Period* (BAR British Series 124) (Oxford: British Archaeological Reports).

Hines, J 1993 *Clasps, hektespenner, agraffen: Anglo-Scandinavian Clasps of Classes A-C of the 3rd to the 6th Centuries A.D. Typology, Diffusion and Function* (Stockholm: Kungl. Vitterhets historie och antikvitets akademien).

Hines, J 1994 The Becoming of the English: Identity, Material Culture and Language in Early Anglo-Saxon England, *Anglo-Saxon Studies in Archaeology and History* 7, 49–59.

Hines, J 1997 *A New Corpus of Anglo-Saxon Great Square-Headed Brooches* (Woodbridge: Boydell for The Society of Antiquaries of London).

Hines, J 2013 The Origins of East Anglia in a North Sea Zone, in D Bates and R Liddiard (eds), *East Anglia and its North Sea World in the Middle Ages* (Woodbridge: Boydell), 16–43.

Hines, J and A Bayliss (eds) 2013 *Anglo-Saxon Graves and Grave Goods of the 6th and 7th Centuries AD: A Chronological Framework* (Society for Medieval Archaeology Monograph 33) (London: Society for Medieval Archaeology).

Hines, J, A Lane and M Redknap (eds) 2004 *Land, Sea and Home: Settlement in the Viking Period* (Leeds: Maney).

Hingley, R 1989 *Rural Settlement in Roman Britain* (London: Seaby).

Hingley, R, H L Moore, J E Truscott and G Wilson 1997 The Excavation of Two Later Iron Age Fortified Homesteads at Aldclune, Blair Atholl, Perth and Kinross, *Proceedings of the Society of Antiquaries of Scotland* 127, 407–466.

Hinton, D A 2000 *A Smith in Lindsey, The Anglo-Saxon Grave at Tattershall Thorpe, Lincolnshire* (Society for Medieval Archaeology Monograph16) (London: Society for Medieval Archaeology).

Hinton, D A 2005 *Gold and Gilt, Pots and Pins: Possessions and People in Medieval Britain* (Oxford: Oxford University Press).

Hinton, D A 2011 Raw Materials: Sources and Demand, in H Hamerow, D A Hinton and S Crawford (eds), *The Oxford Handbook of Anglo-Saxon Archaeology* (Oxford: Oxford University Press), 423–439.

Hinton, D A and R White 1993 A Smith's Hoard from Tattershall Thorpe, Lincolnshire: A Synopsis, *Anglo-Saxon England* 22, 147–166.

Hirst, S M 1985 *An Anglo-Saxon Inhumation Cemetery at Sewerby East Yorkshire* (York University Archaeological Publications 4) (York: University of York, Department of Archaeology).

Hirst, S M and D Clarke 2009 *Excavations at Mucking Volume 3: Anglo-Saxon Cemeteries: Introduction, Catalogues and Specialist Reports* (London: Museum of London Archaeology).

Hodges, R 1982 *Dark Age Economics: The Origins of Town and Trade* (London: Duckworth).

Hodges, R 2012 *Dark Age Economics: A New Audit* (Bristol: Bristol Classical Press).

Holbrook, N and A Thomas 2005 An Early-medieval Monastic Cemetery at Llandough, Glamorgan: Excavations in 1994, *Medieval Archaeology* 49, 1–92.

Holloway, J 2010 Material Symbolism and Death: Charcoal Burial in Later Anglo-Saxon England, in J Buckberry and A Cherryson (eds), *Burial in Later Anglo-Saxon England c. 650–1100 AD* (Oxford: Oxbow), 83–92.

Hooper, J. 2002 Landscape given meaning: an archaeological perspective on landscape history in Highland Scotland (unpub. PhD thesis, University of Glasgow)

Hope-Taylor, B 1977 *Yeavering: An Anglo-British Centre of Early Northumbria* (Department of the Environment Archaeological Report 7) (London: HMSO).

Hope-Taylor, B 1980 Balbridie and Doon Hill, *Current Archaeology* 7(1), 18–19.

Horn, W and E Born 1979 *The Plan of St. Gall*, 2 volumes (Berkeley (CA): University of California Press).

Howe, N 2004 Rome: Capital of Anglo-Saxon England, *Journal of Medieval and Early Modern Studies* 34(1), 147–172.

Hughes, G and G Crawford 1995 Excavations at Wasperton, Warwickshire 1980–1985. Introduction and Part 1: The Neolithic and Early Bronze Age, *Transactions of the Birmingham and Warwickshire Archaeological Society*. 99, 9–45.

Hunter, F 2007a *Beyond the Edge of the Empire – Caledonians, Picts and Romans* (Groam House Lecture) (Rosemarkie: Groam House Museum).

Hunter, F 2007b Artefact Regions and Identities in the Northern British Iron Age, in C Haselgrove and T Moore (eds), *The Later Iron Age in Britain and Beyond* (Oxbow), 286–296.

Hurst, J 1976 The Pottery, in D M Wilson (ed), *The Archaeology of Anglo-Saxon England* (London: Methuen), 283–348.

Hutcheson, A 1903 Notice of the Discovery of a Full-length Stone Cist Containing Human Remains and a Penannular Brooch at Craigie, Near Dundee, *Proceedings of the Society of Antiquaries of Scotland* 37, 233–240.

Hutton, R 2011a Witch-hunting in Celtic Societies, *Past & Present* 212, 43–71.

Hutton, R 2011b Medieval Welsh Literature and Pre-Christian Deities, *Cambrian Celtic Studies* 61, 57–85.

Hvass, S 2011 *Jelling-monumenterne: deres historie og bevaring* (København: Kulturarvsstyrelsen).

Insoll, T 2011a Ancestor Cults, in T Insoll (ed), *Oxford Handbook of the Archaeology of Ritual and Religion* (Oxford: Oxford University Press), 1043–1058.

Insoll, T (ed) 2011b *Oxford Handbook of the Archaeology of Ritual and Religion* (Oxford: Oxford University Press).

Isaac, G R 2005 Scotland, in J De Hoz, E R Luján and P Sims-Williams (eds), *New Approaches to Celtic Placenames in Ptolemy's Geography* (Madrid: Ediciones Clásicas), 189–214.

Jackman, N, C Moore and C Rynne 2013 *The Mill at Kilbegly: An Archaeological Investment on the Route of the M6 Ballinasloe to Athlone National Road Scheme* (NRA Scheme Monograph 12) (Dublin: National Roads Authority), 115–147.

Jackson, A 1993 Further Thoughts on Sueno's Stone, in W D H Sellar (ed), *Moray: Province and People* (Edinburgh: School of Scottish Studies), 91–95.

Jackson, D A, D W Harding and J N L Myres 1969 The Iron Age and Anglo-Saxon Site at Upton Northants, *Antiquaries Journal* 49, 202–221.

Jackson, K H 1950 Notes of the Ogam Inscriptions of Southern Britain, in C Fox and B Dickins (eds), *The Early Cultures of North-West Europe* (Cambridge: Cambridge University Press), 199–213.

Jackson, K H 1953 *Language and History in Early Britain* (Edinburgh: Edinburgh University Press).

Jackson, K H 1964 *The Oldest Irish Tradition: A Window on the Iron Age* (Rede Lecture) (Cambridge: Cambridge University Press, reissued 2010).

Jackson, K H (ed and trans) 1969 *The Gododdin* (Edinburgh: Edinburgh University Press).

Jackson, K H 1971 *A Celtic Miscellany* (Harmondsworth: Penguin).

James, H F 1992 Early Medieval Cemeteries in Wales, in N Edwards and A Lane (eds), *The Early Church in Wales and the West* (Oxford: Oxbow Books), 90–103.

James, H F and P James 2008 *Excavations at St Ethernan's Monastery on the Isle of May, Fife, 1992–97* (Tayside and Fife Archaeological Committee Monograph 6) (Perth: Tayside and Fife Archaeological Committee).

James, H F, I Henderson, S M Foster and S Jones 2008 *A Fragmented Masterpiece: Recovering the Biography of the Hilton of Cadboll Pictish Cross-slab* (Edinburgh: Society of Antiquaries of Scotland).

James, S, A Marshall and M Millett 1985 An Early Medieval Building Tradition, *Archaeological Journal* 141, 182–215.

Jarman, C, M Biddle, T Higham and C Bronk Ramsey 2018 The Great Viking Army in England: New Dates from the Repton Charnel, *Antiquity* 92, 183–199.

Jenkins, C 1949 Christian Pilgrimages, AD 500–800, in A P Newton (ed), *Travel and Travellers of the Middle Ages* (London: Routledge and Kegan Paul), 39–69.

Jesch, J 1991 *Women in the Viking Age* (Woodbridge: Boydell).

Jewell, R H I 1986 Anglo-Saxon Friezes at Breedon-on-the-Hill, Leicestershire, *Archaeologia* 108, 95–116.

Johns, C 2006 An Iron Age Sword and Mirror Cist Burial from Bryher, Isles of Scilly, *Cornish Archaeology* 41–42, 1–79.

Johnson, K M and K S Paul 2016 Bioarchaeology and Kinship: Integrating Theory, Social Relatedness, and Biology in Ancient Family Research, *Journal of Archaeological Research* 24, 75–123.

Johnstone, S A and B Wailes 2007 *Dún Aillinne: Excavations at an Irish Royal Site, 1968–1975* (University Museum Monograph 129) (Philadelphia (PA): University of Pennsylvania Museum of Archaeology and Anthropology).

Jope, E M 1964 The Saxon Building-stone Industry in Southern and Midland England, *Medieval Archaeology* 8, 91–118.

Jørgensen, L 2003 Manor and Market at Lake Tissø in the Sixth to Eleventh Centuries, in T Pestell and K Ulmschneider (eds), *Markets in Early Medieval Europe: Trading and 'Productive' Sites, 650–850* (Macclesfield: Windgather), 175–207.

Jørgensen, L 2010 Gudme and Tissø. Two Magnate Complexes in Denmark from the 3rd to the 11th Century, *Neue Studien zur Sachsenforschung* 1, 273–286.

Karnell, M H 2012 *Gotland's Picture Stones: Bearers of an Enigmatic Legacy* (Gotländskt Arkiv 84) (Visby: Gotland Museum).

Kelly, A 2010 The Discovery of Phocean Red Slip Ware (PRSW) Form 3 and Bii Ware (LR1 Amphorae) on Sites in Ireland: An Analysis in a Broader Framework, *Proceedings of the Royal Irish Academy* 110C, 35–88.

Kelly, D 1993 The relationships of the Crosses of Argyll: The Evidence of Form, in R M Spearman and J Higgitt (eds), *The Age of Migrating Ideas: Early Medieval Art in Northern Britain and Ireland* (Edinburgh: National Museums of Scotland and Stroud: Sutton), 219–229.

Kelly, F 1988 *A Guide to Early Irish Law* (Dublin: Institute for Advanced Studies).

Kelly, F 2000 *Early Irish Farming: A Study Based Mainly on the Law-texts of the 7th and 8th Centuries AD* (Dublin: Institute for Advanced Studies).

Kemp, R 1996 *Anglian Settlement at 46–54 Fishergate* (The Archaeology of York 7/1) (York: Council for British Archaeology).

Kendall, C B and P S Wells (eds) 1992 *Voyage to the Other World: The Legacy of Sutton Hoo* (Minneapolis: University of Minnesota Press).

Kendrick, T D 1949 *Late Saxon and Viking Art* (London: Methuen).

Kermode P M C 1907 *Manx Crosses or the inscribed and sculptured monuments of the Isle of Man* (London: Bemrose).

Kermode, P M C 1994 *Manx Crosses* (Kermode 1907 reissued with an introduction by D M Wilson) (Balgavies: Pinkfoot Press).

Kershaw, J 2017 An Early Medieval Dual-currency Economy: Bullion and Coin in the Danelaw, *Antiquity* 91, 173–190.

Kershaw, J and E C Royrvik 2016 The 'People of the British Isles' Project and Viking Settlement in England, *Antiquity* 90, 1670–1680.

Kilbride-Jones, H E 1980 *Zoomorphic Penannular Brooches* (Report of the Research Committee of the Society of Antiquaries of London 39) (London: The Society of Antiquaries of London).

Kilmurry, K 1980 *The Pottery Industry of Stamford, Lincolnshire c. AD 850–1250: Its Manufacture, Trade and Relationship with Continental Wares, With a Classification and Chronology* (BAR British Series 84) (Oxford: British Archaeological Reports).

King, H (ed) 1998 *Clonmacnoise Studies 1 1994* (Dublin: Dúchas).

King, H (ed) 2003 *Clonmacnoise Studies 2 1998* (Dublin: Dúchas).

King, H 2009 The Economy and Industry of Early Medieval Clonmacnoise: A Preliminary View, in N Edwards (ed), *The Archaeology of the Early Medieval Celtic Churches* (Leeds: Maney), 333–349.

Kinsella, J 2010 A New Irish Early Medieval Site Type? Exploring the Recent Archaeological Evidence for Non-circular Enclosed Settlement and Burial Sites, *Proceedings of the Royal Irish Academy* 110C, 89–132.

Kirton, J 2015 Locating the Cleulow Cross: Materiality, Place and Landscape, in H Williams, J Kirton and M Gondek (eds), *Early Medieval Stone Monuments. Materiality, Biography, Landscape* (Woodbridge: Boydell), 35–61.

Kjølbye-Biddle, B 1992 Dispersal or Concentration: The Disposal of the Winchester Dead Over 2000 Years, in S Bassett (ed), *Death in Towns: Urban Responses to the Dying and the Dead* 100–1600 (London: Leicester University Press), 210–247.

Knight, J 2001 Basilicas and Barrows: The Latin Memorial Stones of Wales and their Archaeological Contexts, in J Higgitt, K Forsyth and D N Parsons (eds), *Roman, Runes and Ogham: Medieval Inscriptions in the Insular World and on the Continent* (Donington: Shaun Tyas), 8–15.

Knight, J 2005 From Villa to Monastery: Llandough in Context, *Medieval Archaeology* 49, 93–107.

Koch, J T 1997 *The Gododdin of Aneirin: Text and Context from Dark Age North Britain* (Cardiff: University of Wales Press).

Koch, J T 2013 Waiting for Gododdin: Thoughts on Taliesin and Iudic-Hael, Catraeth, and Unripe Time in Celtic Studies, in A Woolf (ed), *Beyond the Gododdin: Dark Age Scotland in Medieval Wales* (St Andrews: University of St Andrews), 177–204.

Krogh, K 1982 The Royal Viking Age Monuments at Jelling in the Light of Recent Archaeological Excavations, *Acta Archaeologica* 53, 183–216.

Lacey, B 2011 Three 'Royal Sites' in Donegal, in R Schot, C Newman and E Bhreathnach (eds), *Landscapes of Cult and Kingship* (Dublin: Four Courts Press), 149–162.

Lager, L 2003 Runestones and the Conversion of Sweden, in M O H Carver (ed), *The Cross Goes North: Processes of Conversion in Northern Europe, AD 300–1300* (Woodbridge and Rochester (NY): York Medieval Press), 497–508.

Laing, L 2006 *The Archaeology of Celtic Britain and Ireland AD 400–1200* (Cambridge: Cambridge University Press).

Laing, L and D Longley 2006 *The Mote of Mark, A Dark Age Hillfort in South-West Scotland* (Oxford: Oxbow).

Lamb, H and K Fryendahl 1991 *Historic Storms of the North Sea, British Isles and North-west Europe* (Cambridge: Cambridge University Press).

Lamm, J-P and H-Å Nordström (eds) 1983 *Vendel Period Studies* (Stockholm: Museum of National Antiquities).

Lane, A and E Campbell 2000 *Dunadd: An Early Dalriadic Capital* (Oxford: Oxbow).

Lang, J T 1972 Hogback Monuments in Scotland, *Proceedings of the Society of Antiquaries of Scotland* 105, 206–235.

Lang, J T 1984 The Hogback. A Viking Colonial Monument, *Anglo-Saxon Studies in Archaeology and History* 3, 85–176.

Lang, J T 1990 *The Anglian Sculpture of Deira: The Classical Tradition* (Jarrow Lecture) (Jarrow: Parish of Jarrow).

Lang, J T 1991 *York and Eastern Yorkshire* (Corpus of Anglo-Saxon Stone Sculpture Volume III) (Oxford: Oxford University Press for The British Academy).

Lang, J T 1999 The Apostles in Anglo-Saxon Sculpture, *Early Medieval Europe* 8(2), 271–282.

Lang, J T 2000 Monuments from Yorkshire in the Age of Alcuin, in H Geake and J Kenny (eds), *Early Deira: Archaeological Studies of the East Riding in the Fourth to Ninth Centuries AD* (Oxford: Oxbow), 109–120.

Lang, J T 2001 *Corpus of Anglo-Saxon Stone Sculpture Volume VI Northern Yorkshire* (Oxford: Oxford University Press for The British Academy).

Larsson, L (ed) 2004 *Continuity for Centuries: A Ceremonial Building and its Context at Uppåkra, Southern Sweden* (Uppåkrastudier 10) (Lund: Almqvist & Wiksell).

Larsson, L 2007 The Iron Age Ritual Building at Uppåkra, Southern Sweden, *Antiquity* 81, 11–25.

Lawlor, H C 1925 *The Monastery of Saint Mochaoi of Nendrum* (Belfast: Belfast Natural History and Philosophical Society).

Leahy, K 2011 Anglo-Saxon Crafts, in H Hamerow, D A Hinton and S Crawford (eds), *The Oxford Handbook of Anglo-Saxon Archaeology* (Oxford: Oxford University Press), 440–459.

Leahy, K and R Bland 2009 *The Staffordshire Hoard* (London: British Museum).

Leary, J and G Brown 2004 *Tatberht's Lundenwic: Archaeological Excavations in Middle Saxon London* (London: Pre-Construct Archaeology).

Lebecq, S 2000 The Role of the Monasteries in the Systems of Production and Exchange of the Frankish World Between the Seventh and the Beginning of the Ninth Centuries, in I L Hansen and C Wickham (eds), *The Long Eighth Century* (Leiden and Boston: Brill), 121–148.

Leeds, E T 1945 The Distribution of the Angles and Saxons Archaeologically Considered, *Archaeologia* 91, 1–106.

Lehane, J, M M Pérez, J O'Sullivan and B Wilkins 2010 Three Cemetery-settlement Excavations in County Galway at Carrowkeel, Treanbaun and Owenbristy, in C Corlett and M Potterton (eds), *Death and Burial in Early Medieval Ireland in the Light of Recent Archaeological Excavations* (Dublin: Wordwell), 139–156.

Leigh, D 1984 Ambiguity in Anglo-Saxon Style I art, *Antiquaries Journal* 64, 34–42.

Lelong, O and G MacGregor 2007 *The Lands of Ancient Lothian: Interpreting the Archaeology of the A1* (Edinburgh: Society of Antiquaries of Scotland).

Leslie, S, B Winney, G Hellenthal, D Davison, A Boumertit, T Day, K Hutnik, E C Royrvik, B Cunliffe, Wellcome Trust Case Control Consortium 2, International Multiple Sclerosis Genetics Consortium, D J Lawson, D Falush, C Freeman, M Pirinen, S Myers, M Robinson, P Donnelly and W Bodmer 2015 The Fine-scale Genetic Structure of the British Population, *Nature* 519, 309–314. doi:10.1038/nature14230.

Levison, W 1943 *The Inscription on the Jarrow Cross* (Newcastle-upon-Tyne: Society of Antiquaries of Newcastle-upon-Tyne).

Levison, W 1946 *England and the Continent in the Eighth Century* (Oxford: Clarendon Press).

Ljungkvist, J 2008 The Development and Chronology of the Valsgärde Cemetery, in S Norr (ed), *Valsgärde Studies: The Place and its People, Past and Present* (Occasional Papers in Archaeology 42; Uppsala: Uppsala University, Department of Archaeology and Ancient History), 13–55.

Ljungkvist, J 2010 *Valsgärde Studies: The Place and its People, Past and Present* (Uppsala: Uppsala University).

Ljungkvist, J, P Frölund, H Göthberg and D Löwenborg 2011 Gamla Uppsala – Structural Development of a Centre in Middle Sweden, *Archäologisches Korrespondenzblatt* 41(4), 571–585.

Lloyd-Jones, J 1995 Measuring Biological Affinity Among Populations: A Case Study of Romano-British and Anglo-Saxon Populations, in J Hugget and N Ryan (eds), *Computer Applications and Quantitative Methods in Archaeology 1994* (BAR International Series 600) (Oxford: Tempus Reparatum), 69–74.

Longley, D 1997 The Royal Courts of the Welsh Princes in Gwynedd, in N Edwards (ed), *Landscape and Settlement in Medieval Wales* (Oxford: Oxbow), 41–54.

Longley, D 2002 Orientation Within Early Medieval Cemeteries: Some Data from North-west Wales, *Antiquaries Journal* 82, 309–321.

Longley, D 2009 Early Medieval Burial in Wales in N Edwards (ed), *The Archaeology of the Early Medieval Celtic Churches* (Leeds: Maney), 105–132.

Losco-Bradley, S and G Kingsley (eds) 2002 *Catholme: An Anglo-Saxon Settlement on the Trent Gravels of Staffordshire* (Nottingham: University of Nottingham).

Loveluck, C 2001 Wealth, Waste and Conspicuous Consumption. Flixborough and its Importance for Mid and Late Saxon Settlement Studies, in H Hamerow and A MacGregor (eds), *Image and Power in the Archaeology of Early Medieval Britain, Essays in Honour of Rosemary Cramp* (Oxford: Oxbow), 78–130.

Loveluck, C 2007 *Rural Settlement, Lifestyles and Social Change in the Later First Millenium AD: Anglo-Saxon Flixborough in its Wider Context* (Excavations at Flixborough Volume 4) (Oxford: Oxbow).

Loveluck, C 2012 Central-places. Exchange and Maritime-oriented Identity around the North Sea and Western Baltic, AD 600–1100, in S Gelichi and R Hodges (eds), *From one Sea to Another: Trading Places in the European and Mediterranean Early Middle Ages* (Turnhout: Brepols), 123–166.

Loveluck, C and D Atkinson 2007 *The Early Medieval Settlement Remains from Flixborough, Lincolnshire: The Occupation Sequence, c. AD 600–1000* (Excavations at Flixborough Volume 1) (Oxford: Oxbow).

Loveluck, C and D Tys 2006 Coastal Societies, Exchange and Identity along the Channel and Southern North Sea Shores of Europe, AD 600–1000, *Journal of Maritime Archaeology* 1, 140–169.

Lowe, C 2006 *Excavations at Hoddom, Dumfriesshire: An Early Ecclesiastical Site in South-West Scotland* (Edinburgh: Society of Antiquaries of Scotland).

Lowe, C (ed) 2008 *Inchmarnock An Early Historic Island Monastery and its Archaeological Landscape* (Edinburgh: Society of Antiquaries of Scotland).

Lucy, S 1998 *The Early Anglo-Saxon Cemeteries of East Yorkshire: An Analysis and Reinterpretation* (BAR British Series 272) (Oxford: John and Erica Hedges).

Lucy, S 1999 Changing Burial Rites in Northumbria AD 500–750, in J Hawkes and S Mills (eds), *Northumbria's Golden Age* (Stroud: Sutton), 12–43.

Lucy, S 2000 *The Anglo-Saxon Way of Death. Burial Rites in Early England* (Stroud: Sutton).

Lucy, S 2002 Burial Practice in Early Medieval Eastern Britain: Constructing Local Identities, Deconstructing Ethnicity, in S Lucy and A Reynolds (eds), *Burial in Early Medieval England and Wales* (London: Society for Medieval Archaeology), 72–87.

Lucy, S 2009 Early Medieval Burial at Yeavering: A Retrospective, in P Frodsham and C O'Brien (eds), *Yeavering: People, Power & Place* (Stroud: The History Press), 127–144.

Lucy, S 2011 Gender and Gender Roles, in H Hamerow, D A Hinton and S Crawford (eds), *The Oxford Handbook of Anglo-Saxon Archaeology* (Oxford: Oxford University Press), 688–703.

Lucy, S and A Reynolds (eds) 2002 *Burial in Early Medieval England and Wales* (Society for Medieval Archaeology Monograph 17) (London: Society for Medieval Archaeology).

Lucy, S, J Tipper and A Dickens 2009 *The Anglo-Saxon Settlement and Cemetery at Bloodmoor Hill, Carlton Colville, Suffolk* (East Anglian Archaeology 131) (Cambridge: Cambridge Archaeological Unit).

Łuczaj, Ł and W M Szymański 2007 Wild Vascular Plants Gathered for Consumption in the Polish Countryside: A Review, *Journal of Ethnobiology and Ethnomedicine* 3, www.ethnobiomed.com/content/3/1/17.

Lutovsky, M 1996 Between Sutton Hoo and Chernaya Mogila: Barrows in Eastern and Western Early Medieval Europe, *Antiquity* 70, 671–676.

Lynn, C J 1978 Early Christian Period Domestic Structures: A Change from Round to Rectangular Plans? *Irish Archaeological Research Forum* 5, 29–45.

Lynn, C J 1981–2 The Excavation of Rathmullan, a Raised Rath and Motte in Co. Down, *Ulster Journal of Archaeology* 44–45, 65–171.

Lynn, C J 1986 Lagore, County Meath and Ballinderry No 1 County Westmeath: Some Possible Structural Reinterpretations, *Journal of Irish Archaeology* 3, 47–58.

Lynn, C J 1994 Houses in Rural Ireland AD 500–1000, *Ulster Journal of Archaeology* 57, 81–94.

Lynn, C J 2003 *Navan Fort: Archaeology and Myth* (Bray: Wordwell).

Lynn, C J and J A McDowell 2011 *Deer Park Farms: The Excavation of a Raised Rath in the Glenarm Valley Co. Antrim* (Belfast: Northern Ireland Environment Agency).

Macalister, R A S 1945 *Corpus Inscriptionum Insularum Celticarum* Volume 1, (Dublin: Four Courts Press).

MacGibbon, D and T Ross 1896 *The Ecclesiastical Architecture of Scotland: From the Earliest Christian Times to the Seventeenth Century* (Edinburgh: David Douglas).

MacGregor, A 1985 *Bone, Antler, Ivory and Horn: The Technology of Skeletal Materials Since the Roman Period* (London: Croom Helm).

MacGregor, A and H Hamerow (eds) 2001 *Image and Power in Early Medieval British Archaeology: Essays in Honour of Rosemary Cramp* (Oxford: Oxbow).

MacGregor, A, A J Mainman et al. 1999 *Craft, Industry and Everyday Life: Bone, Antler, Ivory and Horn from Anglo-Scandinavian and Medieval York* (The Archaeology of York 17/2) (York: Council for British Archaeology).

Mackinder, H J 1915 *Britain and the British Seas* (Oxford: Clarendon Press).

Mac Lean, D 1995 Technique and Contact: Carpentry-constructed Insular Stone Crosses, in C Bourke (ed), *From the Isles of the North: Early Medieval Art in Ireland and Britain* (Belfast: HMSO), 167–175.

Mainman, A J and N S H Rogers 2000 *Craft, Industry and Everyday Life: Finds from Anglo-Scandinavian York* (The Archaeology of York 17/14) (York: Council for British Archaeology).

Malcolm, G, D Bowsher and R Cowie 2003 *Middle Saxon London: Excavations at the Royal Opera House, 1989–99* (MoLAS Monograph 15) (London: Museum of London Archaeology Service).

Maldonado Ramírez, A D 2011 Christianity and Burial in Late Iron Age Scotland, AD 400–650 (Unpublished PhD dissertation, University of Glasgow).

Mallory, J P 1992 The World of Cú Chulainn: The Archaeology of Táin Bó Cúailnge, in J P Mallory (ed), *Aspects of the Táin* (Belfast: December Publications), 103–159.

Mango, M M 2009 *Byzantine Trade 4th–12th Centuries the Archaeology of Local, Regional and International Exchange* (Farnham: Ashgate).

Manning, P and P Stead 2006 Excavation of an Early Christian Cemetery at Althea Library, Padstow, *Cornish Archaeology* 41–42, 80–106.

Marcus, G J 1980 *The Conquest of the North Atlantic* (Woodbridge: Boydell and Brewer).

Marshall, A and G Marshall 1993 Differentiation, Change and Continuity in Anglo-Saxon Buildings, *Archaeological Journal* 150(1), 366–402.

Marshall, D 1977 Carved Stone Balls, *Proceedings of the Society of Antiquaries of Scotland* 108, 40–72.

Marshall, D 1983 Further Notes on Carved Stone Balls *Proceedings of the Society of Antiquaries of Scotland* 113, 628–630.

Martin, T 2012 Identity and the Cruciform Brooch in England: An Investigation of Style, Mortuary Context and Use (Unpublished PhD dissertation, University of Sheffield).

Martin-Clark, E 1950 Significant Objects at Sutton Hoo, in C Fox and B Dickins (eds), *The Early Cultures of North-West Europe* (Cambridge: Cambridge University Press), 109–119.

Martiniano, R, A Caffell, M Holst, K Hunter-Mann, J Montgomery, G Müldner, R L McLaughlin, M D Teasdale, W van Rheencn, J II Veldink, L H van den Berg, O Hardiman, M Carroll, S Roskams, J Oxley, C Morgan, M G Thomas, I Barnes, C McDonnell, M J Collins and D G Bradley 2016 Genomic Signals of Migration and Continuity in Britain Before the Anglo-Saxons, *Nature Communications* 7, 10326. doi:10.1038/ncomms.

Marzinzik, S 2003 *Early Anglo-Saxon Belt Buckles (Late 5th – Early 8th Centuries A.D.): Their Classification and Context* (BAR British Series 357) (Oxford: Archaeopress).

Mathiot, D 2011 Person, Family and Community: The Social Structure of Iron Age Societies Seen Through the Organisation of their Housing in North-West Europe, in T Moore and X-L Armada (eds), *Atlantic Europe in the First Millennium BC* (Oxford: Oxford University Press), 358–374.

Maxwell, G S 1987 Settlement in Southern Pictland: A New Overview, in A Small (ed), *The Picts: A New Look at Old Problems* (Dundee: Graham Hunter Foundation), 31–44.

Mays, S 2000 Stable Isotope Analysis in Ancient Human Skeletal Remains, in M Cox and S Mays (eds), *Human Osteology in Archaeology and Forensic Science* (London: Greenwich Medical Media).

McCone, K 2000 *Pagan Past and Christian Present in Early Irish Literature* (Maynooth: Department of Old Irish, National University of Ireland).

McCormick, F 1997 Iona: The Archaeology of the Early Monastery, in C Bourke (ed), *Studies in the Cult of Saint Columba* (Dublin: Four Courts Press), 45–68.

McCormick, F and E Murray 2007 *Excavations at Knowth 3. Knowth and the Zooarchaeology of Early Christian Ireland* (Dublin: Royal Irish Academy).

McCormick, M 2001 *Origins of the European Economy* (Cambridge: Cambridge University Press).

McCormick, M 2007 Where Do Trading Towns Come From? Early Medieval Venice and the Northern Emporia, in J Henning (ed), *Post-Roman Towns, Trade and Settlement in Europe and Byzantium Volume 1: The Heirs of the Roman West* (Berlin and New York: De Gruyter), 40–68.

McCormick, M 2012 Comparing and Connecting: Comacchio and the Early Medieval Trading Towns, in S Gelichi and R Hodges (eds), *From one Sea to Another: Trading Places in the European and Mediterranean Early Middle Ages* (Turnhout: Brepols), 477–502.

McCullagh, R and R Tipping (eds) 1998 *The Lairg Project 1988–96: The Evolution of an Archaeological Landscape in Northern Scotland* (Edinburgh: Scottish Trust for Archaeological Research).

McCullough, D A 2000 Investigating Portages in the Norse Maritime Landscape of Scotland and the Isles (Unpublished PhD dissertation, University of Glasgow).

McErlean, T and N Crothers 2007 *Harnessing the Tides: The Early Medieval Tide Mills at Nendrum Monastery, Strangford Lough* (Norwich: Stationery Office).

McGrail, S 1998 *Ancient Boats in North-West Europe* (London: Longman).

McLure, J and R Collins (eds) 2008 *Bede: The Ecclesiastical History of the English People; The Greater Chronicle; Bede's Letter to Egbert* (Oxford: Oxford University Press).

McNeill, P G B and H L MacQueen 1996 *Atlas of Scottish History to 1707* (Edinburgh: University of Edinburgh).

McOmish, J M and D Petts 2008 Excavations at Fey Field, Whithorn: Excavations by David Pollock and Amanda Clarke, *The Archaeology of York Web Series* (York: York Archaeological Trust), www.iadb.co.uk/yat/publish.htm?PUB=58.

McSparron, C and B Williams 2011 … And They Won Land Among the Picts by Friendly Treaty or the Sword, *Proceedings of the Society of Antiquaries of Scotland* 141, 145–158.

Meaney, A L 1981 *Anglo-Saxon Amulets and Curing Stones* (BAR British Series 96) (Oxford: British Archaeological Reports).

Meaney, A L 1995 Pagan English Sanctuaries, Place-names and Hundred Meeting Places, *Anglo-Saxon Studies in Archaeology and History* 8, 29–42.

Meehan, B 1994 *The Book of Kells: An Illustrated Introduction* (London: Thames & Hudson).

Meeson, R A 1979 The Formation of Tamworth (Unpublished MA dissertation, University of Birmingham).

Milek, K 2012 The Roles of Pit Houses and Gendered Spaces on Viking-age Farmsteads in Iceland, *Medieval Archaeology* 56, 85–130.

Miles, D 2005 *The Tribes of Britain* (London: Orion).

Millett, M 2016 Rural Settlement in Roman Britain and its Significance for the Early Medieval Period, *Haskins Society Journal* 27, 1–14.

Millett, M and S James 1983 Excavations at Cowdery's Down, Basingstoke, 1978–1981, *Archaeological Journal* 140, 151–279.

Mira, I G 2011 Landscape Dynamics, Political Processes, and Social Strategies in the Eastern Iberian Iron Age, in T Moore and X-L Armada (eds), *Atlantic Europe in the First Millennium BC* (Oxford: Oxford University Press), 153–170.

Mitchell, F and M Ryan 1998 *Reading the Irish Landscape* (Dublin: Town House).

Mithen, S J, W Finlayson, S Smith, E Jenkins, M Najjar and D Maričević 2011 An 11,600 Year-old Communal Structure from the Neolithic of Southern Jordan, *Antiquity* 85, 350–364.

Moffett, L 1994 Charred Cereals from Some Ovens/Kilns in Late Saxon Stafford and the Botanical Evidence for the Pre-burh Economy, in J Rackham (ed), *Environment and Economy in Anglo-Saxon England* (York: Council for British Archaeology), 55–64.

MoLAS 2004 *The Prittlewell Prince: The Discovery of a Rich Anglo-Saxon Burial in Essex* (London: Museum of London Archaeology Service).

Moore, T and X-L Armada (eds) 2011 *Atlantic Europe in the First Millennium BC* (Oxford: Oxford University Press).

Morris, C A 2000 *Wood and Wood-working in Anglo-Scandinavian and Medieval York* (The Archaeology of York 17/13) (York: Council for British Archaeology).

Morris, C D 1996 From Birsay to Tintagel: A Personal View, in B E Crawford (ed), *Scotland in Dark Age Britain* (Aberdeen: Scottish Cultural Press), 37–78.

Morris, C D and R Harry 1997 Excavations on the Lower Terrace, Site C, Tintagel Island 1990–1994, *Antiquaries Journal* 77, 1–143.

Morris, R K 1989 *Churches in the Landscape* (London: Dent).

Morris, R K 2004 *Journeys from Jarrow* (Jarrow Lecture) (Jarrow: Parish of Jarrow).

Morrison, I 1985 *Landscape with Lake Dwellings* (Edinburgh: Edinburgh University Press).

Mortimer, C 1990 Some Aspects of Early Medieval Copper-alloy Technology, as Illustrated by a Study of the Anglian Cruciform Brooch (Unpublished DPhil dissertation, University of Oxford).

Mortimer, R, R Regan and S Lucy 2005 *The Saxon and Medieval Settlement at West Fen Road, Ely: The Ashwell Site* (East Anglian Archaeology 110) (Cambridge: Cambridge Archaeological Unit).

Müller-Wille, M 1970–71 Pferdegrab und Pferdeopfer im frühen Mittelalter, *Berichten van de Rijksdienst voor het Oudheidkundig Bodemonderzoek* 20–21, 119–248.

Müller-Wille, M 1974 Boat-graves in Northern Europe, *International Journal of Nautical Archaeology* 3, 187–204.

Müller-Wille, M 1995 Boat-graves, Old and New Views, in O Crumlin-Pedersen and B Munch Thye (eds), *The Ship as Symbol in Prehistoric and Medieval Scandinavia* (Copenhagen: National Museum of Denmark), 101–110.

Müller-Wille, M 2010 Trade and Communication Networks of the First Millennium AD in the Northern Part of Central Europe – Central Places, Beach Markets, Landing Places and Trading Centres, *Neue Studien zur Sachsenforschung* 1, 380–383.

Munch, G S, O S Johansen and E Roesdahl 2003 *Borg in Lofoten: A Chieftain's Farm in North Norway* (Trondheim: Tapir Academic Press).

Murphy, D 2003 Excavation of an Early Monastic Enclosure at Clonmacnoise, in H King (ed), *Clonmacnoise Studies 2* (Dublin: Dúchas), 1–34.

Murphy, K 1992 Plas Gogerddan, Dyfed: A Multi-period Burial and Ritual Site, *Archaeological Journal* 149, 1–38.

Murray, D and I Ralston 1997 The Excavation of a Square-ditched Barrow and Other Cropmarks at Boysack Mills, Inverkeilor, Angus, *Proceedings of the Society of Antiquaries of Scotland* 127, 359–386.

Murrieta-Flores, P and H Williams 2017 Placing the Pillar of Eliseg: Movement, Visibility and Memory in the Early Medieval Landscape, *Medieval Archaeology* 61, 69–103.

Myhre, B 1987 Chieftains' Graves and Chiefdom Territories in South Norway in the Migration Period, *Studien zur Sachsenforschung* 6, 169–197.

Myres, J N L 1936 The English Settlements, in R G Collingwood and J N L Myres (eds), *Roman Britain and the English Settlements* (Oxford: Oxford University Press), 325–461.

Mytum, H 1996 Early Medieval Settlement in Western Britain and Ireland: Cultural Unity and Diversity, *Ruralia* 1, 124–133.

Nash, C 2015 *Genetic Geographies: The Trouble with Ancestry* (Minneapolis: University of Minnesota Press).

Nash-Williams, V E 1950 *The Early Christian Monuments of Wales* (Cardiff: University of Wales Press).

Näsman, U 2008 Scandinavia and the Huns. A Source-critical Approach to an Old Question, *Fornvännen* 103, 111–118.

Neate, S, D Howell, R Ovenden and A M Pollard (eds) 2011 *The Technological Study of Books and Manuscripts as Artefacts: Research Questions and Analytical Solutions* (BAR International Series 2209) (Oxford: Archaeopress).

Neuman de Vegvar, C 2003 Romanitas and Realpolitik in Cogitosus' Description of the Chgurch of St Brigit, Kildare, in M O H Carver (ed), *The Cross Goes North: Processes of Conversion in Northern Europe, AD 300–1300* (Woodbridge and Rochester (NY): York Medieval Press), 153–170.

Newman, C 1995 The Iron Age to Early Christian Transition: The Evidence from Dress Fasteners, in C Bourke (ed), *From the Isles of the North: Early Medieval Art in Ireland and Britain* (Belfast: HMSO), 17–25.

Newman, C 1997 *Tara: An Archaeological Survey* (Discovery Programme Monograph 2) (Dublin: Royal Irish Academy for the Discovery Programme).

Newman, C 2002 Ballinderry Crannóg No 2 Co. Offaly: Pre-crannóg Early Medieval Horizon, *Journal of Irish Archaeology* 11, 99–124.

Newman, C 2011 The Sacral Landscape of Tara: A Preliminary Exploration, in R Schot, C Newman and E Bhreathnach (eds), *Landscapes of Cult and Kingship* (Dublin: Four Courts Press), 22–43.

Newman, J 1999 Wics, Trade and the Hinterlands – The Ipswich Region, in M Anderton (ed), *Anglo-Saxon Trading Centres: Beyond the Emporia* (Glasgow: Cruithne Press), 32–47.

Newman, J 2003 Exceptional Finds, Exceptional Sites? Barham and Coddenham, Suffolk, in T Pestell and K Ulmschneider (eds), *Markets in Early Medieval Europe: Trading and 'Productive' Sites, 650–850* (Macclesfield: Windgather), 97–109.

Newman, R and M Brennand 2007 The Early Medieval Period Research Agenda, *Archaeology North West* 9, 73–94.

Newton, S 1993 *The Origins of Beowulf* (Woodbridge: Boydell).

Nieke, M 1988 Literacy and Power: The Introduction and Use of Writing in Early Historic Scotland, in J Gledhill, B Bender and M T Larsen (eds), *State and Society: The Emergence and Development of Social Hierarchy and Political Centralization* (London: Unwin Hyman), 237–252.

Nielsen, P O, K Randsborg and H Thrane (eds) 1994 *The Archaeology of Gudme and Lundeborg* (Arkaeologiske Studier X) (Copenhagen: Akademisk Forlag), 169–183.

Noble, G 2007 Monumental Journeys: Neolithic Monument Complexes and Routeways Across Scotland, in V Cummings and R Johnstone (eds), *Prehistoric Journeys* (Oxford: Oxbow), 62–73.

Noble, G and M Gondek 2011 Symbol Stones in Context: Excavations at Rhynie, an Undocumented Pictish Power Centre of the 6th–7th Centuries AD? *Medieval Archaeology* 55, 317–321.

Noble, G, M Gondek, E Campbell and M Cook 2013 Between Prehistory and History: The Archaeological Detection of Social Change Among the Picts, *Antiquity* 87, 1136–1150.

Noble, G, M Goldberg, A McPherson and O Sveinbjarnarson 2016 (Re) Discovering the Gaulcross Hoard, *Antiquity* 90, 726–741.

Noble, R 1984 Turf-walled Houses of the Central Highlands. An Experiment in Reconstruction, *Folk Life: A Journal of Ethnological Studies* 22, 68–83.

Noble, R 2003 Earth Buildings in the Central Highlands; Research and Reconstruction, in S Govan (ed), *Medieval or Later Rural Settlement in Scotland: 10 Years On* (Edinburgh: Historic Scotland), 45–52.

Noel, W 1995 *The Harley Psalter* (Cambridge: Cambridge University Press).

Nordeide, S W and S Brink (eds) 2013 *Sacred Sites and Holy Places* (Turnhout: Brepols).

Nylén, E and J P Lamm 1988 *Stones, Ships and Symbols: The Picture Stones of Gotland from the Viking Age and Before* (Stockholm: Gidlunds).

Nyman, Å 1993 Research into the Swedish Shieling System, in H Cheape (ed), *Tools and Traditions: Studies in European Ethnology Presented to Alexander Fenton* (Edinburgh: National Museums of Scotland), 107–114.

Ó Carragáin, E 1989 The Meeting of Saint Paul and Saint Anthony: Visual and Literary Uses of a Eucharistic Motif, in P Wallace and G Niocaill (eds), *Keimeila* (Galway: Galway University Press), 1–58.

Ó Carragáin, T 2003 A Landscape Converted: Archaeology and Early Church Organisation on Iveragh and Dingle, Ireland, in M O H Carver (ed), *The Cross Goes North: Processes of Conversion in Northern Europe, AD 300–1300* (Woodbridge and Rochester (NY): York Medieval Press), 127–152.

Ó Carragáin, T 2009a Cemetery Settlements and Local Churches in Pre-Viking Ireland in Light of Comparisons with England and Wales, *Proceedings of the British Academy* 157, 329–366.

Ó Carragáin, T 2009b New Light on Early Insular Monasteries, *Antiquity* 83, 1182–1186.

Ó Carragáin, T 2010a *Churches in Early Medieval Ireland* (New Haven (CT) and London: Yale University Press).

Ó Carragáin, T 2010b From Family Cemeteries to Community Cemeteries in Viking Age Ireland? in C Corlett and M Potterton (eds), *Death and Burial in Early Medieval Ireland in the Light of Recent Archaeological Excavations* (Dublin: Wordwell), 217–226.

Ó Floinn, R 1998 Clonmacnoise: Art and Patronage in the Early Medieval Period, in H King (ed) *Clonmacnoise Studies 1* (Dublin: Dúchas), 87–100.

Ó Floinn, R 2001 Patterns and Politics: Art, Artefact and Methodology, in M Redknap, N Edwards, S Youngs, A Lane and J Knight (eds), *Pattern and Purpose in Insular Art* (Oxford: Oxbow Books), 1–14.

O'Brien, E 1992 Pagan and Christian Burial in Ireland During the First Millennium AD: Continuity and Change, in N Edwards and A Lane (eds), *The Early Church in Wales and the West* (Oxford: Oxbow), 130–136.

O'Brien, E 2003 Burial Practices in Ireland: First to Seventh Centuries AD, in J Downes and A Ritchie (eds), *Sea Change: Orkney and Northern Europe in the Later Iron Age AD 300–800* (Balgavies: Pinkfoot Press), 63–72.

O'Brien, E 2009 Pagan or Christian? Burial in Ireland During the 5th to 8th Centuries AD, in N Edwards (ed), *The Archaeology of the Early Medieval Celtic Churches* (Leeds: Maney), 135–154.

O'Connell, A 2013 *Harvesting the Stars: A Pagan Temple at Lismullin, Co Meath* (NRA Scheme Monograph 11) (Dublin: National Roads Authority).

O'Connor, T 2001 On the Interpretation of Animal Bone from Wics, in D H Hill and R Cowie (eds), *Wics. The Early Medieval Trading Centres of Northern Europe* (Sheffield: Sheffield Academic Press), 54–60.

O'Droma, M 2008 Archaeological Investigations at Twomileborris, Co. Tipperary, in J O'Sullivan and M Stanley (eds), *Roads, Rediscovery and Research* (Dublin: National Roads Authority), 45–59.

O'Dwyer, P 1981 *Céli Dé. Spiritual Reform in Ireland, 750–900* (Dublin: Tailliura).

O'Grady, O 2014 Judicial Assembly Sites in Scotland: Archaeological and Placename Evidence of the Scottish Court Hill, *Medieval Archaeology* 58, 104–135.

O'Kelly, M J 1958 Church Island Near Valencia Co. Kerry, *Proceedings of the Royal Irish Academy* 59C, 57–136.

O'Leary, C 2015 Memory, Belief and Identity; Remembering the Dead on Iniscealtra, Co. Clare, in H Williams, J Kirton and M Gondek (eds), *Early Medieval Stone Monuments. Materiality, Biography, Landscape* (Woodbridge: Boydell), 114–148.

O'Maidin, U 1996 *The Celtic Monk: Rules and Writing of Early Irish Monks* (Kalamazoo: Cistercian Publications).

O'Riordan, S P 1942 The Excavation of a Large Earthen Ring-fort at Garranes, Co. Cork, *Proceedings of the Royal Irish Academy* 47C, 77–150.

O'Sullivan, A 1998 *The Archaeology of Lake Settlement in Ireland* (Dublin: Royal Irish Academy for the Discovery Programme).

O'Sullivan A and D Boland 2000 The Clonmacnoise Bridge: An Early Medieval River Crossing in Co. Offaly *Archaeology Ireland Heritage Guide 11* (Bray: Wordwell).

O'Sullivan, A, F McCormick, T Kerr and L Harney 2014a *Early Medieval Ireland: Archaeological Excavations 1930–2009* (Dublin: Royal Irish Academy).

O'Sullivan, A, F McCormick, T Kerr, L Harney and J Kinsella 2014b *Early Medieval Dwellings and Settlements in Ireland, AD400–1100* (BAR International Series 2604) (Oxford: Archaeopress).

O'Sullivan, J 1994 Excavation of an Early Church and a Women's Cemetery at St Ronan's Medieval Parish Church, Iona, *Proceedings of the Society of Antiquaries of Scotland* 124, 327–365, fiche A5–D11.

O'Sullivan, J 1999 Iona: Archaeological Investigations 1875–1996, in D Broun and T Clancy (eds), *Spes Scottorum: Hope of Scots: Saint Columba, Iona and Scotland* (Edinburgh: T and T Clark), 215–243.

O'Sullivan, J and T Ó Carragáin 2008 *Inishmurray. Monks and Pilgrims in an Atlantic Landscape Volume 1: Archaeological Survey and Excavations 1997–2000* (Cork: The Collins Press).

O'Sullivan, J and M Stanley (eds) 2006 *Settlement, Industry and Ritual: Proceedings of a Public Seminar on Archaeological Discoveries on National Road Schemes, September 2005* (NRA Scheme Monograph 3) (Dublin: National Roads Authority).

O'Sullivan, J and M Stanley (eds) 2008 *Roads, Rediscovery and Research: Proceedings of a Public Seminar on Archaeological Discoveries on National Road Schemes, August 2007* (NRA Scheme Monograph 5) (Dublin: National Roads Authority).

Oexle, J 1984 Merowingerzeitliche Pferdebestattung: Opfer oder Beigaben? *Frühmittelalterliche Studien* 18, 122–172.

Okasha, E 1993 *Corpus of Early Christian Inscribed Stones of South West Britain* (London and New York: Leicester University Press).

Okasha, E 1999 The Inscribed Stones from Hartlepool, in J Hawkes and S Mills (eds), *Northumbria's Golden Age* (Stroud: Sutton), 113–125.

Okasha, E 2001 Anglo-Saxon Women: The Evidence from Inscriptions, in J Higgitt, K Forsyth and D N Parsons (eds), *Roman, Runes and Ogham: Medieval Inscriptions in the Insular World and on the Continent* (Donington: Shaun Tyas), 79–88.

Olalde, I, S Brace, A Allentoft … D Reich (and 140 additional authors) 2018 The Beaker Phenomenon and the Genomic Transformation of North-West Europe, *Nature* 555, 190–210.

Olaussen, M 1999 Herding and Stalling in Bronze Age Sweden, in C Fabech and J Ringtved (eds), *Settlement and Landscape: Proceedings of a Conference in Århus, Denmark, May 4–7 1998* (Moesgård: Jutland Archaeological Society), 319–328.

Olsen O, J S Madsen and F Riek (eds) 1995 *Ship-shape: Essays for Ole Crumlin-Pedersen*, (Roskilde: Viking Ship Museum), 305–312.

Opie, I and P Opie 1959 [1982] *The Lore and Language of Schoolchildren* (London: Granada).

Ottaway, P 1992 *Anglo-Scandinavian Ironwork from 16–22 Coppergate* (The Archaeology of York 17/6) (York: Council for British Archaeology).

Owen, O 1999 *The Sea Road. A Viking Voyage Through Scotland* (Edinburgh: Canongate with Historic Scotland).

Owen, O and M Dalland 1999 *Scar a Viking Boat Burial on Sanday, Orkney* (East Linton Tuckwell Press with Historic Scotland).

Owen-Crocker, G R 2004 *Dress in Anglo-Saxon England* revised edition (Woodbridge: Boydell).

Page, R I 1987 *Runes* (London: British Museum Publications).

Page, R I 1998 *Runes and Runic Inscriptions: Collected Essays on Anglo-Saxon and Viking Runes* (Woodbridge: Boydell).

Palliser, D M (ed) 2000 *The Cambridge Urban History of Britain* (Cambridge: Cambridge University Press).

Pantos, A 2004 The Location and Form of Anglo-Saxon Assembly-places; Some 'Moot Points', in A Pantos and S Semple (eds), *Assembly Places and Practices in Medieval Europe* (Dublin: Four Courts Press), 155–180.

Pantos, A and S Semple (eds) 2004 *Assembly Places and Practices in Medieval Europe* (Dublin: Four Courts Press).

Parfitt, K and T Anderson 2012 *Buckland Anglo-Saxon Cemetery, Dover Excavations 1994* (The Archaeology of Canterbury New Series 6) (Canterbury: Canterbury Archaeological Trust).

Parfitt, K and B Brugmann 1997 *The Anglo-Saxon Cemetery on Mill Hill, Deal, Kent* (Society for Medieval Archaeology Monograph 14) (London: Society for Medieval Archaeology).

Parker Pearson, M 2007 Further Evidence for Mummification in Bronze Age Britain, *Antiquity* 81 ProjGall/313.html.

Parker Pearson, M, A Chamberlain, O Craig et al. 2005 Evidence for Mummification in Bronze Age Britain, *Antiquity* 79, 529–546.

Paulsen, P 1992 *Die Holzfunde aus dem Gräberfeld bei Oberflacht und ihre kulturhistorische Bedeutung* (Forschungen und Berichten Vor- und Frühgeschichte in Baden-Württemberg 41, 2) (Stuttgart: Theiss).

Peers, C and C A R Radford 1943 The Saxon Monastery at Whitby, *Archaeologia* 89, 27–88.

Pelteret, D 2001 *Slavery in Early Mediaeval England from the Reign of Alfred Until the Twelfth Century* (Woodbridge and Rochester (NY): Boydell Press).

Pelteret, D 2009 The Role of Rivers and Coastlines in Shaping Early English History, *Haskins Society Journal* 21, 21–46.

Penn, K 2000 *Norwich Southern Bypass. Part II: Anglo-Saxon Cemetery at Harford Farm, Caistor St Edmund* (East Anglian Archaeology 92) (Dereham: Norfolk Museums Service).

Penn, K 2011 *The Anglo-Saxon Cemetery at Shrubland Hall Quarry, Coddenham, Suffolk* (East Anglian Archaeology 139) (Bury St Edmunds: Suffolk County Council Archaeological Service).

Penn, K and B Brugmann 2007 *Aspects of Anglo-Saxon Inhumation Burial: Morning Thorpe, Spong Hill, Bergh Apton and Westgarth Gardens* (East Anglian Archaeology 119) (Dereham: Norfolk Museums Service).

Pestell, T 2004 *Landscapes of Monastic Foundation: The Establishment of Religious Houses in East Anglia c. 650–1200* (Woodbridge: Boydell).

Pestell, T 2009 The Styli, in D H Evans and C Loveluck (eds), *Life and Economy at Early Medieval Flixborough c. AD 600–1000. The Artefact Evidence*. (Excavations at Flixborough Volume 2) (Oxford: Oxbow), 123–137.

Pestell, T 2011 Markets, *Emporia, Wics* and 'Productive' Sites: Trade Centres in Anglo-Saxon England, in H Hamerow, D A Hinton and S Crawford (eds), *The Oxford Handbook of Anglo-Saxon Archaeology* (Oxford: Oxford University Press), 556–579.

Pestell, T 2013 Imports or Immigrants? Reassessing Scandinavian Metalwork in Late Anglo-Saxon East Anglia, in D Bates and R Liddiard (eds), *East Anglia and its North Sea World in the Middle Ages* (Woodbridge: Boydell), 230–255.

Pestell, T and K Ulmschneider (eds) 2003 *Markets in Medieval Europe, Trading and 'Productive' Sites, 650–850* (Macclesfield: Windgather).

Petts, D 2002a Cemeteries and Boundaries in Western Britain, in S Lucy and A Reynolds (eds), *Burial in Early Medieval England and Wales* (London: Society for Medieval Archaeology), 24–46.

Petts, D 2002b The Re-use of Prehistoric Standing Stones in Western Britain? A Critical Consideration of an Aspect of Early Medieval Monument Re-use, *Oxford Journal of Archaeology* 21(2), 195–209.

Petts, D 2003 *Christianity in Roman Britain* (Stroud: Tempus).

Petts, D 2009 *The Early Medieval Church in Wales* (Stroud: The History Press).

Persson, K and B Olofsson 2004 Inside a Mound: Applied Geophysics in Archaeological Prospecting at the Kings' Mounds, Gamla Uppsala, Sweden, *Journal of Archaeological Science* 31, 551–562.

Phillips, C 2006 Portages in Early Medieval Scotland. The Great Glen Route and the Forth-Clyde Isthmus, in C Westerdahl (ed), *The Significance of Portages* (BAR International Series 1499) (Oxford: Archaeopress), 191–198.

Phillips, D and B Heywood 1995 *From Roman Fortress to Norman Cathedral: Excavations at York Minster Volume 1* (London: HMSO).

Philpott, R 1991 *Burial Practices in Roman Britain: A Survey of Grave Treatment and Furnishing A.D. 43–410* (BAR British Series 219) (Oxford: Tempus Reparatum).

Porcher, J 1970 Book Painting, in J Hubert, J Porcher and W Volbach (eds), *Carolingian Art* (London: Thames & Hudson).

Porter, C A, G Chiari and A Cavallo 2002 The Analysis of Eight Manuscripts and Fragments from the Fifth/Sixth Century to the Twelfth Century, with Particular Reference to the Use of and Identification of 'Real Purple' in Manuscripts, in Van Grieken, R et al. (eds), *Art 2002: Proceedings of the 7th International Conference on Non-Destructive Testing and Microanalysis for the Diagnostics and Conservation of the Cultural and Environmental Heritage* (Antwerp: University of Antwerp).

Powlesland, D 1999 The Anglo-Saxon Settlement at West Heslerton, North Yorkshire, in J Hawkes and S Mills (eds), *Northumbria's Golden Age* (Stroud: Sutton, 55–65.

Powlesland, D 2000 West Heslerton Settlement Mobility: A Case of Static Development, in H Geake and J Kenny (eds), *Early Deira: Archaeological Studies of the East Riding in the Fourth to Ninth Centuries AD* (Oxford: Oxbow), 19–26.

Powlesland, D 2003 *25 Years of Research on the Sands and Gravels of Heslerton* (Yedingham: Landscape Research Centre).

Preston-Jones, A and E Okasha 2013 *Early Cornish Sculpture* (Corpus of Anglo-Saxon Stone Sculpture XI) (Oxford: Oxford University Press for The British Academy).

Price, J (ed) 2000 *Glass in Britain and Ireland, AD 350–1100* (British Museum Occasional Paper 127) (London: British Museum Press).

Price, N S (ed) 2001 *The Archaeology of Shamanism* (London: Routledge).

Price, N S 2002 *The Viking Way: Religion and War in Late Iron Age Scandinavia* (AUN 31) (Uppsala: Department of Archaeology and Ancient History).

Pritchard, A 2009 The Origins of Ecclesiastical Stone Architecture in Wales, in N Edwards (ed), *The Archaeology of the Early Medieval Celtic Churches* (Leeds: Maney), 245–264.

Proudfoot, E V W 1996 Excavations at the Long Cist Cemetery on the Hallow Hill, St Andrews, Fife, *Proceedings of the Society of Antiquaries of Scotland* 126, 387–454.

Quinnell, H 2004 *Trethurgy. Excavations at Trethurgy Round, St Austell: Community and Status in Roman and Post-Roman Cornwall* (Truro: Cornwall County Council).

Rackham, J (ed) 1994 *Environment and Economy in Anglo-Saxon England* (CBA Research Report 89) (York: Council for British Archaeology).

Rackham, O 2000 *The History of the Countryside* (London: Phoenix).

Radford, C A R 1951 Report on the Excavations at Castle Dore, *Journal of the Royal Institute of Cornwall* new series 1, 1–119.

Radini A, E Nikita, S Buckley, L Copeland and K Hardy 2017 Beyond Food: The Multiple Pathways for Inclusion of Materials into Ancient Dental Calculus, *American Journal of Physical Anthropology* 162 (Suppl. 63), 71–83.

Raftery, B 2000 *Pagan Celtic Ireland: The Enigma of the Irish Iron Age* (London and New York: Thames & Hudson).

Raftery, B and J Hickey (eds) 2001 *Recent Developments in Wetland Research* (Seandálaíocht Volume 2) (Dublin: University College Dublin).

Rahtz, P 1976a Buildings and Rural Settlement, in D M Wilson (ed), *The Archaeology of Anglo-Saxon England* (London: Methuen), 49–98.

Rahtz, P 1976b The Building Plan of the Anglo-Saxon Monastery of Whitby Abbey, in D M Wilson (ed), *The Archaeology of Anglo-Saxon England* (London: Methuen), 459–462.

Rahtz, P 1977 The Archaeology of West Mercian Towns, in A Dornier (ed), *Mercian Studies* (Leicester: Leicester University Press), 107–130.

Rahtz, P A 1979 *The Saxon and Medieval Palaces at Cheddar: Excavations 1960–62* (BAR British Series 65) (Oxford: British Archaeological Reports).

Rahtz, P 1982 Celtic Society in Somerset AD 400–70 (O'Donnell Lecture for 1981), *Bulletin of the Board of Celtic Studies* 30, 176–200.

Rahtz, P and R Meeson 1992 *An Anglo-Saxon Watermill at Tamworth* (CBA Research Report 83) (York: Council for British Archaeology).

Rahtz, P, A Woodward, I Burrow, A Everton, L Watts, P Leach, S Hirst, P Fowler and K Gardiner 1992 *Cadbury Congresbury. A Late/Post-Roman Hilltop Settlement in Somerset* (BAR British Series 223) (Oxford: Tempus Reparatum).

Rahtz, P, S Hirst and S M Wright 2000 *Cannington Cemetery* (Britannia Monograph Series 17) (London: Society for the Promotion of Roman Studies).

Ralston, I 1987 Portknockie: Promontory Forts and Pictish Settlement in the North-East, in A Small (ed), *The Picts – A New Look at Old Problems* (Dundee: Graham Hunter Foundation), 27–30.

Ralston, I 1997 Pictish Homes, in D Henry (ed), *The Worm, the Germ and the Thorn* (Balgavies: Pinkfoot Press) 18–34.

Ralston, I 2004 *The Hill-Forts of Pictland Since the 'The Problem of the Picts'* (Groam House Lecture) (Rosemarkie: Groam House Museum).

Ramqvist, P H 1992 *Högom: The Excavations 1949–1984* (Neumünster: Wachholz).

Randsborg, K 1980 *The Viking Age in Denmark* (London: Duckworth).

Rasmussen, M 1999 Livestock Without Bones. The Long-house as a Contributor to the Interpretation of Livestock Management in the Southern Scandinavian Early Bronze Age, in C Fabech and J Ringtved (eds), *Settlement and Landscape: Proceedings of a Conference in Århus, Denmark May 4–7 1998* (Moesgård: Jutland Archaeological Society), 281–290.

Ravn, M 2003 *Death Ritual and Germanic Social Structure (c. AD 200–600)* (BAR International Series 1164) (Oxford: Archaeopress).

RCAHMS 1990 *North-East Perth: An Archaeological Landscape* (Edinburgh: Royal Commission on the Ancient and Historical Monuments of Scotland).

RCAHMS 2007 *In the Shadow of Bennachie: A Field Archaeology of Donside, Aberdeenshire* (Edinburgh: Royal Commission on the Ancient and Historical Monuments of Scotland).

RCHME 1959 Wareham West Walls. Excavations by the Royal Commission on Historical Monuments (England), *Medieval Archaeology* 3, 120–139.

Redknap, M 1991 *The Christian Celts. Treasures of Late Celtic Wales* (Cardiff: National Museum of Wales).

Redknap, M 2004 Viking-Age Settlement in Wales and the Evidence from Llanbedrgoch, in J Hines, A Lane and M Redknap (eds), *Land, Sea and Home: Settlement in the Viking Period* (Leeds: Maney), 139–175.

Redknap, M 2009 Early Medieval Metalwork and Christianity: A Welsh Perspective, in N Edwards (ed), *The Archaeology of the Early Medieval Celtic Churches* (Leeds: Maney), 351–374.

Redknap, M and J M Lewis 2007 *A Corpus of Early Medieval Inscribed Stones and Stone Sculpture in Wales* Volume I (South-East Wales and the English Border) (Cardiff: University of Wales Press).

Redknap, M, N Edwards, S Youngs, A Lane and J Knight (eds) 2001 *Pattern and Purpose in Insular Art: Proceedings of the 4th International Conference on Insular Art Held at the National Museum and Art Gallery, Cardiff* (Oxford: Oxbow).

Reece, R 1981 *Excavations on Iona 1964–74* (Institute of Archaeology Occasional Papers 5) (London: Institute of Archaeology).

Reed, D 1995 The Excavation of a Cemetery and Putative Chapel Site at Newhall Point, Balbair, Ross and Cromarty, 1985, *Proceedings of the Society of Antiquaries of Scotland* 125, 779–791.

Reed, S, P Bidwell and J Allan 2011 Excavation at Bantham, South Devon and Post-Roman Trade in South-West England, *Medieval Archaeology* 55, 82–138.

Rees, A 2002 A First Millennium Cemetery, Rectangular Bronze Age Structure and Late Prehistoric Settlement at Thornybank, Midlothian, *Proceedings of the Society of Antiquaries of Scotland* 132, 313–355.

Rees, A 2009 The Excavation of an Iron Age Unenclosed Settlement and an Early Historic Multiple Burial and Metalworking Area at Hawkhill, Lunan Bay, Angus, *Tayside and Fife Archaeological Journal* 15, 22–72.

Rees, W 1963 Survivals of Ancient Celtic Custom in Medieval England, in *Angles and Britons: O'Donnell Lectures* (Cardiff: University of Wales Press), 148–168.

Reich, D. 2018 *Who we are and how we got here* (Oxford: Oxford University Press).

Reid, E 2014 *The Scoonie Hunt and Other Horsemen*, www.the pictishartssociety.org.uk/papers, accessed 20 May 2017.

Renfrew, A C 1973 Monuments, Mobilization and Social Organisation in Neolithic Wessex, in C Renfrew (ed), *The Explanation of Culture Change: Models in Prehistory* (London: Duckworth), 539–558.

Renfrew, A C 1985 *Towards an Archaeology of Mind* (University of Cambridge Inaugural Lecture) (Cambridge: Cambridge University Press).

Renfrew, A C and J F Cherry (eds) 1986 *Peer Polity Interaction and Socio-political Change* (Cambridge: Cambridge University Press).

Renfrew A.C. and P. Bahn 2008 *Archaeology: Theories, Methods and Practice* (5th edition. London and New York: Thames and Hudson).

Reuter, T (ed) 2003 *Alfred the Great: Papers from the Eleventh-centenary Conferences* (Farnham: Ashgate).

Reynolds, A 2009 *Anglo-Saxon Deviant Burial Customs* (Oxford: Oxford University Press).

Rhys, G 2015 Approaching the Pictish Language: Historiography, Early Evidence and the Question of Pritenic (Unpublished PhD dissertation, University of Glasgow).

Richards, J D 1987 *The Significance of Form and Decoration of Anglo-Saxon Cremation Urns* (BAR British Series 166) (Oxford: British Archaeological Reports).

Richards, J D 1988 Style and Symbol: Explaining Variability in Anglo-Saxon Cremation Burials, in S Driscoll and M Nieke (eds), *Power and Politics in Early Medieval Britain and Ireland* (Edinburgh: Edinburgh University Press), 145–161.

Richards, J D 1992 Anglo-Saxon Symbolism, in M O H Carver (ed), *The Age of Sutton Hoo: The Seventh Century in North-Western Europe* (Woodbridge: Boydell), 131–147.

Richards, J D 1995 The Viking Barrow Cemetery at Heath Wood Ingleby, Derbyshire, *Medieval Archaeology* 39, 51–70.

Richards, J D 1999 What's So Special About 'Productive Sites'? Middle Saxon Settlements in Northumbria, in T M Dickinson and D Griffiths (eds), *The Making of Kingdoms* (Oxford: Oxford University Committee for Archaeology), 71–80.

Richards, J D 2003 The Anglian and Anglo-Scandinavian Sites at Cottam, East Yorkshire, in T Pestell and K Ulmschneider (eds), *Markets in Early Medieval Europe: Trading and 'Productive' Sites, 650–850* (Macclesfield: Windgather), 155–166.

Richards, J D 2004 Excavations at the Viking Barrow Cemetery at Heath Wood Ingleby, Derbyshire, *Antiquaries Journal* 84, 23–116.

Richards, M P, B T Fuller and T I Molleson 2006 Stable Isotope Palaeodietary Study of Humans and Fauna from the Multi-Period (Iron Age, Viking and Late Medieval) Site of Newark Bay, Orkney, *Journal of Archaeological Science* 33, 122–131.

Rideout, J S 1995 Carn Dubh, Moulin, Perthshire: Survey and Excavation of an Archaeological Landscape 1987–90, *Proceedings of the Society of Antiquaries of Scotland* 125, 139–195.

Rippon, S, A Wainwright and C Smart 2014 Farming Regions in Medieval England: The Archaeobotanical and Archaeological Evidence, *Medieval Archaeology* 8, 195–255.

Ritchie, A 1995 Meigle and Lay Patronage in Tayside in the 9th and 10th Centuries AD, *Tayside and Fife Archaeological Journal* 1, 1–10.

Ritchie, A 2005 Clothing Among the Picts *Costume, The Journal of the Costume Society* 39, 28–42.

Roberts, B K and S Wrathmell 2002 *Region and Place: A Study of English Rural Settlement* (London: English Heritage).

Roberts, C 2009 *Human Remains in Archaeology: A Handbook* (York: Council for British Archaeology).

Roberts, C and M Cox 2003 *Health and Disease in Britain: From Prehistory to the Present Day* (Stroud: Sutton).

Rodwell, W 2011 *St Peter's Barton-upon-Humber, Lincolnshire: A Parish Church and its Community: Volume I.1 History, Archaeology and Architecture* (Oxford: Oxbow).

Romankiewicz, T 2011 *The Complex Roundhouses of the Scottish Iron Age: An Architectural Analysis of Complex Atlantic Roundhouses (Brochs and Galleried Duns), with Reference to Wheelhouses and Timber Roundhouses,* 2 volumes (BAR British Series 550) (Oxford: Archaeopress).

Rowland, J 1995 Warfare and Horses in the Gododdin and the Problem of Catraeth, *Cambrian Medieval Studies* 30, 13–40.

Royman, N 1999 Man, Cattle and the Supernatural in the Northwest European Plain, in C Fabech and J Ringtved (eds), *Settlement and Landscape: Proceedings of a Conference in Århus, Denmark, May 4–7 1998* (Moesgård: Jutland Archaeological Society), 291–300.

Ruggles, C 1999 *Astronomy in Prehistoric Britain and Ireland* (New Haven (CT) and London: Yale University Press).

Ryan, M 2005 Eucharistic Vessels, Architecture and Liturgical Celebration in Early Medieval Ireland, in R Bork (ed), *De Re Metallica: The Uses of Metal in the Middle Ages* (Farnham: Ashgate), 125–145.

Ryan, M and R Ó Floinn 1983 *The Derrynaflan Hoard 1: A Preliminary Account* (Dublin: National Museum of Ireland).

Rynne, C 2000 Water Power in Medieval Ireland, in P Squariti (ed), *Working with Water in Medieval Europe* (Leiden and Boston: Brill), 1–50.

Sagas 2001 *The Sagas of Icelanders* (London: Penguin).

Samson, R 1992 The Reinterpretation of the Pictish Symbols, *Journal of the British Archaeological. Association* 145, 29–65.

Sandmark, A and S Semple 2008 Places of Assembly: New Discoveries in Sweden and England, *Fornvännen* 103(4), 245–259.

Saunders, T 2001 Early Medieval Emporia and the Tributary Social Function, in D H Hill and R Cowie (eds), *Wics. The Early Medieval Trading Centres of Northern Europe* (Sheffield: Sheffield Academic Press), 7–13.

Sayer, D and H Williams (eds) 2009 *Mortuary Practices and Social Identities in the Middle Ages* (Essays in Burial Archaeology in Honour of Heinrich Härke) (Exeter: University of Exeter Press).

SCARF (Scottish Archaeological Research Framework) 2012 www.scottishheritagehub.com/.

SCC (Staffordshire County Council) 2011 *Tamworth Historic Character Assessment* (Stafford: Staffordshire County Council).

Scheschkewitz, J 2006 *Das spätrömische und angelsächsische Gräberfeld von Wasperton, Warwickshire* (Bonn: Rudolf Habelt).

Schiffels, S, W Haak, P Paajanen, B Llamas, E Popescu, L Loe, R Clarke, A Lyons, R Mortimer, D Sayer, C Tyler-Smith, A Cooper and R Durbin 2016 Iron Age and Anglo-Saxon Genomes from East England reveal British Migration History, *Nature Communications* 7, 10408. doi:10.1038/ncomms10408.

Schönback, B 1983 The Custom of Burial in Boats, in J-P Lamm and H-Å Nordström (eds), *Vendel Period Studies* (Stockholm: Museum of National Antiquities), 123–132.

Schot, R 2006 Uisneach Midi a medón Érenn: A Prehistoric 'Cult' Centre and 'Royal Site' in Co. Westmeath, *Journal of Irish Archaeology* 15, 39–71.

Schot, R 2011 From Cult Centre to Royal Centre: Monuments Myths and Other Revelations at Uisneach, in R Schot, C Newman and E Bhreathnach (eds), *Landscapes of Cult and Kingship* (Dublin: Four Courts Press), 87–113.

Schot, R, C Newman and E Bhreathnach (eds) 2011 *Landscapes of Cult and Kingship* (Dublin: Four Courts Press).

Scull, C 1991 Post-Roman Phase 1 at Yeavering: A Reconsideration, *Medieval Archaeology* 35, 51–63.

Scull, C 1992 Before Sutton Hoo: Structures of Power and Society in Early East Anglia, in M O H Carver (ed), *The Age of Sutton Hoo* (Woodbridge: Boydell), 3–24.

Scull, C 1993 Archaeology, Early Anglo-Saxon Society and the Origins of Anglo-Saxon Kingdoms, *Anglo-Saxon Studies in Archaeology and History* 6, 65–82.

Scull, C 2001 Burials at *Emporia* in England, in D H Hill and R Cowie (eds), *Wics: The Early Medieval Trading Centres of Northern Europe* (Sheffield: Sheffield Academic Press), 67–74.

Scull, C 2002 Ipswich: Development and Contexts of an Urban Precursor in the Seventh Century, in B Hårdh and L Larsson (eds), *Central Places in the Migration and Merovingian Periods* (Stockholm: Almqvist & Wiksell International), 303–316.

Scull, C 2009 *Early Medieval (Late 5th – Early 8th Centuries AD) Cemeteries at Boss Hall and Buttermarket Ipswich, Suffolk* (Society for Medieval Archaeology Monograph 27) (London: Society for Medieval Archaeology).

Scull, C 2011 Social Transactions, Gift Exchange and Power in the Archaeology of the Fifth to Seventh Centuries, in H Hamerow, D A Hinton and S Crawford (eds), *The Oxford Handbook of Anglo-Saxon Archaeology* (Oxford: Oxford University Press), 848–864.

Scull, C 2013 Ipswich: Contexts of Funerary Evidence from an Urban Precursor of the Seventh Century AD, in D Bates and R Liddiard (eds), *East Anglia and its North Sea World in the Middle Ages* (Woodbridge: Boydell), 218–229.

Scull, C and A Harding 1990 Two Early Medieval Cemeteries at Millfield Northumberland, *Durham Archaeological Journal* 6, 1–29.

Scull, C, F Minter and J Plouviez 2016 Social and Economic Complexity in Early Medieval England: A Central Place Complex of the East Anglian Kingdom at Rendlesham, Suffolk, *Antiquity* 90, 1594–1612.

Seaby, W A and P Woodfield 1980 Viking Stirrups from England and their Background, *Medieval Archaeology* 24, 87–122.

Seaman, A 2013 Dinas Powys in Context: Settlement and Society in Post-Roman Wales, *Studia Celtica* 47, 1–23.

Seaver, M 2006 Through the Mill – Excavation of an Early Medieval Settlement at Raystown, County Meath, in J O'Sullivan and M Stanley (eds), *Roads, Rediscovery and Research* (Dublin: National Roads Authority), 73–87.

Seaver, M 2010 Against the Grain. Early Medieval Settlement and Burial on the Blackhill: Excavations at Raystown Co. Meath, in C Corlett and M Potterton (eds), *Death and Burial in Early Medieval Ireland in the Light of Recent Archaeological Excavations* (Dublin: Wordwell), 261–279.

Selkirk, A 1973 Chalton The Excavation of an Anglo-Saxon Village, *Current Archaeology* 37, 55–61.

Sellar, W D H 1993a Sueno's Stone and its Interpreters, in W D H Sellar (ed), *Moray: Province and People* (Edinburgh: School of Scottish Studies), 97–116.

Sellar, W D H (ed) 1993b *Moray: Province and People* (Edinburgh: School of Scottish Studies).

Semple, S 2004 Locations of Assembly in Early Anglo-Saxon England, in A Pantos and Sc Semple (eds), *Assembly Places and Practices in Medieval Europe* (Dublin: Four Courts Press), 135–154.

Semple, S 2013 *Perceptions of the Prehistoric in Anglo-Saxon England. Religion, Ritual, and Rulership in the Landscape* (Oxford: Oxford University Press).

Severin, T 1978 *The Brendan Voyage* (London: Arrow Books).

Sharpe, R (ed and trans) 1995 *Adomnán of Iona Life of St Columba* (Harmondsworth: Penguin).

Sharples, N 2005 *Bornais: A Norse Farmstead in the Outer Hebrides: Excavations at Mound 3, Bornais, South Uist* (London: Oxbow Books).

Shephard, J 1979 The Social Identity of the Individual in Isolated Barrows and Barrow-cemeteries in Anglo-Saxon England, in B C Burnham and J Kingsbury (eds), *Space, Hierarchy and Society: Interdisciplinary Studies in Social Area Analysis* (BAR International Series 59) (Oxford: British Archaeological Reports), 47–79.

Sherlock, S J 2011 Anglo-Saxon Cemeteries in the Tees Valley and Associations with Neolithic and Later Monuments, in S Brookes, S Harrington and A Reynolds (eds), *Studies in Early Anglo-Saxon Art and Archaeology: Papers in Honour of Martin G. Welch* (Oxford: Archaeopress, 112–120.

Sherlock, S J 2012 *A Royal Anglo-Saxon Cemetery at Street House, Loftus, North-East Yorkshire* (Tees Archaeology Monograph Series 6) (Hartlepool: Tees Archaeology).

Sherlock, S J and M G Welch 1992 *An Anglo-Saxon Cemetery at Norton, Cleveland* (CBA Research Report 82) (London: Council for British Archaeology).

Sherratt, A 1996 Why Wessex? The Avon Route and River Transport in Later British Prehistory, *Oxford Journal of Archaeology* 15, 211–234.

Sherwood, R J, D L Duren, E W Demerath, S A Czerwinski, R M Siervogel and B Towne 2008 Quantitative Genetics of Modern Human Cranial Variation, *Journal of Human Evolution* 54, 909–914.

Shoesmith, R 1980 *Excavations at Castle Green* [Hereford] (CBA Research Report 36) (York: Council for British Archaeology).

Sigurðardottir, S 2008 *Building with Turf* (Skagafjorður: Skagafjorður Historical Museum).

Simmons, I G 2001 *An Environmental History of Great Britain* (Edinburgh: Edinburgh University Press).

Sims-Williams, P 2003 *The Celtic Inscriptions of Britain: Phonology and Chronology, c. 400–1200* (Publications of the Philological Society, 37) (Oxford: Blackwell).

Sims-Williams, P 2012 Bronze- and Iron-Age Celtic Speakers: What Don't We Know, What Can't We Know, and What Could We Know? Language, Genetics and Archaeology in the 21st Century, *Antiquaries Journal* 92, 427–449.

Sindbæk, S M 2007, Networks and Nodal Points: The Emergence of Towns in Early Viking Age Scandinavia, *Antiquity* 81, 119–132.

Skre, D 2008 Post-substantivist Towns and Trade AD 600–1000, in D Skre (ed), *The Means of Exchange* (Kaupang Excavation Project Publication Series 2) (Aarhus: Aarhus University Press), 327–341.

Skre, D 2010 Comments on Gudme and Tissø. Two Magnate Complexes in Denmark from the 3rd to the 11th Century, in B Ludowici et al. (eds), *Trade and Communication Networks of the First Millennium ad in the Northern Part of Central Europe* (Stuttgart: Theiss), 287–288.

Skre, D 2012 Markets, Towns and Currencies in Scandinavia c. AD 200–1000, in S Gelichi and R Hodges (eds), *From one Sea to Another: Trading Places in the European and Mediterranean Early Middle Ages* (Turnhout: Brepols), 47–64.

Slack, P and R Ward (eds) 1999 *The Peopling of Britain: The Shaping of a Human Landscape* (The Linacre Lectures 1999) (Oxford: Oxford University Press).

Słupecki, L P 1994 *Slavonic Pagan Sanctuaries* (Warsaw: Institute of Archaeology and Ethnology, Polish Academy of Sciences).

Słupecki, L P 1999 The Krakus' and Wanda's Burial Mounds, *Studia Mythologica Slavica* 2, 77–98.

Small, A (ed) 1987 *The Picts: A New Look at Old Problems* (Dundee: Graham Hunter Foundation).

Small, A, C Thomas and D M Wilson 1973 *St Ninian's Isle and its Treasure* (Oxford: Oxford University Press).

Smith, I M 1990 The Archaeological Background to the Emergent Kingdoms of the Tweed Basin in the Early Historic Period (Unpublished PhD dissertation, University of Durham).

Smith, I M 1991 Sprouston, Roxburghshire: An Early Anglian Centre of the Eastern Tweed Basin, *Proceedings of the Society of Antiquaries of Scotland* 121, 261–294.

Smith, I M 1996 The Origins and Development of Christianity in North Britain and Southern Pictland, in J Blair and C Pyrah (eds), *Church Archaeology: Research Directions for the Future* (York: Council for British Archaeology), 19–36.

Smith, J H 2005 *Europe After Rome: A New Cultural History 500–1000* (Oxford: Oxford University Press).

Smyth, A 1984 *Warlords and Holy Men* (Edinburgh: Edinburgh University Press).

Snow, D 2010 *Archaeology of Native North America* (Upper Saddle River: Prentice Hall).

Soderberg, J 2004a Wild Cattle: Red Deer in the Religious Texts, Iconography and Archaeology of Early Medieval Ireland, *Journal of Historical Archaeology* 8, 167–183.

Soderberg, J 2004b Distinguishing the Local from the Regional: Irish Perspectives on Urbanization in Early Medieval Europe, in J R Mathieu and R E Scott (eds), *Exploring the Role of Analytical Scale in Archaeological Interpretation* (BAR International Series 1261) (Oxford: Archaeopress), 67–82.

Sofield, C M 2015 Living with the Dead: Human Burials in Anglo-Saxon Settlement Contexts, *Archaeological Journal* 172(2), 351–388.

Spall, C A 2006 All that Glitters: The Case for Goldworking at the Early Medieval Monastery at Portmahomack, *Historical Metallurgy* 40(1), 42–48.

Spall, C A 2009 Reflections on the Monastic Arts: Recent Discoveries at Portmahomack, Tarbat, Easter Ross, in N Edwards (ed), *The Archaeology of the Early Medieval Celtic Churches* (Leeds: Maney), 315–332.

Spall, C A 2011 Have We Got a Parchmenerie? Identifying Parchment Making at a Dry-preserved Site: The Evidence from Portmahomack, Tarbatness, Ross-shire, in R Thompson and Q Mould (eds), *Leather Tanneries, the Archaeological Evidence* (London: Archetype), 93–102.

Spall, C A and N J Toop (eds) 2005 *Excavations at Blue Bridge Lane and Fishergate House, York: Report on Excavations; July 2000 to July 2002* (APC Monograph Series, Volume 001) (York: Archaeological Planning Consultancy).

Spall, C A and N J Toop 2008 Before Eoforwic: New Light on York in the 6–7th Centuries, *Medieval Archaeology* 52, 1–26.

Speake, G 1980 *Anglo-Saxon Animal Art and its Germanic Background* (Oxford: Clarendon Press).

Speake, G 1989 *A Saxon Bed Burial on Swallowcliffe Down: Excavations by F de M Vatcher* (Swindon: English Heritage).

Spearman, R M 1988a Industrialization and Urbanization in Medieval Scotland: The Material Evidence (Unpublished PhD dissertation, University of Glasgow).

Spearman, R M 1988b Early Scottish Towns: Their Origins and Economy, in S T Driscoll and M R Nieke (eds), *Power and Politics in Early Medieval Britain and Ireland* (Edinburgh: Edinburgh University Press), 79–95.

Spearman, R M and J Higgitt (eds) 1993 *The Age of Migrating Ideas, Early Medieval Art in Northern Britain and Ireland* (Edinburgh: National Museums of Scotland and Stroud: Sutton).

Spring, A P and C Peters 2014 Developing a Low-cost 3D Imaging Solution for Inscribed Stone Surface Analysis, *Journal of Archaeological Science* 52, 97–107.

Staecker, J 2003 The Cross Goes North: Christian Symbols and Scandinavian Women, in M O H Carver (ed), *The Cross Goes North: Processes of Conversion in Northern Europe, AD 300–1300* (Woodbridge and Rochester (NY): York Medieval Press), 463–482.

Stalley, R 1996 *Irish High Crosses* (Dublin: Town House and Country House).

Stanley, M, E Danaher and J Eogan (eds) 2010 *Creative Minds: Production, Manufacturing and Invention in Ancient Ireland* (NRA Scheme Monograph 7) (Dublin: National Roads Authority).

Stead, I M 2000 *The Salisbury Hoard* (Stroud: Tempus).

Stenton, D M 1957 *The English Woman in History* (London: Allen and Unwin).

Stenton, F M (ed) 1957 *The Bayeux Tapestry* (London: Phaidon Press).

Stenton, F M 1971 *Anglo-Saxon England* 3rd edition (Oxford: Oxford University Press).

Stevenson, J B 1991 Pitcarmicks and Fermtouns, *Current Archaeology* 127, 288–291.

Stocker, D and P Everson 2003 The Straight and Narrow Way; Fenland Causeways and the Conversion of the Landscape in the Witham Valley, Lincolnshire, in M O H Carver (ed), *The Cross Goes North: Processes of Conversion in Northern Europe, AD 300–1300* (Woodbridge and Rochester (NY): York Medieval Press), 271–288.

Stokes, W 1905 *The Martyrology of Oengus the Culdee* (London: Harrison and Sons).

Stoodley, N 1999 *The Spindle and the Spear: A Critical Enquiry into the Construction and Meaning of the Gender in the Early Anglo-Saxon Burial Rite* (BAR British Series 288) (Oxford: British Archaeological Reports).

Stout, M 1997 *The Irish Ringfort* (Dublin: Four Courts Press).

Strachan, D 2013 *Excavations at the Black Spout, Pitlochry and the Iron Age Monumental Roundhouses of North West Perthsire* (Perth: Perth and Kinross Heritage Trust).

Suzuki, S 2000 *The Quoit Brooch Style and Anglo-Saxon Settlement: A Casting and Recasting of Cultural Identity Symbols* (Woodbridge and Rochester(NY): Boydell).

Swift, C 1999 Early Medieval Grave-slabs and their Inscriptions, *Durham Archaeological Journal* 14–15, 111–118.

Swift, C 2000 *Ogam Stones and the Earliest Irish Christians* (Maynooth Monograph 2) (Maynooth: St Patrick's College, Department of Old and Middle Irish).

Swift, C 2003 Sculptors and their Customers: A Study of Clonmacnoise Grave Slabs, in H King (ed), *Clonmacnoise Studies 2* (Dublin: Dúchas), 105–203.

Taylor, C 1979 *Roads and Tracks of Britain* (London: Orion).

Taylor, D B 1990 *Circular Homesteads in North West Perthshire* (Dundee: Abertay Historical Society Publication 29) (Dundee: Abertay Historical Society).

Taylor, E G R 1956 *The Haven-Finding Art. A History of Navigation from Odysseus to Captain Cook* (London: Hollis and Carter).

Taylor, H M 1978 *Anglo-Saxon Architecture* Volume III (Cambridge: Cambridge University Press).

Taylor, H M and J Taylor 1965 *Anglo-Saxon Architecture* Volumes I and II (Cambridge: Cambridge University Press).

Taylor, J 2007 *An Atlas of Roman Rural Settlement in England* (CBA Research Report 151) (York: Council for British Archaeology).

Taylor, S 1996 Place Names and the Early Church in Eastern Scotland, in B E Crawford (ed), *Scotland in Dark Age Britain* (Aberdeen: Scottish Cultural Press), 93–110.

Tedeschi, C 2001 Some Observations on the Palaeography of Early Christian Inscriptions in Britain, in J Higgitt, K Forsyth and D N Parsons (eds), *Roman, Runes and Ogham: Medieval Inscriptions in the Insular World and on the Continent* (Donington: Shaun Tyas), 16–25.

Temple, E 1976 *Anglo-Saxon Manuscripts 900–1066* (London: Harvey Miller).

Tester, A, S Anderson and R Carr 2014 *Staunch Meadow, Brandon, Suffolk: A High-status Middle Saxon Settlement on the Fen Edge* (East Anglian Archaeology 151) (Bury St Edmunds: Suffolk County Council Archaeological Service).

Thäte E S 2007 *Monuments and Minds. Monument re-use in Scandinavia in the Second Half of the First Millennium AD* (Acta Archaeologica Lundensia Series in 4° 27) (Lund: Wallin and Dalholm).

Theuws, F 2004 Exchange, Religion, Identity and Central Places in the Early Middle Ages, *Archaeological Dialogues* 10(1), 121–138.

Theuws, F 2012 River-based Trade Centres in Early Medieval North-western Europe. Some Reactionary Thoughts, in S Gelichi and R Hodges (eds), *From one Sea to Another: Trading Places in the European and Mediterranean Early Middle Ages* (Turnhout: Brepols), 25–46.

Theuws, F, M de Jong and C van Rhijn (eds) 2001 *Topographies of Power in the Early Middle Ages* (Leiden: Brill), 9–30.

Thomas, A C 1961 The Animal Art of the Scottish Iron Age and its Origins, *Archaeological Journal* 118, 14–64.

Thomas, A C 1963 The Interpretation of the Pictish Symbols, *Archaeological Journal* 120, 31–97.

Thomas, A C 1967 *Christian Antiquities of Camborne* (St Austell: H.E. Warne).

Thomas, A C 1971 *The Early Christian Archaeology of North Britain* (Edinburgh: Edinburgh University Press).

Thomas, A C 1981 *Christianity in Roman Britain to AD500* (London: Batsford).

Thomas, A C 1994 *And Shall These Mute Stones Speak? Post-Roman Inscriptions in Western Britain* (Cardiff: University of Wales Press).

Thomas, A C and A Boucher (eds) 2002 *Hereford City Excavations Volume IV 1976–1990*: Further Sites and Evolving Interpretations (Hereford: Hereford City and County Archaeological Trust).

Thomas, G 2000 *A Survey of Late Anglo-Saxon and Viking-Age Strap-ends from Britain* (PhD dissertation, University College London), http://discovery.ucl.ac.uk/1317562/1/248475.pdf.

Thomas, G 2001 Strap-ends and the Identification of Regional Patterns in the Production and Circulation of Ornamental Metalwork in Late Anglo-Saxon and Viking Age Britain, in M Redknap, N Edwards, S Youngs, A Lane and J Knight (eds), *Pattern and Purpose in Insular Art: Proceedings of the 4th International Conference on Insular Art Held at the National Museum and Art Gallery, Cardiff* (Oxford: Oxbow), 39–48.

Thomas, G 2010 *The Later Anglo-Saxon Settlement at Bishopstone: A Downland Manor in the Making* (CBA Research Report 163) (York: Council for British Archaeology).

Thomas, G 2013 Life Before the Minster: The Social Dynamic of Monastic Foundation at Anglo-Saxon Lyminge, Kent, *Antiquaries Journal*. 93, 109–146.

Thomas, G 2017 Monasteries as Places of Power in Pre-Viking England: Trajectories, Relationships and Interactions, in G Thomas and A Knox (eds), *Early Medieval Monasticism in the North Sea Zone* (*Anglo-Saxon Studies in Archaeology and History* 20) (Oxford: Oxford University School of Archaeology), 97–116.

Thomas, M G, M P H Stumpf and H Härke 2006 Evidence for an Apartheid-like Social Structure in Early Anglo-Saxon England, *Proceedings of the Royal Society B*, 273, 2651–2657, doi:10.1098/rspb.2006.3627.

Thompson, R and Q Mould (eds) 2011 *Leather Tanneries, the Archaeological Evidence* (London: Archetype).

Tinniswood, A and A F Harding 1991 Anglo-Saxon Occupation and Industrial Features in the Henge Monument at Yeavering, Northumberland, *Durham Archaeological Journal* 7, 93–108.

Tipper, J 2004 *The Grubenhaus in Anglo-Saxon England* (Yedingham: Landscape Research Centre).

Tolkien, J R R 1936 Beowulf: The Monsters and the Critics, *Proceedings of the British Academy* 22, 245–295.

Toolis, R and C Bowles 2013 Excavations at Trusty's Hill, 2012, *Transactions of the Dumfriesshire Galloway Natural History and Antiquarian Society* 87, 27–50.

Toop, N 2005 Dialogues of Power: Early Christian Monumentality around the Northern Irish Sea AD 400–1000 (Unpublished PhD dissertation, University of York).

Toop, N 2011 Northumbria in the West: Considering the Interaction Through Monumentality, in D Petts and S Turner (eds), *Early Medieval Northumbria: Kingdoms and Communities, AD 450–1100* (Turnhout: Brepols), 85–111.

Trench-Jellicoe, R 2002 Manx Sculptured Monuments and the Early Viking Age, in P Davey and D Finlayson (eds), *Mannin Revisited: Twelve Essays on Manx Culture and Environment* (Edinburgh: Scottish Society for Northern Studies), 11–36

Turner, S 2006 *Making a Christian Landscape* (Exeter: University of Exeter Press).

Tweddle, D 1992 *The Anglian Helmet from 16–22 Coppergate* (The Archaeology of York 17/8) (York: Council for British Archaeology).

Tweddle, D, M Biddle and B Kjølbye-Biddle 1995 *Corpus of Anglo-Saxon Stone Sculpture Volume IV: South-East England* (Oxford: Oxford University Press for The British Academy).

Tweddle, D, J Moulden and E Logan 1999 *Anglian York: A Survey of the Evidence* (The Archaeology of York 7/2) (York: Council for British Archaeology).

Tyler, E M (ed) 2000 *Treasure in the Medieval West* (Woodbridge: York Medieval Press).

Ulmschneider, K 2011 Settlement Hierarchy, in H Hamerow, D A Hinton and S Crawford (eds), *The Oxford Handbook of Anglo-Saxon Archaeology* (Oxford: Oxford University Press), 156–171.

Ulriksen, J 2004 Danish Coastal Landing Places and their Relation to Navigation and Trade, in J Hines, A Lane and M Redknap (eds), *Land, Sea and Home: Settlement in the Viking Period* (Leeds: Maney), 7–26.

Urbańczyk, P 2010 What Did Early Medieval Authors Know about Structures of Governance and Religion in Northern Central Europe? (A Comment on M Hardt), *Neue Studien zur Sachsenforschung* 1, 356–361.

Valante, M 1998 Reassessing the Irish Monastic Town, *Irish Historical Studies* 31(121), 1–18.

Van de Noort, R 1993 The Context of Early Medieval Barrows in Western Europe, *Antiquity* 67, 66–73.

Varenius, B 1995 Metaphorical Ships in Iron-Age Contexts, in O Crumlin-Pedersen and B Munch Thye (eds), *The Ship as Symbol in Prehistoric and Medieval Scandinavia* (Copenhagen: National Museum of Denmark), 35–40.

Venclova, N 2002 The Venerable Bede, Druidic Tonsure and Archaeology, *Antiquity* 76, 458–471.

Viking Ship Museum 2007 *Welcome on Board! The Sea Stallion from Glendalough: A Viking Longship Recreated* (Roskilde: Viking Ship Museum).

Vince, A G 1984 The Aldwych: Mid-Saxon London discovered, *Current Archaeology* 93, 310–312.

Vince, A G 1985 The Saxon and Medieval Pottery of London: A Review, *Medieval Archaeology* 29, 25–93.

Vince, A G 1990 *Saxon London: An Archaeological Investigation* (London: Seaby).

Vince, A G 1994 Saxon Urban Economies: An Archaeological Perspective, in J Rackham (ed), *Environment and Economy in Anglo-Saxon England* (York: Council for British Archaeology), 108–119.

Waddell, J 1998 *The Prehistoric Archaeology of Ireland* (Galway: Galway University Press).

Waddell, J 2005 *Foundation Myths: The Beginnings of Irish Archaeology* (Bray: Wordwell).

Waddell, J 2011 Continuity, Cult and Contest, in R Schot, C Newman and E Bhreathnach (eds), *Landscapes of Cult and Kingship* (Dublin: Four Courts Press), 192–212.

Waddell, J, J Fenwick and K Barton 2009 *Rathcroghan: Archaeological and Geophysical Survey in Virtual Landscape* (Dublin: Wordwell).

Wade, K 1983 The Early Anglo-Saxon Period, in A J Lawson (ed), *The Archaeology of Witton Near North Walsham* (East Anglian Archaeology 18) (Dereham: Norfolk Museums Service), 50–69.

Wade, K 1988 Ipswich, in R Hodges and B Hobley (eds), *The Rebirth of Towns in the West AD700–1050* (CBA Research Report 68) (London: Council for British Archaeology), 93–100.

Wainwright, F T 1959 Æthelflæd Lady of the Mercians, in P Clemoes (ed), *The Anglo-Saxons: Studies in Some Aspects of their History and Culture Presented to Bruce Dickins* (London: Bowes and Bowes), 53–69.

Walker, B 1977 *Clay Buildings in North East Scotland* (Dundee and Edinburgh: Scottish Vernacular Buildings Working Group).

Walker, B 2006 *Scottish Turf Construction* (Edinburgh: Historic Scotland).

Walker, B and C McGregor 1996 *Earth Structures and Construction in Scotland* (Edinburgh: Historic Scotland).

Walker, B, C McGregor and G Stark 1996 *Thatch and Thatching Techniques: A Guide to Conserving Scottish Thatching Traditions* (Edinburgh: Historic Scotland).

Walker, I 2000 *Mercia and The Making of England* (Stroud: Sutton).

Wallace, P F 1992 *The Viking Age Buildings of Dublin* (Dublin: National Museum of Ireland).

Walton Rogers, P 2005 The Textiles from Mounds 5, 7, 14 and 17, in M O H Carver *Sutton Hoo: A Seventh Century Princely Burial Ground and its Context* (London: British Museum Press), 262–268.

Walton Rogers, P 2007 *Cloth and Clothing in Early Anglo-Saxon England, AD 450–700* (CBA Research Report 145) (York: Council for British Archaeology).

Watkins, T 1980 Excavation of an Iron Age Open Settlement at Dalladies, Kincardineshire, *Proceedings of the Society of Antiquaries of Scotland* 110, 122–164.

Watson, B, T Brigham and T Dyson 2001 *London Bridge: 2000 Years of a River Crossing* (MoLAS Monograph 8) (London: Museum of London Archaeology Service).

Watt, M 2004 The Gold-figure Foils ('Guldgubbar') from Uppåkra, in L Larsson (ed), *Continuity for Centuries: A Ceremonial Building and its Context at Uppåkra, Southern Sweden* (Uppåkrastudier 10) (Lund: Almqvist & Wiksell), 167–221.

Webley, L 2008 *Iron Age Households. Structure and Practice in Western Denmark, 500 BC–AD 200* (Moesgård: Jutland Archaeological Society).

Webster, C J and R A Brunning 2014 A Seventh-Century AD Cemetery at Stoneage Barton Farm, Bishop's Lydeard, Somerset and Square-Ditched Burials in Post-Roman Britain, *Archaeological Journal* 161(1), 54–81.

Webster, L 2012 *Anglo-Saxon Art: A New History* (London: British Museum).

Webster, L and J Backhouse 1991 *The Making of England: Anglo-Saxon Art and Culture AD 600–900* (London: British Museum Press).

Webster, L, C Sparey-Green, P Périn and C Hills 2011 The Staffordshire (Ogley Hay) Hoard: Problems of Interpretation, *Antiquity* 85, 221–229.

Wedderburn, L M and D M Grime 1984 The Cairn Cemetery at Garbeg, Drumnadrochit, in J G P Friel and W G Watson (eds), *Pictish Studies: Settlement, Burial and Art in Dark Age Northern Britain* (Oxford: British Archaeological Reports), 151–167.

Weitzmann, K 1977 *Late Antique and Early Christian Book Illumination* (London: Chatto and Windus).

West, S 1985 *West Stow: The Anglo-Saxon Village* (East Anglian Archaeology 24) (Ipswich: Suffolk County Planning Department with Scole Archaeological Committee).

West, S 2001 *West Stow Revisited* (Bury St Edmunds: St Edmundsbury Borough Council).

Westerdahl, C 1992 The Maritime Cultural Landscape, *International Journal of Nautical Archaeology* 21, 5–14.

Westerdahl, C 2005 Seal on Land, Elk at Sea: Notes on and Applications of the Ritual Landscape at the Seaboard, *International Journal of Nautical Archaeology* 34, 2–23.

Westerdahl, C (ed) 2006 *The Significance of Portages* (BAR International Series 1499) (Oxford: Archaeopress).

Westerdahl, C 2008 Boats Apart. Building and Equipping an Iron Age and Early Medieval Ship in Northern Europe, *International Journal of Nautical Archaeology* 37(1), 17–31.

Wheatley, P 1971 *The Pivot of the Four Quarters* (Chicago: Aldine).

Whimster, R 1979 *Burial Practices in Iron Age Britain* (PhD dissertation, University of Durham) http://etheses.dur.ac.uk/7999/1/7999_4997-vol1.PDF?UkUDh:CyT and http://etheses.dur.ac.uk/7999/2/7999_4997-vol2.PDF?UkUDh:CyT.

Whimster, R 1981 *Burial Practices in Iron Age Britain: A Discussion and Gazeteer of the Evidence c. 700 BC–AD 43* (BAR British Series 90) (Oxford: British Archaeological Reports).

White, R 1972 Excavations at Arfryn, Bodedern, Long-cist Cemeteries and the Origins of Christianity in Britain, *Transactions of the Anglesey Antiquarian Society* 1971–72, 19–51.

White, S I and G Smith 1999 *A Funerary and Ceremonial Centre at Capel Eithin, Gaerwen, Anglesey* (*Transactions of the Anglesey Antiquarian Society*) (Bangor: Anglesey Antiquarian Society and Field Club).

Whitehouse, D B 1965 Forum Ware: A Distinctive Type of Early Medieval Glazed Pottery in the Roman Campagna, *Medieval Archaeology* 9, 55–63.

Whitelock, D 1951 *The Audience of Beowulf* (Oxford: Oxford University Press).

Whitelock, D (trans and ed) 1961 *The Anglo-Saxon Chronicle* (London: Eyre and Spottiswood).

Whitelock, D 1968 *The Beginnings of English Society* (Harmondsworth: Penguin).

White Marshall, J and G Rourke 2000 *High Island: An Irish Monastery in the Atlantic* (Dublin: Town House).

White Marshall, J and C Walsh 2005 *Illaunloughan Island: An Early Medieval Monastery in County Kerry* (Bray: Wordwell).

Whitfield, N 1999 Design and Units of Measure in the Hunterston Brooch, in J Hawkes and S Mills (eds), *Northumbria's Golden Age* (Stroud: Sutton), 296–314.

Whitfield, N 2006 Dress and Accessories in the Early Irish Tale of 'The Wooing of Becfhola', in R Netherton and G R Owen-Crocker (eds), *Medieval Clothing and Textiles* Volume 2 (Woodbridge: Boydell), 1–34.

Whitfield, N 2014–15 Embedded Animal Heads on the Hunterston, 'Tara' and Dunbeath Brooches: A Reconsideration, *Journal of the Royal Society of Antiquaries of Ireland* 144–145, 60–76.

Wickham, C 1984 The Other Transition: From the Ancient World to Feudalism, *Past & Present* 103, 3–36.

Wickham, C 2005 *Framing the Early Middle Ages: Europe and the Mediterranean, 400–800* (Oxford: Oxford University Press).

Wilkes, E 2007 Prehistoric Sea Journeys and Port Approaches: The South Coast and Poole Harbour, in V Cummings and R Johnstone (eds), *Prehistoric Journeys* (Oxford: Oxbow), 121–130.

Wilkinson, C 2008 *Forensic Facial Reconstruction* (Cambridge: Cambridge University Press).

Willemsen, A and H Kik (eds) 2010 *Dorestad in an International Framework: New Research on Centres of Trade and Coinage in Carolingian Times* (Turnhout: Brepols).

Willey, G and P Phillips 1958 *Method and Theory in American Archaeology* (Chicago: University of Chicago Press).

Williams, H 1997 Ancient Landscapes and the Dead: The Reuse of Prehistoric and Roman Monuments as Early Anglo-Saxon Burial Sites, *Medieval Archaeology* 41, 1–32.

Williams, H 1999 Placing the Dead: Investigating the Location of Wealthy Barrow Burials in Seventh Century England, in M Rundqvist (ed), *Grave Matters* (BAR International Series 781) (Oxford: Archaeopress), 57–86.

Williams, H 2002 Cemeteries as Central Places: Landscape and Identity in Early Anglo-Saxon England, in B Hårdh and L Larsson (eds), *Central Places in the Migration and Merovingian Periods* (Stockholm: Almqvist & Wiksell International), 341–362.

Williams, H 2004 Assembling the Dead, in A Pantos and S Semple (eds), *Assembly Places and Practices in Medieval Europe* (Dublin: Four Courts Press), 109–134.

Williams, H 2006 *Death and Memory in Early Medieval Britain* (Cambridge: Cambridge University Press).

Williams, H 2010 Engendered Bodies and Objects of Memory in Final Phase Graves, in J Buckberry and A Cherryson (eds), *Burial in Later Anglos-Saxon England, c. 650–1100 AD* (Oxford: Oxbow), 26–37.

Williams, H, J Kirton and M Gondek (eds) 2015 *Early Medieval Stone Monuments. Materiality, Biography, Landscape* (Woodbridge: Boydell).

Williams, I and J E Caerwyn Williams (eds) 1968 *The Poems of Taliesin* (Dublin: Dublin Institute for Advanced Studies).

Williams, R J 1993 *Pennyland and Hartigans: Two Iron Age and Saxon Sites in Milton Keynes* (Buckinghamshire Archaeology Society Monograph 4) (Aylesbury: Buckinghamshire Archaeology Society).

Wilmore, H H 1939 Stone Coffins, Gloucestershire, *Transactions of the Bristol and Gloucestershire Archaeological Society*. 61, 135–177.

Wilson, D M 1964 *Anglo-Saxon Ornamental Metalwork 700–1100 in the British Museum* (London: British Museum).

Wilson, D M (ed) 1976 *The Archaeology of Anglo-Saxon England* (London: Methuen).

Wilson, D M 1984 *Anglo-Saxon Art* (London: Thames & Hudson).

Wilson, D M 2008 *The Vikings in the Isle of Man* (Aarhus: Aarhus University Press).

Wilson, D M and O Klindt-Jensen 1966 *Viking Art* (London: Allen and Unwin).

Wilson, P R, P Cardwell, R J Cramp, J Evans, R H Taylor-Wilson, A Thompson and J S Wacher 1996 Early Anglian Catterick and *Catraeth*, *Medieval Archaeology* 40, 1–61.

Winlow, S 2011 A Review of Pictish Burial Practice in Tayside and Fife, in S T Driscoll, J Geddes and M A Hall (eds), *Pictish Progress: New Studies on Northern Britain in the Early Middle Ages* (Leiden: Brill), 335–369.

Wise, P J 1991 Wasperton, *Current Archaeology* 126, 256–259.

Wood, J 2003 The Orkney Hood: An Ancient Recycled Textile, in J Downes and A Ritchie (eds), *Sea Change: Orkney and Northern Europe in the Later Iron Age AD 300–800* (Balgavies: Pinkfoot Press), 171–175.

Wooding, J 1996 *Communication and Commerce Along the Western Sealanes AD 400–800* (BAR International Series 654) (Oxford: Tempus Reparatum).

Woods, K S 1949 *Rural Crafts of England* (London: Harrap).

Woodward, A 1992 *English Heritage Book of Shrines and Sacrifice* (London: Batsford for English Heritage).

Woodward, A 1993 The Cult of Relics in Prehistoric Britain, in M O H Carver (ed), *In Search of Cult. Archaeological Investigations in Honour of Philip Rahtz* (Woodbridge: Boydell), 1–8.

Woodward, A and P Leach 1993 *The Uley Shrines. Excavations of a Ritual Complex on West Hill. Uley, Gloucestershire 1977–9* (London: English Heritage).

Woolf, A 2006 Dún Nechtán, Fortriu and the Geography of the Picts, *Scottish Historical Review* 85, 182–201.

Woolf, A 2007 *From Pictland to Alba 789–1070* (Edinburgh: Edinburgh University Press).

Woolf, A (ed) 2013 *Beyond the Gododdin: Dark Age Scotland in Medieval Wales* (St John's House Papers 13) (St Andrews: University of St Andrews).

Wormald, F 1952 *English Drawings of the Tenth and Eleventh Centuries* (London: Faber).

Wormald, P 1996 The Emergence of the Regnum Scottorum: A Carolingian Hegemony? in B Crawford (ed), *Scotland in Dark Age Britain* (Aberdeen: Scottish Cultural Press), 131–160.

Wormald, P 1999 *The Making of English Law: King Alfred to the Twelfth Century, 1: Legislation and its Limits* (Oxford: Blackwell).

Wreford Watson, J 1964 The Individuality of Britain and the British Isles, in J Wreford Watson and J B Sissons (eds), *The British Isles: A Systematic Geography* (London: Nelson), 1–19.

Wreford Watson, J and J B Sissons (eds) 1964 *The British Isles: A Systematic Geography* (London: Nelson).

Wright, D 1957 *Beowulf: A Prose Translation* (London: Panther Books).

Yeoman, P 2009 Investigations on the May Island, and Other Early Medieval Churches and Monasteries in Scotland, in N Edwards (ed), *The Archaeology of the Early Medieval Celtic Churches* (Leeds: Maney), 227–244.

Yorke, B 1990 *Kings and Kingdoms of Early Anglo-Saxon England* (London: Seaby).

Yorke, B 1995 *Wessex in the Early Middle Ages* (London: Leicester University Press).

Youngs, S (ed) 1989 *'The Work of Angels', Masterpieces of Celtic Metalwork, 6th–9th Centuries AD* (London: British Museum).

Zimmerman, W H 1999 Why Was Cattle-stalling Introduced in Prehistory? The Significance of Byre and Stable and of Outwintering in C Fabech and J Ringtved (eds), *Settlement and Landscape: Proceedings of a Conference in Århus, Denmark May 4–7 1998* (Moesgård: Jutland Archaeological Society), 301–318.

Index

Notes:
Page numbers in bold denote illustrations.
Major topics are in bold small capitals.
A suffix n. indicates a note (299n. refers to an end note on page 299).

For quick access to contents of Chapters, please see: